D0119257

# The Kingfisher YOUNG PEOPLE'S ENCYCLOPEDIA OF THE UNITED STATES

*The Kingfisher*

# YOUNG PEOPLE'S ENCYCLOPEDIA OF THE UNITED STATES

Kingfisher

NEW YORK

KINGFISHER
Larousse Kingfisher Chambers Inc.
95 Madison Avenue
New York, New York 10016

This revised one-volume edition
first published in the United States
in 1994. Originally published in
multiple volumes in 1992.

2 4 6 8 10 9 7 5 3 1



Library of Congress Cataloging-in-Publication Data
The Kingfisher young people's encyclopedia
of the United States/general editor,
William E. Shapiro——1st American ed.
p. cm.
Includes index.
1. United States——Encyclopedias, Juvenile. [1. United States–
–Encyclopedias.] I. Shapiro, William E. II. Title. Young People's
Encyclopedia of the United States.
E156.K56 1994
973'.03——dc20 93-42501 CIP AC

ISBN 1–85697–521–5

Printed in Italy

**GENERAL EDITOR:** William E. Shapiro

**Editorial Director:** Jim Miles

**Senior Editor:** Jennifer Justice

**Editor:** Cynthia O'Brien

**Assistant Editor:** Sian Hardy

**Copy Editor:** Grace Buonocore

**Contributors:** Sean Connolly, Thomas Cussans, Robert Halasz, Elizabeth Longley, Alison Wormleighton, Eleanor Van Zandt

**Design:** Michèle Arron, Allan Hardcastle, Louise Jervis, Nigel Osborne

**Production:** Lucy Cooper, Susan Latham, Oonagh Phelan

**Picture Research:** Tim Russell, Elaine Willis, Su Alexander

**Educational Consultants:**

Alfred B. Bortz, Ph.D.
Director of Special Projects for
Engineering Education
Carnegie Mellon University
Author, *Superstuff: Materials That Have Changed Our Lives*

Charles Alva Hoyt, Ph.D.
Professor of English Literature Adjunct
Marist College

William Jay Jacobs, Ed.D
Coordinator, History and Social Sciences
Darien (Connecticut) Public Schools
Author, *America's Story*

Jeanette Lambert
Librarian
La Vega Independent School District
Waco, Texas

Mary L. Nieball, Ph.D.
Dean of Library Services
San Jacinto College District
Pasadena, Texas

Jenny Tesar, M.A.
Science writer and consultant

# FOREWORD

*The Young People's Encyclopedia of the United States* introduces the people, places, and events that have shaped the nation during its more than 200 years of history. Biographical sketches tell about the people who have contributed to its growth from a British colony into the most powerful—and most democratic—country in the world. Other articles show how the country is governed. And still others describe the many different peoples who live here—from the Native Americans to those of European descent to the recent immigrants from Asia, Latin America, Africa, and elsewhere.

What are these people like? What are their contributions to the country, to its culture? And what of this nation's history, its literature and the arts, science and space, industry and technology? It is all here, along with articles on topics such as religions, education, holidays, health, and sports.

Still other articles tell about the land itself—from the lofty mountain ranges to the mighty rivers—and about the wonderfully varied animals and plant life that inhabit it. Here, too, are portraits of the 50 states and of the cities that have grown up where once there was only wilderness.

*The Young People's Encyclopedia of the United States* is a valuable reference tool. But it is also more than that. It's an exciting journey through our past, our present, and our future.

William E. Shapiro

# ABOUT *your* ENCYCLOPEDIA

This encyclopedia is about the United States and its neighbors. You will not find an entry on ancient Greece, on Napoleon, or on the elephant. But you will find entries on Canada, Mexico, and Central America, and on the geography of North America, because these are all important for understanding our nation's place in the world today. All the entries are arranged in alphabetical order. If the subject you are looking for does not have its own entry, look in the index at the back.

●

Throughout the encyclopedia you will find words printed in small capitals, like this: CIVIL WAR. These words are called *cross-references*. When you see one, you will know that there is a separate entry on the subject in your encyclopedia. That entry may have more information about the subject you are looking up.

●

Subject symbols appear next to each heading. These are helpful when you are browsing through the encyclopedia and want to find entries on states and cities, for instance, or history, or science and space. There are twelve symbols in all.

●

Each volume contains special feature entries, such as American History, Birds of North America, and Government of the United States. These can be used to help you with your school projects, or you can look them up in the same way as the other entries. You will find them listed at the back of the work. You will also find special expanded entries for each of the states, for every U.S. president, and for each of the armed forces.

●

Fact boxes throughout make it easy to find important information and statistics. And the outside column has a host of fascinating bits of additional and often surprising information.

# THE SUBJECT SYMBOLS

Each entry in this encyclopedia has its own easily recognized symbol opposite the heading. This symbol tells you at a glance which area of interest the entry falls into. Below are the 12 subject areas we have used. At the back of the work there is a list of all the articles divided into subject areas.

**HISTORY** Events from before colonial times to the present day.

**LITERATURE AND THE ARTS** Novelists, playwrights, folklore, folk art and crafts, theater, dance, painting, sculpture, architecture of the United States.

**PEOPLE AND CULTURE** Native and immigrant peoples of North America, their languages and customs, education, health and welfare, social issues.

**GEOGRAPHY** The land and climate of North America: geographic regions, mountain ranges, rivers and lakes, coastlines, national parks.

**SCIENCE AND SPACE** Explorations into fields of science and astronomy, famous scientists and innovators.

**INDUSTRY AND TECHNOLOGY** Transportation, natural resources, manufacturing — industries of yesterday and today.

**GOVERNMENT AND LAW** The U.S. government, its branches and how it works; the armed services and other governmental organizations; political parties; laws and treaties.

**RELIGION, PHILOSOPHY, AND MYTH** The wide variety of religious denominations, philosophers and their ideas, myths and legends.

**SPORTS AND PASTIMES** Baseball, football, basketball, and other sports, sports heroes, plus many hobbies.

**COUNTRIES AND PLACES** Our neighbors in North and Central America and places of interest.

**ANIMALS, PLANTS, AND FOOD** North American animals and their habitats, North American plants, agriculture and food, including regional specialities.

**STATES AND CITIES** Descriptions of each U.S. state, major cities, and sites within and around the country.

# HOW TO GET THE MOST *from your* ENCYCLOPEDIA

**This encyclopedia contains many features to help you look up things easily or simply to have fun just browsing through. Almost every page has several illustrations, and there are fact boxes, special feature entries, and literally hundreds of cross-references to help you find your way around. Some of these features are shown here. We hope you will enjoy exploring the pages of your encyclopedia.**

- **Subject symbols**
- **Fact boxes**
- **"Nuggets"**
- **Special feature entries**
- **Cross-references**
- **Expanded entries on U.S. presidents, states, and each of the armed forces**

**THE TEXT** is full of information and yet easy to read. Cross-references appear in SMALL CAPITALS. Turn to these entries for more information on the subject you are looking up.

**OVER 2,000 ILLUSTRATIONS** and photographs have been used, including hundreds of maps and many diagrams.

**STATE SYMBOLS** appear in the left-hand corner of each state spread. These include the state flag, bird, tree, and flower.

**EXPANDED ENTRIES** on such subjects as U.S. presidents, states, and each of the armed forces provide more detailed information on these important topics.

**FACT BOXES** appear throughout the encyclopedia giving you details on historical dates, facts and figures, and other important facts.

ION

...ans the protection and wise use of ... Natural resources are materials ...t are useful or necessary to people. ...esources are being used than ever ...rces, such as *fossil fuels* (coal, natural gas, ...inerals (such as iron and copper), ...d once they are used up. It is impor...ting these *nonrenewable resources*. For ...smaller cars uses less gasoline. Using ...ad of fossil fuels to heat buildings is ... of conservation. Where possible, ...e *recycled*. Aluminum cans, for exam...down and used to make new cans. ...—such as water, farmland, and for...ewed. But here, too, careful conserva...or example, preventing forest fires and ...ives trees, and replanting logged areas ...ovides trees for the future. ...careful use of natural resources, con...means ENVIRONMENTAL PROTECTION ...LUTION. In the United States, the De...griculture, Energy, and the Interior ...ects of conservation as oil production, ..., mining, soil conservation, and the ...The U.S. Environmental Protection ...volved in conservation. But every citi...e natural resources responsibly.

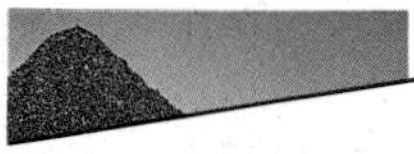

Centennial State

...untains. ...dly and

...do, and ...OINS are ...ne state's ...are based ...nd manu... ...an impor... ...are raised ...ns.

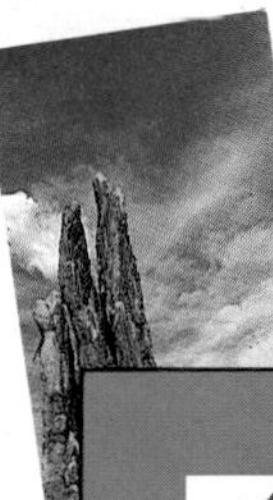

...he Gods is a ...ation created ...e than 50

...idge leads to the ...rt of Vail. ...kiers, including ...ent Gerald Ford, ...do snow because it ...wdery.

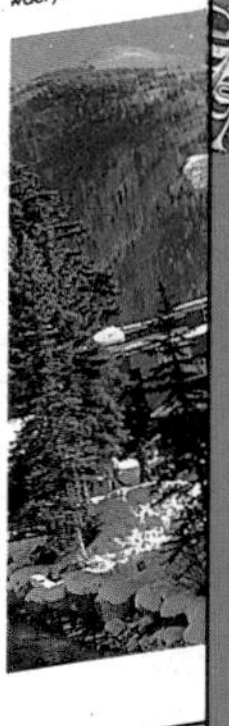



## CONSTITUTION OF THE UNITED STATES

The U.S. Constitution is "the supreme law of the land." It was written in 1787 at a convention held in Philadelphia. The 55 delegates attending became known as the Founding Fathers. They included James MADISON, George WASHINGTON, and Benjamin FRANKLIN. The Constitution replaced the ARTICLES OF CONFEDERATION. After being ratified (approved) by nine states, it went into effect on June 21, 1788. By 1790, the four other states had ratified it.

The Constitution sets out a *federal* system of government. This means that there is a national (federal) government and also state governments.

The Constitution also states that the United States is a *republic*. It has a PRESIDENT elected by the people. There is also a CONGRESS to make the laws, and a SUPREME COURT, the highest court in the land. The Founding Fathers ensured that there was a system of "checks and balances" between these three branches of government.

In 1791 a BILL OF RIGHTS was added to the Constitution. This took the form of ten amendments that set out the rights of individuals. Since then, 16 more amendments have been added.

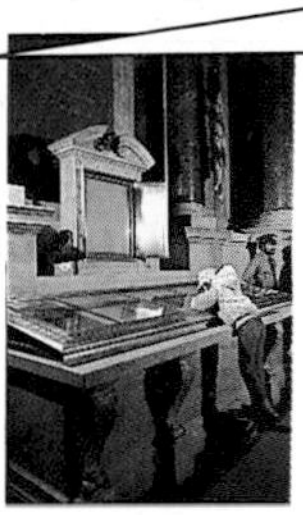

▲ *The Declaration of Independence, Constitution, and Bill of Rights are on display in the National Archives in Washington, D.C.*

## CONSTITUTION ACT

The Constitution Act of 1982 revised the Canadian Constitution. Until that year, the BRITISH NORTH AMERICA ACT of 1867 served as Canada's constitution. Even though Canada has long been an independent country, the British North America Act could be amended only by the British Parliament. In 1982, however, the British Parliament passed the Canada Act. It gave Canada the right to change its own constitution. The Constitution Act of 1982 is part of the Canada Act. One addition is the Charter of Rights and Freedoms, which is similar to the American BILL OF RIGHTS.

**The Constitutional Convention, which wrote the U.S. Constitution, was attended by 55 delegates representing 12 states. Rhode Island did not attend. Thirty-four of the delegates were lawyers; most of the others were merchants or planters. The great majority of the delegates were young men in their twenties and thirties. At 81, Benjamin Franklin was the oldest of those present.**

## CONSTITUTION, U.S.S.

The famous warship U.S.S. *Constitution* was nicknamed Old Ironsides for its ability to withstand enemy fire. Launched in Boston in 1797, it was one of the first frigates built for the U.S. Navy. It measured 204 feet (62 m)



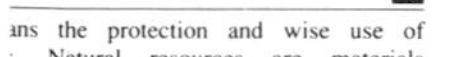

**SUBJECT SYMBOLS** allow you to find quickly those entries on a similar theme. They will make browsing more interesting.

**FASCINATING FACTS** and bits of additional information appear throughout in "nuggets." Many are surprising.

**SPECIAL FEATURE** entries are longer and more detailed than most entries. They will help you with school projects. You will find a list of these special feature entries at the back of the encyclopedia.

## ART

The works of art on these pages show you some of the wonderful variety of American creative styles. Further examples of American art can be found in the articles on PAINTING, SCULPTURE, ARCHITECTURE, and FOLK ART. You might also want to look up the names of individual artists in the Index.

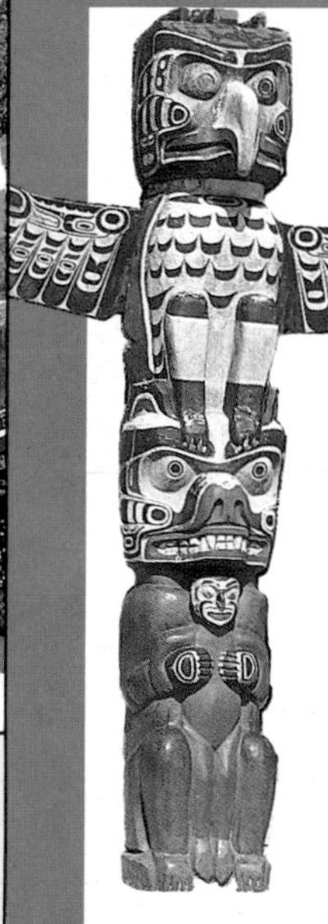

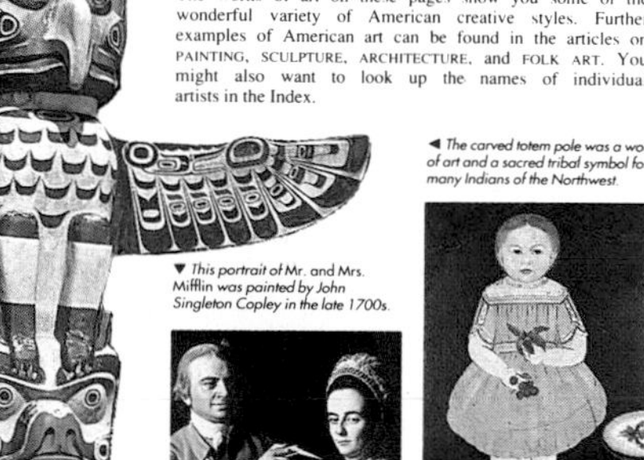

◀ *The carved totem pole was a work of art and a sacred tribal symbol for many Indians of the Northwest.*

▼ *This portrait of Mr. and Mrs. Mifflin was painted by John Singleton Copley in the late 1700s.*

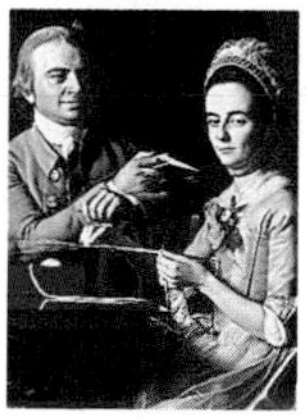

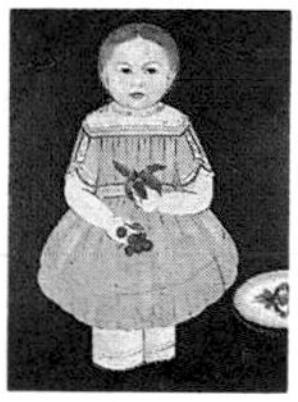

▲ *Girl in Pink, by an unknown artist, is an example of American primitive art from the late 1700s or early 1800s. Primitive art is characterized by its simplicity. This is because most primitive artists were not trained artists.*

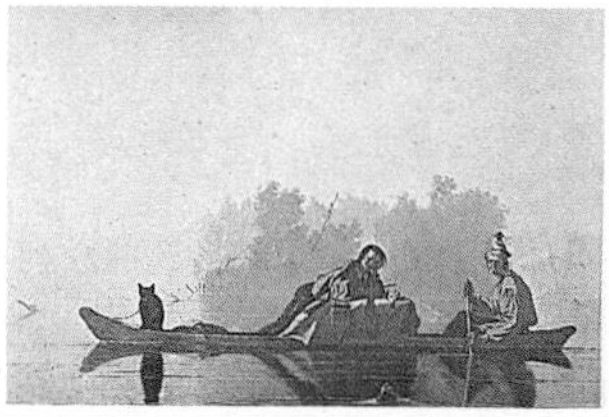

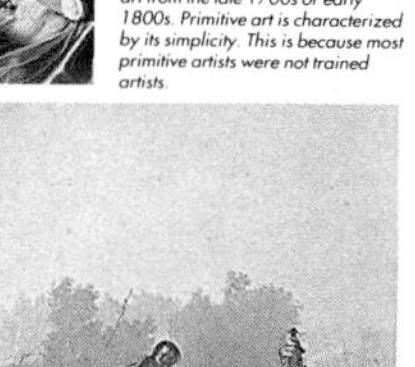

► *George Caleb Bingham recorded this scene of river life, called Fur Traders Descending the Missouri, in the mid-1800s.*

▼ *A statue of George Washington in Philadelphia stands as an example of American civic art for public buildings.*

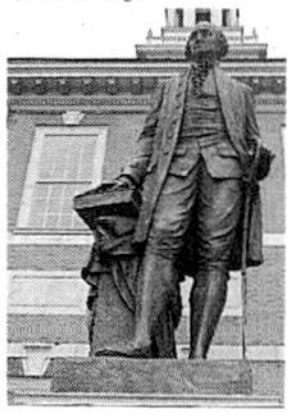

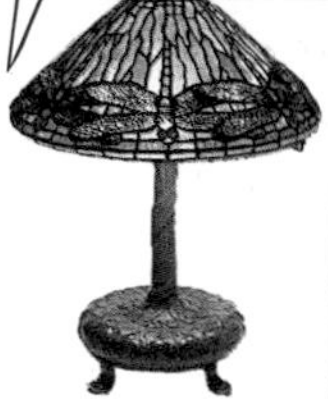

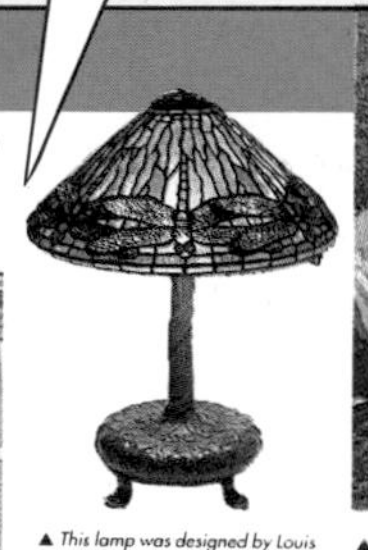

▲ *This lamp was designed by Louis Comfort Tiffany, a major American stained glass designer of the late 1800s. Tiffany helped establish style called art nouveau.*

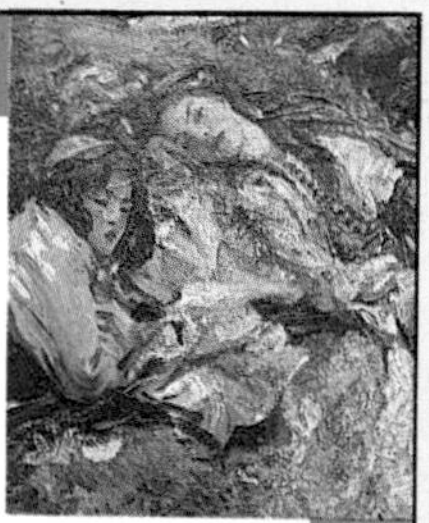

▲ *Although John Singer Sargent was first known for his portraits, in the late 1800s he painted scenes from the countryside, as in this painting The Brook.*

▼ *Built in 1929, the Chrysler Building in New York City shows the influence of the art deco movement with its sleek, streamlined shape and use of geometric patterns.*

► *Mirror Shadow XVI is typical of the work of sculptor Louise Nevelson. Most of her sculptures are made out of wood or use objects from everyday life.*

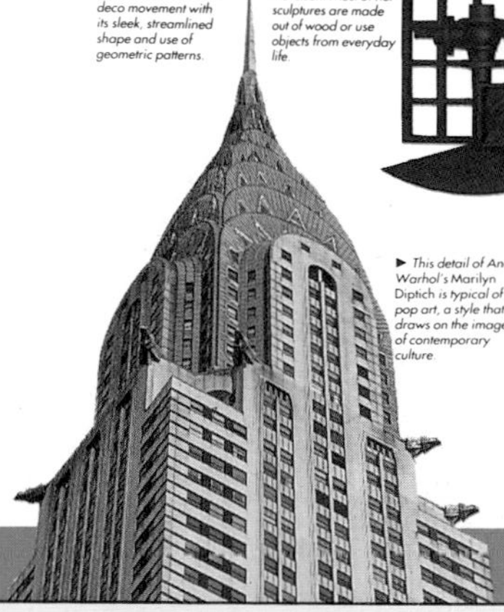

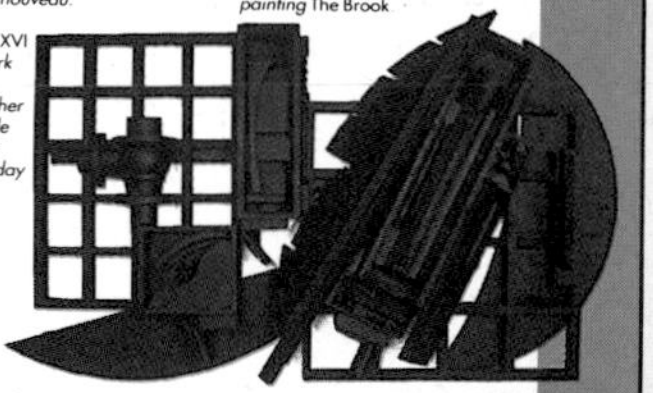

► *This detail of Andy Warhol's Marilyn Diptich is typical of pop art, a style that draws on the images of contemporary culture.*

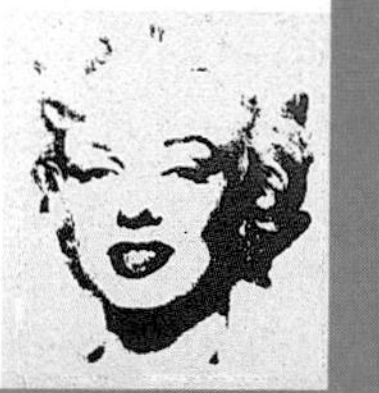

*Products of American* AGRICULTURE *are exported around the world.*

## ABERNATHY, Ralph David 

The Reverend Ralph David Abernathy (1926–1990) was a leader of the CIVIL RIGHTS movement. Born into a poor farming family in Alabama, he graduated from college and became a Baptist minister. Abernathy became friends with Dr. Martin Luther KING, Jr., in Montgomery, Alabama. The two of them led the successful protest against segregation on the buses there. Abernathy and King worked together in many other civil rights demonstrations and sometimes were arrested and went to jail together. After King was murdered in 1968, Abernathy succeeded him as president of the Southern Christian Leadership Conference. He held this position until 1977. Abernathy told the story of his role in the civil rights movement in the book *The Walls Came Tumbling Down.*

## ABOLITIONISTS 

Abolitionists was the name given to people in 19th-century America who urged that SLAVERY be ended, or abolished. In 1808 the importation of slaves was outlawed in the United States. But slavery itself continued to be legal in 11 southern states, where plantation owners depended on it to make a profit. When abolitionists began to condemn slavery more severely, some states responded by passing harsher laws against runaway slaves. They even made it unlawful for masters to free their slaves.

Such actions won more people to the abolitionist cause. By 1840 more than 150,000 people were members of abolitionist societies. It was still not a popular

▼ *Many abolitionists were Quakers or New Englanders, but freed slaves such as Frederick Douglass also joined the movement. William Lloyd Garrison founded a newspaper,* The Liberator, *which tried to make more people aware of the fight against slavery. Lucretia Mott was a Quaker who helped to found the American Anti-Slavery Society. Wendell Phillips, a New England orator, gave up his law practice to join the abolitionist cause.*

**Wendell Phillips**

**Lucretia Coffin Mott**

**William Lloyd Garrison**

**Frederick Douglass**

▲ *Rain Man* stars Tom Cruise and Dustin Hoffman hold two of the four Oscars won by the 1988 film at the Academy Awards. *Rain Man* was named best film, and Hoffman won the best actor award.

▼ *The Oscar was named accidentally in 1931 by an academy librarian, Margaret Hickman. When she saw the statuette she exclaimed, "Why, it looks like my Uncle Oscar!"*

cause, however, even in the North. Abolitionists' meetings were often broken up by mobs, and their printing presses were sometimes destroyed.

The abolitionists themselves did not agree about how slavery should be abolished. One group, led by William Lloyd Garrison, demanded an immediate end to slavery without any payment, or compensation, to the owners. Others wanted a gradual program of freedom, or emancipation, with compensation. Still another group, who came to be called "anti-slavery men," simply opposed the spread of slavery into the new states. Some abolitionists, such as Harriet Tubman, an escaped slave, helped other slaves flee to the North by way of the Underground Railroad.

Among the abolitionists were several famous writers. They included John Greenleaf Whittier, Julia Ward Howe, Harriet Beecher Stowe and the poet and essayist James Russell Lowell. Their works helped to awaken the public's conscience to the evils of slavery.

## ACADEMY AWARDS

The Academy Awards are special tributes to motion pictures released in the previous year and to those involved in making them, including film actors, actresses, writers, and directors. These awards have been presented each year since 1929.

The awards themselves, statuettes called Oscars, are given by the Academy of Motion Picture Arts and

Academy Award Winners: Best Film 1960–1992

| Year | | Year | |
|---|---|---|---|
| 1993 | *Schindler's List* | 1976 | *Rocky* |
| 1992 | *Unforgiven* | 1975 | *One Flew Over the Cuckoo's Nest* |
| 1991 | *The Silence of the Lambs* | 1974 | *The Godfather, Part II* |
| 1990 | *Dances with Wolves* | 1973 | *The Sting* |
| 1989 | *Driving Miss Daisy* | 1972 | *The Godfather* |
| 1988 | *Rain Man* | 1971 | *The French Connection* |
| 1987 | *The Last Emperor* | 1970 | *Patton* |
| 1986 | *Platoon* | 1969 | *Midnight Cowboy* |
| 1985 | *Out of Africa* | 1968 | *Oliver!* |
| 1984 | *Amadeus* | 1967 | *In the Heat of the Night* |
| 1983 | *Terms of Endearment* | 1966 | *A Man for All Seasons* |
| 1982 | *Gandhi* | 1965 | *The Sound of Music* |
| 1981 | *Chariots of Fire* | 1964 | *My Fair Lady* |
| 1980 | *Ordinary People* | 1963 | *Tom Jones* |
| 1979 | *Kramer vs. Kramer* | 1962 | *Lawrence of Arabia* |
| 1978 | *The Deer Hunter* | 1961 | *West Side Story* |
| 1977 | *Annie Hall* | | |

Sciences. All members of the academy are people who actually work as professionals in the film industry. Oscar winners are chosen by a vote among all the members.

Some famous winners of the Best Picture Award include *Gone With the Wind* (1939), *Casablanca* (1943), *Lawrence of Arabia* (1962), and *Rain Man* (1988). People may win an Oscar more than once in a lifetime. Jane Fonda won the Best Actress Award for *Klute* (1971) and for *Coming Home* (1978). Marlon Brando won the Best Actor Award for *On the Waterfront* (1954) and for *The Godfather* (1972).

▲ *Dean Acheson's book,* Present at the Creation: My Years in the State Department, *won a Pulitzer Prize for history.*

## ACHESON, Dean

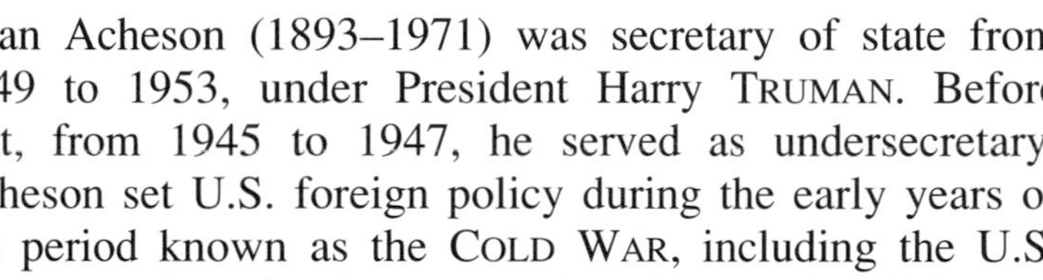

Dean Acheson (1893–1971) was secretary of state from 1949 to 1953, under President Harry TRUMAN. Before that, from 1945 to 1947, he served as undersecretary. Acheson set U.S. foreign policy during the early years of the period known as the COLD WAR, including the U.S. government's refusal to recognize Communist China. In 1947 he helped Secretary of State George C. MARSHALL devise the Truman Doctrine—economic aid aimed at keeping Greece and Turkey free of Soviet domination. He also played a part in setting up the Marshall Plan in 1947. In 1949 he helped create the NORTH ATLANTIC TREATY ORGANIZATION (NATO).

## ADAMS, Ansel

The work of the photographer Ansel Adams (1902–1984) expresses his love of the American landscape. Adams worked almost entirely in black and white. By carefully controlling the black and white tones, he produced powerful, haunting images, especially of the American West. His work helped to establish photography as an art form in its own right—not just a poor relation of painting. The photographs also awakened the public to the need to conserve America's unspoiled land. Adams was a campaigner for conservation, and his photographs helped to persuade people of the rightness of his cause. Adams also wrote a number of books on photography.

In 1940, Adams helped to set up a department of photography at New York City's Museum of Modern Art. Six years later, he founded a photography department at what is now the San Francisco Art Institute.

▼ *In 1946, Ansel Adams established the first college department of photography in California.*

John Adams
**Born:** October 30, 1735, in Braintree (now Quincy), Massachusetts
**Education:** Harvard College
**Political party:** Federalist
**Term of office:** 1797–1801
**Married:** 1764 to Abigail Smith
**Died:** July 4, 1826, in Quincy

John Adams was the first vice president of the United States and the second president. Adams was born in Massachusetts and studied to be a lawyer. He later became a leader in opposing British policies in the American colonies.

Adams was elected to the Massachusetts House of Representatives in 1771 and to the CONTINENTAL CONGRESS in 1774. In Congress he argued for American independence. In 1776 he helped draft the DECLARATION OF INDEPENDENCE.

In 1780, Adams helped draw up the state constitution of Massachusetts. He served as a minister to France, the Netherlands, and Britain. He helped to negotiate the treaty with Britain that ended the American REVOLUTION. In 1789 he became America's first vice president, under George WASHINGTON, the first president.

Two political parties were emerging at this time: the more conservative FEDERALISTS and the liberal Democratic-Republicans. Adams, a Federalist, believed in a strong federal government.

In 1796, Adams was elected president. Thomas JEFFERSON, a Democratic-Republican, became vice president. In office, Adams supported the Alien and Sedition Acts. The aim of these acts was supposedly to curb French revolutionaries who were trying to stir up feeling in the United States. Many people wanted to go to war with France, but Adams avoided it. He was criticized, however, by many people who believed that the Sedition Act was an attack on Americans' basic rights. In the election of 1800, Adams was defeated by Thomas Jefferson. Twenty-five years later he saw his son, John Quincy ADAMS, become president.

▼ *A drawing of the White House made in the early 1800s. The White House was not yet completed when President John Adams and his wife, Abigail, moved into it.*

## ADAMS, John Quincy

John Quincy Adams was the sixth president of the United States. He was the son of John ADAMS, the second president. Trained as a lawyer, he served abroad as a minister and was then elected U.S. senator from Massachusetts in 1803. Adams was a FEDERALIST, but his party forced him to resign his seat because he supported many Democratic-Republican goals.

President James MADISON appointed Adams minister to Russia and Britain, and Adams negotiated the treaty that ended the WAR OF 1812 with Britain. From 1817 to 1825, Adams was President James MONROE's secretary of state. In 1818 he negotiated the treaty with Britain that placed the portion of the U.S.–Canadian border that lies west of the Great Lakes along the 49th parallel.

The next year Adams negotiated a treaty with Spain that gave Florida to the United States. Adams also helped draw up the MONROE DOCTRINE. It stated that the United States would no longer allow European countries to colonize the Americas.

*▼ The Erie Canal was opened at the beginning of President John Quincy Adams's term of office. It enabled ships to pass between New York City and the Great Lakes.*

In the 1824 presidential election, Adams beat Andrew JACKSON by gaining the support of Henry CLAY. Jackson was very bitter and opposed Adams for his entire term of office. Many roads and canals were built during this period, and the country prospered. But for Adams the time was a political failure. In 1828 he lost the election to Jackson. From 1831 until his death in 1848, Adams served in the House of Representatives. There he fought for the protection of Indian tribes and against slavery. For years he argued against the "gag rules," which prevented any discussion of slavery. Finally, in 1844, Adams succeeded in getting them repealed.

**John Quincy Adams**
**Born:** July 11, 1767, in Braintree (now Quincy), Massachusetts
**Education:** Harvard College
**Political party:** National Republican
**Term of office:** 1825–1829
**Married:** 1797 to Louisa Catherine Johnson
**Died:** February 23, 1848, in Washington, D.C.

▲ *The cousin of President John Adams, Samuel Adams was committed to the cause of American independence.*

## ADAMS, Samuel 

Samuel Adams (1722–1803) was one of the driving forces in the American colonists' fight for independence from Great Britain. After his graduation from Harvard and several brief and unsuccessful careers, Adams turned to Massachusetts politics. He soon became convinced that the British Parliament had no right to pass laws for the American colonies, since the colonists had no representatives there. Parliament's power to tax the colonists was especially resented, and Adams was one of the first Americans to protest against this "taxation without representation." His activities ranged from writing articles against Britain to stirring up riots, such as the ones that broke out in Boston in 1765 against the hated STAMP ACT. Adams was also a leader of the BOSTON TEA PARTY. Like his more moderate cousin John ADAMS he was a delegate to the CONTINENTAL CONGRESS and a signer of the DECLARATION OF INDEPENDENCE. From 1794 to 1797, he was governor of Massachusetts.

**Jane Addams's visit to a *settlement house* in London's East End while on a visit to Europe gave her the idea of setting up a similar refuge in Chicago. In its first year, more than 5,000 of Chicago's poor, many of them recent immigrants, passed through the doors of Hull House. Volunteers gave them practical lessons in English and other subjects.**

## ADDAMS, Jane 

Born into a prosperous family, Jane Addams (1860–1935) became an outstanding social reformer. Concern about Chicago's large and poor immigrant population led her and a friend, Ellen Gates Starr, to establish Hull House in 1889. This was America's first settlement house, providing services to the poor. Among the facilities at Hull House were a day nursery, lodging for working girls, a community kitchen, and vocational training. Jane Addams also worked for many other causes, including world peace, factory inspections, an eight-hour working day for women, and women's suffrage (voting rights). In 1931 she was awarded the Nobel Peace Prize.

## ADIRONDACK MOUNTAINS 

The Adirondack Mountains are in northeastern NEW YORK State. They cover about 5,000 square miles (13,000 km$^2$). The region has hundreds of peaks. The highest is Mount Marcy, at 5,344 feet (1,629 m) above sea level.

There are more than 200 lakes, including lakes George

and Placid. Lake Tear of the Clouds, on Mount Marcy, is the highest source of the HUDSON RIVER. There are many gorges, waterfalls, streams, ponds, and swamps in the Adirondacks, and the region is noted for its beautiful scenery. There are a number of parks and resorts. Adirondack Park covers a large portion of the region, and within it is the Adirondack Forest Preserve.

In 1858 this wilderness inspired a poem, "The Adirondacks," by Ralph Waldo EMERSON. The mountains were named after a local Indian tribe in 1609. The word meant "tree eaters." People's activities in the mountains since colonial times can be studied at the Adirondack Museum, near Blue Mountain Lake.

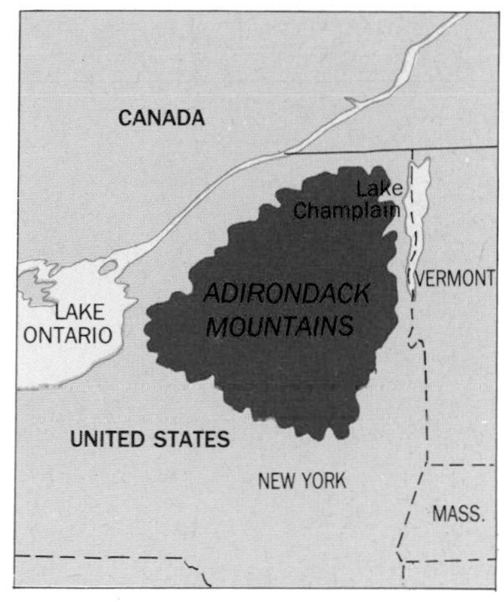


▲ *The Adirondack Mountains of upstate New York are a northern branch of the Appalachian range.*

◀ *Some of the rocks that make up the Adirondack Mountains are more than 1 billion years old.*

## ADOBE *See* Pueblos

## ADVERTISING

The United States has the world's largest advertising industry, with more than 6,500 agencies. Over $100 billion is spent on advertising every year. The center of the industry is New York City, and many of the largest agencies are based there. The term "Madison Avenue" is often used to refer to the advertising business because that is the New York street where most of the agencies were originally located.

The agencies compete with one another to handle advertising for many different businesses. The largest agency is Young & Rubicam. The two largest advertisers are Procter & Gamble, which makes many of the soaps and detergents used

▼ *Posters such as this one, printed in 1895, attract attention from passersby and are still an effective form of advertising.*

► *The bright lights of Broadway in New York City advertise everything from movies to new technology.*

| The Top 10 Advertisers in the U.S. (by spending) |
|---|
| 1. Procter & Gamble |
| 2. Philip Morris |
| 3. Sears, Roebuck |
| 4. General Motors |
| 5. Grand Metropolitan |
| 6. PepsiCo |
| 7. AT&T |
| 8. McDonald's |
| 9. Kmart |
| 10. Time Warner |

in American homes, and the Philip Morris Company, which is involved in the tobacco and food industries. Both spend over $2 billion a year. Sears, Roebuck and General Motors spend over $1 billion.

More than $22 billion is spent on TELEVISION commercials each year. NEWSPAPER advertising costs about $9.7 billion, MAGAZINE advertising about $6.7 billion, and RADIO advertising $766 million.

Advertising laws, both state and federal, protect the public from false advertising. Federal laws are enforced by the Federal Trade Commission. It supervises all types of advertising and tries to make sure that advertising claims are not misleading.

▼ *Engineers use computers to create advanced aircraft designs.*

## AEROSPACE INDUSTRY

The aerospace industry builds and looks after aircraft, missiles, and space vehicles. The term *aerospace* was coined in the 1950s by the U.S. Air Force. It described the first airplanes that could fly outside the Earth's atmosphere. Since then aerospace has become the country's most advanced industry. Aerospace projects cost millions, and sometimes billions, of dollars.

Some aerospace companies, such as Lockheed and BOEING, make complete aircraft. Others, such as General Dynamics and Northrop, specialize in landing gear, in-flight computers, and other instruments. Much of their work is for the armed forces and the government's space program. The 1991 budget of the National

◀ *Aerospace companies have already produced aircraft and spacecraft. Today research is being conducted to create a plane that will travel both in the Earth's atmosphere and in space.*

Aeronautics and Space Administration (NASA) was almost $14 billion. In 1991 the top ten aerospace companies in the United States did over $124 billion worth of business.

Major events affect the aerospace industry directly. The triumphant moon landing in 1969 was a success for the whole industry. But aerospace firms were hurt by the *Challenger* space shuttle disaster in 1986. (See also AVIATION; AIR TRANSPORTATION.)

The Top 10 Aerospace Companies in the U.S. (by sales)

1. Boeing
2. United Technologies
3. McDonnell Douglas
4. Allied-Signal
5. Lockheed
6. General Dynamics
7. Textron
8. Martin Marietta
9. Northrop
10. Grumman

## AGASSIZ, Louis

Jean Louis Agassiz (1807–1873) was a Swiss-born naturalist and geologist. He spent two years in Paris doing research and became a professor in 1832.

Agassiz's great interest was the study of fish (ichthyology). He wrote his first major work on them when he was only 22. Shortly after this, he wrote a *History of the Fresh Water Fishes of Central Europe*.

Agassiz became fascinated by extinct fish—fish that now exist only in fossil form. He wrote a great work on fossil fish which described more than 1,700 species. Agassiz also showed that vast glaciers once covered much of the Northern Hemisphere.

In 1846, Agassiz came to the United States, and became a professor of geology and zoology (the study of animals) at Harvard two years later. Agassiz was an important popularizer of science, and has been called the "best friend that students ever had."

▼ *Louis Agassiz believed that at one time much of the Earth's surface was covered by glaciers. Lake Agassiz, a glacial lake that once covered North Dakota, Minnesota, and southern Manitoba, was named in his honor.*

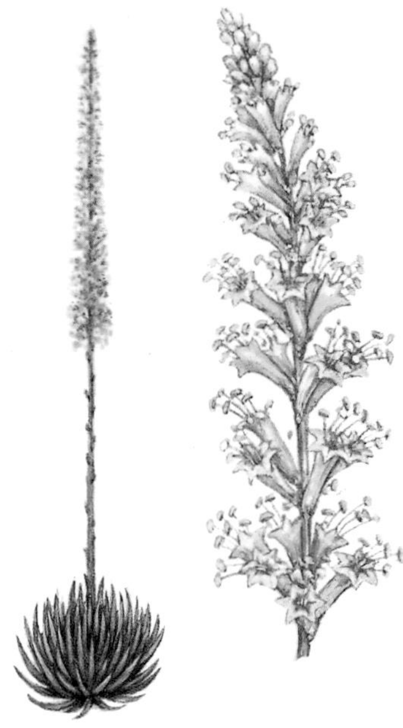

▲ *The agave, or century plant, and its flowers. Mexicans use the sap of some agave plants to make alcoholic drinks such as tequila.*

## AGAVE

Agave is the name of a family of desert plants. In the United States agaves grow in the South and the West. They have thick, sharp-edged leaves, and flowers borne on a tall stalk up to 40 feet (12 m) high. Some varieties live for 60 years before they flower. A common type of agave was once thought to flower only once every 100 years and then die—thus it has also come to be called the century plant.

The leaves of the agave die after the plant has produced flowers, but the base does not die and will produce new plants.

## AGRICULTURE

Agriculture means cultivating the land. It includes not only growing crops but also raising livestock. In the United States more land—over 1 billion acres (400 million ha)—is used for farming than for anything else. Agriculture accounts for only about 2 percent of the total national income, but U.S. produce feeds not only Americans but people in other countries as well. The United States exports about $40 billion worth of food each year.

Many of the more than 2 million farms in the United States have been family farms ever since the days of the pioneers and the HOMESTEAD ACT. The pioneers set the agricultural pattern for the country as they moved

▼ *Dairy farms, such as this one in Pennsylvania, keep Holstein cows because they are the best producers of milk.*

◄ *Combine harvesters are used to cut and separate the grain (seeds) from the rest of the wheat. On large midwestern farms, a combine harvester operated by one person can harvest in a day what it once took many workers weeks to do.*

west. By the early 1900s, different regions, or belts, were specializing in different crops. Many of these belts still specialize today in the same way. Over the last 50 years the number of farms has steadily decreased, while the size of farms has increased. This is largely because of improved farming methods and laborsaving machines that make farm work faster and much more efficient.

CORN is the most important crop grown in the United States. It is grown in most states, but especially in the fertile region known as the Corn Belt, stretching from Indiana to Nebraska. The United States grows 44 percent of the world's corn. The soybean is now the second most important crop, and in several states it is the main crop. The United States grows more than half

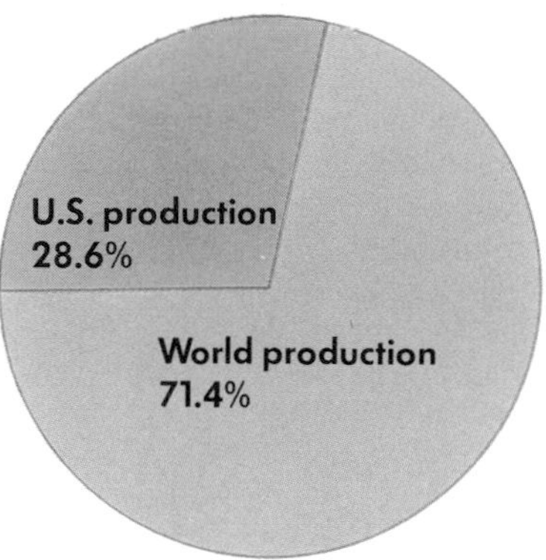


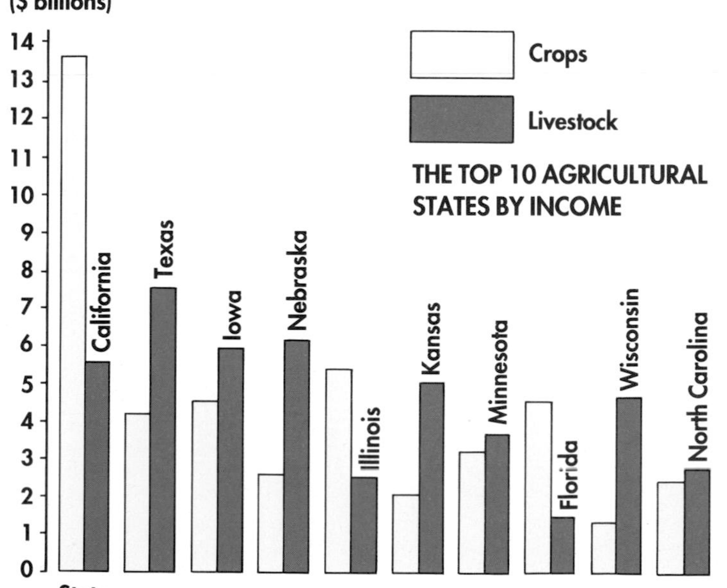


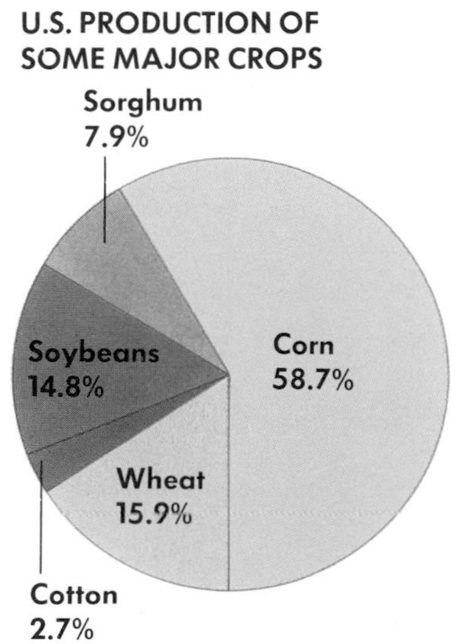

► *Colonial farmers used a homemade plow to prepare their fields for planting. An iron spade on the bottom cut and lifted the soil.*

of all the soybeans in the world.

Many farmers join marketing cooperatives, which help them to find the best markets for their products. Farm organizations lend support to farmers, and federal and state laws set such things as minimum farm prices and standards of quality for farm products.

**Over the last 150 years, new technology has made farming much more productive. In 1850 the average farmer could grow only enough food to feed five people; today the average farmer can produce enough to feed almost 80 people.**

## AILEY, Alvin

The Alvin Ailey American Dance Theater, formed in New York in 1958, is one of the most exciting and popular DANCE companies performing today. Its founder, Alvin Ailey (1931–1989), studied modern dance under such great names as Doris Humphrey and Martha GRAHAM. But he also danced in Broadway shows, and the dances he created for his own company are generally livelier and more colorful than most modern dance. Although the company is now multiracial, many of its dances are about the experiences of black people. The most famous of these is *Revelations.* Basically about religion, it is set to the music of spirituals. Ailey often chose jazz and blues for his dances.

**The Alvin Ailey American Dance Theater has been the starting point for at least one successful career. The pop star Madonna began her career in New York City as a dancer with Ailey's company.**

► Caverna Magica, *one of Alvin Ailey's spectacular dances, is performed here by April Berry and Company. In 1987, Alvin Ailey received the Scripps Dance Award for his lifetime contribution to dance.*

## AIR FORCE, United States

The U.S. Air Force is the youngest branch of the armed forces. Its responsibilities are large and call for a huge number of different types of aircraft (about 7,000 in all) and almost 500,000 airmen and women.

The Air Force has three major jobs. One is to defend the United States and its allies against attack from enemies. A network of radar stations, backed up by airborne radar planes called AWACS, can detect enemy missile or aircraft attacks. Fighter planes can then be called up to destroy them. The second and most important job during war is to attack enemies. Long-range bombers can drop nuclear and other bombs far behind enemy lines, and fighters can attack enemy troops and planes and support U.S. troops. The Air Force also transports U.S. troops to battle zones.

Perhaps its most important role, however, is that of a deterrent force—that is, to prevent the outbreak of war. It does this mainly by possessing large numbers of strategic nuclear weapons on land bases in the United States. Because their destructive power is so great, no enemy wants to risk the possibility that it will be destroyed by them. Originally the Army Air Corps, the Air Force became a separate service in 1947.

▲ *The Air Force was originally a branch of the U.S. Army. It was not until 1947 that it became an independent branch of the armed forces.*

◀ *Air Force uniforms have not changed dramatically in the corps' brief history.*

▼ *The F-15 jet fighter can break through the sound barrier within 19 seconds.*

**During 1927, just over 18,000 people traveled by air in the United States. By 1931, the number had jumped to nearly 400,000. In 1984, world airlines carried nearly 1 billion passengers. Worldwide, about 600 airlines are engaged in passenger and cargo operations, using about 10,000 aircraft.**

## AIR TRANSPORTATION

Air transportation is the fastest way of traveling within the United States. Airline networks connect all major cities with regular flights. There are about 20 scheduled passenger airlines in the United States. In 1991 alone, these airlines carried about 452 million passengers in the United States. Nearly half of those passengers were traveling along the "Northeast Corridor," the stretch of the East Coast from Washington, D.C., to Boston. This is the world's busiest air route.

Remote areas, such as most of Alaska, rely on airplanes to deliver food and medicine. Some "flying doctors" cover thousands of square miles just to make house calls. Their small planes are adapted to landing where there is no airport. Skis or pontoons are put over the wheels so the plane can land on snow or water.

► *Commercial airliners carry passengers and cargo all over the world. Some, such as this TriStar, can carry between 250 and 400 passengers.*

Airports in large cities are very busy. Chicago's O'Hare Airport is the world's busiest. Almost 60 million people pass through it every year. Some airports are so big that buses are needed to connect the terminals. The biggest airport in the United States, Dallas–Fort Worth, covers 17,500 acres (7,082 ha). Atlanta has the fastest growing airport in the United States. All larger airports have one or more additional terminals for handling cargo only. Air transportation in the United States is regulated by the Federal Aviation Administration, a government body. The FAA establishes safety standards for airports, qualifications for pilots, and licenses for aircraft. (See also AEROSPACE INDUSTRY; AVIATION.)

The 10 Busiest Airports in the U.S. (by number of passengers)

1. O'Hare International, Chicago
2. Dallas–Fort Worth Regional
3. Los Angeles International
4. Hartsfield International, Atlanta
5. San Francisco International
6. Stapleton International, Denver
7. John F. Kennedy International, NYC
8. Miami International
9. Newark, New Jersey
10. Boston, Mass.

*► An aircraft ground crewman wears earmuffs to protect his ears from the noise as he refuels an airliner.*

*▼ A plan of Hartsfield International Airport, Atlanta, which is one of the world's busiest airports. Passengers move between its huge terminals on an underground transit system.*

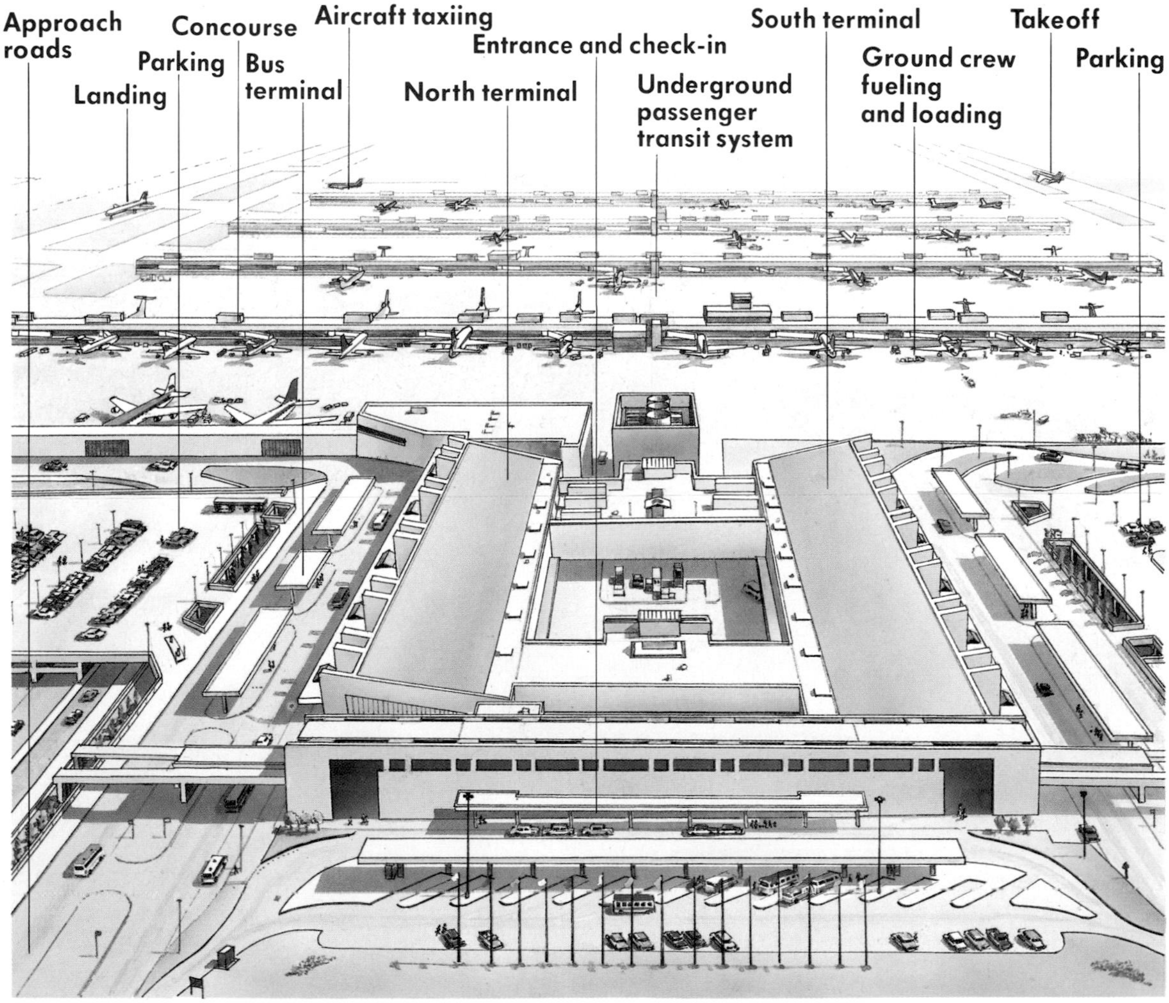

**Approach roads**
**Landing**
**Parking**
**Concourse**
**Bus terminal**
**Aircraft taxiing**
**North terminal**
**Entrance and check-in**
**Underground passenger transit system**
**South terminal**
**Ground crew fueling and loading**
**Takeoff**
**Parking**

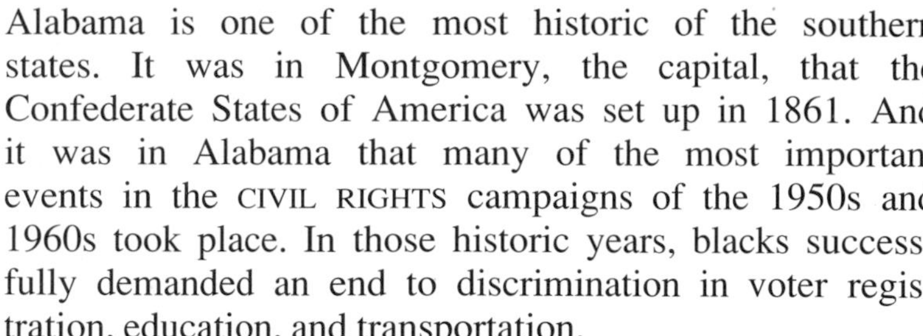

Alabama is one of the most historic of the southern states. It was in Montgomery, the capital, that the Confederate States of America was set up in 1861. And it was in Alabama that many of the most important events in the CIVIL RIGHTS campaigns of the 1950s and 1960s took place. In those historic years, blacks successfully demanded an end to discrimination in voter registration, education, and transportation.

Traditionally, Alabama has been a major farming region of the South. In the 1800s, when Alabama was a slave state, cotton was the most important crop. Right up to the early years of this century, cotton was still the state's major product. When a series of poor harvests struck Alabama, farmers began to plant different types of crops, becoming much more prosperous in the process. Cotton is still important to Alabama, but today crops such as corn, peanuts, and soybeans are also grown, and poultry and livestock are raised. Alabama is

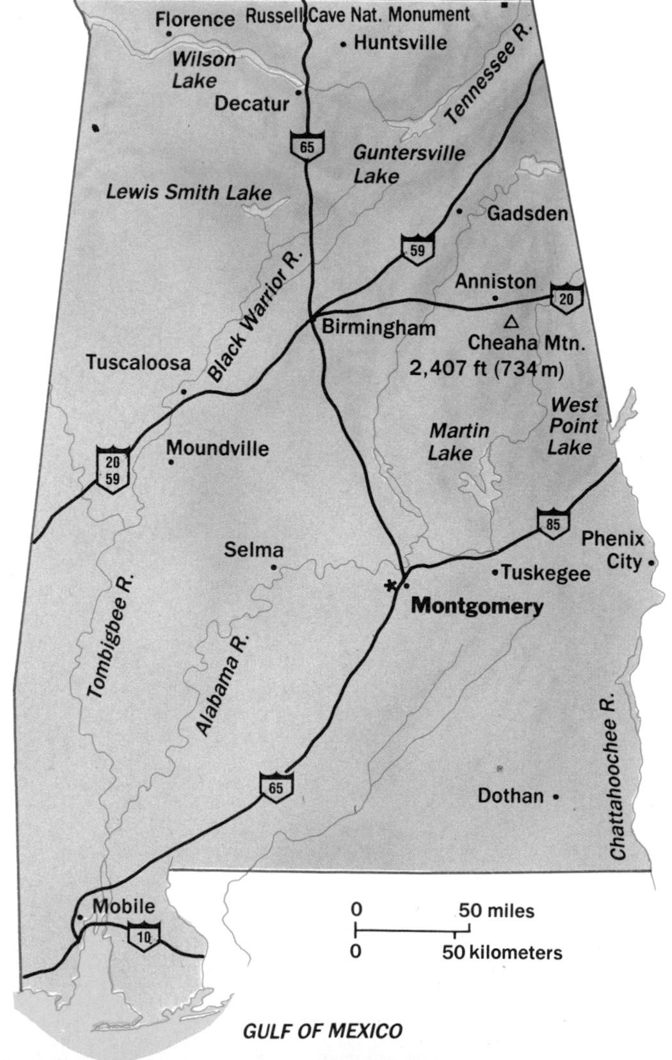


Alabama
**Capital:** Montgomery
**Area:** 50,750 sq mi (131,443 km²). Rank: 30th
**Population:** 4,040,587 (1990). Rank: 22nd
**Statehood:** December 14, 1819
**Principal rivers:** Tombigbee, Alabama, Tennessee
**Highest point:** Cheaha Mountain, 2,407 ft (734 m)
**Motto:** *Audemus Jura Nostra Defendere* (We Dare Defend Our Rights)
**Song:** "Alabama"

▲ *Paddle-wheel steamboats on the Tennessee River in northern Alabama. These steamboats were a common sight on rivers throughout the United States during the 1800s. They gradually disappeared as railroads and other more efficient methods of transportation took over.*

also one of the most important industrial states in the South. It has huge reserves of the three most important raw materials used in steel-making—coal, limestone, and iron ore.

The southern part of Alabama, especially toward the Gulf of Mexico, is fertile and low lying. This is where most of the state's farms are located. The north is hilly and forested, with many rivers and lakes. Many of Alabama's rivers have been dammed to provide power for hydroelectric power stations. The largest city in Alabama is Birmingham, the center of the state's flourishing steel-making industry.

► *White Hall, at Tuskegee University, the nation's oldest seat of learning for black Americans.*

**Places of Interest**

- Alabama Space and Rocket Center, Huntsville, houses the world's biggest collection of missiles.
- Mound State Monument, near Moundville, site of 20 Indian burial mounds.
- Jefferson Davis House, Montgomery, was home to the President of the Confederacy for the first few months of his term.

# ALASKA

Alaska is the largest state in the United States and the most northerly. It is at the northwest corner of North America. Almost a third of the state lies north of the Arctic Circle. Wilderness, glaciers, and mountains cover much of Alaska, and its unspoiled natural beauty attracts hundreds of thousands of visitors every year. MOUNT MCKINLEY, at 20,320 feet (6,194 m), is the highest peak in North America.

Much of Alaska has short summers and long, cold winters. Most Alaskans live along the southern coast, where the climate is mildest. Anchorage, the largest city, and Juneau, the capital, are located here. In the southwest the Aleutian Islands stretch westward for 1,100 miles (1,800 km).

The ancestors of the ALEUT people, the Inuit (ESKIMOS), and the American INDIANS were the first people to settle in the Western Hemisphere. More than 12,000 years ago, they traveled across a land bridge that connected Alaska and Asia. The Russians were the first

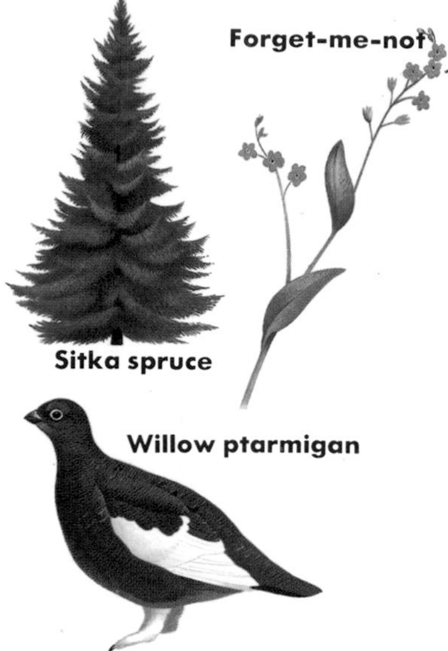

**Places of Interest**

- Klondike Gold Rush National Park commemorates the years of the gold rush.
- Ketchikan is famous for its collection of potlatch houses and totem poles.
- The Alaska Highway covers 1,422 mi (2,288 km) and allows access to much of Alaska's magnificent scenery.
- National parks include Denali National Park, Katmai National Park, and Glacier Bay National Park.

Europeans to settle Alaska. They came in search of furs in the 1700s. In 1867, U.S. Secretary of State William H. Seward bought Alaska from Russia for $7.2 million. Because it was so cold and desolate, many people called Alaska "Seward's Folly." But when gold was discovered in the late 1800s, thousands of Americans flocked there. Alaska became the 49th state in 1959, and less than ten years later oil was discovered along the Arctic coast. Today oil is the state's main source of income.

Alaska's population is just over half a million. It has fewer people than any other state except Wyoming. But between 1980 and 1990, many people moved to the United States' "last frontier," and its population increased by more than a third.

◀ *Cotton grass flowers during Alaska's brief summer, while in the background Mount McKinley remains covered in snow.*

◀ *Most of the 700 million barrels of petroleum produced in Alaska each year are shipped out through the Trans-Alaska Pipeline, which is 800 miles (1,300 km) long.*

▼ *A ride in a dogsled is a good way of enjoying Alaska's magnificent scenery.*

**Alaska**
**Capital:** Juneau, since 1900 (Sitka, 1884–1900)
**Area:** 570,374 sq mi ($1,477,267 \text{ km}^2$). Rank: 1st
**Population:** 550,043 (1990). Rank: 49th
**Statehood:** January 3, 1959
**Principal rivers:** Yukon, Kuskokwim
**Highest point:** Mt. McKinley, 20,320 ft (6,194 m)
**Motto:** North to the Future
**Song:** "Alaska's Flag"

# ALBERTA

Alberta is one of CANADA's three Prairie Provinces. In the south, huge farms and cattle ranches stretch across the rolling prairie lands. Alberta is one of the most ruggedly beautiful regions of North America. Many visitors come to the Canadian Rockies in the south-western part of the province. Here they ski in the winter and walk, swim, and admire the scenery in the summer. Others visit the mountains and forests of the north to hunt and fish.

Alberta produces more than 80 percent of Canada's oil and natural gas and 50 percent of its coal. It is also an important farming area, growing more oats and barley than any other province. Wheat and potatoes are also important crops. Many ranches raise cattle for beef.

EDMONTON is the capital of Alberta, but CALGARY, which is farther south, is the largest city. More than half of all Albertans live in and around these cities. Calgary is famous for its annual rodeo, the Calgary Stampede, which is held every June.

Europeans first settled Alberta during the 1700s. They were mostly fur traders. The building of the Canadian Pacific Railway in the 1800s and the discovery of oil in the 1940s drew many settlers to Alberta. Today it is one of Canada's richest and fastest growing provinces.

▲ *Moraine Lake in Banff National Park, established in 1885.*

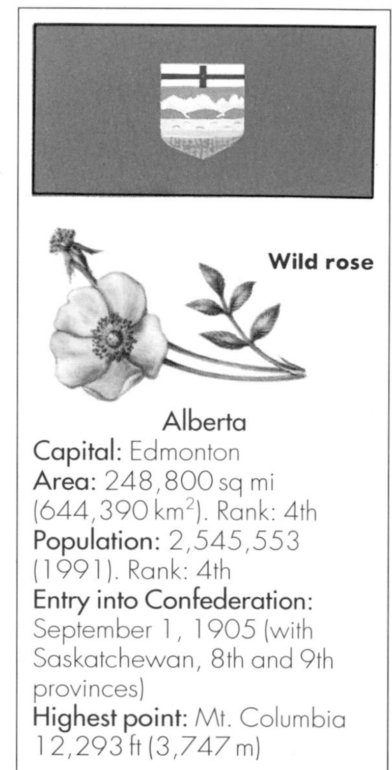


**Alberta**

**Capital:** Edmonton

**Area:** 248,800 sq mi (644,390 km$^2$). Rank: 4th

**Population:** 2,545,553 (1991). Rank: 4th

**Entry into Confederation:** September 1, 1905 (with Saskatchewan, 8th and 9th provinces)

**Highest point:** Mt. Columbia 12,293 ft (3,747 m)

## ALBUQUERQUE 

Albuquerque, with 384,736 people, is the largest city in NEW MEXICO and one of the most important cities in the Southwest. It was founded by Spanish settlers in 1706, and named for the Duke of Alburquerque, a governor of New Spain. Its Spanish and Indian heritage is still obvious in its low, flat-roofed buildings. In 1848, after the MEXICAN WAR, Albuquerque became part of the United States. Before 1945 it was a small city, depending on local farms for its prosperity. Since then it has become a major center for nuclear research and its population has quadrupled. The climate is warm and dry, with sun almost all year round.

▲ *The Church of San Felipe de Nerí, built in 1706 by Spanish missionaries, is one of Albuquerque's landmarks.*

## ALCOTT, Louisa May 

Louisa May Alcott (1832–1888) is best known as the author of *Little Women*, a novel about a family of four sisters at the time of the CIVIL WAR. The story is partly based on her own life.

The Alcotts lived in Concord, Massachusetts, where their friends included such famous writers as Ralph Waldo EMERSON, Henry David THOREAU, and Nathaniel HAWTHORNE. Louisa's father was a teacher and philosopher who tried his hand, unsuccessfully, at several ventures, including a communal farm. Louisa worked from an early age to help support the family. During the Civil War she served as an army nurse, an experience described in *Hospital Sketches*. After the success of *Little Women*, she wrote other books for children, including the sequels *Little Men* and *Jo's Boys*.

▼ *"Buzz" Aldrin stepped onto the moon 18 minutes after Neil Armstrong. Together they set up scientific experiments and collected rock samples.*

## ALDRIN, Edwin, Jr. 

Edwin "Buzz" Aldrin (1930– ) was the second man to walk on the moon. Born in New Jersey, Aldrin graduated from the U.S. Military Academy in 1951. After a career as a pilot he joined the SPACE PROGRAM as an astronaut. In 1966 he set a record with his 5½-hour space walk on the Gemini 12 flight. On July 20, 1969, the Apollo 11 lunar module landed on the moon, carrying Aldrin and Neil ARMSTRONG. Later, the two flew the lunar module back to the command module, and the mission splashed down safely in the Pacific Ocean four days later.

▼ *The United States produces about 85 million tons of alfalfa every year, more than any other country in the world.*

## ALEUTS

The Aleuts are the native inhabitants of the Aleutian Islands, about 70 islands that extend in a curved line from the southwestern corner of ALASKA. They are related to the ESKIMOS and speak a similar language. When Russia began colonizing the islands in the 1700s, about 25,000 Aleuts lived there. They lived by hunting and fishing and were skilled in basketwork and in carving stone, bone, and ivory. Each village had its own chief, an office that was usually hereditary—that is, passed on from father to son. By the mid-1900s the Aleut population had declined to about 1,300.

## ALFALFA

Alfalfa is a plant that is used to feed many types of animals, especially dairy cows and beef cattle. It is rich in the nutrients they need. Because there are many different types of alfalfa and because it is easy to grow, alfalfa is farmed all across the United States. Most farmers feed it to animals as hay; this is alfalfa that has been cut and allowed to dry. Others store it in silos without drying it; this is called silage. Some farmers let their animals graze on alfalfa where it grows.

## ALGER, Horatio

▼ *The Algonquins were farmers as well as hunters and fishermen: They grew beans, squash, and corn. The corn was then ground with a wooden mortar and pestle.*

The "rags-to-riches" stories of Horatio Alger (1832–1899) are generally thought to express the "American Dream." Many people apply the term "Horatio Alger story" to the lives of millionaires who have achieved success through hard work and cleverness. In fact, in Alger's books, virtue and good luck are the main ingredients. The typical Alger hero is a poor, fatherless boy who performs some act of kindness for a rich man, who then gives the boy a fortune. Alger himself was not a success. He earned a modest income as chaplain in a boys' lodging house and sold his books for small fees to publishers who made a fortune from them.

## ALGONQUINS

Algonquin, or Algonkin, is a name that refers to American INDIANS who originally lived in the eastern provinces of CANADA. They included more than one tribe.

The term "Algonquian" (Algonkian) refers to the group of related languages that these tribes spoke. The first Bible that was printed in the American colonies used one of the Algonquian languages called "Natick." During the FRENCH AND INDIAN WAR the Algonquins fought on the side of the French.

## ALI, Muhammad 

▲ *Muhammad Ali combined speed with sudden attacks. He said he could "float like a butterfly but sting like a bee."*

Muhammad Ali (1942– ) was the only boxer to win the world heavyweight title three times. Born Cassius Clay in Lexington, Kentucky, he won an Olympic gold medal in 1960. After turning professional, he defeated Sonny Liston to win the heavyweight title in 1964. In 1967 he joined the Nation of Islam (Black Muslims). When he refused to go into the armed forces for religious reasons, Ali was stripped of his title. The U.S. Supreme Court reversed this decision four years later. Ali regained his title in 1974. He lost it to Leon Spinks in 1978 but regained it later that year. He retired in 1979 but fought again, unsuccessfully in 1980 and 1981.

▲ *In the early hours of May 10, 1775, Ethan Allen and a band of 83 men attacked the British garrison at Fort Ticonderoga.*

## ALLEN, Ethan 

Ethan Allen (1738–1789) was a great patriot during the American REVOLUTION. He gained his first military experience fighting for the British in the FRENCH AND INDIAN WAR. After this he settled in the New Hamp-

**Neither American nor British casualties resulted from the attack on the garrison at Fort Ticonderoga. Ethan Allen's troops surprised the occupants of the garrison during a night raid. Allen is said to have confronted the sleepy British lieutenant Jocelyn Feltham shouting, "Come out of there, you damned old rat." When asked on whose authority he was acting, Allen replied, "In the name of the Great Jehova and the Continental Congress." Lieutenant Feltham surrendered immediately.**

shire Grants, land that became part of Vermont. In the early 1770s the ownership of this land was given by the British to New York. Allen formed the Green Mountain Boys to fight against New York's claim.

In 1775, in one of the first battles of the American Revolution, Allen and his Green Mountain Boys took Fort Ticonderoga from the British. After the war, he continued his fight for Vermont's statehood and eventually retired to the Vermont town of Burlington.

## ALLIGATOR

The American alligator is a large REPTILE that lives in rivers, lakes, and swamps in the southeastern United States. It grows up to 19 feet (5.8 m) long, but most are shorter. Alligators eat fish, frogs, snakes, birds, small mammals, and even young deer. They are strong swimmers and will wait for hours for their prey.

The female alligator lays 20 to 70 eggs in a nest of grass, leaves, and mud. She covers them up and guards them ferociously for about two months until they hatch. Alligators are a protected species, and hunting them is carefully controlled.

▼ *Adult alligators hiss, and males also make bellowing noises. Young alligators croak like frogs.*

**The skin on an alligator's back is tough and ridged with many small bones. The skin on its belly, however, is smooth. Skin from the bellies of farmed alligators is still popular as a material for handbags and other goods.**

## ALVAREZ, Luis

Luis Alvarez (1911–1988) was a physicist who did much important research into the atom. To learn more about *subatomic* particles—particles inside the nucleus of the atom—Alvarez used a device called a bubble chamber in which the tracks of the tiny particles could be identified. He discovered a number of new particles. Some of these existed for only a short time, one for less than a second. In 1968, Alvarez was honored with the Nobel Prize for physics.

**A bubble chamber is basically a container filled with a special liquid under pressure. Particles that are too small to be seen are shot into the liquid. As they pass through it they create tracks of tiny bubbles. From photographs of these tracks scientists are able to measure the properties of the particles.**

◀ *A 17th-century map of Virginia. The first permanent European settlement was founded at Jamestown in 1607, more than 100 years after Columbus first reached the Americas.*

## AMERICA 

The term "America" refers to all the land and islands of the Western Hemisphere. The word comes from *Americus*, the Latin form of the name of the Italian navigator Amerigo VESPUCCI. From the Arctic coast in the north to the southern tip of Argentina in the south, America extends more than 9,500 miles (15,300 km). Together, these lands cover about 28 percent of the Earth's land surface.

America includes the continents of NORTH AMERICA and South America. Central America, which is geographically part of North America, lies between them. The narrowest point in Central America, the Isthmus of Panama, links the continents of North and South America. North and South America are sometimes referred to together as "the Americas."

Another way of dividing up the continent is on a cultural basis. North America includes CANADA and the UNITED STATES. Latin America, so-called because most people there speak the Latin-based languages Spanish or Portuguese, includes all the land and islands to the south of the United States.

**Many scientists believe that millions of years ago America was joined to Africa and Eurasia, forming one big landmass called Pangaea. About 200 million years ago this huge landmass broke up, and the continents began to drift to their present positions. This theory that the continents are moving slowly over the Earth's surface is called the *Continental Drift Theory*. Scientists predict that in about 50 million years the California coast will have broken away and drifted northward toward Alaska.**

# AMERICAN HISTORY
# A Timetable

1

| | |
|---|---|
| 18,000 B.C. | Ancestors of the American INDIANS from Asia are the first people to settle in North America. |
| A.D. 1000 | Vikings led by Leif ERICSSON land on the coast of North America. |
| 1492 | Christopher COLUMBUS lands in the New World. |
| 1607 | English settlers found JAMESTOWN SETTLEMENT in Virginia. |
| 1619 | Ships arrive in Jamestown with the first black slaves. |
| 1620 | Pilgrims found PLYMOUTH COLONY, Massachusetts. |
| 1681 | William PENN is granted a royal charter to set up a colony in what is now Pennsylvania. |
| 1754–1763 | The French and Indian War between France and Great Britain leads to British control of most of eastern North America. |

2

| | |
|---|---|
| 1770 | British troops kill five colonists and injure six others during the BOSTON MASSACRE. |
| 1773 | The BOSTON TEA PARTY takes place. |
| 1774 | The First CONTINENTAL CONGRESS meets in Philadelphia. |
| 1775 | The battles of LEXINGTON AND CONCORD mark the beginning of the American REVOLUTION. |
| 1776 | The DECLARATION OF INDEPENDENCE is adopted at Philadelphia on July 4. |
| 1781 | American forces defeat the British at Yorktown, Virginia. |
| 1783 | Britain recognizes U.S. independence in the Treaty of Paris. |
| 1788 | The U.S. CONSTITUTION comes into effect. |
| 1789 | George WASHINGTON and John ADAMS are elected first president and vice president of the new nation. |
| 1791 | The BILL OF RIGHTS becomes part of the Constitution. |
| 1803 | The United States buys the vast French territory between the Mississippi River and the Rocky Mountains under the terms of the LOUISIANA PURCHASE. |
| 1812–1815 | The United States and Great Britain fight the WAR OF 1812. |
| 1819 | Spain cedes Florida to the United States. |
| 1823 | The MONROE DOCTRINE warns European countries against interference in the Americas. |
| 1825 | The ERIE CANAL is completed. |
| 1836 | Texan revolutionaries defeat the Mexican army and declare Texas an independent republic. |

*The history of America starts with the history of the Indians. Indians of the Pacific Northwest carved this bird's head (1). In the early 1600s people like the Pilgrims settled in America hoping to build a better life for themselves (2). The painting* The Spirit of '76 *by Gilbert Stuart (3) captures the feeling that united the colonists in their fight for independence. Pioneers faced many dangers to open up the West in the early 1800s (4). The Civil War split the young nation in two, causing massive casualties (5). The Great Depression of the 1930s left many people starving and homeless (6). About 58,000 American soldiers lost their lives in the Vietnam War before U.S. troops pulled out in 1973 (7). When George Bush was sworn in as the 41st president of the U.S. in 1989 (8), he became the leader of one of the superpowers of the world.*

3

4

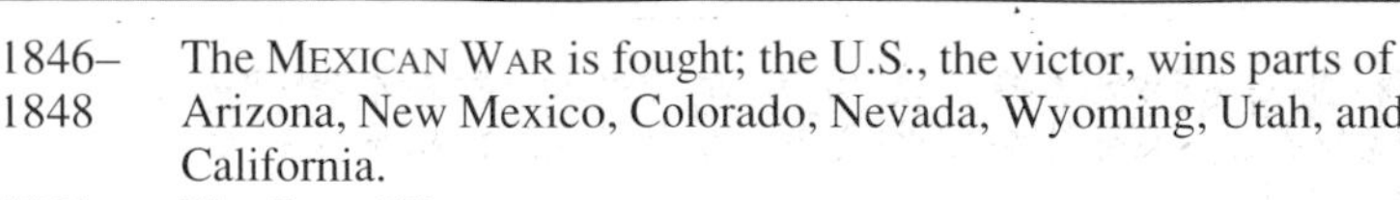

1846–1848 The Mexican War is fought; the U.S., the victor, wins parts of Arizona, New Mexico, Colorado, Nevada, Wyoming, Utah, and California.

5

6

7

8

1861 The Civil War starts.

1863 President Abraham Lincoln issues the Emancipation Proclamation.

1865 The Civil War ends; President Lincoln is assassinated; the 13th Amendment outlaws slavery.

1867 The United States buys Alaska from Russia.

1869 The world's first transcontinental railroad is completed across the United States.

1898 The U.S. defeats Spain in the Spanish–American War.

1914 The Panama Canal is opened.

1917 The United States enters World War I.

1918 World War I ends; the Allies and Germany accept President Woodrow Wilson's Fourteen Points as the basis for the peace negotiations.

1920 The 19th Amendment gives women the right to vote.

1929 The stock market crashes; the Great Depression begins.

1933 President Franklin D. Roosevelt introduces his New Deal program.

1941 The Japanese attack Pearl Harbor, and the United States enters World War II.

1945 The United States drops two atomic bombs on Japanese cities; World War II ends.

1948 Congress approves the Marshall Plan.

1950–1953 The United States, aided by other UN countries, fights in the Korean War.

1954 The Supreme Court rules that racial segregation in public schools is illegal.

1961 Alan Shepard is the first American in space.

1962 The USSR removes its missiles from Cuba, ending the Cuban Missile Crisis.

1963 Martin Luther King, Jr., leads a massive civil rights march on Washington, D.C.; President John F. Kennedy is assassinated.

1965 President Lyndon B. Johnson orders hundreds of thousands of U.S. combat troops into Vietnam.

1969 Neil Armstrong becomes the first person on the moon.

1973 The last American soldiers leave Vietnam.

1974 Richard M. Nixon becomes the first U.S. president to resign from office.

1981 The space shuttle *Columbia* makes its maiden flight.

1987 The United States and the USSR sign the first comprehensive nuclear arms control treaty.

1989 U.S. troops invade Panama and depose military leader Manuel Antonio Noriega.

1990 U.S. troops are sent to the Persian Gulf, following Iraq's invasion of Kuwait.

1991 In the Persian Gulf War, U.S. troops help free the Mideast nation of Kuwait from occupation by its neighbor Iraq.

1992 U.S. troops are sent to Somalia to restore order and help end famine.

The American Legion is one of the sponsors of American Education Week, which it founded in 1921. Every year, for a week during the fall, there are special exhibitions, television programs, and conferences that aim to inform the public about the work of education, its problems, and achievements. The idea of Education Week has now been taken up by a number of other countries.

## AMERICAN INDIANS *See* Indians, American

## AMERICAN LEGION

The American Legion is an organization of veterans of the armed forces—the U.S. Army, Navy, Marine Corps, and Air Force—who served during wartime. It was founded in 1919. Today the Legion has almost 3 million members. There are branches nationwide.

The American Legion provides a meeting place for men and women who are wartime veterans. There are many social activities in which members and their families can take part. But the Legion also tries to help veterans, assisting them with education, housing, or medical care. Some veterans have suffered injuries that make it difficult or impossible for them to go back to their normal lives. To help them, the Legion supports many long-stay hospitals and training programs.

## AMERICAN REVOLUTION *See* Revolution, American

## AMERICA'S CUP

The America's Cup is the world's most important yacht race. It is named after the yacht *America*, which in 1851 won a sailboat race around the Isle of Wight, England, beating 14 British yachts. Between that year and 1983, many attempts were made by British and other yachts to win back the Cup. But the races were always won by American boats. Then in 1983 an Australian boat, *Australia II*, won the Cup. It was the first time in 132 years that an American boat had been defeated. But in Australia in 1987 an American boat, *Stars and Stripes*, won the Cup back. *Stars and Stripes*, won again in 1988, and *America*$^3$ won in 1992.

▼ *In 1987,* Stars and Stripes *beat Australia's* Kookaburra III *to win back the America's Cup — the oldest trophy in international sport.*

## AMPHIBIANS

Amphibians are animals that have moist skin with no scales. Nearly all live part of their lives in the water and part on land. FROGS AND TOADS are amphibians, as are salamanders. One of the most common salamanders in the United States is the spotted salamander.

Most North American salamanders are 4 to 6 inches (10 to 15 cm) long. The hellbender, however, found in the eastern and central United States, is about 30 inches (75 cm) long. It lives in streams and under nearby rocks.

Some salamanders, known as sirens, look like eels. They are found mainly in the Southeast. The greater siren is 20 to 35 inches (50 to 90 cm) long. Salamanders called congo eels also look like eels. The most common species is up to 30 inches (75 cm) long and is found from Virginia to Louisiana. Unlike most other salamanders, congo eels have a vicious bite.

Mud puppies are a type of salamander found in eastern North America. In the South they are called water dogs. The arboreal salamander is found in Oregon, California, and New Mexico. It breathes only through its skin. Up to 30 live together in tree hollows.

▲ *The tiger salamander belongs to the mole salamander family, one of the seven salamander families that live in North America. North America has more species, or kinds, of salamanders than any other continent.*

## ANDERSON, Marian 

Marian Anderson (1902–1993) was the first black singer to perform at the Metropolitan Opera House in New York City. Her talent was discovered when she was only six, while she was singing in her church choir in Philadelphia. The church raised money for her singing lessons. Her voice developed into a rich contralto, and in her twenties she began a successful concert career. In 1939, Marian Anderson was prevented from singing in Washington's Constitution Hall because of her race. Eleanor ROOSEVELT, the wife of President Franklin D. ROOSEVELT, arranged for her to sing at the Lincoln Memorial instead; 75,000 people came to hear her. In 1955 she made her first appearance at New York City's Metropolitan Opera House in Verdi's *A Masked Ball*.

▼ *Although she is best known for her beautiful voice, Marian Anderson was also a delegate to the United Nations.*

▲ *A young prairie dog keeps an eye open for any sign of danger as it feeds.*

## ANIMAL LIFE OF NORTH AMERICA

North America has a rich variety of animals. Some, such as the PRONGHORN, American BISON, and PRAIRIE DOG, exist nowhere else in the world. North America is the home of the world's smallest flesh eater, the least WEASEL, and the largest flesh eater on land, the Kodiak BEAR. Each species lives in the habitat that suits it best. The frozen north is home to very few animals during the winter. But during the brief summer many animals, including the CARIBOU and WOLF, migrate there.

South of the Arctic region are the evergreen forests. Farther south are deciduous forests with broad-leaved trees. Animals of the forests include the elk, MOOSE, white-tailed DEER, wolf, COUGAR, wolverine, bear, FOX, BOBCAT, GROUNDHOG, SKUNK, PORCUPINE, SQUIRREL, CHIPMUNK, and OPOSSUM. Rivers and meadows attract such animals as the RACCOON, BEAVER, OTTER, and MUSKRAT. In the mountains are the Rocky Mountain GOAT and BIGHORN SHEEP.

In the center of the continent are the wide prairies. Here live animals that burrow into the ground, such as the prairie dog and the GOPHER. The BADGER, COYOTE, pronghorn, and even the bison roam the prairies.

Life in the hot, dry deserts includes LIZARDS, RATTLESNAKES, and mammals such as the JACKRABBIT and small RODENTS. And a rich variety of animals, including SEALS and SEA LIONS, WHALES, and sea OTTERS, lives around the coasts. (See also AMPHIBIANS; BIRDS; CRUSTACEANS; FISH; INSECTS; MOLLUSKS; REPTILES; see Index for other animal entries.)

▲ *The cougar is one of North America's largest predators. It is also known as the puma, mountain lion, panther, and catamount.*

► *In 1889 only 540 bison remained of the vast herds that once roamed the American prairies. Today about 15,000 live protected on game preserves.*

## ANNAPOLIS

Annapolis, the capital of MARYLAND, is located on the Severn River near the western shore of CHESAPEAKE BAY. It was founded in 1649 by English settlers and today it has a population of 33,187. Annapolis is one of the oldest and most historic cities in the United States. In 1708 its name was changed from Providence to Annapolis in honor of Queen Anne of England. The suffix *polis* is Greek for "city," so *Annapolis* means "Anne's city." Today, Annapolis is famous as the home of the U.S. Naval Academy and as a sailing base. The city still has many colonial buildings—its State House is the oldest state capitol in the nation. The treaty that ended the American REVOLUTION was signed in Annapolis, and the city was the capital of the United States from 1783 to 1784.

▲ *Students stand to attention at the U.S. Naval Academy, founded in Annapolis in 1845.*

## ANTHONY, Susan B. 

The fact that American women can vote owes a great deal to the work of Susan B. Anthony (1820–1906). She was born into a Quaker family in Massachusetts that believed firmly in the abolition of SLAVERY. As an adult she worked for the American Anti-Slavery Society. With the end of slavery during the Civil War, she began to fight for WOMEN'S RIGHTS. She was a leader of the National Woman Suffrage Association. She also fought for another cause, that of temperance (abstaining from alcoholic beverages). Anthony's work on behalf of women's rights won her international admiration. Fourteen years after her death Congress passed the Nineteenth Amendment giving women the vote.

▲ *Susan B. Anthony was arrested and fined $100 for voting in the 1872 presidential elections, held long before women won the right to vote.*

## ANTS 

Ants are INSECTS that live in groups called colonies. Some, such as thief ants and pharaoh's ants, are household pests, invading buildings in search of food. Carpenter ants chew holes in timber. The fire ant is a serious pest in the South. It builds large nests that get in the way of hay cutting. It also feeds on seeds and young plants and has a painful sting. Legionary ants live in warm parts of the United States and in Latin America. They travel in armies of thousands, devouring any insects that stray into their path.

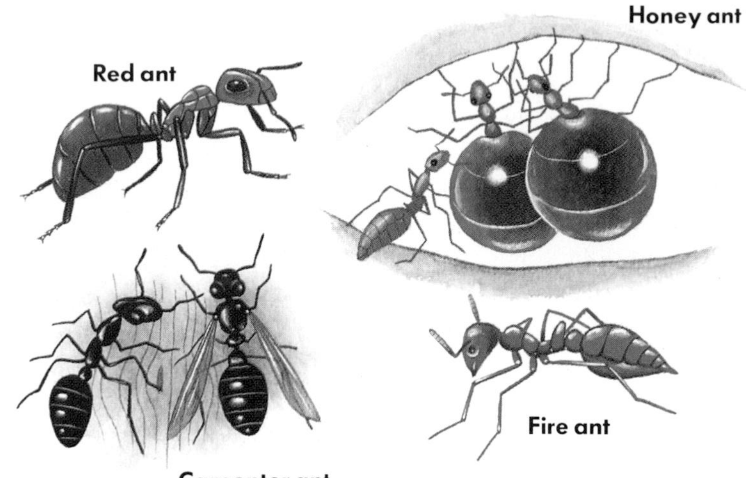


► *Four kinds of ants that are found in North America. Carpenter ants damage buildings by tunneling into wooden beams to make nesting space. Honey ant workers called repletes act as storage jars for the honeydew the ants gather. The back part of each replete's body, called the gaster, swells up as the honeydew fills it. Fire ants have a poisonous stinger that can pierce the skin. They have been known to attack baby birds and sting them to death. Red ants are also aggressive in defending their nests.*

Harvester ants collect and store seeds in their nests. They are found mainly on the Great Plains. Some ants tend small insects known as aphids, rather as people tend cows. They "milk" the aphids for their sweet liquid, or honeydew. Honey ants, found in the western United States, collect honeydew and store it inside certain worker ants called *repletes*. When an ant wants some honeydew, it taps the replete, which regurgitates (throws up) some of the liquid.

Leaf-cutting ants, found in Texas and Louisiana, strip leaves from plants. In their nests the ants use the leaves to grow a fungus that is used as food. There are no fungus-growing ants outside the New World.

Some ants use "slaves" to help with their work. They kidnap the young of a closely related species from a different nest. Many of the red ants and black ants found in North America are slave-maker ants.

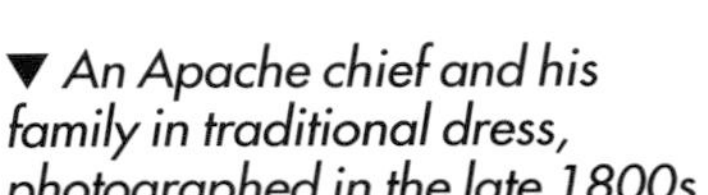
▼ *An Apache chief and his family in traditional dress, photographed in the late 1800s.*

## APACHES

The Apaches are a southwestern INDIAN tribe that originally came from Canada over 1,100 years ago. They were nomads, with no fixed settlements. The Apaches were much feared because they raided other tribes, stealing food and captives for use as slave labor. The very name Apache is thought to mean "enemy."

The Apaches stopped the spread of the Spanish from Mexico. Later they resisted the American settlers who opened the western frontier. A long series of wars under such legendary chiefs as COCHISE, Victorio, and GERONIMO finally ended in 1886. About 10,000 Apaches still live in Arizona, New Mexico, and Oklahoma.

## APOLLO PROGRAM See Space Program

## APPALACHIAN MOUNTAINS

The Appalachians form the great eastern MOUNTAIN range that runs for almost 1,600 miles (2,575 km) from Newfoundland in Canada as far south as Alabama. They are the oldest mountains in the United States. Wind and rain over tens of millions of years have eroded them and worn them down.

The Appalachians contain many smaller ranges of mountains. These include the White Mountains in New Hampshire, the Green Mountains in Vermont, the Catskills in New York, the Alleghenies in Pennsylvania, and the BLUE RIDGE MOUNTAINS, which run from Pennsylvania to North Carolina. The tallest peak in the Appalachians is Mount Mitchell, in the Black Mountains of North Carolina. It is 6,684 feet (2,037 m) high.

The forests of the Appalachians are important sources of lumber and of wood pulp used in papermaking. Coal is another important resource. The soil provides much farmland for apples, grain, potatoes, and tobacco.

The Appalachian National Scenic Trail, from Maine to Georgia, is visited every year by thousands of tourists.

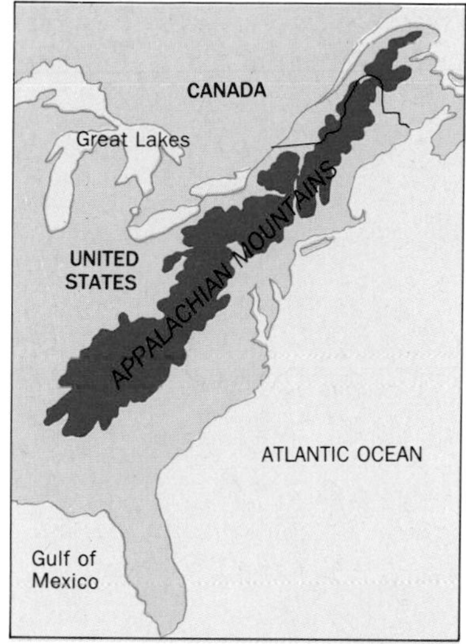


▲ *It is commonly thought that the Appalachians are a very old mountain system. This is only partially true. Most of the Appalachians are less than 25 million years old, which is quite young for a mountain range. Only the highest peaks date from the Permian Period, 200 million years old.*

## APPLESEED, Johnny

Johnny Appleseed is the name by which John Chapman (1774–1845) has become known. As early pioneers moved west and cleared the land, Chapman followed them, planting orchards of apple trees as he went.

Legends grew up about him. Some said he was so eager to encourage the cultivation of apples in the young country that he gave the settlers many gifts of seeds and young trees for planting. Very little is really known about John Chapman, but the legend of Johnny Appleseed lives on as an inspiration to all who care about the land.

▲ *Johnny Appleseed became one of the symbols of the pioneering spirit in America.*

## ARAPAHOS

The Arapahos are one of the INDIAN tribes that lived in the GREAT PLAINS. They moved there from what are now the North Central states. This probably happened in the early 1800s.

▲ *Two Arapaho girls pose in traditional dress in Oklahoma. The Southern Arapaho people were given land in Oklahoma in 1867 by the Treaty of Medicine Lodge.*

Two groups developed. The Northern Arapahos lived along the Platte River in Wyoming; the Southern Arapahos settled in Colorado, around the Arkansas River. Both groups hunted buffalo. Their life-style depended on the horses they got from trading with their neighbors, the KIOWAS. The Arapahos were one of the main tribes involved in the wars that took place as American settlers moved west in great numbers, taking over more and more land from the Indians. After the INDIAN WARS, the defeated Northern and Southern Arapahos were moved onto two separate reservations, in Wyoming and Oklahoma.

## ARBOR DAY

Arbor Day is a day set aside for the planting of trees. It dates from 1872. Arbor Day was the idea of J. S. Morton, a member of the Nebraska State Board of Agriculture. Today it is celebrated in many states, and in a number of them it is a legal holiday.

The ceremonial planting of trees on Arbor Day is often a local school activity. It is a special day on which to remember the importance of trees and forestland. Because of climate differences, Arbor Day is not the same day in every state.

► *A tree is planted during an Arbor Day ceremony. By planting trees young people demonstrate their interest in improving the environment.*

Some Archaeological Sites in the U.S.

- **Folsom, N. Mex.** Flint spearheads have been found dating from 9000–8000 B.C.
- **Koster, Il.** This may be the oldest village in the U.S. The site spans 8,000 years (from 7500 B.C.–A.D. 1000) and covers 11 different Indian cultures.
- **Mesa Verde, Colo.** The most excavated site in the country, Mesa Verde contains remains of cave and cliff dwellings dating from A.D. 350–1300.

## ARCHAEOLOGY

Archaeology is the study of ancient peoples. In the United States, this study began in the late 1700s with the work of Thomas JEFFERSON. This scholar who became president contributed to the early methods of American archaeology. He carefully dug up and studied a large mound of earth on his lands in Virginia, uncovering a number of Indian burials.

In the 200 years since that time, thousands of mounds have been found. Some were for burials, while others were used for religious ceremonies. The MOUND BUILDERS were prehistoric Indians who lived between A.D. 600 and the time of the early Spanish explorers of North America. Some mounds were shaped like animals, such as the Great Serpent Mound in Ohio. Other famous mounds are in Cahokia, Illinois; Adena and Hopewell, Ohio; and Moundville, Alabama.

As pioneers opened up the West, other great Indian cultures were discovered. One of these was the Anasazi. These people built adobe (clay) villages like apartment buildings into the sides of cliffs. Mesa Verde, in Colorado, is the remains of one of these. The Anasazi also lived in pueblos, in which many rooms were joined together around an open space. Each pueblo formed a small village. Pueblo Bonito at Chaco Canyon, New Mexico, was built over 3,000 years ago. The HOPI, Pecos, and Zuni Indians may be descendants of the Anasazi culture.

Archaeologists have found firm evidence that people lived in America at least 12,000 years ago. They came from Asia to Alaska over a strip of land called *Beringia*. That "land bridge" is now under water. Spearheads belonging to the Clovis and FOLSOM cultures, who were wandering hunters, have been found in the West.

The VIKINGS are the first people known to have come from the Old World. The remains of their houses, found at L'Anse aux Meadows in Newfoundland, are almost a thousand years old.

**Hohokum pottery dish A.D. 500-900**

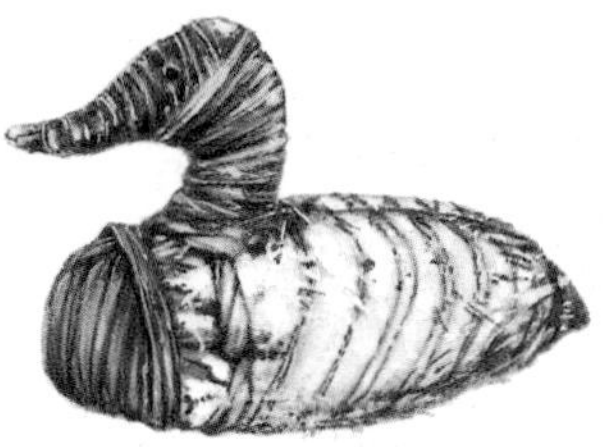

**Decoy duck 200 B.C.**

**Hopewell pipe A.D. 300**

▲ *Archaeological excavations of Indian sites have uncovered a variety of artifacts.*

▼ *In the 1840s dozens of burial mounds were opened in the lower Mississippi Valley. This drawing was made from a painting of one of the excavations in Louisiana.*

**The Great Chicago Fire, which destroyed much of the city in 1871, gave American architects a golden opportunity to experiment with new designs when rebuilding the city. As a result of the fire, Chicago became the center of American architecture in the late 1800s and early 1900s. There is even a style of architecture called the Chicago School.**

## ARCHITECTURE

Architecture is the art of designing buildings. Some buildings are very simple, designed by the people who build them; this is called *vernacular* architecture. The timber houses built by the colonists of New England in the 1600s are examples of this kind of architecture. Most buildings today, however, are designed by trained architects in a chosen style.

Many American architectural styles originally came from Europe. They were then adapted by the colonists to suit the different climate and building materials of their new homeland. For example, the simple, dignified houses called *colonial* and found in the East, are built in a style brought from England during the 1700s. Many missions in California and New Mexico show the influence of the Spanish *baroque* style of the 1600s. American public buildings often have domes and columns derived from the *classical* architecture of ancient Greece and Rome. The CAPITOL building in Washington, D.C., is an example of this *neoclassical* style; so are many of the pre–Civil War plantation houses of the southern states.

▼ *Falling Water, a house in Pennsylvania, is one of Frank Lloyd Wright's most famous buildings. His houses are designed to be in harmony with the landscape.*

Later other, older, European styles were revived. The *gothic* style developed in the 1100s with the building of the great medieval cathedrals. Gothic spires and pointed arches were used for many American churches and university buildings during the late 1800s. The 1800s were also the years of the INDUSTRIAL REVOLUTION, and architects designed many factories and railroad stations as well as country homes and cathedrals.

Practical inventions often influence architecture. The steel frame and the elevator made possible the first tall office buildings, which appeared in Chicago in the 1880s. Today, SKYSCRAPERS tower over most cities in the United States. Reinforced concrete, which contains steel rods or mesh, allows architects greater freedom for their designs.

From the 1930s until recently, architecture tended to be very plain and boxlike. This style is called *modernism* or *functionalism*, because its supporters insisted that a building's form must be determined by its function, or use. Today many architects are turning to more decorative, colorful styles. They use ideas from the past, such as classical columns. This trend is called *postmodernism*.

▲ *Michael Graves's Portland Building was completed in 1982 and is a good example of postmodern architecture.*

▼ *Below are some examples of different styles of American architecture over the last 350 years.*

Some American Structures

| Building | Architect |
|---|---|
| White House, Washington, D.C. | James Hoban (1762–1831) |
| Washington Monument, Washington D.C. | Robert Mills (1781–1855) |
| Trinity Church, Boston | Henry Richardson (1838–1886) |
| Tiffany Building, New York City | Stanford White (1853–1906) |
| Auditorium Building, Buffalo | Louis Sullivan (1856–1924) |
| Harvard University Graduate Center, Boston | Walter Gropius (1883–1969) |
| Museum of Modern Art, New York City | Edward Durrell Stone (1902–1978) |
| Seagram Building, New York City | Philip Johnson (1906– ) and Ludwig Mies van der Rohe (1886–1969) |
| Trans World Airlines Terminal, New York City | Eero Saarinen (1910–1961) |
| National Gallery of Art (East Building), Washington, D.C. | I.M. Pei (1917– ) |

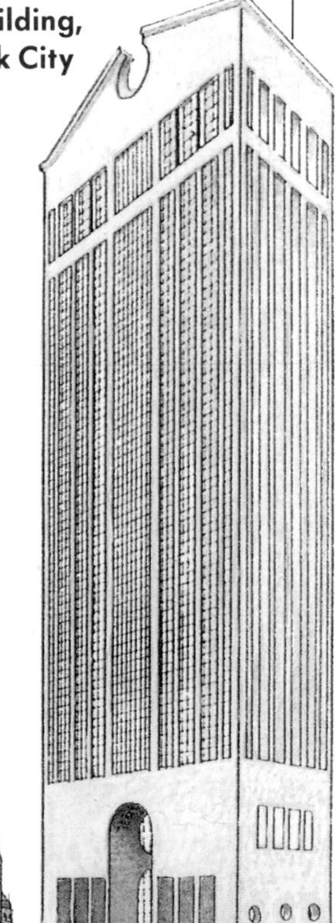

**Monticello, near Charlottesville, Virginia**

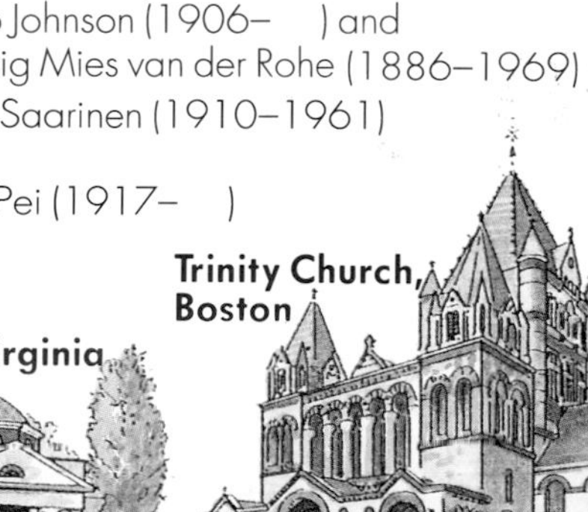

# ARIZONA

Arizona is a state in the Southwest. Much of it is desert, and it was long thought that people would not settle there because of the burning summer heat. But irrigation has made the land productive, and air-conditioning has helped people endure the heat. Today, cotton, vegetables, and other crops are grown in Arizona. And its population has grown by a third since 1980, making it one of the fastest growing states in the nation.

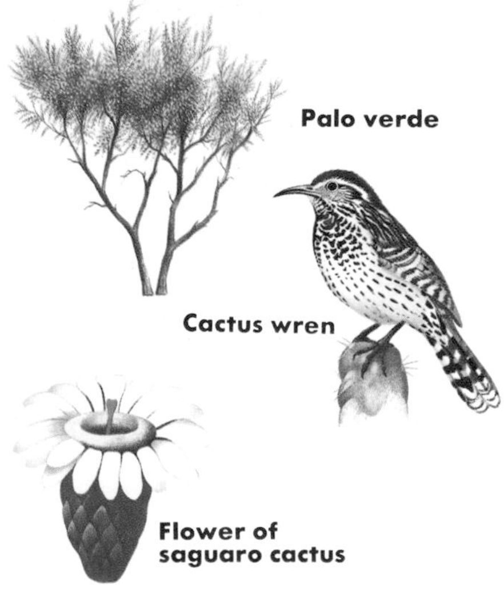


In addition to agriculture, manufacturing, mining, and tourism are important industries. Most of Arizona's factories are located in and around PHOENIX, the capital and largest city, and Tucson. Molybdenum, gold, and silver are mined in Arizona. But its most important mineral is copper. Arizona supplies more than two thirds of the nation's copper. Tourism is second in importance to manufacturing. Tourists visit the state in the winter to enjoy the dry desert air. They also come to wonder at such natural attractions as the GRAND CANYON and the PAINTED DESERT.

The Spanish were the first Europeans to settle in the

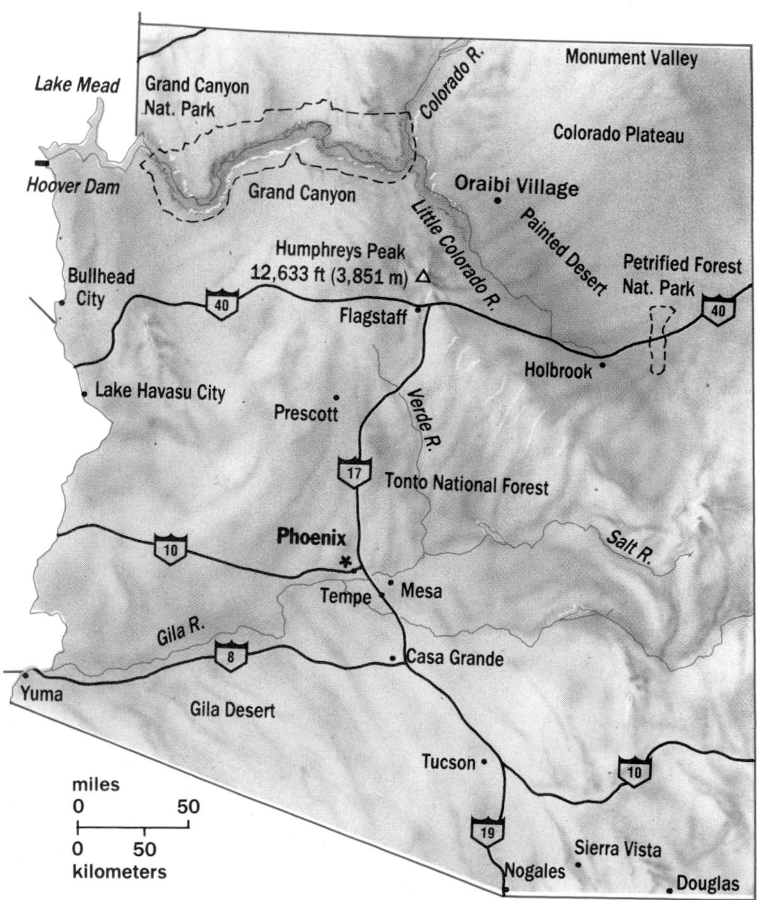


▼ *The Grand Canyon's spectacular rock formations form Arizona's greatest natural wonder.*

region. They ruled it from the 1500s until 1821, when it became part of newly independent Mexico. The United States took possession of Arizona in 1848. Some of the fiercest fighting between Indians and white settlers took place beginning in 1861. The APACHES, led by such men as GERONIMO and COCHISE, and the NAVAJOS were brave foes. They were not defeated until 1886.

Arizona still has one of the largest Indian populations in the country—almost 170,000. But they are far outnumbered by the state's more than 450,000 HISPANIC AMERICANS, most of whom are Mexican.

**Places of Interest**

- The Grand Canyon is one of the natural wonders of the world.
- The Scenic Apache Trail passes through Tonto National Forest.
- Oraibi Village in Navajo County is probably the oldest continuously inhabited settlement in the country and is just one of several Hopi villages in Arizona.
- San Xavier del Bac Mission, near Tucson, is an example of an early Arizona mission settlement.

**Arizona**

**Capital:** Phoenix
**Area:** 114,006 sq mi (295,276 km$^2$). Rank: 6th
**Population:** 3,665,228 (1990). Rank: 24th
**Statehood:** February 14, 1912
**Principal rivers:** Colorado, Gila
**Highest point:** Humphreys Peak, 12,633 ft (3,851 m)
**Motto:** *Ditat Deus* (God Enriches)
**Song:** "Arizona March Song"

◀ *Graves in Boot Hill Cemetery bear witness to Tombstone's violent past. Gunfights were common in the days of the silver-mining boom in the 1800s.*

▼ *When the first Europeans arrived in Arizona, they found well-developed Indian civilizations. Tourists can still visit pueblo villages, some of which date from the 1100s.*

# ARKANSAS

Arkansas is among the most beautiful southern states. It is a major agricultural state, but industry has become important in recent years. Northern and western Arkansas—the Highlands—are mountainous, with forests, lakes, and streams. Southern and eastern Arkansas—the Lowlands—are lower and more fertile. Tourists from all over the United States visit Arkansas every year to hunt in its forests, fish in its lakes, and admire its natural beauty. The Ozark and Ouachita mountain ranges in northern Arkansas are especially popular. Many visitors come to bathe in the state's natural spring waters at resorts such as Mammoth Spring and Hot Springs.

Mockingbird

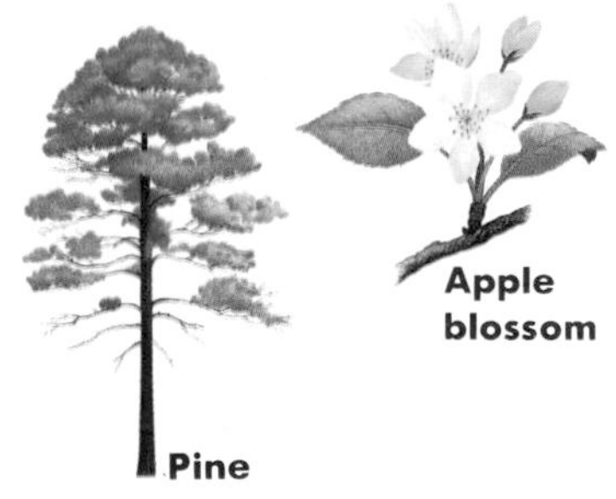

Pine

Apple blossom

The processing of food grown on Arkansas's farms is the state's most important industry. Many factories make electric and electronic equipment. Others make paper and wood products, such as furniture. Bauxite mining—bauxite is used to make aluminum—and petroleum refining also contribute to the state's prosperity. Arkansas also has the only diamond mine in the country, at Murfreesboro. Its farms raise more broiler chick-

▼ *A young visitor digs for diamonds at Crater of Diamonds State Park.*

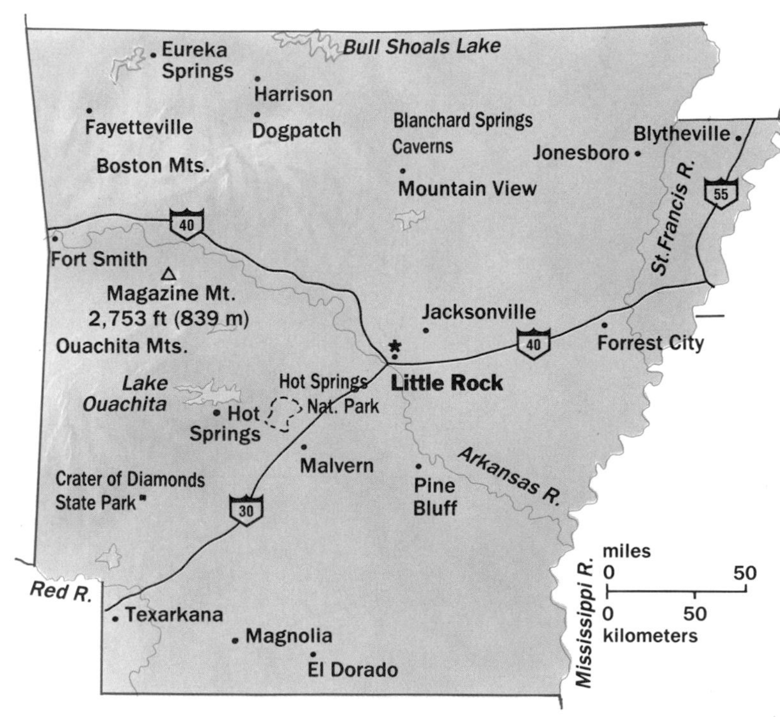

ens than those of any other state and grow one third of the total U.S. rice crop. Soybeans and cotton are also important state crops.

Arkansas belonged to France, Spain, and then France again before it became part of the United States in the LOUISIANA PURCHASE of 1803. It was a slave state before the CIVIL WAR and fought with the Confederacy in the war. Its prosperity was destroyed by the war, and Arkansas remained poor for many years.

Little Rock, located in the center of the state on the banks of the Arkansas River, is the capital and largest city of Arkansas.

**Places of Interest**

- Crater of Diamonds State Park has the only active diamond fields in the U.S.
- Blanchard Springs Caverns, near Mountain View, attracts many visitors with its beautiful rock formations.
- Dogpatch U.S.A., near Harrison, is an amusement park with a zoo, caves, and musical entertainment.
- The steam train of Eureka Springs is one of this popular Victorian resort's many attractions.
- Hot Springs National Park is a popular spa.
- Mountain Village 1890, Bull Shoals, is a reconstruction of an early pioneer town.

▲ *The State Capitol in Little Rock was modeled on the U.S. Capitol.*

▼ *The Ozark Mountains lie in the Highlands of Arkansas. The region's beautiful scenery makes it popular with tourists.*

**Arkansas**
**Capital:** Little Rock
**Area:** 53,182 sq mi (137,742 km²). Rank: 29th
**Population:** 2,350,725 (1990). Rank: 33rd
**Statehood:** June 15, 1836
**Principal rivers:** Arkansas, Mississippi
**Highest point:** Magazine Mountain, 2,753 ft (839 m)
**Motto:** *Regnat Populus* (The People Rule)
**Song:** "Arkansas"

▲ *Although the armadillo has short legs, it can run quite quickly and will scurry away at the first sign of danger.*

## ARMADILLO 

The armadillo is a small, burrowing mammal, covered with bony plates joined together to form a kind of armor. The armadillo hunts at night. It eats roots, small creatures such as insects, worms, and snails, and the carcasses of dead animals.

The only armadillo in the United States is the Texas armadillo. It is also known as the nine-banded armadillo because it has nine thin, movable plates between the fixed plates that cover its shoulders and haunches. The armadillo, which averages under 2 feet (60 cm) long, is edible.

**As a child Louis Armstrong would follow the brass bands through the streets of New Orleans. Later he played the trumpet on the Mississippi riverboats. He got his big break when he was asked to play second trumpet in Joe "King" Oliver's band.**

## ARMSTRONG, Louis 

The dazzling trumpet playing of Louis Armstrong (1900–1971) was one of the glories of JAZZ. Armstrong was nicknamed "Satchmo" after someone observed that he had a mouth like a satchel. In the 1920s he became one of the first jazz players to perform improvised solos. A vocalist with an appealing, gravelly voice, Armstrong popularized a singing style called *scat*, in which nonsense syllables imitate an instrument. He also composed many jazz songs.

Satchmo was born in the birthplace of jazz, New Orleans, and grew up with the sounds of its brass bands in his ears. But his family was poor, and he was often left to fend for himself. While in a home for delinquent boys he learned to play the cornet, a trumpet-like instrument, and decided to become a musician. His talent for comedy as well as music led to parts in many films, including *High Society* and *Hello, Dolly*.

▼ *Neil Armstrong was the first civilian to join the astronaut training program. In 1986 he was asked to chair the commission set up to investigate the* Challenger *space shuttle disaster.*

## ARMSTRONG, Neil 

In July 1969 astronaut Neil Armstrong (1930– ) became the first person to set foot on the moon. Armstrong began his career as a Navy pilot and went on to become a civilian test pilot. He joined the SPACE PROGRAM as an astronaut in 1962, and his first space flight was just four years later. On board Gemini 8 he was involved in the first docking of vehicles in space. Three years later, during the Apollo 11 mission, he stepped onto the surface of the moon and said, "That's one small step for man, one giant leap for mankind!"

## ARMY, United States

The U.S. Army is the largest and the oldest branch of the United States armed forces. Its special responsibilities are for military operations on land, but it also engages in other vital military activities such as search-and-rescue operations and civil defense. In all, the Army employs almost 2 million men and women, of whom more than 660,000 are soldiers on active duty.

The Army was first formed in 1775, as the Continental Army. Its job then was to fight and defeat the British in the American REVOLUTION. Its responsibilities today are much greater. The Army's two primary roles are to defend the United States and, in the event of war, to attack its enemies overseas. The Army's active-service personnel are stationed on bases in the United States and overseas, especially in Europe.

There are many different branches of the Army, but the most important are the combat units, which include the infantry, the armored forces, and the artillery. They are backed up by a wide range of other troops, such as communications and observation units, transportation units, engineers, and logistic units. All Army units must be properly trained and are supplied with the latest equipment. A large part of the Army's work and budget goes to ensuring that these basic priorities are met. The Army is run by the Department of the Army in Washington, D.C.

▲ *The U.S. Army insignia, which is based on the Great Seal of the United States, was adopted in 1778.*

◀ *Some of the uniforms soldiers have worn since Congress created the Continental Army in 1775.*

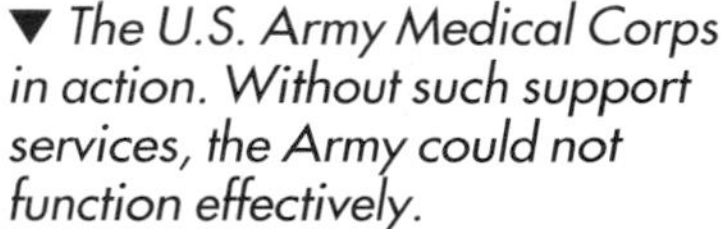

▼ *The U.S. Army Medical Corps in action. Without such support services, the Army could not function effectively.*

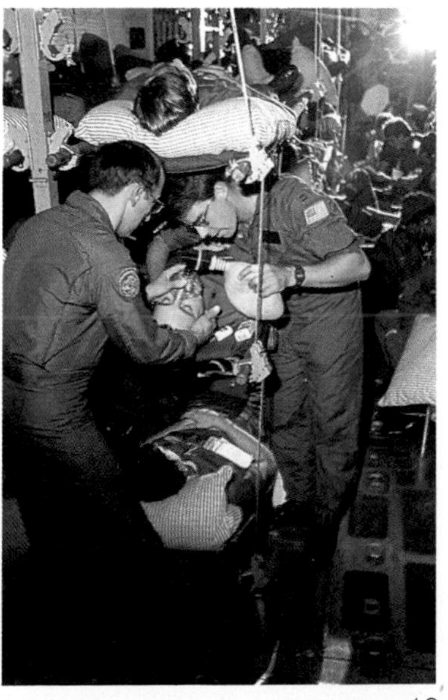

# ART

The works of art on these pages show you some of the wonderful variety of American creative styles. Further examples of American art can be found in the articles on PAINTING, SCULPTURE, ARCHITECTURE, and FOLK ART. You might also want to look up the names of individual artists in the Index.

◄ *The carved totem pole was a work of art and a sacred tribal symbol for many Indians of the Northwest.*

▼ *This portrait of* Mr. and Mrs. Mifflin *was painted by John Singleton Copley in the late 1700s.*

▲ Girl in Pink, *by an unknown artist, is an example of American primitive art from the late 1700s or early 1800s. Primitive art is characterized by its simplicity. This is because most primitive artists were not trained artists.*

► *George Caleb Bingham recorded this scene of river life, called* Fur Traders Descending the Missouri, *in the mid-1800s.*

▼ A statue of George Washington in Philadelphia stands as an example of American civic art for public buildings.

▲ This lamp was designed by Louis Comfort Tiffany, a major American stained glass designer of the late 1800s. Tiffany helped establish style called art nouveau.

▲ In the late 1800s, John Singer Sargent began to use soft, countryside settings for his portraits, as shown in this detail The Brook.

▼ Built in 1929, the Chrysler Building in New York City shows the influence of the art deco movement with its sleek, streamlined shape and use of geometric patterns.

► Mirror Shadow XVI is typical of the work of sculptor Louise Nevelson. Most of her sculptures are made out of wood or use objects from everyday life.

► This detail of Andy Warhol's Marilyn Diptich is typical of pop art, a style that draws on the images of contemporary culture.

Chester A. Arthur was elected vice president of the United States in 1880. He became the 21st president when President James A. GARFIELD was assassinated (murdered) in 1881. As a young laywer, Arthur had been against slavery. He made a name for himself in two cases. In one, he won the freedom of two slaves. In the other, he fought for a free black's civil rights.

After joining the Republican Party, Arthur became active in New York politics. In 1871, President Ulysses S. GRANT made Arthur customs collector for the port of New York City. The customs house provided jobs to party supporters, who were known as "Stalwarts," even if they were not qualified for them. In the late 1800s many politicians were more interested in the spoils of office than in policies or issues. As customs collector, Arthur did nothing dishonest, but he did not change the system either. President Rutherford B. HAYES, who followed Grant, finally forced Arthur out of office.

▼ *The Brooklyn Bridge was opened in 1883, during Chester A. Arthur's term of office. It was hailed as the eighth wonder of the world.*

Arthur and other Republican Stalwarts tried to have Grant renominated as the presidential candidate in 1880. But Garfield won the nomination. To win the support of the Stalwarts, the Republicans chose Arthur as the vice presidential candidate. The Republicans won the election. Many people, however, were nervous about Arthur, especially when he took over as president after Garfield's assassination. He seemed too rooted in the so-called spoils system. After Arthur became president, however, he abandoned the spoils system and reformed the civil service.

**Chester A. Arthur**
**Born:** October 5, 1829, in Fairfield, Vermont
**Education:** Union College
**Political Party:** Republican
**Term of office:** 1881–1885
**Married:** 1859 to Ellen Lewis Herndon
**Died:** November 18, 1886, in New York City

## ARTICLES OF CONFEDERATION 

The Articles of Confederation was a formal compact drawn up by the original 13 states in 1781. It gave the young country a body of laws that it was governed by until the CONSTITUTION was finally drawn up and approved by all the states in 1789.

Each of the states was anxious to guard its own independence and the right to govern its citizens. As a result, some powers were given only to the states and some only to CONGRESS. Matters that affected all the states (in other words, the country as a whole) were dealt with by Congress. These included the powers to declare war and establish armed forces for defense, to carry on relations with foreign countries, and to issue money. The powers to tax the people and regulate the sale of goods were given to the states.

**Under the Articles of Confederation, Congress had so little power that effective government of the new nation was almost impossible. In order to prevent disorder breaking out, a committee was set up to amend the Articles. However, the committee took the bold step of drawing up a completely new constitution. This caused one delegate to remark, "We are razing the foundations of the building, when we need only repair the roof."**

## ASIMOV, Isaac 

Isaac Asimov (1920–1992) was a biochemist and best-selling science fiction writer. He was born in Russia and brought to the United States by his parents at the age of three. After obtaining a Ph.D. in chemistry, he was associate professor at Boston University Medical School from 1955 to 1958.

Asimov's first story was published in 1939. He has written more than 350 books and several hundred articles. He is best known for his science fiction works and has won several Hugo and Nebula awards for them. His Foundation series was given a special Hugo Award as Best All-Time Science Fiction Series. Asimov has also written detective stories, encyclopedias, textbooks, and books on many aspects of science.

## ASTAIRE, Fred 

Fred Astaire (1899–1987), born Frederick Austerlitz, became famous as the star of a number of popular musical movies. Astaire created all his own dances. He was able to make complicated dance steps seem relaxed and easy. His style was smooth and elegant.

Astaire's first dancing partner was his sister Adele, with whom he danced on stage. His film partners included Audrey Hepburn and Cyd Charisse. But the most famous was Ginger Rogers, with whom he made

▼ *Fred Astaire dances in the movie* Finian's Rainbow *(1968). Astaire received a special Academy Award in 1949 in recognition of his talent as a film entertainer.*

ten films. Astaire was also a fine actor, who turned in excellent performances in *On the Beach* and *The Towering Inferno*.

▲ *Nancy Astor dressed for a costume party in 1910. She later became Lady Astor and was elected to the British Parliament.*

## ASTOR FAMILY

In the 1800s the Astors became one of the wealthiest and most prominent families in the United States. When John Jacob Astor arrived in New York City in 1783, he was a penniless 20-year-old German. By the time he died in 1848, he had a fortune of $20 million, made from the fur trade and from real estate. His descendants became even richer. By the 1880s they were making $5 million a year, much of it from tenements occupied by poor immigrants. The Astors themselves lived in great splendor. Mrs. William B. Astor, Jr., was the "queen" of New York society in the late 1800s. The Astor "cottage" in Rhode Island was really a mansion.

One branch of the family moved to England, where they were given titles. The Virginia-born Lady Nancy Astor became the first woman elected to Parliament.

Both the British and the American Astors have also been active in journalism. For many years Vincent Astor owned *Newsweek* magazine. He sold off the Astor real estate holdings in the 1940s and left most of his fortune to charity.

▼ *Downtown Atlanta boasts one of the tallest hotels in the world, the 73-story Peachtree Center Plaza Hotel.*

## ATLANTA

Atlanta, with 394,017 people, is the capital of GEORGIA and its largest city. It is one of the fastest-growing cities in the country and a major industrial and transportation center. Downtown Atlanta has many new high rises and malls, especially around Peachtree Center.

Atlanta was founded in 1837. Then it was called Terminus, because it stood at the southern end, or terminus, of the Western and Atlantic Railroad. Its name was changed to Atlanta in 1845. During the Civil War it was a Confederate supply base and was burned to the ground by General SHERMAN's Union army. The city grew rapidly after the war, when it was also made the state capital. Atlanta became famous in the 1950s and 1960s as a leading center of the CIVIL RIGHTS movement. Martin Luther KING, Jr., was born and buried in the city. Today Atlanta is the commercial and financial center of the Southeast.

## ATLANTIC CHARTER

In August 1941 the United States was not yet in WORLD WAR II. It was, however, supplying arms and other materials to Britain and other Allies. U.S. President Franklin D. ROOSEVELT and British prime minister Winston Churchill met on a warship in the North Atlantic and drew up the Atlantic Charter. It declared, among other things, that the two nations were not seeking any more territory and that they supported self-government for all peoples. The Charter also stated that once the Allies had defeated the Axis powers (Germany, Italy, and Japan), they would work for a world in which nations could live in peace.

**On January 1, 1942, the 26 governments then at war with Germany held a conference in Washington, D.C. They declared that they "subscribed to a common program of purposes and principles in the joint declaration . . . the Atlantic Charter." This agreement was later signed by most of the free nations of the world. It formed the basis of the United Nations, which was founded in San Francisco in April–June 1945.**

## ATTUCKS, Crispus

Crispus Attucks (1723?–1770), a black man, was one of the first colonists to be killed in events that led up to the American REVOLUTION. A runaway slave, he was one of a group of extremists in Boston who protested against the presence of British troops there. On March 5, 1770, Attucks led a mob in goading some British soldiers, who finally opened fire on them. Attucks and two others were killed instantly; two other colonists died later. Attucks's statesmanlike funeral was attended by thousands. A monument to these victims of the BOSTON MASSACRE was built in Boston in 1888.

## AUDUBON, John James

A love of wildlife and a talent for painting led John James Audubon (1785–1851) to undertake an enormous project: painting every known species of bird in North America. Audubon had studied art in Paris (his father was a French sea captain) and then settled in the United States. In 1820 he began traveling around the country, painting birds in their natural habitat. To support his family he also painted portraits, while his wife worked as a governess. The 435 paintings, which took him some 20 years, are remarkable for their detail and realism. To ensure accuracy, Audubon worked from freshly killed specimens, and he also observed the birds in the wild. He used watercolors, sometimes redrawing the work many times before he was satisfied. Audubon's paintings make a unique record of American bird life.

▼ *The wild turkey was just one of the many bird species Audubon painted. His collected paintings were later published in a book called* The Birds of America.

▲ *A view of the Austin skyline. Austin is one of the country's fastest-growing cities.*

## AUSTIN

Austin is the capital of TEXAS and is located in the heart of the state. It is a port on the COLORADO RIVER and is an important center for transporting crops produced in the area. Many conventions are held in Austin, which is the home of the University of Texas and many other colleges. It is named after Stephen Austin, who is sometimes called the "father of Texas." Austin became the capital of the Republic of Texas in 1836 when Texas declared its independence from Mexico. Today 465,622 people live in Austin.

## AUTOMOBILE INDUSTRY

The automobile industry is one of the most important businesses in America. U.S. automobile companies produce more than 5 million cars a year, more than 15 percent of all the cars made in the world, as well as 4 million trucks and buses. Their combined value is more than $130 billion. More than 800,000 people work in this huge industry. Many other industries depend on it, too. More than half the lead and rubber used every year in the United States, and almost 20 percent of all the steel, is bought by the automobile industry.

▼ *The introduction of conveyor belts on automobile assembly lines in 1913 cut the cost of building cars by more than half.*

The leading automobile companies have headquarters in or near DETROIT, Michigan. Their industry is one of the most competitive in the world. U.S. manufacturers have to work hard to keep ahead of overseas competition, especially from Japan. They invest millions of dollars every year to find ways to make their cars more economical. The three largest automobile manufacturers are General Motors, Ford, and Chrysler.

▲ *A machine lowers the body of a truck onto its chassis on a General Motors assembly line. Assembly lines have come a long way from the lines of the early 1900s. Machines now do most of the work, and many lines are even using industrial robots. The first industrial robot was used on an automobile assembly line in 1961.*

Indianapolis 500 Winners

| Year | Driver | Winning Speed (mph) |
|---|---|---|
| 1993 | Emerson Fittipaldi | 157.207 |
| 1992 | Al Unser, Jr. | 134,477 |
| 1991 | Rick Mears | 176.457 |
| 1990 | Arie Luyendyk | 185.984 |
| 1989 | Emerson Fittipaldi | 167.581 |
| 1988 | Rick Mears | 144.809 |
| 1987 | Al Unser | 162.175 |

Daytona 500 Winners

| Year | Driver | Winning Speed (mph) | Car |
|---|---|---|---|
| 1993 | Dale Jarrett | 154.972 | Chevrolet |
| 1992 | Davey Allison | 160.256 | Ford |
| 1991 | Ernie Irvin | 148.148 | Chevrolet |
| 1990 | Derrike Cope | 165.761 | Chevrolet |
| 1989 | Darrell Waltrip | 148.466 | Chevrolet |
| 1988 | Bobby Allison | 137.531 | Buick |
| 1987 | Bill Elliott | 176.263 | Ford |

## AUTOMOBILE RACING 

Automobile racing is one of the most popular sports in the United States. The most famous race is the Indianapolis 500, held each Memorial Day. More than 100 million television viewers worldwide watch the cars speeding at almost 200 miles per hour (320 km/hr). Between them, the two Unser brothers, Al and Bobby, have won this race seven times, and A. J. Foyt has won it four times.

Two types of automobile racing were invented in the United States. Stock car racing uses showroom models with special engines; the top race is the Daytona 500. The South has produced most of the best stock car racers, including Richard Petty and Cale Yarborough. Drag racing cars are like rockets on wheels. They developed in the 1960s from the hot rods raced in California. Modern drag racing cars, called "rails," can reach speeds of 200 miles per hour (320 km/hr).

▼ *The 1989 24-hour endurance race held at the Daytona Speedway. Endurance racing is one of the most popular forms of sports car racing.*

► *The B-2 Stealth bomber is one of the most technologically advanced aircraft in the world. It took seven years to develop and is 69 feet (21 m) long with a wingspan of 172 feet (52.4 m).*

## AVIATION

The United States has always been a leader in aviation. The WRIGHT BROTHERS built the first airplane and flew it in Kitty Hawk, North Carolina, on December 17, 1903. Other Americans were pioneers of aviation. Charles LINDBERGH became the first person to fly solo across the Atlantic in 1927. Five years later Amelia EARHART broke the record for an Atlantic crossing.

Chuck Yeager became the first person to travel faster than the speed of sound in 1947. His flight was one of the first in a jet airplane. Today most airplanes are jets. The fastest planes are used by the U.S. Navy and Air Force. These can break speed records every year. A different sort of record was set in December 1986. Richard Rutan and Jeana Yeager landed their light aircraft *Voyager* in California after flying nonstop around the world without refueling. (See also AEROSPACE INDUSTRY; AIR TRANSPORTATION.)

▼ *Wilbur Wright appeared on a French magazine cover in 1908, after he demonstrated his plane in France. A year later Wilbur and his brother Orville founded the American Wright Company to manufacture planes and train pilots.*

**Some Important Dates in American Aviation**

1903 The Wright Brothers make the world's first successful airplane flight.
1918 The world's first airmail service begins.
1924 U.S. Army pilots make the first round-the-world flight.
1926 Scheduled passenger flights begin.
1927 Charles Lindbergh makes the first solo nonstop flight across the Atlantic.
1947 Air force Captain Charles Yeager makes the first supersonic flight in the X-1 rocket plane.
1949 An Air Force pilot flies a B-50 nonstop around the world.
1959 American Airlines sets up the first transcontinental jet service using Boeing 707s.
1970 Boeing 747 jumbo jets are put in service by Pan Am.
1980 The space shuttle *Columbia* makes its first successful airplane-like landing.

## BADGER

A badger is a member of the WEASEL family. The American badger is found mainly on the western and central plains from southern Canada down to Mexico. Badgers spend the day underground and come out at night to hunt for food. They are 16 to 30 inches (42 to 76 cm) long and weigh about 8 to 25 pounds (3.5 to 11.5 kg). Badgers are fierce when cornered.

Badgers have very strong jaws. They eat small animals such as ground squirrels and mice, as well as insects, roots, and fruits. They have long, heavy, blunt claws on their front feet, which they use for digging. Badgers dig burrows, or dens, to live in. The burrows have tunnels that lead to sleeping and storage chambers.

## BADLANDS 

Badlands are areas where wind, rain, and floods have carved the land into strange shapes. Towering cliffs and ridges alternate with deep ravines and rugged masses of stone. These areas look like the uninviting terrain of some far-off planet. The soil has been eroded away so that little grows here other than a few wildflowers and sagebrush. One such region in South Dakota has been set aside as the Badlands National Park. Many visitors travel here to enjoy the wild scenery and to hunt for fossils in the cliffs. (See map, SOUTH DAKOTA.)

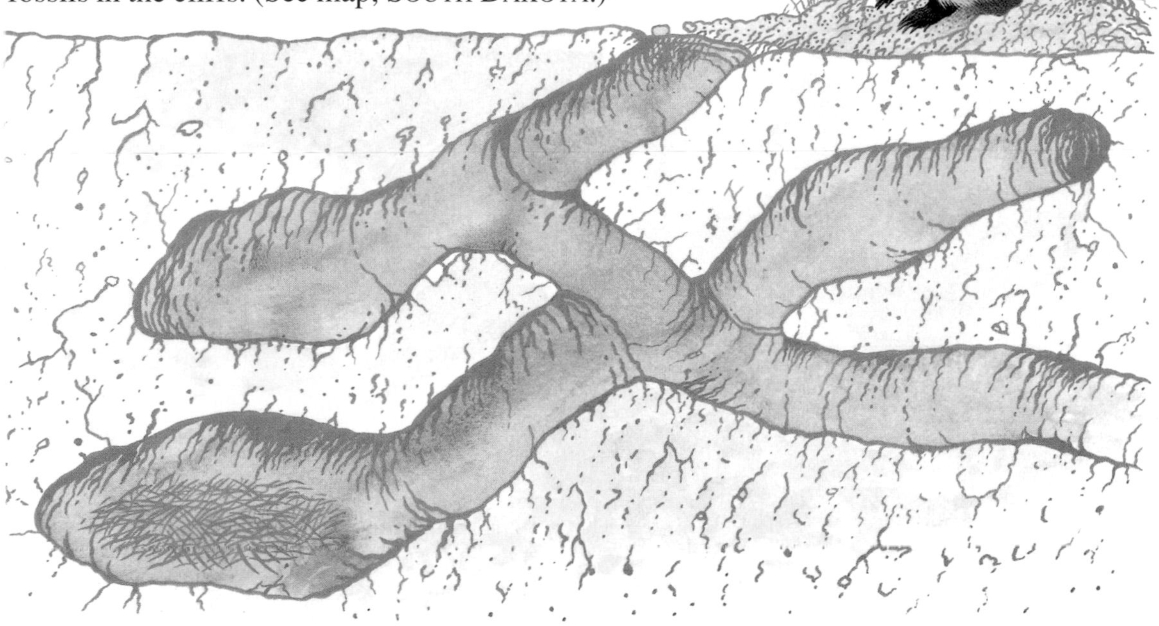

▼ *The chambers in a badger's burrow are used for sleeping and for the young to live in. Badgers keep their burrows very clean.*

▲ *George Balanchine directs a rehearsal of the ballet* The Nutcracker.

## BAEKELAND, Leo

Leo Baekeland (1863–1944) was a Belgian chemist who came to New York in 1889, where he worked for the rest of his life. He is best known for two inventions. One was a light-sensitive coating for photographic plates. This allowed photographs to be developed much faster and more easily than before and with much better results. The other, invented in 1909, was the first form of plastic. It was called Bakelite in honor of him. Bakelite is used in electric switches, pot handles, and pipe stems and as electrical insulation.

## BALANCHINE, George

The most famous name in American BALLET, George Balanchine (1904–1983) was born in St. Petersburg (now Leningrad), in Russia. He studied there at the Imperial School of Ballet. Later he joined the renowned Ballets Russes, in Paris, as a dancer and choreographer (composer of dances).

After moving to the United States in 1933, Balanchine helped to raise the standard of American ballet. The company he founded, the New York City Ballet, is known especially for the brilliant technique of its dancers. Balanchine created many ballets for the company. Although a few tell stories, most are patterns of dance movements inspired by the music. Balanchine also composed dances for stage musicals and films.

▼ *Balboa's discovery of the Pacific Ocean led to further Spanish exploration down the west coast of South America.*

## BALBOA, Vasco Núñez de

Vasco Núñez de Balboa (1475?–1519) was a Spanish explorer. In 1513 he became the first European to sight the eastern shore of the Pacific Ocean.

In 1500, Balboa set sail from Spain to make his fortune in the New World. In 1510 he fled from Hispaniola in the West Indies to escape from people to whom he owed money. The ship on which Balboa sailed arrived in Panama, where he founded a colony called Darién. Balboa became acting governor of the colony. While there, he heard of a huge sea from the local Indians. Balboa set out to discover this body of water. He eventually sighted it from a mountain on the Isthmus of Panama. He named the new ocean the Great South Sea and claimed it for Spain.

## BALDWIN, James

James Baldwin (1924–1987) was a leading novelist, playwright, and essayist. He was born in Harlem in New York City, the eldest of nine children. While still in his teens, he was a part-time preacher in his stepfather's church, an experience he used as the basis of his first novel, *Go Tell It on the Mountain.* His other novels include *Giovanni's Room* and *Tell Me How Long the Train's Been Gone*, which explores the black CIVIL RIGHTS movement of the 1960s.

Baldwin's play *Blues for Mister Charlie* is a bitter attack on whites' oppression of blacks. He took an active part in the struggle for civil rights, and many of his essays deal with this issue. Collections of his essays include *Nobody Knows My Name* and *The Fire Next Time*.

▲ *Many of James Baldwin's novels were a commentary on the civil rights struggle of the 1960s. His first novel,* Go Tell It on the Mountain, *was written while Baldwin was living in Paris.*

## BALLET

Ballet has existed in Europe for more than 300 years, but it did not become well established in North America until this century. During the 1800s, European ballet dancers occasionally visited the United States, and they were generally well received. In the early 1900s the great Russian ballerina Anna Pavlova toured to packed houses. But ballet still seemed very foreign to most Americans at that time.

The first major American company was the American Ballet—now the New York City Ballet—founded by the

**During a tour in the early 1840s, Viennese ballerina Fanny Essler won the hearts of the American people with her dancing. Such was her popularity that congressmen meeting in Washington adjourned so that they would not miss her performance.**

◄ *The American Ballet Theatre in a performance of the ballet* Symphonie Concertante.

**American musical composers have been attracted to ballet. Aaron Copland's music for the ballet *Appalachian Spring* was an inspiration to other composers. Leonard Bernstein adapted the ballet form in his musicals *On the Town* and *West Side Story*.**

wealthy patron Lincoln Kirstein and the choreographer George BALANCHINE in 1933. Balanchine's wife, Maria Tallchief, danced for the New York City Ballet. Today this is one of the world's leading ballet companies.

Many fine companies and schools now flourish in the United States. An outstanding company, the American Ballet Theatre, was founded in 1939. Its choreographers, unlike Balanchine, have generally preferred to create ballets that tell a story. Some, especially Agnes de Mille, brought a distinctively American style to ballet. They did this by combining ballet's traditional elegant steps with freer movements suitable for portraying the life of the Old West, for example, or urban themes. This trend has spread to other countries. Ballets now often include movements drawn from other kinds of dance, including modern dance and disco dancing. Another major ballet company is the Joffrey Ballet, directed by Robert Joffrey.

## BALTIMORE

Baltimore is a port located on the Patapsco River, which flows into CHESAPEAKE BAY. It is the largest city in MARYLAND with 736,014 people. It is a historic city, too, founded as long ago as 1729. During the American REVOLUTION, Baltimore was the capital of the United States for a brief time. It was in Baltimore in 1814 that

▼ *Decked out with flags, the* Pride of Baltimore *sails out of Baltimore harbor, one of the world's largest natural harbors.*

Francis Scott Key wrote the "Star-Spangled Banner" after Fort McHenry held out against an attack by British warships during the WAR OF 1812. Today, the city's most important industries are shipping, iron and steel manufacturing, and tourism. Much of downtown Baltimore has been rebuilt, especially around the historic Inner Harbor area.

**Baltimore was the first American city to have a railway system. The Baltimore and Ohio Railroad (B&O) began carrying passengers in January 1830. At first, passenger carriages were pulled along rails by horses. Later that year, the *Tom Thumb*, the first locomotive built in the United States, was used to push the carriages.**

◀ *Drive-in banks are one of the ways in which banks have developed to try to meet the customer's needs.*

## BANKS AND BANKING

Banks are places where people can deposit their money for safekeeping. The banks make a profit by lending this money to people and businesses and by investing it.

Most people bank at *commercial banks.* Here they can open savings accounts that earn them interest. They can open checking accounts, so that they can pay their bills with checks. And they can borrow money—to buy a car, for example. Many people use bank cards to get cash even when the banks are closed. There are more than 12,000 commercial banks in the United States. About $2.5 trillion is deposited in these banks.

Many people open savings accounts at *savings banks.* There are more than 1,300 of these banks in the United States. They have deposits of about $838 billion.

*Credit unions* and *savings and loan associations* are banks that lend money to their depositors, especially for home mortgages. *Investment banks* lend money to companies in return for stock in the companies. These banks can then resell the stock to make a profit.

The Federal Reserve System serves as the central bank of the United States. There are 12 banks in the system, which was set up in 1913. Its most important role is to help economic growth. It controls the supply of money in the country and keeps watch over all the other banks.

Largest U.S. Commercial Banks (by deposits)

1. Citicorp, New York
2. Chemical Banking Corp., New York
3. BankAmerica, Corp., San Francisco
4. Nationsbank Corp., Charlotte, N.C.
5. J.P. Morgan & Co., New York
6. Chase Manhattan Corp., New York
7. Security Pacific Corp., Los Angeles
8. Bankers Trust New York Corp., New York
9. Wells Fargo & Co., San Francisco
10. First Chicago Corp., Chicago

Washington, D.C., is one of the few cities in the world that was designed before it was built. A French engineer, Pierre Charles L'Enfant, was hired to draw up a plan for the capital. In 1789, Benjamin Banneker and Andrew Ellicott were commissioned by President George Washington to help survey and plan its construction.

## BANNEKER, Benjamin

Benjamin Banneker (1731–1806) was the best-known black person in the early history of the United States. A free black, Banneker taught himself mathematics and astronomy. As a young man, he built a wooden clock that kept nearly perfect time for 50 years. In 1789 he correctly predicted an eclipse of the sun. In 1791 Banneker helped survey the new DISTRICT OF COLUMBIA. At the age of 60 he began providing astronomical calculations, weather forecasts, and times of the tides for an almanac he published every year. He also sent out pamphlets against slavery and war.

## BANTING, Sir Frederick

▲ *Sir Frederick Banting was only 30 years old when he discovered insulin.*

Sir Frederick Banting (1891–1941) was a Canadian doctor who in 1922 discovered a hormone called insulin in the pancreas, one of the body's most vital organs. Insulin helps the body to break down sugar. People whose bodies cannot produce insulin are called diabetics and have a disease called diabetes. Banting's important discovery has helped to prolong the lives of millions of diabetics. In 1923, Banting and a co-worker, John Macleod, shared the Nobel Prize for medicine for the discovery of insulin.

## BAPTISTS

There are more than 31 million Baptists in the United States, making them the largest Protestant group in the nation. The group consists of more than 30 separate churches. The Southern Baptist Convention is the largest of these and contains about half of all Baptists in America. Baptists become full members of their church when they are baptized. This does not usually happen in infancy but when a person is old enough to make the decision to join the church. According to Baptist practice, candidates for baptism are usually immersed in water to mark their entrance into the church.

The Six Major Baptist Denominations (by membership)

1. Southern Baptist Convention
2. National Baptist Convention, U.S.A.
3. National Baptist Convention of America
4. Progressive National Baptist Convention
5. American Baptist Churches in the U.S.A.
6. American Baptist Association

## BARDEEN, John

John Bardeen (1908–1991), an American physicist, was co-winner of the Nobel Prize for physics in 1956 and 1972. Bardeen's first Nobel Prize, shared with two Bell

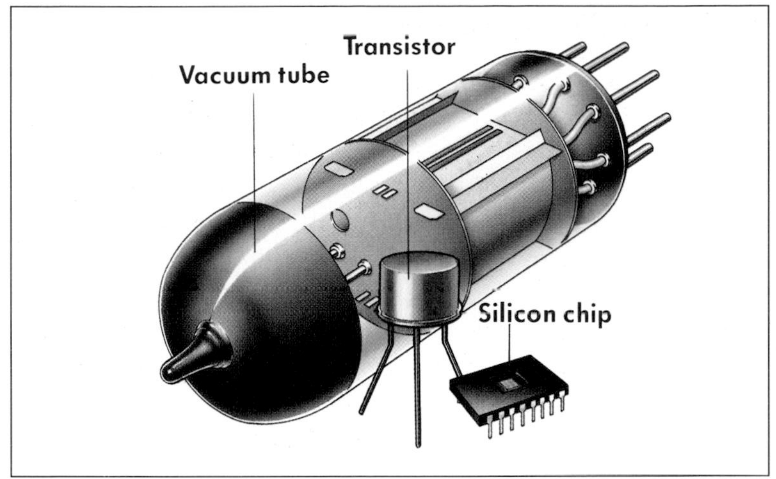


◀ *Before the invention of the transistor, vacuum tubes were used in electronic equipment. In the 1960s and 1970s tubes were replaced by the transistor, which was smaller, used less energy, and cost less. Since then, transistors have gotten even smaller. Today over a million transistors can be put on a silicon chip just 0.25 inch (5 mm) square.*

Telephone Company colleagues, W. B. SHOCKLEY and W. H. BRATTAIN, was for inventing the transistor. This device revolutionized electronics. His second Nobel Prize was shared with L. N. Cooper and J. R. Schrieffer. They further developed the theory of superconductivity. This is the ability of certain substances, called *superconductors*, to conduct electricity without resistance at very low temperatures.

## BARNUM & BAILEY 

Barnum & Bailey is one of the most famous CIRCUS names in the world. The circus grew largely from the work of one man, Phineas T. Barnum (1810–1891) one of the most famous showmen in the world. Barnum began his show business career by exhibiting an elderly slave he claimed was 160 years old and had been George Washington's nurse. He then exhibited Charles Stratton, a midget, as "General Tom Thumb." Later Barnum toured the United States with the famous singer Jenny Lind, the "Swedish Nightingale."

In the 1870s, Barnum set up "The Greatest Show on Earth," a touring circus and sideshow. One of his partners, James Bailey, developed this circus until the Ringling Brothers, a famous circus family, bought it in 1907. Today it is known throughout the world as the Ringling Brothers and Barnum & Bailey Circus.

▲ *An early poster for the Barnum & Bailey circus. P. T. Barnum's life was dedicated to show business, so much so that with his dying words he asked about the day's receipts at the circus.*

**Phineas T. Barnum could be considered a pioneer of modern advertising. He would send "advance men" out to cover a town with posters to advertise the arrival of his traveling show. Brass bands and a spectacular parade would further promote the event.**

## BARRYMORE FAMILY 

Born to actor parents, Ethel (1879–1959), John (1882–1942), and Lionel (1878–1954) Barrymore were

► *From left to right, Lionel, Ethel, and John Barrymore, starring together in the movie* Rasputin and the Empress.

**During the 1920s, moviegoing was fast becoming America's favorite form of entertainment. In 1926 the first motion picture with a synchronized musical score was released. The movie, *Don Juan*, starring John Barrymore, marked what Warner Brothers called "the beginning of the sound era."**

among the leading figures of the American stage and screen for half a century. Ethel first made a name for herself on the London stage. In 1901 she scored a triumph on Broadway in *Captain Jinks of the Horse Marines*. She won an Oscar for her performance in the film *None but the Lonely Heart*. Her brother Lionel appeared in many films, including *Captains Courageous* and *Duel in the Sun*. He is probably best remembered for his annual portrayal, on radio, of Scrooge in *A Christmas Carol*. John, dubbed "the great profile," often played romantic leading men in such films as *Grand Hotel* and *Dinner at Eight*. However, he also gave memorable performances on stage as Shakespeare's Richard III and Hamlet. John's granddaughter, Drew (1975– ), has carried on the family acting tradition.

## BARTON, Clara

Clara Barton (1821–1912) was the founder of the American RED CROSS. When the CIVIL WAR broke out in 1861, she was working in Washington, D.C., as the first woman clerk in the U.S. Patent Office. She set up an organization to take food and supplies to wounded soldiers. She even nursed the wounded herself and was soon being called "the Angel of the Battlefield." At the end of the war, President Abraham LINCOLN asked her to start an office to search for missing soldiers.

On a visit to Switzerland, Clara Barton learned of the work being done there by the International Red Cross, which had been founded in 1864. In 1881, after returning home, she founded the American branch of the Red Cross and served as its president until 1904.

▼ *Clara Barton's suggestion that the Red Cross serve victims of natural disasters became part of the constitution of the Red Cross in 1884.*

## BASEBALL

For many years there was a widespread belief that baseball was invented by Abner Doubleday in Cooperstown, New York, in 1839. But baseball actually developed from other bat-and-ball games that had been played long before 1839. Rules for baseball were drawn up in 1845, and it quickly became popular. The first professional league was the National League, founded in 1876. The American League followed in 1900.

Today each of the major leagues has two divisions, East and West. Each of these National League and American League divisions has seven teams. In the fall the divisional champions have a play-off for the league championship. The winners play for the overall crown in the best-of-seven World Series in October. In early July, about halfway through the season, the best players from each league play each other in the All Star Game.

Top baseball players become national heroes. Some of their records last for decades. Babe Ruth's career record of 714 home runs was only broken in 1974, by Hank Aaron. These two players and other stars, such as Cy Young, Jackie Robinson, Lou Gehrig, Ted Williams, and Ty Cobb, are in Baseball's Hall of Fame in Cooperstown, New York.

▲ *Good pitching is vital to a team's success. Orel Hershiser of the L.A. Dodgers had a record 59 consecutive scoreless innings at the end of the 1988 season.*

Winners of the World Series

| Year | Team |
|---|---|
| 1993 | Toronto Blue Jays |
| 1992 | Toronto Blue Jays |
| 1991 | Minnesota Twins |
| 1990 | Cincinnati Reds |
| 1989 | Oakland Athletics |
| 1988 | L.A. Dodgers |
| 1987 | Minnesota Twins |
| 1986 | New York Mets |
| 1985 | Kansas City Royals |
| 1984 | Detroit Tigers |
| 1983 | Baltimore Orioles |
| 1982 | St. Louis Cardinals |
| 1981 | L.A. Dodgers |
| 1980 | Philadelphia Phillies |
| 1979 | Pittsburgh Pirates |
| 1978 | New York Yankees |

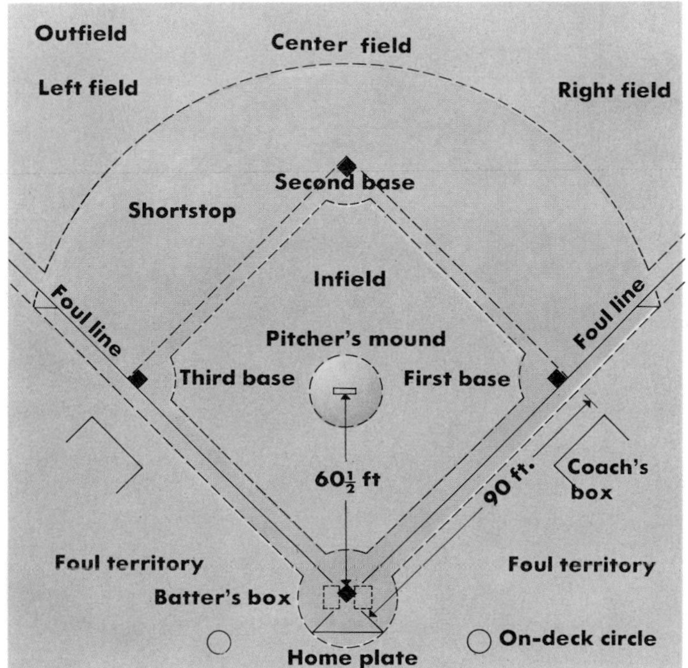


◀ *Although the size of the outfield and foul territory may vary from ballpark to ballpark, the measurements of the infield are always the same.*

## BASIE, Count

Count Basie (1904–1984), born William Basie, was a JAZZ composer and bandleader.

Basie became famous in the 1930s. Perhaps his greatest contribution to the field of jazz was to combine the big band "swing" sound of the 1930s with the sound of the new "modern jazz" that came into being during the early 1940s.

Basie's orchestra had a relaxed and highly colorful style of playing, with the strong use of soloists, both instrumental and vocal. Eventually, Basie concentrated less on solo playing and more on his very personal style of overall musical arrangements.

▲ *Count Basie formed his own band in 1935. Many famous soloists played with the band, including the saxophonist Lester Young and the drummer Jo Jones.*

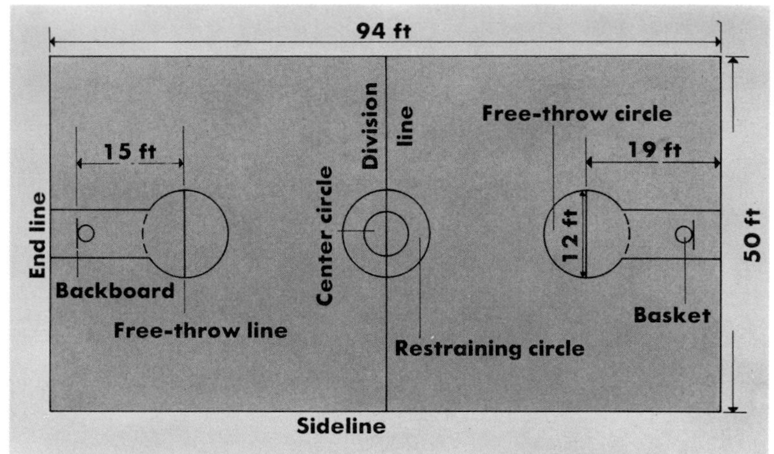


► *A diagram of a regulation basketball court.*

▼ *James Worthy scores for the L.A. Lakers with a "dunk," one of basketball's most spectacular shots.*

## BASKETBALL

In 1891 physical-education instructor James Naismith invented basketball as a game for student athletes to play indoors between the football and baseball seasons. He stuck peach baskets on two poles, divided the players into two teams, and gave them a soccer ball to shoot at the baskets. The rules for the modern sport were soon drawn up, and basketball attracted more and more players. It is now the most popular indoor team sport in the world.

Colleges have always attracted big crowds for their games. The best college players are offered multimillion-dollar contracts to play professionally in the National Basketball Association (NBA). The NBA's Eastern Conference is divided into the Atlantic Division (six teams) and the Central Division (seven teams). The

Western Conference's Midwest Division and Pacific Division have seven teams each. Divisional and conference play-offs take place each May and June to decide the NBA Championships.

Modern players such as Michael Jordan, Magic Johnson, and Larry Bird earn top salaries for their skills. But no one seems likely to reach the scoring heights of Wilt Chamberlain, who scored 100 points in a single game in 1962. Kareem Abdul-Jabbar, another basketball great, scored 38,387 points in his 20-year career.

NBA Play-off Championships

| Year | Team |
|---|---|
| 1993 | Chicago Bulls |
| 1992 | Chicago Bulls |
| 1991 | Chicago Bulls |
| 1990 | Detroit Pistons |
| 1989 | Detroit Pistons |
| 1988 | L.A. Lakers |
| 1987 | L.A. Lakers |
| 1986 | Boston Celtics |
| 1985 | L.A. Lakers |
| 1984 | Boston Celtics |
| 1983 | Philadelphia 76ers |
| 1982 | L.A. Lakers |
| 1981 | Boston Celtics |
| 1980 | L.A. Lakers |
| 1979 | Seattle SuperSonics |
| 1978 | Washington Bullets |
| 1977 | Portland Trail Blazers |

## BATS

Bats are the only mammals that can fly. Their wings are made of skin stretched between their long arms and fingers. Bats are found almost everywhere in North America, from caves and deserted log cabins in the Midwest to New York City's attics. Of the 900 species, or kinds, of bats found in the world, about 40 are found in North America.

There are no vampire bats in North America. Nor are there any of the enormous bats known as flying foxes, which are found in warmer climates. The largest North American bat is the hoary bat, which has a 16-inch (40-cm) wingspan. Many North American bats have a wingspan of about 12 inches (30 cm).

One of the most common North American species, the little brown bat, is found all over the continent except for the extreme north. Another species, the red bat, is found east of the Rocky Mountains.

▲ *Pictured here are four American bats. Not all bats live in big colonies. The Mexican freetail roosts in large numbers. The other three species, however, roost in small colonies or singly.*

## BAUM, L. Frank

L. Frank Baum (1856–1919) was an author of children's fantasy books. He created a magical land called Oz, about which he wrote over a dozen books and short stories. The first of these books was made into the

▲ *A black bear cub. The black bear is the most common bear in North America.*

▼ *Bears of North America. Although the grizzly bear is fiercer, it is not as large as the Alaskan brown bear, which grows up to 9 feet (2.7 m) long and is the largest of all.*

famous 1939 film *The Wizard of Oz.* Judy GARLAND played Dorothy, a young girl who has a whole series of adventures in Oz. In her search for the wizard, she is threatened by a wicked witch and helped by a good witch, and she meets such wonderful characters as the Tin Man, the Scarecrow, and the Cowardly Lion.

These books were so popular that after Baum died, other people continued to write Oz stories. Baum also wrote many books under other names (*pseudonyms*).

## BEARS

Bears are the largest *carnivores* (flesh-eating mammals) in North America. They eat small mammals and fish, as well as fruit, roots, and plants. Bears especially love honey. Most are good swimmers. They usually sleep through much of the winter.

The smallest North American bear is the black bear. A good climber, it lives in forests all over North America. It is often seen in national parks, where it raids trash cans and begs for food. Visitors are forbidden to feed the bears, as black bears can be dangerous, particularly when protecting their cubs.

The grizzly bear is much larger. It used to be found all over the West, but it was hunted a great deal. Today grizzlies are common only in parts of Canada and Alaska and a small area of Montana. The grizzly normally kills only for food, but it has sometimes been known to attack people.

The Kodiak bear, an Alaskan brown bear, is the largest bear in the world and the largest land carnivore. It is related to the grizzly bear. The Kodiak bear is very strong but will not usually attack people if it is left alone. It is expert at catching salmon to eat.

The polar bear lives in the Arctic region of North America, where it eats mainly seals and fish. Its white fur makes it less noticeable against the snow and ice.

▲ The entrances to a beaver lodge are underwater, but the living chamber is above water level.

## BEAVER

A beaver is a RODENT, an animal that has long front teeth for gnawing. Beavers eat bark from trees and can even fell trees by gnawing around the trunks. They cut these trees into logs with their teeth. They use the logs, along with branches, rocks, and mud, to build dams across streams and small rivers.

A pond forms behind a dam, and in it beavers build an island home known as a *lodge*. The lodge is a mound of logs and branches covered with mud, with dry earth and leaves inside. One or more families of beavers live together in the lodge. The members of this *colony* work together, constantly repairing or enlarging the dam.

Beavers are very good swimmers. Their flat, paddle-shaped tails help them swim. They also use their tails to lean on when they are gnawing trees. To warn their families of danger, they slap their tails on the water.

Beavers have been hunted so much for their thick, waterproof fur that now they are protected by the United States and Canadian governments. There are more beavers in North America than anywhere else in the world. They are about 4 feet (1.3 m) long and weigh about 60 pounds (27 kg) or more.

▲ Beavers' teeth never stop growing. Constant gnawing on the branches and trunks of trees keeps them very sharp.

## BEES

Bees are INSECTS that are related to ANTS and wasps. Most kinds are solitary—they live alone. Each female builds a nest. She lays one egg on some pollen in each cell in the nest. This will provide food for the larvae (young bees) after the eggs hatch. With her work done, the female seals up the nest and flies away.

The most common type of solitary bee in North America is the leaf-cutting bee. It cuts out pieces of leaves to make the cells. A relative of the leaf cutter is

▲ The picture shows honeybees swarming. This occurs when a colony becomes overcrowded. The queen bee and many of the workers then leave to start a new colony elsewhere.

▼ *The common, or American, bumblebee lives in a colony in the ground that may contain fifty to several hundred bees.*

the mason bee. It makes a kind of concrete for its nest, using clay and saliva. The mining bee digs burrows in the ground for its nest. The carpenter bee builds a nest in wood or plant stems. The cuckoo bee does not build a nest at all. It lays its eggs in other bees' nests.

Bumblebees and honeybees are social rather than solitary—they live in colonies. A bumblebee colony can have several hundred bees. Most are worker bees. Some are drones, which fertilize the queen. There is one queen in each colony. Honeybee colonies contain 50,000 to 80,000 bees. Honeybees make the cells of their nests, or hives, out of beeswax. After making honey out of plant nectar, they store it in these cells. Some people raise honeybees for their honey and beeswax. Beekeeping is widely practiced in North America.

A fierce new type of honeybee, the so-called "killer bee," has spread throughout South America and as far north as the U.S.–Mexico border.

## BEETLES

▼ *Beetles include the most useful and the most destructive of insects. The ladybug, for example, eats garden pests such as aphids. The Japanese beetle, introduced by accident into North America, destroys cultivated plants and fruits.*

A beetle is an INSECT that has hard sheaths, or wing cases, that cover and protect its wings. There are more kinds of beetles than any other creature in the world. North America has 28,000 species, almost a tenth of the total species in the world. The name beetle means "biter," for beetles have strong mouth parts. The well-

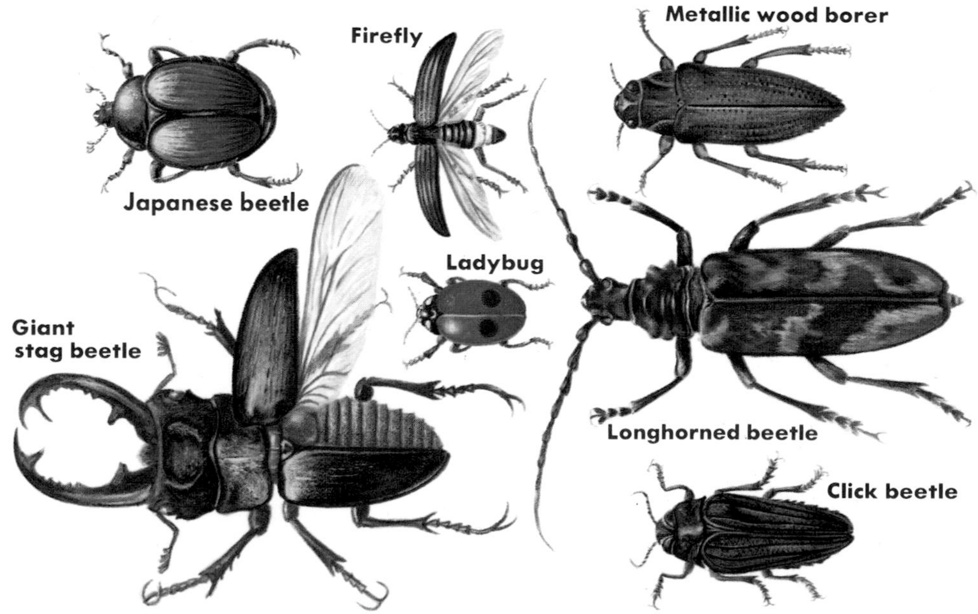

known June bug has particularly strong jaws, as does the fierce-looking stag beetle. Male stag beetles can sometimes be seen fighting, using their large jaws to grip each other. Other well-known North American beetles include the Japanese beetle, the ladybug, the Colorado potato beetle, the boll weevil, and the firefly.

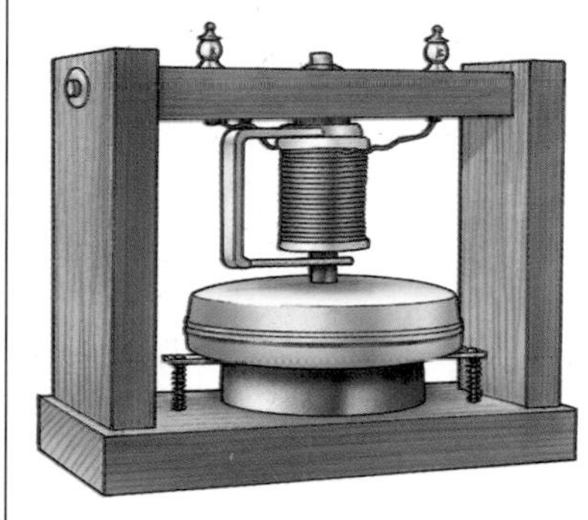

**The First Bell Telephone**
Alexander Bell's telephone worked by changing sound waves produced by the human voice into an electric current. This current could then be transmitted along a wire and changed back into sounds at the other end.

▲ *In 1892, Alexander Graham Bell telephoned Chicago from New York City to demonstrate to businessmen the usefulness of his new invention.*

## BELL, Alexander Graham

Alexander Graham Bell (1847–1922) was a Scottish-born scientist, teacher, and inventor of the telephone. He came to the United States in 1871.

Bell was fascinated by the sound of the voice and how the human ear hears it. He taught the deaf, using a system invented by his father. Bell had also become fascinated with the recently invented telegraph. He believed that if electricity could carry telegraph signals, it could also carry human speech and other sounds. Others had been trying to achieve the same thing, but in 1876, Bell succeeded. The first words ever spoken over a telephone were Bell's request to his assistant: "Mr. Watson, come here. I want you." A year later, Bell established the Bell Telephone Company.

Bell later experimented in other areas, including sheep breeding and the creation of a flying machine. He also started the organization now known as the Alexander Graham Bell Association for the Deaf.

**When President James A. Garfield was shot by an assassin, Alexander Graham Bell developed a device that he hoped would locate the bullet inside the president's body. It was similar to a modern mine detector. Unfortunately, it could not distinguish between the bullet and the iron springs of the president's bed, and so the experiment failed. President Garfield eventually died on September 19, 1881.**

## BELLOW, Saul

The novelist Saul Bellow (1915–  ) was born in the province of Quebec, Canada, of Russian Jewish parents but moved with them to Chicago as a child. He made use of this background in *The Adventures of Augie March.* This

▲ *Saul Bellow won both a Nobel Prize and a Pulitzer Prize for his works. Besides novels, Bellow has written short stories and drama.*

novel relates the sometimes sad, sometimes comic experiences of a poor Jewish boy who refuses to settle for a safe, humdrum existence. Some of Bellow's other books, such as *Henderson the Rain King*, are about individuals who go through crises that force them to examine their lives. Another important theme in his writing is the relationship between Jews and Gentiles. This is the main theme in *The Victim*. Bellow won the 1976 Nobel Prize for literature. Three of his books—*The Adventures of Augie March*, *Herzog*, and *Mr. Sammler's Planet*—won National Book Awards.

## BENÉT, Stephen Vincent

The author and poet Stephen Vincent Benét (1898–1943) acquired in childhood a taste for history and literature. Perhaps his best-known work is his long narrative poem *John Brown's Body*, which vividly describes the events and personalities of the Civil War. Benét won a Pulitzer Prize for this poem. *Western Star*, published after his death, won a second Pulitzer. In addition to poetry, he wrote novels and short stories, including the story *The Devil and Daniel Webster*, which was turned into a play, a film, and an opera. *A Book of Americans*, which he wrote with his wife, Rosemary Carr, consists of portraits in verse of famous historical characters.

▼ *James Gordon Bennett, Jr., who inherited his father's keen sense of news, was the first person to introduce the idea of the "exclusive" news story.*

## BENNETT, James Gordon

James Gordon Bennett (1795–1872) was a Scottish-born newspaper editor who founded the New York *Herald* in 1835. Today's NEWSPAPERS owe much to his new ideas about journalism. He broke with tradition and sent reporters out actively seeking news. During the Civil War, Bennett assigned a number of reporters to provide accurate coverage of the war as it happened. The *Herald* was the first newspaper to publish anything about stocks and finance. Bennett also helped found the Associated Press news agency.

Bennett's son, James Gordon Bennett, Jr. (1841–1918), who was born in New York City, carried on his father's work. He also established newspapers in London and Paris. It was Bennett who sent the journalist Henry M. STANLEY on his legendary expedition to find the explorer Dr. David Livingstone in Africa.

◀ *The strong colors and feeling of movement in Thomas Hart Benton's mural* Independence and the Opening of the West *are typical of the artist's work.*

**Regionalism was an art movement that portrayed life in the United States during the 1930s. It was an attempt to create a completely American style of painting. Regionalist artists painted scenes and people from different regions of the United States. Thomas Hart Benton's subjects were often farmers and other people who lived and worked in small towns or rural areas in the Midwest and South.**

## BENTON, Thomas Hart 

The paintings of Thomas Hart Benton (1889–1975) show life among ordinary American people, especially in the rural parts of the South and Midwest. Benton came from Missouri and was named after a great uncle who had been a U.S. senator from that state.

After studying at the Art Institute of Chicago, Benton went to study further in Paris. But he turned his back on modern European art, which was becoming more concerned with forms. He chose instead to represent simple subjects in ways that the average person could understand. Although Benton's paintings are clear, they are not truly realistic. The colors are very vivid, and the lines are swirling, suggesting movement. Benton painted a number of *murals* (large wall paintings). He also taught in art schools.

## BERING STRAIT 

The Bering Strait is a passage of water that separates ALASKA from Asia. The strait connects the Arctic Ocean and the Bering Sea. At its narrowest point, this barrier between the United States and the Soviet Union is only 36 miles (58 km) wide. In the middle of the Bering Strait are the two Diomede Islands. One belongs to the United States and the other to the Soviet Union. During the Ice Age there was a land bridge where the Bering Strait is now located. The ancestors of the American Indians reached North America by crossing that bridge.

▼ *The Bering Strait is the only place where people in the United States can look across at Soviet territory.*

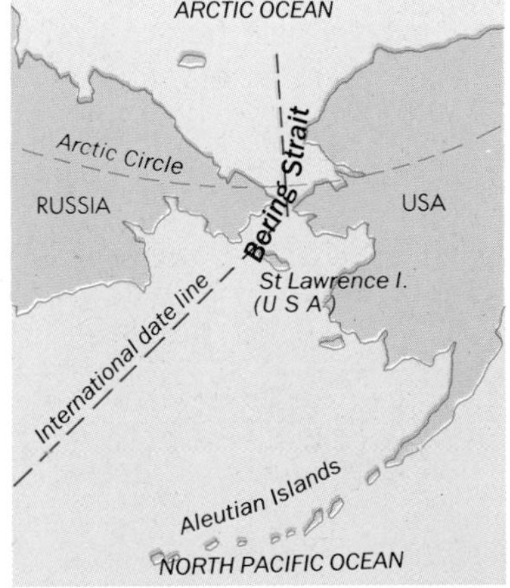

▲ *Irving Berlin on the movie set for* This is the Army, *one of the many musicals he wrote. Others include* Annie Get Your Gun *and* Louisiana Purchase.

## BERLIN, Irving 

Irving Berlin (1888–1989) was one of the most popular American songwriters. He was born in Russia and came to the United States in 1892.

He taught himself music and began writing songs in 1906 under his real name, Baline. By mistake, his name was printed as "Berlin," and he adopted it for the rest of his life. During his career he wrote almost 5,000 songs, some of which are all-time favorites. Among them are classics such as "God Bless America," "White Christmas," and "Alexander's Ragtime Band." He also wrote the songs for *Annie Get Your Gun* and other musicals.

Berlin insisted on publishing his own music so that he could control the money he received. To help other songwriters protect their rights he helped start the American Society of Composers, Authors, and Publishers (ASCAP).

▼ *Leonard Bernstein rehearses the London Symphony Orchestra for a performance in Britain.*

## BERNSTEIN, Leonard 

Leonard Bernstein (1918–1990) was a man of many talents. He was a conductor of some of the world's great orchestras, a composer, a pianist, a writer, and a television personality. He shot to fame in 1943 when, at the last moment, he substituted for the conductor of the New York Philharmonic, who had become ill. Bernstein's conducting impressed the critics and launched him on a brilliant career as a conductor. As a composer he is best known for *West Side Story*. Among his other compositions are the ballet *Fancy Free*; *Chichester Psalms*, a setting of Hebrew psalms for choir and orchestra; and the music for the film *On the Waterfront*. Bernstein also had a gift for communicating in words, which he employed in many television programs and in several books, including *The Joy of Music*.

## BERRIES 

Berries are small fruits that grow on bushes, shrubs, or trailing vines. Some kinds are popular garden plants. Many types of berries are tasty and rich in vitamins. They can be eaten fresh or they can be used to make juices and wines, pastries and pies, and jellies and jams.

Berries grow wild in many parts of North America

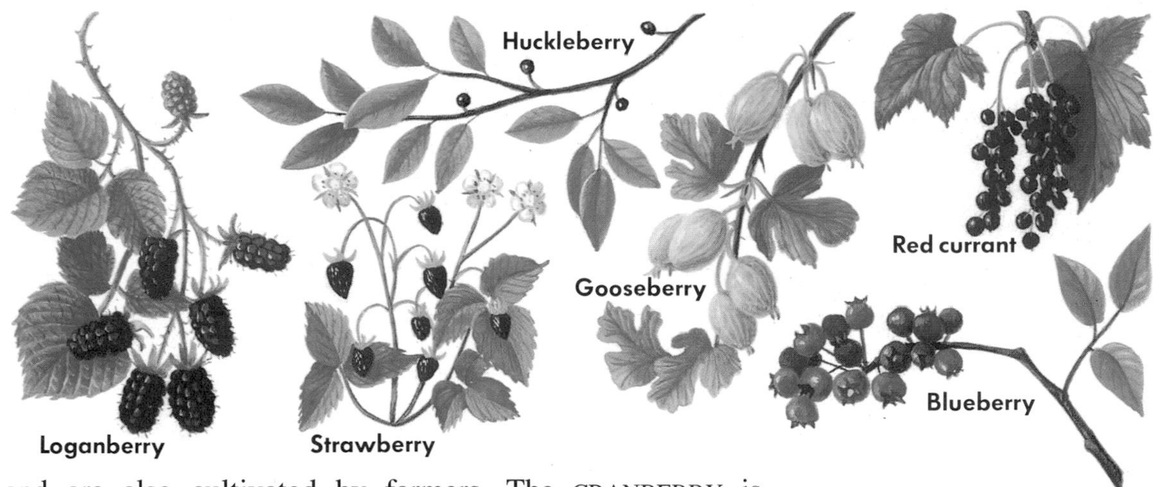


▲ *Some of the many fruits that people call berries. Of the above, only blueberries, gooseberries, huckleberries, and red currants are considered true berries by botanists. They all have seeds inside a single fruit. Strawberries and loganberries are made up of many small fruits.*

and are also cultivated by farmers. The CRANBERRY is an important crop in Massachusetts, Wisconsin, New Jersey, and Washington. A close relative of the cranberry, the lingonberry, is sometimes called the mountain cranberry. Blueberries and huckleberries are also related to the cranberry. Maine is a leading producer of blueberries. Huckleberries grow from New England to the Rockies. Gooseberries and currants are also found across the country.

Blackberries, raspberries, and strawberries are important cultivated crops. They are members of the rose family. Blackberries, which include dewberries, boysenberries, and loganberries, grow best in the warm climate of the South. The three varieties of raspberries—red, black, and purple—are grown along the North Atlantic and Pacific coasts and in the Great Lakes region. The strawberry is the most important cultivated berry. Wisconsin, California, and Oregon are the leading strawberry-producing states.

## BETHUNE, Mary McLeod

Mary McLeod Bethune (1875–1955) was an educator who spent her life working to improve education for black people, especially women.

Her Florida school for black girls later became part of the coeducational Bethune-Cookman College. In 1935 she founded the National Council of Negro Women. Bethune also worked in a number of government positions under presidents Coolidge, Hoover, Roosevelt, Truman, and Eisenhower. Under Roosevelt she was the director of the Division of Negro Affairs of the National Youth Administration.

**The group of advisers who assisted Franklin D. Roosevelt during his presidency was once described by a journalist as "Roosevelt's Brain Trust." The name stuck. From 1935 to 1944, Mary McLeod Bethune served as his special adviser on the problems of minority groups in the United States.**

▲ *Bighorns range in color from dark gray-brown to pale buff. However, all have creamy white patches on their rumps.*

## BIGHORN SHEEP

The bighorn, or mountain sheep, is the only wild sheep found in North America. It lives on remote mountain slopes of the western United States and southwestern Canada. In California it is protected in reserves. There are three species, or kinds, of bighorn: the Rocky Mountain sheep, Dall sheep, and Stone's sheep.

Male bighorns, or rams, have long horns that sweep back in a huge curve of 39 inches (100 cm) or more. The horns of the ewes (females) are shorter and straighter.

► *Bighorn sheep can venture high above the treeline on steep mountainsides. Their lambs can climb up rocky slopes from the day they are born.*

## BILL OF RIGHTS

The first ten amendments to the United States CONSTITUTION form what is known as the Bill of Rights, a summary of the basic rights held by all U.S. citizens. Canada has a similar summary, called the Charter of Rights and Freedoms.

When the Constitution was written, many felt it did not clearly guarantee the rights and freedoms that had been fought for in the American REVOLUTION. As a result, a number of amendments (additions) to the Constitution were proposed. The ten that became the Bill of Rights were passed by Congress in 1789 and became law in 1791, when they were approved by the required number of states.

Since 1791 sixteen other amendments have been

**The first ten amendments to the U.S. Constitution became the law of the land on December 15, 1791. The amendments were known as the Bill of Rights. There were originally 12 amendments, but two that changed the method of electing members of Congress were rejected.**

added, but it is the first ten that stand as a charter for the freedoms of all Americans.

Sometimes there are arguments about just what these rights actually mean. In that case the SUPREME COURT generally decides. This court has the power to interpret what the Constitution says. The court's decision becomes part of the law of the land.

**United States Bill of Rights**

Amendment 1
Congress shall make no law respecting an establishment of religion, or prohibiting the free exercise thereof; or abridging the freedom of speech, or of the press; or the right of the people peaceably to assemble, and to petition the government for a redress of grievances.

Amendment 2
A well-regulated militia, being necessary to the security of a free state, the right of the people to keep and bear arms shall not be infringed.

Amendment 3
No soldier shall, in time of peace, be quartered in any house without the consent of the owner, nor in time of war, but in a manner to be prescribed by law.

Amendment 4
The right of the people to be secure in their persons, houses, papers, and effects, against unreasonable searches and seizures, shall not be violated, and no warrants shall issue, but upon probable cause, supported by oath or affirmation, and particularly describing the place to be searched, and the persons or things to be seized.

Amendment 5
No persons shall be held to answer for a capital or otherwise infamous crime, unless on a presentment or indictment of a grand jury, except in cases arising in the land or naval forces, or in the militia, when in actual service in time of war or public danger; nor shall any person be subject for the same offense to be twice put in jeopardy of life or limb; nor shall be compelled in any criminal case to be a witness against himself, nor be deprived of life, liberty, or property, without due process of law; nor shall private property be taken for public use, without just compensation.

Amendment 6
In all criminal prosecutions, the accused shall enjoy the right to a speedy and public trial, by an impartial jury of the state and district wherein the crime shall have been previously ascertained by law, and to be informed of the nature and cause of the accusation; to be confronted with the witnesses against him; to have compulsory process for obtaining witnesses in his favor, and to have the assistance of counsel for his defense.

Amendment 7
In suits of common law, where the value in controversy shall exceed twenty dollars, the right of trial by jury shall be preserved, and no fact tried by a jury, shall be otherwise reexamined in any court of the United States, than according to the rules of the common law.

Amendment 8
Excessive bail shall not be required, nor excessive fines imposed, nor cruel and unusual punishment inflicted.

Amendment 9
The enumeration in the Constitution, of certain rights, shall not be construed to deny or disparage others retained by the people.

Amendment 10
The powers not delegated to the United States by the Constitution, nor prohibited by it to the states, are reserved to the states respectively, or to the people.

# BIRDS OF NORTH AMERICA

Robin
10 in (25 cm)

Mockingbird
10½ in (27 cm)

Eastern goldfinch
5 in (13 cm)

Black-capped chickadee
5¼ in (13 cm)

Cardinal
8½ in (22 cm)

Birds are animals with feathers. They are warmblooded, like mammals, and they lay eggs, like reptiles. Nearly all birds can fly. There are about 8,700 kinds, or *species*, of birds in the world.

North America is home to many bird species. At times there may be as many as 20 billion birds on the continent. Some are only summer visitors. They raise their young and then *migrate*, or travel, to warmer climates for the winter. But many other birds spend their entire lives in North America.

The land and climate of North America are varied, so there are many different *habitats* for birds. Birds live in the habitat that suits them best. Snow geese, for example, breed along the icy coast of Alaska. Far to the south, in the hot deserts of Arizona, cactus wrens make their nests in cacti.

Sparrows, robins, and jays are among the most commonly seen U.S. birds. But North American birds vary enormously, in size and in other ways. The calliope hummingbird of southern California is only about 2.75 inches (7 cm) long. The California condor measures up to 9 feet (2.6 m) from wing tip to wing tip. It is the largest flying bird in the world.

The California condor is one of several North American birds that are in danger of dying out, or becoming *extinct*. Only about 40 of these birds remain, all in captivity. *Endangered species* such as the condor are protected by law in the United States. The bald eagle, the national bird of the United States, is another of these protected species.

See also BIRDS OF PREY; CARDINAL; CONDOR; DUCKS AND GEESE; EAGLE; ENDANGERED ANIMALS AND PLANTS; GULLS AND TERNS; HAWK; HERON; HUMMINGBIRD; KINGFISHER; MOCKINGBIRD; OWLS; PELICAN; PIGEON; QUAIL; ROBIN; TURKEY; VULTURE; WATER BIRDS; WOODPECKER.

► *A young eagle is banded. Bird banding provides us with useful information about the behavior of different species.*

The roadrunner is a ground-dwelling bird of the Southwest that preys on lizards, snakes, young birds, and mice. It gets its name from the way in which it runs down roads in front of moving vehicles, often as fast as 15 mph (24 km/hr).

Ruffed grouse
17 in (43 cm)

Some Extinct Species
- Passenger pigeon
- Carolina parakeet
- Great auk
- Eskimo curlew
- Labrador duck

Some Endangered Species
- Wild turkey
- California condor
- Whooping crane
- Ivory-billed woodpecker
- Hawaiian goose (nene)
- Bald eagle

In 1903, President Theodore Roosevelt opened Pelican Island in Florida to protect the nesting sites of the brown pelican. This was the first of 400 similar refuges now part of the National Wildlife Refuge System.

Roadrunner
22 in (56 cm)

▼ *Birds can adapt to survive in different habitats. The cactus wren, for example, lives in the desert, nesting among cactus spines.*

Great horned owl
22 in (56 cm)

**Bald eagle**

**Turkey vulture**

**Prairie falcon**

▲ *Although the hooked beaks of the birds of prey pictured above look extremely vicious, the birds depend on their talons as their main weapon. Their beaks are only used when feeding.*

▲ *The bison originally came from Eurasia and migrated to North America in prehistoric times over a land bridge across the Bering Strait.*

## BIRDS OF PREY

Birds that hunt other animals for food are called birds of prey. They all have sharp claws, or talons, for catching and killing their prey and curved beaks for eating.

North America's largest birds of prey are the California CONDOR and the EAGLE. Buzzards, or turkey VULTURES, are birds of prey found all over North America. Most hunt in the daytime, but OWLS are birds of prey that hunt at night. The great horned owl and the screech owl are the most widespread owls in North America.

North America has many species of HAWKS. The sharp-shinned hawk and Cooper's hawk are typical of the group known as "true hawks." They live in woodlands over much of North America. Another group of hawks is the *buteos*. The most common of these is the red-tailed hawk, which lives in woods and open country.

Falcons are a type of hawk, too. One falcon, the American kestrel, or sparrowhawk, is a familiar sight in the western mountains and prairies. The peregrine falcon, which also lives in the West, is the fastest diver of all. It swoops down on its prey at a speed of up to 180 miles per hour (290 km/hr). A relative of the falcon is the osprey, a fish-eating hawk. It is found on the East Coast in particular and is an endangered species, protected by law.

North America has four species of kites. The swallow-tailed kite is the most graceful and elegant of all birds of prey. It lives in the southern swamps, along with the agile Mississippi kite.

## BISON

The bison is a large mammal. It is commonly called the buffalo, although it is not a true buffalo. The bison is similar to the ox, but it is much larger and is covered with long, shaggy fur. It eats grass and leaves, the bark and twigs of trees, and shrubs.

There are two kinds of American bison, the plains bison and the wood bison. The wood bison is slightly larger. Millions of bison once filled the plains and prairies. By the beginning of this century, however, hunters had killed some 50 million bison, and they were almost extinct. Herds are now protected within national parks so that the bison can increase in numbers.

## BLACK AMERICANS

Most Black Americans are descended from African slaves brought to North America in the 17th and 18th centuries. Their original homelands were in West Africa, where we find such countries as Ghana and Sierra Leone. Until recently, they were called Negroes, which is the Spanish word for "black." Today many blacks prefer to be called African-Americans. There are more than 30 million blacks in the United States, making up about 12 percent of the population.

The story of Black Americans is mainly that of a long struggle to win equality in a society dominated by whites. Even after slavery was abolished, blacks who lived in the South were not free in the full sense of the word. They worked for low wages and were generally prevented from getting an education. A few pioneering black educators, such as Booker T. WASHINGTON, established schools and colleges, but educated blacks were treated with more hostility than those who "kept their place." Fear of violence from the KU KLUX KLAN prevented southern blacks from exercising their right to vote. Even in the North, prejudice kept most blacks in low-paying jobs and poor neighborhoods.

Despite the prejudice, blacks have distinguished themselves in government, business, the arts, and the professions. Blacks have also excelled in many sports. JAZZ—possibly the most important musical develop-

▲ *New York City's first black mayor, David Dinkins (left), was elected in 1989. Award-winning author Maya Angelou (right) has written several books based on her own life.*

▲ *Africans were brought to North America to work as slaves on the plantations of the South. By the early 1800s, about 700,000 slaves lived in the southern states.*

Notable Black Americans
(with biographies in this encyclopedia)

*20th-Century Leaders*

Ralph Abernathy
Ralph Bunche
Shirley Chisholm
W.E.B. DuBois
Marcus Garvey
Jesse Jackson
Martin Luther King, Jr.
Malcolm X
Adam Clayton Powell
Colin L. Powell
A. Philip Randolph
Roy Wilkins
Andrew Young
Whitney M. Young

*The Arts*

Marian Anderson
Louis Armstrong
James Baldwin
Gwendolyn Brooks
Countee Cullen
Langston Hughes
Paul Robeson

ment of the 20th century—has its roots in Black American culture.

Thanks to the CIVIL RIGHTS movement, more blacks now get a good education and good jobs than formerly, although there is still a long way to go. At the same time, black leaders, writers, and artists are urging their people to develop a sense of pride in their own culture. The phrase "Black is beautiful" is a reminder to blacks (and whites) that they have much to be proud of.

**Notable Black Americans** (continued)

*Science and Education*

Benjamin Banneker
Mary McCleod Bethune
Luther Burbank
George Washington Carver
Booker T. Washington

*Historical Figures*

Crispus Attucks
Frederick Douglass
Sojourner Truth
Harriet Tubman
Nat Turner

## BLACKFOOT

The Blackfoot are an important group of three tribes which lived in the area where Montana and the Canadian provinces of Saskatchewan and Alberta lie today. They were the Siksika (Blackfoot proper), the Piegan, and the Blood. They spoke an Algonquian language.

Like other PLAINS tribes, the Blackfoot depended on hunting the buffalo. It provided the food they ate. Buffalo hide was made into tents, or tepees. At first the Blackfoot hunted and traveled on foot. They were at the mercy of the SHOSHONI, who moved into the Great Plains with horses. Then the Blackfoot began to take horses from other tribes. With horses and weapons they obtained in trade with the settlers, they became very strong. Today they live as farmers and ranchers.

▼ *A Blackfoot Indian wearing the traditional skin shirt and leggings. In the winter a bison robe was wrapped around the shoulders.*

## BLACK HAWK

Black Hawk (1767–1838) was a Sauk Indian leader who fought to prevent white settlers from taking his people's lands. His Sauk name was *Ma-ka-tai-me-she-kia-kiak*—Black Sparrow Hawk.

In 1804, other chiefs signed away the Sauk lands in Illinois. Most of the Sauk moved by 1830, but Black Hawk and his tribe refused. Armed volunteers forced the Indians to leave their homes. A period of fighting, known as the Black Hawk War, ended in a massacre. Soldiers ignored a flag of truce and killed almost every Indian. Black Hawk himself was taken prisoner for a time and then settled on a reservation.

## BLACKWELL, Elizabeth

Elizabeth Blackwell (1821–1910) was the first woman to obtain a Doctor of Medicine (M.D.) degree from an

American medical school. Born in England, she came to the United States with her family when she was a young girl. She received a good education, but many medical schools rejected her before the Geneva (N.Y.) Medical School agreed to admit her. She graduated first in her class. After training in Paris and London, she opened the New York Infirmary for Women and Children, which provided free health care for the poor and training for women who wanted to become doctors. In 1869, Dr. Blackwell returned to England, where she helped found the London School of Medicine for Women.

▲ *The Blue Ridge Mountains get their name from the blue haze that, from a distance, seems to surround the mountains.*

## BLUE RIDGE MOUNTAINS

Part of the APPALACHIAN MOUNTAINS, the Blue Ridge Mountains are famous for their scenery. The range extends 615 miles (990 km) from southeastern Pennsylvania through Maryland, Virginia, and North and South Carolina to northern Georgia. The highest peaks are in North Carolina. Many rivers and streams run through the mountains. Though famous for their isolation and beauty, the mountains are threatened by POLLUTION and by industrial and housing development.

## BOBCAT

The bobcat, or lynx, is a wild CAT found almost all over the United States, in southwestern Canada, and in northern Mexico. It is at home in most habitats, especially open scrubland and forests with rocky areas. The bobcat generally comes out to hunt at night, feeding on rodents, rabbits, other small mammals, and birds. When it is really hungry, it will even attack deer and sheep.

▼ *Bobcats thrive in the mountain forests and stony terrain of the southwestern states.*

The bobcat is about 24 to 30 inches (60 to 100 cm) long and weighs about 29 pounds (13 kg). It makes a home, or lair, in the hollow of a fallen tree or among the roots of a large bush.

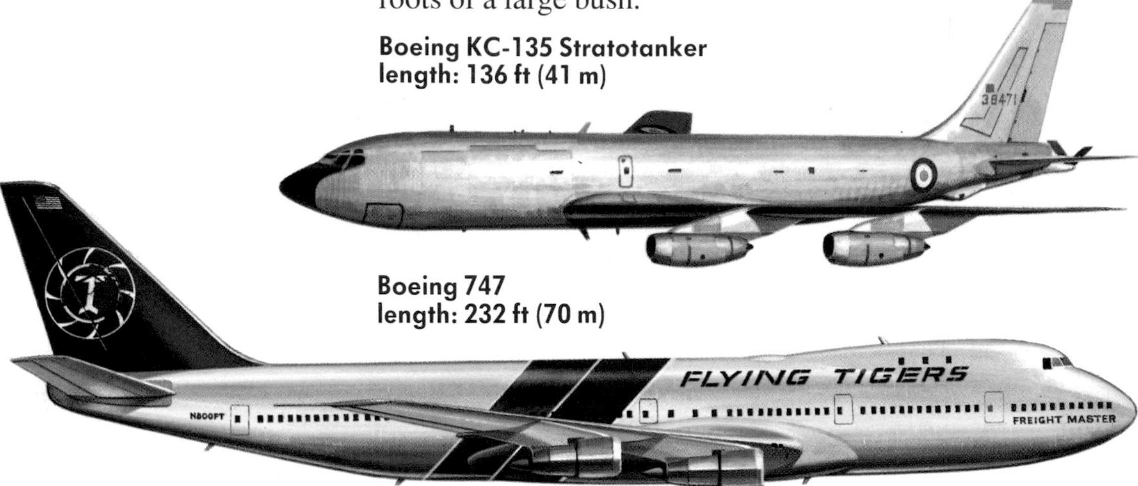


▲ *The Boeing 747 was the first jumbo jet. It can fly 6,000 miles (9,650 km) nonstop. The KC-135 Stratotanker is used to refuel military planes in flight.*

## BOEING, William Edward

William Edward Boeing (1881–1956) is one of the most famous names in aviation. In 1916, in Seattle, Washington, he helped set up the Pacific Aero Products Company. This later became the Boeing Company, with Boeing himself as its president. Today it is the largest AEROSPACE company in the United States, employing more than 100,000 people. Everybody knows Boeing's most famous plane, the 747, or jumbo jet, the most successful commercial airliner ever built. But Boeing has built many other successful jets, including the 707, the 727, and the 737. The company also makes military airplanes and parts for spacecraft.

▼ *Humphrey Bogart won an Academy Award for Best Actor for his performance in* The African Queen.

## BOGART, Humphrey

Humphrey Bogart (1899–1957) was one of America's best-loved film stars. He was best known for his hard-boiled, no-nonsense characters, especially the detectives Philip Marlowe, whom he played in *The Big Sleep*, and Sam Spade, whom he played in *The Maltese Falcon*. These films helped establish a new kind of thriller, one that was glamorous and seedy at the same time. Even today, people love to imitate the rasping voice and world-weary attitude Bogart brought to these parts. His other famous films include *The Treasure of the Sierra Madre* and *The African Queen*.

▲ *While held captive by the Indians, Daniel Boone was forced to "run the gauntlet." This was a test of courage in which Boone had to run unarmed between two rows of fierce warriors.*

## BOONE, Daniel

Daniel Boone (1734–1820) was a famous American pioneer. Just before the American Revolution, he helped blaze the WILDERNESS ROAD through the Cumberland Gap in the Allegheny Mountains. It was along this trail that thousands of settlers made their way westward to Kentucky and beyond, expanding the frontier of the young American nation.

From Boone's earliest childhood, first in Pennsylvania and later in North Carolina, he was at home in the wilderness. He learned how to hunt and trap and to live in the forests like an Indian. In 1775 he led his family and others along the Wilderness Road into Kentucky, where he had already built the settlement of Boonesborough. Three years later Boone was captured by the Shawnee Indians. After learning that the Indians were going to attack Boonesborough, he escaped and led the successful defense against the attack. More and more people were now coming to Kentucky. Boone, who liked the wilderness, moved west to Missouri.

## BOOTH, Edwin

Edwin Booth (1833–1893) was a famous actor of the late 1800s. He was especially admired for his portrayal of Shakespeare's Hamlet. The son of an English actor, Junius Brutus Booth, Edwin was only 15 when he first appeared on stage. By his late twenties he was a star in New York. When Booth's brother, John Wilkes BOOTH, assassinated President Abraham LINCOLN, Edwin retired briefly from the stage.

▼ *Edwin Booth's roles in Shakespeare's plays made him a star on both sides of the Atlantic. He is pictured here dressed as Hamlet.*

▲ *John Wilkes Booth crept into the president's box and shot Lincoln at point-blank range. Brandishing a dagger, he leapt to the stage, breaking his leg, and fled.*

## BOOTH, John Wilkes

John Wilkes Booth (1838–1865) was the person who assassinated President Abraham LINCOLN. Like his brother, Edwin BOOTH, he was an actor. Known for his support of slavery and pro-Southern views, he soon found additional work as a secret Confederate agent. Booth's hatred of Lincoln led him to organize a plot to kill the president. On April 14, 1865, just after the end of the CIVIL WAR, he entered Ford's Theater in Washington, where Lincoln was attending a play, and shot the president in the head. Booth escaped to a farm in Virginia, but Federal troops found him. He was either killed by the soldiers or took his own life.

▼ *The John Hancock towers, old and new, rise up over Boston's Back Bay district.*

## BOSTON

Boston is the capital of MASSACHUSETTS and its largest city, with a population of about 574,200. It is one of the oldest and most historic American cities, founded by PURITAN settlers in 1630. Boston still has many fine old buildings, especially from the colonial period. It was in Boston that many of the events leading up to the American REVOLUTION took place. In the 1800s, Boston grew into a great port and industrial center, where many immigrants, especially from Ireland and Italy, settled. Boston is still an important port, and it has also become a leading financial, business, and transportation center. The many colleges and universities in the Boston area, including Harvard University and the Massachusetts Institute of Technology, have also made the city a major educational center. Boston is on the Atlantic coast, 200 miles (320 km) northeast of New York City.

**Between 1615 and 1617 an epidemic of measles, scarlet fever, and other diseases was responsible for wiping out almost the whole Indian population of the Shawmut peninsula. The diseases had been carried to the region by European explorers. Shawmut was renamed Boston on September 7, 1630, by John Winthrop, governor of Massachusetts.**

## BOSTON MASSACRE

The Boston Massacre was one of the events that led to the American REVOLUTION. On March 5, 1770, a mob of colonists, protesting the presence of British troops in Boston, started hurling snowballs and stones at a soldier who was standing guard at the Boston Customs House. About twenty soldiers joined him and confronted the mob with fixed bayonets. Finally one soldier, who had been hit with a club, opened fire, and others followed. Five colonists were killed. Radical colonists quickly named the incident the "Boston massacre" to whip up resentment against the presence of British troops.

▼ *The event now known as the Boston Massacre occurred when British soldiers were confronted with an unruly mob and lost control. The crowd had been pelting them with snowballs and calling them "lobster-backs," a reference to their red coats.*

## BOSTON TEA PARTY

The Boston Tea Party was one of the events that led to the American REVOLUTION. In 1773, the British Parliament gave the East India Company the right to sell tea to the American colonies at a low price. This meant that the company had a *monopoly*—no one else could match its low price. The colonists feared that the British would try to set up other monopolies, hurting local businesses. They also resented a tax imposed on tea. Some ports refused to admit the British tea ships. In Boston, when two ships arrived, colonists demanded

**The Boston Tea Party inspired a number of copycat "tea parties." In April 1774, a band of New Yorkers, dressed as Indians, dumped British tea in the East River. In October of the same year, the patriots of Annapolis, Maryland, burned the *Peggy Stewart*, a British vessel, and its cargo of tea.**

that the governor order them to leave. When he refused, a group of SONS OF LIBERTY dressed up as Indians and boarded the ships during the night of December 16, 1773. They dumped 342 chests of tea into Boston Harbor. The British then passed more severe laws against the colonists, increasing their anger.

▲ *Samuel Adams led his fellow patriots in the Boston Tea Party. They were disguised as Indians.*

## BOTANICAL GARDENS

A botanical garden is a large park where plants are grown for scientific research or public display. The plants are clearly labeled, and people can examine them and learn more about the way they grow. The plants are also studied by scientists doing research.

One of the largest botanical gardens in the United States is the New York Botanical Garden in New York City. The Brooklyn Botanic Garden, also in New York City, has a special Fragrance Garden for the blind, as well as a children's garden. One of North America's few tropical botanical gardens is the Fairchild Tropical Garden in Miami, Florida. The Missouri Botanical Garden in St. Louis has one of North America's finest collections of orchids, as well as a Japanese Garden.

► *The Brooklyn Botanic Garden, seen here in June, is an oasis of quiet in New York City.*

Some Botanical Gardens in the U.S.

- Arnold Arboretum, Jamaica Plain and Weston, Massachusetts
- Brooklyn Botanic Garden and Arboretum, Brooklyn, New York
- Fairchild Tropical Garden, Miami, Florida
- Longwood Gardens, Kennett Square, Pennsylvania
- Los Angeles City and County Arboretum, Arcadia, California
- Missouri Botanical Garden, St. Louis
- New York Botanical Garden, Bronx, New York
- Rancho Santa Ana Botanic Garden, Claremont, California
- United States National Arboretum, Washington, D.C.

## BOURKE-WHITE, Margaret

The news photographer Margaret Bourke-White (1906–1971) covered many important events of the 20th century. She began her career in 1927, specializing in pictures of buildings and industry. As a photographer for *Life* magazine, she covered some of the battles of WORLD WAR II. She also photographed the horrors of

◄ *Margaret Bourke-White's photographs revealed the beauty that people often ignore around them. This photograph of the George Washington Bridge, which links New York and New Jersey, was taken around the time of the bridge's opening in 1931.*

**Margaret Bourke-White's photograph of Fort Peck Dam in Montana was chosen for *Life*'s first cover as a news magazine. The dam, completed four years later in 1940, was a typical subject for Bourke-White's camera. It represented the national will to fight the Depression with large-scale public works projects.**

the Nazi concentration camps. Later she photographed the struggle for independence in India. Books of her photographs include *Shooting the Russian War* and *Halfway to Freedom.*

## BOWDITCH, Nathaniel

Nathaniel Bowditch (1773–1838) was a mathematician and astronomer. He was raised in the seaport of Salem, Massachusetts. Bowditch had little formal education, but he had a great thirst for knowledge. He taught himself mathematics, French, and Latin. When only in his teens, he wrote a complete almanac. His most important book, *The New American Practical Navigator*, is still a standard reference book for sailors.

▼ *Nathaniel Bowditch's combined skills in mathematics and astronomy made nautical research easy for him.*

▲ *The Bowie knife has a large blade with a curved edge. It was designed as a single all-purpose implement, useful for hunting as well as for defense.*

## BOWIE, James

James Bowie (1796–1836) was a frontiersman, adventurer, Indian fighter, and a hero of the Mexican War. Born in Georgia, Bowie spent much of his life in Texas, which was then part of Mexico. He became a Mexican citizen, but he took part in the Texas Revolution and died at the siege of the Alamo, sharing command of the defense of the fort against the Mexicans. Bowie is often credited with designing the Bowie knife, a weapon favored by American frontiersmen. But some experts believe that his brother, Rezin, actually designed it.

## BOWLING

There are more than 11,000 bowling alleys in the United States. Millions of people bowl each year.

Bowling was introduced to America by the Dutch in the 1600s. They used nine pins, and men would bet on the outcome of the games. The American colonies banned bowling as a result. Bowlers got around the law by using ten pins rather than the nine used before. Today there are many kinds of bowling games, such as duckpins, fivepins, lawn bowling, candlepins, and boccie. But tenpin bowling is the most popular game. Dozens of tournaments organized by such groups as the Professional Bowlers Association and the Ladies Professional Bowlers Tour are televised. Today's champion bowlers include Marshall Holman, Mike Aulby, Earl Anthony, and Robin Romeo.

▼ *Joe Louis became world heavyweight champion in 1937. He defended the title 25 times before his retirement in 1949.*

## BOXING

The sport of boxing has many critics, but it is still extremely popular. More than 750 million people around the world watched heavyweight champion Mike Tyson's defeat in January 1990, when James Douglas defied predictions and knocked him out.

Fears of illegal gambling, as well as the bloody results of bare-knuckle fights, meant that boxing was against the law in most states until early this century. New York became the first state to legalize boxing under the Walker Law, passed in 1920. This called for strict regulations and the use of padded boxing gloves. The Golden Age of boxing over the next two decades brought world fame to fighters such as Jack DEMPSEY,

◀ *Mike Tyson's 30-month reign as undisputed world heavyweight champion began with his victory over Tony Tucker (right) on August 1, 1987.*

Gene Tunney, and Joe LOUIS. After World War II, television made "the Saturday night fight" as popular as "Monday night football" is today. Later, such boxers as Muhammad ALI, George Foreman, and Sugar Ray Leonard further increased the sport's popularity.

Some Famous American Boxers

| Heavyweight Champions | |
|---|---|
| John L. Sullivan | 1882–1892 |
| James J. Corbett | 1892–1897 |
| Jack Johnson | 1908–1915 |
| Jack Dempsey | 1919–1926 |
| Joe Louis | 1937–1949 |
| Rocky Marciano | 1952–1956 |
| Muhammad Ali | 1964–1967<br>1974–1978 |
| Mike Tyson | 1987–1990 |
| **Middleweight Champions** | |
| Sugar Ray Robinson | 1951–1952<br>1955–1957<br>1958–1959 |
| **Welterweight Champions** | |
| Sugar Ray Robinson | 1946–1951 |
| Sugar Ray Leonard | 1980–1982 |

## BOY SCOUTS *See* Scouts

## BRADFORD, William

William Bradford (1590–1657) was a leader of the Pilgrims and governor of PLYMOUTH COLONY for more than 30 years between 1621 and 1656. He helped draw up the Mayflower Compact. This agreement laid the foundations for the colony's self-government. He encouraged the development of democratic institutions, such as the town meeting, and established a generally peaceful relationship with the local Indians. Plymouth Colony prospered under his leadership.

**Governor William Bradford did not approve of celebrations. Despite this, he established the first feast of Thanksgiving to celebrate the successful harvest in the autumn of 1621.**

## BRADLEY, Omar Nelson

Omar Bradley (1893–1981) served in the U.S. Army for more than 35 years. He attained the rank of General of the Army. During WORLD WAR II he proved himself a brilliant commander in North Africa and in the invasion of Sicily in 1943. The next year he was put in charge of the American forces that landed on the beaches at Normandy, France, on D DAY. Bradley was made chief of staff of the Army in 1948, and a year later he became the first chairman of the Joint Chiefs of Staff.

▲ *Marlon Brando played Johnny, the tough leader of a motorcycle gang, in* The Wild Ones.

## BRADY, Mathew

The photographer Mathew Brady (1823–1896) is best known for his pictures of the CIVIL WAR. He began his career as a fashionable portrait photographer, photographing many famous people.

To photograph the Civil War, Brady hired a team of 20 photographers. Brady himself was present at several battles. Action photographs were not yet possible, but Brady's pictures of weary, wounded, and dead soldiers form a moving record of the war. Taking these pictures cost Brady $100,000. But he earned very little from them and died a poor man.

## BRANDO, Marlon

Marlon Brando (1924– ) is one of the most famous actors of this century. He first became known as a powerful stage actor, but he soon went to HOLLYWOOD. Some of his classic film performances include Marc Antony in *Julius Caesar* and Stanley Kowalski in *A Streetcar Named Desire*. He won an ACADEMY AWARD in 1954 for his role in *On the Waterfront*. His rare later roles include Don Corleone in *The Godfather*, which won him another Oscar (1972).

## BRANT, Joseph

Joseph Brant (1742–1807) was a MOHAWK chief. His Indian name was Thayendanegea. Brant was a good friend to the British and fought for them in the FRENCH AND INDIAN WAR. His sister married Sir William Johnson, who became superintendent of the Iroquois tribes in what is now upstate New York. Brant even visited Britain, but he returned to America to fight for the British in the American REVOLUTION. After the war, Britain gave him a grant of land in Canada.

▼ *Walter Brattain's work on semiconductors and transistors opened the world of electronics for modern use.*

## BRATTAIN, Walter

Walter Brattain (1902–1987) was a physicist who invented the transistor in 1947 with fellow scientists William B. SHOCKLEY and John BARDEEN. In 1956 all three, who worked at Bell Telephone Laboratories, were awarded the Nobel Prize for physics for their invention. The transistor revolutionized electronics. It helped make possible many of the electronic products we take for granted today, such as personal computers and communications satellites.

▲ *The Governor Thomas Johnson Bridge spans the Patuxent River in Maryland.*

## BRIDGES 

Bridge building has always been one of the greatest challenges facing engineers and builders in the United States. Most famous bridges are suspension bridges. Suspension bridges are suspended from cables hung between two tall towers. The U.S. bridge with the longest suspended span is the Verrazano-Narrows Bridge, linking Staten Island and Brooklyn in New York City. The span between its towers is 4,260 feet (1,298 m).

The Golden Gate Bridge in San Francisco has a

Some Notable American Bridges

| Kind of Bridge | Total Length | Year Opened | Bridge |
|---|---|---|---|
| Suspension | 26,372 ft (8,017 m) | 1957 | Mackinac Straits, Michigan |
| Suspension | 13,700 ft (4,176 m) | 1964 | Verrazano-Narrows, New York |
| Suspension | 8,981 ft (2,737 m) | 1937 | Golden Gate, California |
| Cantilever | 13,915 ft (4,241 m) | 1974 | Commodore John Barry, Pennsylvania – New Jersey |
| Steel arch | 8,460 ft (2,579 m) | 1931 | Bayonne, New Jersey – Staten Island, New York |
| Combination | 154,387 ft (47,057 m) | 1956 and 1969 | Lake Pontchartrain Causeway, Louisiana |

shorter span, but its two bridge towers are the highest in the world—746 feet (227 m) above the water level. In the 18th and 19th centuries, many covered wooden bridges were built. The roof protected passengers as well as the structure of the bridge itself. Most of these bridges fell victim to fires, but the remaining covered bridges (mainly in New England) are popular with tourists.

Engineers still build drawbridges to raise when tall ships have to pass through. Drawbridges that open on a hinge (like medieval castle drawbridges) are called bascule bridges. Chicago has five bascule bridges with a span of more than 240 feet (74 m).

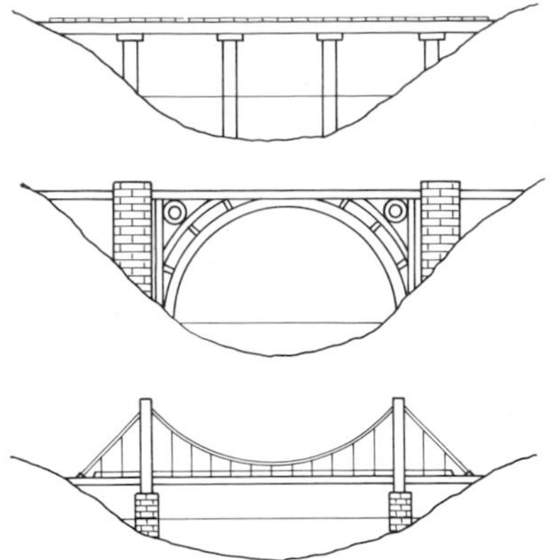

▲ *Standard bridge designs include beam (top), arch (center), and suspension.*

► *The 5-mile (8-km)-long Mackinac Bridge links Michigan's Upper and Lower peninsulas.*

▼ *Nevada's bristlecone pines survive for thousands of years in poor soil and arid conditions. Most other trees would die within a month.*

## BRISTLECONE PINE

Bristlecone pine trees are the oldest living trees in the world. The oldest one of all, named Methuselah, is almost 4,700 years old. These trees grow mainly in mountainous areas in the southwestern states.

The trees grow very slowly and are only about 10 to 30 feet (3 to 8 m) tall. Bristlecone pines that grow in the eastern states are dwarf trees and may grow to only 3 feet (1 m). Gnarled and twisted by the wind, they do not grow at elevations below about 8,000 feet (2,600 m). The few bunches of needles growing on each tree stay on the tree for up to 30 years. This helps the trees endure long droughts.

# BRITISH COLUMBIA

British Columbia is CANADA's westernmost province and the only province on the Pacific coast. It is also the country's third largest province in size and in population.

Much of British Columbia is wild and rugged, with spectacular forests, rivers, and lakes. The Rocky Mountains lie along British Columbia's border with the province of Alberta. Numerous rivers, such as the Fraser, reach inland from the rocky coast. Away from the ocean, the winter climate can be as harsh as the terrain. Settlement in these regions has been difficult. But the province's vast natural resources, especially timber, coal, copper, and lead, have drawn many eastern Canadians to British Columbia since it was opened up in the 1800s. Most people live in the southwestern part of the province, in and around the cities of VANCOUVER, the largest city and port, and Victoria, the capital. Victoria is located on the 285-mile (460-km)-long Vancouver Island. The weather in the southwest is warm, with frequent rain. Parts of the coast here are fertile and low-lying, with many farms. There are also numerous fishing villages and towns.

▲ *Snowcapped mountains loom over the excellent natural harbor of Horseshoe Bay, in west Vancouver.*

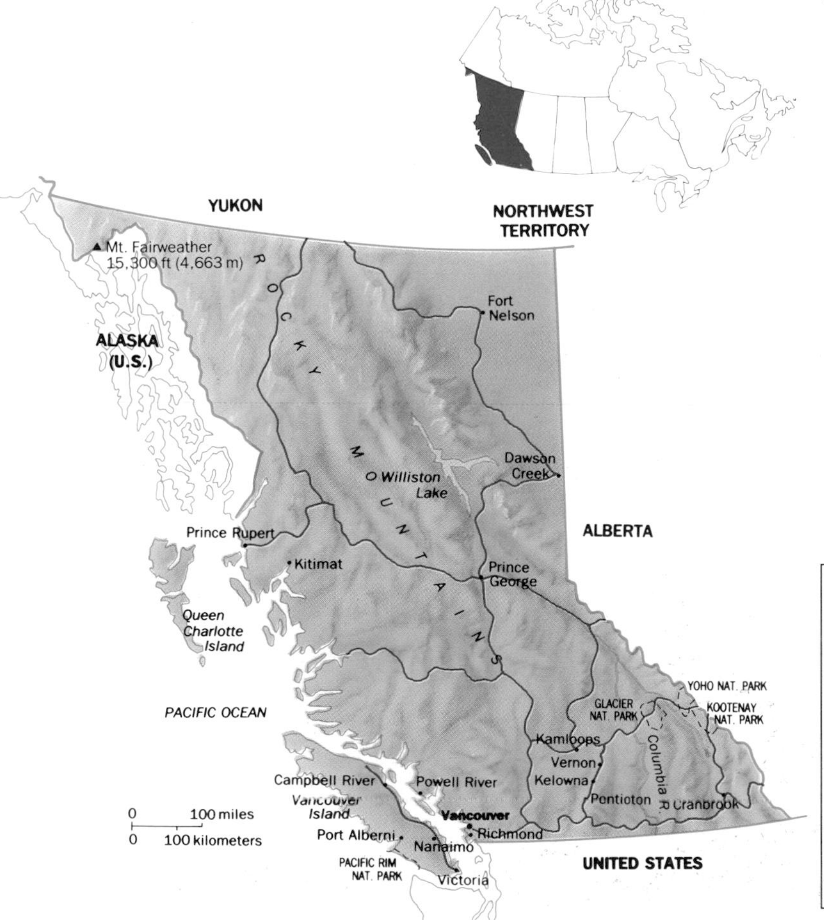

**Flowering dogwood**

British Columbia
**Capital:** Victoria
**Area:** 365,900 sq mi (947,800 km²). Rank: 3rd
**Population:** 3,282,061 (1991). Rank: 3rd
**Entry into Confederation:** July 20, 1871 (6th province)
**Highest point:** Mt. Fairweather, 15,300 ft (4,663 m)

**On April 17, 1982, the British North America Act was replaced with the Constitution Act, the new governing document of Canada.**

## BRITISH NORTH AMERICA ACT 

Passed by the British Parliament in 1867, the British North America Act created the Canadian Confederation. It also served as CANADA's constitution. The new nation consisted of the provinces of Nova Scotia, New Brunswick, Ontario, and Quebec. By 1873 all of the other provinces except Newfoundland had joined. The act provided for a government similar to that of Britain, with a parliament and a prime minister. The British North America Act served as Canada's written constitution until 1982, when the British Parliament passed the Canada Act. This, in effect, transferred Canada's constitution to Canada from Britain.

**Each year since 1947, Broadway has honored its best productions with the Tony Awards. These are given for the best play and musical, best actor and actress, and other achievements.**

## BROADWAY 

Broadway is the best-known street in NEW YORK CITY. From its start at the southern tip of Manhattan it runs 15.5 miles (25 km) north, eventually crossing into the Bronx and ending at the city's northern border. Broadway passes Wall Street and the famous financial district, but its most noted stretch is just north of Times Square, where Broadway becomes the center of the theater district. Most of New York's famous plays and shows have been staged in Broadway theaters. High rents nowadays have closed many theaters.

▼ *The neon lights are always bright on Broadway. Illuminated movie and theater marquees compete with dazzling billboard ads and headlights from passing traffic.*

## BROOKS, Gwendolyn

Gwendolyn Brooks (1917– ) won the PULITZER PRIZE for poetry in 1950 for her collection of poems entitled *Annie Allen*. Brooks has spent most of her life in Chicago. Her observations of racial hatred and discrimination in the Chicago neighborhood where she lived inspired her early work, such as *Bronzeville Boys and Girls*. Using short, sharp phrases and simple rhymes, she wrote of everyday things and experiences as they affected the lives of black people. She became the poet laureate of Illinois in 1968.

▲ *Gwendolyn Brooks was born in Kansas, but her poems deal with ghetto life in Chicago.*

## BROWN, John

John Brown (1800–1859) was an ABOLITIONIST who believed that force was necessary to free the slaves. He was considered a radical by some in the abolitionist movement. In 1856, Brown, four of his sons, and other abolitionists were involved in some bloody fighting between pro- and anti-slavery settlers in Kansas. On the night of October 16, 1859, he and 21 armed co-conspirators captured the federal arsenal at Harpers Ferry, Virginia. Several people were killed on both sides. Two days later, Federal troops commanded by Col. Robert E. LEE forced the band to surrender. Brown was tried and convicted of treason against Vir-

▼ *John Brown lost two sons in the Harpers Ferry raid. His own execution made him a martyr for the anti-slavery movement.*

**At the 1896 Democratic National Convention, Bryan made one of the most famous political speeches in the history of the United States. He was calling for the free coinage of silver at a fixed rate with gold. He believed that if the government issued silver coins as well as gold, it would help the country's farmers and therefore improve the whole economy. Bryan ended his rousing speech with the much quoted words: "You shall not crucify mankind upon a cross of gold."**

ginia, promoting a slave revolt, and murder. He was hanged in December. Many Northerners considered him a martyr, and during the CIVIL WAR "John Brown's Body" was a popular Union song.

## BRUCE, Blanche Kelso

Blanche Kelso Bruce (1841–1898) was the first black American to serve a full term in the U.S. Senate. Bruce was born a slave in Virginia, but was tutored by his master's son and attended Oberlin College in Ohio. He set up two schools for blacks in Kansas and Missouri. After the CIVIL WAR, Bruce became a planter in Mississippi. He later became involved in Republican politics, and in 1874 was elected to the U.S. Senate. As senator he actively promoted the rights of minorities, including Indians and immigrants from Asia.

## BRYAN, William Jennings

William Jennings Bryan (1860–1925) was a great orator and political leader. A lawyer, Bryan entered politics in the 1880s as a Democratic congressman from Nebraska. He ran for president in 1896 as an opponent of the gold standard, a major issue of the day. Although he lost the election, he remained an important Democratic leader. He later served as President Woodrow WILSON's secretary of state. He resigned because he thought Wilson's policies would bring the country into WORLD WAR I. Bryan returned to lecturing and the law until his death in 1925.

▼ *Not long before his death in 1925, William Jennings Bryan was the attorney for the prosecution in the famous Scopes trial in Tennessee. John Scopes, a teacher, had been charged with teaching the theory of evolution in violation of state law. Bryan used his great oratory skill to present a religious view of creation. Scopes was convicted but not before defense attorney Clarence Darrow had put Bryan through some fierce cross-examination.*

# BUCHANAN, James

James Buchanan was the 15th president of the United States. He served during the years just before the CIVIL WAR. Before his election, Buchanan, who was a lawyer, served in the Pennsylvania legislature and the U.S. House of Representatives. He also served as minister to Russia, U.S. senator, secretary of state under President James K. POLK, and minister to Great Britain. A Democrat, he was elected president in 1856.

When Buchanan came to office, the United States was heading toward civil war. In Kansas, pro-slavery and anti-slavery groups were fighting. Buchanan felt that slavery was wrong, but he wanted to preserve the Union. Because pro-slavery people controlled the government of Kansas, Buchanan was ready to allow Kansas to join the Union as a slave state. This angered many Northerners.

In 1857, Buchanan became involved in the Dred Scott case. The Supreme Court had ruled that the slave Dred Scott could not take legal action in a federal (national) court to obtain his freedom, because slaves were not U.S. citizens. Buchanan supported this position, which further annoyed Northerners.

▼ *On January 9, 1861, South Carolina troops fired on the federal ship* Star of the West. *President Buchanan had sent the ship to supply troops stationed around Charleston Harbor.*

In 1859, John BROWN made his famous raid on the arsenal at Harpers Ferry. The United States was on the brink of civil war. The DEMOCRATIC PARTY was split, and Republican Abraham LINCOLN won the election. As a result, seven southern states seceded (withdrew) from the Union during Buchanan's last months in office. He stated that they had no right to secede, but also that he had no power to stop them. In March 1861 he handed over the reins of government to Lincoln.

**James Buchanan**
**Born:** April 23, 1791, near Mercersburg, Pennsylvania
**Education:** Dickinson College, Carlisle, Pennsylvania
**Political Party:** Democratic
**Term of office:** 1857–1861
**Died:** June 1, 1868, in Lancaster, Pennsylvania

▲ *Many of Pearl Buck's 65 books and hundreds of stories tried to foster understanding between Asia and the West.*

## BUCK, Pearl S.

Pearl Buck (1892–1973) was a novelist who wrote about life in China. She spent most of her childhood in that country, where her parents were missionaries. Her best-known book, *The Good Earth*, tells of a Chinese peasant and his wife whose struggles and patience are eventually rewarded with prosperity. This novel won the 1932 PULITZER PRIZE; later writings won her the Nobel Prize for literature in 1938. After World War II, Pearl Buck did charitable work, helping Asian orphans and retarded children. She told the story of her own life in *My Several Worlds*.

## BUFFALO *See* Bison

## BUFFALO BILL *See* Cody, William F.

## BUGS

**The fearsome assassin bug is known for its painful stab and resulting swelling. Despite this, it is very useful as a pest control. Because the assassin bug feeds on the insects that destroy crops, it has proved to be a farmer's friend.**

People often use the word "bug" to refer to any INSECT. But to scientists, bugs are only those insects that have long, pointed, beaklike mouthparts. Bugs use their mouthparts for sucking the juices of plants or the blood of humans or other animals.

Bugs can be found nearly everywhere. Some, such as water boatmen, backswimmers, and water scorpions, live in the water. But most bugs live on land.

Many bugs are helpful because they destroy weeds or insect pests. But often bugs are harmful because they attack crops. Plant bugs, lace bugs, and stinkbugs, for example, are all serious pests. A number of bugs, such

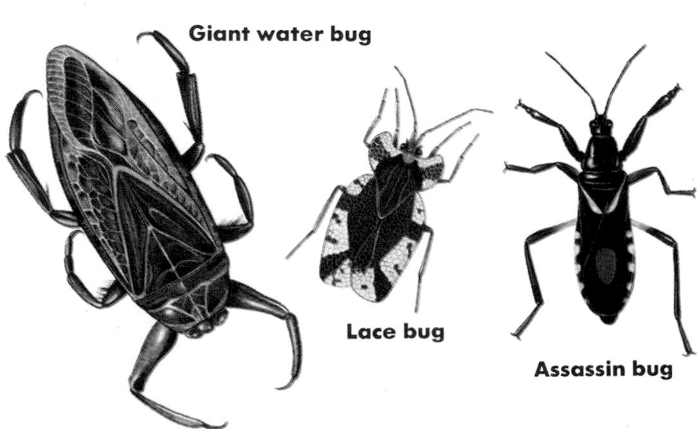


► *Bugs come in all different shapes and sizes. The giant water bug can grow to 2.5 inches (6 cm), while the lace bug grows to a mere 0.25 inch (0.6 cm). Bugs vary in color too. Often the colors are designed to act as camouflage or to warn off predators. All bugs belong to the insect order* Hemiptera.

as the bedbug, bite humans or animals. Some even pass on germs.

To hide from their prey and their enemies, some bugs, such as the ambush bug, are colored to blend in with their background. Others, like the stinkbug, smell nasty or have an unpleasant taste. Many advertise this fact by being brightly colored.

A young bug, after hatching from an egg, is called a *nymph*. It looks very much like an adult bug but does not have wings.

Despite their names, ladybugs, mealy bugs, doodlebugs, and sowbugs are not true bugs.

▲ *Many Northerners thought that the first Battle of Bull Run would end the Civil War quickly. Some Washington residents even took picnics and watched. The fierce battle that followed, with its many casualties, came as a terrible shock.*

## BULL RUN, Battles of 

Two CIVIL WAR battles were fought near the stream called Bull Run, near Manassas, in northern Virginia. They are known in the North as the Battles of Bull Run, and in the South as the Battles of Manassas. The first battle, on July 21, 1861, was the opening engagement of an intended Union attack on Richmond. Both sides were inexperienced. The Union forces seemed at first to have the advantage, but the arrival of Confederate reinforcements stopped them and they retreated to Washington. The battle demonstrated to Northerners that they would not be able to win the war quickly.

The following year, on August 29–30, General LEE's Confederate army met another Union army in the same place and defeated them, with heavy casualties on both sides. More than 27,000 Union and Confederate soldiers were killed, captured, or wounded during the two Battles of Bull Run.

**Casualties at the second Battle of Bull Run were heavy. Following this major Confederate victory, Union troops were cleared out of Virginia for the first time during the Civil War.**

## BUNCHE, Ralph

Ralph Bunche (1904–1971) was a distinguished diplomat. During the 1940s he played an important role in setting up the UNITED NATIONS. His special area of knowledge was in dealing with colonies or former colonies. His skill as a negotiator was also highly prized. After the establishment of the state of Israel in 1948, war broke out in the Middle East between Israel and its Arab neighbors. Bunche conducted talks that led to an armistice. This great achievement won him the Nobel Peace Prize in 1950. He later held several important positions in the United Nations.

**The famous Battle of Bunker Hill actually took place on Breed's Hill, a short distance away. The American troops set up bulwarks on Breed's Hill but lacked the supplies they needed to defeat the British outright. However, the British army was forced to charge the hill three times before the Americans finally withdrew.**

## BUNKER HILL, Battle of

The Battle of Bunker Hill, at Boston, was the first major battle of the American REVOLUTION. It was actually fought on nearby Breed's Hill. British troops controlled Boston, and they planned to occupy the hills across the Charles River from the city. The colonists learned of this plan and sent their forces to Breed's Hill before the British could do so. On June 17, 1775, British troops attacked. The British captured both hills, but 1,000 out of 2,300 British soldiers were killed. Of the 3,200 Americans in the battle, 450 were killed or wounded.

*▼ The American troops at Bunker Hill had very little ammunition. As the British marched toward them in rows, American Colonel William Prescott told his men to wait. He gave his now-famous order: "Don't fire until you see the whites of their eyes."*

## BUNYAN, Paul 

In American FOLKLORE, Paul Bunyan is a legendary figure, a lumberjack of superhuman size and strength. He is the hero of many "tall tales," in which frontiersmen would try to outdo each other in telling ever more incredible stories. In one story, for example, it is claimed that Bunyan created the Grand Canyon by dragging his pickax along the ground. In another, his giant blue ox, Babe, hauled the logs from an entire forest. The character may have been based on a real person, a French Canadian named Paul Bunyon who ran a logging camp in the mid-1800s. The feats of the fictional Paul Bunyan first appeared in print in a lumber company's advertisement in 1914. Since then, they have been celebrated in several books, in poems by Robert Frost and others, and in an operetta by the British composer Benjamin Britten.

▲ *Most Paul Bunyan stories also include tall tales about his blue ox, Babe. Babe was supposed to have measured 42 ax handles long and could drink a river dry.*

## BURBANK, Luther 

Luther Burbank (1849–1926) was a plant breeder who developed hundreds of new kinds of vegetables, fruits, and flowers. Burbank was fascinated by the possibility of creating new kinds of plants from already existing ones. The reason for doing this was so that the new plants would combine the strengths of the older ones—for instance, a vegetable with an interesting flavor and texture that would also withstand harsh weather. Among his most well-known creations are the Burbank (or Idaho) potato and the Shasta daisy.

▲ *Aaron Burr's political career ended when he killed Alexander Hamilton in a duel. By the mid-1800s dueling was banned in most of the United States.*

## BURR, Aaron

Aaron Burr (1756–1836) was an American political leader who became vice president under Thomas JEFFERSON.

A lawyer, Burr entered New York state politics in the 1780s. He was elected to the U.S. Senate in 1791. In the meantime, however, he had acquired a political enemy, Alexander HAMILTON. When Burr and Thomas Jefferson tied in the presidential election of 1800, Hamilton worked to secure Burr's defeat. Burr then served as vice president under Jefferson. But in 1804, before his term was finished, he fought a duel with Hamilton in which Hamilton was killed. Under threat of arrest for murder, Burr joined a friend, General James Wilkinson, in a plot to invade Mexico and found a new country that would have included part of the Louisiana Territory. Wilkinson betrayed Burr, who was tried for treason. He was acquitted, but his political career was finished.

► *Johnny Weissmuller, the first actor to play Tarzan in the movies, wrestles with a young elephant. The Tarzan movies introduced millions of people to Edgar Rice Burroughs's books. They have been translated into 50 languages.*

**Edgar Rice Burroughs had no experience of either English high society or the African jungle before he wrote his Tarzan novels. Instead he had been a storekeeper, gold miner, cowboy, and even light-bulb salesman.**

## BURROUGHS, Edgar Rice

The writer Edgar Rice Burroughs (1875–1950) created Tarzan, one of the most popular characters in fiction. Tarzan, the son of an English nobleman, is abandoned in Africa as a baby when his parents are killed. He is brought up by apes and learns their language. Burroughs wrote the first Tarzan book, *Tarzan of the Apes*, in 1914. It was an immediate success, and he went on to write another 25 Tarzan books.

# BUSH, George

George Bush was the 41st president of the United States. Born in Massachusetts, he served as a U.S. Navy pilot during World War II. Later, after moving to Texas, he helped found an oil company and then entered politics. Between 1967 and 1977, Bush was a U.S. congressman, ambassador to the United Nations, envoy to China, and director of the Central Intelligence Agency (CIA). He served as vice president under Ronald REAGAN from 1981 to 1989.

Bush was elected president in 1988. During his term in office, all the Communist regimes of eastern Europe collapsed, and the Soviet Union fell apart. After more than 40 years of COLD WAR, Americans no longer had to fear the prospect of a nuclear war. In December 1989 Bush ordered U.S. troops to invade Panama and overthrow that country's dictator, General Manuel Noriega. Bush sent U.S. troops overseas again in August 1990 when Iraq invaded the oil-rich country of Kuwait. Because this threatened U.S. oil supplies, Bush organized an armed response. Led by the United States and backed by the United Nations, a force of 28 nations expelled the Iraqis from Kuwait in February 1991.

In domestic affairs, Bush had inherited a huge budget deficit. The government was spending much more than it was taking in from taxes and other sources. When Bush was running for president, he promised "no new taxes." But in 1990 he backed a bill to reduce the deficit by raising taxes. The higher taxes and the poor performance of the U.S. economy during his term in office cost Bush the presidency. In his bid for re-election in 1992 he was defeated by Democrat Bill CLINTON.

George Bush
**Born:** June 12, 1924, in Milton, Massachusetts
**Education:** Yale University
**Political party:** Republican
**Term of office:** 1989–1993
**Married:** 1945 to Barbara Price

*▼ George Bush (center) commanded an X-2 Naval Air fighter plane in World War II.*

*◄ President Bush, seen here with former British Prime Minister Margaret Thatcher. Even before he became president, Bush had met many world leaders during his years as vice president.*

# BUTTERFLIES AND MOTHS

Butterflies and moths are flying INSECTS whose wings are covered in tiny, colored scales. Most feed by sucking sweet juices, known as nectar, from flowers. There are about 12,000 different kinds, or *species*, of butterflies in the world and about 120,000 species of moths. Of these, there are about 700 species of butterflies and 9,000 species of moths in North America.

The colors and patterns on the wings of butterflies and moths help to protect them from being eaten by other ani-

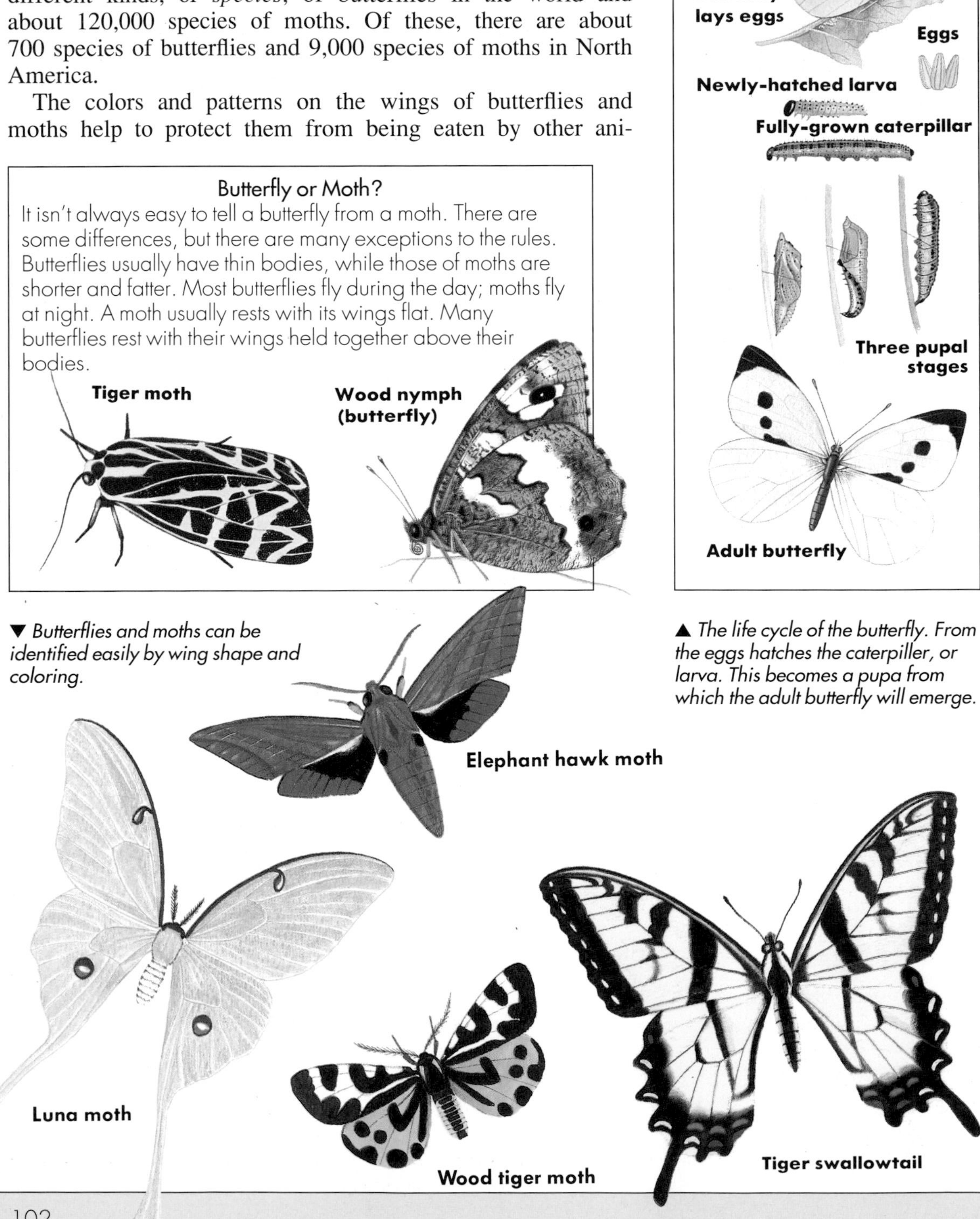


### Butterfly or Moth?

It isn't always easy to tell a butterfly from a moth. There are some differences, but there are many exceptions to the rules. Butterflies usually have thin bodies, while those of moths are shorter and fatter. Most butterflies fly during the day; moths fly at night. A moth usually rests with its wings flat. Many butterflies rest with their wings held together above their bodies.

▼ *Butterflies and moths can be identified easily by wing shape and coloring.*

▲ *The life cycle of the butterfly. From the eggs hatches the caterpiller, or larva. This becomes a pupa from which the adult butterfly will emerge.*

▲ *A cluster of monarch butterflies swarms in a tree during the annual migration from their winter quarters in Mexico to their breeding grounds in the United States and Canada.*

mals. Some, such as hawk moths, look so much like their surroundings that they are practically invisible. Others, such as monarch butterflies, have an unpleasant taste or are poisonous. They are usually brightly colored, so that their enemies will easily remember to avoid them. There are some butterflies and moths that look like (or *mimic*) a poisonous type of butterfly. Their enemies avoid them even though they do not actually taste bad themselves. Viceroy butterflies, for example, mimic monarchs.

Butterflies known as hairstreaks have spots that look like eyes at the tip of each back wing. These false eyes cause their enemies to snap at the wrong part, so that the butterfly escapes.

Because many species are similar in a number of ways, they are grouped into large categories. Skippers are insects that share characteristics of butterflies and moths. They are usually classed as a separate group.

**Butterfly Families**

**Fritillaries:** Regal fritillary
**Blues, Coppers, and Hairstreaks:** American copper, Spring azure
**Brush-footed butterflies:** Mourning cloak
**Sulphurs and Whites:** Common sulphur
**Satyrs and Wood nymphs:** Pearly eye
**Swallowtails:** Black swallowtail
**Metalmarks:** Northern metalmark
**Milkweed butterflies:** Monarch
**Snout butterflies:** Southern snout butterfly

▲ *Charles Lindbergh congratulates Richard Byrd for his flight over the South Pole. Just two years before, in 1927, Lindbergh had made his historic transatlantic flight.*

## BUZZARD *See* Vulture

## BYRD, Richard E.

Richard Byrd (1888–1957) was America's greatest Antarctic explorer. He learned to fly in the Navy, after graduating from the U.S. Naval Academy in 1912. In 1926, during an expedition to the Arctic, he and his co-pilot, Floyd Bennett, became the first persons to fly over the North Pole. Byrd later passed on some advice on navigation to Charles LINDBERGH, who was preparing for his own transatlantic flight. Byrd soon turned his attention to Antarctica. He led an expedition to that frozen continent in 1928, and in the following year he became the first person to fly over the South Pole. Soon after, he was promoted to rear admiral. Byrd led four other expeditions to Antarctica, the last in 1956, to explore and map the continent and to conduct scientific studies. During his 1933–1935 expedition, Byrd stayed alone in a weather station built under the snow and ice for five months. His small hut was located farther south than any human occupation up to that time. He wrote about this adventure in the book *Alone*.

**Despite freezing fingers and an aircraft with an oil leak, Byrd and Bennett circled the North Pole several times. The journey lasted 15 hours and 51 minutes. In 1909, Robert E. Peary and Matthew Henson had taken eight months to reach the North Pole by dogsled.**

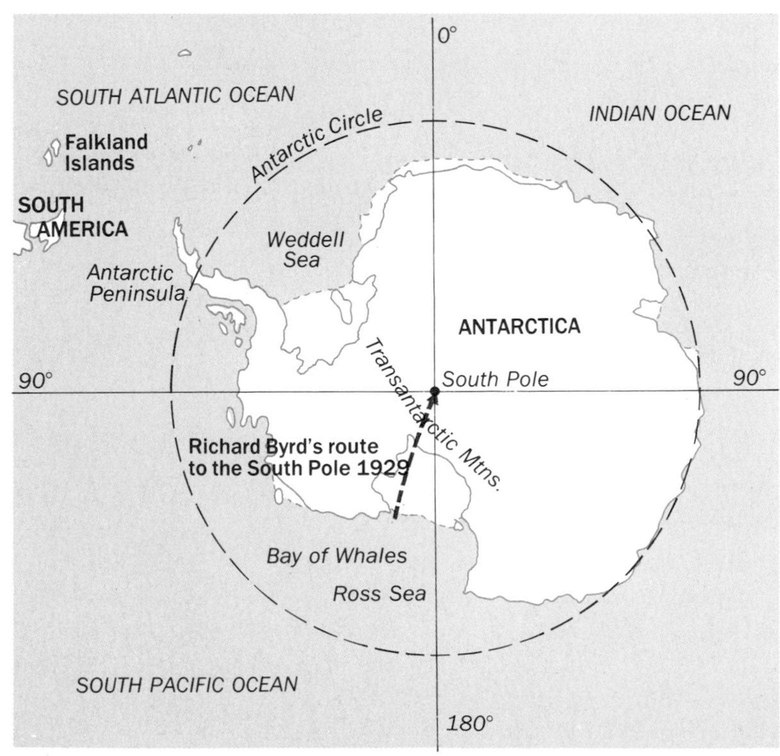


► *On November 28, 1929, Byrd became the first person to fly over the South Pole. He set off from his base camp, called "Little America," on the Ross Ice Shelf at the Bay of Whales, and the round trip took him 19 hours.*

## CABINET

The Cabinet is a group of presidential advisers. It includes the heads, or secretaries, of the major government departments, plus the attorney general. The Cabinet is not the only group that helps shape the government's policies. Some presidents have used their own advisers even more than they have used the Cabinet for decision making.

Though the CONSTITUTION does not call for a Cabinet, over the years it has become a central part of the United States government. The president nominates the members of the Cabinet, and they must then be approved by the Senate. He often chooses them not just because he thinks they will be able to perform their jobs efficiently, but because they share his political goals. As a result, when a new president is elected, the members of the old Cabinet resign, and the new president appoints a new Cabinet.

◀ *President Clinton and the 1993 Cabinet hold the weekly meeting in the Cabinet Room of the White House.*

**Members of the Cabinet**

Secretary of State
Secretary of the Treasury
Secretary of Defense
Secretary of the Interior
Secretary of Agriculture
Secretary of Commerce
Secretary of Labor
Secretary of Health and Human Services
Secretary of Housing and Urban Development
Secretary of Transportation
Secretary of Energy
Secretary of Education
Secretary of Veterans Affairs
Attorney General

## CABLE CAR

A cable car is a passenger vehicle pulled by a cable that is constantly moving. The cable cars of a ski lift hang from the cable that extends up the slope. SAN FRANCISCO has a system of cable cars for public transportation. The cars run on rails, with the cable submerged in a channel below the rails. The American inventor Andrew S. Hallidie developed the first cable car. His cable car system was first used in San Francisco, in 1873. Cable cars remain a popular and effective way of traveling along San Francisco's hilly streets.

**One of the most important outcomes of John Cabot's voyages was his discovery of the dense schools of cod off the southeastern coast of Newfoundland. News of the rich fishing grounds on the Grand Banks spread, and fishing crews have been attracted there ever since.**

## CABOT, John and Sebastian 

John Cabot (1450?–1498?) and his son Sebastian (1476?–1557) were of Italian origin, but they explored the New World for England. In an attempt to compete with Spain's colonizing activities, Henry VII of England commissioned John Cabot to search for new lands. In 1497, Cabot arrived on the coast of Canada (possibly Newfoundland), which he claimed for the English king. Cabot's explorations of this territory prepared the way for England's colonization of Canada. On a second voyage, in 1498, Cabot was lost at sea. His son Sebastian, who had accompanied him on his first voyage, later worked for Spain as well as for England. At one time he was cartographer, or mapmaker, to Henry VIII, and in 1544 he produced a famous map of the world.

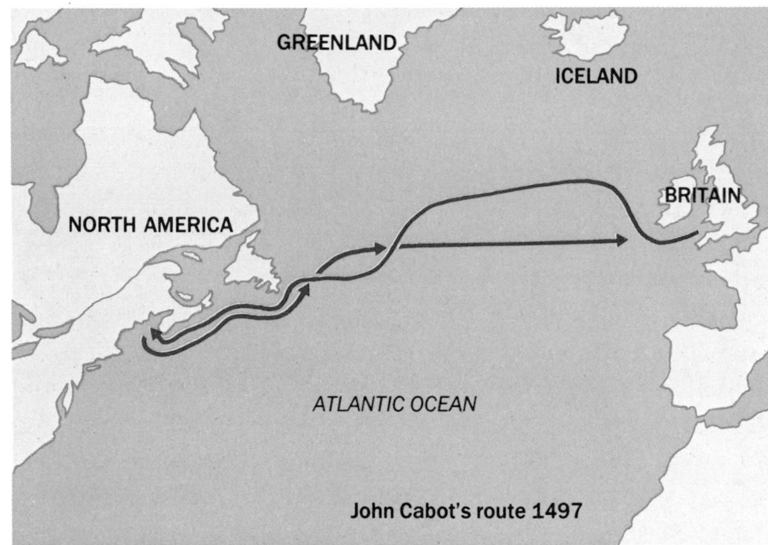


► *John Cabot's exploration of the Canadian coast and the St. Lawrence River opened up present-day Canada for England.*

## CABRILLO, Juan Rodriguez 

Very little is known about the life of the explorer Juan Rodriguez Cabrillo (died 1543?), except that he was the first European to discover California. He may have been born in Portugal, but he fought and explored for Spain. It is believed that he founded the town of Oaxaca, in Mexico, and that he was one of the conquerors of the part of Central America now including Guatemala, Nicaragua, and El Salvador. In 1542 he sailed up the west coast of North America with an exploration party. He explored much of the coast of California, including the areas around San Diego and Monterey.

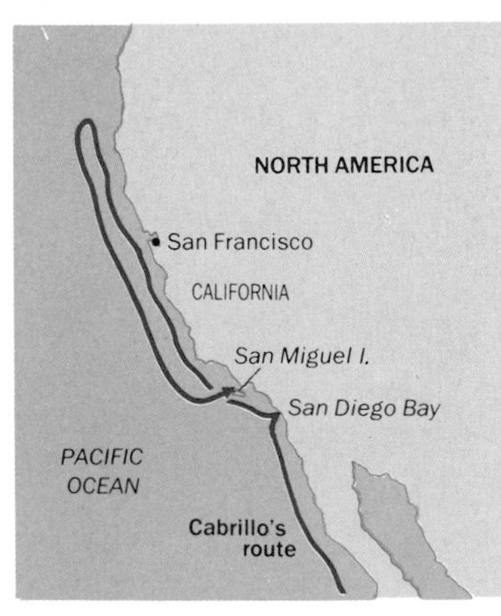


▲ *Juan Rodriguez Cabrillo explored the California coast as far north as what is now the border with Oregon.*

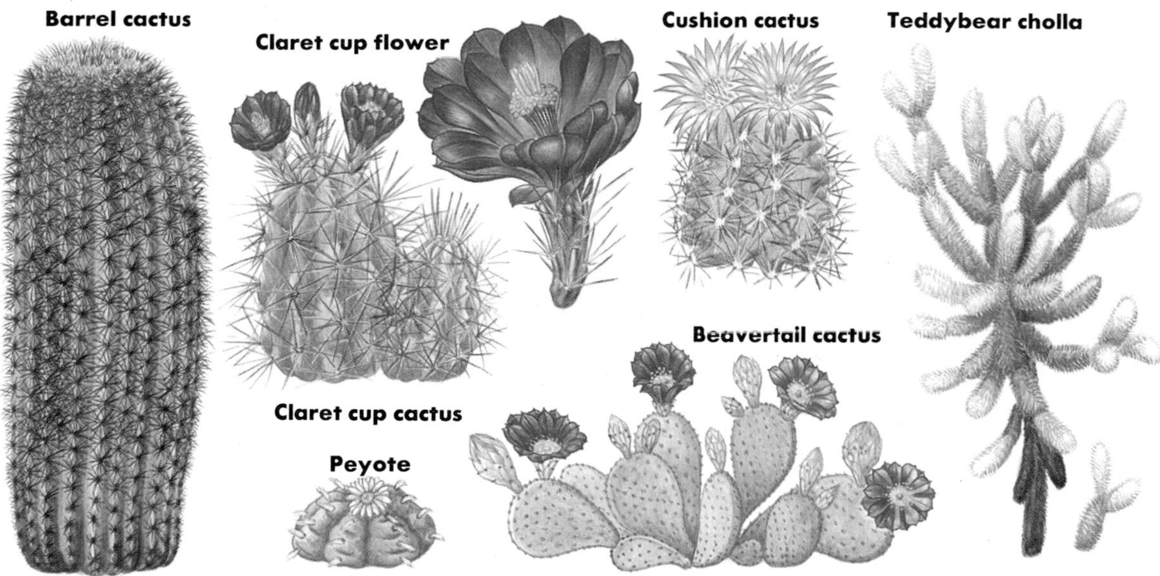


▲ *The 2,000 species of cactuses have developed some unusual shapes to adapt to special conditions of rainfall and elevation.*

## CACTUSES

A cactus is a plant that can store a large amount of water in its stem. Cactuses are native to North and South America, where they are the most common desert vegetation.

Cactuses have developed differently than other plants. The stems and branches do the work that in other plants is done by the leaves. Instead of leaves, a cactus usually has hairs, needles, or spines. These protect it from animals. The thick, waxy skin of the cactus keeps the water in instead of allowing it to evaporate, as in other plants. The roots grow near the surface of the ground and can quickly take in water when it does rain.

The best-known cactuses are the prickly pears. Their fruits look like pears and can be eaten. The largest cactuses are the saguaro cactuses. These can be up to 40 feet (12 m) tall. Pincushion cactuses grow from Mexico to Canada and are often grown as houseplants. Barrel cactuses can be up to 12 feet (3.5 m) tall and several feet thick. One type of barrel cactus, the bisnaga, may live more than 1,000 years.

▼ *The saguaro cactus blossoms for only a few days each spring.*

## CADDOS

The Caddos are an INDIAN people who came from the southeastern plains. They lived largely in what is now Arkansas, Oklahoma, Louisiana, and Texas. Their language, Caddoan, was spoken by a number of other tribes, including the PAWNEE. In the 1500s the Spanish found the Caddos to be fierce warriors. Most Caddos were hunters and farmers, who came into conflict with the nomadic tribes that followed the game as it moved over the plains. When war broke out between Indians and the white settlers, the Caddos offered themselves as scouts to the army as a way of fighting their enemies, the hunting tribes. Today, some 1,200 Caddos live on a reservation in Oklahoma.

▼ *Caddo women were skilled makers of highly decorated pottery, which was traded widely with other tribes.*

## CADILLAC, Antoine de la Mothe

**Mt. Cadillac in Maine, the highest point on the Atlantic coast of the United States, is named for the soldier-explorer, as are Cadillac, Michigan, and the Cadillac automobile.**

Antoine de la Mothe, sieur de Cadillac (1658–1730) was a French soldier and colonist who founded the city of DETROIT. He fought in battles against the IROQUOIS Indians in Canada and for three years served as commandant of the French trading post of Mackinac (in Michigan). In 1701 he founded a new post called Fort Pontchartrain du Detroit, now called simply Detroit. Later, Cadillac was governor of Louisiana. But he made a number of enemies and was recalled to France.

## CAGE, John

**A performance of John Cage's highly original *Imaginary Landscape No. 4* requires 24 musicians, a conductor, and 12 radios. To make sure that no two performances are ever the same, each radio is tuned to a different station and the volume of the radios is changed during the piece.**

John Cage (1912–1992) is a composer who spent much of his career exploring new musical sounds. He placed spoons, pieces of wood, rubber bands, and other objects on piano strings to create new sounds. He called this his "prepared piano." Cage is also known for his chance, or random, music. In this musicians and radios are used. As the musicians play, the radios are tuned in to different stations. Some Cage compositions even include the sound of slamming doors or electrical generators. Many people think that Cage's music is strange. But others regard him as a musical genius.

## CAGNEY, James 

James Cagney (1899–1986) was a great movie actor who is best known for his roles in gangster films of the 1930s. But his early training was as a song and dance man in Vaudeville, skills he also brought to Hollywood. It was for his role as the Broadway musical star George M. Cohan in *Yankee Doodle Dandy* that Cagney won an ACADEMY AWARD as best actor in 1942. Thc toughness that made him ideal as a gangster also made him believable in military and spy roles, such as the World War II film *13 Rue Madeleine*.

▲ *James Cagney was a small, wiry man, but his expression and voice could be wonderfully menacing for the role of "tough guy" that he so often played.*

## CAJUNS

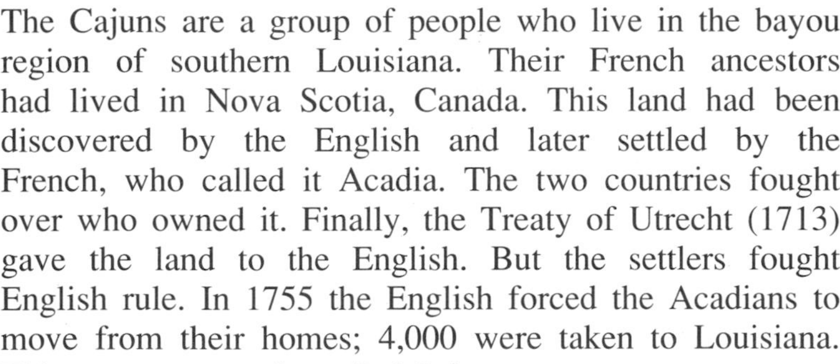

The Cajuns are a group of people who live in the bayou region of southern Louisiana. Their French ancestors had lived in Nova Scotia, Canada. This land had been discovered by the English and later settled by the French, who called it Acadia. The two countries fought over who owned it. Finally, the Treaty of Utrecht (1713) gave the land to the English. But the settlers fought English rule. In 1755 the English forced the Acadians to move from their homes; 4,000 were taken to Louisiana. This group came to be called Cajuns.

**The French-speaking, Roman Catholic Cajuns number about 250,000. They maintain their old traditions and speak an old form of French into which are mixed words taken from English, German, Spanish, and various Indian languages.**

◀ *Cajun music is ideal for open-air dances where the whole community takes part. The words of Cajun songs are often in old-fashioned French.*

▲ *Calamity Jane's fame spread when she showed off her skills in a Wild West touring company.*

## CALAMITY JANE

Calamity Jane (1852?–1903), who was born Martha Jane Canary, was a frontierswoman and adventuress. Although not the glamorous and high-principled heroine portrayed in the popular novels of the late 1800s, the real Calamity Jane was a skilled horsewoman and a crack shot. Most of her adult life was spent in the mining town of Deadwood, South Dakota, where her wearing of men's clothing was cheerfully tolerated. For a while she rode with the 7th U.S. Cavalry, and she may have served as a scout for General Custer. It is believed that her nickname resulted from her warning men that if they offended her they were inviting calamity.

## CALDER, Alexander

Alexander Calder (1898–1976) was one of the most important sculptors of this century and the first American sculptor to be known across the world. He obtained a degree in engineering before enrolling at the Art Students League in New York City in 1923. Calder is most famous for his *mobiles*—sculptures that are made of colored sheets of metal and are wired together so that they gently move in the air. They seem familiar today, but in 1932, when Calder made his first mobiles, people considered them daringly new. Later, Calder created *stabiles*, sculptures that look like mobiles but do not move.

▼ *Alexander Calder created many mobile sculptures. But even his static (nonmoving) art, such as this sculpture in San Diego, California, always has a sense of movement.*

◄ *The Calgary Exhibition and Stampede is Canada's largest rodeo. It features agricultural displays and carnival rides. The Stampede has taken place once a year since 1923.*

## CALGARY

Calgary is the largest city in the province of ALBERTA and the center of the Canadian oil industry. It has a population of 710,000. Founded in 1875, it is located just east of the Canadian Rocky Mountains. Calgary is an important cattle center. The Calgary Stampede, an annual rodeo festival, is world famous. Today, Calgary is also a major industrial, financial, and transportation center. Downtown Calgary, with its malls and high rises, reflects the city's prosperity. In 1988, Calgary hosted the Winter Olympics. Winter sports enthusiasts now take advantage of the city's many fine winter sports facilities.

**Many Americans live in Calgary, largely because there are about 400 oil companies based in the city.**

## CALHOUN, John C.

John C. Calhoun (1782–1850) was an important Southern political leader in the years before the CIVIL WAR. He strongly defended states' rights and believed that an individual state could declare an act of Congress unconstitutional and refuse to obey it. This was known as the theory of *nullification*. Calhoun was from South Carolina. He was a planter and a politician who served for many years in Congress and as vice president under John Quincy ADAMS and Andrew JACKSON. He was also secretary of war under President James MONROE and secretary of state under President John TYLER. Calhoun was an outspoken defender of slavery, and during his 15 years as a senator from South Carolina, he fought to keep slavery alive and to have new slave states admitted to the Union.

▼ *John C. Calhoun's fiery speeches supported the Southern cause in the decades before the Civil War.*

# CALIFORNIA

California is the third largest state. Only Alaska and Texas are larger. It is situated on the Pacific coast and stretches 780 miles (1,260 km) from the Mexican border in the south to the Oregon border in the north. The SIERRA NEVADA and the MOJAVE DESERT cover much of eastern California. California has the largest population of any state. Many people are attracted by the state's sunny climate, great natural beauty, strong economy, and relaxed life-style. In the 1800s, California was a promised land to both Americans and immigrants. Hundreds of thousands made the difficult journey west in covered wagons.

The largest city in California is LOS ANGELES. It is a major manufacturing and financial center and the hub of the motion picture and television industries. SAN DIEGO and SAN FRANCISCO are also thriving cities. The capital is Sacramento. The first Europeans to settle in California were Spaniards, in the 1500s. In 1822, California became part of Mexico, after that country won its independence from Spain. Then, in 1848, after

California valley quail

Golden poppy

California redwood

Places of Interest

- Disneyland, near Anaheim, was designed by Walt Disney. Most of the exhibits and rides are based on characters from his films.
- Yosemite National Park is just one of six national parks in California. Its magnificent scenery includes Yosemite Falls, one of the world's highest waterfalls.
- The Redwood Highway takes you from San Francisco to Oregon through impressive groves of redwood trees. These trees are the tallest in the world.
- The mission at Santa Barbara was founded in 1786 by Franciscan friars. It is one of several similar missions set up to convert the Indians to Christianity.
- Death Valley National Monument is a desert wilderness and includes the lowest point, 282 feet (86 m) below sea level, in the Western Hemisphere.

the MEXICAN WAR, it became an American territory. Two years later, it became the 31st state.

Today, much of California depends on farming, especially along the fertile Central Valley that runs up the middle of the state. Oil is one of the many important industries. Many "high-tech" industries are situated in "Silicon Valley" in northern California. Tourism is important, too. Natural attractions such as parks, forests, and mountains, and man-made attractions such as Disneyland, draw millions of visitors.

◀ *Upper Yosemite Falls in Yosemite National Park is 1,430 feet (436 m) high, the highest waterfall in the country.*

▼ *Malibu, located just west of Los Angeles, is the home of many wealthy celebrities.*

▶ *Laguna Beach is one of California's finest harbors. Its fine sands and safe waters also make it popular with swimmers.*

California

**Capital:** Sacramento

**Area:** 163,707 sq mi (424,002 km²). Rank: 3rd

**Population:** 29,760,050 (1991). Rank: 1st

**Statehood:** September 9, 1850

**Principal rivers:** Sacramento, Colorado

**Highest point:** Mt. Whitney, 14,495 ft (4,418 m)

**Motto:** *Eureka* (I Have Found It)

**Song:** "I Love You, California"

| Canada |
|---|
| **Capital:** Ottawa<br>**Official languages:** English and French<br>**Area:** 3,849,662 sq mi (9,970,610 km$^2$)<br>**Population:** 27,296,800 (1991)<br>**Government:** Parliamentary democracy<br>**Highest point:** Mt. Logan, 19,524 ft (5,951 m)<br>**Principal rivers:** St. Lawrence, 1,900 mi (3,058 km); Mackenzie, 1,071 mi (1,724 km)<br>**National anthem:** "O Canada" |

## CANADA

Canada is the second largest country in the world. Its land area covers more than 3,558,000 square miles (9,215,000 km$^2$). It extends east to west from the Atlantic to the Pacific. The United States forms Canada's southern border. To the north, it extends almost as far as the North Pole. Despite its size, Canada's population is small—only one tenth that of the United States. Most Canadians live in a narrow belt only 125 miles (200 km) from the U.S. border. This is where the largest cities and most important industries are. TORONTO, in the province of ONTARIO, and MONTREAL, in the province of QUEBEC, are the two biggest cities. OTTAWA, the capital, is small by comparison.

The vast forests of Canada's interior have made it the world's biggest producer of pulpwood. There are important mineral reserves, too, especially of oil, iron, nickel, uranium, and gold. These have helped Canada become one of the most important industrial countries in the world. Canada also has huge farms and cattle ranches, especially in the Prairie Provinces of MANITOBA, SASKATCHEWAN, and ALBERTA.

Alaska
Victoria I.
Baffin I.
YUKON TERRITORY
Mackenzie R.
Great Bear L.
NORTHWEST TERRITORIES
Mt. Logan ▲ 19,524 ft (5,951 m)
Whitehorse
Yellowknife
Great Slave L.
NEWFOUNDLAND
Hudson Bay
Queen Charlotte Islands
Coast Mountains
Rocky Mountains
CANADA
Churchill
ALBERTA
Labrador
MANITOBA
St. Lawrence R.
QUEBEC
Edmonton
St. John's
SASKATCHEWAN
L. Winnipeg
Calgary
ONTARIO
NEW BRUNSWICK
PRINCE EDWARD ISLAND
Vancouver I.
Vancouver
Victoria
Regina
Winnipeg
Quebec
Halifax
NOVA SCOTIA
L. Superior
Ottawa
Montreal
UNITED STATES
L. Michigan
L. Huron
Toronto
L. Ontario
Hamilton
L. Erie

▲ *Peggy's Cove in Nova Scotia is typical of the small fishing villages in Canada's Maritime Provinces.*

▲ *The Canadian Parliament meets in the federal capital of Ottawa. The building is patterned on the British Houses of Parliament.*

The first settlers in Canada caught fish in its rivers and lakes and trapped animals in its forests. Many were French, and about 20 percent of all Canadians still speak French. In the province of Quebec, 80 percent of the people speak French. But the largest group of immigrants were British, and Canada still has close links with Britain. Canada is a member of the British Commonwealth.

**Canada has the longest coastline of any country in the world— about 152,000 miles (244,000 km). It is bordered by the Pacific Ocean on the west, the Arctic Ocean on the north, and the Atlantic Ocean on the east.**

◀ *The Canadian Rockies are even wilder and more unspoiled than those in the United States.*

▶ *Many of Canada's first settlers spent whole winters without seeing another family.*

**Important Dates in Canadian History**

**1534** Jacques Cartier claims Canada for France.
**1763** Following a series of wars between French and British colonists, the Treaty of Paris is signed surrendering most of New France to Britain.
**1812–1815** British and Canadian troops protect the colony from American invasion.
**1867** The British North America Act establishes the Canadian Confederation.
**1885** The Canadian Pacific Railway spans the country.
**1931** The Statute of Westminster makes Canada an independent nation.
**1959** The St. Lawrence Seaway is opened.
**1965** The Canadian maple leaf flag is raised for the first time in Ottawa.
**1982** The Constitution Act, including a new Canadian Charter of Rights and Freedoms, becomes the governing document of Canada, removing British involvement in legislation.

## CANADIAN HISTORY

The first Europeans to arrive on Canadian soil were the Vikings. They settled briefly in NEWFOUNDLAND sometime around A.D. 1000. Much later, in 1497, the explorer John CABOT claimed this region for England. But it was the French who first put down roots in the land we know as Canada. French fishermen, fur trappers, and missionaries settled along the St. Lawrence River and in the Great Lakes region. They traded with the Indians and converted many of them to Christianity.

The colony of NEW FRANCE prospered from the beginning of the 1600s until the mid-1700s. In the meantime, however, Britain was also colonizing the region. Several wars broke out between these rival powers, and in 1763 the treaty ending the FRENCH AND INDIAN WAR (Seven Years' War) gave Britain control of Canada.

▶ The Death of Wolfe, *a painting by Benjamin West, depicts the dying British General James Wolfe at the Battle of Quebec, fought against the French during the French and Indian War. Wolfe and the French commander, the Marquis de Montcalm, were killed in the battle, but the British won the day.*

Over the next hundred years, Canada consisted of several provinces, ruled mainly from Britain, though with their own elected assemblies. The population increased rapidly and began to move westward. The growing need for unity led, in 1867, to the BRITISH NORTH AMERICA ACT, which established the Canadian Confederation. Full independence from Britain was achieved in 1931, though Canada remains a member of the British Commonwealth of Nations.

The period after World War II saw a rapid development of Canadian industry and a new level of prosperity. Another wave of immigration, mainly from Europe, added to the nation's cultural diversity.

In recent years the unity of the country has been threatened. Some French Canadians, fearing that their culture is in danger of being submerged by the English-speaking majority, have agitated for independence for the province of QUEBEC. The Canadian government has responded with several measures to preserve the French language and play down the ties with Britain, but Anglo-French tensions remain.

▲ *In 1982, Prime Minister Pierre Trudeau announced the Constitution Act, a milestone for Canadian self-government.*

◀ *The Canadian Pacific Railway, finished in 1885, linked Canada from coast to coast. At the ceremony held to complete the link, the final spike, made of gold, was driven in.*

## CANADIAN SHIELD

The Shield is a geological term used to describe the huge land mass surrounding Hudson Bay in the center of Canada. The Shield is extremely hard land, with a thin layer of topsoil covering bedrock composed mainly of granite. This bedrock was formed as mountains more than 600 million years ago. Natural erosion and several Ice Ages since then have worn it down. A typical Shield landscape is one of low, rolling hills with many small lakes and rivers. Parts of the Shield extend south into the states of Minnesota, Wisconsin, and New York.

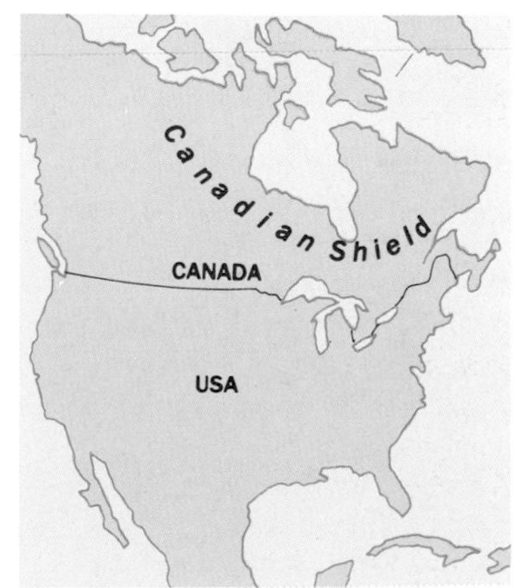


▲ *The rocky Canadian Shield covers more than half of Canada's land area.*

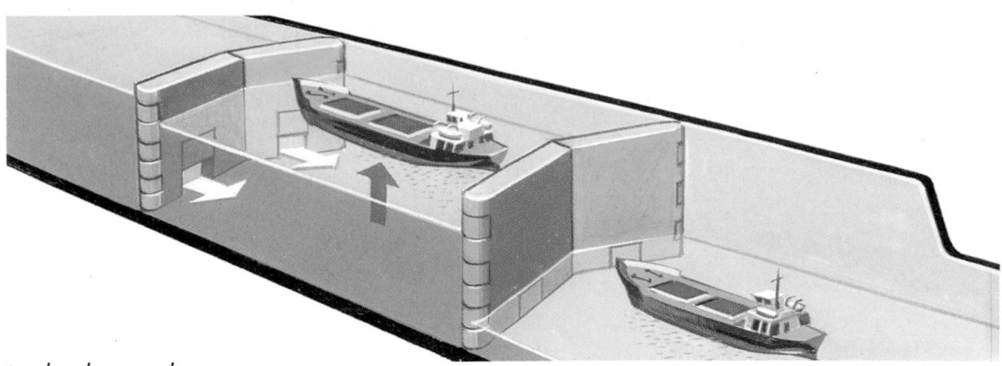

▲ *Ships are raised or lowered through canal locks in a series of steps. Water fills the lock to raise the ship up a level, and the gates are opened to allow the ship through. The gates must then be shut and the water level lowered again through sluice gates before the next ship at the lower level can enter the lock.*

▲ *St. Lambert Lock in Quebec is part of the man-made section of the St. Lawrence Seaway. Ships can carry cargo along the seaway from the Great Lakes to the Atlantic.*

## CANALS

Canals are waterways dug across land. Some are used for supplying water to crops or for drainage. Large canals are used by barges or ships. These inland waterways connect rivers, lakes, seas, or cities.

The first major canal in the United States was the ERIE CANAL, finished in 1825. It joined Lake Erie with the HUDSON RIVER, thus linking the GREAT LAKES with the Atlantic Ocean. This allowed the products of the Great Lakes region to be shipped to Europe by way of the port of New York City. As a result, Rochester, Buffalo, and other cities along the canal grew rapidly, and New York City became North America's greatest port. In 1918 the Erie Canal was made part of the New York State Barge Canal System.

After the Erie Canal, many more canals were built, especially in Ohio and Indiana. They were used by barges pulled along by mules or horses that walked on a

► *The St. Lawrence River is a natural canal as it passes Quebec City. It is deep enough even for huge, seagoing tankers.*

path alongside the canal. Beginning in the late 1800s, however, the railroad proved a faster and less expensive means of transportation. Most of the old canals are no longer used.

Important North American canals in use today include the Sacramento Canal in California and the Houston Ship Canal in Texas. The ST. LAWRENCE SEAWAY is a whole series of canals. It allows large seagoing vessels to travel between the Great Lakes and the Atlantic. The PANAMA CANAL in Central America provides a shortcut for ships between the Atlantic and Pacific oceans.

**The Largest Canyons in the U.S.**

Glen Canyon, Utah, Arizona
Grand Canyon, Arizona
King's Canyon, California
Bighorn Canyon, Wyoming
Canyon de Chelly, Arizona
Black Canyon, Colorado
Walnut Canyon, Arizona

◀ *The Peekaboo Loop Trail winds through the spectacular rock formations of Bryce Canyon in Utah. Water, wind, and weather have eroded away the softer rock, leaving the harder rock behind.*

## CANYONS 

A canyon is a long, narrow valley between high cliffs. It usually has a river or stream flowing through it. The desert region known as the Colorado Plateau, covering parts of Arizona, Utah, Colorado, and New Mexico, is a vast maze of deep canyons. The most spectacular is the GRAND CANYON, which in some places is more than one mile (1.6 km) deep. Canyons are carved out by rivers over millions of years. The layers of exposed rock at the top are the youngest. On the canyon floor, the rock may be hundreds of millions of years old.

## CAPE CANAVERAL 

Cape Canaveral, on the east coast of Florida, is the site of the John F. Kennedy Space Center. The National Aeronautics and Space Administration (NASA) Launch

▼ *The Cape Canaveral launchpad is over 20 stories high. Hundreds of local people are NASA employees.*

▼ *Cape Cod has some of the best beaches along America's Atlantic coast. Surfers prefer the wild waves of the ocean side, facing east. The shallower—and calmer—waters of Cape Cod Bay are ideal for vacationers.*

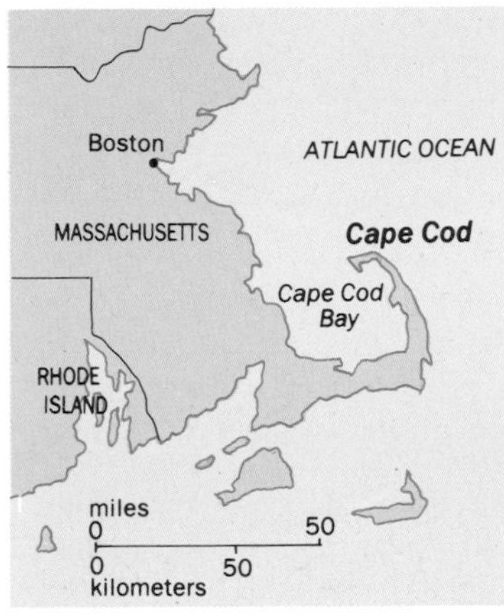


Operations Center is at this space center. Cape Canaveral has been the launching site for most American space vehicles. The first satellite was sent into orbit in 1958. Every manned U.S. rocket, from the tiny Mercury probes in the early 1960s to today's space shuttles, has been launched from Cape Canaveral. The Cape is also the site of the Air Force Missile Test Center.

In 1963, Cape Canaveral was renamed Cape Kennedy, in honor of President John F. Kennedy. In 1973 the name was changed back to Cape Canaveral.

## CAPE COD

Cape Cod is a sandy, hook-shaped peninsula that extends eastward about 65 miles (105 km) from the MASSACHUSETTS mainland. The coastline is irregular, with many bays and harbors. The islands of Martha's Vineyard and Nantucket lie to the south of Cape Cod.

The Pilgrims landed briefly at the tip of Cape Cod in 1620, before continuing across Cape Cod Bay to Plymouth. The site of their first landfall is now called First Encounter Beach. Tourism has replaced fishing as Cape Cod's leading industry. The winter population of about 180,000 rises to more than 1.5 million each summer.

▼ *The Capitol is built according to the architectural rules of ancient Rome. Many state capitols also use the domes and columns that were features of classical Roman buildings.*

## CAPITOL, U.S.

The Capitol is the building in the center of WASHINGTON, D.C., where Congress meets to make the laws of the United States. Its white exterior and huge dome are familiar as a symbol of American democracy. The Capitol takes its name from the Capitoleum, the temple of Jupiter built on the Capitoline Hill in ancient Rome. Rome's senate sometimes met on the Capitoline Hill. The building borrowed more than just its name from Rome. The architecture follows Rome's classical style. Inside the Capitol there are three main areas. In the center, under the dome, is the Great Rotunda, where important ceremonies are held. To the north is the Senate Chamber, where the Senate meets, and to the south is the House Chamber, where the House of Representatives meets.

Work on the Capitol began in 1793, when George WASHINGTON laid the cornerstone. The building was completed in 1800 but was burned down by the British during the WAR OF 1812. It was rebuilt by 1829.

## CARDINAL

The cardinal is one of North America's most colorful songbirds. It is found in hedgerows and at the edges of woodlands. Cardinals can also be spotted in parks, gardens, orchards, and farmland.

The cardinal is about 8 inches (20 cm) long. The male has the well-known bright red coloring. The female is brown with some red on its crest, wings, and tail. The cardinal eats seeds, berries, green shoots, insects, and larvae (young insects). Its song is a clear, whistling sound, either high or low pitched.

Cardinals build their nests in trees or tall bushes. After the nesting season, they merge into small groups and roam through the countryside.

**Sometimes called the redbird, the cardinal is one of the most colorful crested birds of North America. It migrates northward in spring, but rarely goes farther north than the state of Massachusetts.**

▼ *Many Caribbean islands, such as this one in the country of St. Vincent and the Grenadines, are popular vacation spots. Tourism often provides the chief source of income for the islands.*

## CARIBBEAN SEA

The Caribbean Sea is an arm of the Atlantic Ocean. It is bounded by Central and South America and the islands of the West Indies. The sea was named after the Carib Indians, who lived on some of these islands. The Caribbean is one of the world's busiest waterways, because ships using the PANAMA CANAL must pass through it. The climate is tropical, and it is a major winter vacation area, particularly for North Americans. The four largest West Indian islands—Cuba, Hispaniola (Dominican Republic and Haiti), PUERTO RICO, and Jamaica—are known as the Greater Antilles. The Lesser Antilles is made up of hundreds of small islands, including the U.S. VIRGIN ISLANDS. The people of Puerto Rico and the U.S. Virgin Islands are U.S. citizens.

▼ *The Caribbean Sea is a passageway for ships carrying many goods to and from the United States.*

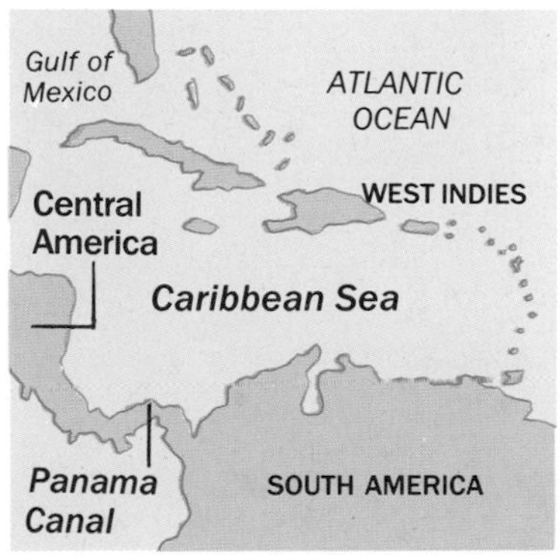

▶ *Two caribou bulls show off their large, branched antlers. Both sexes have antlers, but the female's are smaller and less elaborate. Caribou gather in large herds in the late fall and migrate south to escape the Arctic winter, sometimes traveling over 800 miles (1,300 km). When spring comes, they return north. Their migration routes were taken into account when oil and gas pipelines were laid in Alaska and Canada.*

**As a caribou moves, a tendon in its foot rubs against a bone and makes a clicking noise. This click becomes very noticeable when caribou gather in herds to migrate; the sound of the continuous clicking of more than 100,000 caribou is unforgettable.**

## CARIBOU

The caribou is the North American reindeer. It lives in Alaska and northern Canada. At one time it was also found much farther south, but its numbers have been much reduced. Some Inuit (ESKIMOS) and INDIANS eat caribou meat and use its hide to make clothing.

The caribou, like other reindeer, is the only kind of DEER in which both male and female have antlers. They eat grass, sedges, the shoots of trees, mosses, and lichens. Caribou live in herds, migrating long distances south for the winter. The caribou living in the northern tundra are known as barren-ground caribou. Caribou found in the woodlands farther south are called woodland caribou.

▼ *Stokely Carmichael coined the term "Black Power" during a civil rights march in 1966. He was encouraging blacks to make their voices heard in America by exercising their right to vote.*

## CARMICHAEL, Stokely

Stokely Carmichael (1941– ) was a leader of the black CIVIL RIGHTS movement in the 1960s. Born on the island of Trinidad, Carmichael grew up in Harlem, in New York City. In 1960, as a student at Howard University, he helped to form the Student Nonviolent Coordinating Committee (SNCC). This racially mixed group led peaceful protests against segregation. After Carmichael was elected chairman of the SNCC in 1966, the group adopted the idea of Black Power. Black Power meant the gaining of political power and economic control. Carmichael later led the militant Black Panther Party.

## CARNEGIE, Andrew

Andrew Carnegie (1835–1919) was a famous industrialist and philanthropist. Born in Scotland, he came to the United States with his family when he was 12. He was very successful in the steel industry and became one of the richest men of his time. Carnegie believed that riches should be used for the good of society, so he gave much of his fortune away. He created almost 2,000 public libraries in the United States so that books and knowledge could be within everyone's reach. He also sponsored the building of Carnegie Hall in New York City for concerts. Today, his work continues through such institutions as the Carnegie Corporation and the Carnegie Foundation for the Advancement of Teaching.

▲ *During his lifetime, Andrew Carnegie gave more than $350 million to charitable causes.*

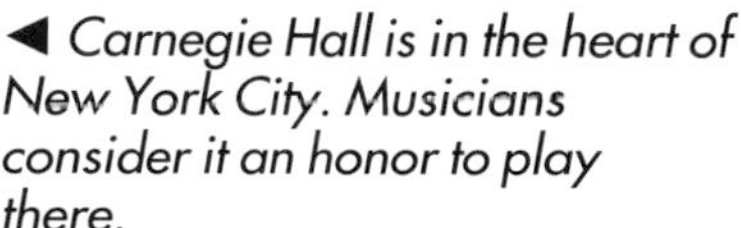

◀ *Carnegie Hall is in the heart of New York City. Musicians consider it an honor to play there.*

## CARSON, Kit

Christopher ("Kit") Carson (1809–1868) was a legendary hero of the American western frontier. At the age of 15 he ran away from his home in Missouri and joined a group of traders headed for Santa Fe. In the West he made his living by trading and fur trapping. He was later asked to serve as a guide for John C. FRÉMONT's expeditions across the Rocky Mountains. As a soldier, he fought bravely in the MEXICAN WAR. During the CIVIL WAR, he was a Union brigadier general and fought Confederate forces in New Mexico. In 1868 the government appointed him superintendent of Indian affairs for the Colorado Territory. Many people admired Carson. Several towns are named after him, including Carson City, the capital of Nevada.

▼ *Legends about Kit Carson sprang up in a series of novels written in the 1860s and 1870s.*

James Earl (Jimmy) Carter, Jr., was the 39th president of the United States. Before he ran for the presidency, Carter, a Democrat, was governor of Georgia (1971–1975).

Soon after taking office as president in 1977, Carter fulfilled an election promise and pardoned those who had avoided the draft during the VIETNAM WAR. Carter's honesty and easygoing manner at first made him a popular figure in the White House. His commitment to human rights, at home and abroad, added to his popularity. Carter's biggest problem within the United States was inflation (rising prices). An energy crisis and the high price of oil were the main causes. Carter created a new Department of Energy.

One of Carter's major achievements was the 1979 Camp David Agreement, when Prime Minister Begin of Israel and President Sadat of Egypt signed a historic peace treaty. Also in 1979, Carter and the Soviet Union signed a treaty known as SALT 2, limiting nuclear weapons. But when the Soviets invaded Afghanistan six months later, Carter withdrew the treaty. The United States also stopped selling grain to the Soviet Union and boycotted the 1980 Moscow Olympic Games.

► *President Carter's informal approach at the Camp David Agreement lessened tension between Egypt and Israel.*

Jimmy Carter
**Born:** October 1, 1924, in Plains, Georgia
**Education:** U.S. Naval Academy
**Political party:** Democratic
**Term of office:** 1977–1981
**Married:** 1946 to Rosalynn Smith

The worst crisis of Carter's presidency came when 63 Americans were taken hostage in Iran. Carter sent a military force to rescue them, but the effort failed. Carter's popularity declined as a result of the crisis, and he was beaten by Ronald REAGAN in the 1980 election. The hostages were finally released on Carter's last day of office.

▼ *Jimmy Carter's hometown of Plains, Georgia, was a quiet rural community when he was a boy in the 1920s.*

## CARTIER, Jacques

The French navigator Jacques Cartier (1491–1557) made three voyages to Canada. He was the first European to sail the whole navigable length of the ST. LAWRENCE RIVER. Cartier claimed the region for France.

Cartier first sailed to Canada in 1534. On his second voyage, in 1535, he was told by the Indians of a land farther west that was rich in gold and precious stones. In 1541, King Francis I of France sent Cartier back to Canada, along with a nobleman named de Roberval, to establish a colony there. The venture was unsuccessful. And the supposed gold and diamonds that he took back to France proved worthless. But Cartier's voyages paved the way for the French empire in North America.

▲ *George Washington Carver's studies into soils and crops led to many breakthroughs in farming. He developed more than 300 by-products from different crops.*

## CARTOON *See* Comic Art; Motion Pictures

## CARVER, George Washington

The son of slave parents, George Washington Carver (1864?–1943) became a leading agricultural chemist. As an orphaned boy, living on a Missouri plantation, Carver developed an interest in plants and animals. He recieved a masters degree in science from Iowa State Agricultural College in 1896. Carver then went to Tuskegee Institute, in Alabama, where he taught and experimented with different crops. He discovered that peanuts and soybeans could enrich soil that had been exhausted by many years of growing cotton. He also discovered many uses for these crops, and so helped southern farmers to become more prosperous. Carver's work earned him honors in the United States and abroad and the respect of world leaders.

## CASSATT, Mary

Mary Cassatt (1844–1926) was an important painter. Born in Pennsylvania, she moved to France when she was 22. There she met a group of painters called the Impressionists, who strongly influenced her work. They painted scenes from everyday life and tried to give their *impression* of them. Their aim was to create a sense of scenes glimpsed rather than studied.

▼ Mother and Child, *a painting by Mary Cassatt. Many of her finest works were tender studies of motherhood.*

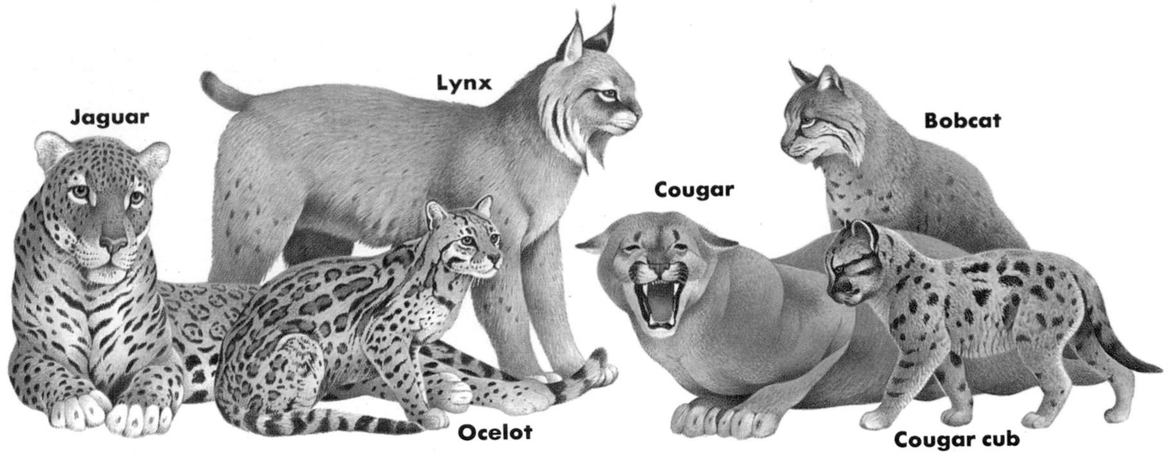


▲ *Most North American wild cats live in undeveloped areas west of the Mississippi River. People are their worst enemy. The jaguar was found in the Southwest up until the early 1900s, though now it is restricted to Central and South America.*

## CATS

Wild cats and domestic cats are all part of the same family. Domestic cats are extremely popular in the United States as pets. There are more than 58 million cats in U.S. households. Popular breeds of domestic cats include the American short-hair, the Siamese, the Maine Coon, and the Persian.

Of the several wild cats found in North America, the COUGAR (also known as the mountain lion or puma) is the most common. It lives in wilderness areas from British Columbia to South America. The smaller BOBCAT, or lynx, lives in forested areas and scrubland all over the United States. The jaguar was once the largest wild cat to be found in North America. Today, however, it is an endangered species and is found only in Mexico and Central and South America.

▼ *Carrie Catt's tireless work over three decades helped secure the vote for women.*

## CATHER, Willa Sibert

Willa Cather (1873–1947) was a great American writer of short stories and novels. She was raised in Nebraska, and many of her stories painted a realistic picture of the harsh life of immigrants living on the prairies in the late 1800s. Among her best-known stories are *My Antonia* and *O Pioneers!*. *One of Ours*, the story of a young Nebraska farmer who is killed in World War I, won a Pulitzer Prize.

## CATT, Carrie Chapman

Carrie Chapman Catt (1859–1947) was a leader in the fight for WOMEN'S RIGHTS. A teacher by profession, and one of the first woman school superintendents in the country, she began to work for the Iowa Woman Suffrage Association in 1887. Her husband, George Catt, encouraged her in this work. From 1900 to 1904 and from 1915 to 1920 she was president of the National American Woman Suffrage Association. When women finally won the vote in 1920, she reorganized this group into the League of Women Voters.

## CAVES

Caves are usually found in rocks such as limestone and gypsum, which are easily dissolved by water. The most extensive caves, usually called caverns, extend for miles underground. About 130 caves in the United States are open to the public. Some of the most dramatic are located in the Appalachian Mountains. Mammoth Cave, in central Kentucky, was discovered in 1799. Its 194 miles (312 km) of explored passages form a national park. Carlsbad Caverns in New Mexico make up another national park. The caverns extend for 68 square miles (177 $km^2$) and are said to be the largest in the world. They include a stalagmite that is 62 feet (19 m) tall.

▲ *Carlsbad Caverns in New Mexico are a national park. Visitors can go 829 feet (253 m) below ground.*

## CENSUS

The Constitution called for a population census "within three years after the first meeting of the Congress of the United States and within every subsequent term of ten years." The first census, held in 1790, counted 3,929,214 Americans. The 1990 census found the U.S. population to be 248,709,873.

The Bureau of the Census, founded in 1902, conducts this research. The population figures are used to determine how many members each state will have in the U.S. House of Representatives. Some government aid to states is also determined by these population figures. The Census Bureau also conducts censuses of manufacturing, businesses, transportation, agriculture, and fishing. These censuses are conducted more frequently than the population census.

Caves to Visit in the U.S.

**Carlsbad Caverns, New Mexico**, are spread over three different levels.
**Luray Cavern, Virginia**, contains many stalactites and stalagmites of different colors.
**Mammoth Cave, Kentucky**, has 194 miles (312 km) of underground passageways.
**Wind Cave, South Dakota**, is a series of limestone caverns with interesting "boxwork" crystal formations.
**Wyandotte Cave, Indiana**, contains the highest known underground mountain, Monumental Mountain.

## CENTRAL INTELLIGENCE AGENCY

The Central Intelligence Agency (CIA) collects intelligence (information) about other countries that is important to the security of the United States. It also conducts covert (secret) operations against the enemies of the United States. Many countries have similar agencies. Although Congress has to be informed about the work of the CIA, little information is made public.

The CIA was set up in 1947. Its headquarters are in Washington, D.C., but many CIA agents work overseas. The CIA also employs many foreign agents. While the CIA is important to U.S. security, not all its operations are successful. The failure of some has caused embarrassment to the government.

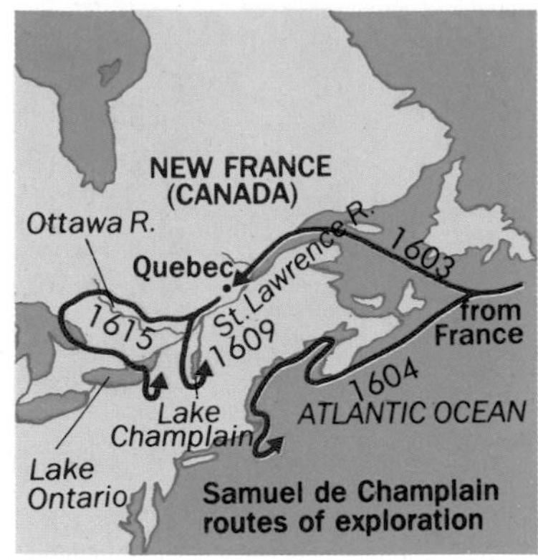


▲ *Samuel de Champlain's expeditions opened up valuable fur-trading routes into the heart of North America.*

► *Samuel de Champlain charted the course of the St. Lawrence River in 1603. A century later, when this map was made, more than 95 percent of all French settlers lived along the river.*

**As Samuel de Champlain explored the St. Lawrence River, he had more than fur trading in mind. He was convinced that a Northwest Passage to Asia branched off the river.**

## CHAMPLAIN, Samuel de

Samuel de Champlain (1567?–1635) was a French navigator and explorer who founded the city of QUEBEC in Canada. He first visited North America in 1603, when he explored the ST. LAWRENCE SEAWAY. Later he explored the northeastern coast from Nova Scotia south to Cape Cod. In 1608 he set up a trading post at Quebec. Champlain managed to establish friendly relations with the local Algonquin and Huron Indians, which helped the settlement to prosper. In 1609, he discovered Lake Champlain. Three years later, he was appointed governor of French Canada. By the time Champlain died, the colony extended the length of the St. Lawrence River.

**One of Raymond Chandler's most famous thrillers, *The Big Sleep*, was made into a film in 1946 starring Humphrey Bogart. The script for the film, however, was written by another novelist, William Faulkner.**

## CHANDLER, Raymond

Raymond Chandler (1888–1959) was a leading writer of crime stories. The hero of his books was Philip Marlowe, a tough private eye. The stories are set in the seedy world of Los Angeles crime. Some of his best-known books include *The Big Sleep*, *The Long Goodbye*, and *Farewell, My Lovely*. Chandler also wrote a number of movie scripts, mostly based on his own books. Humphrey BOGART played Philip Marlowe in the movie *The Big Sleep*.

## CHAPLIN, Charlie 

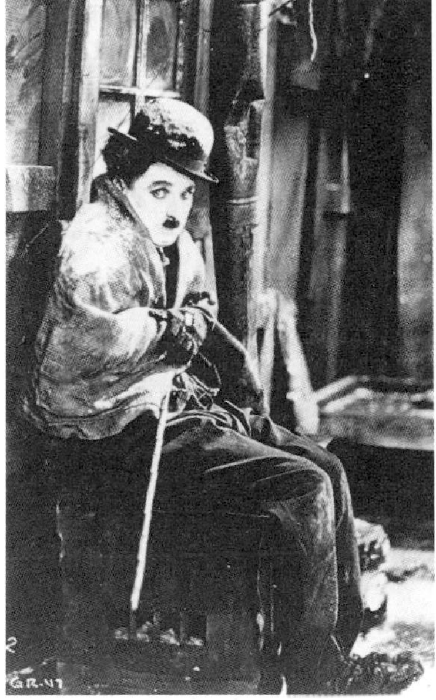

▲ *A scene from* The Gold Rush, *one of Charlie Chaplin's best-known films.*

Charlie Chaplin (1889–1977) was the most successful comedian in the age of silent movies. At the height of his fame in the 1920s, he was known and loved throughout the world for his portrayal of the Little Tramp in films such as *The Kid* and *The Gold Rush*. Later, Chaplin wrote, directed, and starred in a number of serious films. Charlie Chaplin was born in England. He came to the United States in 1910 where he lived until 1952. Chaplin died in Switzerland.

## CHEROKEES 

The Cherokees are an INDIAN people who originally lived as farmers and hunters in what is now North Carolina and northern Georgia. Because colonists tried to take their land, the Cherokees sided with the British during the American REVOLUTION. Later, the Army

▼ *The U.S. government offered the Cherokee nation $5.7 million to resettle in Oklahoma. More than 90 percent of the Cherokees refused, so troops were used to force them to move.*

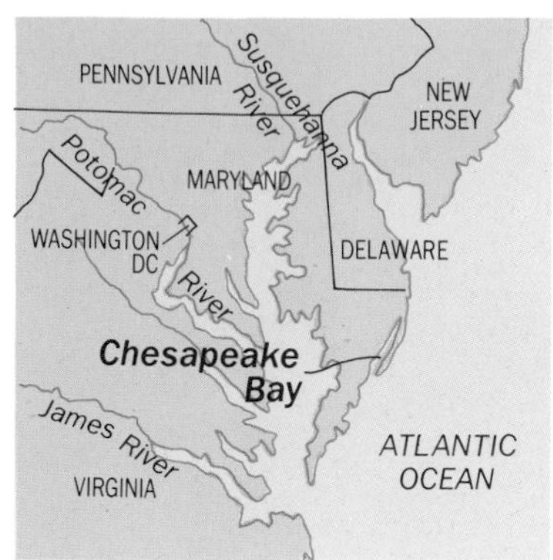


▲ *Chesapeake Bay's many harbors are ideal for pleasure boats. The bay is also an important source of seafood, particularly oysters and crabs.*

**The Chesapeake Bay Retriever is the only retriever developed in the United States. According to legend, an English ship with dogs aboard was shipwrecked on the Maryland shore of the bay in 1807. The dogs were given by the ship's crew to their rescuers, and the new breed was developed from them.**

forcibly removed some 15,000 Cherokees from their land and resettled them in Oklahoma. Four thousand died from disease, starvation, and the cold as they were made to march across the country during the brutal winter of 1838–1839. This terrible journey has become known as the "Trail of Tears." In Oklahoma the Cherokees, CHICKASAWS, CHOCTAWS, CREEKS, and SEMINOLES were known as the Five Civilized Tribes. There are more than 100,000 Cherokees today. Nearly half of them live in Oklahoma.

## CHESAPEAKE BAY

Chesapeake Bay is an inlet of the Atlantic Ocean. It is 200 miles (320 km) long and is bounded by Virginia and Maryland. "Chesapeake" is an Algonquian word meaning "country on a big river." When John SMITH, who helped found JAMESTOWN SETTLEMENT, explored the bay in 1608, he said, "Heaven and earth never agreed better to frame a place for man's habitation." Several rivers, including the Potomac and Susquehanna, run into it. BALTIMORE, Maryland, and Norfolk, Virginia, are the two most important ports on the bay. The city of ANNAPOLIS, on the bay's western shore, is the site of the U.S. Naval Academy.

## CHEVROLET, Louis

Louis Chevrolet (1879–1941) was an automobile racer and manufacturer. Born in Switzerland, he emigrated to the United States in 1900. Fascinated by cars, he became a racing driver. In his first race, in 1905, he defeated a famous American driver named Barney Oldfield, and he went on to set many speed records. He designed the first Chevrolet car in 1911.

► *Louis Chevrolet (with black hat and mustache) stands beside the* Frontenac, *the car he designed for the 1921 Indianapolis 500 automobile race. Tommy Milton (left) drove the* Frontenac *to victory that year. Another Chevrolet automobile had won the previous year's race.*

## CHEYENNES 

The Cheyennes are an important PLAINS INDIAN tribe. In 1851 they divided into two groups, the Northern and Southern Cheyennes. The Northern lived in South Dakota, the Southern along the Arkansas River. The Northern Cheyennes fiercely resisted white settlement. In 1876 they were at the Battle of the Little Bighorn, where General George CUSTER was killed. They were finally defeated. In 1884 the government granted them a reservation on the Tongue River in Montana. Today, several thousand still live there. The Southern Cheyennes have a reservation in Oklahoma.

▲ *This man is a Northern Cheyenne, one of a group that lives on a reservation in Montana set up by the U.S. government in 1884.*

◀ *Chicago is the birthplace of the skyscraper. The John Hancock Center (top left) and the Standard Oil Building (top right) are two of the city's tallest buildings. The Sears Tower, also in Chicago but not shown in this picture, is the world's tallest building at 110 stories.*

## CHICAGO 

Chicago, ILLINOIS, is the third largest city in the United States, with a population of almost 3 million. Situated on the southwestern shore of Lake Michigan, it is one of the most important transportation centers in the country. Vast quantities of industrial goods and raw materials flow through Chicago's huge railroad yards. Its O'Hare Airport is the busiest airport in the country. The city is also a major financial center. Chicago began as a trading settlement outside Fort Dearborn, which was built in 1803. It grew rich as a cattle town. A fire destroyed downtown Chicago in 1871, but the city was rebuilt and it became a major industrial center.

**In 1871, Chicago was swept by a devastating fire that started in a barn and left almost 100,000 people homeless. In two days it caused tens of millions of dollars in damage. When the city was rebuilt, wooden buildings were replaced with stone ones.**

▲ *The Chinooks were skillful fishermen. In this old photograph a Chinook is spearing salmon in the rapids of the Columbia River.*

## CHINOOKS

The Chinooks were a tribe of INDIANS of the Pacific Northwest. They lived along the shores of the Columbia River in Washington and Oregon. In the past, the Chinooks lived simply, fishing mostly for salmon and gathering food from the forest. When European explorers seeking goods first came to the Northwest, the Chinooks traded with them. There are very few Indians of pure Chinook stock left; their descendants live mainly in the state of Washington.

## CHIPMUNK

The chipmunk is a type of GROUND SQUIRREL. The eastern chipmunk is larger than the various types of western chipmunks. Chipmunks make a shrill chirping noise, and most types live in burrows they dig in the ground. Chipmunks are good climbers; they often climb trees and bushes looking for nuts, seeds, berries, and insects to eat. The food is carried in the large pouches in their cheeks, then stored in their burrows until they need it.

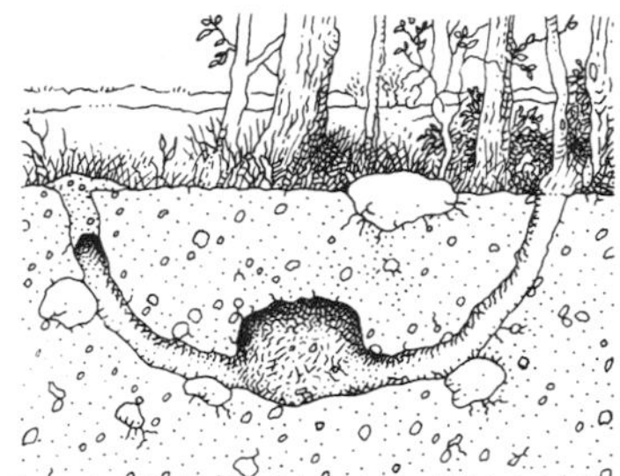

► *Chipmunks are related to squirrels and woodchucks. They have large pouches in their cheeks to carry food. Their burrows are used for protection and food storage.*

## CHIPPEWAS

The Chippewas are one of the Great Lakes Algonquian INDIAN tribes. They originally lived around Lake Superior, in both the United States and Canada. (In Canada they are called the Ojibway or Ojibwa.) The Chippewas lived in small groups of houses. For their food they hunted, fished, and gathered wild rice. They have a history of conflict with the SIOUX. There is a record from 1678–79 of a Frenchman named Duluth negotiating a treaty between the two tribes. During the FRENCH AND INDIAN WARS the Chippewas supported the

**The name Manitoba is thought to have come from the Chippewa Indian word *manitou*, meaning "Great Spirit." Wisconsin's name comes from a Chippewa word meaning "gathering of the waters."**

▲ *The Chippewas bent branches to make the frames for their wigwams. The outer layer was made from either birchbark or animal hides.*

French. Today they are active in many professions. Some Chippewas live on reservations in North Dakota and Minnesota.

## CHISHOLM, Shirley

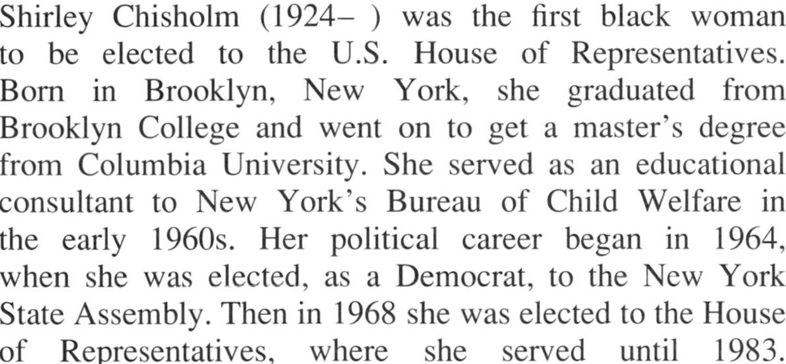

Shirley Chisholm (1924– ) was the first black woman to be elected to the U.S. House of Representatives. Born in Brooklyn, New York, she graduated from Brooklyn College and went on to get a master's degree from Columbia University. She served as an educational consultant to New York's Bureau of Child Welfare in the early 1960s. Her political career began in 1964, when she was elected, as a Democrat, to the New York State Assembly. Then in 1968 she was elected to the House of Representatives, where she served until 1983. She has promoted the rights of women and minorities.

▲ *Shirley Chisholm campaigned for the Democratic presidential nomination in 1972. Although she lost, she showed that a black woman could aim for the top job in the nation.*

## CHOCTAWS

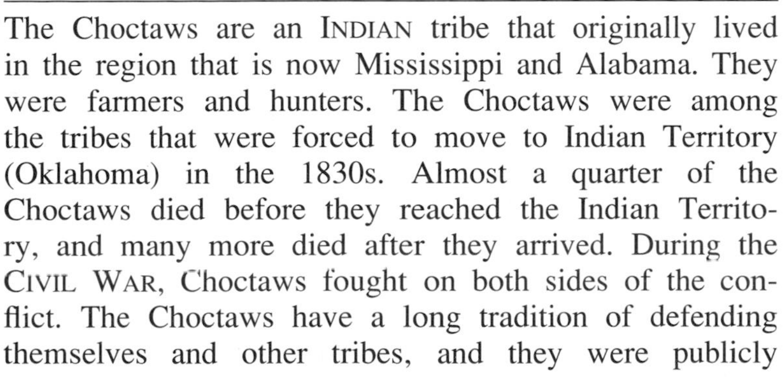

The Choctaws are an INDIAN tribe that originally lived in the region that is now Mississippi and Alabama. They were farmers and hunters. The Choctaws were among the tribes that were forced to move to Indian Territory (Oklahoma) in the 1830s. Almost a quarter of the Choctaws died before they reached the Indian Territory, and many more died after they arrived. During the CIVIL WAR, Choctaws fought on both sides of the conflict. The Choctaws have a long tradition of defending themselves and other tribes, and they were publicly

▲ *George Catlin painted this scene of Choctaw Indians performing a ceremonial dance. Dances and ceremony played an important part in the cultural life of the Choctaws.*

active in the struggle for Indian rights that took place earlier this century. Today there are some 10,000 Choctaws. Most live on reservations in Oklahoma.

## CHRISTIANITY

Christianity, the religion based on the teachings of Jesus Christ, is the major religion in the United States. Of the 250 million people in the United States, just under 60 percent belong to some religious group. Of these, more than 90 percent are members of a religious group that holds Christian beliefs.

The ROMAN CATHOLIC CHURCH is the largest single group (about 58.6 million). Its head is the Pope in Rome. In the United States there are 34 archdioceses (a district that comes under the control of an archbishop).

The second largest group is the BAPTISTS (over 31 million). METHODISTS number about 12.5 million. Their beliefs are based on the teachings of John Wesley, a preacher in England in the 1700s. They baptize both infants and adults.

There are about 8.3 million LUTHERANS in America. They follow the teachings set down by Martin Luther in Germany in the early 1500s. Episcopalians number about 2.4 million, but they are part of the larger Anglican Communion, which has many member churches throughout the world.

In addition, there are other significant Christian groups, including the Orthodox churches, the Pentecostals, the Presbyterians, the Church of Christ Disciples, and the United Church of Christ. Smaller groups in-

Christian Churches in the U.S.

| Church | Membership |
|---|---|
| Roman Catholic | 58,568,015 |
| Baptist | 31,040,661 |
| Methodist | 12,445,020 |
| Lutheran | 8,319,869 |
| Churches of God | 5,744,879 |
| Latter-day Saints | 4,459,231 |
| Presbyterian | 4,225,736 |
| Eastern Orthodox | 4,205,453 |
| Pentecostal | 3,285,500 |
| Episcopal | 2,446,050 |
| Churches of Christ | 1,683,346 |
| United Church of Christ | 1,599,212 |
| Christian Churches and Churches of Christ | 1,070,616 |
| Christian Church (Disciples of Christ) | 1,039,692 |
| Jehovah's Witnesses | 858,367 |
| Adventist | 745,375 |
| Christian Methodist Episcopal Church | 719,922 |
| Church of Christ, Scientist | 700,000 |
| Reformed | 571,115 |
| Salvation Army | 445,566 |
| Mennonite | 364,739 |
| Friends (Quaker) | 122,957 |

clude the Reformed churches, the MENNONITES (and Amish), the Society of Friends, and the Adventists. (See also PROTESTANTISM.)

▼ *A church service in Tucson, Arizona, unites three generations of one family.*

▼ *Church weddings are solemn but happy occasions.*

## CHRISTIAN SCIENCE 

Christian Science is a religious movement that was founded by Mary Baker EDDY (1821–1910). In 1879, in Boston, she founded what is called the Mother Church—The First Church of Christ, Scientist. This church is still the headquarters of the movement, which has now spread throughout the world.

Christian Science emphasizes healing by purely spiritual means. It holds that God is goodness. Sickness and evil mean that this goodness has temporarily been lost. People can regain the goodness by prayer. Christian Scientists believe that through reading God's word in the Bible, people can come closer to God and eventually destroy physical and spiritual illness. Christian Science beliefs are contained in Mrs. Eddy's book, *Science and Health with Key to the Scriptures.*

▼ *The Mother Church in Boston's Christian Science Center is the headquarters of the Christian Science movement.*

## CIRCUS 

A circus is a touring show with trained animals, clowns, acrobats, and other performers. Some circuses still perform under a large tent called the "Big Top." The various acts are performed in a round area, or ring.

▲ *Circus posters have always attracted audiences who are drawn to the spectacle of such daring acts as walking the tightwire.*

The first real circus in North America performed in 1793 in Philadelphia. President George Washington was one of the spectators. The most famous circuses were the Ringling Brothers Circus and the BARNUM & BAILEY Circus. At one time the Ringling Brothers Circus toured for six months of the year, covering 15,000 miles (24,000 km). The two circuses are now one; it performs in permanent indoor arenas.

Trained animals, clowns, and trapeze and tightwire artists are the most popular performers in a circus. In North America, many circuses begin with a big parade, or "spec" (for spectacle). All of the performers wear dazzling costumes and march around the arena as the band plays and the clowns entertain.

Large circuses that are still performed outside may have many smaller tents housing wild animals in cages. But the main show always takes place in the Big Top.

► *Modern circus animals are as highly trained as the human performers.*

**City planning in English-speaking North America began in 1692 when William Penn worked out a plan for the city of Philadelphia. In 1807, town planners divided Upper Manhattan into 2,000 rectangular blocks, 200 feet (61 m) wide. This monotonous but convenient design became the pattern for many other U.S. cities.**

## CITIES

A city is a community in which large numbers of people live. The U.S. government defines a city as a community of more than 2,500 people having an agreed form of local government. In the United States, there are more than 2,300 cities with 10,000 or more people. About half of all Americans live in these communities.

People live in cities for many reasons. There are many kinds of businesses in cities, so many people work there. Cities are also cultural and recreational centers. City life, however, has many problems. Many cities have high pollution levels

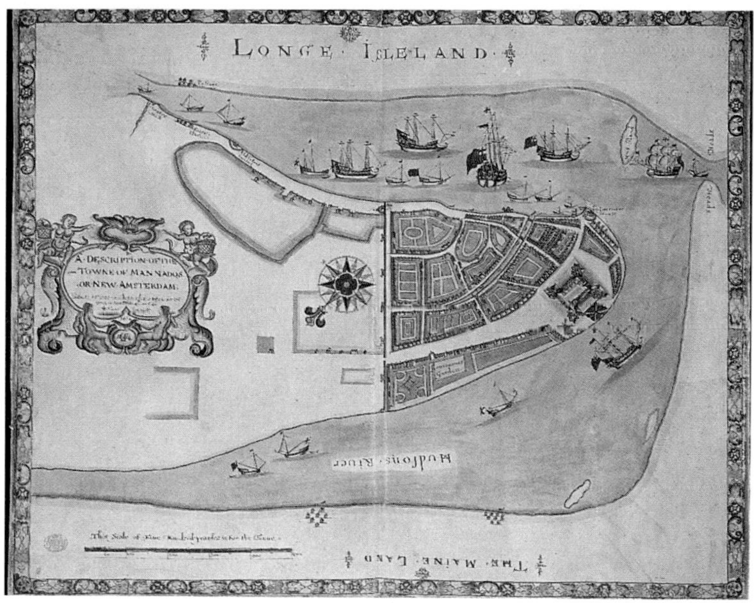

◀ *This map of the southern tip of Manhattan was drawn in 1664. In that same year it ceased to be Dutch New Amsterdam and became British New York.*

caused by traffic and factories. Noise, crime, and racial conflicts also detract from the quality of life. The lack of decent housing is another problem.

Because of these problems, many people have moved away from cities to the surrounding suburbs. Others have moved from the older cities of the North to developing cities in the South and the Southwest, in the area called the Sunbelt.

ST. AUGUSTINE, Florida, is the oldest city in North America. It was founded by the Spanish in 1565. The next cities to be established were BOSTON, New Amsterdam (which became NEW YORK), PHILADELPHIA, and BALTIMORE. Today, New York is the country's largest city. It has 7.3 million people. LOS ANGELES has 3.5 million, and CHICAGO has almost 3 million.

The 25 Largest Cities in the U.S.

| City | Population |
|---|---|
| New York, N.Y. | 7,322,564 |
| Los Angeles, Calif. | 3,485,398 |
| Chicago, Ill. | 2,783,726 |
| Houston, Tex. | 1,630,553 |
| Philadelphia, Pa. | 1,585,577 |
| San Diego, Calif. | 1,110,549 |
| Detroit, Mich. | 1,027,974 |
| Dallas, Tex. | 1,006,877 |
| Phoenix, Ariz. | 983,403 |
| San Antonio, Tex. | 935,933 |
| San Jose, Calif. | 782,248 |
| Indianapolis, Ind. | 741,952 |
| Baltimore, Md. | 736,014 |
| San Francisco, Calif. | 723,959 |
| Jacksonville, Fla. | 672,971 |
| Columbus, Ohio | 632,910 |
| Milwaukee, Wis. | 628,088 |
| Memphis, Tenn. | 610,337 |
| Washington, D.C. | 606,900 |
| Boston, Mass. | 574,283 |
| Seattle, Wash. | 516,259 |
| El Paso, Tex. | 515,342 |
| Nashville-Davidson, Tenn. | 510,784 |
| Cleveland, Ohio | 505,616 |
| New Orleans, La. | 496,938 |

**The national population census of 1920 was a turning point in U.S. history. It marked the first time that city dwellers outnumbered rural residents.**

◀ *Cincinnati's location along the Ohio River made it a bustling port during the 1800s. Today it is a major industrial center.*

**Citizenship Day has been celebrated on September 17 every year since 1952. This date marks the signing of the Constitution in 1787. Ceremonies held on that day honor native-born Americans who have reached voting age as well as newly naturalized foreign-born American citizens.**

## CITIZENSHIP

A citizen is a full member of a country. By holding citizenship, a person is entitled to certain rights and privileges. A citizen also has certain duties and obligations. U.S. citizens, for example, have the right to vote beginning at the age of 18 and the right to protection while living abroad. In return, they owe allegiance to the U.S. government. In the event of war, they may have to serve in the armed forces.

The Fourteenth Amendment to the U.S. Constitution states that all persons born in the United States are citizens. (Children whose parents are foreign diplomats are exceptions.) People not born in the United States can become naturalized citizens. This is a legal process in which the person swears allegiance to the United States and gives up loyalty to his or her country of birth. Naturalized citizens have the same rights and duties as other citizens. They may not, however, become president or vice president.

▼ *Many pickers are needed to harvest the oranges grown around Bakersfield in California. Much is still done by hand.*

## CITRUS FRUIT

Citrus fruits have thick rinds with juicy pulp inside. They grow on trees in warm regions. Citrus fruits include oranges, grapefruits, and lemons. Less well known citrus fruits include the mandarin, kumquat, and tangelo.

The United States is the world's leading grower of citrus fruits. Florida produces about two thirds of the sweet oranges and grapefruits grown in the United States. The Dancy tangerine is the most important type of mandarin grown in Florida. California and Arizona are also important grapefruit producers, and California produces more fresh lemons than anywhere else in the United States.

▼ *The United States produces many types of citrus fruit. They are all rich in Vitamin C.*

## CIVIL RIGHTS 

Civil rights are those rights guaranteed to an individual by law and custom. The American BILL OF RIGHTS, for example, guarantees freedom of speech and religion. It also guarantees a free press, the right to own property, and the right to a speedy trial by jury.

BLACK AMERICANS were long denied many civil rights. The Thirteenth Amendment to the U.S. Constitution abolished slavery. The Fourteenth Amendment made blacks citizens, and the Fifteenth Amendment gave black men the right to vote. Still, many states kept blacks from voting. And in the late 1800s, many states passed laws that required the segregation (separation) of races in everything from transportation to schools. In 1896 the Supreme Court ruled that "separate but equal" facilities were constitutional.

In 1954, however, the Supreme Court ruled that separate facilities were, by their very nature, unequal and therefore unconstitutional. This ruling launched the civil rights movement of the 1950s and 1960s. In 1957 the government set up a Commission on Civil Rights. And the Civil Rights Act of 1964 banned discrimination in public places and in employment. Other minorities, such as the elderly and the handicapped, have also relied on these laws to preserve their rights.

Women in the United States also have suffered from discrimination. They fought for many years before the Nineteenth Amendment to the Constitution gave them the right to vote in 1920. The Civil Rights Act of 1964 protects them, as well as blacks, from job discrimination. The women's movement continues to fight for WOMEN'S RIGHTS.

▲ *Neighborhood rallies and marches help keep civil rights issues in the public eye.*

**Some Important Dates in Civil Rights Legislation**

**1791** The first ten amendments to the Constitution, now known as the Bill of Rights, become law.
**1865** The Thirteenth Amendment abolishes slavery in the U.S.
**1868** The Fourteenth Amendment grants citizenship to all former slaves.
**1870** The Fifteenth Amendment prohibits all states from denying a person the vote because of his race.
**1920** The Nineteenth Amendment gives women the right to vote.
**1955** The U.S. Supreme Court orders all schools to desegregate with "all deliberate speed."
**1957** The Commission on Civil Rights is set up to investigate charges of denial of civil rights.
**1964** The Civil Rights Act prohibits discrimination on the basis of race, color, religion, natural origin, or sex. The Equal Employment Opportunity Commission is set up.
**1969** The Supreme Court orders schools to desegregate.

## CIVIL SERVICE 

People who work for the government and are not in the military and not elected to office are in the civil service. These people are called civil servants. Civil servants work for the federal, state, and local governments. They carry out the everyday work of the government. More than 3 million people work for the federal government, and almost 14 million people work for state and local governments. Almost three fourths of the people the federal government employs work for the Department of Defense and the Postal Service.

# CIVIL WAR

◀ *This recruiting poster offers a $100 bounty (award), payable at the end of the war.*

▲ *The attack on Fort Sumter in South Carolina triggered the Civil War.*

▼ *Union General Ulysses S. Grant.*

The Civil War (1861–1865) was fought between the northern states (the Union) and those southern states (the Confederacy) that had seceded, or withdrawn, from the Union. The war was fought over the issues of states' rights and slavery. The southern states believed that they had the right to make their own laws without interference by the federal government—especially laws that had to do with slavery. They needed slaves to work on their large farms, or plantations, and felt that the southern economy would be ruined if slaves were freed. Many Northerners wanted to abolish, or end, slavery.

When Abraham Lincoln was elected president in 1860, the South feared that he would abolish slavery. Beginning in December 1860, 11 southern states seceded. They formed the Confederate States of America.

**Major Battles of the Civil War**

| Battle | Date | Location | Total Casualties | Victory |
|---|---|---|---|---|
| Bull Run | | | | |
| First | 1861 | Virginia | 4,600 | Confederate |
| Second | 1862 | Virginia | 25,300 | Confederate |
| Shiloh | 1862 | Tennessee | 23,700 | Union |
| Antietam (Sharpsburg) | 1862 | Maryland | 26,100 | Union |
| Fredericksburg | 1862 | Virginia | 17,900 | Confederate |
| Chancellorsville | 1863 | Virginia | 30,000 | Confederate |
| Vicksburg, Siege of | 1863 | Mississippi | 17,400 | Union |
| Gettysburg | 1863 | Pennsylvania | 43,400 | Union |
| Chickamauga | 1863 | Georgia | 34,000 | Confederate |
| Wilderness | 1864 | Virginia | 25,400 | Union |
| Petersburg, Siege of | 1864 | Virginia | 70,000 | Union |

**During the Civil War, more than twice as many soldiers died of diseases such as typhoid, malaria, and dysentery than were killed in battle. The North lost 364,000 soldiers (about one in five); the South lost 258,000 soldiers (about one in four).**

► *The Battle of Chickamauga, fought in Georgia in 1863, was the Confederacy's last important victory in the war.*

The war started on April 12, 1861, when Confederate troops fired on Fort Sumter, South Carolina. The Confederates won a number of victories early in the war. In July 1863, however, the tide turned at the Battle of Gettysburg in Pennsylvania. This Confederate defeat was followed by others, and in the fall of 1864 Union General William T. Sherman captured Atlanta, Georgia. He followed this victory with a "march to the sea," during which he destroyed much of the countryside. On April 9, 1865, Confederate General Robert E. Lee surrendered to Grant.

The cost of the Civil War was staggering. More than 600,000 Americans died—almost as many as in all other American wars combined. But the Union was preserved. See also BOOTH, John Wilkes; BULL RUN; CONFEDERATE STATES OF AMERICA; EMANCIPATION PROCLAMATION; GETTYSBURG, Battle of; GRANT, Ulysses S.; LEE, Robert E.; LINCOLN, Abraham; SHERMAN, William Tecumseh.

*The photographs of wounded soldiers (left) and Confederate General Robert E. Lee (right) were taken by Mathew Brady. He was a pioneer of photography and took more than 3,500 pictures of Civil War battles and camp life. Some were posed portraits of officers, but most showed ordinary soldiers in terrible conditions.*

▲ *These butter clams have been gathered from mudflats along the Pacific Northwest coast. Clams suck in water and filter it for food.*

## CLAM

A clam is a saltwater shellfish. There are more than 12,000 species of clams worldwide. Clams are called bivalves. They have two shells, called valves, held together by a type of hinge called a ligament. Several types of clams are collected for eating in the United States. The most popular Pacific variety is the long and narrow razor clam. Atlantic soft-shell clams are fried, steamed, or used in thick soup called chowder. They are found mainly along muddy New England beaches. The shells of hard-shell clams, called quahogs, were made into wampum, a type of money used by ALGONQUIN Indians.

## CLARK, George Rogers

George Rogers Clark (1752–1818) was a soldier and frontier leader during the American REVOLUTION. Clark was born in Virginia and settled in what is now Kentucky.

When war broke out, Clark obtained permission from Virginia's governor, Patrick HENRY, to organize troops for the defense of the frontier. In 1778 his forces, numbering about 175, marched through the wilderness and captured the British posts of Kaskaskia and Cahokia, on the Mississippi River. The following year, they took Vincennes, in Indiana. Because promised reinforcements failed to arrive, Clark had to abandon his conquests. But these victories ensured that this area, then called the Northwest Territory, was given to the United States by Britain after the Revolution.

▼ *In 1779, George Rogers Clark forced the British to surrender Fort Sackville, which controlled the town of Vincennes.*

## CLAY, Henry

Henry Clay (1777–1852) was one of the ablest political leaders during the years before the CIVIL WAR. He ran for president three times but was never elected. However, he made his mark in other ways. 'Clay represented Kentucky in the House of Representatives and the Senate for many years, first as a Jeffersonian Republican and then as a Whig. He also served as secretary of state under John Quincy ADAMS.

Clay is best remembered for steering through Congress a series of compromises that held the Union together in the stormy years before the Civil War.

Because of his work, Clay became known as the Great Compromiser. In the Missouri Compromise (1820), Missouri was admitted to the Union as a slave state with Maine as a free state. This preserved the existing balance between slave and free states. Clay's compromise tariff of 1833 managed to prevent South Carolina from leaving the Union. Two years before he died, Clay authored the Compromise of 1850. This series of laws admitted California as a free state but made concessions to the South that helped to postpone the Civil War for another 11 years.

▲ *Henry Clay was known in the Senate as the Great Compromiser because he understood both the North and the South. The Civil War might have been prevented if he had lived longer.*

## CLEMENS, Samuel L. *See* Twain, Mark

## CLEVELAND

Cleveland is the second largest city in OHIO, with a population of more than 505,000. It is located on the southern shore of Lake Erie and is a major Great Lakes port and transportation center. Founded in 1796, Cleveland prospered in the 1900s because of its steelworks and became one of the largest cities in the Midwest. Today, it is an important center for the manufacture of automobile parts, machine tools, plastics, and paints. Downtown Cleveland today is modern and busy, with fine buildings and parks. In 1967, with the election of Carl Stokes, Cleveland became the first major U.S. city to have a black mayor.

**Cleveland's role as an industrial leader was confirmed during the Civil War. The city's iron ore and coal were mined for steel production. This was to meet the Union's growing demands for railroad equipment, heavy machinery, and ships.**

◀ *Cleveland is an important Great Lakes port. It is also the home of one football team, the Cleveland Browns (NFL), one baseball team, the Cleveland Indians (AL), and the Cleveland Symphony, one of the nation's leading orchestras.*

## CLEVELAND, Stephen Grover

Grover Cleveland
**Born:** March 18, 1837, in Caldwell, New Jersey
**Education:** Left school at 14; legal training
**Political party:** Democratic
**Terms of office:** 1885–1889 and 1893–1897
**Married:** 1886 to Frances Folsom
**Died:** June 24, 1908, in Princeton, New Jersey

Grover Cleveland was president of the United States twice. These two separate terms of office meant that he was both the 22nd and 24th president. Cleveland, a lawyer, had been mayor of Buffalo, New York, and then governor of New York. He was the first Democrat to be elected president in 28 years.

After his election in 1884, Cleveland maintained his record of honesty and integrity. He proved that he was not afraid to do what he considered right even if it made him unpopular. One of his aims was to reduce the very high tariff (tax on imported goods) that was creating economic problems. However, the Republican-controlled Senate resisted this. In 1888, Cleveland lost the election to the Republican candidate, Benjamin HARRISON, but in 1892 he won by a large margin.

Early in his second term there was a severe economic depression. Cleveland wanted to end the issuing of silver (rather than gold) money, which he believed would cause inflation (rising prices). But the measures he took upset the supporters of silver. Cleveland had other problems as well. In 1894 police broke up a march of the unemployed on Washington. During a railroad strike in Chicago, Cleveland sent in federal troops.

*► France's gift of the Statue of Liberty in 1886 was a highlight of the Cleveland presidency.*

During this term, British Guiana and Venezuela were involved in a boundary dispute. Cleveland warned the British that their claims went against the MONROE DOCTRINE. Finally, they backed down.

Because of Cleveland's support for the gold standard and for a lower tariff, the Democrats did not renominate him in 1896.

*▼ Frances Folsom was 21 years old when she married Grover Cleveland. He was 49. The wedding was held in the White House.*

## CLIFF DWELLERS 

The cliff dwellers were INDIAN tribes in the Southwest who lived in caves or homes built in cliff overhangs. Eventually these homes were built in layers on top of each other, so that the cliff wall looked like a strange apartment complex. The only way to reach the homes was by a ladder that was taken away when not in use to protect the Indians from attack. There were watchtowers from which possible invaders could be seen. The cliff complexes also had large, decorated underground rooms called *kivas* that were used as community meeting places and for special ceremonies.

The best known of the cliff dwellers were the Anasazi Indians. They were the ancestors of the PUEBLO Indians. The Anasazi abandoned their cliff dwellings about A.D. 1300. The Cliff Palace at Mesa Verde in Colorado has over 200 rooms and 23 kivas. It is a United States National Park.

## CLIMATE 

The climate is an average of weather conditions occurring over several decades. The United States, with its vast area, contains examples of the main types of world climates. At one extreme is the wet, semi-tropical climate, seen mainly in the Hawaiian Islands and southern Florida. Annual rainfall in that climate often exceeds 100 inches (250 cm). At the other extreme are the polar climates of northern Alaska. Here winter temperatures dip below –50°F (–45°C). Arizona, New Mexico, and eastern California are arid. Rainfall can be less than 10 inches (25 cm) a year, and summer temperatures soar to 120°F (50°C). The MOJAVE and other DESERTS are in this region. By contrast, the coasts of Washington and Oregon, in the northwest, are among the rainiest places in the United States. Most of the United States, however, has a temperate climate. There is regular rainfall and temperatures are not extreme during most of the year.

Many different kinds of dangerous weather conditions can be seen in the United States. Hurricanes often batter the coasts along the Gulf of Mexico and Atlantic Ocean. Tornadoes hit the central part of the country and the southeastern coast. And flooding is common in the central and eastern states. In contrast, the western states often suffer from severe drought.

▼ *Information collected by weather stations and satellites provides an accurate picture of temperature patterns across the country.*

**Average January temperatures**

| Degrees Fahrenheit | Degrees Celsius |
|---|---|
| Over 60 | Over 16 |
| 45 to 60 | 7 to 16 |
| 30 to 45 | –1 to 7 |
| 15 to 30 | –9 to –1 |
| 0 to 15 | –18 to –9 |
| –15 to 0 | –26 to –18 |
| Below –15 | Below –26 |

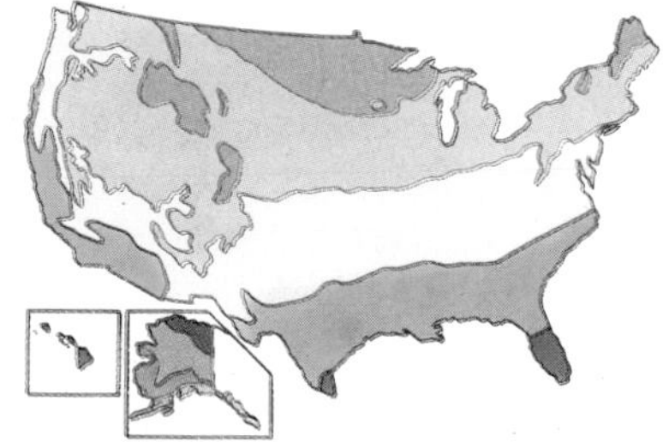

**Average July temperatures**

| Degrees Fahrenheit | Degrees Celsius |
|---|---|
| Over 90 | Over 32 |
| 75 to 90 | 24 to 32 |
| 60 to 75 | 16 to 24 |
| 45 to 60 | 7 to 16 |
| Below 45 | Below 7 |

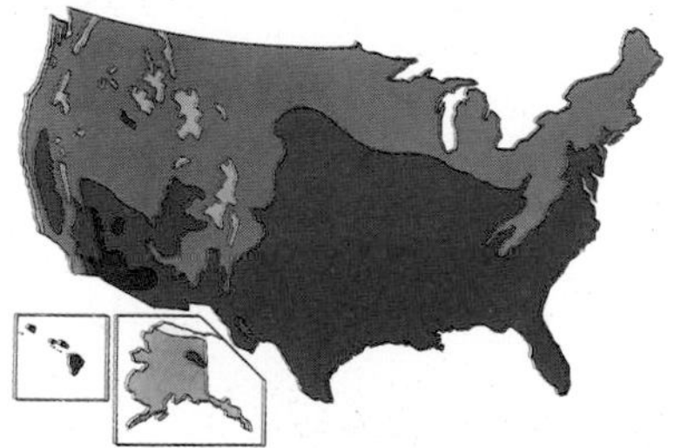

# CLINTON, William (Bill) J.

William (Bill) Jefferson Clinton is the 42nd president of the United States. After graduating from Yale University Law School, he returned home to Arkansas. Six years later, at the age of 32, he became governor of that state. He was the nation's youngest governor. As the Democratic presidential candidate in 1992, he promised to revive the United States weakened economy. He defeated President George BUSH and independent candidate Ross Perot, winning more than 45 percent of the vote in 20 states.

Soon after taking office, Clinton presented a plan to reduce the government's budget deficit by increasing taxes and cutting government spending. Congress approved the plan by a narrow margin. But it rejected his plan to raise money by taxing all forms of energy. Clinton's other major initiative was a proposal to provide every American with health insurance. If passed by Congress, it would be the most sweeping national program since Social Security was enacted in 1935. President Clinton also successfully urged Congress to approve the North American Free Trade Agreement which will remove barriers to trade and investment between the United States, Canada, and Mexico.

In foreign affairs, Clinton sent American troops to the African country of Somalia. The goal was to halt the fighting between various groups and bring an end to starvation in the country. Another concern during Clinton's first year in office was to find a way to end the war in Bosnia. He strongly supported President Boris Yeltsin in his bid to bring democratic and economic reforms to Russia. And he supported the peace agreement between Israel and the Palestine Liberation Organization.

Bill Clinton
**Born:** August 19, 1946, in Hope, Arkansas
**Education:** Georgetown University, Oxford University, Yale University Law School
**Political party:** Democratic
**Term of office:** 1993–
**Married:** 1975 to Hillary Rodham

▼ *First lady Hillary Clinton plays an active role in the president's administration.*

◀ *President Clinton, seen here with cabinet colleagues, faced many problems during his first few months of office.*

## COAL *See* Mining Industry

## COAST GUARD, U.S.

The U.S. Coast Guard is a branch of the armed services. It does exactly what its name suggests: it guards the coasts of the United States.

Among the Coast Guard's most important jobs are helping in emergencies and arresting smugglers. But its many day-to-day tasks include maintaining navigational aids such as buoys and lighthouses, reporting weather for the National Weather Service, and overseeing safety regulations for every kind of seagoing vessel. The Coast Guard was founded in 1790. It is part of the Department of Transportation. During a war, however, the Coast Guard operates under the Department of the Navy.

## COCHISE

Cochise (1812?–1874) was a great chief of the Chiricahua APACHES, an Indian tribe that lived in what are now New Mexico and Arizona. In 1861 he and his people were mistakenly accused of stealing and of kidnapping a white child. Cochise denied the charges, but he was imprisoned. He escaped, taking some hostages because the Army was holding some of his relatives. Eventually both sides killed their hostages. A war broke out that involved other tribes and led to great loss of life over a number of years.

In 1872, General Oliver Howard, with the help of Thomas Jeffords, a frontiersman, finally negotiated peace with Cochise.

**A remarkable friendship grew between the Apache Indian chief Cochise and a mail contractor, Thomas Jeffords. In an attempt to stop some of the violence between his couriers and the Apaches, Jeffords met with Cochise alone and the two men declared peace, although the war with the settlers went on. When Cochise signed the treaty that ended his raids in exchange for a reservation, he insisted that Thomas Jeffords be appointed the Indian agent.**

## COCHRAN, Jacqueline

Jacqueline Cochran (1910?–1980) was a famous aviator. During her career she held more flying records than anyone else. In 1938 she set two speed records and became the first woman to win the Bendix Transcontinental Air Race. During World War II, Cochran organized the Women Airforce Service Pilots (WASPS). In 1953, she broke the men's and women's world speed records. She later became the first woman to fly faster than the speed of sound.

▼ *The pilot Jacqueline Cochran was the first civilian woman to be awarded the Distinguished Service Medal.*

**Buffalo Bill Cody's Wild West Shows were more popular with easterners and Europeans than with natives of the American West itself. His first show, at Omaha, Nebraska, in 1883, was only a partial success. Many customers complained about paying for action they could normally see for free.**

## CODY, William F. 

William F. Cody (1846–1917), better known as "Buffalo Bill," was a frontier scout and showman. Cody led an adventurous life. He carried mail for the PONY EXPRESS and was a scout for the Union during the CIVIL WAR. He became a buffalo hunter and was credited with having killed 4,000, a feat that led to his nickname. After a brief time as an Army scout and Indian fighter, he began a career as an entertainer. He eventually formed a company called "Buffalo Bill's Wild West Show." The show toured the United States and Canada and even performed in Europe. During the show, Buffalo Bill reenacted some of his legendary exploits against the Indians and demonstrated his skill as a marksman. The city of Cody, Wyoming, is named after him.

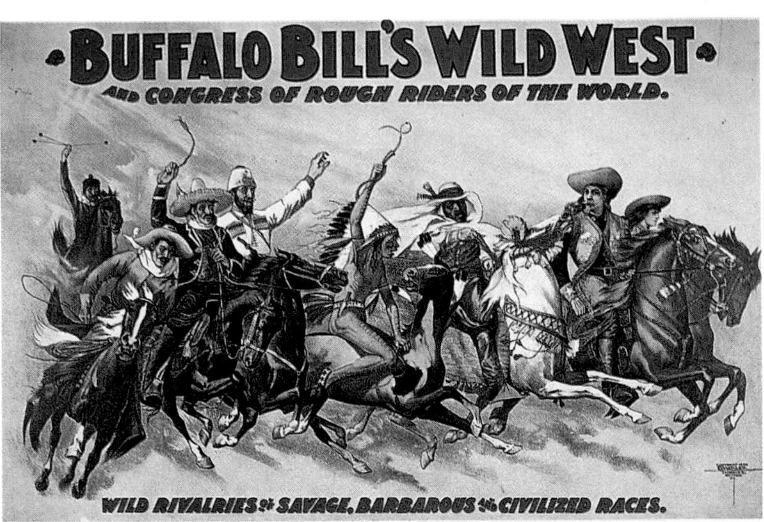


► *Buffalo Bill's Wild West Show included other legendary figures, such as Calamity Jane and the Apache chief Geronimo.*

## COHAN, George M. 

**Written on April 6, 1917, the day the United States declared war against Germany and entered World War I, the song "Over There" by George M. Cohan was an immediate hit. Its stirring words, "The Yanks are coming," probably made it one of the most inspiring calls-to-arms ever written.**

George M. Cohan (1878–1942) wrote many famous songs and plays. He was born in Providence, Rhode Island. As a child he performed in a vaudeville act with his family and began writing when he was a teenager. He also acted in plays and produced them. He was a well-known figure on BROADWAY. The 1942 movie *Yankee Doodle Dandy* and the 1968 musical *George M!* were about his life. Some of Cohan's most famous songs are "You're a Grand Old Flag," "Give My Regards to Broadway," and "I'm a Yankee Doodle Dandy." He was given a special medal by Congress for his World War I song "Over There." His best-known performances were in *Ah, Wilderness!* and *I'd Rather Be Right*.

## COINS 

The United States issues more than 15 billion coins each year. The coins are produced in the federal mints in Philadelphia, Denver, and San Francisco. Individual states cannot issue their own coins. Six types of coins are in current use: the cent (penny), 5-cents (nickel), 10-cents (dime), 25-cents (quarter), 50-cents (half-dollar), and dollar. Nearly 173 billion coins are in circulation, including 129 billion pennies, 11.5 billion nickels, 16.4 billion dimes, and 15.6 billion quarters. Many other U.S. coins, such as the half-cent and the $20 gold piece, are no longer produced.

▼ *Coins commemorate famous people and places, such as presidents Washington, Lincoln, and Roosevelt, and Jefferson's home, Monticello.*

## COLD WAR

The term Cold War describes the tension between democratic and Communist countries that began after

◀ *The friendly relations between President Ronald Reagan and Soviet leader Mikhail Gorbachev helped reduce Cold War tensions in the late 1980s.*

▲ *This commencement ceremony at State University of New York at Stony Brook is one of thousands that take place each spring in the United States.*

WORLD WAR II. The United States and its allies in the West felt threatened by the Soviet Union's efforts to promote Communism and extend its control and influence around the world. Both sides built up large military arsenals. Actual fighting, or "hot war," nearly broke out over a number of incidents, including the CUBAN MISSILE CRISIS of 1962. In addition, conflicts such as the KOREAN WAR and the VIETNAM WAR were seen as part of the effort to contain Communism. In 1989, however, Soviet leader Mikhail Gorbachev allowed the Communist countries of Eastern Europe to elect democratic governments. Then, in 1991, the Soviet Union broke up into 15 republics, and the Cold War came to an end.

## COLLEGES AND UNIVERSITIES

Colleges and universities are schools where students go to continue their education after they graduate from high school. Students may go to a four-year college or to a two-year junior, or community, college.

The oldest university in the United States is Harvard University. It was founded in 1636. Today there are more than 3,500 colleges and universities in the country. About 14 million students are enrolled in these schools, including 420,000 foreign students. More than three quarters of all students go to public schools, those sponsored by local and state governments and the federal government. The average cost of tuition and

The 10 Oldest Universities and Colleges in the U.S.

| University | Founded |
|---|---|
| Harvard University, Cambridge, Mass. | 1636 |
| College of William and Mary, Williamsburg, Va. | 1693 |
| Yale University, New Haven, Conn. | 1701 |
| University of Pennsylvania, Philadelphia, Pa. | 1740 |
| Princeton University, Princeton, N.J. | 1746 |
| Washington and Lee University, Lexington, Va. | 1749 |
| Columbia University, New York, N.Y. | 1754 |
| Brown University, Providence, R.I. | 1764 |
| Rutgers, The State University of New Jersey, New Brunswick, N.J. | 1766 |
| Dartmouth College, Hanover, N.H. | 1769 |

► *College courses in science and engineering make use of fully equipped laboratories.*

◄ *Some college classes are conducted in an informal manner, even outdoors if the weather permits.*

| 10 Most Popular Degrees |
|---|
| Business and management |
| Social sciences (including history) |
| Education |
| Engineering |
| Health sciences |
| Communications |
| Psychology |
| Literature |
| Life sciences |
| Visual and performing arts |

room and board at a four-year public school is about $6,000 per year for state residents and $9,500 per year for nonresidents. About one quarter of all students attend private colleges and universities. The average cost per year at these institutions is about $13,000, but some can cost more than $20,000.

More than 1.3 million degrees are awarded each year; 75 percent of these are bachelor's degrees, and 23 percent are master's degrees. More than 35,000 doctoral degrees are earned each year. For many students, a higher education is a means to getting a good job, which is why more people earn business degrees than any other kind.

Students who want to go to college take national tests called SATs (Scholastic Aptitude Tests) and ACTs (American College Tests). The results show how good a student's basic skills are. Some colleges also give an entrance examination of their own.

## COLLINS, Michael

Michael Collins (1930– ) was the astronaut who piloted the command module during the Apollo 11 mission to the moon in July 1969. Collins remained in the command module, circling the moon, while Neil ARMSTRONG and Edwin ALDRIN landed on the moon's surface in the lunar module.

Before the Apollo 11 mission, Collins was the co-pilot of the Gemini 10 flight, with John Young, in July 1966. During this flight he walked in space. In 1971, Collins became the director of the National Air and Space Museum in Washington, D.C.

▼ *During the Apollo 11 mission, Michael Collins manned the command module* Columbia *while Neil Armstrong and Buzz Aldrin made their historic landing on the moon.*

# COLORADO

Colorado is known as the Centennial State. This is because it became a state in 1876, 100 years after the signing of the Declaration of Independence. Colorado is one of the ROCKY MOUNTAIN states. Over half the state is ruggedly mountainous. The eastern part of the state, which is flatter, forms the western edge of the Great Plains. These plains are where most of Colorado's people live, especially in and around the city of DENVER, the capital and largest city.

Towering mountains make Colorado one of the most dramatically beautiful states in the country. In winter, visitors come to ski at famous resorts such as Aspen and Vail. In summer, they come to walk, camp, hunt and fish, and to admire the scenery. Tourism is one of the most important businesses in Colorado.

The eastern part of Colorado became part of the United States in 1803, as part of the LOUISIANA PURCHASE. After the western half was taken from Mexico in 1848, settlers began to flock to the area.

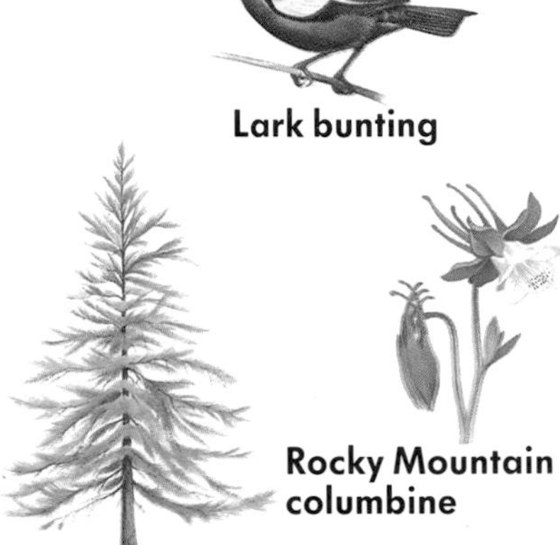

Lark bunting

Rocky Mountain columbine

Blue spruce

► *Pikes Peak, in Colorado's eastern Rockies, was one of the most famous landmarks for the wagon trains of the pioneers. It is named for Zebulon Pike, the explorer who first traveled through there in the early 1800s.*

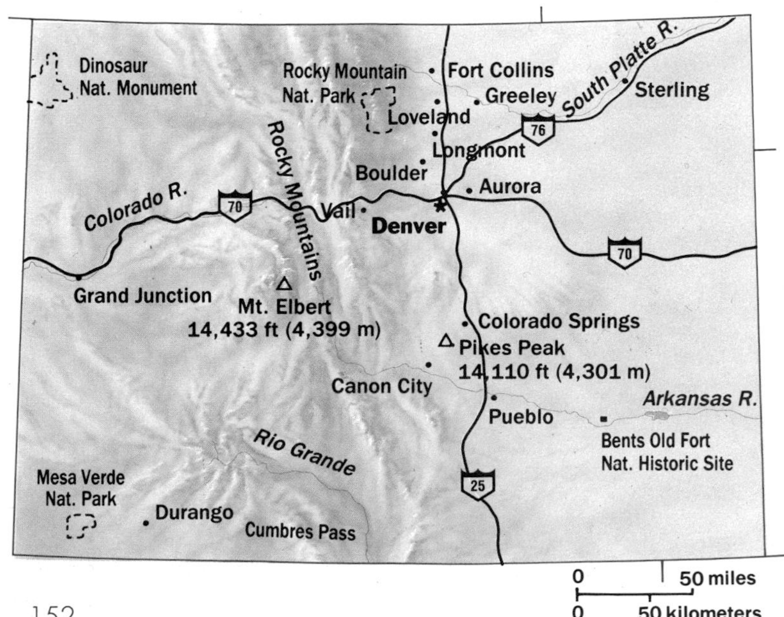


**Colorado**

**Capital:** Denver
**Area:** 104,100 sq mi (269,620 km²). Rank: 8th
**Population:** 3,294,394 (1991). Rank: 26th
**Statehood:** August 1, 1876
**Principal rivers:** Colorado, South Platte, Arkansas
**Highest point:** Mt. Elbert, 14,433 ft (4,399 m)
**Motto:** *Nil Sine Numine* (Nothing Without Providence)
**Song:** "Where the Columbines Grow"

Many were drawn by tales of gold in its mountains. Through the 1850s, thc population swelled rapidly and many mining communities were founded.

Gold and silver are still mined in Colorado, and Denver is the site of a U.S. Mint, where COINS are produced, or minted. But today petroleum is the state's most important mineral. Many oil companies are based in Denver. Other industries include finance and manufacturing, especially in Denver. Colorado is an important agricultural state, too. Cattle and sheep are raised all over the state, and wheat is grown on the plains.

► *The Garden of the Gods is a colorful rock formation created by volcanoes more than 50 million years ago.*

**Places of Interest**

- Mesa Verde National Park, near Cortez, has Indian cliff dwellings that are almost a thousand years old.
- The U.S. Mint, in Denver, produces millions of coins every year.
- Bent's Old Fort, near La Junta, is a reconstruction of a trading post originally completed in 1833. The fort was Colorado's first permanent settlement.

▼ *A covered bridge leads to the famous ski resort of Vail. Thousands of skiers, including former president Gerald Ford, prefer Colorado snow because it is dry and powdery.*

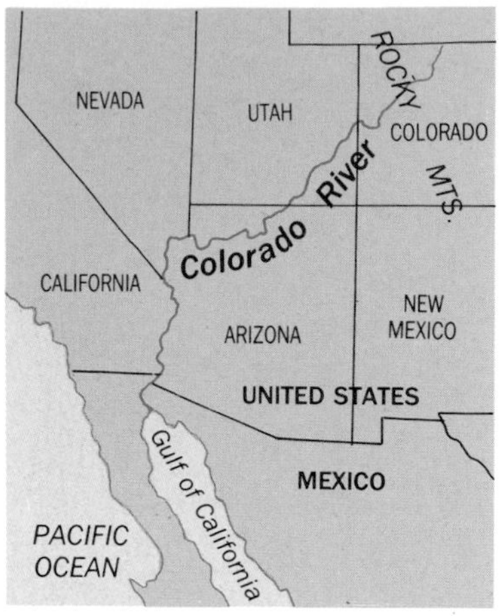


▲ *Dams in four states harness the waters of the Colorado River. The dams provide irrigation for farming and reduce erosion caused by the river.*

► *The Powell Expedition of 1869 (right) explored the Colorado River through the Grand Canyon. Over millions of years, the waters of the river have eaten through the layers of surrounding rock to create deep canyons with vertical walls (far right).*

▼ *The famous Lewis and Clark Expedition followed the Columbia River to reach the Pacific Ocean in 1805. For nearly three weeks they braved dangerous rapids and hostile Indians along the Columbia River.*

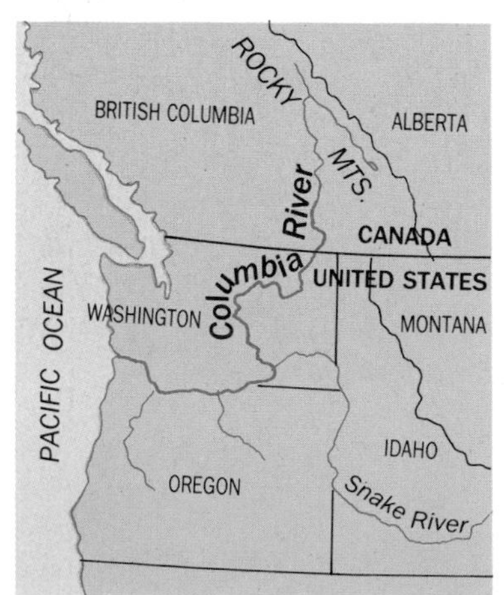


## COLORADO RIVER

The Colorado River is one of the longest rivers in the United States. It is along the Colorado River, in Arizona, that the GRAND CANYON, America's most famous natural wonder, is located. The Colorado River is 1,450 miles (2,333 km) long. It flows southwest from the Rocky Mountains through Colorado, Utah, and Arizona to the Gulf of California in Mexico. Seven other rivers flow into it, including the Little Colorado River and the Gila River. A number of DAMS have been built across the Colorado River to regulate its flow and to provide power for electricity. The most famous is the Hoover Dam, built by the federal government in 1936.

## COLUMBIA RIVER

The Columbia River is one of the longest and most important rivers in North America. It flows north through British Columbia in Canada and then south to Washington state before heading west to the Pacific Ocean. This westernmost section of the river forms most of the border between Washington and Oregon. Portland, Oregon's most important port, is on the Williamette River, a tributary of the Columbia. In all, the river is 1,243 miles (2,000 km) long. The Columbia River is the single largest source of electricity in the northwestern United States. Thirteen huge DAMS have been built on the river. The largest is the Grand Coulee Dam, in Washington. It provides more electricity than any other power plant in the country.

## COLUMBUS

Columbus, the capital of OHIO, is located on the Scioto River near the center of the state. This central location was the main reason the site was chosen as the state capital. Construction began in 1812 and Columbus became the capital in 1816. About 632,900 people live in the city today. The state government employs many people in Columbus, but even more work in the manufacturing industries there. Heavy machinery such as coal-mining equipment is produced, as well as paints, shoes, refrigerators, and many other household items. Columbus was one of the first U.S. cities to recognize environmental problems. Since 1952 the city's downtown area has been redeveloped, new housing has been built, and tough anti-pollution laws have been enacted.

▲ *The Columbus Civic Center has a riverside location. It contains city and state government buildings and the 555-foot (168-m) Lincoln–Leveque Tower.*

## COLUMBUS, Christopher

Christopher Columbus (1451–1506) was a great explorer and seaman. Born in Genoa, in Italy, he sailed for the Spanish King Ferdinand and Queen Isabella. In 1492 Columbus made the historic voyage in which he reached the New World.

Columbus had become convinced that it would be possible to reach Asia by sailing west from Europe in-

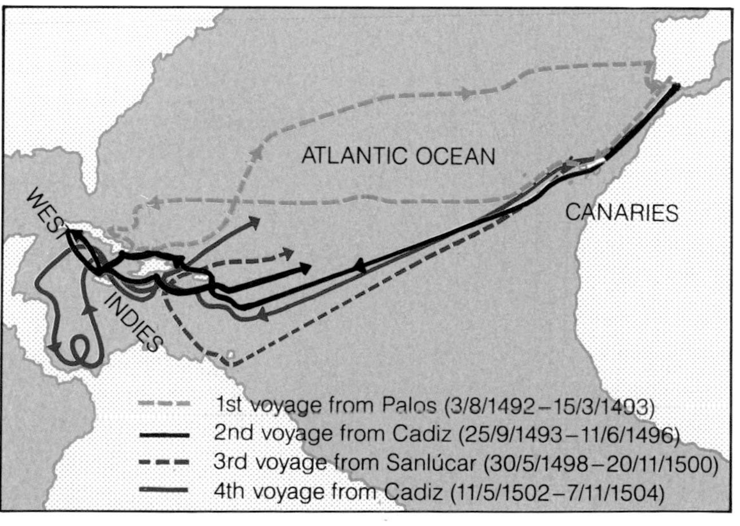


◀ *Christopher Columbus made four voyages to the Americas between 1492 and 1504. He explored the islands of the Caribbean as well as the coast of Central and South America.*

▼ *Columbus sought honors and riches so that his descendants would be spared the poverty he faced as a child in Genoa.*

**Columbus very nearly failed to reach America. His sailors, tired and disheartened after so many weeks at sea without any sign of land, threatened to mutiny on October 10, 1492. Columbus managed to convince them to sail on for three more days. Just over a day later, on October 12 at 2 A.M., the fleet sighted one of the islands of the Bahamas. By noon, Columbus had set foot on San Salvador.**

stead of east. He set out in 1492 with three small ships, the *Santa Maria*, the *Niña*, and the *Pinta*, and a crew of 90. The first land he reached was an island in the Bahamas, southeast of Florida. But Columbus was sure he had reached Asia. On later voyages he discovered other Caribbean islands and parts of Central and South America, while searching for gold. He founded several Spanish colonies in these lands. But his inability to get along with people involved him in several conflicts, and the Spanish monarchs took away his command. He died less than two years after he returned to Spain from his fourth voyage. But his voyages opened up the settlement of the Western Hemisphere.

## COMANCHES

The Comanches are an INDIAN tribe that originally lived on the southern Great Plains. Their skill with horses made them successful hunters of buffalo. The Comanches often raided other tribes to obtain horses and slaves. Beginning in the 1700s, the Comanches fought to keep white settlers out of their lands. When the Americans tried to restrict the Comanches to land in southwestern Oklahoma, war broke out. The Texas Rangers were formed to control the Comanches, but they did not have much success at first. In 1858 the Rangers started a major campaign against the tribe. The Comanches finally surrendered in 1875. Chief QUANAH PARKER led his people to the reservation. Today thousands of Comanches live on a reservation in Oklahoma.

▼ *In this painting by George Catlin a Comanche ropes a wild stallion. The Comanches were skilled riders and depended on horses for hunting buffalo.*

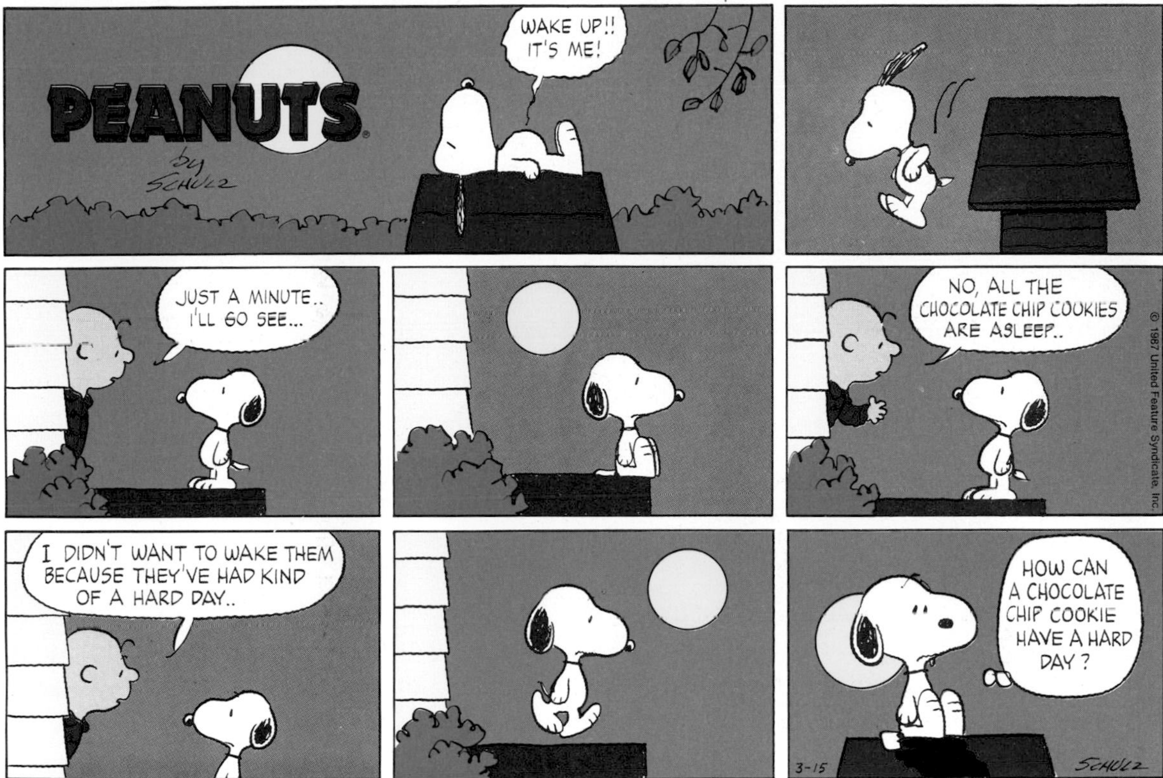


▲ *The "Peanuts" characters were originally called "Li'l Folks" by their creator, Charles Schulz. The strip appears in newspapers in more than 60 countries.*

## COMICS

Comic strips have been a popular feature of newspapers for nearly a century. A strip is a series of several cartoons. Comic books developed as collections of comic strips. The first comic strips, nicknamed the "funnies," appeared in newspapers in the 1890s. William Randolph HEARST's *New York Journal* introduced the first color comic pages in 1896. The Golden Age of comic art lasted from then until World War II, with millions of readers following their favorite cartoons each day. Superheroes such as Superman, Spiderman, and Batman were created in the 1930s as an escape from the hard times of the Great DEPRESSION. Television lessened demand somewhat, but in the 1960s a small group of artists, such as Roy Lichtenstein, claimed that comics were true modern art. The tradition of the funnies continues with Peanuts, Garfield, and Doonesbury.

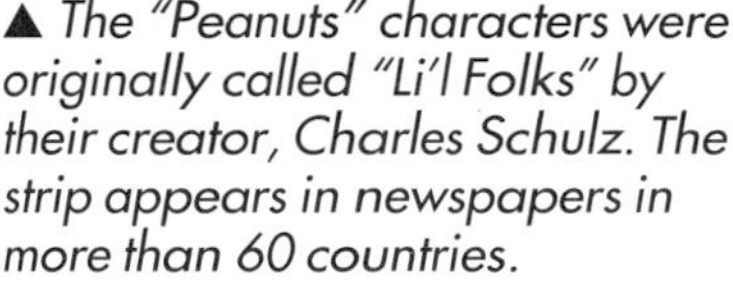

▼ *Communications satellites such as Telstar use electronic equipment to increase the strength of telephone signals.*

## COMMUNICATIONS INDUSTRY

The size of the United States has always made it important to convey information as fast as possible. There was no real communications industry until after Samuel

| | Some Important Dates in History of American Communication |
|---|---|
| 1673 | The first regular mail service in the colonies begins between Boston and New York City. |
| 1704 | The *Boston News-Letter* is the first regularly produced newspaper in the colonies. |
| 1844 | Samuel F. B. Morse sends the first telegraph message from Washington, D.C., to Baltimore, Maryland. |
| 1858 | The first successful transatlantic telegraph cable is laid. |
| 1860 | The Pony Express begins. |
| 1861 | The first transcontinental telegraph service is completed at Salt Lake City, Utah. |
| 1876 | Alexander Graham Bell patents the first telephone. |
| 1918 | The first scheduled airmail service begins between Washington, D.C., and New York City. |
| 1919 | The Radio Corporation of America is established. |
| 1946 | Start of the television boom in the United States. By 1960, almost every household will own a television set. |
| 1965 | America launches the Early Bird satellite over the Atlantic to relay telephone and television signals between the U.S. and Europe. |
| 1980 | *The Columbus Dispatch* of Columbus, Ohio, becomes the first electronic newspaper. It can transmit some of its contents directly to office and home computers. |
| 1980s | Satellite broadcasting widens the choice of television channels and programs. |

**The speed of communication has increased enormously over the past hundred years. It has been estimated that within 35 minutes after the assassination of President John F. Kennedy in 1963, more than 90 percent of the U.S. population had received the news. It took over eight months for the same proportion of the public to learn of President Abraham Lincoln's assassination in 1865.**

MORSE invented the telegraph in 1837. Alexander Graham BELL's telephone, invented in 1876, took instant communications a step further. The first long-distance telephone lines between New York City and Chicago were opened in 1892.

This century has seen these inventions develop into multimillion-dollar industries. New developments in electronics, such as computers and microchips, make communications systems cheaper and more efficient.

Broadcasting, which includes RADIO and TELEVISION, is a branch of communications. Cellular telephones, used in automobiles, ships, and airplanes, broadcast using radio waves. And early in the next century, communications experts expect that videophones will allow people to see each other on television screens while they talk on the telephone.

► *Fiber-optic technology was introduced in 1980. It is the latest development in communications. Telephone messages travel on laser beams along fine strands of glass.*

## COMMUNITY COLLEGES

Community colleges are also known as "junior colleges." Most of their study programs last two years. These colleges provide training in a number of fields, such as accounting, bookkeeping, computing, laboratory analysis, nursing, and secretarial work. Instead of going to a four-year college, some high school graduates may choose to go to a community college, where they can obtain associate of arts (A.A.) or associate of science (A.S.) degrees. If such students then decide to go on and study for a full bachelor's degree, they can often transfer the credits they earn at a community college toward a degree at a four-year college.

**The first public junior college was Joliet Junior College, established in 1901 in Joliet, Illinois, partly as a result of the influence of the educator William Rainey Harper. He is commonly regarded as the father of the junior college.**

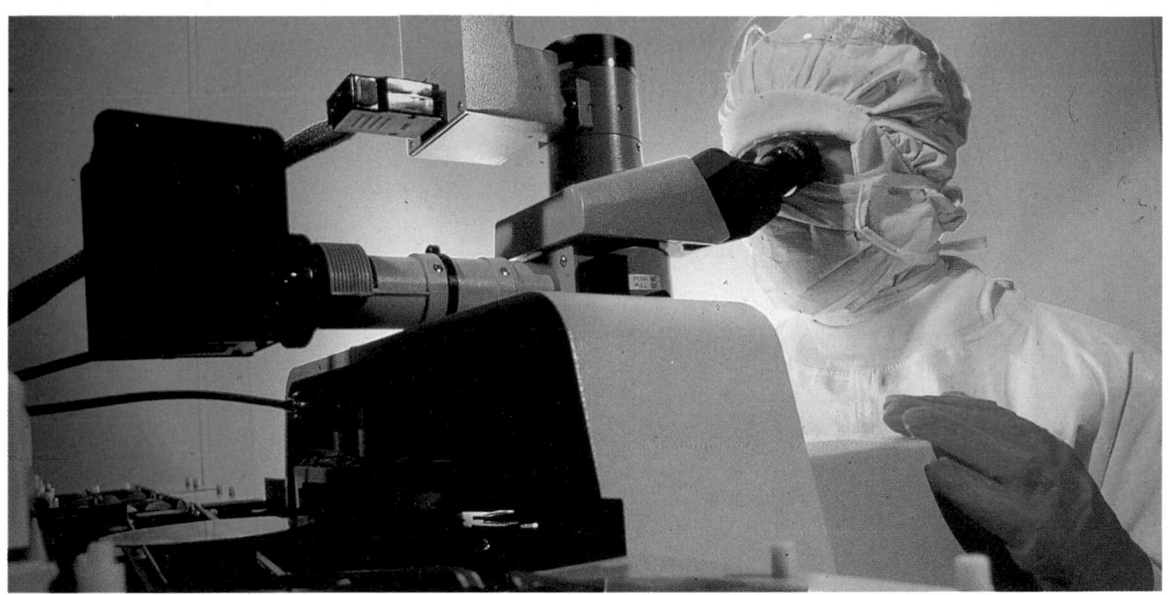

*▲ Powerful microscopes are needed to examine the circuitry on a silicon microchip, the miniature coding inside electronic equipment. The technician wears protective clothing to prevent particles from his body from getting on the chip.*

## COMPUTER INDUSTRY

The computer industry is one of the largest and fastest-growing sections of the U.S. economy. Early computers, used in universities and scientific companies since World War II, were bulky and expensive. New developments in microelectronics changed the industry in the 1970s. Computers became smaller and less expensive. More important, the new computers could hold hundreds of times the amount of information.

The 1980s saw the real boom in computers. By the end of the decade more than $50 billion worth of computers were being sold each year in the United States. Companies such as Apple and IBM also opened

► *Photographs of a computer circuit board are magnified hundreds of times for checking. A broken element the thickness of a human hair can cause a computer to fail.*

Some of the Major Computer Companies in the U.S.

Mainframe Computers
1. IBM
2. Unisys Corp.
3. Amdahl Corp.
4. Cray Research Inc.

Minicomputers
1. IBM
2. Digital Equipment Corp.
3. Hewlett-Packard
4. Wang Laboratories

Microcomputers
1. IBM
2. Apple Computer Inc.
3. Compaq Computer Corp.
4. Tandy Corp.

up the market for personal computers (PCs). There are now more than 100 million PCs in use in the United States. Half of these are for home use; most of the rest are used for work. Annual spending on PCs rose from $3.1 billion in 1981 to almost $50 billion in the early 1990's.

## CONDOR

The California condor, a type of VULTURE, is one of the world's largest flying birds. It is about 50 inches (130 cm) long, and its wingspan can be as much as 10 feet (3 m). Once, condors were found all along the west coast of North America. But today, the species is in danger of becoming extinct (dying out) and is protected by law. As of mid-1990, there were only 40 California condors.

In the wild, condors usually eat the carcasses of dead animals. But sometimes they kill small animals.

▼ *A pair of condors nests only once every two years and lays only one egg. In hopes of ensuring successful breeding the 40 remaining condors are being held in captivity. There are plans to return them to their natural habitat in 1992.*

## CONFEDERATE STATES OF AMERICA

The Confederate States of America, or Confederacy, was the name adopted by the Southern states that seceded (withdrew) from the United States just before the start of the CIVIL WAR in April 1861. These states seceded from the United States because they thought that the country's new Republican president, Abraham LINCOLN, would halt the expansion of slavery, thus threatening the Southern way of life.

Jefferson DAVIS was elected president of the Confederacy. Originally based in Montgomery, Alabama, the government later made Richmond, Virginia, its capital. The Confederacy's constitution was similar to that of the United States, but it gave more power to individual states and protected the system of slavery.

**The First Members of the Confederate Cabinet**

| | |
|---|---|
| President | Jefferson Davis |
| Vice president | Alexander H. Stephens |
| Secretary of state | Robert Toombs |
| Secretary of the treasury | Christopher Memminger |
| Secretary of war | Leroy P. Walker |
| Secretary of the navy | Stephen R. Mallory |
| Postmaster general | John H. Reagan |
| Attorney general | Judah P. Benjamin |

▲ *The Confederacy was formed in February 1861 by South Carolina, Alabama, Florida, Georgia, Louisiana, and Mississippi. Texas joined in March, while Arkansas, North Carolina, Tennessee, and Virginia joined soon after the start of the war.*

▲ *The Confederacy issued so much currency — $1.3 trillion worth — that inflation soared. By 1865, a pair of shoes cost as much as a soldier's wages for the entire four-year war.*

President Lincoln refused to accept the new nation, and war broke out between the Union and the Confederacy on April 12, 1861. The relative weakness of the Confederate government was to prove a drawback in conducting the Civil War. Jefferson Davis often had

**Today the average member of Congress is in his or her fifties, the number of younger members having increased in recent years. The U.S. Congress is served by a larger staff than any other legislature in the world. There are more than 7,500 staff employees who work for members of the House of Representatives, and more than 3,600 for the senators. House and Senate committees also employ more than 3,000 staff. Other staff members bring the total serving Congress to more than 23,000.**

problems getting the soldiers and equipment he needed from the individual states.

The Confederacy ended when Union troops captured President Davis a month after General Robert E. LEE surrendered at Appomattox on April 9, 1865.

## CONGRESS OF THE UNITED STATES 

The Congress is the lawmaking, or legislative, branch of the United States GOVERNMENT. The laws it passes apply to everyone in the country. Congress meets in the Capitol Building in Washington, D.C.

Congress is made up of the Senate and the House of Representatives. There are 100 senators, two for each state. Senators are elected for terms of six years. There are 435 representatives, each of whom is elected for a term of two years. Representatives are elected according to how many people live in a state; every state has to have at least one. The states with large populations, such as California, can have as many as several dozen.

The vice president of the United States serves as president of the Senate during the sessions. The vice president is not actually a member of the Senate, but if there is a tie vote, the president of the Senate then has the right to cast the deciding vote. The House of Representatives is headed by the speaker of the House. This important representative is chosen from the party that has the most members in the House.

Bills must be approved in both houses before going to the president of the United States for final approval. All bills that deal with finance and taxation must be introduced in the House of Representatives. The president can request military action, but only Congress (both houses sitting in a joint session) can declare war.

▼ *Committees in both houses discuss bills (proposed laws) in detail. Their reports save discussion time in Congress and help senators and representatives form opinions for voting. Sometimes nearly two years may pass before a bill becomes law.*

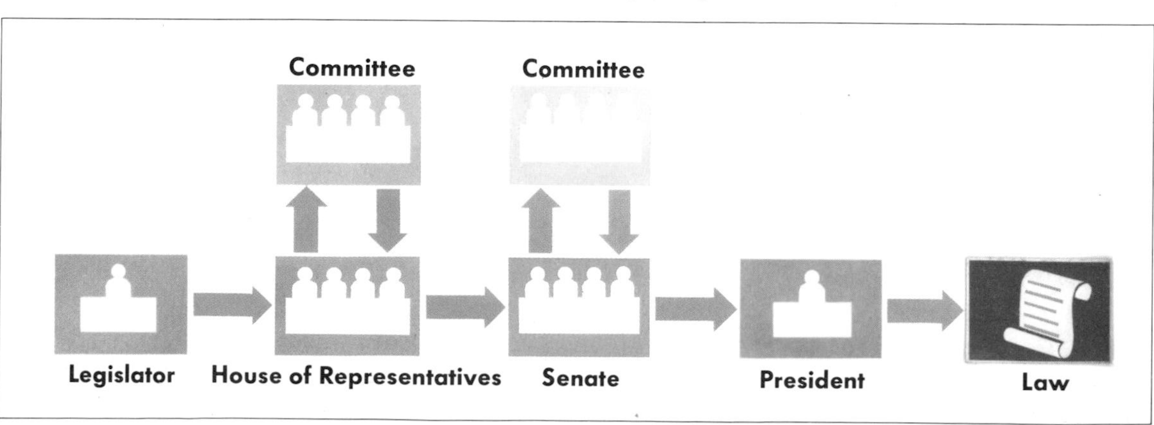

◀ *A lumberjack uses a back-cut technique to fell a Douglas fir. This valuable conifer accounts for one fourth of all lumber in the United States.*

## CONIFER

A conifer is a TREE or shrub that bears cones. Seeds and pollen are produced on the cones. Most conifers are evergreen and have needle-shaped leaves. Common North American conifers include firs, cedars, spruces, redwoods, yews, cypresses, junipers, larches, pines, and hemlocks.

The tallest type of conifer in the world is the SEQUOIA, or redwood, which grows in California and Oregon. Another conifer, the BRISTLECONE PINE, found in California and Nevada, is the oldest tree in the world.

Conifer forests, especially those in Oregon and Washington, provide lumber, wood pulp for papermaking, and other products. Douglas fir is the most valuable conifer commercially grown in North America.

▼ *A conifer cone does the same job as fruit or berries on other types of trees. Each scale has a seed at its base.*

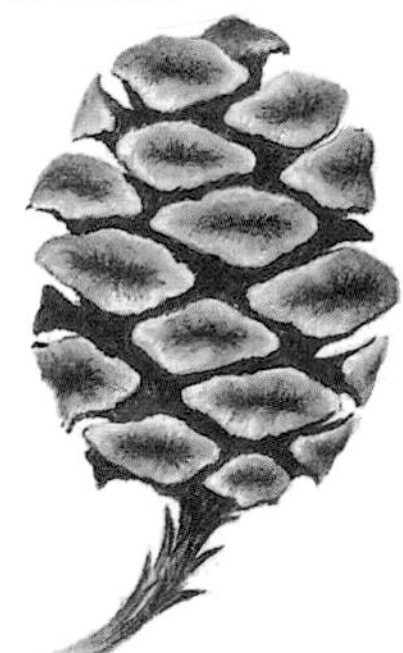

**Mature female cone of the giant sequoia**

▼ *The cones of a white spruce are usually grouped about 4 inches (10 cm) from the tip of the branch.*

**Mature female cones of the Sitka spruce**

▼ *The redwood is the tallest tree in the world. One California specimen was more than 375 feet (112 m) tall.*

**Coast redwood**

Connecticut is one of the NEW ENGLAND states. It is located on the northeastern seaboard, between NEW YORK State, MASSACHUSETTS, and RHODE ISLAND. It is one of the most historic states in the country, as well as one of the most important industrially. It is also one of the smallest states (only Delaware and Rhode Island are smaller). Connecticut is a popular vacation area. Its sandy beaches and small towns, many with fine colonial buildings, attract many visitors.

Connecticut was one of the first areas of the United States to be settled. The first Europeans arrived as early as 1614. By the mid-1600s, English settlements had been established in many parts of Connecticut. Connecticut played an important role in the American REVOLUTION. After the war, in 1787, delegates from

**Mountain laurel**

**White oak**

**American robin**

► *Sea captains' houses and shops line the harbor front at Mystic Seaport. New England's 19th-century whaling fleets set sail from ports such as Mystic.*

**Connecticut**
**Capital:** Hartford
**Area:** 5,544 sq mi (14,358 km$^2$). Rank: 48th
**Population:** 3,287,116 (1990). Rank: 27th
**Statehood:** Jan. 9, 1788
**Principal rivers:** Connecticut, Housatonic, Thames
**Highest point:** Mt. Frissell, 2,380 ft (725 m)
**Motto:** *Qui Transtulit Sustinet* (He Who Transplanted Still Sustains)
**Song:** "Yankee Doodle"

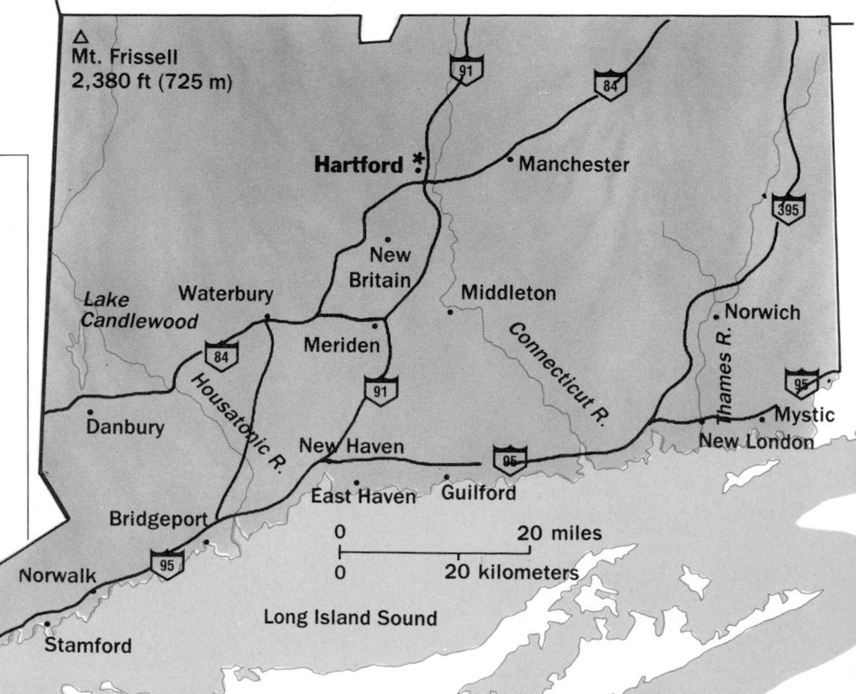

Connecticut played an important part in drawing up the U.S. CONSTITUTION. They proposed a solution, or compromise, known as the Connecticut Compromise, under which all states would have equal representation in the Senate but representation based on population in the House of Representatives. In 1788, Connecticut became the fifth state to sign, or *ratify*, the Constitution.

Through the 1900s, Connecticut grew to become an important industrial as well as agricultural state. Today, there are many major industrial plants and centers throughout the state. The state capital is Hartford. It is one of the leading centers in the country of the insurance business. Because the southern half of the state is close to New York City, many people who work in New York live in Connecticut, commuting to work every day.

▲ *The elegant state capitol building in Hartford was built in 1879. It contains mementos of the Revolutionary War.*

### Places of Interest

- Whitfield House, Guilford, was built in 1639 and is the oldest stone house in New England. It is just one of many colonial buildings that can be visited.
- Mark Twain Mansion, Hartford, was home to the author of *Tom Sawyer* for some years. It contains many personal belongings of the Twain Family.
- Mystic Seaport, Mystic, is a reconstruction of a whaling village of the 1800s. Today hundred-year old ships are moored in the harbor.
- Shore Line Trolley Museum, East Haven, exhibits trolleys that date from the late 1800s. Visitors may ride on some of the exhibits in the museum.

▼ *This traditional bridge crosses the Housatonic River in western Connecticut. Covered bridges kept rain and snow off travelers.*

▲ *Solar panels use sunshine to heat water and provide electricity. They help conserve fuels that would do the same job.*

# CONSERVATION

Conservation means the protection and wise use of natural resources. Natural resources are materials found in nature that are useful or necessary to people.

More natural resources are being used than ever before. Some resources, such as *fossil fuels* (coal, natural gas, and oil) and minerals (such as iron and copper), cannot be replaced once they are used up. It is important to avoid wasting these *nonrenewable resources*. For example, driving smaller cars uses less gasoline. Using solar energy instead of fossil fuels to heat buildings is another example of conservation. Where possible, minerals should be *recycled*. Aluminum cans, for example, can be melted down and used to make new cans.

Other resources—such as water, farmland, and forests—*can* be renewed. But here, too, careful conservation is needed. For example, preventing forest fires and recycling paper saves trees, and replanting logged areas with young trees provides trees for the future.

As well as the careful use of natural resources, conservation also means ENVIRONMENTAL PROTECTION and avoiding POLLUTION. In the United States, the Departments of Agriculture, Energy, and the Interior supervise such aspects of conservation as oil production, land management, mining, soil conservation, and the forest service. The U.S. Environmental Protection Agency is also involved in conservation. But every citizen has a duty to use natural resources responsibly.

▲ *Mountain firs and rare wildflowers are protected in Mount Rainier National Park in Washington State.*

► *This mountain of scrap metal in Long Beach, California, will be melted down for recycling.*

## CONSTITUTION OF THE UNITED STATES

The U.S. Constitution is "the supreme law of the land." It was written in 1787 at a convention held in Philadelphia. The 55 delegates attending became known as the Founding Fathers. They included James MADISON, George WASHINGTON, and Benjamin FRANKLIN. The Constitution replaced the ARTICLES OF CONFEDERATION. After being ratified (approved) by nine states, it went into effect on June 21, 1788. By 1790, the four other states had ratified it.

The Constitution sets out a *federal* system of government. This means that there is a national (federal) government and also state governments.

The Constitution also states that the United States is a *republic*. It has a PRESIDENT elected by the people. There is also a CONGRESS to make the laws, and a SUPREME COURT, the highest court in the land. The Founding Fathers ensured that there was a system of "checks and balances" between these three branches of government.

In 1791 a BILL OF RIGHTS was added to the Constitution. This took the form of ten amendments that set out the rights of individuals. Since then, 16 more amendments have been added.

▲ *The Declaration of Independence, Constitution, and Bill of Rights are on display in the National Archives in Washington, D.C.*

## CONSTITUTION ACT

The Constitution Act of 1982 revised the Canadian Constitution. Until that year, the BRITISH NORTH AMERICA ACT of 1867 served as Canada's constitution. Even though Canada has long been an independent country, the British North America Act could be amended only by the British Parliament. In 1982, however, the British Parliament passed the Canada Act. It gave Canada the right to change its own constitution. The Constitution Act of 1982 is part of the Canada Act. One addition is the Charter of Rights and Freedoms, which is similar to the American BILL OF RIGHTS.

**The Constitutional Convention, which wrote the U.S. Constitution, was attended by 55 delegates representing 12 states. Rhode Island did not attend. Thirty-four of the delegates were lawyers; most of the others were merchants or planters. The great majority of the delegates were young men in their twenties and thirties. At 81, Benjamin Franklin was the oldest of those present.**

## CONSTITUTION, U.S.S.

The famous warship U.S.S. *Constitution* was nicknamed Old Ironsides for its ability to withstand enemy fire. Launched in Boston in 1797, it was one of the first frigates built for the U.S. Navy. It measured 204 feet (62 m)

► *The 44-gun U.S.S.* Constitution *remains on active duty. On each Independence Day it is taken on a "tour of duty" around Boston Harbor.*

**Oliver Wendell Holmes, Sr., wrote the famous poem "Old Ironsides" when he heard about plans to scrap the U.S.S.*Constitution.* Published in 1830, the poem became popular across the country and helped preserve the ship as a national monument. It also gave the ship its nickname.**

in length and carried 44 guns. It carried a crew of 80 sailors.

The *Constitution* first distinguished itself in 1803–1804, in the war against the Barbary pirates who controlled Tripoli (Libya). During the WAR OF 1812 it won several victories over British ships. In 1829 the *Constitution* was declared unseaworthy. Plans to scrap it were abandoned, and the ship, restored in 1927–1931, is now docked on the Charles River near Boston.

## CONSTRUCTION INDUSTRY

The construction industry is one of the largest industries in the United States. Almost 5 million people are employed in some form of construction. There are three

▼ *Steel girders form the skeleton of skyscrapers such as this one in Philadelphia. Construction workers use bolts to fasten girders to other girders and concrete floors.*

main types of construction. Heavy construction sees that the biggest projects, such as hydroelectric dams and other power plants, are built. The federal government and state governments, or some of the largest corporations, pay for these projects, which cost many millions of dollars. Highway construction is another large area, again funded by government. The third type, general construction, can vary in size from skyscrapers and large hotels to private houses. Total annual earnings for the construction industry come to more than $230 billion. Most construction workers belong to unions.

▲ *Construction workers repair cable car tracks on a San Francisco street. Transportation and maintenance contracts can be worth millions of dollars to construction companies.*

## CONSUMER PROTECTION

Consumer protection is the idea of protecting the general public, which *consumes* (buys and uses) goods, from dangerous products and misleading advertising. This idea goes back to the beginning of the 1900s, when bad business practices were exposed by writers such as Upton SINCLAIR, who risked his life exposing the meat-packing industry. Government legislation during the DEPRESSION of the 1930s sought to protect small investors. The modern consumer movement began in the 1960s, with the crusading work of reformers such as Ralph NADER.

Consumer protection is now ensured at three levels. Most important are the government agencies such as the Food and Drug Administration, the U.S. Department of Agriculture, and the Federal Trade Commission. Many industries monitor themselves through the Committee of Better Business Bureaus or local Chambers of Commerce. Finally, private individuals and organizations, such as the Consumer Federation of America, look after the public interest.

**In 1938 an act was passed empowering the Food and Drug Administration to test the safety of all new drugs before they are placed on the market. Then, during the 1950s and 1960s, safety standards were set up to cover many products, including household chemicals, toys, flammable fabrics, and motor vehicles.**

## CONTINENTAL CONGRESS

The Continental Congress was a group of delegates from the 13 American colonies that made the decision to declare independence from Britain and served as the young nation's first government. The First Continental Congress met in 1774 in Philadelphia. It met in response to the Intolerable Acts, which the British Parliament had passed to punish Massachusetts for the BOSTON TEA PARTY and to assert British power; one of these acts had closed Boston Harbor. The Congress

▲ *The members of the First Continental Congress represented the interests of American colonists but made no move toward independence. British flags and banners hung over their debating chamber.*

passed a declaration of personal rights, petitioned the king to consider their grievances, and called for a boycott of British goods.

When the Congress met again in 1775, Britain had increased its repressive measures, and fighting had broken out at LEXINGTON AND CONCORD, Massachusetts. Congress adopted the New England militia as the "Army of the United Colonies," with George WASHINGTON as its commander. When further petitions to the king proved useless, the delegates resolved to separate from Britain. On July 4, 1776, they adopted the DECLARATION OF INDEPENDENCE.

The Congress continued to function as the national government throughout the American REVOLUTION and after it, under the ARTICLES OF CONFEDERATION, until the CONSTITUTION was adopted.

## CONTINENTAL DIVIDE

The Continental Divide, or Great Divide, runs north–south along the crest of the Rocky Mountains. Its name comes from the fact that all the rivers and streams on the west side of the crest run west into the Pacific Ocean, and all the rivers and streams on the east side of the crest flow east into the Atlantic Ocean or one of its arms, such as the Gulf of Mexico. In other words, this is the highest point of the United States, one that "divides" most of the country's major natural waterways.

▼ *The Continental Divide is often called "America's Watershed" because it feeds so many rivers. Melting snow from the mountains fills the headwaters of the rivers each spring.*

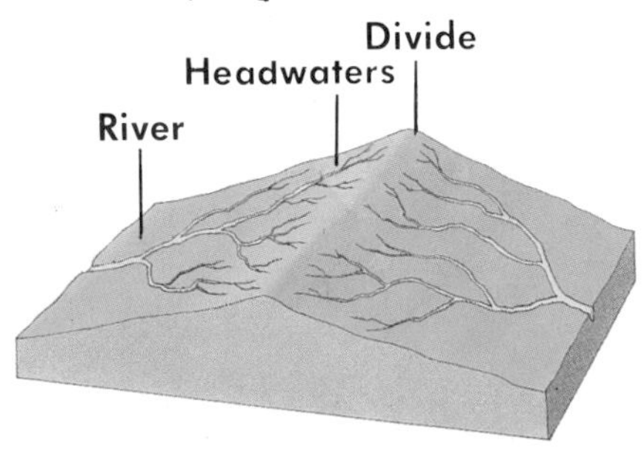

## COOLIDGE, Calvin

Calvin Coolidge was the 30th president of the United States. He served during the period of great prosperity between WORLD WAR I and the Great DEPRESSION which began with the stock market crash of 1929. A cautious, thrifty man, he was famous for using few words and was nicknamed Silent Cal.

Coolidge believed that government should interfere as little as possible in private business. The nation was very prosperous as this time. This was also the time of PROHIBITION, when the sale of alcoholic beverages was banned. Organized crime flourished, and Coolidge could not control it.

▲ *President Coolidge opened the 1925 World Series. "Silent Cal" once spoke only four words during a baseball game: "What time is it?"*

A Republican, Coolidge had been vice president under Warren G. HARDING. He became president when Harding died in office in 1923. Coolidge was visiting his father in Vermont when he learned of Harding's death. Coolidge's father, a notary public, swore him in.

Coolidge's first task was to clean up the corrupt administration he had taken over from Harding. His honesty and common sense were much admired, and in 1924, Coolidge was elected president with a very large majority. During his administration, Coolidge cut taxes and reduced government spending. He vetoed payment of a bonus to war veterans, but Congress passed the measure over his veto. He also vetoed bills to give financial aid to farmers, after a severe drop in farm prices. Coolidge did not take much interest in foreign affairs and was against the United States joining the League of Nations. At the end of his term in office he was very popular but refused to run for reelection in 1928.

**(John) Calvin Coolidge**
**Born:** July 4, 1872, in Plymouth Notch, Vermont
**Education:** Amherst College, Massachusetts
**Political party:** Republican
**Term of office:** 1923–1929
**Married:** 1905 to Grace Anna Goodhue
**Died:** Jan. 5, 1933, in Northampton, Massachusetts

▲ *James Fenimore Cooper began writing after boasting to his wife that he could write a better book than the novel she was reading.*

## COOPER, James Fenimore

James Fenimore Cooper (1789–1851) was born in Burlington, New Jersey, but spent most of his life in New York State. Cooper wrote many novels, some of which drew on his five years in the Navy. His most famous books are a series called *The Leatherstocking Tales*—including *The Deerslayer*, *The Pathfinder*, and *The Last of the Mohicans*. These tell of a frontiersman, Natty Bumppo, who lived among the Indians, and tales of people who settled the new country. Cooper also wrote a great deal about the values of American society.

## COPLAND, Aaron

Aaron Copland (1900–1990) was one of the most famous American composers of this century. He studied in New York City and in Paris. Some of his earlier works were influenced by European music. Later he used American folk music and JAZZ in his compositions. The quality of Copland's music did much to raise the standing of American music in international circles. He wrote ballets based on American folklore, such as *Billy the Kid* and *Appalachian Spring*, as well as works to be performed by a full orchestra. Copland wrote a number of books on music, especially to encourage understanding of modern music.

▲ *Aaron Copland conducted his own works in some of the first recordings of symphonic music.*

## COPLEY, John Singleton

John Singleton Copley (1738–1815) was a great painter during America's colonial period. He painted portraits of many colonial leaders. Copley completed his first signed painting when he was only 15 years old. But his real fame dates from 1766, when his portrait of his brother, *The Boy with Squirrel*, was sent to London and highly praised. Copley's mixed loyalties in the days after the Boston Tea Party made him a traitor in many patriots' eyes. In 1775, Copley moved to London where he developed his vivid and colorful style of portraits. He also painted many historical subjects. (See ART.)

**One of John Singleton Copley's most famous paintings is *Watson and the Shark*, now in the Museum of Fine Arts, Boston. It shows a young man being attacked by a shark while his friends try to aid him. Copley actually saw this event in Havana harbor.**

## CORN

Corn is the most important cereal crop in North America. It was cultivated by the Indians for centuries before

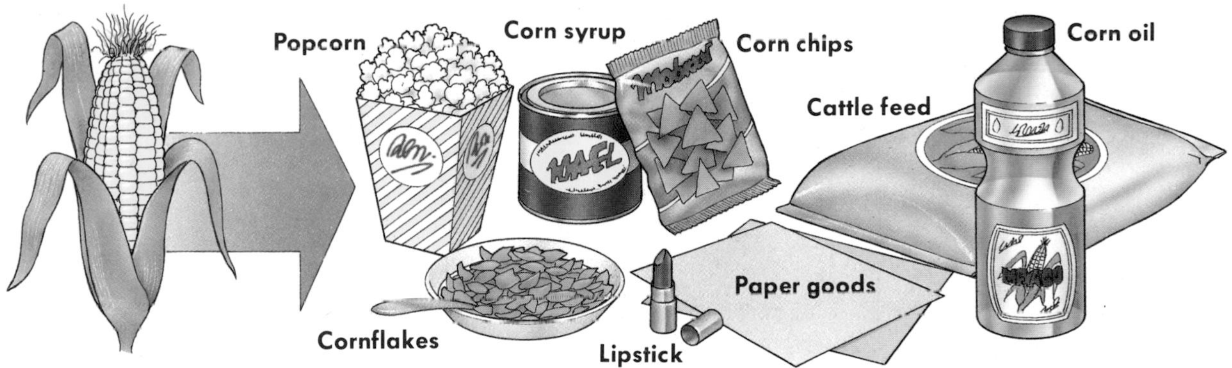


▲ *Corn kernels can be refined (taken apart) to obtain by-products like popcorn.*

Christopher Columbus's men first sampled it. The United States produces almost half of all the corn grown in the world. About 60 percent of the crop is used as feed for livestock. The rest is used as food in the United States or is sold to other countries. Most corn is grown in the area known as the Corn Belt. This is made up of the states of Iowa, Illinois, and Indiana, western Ohio, and parts of Minnesota, Nebraska, Missouri, Kansas, and South Dakota. The United States produces more than 7.5 million bushels of corn each year.

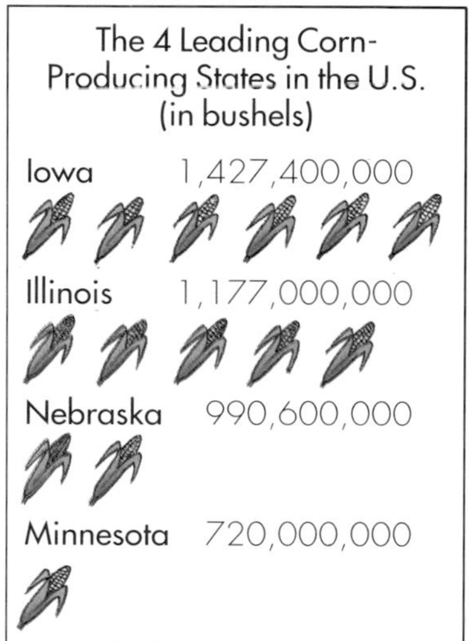


## CORONADO, Francisco Vásquez de

Francisco Vásquez de Coronado (1510?–1554) led the first expedition to explore the American Southwest. He set out to discover the legendary "Seven Golden Cities of Cibola" and bring back the gold to New Spain (Mexico). The cities turned out to be merely the Zuni Indian villages, which the Spaniards captured. Coronado's main force reached as far north as Kansas. Two other units explored the Gulf of California and the Colorado River, including the Grand Canyon. Although he failed to find gold, Coronado added greatly to Europeans' knowledge of North America.

▼ *Some of Coronado's men went west to the Grand Canyon. They were the first Europeans to lay eyes on this natural wonder.*

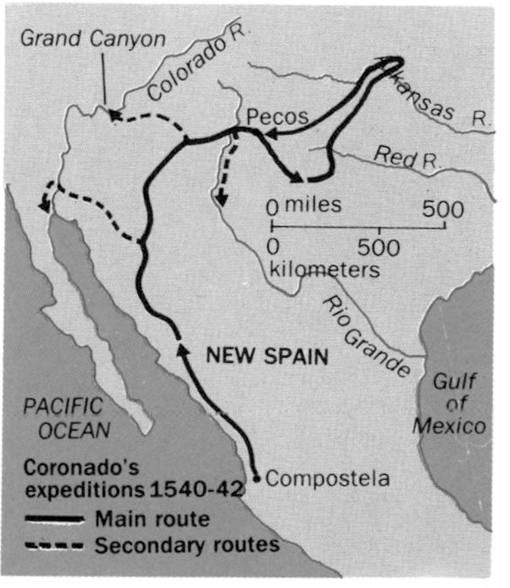


## CORPORATION

The corporation is the single most important type of business grouping in the United States. A corporation can own land, earn and spend money, and go to court just as if its members were one person. There are about 4 million corporations in the United States.

There are special rules governing corporations. For example, a corporation must be *chartered*, or incorporated, by the state or federal government. This forms a

| The 10 Largest U.S. Industrial Corporations (by sales) |
|---|
| 1. General Motors |
| 2. Exxon |
| 3. Ford Motor |
| 4. IBM |
| 5. General Electric |
| 6. Mobil |
| 7. Philip Morris |
| 8. E. I. du Pont |
| 9. Chevron |
| 10. Texaco |

contract between the company and the government. The new corporation must also hold annual meetings and issue reports, so that its investors can study its spending and tax officials can assess corporate tax.

Many corporations sell shares of stock to investors, who are then part owners. This provides the money corporations need to expand. Enormous amounts of money are involved. Total corporate assets are more than $12 trillion.

Some of the first colonies, such as the Massachusetts Bay Colony and Virginia, were corporations. In the 1800s, corporations raised the millions of dollars required to build many of the nation's railroads. Some of today's richest corporations are General Motors, Ford, General Electric and Exxon.

▼ *Indian tribes opposing the Aztecs helped Cortés reach Tenochtitlán, the Aztec capital.*

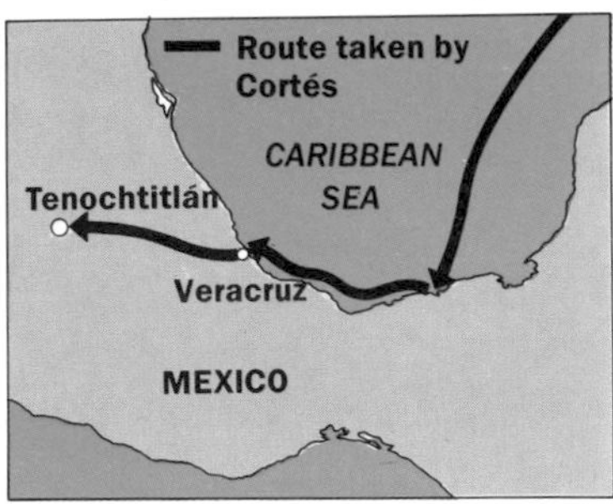


## CORTÉS, Hernán

Hernán Cortés (1485–1547) was one of the Spanish *conquistadores* (conquerors) of the Americas. He first sailed to the New World in 1504. He helped Spain conquer Cuba in 1511 and later became mayor of the town of Santiago. In 1519 he led an expedition of 600 men to Mexico and landed on the Yucatán peninsula.

▼ *The Aztecs were very religious. When they first saw Cortés, they believed him to be a white-skinned god and welcomed him with gifts.*

To prevent his men from deserting, he burned all but one of the party's 11 ships.

The Aztec civilization that Cortés found in Mexico was highly developed but politically weak. Cortés took advantage of this. With the help of an Indian princess, Malinche, he captured the Aztec emperor, Montezuma, and seized control of the capital of Tenochtitlán. Cortés was made governor of the colony of New Spain (Mexico). At home, however, Cortés had enemies who plotted his downfall. In 1540 he returned to Spain.

▲ *An Arizona cotton worker prepares raw cotton to be sucked into a yarn-spinning machine.*

## COTTON

Cotton is the soft white hairs, or fibers, that grow on the seeds of the cotton plant. After harvesting, the cotton fibers are separated from the seeds and spun into yarn. The yarn is generally woven into cotton fabric, which is used for clothing, sheets, and many other items.

Cotton is one of the world's most important crops. The United States is one of the leading producers, growing almost 18 percent of the world's cotton. Most of the cotton is grown in the Cotton Belt, which stretches across the south from Florida to California. Texas is the main cotton-growing state.

The Indians grew cotton in many places, including the Southwest. The colonists cultivated it too. Later it was grown on plantations in the South. The cotton gin, invented in 1793 by Eli WHITNEY, increased production greatly. This machine separates the cotton fiber from the seed very quickly. Insect pests such as the boll weevil cause great damage to cotton crops.

The 4 Leading Cotton-Producing States in the U.S. (in bales)

|  |  |
|---|---|
| Texas | 3,322,000 |
| California | 3,111,000 |
| Mississippi | 2,131,000 |
| Arkansas | 1,681,000 |

▼ *Hundreds of field workers were needed to pick cotton in the 1800s. Mechanical pickers were not invented until 1940.*

▲ *Cougars save their energy for hunting. They will sometimes sleep up to 22 hours a day digesting their last kill.*

## COUGAR

The cougar is North America's largest cat. It can grow to 5 feet (1.5 m) and have a 3-foot (1-m) tail. The cougar, which is also called the puma or mountain lion, is most common in the western United States and in northwestern Canada. But it can also be found in other parts of the continent. It prefers a rocky habitat and sparse woodland, particularly in the mountains. The eastern cougar is an endangered species.

The cougar is a carnivore, or meat eater. It preys on many animals, including deer, cattle, birds, mice, and rabbits. An expert climber, the cougar may lie in wait for its prey for hours before pouncing on it from above.

► *Dolly Parton is one of country music's biggest stars. She is a songwriter as well as a singer.*

**In 1925, radio station WSM in Nashville, Tennessee, began broadcasting a weekly hillbilly music show named the *Grand Ole Opry*. The first star of this show was "Uncle" Dave Mason, who sang 19th-century country ballads. Roy Acuff joined the show in 1938, and during the 1940s the *Grand Ole Opry* was broadcast nationally over NBC radio. By 1950 it had become a supershow with over a hundred performers. The *Grand Ole Opry* was largely responsible for Nashville becoming the center of the country music industry.**

## COUNTRY MUSIC

Country music has its roots in rural mountain music, especially from the southern United States. In the 1920s many new U.S. radio stations began playing rural music, and it became widely popular. In 1925 the *Grand Ole Opry* was first broadcast on radio. The Carter Family and Jimmy Rodgers were among the first of these country musicians. Gradually the music changed. By the 1930s western music had developed, sung by film-star cowboys such as Gene Autry. Another variation was honky-tonk, made famous by such musicians as Bob Wills and Ernest Tubb. Bluegrass music, originating in Kentucky, was developed by the Monroe Brothers and later made famous by Flat and Scruggs.

Country music had become big business by the 1950s and 1960s, with Nashville, Tennessee (home of the *Grand Ole Opry*), its capital. But by the late 1960s country music had gotten closer and closer to pop music. A number of musicians reacted against this and began producing country music more like the original sound. These "new country" musicians included Emmylou Harris, the Judds, Ricky Skeggs, George Strait, and Randy Travis.

## COURTS *See* Government of the United States; Laws and Legal System

## COWBOY

For many Americans, cowboys occupy a central role in United States history. They represent the brave frontier spirit that tamed the West. Thousands of films, television programs, and books have celebrated their deeds in the Wild West. In fact, most cowboys led monotonous, uncomfortable lives. But without cowboys, the West would have been much harder to settle.

Cowboys thrived from about 1865 to 1885. Later, when the new railroads were used to transport cattle and ranches were fenced in with barbed wire, no more than a handful of cowboys were needed. The main job of cowboys was to look after the huge herds of cattle that roamed across Texas and other parts of the Southwest and West. The cowboys rounded up the cattle, usually in the spring, and drove them north to towns

▲ *The clothes that a cowboy wore were designed for a life in the dusty prairie. The bandanna, for example, could be worn over the mouth and nose to filter dust and the smell of cattle.*

**Most cowboys came from the South, and many of them had fought in the Civil War. About a third of them were blacks or Mexican Americans.**

◀ *Young cattle are branded before they are turned loose to graze. Each ranch has a different brand, with symbols or initials to identify the cattle owner.*

**Between 1865 and 1880 cowboys drove at least 3.5 million cattle in herds of between 1,500 and 3,000 from southern Texas to towns in Kansas and Nebraska and to ranges in Wyoming, Montana, and elsewhere. Working up to 20 hours a day, the cowboy drove the animals from one watering hole to the next. For this hard and dirty work he earned between $25 and $40 a month.**

such as Abilene and Dodge City, Kansas, where they could be transported east by railroad. Cowboys had to be skillful riders—they might need to spend days at a time on horseback—and be able to use a rope called a *lariat* to rope individual cattle. All cowboys owned a saddle, but few had their own horses; these usually belonged to the ranch owners. The toughest part of a cowboy's life was a trail drive, when the cattle had to be taken north. Some trail drives were up to 1,000 miles (1,600 km) long.

► *Coyotes have excellent eyesight and can run as fast as 40 miles per hour (65 km/hr).*

## COYOTE

The coyote is a type of wild dog. It is closely related to the wolf and is sometimes called the prairie wolf. The coyote is most common in the prairies of the western United States, but it is found all over North America, even as far east as New England. Smaller than a wolf, it is about 3 feet (1 m) long, not counting the tail. The coyote's long howl can often be heard at night.

Coyotes spend most of their time hunting. They used to follow BISON and PRONGHORNS. Today they hunt smaller animals, such as rabbits, birds, rats, frogs, and occasionally domestic animals. They also eat the remains of dead deer and other large animals. Coyotes usually hunt alone.

▼ *Cranberries are grown commercially in bogs, which are like shallow marshes. Farmers flood the bogs each winter to protect the plants from the extreme cold.*

## CRANBERRY

A relative of the blueberry, the cranberry is traditionally served as a sauce or relish with turkey at Thanksgiving and Christmas dinners. Cranberries are also used in pies and in drinks. The American, or large, cranberry grows wild in the northeastern United States. It is cultivated in Massachusetts, New Jersey, Wisconsin, Oregon, and Washington. The small cranberry, which has smaller fruit, grows in wild marshy ground in northern North America. More than 94,000 tons of cranberries are produced every year in the United States.

**Stephen Crane was an adventurous reporter. In 1897, during a gun-running expedition to Cuba, he was shipwrecked and spent two days in an open boat with three other men. He wrote about this experience in one of his finest short stories, *The Open Boat*, published in 1898.**

## CRANE, Stephen

Stephen Crane (1871–1900) was a journalist and a writer. In his early twenties, Crane wrote newspaper articles about slum life in New York City during the 1890s. His first novel, *Maggie: A Girl of the Streets*, continued this theme. Cranc also wrote about war. He saw this not as romantic or heroic but as brutal and cruel. His most famous work, *The Red Badge of Courage*, tells the story of a Union soldier in the Civil War. Later, Crane traveled to Europe to work as a war correspondent. He died there of tuberculosis at the age of only 28.

## CRAZY HORSE

Crazy Horse (1849?–1877) was a great leader and war chief of the Oglalas, a band of the Teton SIOUX who lived in South Dakota and other parts of the northern plains. Crazy Horse fought against whites who tried to settle on Indian lands and against the army's efforts to force the Indians onto reservations. In 1876 he fought alongside SITTING BULL at the Battle of the Little Bighorn, better known as "Custer's Last Stand." Crazy Horse finally surrendered to the U.S. cavalry in May 1877. He was killed trying to escape in September of that year. Today a large sculpture of Crazy Horse is being created in South Dakota as a memorial.

## CREES

The Cree INDIANS are a North American tribe. There are two groups of Crees, the Woodland Crees from the northern regions of Canada and the Plains Crees. The Plains Crees migrated south (some into the northern United States) after the spread of the horse, which made hunting buffalo much easier. During the 1600s thc Crees in Canada worked with French fur traders. Some of them intermarried. Their descendants are called Métis. Today there are fewer than 3,000 Crees.

▼ *Poundmaker, a famous Cree chief, joined the rebellions led by Louis Riel in Canada during the 1880s. They were defeated in Saskatchewan in 1885.*

▲ *Images of the sun, which the Creek Indians worshiped, were turned into abstract designs on their pottery.*

## CREEKS 

The Creek Indians were one of the largest and most powerful tribes of the southeastern United States. They lived in what is now Georgia, Alabama, and northern Florida. Together with the Cherokees, Chickasaws, Choctaws, and Seminoles, they formed a group that the white settlers called the Five Civilized Tribes. In 1813–1814 the Creeks, under Tecumseh, fought against the new settlers. This was known as the Creek War. They were crushed by Andrew Jackson, who took 23 million acres of their lands. In the 1830s they were moved west to Indian Territory. They suffered much hardship, and in 1901 a Creek Indian led the Snake Uprising to fight against unjust land distribution. Today there are about 13,000 Creeks.

## CRIME 

Crime is one of the biggest problems facing the United States. There are more than 20,000 murders each year in the United States, and in 1991 there were more than 1.9 million violent crimes. Violent crimes increased by almost 45 percent between 1983 and 1990. During the same period, property crimes, such as break-ins, vandalism, and "car-jacking" and auto theft, increased by almost 17 percent. People who do not declare all their taxes or who defraud people in business are committing a "white collar" crime.

People disagree about the best ways to prevent crime. Some argue that the death penalty is a deterrent—a way of making people afraid to commit a murder. Others argue that rehabilitation—teaching criminals how to become better citizens—is the answer. Apart from local and state police forces, the most famous anti-crime organization in the United States is the Federal Bureau of Investigation (FBI). It fights all types of crime, including organized crime, illegal gambling, drug dealing, and blackmail.

**Most common crimes in the United States**

**Robbery 4.4%**
**Aggravated assault 7.3%**
**Motor vehicle theft 11.3%**
**Burglary 21.2%**
**Rape 0.7%**
**Murder 0.2%**
**Larceny-theft 54.9%**

▲ *The most common crimes committed in the United States. In some states, serious crimes are punishable by death.*

## CROCKETT, Davy 

Even in his own lifetime, the frontiersman David Crockett (1786–1836) was something of a legend. He had little formal schooling. Instead, he learned the skills of life on the frontier, such as hunting bear and raccoon.

In 1813 he joined the army and fought under Andrew JACKSON against the CREEK Indians. He later was a member of the Tennessee state legislature and served several terms in the U.S. Congress.

Crockett's early association with Andrew Jackson came to an end in the late 1820s, and he was taken up by the new Whig Party. The Whigs built up his image as a folk hero, as a counter to President Jackson's appeal.

After his political career ended in 1835, Crockett went to Texas, which had recently declared its independence from Mexico. Crockett was one of the men who fought to defend the Alamo when Mexican soldiers laid siege to it on February 23, 1836. He and all the other defenders, including James BOWIE, were killed in the Mexicans' final assault on March 6, 1836.

▲ *Davy Crockett used his rifle as a club when he ran out of ammunition at the Alamo. He had been in Texas only two weeks when he was called into battle there.*

▼ *Bing Crosby was modest about his talent. He once said that he was "just another guy who likes singing in the shower."*

## CROSBY, Bing 

Harry Lillis "Bing" Crosby (1904–1977) was a movie star known around the world for his easy charm and casual, "crooning" style of singing. Many regard him as one of the most talented entertainers of the 20th century. He began his career as a singer with dance bands, including that of Paul Whiteman, the "King of Jazz." In the 1930s, Crosby began making movies. Most of his films were comedies and musicals, although he could also be a serious actor. Crosby made many records as well; the most famous was "White Christmas," which sold 30 million copies. In 1944 he won the Academy Award as best actor for *Going My Way*.

▲ *Crow medicine men prepared cures for the tribe and also helped in religious and magical ceremonies.*

## CROWS

The Crows, a nomadic INDIAN tribe of the Great Plains, lived mainly in Montana, around the Yellowstone River. They were hunters of bison. When the United States began to expand, the Crows fought the white settlers who came to the northwest along the Oregon Trail. They soon saw that they could not win in the end and made peace with the army. The Crows fought with the whites against other Indian tribes. In 1876 they helped to defend the troops of General Crook at the battle of Rosebud Creek. Crook's troops had been attacked by Sioux and Cheyenne warriors under CRAZY HORSE.

In 1877 the Crows and the army tracked down the NEZ PERCÉ Indians on their march toward Canada. Today about 3,500 Crows live on a reservation in Montana.

► *Shrimp are small crustaceans. This banana shrimp, found in Hawaii, has a delicate, striped body.*

## CRUSTACEANS

A crustacean is an animal that has a hard shell and no bones. It also has many jointed legs. Most crustaceans live in the water, but some, such as wood lice, live on land. Some crustaceans, called shellfish, are popular foods. These include LOBSTERS AND CRABS, crayfish, and especially shrimp. Shrimp are the most valuable fishing catch in the United States, which is the world leader in shrimp production. Shrimp are found in both salt water and fresh water. The main shrimp-producing states are Alaska, Florida, Louisiana, and Texas. Large species of shrimps are often called prawns.

The crayfish is similar to the lobster, but it is smaller and lives in fresh water. Most of the world's crayfish come from Louisiana.

Barnacles and water fleas are also crustaceans.

**Many crustaceans are very sensitive to natural and industrial pollution. One type of natural pollution, a type of algae called "red tide," can wipe out shellfish beds in just a few days.**

## CUBAN MISSILE CRISIS

The world held its breath for a whole week in October 1962. President John F. KENNEDY had received Air Force photographs showing that the Soviet Union was building missile launch sites in Cuba. The nuclear missiles could reach and destroy many U.S. cities. On October 22, after a secret meeting with his Cabinet, the president ordered a naval blockade of Cuba, demanding that the Soviet Union remove the missiles. On October 24, Soviet Premier Nikita Khrushchev angrily threatened to fight this act of "piracy."

Days passed, and neither side gave in. The United States made plans to invade Cuba, and the world braced itself for nuclear war. Finally, on October 28, Khrushchev agreed to remove the missiles and destroy the launch sites if the United States agreed not to invade Cuba. The crisis was over.

**The high-flying U-2 aircraft was responsible for supplying the United States with accurate photographs of Soviet missile sites in Cuba during the Cuban missile crisis. This remarkable plane could fly at a height of about 90,000 feet (27,000 m). From this great height it could take very detailed pictures of ground installations. The U-2's job has now been taken over by satellites.**

## CURRIER AND IVES

In the mid- to late-1800s the firm of Currier and Ives published thousands of printed pictures showing scenes of American life. The business was started in New York in 1835 by Nathaniel Currier (1813–1888). In 1857 his bookkeeper, James Ives (1824–1895), who was also an artist, became a partner. The pictures were drawn by various artists, printed by lithography, and colored by hand. The subjects included sports events, frontier life, Mississippi River steamboats, great disasters, and other historic events. Between 1840 and 1890 more than 7,000 different pictures were produced.

**Currier and Ives prints were not sold as great art, but they were very popular. Many of them sold for as little as 15 cents. These prints are now rare and costly. The prints often depicted current events. In 1840, three days after the burning of the steamship *Lexington*, Currier's artists and lithographers published a thrilling picture of the burning ship.**

◀ *Currier and Ives lithographs often celebrated great events. In 1881, Nathaniel Currier honored the yacht* America, *which 30 years before had won the race that later became known as the America's Cup.*

▼ *During the Civil War, George Armstrong Custer was promoted briefly to the rank of brigadier general. He was only 24. Some historians blame this early success, and Custer's own vanity, for his downfall.*

## CURTISS, Glenn Hammond

Glenn H. Curtiss (1878–1930) was a pioneer of the U.S. aviation industry. As a boy, an interest first in bicycles and then in motorcycles led him to design and build airplane engines. In 1908 he began building airplanes as well. In 1910, Curtiss became the first person to fly from Albany, New York, to New York City. Curtiss then designed airplanes for the U.S. Navy. During World War I, his factories produced thousands of planes. After the war, one of his seaplanes became the first airplane to fly the Atlantic Ocean.

## CUSTER, George

George A. Custer (1839–1876) was an American cavalry officer. After the Civil War, where he served in the Union army, Custer was sent west with the 7th Cavalry to help subdue the Plains Indians. In 1874 he led an expedition that discovered gold in the Black Hills, in Dakota Territory. This area had been guaranteed to the Indians. But the U.S. government issued an order stating that any Indians who had not moved onto reservations by January 31, 1876, would be considered hostile.

The Indians may not have received the order, and they gathered that spring as usual for their hunting, near Little Bighorn, in Montana. Custer was ordered to go there and await General Alfred Terry's forces. Instead, he ordered his men to attack on June 25. Custer and all of his 265 soldiers were killed.

▼ *The 2,000 Indians who defeated Custer at Little Bighorn were led by Crazy Horse and Sitting Bull. "Custer's Last Stand," as it came to be known, probably lasted less than an hour.*

## DAIRY INDUSTRY 

The dairy industry produces milk from cows. It also processes and markets this milk, as well as milk by-products such as butter, cream, ice cream, and cheese. There are almost 10 million milk cows on dairy farms in the United States. They produce about 20 billion gallons (75 billion liters) of milk every year. Dairying is a sophisticated industry that makes wide use of the latest agricultural technology. This helps it to meet the enormous demand for milk products while keeping its costs low, and to ensure that its products are always fit for humans to eat and drink. Strict regulations cover the way cows are kept, the food they eat, and the barns they live in. Wisconsin, California, New York, Minnesota, and Pennsylvania are the leading dairy states. The size of dairy farms varies enormously. Some have almost 1,000 cows, but most have fewer than 50. Most cows can produce around 1,500 gallons (5,677 liters) of milk a year.

▲ *Strict health laws govern the bottling of milk. More than 17 billion gallons (64 billion liters) are produced in the United States each year.*

## DAKOTA INDIANS *See* Sioux

◄ *The modern Dallas skyline reflects the building boom of the 1970s and early 1980s. During that time the population of Dallas rose by more than 20 percent.*

## DALLAS 

Dallas is the second largest city in TEXAS and one of the largest cities in the country. Over a million people live in Dallas. Located in the northeastern part of the state, it is a busy, bustling city. There are many spectacular high rises and elegant shops in its downtown area. The 72-story InterFirst Plaza building and the 50-story Reunion Tower are the best-known city landmarks.

Dallas was founded in 1841 and quickly became a

**Since a dam blocks the passage of fish, many dams have stepped pools at their sides that allow the fish to bypass the dam.**

major transportation and trading center. But it wasn't until after 1940 that Dallas became anything like today's huge city. Between 1940 and 1970, its population tripled. Oil is the city's major business, but there are numerous important manufacturing industries based here, too. Dallas is also a major cotton market. President John F. KENNEDY was assassinated in Dallas on November 22, 1963.

## DAMS

A dam is a barrier built across a river or stream to control the flow of the water. This is done for a number of reasons. Dams stop flooding. They create reservoirs that hold a water supply for household and industrial use. And they provide water for the irrigation of farmland. The water stored in a dam's reservoir can also be used to create HYDROELECTRIC POWER.

There are many dams in the United States. One of the largest dam projects was the Tennessee Valley Authority (TVA). The authority built several dams along the Tennessee River. These created large lakes and helped to control the water supply.

The New Cornelia Tailings Dam, Arizona, is the second largest earth-fill dam in the world. The Fort Peck Dam, which is 4 miles (6.4 km) long, spans the Missouri River in Montana. The Grand Coulee across the Columbia River in the state of Washington is the largest concrete dam in the United States. It supplies water for irrigation. It also provides more hydroelectric power than any other source in the country.

The 7 Largest Dams in the U.S. (by volume)

| Dam | Location |
|---|---|
| New Cornelia Tailings | Ten Mile Wash, Arizona |
| Fort Peck | Missouri River, Montana |
| Oahe Tailings | Missouri River, South Dakota |
| Oroville | Feather River, California |
| San Luis | San Luis River, California |
| Garrison | Missouri River, North Dakota |
| Cochiti | Rio Grande, New Mexico |

► *Hoover Dam, on the Arizona-Nevada border, backs up the Colorado River to create Lake Mead, the largest artificial lake in the United States. The dam was finished in 1936 after three years of construction costing $120 million. It provided many jobs during the worst years of the Depression.*

## DANCE

Dance is probably the oldest of all art forms. Since ancient times, people have danced for many reasons: as recreation, as a courtship ritual, as entertainment, to tell a story, and as an act of worship. Religious dance is still part of the culture of some American Indian tribes.

Many different dance traditions have flourished, and some have originated, in North America. During Colonial times, American society danced the minuet and refined forms of English country dances; in the 19th century it took up a new European dance, the waltz. On the frontier, square dancing became a popular social activity. In this century Americans have created such dances as the Charleston, the jitterbug, and the twist. Many modern ballroom dances, however, like the rhumba, tango, and cha-cha, come from Latin America.

▲ *The Apache round dance is a ritual celebrating tribal history and famous battles.*

◀ *Merce Cunningham's troupe has led modern dance into a new era of free expression.*

▼ *Dance routines by Fred Astaire and Ginger Rogers were the highlights of many movie musicals in the 1930s and 1940s.*

American stage and film musicals have nourished a variety of dance styles, from solo tap dancing (originally developed by black Americans) to lavish numbers based partly on BALLET. And classical ballet itself has a huge following. Some American ballet companies, such as the New York City Ballet and the Dance Theater of Harlem, are among the best in the world.

As a reaction against the formality of ballet, some American dancers have developed freer styles, known collectively as "modern dance." Pioneers of modern dance include Isadora DUNCAN and Martha GRAHAM.

▼ *Bette Davis was furious when Vivien Leigh was chosen to play Scarlett O'Hara in* Gone With the Wind. *Instead, her studio offered her the lead role in* Jezebel. *This gave Bette Davis the chance to play a similar strong southern heroine. The Oscar that she won helped make up for her earlier disappointment.*

▼ *Jefferson Davis's birthday, June 3, is a public holiday in seven southern states. The date is also known as Confederate Memorial Day.*

## DARROW, Clarence

Clarence Darrow (1857–1938) was a brilliant criminal defense lawyer. He also fought for many causes during his career, including freedom of expression and the abolition of the death penalty. Born in Ohio, he practiced mainly in Chicago. During the early part of his career he successfully defended several labor leaders; later, he turned to criminal cases. Darrow is perhaps best known for his role in a case he lost: the trial of John Scopes. In 1925, Scopes was tried for teaching evolution in Tennessee. At the time, this was against the law. Darrow's eloquent defense of Scopes was one of the most dramatic in U.S. legal history. Darrow wrote his autobiography, *The Story of My Life*, in 1932.

## DAVIS, Bette

Born in Lowell, Massachusetts, the actress Bette Davis (1908–1989) was one of the great stars of motion pictures. She often played women who were strong and determined, including *Jezebel*, for which she won her second Oscar in 1938. She won her first in 1935 for her role in *Dangerous*. Perhaps her greatest role was as Margo Channing in *All About Eve* in 1950. In the 1960s she starred in a number of horror films, including *Hush, Hush, Sweet Charlotte, Whatever Happened to Baby Jane?*, and *The Nanny*.

## DAVIS, Jefferson

Jefferson Davis (1808–1889) was the only president of the CONFEDERATE STATES OF AMERICA. He was born in Kentucky and grew up in Mississippi. Davis was first elected to the U.S. House of Representatives in 1845. Later he served as a U.S. senator from Mississippi and as secretary of war under President Franklin PIERCE.

Davis took a moderate line in the dispute between North and South. He was not in favor of secession, but he thought that states had a constitutional right to secede if they wished. He also supported slavery. After Abraham LINCOLN was elected president in 1860, Mississippi was among the states that seceded and formed the Confederate States of America. In February 1861, Davis was named president of the Confederacy.

After the South was defeated, in 1865, Davis was captured by Union troops and charged with treason. He spent two years in prison, but the case was never brought to trial. His last years were spent in Mississippi.

## D DAY

June 6, 1944, called "D Day," was the date of the Allied invasion of German-occupied France in WORLD WAR II. A combined British, American, Canadian, and Free French force crossed the English Channel and landed on the coast of Normandy. Some 176,000 troops took part in Operation "Overlord," making it the largest invasion force in history.

The forces were commanded by the American General Dwight D. EISENHOWER. The five landing beaches—called Utah, Omaha, Gold, Juno, and Sword—were spread along a 40-mile (65-km) stretch of the Normandy coast. The worst fighting took place at Omaha Beach, where 2,000 Americans lost their lives. However, by the end of D Day the Allies controlled all five beaches.

▲ *The D Day landings in Normandy took the Germans by surprise. They had expected the Allies to cross the narrowest stretch of the English Channel, farther north at Calais.*

◀ *Death Valley was named by gold seekers, many of whom died crossing the valley during the 1849 gold rush.*

## DEATH VALLEY

Death Valley is a desert in southeastern California. It is about 140 miles (225 km) long. It forms part of the much larger Death Valley National Monument. Its lowest part is Badwater, 282 feet (86 m) below sea level. Movements in the earth's crust created Death Valley. These forced the surrounding lands up and forced down the area between them. Death Valley is extremely hot and receives almost no rain. In 1913 the highest temperature ever recorded in the United States was in Death Valley, a searing 134°F (57°C). Few plants and animals can live in these arid conditions.

▼ *The lowest part of Death Valley is the lowest piece of land in the Western Hemisphere.*

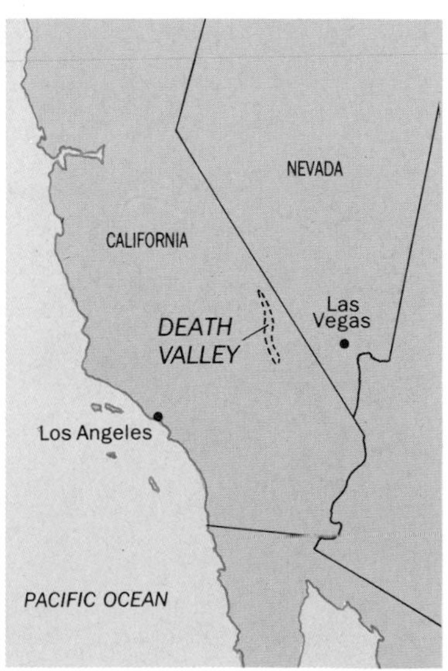

## DEBS, Eugene V.

Eugene V. Debs (1855–1926) was a labor and political leader. Born in Terre Haute, Indiana, he began working for the railroads while still in his teens. Debs joined the Brotherhood of Locomotive Firemen and in 1893 formed the American Railway Union. A year later he was jailed after involvement with a strike. While there, he became a socialist. He ran for president as a socialist five times. His 1920 campaign was run from prison, to which he had been sent after his outspoken opposition to war during World War I.

**The Declaration of Independence was written almost entirely by Thomas Jefferson. Only two passages in Jefferson's draft were rejected by the Congress — a very strong denunciation of the slave trade and an impolite reference to the English people.**

► The Declaration Committee, *a Currier and Ives print, was a popular memento of the U.S. Centennial in 1876, held to mark the 100th anniversary of the signing of the Declaration of Independence.*

## DECLARATION OF INDEPENDENCE

The Declaration of Independence marked the birth of the United States. It was adopted on July 4, 1776, by representatives of the 13 colonies attending the Second Continental Congress. This was held in Philadelphia, at the Pennsylvania State House, which became known as INDEPENDENCE HALL. Messengers carried copies of the Declaration to different states. It was later signed by the 56 delegates to the Congress. July 4 is still celebrated as the nation's birthday.

The document was drafted by Thomas JEFFERSON. He was assisted by John ADAMS, Benjamin FRANKLIN, Robert Livingston, and Roger Sherman. The Declaration proclaimed that the 13 British colonies in North America were no longer under British rule. It also said that although they were independent states, they were also united.

▼ *The Declaration was read out at state houses within days of its signing. Most of the public was wildly in favor of it.*

The first part of the Declaration sums up the rights of all people. It states that all men are born equal—that is, they all have the same rights. It also says that governments exist to protect each citizen's right to life, liberty, and happiness. The rest of the document lists the colonies' grievances against King George III of Britain.

Written on parchment, the Declaration of Independence can be seen in the National Archives building in Washington, D.C.

▲ *The original Purple Heart was called the Badge of Military Merit. It honored bravery in the Revolutionary War. This modern version, established in 1932, is awarded to members of the armed forces who have been killed or wounded in action.*

## DECORATIONS AND MEDALS 

The Purple Heart is the oldest U.S. military medal. George Washington issued the first three in 1782, and the medal still bears his profile. This award is for being killed or wounded in action. A member of any branch of the armed forces can receive the Purple Heart, as well as other medals such as the Silver Star and Bronze Star. Other medals, such as the Distinguished Flying Cross (Air Force) and the Distinguished Service Cross (Army), can be issued by only one branch. The highest military award is the Medal of Honor. This can be awarded to any military person and honors bravery and risk of life to help others.

The government also recognizes the value of great actions in peacetime. The highest nonmilitary award is the Presidential Medal of Freedom. It honors important contributions to the interests of the United States or the cause of world peace.

## DEER 

Deer are animals that chew the cud and have *cloven* hoofs (hoofs that are divided in half). The males usually have antlers. No other animal has antlers. Deer eat

▼ *Deer antlers develop each year from tender stumps, covered in a layer of soft, hair-covered skin, to fully grown branches. The four stages show the period from spring to fall.*

▲ *Deer of North America. Male deer, or stags, use their antlers mainly for fighting one another. Speed is a deer's greatest defense against predators. A white-tailed deer can run at 40 miles per hour (64 km/hr). Even the moose, which can weigh nearly a ton, can reach speeds of up to 20 miles per hour (32 km/hr).*

leaves, fruit, grass, and sometimes moss, bark, and twigs.

The largest deer in the world is the MOOSE. It lives in Alaska, northern Canada, the Great Lakes region, New York, Montana, and Idaho. The male moose has massive antlers. The male wapiti, or elk, also has spectacular antlers. It was once found from central Canada to New Mexico but now lives only in the northern part of this range.

The white-tailed, or Virginia, deer is the most common deer in North America. It is found in forests and open country through most of the United States from the Atlantic coast to the Rocky Mountains, as far south as Mexico. A close relative, the black-tailed, or mule, deer, lives in the western United States.

The CARIBOU is the North American reindeer. It is found in Canada and Alaska. Both the female and the male have antlers. Herds of caribou migrate from summer ranges to winter ranges.

**The Department of Defense employs about 2 million men and women on active duty and about 1 million civilian employees. It takes more than one fourth of the total U.S. annual budget.**

## DEFENSE, DEPARTMENT OF

The U.S. Department of Defense was set up in 1949 as a way of centralizing the three main branches of the armed forces. It is part of the executive branch of the federal GOVERNMENT. The secretary of defense is a Cabinet member. The Army, Navy, and Air Force make up the three military departments of the Department of Defense. Each of these services is led by a chief of staff. Together these three are known as the Joint Chiefs of Staff (JCS). Their job is to meet with and advise the secretary of defense and the president.

Important military orders begin with the president, who is commander in chief of the armed forces. They are passed on to the secretary of defense and then to the JCS. This elaborate system ensures that civilians, represented by the president and the secretary of defense, have ultimate control over military action. The responsibility is great. The Department of Defense has an annual budget of about $262 billion, or 20 percent of the federal budget. With the apparent end of the COLD WAR in 1990, it is expected that this percentage will decrease in the years ahead.

▼ *The five-sided Pentagon in Washington, D.C., is the headquarters of the Department of Defense. Covering 29 acres (12 ha), it is one of the world's largest office buildings. More than 20,000 people work in the Pentagon.*

## DE FOREST, Lee 

Lee de Forest (1873–1961) was a pioneer of the early days of radio. In 1907 he invented a vacuum tube known as a *triode*. Because of its ability to boost, or amplify, weak electrical signals, the triode played a crucial role in the development of long-distance radio. De Forest resoundingly demonstrated its success in 1910, when he broadcast a concert from the Metropolitan Opera House in New York City. He also worked for the U.S. Navy. His early naval radio stations revolutionized communications at sea. Later, he did important work on sound waves, paving the way for talking pictures.

**Lee de Forest took out more than 300 patents on radio and electronic devices. But the one invention that some people say was as great as the invention of radio itself was the vacuum tube called a *triode* or *audion*. Before this invention, the only radio signals were the "dot-dash" of Morse code.**

# DELAWARE

Delaware lies on the Atlantic coast between Maryland, Pennsylvania, and New Jersey. It is the second smallest state (only Rhode Island is smaller). It is also the oldest state. On December 7, 1787, Delaware became the first state to ratify, or approve, the new U.S. Constitution. Delaware's nickname, The First State, commemorates this historic action.

The region occupied by Delaware was one of the first to be visited, and later settled, by Europeans. Henry HUDSON, an Englishman, reached it in 1609. The following year, another Englishman, Samuel Argall of the Virginia Colony, also reached it. He named the bay he found for Lord De La Warr, governor of Virginia. Delaware was settled by both the Swedish and the Dutch, but by 1664 it had become an English colony. Delaware played a small but significant role in the American REVOLUTION. Later it fought on the Union side throughout the CIVIL WAR even though it was a slave state.

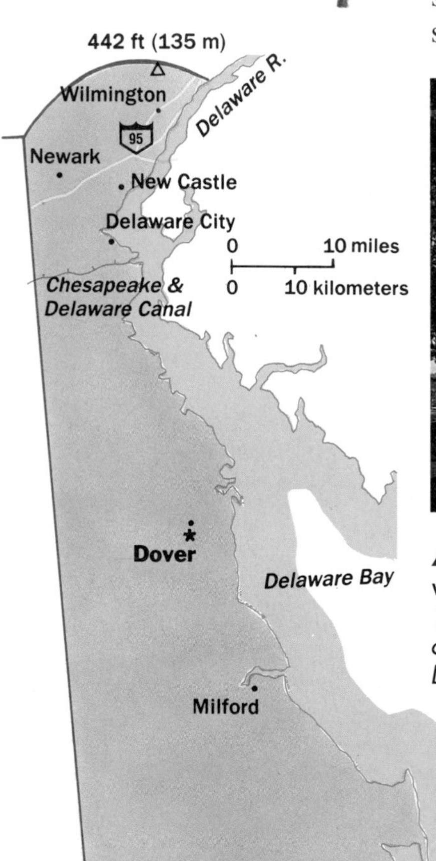

▲ *The Old State House, in Dover, was Delaware's capitol from 1792 until 1933. Today it contains exhibits relating to Delaware's history.*

**Places of Interest**

- Fort Delaware stands on Pea Patch Island and can only be reached by boat from Delaware City. It was used as a prison during the Civil War.
- Hagley Museum and Eleutherian Mills, near Wilmington, features the original powder mills of Éleuthère Irénée du Pont as well as models showing the development of industry in Colonial America.
- The town of New Castle contains many interesting colonial buildings, cobblestone streets, and an old village green.
- Henry Francis Du Pont Winterthur Museum, near Wilmington, houses a collection of Early American furniture, china, and silver dating from 1640 to 1840.

Delaware today is an important business area. The state's favorable laws governing registered companies have led almost 200,000 U.S. companies to establish themselves here, even though many trade in other areas of the country. Numerous law firms in particular are registered in Delaware. Few industries are based in the state. The most important are in the chemical business, especially in Wilmington, Delaware's largest city. Farms cover much of the state, especially the fertile plains that stretch inland across southern Delaware. The sandy beaches of the southeastern coast of the state draw many summer vacationers.

**Delaware**
**Capital:** Dover
**Area:** 2,489 sq mi (6,447 km$^2$). Rank: 49th
**Population:** 666,168 (1990). Rank: 46th
**Statehood:** Dec. 7, 1787
**Principal rivers:** Delaware, Mispillion, Nanticoke
**Highest point:** Centerville, 442 ft (135 m)
**Motto:** Liberty and Independence
**Song:** "Our Delaware"

◀ *Delaware's only major city, Wilmington, is within 10 miles (16 km) of New Jersey, Pennsylvania, and Maryland. It is the center of Delaware's chemical industry.*

▼ *The Brandywine Valley in northern Delaware is the highest region of the state.*

▲ *The donkey first appeared as the Democratic Party symbol in this 1870 political cartoon by Thomas Nast. The donkey was meant to represent only a faction of the party, but the Democrats adopted it as the party mascot.*

## DEMOCRATIC PARTY

The Democratic Party is one of the two major POLITICAL PARTIES in the United States. The beginnings of the Democratic Party were in 1792, when supporters of Thomas JEFFERSON formed the Democratic-Republican Party. They believed in states' rights and government by the people. In the 1830s it became known as the Democratic Party.

In 1860, after nearly 60 years of being in office, the party split over the issues of states' rights and slavery. For the next half century, there was only one Democratic president, Grover CLEVELAND. In 1896 the party split between supporters of gold coins and silver. The Democrats won in 1912 and 1916 with Woodrow WILSON, then not again until 1932, with Franklin D. ROOSEVELT. He was followed by Harry S. TRUMAN. The next Democratic victory was in 1960, when John F. KENNEDY was elected president. Lyndon B. JOHNSON succeeded him, serving from 1963 till 1969. After Jimmy CARTER was elected in 1976, the next Democrat to win a presidential election was Bill CLINTON in 1992.

## DEMPSEY, Jack

Jack Dempsey (1895–1983), whose real name was William Harrison Dempsey, was heavyweight BOXING champion from 1919, when he beat Jess Willard, to 1926, when he lost to Gene Tunney. In 1927, Dempsey fought Tunney again. This time Dempsey knocked Tunney down, but the referee didn't start counting Tunney out until Dempsey got to the neutral corner. As a result, Tunney was able to get up at the count of 9. He went on to win the fight. This "long count" became one of the most famous incidents in boxing history.

▼ *Denver's bustling commercial center is located only 10 miles (16 km) east of the Rocky Mountains. The Great Plains lie on the other side of the city.*

## DENVER

COLORADO's capital, Denver, is known as the Mile-High City because the state capitol is exactly 5,280 feet (1,610 m) above sea level. Denver is located on the western edge of the Great Plains. It is the industrial, commercial, and transportation center of the Rocky Mountain region and has a population of over 467,000. Denver's most important employers are the state and federal governments. It is also the site of a federal mint.

## DEPRESSION, GREAT 

The Great Depression was a severe economic slump that occurred in the United States, and later in other countries, in the 1930s. It was triggered by the stock market crash of 1929, when share prices plunged.

The sudden drop in prices affected almost every part of the economy. Many farmers, for example, now received so little for their crops that they were unable to pay their debts. Many lost their farms. The reduced demand for goods and services forced most businesses to lay off some of their employees. By 1933, the worst year of the Depression, 12 million Americans were unemployed—about one quarter of the work force. Many unemployed, homeless people took shelter in shantytowns, managing to keep alive through odd jobs, charity, and begging.

◀ *The New Hope Mission in New York City, and thousands like it around the country, gave food to the poorest families during the Depression.*

Among the many businesses that failed were thousands of banks. There was no federal deposit insurance, and when people feared that a bank was in trouble they would rush to withdraw their savings. With all its assets wiped out, the bank would be forced to close.

For the first two years of the Depression, the government took little direct action, believing that the economy would recover naturally. Then the election of Franklin D. ROOSEVELT as president brought the NEW DEAL. This was a set of laws designed mainly to ease the worst of the poverty, provide support for the banks, and create new jobs. This helped considerably. But it was not until 1939, when the outbreak of WORLD WAR II gave an enormous boost to heavy industry, that the Depression came to an end.

**The Great Depression changed the way the public and the government viewed the U.S. economy. Before the Depression, people looked to bankers and business executives as the leaders of the nation's economy, and the government kept federal involvement to a minimum. After the stock market crashed, the public lost faith in the business tycoons and looked to the government to solve the crisis. Since then the government has been more involved in the way the economy is run.**

**During the Depression the total earnings of everyone in the country fell by half. Top stenographers in New York saw their pay drop from $35.45 a week to $16. There were more than 85,000 business failures. The Depression years saw a burst of union organizing. Total union membership rose from about 3 million to over 10 million in 1941. In other countries the Depression had an even more profound effect. It strengthened the hold of Adolf Hitler in Germany and added to the tensions that led to World War II.**

# DESERTS

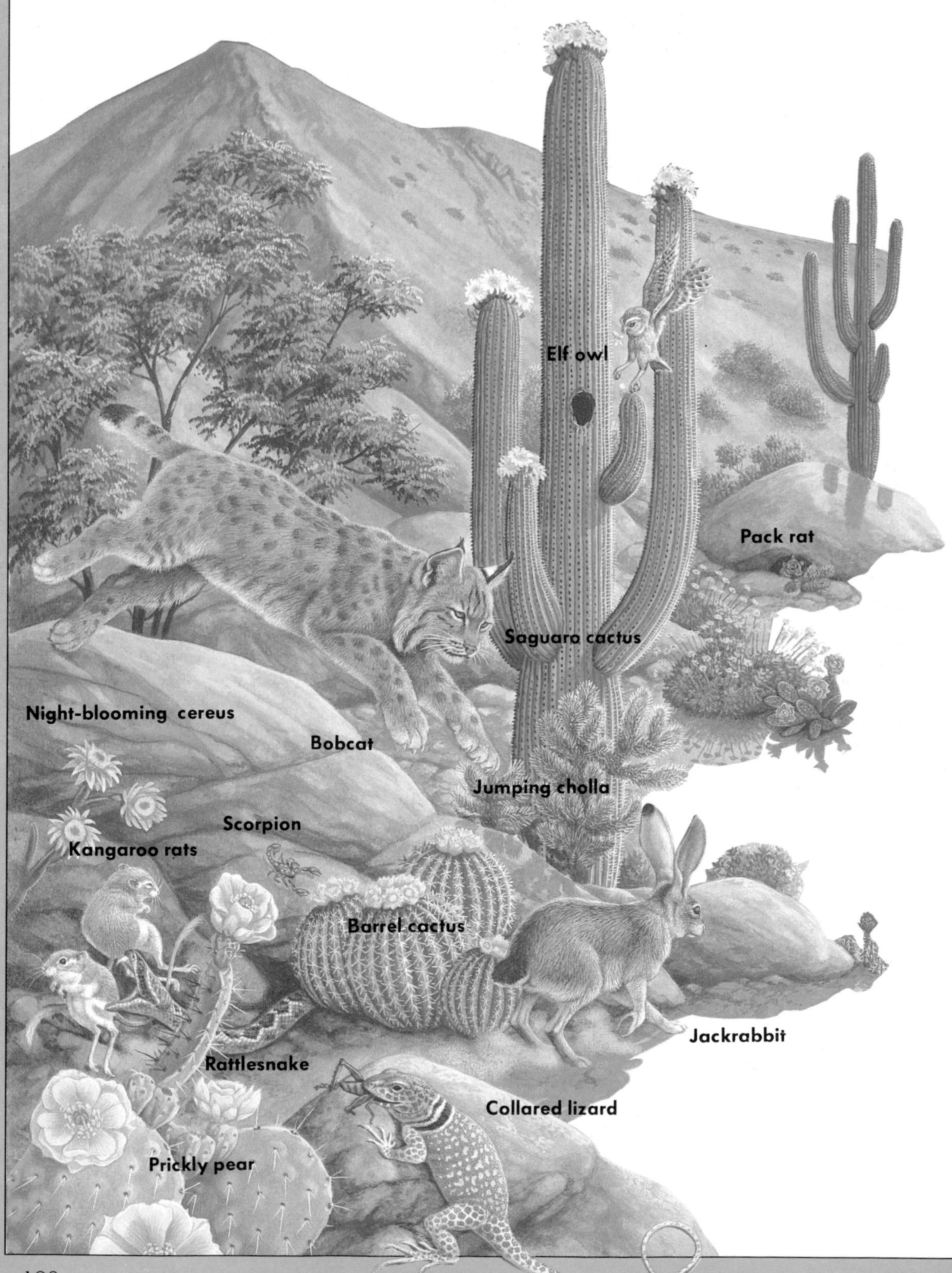

Elf owl
Pack rat
Saguaro cactus
Night-blooming cereus
Bobcat
Jumping cholla
Scorpion
Kangaroo rats
Barrel cactus
Jackrabbit
Rattlesnake
Collared lizard
Prickly pear

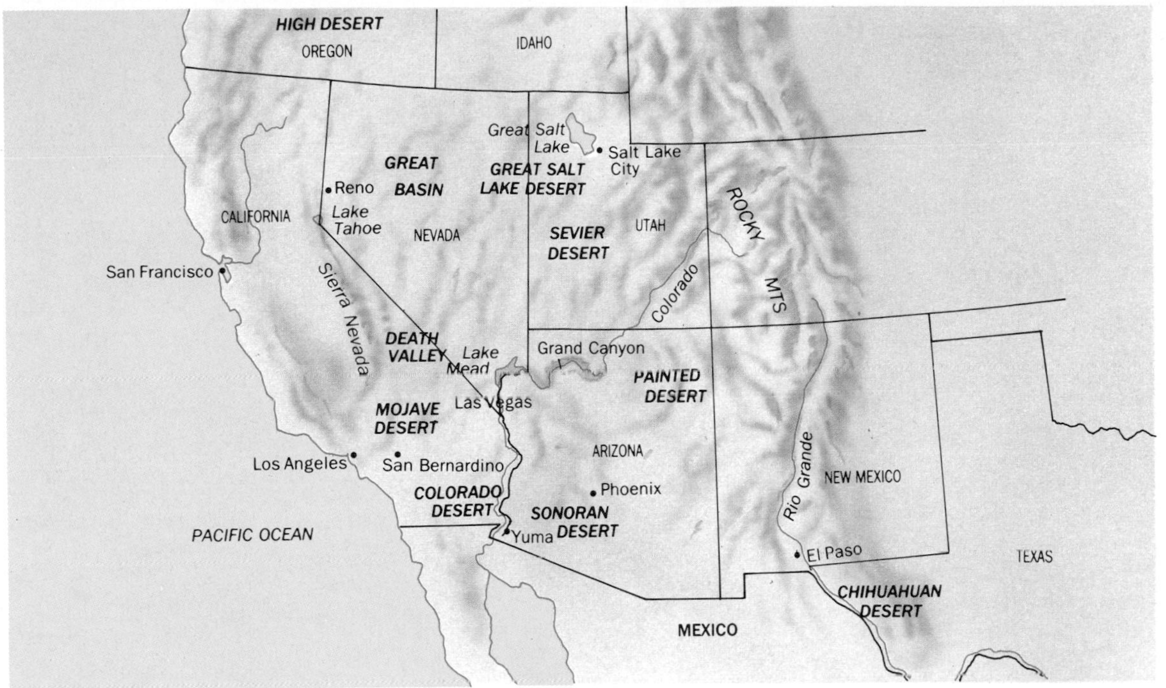


▲ *Most deserts in the United States are located west of the Rocky Mountains.*

**Desert areas of the United States**

**Sometimes several inches of torrential rain might fall in desert areas within a few hours, but usually rain falls only at very long intervals. Records at Iquique in the Atacama Desert of northern Chile showed no rain at all for a period of four years. Death Valley in California has an average annual rainfall of only 1.5 inches (38 mm) compared with New York City's 42 inches (1,067 mm).**

A desert is a barren region of limited rainfall. The soil is too dry for many plants to grow. There are large desert regions in the western United States and in Mexico. They are caused by mountains to the west that block moist air moving in from the Pacific Ocean. Conditions in many deserts are extreme, usually with hot days and cold nights. DEATH VALLEY, in California, is one of the hottest places in the world during summer. Temperatures there have been known to soar to over 130°F (54°C). A "cold desert," such as that in northern Canada and Alaska, is a place where the barrenness is caused by low temperatures.

Deserts are not always covered in sand dunes. Much of North America's largest desert region, the Great Basin, is high, dry sagebrush country.

North American deserts have more plants than other deserts in the world. These include many kinds of CACTUS and the famous Joshua trees, which are found in the MOJAVE and other deserts of the Southwest.

Some animals have adapted to desert life in North America. Birds include the roadrunner, cactus wren, and sage hen. Other desert animals include the Gila monster, kit fox, collared peccary, and kangaroo rat. Tiny insects live in some desert ponds. They are dormant (temporarily inactive), sometimes for months, until some rainfall creates a tiny pond in which they reproduce.

Some deserts are rich in minerals and other natural resources. Uranium and copper, for example, are mined in North American deserts. If irrigated (artificially watered), deserts can be made suitable for farming. Part of the Colorado River has been used to irrigate areas of the Sonoran Desert to produce fertile farmland.

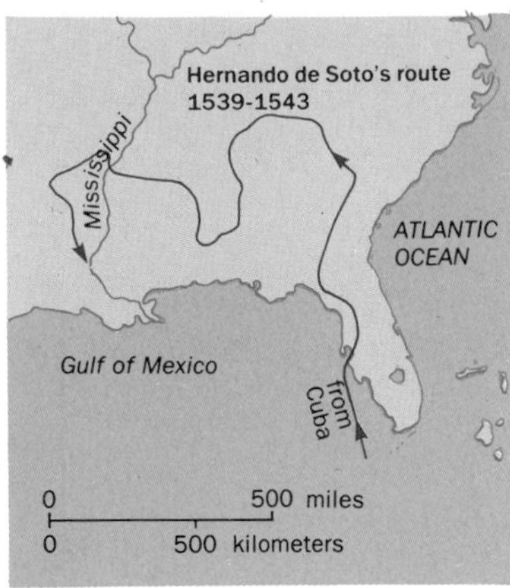


▲ *De Soto arrived at the Mississippi River at what is now the border between Mississippi and Arkansas.*

## DE SOTO, Hernando

The Spanish *conquistador* (conqueror) Hernando de Soto (1500?–1542) explored the southeastern part of what is now the United States and discovered the Mississippi River.

Between 1516 and 1536, de Soto took part in various expeditions in Central America and Peru. His last and most important expedition took him to the lands north of Mexico where he hoped to find gold. He arrived in Florida in 1539, with 1,000 men, and began a three-year-long exploration that took him as far north as Tennessee and as far west as Oklahoma. He died of a fever and his body was sunk in the Mississippi.

## DETROIT

Detroit, Michigan, is a major manufacturing center and the country's leading automobile-producing city. It is one of the largest cities in the country, with a population of more than 1 million. The city is also a major port and transportation center. It lies on the Detroit River, in southeastern Michigan, facing Canada across the river. Detroit was founded by a Frenchman, Antoine CADILLAC, in 1701. It quickly became a leading center of the fur trade. In the early years of this century, Detroit became the headquarters of the automobile industry. Thereafter, it grew rapidly. Almost 60 percent of the

▼ *Older buildings, such as Christ Church, are dwarfed by Detroit's Renaissance Center. Four 39-story office towers flank a 73-story hotel.*

population is black, and the city has suffered from racial tensions for many years. These are often worst when economic conditions are also poor.

▲ The educator John Dewey believed that knowledge came from dealing with new experiences. He argued that students should learn from experiments, rather than by memory.

## DEWEY, George

George Dewey (1837–1917), an American naval officer, was a hero of the SPANISH-AMERICAN WAR. Dewey graduated from the U.S. Naval Academy at Annapolis in 1858 and, as a young officer, fought in the CIVIL WAR. When the Spanish-American War broke out in 1898, Dewey was a commodore. He was in charge of the six ships that formed the Asiatic Squadron. Dewey and his fleet sailed from Hong Kong to Manila in the Philippines. In spite of being outnumbered, he destroyed ten ships of the Spanish fleet and seized the harbor. Not one American life was lost in the battle. Dewey was made an admiral of the navy the following year.

## DEWEY, John

John Dewey (1859–1952) was a philosopher and educator who strongly influenced educational practices in the United States. He believed that intelligence needed to be stimulated by new and different problems if people, especially young people, were to develop their full potential. Earlier education had often focused on teaching largely by memory. Dewey called on educators to set problems that would challenge children and make them think for themselves. He believed, too, that education should aim to do more than instill knowledge: it should also ensure the moral development of children.

## DICKINSON, Emily

Emily Dickinson (1830–1886) was a famous American poet. Born in Amherst, Massachusetts, she grew up in a prosperous, educated family. Her father was a lawyer and congressman. Her home was strict and rules were rigid. She rarely left it. She created her own world in her poetry. Only about ten of 1,800 poems she wrote were published during her lifetime; the rest appeared over many years only after her death in 1886. Dickinson's poems are short and simple, but they are full of passion. She tended to use single, sharp images. Many of her poems were about feelings and nature.

▼ Emily Dickinson believed it was the poet's duty to produce "amazing sense from ordinary meaning." Her poems are considered among the greatest in American literature.

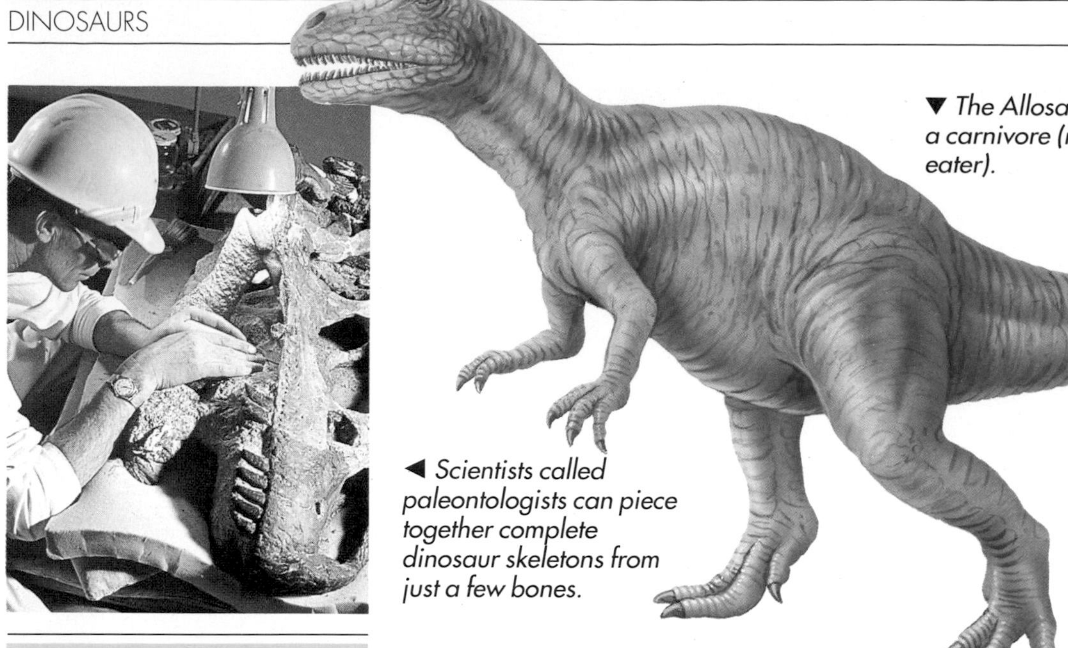

▼ *The Allosaurus was a carnivore (meat eater).*

◀ *Scientists called paleontologists can piece together complete dinosaur skeletons from just a few bones.*

**During the early part of the age of the dinosaurs, 200 million years ago, the continents were all joined together in one great land mass. This is why dinosaurs have been found on every continent except Antarctica. Remains of about 300 different species of dinosaurs have been found, but some of these are known only from a single tooth or a small bone fragment.**

▼ *The Stegosaurus ate mostly plants. Its armor plates and spiked tail were good defenses against attack.*

## DINOSAURS

Dinosaurs were reptiles that lived for millions of years on most parts of the earth. The word dinosaur means "thunder lizard" in Greek. Dinosaurs died out mysteriously about 65 million years ago. We know about dinosaurs because people have discovered and preserved fossils, the remains of dinosaurs found in rock. Dinosaur fossils have been found all over North America, but the best finds have been in the western states and Canadian provinces. Some outstanding displays of dinosaur fossils are in the Dinosaur National Monument, on the border between Utah and Colorado.

In general, North American dinosaur fossils are similar to those found on other continents. This is because many of the continents were still attached to each other during the early part of the age of the dinosaur.

American dinosaur specialist Jim Jensen was examining an arm and shoulder bone in 1979 and found that they were from an undiscovered large species. He calculated that such a dinosaur, which he named Ultrasaurus, would be 100 feet (30 m) long and would weigh 143 tons, as much as the weight of 20 large elephants. That would make Ultrasaurus the largest animal that ever roamed the earth. It would have looked like a larger version of the more familiar Brachiosaurus.

◀ *Disneyland, in Anaheim, California, was the creation of Walt Disney (below). It opened in 1955.*

## DISNEY, Walt

Walter Elias Disney (1901–1966) was a cartoon artist and a producer of cartoon films. He was born in Chicago and raised in Missouri. In 1923 he began to experiment with cartoon *animation*. Disney's "stars" became famous around the world—Mickey and Minnie Mouse, Donald Duck, and a host of others. *Snow White and the Seven Dwarfs*, *Cinderella*, *Fantasia*, and *101 Dalmatians* are just a few of the feature-length cartoons turned out by Disney's animation team. He later went on to produce nature films and TV programs. Two theme parks —Disneyland, in California, and Disney World, in Florida—pay tribute to Disney's creative genius.

▶ *The first Mickey Mouse cartoon, called* Plane Crazy, *appeared in 1928.*

▼ *The fantasy atmosphere of* Snow White and the Seven Dwarfs *(1937) offered audiences an escape from the Depression.*

# DISTRICT OF COLUMBIA

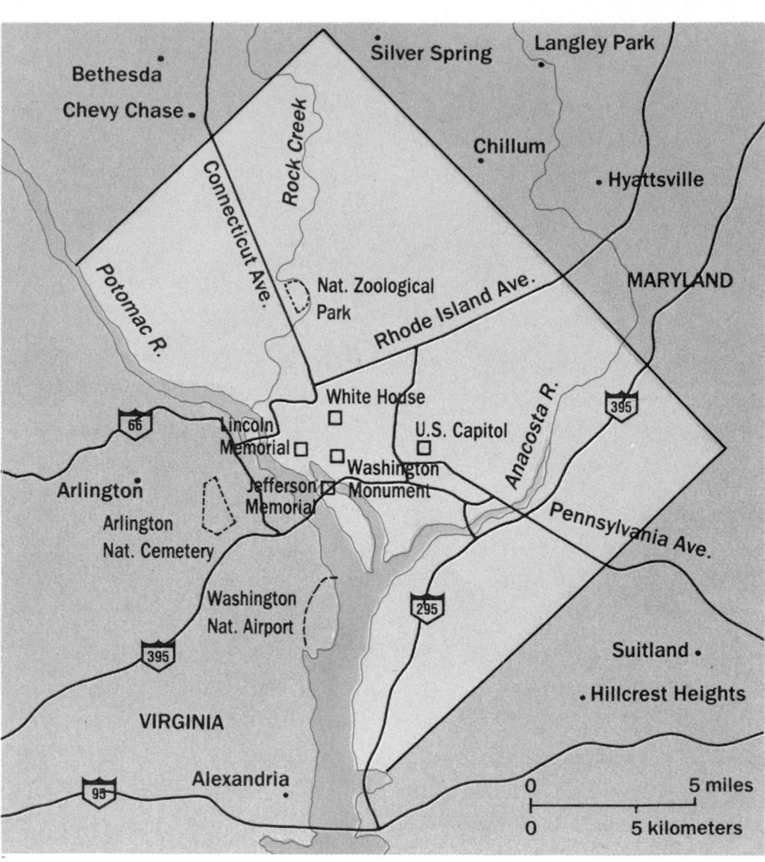


▼ *The Jefferson Memorial is built in the same architectural style that Jefferson used for his own home, Monticello.*

The District of Columbia is the seat of the government of the United States. Since 1890 it has also covered the same area as the city of WASHINGTON, D.C. The Constitution provided that a tract of land be set aside for the new nation's capital. Congress authorized it in 1790. In 1791, George WASHINGTON himself chose the site of the new city, and he hired a French architect, Pierre Charles L'Enfant, to design it. It was to be built on land ceded by Maryland and Virginia. In 1800, the federal

Places of Interest

- The Capitol is the building where the U.S. Congress meets. Visitors to the Capitol can see Congress in action and enjoy the works of art that hang in the Great Rotunda.
- The White House was begun in 1792 and has been home to every U.S. president except George Washington.
- The Air and Space Museum has many interesting exhibits, including the Wright brothers' first airplane.
- The Washington Monument, Lincoln Memorial, and Jefferson Memorial pay tribute to three of America's great presidents.

government moved to the new city from Philadelphia. In 1846 the land given by Virginia was returned to that state. Confederate territory in the CIVIL WAR began just over the Potomac River, in Virginia.

Today Washington, D.C., is probably the most important center of government in the world. The WHITE HOUSE, the CAPITOL, and the SUPREME COURT are all located in the city.

District of Columbia
**Area:** 68.25 sq mi (176.75 km$^2$)
**Population:** 606,900 (1990)
**Principal river:** Potomac
**Highest point:** Tenleytown, 410 ft (125 m)
**Motto:** *Justitia Omnibus* (Justice for All)

## DOGS

In the United States, 128 breeds of purebred dogs are registered with the American Kennel Club, the organization of U.S. dog breeders. The breeds are divided into seven groups: sporting, hound, toy, working, herding, terrier, and nonsporting breeds. Seven breeds were originally developed in the United States. The first was the Alaskan malamute, bred by the Inuits (Eskimos) 3,000 years ago. Others are the American water spaniel, Chesapeake Bay retriever, American foxhound, black-and-tan coonhound, American Staffordshire terrier, and Boston terrier. Many pets are not purebred but are crosses between more than one breed. North American relatives of the dog are the COYOTE, FOX, and WOLF.

▼ *The names of North American dog breeds give a clue to why they have been called man's best friend. An Eskimo sled dog (above) is used to pull sleds in the Arctic.*

► *The first Douglas DC-3s were built especially for American Airlines in 1935. The DC-3 soon became the world's most popular transport plane.*

**The famous Douglas DC-3, the Dakota, carried 21 passengers at a speed of 192 miles per hour (309 km/hr) and accounted for most of the world's passenger traffic for many years. The DC-3 was modified for military use and named the C-47 during World War II. It was the mainstay of U.S. troop and cargo transport.**

## DOUGLAS, Donald W.

Donald W. Douglas (1892–1981) was an aircraft designer. In 1921 he founded the Douglas Aircraft Company, which became part of the McDonnell Douglas Corporation in 1967. Douglas planes include commercial transports, bombers, and jet airliners.

## DOUGLAS, Stephen A.

Stephen A. Douglas (1813–1861) is remembered today mainly as the Democratic opponent of Abraham LINCOLN in a series of debates during their race for an Illinois Senate seat in 1858. An excellent speaker, he was especially eloquent in the causes of U.S. westward

▼ *Although Stephen A. Douglas was a short man, his powerful speaking voice and strong build gained him the nickname the Little Giant.*

expansion and "popular sovereignty." This was the principle that the people settling a territory should be allowed to decide for themselves whether or not to allow slavery.

Douglas won the 1858 senatorial election, but two years later he came in second to Lincoln in the presidential race. Douglas supported the new president, but he died soon after Lincoln's inauguration.

**In addition to his prominent political career, Stephen A. Douglas was a wealthy land speculator around the Chicago area. He helped make that city a major railroad terminus.**

## DOUGLASS, Frederick

Born of a slave mother and a white father (whom he never knew), Frederick Douglass (1817–1895) became one of the most outstanding CIVIL RIGHTS leaders in U.S. history. As a child he was taught to read by a kindly white mistress; when the master forbade this, Frederick secretly continued his education on his own. In 1838 he escaped to the North. Here, his gift with words soon brought him to the forefront of the ABOLITIONIST movement. During the Civil War he was an adviser to President Abraham LINCOLN. Afterward, he worked for full civil rights for blacks and women and held several important jobs in the U.S. government. His autobiography is *Life and Times of Frederick Douglass*.

**During the Civil War, President Lincoln's government passed a law that all able-bodied males aged 20 to 45 were liable for the draft unless they paid $300. This law caused many riots, especially in New York City. Workers, largely of Irish descent, battled with police and militiamen. There were about 1,000 casualties.**

## DRAFT

The draft, also called conscription, is a method of calling men for service in the armed forces. During the CIVIL WAR, the South was forced to draft soldiers beginning in 1862; the North followed in 1863. Before

*▼ Secretary of War Newton Barker drew the first draft number of World War I on June 27, 1918. About 2.5 million Americans were drafted over the remaining five months of the war.*

**When Theodore Dreiser published his first book, *Sister Carrie*, in 1900, it sold only 456 copies. It was considered immoral, and the publisher refused to distribute or advertise it.**

the United States entered WORLD WAR I, the U.S. Army had only just over 125,000 men. A draft was started, and 2.5 million more soldiers were called up. During WORLD WAR II, 10 million of the 18 million U.S. soldiers were drafted. Two million men were drafted to fight in Korea, and about 1.75 million drafted soldiers fought in the VIETNAM WAR. The United States has had a volunteer army since 1973. But young men must register for the draft with the Selective Service System when they reach the age of 18.

▼ *The government's anti-drug efforts are aimed mainly at young people in the inner cities. This poster in Harlem, New York City, is part of the "Say NO to Drugs" campaign.*

## DREISER, Theodore 

The novelist Theodore Dreiser (1871–1945) is best known for two books, *Sister Carrie* and *An American Tragedy*. Dreiser earned a good living as a magazine editor. But he achieved little success as a writer until 1925, when *An American Tragedy* was published. This book, based on a real murder case, was hailed as a masterpiece. Dreiser had a pessimistic view of American society. His books often portray individuals who are helpless against this society.

## DRUG ABUSE 

The harmful use of mind-altering drugs is called drug abuse. Some people start to use drugs for a thrill or as an escape from stress or poverty. Sometimes these drugs are legal, such as alcohol, sleeping pills, or prescription drugs. In the 1960s a wide range of illegal drugs began to appear. Officials seize about $600 million worth of drugs each year, but many times that amount reach the country. The most dangerous are heroin and crack, a type of cocaine. Both are addictive and can lead to death from overdoses. Marijuana and amphetamines (mood lifters) are not physically addictive but can cause users to crave them and resort to crime to obtain them. Clinics and halfway houses, supported privately or by the government, help drug abusers "kick the habit."

▼ *W.E.B. Du Bois once described his civil rights beliefs as "the recognition of the principle of human brotherhood as a practical present creed."*

## DU BOIS, W.E.B. 

W.E.B. Du Bois (1868–1963) was an important black-American leader and historian. He became the first black to obtain the degree of doctor of philosophy (Ph.D.) from Harvard University. Du Bois believed that black people must actively fight prejudice and injustice. In 1909 he was one of the founders of the NATIONAL ASSOCIATION FOR THE ADVANCEMENT OF COLORED PEOPLE (NAACP). After decades of work DuBois saw little progress and began to look for new solutions. He joined the Communist Party in 1961. Du Bois lived in Ghana for the last years of his life.

## DUCHAMP, Marcel

Marcel Duchamp (1887–1968) was a French artist who moved to the United States in 1942. He dramatically expanded the frontiers of modern art—though even today many people believe Duchamp was a clever showman rather than a true artist. During his life, his works angered critics and the public. Duchamp maintained that art was whatever an artist said it was, however ridiculous. A well-known work is his *Mona Lisa*, a copy of the famous painting with a beard and mustache added.

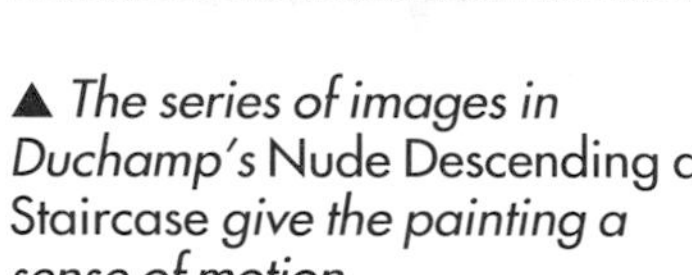

▲ *The series of images in Duchamp's* Nude Descending a Staircase *give the painting a sense of motion.*

## DUCKS AND GEESE

Ducks and geese are birds that swim. They have webbed feet and flat bills. Ducks are smaller than geese and have shorter necks. Male ducks, or drakes, are usually more brightly colored than females. The male goose, or gander, has the same coloring as the female. Ducks

▼ *Ducks and geese are migratory birds. Some will travel huge distances, even all the way from Alaska to Texas.*

▲ *The plumage colors of ducks and geese often act as camouflage. The snow goose is well suited to its Arctic home.*

spend more time in the water than geese, and their legs are set farther back.

Ducks and geese nest in the north and travel south in the winter. In North America, many species of ducks and several species of geese nest along the northern coast of North America. South of this Arctic region, the lakes and rivers of the spruce belt that runs from east to west across Canada and Alaska provide nesting grounds for millions of ducks. The marshes, ponds, and lakes of the northern prairies are also the main breeding grounds for enormous numbers of ducks. Many ducks and geese spend the winter on the east coast, and many millions more winter in the marshes and ponds of the California valleys.

## DULLES, John Foster

John Foster Dulles (1888–1959) was secretary of state between 1953 and 1959 under President Dwight D. EISENHOWER. He helped formulate U.S. foreign policy during the COLD WAR. Dulles strongly opposed communism. He urged that the United States respond actively to Communist expansion. He even called for the "liberation" of countries of the Soviet bloc. Earlier, he had served as a U.S. delegate to the UNITED NATIONS and as a senator from New York.

## DUNCAN, Isadora

Isadora Duncan (1878–1927) was a famous dancer. As a child in San Francisco, she decided that the movements of classical ballet were too stiff, too artificial. Later, in Europe, she saw artwork showing the ancient Greeks. She soon developed dances based on how she thought the Greeks had danced. She danced barefooted, had long, flowing hair, and wore flowing garments. And her dancing flowed too. She used very free

▼ *Isadora Duncan caused a sensation dancing barefoot in loose tunics or Grecian-style robes. She again caused a sensation when she declared herself a Communist. Boston banned her from dancing there in 1922.*

movements, like the movements she saw in nature, such as rolling waves. Duncan's dancing helped launch modern dancing. She died in France, strangled when her long scarf was caught in the wheel of a car.

▲ *Charles Duryea demonstrated the one-horsepower car that won the first U.S. automobile race. In February 1896 the Duryea brothers sold the first automobile in the United States.*

## DU PONT, Éleuthère

Éleuthère Irénée du Pont (1771–1834) was a Frenchman who came to the United States in 1800 and founded a company that was to become world famous. In 1802, near Wilmington, Delaware, du Pont built a gunpowder plant, later known as E. I. du Pont de Nemours and Co. The company prospered, especially during the War of 1812. After du Pont's death, members of the family continued to run the business. The company expanded into a wide range of products, including plastics, chemicals, and synthetic fibers.

## DURYEA, Charles E. and J. F.

The Duryea brothers, Charles E. (1861–1938) and J. Frank (1869–1967), were trailblazers in the U.S. automobile industry. They built the first gasoline-powered automobile in the United States. This was demonstrated in Springfield, Massachusetts, in 1893. Two years later they won the first gasoline-powered automobile race, in Chicago, with a similar one-cylinder model. They invested some of their $2,000 prize in a workshop and set up the Duryea Motor Wagon Company that same year. Three years later Frank merged this company with the larger Stevens Arms Company. With more money and a larger factory he helped to design Stevens-Duryea cars, which were some of the first four- and six-cylinder automobiles.

▼ *The conditions in the Dust Bowl caused terrible poverty for many farmers and their families. Many had to give up their livelihood and seek employment elsewhere. The story of one such family is movingly told in John Steinbeck's novel* The Grapes of Wrath.

## DUST BOWL

In the mid-1930s, a series of terrible dust storms swept across the southern Great Plains. This area, centered in Kansas, Oklahoma, Texas, New Mexico, and Colorado, became known as the Dust Bowl. In the 1930s the soil was dry because of a long drought. Hundreds of millions of tons of topsoil were carried off by the winds, destroying the land. Many people lost their farms. Improved farming methods brought some relief, but dust storms are still a problem in this region.

## EAGLE

Eagles are large BIRDS OF PREY. Two species, the bald eagle and the golden eagle, breed in North America. The bald eagle is found nowhere else in the world. It ranges from Alaska to British Columbia and the western Great Lakes region and is also found in parts of the East. At one time it was found all over the continent, but it has become very rare. A type of sea eagle, it eats fish. The golden eagle lives in open country, mountainous regions, and prairies, from Alaska to Mexico. The numbers of both species have been reduced by hunting, and now they are protected by law.

*► The bald eagle, the U.S. national symbol, is not really bald; it has white feathers on its head. Similarly, Mexico's national symbol, the golden eagle, is not really gold. It has just a few gold flecks on the back of its neck.*

*▼ "Gas is low" were the last words heard from Amelia Earhart before her plane disappeared over the Pacific.*

## EARHART, Amelia

Amelia Earhart (1897–1937) was a famous American aviator who broke several world flying records. She worked to open aviation to women. In 1928 she became the first woman to cross the Atlantic Ocean by air. This was as a passenger, but in 1932 she became the first woman to fly across the Atlantic alone. In 1935 she became the first woman to fly from Hawaii to California. In 1937 she and a navigator attempted to fly around the world. With less than one third of the journey to go, her plane disappeared in the Pacific Ocean. No trace of the plane or aviators has ever been found.

## EARP, Wyatt

Wyatt Earp (1848–1929) was a legendary frontiersman and peace officer of the Old West. He worked as a stagecoach driver, a railroad construction worker, a gambler, a surveyor, and a buffalo hunter before becoming a lawman. In 1876 he became chief deputy marshal in Dodge City, Kansas. In 1879 he settled in Tombstone, Arizona Territory. Earp and his brothers participated in the famous "Gunfight at the O.K. Corral," in which they killed several suspected cattle rustlers.

▲ *The "Gunfight at the O.K. Corral" took place on October 26, 1881, in Tombstone, Arizona. Wyatt, Virgil, and Morgan Earp, and town dentist Doc Holliday killed four members of the Clanton gang.*

## EARTHQUAKES

The Earth's crust is made up of "plates" of rock. Huge pressures within the Earth push the plates against and over each other at the edges, which are known as faults. An earthquake occurs when two plates suddenly lurch against each other.

Most major quakes in the world have occurred in the earthquake "belt" that circles the Pacific. In North America, this belt runs along the west coast. The San Andreas fault runs through California from north to south. In the San Francisco Bay area, there are three more faults—the Hayward, Calaveras, and Sargent faults. They often have tremors, or small quakes.

A quake measuring 6.9 on the Richter scale (which

▼ *The older buildings of San Francisco's Marina district had no earthquake protection. They suffered the worst in the 1989 earthquake.*

**The Worst 20th-Century Earthquakes to Hit the U.S.**

**1906, April 18** San Francisco is destroyed by an earthquake. More than 500 people are killed or missing.
**1933, March 10** An earthquake at Long Beach, California, kills 117 people.
**1964, March 27** The strongest earthquake to hit North America strikes 80 miles (130 km) east of Anchorage, Alaska. It is followed by a tidal wave 50 ft (15 m) high. A total of 117 people are killed.
**1989, October 17** An earthquake measuring 6.9 on the Richter scale hits San Francisco, destroying parts of the Bay Bridge and the Interstate 880. Nearly 100 people are killed.

records the magnitude, or strength, of an earthquake) hit the San Francisco area in October 1989. An elevated freeway and part of the Bay Bridge collapsed, as did many buildings.

Although many minor earthquakes have taken place in the region, the most damaging quake there was the 1906 San Francisco earthquake. During the quake, the land along the San Andreas fault lurched 21 inches (53 cm). It was one of the most devastating earthquakes ever.

► *In 1912, Eastman Kodak became one of the first companies to build a research laboratory. Before that, firms kept their products unchanged and hoped they would continue selling.*

## EASTMAN, George 

George Eastman (1854–1932) did more to bring photography within the reach of ordinary people than any other pioneer of photography. The company he founded in 1880, Eastman Kodak, is still one of the largest photographic businesses in the world. One invention of Eastman's — roll film — revolutionized photography. Before that, pictures could only be taken using cumbersome glass plates. By 1888, Eastman had produced his first all-purpose camera. It cost $25. By 1900 he was making a camera that cost only $1.

▼ *The first amateur photographers sent their cameras, with exposed film inside, to this Eastman plant in Rochester, New York. In return they would receive a new loaded camera.*

## ECKERT, John P., Jr. 

John Presper Eckert (1919– ) and the physicist John W. Mauchly (1907–1980) created the first electronic digital computer. This machine, called ENIAC (*E*lectronic *N*umerical *I*ntegrator *a*nd *C*omputer), was made for the U.S. Army and completed in 1946. It weighed

60,000 pounds (27,000 kg) and almost filled a room 50 by 30 feet (15 by 9 m). Eckert and Mauchly formed their own computer manufacturing company. Over the next two decades they made many discoveries. Their research and work provided the basis for most of the computers that are in use today.

## ECONOMY, U.S.

The U.S. economy is the most powerful in the world. Economists judge its performance by examining the Gross National Product (GNP), which is the total monetary value of goods and services produced annually. The U.S. GNP is about $6 trillion. SERVICE INDUSTRIES, worth about $1 trillion each year, are the largest element, with MANUFACTURING close behind. Government spending comes to about $625 billion each year. Compared with some other countries, the U.S. government plays a smaller role in national economic affairs. The American free market system favors individuals or private companies.

Colonial America's economy was largely agricultural. Manufacturing took the lead in the 1800s, but in the past ten years service industries have been in first place.

▲ *Traders at the New York Stock Exchange scramble to handle orders on a busy trading day. Stock market trading often reflects the health of the national economy.*

Some Economic Terms

**Boom** is a time of fast economic growth. During a boom, unemployment is low and people have plenty of money.
**Capitalism** is an economic system where private individuals control most of a country's industries.
**Consumer** is anyone who buys goods and uses services.
**Cost of living** is the cost of buying the products and services that are used in everyday life.
**Depression** is a time when business activity is very low and unemployment is high.
**National income** is the total amount of money earned in a nation over a period of time.
**Standard of living** is a term used to describe the level at which a family or country lives.

## EDDY, Mary Baker

Mary Baker Eddy (1821–1910) was the founder of the CHRISTIAN SCIENCE religion. From childhood she suffered from a spinal illness that often prevented her from going to school. As an adult she was cured, temporarily, by a faith healer. After his death and the return

▼ *Mary Baker Eddy believed that the practice of medicine was not the route to healing. Healing could only begin when a patient had faith in God.*

**At the age of 12, Thomas Edison became a train boy, selling candy and magazines on the Grand Trunk Railroad. In his spare time, he experimented with chemicals in the baggage car. He even printed a newspaper on the moving train.**

of her illness, she turned to the New Testament, and her reading and meditation on it produced a cure. She described her system of faith healing in a book called *Science and Health with Key to the Scriptures* (first published in 1875). Soon she had many followers, including Asa G. Eddy, whom she married. In 1879 she founded the First Church of Christ, Scientist, in Boston. In 1908, Mary Baker Eddy founded the highly respected *Christian Science Monitor.*

## EDISON, Thomas Alva

▼ *The hardworking Edison once decribed genius as "1 percent inspiration and 99 percent perspiration."*

Thomas Alva Edison (1847–1931) was perhaps the most successful inventor of all time. Though largely self-taught, he devised thousands of new and different machines. Many were improvements to existing inventions —Edison was primarily interested in helping improve the quality of people's lives, not in being a great inventor—but a number, such as the phonograph, were entirely original. His impact on the modern world was immense and recognized in his own lifetime.

Edison's interests knew no limits. Even as a boy in Ohio, he was interested in everything around him. His major work included perfecting the electric light; a new, more reliable typewriter; an improved version of the telephone; movie cameras; electric generators; and the dictaphone. To many, he personified the questing spirit of America. His laboratory in New Jersey is now a national monument.

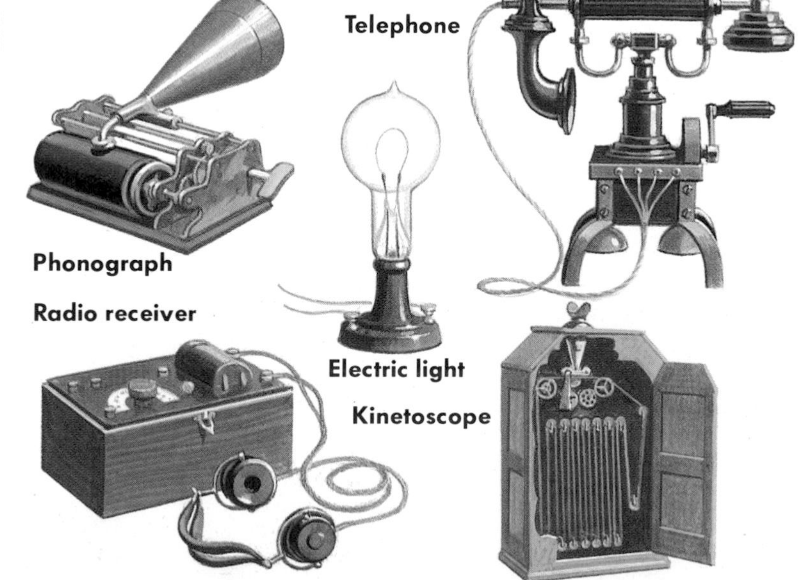


► *Thomas Edison showed his skill at improving other inventions as well as devising his own. His work improved the performance of the telephone and the radio receiver. The phonograph, electric light, and kinetoscope were his own creations.*

## EDMONTON

Edmonton is the capital and second largest city of the Canadian province of ALBERTA. It has a population of over 600,000. Located on the North Saskatchewan River, it is the most northerly city in Canada and is known as the Gateway to the North. Edmonton began as a fur-trading post in 1795. Today it is an important center of Canada's oil industry. Most of Alberta's oil fields are within 100 miles (160 km) of the city. Edmonton is also a major distribution center for goods being transported to and from Alaska and the Canadian northwest. Downtown Edmonton has malls, parks, and high rises.

▲ *The 3,000-acre (1,200-ha) Capital City Recreation Park is just across the river from downtown Edmonton.*

◀ *Most schools in the country had only one room and one teacher. Some children had to walk more than 10 miles (16 km) to get to school. The teacher had to teach children of all ages and grades. One-room schools existed well into this century.*

## EDUCATION

About 60 million people are enrolled in all public (tax-supported) and private schools in the United States. More than 46 million of this total attend elementary and secondary schools. The rest attend institutions of higher education—which is everything beyond high school. Public schooling is funded and controlled at the state and local level. The federal Department of Education provides mainly guidance and some money—about 6 percent of the total cost of $372 billion each year. Federal funds also pay for special programs for the handicapped and bilingual education.

A completed high school education is important for getting a good job, but more than 30 percent of high school students leave before graduation. States decide at what age students are allowed to leave school—

**Public education in the United States takes place in more than 83,000 elementary and secondary schools, on which about $226 billion a year is spent. There are more than 3,500 private and public colleges, community and junior colleges, and universities, on which almost $150 billion a year is spent. Almost 90 percent of regular day-school students and almost 75 percent of students in higher education are in public institutions.**

*► High schools offer a course of study that allows students to prepare for college or university. Vocational courses are also offered for students who intend to get a job when they graduate from secondary school.*

Some Important Dates in the History of U.S. Education

**1635** The first secondary school in the colonies, The Boston Latin School, is opened.
**1636** Harvard College (now Harvard University) is founded near Boston.
**1647** Massachusetts passes a law that requires towns to establish public elementary and secondary schools.
**1833** Oberlin College is the first U.S. coeducational college.
**1852** Massachusetts is the first state to pass a law making school attendance compulsory.
**1901** Joliet Junior College opens in Illinois. It is the country's oldest junior college.
**1954** The U.S. Supreme Court rules that segregation by race in public schools is unconstitutional.
**1965** Congress passes the Elementary and Secondary Education Act to improve education for children from low-income families.
**1979** Congress establishes the U.S. Department of Education.

usually 15 to 16 years of age. About 2.3 million students graduate from high school annually, and more than 1 million from four-year colleges.

The curriculum—exactly what is taught—has changed greatly since the first American public schools more than 150 years ago. It was enough then to teach reading, writing, and arithmetic. The modern world calls for such subjects as computer science. And to enable the United States to compete better in the world economy, more schools are offering a wider variety of language courses, including Japanese. They are also offering courses in global studies, so that Americans can learn about other countries and cultures. At the same time, traditional nonacademic studies such as home economics and industrial arts continue to be important.

*► Here pupils from a New York City elementary school learn about their city. Field trips are an important part of education.*

◀ *On average, more than $4,000 is spent on every pupil in the United States each year. Some of this money goes toward simple items such as the dry cells needed to teach basic electricity. Computers and similar equipment cost much more.*

Some high schools even specialize in these subjects, which are also called vocational skills. These skills must keep pace with the changing machinery and technology the students must face. Another recent trend is the changing of the curriculums to reflect the contributions of non-European ethnic groups to American society.

**Boys and girls in Colonial America had very different educations. Six- and seven-year-olds would learn the alphabet at the same school. After that boys would continue their "book learning" in the hope of attending college. Girls would stay at home to be taught domestic skills such as cooking and weaving.**

## EINSTEIN, Albert

Albert Einstein (1879–1955) was one of the greatest physicists of all times. He won the 1921 Nobel Prize for physics for his work on the photoelectron effect—the release of electrons by a metal that is struck by light. Einstein was born in Germany and went to school there and in Switzerland. In 1914 he became director of the Kaiser Wilhelm Institute in Berlin. In 1933, however, the Nazis came to power in Germany, and they took away Einstein's citizenship because he was Jewish. He then joined the Institute for Advanced Study in Princeton, New Jersey. He worked there for the rest of his life and became a U.S. citizen in 1940.

Einstein is best known for his general theory of relativity, which he published in 1916. This incorporated the work of many years and explained the way space, time, motion, mass, light, and gravitation are related. His theory also states that mass and energy are two forms of the same thing. This is the basic idea behind atomic energy. During the last 25 years of his life, Einstein continued his work on the theory of relativity. Sadly, he died before he felt that his work had been completed.

▼ *Albert Einstein was a brilliant scientist but could sometimes be an "absent-minded professor." Once he was found walking up and down a street in Princeton, New Jersey, where he lived, looking puzzled. He had forgotten his address.*

# EISENHOWER, Dwight D.

Dwight D. Eisenhower
**Born:** Oct. 14, 1890, in Denison, Texas
**Education:** West Point Military Academy, New York
**Political party:** Republican
**Term of office:** 1953–1961
**Married:** 1916 to Mamie Geneva Doud
**Died:** Mar. 28, 1969, in Washington, D.C.

Dwight David ("Ike") Eisenhower (1890–1969) was elected president in 1952. Previously he had been Supreme Allied Commander during WORLD WAR II and the first Commander of the NORTH ATLANTIC TREATY ORGANIZATION (NATO) forces. His bravery, integrity, warmth, and sincerity made him enormously popular both before and after his election.

Elected on the Republican ticket, Eisenhower introduced a domestic program he called "Modern Republicanism." He introduced social welfare programs that included more social security benefits; government aid in building schools; and a new Department of Health, Education, and Welfare. In 1954 the Supreme Court ruled that racial segregation in public schools was unconstitutional. When violence broke out at some newly integrated schools in the South, Eisenhower sent troops into Little Rock, Arkansas, to enforce the law.

► *Eisenhower negotiated an end to the Korean War.*

▼ *During World War II, General Eisenhower made many of his decisions jointly with Britain's Field Marshal Montgomery.*

Eisenhower worked hard to achieve peace, and in 1953 he negotiated an end to the KOREAN WAR. But he also was firmly against communism. In 1954 he helped create the Southeast Asia Treaty Organization (SEATO) to prevent the spread of communism. In 1957 he promised military and economic aid to any Middle Eastern countries that asked for it, to help them resist Communist aggression. This became known as the Eisenhower Doctrine. The next year, he sent marines into Lebanon, after its president appealed for help. In 1961, Eisenhower broke off diplomatic relations with Cuba, which had become Communist under the dictator Fidel Castro.

## ELECTIONS

▲ *Modern voting machines have largely replaced the traditional ballots that voters marked in ink. Election results can now be known in hours rather than days.*

Many government positions at local, state, and national levels are held by people who are chosen by voters in elections. The elections are held at intervals laid down by law, which vary depending on the position.

Nationwide, presidential elections draw the most attention. They are held every four years on the first Tuesday after the first Monday in November. Presidential candidates are nominated at national party conventions. The voting is done by delegates who are chosen, usually in *primary elections*, to represent their states. The candidates for each party then campaign throughout the nation to explain what they would do if elected. Finally, all registered voters in each state cast their ballot in the national election. The results of presidential elections are decided by the ELECTORAL COLLEGE. The candidate who wins the majority of the electoral votes is declared president.

## ELECTORAL COLLEGE

The electoral college is a group of individuals who elect the president and vice president of the United States. Each state has a certain number of electors. This number equals the number of the state's congressional representatives and senators combined. The electors meet in state capitals on the first Monday after the second Wednesday in December in presidential election years. They vote for whichever candidates, presidential and vice presidential, got the most votes in their state. On January 6 (or the next day, if January 6 is a Sunday), the president of the Senate announces the winners. This never comes as a surprise because the electors usually follow their states' voting patterns. The popular vote is often closer than the electoral vote because the electors use a winner-take-all system. In the 1992 election, Bill CLINTON got 43.7 million votes and 370 electoral votes. George BUSH received 38.1 million votes but only 168 electoral votes because he won in only 17 states.

▼ *Electric power plants must operate 24 hours a day. Any time when they are off — called downtime — is expensive for the power companies.*

## ELECTRIC POWER INDUSTRY

The electric power industry in the United States produces more electricity than any other country in the world and supplies the nation with energy. Electric

▲ *T. S. Eliot used diagrams and symbols to explain some of his work to students at Princeton University.*

power is generated in large factories, called plants. About 57 percent of electric power comes from burning coal. Other sources are nuclear energy, natural gas, and hydroelectric plants. Hydroelectric power is usually produced in areas where there are few people, such as at the dams in Washington State, so long cables are used to take the electricity to big cities. Some oil is also burned to produce electricity. The demand for electricity in the United States continues to grow. Soon new ways of producing it will have to be found as many of the fossil fuels used today, such as coal and natural gas, will soon run out. Some electric companies have already started to experiment with solar and wind power to generate electricity.

Some electric companies supplying power are owned by state governments, but most (about 80 per cent) are owned by private investors.

## ELIOT, T. S.

The poet, playwright, and literary critic Thomas Stearns Eliot (1888–1965) was one of the most important writers of the 20th century. He received the 1948 Nobel Prize for literature. Eliot was born in St. Louis, Missouri, but as a young man he settled in England and became a British citizen in 1927. Eliot's poetry deals mainly with the problems of living in a purposeless, modern world. Most of his poems, including *The Waste Land* and *Four Quartets*, are not easy to read. In a lighter vein, Eliot wrote *Old Possum's Book of Practical Cats*, which was later used for the musical *Cats*.

▼ *Musicians were always loyal to "the Duke." Clarinetist Jimmy Hamilton (right), a top soloist, played with Ellington (left) for nearly 30 years.*

## ELLINGTON, Duke

Edward Kennedy ("Duke") Ellington (1899–1974) was a jazz pianist, songwriter, and bandleader. He is considered one of the most important people in the history of JAZZ. He came to public attention in the late 1920s, when his band was playing in New York City at Harlem's famous Cotton Club. His band sound was unique in music. His song, "Take the A Train," was one of the best-selling records of the 1930s. He helped other musicians by changing the lineup of his band. A number of his works were composed to highlight solo jazz musicians. But he also wrote large works, some of which were religious, intended to be performed as concerts.

## EL PASO 

El Paso, with a population of more than 515,000, is the largest city on the Mexican border. It is located on the north bank of the RIO GRANDE in the extreme west of TEXAS. More than 30 percent of the country's copper refining takes place in El Paso. Clothing manufacture and the military also provide employment. Fort Bliss, located just northeast of the city, is the headquarters of the Army Air Defense Center. El Paso was founded by the Spanish in 1659. It began to grow from 1849, when the MEXICAN WAR established the Rio Grande as the U.S.–Mexican border.

▲ *The El Paso Civic Center was built during the 1970s, when El Paso's population grew by more than 30 percent.*

## EMANCIPATION PROCLAMATION 

Many people believe that the Emancipation Proclamation, issued on January 1, 1863, freed all the slaves in the United States. But this came after the CIVIL WAR, by the Thirteenth Amendment to the Constitution.

President Abraham LINCOLN opposed slavery, but he had been elected on a platform that promised not to interfere with slavery within the slave states. His primary aim was to save the Union. He first issued the Proclamation, in rough form, just after the Union victory at Antietam, in September 1862. It declared that all the slaves in the Confederacy were free (*not* those in the loyal border slave states, whose support Lincoln badly needed). At the time, of course, Lincoln had no power over the Confederate states. But nearly 200,000 of their slaves went north as free men and joined the Union army. The Proclamation also identified the Union's cause firmly with the fight against slavery.

▼ *Ralph Waldo Emerson came from a long line of clergymen. Trained as a minister, he resigned in 1832 to become a writer and public figure.*

## EMERSON, Ralph Waldo 

Ralph Waldo Emerson (1803–1882) was one of the most important American writers of the 19th century. He is best known for his essays written on such subjects as "Politics," "Friendship," and "Self-Reliance." These reveal Emerson's belief in a divine spirit within humans. His essay *Nature* affirms the power of nature to reveal spiritual truths (a philosophy known as *transcendentalism*). Many of Emerson's beliefs were shared by other American writers of the time such as Henry David THOREAU. Emerson also wrote poetry.

## ENDANGERED ANIMALS AND PLANTS

These are species, or types, of animals and plants that will soon become extinct (die out) unless they are protected. Most are at risk because of people. Animals are often hunted and plants are collected so much that they disappear forever. More animals are trapped in the United States than in any country in the world except the Soviet Union.

Many species have been threatened because the growth of cities, agriculture, and industry has destroyed their *habitat* (the place where animals live naturally). POLLUTION has affected many species too. Pesticides in rivers collect in the bodies of fish, which are then eaten by birds. The pesticides make the birds' eggs break too easily. This is one reason why the osprey and southern bald EAGLE are endangered.

Some Endangered U.S. Animals and Plants

**Mammals**
Ocelot
Southern sea otter
Red wolf
Grizzly bear

**Birds**
California condor
Whooping crane
Ivory-billed woodpecker

**Reptiles and Fish**
American crocodile
Red-bellied turtle
Gila trout

**Plants**
Arizona hedgehog cactus
Dwarf bear poppy
Antioch Dunes evening primrose

► *Some native plants, such as the Knowlton's cactus, have become endangered as more people move to the southwestern states.*

Federal and state laws protect wild animals and plants that are listed as endangered. They cannot be hunted, collected, bought or sold, or threatened in any way. Their habitats are protected in NATIONAL PARKS and wildlife refuges and by government controls over land use and pollution. Sometimes animals that are nearly extinct, such as the California CONDOR, are captured to be bred in captivity so that possibly one day they can be returned to the wild.

▼ *The brown pelican can hold twice its body weight in its bill pouch. Pollution in the Gulf of Mexico threatens its fishing grounds.*

## ENVIRONMENTAL PROTECTION

The environment is the surroundings in which people, animals, and plants live. Environmental protection means keeping our environment safe for the future.

In North America many measures are being taken to protect the environment. POLLUTION is controlled by

◀ *More than 35,000 tons of toxic petroleum were released in 1989 when the* Exxon Valdez *ran aground off the coast of Alaska. Environmental disasters such as this destroy much wildlife. Seabirds die when their feathers are soaked with oil.*

law, and CONSERVATION of NATURAL RESOURCES is encouraged. However, many people believe that more could be done.

ENDANGERED ANIMALS are protected by law. These are the types of animals that have been hunted so much by people that they are in danger of disappearing forever. NATIONAL PARKS and nature reserves protect wildlife in its natural environment. Plants and trees that are at risk are protected in much the same way.

The countries of the world cooperate in protecting the environment. A good example is the proposed Bering Land Bridge National Preserve, in the Bering Strait between Alaska and Siberia. This national park and wilderness preserve will be managed by the United States and the Soviet Union together.

**Some Important Dates in the History of U.S. Environmental Protection**

1872 Yellowstone National Park, the first national park in the world, is established.
1899 The first important pollution law is passed making it illegal to dump any liquid waste (except from sewers) into navigable waters. This law was not enforced.
1903 Pelican Island, Florida, becomes the first federal wildlife refuge.
1916 Congress sets up the National Park Service.
1933 The Civilian Conservation Corps is set up to plant trees and perform other conservation tasks.
1966 The National Wildlife Refuge System comes into being.
1970 The Environmental Protection Agency is set up to guard against pollution.
1972 DDT is banned from general use as a pesticide because it is discovered that it poisons the food chain.
1973 The Endangered Species Act provides more protection for threatened animals and plants.
1990 The U.S. and 69 other countries agree to phase out CFCs (chlorofluorocarbons) by the year 2000. CFCs are one of the major causes of the destruction of the ozone layer.

## EPISCOPALIANS

Episcopalians are members of the Episcopal Church, which is part of the worldwide Anglican Communion. Before the American REVOLUTION, Episcopalians belonged to the Church of England. The Revolution severed the ties between the Church in the United States and the Church of England. There are three Episcopal churches. The largest, the Episcopal Church, has almost 2.5 million members. The other two churches are very small and together have only about 12,000 members between them. Episcopalians are Protestant. Their services are often based on those that were developed in the Church of England.

▲ *Leif Ericsson's accounts of a new land called Vinland seem to describe the east coast of North America.*

**According to old Icelandic stories called *sagas*, Leif Ericsson and his men put ashore on a barren tableland of flat rocks backed by icy mountains. They then sailed south and finally landed on a shore where the land was green with trees and sweet "grapes." Ericsson named this place Vinland (Wineland), and they spent the winter there. The "grapes," which were probably cranberries or gooseberries, were used to make wine.**

## ERICSSON, Leif

Christopher COLUMBUS is hailed as the man whose explorations led to the permanent settlement of North America. But he was not the first European to reach the Americas. That achievement probably belongs to Leif Ericsson (about A.D. 980–1025), a Norseman, or Viking, originally from Iceland. Around the year A.D. 1000, he sailed west from Greenland with 35 men in search of a land said to have been seen by another Norseman. No one is quite sure where Ericsson made landings. Some say northern Newfoundland, where remains of a Norse settlement have been found. But Ericsson and his men are known to have spent the winter in this new land before returning to Greenland.

## ERIE CANAL

The Erie Canal stands as one of the greatest engineering and construction feats in U.S. history. It was built between 1817 and 1825 to provide a waterway from the

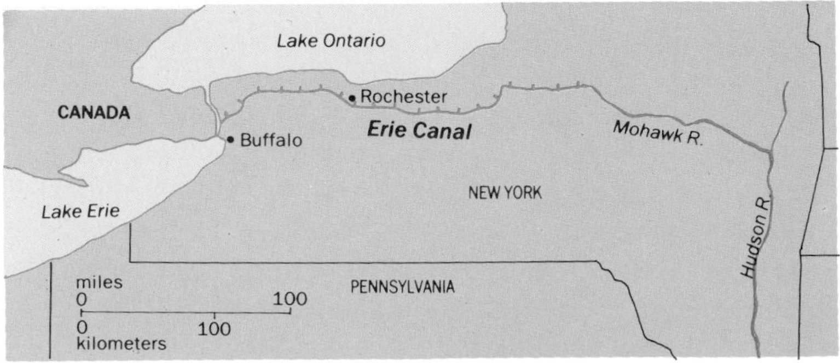


► *By providing a link with the Great Lakes and the Midwest, the Erie Canal made New York City the chief port of the U.S. east coast.*

East to the GREAT LAKES. The canal runs 363 miles (585 km) from Albany on the HUDSON RIVER to Buffalo on Lake Erie. The original canal was 40 feet (12 m) wide and 4 feet (1.2 m) deep. This narrow and shallow design was chosen so that wide, flat-bottomed barges could be drawn by horses on either side of the canal. The $7 million cost to build the canal was quickly paid back by the canal fees paid by barges. Today road and rail traffic have taken over from the canal, but it remains open. It is part of the New York State Barge Canal system.

**The Erie Canal remains an active commercial waterway. More than 5 million tons of cargo are still shipped through the canal each year.**

## ERIE, LAKE *See* Great Lakes

## ESKIMOS

The Eskimos are not related to the American Indians. They are descendants of people who crossed the BERING STRAIT and spread across the Arctic and subarctic regions of North America. They did this between 5,500 and 3,000 years ago. "Eskimo" is an Algonquian Indian name that means "raw meat eaters." Eskimos prefer the name *Inuit* ("the people").

▲ *Eskimo girls make the most of the short summer months in Inuit Kangirsuk, northern Quebec.*

◀ *Fewer and fewer Eskimos live in the traditional way, ice fishing and hunting according to the season.*

There are a number of different groups of Eskimos within three main large groups: the Alaskan, the Central, and the Greenland Eskimos. The Eskimos have a hunting and fishing style of life that is suited to their cold environment. They can make houses, called igloos, very quickly out of the ice and snow. For hunting in snow they use snowmobiles or special sleds. And for traveling on the rivers they use kayaks (completely covered except for a hole where the rider sits) and umiaks (larger open boats). Today many Eskimos live in settlements with buildings made of wood.

**Although some Eskimos still live by hunting and trapping, most Canadian and Alaskan Eskimos now live in towns and settlements. The exploitation of oil and natural gas in northern areas has vitally changed their way of life, not always for the better. However, the arts and handicrafts of the Eskimos are becoming more widely known.**

► *Ethnic differences seem unimportant when children get to know each other at school.*

## ETHNIC GROUPS

An ethnic group is any group of people who have certain things in common that set them apart from the larger society in which they live. For example, these people, or their ancestors, might have come from the same country. Or they may speak the same language, be of the same race, or practice the same religion.

The United States is especially rich in the number of different ethnic groups that make up its population. The people of American ethnic groups have come from almost every other country in the world.

People in the same ethnic group often tend to live in the same areas. This gives them a sense of belonging in their new land. Others try to become part of the larger society. But even when they do this, they like to hold on to their ethnic identity in some way, so that they can continue to share their common heritage. Special groups teach and preserve the cultural legacy of different ethnic groups. American life is rich in festivals and other events that reflect this ethnic variety.

There are many reasons why people of different ethnic groups have migrated to the United States. They have come to find religious freedom, to escape from wars, and to build better lives for themselves and their families. BLACK AMERICANS, however, were forced to come here—as slaves. And Native Americans—the American INDIANS, ESKIMOS, and ALEUTS—were here long before the Europeans. Ethnic groups have become a strong presence in all areas of American society.

Largest Ethnic Groups in the U.S. (by ancestral region and country)

**American**
American Indian

**African**
Black Americans

**European**
Germans
Irish
English
Italians
French
Polish
Scotch-Irish

**Asians**
Chinese
Filipinos
Japanese
Indians
Koreans
Vietnamese
Turks

**Latin Americans**
Mexicans
Puerto Ricans
Cubans
Dominicans
Colombians
Haitians

## EVERETT, Edward

Edward Everett (1794–1865) was an important politician and an outstanding orator in the 1800s. Between 1825 and 1854 he had a distinguished career as a congressman, governor of Massachusetts, U.S. minister to Great Britain, secretary of state under President Millard FILLMORE, and Massachusetts senator. He was also president of Harvard College. Everett delivered a brilliant speech at Gettysburg the day that Abraham LINCOLN made his famous GETTYSBURG ADDRESS.

**Edward Everett gave his speech at Gettysburg immediately before Abraham Lincoln delivered his famous Gettysburg Address. Everett was so amazed at Lincoln's ability to say so much in so few words that he declared then and there that Lincoln's speech would live for generations, while his own would be forgotten.**

## EVERGLADES

The Everglades is a huge swamp that covers 4,000 square miles (10,000 km$^2$) of southern FLORIDA. Much of it consists of glades, or prairies of sawgrass, a grass-like plant. The swampy water flows very slowly from Lake Okeechobee in the north to Florida Bay in the south. Many low islands, or hammocks, are covered with mangroves and other tropical trees. The animal life includes snakes, turtles, alligators, and many kinds of mammals and birds. The northern part of the Everglades has been drained and is used for farming. The Everglades National Park is in the southern part.

▼ *The Florida Everglades extend from Lake Okeechobee south to the Florida Keys.*

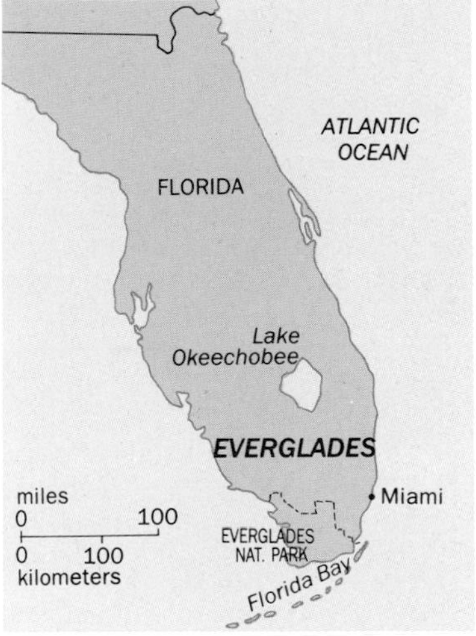


◀ *The anhinga, a bird of prey related to the cormorant, is native to the sluggish waters of the Everglades. It feeds on frogs, small fish, and even baby alligators.*

# EXPLORATION OF NORTH AMERICA

The first Europeans to explore North America were probably the Vikings. Around the year 1000, the Viking Leif Ericsson probably started a colony on the northern tip of Newfoundland, in an area called Vinland.

It was the Spanish, however, who began intensive exploration of the Americas at the beginning of the 1500s. They were searching mainly for gold and for a short route to the Far East. Some of them, such as Hernando De Soto and Ponce De Leon, explored Florida; others, including Francisco Coronado, traveled through Mexico into what is now the southwestern United States.

**The earliest map showing the New World was drawn in 1500 by the Spanish explorer Juan de la Cosa who sailed with Christopher Columbus on his second voyage in 1493. In 1507, Martin Waldseemuller, a German mapmaker, drew the first map on which the word America appeared. He named it after the explorer Amerigo Vespucci.**

◀ *This map, drawn in Antwerp in 1570, was one of the first guides to the New World.*

French exploration was centered mainly in the North, and the main attraction was the fur trade. French-Canadian traders and trappers had journeyed far into the Great Lakes region by the early 1600s. Later in the century the French explored the whole length of the Mississippi River and founded settlements in that region. Later explorers, thinking they were in unchartered territory, would often find French-Canadian fur trappers already trading there.

British victory in the French and Indian War (1755–1763) opened up the land west of the Appalachian Mountains to exploration and settlement by its colonists. Thus began a push westward that was to continue for the next hundred years or so.

A great stimulus to American exploration was the Louisiana Purchase in 1803, which doubled the size of the United States. Lewis and Clark and Zebulon Pike led expeditions which opened up the West. And in the 1840s, John Charles Fremont explored the Rocky Mountains and pushed into California and Oregon.

▼ *Lewis and Clark used their Shoshoni interpreter, Sacagawea, to speak to the Indians they met on their mission.*

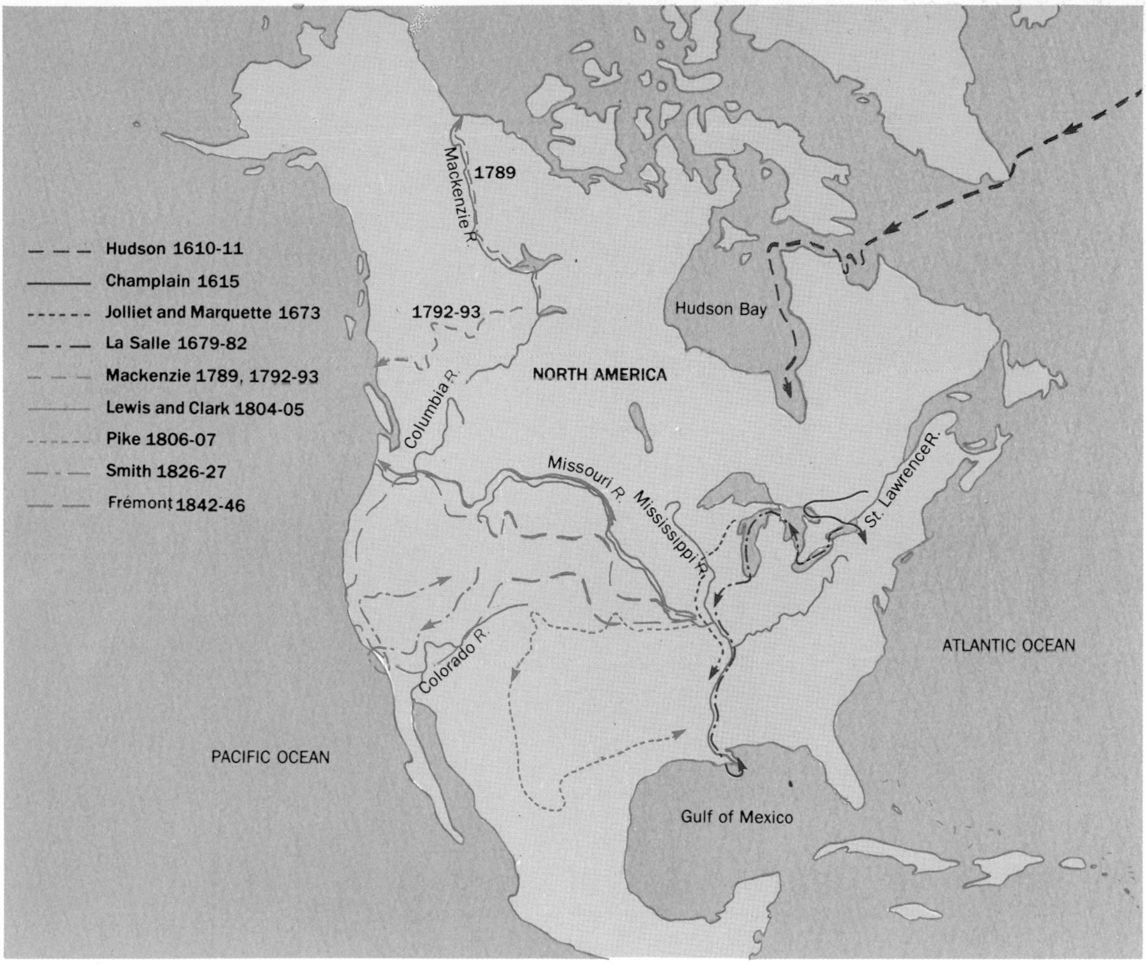

Hudson 1610-11
Champlain 1615
Jolliet and Marquette 1673
La Salle 1679-82
Mackenzie 1789, 1792-93
Lewis and Clark 1804-05
Pike 1806-07
Smith 1826-27
Frémont 1842-46

Mackenzie R.
1789
1792-93
Hudson Bay
NORTH AMERICA
Columbia R.
Missouri R.
Mississippi R.
St. Lawrence R.
Colorado R.
ATLANTIC OCEAN
PACIFIC OCEAN
Gulf of Mexico

▲ *Some of the exploration routes that opened up the North American interior.*

## A Chronology of North American Exploration

**1535** Jacques Cartier sails up the St. Lawrence River.
**1539–1542** Hernando de Soto explores the Southeast and discovers the Mississippi River.
**1603–1616** Samuel de Champlain explores the eastern coast of North America. He sails up the St. Lawrence River as far west as Lake Huron.
**1609–1611** Henry Hudson explores Hudson Bay, the Hudson River, and Hudson Strait.
**1673** Jacques Marquette and Louis Jolliet explore the area of the northern Mississippi river.
**1679–1682** Sieur de la Salle and Henri de Tonti explore the Great Lakes and follow the Mississippi to the Gulf of Mexico.
**1789–1793** Sir Alexander Mackenzie follows the Mackenzie River to the Arctic Ocean and explores western Canada.
**1804–1806** Meriwether Lewis and William Clark cross the Rocky Mountains and reach the Pacific Ocean.
**1805–1807** Zebulon Pike explores the Midwest, Rocky Mountain region, and the Southwest.
**1842–1846** John Charles Fremont explores the West.

▼ *Zebulon Pike's explorations stimulated American settlement in the Southwest.*

## FAIRBANKS, Douglas

Douglas Fairbanks (1883–1939) was a leading motion picture actor and producer from the silent screen era. Romantic and athletic, Fairbanks was well suited to the swashbuckling leading men he portrayed. His first motion picture was *The Lamb* (1915). In 1919, Fairbanks founded the United Artists Studio with Mary PICKFORD (his wife from 1920–1935), Charlie CHAPLIN, and the director D. W. Griffith. Douglas Fairbanks, Jr., his son by his first wife, played similar roles in 1930s and 1940s.

► *Douglas Fairbanks never had fencing lessons, but he became famous by portraying masters of swordplay.*

▼ *During the Civil War, Admiral Farragut got the nickname "Old Salamander" for navigating ships past the forts at New Orleans and Mobile.*

## FARRAGUT, David

David Farragut (1801–1870) was an admiral in the U.S. Navy. He fought in the WAR OF 1812 and the MEXICAN WAR (1846–1848). During the CIVIL WAR he fought for the Union side even though he came from the South. In 1862 he sailed his ships past Confederate fortifications to capture New Orleans. He then sailed up the Mississippi River to attack the Confederate forces at Vicksburg, Mississippi. In 1864, Farragut led a fleet into Mobile Bay, Alabama, forcing that Confederate port to close down. During the battle, an officer spotted some mines, which were then called torpedoes. Farragut's defiant cry, "Damn the torpedoes! Full speed ahead!" made him a hero of the Union navy.

## FASHION

Until well into the 20th century, the United States looked to the designers of Paris for the fashionable "look" of the year. But even in the 1800s there were some purely American ideas that set popular trends. Bloomers, the loose, gathered pants worn under short skirts, were named after the social reformer Amelia Bloomer. In the 1890s the illustrator Charles Dana Gibson created a distinctive female look. From 1890 to about 1910, women everywhere copied the "Gibson Girl" look with its long neckline and upswept hair.

The single biggest contribution of the United States has been not a style, but a fabric—denim. Levi Strauss first created a garment using denim and copper studs in 1850. This became widely used by workers who needed tough clothing, such as farmers and cowboys. But a clothing revolution started in the 1960s that carried on into the 1980s. Denim became high fashion. It fitted in well with the new "unisex" look. It was used for pants, jumpsuits, jackets, dresses, suits, and hats. And denim was not just American; it was world fashion.

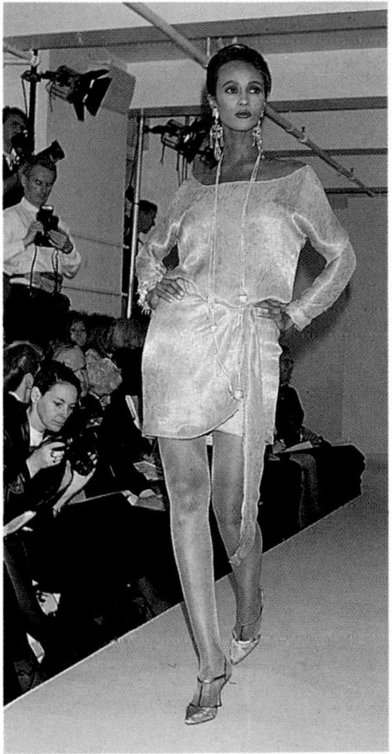

▲ *Fashion models display the works of leading designers such as Donna Karan at each spring's fashion shows.*

**Long pants for men arrived in the United States around the year 1820. The fashion had begun with the peasants who came to power during the French Revolution. The first wearers of long pants in the United States were seen as "revolutionary" as a result.**

◄ *Over the past 200 years, everyday American fashions for men and women have become simpler. Styles were often based on what was fashionable in Europe at the time. Gradually American fashion developed its own characteristics.*

▲ *Denim clothes are a popular choice for all ages. It is durable, comfortable, and fashionable.*

Americans like to be comfortable in their clothing, whether it is for business, entertaining, or relaxing. The clothing designs of Halston, Oscar de la Renta, and Anne Klein dominated in the 1960s and 1970s. Today the strong styles of Calvin Klein, Ralph Lauren, Donna Karan, and Norma Kamali influence U.S. fashion.

## FATHERS OF CONFEDERATION

The Fathers of Confederation were the "founding fathers" of Canada. By the early 1860s, the British colonies in Canada had been given a large measure of self-government. But some of their leaders, including John MACDONALD, of Upper Canada (Ontario), and George Etienne Cartier, of Lower Canada (Quebec), felt that the colonies would be stronger if they were confederated, or united.

In September 1864, 23 representatives from Upper and Lower Canada, Nova Scotia, New Brunswick, Newfoundland, and Prince Edward Island (P.E.I.) met in Charlottetown, P.E.I. They agreed to confederation. The following month they met again in Quebec City and drew up proposals for the new government. The British government favored the plan, and on July 1, 1867, Parliament passed the BRITISH NORTH AMERICA ACT, creating the Dominion of Canada.

▼ *The agreements reached by the Fathers of Confederation were legally binding in Canada until the Constitution Act replaced them in 1982.*

## FAULKNER, William 

William Faulkner (1897–1962) was a famous writer. He was born in New Albany, Mississippi, and spent most of his life in that state. He wrote short stories and novels. His fame stems from the novels that were set in the imaginary Yoknapatawpha County (based on Oxford, Mississippi, where he lived). In these novels, Faulkner dealt with the values and morals of southern society. He wrote about race and prejudice, crime and violence, love and concern, honor and pride. Faulkner won the Nobel Prize for literature in 1949 and the Pulitzer Prize in 1955 and 1963. *The Sound and the Fury*, *The Reivers*, *Absalom, Absalom!*, and *Go Down, Moses* are among his greatest works. He also wrote many film screenplays.

▲ *William Faulkner came from a wealthy background. Many family friends were shocked by the controversial themes of his novels and short stories.*

## FEDERAL BUREAU OF INVESTIGATION 

The Federal Bureau of Investigation (FBI) is the chief law-enforcement arm of the United States Department of Justice. Its 9,600 special agents investigate bank robberies, hijackings, kidnappings, and other federal crimes. They also work closely with state law-enforcement agencies. Other FBI duties include tracking organized crime gangs such as the Mafia and investigating people it thinks are a risk to the country's security. In the past, the FBI has tracked down many enemy agents operating within the United States. The FBI also investigates drug dealing, terrorism, and white collar crime such as financial fraud.

The FBI was founded in 1908, though it got its name only in 1932. Its headquarters are in Washington, D.C., and its director is appointed by the president.

▼ *FBI agents wear a badge that features the American eagle and the scales and sword of justice.*

## FEDERALISTS 

The Federalists were those people who vigorously supported the adoption of the new Constitution, with its federal form of government. They included Alexander HAMILTON, James MADISON, and John JAY. During George WASHINGTON's government, a split occurred between those who believed in a strong central government and those who believed that the states and the individual should retain as many rights as possible. Those who believed in a strong federal government formed the Federalist Party under Alexander Hamilton.

**_The Federalist_ is the title given to 85 essays published in 1787–1788 in various New York newspapers to convince voters to support ratification of the new Constitution of the United States. These essays were published in book form in 1788. It is believed that Alexander Hamilton wrote 51 of the essays, Madison 29, and John Jay 5. The essays are still a classic example of an analysis of federalism and free government.**

It was the first political party in the United States. Among the policies it favored were the creation of a central bank, a system of tariffs and excise (indirect) taxes, and neutrality in the war between Britain and France that broke out in 1793. The Federalists achieved the election of John ADAMS in 1796, but by 1800 they had been overtaken by the new Democratic-Republican (later DEMOCRATIC) Party, led by Thomas JEFFERSON. By 1815, the Federalist Party had disintegrated. But the Federalists had done a great deal to strengthen the central government of the United States and give it its present form.

## FEDERAL RESERVE *See* Banking

## FEDERAL TRADE COMMISSION *See* Trade

## FERBER, Edna

Edna Ferber (1885–1968) was a famous writer. She was born in Kalamazoo, Michigan, and raised in Wisconsin. She started work as a journalist when she was 17, but soon started writing successful novels and plays. These were largely about American life in the 19th century. Ferber claimed that her books were intended as social criticisms as well as entertainment. She won the Pulitzer Prize for fiction in 1925 for *So Big*. A number of her books, including *Cimarron*, *Giant*, *Ice Palace*, and *Show Boat*, were made into movies. She wrote a number of plays with George S. Kaufman. Some of these, such as *Dinner at Eight* and *Stage Door* were also made into films.

▼ *James Dean starred in the 1956 movie version of* Giant, *Edna Ferber's tale of 20th-century Texas.*

## FERMI, Enrico

In 1934, Enrico Fermi (1901–1954) became the first person to split the atom. At that time, however, he did not know just what he had done. The process of splitting an atom is called *nuclear fission.* Born in Italy, Fermi settled in the United States in 1938. That same year he was awarded the Nobel Prize for physics for his work in the United States. In 1939, Fermi became a professor of physics at Columbia University, but he moved to the University of Chicago in 1942. That same year he produced a nuclear chain reaction. This led to both the atomic bomb—which Fermi helped develop during World War II—and nuclear power plants. After World War II, Fermi began research on high-energy particles. The Fermi National Accelerator Laboratory, in Batavia, Illinois, is named after him. So, too, is fermium, an artificially made radioactive element.

**The chemical element fermium was named after Enrico Fermi. It was first discovered in the debris from the first H-bomb explosion. It is a radioactive element and has to be made artificially. The total amount of fermium that has been made since it was discovered in 1952 is less than one-millionth of a gram.**

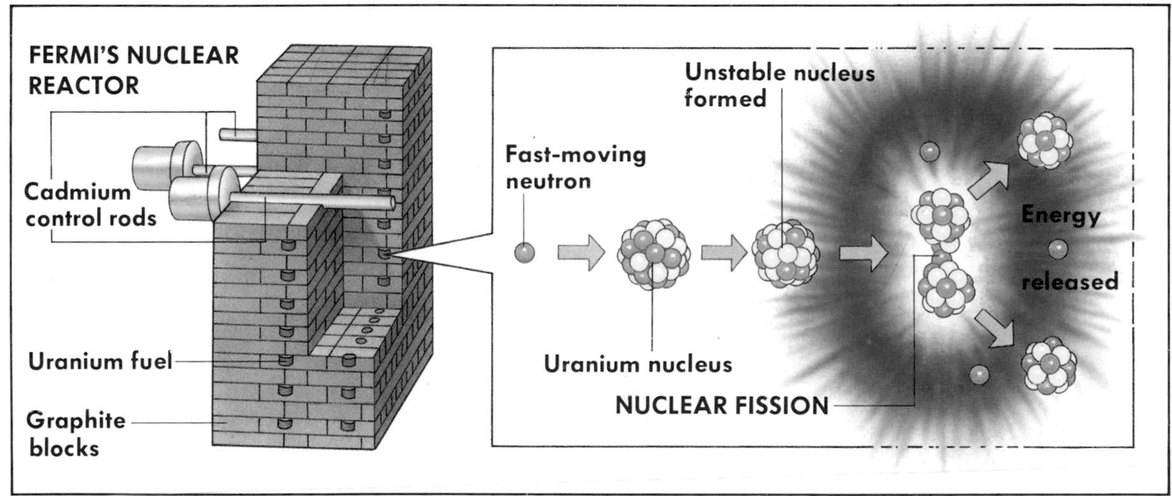


▲ *Nuclear fission provides the energy for both nuclear power and atomic weapons. A neutron splits the nucleus of a uranium atom, giving off energy and releasing more neutrons. Each neutron can go on to split another uranium nucleus, which in turn gives off more heat and releases more neutrons in a chain reaction.*

## FIELD, Marshall

Marshall Field (1834–1906) was a U.S. businessman who founded the world-famous Chicago department store Marshall Field and Company. He introduced sales methods, such as marking prices on goods and allowing customers to exchange merchandise if they were dissatisfied. On his death, Field left money to create Chicago's Field Museum of Natural History, and he provided land for the new University of Chicago. Field's grandson, Marshall Field III, set up the family publishing business, which included the *Chicago Sun-Times.* The Field Corporation was established by Marshall Field V.

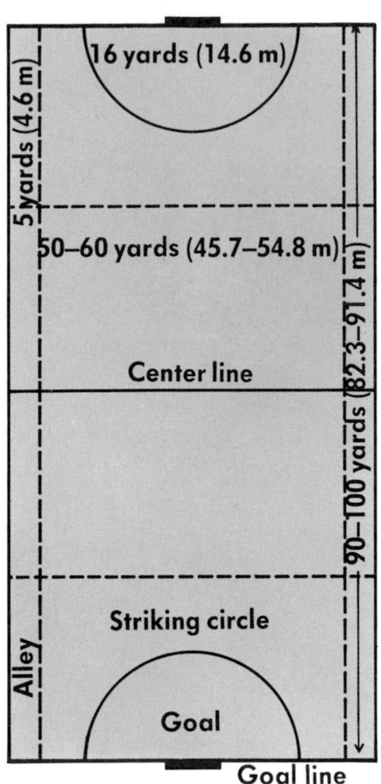


▲ *Field hockey teams have 11 members. Goals can only be scored from within the striking circle and are worth one point.*

## FIELD HOCKEY

Field hockey is a team sport. In the United States, it is usually played by girls. Each team tries to knock a ball into the opposing team's goal by using a stick with a curved end. Early in the 20th century the game was brought to the United States from Great Britain by Constance Applebee. The United States Field Hockey Association (for women) and the Field Hockey Association of America (for men) were formed in the 1920s.

Men and women play according to the same rules. Men first played field hockey in the Olympics in 1908; women have played in the Olympics only since 1980.

## FIELDS, W. C.

W. C. Fields (1879–1946) was one of the great movie comedians. His real name was William Claude Dukenfield. Fields's strange way of speaking out of the side of his mouth is widely imitated by comedians even today. Fields was born in Philadelphia. When asked his opinion of things he found boring, he would say, "On the whole, I'd rather be in Philadelphia." This line became one of his trademarks. He was also known for his strong dislike for children and animals and made this part of his comic roles. *My Little Chickadee* and *The Bank Dick* are two of his best-known films. He also wrote movie scripts using made-up names such as Mahatma Kane Jeeves and Otis T. Cricklecobis.

**W. C. Fields ran away from home at the age of 11 and within three years had begun a stage juggling act. He was well known for his tricks with a corkscrew-shaped billiard cue!**

► *W. C. Fields and Mae West teamed up in* My Little Chickadee, *one of the most successful movies of 1940.*

## FILLMORE, Millard

Millard Fillmore was the 13th president of the United States. He became president in 1850, when the issue of slavery was dividing the country. Fillmore had been elected vice president on the Whig ticket with Zachary TAYLOR. When Taylor died in office, Fillmore became president. At that time, the Compromise of 1850 was being debated in Congress. This concerned whether slavery should be allowed in the lands won from Mexico in the MEXICAN WAR (1846–1848).

Even though he did not approve of slavery, Fillmore was in favor of the compromise. He felt slavery had to be permitted until it could be abolished without leading to civil war. He got the compromise passed very quickly. California was admitted to the Union as a free state (in which slavery was against the law), and the slave trade was abolished in Washington, D.C. The new territories of New Mexico and Utah were created; they both banned slavery. The boundary of Texas was also settled.

▼ *Slavery was the subject of fierce Senate debates in the late 1840s. As vice president, Millard Fillmore was also president of the Senate at that time.*

The other main section of the compromise was the Fugitive Slave Law. Under this law, people could be jailed or fined if they helped runaway slaves. Also, runaway slaves were to be returned to their owners without trial. The compromise postponed the Civil War by about ten years. But Fillmore's strict enforcement of the Fugitive Slave Law made him very unpopular in the North, where the ABOLITIONIST movement was strong.

Fillmore's major achievement was opening up Japanese ports to U.S. trade. In 1853 he sent Commodore Matthew PERRY and a U.S. fleet on this historic mission to negotiate trading terms with Japan.

Millard Fillmore
**Born:** January 7, 1800, in Locke, New York
**Education:** Received little formal education; legal training
**Political party:** Whig
**Term of office:** 1850–1853
**Married:** 1826 to Abigail Powers
**Died:** March 8, 1874, in Buffalo, New York

► *These Los Angeles fire fighters wear helmets, goggles, gloves, and waterproof suits. This special equipment helps protect them from smoke, flames, and falling debris.*

The Worst Fires in U.S. History

**1871** Chicago Fire: 17,450 buildings destroyed; 250 dead
**1876** Brooklyn, New York: 295 dead
**1894** Minnesota forest fire: 6 towns destroyed; 413 dead
**1900** Hoboken, New Jersey: 326 dead
**1903** Chicago: 602 dead
**1918** Minnesota forest fire: 400 dead
**1930** Columbus, Ohio: 320 dead
**1942** Boston: 491 dead

## FIRE FIGHTING

In 1679, Boston became the first city in the colonies to set up a paid group to fight fires. Today there are tens of thousands of fire-fighting companies all over the country. Fire fighters have to be prepared to deal with fires in many different and difficult circumstances—in cities and towns, in the country, and in forests. Some fire departments have paid crews; others are staffed by volunteers. (Women were first accepted as paid fire fighters in the 1970s.) They receive special training, including first aid.

Today fire departments spend much time on preven-

▼ *Chemicals dumped by air tankers help check the progress of a forest fire in California's Sierra Nevada mountains. Each year about 3 million acres (1.3 million ha) of forest are destroyed by fire.*

tion and education—trying to prevent fires from happening in the first place. They have inspectors who regularly check public buildings to make sure there are no fire hazards. Fire fighters also speak to public groups. They warn them of the danger of fire and tell them how they can prevent it. There are clear guidelines for behavior in case of a fire—what to do and how to get out of the building as quickly as possible. Schools have regular fire drills so pupils will know how to cope in a real emergency.

## FIRESTONE, Harvey

Harvey Firestone (1868–1938) was a businessman and manufacturer. Firestone was active in the early days of the automobile industry. Born in Ohio, he set up the Firestone Tire and Rubber Company in Akron, Ohio, in 1900. Early in his life Firestone saw how useful rubber could be. He devoted most of his life to working with this substance—not only making tires, but also improving the rubber and discovering new uses. As rubber began to be used more widely, he and Henry FORD carried out research to find an artificially made substitute that would be as good.

▲ *The first tires made by the Firestone Tire and Rubber Company were solid. The company pioneered later developments, such as tubeless and radial tires.*

## FISH

Fish are *vertebrates*, or animals with backbones, that live in the water. Every fish lives in the region that suits it best. About two thirds of all species of fish live in salt water, and one third in fresh water.

North America is rich in freshwater species of fish. Some of the freshwater fish, such as minnows and trout, prefer fast-flowing streams. Others, including carp and catfish, do better in warm, muddy rivers. Still others, such as bluegills, lake trout, white perch, and whitefish, live in lakes. Some fish are found in lakes, rivers, *and* streams. These include black bullheads, largemouth bass, muskellunge, northern pike, rainbow trout, and yellow perch.

Many fish migrate from one area to another. Some trout leave their lakes to spawn (lay eggs) in rivers. Many types of alewives, salmon, and white sturgeon swim from salt water to fresh water to spawn. The North American eel migrates in the other direction. It lives in fresh water and spawns in salt water.

### Some Unusual Fish

**Atlantic croakers** make croaking noises (like frogs) at dawn and dusk.
**Catfish**, like other bottom-dwelling fish, use feelers to search for food.
**Flying fish** don't really fly; they glide, using their long, stiff fins as wings.
**Goose fish** can open their mouths wide enough to swallow some seabirds.
**Pilot fish** swim alongside sharks and feed on their leftovers.
**Porcupine fish** puff up their spiny skin like balloons when they are threatened or attacked.

► *Salmon brave waterfalls and hungry bears on their way upstream to spawn.*

▼ *Some freshwater fish, such as the walleye perch and largemouth bass, are common throughout North America. Others thrive in special environments: the northern pike in cold northern lakes and the coho salmon along the Pacific northwest coast.*

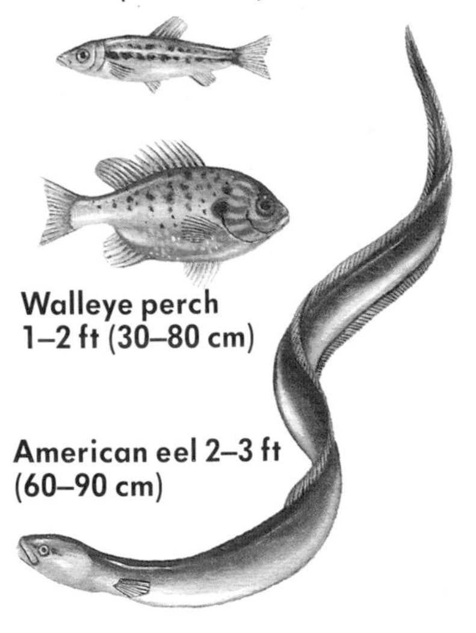


Some saltwater fish live only along the coasts and are referred to as coastal fish. Others live away from the coast, at various depths, and are known as oceanic fish. As with freshwater fish, certain saltwater fish migrate. For example, mackerel and many types of haddock migrate from coastal waters to deeper waters.

## FISHING INDUSTRY

The United States fishing industry is involved in catching fish and shellfish so that they can be processed into food. The industry's catch in U.S. waters totaled 7.2 billion pounds in 1988 and was valued at $3.5 billion. About 360,000 people are employed by the industry. Of these, about 250,000 are fishermen who work on about 125,000 ships and boats.

Commercial fishing takes place off the eastern, southern, and western coasts and in the Great Lakes. Alaska is the leading fishing state, followed by Louisi-

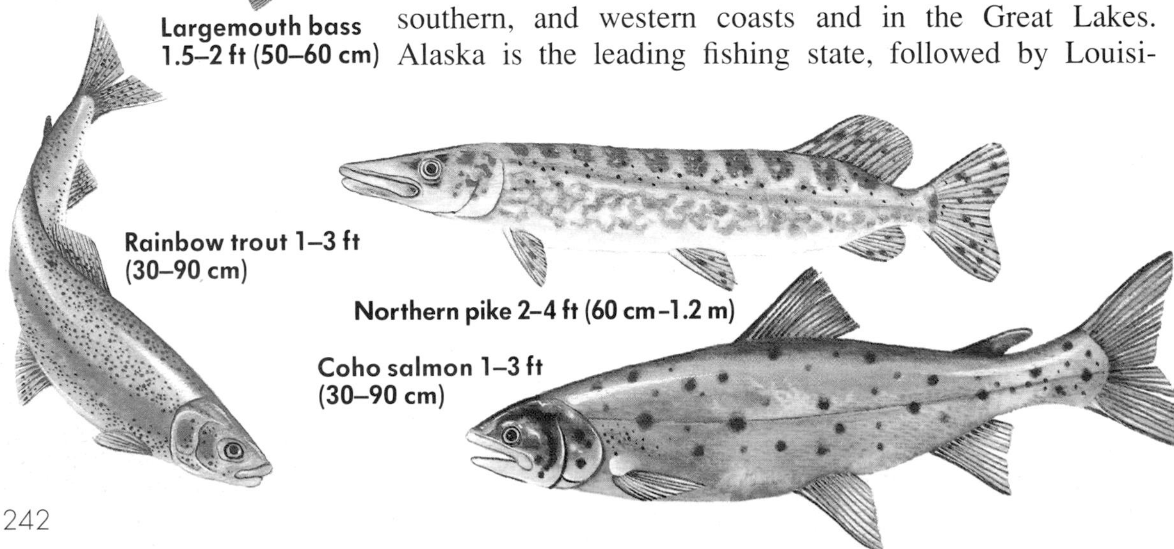

◀ *This New England fishing vessel has used sonar to locate a school of butterfish. U.S. fishermen have had exclusive fishing rights to waters up to 200 miles (320 km) off the coast since 1977.*

ana and Virginia. In quantity, the most important fish caught is menhaden. In terms of value, however, salmon is the most important fish. Shrimp and crabs are the most valuable shellfish caught. Water pollution and overfishing are threats to the future of the industry. As a result, there are now restrictions on fishing in U.S. waters.

Fish and shellfish for human consumption are sold fresh, frozen, or canned. Only half the catch is eaten by people. Menhaden, for example, is used for its oils or as fertilizer or animal feed. And only half the fish eaten by Americans comes from the U.S. fishing fleet. The other half is imported.

Most Important Commercial Fish

1. Sockeye salmon
2. Halibut
3. Chinook salmon
4. Gulf menhaden
5. Sablefish
6. Pink salmon
7. Silver salmon
8. Yellowfin tuna
9. Pacific herring
10. Alaska pollock

## FITZGERALD, F. Scott

F. Scott Fitzgerald (1896–1940) was a novelist and short-story writer. He wrote about the United States in the 1920s. Fitzgerald called this period the "Jazz Age." Others called it the "Roaring Twenties." It was a time of wild parties, drinking, and seemingly glamorous society. It was a time when wealthy people looked for excitement to ease the boredom in their lives. Fitzgerald wrote about these people in such books as *The Beautiful and Damned* and *The Great Gatsby*. In fact, he and his wife Zelda lived their own lives like the characters in his books. But they, like other people, and like some of his fictional characters, found that a life of pleasure-seeking could be very empty. His wife became mentally ill, and he became an alcoholic. Fitzgerald's last novel, *The Last Tycoon*, was about Hollywood. It was published in 1941, the year after he died.

▼ *F. Scott Fitzgerald once observed that "the rich are different." But he later learned that money alone could not make people happy.*

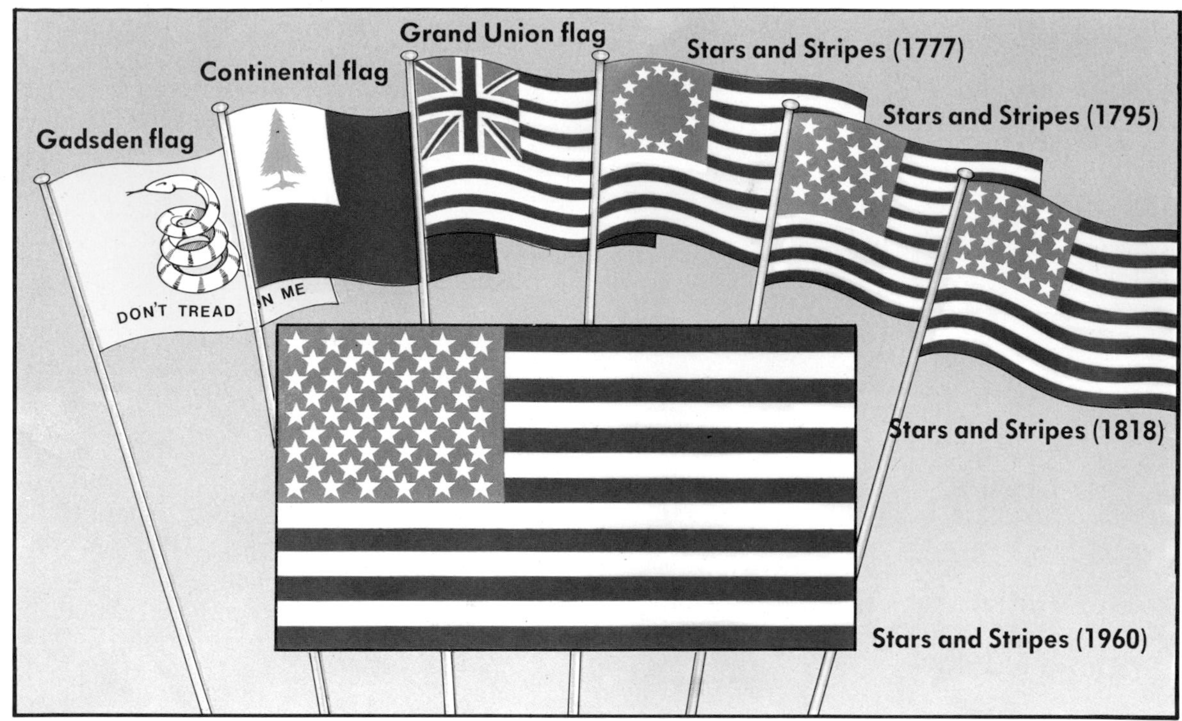


▲ *Rattlesnake and pine tree symbols on the first American flags were signs of anger and strength. The stripes, symbols of the original 13 colonies, shared space with the British Union flag on the first national flag. In 1777 the Continental Congress replaced this flag with the first version of the Stars and Stripes.*

**The American flag that inspired Francis Scott Key to write *The Star-Spangled Banner* had 15 stripes and 15 stars. Vermont and Kentucky had just joined the Union, so two stars and two stripes had been added to the original 13. Altogether the Stars and Stripes has been through 27 different versions.**

## FLAG

Popularly known as the "Stars and Stripes" or "Old Glory," the flag of the United States has changed many times, but the basic elements have remained the same.

In June 1777, after the DECLARATION OF INDEPENDENCE, the CONTINENTAL CONGRESS decided what the flag of the new country would look like. It had 13 stripes in alternating red and white, to stand for the 13 states. Also representing the states were 13 white stars on a blue background. The Congress said these represented "a new constellation." In other words, the new country in the world was like a new group of stars in the sky.

The colors were the same as those chosen in 1782 for the GREAT SEAL of the United States, in which red stood for hardiness and courage, white for purity and innocence, and blue for vigilance, perseverance, and justice, representing the qualities of the new nation.

As new states joined the Union, more stars were added, in different arrangements. The flag was changed to include 15 stripes when the first two new states joined. But since 1818 it has had 13 stripes. These represent the first 13 states. Since 1960 the flag has had 50 stars, for the 50 states of the Union. Before that no star had been added since 1912.

## FLANAGAN, Edward J.

Father Edward Flanagan (1886–1948) was a Roman Catholic priest who founded Boys Town near Omaha, Nebraska. Born in Ballymoe, Ireland, he later was a priest in Nebraska. There he started taking in homeless and delinquent boys in 1917. In 1921 he bought a large farm and built living, study, and training areas. He called this community Boys Town. In 1979, Boys Town began to take in girls. About 560 children live in Boys Town. But through other programs, including foster care and hospital care, Boys Town assists more than 13,000 children a year.

## FLOOD

The first pioneers called America "the land of a thousand rivers." We know now that there are even more rivers and that they can be killers when they flood. In 1889, for example, the Johnstown, Pennsylvania, flood caused the deaths of 2,200 people when a dam broke.

Beginning in the late 1920s, Congress set up a nationwide system of flood defenses. In Louisiana, where the land around the Mississippi River is the lowest, a network of channels, reservoirs, and levees (raised banks) was built. In California's Central Valley dams were built to protect against floods as well as to provide water for irrigation and hydroelectric power.

**The Worst Floods in U.S. History**

**1889** Johnstown, Pennsylvania: 2,200 dead
**1900** Galveston, Texas: 5,000 dead
**1903** Heppner, Oregon: 325 dead
**1913** Ohio, Indiana: 732 dead
**1915** Galveston, Texas: 275 dead
**1928** Saugus, California: 450 dead
**1928** Lake Okeechobee, Florida: 2,000 dead
**1972** Rapid City, South Dakota: 236 dead
**1993** The Midwest: $10 billion in property damage

▼ *The James River overflowed and flooded thousands of acres in Richmond, Virginia, in 1985. Parts of the city were cut off by flood waters.*

# FLORIDA

Florida's nickname is the Sunshine State. Its blue skies, high temperatures, and almost year-round sun have made it a favorite vacation area for over 40 million Americans every year. Millions of senior citizens have retired there. In fact, Florida's population is growing faster than that of almost every other state. Its economy is developing rapidly, too. Agriculture remains one of its most important businesses—especially the cultivation of oranges and grapefruits. But many high-tech industries have also been established in the state recently. Electronic engineering, especially of computers, is increasingly important to Florida.

Except for Hawaii, Florida is the most southerly state. On a map it looks like a finger of land that juts out from the southeast corner of the United States. It extends almost 450 miles (725 km) from north to south. The Atlantic Ocean is to the east and the warm waters of the Gulf of Mexico are to the west. The state has many natural attractions, such as sandy beaches, the strange swamps of the EVERGLADES National Park, and the little islands that make up the Florida Keys. It also offers a host of man-made attractions, including sophisticated resorts, Walt Disney World, and Sea World in Orlando. The largest city is JACKSONVILLE; the capital is Tallahassee, located in the northern part of the state.

The first Europeans to settle Florida were Spaniards, in the 1500s. In 1763, Florida became a British colony, but in 1783 it was regained by Spain. It became an American territory in 1822 and a state in 1845.

▲ *Specially trained guides conduct airboat tours of the Everglades.*

► *Modern hotels line the Strand at Miami Beach. This strip of land constitutes some of the most expensive real estate in the United States.*

▲ *The Florida Keys, a string of islands, stretches south into the Gulf of Mexico. Many of the smaller keys make up the Great White Heron National Wildlife Refuge.*

**Places of Interest**

- St. Augustine was founded in 1565 and is the oldest city in the United States. Many colonial houses have been restored.
- Walt Disney World in Orlando offers an amusement park, a recreational center, a fairy-tale castle, and the futuristic Epcot Center as some of its many attractions.
- Marineland, near St. Augustine, was the world's first oceanarium. It includes more than 100 kinds of marine creatures – all living in natural surroundings.
- Everglades National Park is one of several national parks in Florida. The Everglades are home to many interesting and rare species of animals, birds, and plants.

**Florida**

**Capital:** Tallahassee
**Area:** 65,758 sq mi (170,313 km$^2$). Rank: 22nd
**Population:** 12,937,926 (1990). Rank: 4th
**Statehood:** Mar. 3, 1845
**Principal rivers:** St. Johns, St. Marys, Suwannee, Apalachicola
**Highest point:** A hilltop in Walton County, 345 ft (105 m)
**Motto:** "In God We Trust."
**Song:** "Swanee River"

# FOLK ART, AMERICAN

▼ *Common household items from the 18th and 19th centuries (below) have become collector's items as folk art. In 1990 a 19th-century metal weather vane was sold for more than $100,000 in New York. Naive (or Primitive) art (right) was considered worthless until modern painters came to appreciate its bold simplicity.*

**Earthenware plate**

**Tole ware**

**Weathervane**

Folk art is the art of ordinary people—people who are not professional painters, sculptors, furniture makers, or the like. North American folk art includes the work of people of European and African ancestry. Indian folk art, such as totems and beadwork, is usually considered separately. Useful objects can be folk art, but the decorative element must be the foremost consideration. Folk art is still being made. A 20th-century example is the Watts Tower in Los Angeles, which is made of found objects such as broken bottles. As early as the 1670s, folk artists, who were usually untrained and anonymous, were painting portraits of merchant families and other well-to-do middle-class people. Other popular subjects included landscapes, everyday (genre) scenes, and historical and religious subjects. These works are examples of what is called naive or primitive art.

The first American folk sculptors carved images on gravestones, but most later carvers worked in wood. They made ship carvings, weather vanes, and trade signs such as life-size Indians for tobacco dealers. In the Southwest, some Hispanic wood carvers made impressive *bultos* (holy figures). New

England seamen made some objects from the teeth and bones of whales — work that is known as scrimshaw.

Some everyday pottery achieved the status of art. Examples include redware dishes in the Pennsylvania Dutch tradition and stoneware face jugs made by black potters. Some quilts and hooked rugs are examples of abstract art.

The Museum of American Folk Art and the Metropolitan Museum of Art, both in New York City, exhibit folk art.

**Cigar-store figure**

▲ *Life-size wooden sculptures stood outside many cigar stores in the 1800s. They were symbols of the Indians who introduced the white settlers to tobacco.*

### Influences on American Folk Art

**British:** shop signs, boat figureheads, wood carving, needlecraft, leatherwork.
**Dutch:** portraits and biblical painting.
**Scandinavian:** wood carvings, furniture, household utensils, inlaid wood pictures.
**German:** Pennsylvania Dutch tole ware, quilting, barn signs, painted chests.
**Hispanic:** carved religious figures (*bultos*), altar paintings (*retablos*).
**African:** baskets, ceramics, musical instruments, ironwork, wood carving, gravestones.

◀ *This North Carolina quilter is carrying on a 250-year-old tradition. These quilts are made of patchwork, a decorative way of using scraps of cloth so that nothing goes to waste.*

### Some Features of American Folk Art

**Figureheads** were elaborately carved wooden statues placed on the bows (fronts) of sailing ships.
**Limners** were traveling American folk artists who specialized in painting portraits.
**Samplers** were embroidered "diplomas" showing that a girl had mastered many needlework stitches.
**Tole ware** household utensils were made of sheet metal and painted with vivid colors.

▼ *New England whalers made intricate carvings on their long voyages. The pictures, called scrimshaw, were often carved from whales' teeth.*

▲ *Superstitions are part of folklore. Long ago the Pennsylvania Dutch painted hex signs on their barns to ward off witches. Today they are used as good-luck symbols.*

## FOLKLORE, American

The word "folklore" means "knowledge, or learning, of the people." But it is a special kind of knowledge—the kind that has been passed down by word of mouth from generation to generation. There are many kinds of folklore. There are folk songs and folk dances, folk tales and folk art. Fairy tales and nursery rhymes and myths and legends are also folklore. So, too, are many superstitions, children's games, and riddles.

One of the most popular types of folklore is the folk tale. Many American folk tales are really tall tales. They are about bigger-than-life cowboys, lumberjacks, miners, or other people. Folk tales are often based on real people, but they are more fiction than fact. For example, there probably was a lumberjack with a name like Paul BUNYAN, but the tall tales invented about him have turned him into a superhuman folk hero who could chop down entire forests by himself. The folk hero PECOS BILL was based on cowboys of the Old West. But he was entirely made up by a journalist in the 1920s. Many ballads have been written about John Henry, that "steel drivin' man" who could work faster than a steam drill. And in terms of boasting, few could match Mike Fink, who bragged that he was the fastest shot and best fighter along the entire Mississippi River. Davy CROCKETT, a real-life hero, has become one of America's best-loved folk heroes.

▼ *Plains Indians valued storytelling, an important part of folklore. Tribal lore and customs passed from one generation to the next in long evening sessions.*

◀ *Mike Fink's life as a frontiersman — and death in a shooting contest — led to many legends and stories.*

**The poem *The Courtship of Miles Standish*, by Henry Wadsworth Longfellow, has become part of American folklore. According to the poem, the famous Pilgrim leader was too timid to ask Priscilla Mullens to marry him, and he sent his friend John Alden to ask on his behalf. This account was not true, but it helped preserve Standish's memory.**

Animal tales are another type of folklore. Black Americans brought many animal tales with them from Africa when they were forced into slavery in the Americas. In the late 1800s, Joel Chandler HARRIS made these tales popular when he wrote the Uncle Remus stories. These were humorous tales about animals, such as Brer Rabbit, that have human qualities.

The American INDIANS also have their folklore. Many of their folk tales, myths, and legends are about the origins of people. One tribe, the Algonquins, even has a story like the well-known Cinderella fairy tale. (See MYTHS AND LEGENDS.)

▼ *The songs children sing while jumping rope and other street rhymes and songs are part of the folklore tradition.*

### The Story of John Henry

The black laborer John Henry worked on a team digging the Big Bend railroad tunnel in West Virginia in the 1870s. The railroad workers used sledgehammers to dig the rock. When a steam drill was brought in to replace some workers, John Henry had a race with it. He won but died of exhaustion immediately afterward. This story of man against machine became the subject of many songs and ballads.

▲ *Pete Seeger has been collecting and singing folk songs since the 1930s. His music covers many themes, from songs of protest to traditional melodies.*

## FOLK MUSIC

Like other types of FOLKLORE, folk music usually originates among rural people. The songs are passed on orally long before they are written down. Some folk songs, called ballads, tell a story. Many of these were brought to North America by settlers from Great Britain and Ireland.

Other kinds of folk songs include lullabies, work songs, and religious songs. The hymn "Amazing Grace" and the lovely Appalachian Christmas carol "I Wonder as I Wander" are native North American folk songs. Among the best loved of all folk songs are black American spirituals, such as "Deep River" and "Steal Away."

Work songs have often helped to keep people's spirits up during long hours of toil and to help them work rhythmically. On sailing ships, teams of sailors performed many tasks to the strong beat of sea chanteys. The songs of American cowboys, such as "Red River Valley" and "Git Along, Little Dogie" are a distinctively American form of folk music.

Folk music has remained popular in the 20th century. American folk singers and composers have beocme internationally known for dealing with social issues through their music. Pete Seeger, who began performing in the 1930s, has influenced many other musicians, including Bob Dylan, Joan Baez, and Arlo Guthrie.

▼ *Scientists were able to date the Folsom culture by dating the bones of mammoths that lay near a Folsom spearhead. The notches on the spearhead exactly matched the grooves on the mammoth bones.*

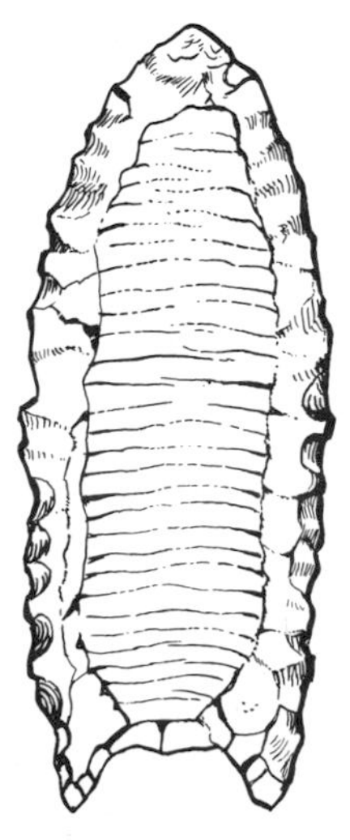

## FOLSOM CULTURE

The Folsom culture is the name given to some prehistoric people who lived in North America about 10,000 years ago. Evidence of these people was first found at Folsom, New Mexico, in 1926. The Folsom culture came after the Clovis culture. These people hunted large game such as mammoths. The Folsom were also hunters, and many of their spearheads have been found. Although there was still some large game, the Folsom seem to have hunted smaller game such as the long-horned bison, now extinct (no longer existing).

The main Folsom site is Lindenmeier in Colorado. It shows that the Folsom were more advanced than the Clovis. Their spearheads were smaller and more carefully made. They also made different kinds of tools, such as special needles for sewing and possibly basket making, and scrapers used to prepare animal skins.

◀ *In The Grapes of Wrath, Henry Fonda played Tom Joad, one member of a proud but poor family escaping from the Oklahoma Dust Bowl to a new life in California.*

## FONDA, Henry

Henry Fonda (1905–1982) was a U.S. stage and screen actor. He was in more than 80 motion pictures and many BROADWAY productions. In 1982 he was awarded an Oscar as Best Actor for his performance in the motion picture *On Golden Pond.* His actress daughter, Jane, starred with him in the film. His best-known stage appearance was in the Broadway production of *Mr. Roberts*, for which he was awarded a Tony. This was made into a film in which Fonda starred. His other films include *The Grapes of Wrath*, *My Darling Clementine*, and *Twelve Angry Men.*

## FOOD INDUSTRY

The average American family spends more than $3,300 each year on food. The people and companies that take the "raw materials" (such as meat, fish, and crops) and then prepare them for sale make up the food industry. Every canning factory, bakery, and refrigerated trailer truck is part of this industry. About 1.6 million people are employed in the food industry. That number is less than 10 percent of all manufacturing workers.

The government pays careful attention to the food industry because its products can affect people's health. The Department of Agriculture and the Food and Drug Administration watch over food factories and check on products that will be sold in stores. Even the simplest foods are tested to make sure they do not contain harmful ingredients. These government bodies also ensure that companies list their products' ingredients.

Business in the food industry was worth $308 billion in 1988, and profits were nearly $25 billion.

▼ *This chart shows the amount of every major food consumed per person per year in the United States. The U.S. population consumes more sugar and protein than nearly every other country in the world.*

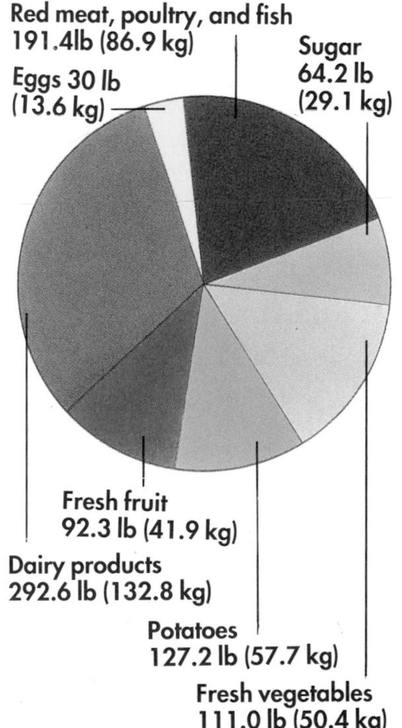

# FOOTBALL

► *Jim Thorpe, an Indian from Oklahoma, was an All-America football player at school and an outstanding professional from 1915 to 1930.*

◄ *Modern goalposts are supported by a single padded upright (to protect players) and a crossbar that is 10 feet (3 m) above the ground.*

▼ *This diagram shows the field marked out for pro football. Goalposts are on the goal line.*

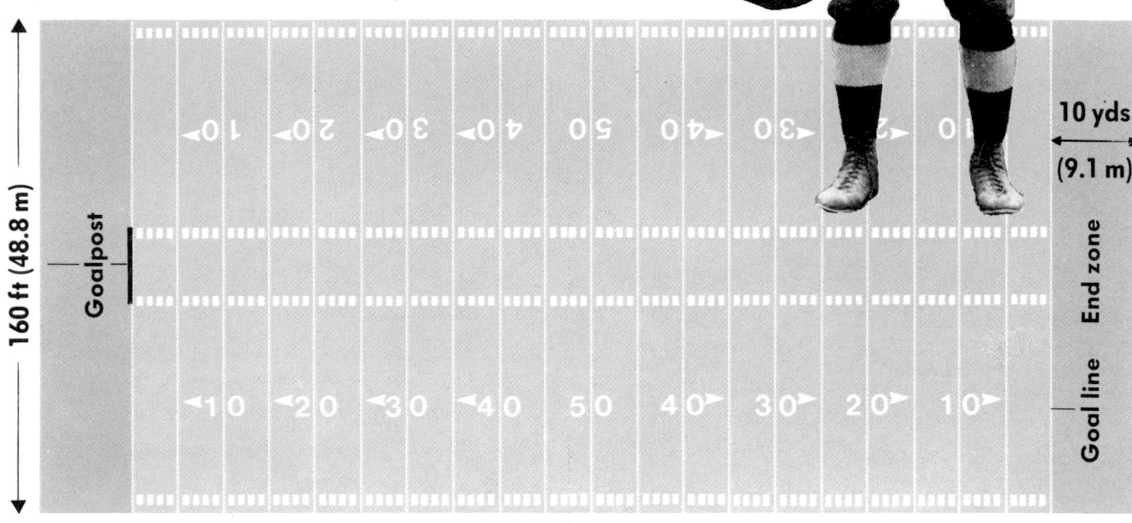


| Superbowl Winners (NFL Champions) | |
|---|---|
| 1994 | Dallas Cowboys |
| 1993 | Dallas Cowboys |
| 1992 | Washington Redskins |
| 1991 | New York Giants |
| 1990 | San Francisco 49ers |
| 1989 | San Francisco 49ers |
| 1988 | Washington Redskins |
| 1987 | New York Giants |
| 1986 | Chicago Bears |
| 1985 | San Francisco 49ers |
| 1984 | Los Angeles Raiders |
| 1983 | Washington Redskins |
| 1982 | San Francisco 49ers |
| 1981 | Oakland Raiders |
| 1980 | Pittsburgh Steelers |
| 1979 | Pittsburgh Steelers |

| Heisman Trophy Winners (Annual award to best college player) | |
|---|---|
| 1992 | Gino Torretta, U. of Miami |
| 1991 | Desmond Howard, U. of Michigan |
| 1990 | Ty Detmer, Brigham Young U. |
| 1989 | Andre Ware, U. of Houston |
| 1988 | Barry Sanders, Oklahoma State U. |
| 1987 | Tim Brown, U. of Notre Dame |
| 1986 | Vinny Testaverde, U. of Miami |
| 1985 | Bo Jackson, Auburn U. |
| 1984 | Doug Flutie, Boston College |
| 1983 | Mike Rozier, U. of Nebraska |
| 1982 | Herschel Walker, U. of Georgia |
| 1981 | Marcus Allen, U. of Southern California |
| 1980 | George Rogers, U. of South Carolina |
| 1979 | Charles White, U. of Southern California |
| 1978 | Billy Sims, U. of Oklahoma |
| 1977 | Earl Campbell, U. of Texas |

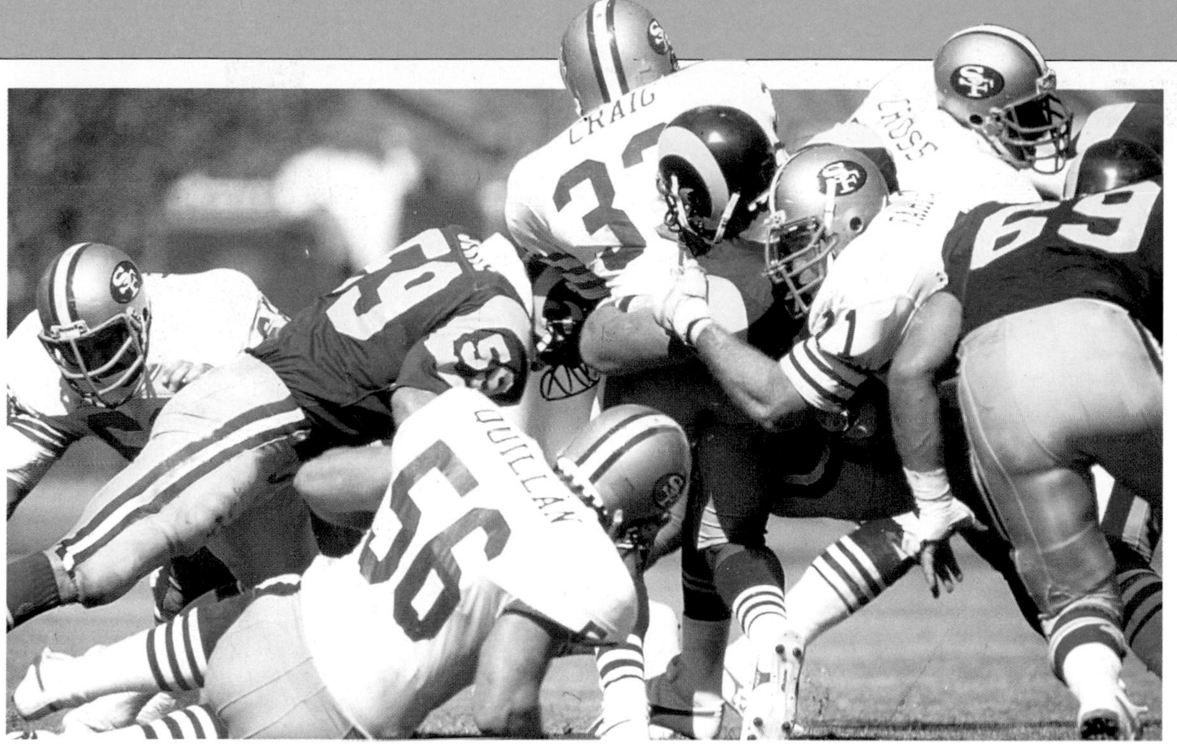


▲ *The NFL's San Francisco 49ers (in white shirts) have won four Superbowls since 1982.*

Football has become so popular that many people claim that it—not baseball—is the national sport of the United States. Much of its popularity is because of television. TV coverage has even introduced football to many foreign countries. In Europe and elsewhere it is known as American football. This is to avoid confusion with soccer, which is called football everywhere except in the United States.

Football developed in the mid-19th century. At that time it was similar to soccer. A round ball was used, and players tried to kick it across their opponents' goal lines. The sport became a favorite among college students. The first college football game was between Rutgers and Princeton, in 1869. After this, Americans started playing a game that was more like the English sport of rugby football, which had also developed from soccer. In this game the ball was oval. Players could kick or carry it over the goal line. The forward pass was added to the game in 1906.

Professional football first became organized in the 1920s. Today the National Football League (NFL) has 28 teams. The NFL is divided into two conferences, the American Football Conference and the National Football Conference. The champions of the two conferences play in the Superbowl each January. More than 850 million television viewers around the world watched the Dallas Cowboys defeat the Buffalo Bills in Superbowl XXVII in 1993.

Television has brought the sport to the public, but 15 million spectators still watch NFL games live each year. More than 36 million attend college games. The average salary for an NFL player is over $300,000 per year.

▼ *Quarterbacks put a spiral spin (A) on their forward passes so the ball will go where it is aimed. Placekickers send the ball end-over-end (B) for field goals and kickoffs.*

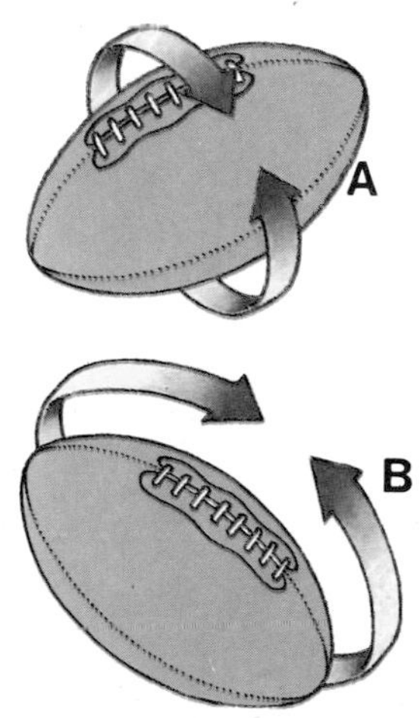

# FORD, Gerald R.

**Gerald Ford**
**Born:** July 14, 1913, in Omaha, Nebraska
**Education:** University of Michigan
**Political party:** Republican
**Term of office:** 1974–1977
**Married:** 1948 to Elizabeth Bloomer

Gerald Ford, 38th president of the United States, was the only president not elected to this office. Ford's 2½ years as president (1974–1977) were troubled because of the way he took office and the problems that he inherited once in power.

Ford was the Republican leader in the U.S. House of Representatives when Vice President Spiro Agnew resigned office in October 1973. President Richard NIXON appointed Ford to fill the vacant position. Ten months later, it was Nixon who resigned, because of his involvement in the Watergate scandal. Ford then succeeded Nixon as president. A month later, he pardoned Nixon for any crimes the former president might have committed in office. This action angered the many Americans who were disturbed by Watergate.

► *In 1976, President Ford led six other world leaders at an economic summit in Puerto Rico.*

Ford inherited serious economic problems. The cost of living had risen sharply, partly because of increased prices for foreign oil. In addition, the percentage of people out of work was higher than at any time since the Great Depression of the 1930s. These conditions gradually improved. However, Ford did not get along well with the Democratic-controlled Congress. He vetoed 55 bills passed by Congress.

In foreign affairs, Ford relied heavily on Secretary of State Henry KISSINGER. Ford signed an arms agreement with the Soviet Union. But the prestige of the United States was hurt when the VIETNAM WAR ended with the defeat of America's ally, South Vietnam. Ford narrowly lost the 1976 presidential election to the Democratic Party nominee, Jimmy CARTER.

▼ *Gerald Ford had good support in his bid for the 1960 nomination for vice president, but Henry Cabot Lodge, Jr., of Massachusetts became the Republican candidate.*

*◀ The "Tin Lizzie" of 1909 was one of the first Model T Fords. It was cheap to run and had a top speed of about 40 miles per hour (64 km/hr).*

**Henry Ford knew that lowering the price of his automobiles made good business sense. He said, "Each time I lower the price by one dollar I sell another thousand cars."**

**When Henry Ford began producing his automobiles on an assembly line, he knew that workers would remain loyal if their wages were good. The average wage in 1914 was $2.40 a day. Ford paid $5.00 a day minimum. By 1926 he was paying his workers $10.00 a day.**

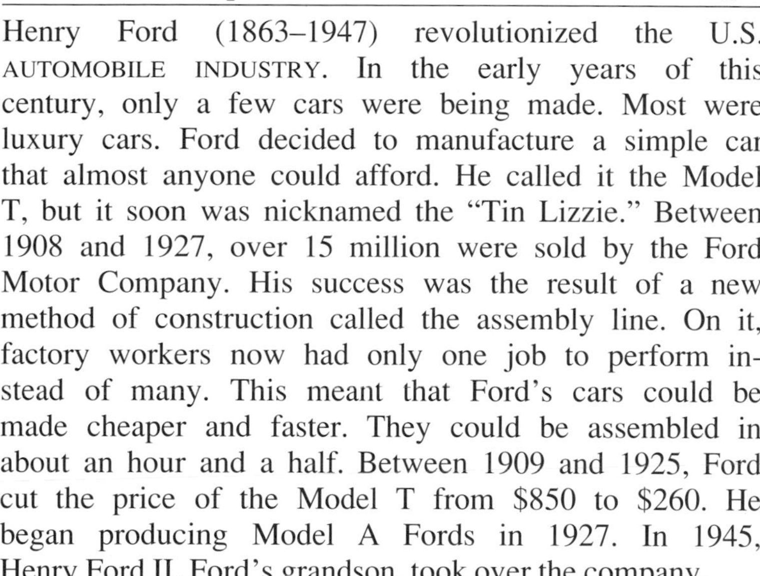

## FORD, Henry

Henry Ford (1863–1947) revolutionized the U.S. AUTOMOBILE INDUSTRY. In the early years of this century, only a few cars were being made. Most were luxury cars. Ford decided to manufacture a simple car that almost anyone could afford. He called it the Model T, but it soon was nicknamed the "Tin Lizzie." Between 1908 and 1927, over 15 million were sold by the Ford Motor Company. His success was the result of a new method of construction called the assembly line. On it, factory workers now had only one job to perform instead of many. This meant that Ford's cars could be made cheaper and faster. They could be assembled in about an hour and a half. Between 1909 and 1925, Ford cut the price of the Model T from $850 to $260. He began producing Model A Fords in 1927. In 1945, Henry Ford II, Ford's grandson, took over the company.

## FOREIGN AID

Foreign aid is the term used for the money and goods that the United States government provides to other countries. Some of this is in the form of loans and some in outright donations (grants). Money, food, and equipment go for such purposes as farming, housing, health, and industrial development. Other foreign aid is in the form of military goods, such as tanks and warplanes. Since World War II, foreign aid mainly has been

Countries Receiving Most U.S. Foreign Aid

1. Egypt
2. Israel
3. Turkey
4. Nicaragua
5. Philippines
6. Pakistan
7. El Salvador
8. Poland
9. Zimbabwe
10. Honduras
11. Bolivia
12. Bangladesh
13. Panama
14. Jamaica
15. Kenya

intended to help nations resist the spread of Communist influence, especially from the Soviet Union or China. A total of $374 billion was spent on foreign aid between 1946 and 1990.

**Landmarks in U.S. Foreign Policy**
**1823** Monroe Doctrine protects the Americas
**1898** U.S. gains territories after defeating Spain
**1904** "Big Stick" diplomacy strengthens Monroe Doctrine
**1946** Marshall Plan helps rebuild Europe
**1949** U.S. enters NATO; Truman Doctrine pledges U.S. support for anticommunists
**1970** U.S. renews ties with China
**1991** Cold War between the U.S. and the Soviet Union comes to an end.

## FOREIGN POLICY

The foreign policy of a nation is based on what its government considers to be in the interests of the nation and its people. Foremost is securing lives and property against possible foreign invasion. Countries also want to sell their products abroad on fair terms. Governments try to achieve these aims through negotiations, but sometimes they go to war. The president of the United States is mainly responsible for foreign policy. He is assisted chiefly by the Department of State. Congress also has a role. For example, the Senate must ratify treaties. Public opinion on international affairs also helps decide foreign policy.

## FOREIGN SERVICE

The Foreign Service of the United States has the job of carrying out American policies in other countries. Its members also provide information to help the president and secretary of state establish foreign policy. In addition, they provide help for U.S. citizens and businesses in foreign lands. The Foreign Service is part of the State Department, and its members are civil servants. Personnel work in about 180 embassies and missions abroad and in more than 150 consulates, consulates general, and consular agencies. They rank from clerks to important diplomats. The highest rank is ambassador, but not all ambassadors are members of the Foreign Service. The Foreign Service was formed in 1924, when the diplomatic and consular corps were combined.

*▼ The Forest Service has a duty to inform the public as well as protect the environment. This forest ranger's photo was taken while she was conducting a tour of Zion National Park in Utah.*

## FORESTS AND FORESTRY INDUSTRY

Forests cover 728 million acres (295 million ha) of the United States. These range from the vast tracts of spruce and other evergreens in Alaska to the subtropical forests of southern Florida. About two thirds of this forested area is considered timberland. This means that it is capable of producing lumber or wood pulp.

The U.S. government owns about a third of all for-

◄ *Each year thousands of forest trees are lost as a result of natural causes and people's carelessness. Tree nurseries such as this one help maintain stocks of trees.*

ested land. It is managed by the Forest Service, a branch of the Department of Agriculture. Much of the remaining forest is owned by lumber corporations or leased to them by individual owners. The Forest Service and the lumber companies employ specialists in fire prevention and soil protection to ensure that forests will remain a source of business and recreation. (See LUMBER INDUSTRY.)

**The gold at Fort Knox is stored in concrete and steel vaults inside a 12,700 sq ft (1,168 m$^2$) bombproof building, protected by armed guards. The vaults are also protected by electronic devices, and the interiors are constantly visible to security guards.**

## FORT KNOX

Fort Knox is a large U.S. Army base south of Louisville, Kentucky. It is the site of the Armor Center, the Army's principal training base for its armored forces. It was established in 1918.

Most people know Fort Knox best as the home of the U.S. Treasury Department's gold depository, probably the most secure building in the country. More than $50 billion worth of gold is stored here. During World War II, it was also used to store some of the nation's most precious papers, including the original copies of the Declaration of Independence and the Constitution.

## FORT WORTH

Fort Worth is an important industrial city in north-central TEXAS. It was established as a fort in 1849 to protect settlers from Indians. Fort Worth began to grow rapidly when large amounts of oil were found in the

▼ *The Tarrant County Courthouse, built in the last century, is dwarfed by Fort Worth's modern skyline.*

▲ *The modern 4-H emblem was first used by branches in Iowa around 1910.*

The 4-H Motto
"To Make the Best Better"
I pledge
My *Head* to clearer thinking,
My *Heart* to greater loyalty,
My *Hands* to larger service, and
My *Health* to better living, for my club, my community, my country, and my world.

▼ *A young 4-H club member poses with his prizewinning animal. Contests and competitions help develop the successful 4-H "learn by doing" approach to life.*

surrounding area in 1917. Oil refining is still a major industry; more than 30 oil companies have offices in Fort Worth. The other big industry is aircraft manufacture, which began during World War II. General Dynamics is now the largest aircraft company. The Dallas–Fort Worth International Airport, opened in 1974, is located between the two cities. More than 447,000 people live in Fort Worth.

## FOSTER, Stephen

Stephen Foster (1826–1864) wrote some of the best-known songs in America. Born on July 4, 1826, in what is now Pittsburgh, Pennsylvania, he loved music from an early age. He learned to play the clarinet when he was only six and began composing music and writing songs when he was a teenager. Although he wrote many successful songs that are classics, he made almost no money. He died, sick and broken in spirit, in 1864. Some of Foster's most famous songs include *Oh! Susanna* and *Swanee River* (he wrote it as *Old Folks at Home*).

## 4-H CLUBS

4-H clubs are clubs for young people over the age of nine. About 5.8 million youths belong to 4-H. They "learn by doing," through a wide range of individual and group projects. 4-H stands for "head, heart, hands, and health." The emblem is a green four-leaf clover with a white "H" on each leaf.

Every 4-H member works on at least one project a year. There are more than 50 approved projects to choose from. Projects range over such subjects as home economics, conservation, agriculture, forestry, photography, woodworking, horsemanship, dog care and training, automobile care, health, and indoor gardening.

Local clubs meet at least once a month. They also organize activities such as picnics and hikes. Most clubs serve their communities in various ways. For example, they might plant trees or help fight pollution.

## FOURTEEN POINTS

The Fourteen Points formed President Woodrow WILSON's program for a just and lasting peace after World War I. He outlined this program in January 1918

in a speech to Congress. Wilson hoped that these points would be used as a basis for peace talks. The first point said that countries should not make secret treaties, such as those that had helped bring about World War I. Wilson also called for freedom of the seas and freedom of trade. He said that countries should reduce their armaments. Germany, he said, should take its troops out of other European countries. He also called for changes in certain European boundaries. The 14th point called for the formation of an association of nations. This led to the formation of the League of Nations in 1920. But the United States never joined the League. Wilson fought for his program at the Paris Peace Conference of 1919.

**Kit fox**

**Gray fox**

▲ *The kit fox is sometimes called the swift fox because of the speed with which it moves around the deserts and plains where it lives. The gray fox is the only member of the dog family that can climb trees. It is the most common fox of the southern United States.*

## FOX 

The fox is the smallest member of the DOG family. It has long fur, pointed ears and snout (nose), and a bushy tail. Most North American foxes are about 23 to 27 inches (58 to 69 cm) long, excluding the 14- to 16-inch (36- to 41-cm) tail.

The red fox is the most common fox of North America. It is found all over the continent north of Mexico. The silver fox, black fox, and cross fox are actually types, or *color phases*, of red foxes. One litter of red fox cubs may include all of these color phases.

The gray fox lives from southern Canada to northern South America. It is the most common fox of the southern United States. The kit fox is found in the plains and deserts of the West. The Arctic fox lives in the far north. Its thick coat and pads of fur under its feet help to keep it warm.

## FRANKLIN, Benjamin 

Benjamin Franklin (1706–1790) was one of the most multi-talented men in American history. He was a printer, author, scientist, inventor, civil servant, and diplomat and one of the Founding Fathers of the United States. Franklin was born in Boston. After only a few years of formal education, he was apprenticed to an elder brother, who was a printer. By the age of 23, Franklin had his own printing business, in Philadelphia, and was publisher of the respected *Pennsylvania Gazette*. Another success was *Poor Richard's Almanack*. Franklin

▼ *Benjamin Franklin was described by Thomas Jefferson as "the greatest man and ornament of the age and country in which he lived."*

▲ *Franklin was proud of the first issue of the* Pennsylvania Gazette. *He had written, edited, and printed most of it himself.*

expressed his beliefs in this publication by using witty sayings, such as "Early to bed and early to rise, makes a man healthy, wealthy, and wise."

Franklin's interest in civic welfare led him to establish Philadelphia's first lending library and a volunteer fire department. His inventive genius produced the efficient Franklin stove, bifocal eyeglasses, and the lightning rod. This last came about because of his famous experiments with lightning, which he proved was electricity.

Between 1757 and 1775, Franklin lived mostly in London. He represented the interests of Pennsylvania and tried in vain to mend the growing rift between Britain and the colonies.

Just before the war broke out, he returned to Philadelphia to sit in the CONTINENTAL CONGRESS. Later, he was sent to France to obtain military and economic aid, which had a vital role in the American victory.

Franklin's last public service was as a delegate to the Constitutional Convention, where he worked hard to get the Constitution adopted.

## FRÉMONT, John C.

The mapmaker and explorer John Charles Frémont (1813–1890) played an important role in the settling of the Far West. Frémont learned to make maps while he was a young officer in the Army. Later, through the influence of his father-in-law, Senator Thomas Hart Benton, Frémont was sent to explore and map a large part of the territory between the Mississippi and the Pacific. His accounts of these explorations—which

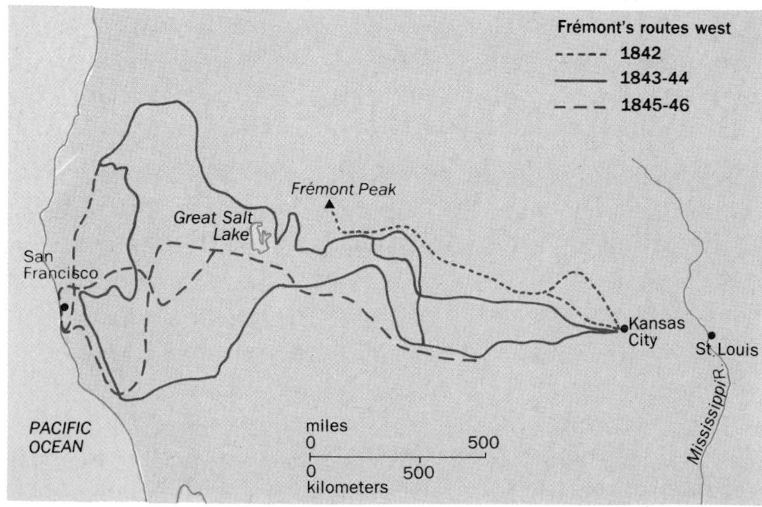


► *John Frémont had been a surveyor in the Appalachian mountains of the Carolinas. That experience, plus his teaming up with frontier explorer Kit Carson, helped him compile detailed maps of the Rockies.*

yielded much valuable information—won him great public esteem, and he became known as the "Pathfinder." Pioneer wagon trains relied on his maps.

When the MEXICAN WAR broke out in 1846, Frémont helped to win California for the United States. He later settled there and served as one of its first senators. After the 1849 gold rush he became a multimillionaire.

Although born in Georgia, Frémont opposed slavery, and in 1856 the newly formed Republican Party nominated him for the presidency. He lost to the Democratic candidate, James BUCHANAN.

**John C. Frémont's presidential campaign in 1856 used the slogan "Free Soil, Free Speech, Frémont." He wanted any new U.S. lands to be free (not slave) territories. The "free speech" referred to his opposition to Southern efforts to ban abolitionist literature.**

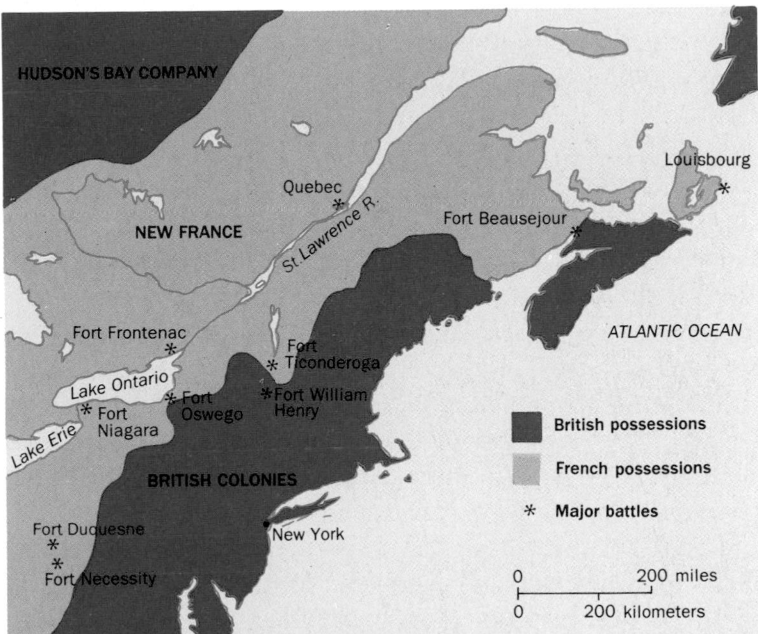


◀ *This map shows the colonial boundaries in 1755, at the beginning of the French and Indian War. Although Great Britain controlled most of the Atlantic coast, France had the St. Lawrence River, which led to the center of the continent. Eight years later Britain controlled nearly all of the territory shown on the map.*

## FRENCH AND INDIAN WAR

The French and Indian War (1754–1763) was fought between Britain and its American colonies, on one side, and France and its Canadian colony and some Indian tribes on the other. It became part of a wider conflict, known as the Seven Years' War, which took place in Europe, India, and the West Indies. In Europe, other countries and issues were involved. In North America, however, it was mainly a struggle between France and Britain for colonial power.

The war began when colonial troops, led by the young George WASHINGTON, attempted to capture some forts that the French had built on frontier land claimed by Britain. Washington was defeated. The following year British General Edward Braddock was

▼ *Colonel George Washington was among the British officers who captured Fort Duquesne (now Pittsburgh) in 1758. The retreating French troops had abandoned the fort.*

▲ *Quakers are opposed to war. These peaceful demonstrators in Washington, D.C., are showing their opposition to the violence in Latin America.*

also defeated when he tried to capture Fort Duquesne (now Pittsburgh). The war went badly for Britain until 1759. In that year, the British won a series of victories on land and at sea. In September, General James WOLFE captured Quebec. This victory marked the end of French power in North America. The Treaty of Paris (1763) gave Britain French Canada and all the French-held territory east of the Mississippi River. This opened up a vast area for settlement by the American colonists.

However, the war was to become a contributing factor in the friction between Britain and the colonies. Measures passed by Britain to get the colonies to pay some of the cost of the war—notably the hated STAMP ACT of 1765—met with strong opposition.

## FRIENDS, Society of

The Religious Society of Friends, more commonly known as the Quakers, was founded in England in the 1600s by George Fox. At that time, Quakers were persecuted for their beliefs. In 1682, William PENN founded Pennsylvania as a colony in which the Quakers and people of other faiths could practice their beliefs. Today there are about 123,000 Quakers in the United States. There are smaller groups of Quakers in Kenya, Great Britain, and other countries.

Except for their belief in the "inner light" ("that of God" in each person), Quakers have no rigid structure to their beliefs or their manner of worship. Most Quaker groups come together in meetinghouses where they worship informally. They may meditate silently or, if they feel they have had a communication from God, they may rise and speak to the assembled group.

Quakers reject war, and they have sponsored many organizations to promote peace. They have also worked for the causes of racial equality and prison reform.

**Frogs are important for many reasons. They eat insects that would otherwise destroy crops. They are a source of food for people — their meaty hind legs are considered a delicacy. And they are important as laboratory animals.**

## FROGS AND TOADS

Frogs and toads are AMPHIBIANS. At different times of their life cycle, amphibians live in water and out of water, but they must always keep their skin moist. Toads are heavier than frogs and have a drier skin with warts. And their legs are shorter, so they cannot jump as far. Some toads walk instead of jump.

The largest North American toad is the Colorado

River toad. The largest North American frog is the bullfrog, which may be up to 8 inches (20 cm) long. The leopard, or grass, frog is found throughout most of North America north of Mexico. Close relatives of these frogs are the green, pickerel, and wood frogs.

Tree frogs, which live mostly in trees, are usually less than 2 inches (5 cm) long. There are about 25 species of tree frogs in North America. Chorus frogs and cricket frogs are North American tree frogs that live in marshy places and don't actually climb trees.

Spade-foot toads live in the dry areas of the Great Plains and the Southwest. They prevent their skin from drying out by spending most of their lives underground. When it rains they come out to breed.

▲ *Young frogs and toads are called tadpoles. Adults of both species use protective skin coloring to blend into a natural background. For years people incorrectly thought they could get warts from touching the bumps on a toad.*

## FROST, Robert

Robert Frost (1874–1963) was one of the best loved of American poets. He was born in San Francisco but spent most of his life in rural New England. Many of his poems are about this part of the country. Among them are "Mending Wall," and "The Death of a Hired Man."

Frost's poems are simple in style and language. But they usually contain a deeper meaning. Four of his collections of poetry were awarded the Pulitzer Prize. In addition to writing poetry, Frost taught at several colleges and gave many public readings of his poems.

▼ *In 1961, Robert Frost read his poem "The Gift Outright" at the inauguration of President John F. Kennedy. He published his last volume of poems the following year, when he was 88 years old.*

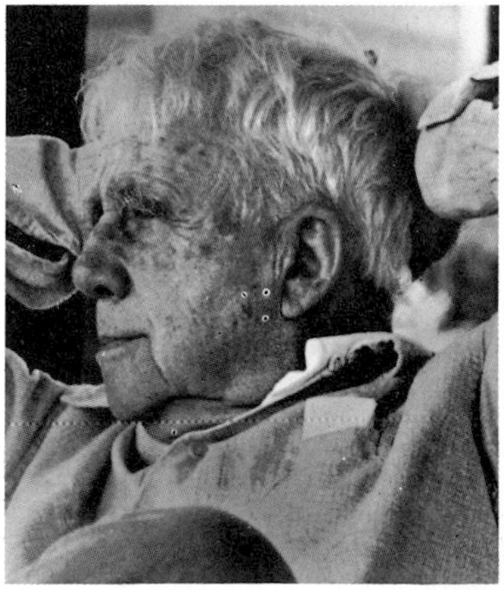

▲ *Cultivated fruits thrive in the varied terrain of North America. Some North American grape varieties can withstand the plant louse phylloxera, which destroyed France's wine production in the 19th century.*

## FRUIT

The United States is the main fruit-producing country in the world. California grows the most fruit of any state. The most valuable fruit crop in the United States is oranges. Like other CITRUS FRUITS, these grow on trees in warmer parts of the country, such as Florida, California, and Arizona. The United States grows more citrus fruits than any other country, but severe cold spells sometimes threaten the crops.

Apples, apricots, cherries, peaches, pears, and plums also grow on trees. These fruits grow in parts of North America that have a cold season each year. California, Washington, Michigan, and Oregon are important growers of these fruits.

After oranges, the most important fruit grown in the United States is the grape. It grows on woody vines. California is the leading grower of grapes. Most other small fruits, including most BERRIES, grow on bushes.

Berries thrive in the harsh conditions of some northern states. Cranberries are grown in the marshy areas of Massachusetts, New Jersey, and Wisconsin. Blueberries are important crops in Michigan and Maine.

## FULBRIGHT, James William

J. William Fulbright (1905– ) was born in Sumner, Missouri. He became a lawyer and the president of the University of Arkansas. Fulbright entered the U.S. House of Representatives in 1942 and the Senate in 1945. He served there until 1974. Fulbright was the chairman of the Senate Foreign Relations Committee and wrote several books on American foreign policy. He opposed U.S. involvement in the VIETNAM WAR. Fulbright started the famous Fulbright scholarships. These yearly awards make it possible for Americans to study or do research in other countries.

**Buckminster Fuller was not disappointed if his inventions failed to be used immediately. He once wrote, "I just invent. Then I wait until man comes around to needing what I have invented."**

## FULLER, Buckminster

Buckminster Fuller (1895–1983) was an inventor. He was born in Milton, Massachusetts. Fuller wanted to create designs that would suit the conditions of the 20th century. He looked at ways of using building materials so that people could feel part of nature and the world about them. Shape was an important factor in his de-

◀ *Geodesic domes are easily assembled and lightweight. The huge dome of the U.S. Pavilion was a highlight of the Expo '67 World's Fair in Montreal.*

signs. One for which Fuller was best known was the geodesic dome. This large structure was shaped like a ball. It was made of light metal and glass forming a framework that looked like mesh.

## FULTON, Robert

The American inventor Robert Fulton (1765–1815) was the first to build a commercially successful steamboat, the *Clermont*. After abandoning his early plans to be a painter, Fulton turned to engineering. He invented a torpedo and an early form of submarine, neither of which attracted much interest. Success came when he designed a steam-powered boat for travel up the Hudson River between New York City and Albany. Fulton's boat was 150 feet (45 m) long and had two side paddlewheels. It made its first trip in August 1807. The

**Robert Fulton's submarine *Nautilus* was the first practical undersea vessel. The craft carried a crew of four and had a hand-operated screw propeller at the stern. It had water ballast tanks to raise or lower the craft and horizontal rudders to make the craft dive or surface. Fulton could keep his submarine submerged for up to six hours, but the French, British, and U.S. governments were not interested.**

◀ *Robert Fulton's* North River *(or* Clermont*) opened the world's first profitable steamship line in 1807. The service ran on New York's Hudson River.*

journey took 32 hours—one third of the four days required by sailing sloops. The *Clermont* went into regular service in 1808. Other Fulton-designed boats were used on the Mississippi River.

## FUR TRADE

The fur trade played a key role in the settlement of North America. Europeans had begun trading goods for furs with Indians as early as the 1500s. As the demand for furs grew in Europe, fur traders explored ever larger areas in search of fur-bearing animals such as otter, mink, fox, and beaver. Throughout the 1600s, French traders explored along the St. Lawrence River to the Great Lakes. Some of their trading posts, such as Quebec and Montreal, became important cities. The British traded furs, too, in New England and Virginia as well as in Canada. In 1670 the British formed the HUDSON'S BAY COMPANY to trade in furs. Its trappers went deep into the wilderness. In the 1700s, Britain and France went to war over control of the trade. Britain's victory helped ensure that Canada remained a British colony. By the early 1800s, traders and trappers had moved well into the West. Mountain men such as Kit CARSON gained fame as intrepid trappers. By the mid-1800s the demand for furs in Europe had all but ended, and the fur trade dwindled to almost nothing.

▲ *The fur trapper's hunting rifle was longer than army weapons. Although the rifle was more difficult to handle, its better aim meant that the hunter could save gunpowder.*

▼ *This Currier and Ives print depicts the life led by fur trappers. They would often spend months in the wilderness along the Missouri River.*

◀ *The architect Frank Lloyd Wright designed furniture specially for his offices.*

▲ *Shaker furniture, such as this rocking chair, reflected the simplicity of the Shaker religion.*

## FURNITURE

Furniture has been produced in America since the arrival of the first European colonists. Craftsmen known as cabinetmakers made beds, chairs, and tables. They relied on memory or designs from Europe, such as Renaissance style and Elizabethan and Tudor models from England.

During the 18th century, neoclassical designs, based on those of ancient Greece and Rome, became the fashion. In the United States, they were known as the Federal and Empire styles. Foremost among American cabinetmakers in this style was Duncan Phyfe, whose career began in the 1790s. Later styles included Gothic Revival (1820–1850) and Art Nouveau (1880–1910). There were also purely American styles. Shaker furniture was plain and undecorated but it had a severe beauty. The Pennsylvania Dutch decorated furniture with animal, bird, or geometric forms. At the same time, the Industrial Revolution of the 1800s made it easier to mass-produce furniture, especially simple styles.

American 20th-century furniture has been heavily influenced by streamlined European styles such as Art Deco and Bauhaus designs. With their popularity came materials lighter than wood, such as aluminum, chrome, and plastics. Charles Eames (1907–1978) became known for his formfitting chairs. The center of the U.S. furniture industry has moved from the Northeast to the South. In 1987 furniture makers in the United States turned out $37 billion worth of merchandise and employed 530,000 people.

▼ *This Federal-style chest features the images and proportions of ancient Greek and Roman design.*

## GABLE, Clark

Clark Gable (1901–1960) was one of the great romantic screen heroes. Born in Cadiz, Ohio, he appeared in dozens of movies. His Hollywood career spanned 30 years. He often played the role of what might be called a "loner"—an independent man who has a strong impact on people and events around him. Gable won an Oscar for the 1934 comedy *It Happened One Night*. But he will always be best remembered for his role as Rhett Butler in the great Civil War movie *Gone With the Wind*. Gable died in 1960 after filming *The Misfits*, which also starred Marilyn MONROE.

► *Clark Gable played the roguish Southern hero Rhett Butler in the movie* Gone With the Wind.

▼ *As a railroad president, James Gadsden knew that his purchase was a possible train route. He had no idea that the land was also rich in gold and silver.*

## GADSDEN PURCHASE

The United States negotiated the Gadsden Purchase with Mexico in 1853. Under its terms, the United States bought a strip of land lying just south of the boundary fixed in 1848 after the MEXICAN WAR. The 30,000-square-mile (78,000 km$^2$) strip of land lies south of the Gila River. It now forms part of New Mexico and Arizona. The United States wanted to build a railroad to the Pacific coast on the land. Mexico did not want to give up any more territory, but it badly needed money. The United States paid $10 million for the land. The purchase was named for the U.S. minister to Mexico, James Gadsden. He arranged the purchase with Mexican President Antonio López de Santa Anna.

## GALBRAITH, John Kenneth

Canadian-born John Kenneth Galbraith (1908– ) has been one of the most influential American economists of this century. His teachings and writings on the management of money, especially by governments, have had enormous impact. Between 1949 and 1975, he was professor of economics at Harvard. During this time, he often advised the government on economic policy. From 1961 to 1963, he also acted as U.S. ambassador to India. He has always maintained that the government must play an important part in directing the national economy but without interfering with people's right to spend their money as they choose.

▲ *John Kenneth Galbraith addressed a press conference in 1979 on the subject of inflation. His stern proposals, which were not taken up by President Jimmy Carter, called for wage controls and gas rationing.*

## GALLATIN, Albert

Born in Geneva, Switzerland, Albert Gallatin (1761–1849) moved to the United States at the age of 19. He went into business and then into politics. Gallatin was a member of the Republican, or Democratic-Republican, Party. In 1795 he was elected to the U.S. House of Representatives. A financial expert, he established what is now called the House Ways and Means Committee, which deals with expenditure. He later served as secretary of the treasury under presidents Jefferson and Madison. In that office, he managed to reduce the national debt from $80 million to $45 million in the space of ten years. Later, he revealed equal skill as a diplomat, playing a leading part in the negotiations that ended the WAR OF 1812.

▼ *Albert Gallatin was born in Switzerland but believed that the United States should turn away from Europe. He was against war mainly because it was expensive.*

## GALLUP, George

George Gallup (1901–1984) was a statistician—a person who gathers and interprets numerical information. He conducted public opinion polls to find out what people thought about different issues. His best-known polls were about politics. Gallup began conducting polls in 1932. His poll, along with two others, correctly predicted that Franklin D. ROOSEVELT would win the 1936 presidential election. This boosted people's faith in polls. Gallup founded the American Institute of Public Opinion in 1935. Gallup polls are still considered accurate reflections of public attitudes toward politics and social issues.

## GARFIELD, James

James Garfield, the 20th president of the United States, had served less than four months when he was assassinated by someone to whom he had refused to give a job.

After a very poor childhood, Garfield worked his way through college, became a teacher, and studied law. He was elected to the Ohio Senate as a Republican. He served in the Union Army during the Civil War, rising to the rank of major general. Ohio elected him to the U.S. House of Representatives in 1862. He served there from 1863 to 1880.

In 1874 a serious scandal occurred during the administration of President Ulysses S. GRANT. In those days, many politicians bought votes and accepted bribes. Garfield was accused of taking $329 as a bribe, but the charge was never proved.

**President James A. Garfield's assassination led Congress to pass the Pendleton Act in 1883. This measure ended the patronage system by "classifying" about 10 percent of all federal jobs. It also created a Civil Service Commission to supervise examinations for these federal posts.**

► *President Garfield was fatally wounded in the train station in Washington, D.C., on the way to his 25th reunion at Williams College in Massachusetts.*

In 1880, Garfield was nominated by the Republicans for president. The party had split into two rival groups called the Stalwarts and the Half-Breeds. Garfield was chosen in order to prevent the Stalwarts from nominating former president Ulysses S. Grant. He narrowly won the election.

At that time, under the spoils system, government employees were turned out of their jobs when a new president took over. Garfield gave the government jobs to his supporters. Many Stalwarts were disappointed. It was one of these Stalwarts who shot Garfield, but there was no proof of a conspiracy. Garfield's assassination shocked the nation into action. Two years later Congress passed a bill reforming the civil service system.

James Garfield
**Born:** November 19, 1831, in Orange, Ohio
**Education:** Williams College
**Political party:** Republican
**Term of office:** 1881
**Married:** 1858 to Lucretia Rudolph
**Died:** September 19, 1881, in Elberon, New Jersey

## GARLAND, Judy

Judy Garland (1922–1969) was one of America's best-loved actresses. Born in Grand Rapids, Minnesota, she began her career on stage at the age of five. She made her first movie only nine years later. Garland had a soft, emotional quality that showed in her roles and gave her a special appeal. She used her distinctive singing voice in *The Wizard of Oz*, *Meet Me in St. Louis*, and *A Star is Born*. Garland also proved herself to be a strong dramatic actress in such films as *Judgment at Nuremberg*.

▲ *Judy Garland is known all over the world for her portrayal of Dorothy in* The Wizard of Oz.

## GARRISON, William Lloyd

William Lloyd Garrison (1805–1879) was a famous ABOLITIONIST. He expressed his views in *The Liberator*, a newspaper he founded in 1831. The following year, he founded the New England Anti-Slavery Society. It was the first abolitionist group that insisted on freeing the slaves immediately. Shortly afterward he helped to form the American Anti-Slavery Society. Later, Garrison became more extreme in his views. In *The Liberator* in 1844 he urged that the North secede from the slaveholding South. He also denounced the compromises that held the Union together during the 1850s. After slavery was abolished by the Thirteenth Amendment in 1865, Garrison continued to fight for equality for blacks.

**William Lloyd Garrison's newspaper, *The Liberator*, was launched with the words, "*I will be* as harsh as truth, and as uncompromising as justice—I will not excuse—I will not retreat a single inch—AND I WILL BE HEARD."**

## GARVEY, Marcus

Born in Jamaica, Marcus Garvey (1887–1940) was the founder of the Universal Negro Improvement Association (UNIA). Its aims were to increase black people's pride in their race and help them to achieve economic independence. When Garvey moved to the United States in 1916, his movement began to flourish. Garvey's inspiring speeches, given in UNIA's Liberty Hall in Harlem, and his newspaper, *Negro World*, attracted 2 million followers, most of them poor blacks. Garvey set up several blacks-only businesses. And he preached that blacks should return to Africa. Many middle-class black leaders disapproved of Garvey's goal of separating the races. Garvey was convicted of dishonest business dealings in 1925. He served two years of his prison sentence and was then deported. Garvey spent his last years in Jamaica and London.

▼ *Marcus Garvey was a stirring leader but a poor businessman. His attempts to found an independent black African country failed when his businesses ran out of cash.*

▲ *Satellites can monitor weather over large parts of the globe. This photograph shows an area of clear weather over the U.S. Southwest and northern Mexico.*

# GEOGRAPHY

Geography is the study of the Earth and its relationship to the people who live in it. A country's geographic location and its physical geography are important factors in how that country will develop. The United States' location, for example, with oceans and seas on three sides, has enabled it to become one of the world's great trading countries. Its great rivers, such as the MISSISSIPPI-MISSOURI RIVER SYSTEM have served as internal transportation routes. Its vast central plain, with its fertile soil, has produced agricultural products in great abundance. And the country's wealth of natural resources and generally temperate climate have enabled Americans to build a prosperous nation.

The United States has several major geographical regions. Many of the early settlers established colonies on the eastern *Coastal Plain*, which extends from New York to the Mexican border. To the west of the coastal plain is another physiographic region—the *Appalachian Highlands*. This mountainous region extends from the United States–Canadian border south to central Alabama. The APPALACHIANS were a barrier that kept settlers, at first, from moving westward. Today this beautiful region is also an important mining area.

After Daniel Boone blazed a trail through the Appalachians, settlers by the thousands made their way west. There they encountered the continent's vast *Interior Plains*. The Mississippi River and its tributaries, including the Missouri, drain this region. It is the agricultural heartland of the United States. The GREAT LAKES are in the northern part of the plains. Great industrial cities grew up in this area.

West of the plains are the ROCKY MOUNTAINS, which extend from New Mexico into Canada. Like the Appalachians in the east, these western mountains are rich in minerals. West of the Rockies is an area of high plateaus cut by deep river gorges. Much of this river is arid. DEATH VALLEY, the lowest point in the United States—and the hottest—is located here. Farther to the west is the *Pacific Mountain System*. Here, fertile valleys nestle between towering mountains.

The western edge of the United States, along the Pacific coast, has many volcanoes and earthquake faults. This region is part of the Ring of Fire that encircles the Pacific Ocean. Hawaii, far to the west in the Pacific, and Alaska, to the north beyond Canadian territory, are also part of this earthquake and volcano area.

**Extremes of U.S. Geography**

**Highest point**
Mt. McKinley, Alaska, 20,320 ft (6,194 m)

**Lowest point**
Death Valley, California, 282 ft (86 m) below sea level

**Highest state**
Colorado, average mean elevation, 6,800 ft (2,040 m)

**Lowest state**
Delaware, average mean elevation, 60 ft (18 m)

**Geographic center**
48 states: near Lebanon, Kansas; all 50 states: Butte County, South Dakota

## GEOLOGY

Geologists study rocks and other parts of the Earth's surface to learn how it was formed. The oldest part of North America's surface, the CANADIAN SHIELD, was formed many hundreds of years ago. This mass of rock covers eastern Canada and the northeastern United States. The mountains on the East Coast—the APPALACHIANS—began to form about 500 million years ago. They formed as the result of continental drift. Scientists believe that all of the continents once were a single giant continent. It broke apart, and the separate smaller continents started drifting. Sometimes they drifted into one another. When this happened to North America, the collision forced up the edges of the continent to form the Appalachians. A later collision created the western ranges such as the Rockies.

Huge ice sheets also changed the face of North America. About two million years ago glaciers covered much of the continent. When the ice melted, great rivers and river valleys were formed. The GREAT LAKES were also formed from melting ice.

▼ *A geologist carries out a controlled explosion to test soil in the search for petroleum deposits.*

# GEORGIA

Brown thrasher

Live oak

Cherokee rose

Georgia is the largest state east of the Mississippi River. Located in the southeastern United States, it borders on the Atlantic Ocean. Georgia is a prosperous state. Farming, especially of soybeans, peanuts, tobacco, corn, and wheat, has been important to Georgia for many years. It is a major manufacturing state, too. Many industries are located in and around ATLANTA, the state's capital and largest city. Atlanta is the center of Georgia's thriving textile business.

Many think of Georgia as one of the most beautiful states. Lofty pine forests grow across much of Georgia. These are important sources of timber as well as a leading leisure resource. Hunters, fishermen, and walkers love to explore them. Magnolia trees and flowers flourish in the state's sunny climate.

The first Europeans to visit Georgia were Spanish and French settlers in the 1500s. But in 1733, James OGLETHORPE founded an English colony. It was named for King George II of England. In the Revolutionary War, British troops captured the city of Savannah in 1778. They were defeated only in 1782. In the first half

**Places of Interest**

- The Dahlonega Gold Museum is built on the site of the first United States gold rush. Visitors can pan for gold and keep what they find!
- Etowah mounds, near Cartersville, is one of the largest Indian mound complexes in the country. A museum displays pottery, sculptured images, and other artifacts.
- Okefenokee National Wildlife Refuge offers guided boat tours around the largest freshwater swamp in the country.
- The Little White House in Warm Springs is the house in which President Franklin D. Roosevelt lived and died. It is full of Roosevelt mementos.

► *The houses around Monterey Square in Savannah were built in the colonial era by wealthy merchants and shipowners.*

of the 1800s, Georgia became one of the leading cotton-growing states in the South and a major slave state. The invention of the cotton gin by Eli WHITNEY in Georgia in 1793 had made cotton growing much more profitable. Georgia was the fifth state to leave the Union just before the start of the CIVIL WAR in 1861. In 1864, Union forces under General William SHERMAN burned Atlanta and destroyed huge areas of the state. In 1976, Jimmy CARTER became the first Georgian to be elected president of the United States.

▲ *Okefenokee Swamp extends 45 miles (72 km) across southeastern Georgia. Much of it is a wildlife refuge.*

▲ *Statues of Confederate heroes have been carved from the granite of Stone Mountain.*

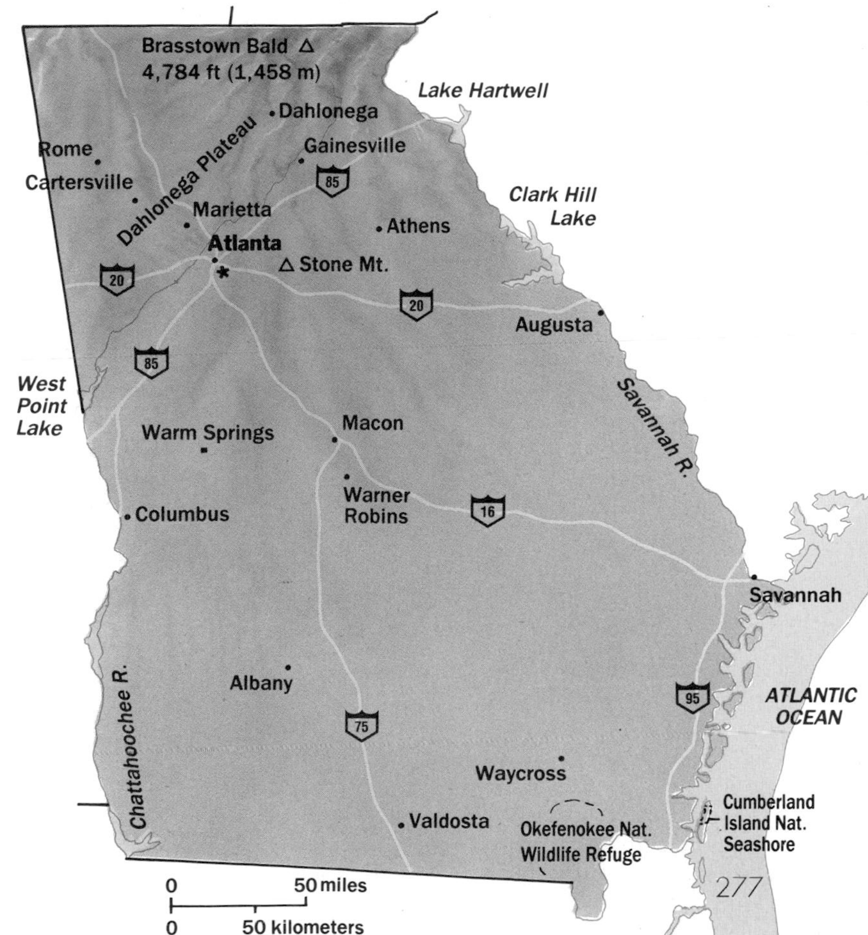


| Georgia |
|---|
| **Capital:** Atlanta |
| **Area:** 59,441 sq mi (153,953 km²). Rank: 24th |
| **Population:** 6,478,216 (1990). Rank: 11th |
| **Statehood:** Jan. 2, 1788 |
| **Principal rivers:** Chattahoochee, Savannah, Suwannee |
| **Highest point:** Brasstown Bald, 4,784 ft (1,458 m) |
| **Motto:** "Wisdom, Justice, and Moderation" |
| **Song:** "Georgia on My Mind" |

▲ *Geronimo's fierce resistance to white rule began in 1858, when Mexican bandits killed his mother, wife, and children.*

## GERONIMO

Geronimo (1829–1909) was a famous warrior and leader of the Chiricahua Apache Indians. He was born in Arizona, when it was part of Mexico. In the late 1870s, the U.S. Army put his people in the San Carlos reservation in Arizona. Geronimo escaped and with other Indians fought on both sides of the U.S.–Mexican border. He became the best fighter and strongest leader. The Army brought in General George Crook, who had successfully fought against other Apaches. Geronimo was captured several times and managed to escape. General Nelson Miles replaced Crook, and in 1886 Geronimo gave himself up. He was kept a prisoner in Florida, Alabama, and, finally, Fort Sill, Oklahoma.

## GERSHWIN, George and Ira

George (1898–1937) and Ira (1896–1983) Gershwin were brothers, born to Russian immigrant parents in New York. Together, they produced some of the most memorable songs of the century. George wrote the music, Ira the words. Their first hits were musical comedies. These included *Lady, Be Good!*, *Oh, Kay!*, and *Funny Face*. At the same time, George was already writing serious musical pieces such as *Rhapsody in Blue* and *An American in Paris*. These used jazz and blues to create a striking and unmistakably modern effect. The Gershwins' last great success before George's early death was the American folk opera *Porgy and Bess*. It is still often produced today.

**George Gershwin dropped out of school when he was 15 years old in order to write songs. He was paid $15 a week. His first hit, *Swanee*, was recorded in 1920 by Al Jolson. The song was very popular and earned Gershwin $10,000 in royalties for 1920 alone.**

► *The musical film* An American in Paris *was inspired by Gershwin's 1928 composition of the same name.*

## GETTY, J. Paul

Jean Paul Getty (1892–1976) was one of the richest men in the world. Getty was born in Minneapolis, Minnesota. He came from a successful oil family and, with a loan from his father, made his own fortune in the oil business. He made his first $1 million when he was in his early twenties. Getty kept the extent of his wealth secret, but he is thought to have been worth over $3 billion dollars. He spent much of his life in England.

## GETTYSBURG ADDRESS

In November 1863, President Abraham LINCOLN was invited to make a "few appropriate remarks" at the dedication of a national cemetery at Gettysburg, Pennsylvania. A few months earlier, thousands of Union soldiers had died there, at the Battle of Gettysburg.

The main address was given by the famous orator Edward Everett. It lasted two hours and was hailed as one of the finest of his career. Lincoln's lasted about two minutes. Today Lincoln's Gettysburg Address is regarded as a masterpiece. In a few sentences Lincoln expressed the central issue of the war: the survival of any nation that is dedicated to human freedom.

Legends about the Gettysburg Address sprang up soon after Lincoln's assassination. One story said that the president had written the speech on the back of an envelope while traveling to Gettysburg by train. In fact he had chosen his words with great care, writing several versions beforehand.

**The Closing Passages of the Gettysburg Address**

"... It is rather for us to be here dedicated to the great task remaining before us—that from these honored dead we take increased devotion to that cause for which they gave the last full measure of devotion—that we here highly resolve that these dead shall not have died in vain—that this nation, under God, shall have a new birth of freedom—and that government of the people, by the people, for the people, shall not perish from the earth."

▼ *President Lincoln's Gettysburg Address expressed his belief that the Civil War was being fought to preserve American ideals of liberty and freedom.*

▲ *A geyser is like a pressure cooker. The higher the pressure, the hotter the water has to be to boil. The superheated steam and water are pushed out as a powerful jet. When water has seeped back and heated up, the process starts again.*

▼ *Castle Geyser in Yellowstone National Park erupts at irregular intervals. However, you can set your watch by its neighbor, "Old Faithful," which erupts every 73 minutes.*

## GETTYSBURG, Battle of

The Battle of Gettysburg (July 1–3, 1863) was a turning point of the CIVIL WAR. This important Union victory by General George MEADE stopped an invasion of the North by General Robert E. LEE's Confederate Army. From this point onward, the South's chances of winning the war declined.

Gettysburg, a small town in Pennsylvania, was of strategic importance because ten roads met there. The battle was the bloodiest ever fought on American soil: more than 21,000 Confederate soldiers and more than 22,000 Union soldiers were killed or wounded in it. The most severe losses for the South occurred during General George PICKETT's charge, when 15,000 Confederate troops attempted to break through the Union lines; only 8,000 returned from this ill-fated attack. Lee's army retreated to Virginia.

## GEYSERS

A geyser is a spring that spurts hot water and steam into the air. It consists of a very narrow, deep hole, like a tube, that goes down into the earth into hot rock. Cold water seeps down to the hot rocks, where it is heated. The steam that is formed builds up pressure and makes the water shoot out of the hole for a short while.

Geysers are found in volcanic regions, near rivers and lakes. Most of the world's geysers are in WYOMING, Iceland, and New Zealand. Wyoming's Yellowstone National Park has over 200 geysers, including the most famous geyser in the world, "Old Faithful."

## GIRL SCOUTS *See* Scouts

## GLENN, John H.

John Glenn (1921–   ) was the first American astronaut to orbit the earth. Today he is a Democratic senator from Ohio, the state where he was born. In 1962, Glenn orbited the earth in the spacecraft *Friendship 7*. The whole space voyage took just under five hours. Glenn had to handle the space capsule controls when the automatic controls failed. Two years later Glenn resigned from the space program and started a career in

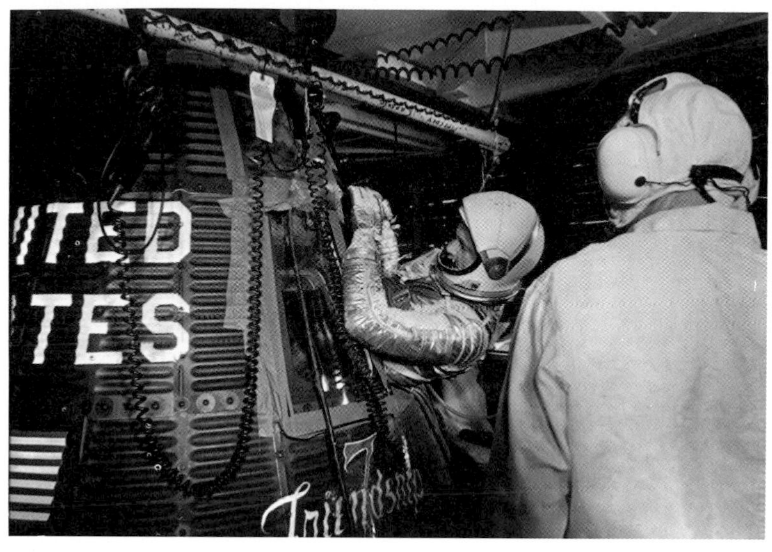

◀ *John Glenn and his fellow astronauts insisted on having controls and a windshield on the Mercury spacecraft. Glenn used his own experience as a jet pilot to land the Mercury* Friendship 7 *manually when the automatic controls broke down.*

politics. He was elected to the U.S. Senate in 1974 and reelected in 1980, 1986, and 1992. He made an unsuccessful bid for the Democratic presidential nomination in 1984.

## GOATS

In the United States goats are raised for their milk and their wool. The most popular breeds for milk in North America are the Anglo-Nubian, or Nubian, Saanen, and Toggenburg. Nearly half the goats in the United States are Angoran. These are raised for their shaggy, white wool, known as mohair.

There are no wild goats in North America. The Rocky Mountain goat is wild, but it is not a true goat. It is a goat-antelope. It lives above the timberline in rocky, mountainous areas of Montana, western Canada, and southwestern Alaska. It is protected by law.

▼ *The surefooted Rocky Mountain goat must scramble along steep hillsides to feed on twigs and shrubs. The billy (male) weighs up to 200 pounds (91 kg).*

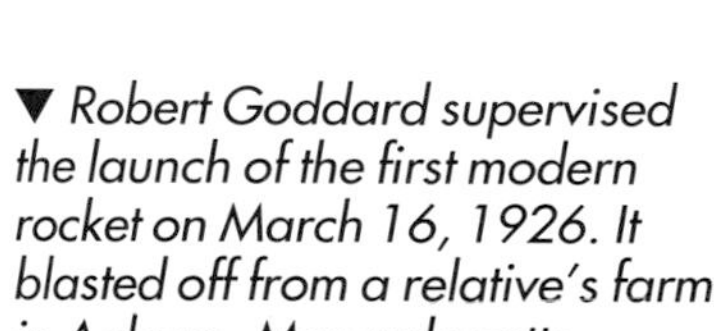

## GODDARD, Robert H.

Robert Goddard (1882–1945) was the United States' leading pioneer of rocket flight. Only after Goddard's death did scientists realize the importance of his work. He was the first to think about using liquid gases such as hydrogen and oxygen for rocket fuel rather than the conventional solid fuels. He launched his first successful liquid-propelled rocket in 1926. Throughout the 1930s, he experimented with larger and more powerful rockets. Much of Goddard's work bore fruit with the United States' successful spaceflights of the 1950s and 1960s.

▼ *Robert Goddard supervised the launch of the first modern rocket on March 16, 1926. It blasted off from a relative's farm in Auburn, Massachusetts.*

▲ *Goethals was a demanding organizer but he treated his workers fairly. He helped establish the eight-hour limit to the working day.*

## GOETHALS, George Washington 

George Washington Goethals (1858–1928) was an engineer and U.S. Army officer. His greatest achievement was to build the Panama Canal between the Caribbean Sea and the Pacific Ocean. This task, which lasted from 1907 to 1914, had seemed impossible to many. But Goethals solved the complex engineering problems. He also overcame the difficult supply and sanitation problems of working in a remote jungle region. From 1914 to 1916, Goethals was governor of the Panama Canal Zone. He was director of supplies for U.S. troops during World War I and later ran a successful engineering company.

## GOLD RUSH 

A gold rush is a sudden movement of fortune seekers into an area where gold has been discovered. Perhaps the most famous gold rush took place in California in the mid-1800s. On January 24, 1848, a workman at Sutter's Mill in the northern part of California discov-

▼ *Prospectors pan for gold at a mining camp in California. Some people made their fortunes indirectly from the Gold Rush. Levi Strauss began by selling his denim "Levis" to prospectors, and the Ames Shovel Company supplied hardware.*

ered nuggets of gold. Within months the news had spread all over the country and abroad. Men abandoned their jobs and families and headed west to make their fortunes. In 1849 some 80,000 prospectors arrived in California. They even included many Europeans.

Because the overland route was difficult and dangerous, many of these "forty-niners" chose the long sea voyage around the southern tip of South America, arriving in the port of San Francisco. A village of 800 people in 1848, it grew to 50,000 by 1855. Saloons and gambling palaces sprang up on every side to part the lucky prospectors from their new-found wealth.

Most of the forty-niners found nothing. The ramshackle mining camps they built were abandoned. But some fortunes were made, and by 1900 more than $1 billion worth of gold had been mined in California.

Other gold rushes took place in Colorado in 1858 and in the Klondike section of Canada's Yukon Territory in 1896.

▲ *Top women golfers such as Jan Stephenson can win up to $400,000 each year.*

## GOLF 

The United States produces more top golfers than any other country. One reason is the large number of public courses, where anyone can play. There are 12,500 golf courses in the United States, and 7,500 of those are open to the public. Some are even owned and run by towns and cities. These are called municipal courses.

The U.S. Open is the oldest tournament in the country. In 1995 it will celebrate its 100th birthday. It has produced some memorable success stories. In 1913 an unknown 20-year-old former caddie named Francis Ouimet beat the famous British champion Harry Vardon. In 1988 and 1989, Curtis Strange became the first man to win the U.S. Open two years in a row since Ben Hogan did it in 1950 and 1951. The PGA tournament, organized by the Professional Golfers' Association, dates from 1916. Like the U.S. Open, it is played at a different course each year.

The third important championship, or "Major," in the United States is the Masters Tournament. This is always played on the course in Augusta, Georgia, that was designed by the tournament's founder, Bobby JONES, in 1934. Today top golfers can win hundreds of thousands of dollars a year. And they can earn even more through advertising because of their fame.

**Bobby Jones**

**Jack Nicklaus**

▲ *Bobby Jones, an amateur, retired as world champion in 1930. Jack Nicklaus became the first golfer to win more than $2 million in prize money.*

**When Samuel Gompers was 13, his parents brought him to New York City. He got work in a cigar factory where the workers had a self-education plan. Each worker in turn read aloud while the others rolled cigars.**

## GOMPERS, Samuel

Samuel Gompers (1850–1924) was one of the most important U.S. labor leaders. Born in England, he moved to the United States when he was 13 and soon started work as a cigar maker. In the late 1800s, pay and working conditions in industry were very poor. LABOR UNIONS had little bargaining power. Gompers campaigned for an end to crowded sweatshops and for the right to strike. And he sought better wages and shorter working hours. In 1886 he became the first president of the American Federation of Labor (AFL). Except for one year, he held this position until his death.

▲ *Benny Goodman helped open up New York's Carnegie Hall to jazz in 1938. In 1962 he led the first jazz tour of the Soviet Union since the 1920s.*

## GOODMAN, Benny

Benny Goodman (1909–1986) was a JAZZ musician and bandleader. Born in Chicago, he showed a gift for music when only a child. He made his first public appearance at the age of 12 and joined a professional band four years later. Goodman's instrument was the clarinet. He played with jazz bands and also with full symphony orchestras—the first jazz musician to do so. He was one of the pioneers of the "swing" sound in jazz that became popular during the 1930s.

## GOOD NEIGHBOR POLICY

The Good Neighbor policy was proposed by President Franklin D. ROOSEVELT in his first inaugural address in 1933. He wanted to establish better relations with Latin American countries. These countries had come to distrust the United States because of its frequent intervention in their affairs. Roosevelt's policy was made clear at the Pan American conference in Montevideo, Uruguay, later in 1933. The nations that attended promised not to interfere in each others' affairs.

The United States honored its promise, and it gave a great deal of economic aid to Latin America. Those countries responded by supporting the United States in World War II. In 1949 the United States and the nations of Latin America formed the Organization of American States. And during the 1960s, under the Alliance for Progress, the United States gave Latin America much economic aid. U.S. relations with Latin America have not always been good in recent years.

## GOODYEAR, Charles

Charles Goodyear (1800–1860) was an inventor who developed a method of making rubber usable for everyday operations. Born in New Haven, Connecticut, Goodyear spent his early career working on inventions that he hoped would help industry. In 1832 he turned his attention to the basic form of rubber called India rubber. This has the familiar rubbery qualities at room temperature but becomes sticky when heated and brittle when cooled. Goodyear accidently added sulfur to this rubber while heating it. He found that the rubber retained its natural qualities even at this higher heat. Goodyear perfected this system of "vulcanizing" rubber, which led to many uses, particularly in car tires. He patented this invention, but later died in poverty.

## GOPHER

The gopher, or pocket gopher, is a RODENT. It is about 10 inches (25 cm) long. The gopher is found in many parts of North America. There are many different species of gophers. The most common are the eastern pocket gopher (found in Florida and the midwestern United States) and the western pocket gopher (found in western North America). The gopher spends most of its time underground in long tunnels it has dug with its large front claws and front teeth.

▲ *The gopher uses its sensitive tail to feel its way in the dark tunnels it digs with its teeth and large front claws.*

## GOULD, Jay

Jay Gould (1836–1892) was a businessman who owned many railroads in the United States. He made millions of dollars using questionable business practices. Most of his money was made in buying railroads. Gould took advantage of the fact that in his time there was no law about the way stocks and shares were issued. He got more and more people to invest. The effect of this was that each share was worth much less than it was bought for. Gould made a fortune, but many went bankrupt.

**Jay Gould made his fortune in the 1860s, when there were few controls to safeguard investors' money and to regulate business practices. Gould and other powerful multimillionaires, such as Cornelius Vanderbilt and John D. Rockefeller, came to be known as "Robber Barons."**

## GOURD

A gourd is a trailing or climbing plant that produces fruit very similar to squashes and pumpkins. The fruit, also called gourds, have hard shells. Gourds come in

**Bottle gourds, which may reach a length of 5 feet (1.5 m), were used by American Indians as utensils.**

many different shapes, sizes, and colors. A few gourds can be eaten. But most are used as decorations. One popular gourd is the loofah, or dishcloth gourd. The inside of the dried loofah can be used as a dishcloth or bath sponge. Originally the term "gourd" referred to only two plants, the yellow-flowered gourd and the bottle gourd.

*▼ All kinds of colorful and strangely shaped gourds can be grown at home in a sunny patch of the garden. The inside of a loofah gourd can be dried and used as a fragrant dishcloth.*

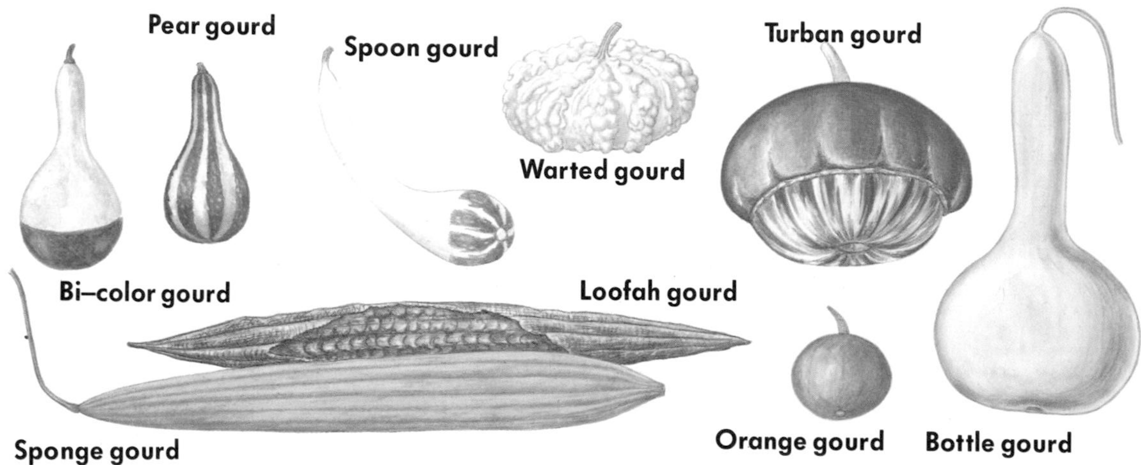


## GOVERNMENT, Canadian

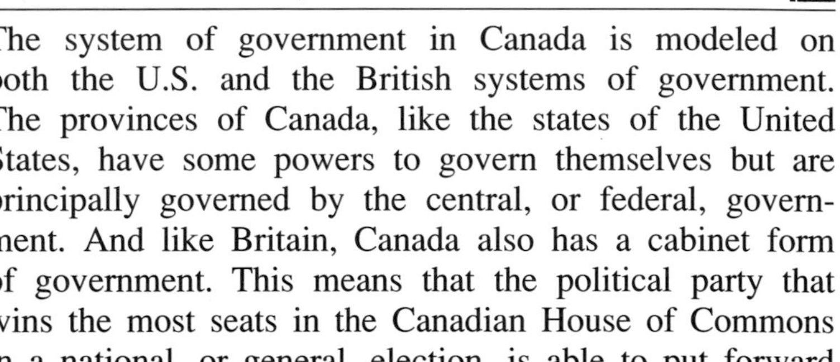

The system of government in Canada is modeled on both the U.S. and the British systems of government. The provinces of Canada, like the states of the United States, have some powers to govern themselves but are principally governed by the central, or federal, government. And like Britain, Canada also has a cabinet form of government. This means that the political party that wins the most seats in the Canadian House of Commons in a national, or general, election, is able to put forward

**For 15 years, from 1895 to 1911, Canada had only one prime minister, Wilfred Laurier. During these years, Canada expanded rapidly. Two transcontinental railroads were built, and the population increased by more than 30 percent between 1901 and 1911.**

*► Pierre Trudeau was prime minister in 1982 when Canada's modern constitution was introduced.*

◀ *The members of the leading political parties face each other in the Canadian Parliament in Ottawa. Those from the majority, or government, party sit on the left of the House. Opposition parties sit on the right.*

its leader to be the national leader, or PRIME MINISTER. With the support of Parliament, he then governs through his chief ministers, who collectively form the cabinet. And again like Britain, Canada is a constitutional monarchy. The queen of England is its head of state. She appoints a governor-general as her representative. Laws can only be passed if they are agreed on by both houses of Parliament. They must then be signed by the governor-general. Canada's legal system is independent of the government and is headed by the Supreme Court. (See also CONSTITUTION ACT.)

**In 1976, Quebec's provincial elections were won by the Parti Québecois, a party committed to making Quebec an independent republic. In 1980 a referendum in Quebec turned down the proposal.**

The Three Branches of Canadian Government (Federal and Provincial)

| EXECUTIVE | LEGISLATIVE | JUDICIAL |
|---|---|---|
| **Federal Level** | **Federal Level** | **Federal Level** |
| Sovereign (English monarch)<br>Governor-General (appointed by monarch)<br>Prime Minister (leader of majority party in House)<br>Cabinet (chosen from Prime Minister's party in Senate and House) | Senate (104 members chosen by Governor-General)<br>House of Commons (295 elected members) | Supreme Court of Canada (nine judges form highest court of appeal)<br>Federal Court of Canada A. Trial Division: 14 judges B. Court of Appeal: 10 judges |
| **Provincial Level** | **Provincial Level** | **Provincial Level** |
| Lieutenant-General (chosen by Governor-Gen.)<br>Premier (majority leader in legislature)<br>Cabinet (members of Premier's party) | Legislature* (members elected from local constituencies)<br><br>*Quebec's Legislature is called the National Assembly | Provincial Courts (number of judges varies by province)<br>Local justice provided by police magistrates, justices of the peace |

# GOVERNMENT, UNITED STATES

The United States has a federal form of government. This means that governmental power is shared by the federal, or central, government and the state governments. This article deals with the federal government. (See also LOCAL GOVERNMENT and STATE GOVERNMENT.)

The CONSTITUTION of the United States is the highest law of the land. It details some of the powers of the federal government. These include the power to make treaties, maintain an armed force, engage in war, coin money, and place a tariff (tax) on imports and exports.

The federal government is made up of the executive, legislative, and judicial branches. Each of these branches is separate. But there is a system of checks and balances that makes sure that no single branch becomes too powerful. The president, for example, can increase the size of the armed forces. But only CONGRESS can appropriate money for this purpose.

**James Madison, who has been called the Father of the American Constitution, said of government: "If men were angels, no government would be necessary. If angels were to govern man, neither external nor internal controls on government would be necessary."**

CONSTITUTION

Legislative Branch — House of Reps.; Senate

Executive Branch

Judicial Branch — Supreme Court; Appeals Court

**Executive Office**
President of the United States
Council of Economic Advisers
National Security Council
Office of Management and Budget

**Executive Departments**
Agriculture
Commerce
Defense
Education
Energy
Health and Human Services
Housing and Urban Development
Interior
Justice
Labor
State
Transportation
Treasury
Veterans Affairs

**Some Independent Agencies of the Executive Branch**
Central Intelligence Agency
Commission on Civil Rights
Environmental Protection Agency
Federal Communications Commission
Federal Reserve System
Federal Trade Commission
Interstate Commerce Commission
National Aeronautics and Space Administration
National Labor Relations Board
National Science Foundation
Peace Corps
Securities and Exchange Commission
United States Information Agency
United States Postal Service

◀ *The three branches of the federal government have their duties defined by the Constitution. This system of "checks and balances" prevents one branch from becoming too powerful.*

The executive branch enforces the nation's laws. The president heads this branch and is known as the chief executive of the United States. This branch includes 14 executive departments, such as the Department of Defense. The heads of these departments, and sometimes other officials, make up the CABINET, which advises the president. Many independent agencies, such as the Central Intelligence Agency, are also part of the executive branch.

The legislative branch—the Congress—originates and passes laws. It is made up of the SENATE and the HOUSE OF REPRESENTATIVES. There are 100 elected senators, two from each state. There are 435 elected representatives. The number of representatives from each state is determined by the state's population.

The judicial branch consists of the SUPREME COURT and other federal courts. The Supreme Court hears appeals cases from other federal courts and from the highest state courts. It interprets laws and determines whether federal, state, and local laws are constitutional.

▲ *President Bush, head of the executive branch, addresses Congress (legislative branch) by invitation only.*

**The United States was the first nation in the world to plan a capital city — Washington, D.C. — specially for its seat of government.**

▼ *The Constitution imposes limits on the types of federal responsibilities. State and local governments deal with most other matters, such as education, police, licenses, and public transportation.*

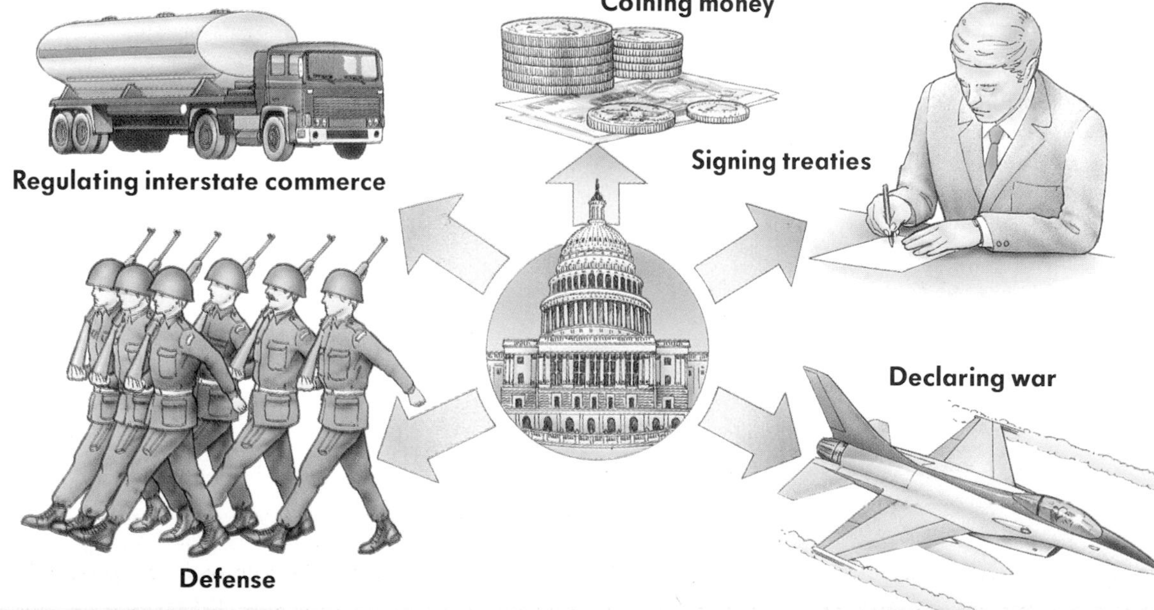

▲ *Billy Graham's religious mission since 1949 has extended beyond the United States to Africa, Asia, and Europe, including the Soviet Union.*

▼ *Martha Graham shocked audiences that expected traditional smooth and demure dancing. Her dances included sudden and dramatic movements, often expressing strong feelings.*

## GRAHAM, Billy

Billy Graham (1918– ) is a world-famous American religious leader. Born in Charlotte, North Carolina, he was ordained as a minister at 22. He has spent all his life as an evangelist—spreading the word of Christ by preaching. Graham has made many religious campaigns within the United States and in places as far away as Asia and Africa. He has also made many appearances on television and has written several books. Since 1955 Americans have voted him among the "ten most admired men in the world" some 30 times.

## GRAHAM, Martha

Of all the leaders of the modern dance movement, Martha Graham (1894–1991) has had the greatest influence. She trained at the important Denishawn School in California, which had been founded by Ruth St. Denis and Ted Shawn. There she learned about the dance traditions of many countries. Graham began developing her own style of dance in the 1920s. Her aim was to express feelings through dance. For this purpose she created a whole new way of dancing. It involved movements that were very expressive. Graham founded the Martha Graham School of Contemporary Dance in 1927 and produced very theatrical works. Among her most successful works are *Letter to the World*, a portrait of the poet Emily Dickinson, and *Appalachian Spring*, which portrays life on the American frontier.

## GRAINS

Grain is the seed of cereal grasses. The prairies and plains of North America are among the main regions of the world that grow grain. Wheat is the most important grain crop in the world. It is used for meal, breakfast cereal, and flour. CORN is another of the world's most important crops. It is used mainly as animal feed but also for cooking and in breakfast cereal. The United States is the biggest corn producer in the world.

Oats and barley are also widely grown in North America. These are used mainly for animal feed. But oats are also eaten as porridge, and barley is used to brew beer and for breakfast cereal. Other grains grown in North America are rye, millet, and rice.

## GRAND CANYON

Located in northwestern ARIZONA, the Grand Canyon is one of the most spectacular canyons in the world. It was carved out of rock over the past 6 million years by the COLORADO RIVER, which flows through it. The canyon is 277 miles (443 km) long, up to 1 mile (1.6 km) deep, and up to 18 miles (29 km) wide.

Layers of rock—sandstone, limestone, shale, and granite—are exposed in the sides of the canyon. There are many fossils in the rock, including shells, bones, and the tracks of camels, elephants, dinosaurs, and other animals. The rocks at the bottom of the canyon are the oldest rocks. They are at least 1 billion years old.

The deepest and most beautiful part of the canyon is within Grand Canyon National Park. Visitors drive or hike through it, ride mules down into the canyon, or travel by boat or raft down the Colorado River.

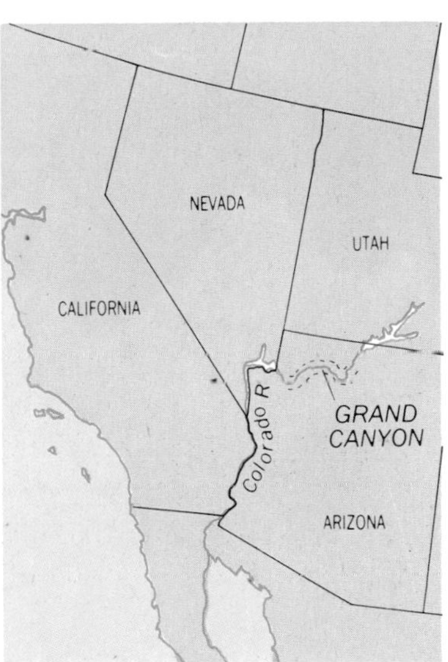


▲ *The Colorado River, which formed the Grand Canyon, is one of the major rivers in the United States.*

**The Grand Canyon gorge carved by the Colorado River reveals over a billion years of the earth's history. The North Rim of the gorge is more than 1,000 feet (300 m) higher than the South Rim in places. In 1540, García López de Cárdenas, a Spanish explorer, became the first European to see the Grand Canyon.**

◀ *The Grand Canyon has been preserved as a national park since 1919; its size was doubled in 1975. About 300 members of the Havasupai Indian tribe live in one of the side canyons.*

# GRANT, Ulysses S.

Ulysses S. Grant
**Born:** April 22, 1822, in Port Pleasant, Ohio
**Education:** West Point Military Academy
**Political party:** Republican
**Term of office:** 1869–1877
**Married:** 1848 to Julia Dent
**Died:** July 23, 1885, in Mount McGregor, New York

Ulysses S. Grant was the 18th president of the United States. He was elected president because of the popularity that grew out of his success as commander of the Union Army during the CIVIL WAR. Grant was an excellent general but did not have the qualities needed to make a good president. Scandal and corruption dominated his administration.

Grant won many crucial battles in the Civil War. He was given command of the Union Army in 1864. In 1865 the Confederate commander, General Robert E. LEE, surrendered at Appomattox Court House in Virginia.

Grant's fame led the Republicans to nominate him for president in 1868. He narrowly beat the Democratic candidate. In 1872 he was reelected by a larger margin. As president, Grant had to deal with many postwar problems. The KU KLUX KLAN terrorized the freed blacks. Congress passed two acts to try to protect black voting rights. There were also economic problems. Grant's leadership was too weak to cope with most of these problems. He appointed relatives, supporters, and other inexperienced people to important positions.

► *The Transcontinental Railroad was completed during Grant's presidency, on May 10, 1869. The last spike was driven in at Promontory Point, Utah.*

▼ *Grant's last year was spent in Mount McGregor, New York.*

Grant's time in office is most remembered for its scandals. He himself was honest, but he was unable to prevent widespread corruption at all levels of government. One scandal involved Grant's brother-in-law. His private secretary was involved in another, and members of Congress in yet another. In 1876, Grant refused to run for a third term. In 1880 a group within the Republican Party tried to nominate him, but the nomination went to James GARFIELD.

## GRASSHOPPERS

Grasshoppers are a type of INSECT. They can fly but they usually leap—and they can leap incredible distances. There are two main kinds. Long-horned grasshoppers have long antennas, and short-horned grasshoppers have shorter, thicker antennas. Grasshoppers, like other insects, use their antennas, or feelers, to feel, taste, and smell. Katydids and Mormon crickets are long-horned grasshoppers.

A few kinds of grasshoppers are pests. Some short-horned grasshoppers, called locusts, migrate in huge groups known as swarms in search of food. Swarms of locusts damage crops by eating the leaves of the plants. In the western United States, they cause millions of dollars worth of damage every year. Insecticides (chemicals that kill insects) are used to try to keep the numbers down. But little can be done to control a plague of locusts once a swarm develops.

▲ *Lubber grasshoppers are almost wingless. They live mainly in the southwestern states.*

## GREAT LAKES

The five Great Lakes—Superior, Michigan, Huron, Erie, and Ontario—make up North America's most important inland waterway. Ships can travel between the lakes and the Atlantic Ocean by way of the ST. LAWRENCE SEAWAY or other CANALS. This allows goods from the heartland of North America to be shipped all over the world.

Lake Superior is the world's largest freshwater lake.

▼ *Point Pelee is a Canadian National Park at the western end of Lake Erie. The different colors of the water on either side of the point indicate the varied depths of the lake.*

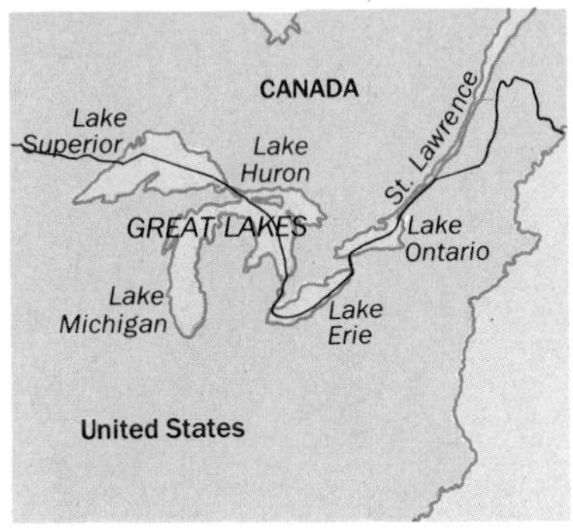


▲ *Cargo is often shipped more than 2,000 miles (3,200 km) from the Great Lakes to the Atlantic. The St. Lawrence Seaway takes all this trade.*

Lake Michigan is entirely within the U.S. boundary. Lakes Superior, Huron, Erie, and Ontario form a natural boundary between Canada and the United States, and the two countries share them.

Most of Canada's manufactured goods and half of those of the United States are produced in the Great Lakes area. The industry is extremely varied. It includes steel mills in Illinois, Indiana, Ohio, and Ontario and the automobile industry in Detroit. There are about 50 large ports and 150 smaller ones on the Great Lakes. Ocean-going ships can use the larger ports. Limestone, coal, iron ore, copper, and steel from the Great Lakes region are shipped on the lakes. Ships also carry timber and wood pulp from the forests north of the lakes, and grain from the prairies west and northwest.

POLLUTION of the lakes has been one of the reasons the commercial FISHING INDUSTRY has declined. However, progress is being made in fighting pollution, especially in lakes Michigan and Erie. The lakes are also much used for recreation.

Areas and Depths of the Great Lakes

**Superior:** 31,820 sq mi (82,414 km²).
Depth: 1,333 ft (406 m)
**Huron:** 23,010 sq mi (59,596 km²).
Depth: 750 ft (229 m)
**Michigan:** 22,400 sq mi (58,016 km²).
Depth: 923 ft (281 m)
**Erie:** 9,940 sq mi (25,745 km²).
Depth: 210 ft (64 m)
**Ontario:** 7,540 sq mi (19,529 km²).
Depth: 802 ft (244 m)

## GREAT PLAINS

The Great Plains are a high *plateau* (raised area of flat land) of dry grassland. They stretch from the Rocky Mountains eastward for about 400 miles (640 km) into the prairies. From north to south, they extend from southern Canada to southern Texas. They cover an area of about 1,125,000 square miles (2,900,000 km$^2$). Much of the region has cold winters and warm summers. There is little rain and a lot of wind. Most of North

► *Farms on the Great Plains are often located near rivers. This makes crop irrigation easier, and the trees that line the riverbanks act as windbreaks.*

America's wheat is grown in the eastern part of the plains. The rest of the land is used for other crops and for cattle and sheep grazing. The weather there is too harsh for large-scale agriculture.

At one time the Great Plains were the home of large herds of bison. Today the wildlife includes the PRAIRIE DOG, prairie falcon, PRONGHORN, COYOTE, and a small number of bison. In the woods of the northern Great Plains, timber wolves, CARIBOU, and MOOSE are still found.

▲ *Great Salt Lake is fed by freshwater streams from the Rocky Mountains. Much of this water evaporates, leaving behind salt deposits.*

## GREAT SALT LAKE

Great Salt Lake, in northwestern UTAH, is an inland sea. It is seven times saltier than the ocean. The lake is salty because the water does not drain away. Instead, it dries up, leaving salt behind. There is very little rainfall. The water in the lake—and the salt—comes from the three rivers that feed into it.

▲ *The white crust along the shore of Great Salt Lake is the salt that remains after the water evaporates. About 200,000 tons of salt are taken each year from the lake.*

Great Salt Lake is about 75 miles (120 km) long and 50 miles (80 km) wide, but the size varies at any particular time. It is less than 15 feet (4.5 m) deep in most places. It is so salty that a swimmer cannot sink. No fish can live in the water. However, the islands, marshes, and mudflats attract many waterfowl.

SALT LAKE CITY, Utah's capital, is 5 miles (8 km) southeast of the lake.

▲ *The two sides of the Great Seal appear on the dollar bill. The scroll reads* E pluribus unum, *which means "From many [states], one [nation]."*

## GREAT SEAL OF THE UNITED STATES

The Great Seal is the official symbol of the United States. The face of the seal is used on important documents. It shows the American bald eagle. On its breast is a shield with 13 red and white stripes. In its right talon the eagle clutches an olive branch with 13 leaves and 13 olives. This symbolizes peace. In its left talon are 13 arrows, symbolizing might. The scroll in its beak reads *E pluribus unum* ("From many [states], one [nation]"). Above the eagle's head are 13 stars, one for each of the 13 original states. On the reverse of the seal is a pyramid, surmounted by an eye, representing Providence. The words *Annuit coeptis* mean "He [God] has favored our undertakings." Below the pyramid are the words *Novus ordo seclorum*, which translate as "a new order of the ages"—that is, the new American republic.

▲ *Horace Greeley popularized the phrase "Go west, young man" as advice to the unemployed of New York City.*

## GREELEY, Horace

The newspaper editor Horace Greeley (1811–1872) was the founder of the *New York Tribune*, a forerunner of today's *Herald Tribune*. He used his newspaper to campaign for various reforms, especially the abolition of slavery. He supported public education and an end to the death penalty. Greeley also fought for equality for women in jobs, but he opposed giving them the vote.

Not satisfied with merely influencing public opinion, Greeley tried several times to win public office. In 1872 he ran against President GRANT. Although Grant won, Greeley polled almost as many popular votes.

▼ *Before leaving its burrow, the groundhog sits up on its haunches to look and listen for signs of danger.*

## GROUNDHOG

The groundhog, or woodchuck, is a member of the SQUIRREL family. It lives in woodlands in much of Canada and in eastern parts of the United States. About 25 inches (65 cm) long, it has a bushy tail and feet with sharp claws that are good for digging. Groundhogs dig underground burrows. They sleep in them at night and also run to them in case of danger. During the day groundhogs feed on grass, leaves, shoots, seeds, and fruits. Farmers regard them as pests because they eat crops. In autumn they fill the entrance to their burrows with stones and grass and hibernate until late winter or early spring.

## GROUND SQUIRREL

The ground squirrel is a SQUIRREL that lives in burrows it digs underground. It sleeps in its burrow at night. Ground squirrels that live in cold areas hibernate in the burrows during the winter. North America has many different types of ground squirrels.

The antelope ground squirrel lives on the dry plains and low mountainsides of the southwestern United States. The underside of its tail is white. It holds its tail over its back, which is the reason for its name.

The thirteen-lined ground squirrel is found west of the Great Lakes. It has 13 white stripes on its back and sides. The California ground squirrel lives in Oregon and California. It eats crops. Its fleas transmitted bubonic plague in San Francisco in 1900. The Arctic ground squirrel is found in northern Canada and Alaska. It is as long as 20 inches (50 cm). It is a traditional source of food and clothing for Eskimos. The golden-mantled ground squirrel lives in the mountains and forests of the western United States and southwestern Canada. The ruck ground squirrel is common in the western United States.

▲ *Ground squirrels hibernate most of the winter, partly because their dark coats show up so clearly against the snow.*

## GUAM

Guam is a small island in the western Pacific Ocean. It is 30 miles (48 km) long and 8 miles (13 km) wide. Guam has been a U.S. territory since 1898, when Spain ceded it to the United States after the SPANISH-AMERICAN WAR. Since 1950 the people of Guam have been U.S. citizens. They have a government of their own and also elect one nonvoting delegate to the House of

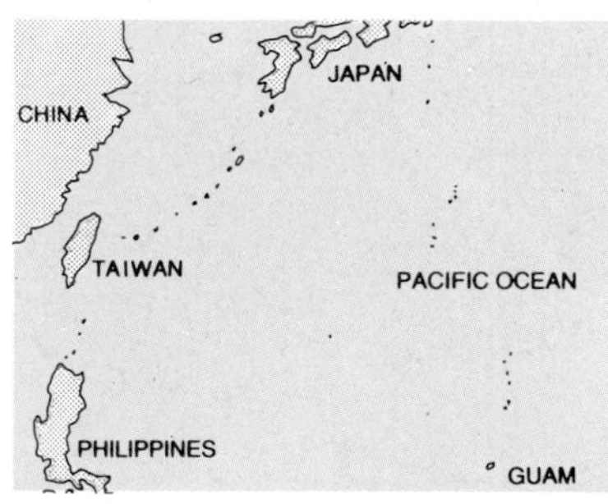


▲ *Guam is the largest and southernmost of the Mariana Islands in the western Pacific.*

**Guam**
**Capital:** Agana
**Area:** 209 sq mi (541 km²)
**Population:** 133,000
**Status:** self-governing territory of the United States
**Location:** Mariana Islands in the western Pacific Ocean
**Sources of income:** military installations, tourism, chicken farming, fishing

◀ *Guam's Andersen Air Force Base is an important U.S. military installation in the Pacific Ocean.*

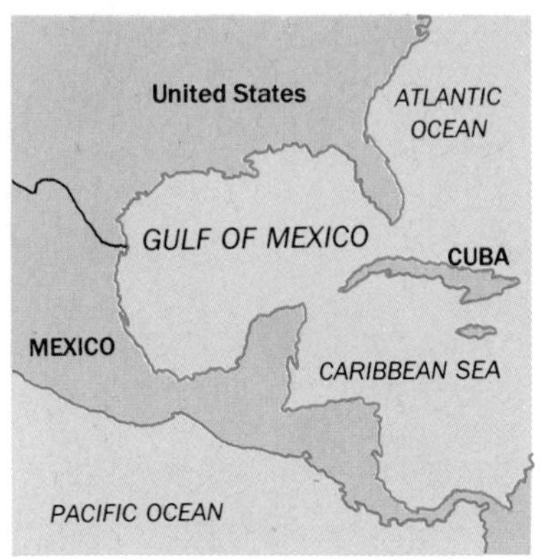


▲ *The warm waters of the Gulf of Mexico breed most of the hurricanes that hit North and Central America.*

▼ *Some common American gulls and terns. As well as being normally smaller than gulls, terns can be identified by their swallowlike forked tails.*

Representatives in Washington, D.C. Guam is strategically important to the United States and much of its economy depends on the air force and naval bases there. About one fifth of the 133,000 people living on Guam are American servicemen and women. In December 1941, three days after it attacked PEARL HARBOR, Japan captured Guam; in 1944 it was retaken by the U.S. Marines.

## GULF OF MEXICO

The Gulf of Mexico is a huge area of water almost entirely surrounded by Mexico and the southern coast of the United States. Texas, Louisiana, Mississippi, Alabama, and Florida all border it. Cuba is the only large land mass on its southeastern corner. The Caribbean Sea and the Atlantic Ocean both flow into it. Much of it is shallow and warm, and most of the land that faces it is marshy and low-lying, with few good harbors. Water flowing out from the Gulf of Mexico into the Atlantic forms the Gulf Stream, a warm-water current that runs up the east coast of the United States.

## GULLS AND TERNS

Gulls and terns are two closely related types of seabirds. Gulls can swim better, but terns are faster, more graceful fliers. Both are usually mixed white, gray, and black in color. They are found almost everywhere in the world, even well inland.

From bill to tail, gulls range in size between 11 and 31 inches (28 and 78 cm). Best known in the United States is the herring gull, which is often seen eating discarded food at ports and garbage dumps. Terns are smaller on average, ranging in length from 8 to 21 inches (20 to 53 cm). The arctic tern is the greatest traveler of all birds. It flies from the far north to the Antarctic each autumn.

## GUNS

Guns have played an important part in American history since colonial times. Settlers relied on firearms to protect themselves against Indians and wild animals. These guns were made primarily in England and other European countries. By the time American pioneers began to settle the West, American guns were being made. One of the most reliable was the Colt revolver, manufactured by Samuel Colt beginning in 1836. It was known as the six-shooter because it could fire six shots without being reloaded. The Winchester rifle, another favored weapon in the West, was first made in 1866. It could fire 15 bullets without reloading.

Article II of the U.S. Constitution protects "the right of the people to keep and bear arms." But today more and more guns are falling into the hands of criminals. The National Rifle Association argues for the continued right to bear arms. It helps train people in the proper use of weapons. However, the number of murders committed with guns increases every year in the United States.

**Colt navy revolver 1851**

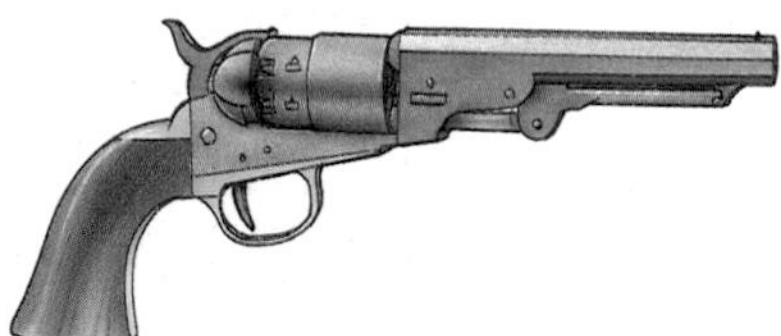

**Gatling gun 1861**

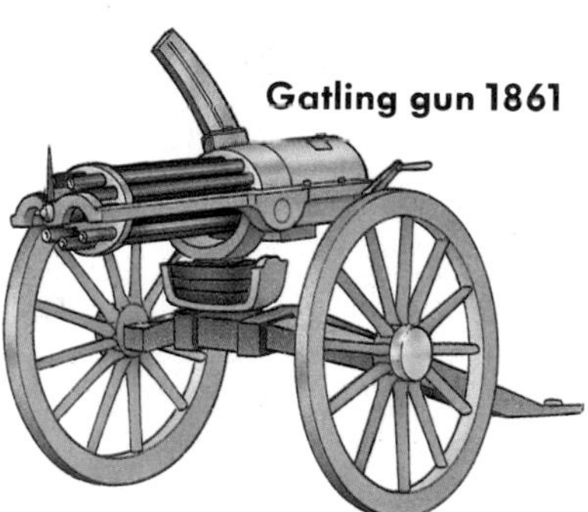

▲ *The Colt revolver was the ultimate law enforcer in the Wild West. The Gatling gun, an early machine gun, was developed during the Civil War.*

## GYMNASTICS

Gymnastics is an important part of physical education in schools in the United States. Gymnastic exercises help students increase their strength, coordination, balance, agility, and flexibility. Gymnastic events are popular in the summer Olympic Games.

In men's Olympic competition, there are six events. Two are performed on "horses," which are leather-covered objects. The competitor performs athletic maneuvers on and around these horses, using only his hands for support. The same applies to routines conducted on parallel bars, the horizontal bar, and rings. The floor exercise consists of maneuvers on a mat. Women compete in the horse vault, uneven bars, balance beam, and floor exercise.

▼ *Mary Lou Retton is shown here on the balance beam, one of the most difficult women's gymnastic events. They must jump, somersault, and do cartwheels on a beam that is only 4 inches (100 mm) wide.*

## HALE, Nathan

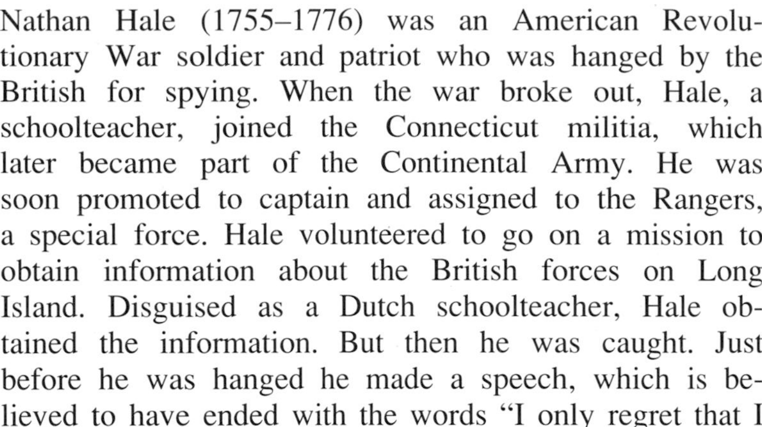

Nathan Hale (1755–1776) was an American Revolutionary War soldier and patriot who was hanged by the British for spying. When the war broke out, Hale, a schoolteacher, joined the Connecticut militia, which later became part of the Continental Army. He was soon promoted to captain and assigned to the Rangers, a special force. Hale volunteered to go on a mission to obtain information about the British forces on Long Island. Disguised as a Dutch schoolteacher, Hale obtained the information. But then he was caught. Just before he was hanged he made a speech, which is believed to have ended with the words "I only regret that I have but one life to lose for my country."

► *Nathan Hale was hanged in New York City. British Major Cunningham refused his last request for a Bible.*

▼ *A statue of a young player stands outside the Baseball Hall of Fame and Museum in Cooperstown, New York.*

## HALL OF FAME

A hall of fame is designed to pay honor to a special group of people. There are many different halls of fame. Some contain busts of the honored people. Others contain actual mementos. The Hall of Fame for Great Americans is in New York City. It contains busts of Americans from many different fields: presidents, including George Washington and Thomas Jefferson; writers such as Henry Wadsworth Longfellow, Harriet Beecher Stowe, and Edgar Allan Poe; and inventors, among them Elias Howe and Thomas Edison. Other halls of fame include those for baseball, football, American Indians, American women, and space travel.

◀ *The tradition of Halloween goes back to ancient pagan (pre-Christian) festivals of witches and spirits.*

**The word "Halloween" is a shortened form of All Hallows Eve. All Hallows, now known as All Saints, is the day when many Christians honor the memory of all the saints. The Christian Church in Medieval Europe used this religious purpose to take the place of the witching festival that already existed.**

## HALLOWEEN 

Halloween is celebrated on October 31, when children dress up in costumes and "trick-or-treat"—going from house to house to ask for a treat in return for not playing a prank. These days the "trick" is not normally done. The treat is often candy. Some children collect money for UNICEF (the United Nations Children's Fund), instead of a treat. A jack-o'-lantern is traditionally made on Halloween. It is a hollowed-out pumpkin with a face carved in it and a candle or other light inside. Halloween parties are often held. Costumes are worn and traditional games like bobbing for an apple are played.

## HAMILTON, Alexander 

Alexander Hamilton (1755–1804) was one of the Founding Fathers of the United States. More than any other leader, he was responsible for the ratification of the U.S. Constitution and the establishment of a strong central government. Hamilton was also the country's first secretary of the treasury.

Hamilton was born on the British West Indies island of Nevis. While in his teens, he traveled to North America, where he studied at King's College (now Columbia University). When the American REVOLUTION started, Hamilton joined the Continental Army. He fought brilliantly in several battles and was soon made an aide to General George WASHINGTON.

After the war, Hamilton became a leading lawyer in

▼ *Alexander Hamilton favored the creation of a national bank. He succeeded in this aim, despite opposition from Secretary of State Thomas Jefferson.*

▲ *Hamilton's location on the shore of Lake Ontario has made it a trading and industrial center.*

New York. He was a delegate to the CONTINENTAL CONGRESS in 1782 and the Constitutional Convention in 1787. At both he fought for the establishment of a strong central government. Hamilton felt that the Constitution left too much power to the states. Still, with John JAY, and James MADISON, Hamilton wrote the *Federalist* papers, urging ratification.

After Washington became president, he named Hamilton secretary of the treasury. During this period (1789–1795), the United States' first two political parties were formed. The FEDERALIST Party, led by Hamilton, wanted a strong central government. The Democratic-Republican Party, led by Thomas JEFFERSON, wanted less control from a national government.

Hamilton believed that for the new nation to prosper, it needed to be strong financially. To this end he began a system of federal taxes.

Hamilton remained influential even after leaving office. One of his long-time political opponents was Aaron BURR. Hamilton's opposition was the main reason for Burr's defeat in the presidential election of 1800 and the election for New York governor in 1804. Following this second defeat, Burr challenged Hamilton to a duel. On July 11, 1804, Burr shot Hamilton. Hamilton died the next day.

▼ *Oscar Hammerstein modernized musical comedies by combining catchy songs with good plots and dancing.*

## HAMILTON

Hamilton is an important port in the Canadian province of ONTARIO. It is located on the western end of Lake Ontario, which is part of the ST. LAWRENCE SEAWAY. Hamilton is a major port along the seaway. More than 10 million tons of cargo pass through Hamilton each year. Train connections link it with western Canada and most of the United States. As a result, cargo transport is the largest source of work. Hamilton is also an important financial and steel-producing center. More than half of Canada's steel is produced there.

## HAMMERSTEIN, Oscar, II

Oscar Hammerstein (1895–1960) is one of the key names in the history of musical comedies. Born in New York City, he had written the lyrics (words) for his first musical by the age of 25. His musicals had strong stories with a good script. The songs and dances were carefully worked to be part of the action. He worked with Sigmund ROMBERG and Jerome KERN, but his most famous partnership was with Richard RODGERS. They wrote *Oklahoma!*, *Carousel*, *South Pacific*, *The King and I*, and *The Sound of Music*.

## HANCOCK, John 

▲ *In 1780, John Hancock was elected governor of Massachusetts. He held that office almost without interruption until his death.*

John Hancock (1737–1793) was a leader of the American REVOLUTION. He was the first to sign the Declaration of Independence. He wrote his name in very large letters. This is the origin of the term "John Hancock" for a person's signature.

Hancock was born into a prominent Massachusetts family. He graduated from Harvard and went into an uncle's business. Later he entered local Boston politics and joined with Samuel Adams in opposing the presence of British troops in the colony. He was a delegate to the Continental Congress between 1775 and 1780 and its president in the crucial time when it decided on independence.

► *Hancock's signature is famous because, as president of the Continental Congress, he was first to sign the Declaration of Independence. His was also the largest signature.*

John Hancock

▼ *The "Saint Louis Blues" was released in 1914. Handy achieved musical and publishing success by overcoming racial prejudice and the handicap of being blind during his later years.*

## HANDY, William Christopher 

Many people consider the black composer and bandleader W. C. Handy (1873–1958) to be the "father of the blues." He did not invent the blues, which developed from black folk music. But he did a great deal to popularize the songs, arranging them for his own orchestra. He also wrote some of the best blues of all time, including "Memphis Blues" and "Saint Louis Blues," as well as marches and some symphonic pieces. Because he couldn't find a publisher for "Saint Louis Blues," he started his own music publishing business, which helped bring black music to a wider public.

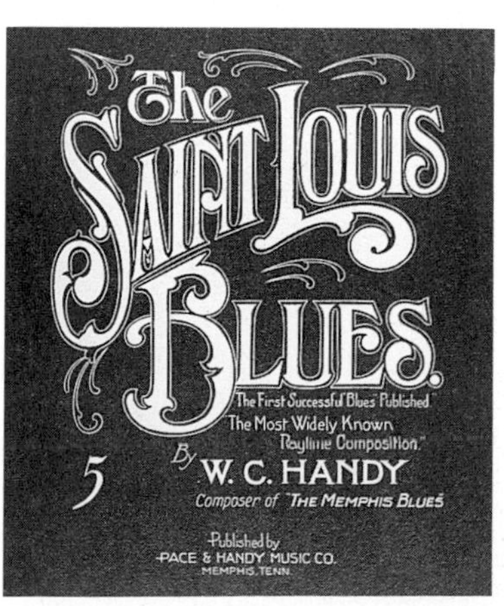

# HARDING, Warren

Warren Gamaliel Harding was the 29th president of the United States. In the presidential election of 1920, he received seven million more votes than his Democratic opponent. This was a wider margin than any previous president had won by. Harding offered people a "return to normalcy" after the difficult years of World War I. Unfortunately, there was a great deal of corruption during his administration.

Harding was a good-natured, easygoing man. He was very popular with the public. A conservative Republican, he was selected as the presidential nominee by party bosses.

► *Prohibition, or the banning of alcoholic beverages, began under President Harding.*

**Warren Harding**
**Born:** November 2, 1865 near Corsica, Ohio
**Education:** Ohio Central College
**Political party:** Republican
**Term of office:** 1921–1923
**Married:** 1891 to Florence King DeWolfe
**Died:** August 2, 1923, in San Francisco, California

After he was elected, Harding made some poor choices for his Cabinet. Many other important government jobs went to unqualified or dishonest people, who took advantage of their positions for personal gain. There were many scandals. The worst of the scandals was the Teapot Dome oil scandal. The Secretary of the Interior had taken bribes to lease some of the Navy's oil reserves. The scandals overshadowed everything else about Harding's administration.

In foreign policy, Harding refused to allow the United States to join the League of Nations or to cooperate with Europe on defense. At home, the government cut taxes and set a high protective tariff (tax on imported goods). It also established a federal budget system. For the first time ever, the United States drastically reduced the number of immigrants allowed into the country. Harding died in office, before people had become aware of how much corruption there was.

▼ *The Teapot Dome scandal helped ruin President Harding's reputation.*

## HARPER, Frances

Frances Harper (1825–1911) was an author and leading black poet of her time. She was born Frances Ellen Watkins to free parents in Baltimore. They died when she was only two, so she was reared and educated by an uncle. From 1854 she wrote poetry and delivered lectures in northern states. Her arguments helped convince many people of the evils of slavery. In 1860 she married a farmer, Fenton Harper, and took his name. She stopped lecturing four years later when he died, but she continued writing. *Moses: A Story of the Nile*, written in 1869, was seen as a triumph. Frances Harper's later years were spent campaigning against the drinking of alcoholic beverages and for women's right to vote.

▲ *In her later years, Frances Harper combined her work for racial equality with the movement to support women's right to vote.*

## HARRIMAN, W. Averell

W. Averell Harriman (1891–1986) was an important U.S. statesman. Born in New York, he became a millionaire before entering government service. From 1948 to 1953 he was the administrator of the Marshall Plan, the vast U.S. economic aid program in Europe after the end of World War II. During the war itself, he had helped arrange U.S. military aid to Britain and the Soviet Union. In 1963, he also helped negotiate the first nuclear test ban treaty between the United States, the Soviet Union, and Great Britain. Harriman was also governor of New York from 1955 to 1958.

**During his long and distinguished career as a statesman and diplomat, W. Averell Harriman served under four presidents — Franklin D. Roosevelt, Harry Truman, John F. Kennedy, and Lyndon Johnson.**

## HARRIS, Joel Chandler

Joel Chandler Harris (1848–1908) was the creator of the Uncle Remus stories. These were based on folk legends of black Americans. Harris learned about these legends when he worked on *The Countryman*, a newspaper published by a plantation owner in Georgia. Harris began writing for the *Atlantic Constitution* in 1876. Three years later he published the first of the Uncle Remus stories, "The Tar Baby." In this story, and in those that followed, Uncle Remus, a former slave, tells stories to the son of the family he works for. The stories are about the adventures and mishaps of various animal characters, including Brer Rabbit and Brer Fox. They are full of humor and wisdom and capture the speech patterns of rural blacks of the 1800s.

**Joel Chandler Harris's "Uncle Remus" stories were immediately popular across the country. Ordinary readers identified with the homespun humor and vivid descriptions of the characters. Serious critics praised Harris for his study of black American speech.**

## HARRISON, Benjamin

Benjamin Harrison
**Born:** August 20, 1833, in North Bend, Ohio
**Education:** Miami University, Ohio
**Political party:** Republican
**Term of office:** 1889–1893
**Married:** 1853 to Caroline Lavinia Scott; 1896 to Mary Dimmick
**Died:** March 13, 1901, in Indianapolis, Indiana

Benjamin Harrison was the 23rd president of the United States. His grandfather was William Henry HARRISON, the ninth president.

Harrison became a lawyer while in his early twenties and soon entered politics. When the CIVIL WAR started in 1861, he became commander of the 70th Regiment of Indiana Volunteers. After the war he returned to politics and his law practice. Harrison was elected to the U.S. Senate from Indiana in 1881 and ran for president in 1888 against President Grover CLEVELAND. Cleveland got more popular votes than Harrison, but Harrison won the election because he had more electoral votes. (See ELECTORAL COLLEGE.)

During Harrison's administration, his party, the Republican Party, controlled Congress. The Congress raised tariffs (taxes on imported goods) to protect American manufacturers. But this also made it more expensive for people to buy things.

► *The United States saw some of its greatest waves of immigrants during the presidency of Benjamin Harrison.*

▼ *Harrison's wife Caroline, shown here in a White House photo, died in 1892.*

Under Harrison, the United States became more involved in foreign affairs. It set up a conference in Washington, D.C., with most of the Latin American countries. This led to the formation of the Pan-American Union, whose aim was to promote cooperation between the United States and Latin America. (See ORGANIZATION OF AMERICAN STATES.) And the United States, along with Great Britain and Germany, made the Samoan Islands a protectorate.

Harrison's high tariffs and heavy government spending were not popular. In the 1882 presidential election, he lost to Grover Cleveland.

# HARRISON, William Henry

William Henry Harrison was the ninth president of the United States. He held the office for one month—the shortest time in U.S. history. He was the first president to die in office.

Harrison fought in the Indian wars during the 1790s, and then became the first governor of the new Indiana Territory in 1800. He negotiated treaties with the Indians that gave settlers millions of acres of land. The Indians, led by the Shawnee chief TECUMSEH, resisted. In 1811, Harrison and his men defeated the Indians at the Battle of Tippecanoe. During the WAR OF 1812, in the Battle of the Thames, in Ontario, Canada, General Harrison and his troops defeated the British and their Indian allies. After the war, Harrison settled in Ohio and became a leader in Whig politics. He served in the U.S. House of Representatives, the Ohio Senate, the U.S. Senate, and as minister to Colombia. In 1836 he ran unsuccessfully for president against the Democratic candidate Martin VAN BUREN.

In 1840 Harrison ran once again against Van Buren. This time the Whigs exploited Harrison's "old soldier" and frontiersman image. The vice presidential candidate was John Tyler. "Tippecanoe and Tyler, too" became the rallying cry. Harrison—or "Old Tip," as he was called—won easily.

On the day he was inaugurated, Harrison insisted on standing in the drizzle wearing no hat or coat. He caught a cold that turned into pneumonia. He died one month later.

**William Henry Harrison**
**Born:** February 9, 1773, in Charles City County, Virginia
**Education:** University of Pennsylvania
**Political party:** Whig
**Term of office:** 1841
**Married:** 1795 to Anne Symmes
**Died:** April 4, 1841, in the White House

◄ *William Henry Harrison caught a cold while delivering his inaugural address in 1841. He died 30 days later.*

▼ *Harrison's 1840 presidential campaign relied on his military victories of 30 years before.*

# HAWAII

Hawaii is the youngest state in the United States. It is also the southernmost state and the only state that is not part of the North American continent. Hawaii is a chain of 132 volcanic islands in the Pacific Ocean. It is located about 2,400 miles (3,900 km) from the nearest point of the continental United States. Most people in Hawaii live on the eight largest islands. These are Hawaii, Maui, Oahu, Kauai, Molokai, Lanai, Nihau, and Kahoolawe. Hawaii is the largest island. But almost 80 percent of the people live on Oahu. It is the site of Honolulu, the state's capital and largest city.

Tourism is the main source of the islands' prosperity. Millions of people visit Hawaii every year to enjoy its warm, sunny climate, its coral reefs and sandy beaches, its lush mountain scenery, and its relaxed, friendly lifestyles. The Hawaiians are known for their warmth and charm; they greet visitors with garlands of flowers called *leis*. Traditional Hawaiian feasts called *luaus* are also popular with visitors and locals alike.

The original Hawaiians were Polynesians who sailed to the islands over 2,000 years ago in great canoes. Today, pure Hawaiians make up only 1 percent of the population. Many people from Japan, the Philippines, China, and other parts of Asia live in Hawaii. Many make their living from food processing, especially of pineapples, the islands' largest crop.

Hawaii became a U.S. territory in 1900 and a state in 1959. There has been a major naval and air force base at PEARL HARBOR on Oahu since before World War I. When Japanese planes attacked Pearl Harbor on December 7, 1941, the United States entered World War II.

Hawaii
**Capital:** Honolulu
**Area:** 10,932 sq mi (28,313 km$^2$). Rank: 43rd
**Population:** 1,108,229 (1990). Rank: 41st
**Statehood:** Aug. 21, 1959
**Principal rivers:** Wialuku (Hawaii), Anahulu (Oahu)
**Highest point:** Mauna Kea, 13,796 ft (4,205 m)
**Motto:** *Ua Mau Ke Ea O Ka Aina I Ka Pono* ("The Life of the Land is Perpetuated in Righteousness")
**Song:** "Hawaii Ponoi"

► *Taro, grown mainly for its edible root, is cultivated on small Hawaiian farms.*

▶ *The Hawaiian islands were formed by volcanoes. Much of Hawaii's shoreline rises abruptly from the Pacific Ocean.*

Places of Interest

- Kealakekua Bay, on the island of Hawaii, is where Captain James Cook was killed in 1779.
- Pearl Harbor, on Oahu, is a U.S. naval base and scene of the famous bombing by the Japanese in 1941.
- Waimea Canyon, on Kauai, is a deep gorge colored with tropical foliage. A highway nearby offers excellent views.

▶ *Waikiki Beach, with its famous Diamond Head mountain in the background, is one of the most popular tourist attractions in the United States.*

▲ *Most hawks soar high above the ground looking for prey below. Their keen eyesight enables them to see prey such as rabbits nearly a mile away.*

## HAWK

The hawk is a BIRD OF PREY. It is related to the eagle. One type of hawk is called a true hawk, or bird hawk, or chicken hawk. True hawks' bodies are streamlined and they have long, pointed wings. This makes them good at flying low and fast through the woods. Another type of hawk is the buteo, or buzzard hawk. Buteos are large and heavy, with broad wings and wide tails. They may perch high up on a tree, or soar in circles in the sky. When they spot their prey, they swoop down. The American red-tailed hawk, the sharp-shinned hawk, and Cooper's hawk are all found in the United States. Sometimes other birds of prey, such as the marsh hawk and other falcons, are also regarded as types of hawks.

▼ *Nathaniel Hawthorne's works painted a grim picture of life in colonial Massachusetts, where his ancestors had been prominent Puritan leaders.*

## HAWTHORNE, Nathaniel

Nathaniel Hawthorne (1804–1864) was an important novelist. Sin and guilt are major themes in his writing. *The Scarlet Letter* is considered Hawthorne's finest book. It is the moving story of a young woman who is persecuted for adultery. In *The House of Seven Gables*, Hawthorne tells the story of a family who for generations have lived under a curse.

Success as a writer did not come easily to Hawthorne. He was in his early thirties when *Twice-told Tales*, his first book under his own name, was published; and the last ten years of his life were not very productive. But he was one of the major figures in the first flowering of American literature, in the early 1800s. Hawthorne also had a strong influence on the work of his friend Herman MELVILLE and other writers.

## HAYES, Rutherford B.

Rutherford B. Hayes was the 19th president of the United States. He ended the RECONSTRUCTION in the South after the CIVIL WAR. But he is most remembered for the circumstances of his election in 1876. Some people described it as the "stolen election."

In the election, Hayes's Democratic opponent, Samuel Tilden, received a majority of the popular votes. He needed one more electoral vote in the ELECTORAL COLLEGE to win. However, there were a further 20 electoral votes that the Republicans said did not count because of voting procedures in those states.

An Electoral Commission was set up to break the deadlock. The commission decided to give all 20 votes to Hayes. He therefore won the election. In fact, the Republicans had secretly come to an agreement with the Southern Democrats. In return for the Southern Democrats' support for Hayes, the Republicans promised to remove federal troops from the South. Hayes had nothing to do with the compromise, but he did fulfill its promises.

When Hayes took office, the country was in an economic depression. Hayes was a supporter of "sound money." This meant he did not want to increase the amount of paper money or silver coins in circulation. By the end of his term, the country was more prosperous. Hayes also started reforming the civil service. During his time in office, Hayes restored faith in the presidency. However, he did not run for another term.

**Rutherford B. Hayes**
**Born:** October 4, 1822, in Delaware, Ohio
**Education:** Kenyon College, Ohio, and Harvard Law School
**Political party:** Republican
**Term of office:** 1877–1881
**Married:** 1852 to Lucy Ware Webb
**Died:** January 17, 1893 in Fremont, Ohio

▼ *Railroad workers called a national strike in 1877, shortly after Hayes became president. He called out federal troops to crush the strike.*

► *This intensive care unit in Cleveland, Ohio, uses modern computers to monitor the progress of patients.*

**More than 7 million people work in the U.S. medical care system — the country's largest employer. There are 650,000 physicians, 1,666,000 nurses, and 168,000 dentists. There are almost 6,700 hospitals, with 1,210,000 beds. The majority of the population relies on private insurance, which on average covers less than 40 percent of health costs.**

## HEALTH

Good health is the state of being physically and mentally fit. Physical fitness means having enough energy to carry out everyday tasks and leisure activities without becoming unusually tired. Regular exercise helps people stay physically fit. They also need to get enough sleep and to eat properly. In addition, it is important to visit the doctor and dentist for regular check-ups and to avoid such bad habits as smoking, drinking alcoholic beverages, and taking illegal drugs. Mental health means feeling good about oneself and getting along with others. Being mentally healthy gives people the chance to get what they want out of life.

Being healthy, however, needs more than individual effort. Community action, mainly by government agencies, protects the public from health hazards. For example, requiring everybody to be vaccinated prevents certain infectious diseases. Food sold to the public is checked carefully to make sure it is fit to eat. Laws keep the air we breathe and the water we drink from being fouled by pollution.

Finally, people need access to medical care. The United States has one of the best health-care systems in

▼ *Medical professionals offer reassurance to young patients. A doctor checks this boy's tonsils with a small flashlight.*

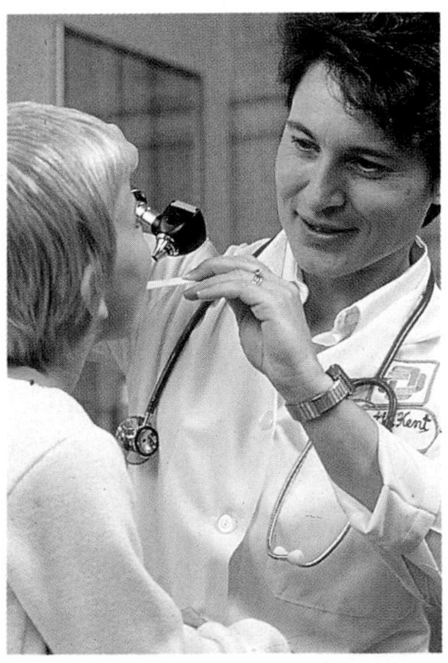

the world. But different regions and different ethnic groups sometimes get unequal treatment. The infant mortality rate for non-whites, for example, is nearly double that for whites. Another major problem is the rising cost of health care. Today the cost is more than double that of 1980. Health care costs about $2,566 per person each year. The total spent each year is about $666 billion. The government spends nearly $269 billion of this. Most Americans are covered by public or private health insurance. But 14 percent of the people are not covered or need public assistance to pay their bills.

Almost 70 percent of all deaths in the United States are caused by diseases of the heart and blood vessels and by cancer. Accidents, lung diseases, and pneumonia and flu are other leading causes of death. During the 1980s, AIDS became a leading cause of death. This disease, *A*cquired *I*mmune *D*eficiency *S*yndrome, has become a major public health problem.

▲ *William Randolph Hearst's power as a newspaper owner has never been matched. His newspaper crusade led the United States into the Spanish-American War in 1898.*

## HEARST, William Randolph

William Randolph Hearst (1863–1951) was one of the most successful American newspaper and magazine publishers. He pioneered a new kind of journalism. It used large headlines and a no-holds-barred style of writing. Popular journalism, or "yellow" journalism, as people called it, had an enormous impact, and Hearst was able to influence public opinion. But many disliked his bullying personality and unscrupulous business methods. He was never afraid to lower the prices of his papers to put rivals out of business, and he often used his papers to put forward his own ideas and to help his political ambitions.

▼ *Coast Guard helicopters use winches to rescue people from the decks of ships in high seas.*

## HELICOPTER

Helicopters are useful aircraft because they can take off and land almost anywhere. Radio stations in large U.S. cities use helicopters to report on traffic conditions. Military helicopters are used to transport troops and supplies, and U.S. Navy helicopters have been used to pluck astronauts from the sea after space missions. Large helicopters are sometimes used in construction projects to lower heavy girders into place. The Russian-born American engineer Igor SIKORSKY built the first successful helicopter in the United States in 1939.

▼ *These lightweight Bell helicopters are designed for combat or civilian use.*

History was made in 1982 when H. Ross Perot, Jr., set a round-the-world speed record in a helicopter. He took just over 29 days.

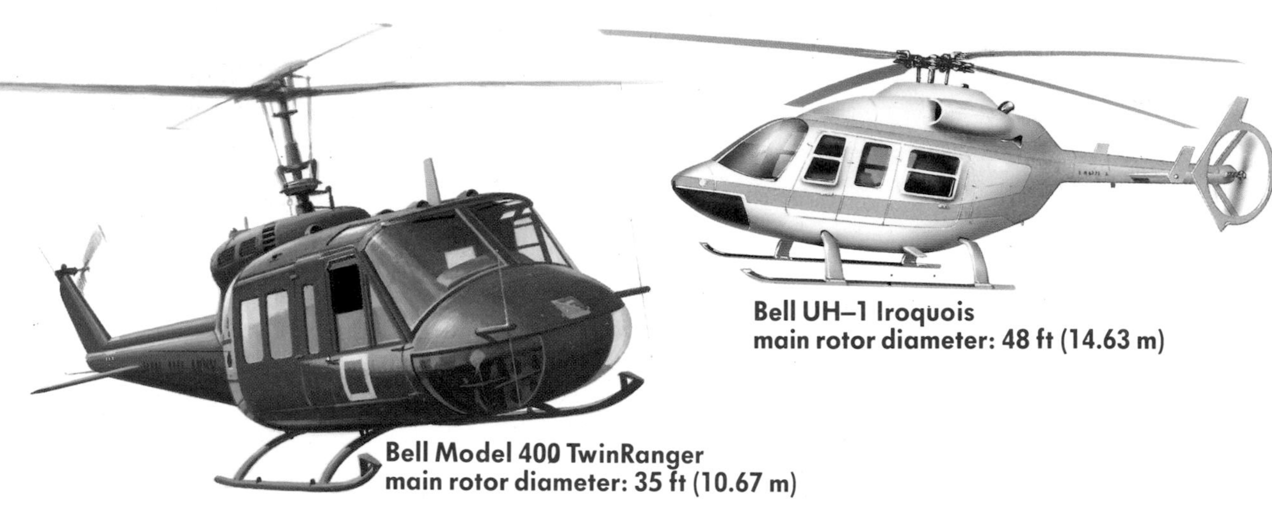

**Bell UH–1 Iroquois**
**main rotor diameter: 48 ft (14.63 m)**

**Bell Model 400 TwinRanger**
**main rotor diameter: 35 ft (10.67 m)**

## HEMINGWAY, Ernest 

▼ *Hemingway's taste for adventure reflected his view that writing must come from personal experience.*

The life of the novelist and short-story writer Ernest Hemingway (1899–1961) was full of action. Hemingway loved sports—especially hunting, deep-sea fishing, and bullfights. Courage, death, and war were the subjects of many of his books. One of them, *A Farewell to Arms*, is based on his experiences as an ambulance driver in Italy during World War I. Another, *For Whom the Bell Tolls*, is about an American volunteer fighting in the Spanish Civil War—a conflict that Hemingway covered as a foreign correspondent.

It was while working in Paris as a journalist in the 1920s that Hemingway first achieved success as a writer of fiction. His novel *The Sun Also Rises* is about the lives of Americans in Europe between the two world wars.

A short novel, *The Old Man and the Sea*, won the Pulitzer Prize in 1953. The following year, Hemingway was awarded the Nobel Prize for literature.

After a period of being hospitalized for mental illness, Hemingway took his own life with a shotgun.

## HENRY, O. 

O. Henry (1862–1910) was one of the most famous American short-story writers. His real name was William Sydney Porter. Porter's stories were about simple people who led ordinary lives. But he wrote with honesty, and his stories became very popular. One of the most touching, *The Gift of the Magi*, is about a poor young couple who sell the only things they possess to buy each other a Christmas present. The wife sells her long hair to buy her husband a watch chain; the husband sells his watch to buy an ornament for his wife's hair.

▲ *O. Henry has been commemorated by the modern O. Henry Awards. These go each year to the country's best short story writer.*

## HENRY, Patrick

The Virginia lawyer and legislator Patrick Henry (1736–1799) was one of the first and most eloquent supporters of the cause of American independence. In 1765, Henry was elected to the Virginia legislature. He soon shocked some delegates with angry attacks against Britain's passage of the Stamp Act. Later he was a delegate to the Continental Congress. In a famous speech to the Virginia legislature in 1775, he ended with the ringing words "I know not what course others may take, but as for me, give me liberty or give me death!"

Henry served on the committee that drafted the Virginia state constitution and was the state's governor during the early years of the war and again for two years after it. Fearing the power of a strong central government, he opposed ratification of the U.S. Constitution in 1787. It was partly in response to pressure from Henry that the Constitutional Convention passed the first ten amendments—the BILL OF RIGHTS.

▼ *Patrick Henry's fiery orations convinced many Virginians to stop sitting on the fence and to join the Revolutionary cause. Many landowners had been comfortably well-off and content to let things stay as they were.*

► *Katharine Hepburn usually plays confident but sensitive heroines. She is equally at home in comedy and drama.*

**Katharine Hepburn was an obvious choice to star in the "screwball" comedies of the 1930s. These movies relied on quick wit and clever dialogue rather than the slapstick antics of the silent comedies.**

## HEPBURN, Katharine

Katharine Hepburn (1909– ) is one of the screen's great actresses. She has won four Oscars. As a young actress, Hepburn gained recognition in such roles as Jo in *Little Women* and Tracy Lord in *The Philadelphia Story*. Later, she played opposite Spencer Tracy in a series of memorable films including *State of the Union* and *Adams Rib*. Among her other film performances are those in *The African Queen*, *Long Day's Journey into Night*, *The Lion in Winter*, and *On Golden Pond*. She has also appeared in stage productions, including *As You Like It* and the musical *Coco*, about the life of dress designer Coco Chanel.

## HERON

The heron is a wading bird. Herons are most common in the tropics, but a number of species live in North America. They are found in regions with many lakes, rivers, and swamps. The largest North American heron is the great blue heron. It is found all over North America. The little blue heron and the Louisiana heron live along the Gulf of Mexico. The little green heron is found from the tropics to Canada. These are all "typical herons," which feed during the day. Other herons feed at twilight or at night. These include the black-crowned night heron, which is found all over North America, and the yellow-crowned night heron, which lives in the central and eastern United States.

▼ *Great blue herons have a wingspan of 6 feet (1.8 m). A headdress of bright feathers extends down their backs every mating season.*

## HESSIANS

Hessians were German soldiers hired to aid the British during the American REVOLUTION. They were called Hessians because many of them came from the German province of Hesse-Kassel. Hessians fought in many European conflicts and were respected as fighters. But their defeat by General George WASHINGTON at the Battle of Trenton, New Jersey, on December 29, 1776, helped give the new American Army confidence. Many Hessians had no love for the British cause and either deserted or switched sides to fight with the colonists.

▲ *American cartoonists often portrayed the Hessian soldiers as clowns because of their uniforms and their difficulty with the English language.*

◀ *Hiawatha was able to convince other Iroquois tribes to unite in 1570 because they all felt threatened by the Algonquins.*

## HIAWATHA 

Hiawatha was a MOHAWK Indian leader who lived in the 1500s in what is now northern New York State. He and his teacher, Deganawidah, a Huron, founded the IROQUOIS LEAGUE. It included the Cayugas, Mohawks, Oneidas, Onondagas, and Senecas. This pact ended war among the Iroquois tribes and enabled them to fight off the Algonquins. In 1855, Henry Wadsworth LONGFELLOW wrote *The Song of Hiawatha*. The Indian in this poem was not based on the real Hiawatha.

▼ *Frontiersmen agreed that Wild Bill Hickok was the "fastest gun in the West." He always carried two pearl-handled pistols.*

## HICKOK, James "Wild Bill" 

Despite his lawless nickname, James Butler Hickok (1837–1876) was a U.S. marshal. Hickok was born in Illinois but later moved to Kansas. During the Civil War

▲ *The Flamingo Hotel is a Las Vegas landmark. The Hilton chain has hotels in 38 countries.*

he served as a scout and spy for the Union Army. He later became an Indian fighter.

As U.S. marshal of several Kansas frontier towns, he was responsible for keeping law and order. Hickok was known for his courage. On one occasion he fought a notorious gang single-handedly, killing three of them.

In 1872, Hickok displayed his legendary marksmanship in Buffalo Bill's Wild West Show. He was killed in a poker game by someone who shot him from behind.

## HILTON, Conrad

Conrad Hilton (1887–1979) was America's most famous HOTEL owner. He became known as the "king of the innkeepers." He was born in San Antonio, New Mexico. Part of his house was used as a small hotel, so young Conrad learned many things about running hotels. In 1919 he bought his own hotel, the Mobley, in Cisco, Texas. It was successful and he was able to use the money he made to buy more hotels. By 1966, Hilton owned more than 60 hotels in the United States. These included the Waldorf-Astoria in New York City and the Beverly Hilton in Beverly Hills, California.

## HISPANIC-AMERICANS

The U.S. Hispanic population is about 22.4 million. This represents approximately 9 percent of the total U.S. population. The United States has the fifth largest Hispanic population in the world.

Hispanic-Americans can trace their origins to almost every Spanish-speaking country in the world. The largest group is Mexican-American (60.4 percent), followed by Puerto Rican (12.2 percent), Cuban (4.7 percent), and Central and South America (22.7 percent).

About 90 percent of Hispanic-Americans live in just nine states. Most live in California (34 percent), Texas (19 percent), New York (10 percent), and Florida (17 percent). The states of Illinois, Arizona, New Jersey, New Mexico, and Colorado also have large Hispanic populations.

Hispanic-Americans tend to have the same religious beliefs. The majority are Roman Catholics. They share several other characteristics as well. For example, they are younger and have larger families than the U.S. population as a

Famous Hispanic-Americans

**Toney Anaya** was governor of New Mexico from 1983 to 1987.

**Romana Bañuelos** was treasurer of the United States from 1971 to 1974.

**Cesar Chavez** organized California grape pickers in the 1960s.

**Gloria Estefan** is one of the world's most popular singers.

**Lee Trevino** has been a professional golf star for more than 25 years.

**Fernando Valenzuela** won baseball's Cy Young Award as the National League's best pitcher in 1981.

whole. It is estimated that Hispanic Americans will be the number one minority in the United States by the year 2015.

▲ *Hispanic-American children have the advantage of a dual culture—Spanish language and traditions in the United States.*

## HISTORY OF CANADA *See* Canadian History

## HISTORY OF THE UNITED STATES *See* American History

## HOLIDAY, Billie 

Billie Holiday (1915–1959) was a famous JAZZ singer. She was born in Baltimore and spent her early years in poverty. Her voice had a haunting, emotional quality. She worked through the 1930s and 1940s and made many recordings. Her work is still popular, and her records are collector's items. Holiday's personal life was tragic. She had a number of unhappy relationships. She became so dependent on drugs that her voice was affected and her career was ruined. Holiday wrote the story of her life and called it *Lady Sings the Blues*. This was the title of a film about her life made in 1972.

## HOLIDAYS 

A holiday is a day celebrating a certain event or occasion or honoring a famous person. The word comes from "holy day" and indicates that holidays were origi-

**Federal Holidays**

New Year's Day (January 1)
Martin Luther King, Jr., Day (3rd Monday in January)
George Washington's Birthday, or Presidents' Day (3rd Monday in February)
Memorial Day (last Monday in May)
Independence Day (July 4)
Labor Day (1st Monday in September)
Columbus Day (2nd Monday in October)
Veterans' Day (November 11)
Thanksgiving Day (4th Thursday in November)
Christmas Day (December 25)

▲ *Independence Day celebrations on July 4 had already become a tradition by 1812.*

nally religious in nature. In the United States few people work on Sunday, for example, because Christians consider it the Sabbath day. Christmas is a legal holiday in all states. Other legal holidays, such as Independence Day or George Washington's birthday, are meant to remind people of the American past. Schools, public offices, and most private businesses are closed on these days. The president and Congress declare legal holidays for the District of Columbia, the federal territories, and federal employees. Each of the states, however, decides what will be a legal holiday within its borders.

▼ *The "Hollywood" sign was built in 1922 and restored in 1978. Each letter is 45 feet (14 m) high.*

## HOLLYWOOD

Hollywood is regarded as the center of the motion picture industry. It is a district of LOS ANGELES, Cali-

fornia. In the early 1900s, moviemakers discovered how well suited southern California was to making motion pictures. It had a sunny climate, varied scenery, and a large labor market. The first studio was built in 1911. The early motion pictures were silent films. In the late 1920s, the first sound films were produced. Now many of the studios are used for making television films.

**Hollywood now produces far more television movies, series, and commercials than it does motion pictures. In the golden age of Hollywood, a major studio such as MGM had a lot the size of a small town. It included studio offices, film laboratories, thousands of expensive costumes, prop-making shops, vast outdoor sets, editing rooms, restaurants, and many sound stages.**

## HOLMES, Oliver Wendell

Oliver Wendell Holmes (1809–1894) was a physician, university professor, poet, novelist, and essayist. Holmes came from a prominent Boston family. He received his medical degree from Harvard in 1836. After practicing medicine for ten years, he taught medicine and later became dean of the Harvard Medical School.

Holmes was the author of such popular poems as "Old Ironsides" and "The Chambered Nautilus." He also wrote three novels, including *Elsie Venner*. For the *Atlantic Monthly* he wrote a series of essays in the form of witty conversations around an imaginary breakfast table. Twelve of these essays were published as *The Autocrat of the Breakfast-Table* in 1858.

## HOLMES, Oliver Wendell, Jr.

Oliver Wendell Holmes, Jr. (1841–1935), had at least as distinguished a career as his father. He was a lawyer, legal historian, philosopher, and a justice of the U.S. Supreme Court for nearly 30 years.

Holmes obtained his law degree from Harvard Law School in 1866. While practicing law, he also wrote and lectured on it. His book *The Common Law* expressed his belief that the law should grow out of the experiences of society. It should not, he said, be considered a fixed, absolute system.

After serving as a justice and chief justice on the Massachusetts Supreme Court, Holmes was appointed to the U.S. Supreme Court in 1902. He was, and still is, considered one of the great legal minds of his age.

▲ *Oliver Wendell Holmes, Jr., continued giving lectures and publishing until he was in his eighties.*

## HOMER, Winslow

Winslow Homer (1836–1910) was one of America's greatest painters. He began painting scenes of country life. Many of these paintings were used in the magazine

**The Cooper-Hewitt Museum in New York City contains the largest collection of Winslow Homer drawings in the world.**

▲ *Winslow Homer's* Snap the Whip, *painted in 1872, captured the innocence of children playing in a New England meadow.*

*Harper's Weekly*. Homer's paintings became famous in Europe and he lived in England from 1881 to 1882. There he began painting pictures of the sea. When he returned to the United States, he lived in Maine and painted scenes of that state's seacoast. Homer's paintings were very realistic. He said, "When I have selected the thing carefully, I paint exactly what appears." Two of his best paintings are *The Northeaster* and *Cannon Rock*.

## HOMESTEAD ACT

The Homestead Act was passed in 1862. It followed decades of pressure on Congress by the homestead movement. The people in this movement said that public land belonged to the people, and that the head of every family should be given a small farm, or homestead. Southerners opposed the Homestead Act. They feared that free land would lead to the creation of nonslave states. The Homestead Act was passed by Congress only after the Southern states seceded from the Union and the CIVIL WAR began.

The act of 1862 offered 160 acres (65 ha) of land in what is now the Midwest for a small fee to anyone who would occupy and cultivate it for five years. By 1900, as many as 600,000 homesteads were awarded. Many of the settlers failed, through lack of experience, to make a success of their farms. But others prospered, and the North's harvests increased dramatically as a result.

**One of the largest movements west in U.S. history occurred in 1889. The government opened up 2 million acres (800,000 ha) of former Indian land in the Oklahoma Territory for settlement. As soon as the starting gun was fired on April 22, thousands of homesteaders raced to claim the land. By sunset all the land was gone. Those homesteaders who jumped the gun were called "Sooners," still a nickname for Oklahomans.**

## HOOVER, Herbert

Herbert Clark Hoover was the 31st president of the United States. The worst DEPRESSION in U.S. history occurred during his presidency. Before he left office, one out of every four wage earners was out of work.

Hoover was an engineer and businessman before entering public affairs. During and after World War I, his relief work in Europe kept millions of people from starving to death. From 1921 to 1928 he was secretary of commerce under President Warren G. HARDING.

With the election of Hoover, a Republican, in 1928, the country expected the prosperity of the previous years to continue. But in October 1929, prices on the New York Stock Exchange, which had reached record levels, suddenly dropped. Soon businesses all over the United States were closing in record numbers.

▲ *Public confidence in banks hit an all-time low during President Hoover's administration. By the end of 1932 more than 5,000 banks had gone out of business.*

Under Hoover's direction, the federal government provided loans to banks and other firms, home owners, and farmers. He supported public works and conservation programs. But he refused to support government "handouts" such as federal aid to those out of work. Hoover felt that help for the poor should come from charities, private companies, and state and local governments. By 1933, 13 million Americans were out of work. Many people lost their homes and became squatters living in shantytowns known as Hoovervilles.

Most Americans felt that Hoover had not done enough to end the Depression. As a result, he lost the 1932 election to Franklin D. ROOSEVELT. In retirement, Hoover headed commissions that proposed ways to make the federal government more efficient.

Herbert Hoover
**Born:** August 10, 1874, in West Branch, Iowa
**Education:** Stanford University
**Political party:** Republican
**Term of office:** 1929–1933
**Married:** 1899 to Lou Henry
**Died:** October 20, 1964, in New York City

▲ *J. Edgar Hoover set up an efficient anticrime organization, but he was accused of neglecting the civil rights of many suspects.*

## HOOVER, J. Edgar

J. Edgar Hoover (1895–1972) was head of the FEDERAL BUREAU OF INVESTIGATION (FBI) for 48 years. He served under every president from Calvin Coolidge to Richard Nixon. Hoover was born in Washington, D.C. After becoming a lawyer, he took a job with the U.S. Department of Justice. Just seven years later he was made director of the FBI, the branch of the Justice Department that investigated federal crimes. When Hoover took charge of it, it was badly run. Hoover changed it into a strong and effective organization. He set up the FBI National Academy at Quantico, Virginia, and established the FBI Laboratory. Under Hoover, the FBI waged a war against organized crime in the 1930s. And during World War II, it captured many foreign spies. However, Hoover became obsessed with power and his ability to influence people and events. He became one of the most powerful people in the nation. It was only after his death in 1972 that Congress revealed that Hoover had abused his power.

▲ *Kachina dolls represent Hopi gods who live in a mysterious country hidden in neighboring mountains.*

## HOPI

The Hopi are an INDIAN tribe of the southwestern United States. Their name comes from the word *hopitu*, which means "the peaceful ones." They are descended from an ancient Indian people called the Anasazi, who came to the area around 1000 B.C. The Hopi are farmers, and their religion is tied to their environment. Religious ceremonies are centered around the growing cycle of maize, or corn. Winter is considered the most sacred season. At this time ceremonies are held using the kachina doll. These dolls are made of wood and horsehair and represent spirits. Today about 8,000 Hopi live on a reservation in Arizona.

## HOPPER, Edward

Edward Hopper (1882–1967) was one of the greatest American painters of this century. His paintings are realistic and use ordinary settings such as bedrooms, city streets, and empty theaters as their subjects. Many of them show the sadness of everyday life. *Nighthawks*, for example, shows what seem to be lonely people late at night in a mostly empty diner. His paintings contain no

**Edward Hopper was one of the modern artists whose works were displayed in 1913 at the famous Armory Show in New York City. But few people recognized Hopper's genius, and he was forced to earn his living as a commercial artist until 1925.**

◀ *In paintings such as* Pennsylvania Coal Town, *Edward Hopper showed his feeling for people and places that other artists ignored.*

unnecessary details to distract from the real subject of the painting. *Cape Cod Afternoon* is typical of his later work. He began to observe nature with the same attention he gave to his city works.

## HORSE RACING

In the United States, horse racing is the best attended of any sporting event. In *flat racing*, jockeys ride Thoroughbred horses around a flat track. The most famous flat race is the 1¼-mile (2-km) KENTUCKY DERBY. Horses that win the Kentucky Derby, Belmont Stakes, and Preakness Stakes win the Triple Crown.

In *harness racing*, the horse pulls a driver in a sulky, a two-wheeled carriage. Important harness races take place at Yonkers Raceway, in New York, and Meadowlands Raceway, in New Jersey. Standardbred horses are used for harness racing.

Triple Crown Winners (Kentucky Derby, Preakness, and Belmont Stakes)

|  |  |
|---|---|
| 1978 | Affirmed |
| 1977 | Seattle Slew |
| 1973 | Secretariat |
| 1948 | Citation |
| 1946 | Assault |
| 1943 | Count Fleet |
| 1941 | Whirlaway |
| 1937 | War Admiral |
| 1935 | Omaha |
| 1930 | Gallant Fox |
| 1919 | Sir Barton |

◀ *Harness racing developed in the United States in the 1700s. Most modern harness trotters (a type of racehorse) are descendants of Hambletonian, a famous 19th-century trotter.*

**The life span of the horse is 20 to 30 years, but a few reach 40 years. Usually only one foal is born; twins are very rare.**

## HORSES AND THEIR RELATIVES 

The United States has a number of unique breeds of horses. All are descended from the horses of the Europeans. The Morgan is one of the most popular. Small but strong, it was once used as a harness horse and now makes a good saddle horse.

The quarter horse is the fastest horse over a short distance. Originally the horse was bred for quarter races, which were a quarter of a mile long. Some quarter horses are still raced today because they can start, stop, and turn quickly. They are also used for ranch work and as polo ponies.

► *Some Plains Indian tribes, such as the Cheyenne and Pawnee, quickly learned how to tame and ride horses for hunting and war.*

The Appaloosa was originally bred from mustangs (wild horses) in the Palouse River region of Idaho by the Nez Percé Indians. It is an excellent saddle horse.

The American saddle horse is a high-stepping show horse. The Tennessee walking horse is known for its steady running walk, which makes it comfortable to ride. The standardbred horse, also called the American trotting horse, is used in harness racing. Today, thousands of wild horses, or mustangs, roam the open spaces of the West. They are descended from horses that escaped captivity a hundred or more years ago.

Donkeys are small, sturdy, surefooted relatives of horses. They are used for riding, pulling carts, or carrying loads. Small donkeys, or burros, are used as pack animals. The offspring of a male donkey (jackass) and a female horse (mare) is a mule. It is as large as a horse but has long ears and is stronger and more surefooted. Mules cannot usually reproduce. In the United States nearly all mules are used on farms, especially in the southern states.

Special Horse Terms

**Bronco:** an untamed horse in the American West
**Colt:** a male horse less than four years old
**Filly:** a female horse less than four years old
**Hand:** unit of measurement (4 in, or 10 cm) used to determine a horse's height
**Mare:** a female horse more than four years old
**Mustang:** a wild horse on the western plains

## HOTELS AND MOTELS

Hotels and motels serve people who travel and need a temporary place to stay.

Hotels developed from inns, which provided food, entertainment, and a place to sleep for travelers. The first American inn was built in Jamestown, Virginia, in 1610. The first building to be designed as a hotel was the City Hotel in New York City. It was built in the late 1700s. Motels, in which rooms can be reached directly from a parking area, developed later, along with automobile travel.

Today the largest hotels may have as many as 3,000 rooms. These are usually resort hotels, such as those by the seashore, that attract many tourists. Often hotels and motels are part of a chain.

▲ *The Breakers Hotel in Palm Beach, Florida shows the splendor of hotels that were modeled on the European tradition.*

## HOUDINI, Harry

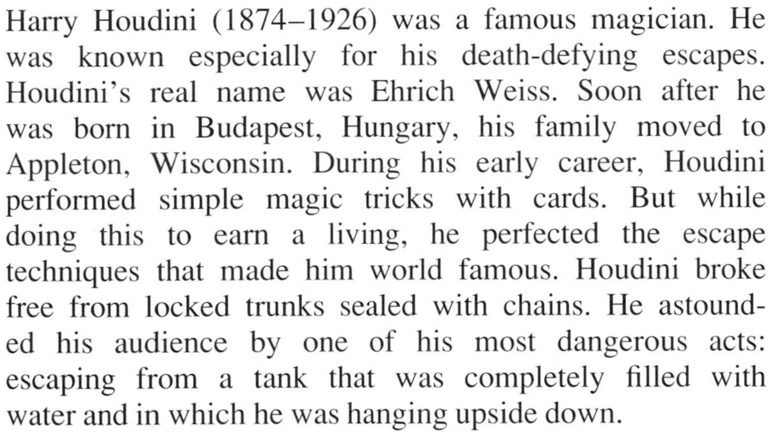

Harry Houdini (1874–1926) was a famous magician. He was known especially for his death-defying escapes. Houdini's real name was Ehrich Weiss. Soon after he was born in Budapest, Hungary, his family moved to Appleton, Wisconsin. During his early career, Houdini performed simple magic tricks with cards. But while doing this to earn a living, he perfected the escape techniques that made him world famous. Houdini broke free from locked trunks sealed with chains. He astounded his audience by one of his most dangerous acts: escaping from a tank that was completely filled with water and in which he was hanging upside down.

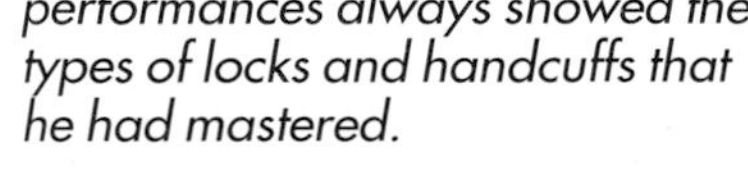

▼ *Posters for Harry Houdini's performances always showed the types of locks and handcuffs that he had mastered.*

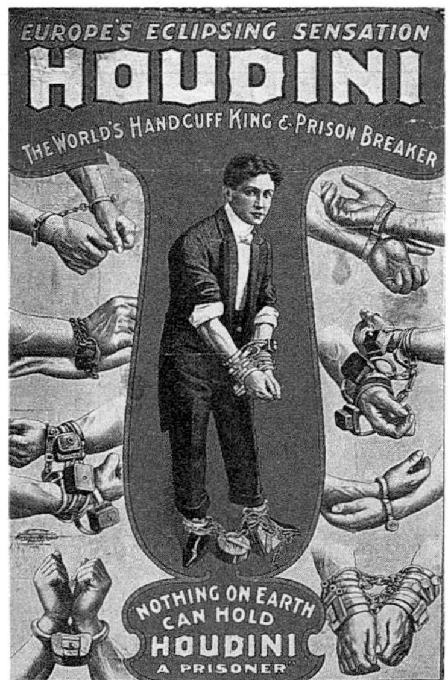


## HOUSE OF REPRESENTATIVES

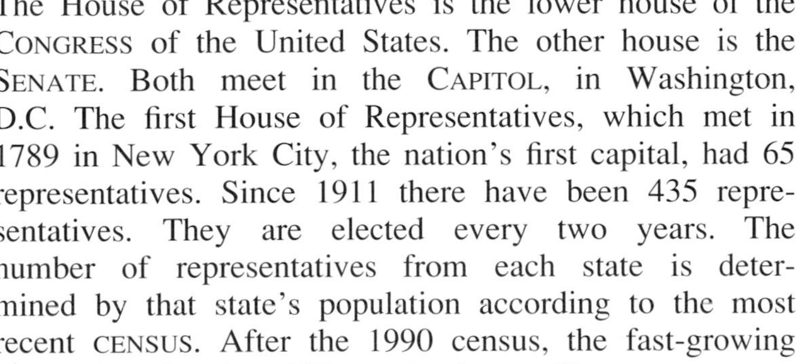

The House of Representatives is the lower house of the CONGRESS of the United States. The other house is the SENATE. Both meet in the CAPITOL, in Washington, D.C. The first House of Representatives, which met in 1789 in New York City, the nation's first capital, had 65 representatives. Since 1911 there have been 435 representatives. They are elected every two years. The number of representatives from each state is determined by that state's population according to the most recent CENSUS. After the 1990 census, the fast-growing states of the South and West gained many House seats.

Members of the House of Representatives must be

| States with Most Representatives | |
|---|---|
| California | 45 |
| New York | 34 |
| Texas | 27 |
| Pennsylvania | 23 |
| Illinois | 22 |
| Ohio | 21 |
| Florida | 19 |
| Michigan | 18 |
| New Jersey | 14 |
| North Carolina | 11 |
| Massachusetts | 11 |
| Georgia | 10 |
| Virginia | 10 |
| Indiana | 10 |

residents of the state from which they are chosen. They must be 25 years old or older. And they must have been U.S. citizens for at least seven years.

The speaker of the House presides over sessions and appoints members of important committees. The speaker is a member of the party—Democratic or Republican—that has the most seats in the House.

## HOUSING

From the time of the first settlers, Americans have dreamed of owning their own home. Today there are more than 93 million housing units in the United States. About two thirds of them are owned by the people who live in them. These include detached houses, condominiums, and cooperative apartments. Still, many millions of people live in rented apartments and houses.

Between 4 million and 5 million homes are sold each year. The average cost of a new house passed $100,000 in 1987. Affordable housing has become an important concern. The U.S. Department of Housing and Urban Development supplies billions of dollars in loans each year. This money is used to build low-cost housing.

## HOUSTON

Houston is the largest city in TEXAS, and the fourth largest in the country, with a population of 1,630,553. It was founded in 1836 and named after General Sam HOUSTON, hero of the Texan war of independence from Mexico. The city began to grow quickly in the early 1900s when oil was discovered nearby. It is an important port, manufacturing and transportation center, as well. The Houston Ship Canal connects the city with the Gulf of Mexico. In the 1960s, NASA built the Manned Spacecraft Center southeast of the city. It was later renamed the Lyndon B. Johnson Space Center.

▲ *Houston's modern skyline is reflected in the Buffalo Bayou, which flows through the center of the city.*

## HOUSTON, Samuel

Sam Houston (1793–1863) was a giant of American history. He was a military hero, a U.S. representative and senator, the first president of the Republic of Texas, and the governor of both Tennessee and Texas.

Houston grew up on a farm in Tennessee. While in his teens, he lived with the Cherokee Indians, who called him Black Raven. After the WAR OF 1812, Houston studied law and began to build a career in politics. He was elected to Congress from Tennessee in 1823 and was elected governor four years later. In 1829, however, Houston resigned and once again went live with the Cherokees, who adopted him into the tribe.

In 1832, President Andrew JACKSON sent Houston on a special mission to Texas, which was then part of Mexico. American settlers revolted against Mexican rule in 1835. A year later Houston was made commander of the Texas army and in the Battle of San Jacinto, he and his troops, outnumbered two to one, defeated the Mexicans. Texas became independent, and Houston became the first president of the Republic of Texas.

Texas became the 28th state of the Union in 1845, and Houston was elected U.S. senator. He became governor in 1859. Just before the start of the CIVIL WAR in 1861, Texas seceded from the Union and joined the Confederacy. Houston opposed this and was forced out of office. He died two years later.

▲ *Sam Houston had the distinction of being elected governor of the states of Tennessee and Texas.*

**Sam Houston, famous as one of the founders of independent Texas, grew up with Cherokees and went through tests to become a tribe member. He promised equal rights for Cherokees and other tribes when he became president of Texas in 1848. These freedoms were taken away two years later when his term of office ended.**

## HOWE, Elias

Elias Howe (1819–1867) invented the sewing machine. He patented it in 1846, sold an English company the British rights to the machine and moved to England so that he could improve the design. In 1849, Howe returned to the United States. His machine had not done well in England and he was now very poor. He soon found that Isaac SINGER and others had manufactured and sold sewing machines based on his invention. Howe sued them and won. After years of poverty, Howe became a rich man.

▼ *Elias Howe's sewing machine was operated by hand. Later sewing machines used pedals and finally electricity.*

## HOWE, Julia Ward

Julia Ward Howe (1819–1910) was a writer and social reformer. She and her husband, Samuel Gridley Howe, published the ABOLITIONIST newspaper the *Commonwealth* in Boston. Early in the Civil War she wrote "The Battle Hymn of the Republic." Set to the tune of "John Brown's Body," this stirring song became the favorite war song of the Union Army. After the war and the freeing of the slaves, she fought to get women the right to vote. She was the first president of the New England Woman Suffrage Association.

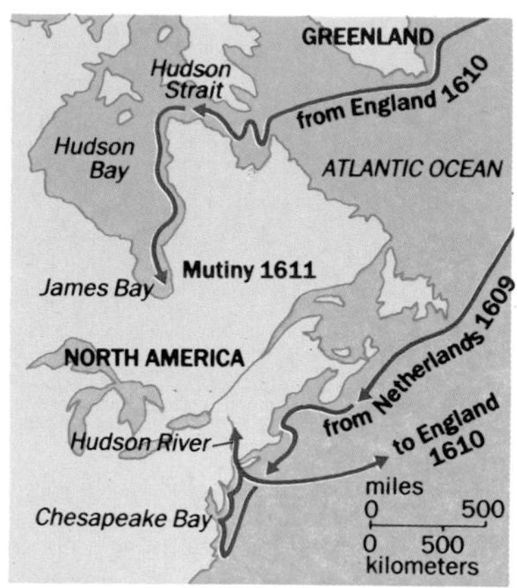


▲ *Henry Hudson's explorations helped set the stage for English and Dutch colonization.*

## HUBBLE, Edwin

Edwin Hubble (1889–1953) was a great astronomer. He studied galaxies, distant bodies of stars like our Milky Way. By measuring their spectra (the colors in their light), he was able to tell how fast their distance from us was changing. In 1924 he announced that his measurements showed that the farther apart two galaxies are, the faster they tend to be moving away from one another. This became known as Hubble's Law. It led some astronomers to a theory that the universe began billions of years ago at a single point with a great explosion called the "Big Bang." The resulting matter is still expanding outward at enormous speeds in all directions. The Hubble Space Telescope is named for Edwin Hubble.

## HUDSON, Henry

The English explorer Henry Hudson (?–1611) made four voyages to the Arctic and North America. He was searching for a northern sea route between Europe and Asia. The HUDSON RIVER, Hudson Bay, and Hudson Strait are named for him.

Hudson made his first voyage in 1607. He reached the east coast of Greenland but turned back after coming upon huge ice floes. A second attempt in 1608 also failed to find the Northwest Passage. In the following year, Hudson sailed with a crew of 20 men aboard his ship, the *Half Moon*. He explored the Atlantic coast of North America as far south as present-day North Carolina. He then traveled far up a river. The river was later named after him.

Hudson's last voyage was in 1610. He sailed through Hudson Strait into Hudson Bay. It soon became ice clogged, and he had to spend the winter there. In the following spring, when the ice melted, his crew mutinied. Hudson, his son, and several others were set adrift in a small boat. They were never heard from again.

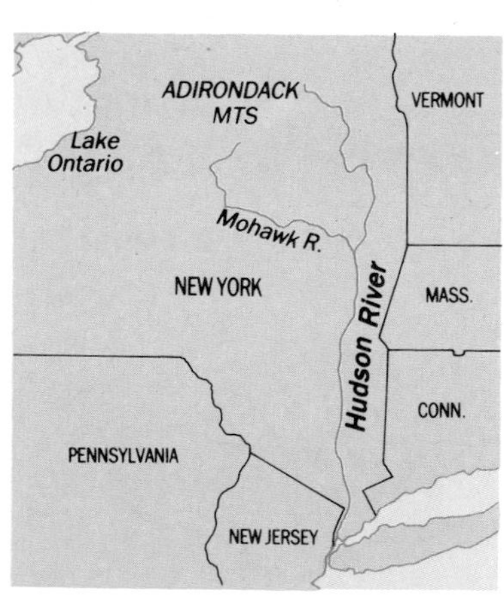


▲ *The source of the Hudson River is in the Adirondack region, one of the least populated areas of New York State. But its mouth, in New York City, is one of the busiest waterways in the world.*

## HUDSON RIVER

The Hudson River is 306 miles (492 km) long. It rises in the ADIRONDACK MOUNTAINS in Lake Tear-of-the-Clouds, in New York State. The river flows south into New York Bay, the large natural harbor at New York

City. The Italian Giovanni da VERRAZANO discovered New York Bay and the mouth of the river in 1524. (The Verrazano-Narrows Bridge is named after him.) The Hudson River itself was first explored in 1609 by the English navigator Henry HUDSON, who was working for the Dutch. The Hudson is an important route for travel and trade. Robert FULTON's steamships began to carry passengers on the Hudson in 1807.

**During the 1800s the Hudson's Bay Company was the only source of goods for many Canadians.**

## HUDSON'S BAY COMPANY 

The Hudson's Bay Company was founded in 1670. Its original purpose was to search for a Northwest Passage to the Pacific Ocean and to establish a fur trade in the lands surrounding Hudson Bay.

For a short time in the early 1800s, the company held a monopoly on the fur trade. It ruled a vast territory in Canada that stretched from the Atlantic Ocean to the Pacific. In 1870 it was required to sell most of its holding to the newly created Dominion of Canada. Today the company is still one of the world's leading fur traders, and it owns many retail stores.

*▼ Langston Hughes found respect as a writer early on, but his struggle as a black American continued all his life.*

## HUGHES, (James) Langston 

The poetry and prose of Langston Hughes (1902–1967) are among the most eloquent expressions of what it is to be black in a white-dominated society.

Hughes published his first collection of poems, *The Weary Blues*, in 1926, to an enthusiastic reception. Among his many other books are a collection of short stories, *The Ways of White Folks*, and *A Pictorial History of the Negro in America*, which was written for children. The poems in *The Panther and the Lash* are concerned with the militant black movements of the 1960s. In *The Big Sea*, Hughes told the story of his life up to the age of 28. *Simple Speaks His Mind* and *The Best of Simple* are collections of humorous sketches.

*▼ The hummingbird's long, hollow tongue darts in and out of its beak. It is forked to help the bird collect nectar.*

**Ruby-throated hummingbird**

## HUMMINGBIRD 

Hummingbirds include the smallest BIRDS in the world. They get their name from the sound their wings make. The birds fly very fast. Like a helicopter, they can fly up or down or forward, backward, or sideways. And they can hover in one place. They hover over plants to feed

▲ *Some Huron tomahawks could also be used as peace pipes. Other tribes agreed that Huron tobacco was the best.*

on nectar from flowers and also insects.

These small, brightly colored birds live only in the New World, mostly in Latin America. The smallest in the United States is the calliope hummingbird. It is only 3 inches (8 cm) long. The ruby-throated hummingbird is the only species that breeds east of the Mississippi. All the others are found in the West and Southwest. Among other species found in North America are the black-chinned, blue-throated, rufous, broad-billed, and broad-tailed hummingbirds.

## HURON, Lake *See* Great Lakes

## HURONS

The Huron INDIANS lived in New York State and Ontario, Canada. The Hurons were related to the IROQUOIS. They were farmers, growing corn, beans, and other crops. The Hurons were very active in the French fur trade. Quebec City is founded on the site of an old Huron trading post. In the mid-1600s, the Iroquois waged war against the Hurons. By the mid-1700s, the Hurons had fled to Ohio. In 1867 they were forced to move again, to Indian Territory in Oklahoma. The few hundred who still live there are called Wyandot.

**The name "hurricane" comes from a West Indian word, *huracán*, which means "evil spirit of the sea."**

## HURRICANE

A hurricane is a powerful storm. Near the storm's center, or eye, the winds are 74 miles per hour (119 km/hr) or more. Some hurricanes have winds of 150

► *Hurricane Hugo swept its way across the Caribbean region toward South Carolina in September 1989.*

miles per hour (241 km/hr). The storm takes shape in the tropics over the ocean and builds in strength. It is circular in shape and can be between 300 and 500 miles (500 and 800 km) across. Hurricanes generally occur from June to October. In the United States, they affect the states along the Atlantic coast, especially in the South, and on the Gulf of Mexico. In the past century there have been over 500 hurricanes. Hurricanes were once given female names, but now male and female names alternate. Hurricanes can cause enormous damage. In 1979, Hurricane Frederic caused $2.3 billion in damage in the United States.

**Some Recent Hurricanes**

1992 "Andrew" kills 38 in Florida and Louisiana and causes $15 billion damage
1989 "Hugo" kills 51 in the Caribbean and the southeastern U.S.
1983 "Alicia" kills 21 and causes $2 billion damage in Texas
1979 "David" hits Puerto Rico and the southeastern U.S.: 2,000 dead
1970 "Celia" causes 11 deaths and $500 million damage in Texas
1955 "Diane" kills 184 between North Carolina and New England

## HYDROELECTRIC POWER

Hydroelectric power is electricity that is produced by the energy of falling water. Some natural waterfalls are used for this purpose. But most hydroelectric power plants are parts of DAMS. The water is stored in the dam's reservoir. It is used to turn turbines, which in turn run generators that produce electricity.

Hydroelectric power supplies less than 5 percent of the energy produced in the United States. Most energy is produced in thermal plants—those plants that use coal, natural gas, oil, and nuclear power to produce electricity. These types of plants cause pollution; hydroelectric plants do not. But the artificial lakes formed by dams destroy the habitats of plants and animals.

The Grand Coulee Dam, on the Columbia River in Washington State, is the largest hydroelectric plant in the United States.

**Largest Hydroelectric Plants in North America**

Grand Coulee (Washington State)
La Grande 2 (Canada)
Churchill Falls (Canada)
Brumley Gap (Virginia)
John Day (Oregon/Washington)
Revelstoke (Canada)
La Grande 4 (Canada)
Mica (Canada)
Bennett W.A.C. (Canada)
La Grande 3 (Canada)

◀ *The Roosevelt Dam, built in 1911, is part of the Salt River irrigation project in south-central Arizona. It is used for water supply, flood control, and power production.*

# ICE HOCKEY

Ice hockey is one of the most popular WINTER SPORTS in the northern United States. It is also the national sport of Canada. Many people play on frozen lakes and ponds, but organized teams usually play on indoor rinks. It is played between two teams of six players each. Goals are scored when the hard rubber disk, called the *puck*, is shot into the other team's goal. The goal is 6 feet (1.8 m) wide and 4 feet (1.2 m) high. Skillful skating makes ice hockey one of the world's fastest team sports.

Professional hockey teams throughout Canada and the United States belong to the National Hockey League. The league is divided into two conferences, which are like the two leagues in baseball. Each conference is then divided into two divisions, each with five or six teams. End-of-season play-offs each May decide which team wins the Stanley Cup and becomes the champion. Famous hockey players of the past include

► *Ice hockey goalies wear masks to protect them against the hard rubber pucks, which travel more than 100 miles per hour (160 km/hr).*

| Stanley Cup Winners (NHL Champions) | |
|---|---|
| 1993 | Montreal Canadiens |
| 1992 | Pittsburgh Penguins |
| 1991 | Pittsburgh Penguins |
| 1990 | Edmonton Oilers |
| 1989 | Calgary Flames |
| 1988 | Edmonton Oilers |
| 1987 | Edmonton Oilers |
| 1986 | Montreal Canadiens |
| 1985 | Edmonton Oilers |
| 1984 | Edmonton Oilers |
| 1983 | New York Islanders |
| 1982 | New York Islanders |
| 1981 | New York Islanders |

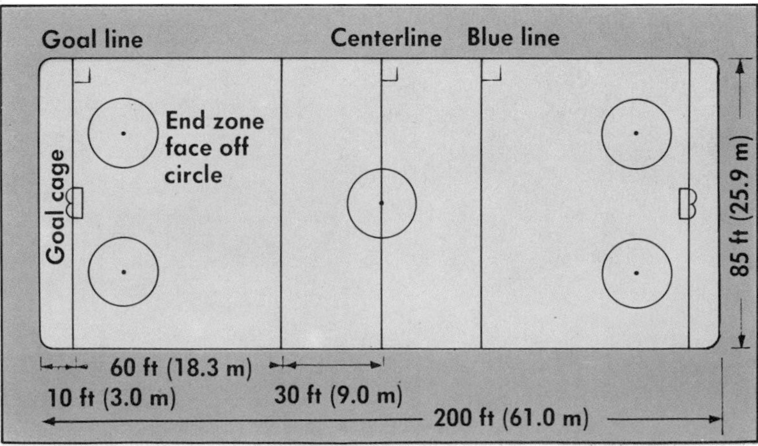


► *Lines divide an ice hockey rink into three zones. Play starts in one of the five face-off circles. Most rinks are 200 feet (61 m) long and 85 feet (25.9 m) wide.*

Guy Lafleur, Bobby Orr, Gordie Howe, and Ken Dryden. Top players today include Mario Lemieux, Ray Bourque, and Wayne Gretzky, who led the Edmonton Oilers to four Stanley Cups in the 1980s.

◀ *Ice-skating is a popular recreational sport. Both New Yorkers and tourists enjoy the rink at Rockefeller Center in New York City.*

**Eric Heiden of the United States made Olympic history in 1980 by winning all of the men's speed skating gold medals. He took first place in five finals — 500 m, 1,000 m, 1,500 m, 5,000 m, and 10,000 m.**

## ICE-SKATING 

Ice-skating is a popular recreational and competitive sport. There are two basic kinds, figure skating and speed skating.

Figure skating is the artistic form. It includes singles, pairs, and ice dance. Ice dance is a cross between skating and ballroom dancing. Figure skating is a popular spectator sport. Many figure skating champions go on to skate professionally in touring groups.

Speed skating involves racing on ice-covered tracks using skates with very long blades. The most popular type in North America is pack, or American-style, skating, in which a number of skaters race at once. Internationally, the most popular is Olympic-style speed skating. In this event, two skaters race each other on a two-lane track. A third type is short-track skating, in which skaters must use the skills of a sprinter.

North American and world figure skating and speed skating championships are held every year. Figure skating and speed skating events are also held at the Winter Olympic Games.

▼ *Speed skater Leslie Bader represented the United States in the 5,000-meter event at the 1987 World Cup.*

# IDAHO

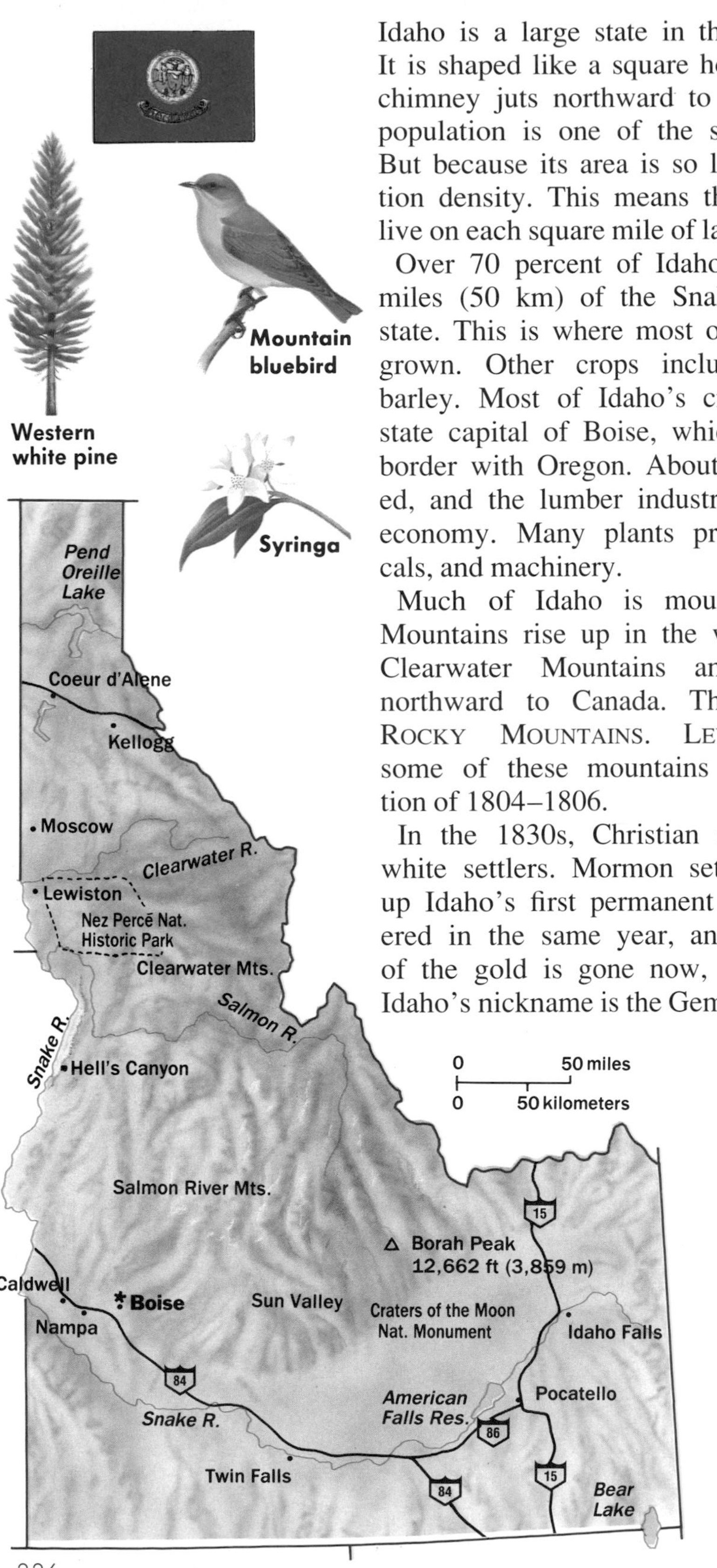


Idaho is a large state in the northwestern United States. It is shaped like a square house with a tall chimney. This chimney juts northward to the Canadian border. Idaho's population is one of the smallest of the United States. But because its area is so large, Idaho has a low population density. This means that a small number of people live on each square mile of land in Idaho.

Over 70 percent of Idaho's population lives within 30 miles (50 km) of the Snake River in the south of the state. This is where most of Idaho's famous potatoes are grown. Other crops include wheat, sugar beets, and barley. Most of Idaho's crops are shipped through the state capital of Boise, which is near the state's western border with Oregon. About two fifths of Idaho is forested, and the lumber industry is an important part of the economy. Many plants produce food products, chemicals, and machinery.

Much of Idaho is mountainous. The Salmon River Mountains rise up in the western part of the state. The Clearwater Mountains and Bitterroot Range extend northward to Canada. These ranges are part of the ROCKY MOUNTAINS. LEWIS AND CLARK explored some of these mountains during their famous expedition of 1804–1806.

In the 1830s, Christian missionaries became the first white settlers. Mormon settlers arrived in 1860 and set up Idaho's first permanent settlement. Gold was discovered in the same year, and more settlers arrived. Most of the gold is gone now, but mining is still important. Idaho's nickname is the Gem State.

Idaho
**Capital:** Boise
**Area:** 83,574 sq mi ($216,456 \text{ km}^2$). Rank: 14th
**Population:** 1,006,749 (1990). Rank: 42nd
**Statehood:** July 3, 1890
**Principal rivers:** Snake, Salmon, Clearwater, Kootenai
**Highest point:** Borah Peak, 12,662 ft (3,859 m)
**Motto:** *Esto Perpetua* (May It Endure Forever)
**Song:** "Here We Have Idaho"

▲ *The submerged rocks in Hell's Canyon National Recreation Area are covered with silt carried by the Snake River.*

► *Cattle farmers collect hay for the winter. Idaho produces nearly 5 million tons of hay each year.*

▼ *Silver City Ghost Town is a relic of Idaho's mining boom in the mid-1800s.*

**Places of Interest**

- Hell's Canyon, on the Snake River, has an average depth of about 1 mi (1.6 km).
- Nez Percé National Historical Park, near Lewiston, honors the Nez Percé Indians and the Lewis and Clark Expedition.
- Sun Valley, in southern Idaho, is one of the country's most famous ski resorts.

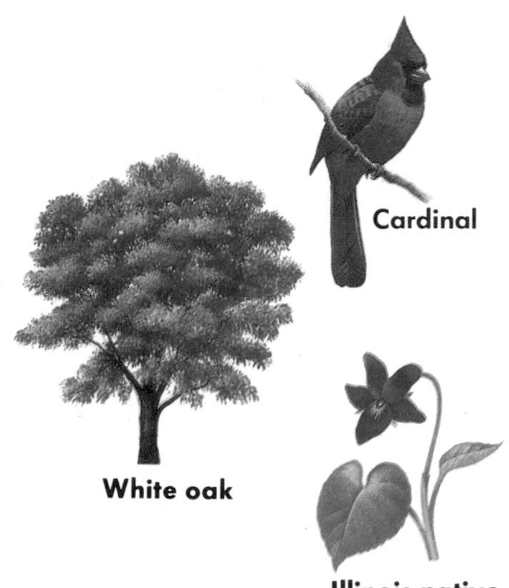
Cardinal

White oak

Illinois native violet

Illinois is a leading farming and industrial state. It is located in the Midwest. Its largest city, CHICAGO, is a major port on Lake Michigan. The state's western border is the Mississippi River, so goods can be sent easily and cheaply from Illinois. Much of the land of Illinois is flat and fertile, and one of its nicknames is the Prairie State. Large quantities of corn, soybeans, wheat, oats, barley, rye, and sorghum are grown in Illinois. Cattle farming is also practiced on a large scale. There are more than 2.5 million cattle in Illinois.

Many different types of goods are produced by Illinois factories. Manufactured goods account for more than ten times the income provided by farming. The state's major products include machinery, petroleum products, electronic equipment, and chemicals. Mining is an important industry in the southern part of the

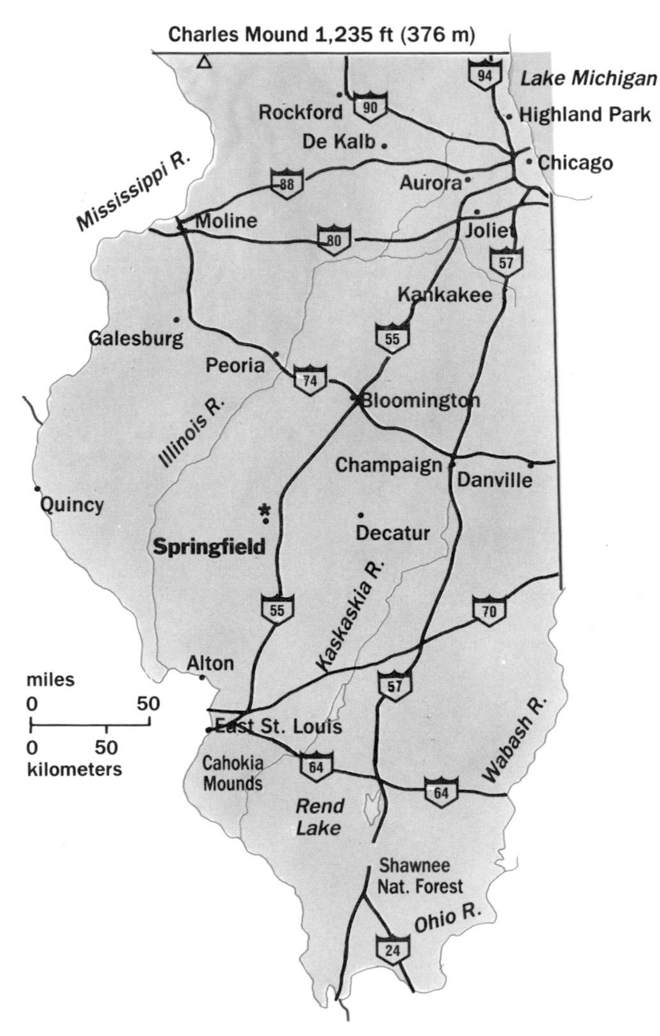


### Places of Interest

- Abraham Lincoln's home, in Springfield, has been preserved as a national historic site.
- Monk's Mound, one of the Cahokia Mounds, is the largest Indian mound in the country.
- Chicago has all the cultural and sporting attractions expected of one of the world's great cities.
- Shawnee National Forest stretches across nine counties of southern Illinois.

state. The factories and stockyards of Illinois were also important for the labor movement in the United States. Many of the modern labor unions were formed in the 1800s or early 1900s in Illinois.

The name "Illinois" comes from the Indians who lived in the area long ago. They called themselves *Illinewek*, or "superior men." The first white settlers were French fur traders in the early 1600s. After the FRENCH AND INDIAN WAR, Great Britain gained control of the region. Illinois grew in population and importance because of its location and good farmland. After the opening of the ERIE CANAL, Illinois attracted many settlers from the east. Abraham LINCOLN grew up in Illinois, and the state is known as the Land of Lincoln.

▲ *The 110-story Sears Building in Chicago is the world's tallest skyscraper.*

◀ *Many goods from Illinois are shipped from Lake Michigan. A series of drawbridges lets ships enter downtown Chicago.*

| Illinois |
| --- |
| **Capital:** Springfield |
| **Area:** 57,918 sq mi (150,007 km$^2$). Rank: 25th |
| **Population:** 11,430,602 (1990). Rank: 6th |
| **Principal rivers:** Mississippi, Ohio, Illinois, Wabash |
| **Highest point:** Charles Mound, 1,235 ft (376 m) |
| **Motto:** State Sovereignty, National Union |
| **Song:** "Illinois" |

◀ *Illinois farmers harvest more than 1 billion bushels of corn each year. Only Iowa produces more.*

► *Many long or difficult names were changed by 19th-century immigration officials at Ellis Island, New York.*

**Immigration Facts**

- Of the 250 million Americans, almost 140 million trace their ancestry to the United Kingdom, Germany, and Ireland.
- In recent years, some 500,000 to 600,000 immigrants have entered the United States annually.
- From 1901 to 1910, the United States received 8.8 million immigrants—more than in any other decade.

## IMMIGRATION

Immigration takes place when people come to live in a country from another one. Because more immigrants have come to the United States than any other country, it is known as a "nation of immigrants." Between 1820 and 1990, more than 56 million immigrants entered the United States legally. Most of them eventually obtained U.S. CITIZENSHIP through a process called naturalization. Millions more have come as illegal immigrants—without papers giving them the right to stay permanently. A law passed in 1986 makes it easier for them to stay in the United States and become citizens.

Before World War I, almost anyone could enter the United States legally. A series of laws then made immigration more difficult. Most immigrants landed at Ellis Island in New York Harbor, where they were investigated by agents of the U.S. Immigration and Naturalization Service. Between 1920 and 1965, immigration was restricted in such a way that people from northern and western Europe had the best chance of entering. Now people with skills that are needed and relatives of U.S. citizens are admitted first, regardless of what country they come from.

In a sense, the American Indians were the first American immigrants. They migrated to the Americas from Asia in the far-distant past. Every other American either was born in another country or descends from people who came from another country. Before 1965, most immigrants came from Europe. Since then, most have come from Latin America and Asia.

**Immigrants to the U.S. in 1987 by Place of Birth**

| | |
|---|---|
| Mexico: | 947,900 |
| Asia: | 342,200 |
| Latin America (Except Mexico): | 329,800 |
| Europe: | 146,700 |
| Africa: | 33,500 |
| Canada: | 19,900 |
| Oceania (including Australia and New Zealand): | 7,100 |
| Others: | 200 |

## IMPEACHMENT

Impeachment is a process that is followed when a government official is accused of a crime or abuse of his or her office. Legally, an impeachment is an accusation. But the term is also used for the trial. In the United States, at the federal level, only the House of Representatives can impeach an official. The Senate then tries the impeached official; a two-thirds vote is necessary for conviction. Impeachment is rarely used. The most famous impeachment was that of President Andrew JOHNSON in 1868. He was found to be not guilty—by one vote. In 1974, President Richard NIXON resigned when it became clear that he was to be impeached.

**In the history of the United States, the Senate has sat on only eleven impeachment trials. Only four of the accused, all federal judges, were convicted. Conviction in an impeachment results in the person being removed from office and disqualified to hold "any office of honor, trust, or profit under the United States."**

## INDEPENDENCE DAY

Independence Day, July 4, is the birthday of the United States. That was the day, in 1776, when the CONTINENTAL CONGRESS adopted the DECLARATION OF INDEPENDENCE. The first celebration of Independence Day was in Philadelphia, on July 8, 1776, when the Declaration of Independence was first read to the public. The LIBERTY BELL rang out from the tower of the State House (now INDEPENDENCE HALL). From then on, the idea of celebrating Independence Day spread throughout the growing country. Independence Day has been a legal federal holiday since 1941.

## INDEPENDENCE HALL

Independence Hall, in PHILADELPHIA, is considered the birthplace of the United States. Delegates to the Second CONTINENTAL CONGRESS met there in 1775 and appointed George WASHINGTON commander in chief of the Continental Army. The following year the delegates met there again to declare the American colonies independent and sign the DECLARATION OF INDEPENDENCE. On July 8, 1776, the LIBERTY BELL, then in the hall's tower, rang out to proclaim the news. The ARTICLES OF CONFEDERATION were adopted in Independence Hall in 1781, and six years later the U.S. CONSTITUTION was drafted there.

Independence Hall was built in 1732 and originally served as the Pennsylvania State House. Today it is part of the Independence National Historical Park.

*▼ On July 8, 1776, the Liberty Bell proclaimed the news of the Declaration of Independence from the tower of Independence Hall in Philadelphia.*

# INDIANA

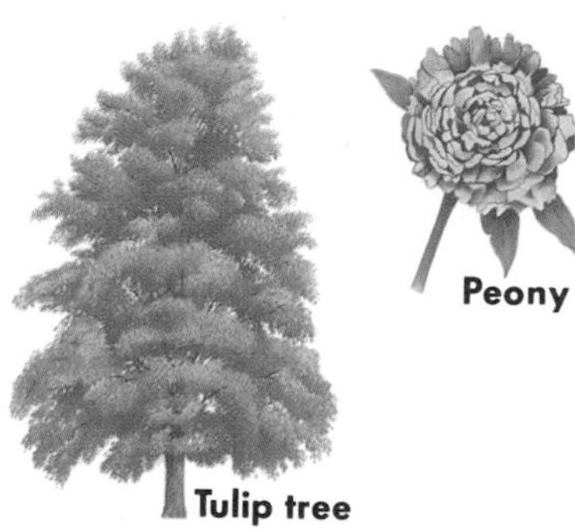

Peony

Tulip tree

Cardinal

Indiana
**Capital:** Indianapolis
**Area:** 36,420 sq mi (94,328 km$^2$). Rank: 38th
**Population:** 5,554,159 (1990). Rank: 14th
**Statehood:** Dec. 11, 1816
**Principal rivers:** Ohio, Wabash, White, Tippecanoe
**Highest point:** Wayne County, near Richmond, 1,257 ft (383 m)
**Motto:** The Crossroads of America
**Song:** "On the Banks of the Wabash, Far Away"

Indiana is an important farming and industrial state in the Midwest. In the northwest, it borders Lake Michigan. The Ohio River forms the state's southern boundary. Indiana has rich farmlands. Corn is the chief crop, but soybeans and wheat are also grown on Indiana farms. Over 4 million hogs and pigs and 1.5 million head of cattle are raised in Indiana. Nearly 95 percent of Indiana's farm goods are sent to other parts of the country.

Industry is even more important than agriculture for Indiana. Industrial income first passed farming income early in the 1900s. Coal mines and limestone quarries were among the first industrial ventures in Indiana. Then oil refineries, steel mills, and factories were built in the northern Indiana cities of Gary, Fort Wayne, and South Bend. The Lake Michigan lakefront became a major industrial region. The factories there provided many people with jobs. But they also caused pollution. New laws have begun to control much of the dangerous pollution and preserve wild areas on the Lake Michigan shoreline. Visitors can now relax in the dunes and forests of the Indiana Dunes National Lakeshore.

Indiana got its name because so many Indian tribes once lived there. Some fierce battles between the U.S. Army and Indian tribes took place in Indiana. The last battle was in 1811. General William Henry HARRISON defeated the Miami Indians in the Battle of Tippecanoe. This cleared the way for permanent white settlements. The victory at Tippecanoe later helped Harrison become U.S. president.

► *The well-managed farms of Steuben County, near the borders with Michigan and Ohio, produce hogs, poultry, and vegetables.*

▲ *Memorial Day parades held in Indianapolis also celebrate the Indianapolis 500, one of the world's greatest and most popular automobile races.*

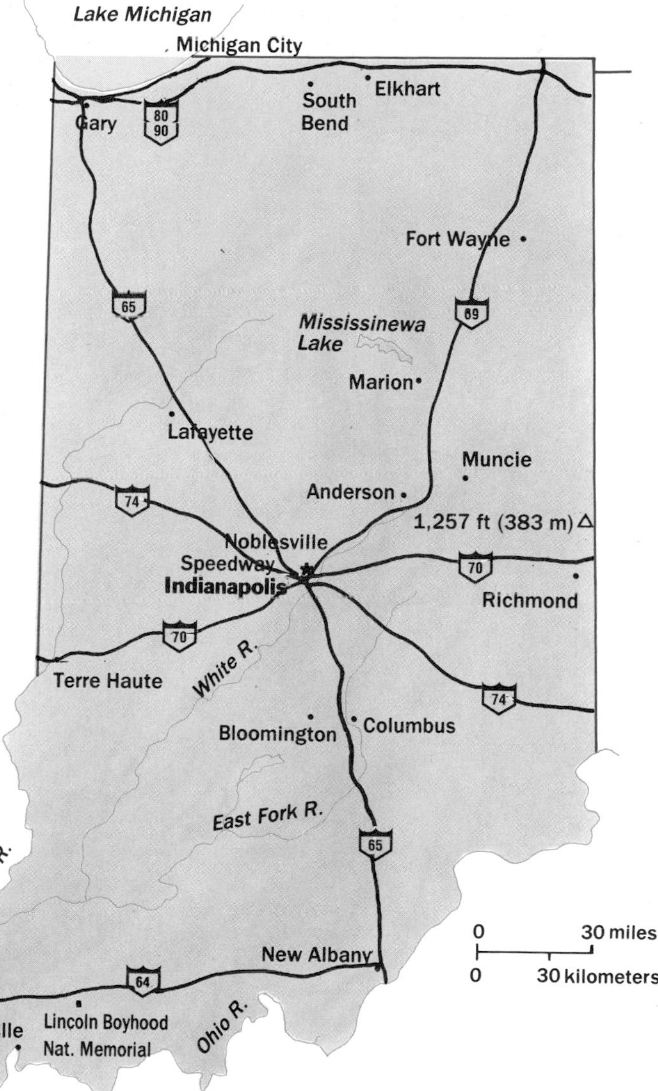


▼ *Lake Tippecanoe is located in the northern part of Indiana, between South Bend and Fort Wayne. Dozens of lakes around the state offer good swimming, boating, and fishing.*

### Places of Interest

- The Indianapolis Motor Speedway, in Speedway, is the home of the Indianapolis 500 automobile race.
- Historic Fort Wayne, a reconstructed fortress, stands on the site of an American Army fort of 1816.
- Conner Prairie Settlement, in Noblesville, is a glimpse into the Indian way of life of the early 1800s.

▲ *Indiana's state capitol, built in 1878, is located in the heart of Indianapolis.*

## INDIANAPOLIS

Indianapolis is the capital and largest city of INDIANA, with a population of 741,952. It is at the geographic heart of the state. It is an important transportation center for the surrounding farming area. Most goods passing between Ohio and Illinois go through Indianapolis. Meat packing is also important. Stockyards cover more than 210 acres (85 ha). Indianapolis is the Midwest regional center for many insurance companies. It is the home of Indiana University and a campus of Purdue University. College football, professional basketball, and the famous Indianapolis 500 automobile race are top sports attractions.

## INDIANS, American

American Indians are the native peoples of the Western Hemisphere. They have been living in the Americas for many thousands of years. When Christopher Columbus arrived in America, he thought he was in the East Indies and called the people he met "Indians." At that time there were between 1 million and 6 million Indians in what is now the United States and Canada. They had come to America from Asia by crossing from Siberia to Alaska and then moving south. This migration started about 30,000 years ago.

Many of the Indians in North America north of Mexico lived by hunting and fishing, growing maize (corn), and gathering nuts, berries, and wild grains. Those who lived east of the Mississippi River included

▼ *A Navajo Ganado rug usually has a deep red background and gold designs.*

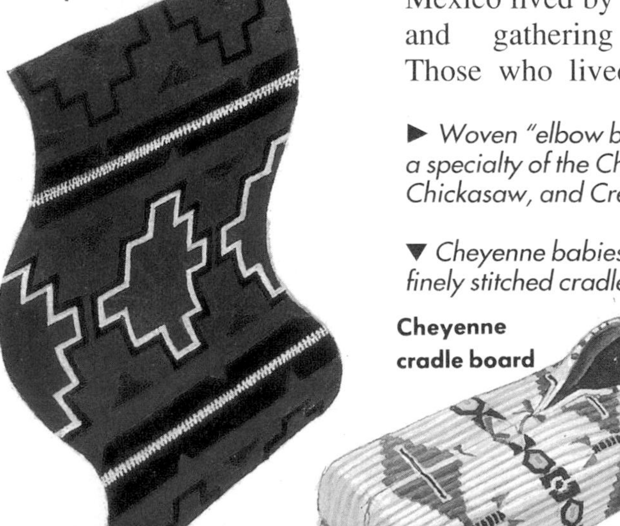


► *Woven "elbow baskets" were a specialty of the Choctaw, Chickasaw, and Creek tribes.*

▼ *Cheyenne babies were put in finely stitched cradle boards.*

◀ *Eastern moccasins were made of a single piece of leather. Plains Indians often decorated their pipes with colorful patterned weavings.*

▼ *Traditional Indian houses suit the climate and terrain of various tribes.*

Major Regions of Indian Tribes and Culture

**Eastern Woodland:** the forests and fields of the East.
**Plains:** the open plains — home of the buffalo.
**Plateau:** along the Columbia River of the Pacific Northwest.
**Great Basin:** the desert regions between the Rockies and the Sierra Nevadas of eastern California.
**Southwest:** the dry highlands of Arizona and New Mexico.
**Northwest Coast:** the fishing area of the northern Pacific coast of Oregon and Washington.
**California:** mountains, forest, rich farmland, and desert.

◀ *Frederic Remington's painting of a Cheyenne brave shows how naturally the Plains Indians took to horseback riding.*

► *The Apache warrior Geronimo, seen here behind the wheel of an early Ford automobile, was a cattle rancher in his last years.*

**Many Indian place-names are clues about local geography: Connecticut ("long river place"); Massachusetts ("large hill place"); Michigan ("great water"); Mississippi ("great river"); Missouri ("muddy water"); Ohio ("fine or good river"); and Wisconsin ("grassy place").**

Algonquian-speaking peoples, the IROQUOIS League, or Confederacy, and what became known as the Five Civilized tribes of the Southeast. The Indians of the Great Plains, with their tepees and feathered head-dresses, are the Indians most often seen in movies. Among these people were the Sioux. They hunted the bison (buffalo), riding horses after they were brought to the New World by Europeans.

The Indians of the Northwest became famous for their totem poles and other wood carvings. The Pueblo Indians of the Southwest were farmers noted for their woven baskets and pottery.

▼ *Indians occupied all of North America before the arrival of Europeans. Each tribe was composed of many smaller tribes sharing the language and customs.*

Territories
Arctic
Subarctic
Northwest Coast
California
Plains
Eastern Woodlands
Southwest

Aleut
Cree
Cree
Chippewa
Blackfoot
Algonquin
Chinook
Crow
Mandan
Sioux
Huron
Mohawk
Iroquois
Nez Percé
Shoshoni
Cheyenne
Pawnee
Miami
Mohican
Ute
Arapaho
Powhatan
Paiute
Kiowa
Cherokee
Navajo
Hopi
Pueblo
Comanche
Creek
Caddo
Choctaw
Apache
Seminole

◀ *Kwakiutl craftsmen of the Pacific Northwest continue the tradition of carving totem poles from cedar logs.*

Many Indian tribes in the East lost their lands to white settlers. In the West, however, many were put on reservations. There are now about 1.5 million Indians in the United States. About one third of them live on reservations. Almost 500,000 Indians live in Canada. The states with the largest numbers of Indians are Oklahoma, Arizona, New Mexico, North Carolina, and California. One half of the total Indian population lives in these five states. The Navajos form the largest Indian

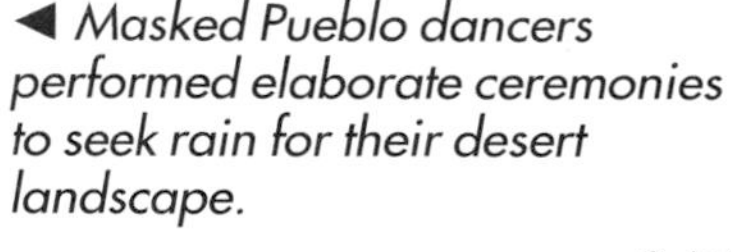

▲ *Young Indians learned crafts and skills such as weaving and hunting. But they still had time for games and sports.*

◀ *Masked Pueblo dancers performed elaborate ceremonies to seek rain for their desert landscape.*

▲ *This Navajo ranger at Grand Canyon National Park can teach visitors about her tribe's long history in the area.*

Indian Loss of Lands:
Some Important Dates

1768: Colonial treaties with Iroquois, Creeks, and Cherokees give settlers more land.
1795: United States gains territory in Ohio from Delaware, Shawnee, Wyandot, and Miami tribes.
1818: Chickasaws sell all their land above Tennessee's southern border.
1825: Georgia gains large areas from Creeks; Osage and Kansas tribes give up land in Missouri Territory.
1828: Arkansas Territory gains Cherokee land.
1832: Sauk (or Sac) Indians give up lands east of Mississippi River.
1851: Sioux sign away lands in Iowa and Minnesota.
1863: Congress removes all Indians from Kansas.
1885: Ahantchuyuks give up land in Oregon.

nation. Their reservation covers all the northeastern corner of Arizona and extends into Utah and New Mexico. Many Sioux live in South Dakota and Oklahoma and Cherokees in North Carolina.

The Indians have been wards of the U.S. government since 1871. Their affairs have been managed by the Bureau of Indian Affairs, a division of the U.S. Department of the Interior. In the 1970s, the Indians began to make strong demands to manage their own affairs. And they began fighting to have their lands returned to them or to get financial settlement. In many cases, their lands had been taken away from them in violation of treaties.

Poverty is widespread among Indians. Their unemployment rate far exceeds that of the general population. Fewer than 50 percent graduate from high school. And their birth, death, and suicide rates are probably the highest in the nation. But with the return of some of their lands, it is hoped that many Indians will be able to achieve a better way of life. The Bureau of Indian Affairs is trying hard to accomplish this. Its staff is now two-thirds Indian, and they are providing better educational opportunities, as well as job training.

This encyclopedia contains articles on many Indian tribes and their great leaders. You may want to look them up in the Index.

## INDIAN WARS

When the Europeans discovered the New World, they claimed the land and all its riches. When white settlers moved onto the lands occupied by Native Americans, war became inevitable. In what is now the United States, these wars began in the early 1600s in Virginia and New England. When France and England fought for control of North America in the 1700s, most Indian tribes supported the losing side, the French. During the American REVOLUTION, most tribes again backed the losing side, the British.

After the WAR OF 1812, the Indians had no European allies to help them. The Black Hawk War (1831–1832) ended with the Sauk and Fox expelled from the upper Mississippi Valley. Most of the Seminoles of Florida were defeated by 1842 and moved west of the Mississippi River. There, also, the Indians had their lands taken by white settlers. Tribes like the

Apaches and the Sioux resisted. The Sioux defeated U.S. troops under General George A. CUSTER at the Battle of the Little Bighorn in 1876. The last battle between U.S. troops and Indians was at Wounded Knee, South Dakota, in 1890, where Sioux men, women, and children were massacred.

▲ *Fierce battles between Indian warriors and the U.S. Army were common in the 1800s. The Indians were outnumbered and defeated by modern weapons.*

## INDUSTRIAL REVOLUTION

Industrial Revolution is the name given to the change from an economy based mostly on growing crops and raising livestock to one based on turning out large amounts of manufactured goods.

The Industrial Revolution first took place in England. It started in the mid-1700s. James Watt's steam engine freed factories from depending on waterpower. Improvements in iron making made it possible to make good, durable machines and parts. With the growth of factories, the nature of work also changed. People had to perform the same tasks over and over again with little or no rest.

Even before independence, Americans were making iron, ships, and small arms. Eli WHITNEY's invention of the cotton gin in 1793 and Robert FULTON's first steamboat in 1807 were important steps in the U.S. Industrial Revolution. The first big factories were mostly textile mills in New England that still depended on water for power. By 1850, however, the United States was on the way to becoming the greatest manufacturing nation in the world.

▼ *The Industrial Revolution in the United States initially centered around textile mills in New England. This woodcut shows a woman spinning yarn.*

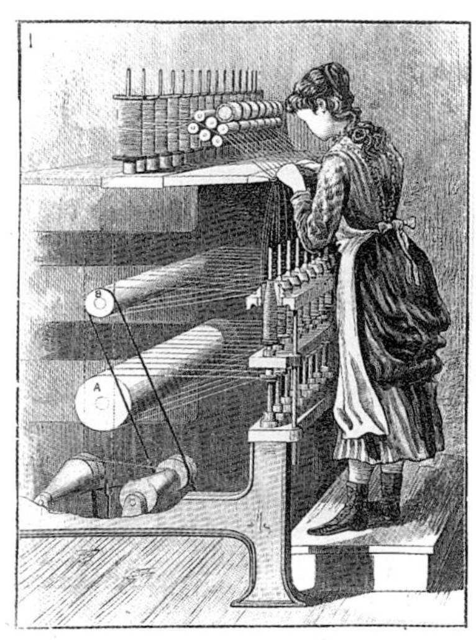

# INSECTS

An insect is a small animal with six legs and a body divided into three parts. Insects are found everywhere, from deserts to glaciers, from hot springs to cold waterfalls. Scientists know of more than 800,000 species, or kinds, of insects in the world. About 80,000 of these are found in North America. One of the largest is the cecropia moth, of eastern North America. It has a wingspan of up to 6 inches (15 cm). The smallest is a type of fairy fly found on the Pacific coast. It is less than 1/100th of an inch (0.5 mm) long.

▼ *An insect has three body sections, the head, thorax, and abdomen. Inside the abdomen are the stomach, reproductive organs, and breathing tubes.*

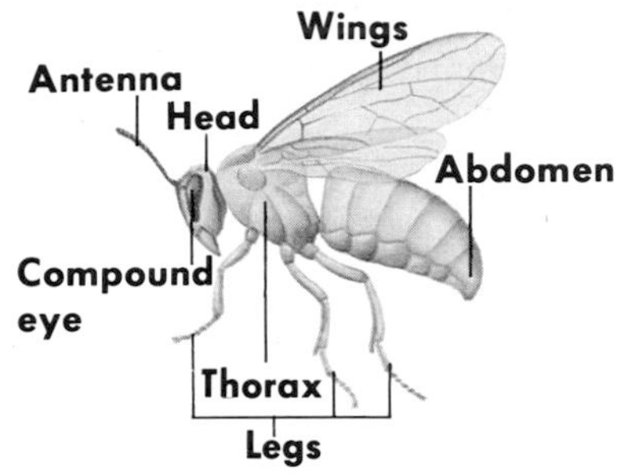


Insects are divided into major groups, or orders. The orders that include the most species are the BEETLES, BUTTERFLIES AND MOTHS, ANTS, BEES and wasps, and true flies. In one square yard of soil, up to 2,000 insects can be found. Most of these are less than ¼ inch (6 mm) long.

Insects are important in the balance of nature. A few, such as honeybees, also provide products people need. Only a few hundred species of North American insects are harmful. But these insects destroy about a tenth of the crops grown in a year. This damage, along with various methods of preventing it, costs the United States billions of dollars every year. Serious pests include the boll weevil, which feeds on cotton, and the Colorado potato beetle, which feeds on potatoes. The Japanese beetle attacks plants in farms, orchards, and gardens. The Hessian fly, corn earworm, flour beetle, and chinch bug destroy grain crops.

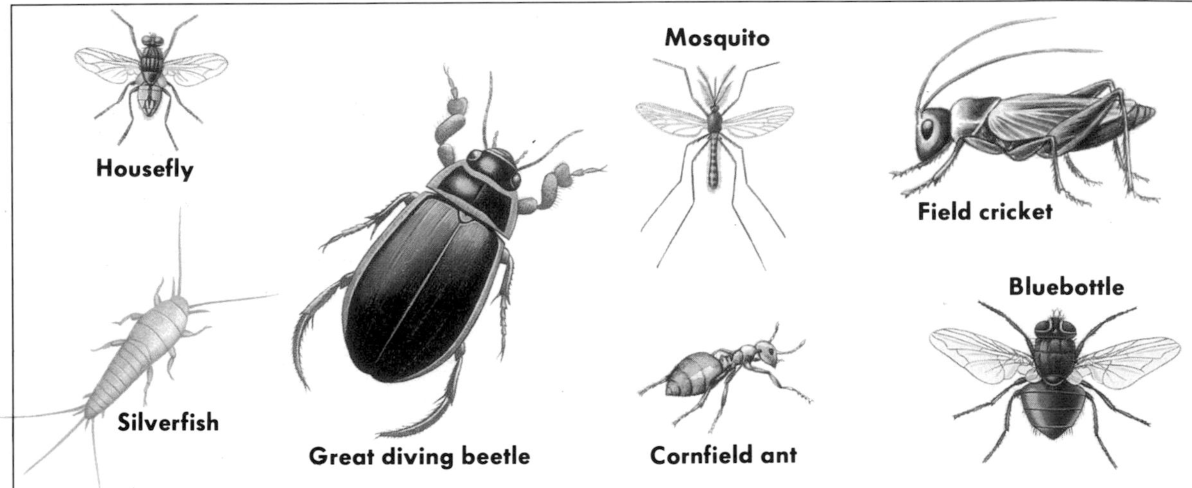


**Because insects are cold-blooded, their pulse rate may range from 140 per minute in an active insect to 1 pulse per *hour* in chilled insects. Insects may vibrate their wings at speeds up to 1,000 beats per second, which is about 12 times faster than the wing beat of the hummingbird.**

Some insects are household pests. These include the silverfish, clothes moth, carpet beetle, ant, and termite. A few insects, such as the human louse, some mosquitoes, and the common housefly, carry disease. Still others, like the "no-see-'em" (a type of midge) of New England, give unpleasant bites. Insecticides (chemicals that kill insects) are one method of controlling insect pests, but many farmers prefer using natural methods, such as using other insects to eat pests.

Insect Pests

**Aphids** damage plants by sucking juices and spreading viruses.

**Corn earworms** are young moths that feed on corn and other crops.

**Head lice** spread typhus to humans.

**Mormon crickets** eat everything in their path, including each other.

**Mosquitoes** transmit harmful diseases such as yellow fever and malaria.

**Weevils** are small beetles that eat their way through crops and grains.

Useful Insects

**Apanteles wasps** lay their eggs in caterpillar pests. The young then feed on the caterpillars and kill them.

**Carrion beetles** help the environment by eating decaying animal matter.

**Honeybees** spread pollen for many plants. They also produce honey and wax.

**Lacewing** larvae feed on destructive insects and provide food for birds.

**Ladybugs** eat harmful insects such as aphids.

**Tachinid flies** eat many dangerous insect pests.

**We now know that many of the chemicals once used to kill insect pests have serious side effects on humans. Safer, "natural" methods have become common. For example, the insect-eating mosquitofish has been introduced to many farming districts.**

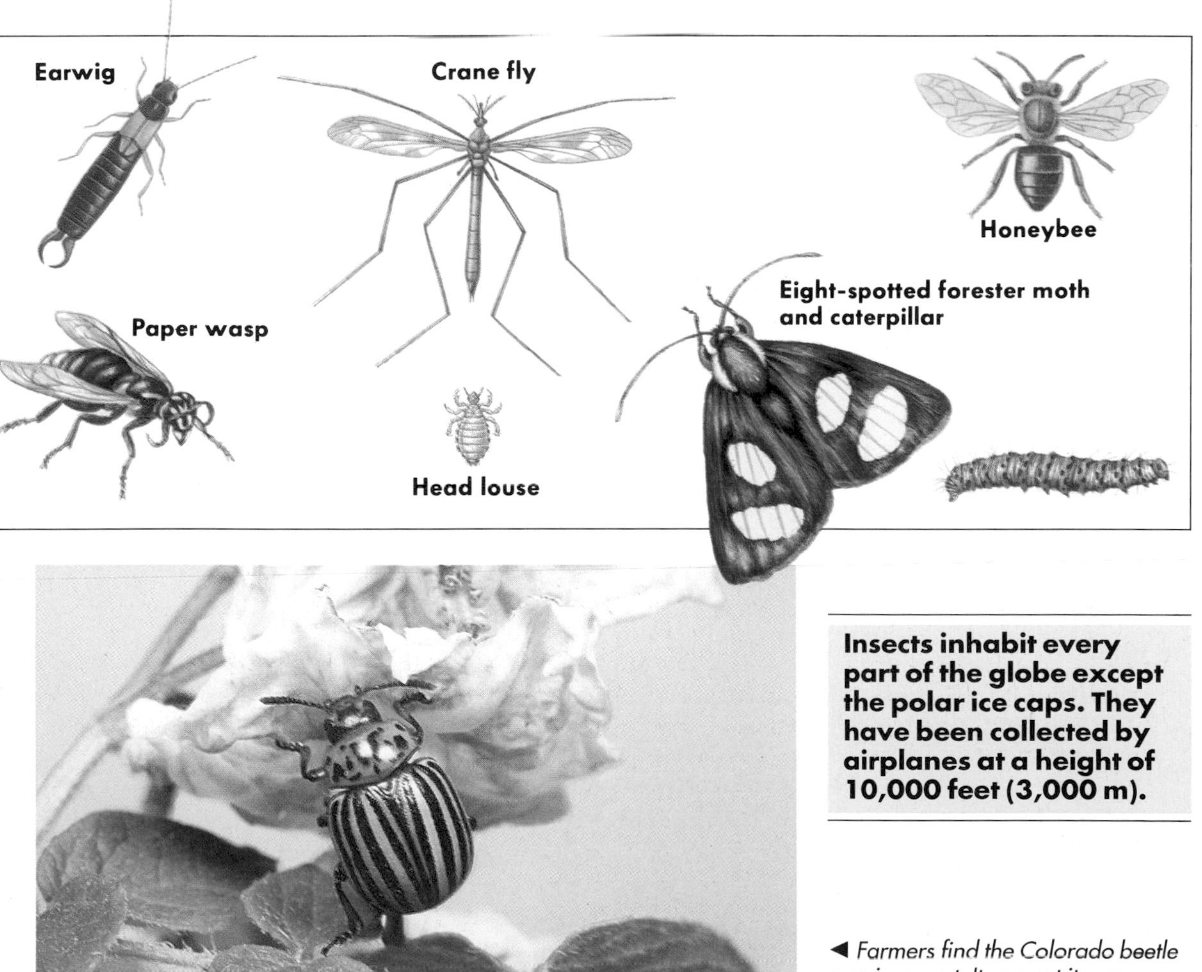


**Insects inhabit every part of the globe except the polar ice caps. They have been collected by airplanes at a height of 10,000 feet (3,000 m).**

◀ *Farmers find the Colorado beetle a serious pest. It can eat its way through the leaves and flowers of trees and crops.*

## INSURANCE INDUSTRY

Insurance exists to provide people with protection against unforeseen events. People pay a certain sum (called a premium) to insurers. In return the insurer assumes the risk of paying compensation for the loss of life or damage to health or property. Life insurance provides payments to the next of kin in the event of the policyholder's death. In the United States, the average family has about $98,400 in life insurance. Health insurance pays doctor and hospital bills and other medical expenses. The most important kinds of property insurance are auto and home-owners insurance.

There are private insurers and government insurers. Among the latter is the federal government, which provides health insurance for the elderly through Medicare. More than 2 million people work in the U.S. insurance industry.

The Top Ten U.S. Insurance Companies

1. Prudential of America
2. Metropolitan Life
3. Teachers Insurance & Annuity
4. Aetna Life
5. Equitable Life Assurance
6. New York Life
7. Connecticut General Life
8. John Hancock Mutual Life
9. Northwestern Mutual Life
10. Travelers

## INTERIOR, Department of the *See* Government, U.S.

## INVENTIONS

An invention is something that has been made for the first time. Americans have invented many useful things, from the safety pin, zipper, and sewing machine to the airplane, nuclear reactor, and laser. Following is a list of some of the most important American inventors and their inventions.

Famous American Inventions and Inventors

| Invention | Inventor | Date |
|---|---|---|
| Air brake | George Westinghouse | 1869 |
| Air conditioning | Willis H. Carrier | 1902 |
| Airplane | Orville and Wilbur Wright | 1903 |
| Bakelite (plastic) | Leo Baekeland | 1907 |
| CAT scanner | Allan Cormack | 1968 |
| Computer, electronic digital | J. Presper Eckert, Jr., and John W. Mauchly | 1946 |
| Cotton gin | Eli Whitney | 1793 |
| Cyclotron | Ernest O. Lawrence | 1931 |
| Electromagnet | Joseph Henry | 1828 |
| Electronic flash | Harold E. Edgerton | 1931 |
| Elevator | Elisha G. Otis | 1853 |
| Escalator | Jesse Reno | 1892 |
| Gyrocompass | Elmer Sperry | 1911 |
| Helicopter | Igor Sikorsky | 1939 |

▼ *The safety razor and sewing machine were invented in 19th-century America.*

Safety razor

Sewing machine

| | | |
|---|---|---|
| Incandescent lamp | Thomas Alva Edison | 1879 |
| Laser | Theodore Maiman | 1960 |
| Lightning rod | Benjamin Franklin | 1752 |
| Lock, pin-tumble | Linus Yale, Jr. | 1865 |
| Locomotive (first U.S.) | Peter Cooper | 1830 |
| Machine gun | Richard Gatling | 1861 |
| Motion-picture projector | Thomas Alva Edison | 1888 |
| Motor, AC | Nikola Tesla | 1887 |
| Nuclear reactor | Enrico Fermi and others | 1942 |
| Nylon | Wallace H. Carothers | 1936 |
| Pen, fountain | Lewis E. Waterman | 1884 |
| Pen, ball-point | John Loud | 1888 |
| Phonograph | Thomas Alva Edison | 1877 |
| Polaroid camera | Edwin H. Land | 1947 |
| Reaper | Cyrus McCormack | 1834 |
| Revolver | Samuel Colt | 1835 |
| Rocket, liquid-fuel | Robert Goddard | 1926 |
| Safety pin | Walter Hunt | 1849 |
| Sewing machine | Elias Howe | 1846 |
| Sleeping car (train) | George Pullman | 1865 |
| Steamboat | Robert Fulton | 1807 |
| Submarine, power-driven | John. P. Holland | 1887 |
| Telegraph | Samuel F.B. Morse | 1837 |
| Telephone | Alexander Graham Bell | 1876 |
| Television | Vladimir Zworykin | 1923 |
| Transistor | John Bardeen, Walter Brattain, William Shockley | 1948 |
| Trolley car, electric | Frank Sprague | 1887 |
| Typewriter | Christopher L. Sholes, Carlos S. Glidden, and Samuel W. Soule | 1868 |
| Videotape recorder | Charles Ginsberg and Charles Anderson | 1956 |
| Vulcanization of rubber | Charles S. Goodyear | 1839 |
| Xerography (photocopying) | Chester Carlson | 1942 |
| X-ray tube | William D. Coolidge | 1913 |
| Zipper | W.L. Judson | 1896 |

**One day in 1849, New York inventor William Hunt was twisting wire while thinking of a way to repay a $15 debt. After three hours he had designed the modern safety pin, which he patented that year.**

**There is always a need for new inventions. One 1990 invention was a "garbage collector" for space vehicles. This device can prevent spacecraft from colliding with other orbiting material.**

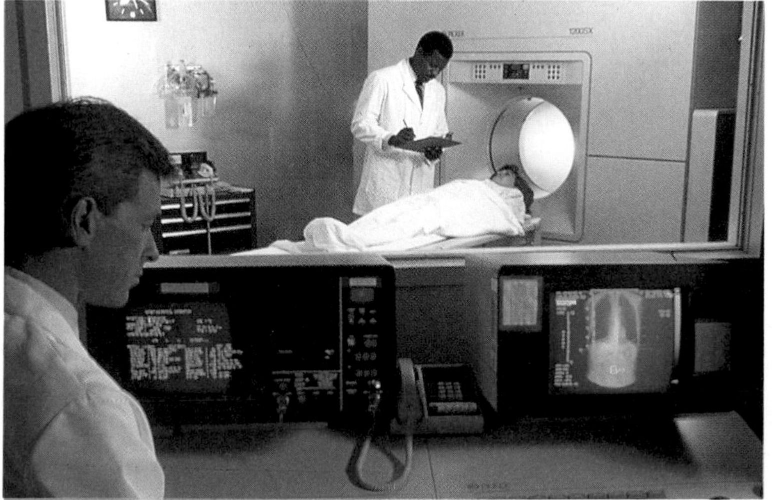

◄ *CAT scanners use X rays to provide doctors with a picture "slice" of a patient's body. Allan Cormack of the United States and Geoffrey Hounsfield of the United Kingdom shared the 1979 Nobel Prize for medicine, awarded for their work in developing the CAT scanner.*

IOWA

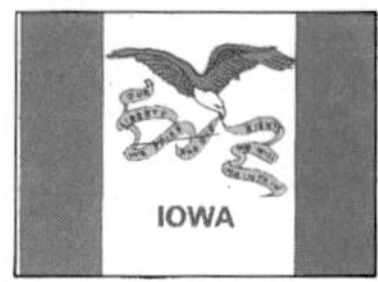

When people think of the Midwest state of Iowa, they usually think of fields of corn, tassels swaying in the breeze. The Hawkeye State, as it is called, is known for rich farmland. It usually ranks first (or second to Illinois) among states each year in the amount of corn grown. Feeding on the corn, and also on soybeans, are

Wild rose

Eastern goldfinch

Oak

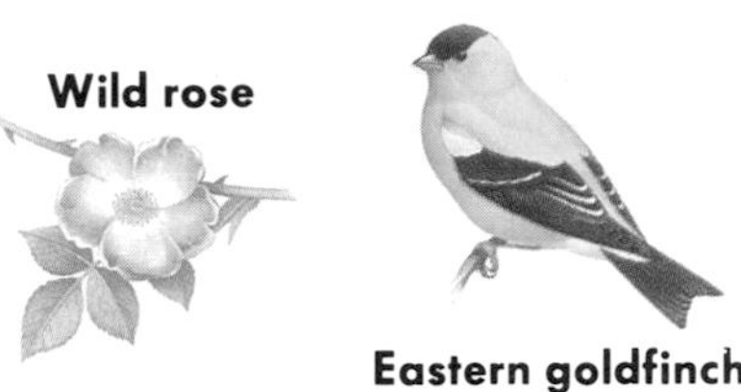

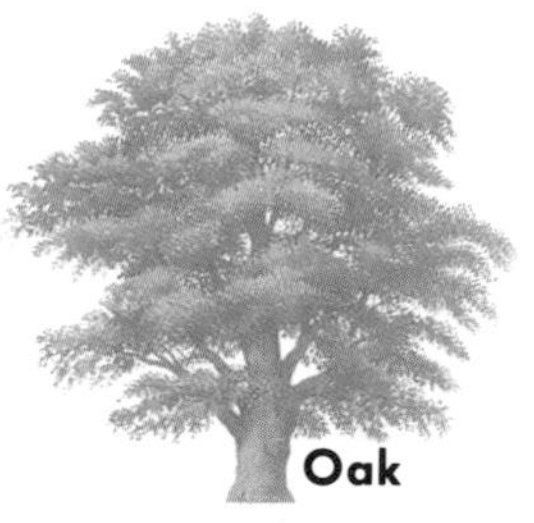

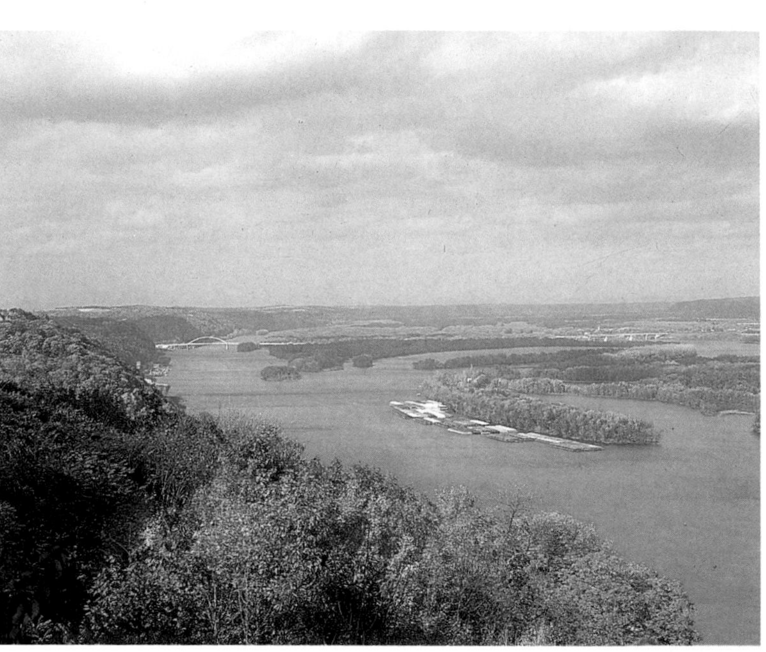

► *The mighty Mississippi River forms Iowa's eastern border and irrigates its fertile farms.*

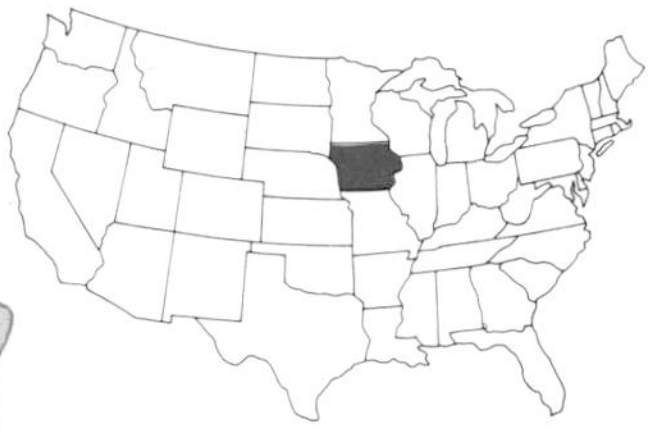

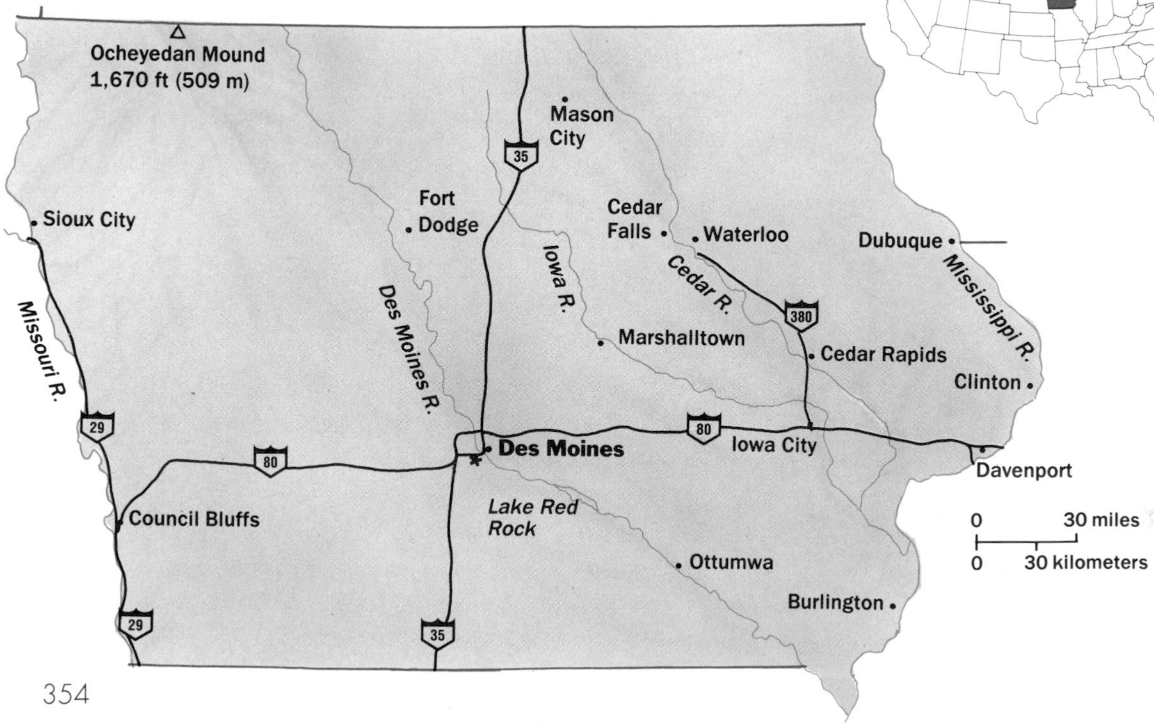
Ocheyedan Mound
1,670 ft (509 m)
Mason City
35
Fort Dodge
Sioux City
Cedar Falls
Waterloo
Dubuque
Iowa R.
Cedar R.
Mississippi R.
Des Moines R.
Missouri R.
380
Marshalltown
Cedar Rapids
Clinton
29
80
80
Des Moines
Iowa City
Davenport
Council Bluffs
Lake Red Rock
0 30 miles
0 30 kilometers
Ottumwa
Burlington
29
35

large numbers of hogs and cattle. Iowa raises more hogs and pigs than any other state. Once the crops and livestock leave the farms, Iowa factories turn them into meat, breakfast cereals, animal feeds, and other food products. But many other goods—especially farm machinery—are made in Iowa. And Des Moines, the state capital and Iowa's biggest city, is a center of the insurance industry.

One reason Iowa is good for growing crops is that the land is flat or gently rolling. The other reason is that glaciers melted at the end of the last Ice Age and left behind fertile rock and soil. The two longest rivers in North America provide irrigation water in case of drought. The Mississippi borders Iowa on the east, and the Missouri on the west. Both allow cheap transport of bulk goods such as grain to other parts of the country.

The first Europeans to visit Iowa were the French explorers and fur trappers. In 1803 it was sold to the United States as part of the LOUISIANA PURCHASE. In 1832 an uprising by Sauk (or Sac) and Fox Indians was put down, and eastern Iowa soon filled with settlers. It became a U.S. territory in 1838 and was admitted to the Union as the 29th state in 1846.

Iowa

**Capital:** Des Moines
**Area:** 56,276 sq mi (145,754 km$^2$). Rank: 26th
**Population:** 2,776,755 (1990). Rank: 30th
**Statehood:** Dec. 28, 1846
**Principal rivers:** Missouri, Mississippi, Des Moines
**Highest point:** Osceola County, border with Minnesota, 1,670 ft (509 m)
**Motto:** Our Liberties We Prize and Our Rights We Will Maintain
**Song:** "The Song of Iowa"

Places of Interest

- Living History Farms, near Des Moines, is a working farm with buildings and implements from the late 1800s.
- Floyd Monument, a 100-foot (30-m) stone shaft in Sioux City, honors Charles Floyd of the Lewis and Clark Expedition.
- The Iowa State Fair, held each August in Des Moines, is one of the largest in the country.

◀ *The gilded dome of the Capitol Building in Des Moines dominates the skyline. Inside are murals and mosaics.*

## IRON AND STEEL INDUSTRY

Iron and steel production is one of the world's most important industries. Between 1896 and 1970 the United States was the leading producer of iron and steel in the world. In 1971 it was overtaken by the Soviet Union. Today Japan also produces more steel than the United States. More than two thirds of U.S. steel is produced by just five states: Pennsylvania, Indiana, Ohio, Illinois, and Michigan.

**The United States produces about 10 percent of the world's steel, down from 20 percent in 1970. But it imports more steel than any other country.**

Steel is made from iron ore. In the United States, most iron ore is mined in Minnesota and Michigan, near Lake Superior. California, Missouri, and Wyoming are other important sources.

The first successful ironworks in the United States was established in 1646, at Saugus, Massachusetts. The U.S. steel industry began in the late 1800s, following the discovery of the iron ore deposits near Lake Superior. In 1873, Andrew CARNEGIE built the first large steel plant in the country, in Pennsylvania. There are now about 160 steel plants in the United States, owned by about 80 private companies. The United States Steel Corporation is the largest. The automobile and construction industries are major users of steel.

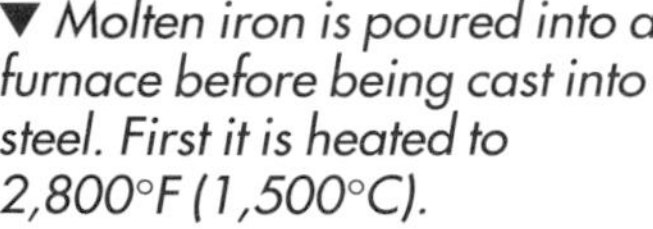

▼ *Molten iron is poured into a furnace before being cast into steel. First it is heated to 2,800°F (1,500°C).*

◀ *Iroquois longhouse villages lined the shores of Lakes Erie and Ontario. Their strange wooden masks represented mythological beings and were worn during tribal ceremonies.*

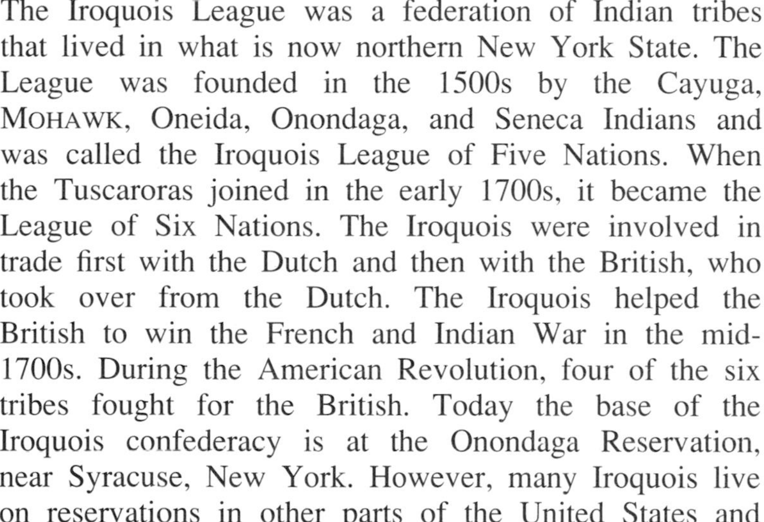

## IROQUOIS LEAGUE

The Iroquois League was a federation of Indian tribes that lived in what is now northern New York State. The League was founded in the 1500s by the Cayuga, MOHAWK, Oneida, Onondaga, and Seneca Indians and was called the Iroquois League of Five Nations. When the Tuscaroras joined in the early 1700s, it became the League of Six Nations. The Iroquois were involved in trade first with the Dutch and then with the British, who took over from the Dutch. The Iroquois helped the British to win the French and Indian War in the mid-1700s. During the American Revolution, four of the six tribes fought for the British. Today the base of the Iroquois confederacy is at the Onondaga Reservation, near Syracuse, New York. However, many Iroquois live on reservations in other parts of the United States and in Canada. (See also HIAWATHA.)

## IWO JIMA, Battle of

Iwo Jima is a volcanic island about 750 miles (1,450 km) south of Tokyo, Japan. It was the scene of one of the fiercest battles of WORLD WAR II. The American victory was vital for the Allies. The Japanese had used Iwo Jima as an air base throughout the war. The U.S. MARINES finally captured the island near the end of the war, on March 17, 1945. But during the month of fighting, 6,800 Marines were killed and more than 18,000 were wounded. After the war the United States governed the island. It was returned to Japan in 1968.

▼ *Iwo Jima's location made it an important air base for U.S. forces on their way toward Japan. Military leaders used the term "island hopping" to describe this path to Japan.*

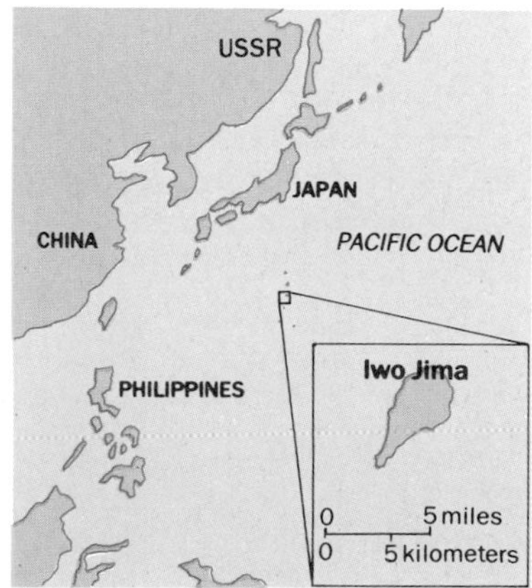

## JACK-IN-THE-PULPIT

The jack-in-the-pulpit is a North American wildflower that grows in damp places. It gets its name from the way it looks. The plant's small flowers are on a stalk-like structure called a spadix. Another part of the plant, the spathe, forms a hood over the spadix. The two structures resemble a person standing in a pulpit.

The jack-in-the-pulpit is sometimes called "Indian turnip" because early white settlers saw Indians cooking the root in the same way that they cooked turnips. But it is dangerous to eat this plant because some parts are poisonous if not cooked properly.

▲ *Some Indian tribes ate jack-in-the-pulpits, but only after carefully preparing them to remove poisonous crystals.*

## JACKRABBIT

The jackrabbit is a large HARE that lives on the grassy plains of the western United States. Most jackrabbits eat crops and are considered pests by farmers. Like other hares, jackrabbits have long hind legs, long ears, and short tails.

Jackrabbits have brownish-gray fur. But the fur of the white-tailed jackrabbit, which lives in the Northwest, turns white during the winter. The black-tailed jackrabbit is the largest jackrabbit. It can grow up to 2 feet (60 cm) in length and weigh 9 pounds (4 kg). Because it has long, donkeylike ears, it is also known as the jackass hare. Other North American jackrabbits include the antelope, California, and white-shouldered jackrabbits.

► *The jackrabbit needs its speed (up to 35 miles per hour, or 60 km/hr) to escape from coyotes. It can jump 20 feet (6 m).*

# JACKSON, Andrew

Andrew Jackson was the seventh president of the United States. He was the first president to rise from humble origins. He campaigned under the slogan "Let the people rule" and founded the modern Democratic Party. A strong leader, Jackson expanded the power of the presidency.

Jackson was a frontiersman who was called "Old Hickory" because of his toughness. He was also a successful businessman and served in Congress and as a judge. As a major general in the WAR OF 1812, he defeated the Creek Indians and routed the British in the Battle of New Orleans. Jackson became a national hero. He was made governor of the Territory of Florida and was then elected senator from Tennessee. In 1828 he was elected president.

Andrew Jackson
**Born:** March 15, 1767, in Waxhaw Settlement, South Carolina
**Education:** Legal studies in law office
**Political party:** Democratic
**Term of office:** 1829–1837
**Married:** 1791 to Mrs. Rachel Donelson Robards
**Died:** June 8, 1845, in Nashville, Tennessee

◄ *Jackson's troops repelled the British attack on New Orleans in 1815.*

Jackson said he was in favor of states' rights. As president, he supported the southern states that forcibly expelled their Indian populations in spite of federal treaties and court decisions. But he threatened to send troops to South Carolina if the state ignored or nullified an unpopular federal tariff law.

Jackson's biggest battle was against the Bank of the United States. This bank dominated banking in the country, and Jackson felt that it was unfair to the West. He crippled the bank by withdrawing federal funds and placing them in state banks. Many of these banks were unsound, however. A financial panic in 1837 caused great damage to the national economy.

In 1837, after serving two terms as president, Jackson retired to his home, the Hermitage, in Tennessee.

▼ *Andrew Jackson was captured by the British during the Revolutionary War. An officer slashed him with a sword for refusing to polish his shoes.*

▲ *Jesse Jackson's hard work on behalf of the poor led to his having a strong voice in national politics. His missions to Syria and Cuba helped secure the release of American prisoners.*

## JACKSON, Jesse

The Reverend Jesse Jackson (1941– ) is a political and CIVIL RIGHTS leader. He was born in Greenville, South Carolina. Jackson, a Baptist minister, took part in the civil rights protests in the South with Martin Luther KING, Jr., in the 1960s. He founded PUSH (People United to Save Humanity) in 1971. Its aim was to increase economic opportunities for blacks. Jackson also encouraged black youths to get a good education. In 1984 and 1988, he sought the Democratic nomination for president. He did not succeed. But by the time of the 1988 campaign, he had many followers and was in a position to influence Democratic policy at the nominating convention.

## JACKSON, Mahalia

Mahalia Jackson (1911–1972) was the most famous gospel singer in the world. She was born in New Orleans and began singing in the choir of the church where her father preached. She moved to Chicago when she was 17, taking jobs in factories and as a hotel chambermaid. In her free time she continued singing in a local Baptist church. Jackson's strong voice and spirited style attracted many admirers. She began making records in the 1930s and continued until her death 40 years later.

## JACKSON, Thomas Jonathan "Stonewall"

▼ *Stonewall Jackson's brilliant victory at Bull Run silenced any Northerners who thought the war would be over in days. His death in 1863 was a severe loss for the Confederate cause, and in particular for General Lee, who called Jackson "my right arm."*

Thomas "Stonewall" Jackson (1824–1863) was a brilliant Confederate general. He was born in Clarksburg, Virginia (now West Virginia). He attended West Point and fought with distinction in the MEXICAN WAR (1846–1848). Later, he taught at the Virginia Military Institute. There his serious nature made him somewhat unpopular with cadets. But later, as a combat officer, he won the respect and love of his troops.

After the start of the CIVIL WAR, Jackson was made a brigadier general in the Confederate Army. He acquired the nickname "Stonewall" at the first BATTLE OF BULL RUN in July 1861. Jackson held his troops in a strong line, resisting heavy enemy fire. "There is Jackson standing like a stone wall!" cried another officer to his own retreating troops. "Let us determine to die here and we will conquer!"

Later, in such important battles as Fredericksburg (1862) and Chancellorsville (1863), Jackson's cool head and mastery of surprise tactics helped to achieve Southern victories. At Chancellorsville he was accidentally shot by his own men.

## JACKSONVILLE

Jacksonville is FLORIDA's largest city, with a population of 672,971. It is located on the St. Johns River in the northeastern corner of the state. Jacksonville was founded in 1822 when Florida became a U.S. territory. It is named after Andrew JACKSON, who was the first territorial governor of Florida. Modern Jacksonville is a trading and financial center. It is also an important port and transportation center.

▲ *The Rouse Project is an imaginative and attractive district to help house Jacksonville's growing population.*

## JAMES, Henry

Henry James (1843–1916) was a major American writer. He wrote 20 novels, including *Daisy Miller*, *The Portrait of a Lady*, and *The Ambassadors*. He also wrote plays and short stories, including the ghost story *The Turn of the Screw*. The philosopher William JAMES was his brother. From early childhood, Henry James traveled widely in Europe, and in 1876 he settled in England. Many of his books are about the conflict between American and European attitudes and moral codes.

**Henry James was a tireless writer, with at least one of his books published each year from 1876 until his death in 1916. He was also a popular member of society. In the winter of 1878–1879 he accepted 140 dinner invitations.**

◄ *Daisy Miller, heroine of one of Henry James's first novels, proved to be popular with American readers.*

▲ *The James gang, led by Jesse James (below) and his brother Frank, staged about 25 violent robberies in Missouri. Innocent railroad workers were often killed.*

## JAMES, Jesse

Jesse James (1847–1882) was a famous outlaw. He and his brother Frank were born in Missouri. They fought on the Southern side during the Civil War, with a band of guerrillas known as Quantrill's Raiders. After the war, James and Frank formed a gang that held up banks and robbed trains. When the governor of Missouri offered a reward for the James brothers, dead or alive, one of the gang shot Jesse dead. Frank James was tried but acquitted and he gave up crime.

## JAMES, William

William James (1842–1910) was a famous psychologist and philosopher. His brother was the writer Henry JAMES. Born in New York City, William James earned a degree in medicine at Harvard University in 1869 and later taught there. He then became interested in how the mind works. In 1890 he wrote *The Principles of Psychology*. (Psychology is the study of the mind.) James's book *Pragmatism* (1907) contains the core of his philosophical theories.

**William James was not afraid to express his professional opinions publicly. In 1899 he offered a description of Theodore Roosevelt, who at the time was a war hero running for president. James said that Roosevelt "gushes over war as the ideal condition of human society."**

## JAMESTOWN SETTLEMENT

Jamestown was the first permanent settlement in North America. It was founded in 1607 on a small island in the James River, in Virginia. Most of the colonists died of disease or famine by the end of the year. Captain John Smith restored morale and discipline the next year by making everyone work. Smith returned to England in 1609. The following winter, 90 percent of the settlers died of starvation. But in 1612, John Rolfe (who later married POCAHONTAS) started growing tobacco. With a cash crop for sale to England, Jamestown thrived.

In 1619 the colonists were allowed to elect members to the Houses of Burgesses—the first legislative body in North America. In 1699 the capital of Virginia was moved to Williamsburg, and Jamestown was abandoned. Most of the island is now part of Colonial National Historical Park.

▲ Jamestown's tobacco exports kept the settlement from starvation in the early years.

## JANSKY, Karl

Karl Jansky (1905–1950) was an engineer. He was born in Norman, Oklahoma. In 1931, Jansky searched for the source of static that was affecting transatlantic messages. He came to the conclusion that some of the static came from outside the solar system. It was radio waves from outer space. Jansky's important discovery led to the development of radio astronomy. This field of science uses radio telescopes to study space by "listening" rather than using optical telescopes.

## JAY, John

John Jay (1745–1829) was a distinguished diplomat during the early history of the United States and the first chief justice of the U.S. Supreme Court.

Born in New York City, Jay began practicing law when he was 23 years old. He was a member of the First CONTINENTAL CONGRESS and president of the Second. After the American REVOLUTION he helped negotiate the Treaty of Paris, in which Britain recognized U.S. independence. Jay believed in a strong central government, and he wrote five of *The Federalist* papers, which urged the ratification of the U.S. CONSTITUTION.

President George WASHINGTON appointed Jay as the first chief justice of the U.S. Supreme Court. He served in that position from 1789 to 1795. In 1794, Jay was sent to England on a special mission—to avoid war with that country. The British still occupied forts in U.S. territory, and they were seizing American ships on the high seas. Under the terms of Jay's Treaty, the British agreed to leave the forts. Jay later served as governor of New York from 1795 to 1801.

▼ Jay's Treaty, signed in 1794, resolved some issues between the United States and Britain. But it did not protect American ships from being searched. This angered many Americans. It passed by a bare two-thirds majority in the Senate in 1795.

# JAZZ

► *Harlem's Cotton Club, jazz mecca of the 1920s*

◄ *Dizzy Gillespie is one of the world's favorite trumpet players.*

Jazz is the kind of music in which players *improvise*—start with a tune and make changes in the melody and rhythm. Jazz has a *syncopated* rhythm—that is, the accent (beat) falls in unexpected places. The basis of jazz is the blues, a form of black American folk music.

Jazz developed around 1900 in NEW ORLEANS. By the 1920s this music was called Dixieland. The most important jazz musician of this era was the trumpeter and singer Louis ARMSTRONG. By the 1930s, Chicago and New York were the centers of jazz. Duke ELLINGTON, Count BASIE, and Benny GOODMAN perfected big-band jazz. Their music was often called "swing" for its inventive rhythms. The most important musician of the 1940s was saxophonist Charlie Parker. The fast tempos and complex chords and rhythms of Parker and his followers were called "bebop." Even more complex and innovative is the jazz of later musicians such as John Coltrane, Ornette Colman, and Charlie Mingus.

▲ *Jazz singer Ella Fitzgerald*

◄ *Charlie Parker (far left), Miles Davis*

**Types of Jazz**

**Bop**, or bebop, is a type of jazz played by smaller bands. Complex rhythms are played with strong feeling.

**Dixieland** continues the New Orleans jazz of the early 1900s. It is loud and cheerful and uses the band as a team.

**Fusion**, developed by musicians such as Miles Davis, combines jazz techniques with those of rock music.

**Swing** was the "big band" music of the 1930s and early 1940s. Soloists were backed up by repeated melodies from the band.

◀ *Louis Armstrong (trumpet) played with King Oliver's Creole Jazz Band in 1920.*

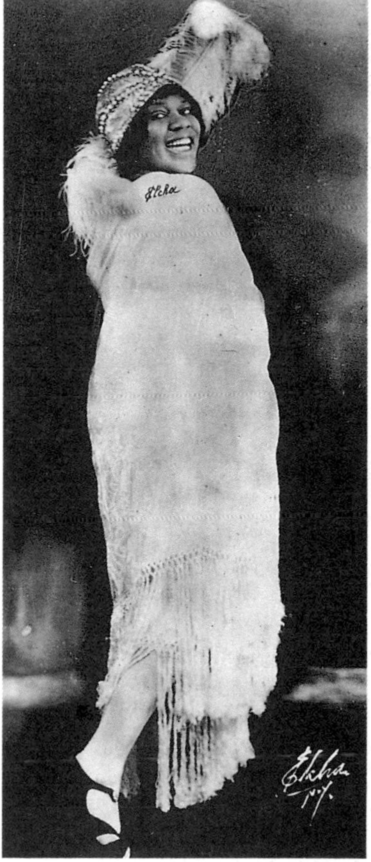

▲ *Many jazz lovers consider Bessie Smith to be the greatest singer ever produced by America.*

### Giants of the Jazz World

**Louis Armstrong** (1900–1971) was an accomplished trumpet player and perhaps the greatest figure in jazz. His gruff but good-natured singing added to his popularity.
**Count Basie** (1904–1984) was a popular and innovative bandleader and pianist.
**Bix Beiderbecke** (1903–1931) was a cornetist and the greatest white jazzman of the 1920s.
**Miles Davis** (1926–1991) is a trumpeter who developed a soft but complex style known as "cool jazz."
**Duke Ellington** (1899–1974) was a bandleader and pianist who composed and arranged his own music.
**Benny Goodman** (1909–1986) was known as the "King of Swing." (Swing is a type of big-band jazz.)
**Wynton Marsalis** (1961–) is a trumpeter who is equally happy playing jazz or classical music.
**Charlie Parker** (1920–1955) was a brilliant saxophone player who changed the face of jazz after World War II.

**Some of the greatest jazz musicians have led unconventional lives and received funny nicknames along the way—such as "Cannonball" Adderley, Eddie "Lockjaw" Davis, "Jelly Roll" Morton, Clarence "Pinetop" Smith, and "Fats" Waller.**

◀ *Preservation Hall in New Orleans is the famous home of New Orleans jazz.*

# JEFFERSON, Thomas

Thomas Jefferson
**Born:** April 13, 1743, in Shadwell, Virginia
**Education:** College of William and Mary
**Political party:** Democratic-Republican
**Term of office:** 1801–1809
**Married:** 1772 to Martha Wayles Skelton
**Died:** July 4, 1826, at Monticello, Virginia

Thomas Jefferson was the third president of the United States and the main author of the DECLARATION OF INDEPENDENCE. Jefferson was talented in many areas. He was not only a politician but also a lawyer, writer, scientist, inventor, farmer, educator, and architect.

Jefferson came from a wealthy Virginia family. After serving in the CONTINENTAL CONGRESS, he was governor of Virginia and the first U.S. envoy to France. Although he opposed the adoption of the U.S. CONSTITUTION, Jefferson joined President George WASHINGTON's Cabinet as the first secretary of state (1790–1794). He often opposed the secretary of the treasury, Alexander HAMILTON, who wanted a strong central government. Jefferson and his followers formed the Democratic-Republican (later Democratic) Party. They believed in individual freedom and as little government as possible.

► *Jefferson's action against the Barbary pirates led to the first U.S. foreign military action.*

▼ *An architectural drawing of Monticello.*

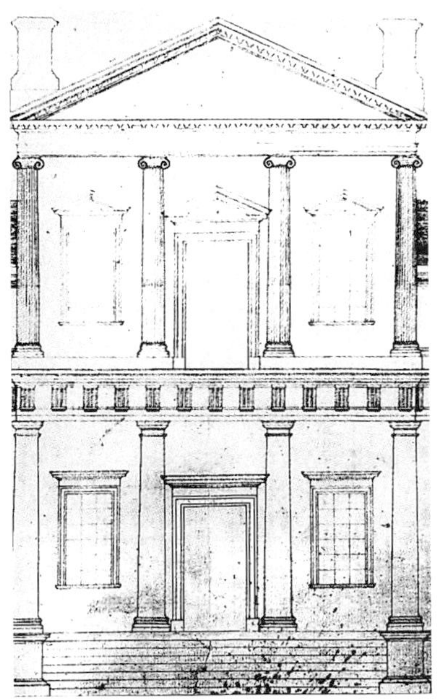

Jefferson was defeated in the 1796 presidential election but became vice president. In 1800 he was elected to the first of two terms as president. His most important achievement as president was the LOUISIANA PURCHASE, which doubled the size of the United States. Jefferson's biggest problem during his presidency was keeping the United States neutral in the war being waged by Britain and France.

In retirement Jefferson lived in Monticello, the house he had designed. On his tombstone he listed the three achievements he was most proud of. One was the Declaration of Independence. The other two were the founding of the University of Virginia and drafting the Statute of Virginia for Religious Freedom.

## JEWS AND JUDAISM

Judaism is the oldest of the world's RELIGIONS that believe in montheism—that there is a single, all-powerful god. It is based on the Torah, the first five books of the Old Testament. In the Torah, God promises the land of Israel (also known as Palestine) to the Jewish people. He sets down the rules by which the Jews should live. The Ten Commandments are the most basic and familiar of these rules.

There are nearly 6 million Jews in the United States. They form the largest non-Christian community in the country and the largest Jewish community in the world. There are three branches of American Judaism—Orthodox, Conservative, and Reform. They differ on such customs as Sabbath observance and the dietary (kosher) laws.

The first Jews in North America arrived in New Amsterdam (now New York City) in 1654. By the mid-1700s, the Jews in the 13 colonies were enjoying greater freedom than anywhere else in the world. In 1880 there were about 250,000 Jews in the United States, mostly of German birth or extraction. Between 1881 and 1924, when immigration laws were tightened, nearly 2.4 million Jews came to the United States. Most of these were from Russia and Poland. In the 1930s and 1940s, Jewish people fled Nazi Germany. Now, however, the Jewish population is overwhelmingly native born.

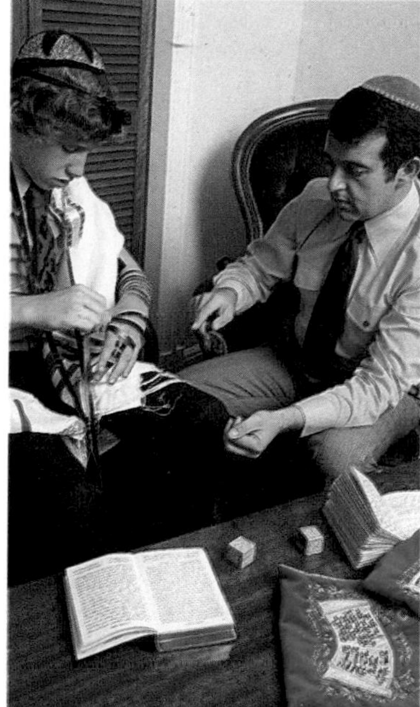

▲ *Jewish boys preparing for their bar mitzvah must study scriptures and learn how to wear special religious garments such as the* Teffi.

## JOHNS, Jasper

Jasper Johns (1930– ) is a leading American artist. His early style of art was known as pop art. This trend of the 1960s concentrated on depicting familiar, everyday objects. In Johns's work these were often letters, numerals, targets, or the American flag. His inspiration for these works came from dreams. Paint and other materials were applied thickly, so that the paintings became almost like sculptures. He also did pop art sculptures. One of these, *Painted Bronze*, consists of two beer cans.

Johns was born in Georgia and studied at the University of South Carolina. After moving to New York he worked for a while designing window displays for Tiffany's jewelry store. Johns destroyed his earliest works when he became famous in the 1950s. He also designed sets for the Merce Cunningham Dance Company.

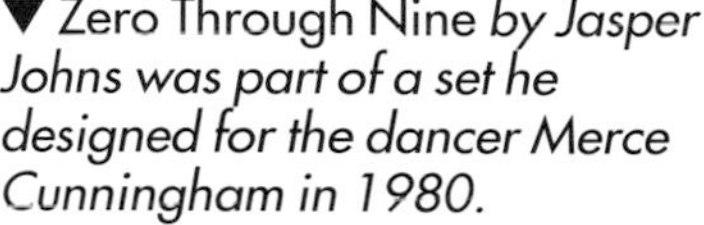

▼ Zero Through Nine *by Jasper Johns was part of a set he designed for the dancer Merce Cunningham in 1980.*

Andrew Johnson
**Born:** December 29, 1808, in Raleigh, North Carolina
**Education:** Self-taught
**Political party:** National Union
**Term of office:** 1865–1869
**Married:** 1827 to Eliza McCardle
**Died:** July 31, 1875, at Carter Station, Tennessee

► *The Civil Rights Act of 1866 made black people full U.S. citizens for the first time.*

▼ *Publications such as* Harper's Weekly *poked fun at President Andrew Johnson's planned Reconstruction of the South.*

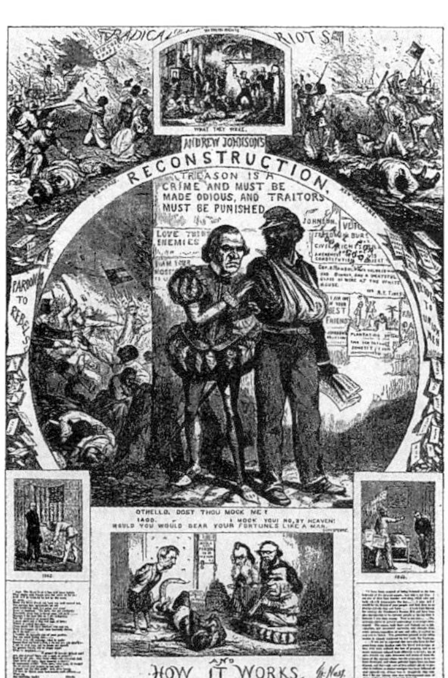


Andrew Johnson was the 17th president of the United States. As vice president he took over the presidency when Abraham LINCOLN was assassinated in 1865. Johnson was the only president never to have gone to school. Johnson became a member of the U.S. House of Representatives, governor of Tennessee, and a U.S. senator. He was the only Southern senator who remained loyal to the Union during the CIVIL WAR. He was made military governor of Tennessee and in 1864 was elected vice president. A little more than a month after taking office, he became president.

As president, Johnson stuck rigidly to policies that treated the South gently during the RECONSTRUCTION period that followed the end of the Civil War. Congress had a majority of Republicans and wanted more drastic

measures taken. It wanted, for example, to punish the leaders of the Confederacy and give the vote to Southern blacks. Johnson vetoed (refused to approve) a number of congressional bills. He believed that the Southern states should deal with their postwar problems with little federal interference. His veto of the Civil Rights Bill in 1866 was overruled by Congress.

When Johnson dismissed the secretary of war without the approval of the Senate, Congress tried to remove him from office. This process is known as IMPEACHMENT. The impeachment failed by one vote, and Johnson finished his term of office. His major achievement was the purchase of Alaska from Russia.

In 1875, Tennessee again elected Johnson U.S. senator. He died a few months later.

## JOHNSON, Lyndon B.

Lyndon B. Johnson was the 36th president of the United States. He took office in 1963 when President John F. KENNEDY was assassinated in Dallas, Texas.

A Democrat from Texas, Johnson served in Congress for 24 years. As leader of the Senate Democrats, he was a powerful political figure. In 1960 he was elected vice president as Kennedy's running mate. Johnson won the presidential election of 1964 easily. He set a record by winning 61 percent of the vote in defeating Republican Barry Goldwater.

A heavily Democratic Congress passed almost all the "Great Society" legislation that Johnson requested. First came a tax cut and a "war on poverty" to promote economic development in poor areas of the country.

Other bills established the Medicare program for the elderly and increased federal funding for education and housing. There were also new IMMIGRATION and CONSERVATION measures.

Racial tensions were high at this time. The CIVIL RIGHTS movement, led by Martin Luther KING, Jr., held peaceful protests. In response, Johnson promoted measures against racial discrimination in voting, housing, employment, and public accommodations. Nevertheless, riots broke out in the black neighborhoods of many cities.

In 1965, Johnson sent U.S. troops to fight the VIETNAM WAR. After three years of bloody fighting, the Communists seemed as strong as ever. With opposition to the war growing at home, Johnson called for peace talks and chose not to run for reelection in 1968.

Lyndon Johnson
**Born:** August 27, 1908, in Stonewall, Texas
**Education:** Southwest Texas State Teachers College
**Political party:** Democrat
**Term of office:** 1963–1969
**Married:** 1934 to Claudia Alta Taylor
**Died:** January 22, 1973, in Johnson City, Texas

◀ *Lyndon Johnson signing his "Great Society" measures. These aimed to improve conditions for racial minorities, the poor, and the elderly.*

▼ *Lyndon Johnson was sworn in as president on board Air Force One, the presidential jet.*

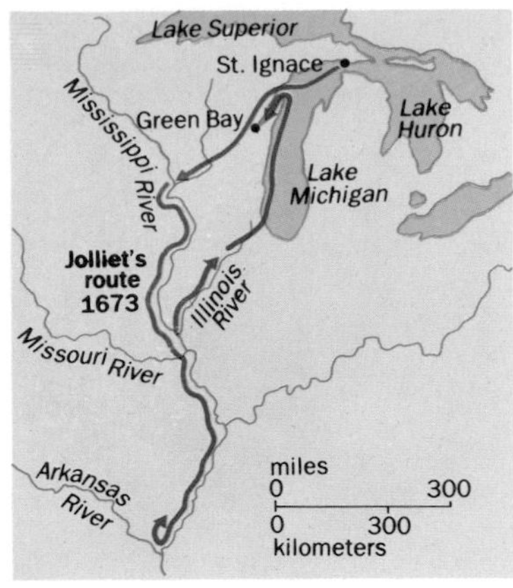


▲ *On his way back to Montreal, Jolliet's canoe overturned and he lost his journal and maps of the area he had explored. He later redrew the maps from memory.*

## JOLLIET, Louis

Louis Jolliet (1645–1700) was a French Canadian explorer. In 1673 he and a priest, Father Jacques MARQUETTE, led an expedition to find the Mississippi River, which they had heard of from the Indians.

The government of New France had hoped that the Mississippi flowed westward to the Pacific Ocean. If this was the case, it would be a route to Asia. But Marquette and Jolliet's five-month journey, which followed the river by canoe as far as southern Arkansas, proved that it flowed south. From friendly Indians they learned that the Spanish occupied land farther south, and they realized that the river flowed into the Gulf of Mexico. Jolliet explored many other territories of North America.

## JOLSON, Al

Al Jolson (1886–1950) was one of the most famous singers and entertainers of this century. His real name was Asa Yoelson. He was born in Russia, but his family moved to the United States when he was seven. Jolson learned English and began singing on stage when he was only 11 years old. By the time he was 25, he was one of America's highest-paid performers. In 1927, Jolson starred in *The Jazz Singer*, the first feature-length movie to have sound. His song-and-dance routine became world famous. "Swanee," "Mammy," and "April Showers," were some of his most famous songs.

▼ *Thousands of copies of the sheet music to "My Mammy" were sold in the 1920s.*

## JONES, Bobby

Bobby Jones (1902–1971) was one of GOLF's greatest players. He won 13 major championships in the eight years that he played, but he never became a professional. Jones shocked the golfing world by winning the British Open in 1926. He was the first amateur to win that title. He won it three more times before he retired in 1930. Jones organized the Masters Tournament as a way of inviting the best players to Georgia.

## JONES, John Paul

John Paul Jones (1747–1792) was a great naval hero of the American REVOLUTION. He is called the "father of the United States Navy." Jones was born in Scotland

and served on British ships. He moved to the United States in 1773.

When the Revolutionary War broke out, Jones offered his services and was commissioned an officer in the Continental Navy. Over the next six years, he scored a string of brilliant successes, capturing, sinking, and burning many British ships. His most spectacular victory took place in 1779, off the coast of England. As captain of the *Bonhomme Richard*, he captured a British man-of-war, the *Serapis*, after a four-hour battle. Jones's ship was so badly damaged that it sank two days after the battle. He and his crew sailed away in the *Serapis*.

After the war, Jones did not receive the recognition that he had expected and moved to Europe. He fell ill and died in Paris. A century later, however, he was given an appropriate grave at the U.S. Naval Academy in Annapolis.

▲ *John Paul Jones was given command of his first American ship, the sloop* Providence, *in 1776. On his first cruise with the ship he destroyed the British fisheries in Nova Scotia and captured 16 British ships.*

◀ *In 1779, Jones's ship the* Bonhomme Richard *captured the British ship* Serapis. *They had been so close that their riggings became entangled.*

## JOPLIN, Scott

Scott Joplin (1868–1917) was a great pianist and composer of ragtime music. Joplin was born in Texarkana, Texas, where his mother had been a slave. He taught himself piano in the house of his mother's employer. By the 1890s he was a popular piano player in the bars and music halls of Missouri. Joplin played ragtime, a type of piano music with a catchy beat. His ragtime compositions, such as "Maple Leaf Rag" and "The Entertainer," are still popular today. Joplin also composed two operas. *Treemonisha* was finally produced in 1972, years after Joplin's death.

**Scott Joplin published some 60 compositions, of which 41 are piano rags. During his lifetime, Joplin was never recognized as a serious composer. In 1971, interest in his music was revived, and in 1976 the Advisory Board on the Pulitzer Prizes awarded Joplin a special citation for his contribution to American music.**

▲ *When Chief Joseph surrendered to the U.S. Army, he said, "My heart is sick and sad. From where the sun now stands, I will fight no more forever."*

## JOSEPH, Chief

Chief Joseph (1840?–1904) was a leader of a band of NEZ PERCÉ Indians in northeastern Oregon. Beginning in 1863, when gold was discovered, whites swarmed into the area. In May 1877 the federal government ordered Chief Joseph's people to be moved. At first the chief agreed. But his people were angry, and war broke out. The Nez Percé won several victories over U.S. Army troops. But when a force of 600 men was sent to capture him, Joseph decided to retreat. He led his band of 750 people toward Canada. After a journey of 1,500 miles (2,400 km), they were forced to surrender in October 1877. Chief Joseph never saw his homeland again. He died on a reservation in the state of Washington.

## JOURNALISM

Journalism is the providing of news and information for the public. It can be divided into two types. The *press*, mainly newspapers and magazines, uses accounts written by reporters to present the news. The system of news reporting on television and radio is often called the *news media.* It is part of the broadcasting industry. Big-city newspapers and national radio and television networks can afford to send reporters to cover news stories. The local press and media rely on *news services*, news-gathering organizations that supply news reports for a fee.

The best American journalism is honored by the PULITZER PRIZES. They go to outstanding examples of public service, news photography, national and international reporting, and many other fields of journalism.

## JUVENILE DELINQUENCY

Juvenile delinquency is the breaking of laws by young people under the age of 18. In 1990, nearly 16 percent of all arrests were of juveniles. Juvenile delinquents are tried in juvenile courts. These courts try to help the young people rather than punish them. Juvenile delinquents who are convicted are sent to such facilities as detention centers, camps, and halfway houses. Here again the justice system tries to help them by providing education and work training. Two major causes of juvenile delinquency are poverty and broken homes.

**NUMBER OF JUVENILE ARRESTS (in thousands)**

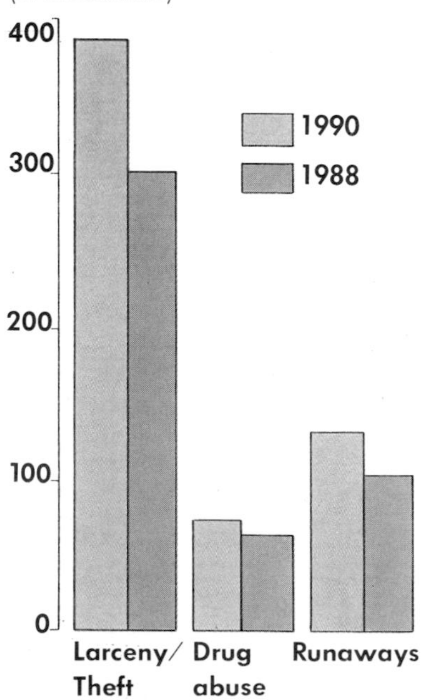

## KAHN, Louis 

Louis Isadore Kahn (1901–1974) was a famous architect. He was born in Estonia, now part of the USSR, but came to the United States when he was only four. He studied and lived most of his life in Philadelphia. He taught architecture at the University of Pennsylvania from 1957 until 1974. Kahn believed that the "useful" parts of buildings, such as staircases and air ducts, should be shown and not hidden. His first major work was the Yale University Art Gallery (1953).

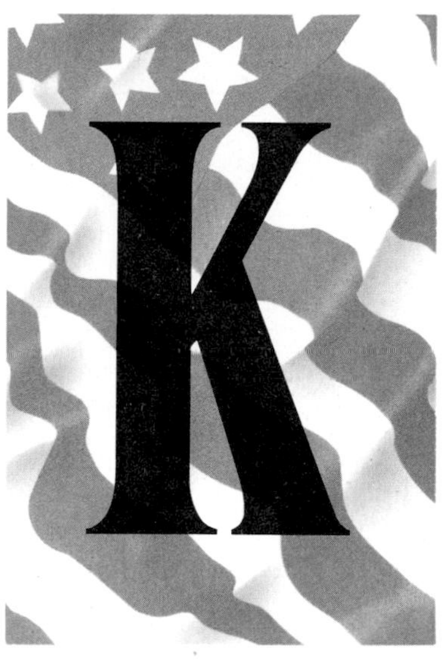

◀ *The Salk Institute in La Jolla, California, displays Kahn's love of concrete and open spaces.*

## KAMEHAMEHA I 

Kamehameha I (1758?–1819) united the Hawaiian islands to form the Kingdom of Hawaii. He was known as Kamehameha the Great, and his birthday, June 11, is a state holiday in HAWAII.

In 1792, Kamehameha defeated a cousin in battle to gain control of most of the island of Hawaii. Between then and 1810, he gained control of the other islands. Some were conquered while others were obtained by peaceful means. Kamehameha worked very hard to make Hawaii strong and wealthy. He also tried to maintain the native customs and religious beliefs of his people. Two of Kamehameha's sons and two of his grandsons ruled Hawaii until 1872.

**Kamehameha's formation of the Kingdom of Hawaii came at a time when other Pacific islands were falling under European control. Kamehameha called on Hawaiians to set aside their differences in order to resist the colonial threat.**

# KANSAS

Kansas, nicknamed the Sunflower State, is located in the very center of the United States. Farming and meat packing are two of the state's most important industries. Large farms are located in the flat central plain of Kansas. In the east there are rolling hills. The western part of the state rises up to become part of the high plains of the western United States.

Kansas produces more wheat than any other state. The wheat is stored with other grains in huge grain silos. Grains from other states are also sent to Kansas for storage. More than 200 million bushels of grain are held in the storage silos of Wichita and Topeka.

The Spanish explorer Francisco Vásquez de CORONADO was the first European to see the land that

**Cottonwood**

**Western meadowlark**

**Sunflower**

Kansas
**Capital:** Topeka
**Area:** 82,282 sq mi (213,110 km$^2$). Rank: 15th
**Population:** 2,477,574 (1990). Rank: 32nd
**Statehood:** Jan. 29, 1861
**Principal rivers:** Kansas, Republican, Smoky Hill, Arkansas, Missouri
**Highest point:** Mt. Sunflower, 4,039 ft (1,231 m)
**Motto:** *Ad Astra per Aspera* (To the Stars Through Difficulties)
**Song:** "Home on the Range"

Places of Interest

- The Eisenhower Center in Abilene is located at the boyhood home of President Dwight D. Eisenhower.
- Kansas Cosmosphere and Space Center, in Hutchinson, is a science museum with special exhibits on space exploration.
- Dodge City has preserved many storefronts made famous in its Wild West frontier days.

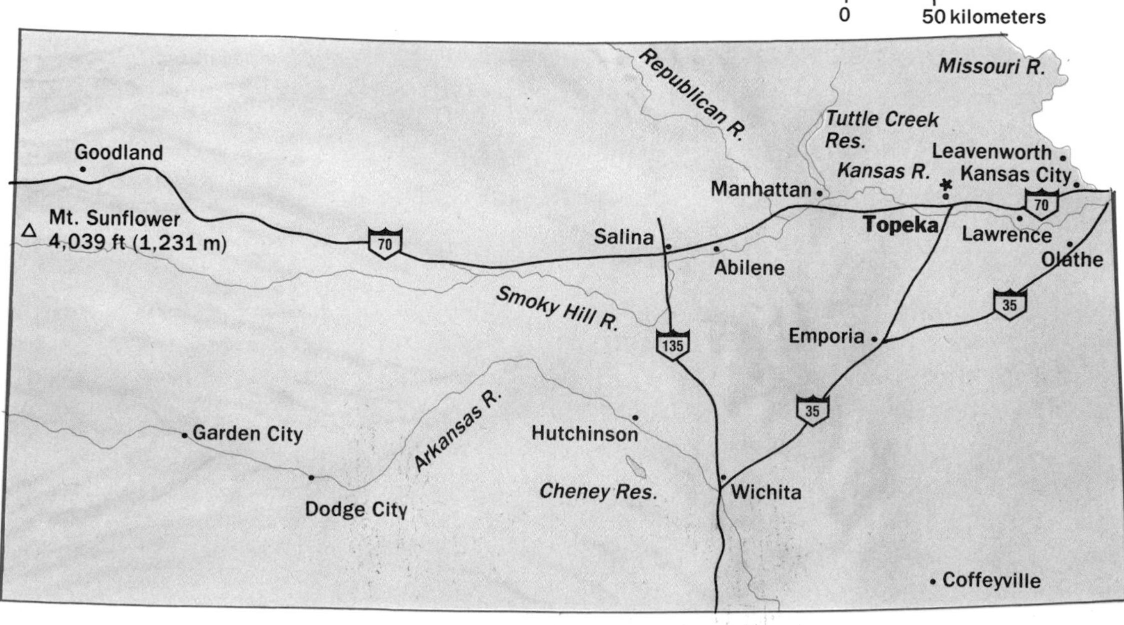

▲ *A reconstruction of Texas Street gives a Wild West flavor to Old Abilene Cow Town in Abilene.*

◀ *Modern combines harvest the important Kansas wheat crop. Kansas is the leading state in wheat production, with about 300 million to 400 million bushels each year.*

▼ *The Monument Rocks are reminders that glaciers covered most of Kansas in the last Ice Age of 10,000 years ago.*

is now Kansas. He traveled there from Mexico in 1541, looking for gold. Later, the French had control over the territory. In 1803, Kansas was part of the huge parcel of land sold by the French to the United States in the LOUISIANA PURCHASE. It became a territory. In the years before the CIVIL WAR, no slaves were allowed in Kansas, so Southern states would not let it become a state. Kansas finally became the 34th state in 1861, just as the Civil War was starting.

Kansas developed quickly after the Civil War. The new railroad lines built across the United States ran through Kansas. The railroads allowed farmers to ship crops and livestock easily and cheaply. Abilene and Dodge City started out as railroad junctions for cattle trains. Today Kansas has a large aircraft industry. Automobiles are also produced there.

▲ *Modern office buildings rise in downtown Kansas City.*

## KANSAS CITY, Missouri

Kansas City is MISSOURI's largest city, with a population of 435,146. It is on the state's western border, where the Kansas and Missouri rivers meet. A different Kansas City, in Kansas, is just across the Missouri River. Because of its river location, Kansas City has long been an important shipping center. Grain and cattle from the central Midwest are shipped through Kansas City. Huge grain elevators are used for storage of the wheat. The world price of wheat is decided in Kansas City.

Kansas City began as a trading post in 1821. It began to grow after the start of the California gold rush of 1849. Prospectors needed clothing and equipment, and Kansas City was used as their major trading center. Today Kansas City is an important industrial city. Only Detroit produces more automobiles. Meat packing and food-processing are also important industries.

## KEATON, Buster

Buster Keaton (1895–1966) was an American motion-picture actor. He was best known for his silent-film comedies. His trademark was an unsmiling, deadpan expression. Keaton went into films in 1917. He had already had a successful career on the stage, having

**Buster Keaton was a superb acrobat. In his films he was always a loner who triumphed over the most mind-boggling disasters.**

► *Buster Keaton's unsmiling expression in all his comedies earned him the nickname "the Great Stone Face."*

joined his parents' vaudeville act before the age of four. Keaton also wrote and directed films. His best motion pictures were *The Navigator*, *The General*, and *The Cameraman*. When sound films began to be made during the late 1920s, Keaton's success declined.

## KELLER, Helen

As the result of an illness when she was not yet two years old, Helen Keller (1880–1968) became deaf and blind. Because of this, she could not speak. When Keller was almost seven, Anne Sullivan became her teacher. She taught Keller to read and write braille, a special alphabet for people who are blind. Keller eventually learned to speak also. (The story was made famous in the 1960s award-winning play and film *The Miracle Worker*.) Keller went to Radcliffe College and graduated with honors in 1904. She then devoted herself to helping other people who were blind and deaf. Among the many books she wrote are *The Story of My Life* and *Midstream: My Later Life*.

▲ *Helen Keller learned to talk from her friend and teacher Anne Sullivan. First she had to learn what talking was.*

## KELLOGG, Frank

Frank Billings Kellogg (1856–1937) was prominent in both national and international politics. He was born in Potsdam, New York, and studied law. He became a U.S. senator from Minnesota in 1917. Kellogg was the U.S. ambassador to Great Britain from 1923 to 1925, and secretary of state under President Calvin COOLIDGE from 1925 to 1929. He also helped negotiate the Kellogg-Briand Pact of 1928. This international agreement to outlaw the use of war to solve international disputes was signed by 64 countries. To honor his work, Kellogg was given the Nobel Peace Prize in 1929. From 1930 he served as a judge of the Permanent Court of International Justice.

**The Kellogg-Briand Pact was formally known as the Treaty for the Renunciation of War. It failed in this purpose, however, because the pact did not provide a way to punish aggressors.**

## KELLY, Gene

Gene Kelly (1912– ) is a dancer, singer, and actor. He is best known for his work in the lavish Hollywood musicals of the 1940s and 1950s. The dance numbers he created were enormously entertaining. They helped to reveal the characters and tell the story. Kelly's style of dance, though based on ballet, was highly athletic. (As a

**Unlike many other Hollywood dancers, who came from a background of vaudeville or theater, Gene Kelly has been totally involved with moviemaking. He codirected *On the Town* and *Singin' in the Rain,* two classic musicals in which he also starred.**

boy in Pittsburgh he had excelled at ice hockey and other sports.) Among the best known of his films are *An American in Paris* and *Singin' in the Rain.*

In 1951, Kelly received a special Oscar for his achievements as dancer, singer, actor, choreographer, and director.

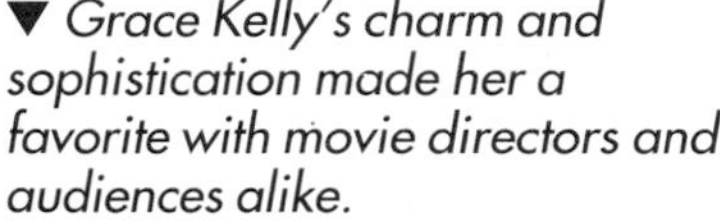

► Les Girls *gave Gene Kelly the chance to show off all his talents as a singer and dancer.*

▼ *Grace Kelly's charm and sophistication made her a favorite with movie directors and audiences alike.*

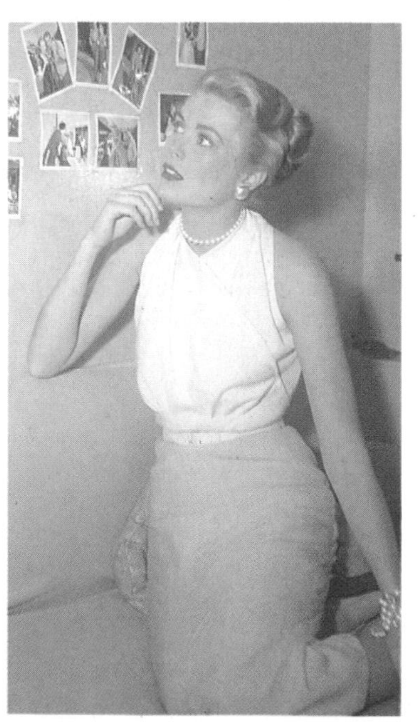

## KELLY, Grace

Grace Kelly (1929–1982) was a motion-picture actress and princess of Monaco. She began her career as a stage actress in 1949. Her first film was *Fourteen Hours.* Three years later, in 1954, her performance in *The Country Girl* won her the Academy Award for best actress. During her six-year Hollywood career, she starred in 11 films. Possibly her best roles were in the Alfred Hitchcock films *Dial M for Murder*, *Rear Window*, and *To Catch a Thief.* Her other films included *High Noon*, *The Swan*, and *High Society.*

Grace Kelly gave up acting in 1956 and married Prince Rainier III, the ruler of Monaco, a small country along France's southern border. Princess Grace died as a result of an automobile accident.

## KENNEDY FAMILY

The Kennedy family is one of the most famous in U.S. history. It has provided the country with a president, three senators, a congressman, a U.S. attorney-general, and an ambassador to Great Britain.

Joseph Patrick Kennedy (1888–1969) was born in Boston, the son of Irish immigrants. He married Rose Fitzgerald (1890– ), the daughter of the mayor of Boston, in 1914. Kennedy became the country's youngest bank president when he was 25 and amassed a fortune by the time he was 30. He was ambassador to Great Britain from 1937 to 1940.

Joseph and Rose Fitzgerald Kennedy had nine children. All four sons went to Harvard University. Joseph, Jr. (1915–1944), a U.S. Navy pilot, was killed in World War II. John (1917–1963) was also a war hero. He later became a congressman, then a senator, and, in 1961, the first Roman Catholic president of the United States. He was assassinated in 1963. Robert (1925–1968) was U.S. attorney-general in his brother's Cabinet. After John's assassination, Robert was elected to the U.S. senate from New York in 1964. While campaigning for the Democratic presidential nomination in 1968, he was assassinated. Edward (1932– ), the youngest Kennedy child, is the senior senator from Massachusetts. Joseph P. Kennedy II (1952– ), Robert's son, was elected a congressman from Massachusetts in 1986.

▲ *Robert Kennedy was campaigning for the presidency when he was assassinated in June 1968.*

▲ *Edward Kennedy was only 30 years old when he was elected U.S. senator from Massachusetts in 1962.*

◄ *The Kennedy family gathered for this photograph in November 1960, the day after John F. Kennedy (center) had been elected president.*

**John F. Kennedy**
**Born:** May 29, 1917, in Brookline, Massachusetts
**Education:** Harvard University
**Political party:** Democratic
**Term of office:** 1961–1963
**Married:** 1953 to Jacqueline Lee Bouvier
**Died:** Nov. 22, 1963, in Dallas, Texas

John Fitzgerald Kennedy was the 35th president of the United States and the first Roman Catholic to become president. Kennedy and his wife, Jacqueline, brought to the White House a special combination of youth and informality, glamour, and style.

John Kennedy was a hero during World War II. Later, he drew on his war record and his father's wealth and Democratic Party connections to enter politics. He was elected to the U.S. House of Representatives from Boston in 1946 and to the Senate from Massachusetts in 1952. In 1960, Kennedy became the Democratic Party nominee for president. He and the Republican nominee, Richard NIXON, held four television debates on the issues. Kennedy impressed the viewers with his intelligence and force of personality. At 43, he became the youngest elected president, narrowly defeating Nixon.

► *On August 28, 1963, John F. Kennedy met with civil rights leaders (including Martin Luther King, Jr.) who had marched to Washington.*

▼ *First Lady Jacqueline Kennedy with Caroline and John, Jr.*

Once in office, Kennedy stepped up the U.S. SPACE PROGRAM in order to put a man on the moon. He established the PEACE CORPS and supported CIVIL RIGHTS for black people. Kennedy also favored a government programs for the elderly and more federal aid to education. Kennedy's greatest challenge came in 1962, when the Soviet Union installed nuclear missiles in Cuba. He insisted that the missiles be removed and stopped ships from entering or leaving Cuba. The world seemed on the brink of nuclear war, but the Soviets backed down and removed the missiles.

Kennedy was assassinated on November 22, 1963, in Dallas, Texas, by Lee Harvey Oswald. Vice President Lyndon B. JOHNSON then became president.

## KENT, Rockwell 

Rockwell Kent (1882–1971) was an explorer and travel writer who gained greater fame as a painter and illustrator. He was born in Tarrytown Heights, New York, and studied architecture at Columbia University. He traveled to the two ends of the American continents, from Alaska to Cape Horn. He wrote and illustrated books about these and other adventures. He also illustrated books by other authors, such as Herman MELVILLE's *Moby Dick*. Kent's illustrations, often in stark black and white, were bold and eye-catching.

**Rockwell Kent was a leading campaigner for world peace, even though his views were unpopular during the Cold War. He visited the Soviet Union many times and even led a committee to promote friendship between the Soviet Union and the United Sates.**

◀ *A detail of Rockwell Kent's* Sundown, Greenland. *Kent's paintings were based on his own experience traveling in the polar regions.*

## KENTON, Stan 

Stanley Newcomb Kenton (1912–1979) was a JAZZ pianist, composer, and bandleader. He was born in Wichita, Kansas, and began playing in jazz bands in the 1930s, when he was in his twenties. He organized a band of his own in 1941. This wartime period was the era of the big bands, which played swing music such as that of Benny Goodman and Glenn Miller. Kenton's band could swing, but he preferred to experiment rather than play just one sort of music. Over the next 35 years he mixed jazz with South American and African music. His love of new sounds led him to introduce a new instrument, the mellophone, to his trumpet section. Stan Kenton's experiments helped keep jazz alive.

▼ *Stan Kenton's intelligent love of music led him to experiment constantly. The size of his band would change from almost orchestra size to just a few players.*

## KENTUCKY

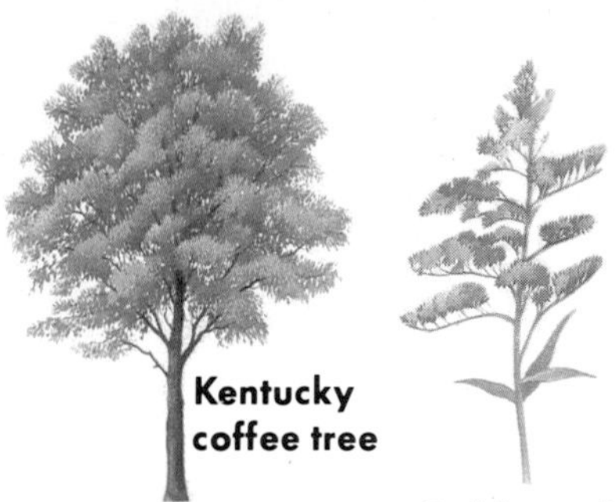

The state of Kentucky is located on the border between the South and the Midwest. Its nickname is the Bluegrass State. The name Kentucky comes from an Indian word meaning "land of tomorrow."

Kentucky was the first frontier for the United States. The original 13 colonies, which became the United States, were all on the Atlantic coast. People knew that there was land to the west, but the APPALACHIAN MOUNTAINS blocked the way. In 1775, Daniel BOONE blazed his way through the Cumberland Gap in the mountains of Tennessee. Settlers soon followed and cleared the forests to make farms. This new territory became the state of Kentucky. Kentucky is still an important farming state. More than 15 million acres (6 million ha) of its land are farmed. Most farms are small compared with the farms of the Midwest. Many date

**Places of Interest**

- The John James Audubon Memorial Museum, near Henderson, contains many of the naturalist's famed bird prints.
- Mammoth Cave National Park, in central Kentucky, includes the world's largest known cave system.
- The Abraham Lincoln Birthplace National Historic Site is located near Hodgenville.
- Horse farms in the "Bluegrass" region near Lexington.

**Kentucky**

**Capital:** Frankfort
**Area:** 40,411 sq mi (104,665 km$^2$). Rank: 37th
**Population:** 3,685,296 (1990). Rank: 23rd
**Statehood:** June 1, 1792
**Principal rivers:** Ohio, Mississippi, Cumberland, Kentucky, Green
**Highest point:** Black Mountain, 4,145 ft (1,263 m)
**Motto:** United We Stand, Divided We Fall
**Song:** "My Old Kentucky Home"

► *Mammoth Cave contains almost 200 miles (320 km) of explored and mapped passages and rooms that are 200 feet (60 m) wide.*

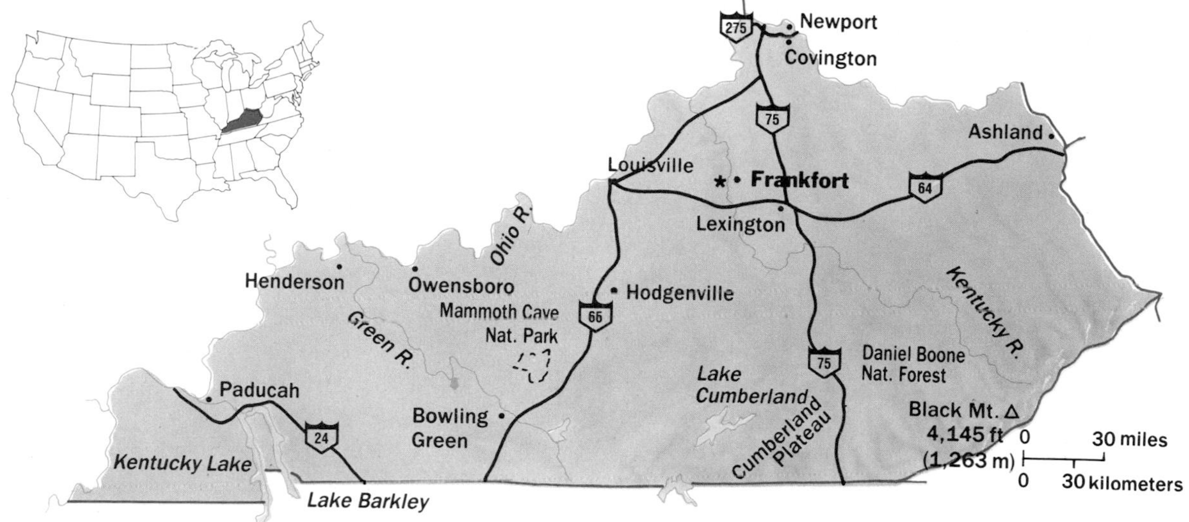


from the time of the first settlers of Kentucky. Abraham Lincoln was born on one of these small Kentucky farms. Kentucky's major crops are tobacco, corn, soybeans, and wheat.

Kentucky is the leading coal mining state. There are many mines in the hilly eastern part of the state. The coal found in this area is called anthracite. It is a hard variety and considered high-quality by the industries that use it. Among the many products made in Kentucky are whiskey, trucks and autos, food products, and chemicals.

Much of the lower land has richer soil. Horses are raised where the famous bluegrass grows. Many of the country's best racehorses come from Kentucky. The KENTUCKY DERBY, one of the world's most famous horse races, is held at Churchill Downs in Louisville.

▲ *Small-scale tobacco farming is still an important part of Kentucky's agriculture.*

◄ *Crops and industrial goods from Louisville, Kentucky, are easily shipped from its port along the Ohio River.*

| Recent Kentucky Derby Winners | |
|---|---|
| 1993 | Sea Hero |
| 1992 | Lil E. Tee |
| 1991 | Strike the Gold |
| 1990 | Unbridled |
| 1989 | Sunday Silence |
| 1988 | Winning Colors |
| 1987 | Alysheba |
| 1986 | Ferdinand |
| 1985 | Spend a Buck |
| 1984 | Swale |
| 1983 | Sunny's Halo |

## KENTUCKY DERBY

The Kentucky Derby is the most famous horse race in the United States. It has been held each year, on the first Saturday in May, since 1875. The race takes place at Churchill Downs in Louisville, Kentucky. The distance is 1¼ miles (2 km). Only three-year-old Thoroughbred horses can be entered, so even the best racehorses have only one chance to win. The winning horse can earn more than $700,000. And the value of the horse itself rises by millions. The Kentucky Derby, along with the Belmont Stakes and the Preakness, is part of the Triple Crown of horse racing in the United States.

▲ *Jerome Kern wrote the music for almost 50 musical comedies.*

## KERN, Jerome

The songs of Jerome Kern (1885–1945) are loved by people the world over. They include "Ol' Man River" (from his greatest musical, *Show Boat*), "Look for the Silver Lining" (from *Sally*), and "Smoke Gets in Your Eyes" (from *Roberta*).

Kern was born in New York City. He learned to play the piano from his mother and studied music in New York and Germany. His early songs were written for revivals of European operettas. He later developed a new, American style of musical comedy, with more realistic characters and songs that helped to tell the story. He also wrote music for films. His own life story is told in the film *Till the Clouds Roll By*.

## KEROUAC, Jack

The novels of Jack Kerouac (1922–1969) are about the Beat generation of the 1950s and 1960s. These were young people who had turned their backs on conventional life. They wandered around the country in search of a good time. It was Kerouac who first called them "Beat"—meaning both "exhausted" and "beatified," or blessed.

Kerouac was born in Massachusetts, of French Canadian parents. He published his first novel, *The Town and the City*, in 1950. In his next novel, *On the Road*, Kerouac described the drifting, pleasure-seeking life he had taken up. Written in a rambling style, it made Kerouac a spokesman of the Beats. Kerouac's other novels include *The Dharma Bums* and *Big Sur*.

## KING, Martin Luther, Jr. 

The Reverend Martin Luther King, Jr. (1929–1968), was a Baptist minister and the main leader of the CIVIL RIGHTS movement of the 1950s and 1960s. Born in Atlanta, Georgia, King started his career as pastor of a church in Montgomery, Alabama. There, in 1955–1956, he led the successful struggle to end segregation on the city's buses.

In 1957, King helped found the Southern Christian Leadership Conference (SCLC). Its aim was to continue the civil rights struggle on a larger scale. King and the SCLC adopted a policy of nonviolent protest. They staged peaceful voter-registration drives in Selma and Birmingham, Alabama, and Albany, Georgia. They also encouraged blacks to engage in peaceful sit-ins, marches, and boycotts. Still, these civil rights workers were often the targets of violence, and King was imprisoned several times. But his courage and eloquence were a constant inspiration to blacks and whites alike.

In August 1963, King led more than 200,000 people in a march on Washington, D.C. There, at the Lincoln Memorial, he gave his famous "I have a dream" speech. In 1964, the same year that the Civil Rights Act was passed, King was awarded the Nobel Prize for Peace.

In April 1968, King traveled to Memphis, Tennessee, to help that city's mostly black workers get better working conditions. He was assassinated there by a white man, James Earl Ray. In 1983, his birthday in late January was designated a federal, legal holiday.

▼ *In 1965, Martin Luther King, Jr., risked personal violence to lead a peaceful march from Selma, Alabama, to the state capitol building in Montgomery.*

## KING, W. L. Mackenzie 

The statesman William Lyon Mackenzie King (1874–1950) was PRIME MINISTER of Canada three times. He served for a total of 21 years. King intended from childhood to enter public life. After studying at the universities of Toronto, Chicago, and Harvard, he entered the civil service as deputy minister of labor. In 1908 he was elected to Parliament. After Sir Wilfrid Laurier's death, in 1919, King became leader of the Liberal Party. King was first elected prime minister in 1921, but it was during his last term (1935–1948) that he most fully showed his qualities of leadership. During World War II, he united the country in the war effort. He then prepared the way for economic and social advances in the postwar period.

**William Lyon Mackenzie King helped build Canadian pride during his 21 years as prime minister. Within Canada he supported efforts to improve relations between French speakers and English speakers. In conducting foreign policy, Mackenzie King always stressed the importance of "intermediate powers"—such as Canada—in maintaining world peace.**

▼ *A painted Kiowa shield shows a bear charging out from between two thunderclouds toward a row of hunters' bullets.*

## KINGFISHER

There are about 85 species of kingfishers in the world. However, only one, the belted kingfisher, is common in the United States. Some belted kingfishers migrate to Latin America in the winter. The belted kingfisher lives near rivers, lakes, and streams, and it feeds mainly on fish. During the nesting season a male and female dig a tunnel in a sandbank or claybank. They build their nest at the end of the tunnel. After the female lays its eggs, it and the male take turns sitting on them.

## KIOWAS

The Kiowas were one of the Great Plains tribes. They were attracted to the plains by the horses that roamed there. Some Kiowas joined with tribes of the Athapascan culture in the southwest. They became known as the Kiowa-Apaches. Like many of the PLAINS INDIANS, the Kiowas fought to protect their land from the white settlers who began to come in great numbers. During the 1840s they fought in Texas. In the Southern Plains War of 1868–1869, the Kiowas were defeated by General Philip Sheridan, the Civil War commander. They were moved to the Indian Territory in the 1870s. Today they number about 8,000, and most live in Oklahoma.

**In 1973, Henry Kissinger shared the Nobel Peace Prize with the North Vietnamese negotiator Le Duc Tho for bringing about a cease-fire in the Vietnam War.**

## KISSINGER, Henry

Henry Kissinger (1923– ) was U.S. secretary of state from 1973 to 1977. He was largely responsible for determining U.S. foreign policy during the 1970s.

Kissinger was born in Germany. When he was 15, his family, which was Jewish, fled the Nazis and settled in New York. Kissinger fought with the U.S. Army during World War II. He then studied political science at Harvard University, receiving a Ph.D., and taught there.

Beginning in 1969, Kissinger served as national security adviser to presidents Richard NIXON and Gerald FORD. Nixon also made him secretary of state in 1973. Kissinger helped restore friendly relations with Communist China and arranged a cease-fire between the Arabs and Israelis during the 1973 war. He also negotiated a cease-fire in the VIETNAM WAR. For this, he and the North Vietnamese negotiator, Le Duc Tho, shared the 1973 Nobel Peace Prize.

▼ *Henry Kissinger visited the Great Wall during his 1971 trip to China. He was organizing President Nixon's famous visit the following year.*

## KITCHEN CABINET

The term Kitchen Cabinet can refer to any informal group of presidential advisers. It originated during the presidency of Andrew JACKSON. Jackson came to rely on a group of friends and associates more than he did his official Cabinet. His political opponents did not like this. They referred to the group as the Kitchen Cabinet. One Kitchen Cabinet member, Martin VAN BUREN, went on to become president himself.

## KOREAN WAR

The Korean War (1950–1953) began when North Korea, a Communist country, attacked South Korea, a pro-Western country. Nearly 3 million people died, including more than 50,000 Americans.

Korea, a peninsula in East Asia, was annexed by Japan in 1910. At the end of World War II, the Soviet Union occupied the northern part of Korea and set up a Communist government. The United States occupied the southern part and set up an anti-Communist government. In 1948 the north and the south became the independent countries of North Korea and South Korea. The boundary was formed by the 38th parallel of latitude. The government of each country claimed to be the legitimate leader of all of Korea.

On June 25, 1950, the North Korean Army invaded South Korea. Two days later the United Nations (UN) authorized its members to aid South Korea. The United

Stages of the Korean War

**June–Sept. 1950:** North Korean troops capture nearly all the peninsula.
**Sept.–Oct. 1950:** UN troops recapture most of the Korean peninsula.
**Nov. 1950–Jan. 1951:** Chinese and North Korean troops push south and capture Seoul (South Korea's capital).
**Jan. 1951–July 1953:** Seoul recaptured; armistice settles border.

▼ *South Korean civilians were forced to flee with few belongings after the North Koreans invaded in 1950. South Korean troops are shown here on their way to the front.*

▲ *U.S. troops at the front in 1950. Late in that year they reached the Chinese border.*

States began sending troops. Sixteen other countries also sent troops. General Douglas MACARTHUR was made commander in chief of the UN forces.

Within two months, North Korean troops captured most of South Korea, including Seoul, the capital. But in September, MacArthur mounted a brilliant amphibious (a combination of land, sea and air) assault at Inchon, near Seoul, on the northwestern coast. The UN forces recaptured most of South Korea and advanced into North Korea. By November 1950 they were at the North Korean border with China. Chinese troops then entered the fighting and forced the Americans and their allies to retreat south of the 38th parallel.

Cease-fire talks began in July 1951. They dragged on for two years, as battles raged near the border. A cease-fire was finally achieved on July 27, 1953. Today there are still more than 40,000 U.S. troops in South Korea.

## KOSCIUSZKO, Tadeusz

The Polish patriot and soldier Tadeusz Kosciuszko (1746–1817) is remembered in the United States for his help in the Revolutionary War. Born into the aristocracy, Kosciuszko sailed for America in 1776 and volunteered for the Continental Army. His work designing fortifications contributed greatly to several American victories, including the Battle of Saratoga (1777). At the end of the war he was made a brigadier general and given American citizenship. For the rest of his life, Kosciuszko fought to keep Poland free from Russia, Prussia (Germany), and Austria, but he was defeated in that effort. He died in exile in Switzerland.

▲ *Tadeusz Kosciuszko is often called the "Hero of Two Worlds" because of his freedom fighting in the United States and Poland.*

## KU KLUX KLAN

The Ku Klux Klan was formed in 1866 by soldiers from the defeated Confederate Army. They would threaten and attack black people who were beginning to use their right to vote. Although the Klan was disbanded in 1869, it was re-formed in 1915. This time the Ku Klux Klan targets included Catholics, Jews, and immigrants, as well as black people. By 1925 it claimed membership of 4 million to 5 million. The public turned against the Klan, and new CIVIL RIGHTS laws made it harder for it to operate. Although its numbers have dwindled, the Klan is still active in some states.

◀ *Peaceful labor union demonstrations, such as this one organized by teachers, are designed to gain public support.*

## LABOR UNIONS

The first nationwide labor unions in the United States, such as the Knights of Labor, were formed in the mid-1800s. They were organized by skilled workers, such as ironworkers, printers, and blacksmiths. But the labor movement really got under way in 1886, when Samuel GOMPERS organized some unions of skilled workers into the American Federation of Labor (AFL). The AFL established the process of collective bargaining to achieve better wages and working conditions.

In the late 1800s and early 1900s, there was strong opposition to organized labor. But during the DEPRESSION, people realized that unions were necessary to give workers some security. Congress passed several laws protecting the rights of unions, including the right to go on strike. In 1935, John L. LEWIS founded the Committee for Industrial Organization (later renamed the Congress of Industrial Organization, CIO). It was generally more aggressive in its policies than the AFL. In 1955 the AFL and CIO merged.

In recent years, new groups of workers—including migrant farm workers—have become unionized. But membership as a whole has declined. Today, only about 18 percent of the work force belong to labor unions.

▲ *David Dubinsky, seen here at a 1957 rally, was a labor leader in the clothing industry for more than 25 years.*

▲ *Bagataway, the original Indian version of lacrosse, gave young braves a chance to demonstrate their skill.*

## LACROSSE

Lacrosse is a sport in which team members use a stick with a net on the end to throw a ball into their opponents' goal. There are ten players on each team. Lacrosse was invented by the Indians of Canada, where it remains a national sport. The National Lacrosse Association of Canada and the U.S. Intercollegiate Lacrosse Association are important governing bodies. In the United States, the University of Maryland and John Hopkins University are among the top teams.

## LAFAYETTE, Marquis de

A French aristocrat, the Marquis de Lafayette (1757–1834) fought with the American colonists in the Revolutionary War and later played a leading role in the French Revolution.

In July 1777 the young Lafayette went to Philadelphia and volunteered for duty. He was commissioned a major general and fought in several important battles. In 1779 he helped persuade the French king, Louis XVI, to send aid to the American colonists. As commander of an army in Virginia, Lafayette contributed significantly to the victory at Yorktown.

When Lafayette returned to France in 1782, he tried to steer his country's own revolution in a moderate course. He was unpopular with those who wanted more extreme changes. Lafayette played an important part in the French Revolution of 1789 and later sat in the French Chamber of Deputies.

▼ *In the siege of Yorktown in 1781, Lafayette sent a courier to his friend General George Washington with important news of the British defenses.*

## LA FOLLETTE, Robert M.

Robert La Follette (1855–1925) was a Wisconsin political leader and reformer. He served as a U.S. congressman, state governor, and U.S. senator. A Republican, La Follette belonged to his party's progressive wing. He fought for workers' rights and against big business. He tried to check the power of the railroads and other large corporations and to have fair taxation. The reform measures introduced by La Follette became known as the Wisconsin Idea.

In the U.S. Senate (1906–1925), La Follette continued to fight against "special interests." He also opposed U.S. entry into World War I and the League of Nations. He broke with the Republican Party in 1924 and was nominated for the presidency by the Progressive Party. La Follette received 5 million votes, but he won only the electoral votes of his home state.

▲ *Robert La Follette's campaigns against "big business" and corruption earned him the nickname "Battling Bob."*

## LAKES

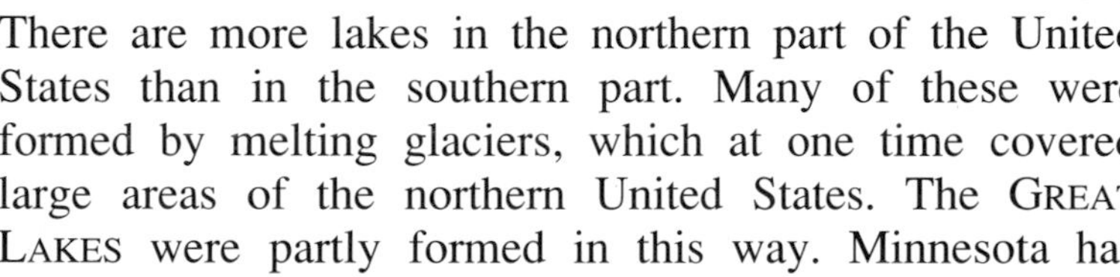

There are more lakes in the northern part of the United States than in the southern part. Many of these were formed by melting glaciers, which at one time covered large areas of the northern United States. The GREAT LAKES were partly formed in this way. Minnesota has about 11,000 glacial lakes. Lakes often form in limestone areas, when water drains into deep hollows in the ground. Lake County, Florida, has more than 1,400 of

▼ *The wooded shores of Lake Tahoe are only a short drive away from Carson City, Nevada, and California's Squaw Valley ski resort.*

**Largest Lakes in North America (sq mi/km²)**

|  |  |
|---|---|
| Superior | 31,820/82,414 |
| Huron | 23,010/59,596 |
| Michigan | 22,400/58,016 |
| Great Bear | 12,000/31,080 |
| Great Slave | 11,170/28,930 |
| Erie | 9,930/25,719 |
| Winnipeg | 9,094/23,553 |
| Ontario | 7,520/19,477 |

these. The deepest lake in North America, Oregon's Crater Lake, is more than one third of a mile (half a kilometer) deep. It was formed by rainwater collecting in the crater of an extinct (dead) volcano. Lake Superior, one of the Great Lakes, is the largest lake in North America and the second largest in the world. North America's largest salt lake, GREAT SALT LAKE, is only about 15 feet (4.5 m) deep. Lake Mead, in Nevada and Arizona, is the United States' largest artificial lake. It was formed by the building of Hoover Dam on the COLORADO RIVER.

## LAND, Edwin Herbert

The physicist Edwin Herbert Land (1909–1991) invented the Polaroid camera. This camera takes and prints photographs in a minute or so. The invention grew out of Land's earlier studies, at Harvard University, in the polarization of light. In 1932 he invented a material that reduced glare. Land founded the Polaroid Corporation in 1937. Some of its products, such as sights for anti-aircraft guns and night-adaptable goggles, were used during World War II. The Polaroid camera appeared in 1947. A model that takes color photographs was introduced in 1963.

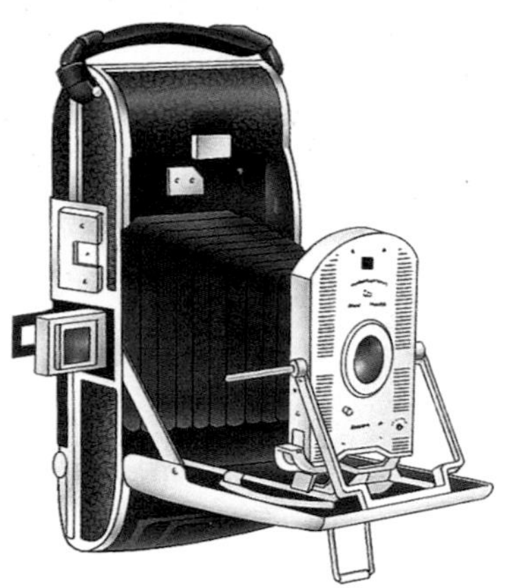

▲ *Even the first Polaroid Land cameras were lightweight and designed for everyday use.*

## LANGLEY, Samuel Pierpont

Samuel Langley (1834–1906) was the first person to build a successful heavier-than-air flying machine. Langley was a civil engineer and architect. He later

► *Langley's pilotless aircraft of 1896 was a forerunner of the Wright brothers' airplane seven years later.*

taught mathematics and became a professor of physics and astronomy at the University of Pittsburgh. He was especially interested in solar activity and its effect on the weather. Langley also made important studies on the nature of flight. His flying machine was first tested in 1896, in a flight over the Potomac River. It weighed 26 pounds (9.7 kg) and was powered by a steam engine. Langley also worked on a manned aircraft but lost this race to the Wright brothers. He served as secretary of the Smithsonian Institution from 1887 until his death.

▼ *Some of Irving Langmuir's later experiments developed "cloud seeding," or using chemicals to promote rain.*

## LANGMUIR, Irving

Irving Langmuir (1881–1957) was an important scientist of this century. He was born in Brooklyn and studied at Columbia University and in Germany. Langmuir worked at the General Electric Research Laboratory from 1909 to 1950. There he did research in many areas. He studied how chemicals react at high temperatures and low pressure. His findings led to the development of the gas-filled tungsten lamp. His work also led to the improvement of electron tubes. Langmuir also invented an atomic hydrogen welding torch and discovered how to produce rain by seeding clouds with dry ice. Langmuir received the Nobel Prize for chemistry in 1932 for his studies that were related to work with the tungsten bulb. He also helped to develop radar in World War II.

**In different parts of the United States, a long sandwich filled with cold cuts, onions, tomatoes, or other ingredients is known as a "hero," "submarine," "grinder," "torpedo," "hoagy," "wedge," or even "spuky." These words are called regional variations of American English.**

## LANGUAGE

English is the main language spoken in North America, even though only about 15 percent of U.S. citizens have English ancestors. In Quebec and some other parts of Canada, French is the main language of a majority of people. Mexicans, along with most other Latin Americans, speak Spanish.

Many Indians and Inuits (Eskimos) still speak their native languages. When the Europeans first arrived in North America, they found hundreds of tribes speaking a variety of languages. By the 1800s, many of these languages had died out.

Today, most U.S. immigrants (people coming to live in the United States) come from developing countries, and English is not their first language. Some people believe that education for these people should be *bilingual*—in their own language as well as in English.

**There are more than half a million words in a large English dictionary. Most people use fewer than 10,000.**

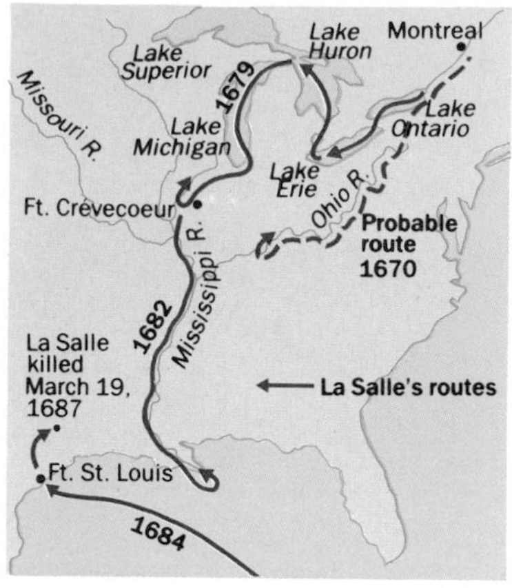


▲ *La Salle's expeditions, like those of Lewis and Clark 120 years later, followed major rivers into the heart of the continent.*

## LARDNER, Ring

Ring Lardner (1885–1933) was a well-known sports journalist and writer of humorous short stories. He was born in Niles, Michigan, and got his first job as reporter on the *South Bend Times*, a newspaper in Indiana. He soon moved to Chicago where he worked as a reporter. Lardner's baseball stories for the *Chicago Tribune* were so popular that they were sold to other newspapers around the country. The *Saturday Evening Post*, a magazine based in New York, began to use Lardner's stories on baseball and ordinary life. He also published several collections of his stories and short plays.

## LA SALLE, Robert Cavelier, Sieur de

The explorer Robert Cavelier, Sieur de La Salle (1643–1687), was the first European to travel the length of the Mississippi River. La Salle was born in France and went to Canada at the age of 23. Having made friends with local Indians, he made several journeys with them, exploring as far as present-day Wisconsin. In February 1682 he led a party of French and Indians down the Mississippi. Arriving at the Gulf of Mexico on April 9, 1682, he claimed the whole Mississippi Basin for France and named it Louisiana, for King Louis XIV. In 1684, La Salle sailed again to the Americas to start a colony there. But the expedition was beset by disasters, and La Salle was killed by mutineers.

▼ *On April 9, 1682, La Salle reached the mouth of the Mississippi River. He claimed all the land in the Mississippi Basin for France, calling it Louisiana.*

## LAUREL AND HARDY

Stan Laurel (1890–1965) and Oliver Hardy (1892–1957) formed one of the best-loved comedy teams of this century. Laurel was born in England, Hardy in Harlem, Georgia. Eventually they both went to Hollywood. Between 1926 and 1952 they made over 60 short movies and 27 full-length features. Laurel played a shy, bumbling, rather stupid man. Hardy ("Ollie") was his fat, pompous friend. Their comedy stems from things going out of control, the tension between the two friends, and finally something unexpected happening to save them. Some of their best-known films are *Babes in Toyland, Sons of the Desert*, and *Blockhead*.

**Between 1926 and 1950, Laurel and Hardy made over 200 slapstick films. One of them, *The Music Box*, won an Academy Award as best comedy short subject. The fat Ollie is perhaps best remembered for his long-suffering glances at the camera.**

◀ *Stan Laurel wrote and directed some of the duo's best material, but his contributions were rarely credited.*

## LAURIER, Sir Wilfrid

Sir Wilfrid Laurier (1841–1919) was the first French Canadian PRIME MINISTER of Canada. Born in a farming community in the province of Quebec, Laurier was educated by both French- and English-speaking teachers. Later he studied law at McGill University in Montreal. Laurier was elected to the Canadian House of Commons in 1874 as a member of the Liberal Party. He became prime minister in 1896 and served until 1911. Laurier successfully promoted the settling of the western territories and the expansion of the railroad system. Although he admired Britain, he resisted any moves to strengthen the ties between that nation and his own. Throughout his career, Laurier worked for harmony between the French and the British populations, and closer trade links with the United States. In later years, his moderate policies were attacked by extremists on both sides, and he was forced to retire in 1911.

▼ *The election of the Roman Catholic and French-speaking Sir Wilfrid Laurier as prime minister helped strengthen Canadian unity.*

▲ *Ernest O. Lawrence's cyclotron was soon nicknamed the "atom smasher."*

## LAWRENCE, Ernest O.

Ernest Orlando Lawrence (1901–1958) was an important physicist. Born in Canton, South Dakota, he began working on atomic energy before World War II. While at the University of California at Berkeley, he was awarded the 1939 Nobel Prize for physics for the invention and development of the cyclotron. Lawrence continued working on the atom and was involved in several major discoveries. In 1957, in recognition of all his work, the U.S. Department of Energy gave him the Enrico Fermi Award. The Lawrence Berkeley Laboratory and the Lawrence Livermore Laboratory are named for him. These centers for nuclear research are operated by the University of California.

## LAWS AND LEGAL SYSTEM

Laws are rules that govern society. In the United States, written laws (or statutes) are made by representative assemblies, such as the U.S. CONGRESS, state legislatures, and city councils. In addition, executive and administrative branches of government may issue administrative acts that have the effect of laws. And courts, through decisions in individual cases, also establish rules. Such rules are sometimes called case law.

There are two basic kinds of law—civil and criminal. Civil law generally deals with disputes between individuals. For example, someone who does not live up to the terms of a contract can be sued in a civil court. Criminal laws are designed to protect the entire community. A person who breaks a criminal law—by robbing a bank, for example—faces trial in a criminal court.

The court system in the United States consists of federal and state courts. The U.S. SUPREME COURT is the highest federal court and the highest court in the country. It hears appeals of cases that were tried in federal courts and the highest state courts. There are 94 federal district courts.

State courts are independent of the federal courts. The highest state court is usually called a supreme court. Other state courts include appellate courts and courts of general trial jurisdiction. There are also county and municipal courts. Along with courts, police departments and government agencies such as the FEDERAL BUREAU OF INVESTIGATION enforce laws.

Some Important Laws in U.S. History

**Northwest Ordinance (1787):** set out how growing territories could become new states.

**Interstate Commerce Act (1887):** created the first federal "watchdog", the Interstate Commerce Commission.

**Income Tax Act (1913):** established the federal income tax still used.

**Social Security Act (1935):** set up an old-age pension scheme and unemployment insurance.

**Civil Rights Act (1964):** banned discrimination in employment, public accommodations, and other areas.

## LEAGUE OF NATIONS

The League of Nations developed from the ideas of President Woodrow WILSON at the end of World War I. He and other world leaders hoped to form an organization that would solve problems between countries and prevent wars. The League was set up in 1920, with its headquarters in Geneva, Switzerland. The United States never joined, however, and the League was powerless when Japan invaded Manchuria, Germany annexed Austria, and Italy invaded Ethiopia in the 1930s. It was dissolved in 1946 and the UNITED NATIONS took its place.

**Speaking in defense of the League of Nations, President Woodrow Wilson told a Midwest audience: "Some people call me an idealist. Well that is the way I know I am an American. America is the only idealist nation in the world."**

## LEE, Robert E.

Robert E. Lee (1807–1870) was a general in the Confederate Army during the CIVIL WAR. Many military historians believe that he was one of the greatest generals in history. Lee graduated from West Point in 1829 and later fought in the MEXICAN WAR (1846–1848).

Although opposed to secession, Lee turned down an offer to command the Union Army in 1861. He could not, he said, raise his hand against his relatives. and home. When Virginia seceded, Lee offered his services to the Confederacy. Lee's Army of Northern Virginia won a number of victories over more numerous and better equipped Union forces. Ultimately, however, he could not match the superior resources of the North. Lee was made general in chief of the Confederate Army in February 1865. But two months later he surrendered to Union General Ulysses S. GRANT.

**Robert E. Lee was a commanding figure. He was almost 5 feet 11 inches tall, weighed 170 pounds, and had wide shoulders and an erect posture. Lee was never known to drink alcohol, smoke, or use bad language.**

▼ *Robert E. Lee's boldness and keen sense of strategy earned him the loyalty of the Confederate Army.*

▲ *William Clark (top) and Meriwether Lewis (bottom).*

## LEND-LEASE ACT

The Lend-Lease Act enabled the United States to aid Britain, the Soviet Union, and other Allies fighting against Germany, Italy, and Japan in WORLD WAR II. The act was passed by Congress in March 1941, nine months before the United States entered the war. At that time, many Americans believed that the United States should stay out of the war. Others, including President Franklin D. ROOSEVELT, believed that the Axis powers must be stopped. Lend-Lease was a way of helping this cause, short of actually fighting.

Lend-Lease aid went first to Britain. By the end of the war, a total of nearly $50 billion in aid had been given to 38 countries, including China and the Soviet Union.

## LEWIS AND CLARK EXPEDITION

The United States acquired the Louisiana Territory from France in 1803 in what is known as the LOUISIANA PURCHASE. In 1804, President Thomas JEFFERSON sent two army officers, Meriwether Lewis and William Clark, to explore this vast area. Their instructions were to find the source of the Missouri River, to reach the Pacific Ocean, and to report on the Indians they met there and on the natural history of the land itself.

The party, which numbered 44, set off from St. Louis, Missouri, in May 1804. Their route along the Missouri River took them as far north as present-day Bismarck, North Dakota. There they built a fort and enlisted the aid of a French Canadian trapper and his Indian wife, SACAGAWEA, as guides and interpreters. Heading west,

▼ *Lewis and Clark used the Shoshoni Indian Sacagawea to convey their message of peace to Indian tribes they met. They also exchanged gifts as a gesture of good will.*

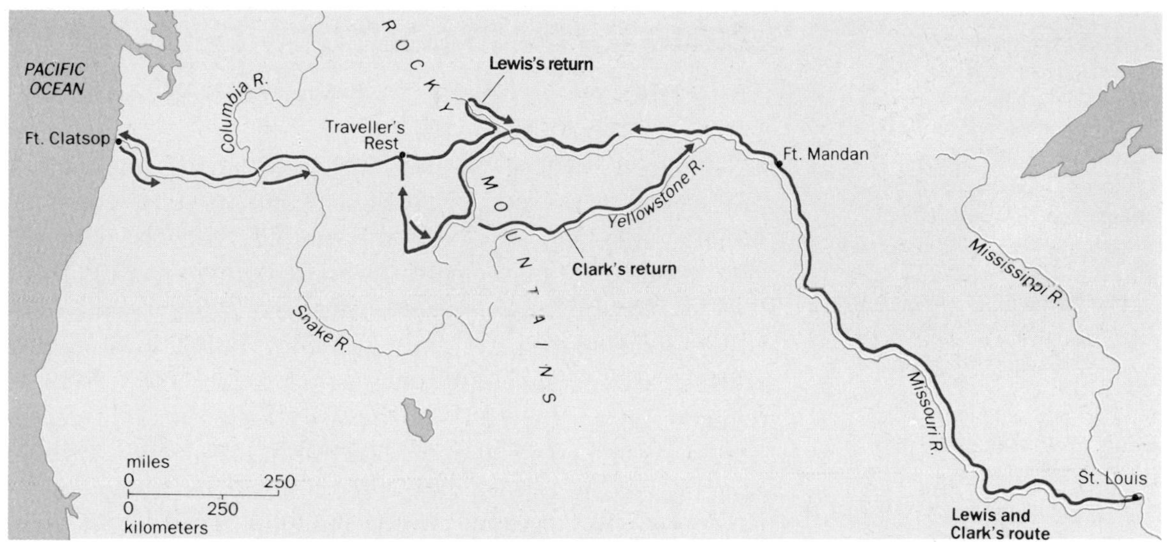


the expedition crossed the Rockies and traveled down the COLUMBIA RIVER to the Pacific Ocean. On the way the explorers established friendly relations with several Indian tribes and collected plant and mineral specimens. They returned to St. Louis in September 1806.

▲ *Lewis and Clark reached the Pacific Ocean in November 1805. Their 18-month journey had taken them nearly 4,000 miles (6,400 km).*

**Some of the most popular gifts carried by Lewis and Clark for the Indians were medals featuring the face of President Thomas Jefferson. The explorers described the president as the "Great White Father in the East" who had sent them.**

## LEWIS, John L.

John L. Lewis (1880–1969) was an American LABOR UNION leader. He was president of United Mine Workers of America (UMW) from 1920 to 1960. He also held positions in the American Federation of Labor (AFL). In 1935, Lewis helped found the Committee for Industrial Organization. It was later named the Congress of Industrial Organizations (CIO). The CIO and the AFL merged in 1955. Lewis fought hard for workers' rights. But his methods sometimes led to violent strikes. And during World War II, he led the mine workers on strikes, even though coal was needed for the war effort. In the 1950s, Lewis successfully campaigned for federal safety standards in coal mines.

## LEWIS, Sinclair

Sinclair Lewis (1885–1951) was an important novelist. He often wrote about the limitations of middle-class life in small-town America. He compared the values people claimed to live by with the values they really practiced. His novels include *Main Street, Babbitt, Arrowsmith* (for which he won a 1926 Pulitzer Prize), and *Elmer Gantry*.

**Sinclair Lewis was the first American to win the Nobel Prize for literature (1930). He wrote steadily, producing 22 novels and three plays.**

**When the redcoats reached Lexington on April 19, 1775, Captain John Parker told his minutemen: "Don't fire unless fired upon!" He later said, "But if they want a war, let it begin here." The battle is still commemorated as Patriot's Day in Maine and Massachusetts.**

## LEXINGTON AND CONCORD, Battles of

The battles of Lexington and Concord, on April 19, 1775, marked the beginning of the American REVOLUTION. These battles, in two small Massachusetts towns, followed a British decision to seize colonial military supplies at Concord. Alerted that the British were coming by messengers from Boston, including Paul REVERE, the colonists hid or destroyed the supplies and prepared for battle. At Lexington they failed to stop the redcoats, and eight militiamen were killed. The British marched on to Concord, 6 miles (10 km) away, where they were met by about 350 militiamen, who finally forced them to retreat. The march back to Boston was punctuated by sniping from colonial farmers, which brought the total British deaths to more than 70. The Americans lost 49 men.

► *The Americans turned back three companies of British soldiers at Concord's North Bridge. The British were attacked constantly on their retreat to Boston.*

▼ *The Liberty Bell was originally cast in England. It cracked during its first use and was recast in Philadelphia in 1753.*

## LIBERTY BELL

The Liberty Bell, weighing just over a ton, symbolizes American independence. The bell was cast in England in 1752 and hung in the Pennsylvania State House in PHILADELPHIA the following year. On July 8, 1776, it was rung when the DECLARATION OF INDEPENDENCE was adopted. It was rung on the same day every year after that until 1835. While being rung for the funeral of John MARSHALL, chief justice of the United States, the bell cracked. It was recast, but it cracked again in 1849. Today the bell hangs in Liberty Bell Pavilion in Philadelphia. On the bell is an inscription from the Bible: "Proclaim Liberty throughout all the land unto all the inhabitants thereof."

◀ *Library books are grouped together by subject using the Dewey Decimal System. Books on any one subject have the same number on their spine.*

## LIBRARIES

There are more than 31,000 libraries in the United States. About half of them are public libraries in cities and towns. The Boston Public Library was the first of the great city public libraries. The New York Public Library is the busiest library in the world.

Schools have libraries too, and there are also several thousand college and university libraries in the United States. The library at Harvard University is the world's largest university library. Founded in 1638, it was the first library in the English-speaking colonies. The United States also has many special libraries, such as the Folger Shakespeare Library in Washington, D.C.

**The Library of Congress has the Western Hemisphere's largest collection of books printed before 1501. There are about 5,600 of these old books, including a copy of the Gutenberg Bible, the first important book that was printed with movable type.**

## LIBRARY OF CONGRESS

The Library of Congress is the world's largest library. It contains more than 80 million items in 470 languages. It was established in Washington, D.C., in 1800 by an act of CONGRESS. Originally it was meant to help government researchers. The library was destroyed during the War of 1812, when the British burned the Capitol. It was replaced the next year with 6,000 volumes from the library of Thomas Jefferson. The Library of Congress has remained a public library since that time. The Library of Congress administers the country's copyright laws. These laws protect authors' writings; other people cannot copy their writings. A special section of the Library of Congress contains material for blind and other handicapped people.

▼ *The Library of Congress covers about 70 acres (29 ha) of floor space.*

► *Portland Head Light is one of several lighthouses warning ships about Maine's rocky coast.*

**Minot Lighthouse in Massachusetts flashes out a pattern known as "1-4-3," one burst of light followed by four bursts, and then three. Sailors remember the pattern as "I love you" and sometimes inscribe the numbers on wedding rings.**

## LIGHTHOUSES

Lighthouses are aids for navigation along rocky or dangerous coastlines. Their powerful lights can be seen more than 20 miles (32 km) out at sea. Lighthouses in the United States are operated by the Coast Guard. Boston Light, the country's oldest lighthouse, has been flashing since 1716. It was destroyed by the British in 1776 but rebuilt in 1783. Ships soon came to rely on a string of lighthouses along the Atlantic coast. By 1900 there were 1,500 lighthouses on the Atlantic and Pacific coastlines. Ships could tell them apart because the flashes of light from each lighthouse formed a distinctive pattern. Today, new techniques such as radio signals have replaced lights and foghorns. There are now only 340 active lighthouses in the United States.

▼ *Queen Liliuokalani was an accomplished author, with books published in both English and Hawaiian.*

## LILIUOKALANI, Lydia

Lydia Liliuokalani (1838–1917) was the last queen of Hawaii. When she inherited the throne from her brother in 1891, American settlers controlled the economy of Hawaii. When the queen tried to curb their power and re-establish a strong monarchy, she was overthrown. The settlers, led by Sanford B. Dole, established the Republic of Hawaii in 1894. A political battle began. The queen was supported by President Grover CLEVELAND, who was against American expansionism. But in 1898, the Senate agreed to annex Hawaii.

## LINCOLN, Abraham

Abraham Lincoln was the 16th president of the United States. Many people believe that he was the greatest of all the presidents. His firm leadership during the CIVIL WAR, which lasted for practically his entire time in office, determined the future of the United States.

Lincoln was born in a log cabin on his father's farm in Kentucky. He largely educated himself and eventually became a lawyer and politician. "Honest Abe" was known for his integrity and the force of his arguments. In 1860 he won the presidential election as an anti-slavery Republican. The Southern states then seceded from, or left, the Union. Six weeks after his inauguration, on March 4, 1861, the Civil War began.

Lincoln fought the Civil War in order to save the Union. If the Union had failed, the world might have decided that democracy did not work. Lincoln had great wisdom and determination. He also had the ability to express his beliefs so that they were understood and accepted. He made many great speeches, including his GETTYSBURG ADDRESS, delivered at a dedication of a cemetery on the site of a Union military victory. Lincoln is probably best remembered for his EMANCIPATION PROCLAMATION in which he freed the slaves in the rebellious Southern states. (Slavery all over the United States was abolished by the Thirteenth Amendment to the CONSTITUTION, in December 1865.)

Lincoln was re-elected in 1864. In April 1865, five days after the Confederate surrender, he was shot while at the theater by John Wilkes BOOTH. He died the next morning. He was the first president of the United States to be assassinated.

Abraham Lincoln
**Born:** February 12, 1809, near Hodgenville, Kentucky
**Education:** Little formal schooling
**Political party:** Republican
**Term of office:** 1861–1865
**Married:** 1842 to Mary Todd
**Died:** April 15, 1865, in Washington, D.C.

▼ *President Lincoln met General George McClellan after the Battle of Antietam in September 1862. McClellan had succeeded in turning back the Confederate forces. But he failed to follow up on his victory and was later relieved of his command.*

► *Charles Lindbergh helped design the* Spirit of St. Louis. *Its light weight and powerful engine made him confident about the 3,600-mile (5,800-km) Atlantic crossing.*

## LINDBERGH, Charles

Charles Lindbergh (1902–1974) was the first person to fly solo nonstop across the Atlantic Ocean. He was born in Detroit and grew up in Minnesota. Lindbergh studied engineering at the University of Wisconsin but left college to become a pilot. He toured the country as a "barnstormer," performing daredevil stunts, such as walking along the plane's wings. Lindbergh convinced a group of businessmen to invest money in him when he heard of a $25,000 prize for flying the Atlantic. On May 20–21, 1927, Lindbergh flew from New York to Paris in the *Spirit of St. Louis*. He became a hero to people around the world. Five years later tragedy struck the Lindbergh family when their young son was kidnapped and killed.

**Charles Lindbergh, nicknamed the Lone Eagle, returned to a hero's welcome in the United States. A parade honoring him in New York City dumped 1,800 tons of ticker tape onto the streets. He then toured 48 of the cities with his plane, the *Spirit of St. Louis*.**

## LITERATURE

There are two main kinds of literature, nonfiction and fiction. Biographies, autobiographies, history, and essays are examples of nonfiction writing. Fiction includes novels, short stories, drama, and poetry.

A distinctively American literature began to emerge after the American Revolution. In the more than two hundred years since, American writers have distinguished themselves in all areas of writing. This encyclopedia contains biographies of the most important writers. Some of these writers are listed here. You may

**Some American books have had a profound effect on society. *Uncle Tom's Cabin* (1852), by Harriet Beecher Stowe, opened people's eyes to the evils of slavery. *The Jungle* (1906), by Upton Sinclair, led to strict hygiene in the food industry.**

want to look up the others in the Index. Several important American poets also have biographies in this encyclopedia. See the entry POETRY.

▼ *Eugene O'Neill's own life was as dramatic as his plays about society in early 20th-century America.*

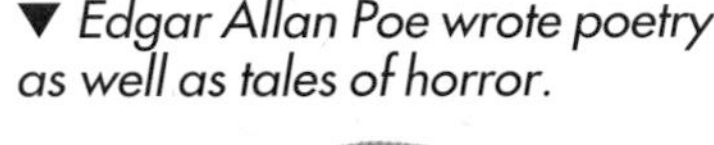

▼ *Edgar Allan Poe wrote poetry as well as tales of horror.*

▼ Little Women, *by Louisa May Alcott, has been loved by generations of readers.*

| American Winners of the Nobel Prize for Literature | |
|---|---|
| 1987 | Joseph Brodsky (Russian-American) |
| 1980 | Czeslaw Milosz (Polish-American) |
| 1978 | Isaac Bashevis Singer (Yiddish) |
| 1976 | Saul Bellow |
| 1962 | John Steinbeck |
| 1954 | Ernest Hemingway |
| 1949 | William Faulkner |
| 1938 | Pearl Buck |
| 1936 | Eugene O'Neill |
| 1930 | Sinclair Lewis |

**Novelists, Short Story Writers, and Essayists**

Louisa May Alcott
James Baldwin
Saul Bellow
Gwendolyn Brooks
Pearl Buck
James Fenimore Cooper
Theodore Dreiser
Ralph Waldo Emerson
William Faulkner
F. Scott Fitzgerald
Joel Chandler Harris
Nathaniel Hawthorne
Ernest Hemingway
O. Henry
Washington Irving
Sinclair Lewis
Jack London
Herman Melville
Edgar Allan Poe
John Steinbeck
Harriet Beecher Stowe
Mark Twain
Richard Wright

**Playwrights**

Edward Albee
Moss Hart
Lillian Hellman
Arthur Miller
Eugene O'Neill
Neil Simon
Tennessee Williams

◀ *James Russell Lowell, a 19th-century "man of letters," was an author, editor, and social critic.*

▼ *Joel Chandler Harris's* Uncle Remus *stories, with characters such as Tar Baby and Brer Rabbit, are still popular today.*

▶ *A good coach is important to Little League baseball. The coach teaches teamwork and good sportsmanship as well as the techniques of the game.*

▼ *Lizards' coloring blends into that of the rocks where they lie for hours in the sun. The Gila monster is one of only two poisonous lizards in the world.*

## LITTLE LEAGUE

Little League Baseball is an organized league for baseball players between the ages of 6 and 18. It was formed in Williamsport, Pennsylvania, in 1939. Today there are Little Leagues in more than 30 countries around the world, and more than 2.5 million young people play the game. Girls have been allowed on Little League teams since 1974. A division for handicapped players was started in 1989.

Each year, a Little League World Series is held in Williamsport for players between the ages of 8 and 12. Four teams from the United States play each other for the U.S. championship. And four other teams, from Asia, Canada, Latin America, and Europe, play for the international championship. Then those two teams play for the world championship. In 1993 the team from Long Beach, California, won the World Series.

## LIZARDS

A lizard is a REPTILE. It is cold-blooded, which means that its body temperature changes with the temperature of its surroundings. Most lizards, therefore, live in warm places, such as the southern part of the United States. One well-known lizard is the gecko. It has toe pads that enable it to run up walls and across ceilings. Many lizards have legs, but some, such as skinks, do not. Skinks are sometimes confused with snakes. The glass snake, or glass lizard, of the East is really a skink. The largest North American lizards are the iguanas. They may grow to more than 6 feet (1.8 m). The Gila monster is the only poisonous lizard in the United States. It lives in the southwestern deserts.

## LLOYD, Harold

Harold Lloyd (1894–1971) was a comedy star of the silent movies. Born in Nebraska, he grew up in California. After beginning as a movie "extra" in 1913, Lloyd created such characters as "Willie Work," "Lonesome Luke," and "Harold," a shy young man who wore horn-rimmed glasses and a straw hat and was eager to succeed in the big city. Many of Lloyd's 300 films were "thrill-comedies," which combined humor and daredevil stunts. In the film *Safety Last*, for example, Lloyd tries to impress a girl and accidentally ends up dangling from the hands of a clock on top of a building.

▲ *Unknown to the audience of* Safety Last, *Harold Lloyd had lost two fingers while making a movie the previous year.*

## LOBSTERS AND CRABS

Lobsters and crabs live in the ocean near the shore. Both are popular seafood. Two main kinds of lobsters are found in North American waters. The American lobster, from the North Atlantic, has the best meat. The spiny lobster is found off the coasts of California and Florida. Its meat is sold as lobster tail. Some people also eat the lobsterlike crayfish. The blue crab is the most valuable crab in eastern North America. It is caught just after it sheds its old shell. Its new shell is still soft, and it is sold as soft-shelled crab. Dungeness crab and Alaska king crab are caught off the Pacific coast.

▼ *Lobsters and crabs are caught near the shore with traps baited with fish.*

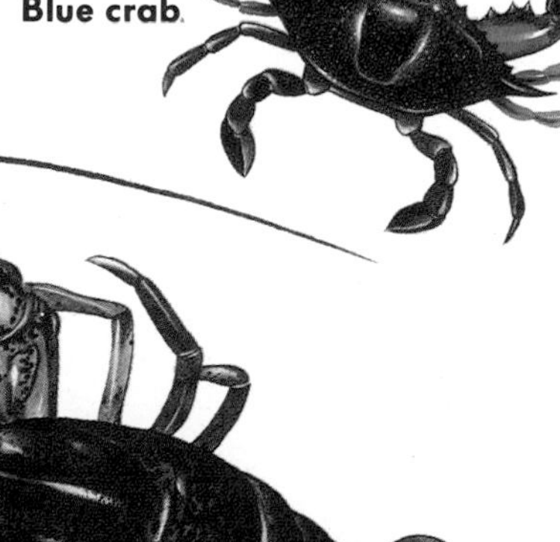

▲ *A diesel locomotive leads a freight train of boxcars and tankers. Many passenger lines in the East use electric locomotives.*

## LOCAL GOVERNMENT

Government bodies for areas smaller than states are called local governments. They provide such services as law enforcement, fire protection, sewage disposal, schools, hospitals, and roads. There are more than 80,000 units of local government in the United States. The largest in area are counties (or boroughs in Alaska and parishes in Louisiana). All states except Connecticut and Rhode Island have county governments. Townships are smaller local government units. They are usually found in the Northeast and Midwest. In some areas, townships are called "towns." Other kinds of local government units are school districts and special districts for a single purpose, such as providing water.

## LOCOMOTIVE

The *Best Friend of Charleston* and the *Peter Cooper* (also known as the "Tom Thumb") were the first American-built locomotives. They began running in 1830. An extra set of movable front wheels was added to later locomotives to help guide them over curving tracks. Until the 1890s, locomotives used steam to turn the turbines that drove the wheels. Wood and, later, coal were burned to provide steam. Electric locomotives, which get power from overhead wires or electrified third rails, began operating in 1895. They are quiet, clean, powerful, and efficient but expensive to maintain. Diesel-electric locomotives were introduced in 1925. They use diesel engines to power generators that then transmit electricity to motors, which in turn drive the wheels.

▼ *Locomotives can be identified by their profiles and by the number of wheels in each section.*

## LOCOWEED

Locoweed is a plant that grows wild in dry regions of western North America. Some types of locoweed are poisonous to animals. The plant is called "locoweed" because animals that have eaten it sometimes run around in a wild, frantic way. (*Loco* is the Spanish word for "crazy.") The animals may lose control of their muscles and eventually die. Horses, sheep, and cattle do not usually eat locoweed if there is other food on the range. Ranchers destroy the plant with weed killer or by cutting the roots.

▲ *Locoweed is addictive. If forced to eat it because of drought or overgrazing, cattle will continue to feed on it until they become ill.*

## LODGE, Henry Cabot, Jr.

Born into a distinguished Massachusetts family, Henry Cabot Lodge, Jr. (1902–1985), had a long career in Republican politics and in diplomacy. After graduating from Harvard, Lodge worked as a journalist and then spent four years (1933–1937) in the Massachusetts legislature. In 1936 he was elected to the U.S. Senate. Except for a period of time in the Army during World War II, he served in the Senate until 1952, when he lost his seat to John F. KENNEDY. Lodge was appointed U.S. ambassador to the United Nations by President Dwight D. EISENHOWER. He held several other diplomatic posts, including that of ambassador to South Vietnam. In 1969, President Richard NIXON sent him to Paris as the chief American negotiator at the Vietnamese peace talks.

## LONDON, Jack

Jack London (1876–1916) was an American novelist who often wrote about the struggle for survival. *The Call of the Wild* and *White Fang* are probably his most famous books. These were based on his adventures in the Klondike during the gold rush of 1897. His book *The Sea Wolf* is about a brutal sea captain. *Martin Eden*, another novel, is based partly on his own life. For much of his life London was poor, and he understood and sympathized with poor people. London had little formal education. He educated himself, mainly at public libraries. He wrote 50 books in 17 years and became the most highly paid American writer of his time. His books have been translated into many languages.

▼ *Jack London lived an adventurous life and liked sailing in particular. He traveled all around the Pacific by boat, sometimes by himself.*

▲ *Most of Long Beach's buildings were built after an earthquake destroyed much of the city in 1933.*

## LONG BEACH

Long Beach is an important port in southern CALIFORNIA, with a population of about 430,000. It is located 20 miles (32 km) south of LOS ANGELES, on San Pedro Bay. Each year more than 40 million tons of goods pass through Long Beach. Oil production, the manufacture of aircraft and machinery, and tourism are important industries. The U.S. Navy sends many of its ships to be repaired at the Los Angeles–Long Beach Naval Shipyard. On the other side of the harbor is the city-run marina, full of pleasure craft.

## LONGFELLOW, Henry Wadsworth

Henry Wadsworth Longfellow (1807–1882) was one of the most popular American poets of the 1800s. He was born and raised in Portland, Maine. After traveling in Europe for several years, he returned to New England and taught. He eventually became professor of modern languages at Harvard University. Longfellow wrote many articles. But he had published his first poem when he was only 13, and poetry was his love. He was greatly influenced by his travels and by personal tragedy. His first wife died in childbirth, the second in a fire. Longfellow had the ability to tell a story. He could make serious ideas easy to understand and make American epics popular. Among his most loved works are *The Song of Hiawatha, Evangeline, The Wreck of the Hesperus*, *Paul Revere's Ride*, and *The Village Blacksmith*.

▼ *Longfellow's knowledge of other countries and cultures inspired many of his poems.*

► *The Indian woman Minnehaha and her father, the arrow maker, featured in Longfellow's* Song of Hiawatha. *Minnehaha was the wife of Hiawatha.*

## LONG ISLAND

Long Island is the southeastern part of NEW YORK. It is 120 miles (190 km) long and 20 miles (32 km) wide at its widest. Long Island Sound is to the north, and the Atlantic Ocean is to the east and south. The New York City boroughs of Queens and Brooklyn form the western part of Long Island. This is the most heavily populated part. New York City's two main airports, Kennedy and La Guardia, are located in Queens. The eastern districts are rural, with potato farms common near the eastern tip at Montauk Point. In between are many suburbs of New York City. Fire Island, along the southern edge, is protected as a national seashore.

**The Long Island community of Levittown was built in 1949 and features similar affordable houses. Not far away are the Hamptons, coastal villages where waterfront houses cost millions of dollars.**

◀ *Pleasure craft line the dock of the Oyster Bay Yacht Club on Long Island.*

## LONGSTREET, James

Born in South Carolina and educated at West Point, James Longstreet (1821–1904) was one of the leading Confederate generals during the CIVIL WAR. As commander of the I Corp of Lee's Army of Northern Virginia, he fought at the battles of Fredericksburg (December 1862—a Confederate victory) and Gettysburg (July 1863). There, his method of attacking brought him some of the blame for the Confederate defeat. A few months later, Longstreet successfully led the attack on Federal lines at Chickamauga, Georgia. He was with Lee when he surrendered at Appomattox in April 1865. After the war, Longstreet served as U.S. minister to Turkey.

▲ *Called "Old Pete" by his men, James Longstreet was General Robert E. Lee's second in command at the Battle of Gettysburg. He was wounded in a later battle and his right arm was paralyzed, but he continued to serve until the end of the Civil War.*

▲ *The call of the common loon is frequently heard echoing over the water. The red-throated loon has a slender, upturned bill.*

▼ *Many of the tallest buildings in Los Angeles were built between 1980 and 1990. During that time the city's population boomed and Los Angeles overtook Chicago as America's second largest city.*

## LOON

The loon is a WATER BIRD. It is also known as the *diver*, because it dives underwater for fish. It has been found enmeshed in nets at over 200 feet (60 meters). The loon most often found in North America is the common loon, or great northern diver. It nests at the edge of small, deep lakes from the northern United States to the Arctic and spends winters near the sea. It has a loud, yodel-like call. Other North American loons are the yellow-billed, Arctic, and red-throated loons, which live on the shores of Arctic lakes.

## LOS ANGELES

Los Angeles, CALIFORNIA, is the second largest city in the United States. Its location on the Pacific coast of southern California, its pleasant climate, and its many cultural attractions continue to draw tourists and settlers. Today Los Angeles has a population of about 3.5 million.

Los Angeles was taken from Mexico in 1846, during the MEXICAN WAR. It began to grow rapidly in the late 1800s after the discovery of gold and oil. The movie industry was established there in the early 1900s, and HOLLYWOOD, a section of Los Angeles, became the

movie capital of the world. Today Los Angeles has many other industries, including aerospace, electronics, and clothing manufacturing. It is also an important port and financial center. One of its major problems is smog. Public transportation is poor, and almost everyone drives a car, creating a severe air pollution problem.

▲ *"Croatoan," the word carved on a tree, was also the name of an Indian tribe that lived near the Lost Colony. Some historians believe that the settlers went to live with these Indians.*

## LOST COLONY 

The Lost Colony was England's second settlement in the Americas. The more than one hundred settlers disappeared, and what happened to them is one of the great mysteries of history. John White founded the settlement in July 1587 on Roanoke Island, off the coast of what is now North Carolina. His granddaughter, Virginia Dare, was born there. She was the first English child born in America. White sailed to England in August for supplies. He returned in 1590 to find no trace of the colonists. The only clues were the words "Cro" and "Croatoan" carved on two trees.

## LOUIS, Joe 

Joe Louis (1914–1981) was one of the greatest American boxers. Born in Alabama and raised in Detroit, Louis began BOXING as a teenager. He became a professional fighter at the age of 20. Three years later he won the world heavyweight title. Over 12 years, Louis successfully defended his title in 25 championship bouts. Twenty of these ended in knockouts. He retired undefeated in 1949, but later fought twice more and was beaten by Ezzard Charles and Rocky Marciano.

**Joe Louis, nicknamed the Brown Bomber, was the longest-reigning world heavyweight champion in history. During his professional career he recorded 68 victories (54 by knockout) and lost only 3 fights.**

# LOUISIANA

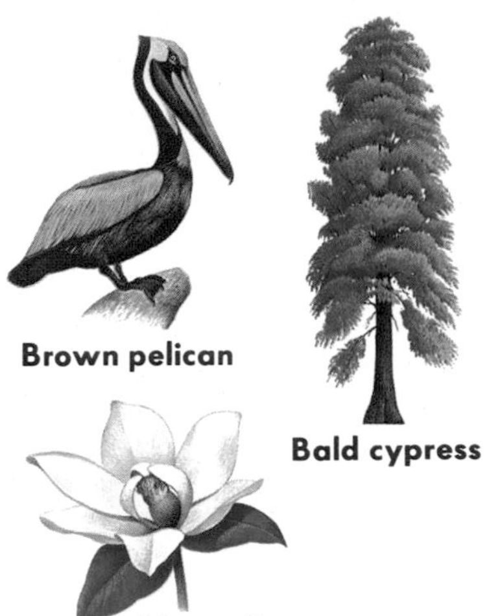

Brown pelican

Bald cypress

Magnolia

Louisiana
**Capital:** Baton Rouge
**Area:** 51,843 sq mi (134,275 km²). Rank: 31st
**Population:** 4,219,973 (1990). Rank: 21st
**Statehood:** April 30, 1812
**Principal rivers:** Atchafalaya, Mississippi, Red
**Highest point:** Driskill Mountain, 535 ft (163 m)
**Motto:** Union, Justice, and Confidence
**Songs:** "Give Me Louisiana," "You Are My Sunshine"

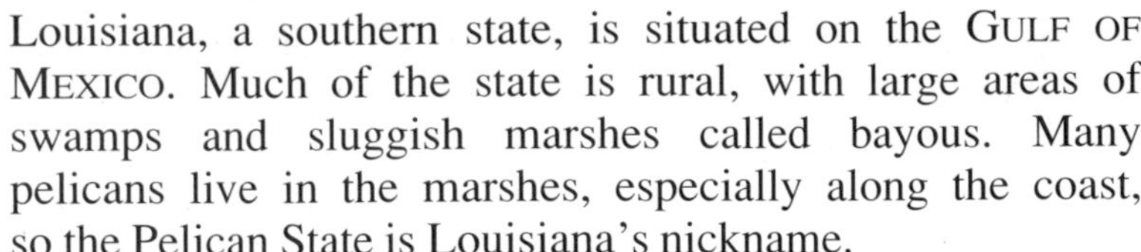

Louisiana, a southern state, is situated on the GULF OF MEXICO. Much of the state is rural, with large areas of swamps and sluggish marshes called bayous. Many pelicans live in the marshes, especially along the coast, so the Pelican State is Louisiana's nickname.

The Gulf of Mexico and the Mississippi River have played an important role in Louisiana's history and culture. The state's three largest cities, NEW ORLEANS, Baton Rouge, the capital, and Shreveport, are located on the Mississippi. The river itself forms part of Louisiana's eastern border and flows through the southeastern part of the state before emptying into the Gulf.

The Spanish were the first Europeans to explore the coast of Louisiana. Hernando DE SOTO sailed up the lower Mississippi as early as 1541. Almost a hundred and fifty years later, the French explorer, Robert Cavelier, Sieur de LA SALLE, sailed down the Mississippi and claimed the region for France. He named it Louisiana for King Louis XIV. The early French settlers, who were called Creoles, were joined in the late 1700s by 10,000 other French-speaking people—the Acadians. They had been forced out of NOVA SCOTIA (Acadia) in Canada by the British. The word "Acadian" soon became shortened to CAJUN.

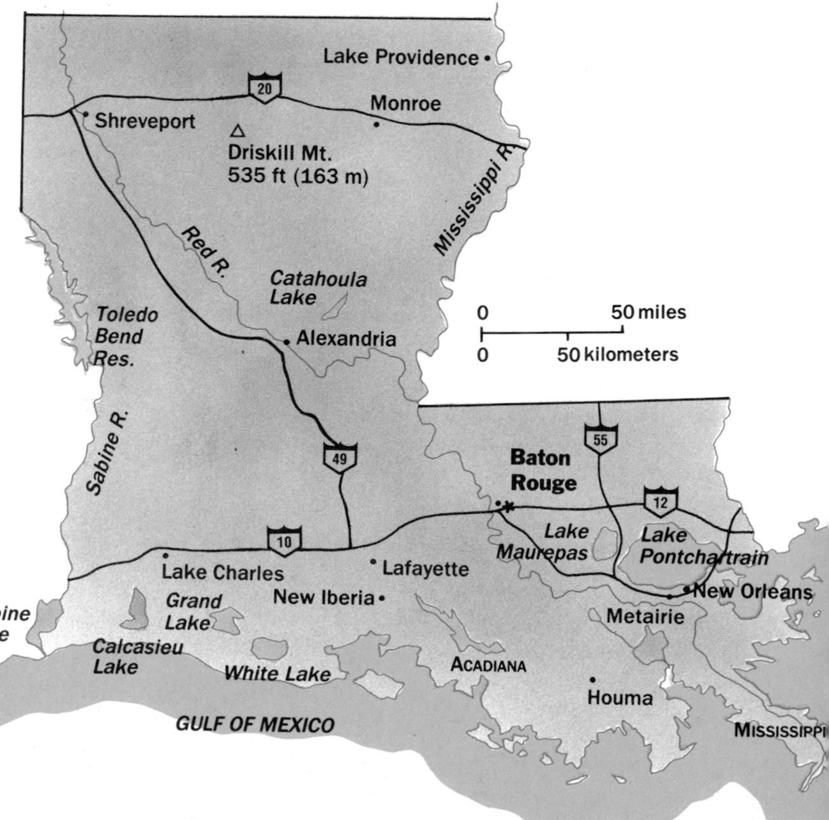

The United States purchased Louisiana from France in 1803, as part of the LOUISIANA PURCHASE. It became a state nine years later. In 1814–1815, during the last battle of the War of 1812, Andrew JACKSON defeated the British at New Orleans. During the CIVIL WAR, Louisiana joined the Confederacy, and it suffered great destruction. Today, however, it is an important agricultural and industrial state. Rice, soybeans, and cotton are the state's most important crops. Oil and natural gas are produced, and petroleum refining provides much of the state's income. Louisiana leads all other states in the production of salt. It is also the country's leading state in fishing, with most of the catch being shellfish. Much of the state's production is shipped through New Orleans, one of the busiest ports in the country.

▲ *Cypresses covered in Spanish moss are a common sight in and around Louisiana's wetlands.*

▲ *Informal Dixieland jazz concerts always draw a crowd in music-loving New Orleans, where jazz is king.*

Places of Interest

- New Orleans blends French architecture, lively jazz, and spicy food.
- The bayou region of Acadiana is the home of many Cajuns, descendants of French-speaking people expelled from Canada.
- The Gulf of Mexico coast has wildlife refuges and offers good sea fishing.

► *Old-time riverboats recall the days when Louisiana became the Mississippi gateway to America's heartlands.*

**The Louisiana Territory stretched from the Mississippi River in the east to the Rocky Mountains in the west, and from the Gulf of Mexico in the south to British North America in the north. Eventually, all or parts of 15 states were formed from the Louisiana Territory.**

## LOUISIANA PURCHASE 

In 1803 the United States purchased the Louisiana Territory from France. This territory had an area of 828,000 square miles (2,144,500 km$^2$). The Louisiana Purchase doubled the size of the United States.

In the late 1700s, France gave the Louisiana Territory to Spain. In 1802, however, the territory was transferred back to France. President Thomas JEFFERSON did not want a strong French presence on the United States' western border. He also worried that Americans would not be allowed to use the Mississippi River for trade or as an outlet to the Gulf of Mexico. He told his ambassador to France, Robert Livingston, and special envoy James MONROE to try to buy the port of NEW ORLEANS. To their surprise, the French offered to sell them the entire Louisiana Territory for about $15 million. The purchase, dated April 30, 1803, opened the way for American settlement of the West.

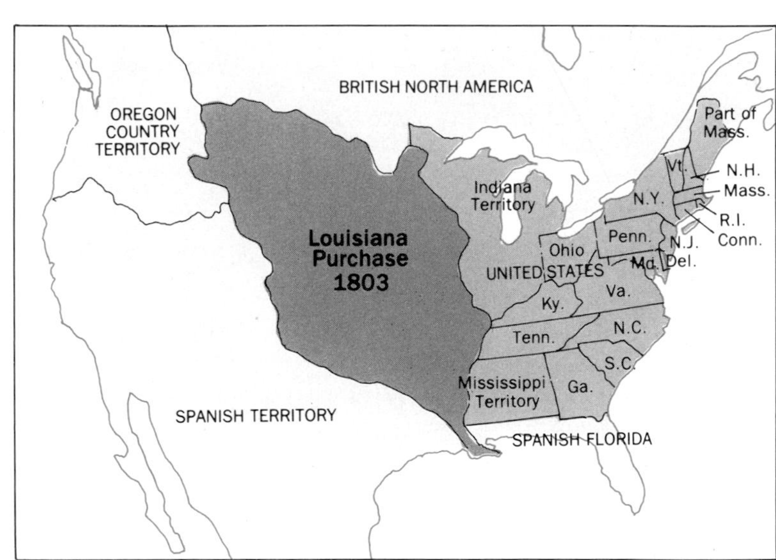


► *Much of the area of the Louisiana Purchase remained unexplored until the Lewis and Clark Expedition of 1804–1806.*

## LOWELL, James Russell 

James Russell Lowell (1819–1891) was a poet, editor, teacher, and diplomat during the 1800s. He had a strong influence on American culture. Lowell was an ABOLITIONIST, and some of his early poems were antislavery. His best-known long poems are *The Vision of Sir Launfal* and the witty *A Fable for Critics*. In 1856, Lowell began teaching modern languages at Harvard University. In the following year he became the first

▼ *James Russell Lowell joined fellow New Englanders Henry Wadsworth Longfellow and Ralph Waldo Emerson in condemning slavery.*

editor of the literary magazine *Atlantic Monthly*. From 1877 to 1885, Lowell was U.S. ambassador to Spain and then to Britain.

◀ *A lumberman sorts trunks at a collecting point in Oregon. Rivers are sometimes used to transport lumber to the mill.*

## LUMBER INDUSTRY

The lumber industry provides wood for construction of such things as buildings and furniture. U.S. lumber companies produce more than 41 billion board feet of lumber each year. Fir, pine, and other softwoods account for 80 percent of production.

The U.S. lumber industry began in New England during Colonial times. As more and more trees were cut down, the industry shifted first to the Midwest and then to the South after the Civil War. It shifted once again in the early 1900s, this time to the West. Today, more than 600,000 people work in the lumber industry.

States with Highest Volume of Timber

1. Oregon
2. Washington
3. California
4. Alaska
5. Idaho
6. Montana
7. Georgia
8. North Carolina
9. Alabama
10. Louisiana

## LUTHERANS

The Lutheran churches are the oldest and largest group of Protestant churches in the world. About 12 percent of the world's Lutherans live in the United States. It is the fourth largest Christian group in the country. Lutheran beliefs are based on the teachings of Martin Luther, a German religious leader during the 1500s. Lutherans believe that only through faith can a person be saved. The largest Lutheran church in the United States is the Evangelical Lutheran Church in America, with about 5.2 million members. Immigrants from Germany and Scandinavia brought Lutheranism to the United States in the 1700s and 1800s.

The Largest Lutheran Churches in the U.S.

1. Evangelical Lutheran Church in America
2. Lutheran Church – Missouri Synod
3. Wisconsin Evangelical Lutheran Synod
4. Association of Free Lutheran Congregations
5. Evangelical Lutheran Synod

## MacARTHUR, Douglas

Douglas MacArthur (1880–1964) was an American general who distinguished himself in WORLD WAR II and the KOREAN WAR.

Early in World War II, MacArthur organized the defense of the Philippines against the Japanese. When forced to withdraw his troops, he made his famous promise to the Filipino people: "I shall return." As Allied commander in the southwest Pacific, he liberated the Philippines in 1944 and later supervised the occupation of Japan.

In 1950, when the Korean War started, MacArthur led the defense of South Korea as commander of the United Nations forces. After disobeying President Harry S. TRUMAN's order not to speak out about carrying the war to China, he was relieved of his command.

► *General Douglas MacArthur led the Allied reconquest of the Philippines in 1944. Two years before, when the Japanese drove the U.S. forces out, MacArthur had promised: "I shall return."*

▼ *Macdonald worked tirelessly to enlarge and strengthen the Dominion of Canada, which he had helped to create.*

## MACDONALD, Sir John Alexander

John Macdonald (1815–1891), the first prime minister of Canada, is known as the Father of Canadian Federation. When he and his parents emigrated from Scotland in 1820, Canada consisted of several separate British provinces. As a legislator in the assembly of Upper Canada (now Ontario), Macdonald worked for Canadian unity. When the Dominion of Canada was created in 1867, Macdonald was named prime minister. He served in this position for almost 19 years. The country prospered under his leadership. The Canadian Pacific Railway was completed in 1855, and the country grew to reach the Pacific Ocean.

## MACKENZIE, Sir Alexander 

Sir Alexander Mackenzie (1764?–1820) was a Scottish fur trader who explored Canada. His base of operations was Fort Chipewyan, a trading post on Lake Athabasca in what is now northern Alberta. In 1789, Mackenzie and his party set out by canoe to reach the Pacific Ocean. But the river that he followed flowed north to the Arctic Ocean. Unhappy with this discovery, he called the river the "River of Disappointment." It is now known as the Mackenzie River. In 1783, Mackenzie tried again. His party canoed down the Peace, Fraser, and other rivers and crossed the Canadian Rockies. They finally reached the Pacific at what is now southwestern British Columbia.

**In 1801, Sir Alexander Mackenzie published an account of his explorations. It was called *Voyages on the River Saint Lawrence and Through the Continent of North America to the Frozen and Pacific Oceans in the Years 1789 and 1793.***

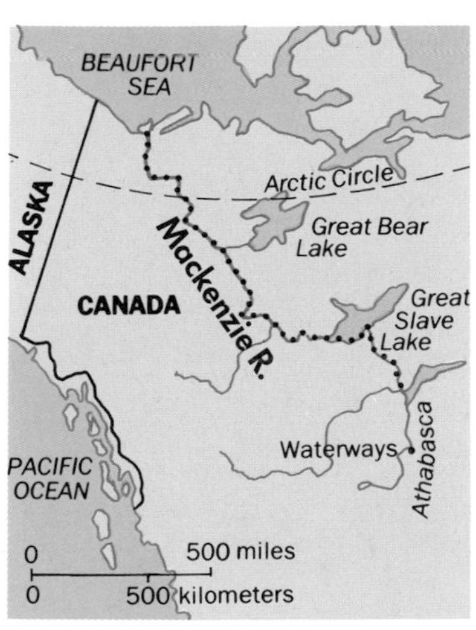

◄ *Sir Alexander Mackenzie was the first European to cross the North American continent north of Mexico on an overland expedition.*

▼ *William Lyon Mackenzie died six years before his dream of Canadian self-determination became reality.*

## MACKENZIE, William Lyon 

The Canadian political leader William Lyon Mackenzie (1795–1861) was born in Scotland. After settling in Upper Canada (Ontario) in 1820, he began publishing a newspaper, the *Colonial Advocate*. In it he argued for democratic reforms. In 1828, Mackenzie was elected to the Legislative Assembly, but he was expelled several times for his attacks on the Tory government. In 1836 he lost his parliamentary seat. By now, however, Mackenzie had many followers. In 1837, with 800 troops, he attempted to seize control of the government. The rebellion was badly organized and quickly suppressed. Mackenzie fled to the United States. In 1849 he was pardoned and returned to Canada where he served again in the Legislative Assembly until 1858.

James Madison
**Born:** March 16, 1751, at Port Conway, Virginia
**Education:** College of New Jersey (now Princeton University)
**Political party:** Democratic-Republican
**Term of office:** 1809–1817
**Married:** 1794 to Dolley Payne Todd
**Died:** June 28, 1836, at Montpelier, Virginia

James Madison was the fourth president of the United States. Born in Virginia, he was one of the founding fathers and one of the Constitution's principal authors.

Madison was a delegate to the CONTINENTAL CONGRESS. And at the Constitutional Convention in Philadelphia in 1787, he helped draft the U.S. CONSTITUTION. He believed that the United States should have a federal form of government. The states, he argued, should control their own local matters, but the federal, or national, government should manage national affairs. With Alexander HAMILTON and John JAY he wrote *The Federalist Papers*, which explained the proposed new constitution to the people and helped win its passage in crucial states, such as New York.

► *Though a treaty with Britain had already been signed, victory at the Battle of New Orleans, during the War of 1812, boosted national pride.*

▼ *President James Madison's wife Dolley rescued the original Declaration of Independence when the British burned Washington, D.C., in 1814.*

Madison was elected to the country's first HOUSE OF REPRESENTATIVES. He proposed the first ten amendments to the Constitution, the BILL OF RIGHTS. In 1800, President Thomas JEFFERSON made Madison secretary of state. While in this position, Madison was involved in the LOUISIANA PURCHASE.

In 1808, Madison was elected president. Britain and France were at war at this time. To protect American ships, Madison banned trade with Britain and France. Finally, however, the United States was forced to declare war on Britain. Madison was re-elected the same year. The WAR OF 1812, or "Mr. Madison's War" as it was sometimes called, ended in 1815. Most Americans felt that the United States had won the war, and Madison was more popular than ever. In 1817 he retired to Montpelier, Virginia. For the next 19 years he managed his estate and worked for the abolition of slavery.

◀ *Some successful magazines are aimed at certain groups of readers, such as children (*Cricket*) or teenagers (*Seventeen*). Others, such as* Time, Life, *and* Reader's Digest, *cover a wide range of subjects in order to attract a large readership.*

## MAGAZINES 

About 11,000 magazines are published in the United States. Some appear weekly, but most are published either monthly, bimonthly (every two months), or quarterly (every three months). Some, like *Reader's Digest* and *Life*, are aimed at millions of people of all ages and interests and have articles on many different topics. Others, like *Business Week*, *Scientific American*, *Sports Illustrated*, and *TV Guide*, are aimed at people with particular interests. Professional, trade, and technical magazines are intended for even smaller groups of readers with interests in these areas.

Most magazines make money either by distributing copies to be sold at newsstands and other outlets, by selling mail subscriptions, or by selling space to advertisers. Some magazines, however, are sent free of charge. For example, *Modern Maturity*, the U.S. magazine with the highest circulation (over 22 million), is sent free to members of the American Association of Retired Persons.

**The first American magazine was published on February 13, 1741. It was the *American Magazine* of Philadelphia. Three days later, Benjamin Franklin published the first issue of his *General Magazine and Historical Chronicle.* It is estimated that today three out of four American adults buy at least one magazine in the course of a year.**

Leading U.S. Magazines
(Circulation in millions)

1. *Modern Maturity* (22.5)
2. *Reader's Digest* (16.3)
3. *TV Guide* (15.4)
4. *National Geographic* (9.9)
5. *Better Homes and Gardens* (8.0)
6. *Family Circle* (5.2)
7. *Good Housekeeping* (5.0)
8. *McCall's* (5.0)
9. *Ladies Home Journal* (5.0)

## MAIMAN, Theodore 

Theodore Maiman (1927– ) is an important scientist and inventor. He developed the first laser, one of the most significant devices of this century. Maiman was educated at Stanford University, where he received a Ph.D. in physics. He joined the Hughes Research Laboratories in 1953. There he became interested in masers—devices that amplify microwaves. Maiman adapted masers to amplify light. His new invention was called a laser. Lasers have many uses. Their powerful beams of light are used in eye surgery and to remove cancers. They are also used to cut through metal and to measure the vast distances in space.

# MAINE

Maine is the easternmost state of the United States. It forms the northeastern corner of the country and is bordered by the Canadian provinces of New Brunswick and Quebec and the state of New Hampshire. The southern border of Maine is a long and rocky coastline on the Atlantic Ocean.

Maine is nicknamed the Pinetree State because giant pines once covered the land. Most were cut down long ago, but new trees grew to replace them. Today there are 17 million acres (almost 7 million ha) of forest in the state, and the manufacture of wood products, especially paper, is Maine's most important industry.

The northern part of the state is a wilderness of forests, mountains, and lakes. Most of the people live in the southeast, within 25 miles (40 km) of the Atlantic coast. PORTLAND, the largest city, and Augusta, the capital, are in the southeast.

It is possible that the Vikings reached Maine around the year 1000, and John CABOT, the English explorer, around 1498. The first permanent settlement was established by the English in 1607. Later in that century, Maine became part of the Massachusetts Bay Colony. It remained part of Massachusetts even after the American Revolution, and did not become a state until 1820.

In its early days, Maine was an important shipbuilding and fishing state. Today, fishing is still important. Maine seafood, especially lobster, is world famous. Potatoes are an important crop. And footwear, electrical and electronic equipment, machinery, and textiles are produced in the state's factories. Thousands of people visit the state to ski, fish, and hunt.

► *A lighthouse stands on Cape Neddick to guide ships safely through the treacherous waters off the Maine coast.*

**Places of Interest**

- Cadillac Mountain, in Acadia National Park, is the highest peak on the U.S. east coast.
- Baxter State Park, in Maine's highland forests, is ideal for camping, hiking, and winter skiing.
- The coastal resort of Kennebunkport is the summer home of President George Bush.
- West Quoddy Head, a small peninsula near Lubec, is the most easterly point in the U.S.

► *Boothbay Harbor is one of Maine's many excellent harbors. The lobster traps on the dock bear witness to the state's valuable lobster catch.*

Maine
**Capital:** Augusta
**Area:** 35,387 sq mi (91,653 km$^2$). Rank: 39th
**Population:** 1,227,928 (1990). Rank: 38th
**Statehood:** March 15, 1820
**Principal rivers:** Androscoggin, Kennebec, Penobscot
**Highest point:** Mt. Katahdin, 5,268 ft (1,606 m)
**Motto:** *Dirigio* (I Guide)
**Song:** "State of Maine Song"

▼ *Craft shops line a street on Mt. Desert Island, a popular tourist resort.*

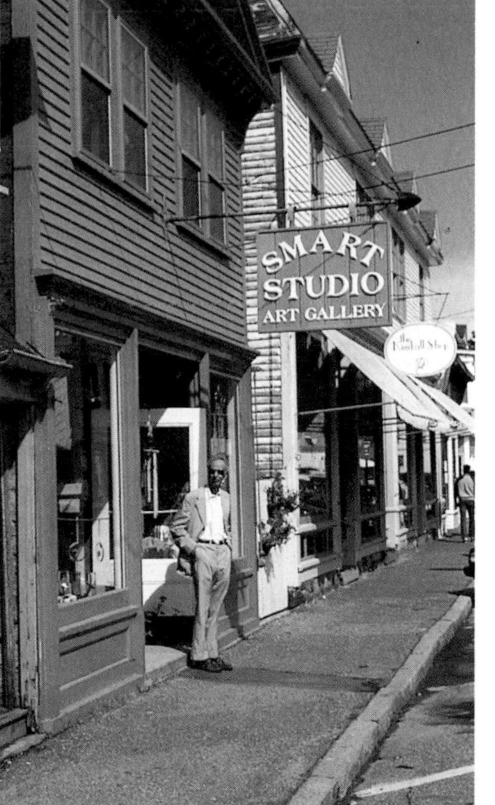


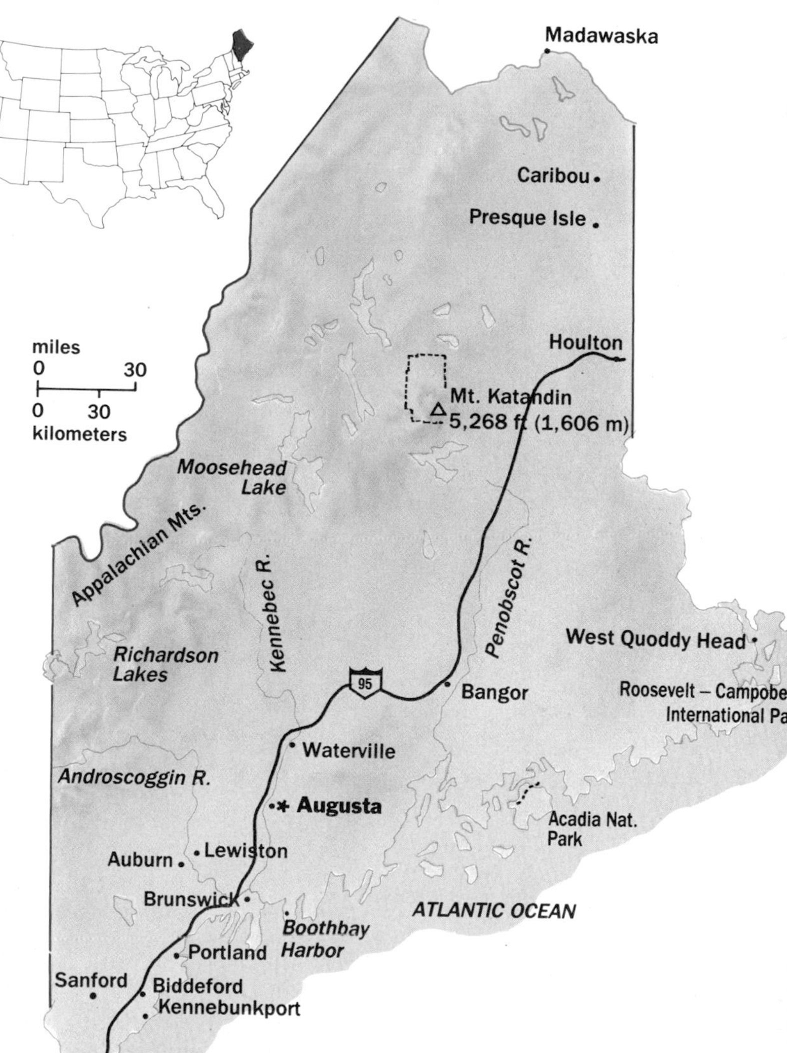

▲ *In 1963, Malcolm X disagreed with the leader of the Black Muslims. He formed a new group in 1964 called the Organization for Afro-American Unity, but he was killed before it was firmly established.*

## MALCOLM X

Malcolm X (1925–1965), who was born Malcolm Little, was an American black nationalist. He became a member of the Black Muslims, a group that believed in the separation of the races and black economic development. Malcolm X attracted many followers to the Black Muslim cause with his strong speeches. But he soon disagreed with them on some issues, such as their refusal to take part in the CIVIL RIGHTS campaigns of the 1960s. Malcolm X left the Black Muslims in 1964 and formed a rival group, the Organization for Afro-American Unity. He was murdered in 1965 by three assassins, two of whom were Black Muslims. His *Autobiography of Malcolm X* was published that same year.

## MANDANS

The Mandans were one of the American INDIAN tribes of the GREAT PLAINS. They lived around the Missouri River valley in South Dakota. The Mandans were farmers. If the land became poor, they would move on and make another settlement. The Mandans used bullboats, round, bowl-shaped boats made of hide stretched over a wooden frame. As horse trading spread among the various Indian tribes, Mandan settlements became bases for buying and selling in the northern part of the country. Today, a few thousand Mandans live on a reservation in North Dakota.

▼ *The artist George Catlin visited the Mandans in 1832, about 30 years after they had met Lewis and Clark. His portrait of Minet was one of his many Mandan portraits.*

## MANIFEST DESTINY

The phrase "manifest destiny" was coined in 1845 by the journalist John L. O'Sullivan. He wrote about "our manifest destiny to overspread the continent allotted by Providence for the free development of our multiplying millions." O'Sullivan was referring to the annexation of Texas that year by the United States. But his phrase was taken up by many Americans who believed that God had given the United States the right to expand. The idea of manifest destiny was used to justify the taking of land from Mexico in the MEXICAN WAR (1846–1848) and the purchase of Alaska (1867). It was also used to justify the annexation of the Philippines, Puerto Rico, and Guam after the SPANISH-AMERICAN WAR in 1898 and of Hawaii the same year.

# MANITOBA

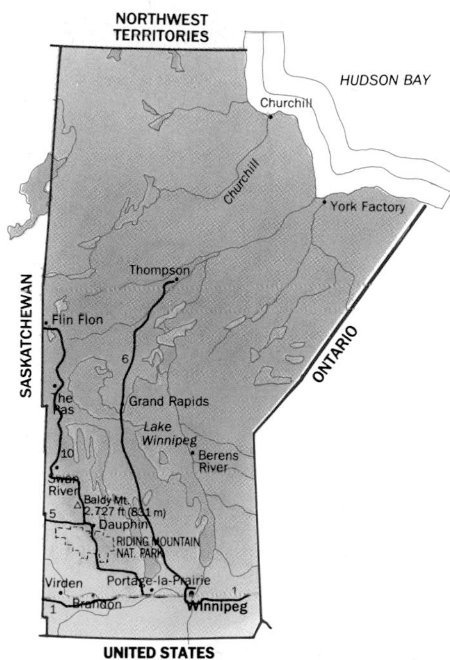


Manitoba is one of Canada's three Prairie Provinces. It is located in the center of Canada, just north of the states of North Dakota and Minnesota. The prairie lands of southern Manitoba have many farms and cattle ranches. Northern Manitoba is a beautiful wilderness with millions of acres of forests. Hudson Bay lies off Manitoba's northeastern border, and lakes, ponds, and rivers cover more than 15 percent of the land.

The British HUDSON'S BAY COMPANY competed with the French in the fur trade during the 1700s. In 1763, however, the French were forced out of Canada after being defeated by the British in the FRENCH AND INDIAN WAR. The first permanent farming settlement, the Red River colony, was established in 1812. Manitoba joined the new Canadian confederation in 1870, becoming the fifth province. At that time it included only the area around the capital city of Winnipeg. Land was added over the years, and Manitoba obtained its present size by 1912.

Today, Manitoba's farms grow wheat, barley, oats, and other crops. Food products, electrical items, chemicals, and other goods are manufactured in the province's factories. Lumbering is also an important industry, and Manitoban mines produce large quantities of nickel, copper, and zinc. The discovery of oil in the 1950s added greatly to Manitoba's prosperity.

**Pasqueflower**

Manitoba
**Capital:** Winnipeg
**Area:** 211,723 sq mi (548,360 km²)
**Population:** 1,091,942 (1991). Rank: 5th
**Entry into Confederation:** July 15th, 1870 (5th province)
**Highest point:** Baldy Mountain, 2,729 ft (832 m)

▲ *Lake Winnipeg, over 250 miles (400 km) long, is the largest body of water in North America to be completely contained in one state or province.*

▲ *In his last speech, Horace Mann, the "Father of Public Education," said, "Be ashamed to die until you have won some victory for humanity."*

## MANN, Horace

Horace Mann (1796–1859) was a great American educational reformer and legislator. He supported many good causes but is best known for his work in making education available to everyone. He said that for a country to remain democratic, all children must receive a free education. While serving in the Massachusetts state legislature, Mann helped to establish the first state board of education in the United States. He also worked to improve the quality of education at all levels. Mann was president of Antioch College (now Antioch University) in Yellow Springs, Ohio, from 1853 until his death.

## MANUFACTURING

Manufacturing is the branch of industry that makes things. It is one of the most important parts of the U.S. economy, although not as important as in the recent past. There are more than 350,000 manufacturing companies in the United States. They turn out products valued at more than $2.5 trillion a year. Profits exceed $100 billion each year. More than 19 million people in the United States are employed in manufacturing.

▼ *Major manufacturers set themselves high standards. This quality controller examines thousands of aluminum cans in a single day.*

There are two types of manufactured goods—durables and nondurables. Durable goods include metals and metal products, machinery, and transportation equipment. In terms of value, the most important kind of durable goods are motor vehicles and parts, which include automobiles. Nondurable goods—goods that are used up—include foods, fuel, chemicals, plastics, paper products, and published materials. The FOOD INDUSTRY is the largest nondurable manufacturing area in the United States.

The largest manufacturing centers are the metropolitan areas of New York City, Los Angeles, Chicago, Detroit, Philadelphia, and Houston. The biggest manufacturing companies include General Motors and Ford (motor vehicles), Exxon (energy products), and International Business Machines (office and communications equipment). In 1991, these four companies had combined sales of about $408 billion, of which General Motors accounted for $124 billion.

**U.S. MANUFACTURING INDUSTRIES**

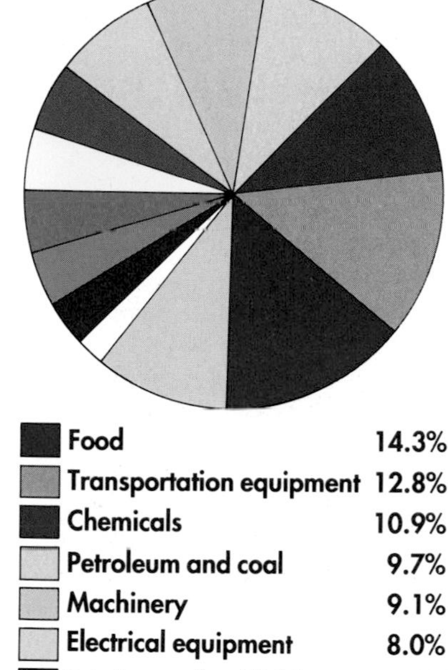

| | |
|---|---|
| Food | 14.3% |
| Transportation equipment | 12.8% |
| Chemicals | 10.9% |
| Petroleum and coal | 9.7% |
| Machinery | 9.1% |
| Electrical equipment | 8.0% |
| Printing and publishing | 5.4% |
| Fabricated metal products | 4.7% |
| Paper | 4.4% |
| Primary metals | 4.1% |
| Instruments | 3.7% |
| Textiles | 2.1% |
| Others | 10.8% |

The Largest U.S. Manufacturers

| Company and Rank | Products |
|---|---|
| 1. General Motors | Motor vehicles/equipment |
| 2. Exxon | Petroleum refining |
| 3. Ford Motor | Motor vehicles/equipment |
| 4. IBM | Computers/office equipment |
| 5. General Electric | Electronics/electrical goods |
| 6. Mobil | Petroleum refining |
| 7. Philip Morris | Tobacco products/food |
| 8. Du Pont | Chemical goods |
| 9. Texaco | Petroleum refining |
| 10. Chevron | Petroleum refining |
| 11. Chrysler | Motor vehicles/equipment |
| 12. Boeing | Aerospace |
| 13. Procter & Gamble | Soaps and cosmetics |
| 14. Amoco | Petroleum refining |
| 15. Shell Oil | Petroleum refining |

## MAPLE

The maple is one of the most common trees in the United States and Canada. The maple leaf even appears on the Canadian flag, and maple trees are the state trees of Rhode Island (red maple), New York, Vermont, and Wisconsin (all sugar maples). Maple trees have many uses. They grow fast and provide good shade in summer. Farmers use them as windbreaks. Maple is a favorite wood of furniture makers because it is strong

▼ *Winged maple seeds grow from a branch in pairs. They separate and float to the ground like propellers.*

and can be polished to a good shine. Its strength is also useful in tools; many ax and hammer handles are made of maple. MAPLE SYRUP is made from the sap of sugar maple trees.

► *In the fall, the leaves of the maple tree become a mass of brilliant reds and golds.*

**Maple sugar was an important trading product in the American northeast and Canada until the late 1800s. At that time cane sugar became much less expensive.**

## MAPLE SYRUP

The Indians taught the first white settlers of North America how to boil down the sap of sugar maples until a sweet syrup was produced. This technique has been preserved, and maple syrup is still an important agricultural product in the states of Vermont and New York and the Canadian province of Quebec. More than 35 gallons (133 liters) of sap are needed to produce one gallon (3.8 liters) of syrup. Because of this, maple syrup is expensive. Most pancake syrups use mainly cane sugar and corn syrups. Less than 3 percent of pancake syrup is maple syrup.

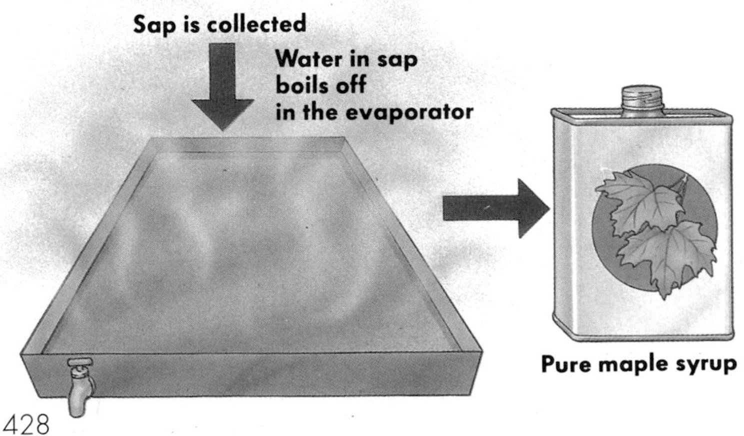


◄ *Sap for maple sugar is collected in the early spring, when there are warm days and cold nights. The sap is "sugared down" in special buildings. A spoonful of hot, new maple syrup poured over snow makes delicious ice candy.*

# MARINE CORPS, United States

The U.S. Marine Corps is the only branch of the armed forces that is trained for combined land, sea, and air action. The Marine Corps was established by the Continental Congress in 1775.

Marines go through a difficult training program known as boot camp. During this time they must learn to react quickly and to obey orders without question or delay. By the time a marine passes this basic training, he feels he is part of a select group of professional fighters. This sense of loyalty is important in combat.

The Marine Corps is divided into three parts. The actual fighting is done by the Operating Forces. These marines are assigned to either the Atlantic or Pacific Naval fleets. Acting as a backup for the Operating Forces is the Supporting Establishment. This is the term used to describe all the marines who are still in the many bases located around the coast of the country. Finally, there is the group known as the Reserves, marines who can be summoned from desk jobs or basic training to join the action. With almost 200,000 troops on active duty, the Marine Corps is the smallest branch of the U.S. armed forces. Marines have fought in every U.S. armed conflict since independence. (*See* AIR FORCE, ARMY, NAVY.)

▼ *The Marine Corps emblem.*

▼ *The Marine Corps War Memorial portrays the raising of the American flag on Iwo Jima during World War II.*

*The Marine Corps uniform has changed over the years as the corps itself has developed.*

# MARINE LIFE

Where Marine Life is on Display

**Marineland** (St. Augustine, Florida)
**Marineland of the Pacific** (Los Angeles, California)
**Miami Seaquarium** (Miami, Florida)
**Monterey Bay Aquarium** (Monterey, California)
**New England Aquarium** (Boston, Massachusetts)
**New York Aquarium** (Brooklyn, New York)
**Shedd Aquarium** (Chicago, Illinois)
**Steinhart Aquarium** (San Francisco, California)

The marine life of North America includes the huge variety of animals and plants that live in the oceans surrounding the continent. Even the shoreline is home to many marine creatures, which live buried in the sand or in rock pools.

Life in the ocean itself varies with depth. Seaweed and other plants that need sunlight grow near the surface. Jellyfish float near the surface. So does plankton, a kind of ocean "soup" made up of tiny plants and animals. Many animals in the sea eat this plankton. The largest fish live near the surface. These include swordfish, tuna, sharks, and marlin. Such creatures as sea urchins, starfish, flounders, and sea anemones live on the ocean floor where the water is shallow. Many strange and unusual fish live at greater depths, where the light is dim or there is no light at all. Some even have light organs, which provide light or frighten predators.

Many organisms that live in the sea are valuable to human beings. Fish and shellfish, for example, are high in protein and are important sources of food. Some types of marine life, such as sponges and seaweed, produce substances that are used to treat diseases. Marine biologists, scientists who study the plants and animals that live in the sea, are constantly searching for other uses of marine life.

*▼ North American seas are rich in animal and plant life. Some, such as the flounder, provide us with food. Others, such as coral and sponge, are made into jewelry and household items.*

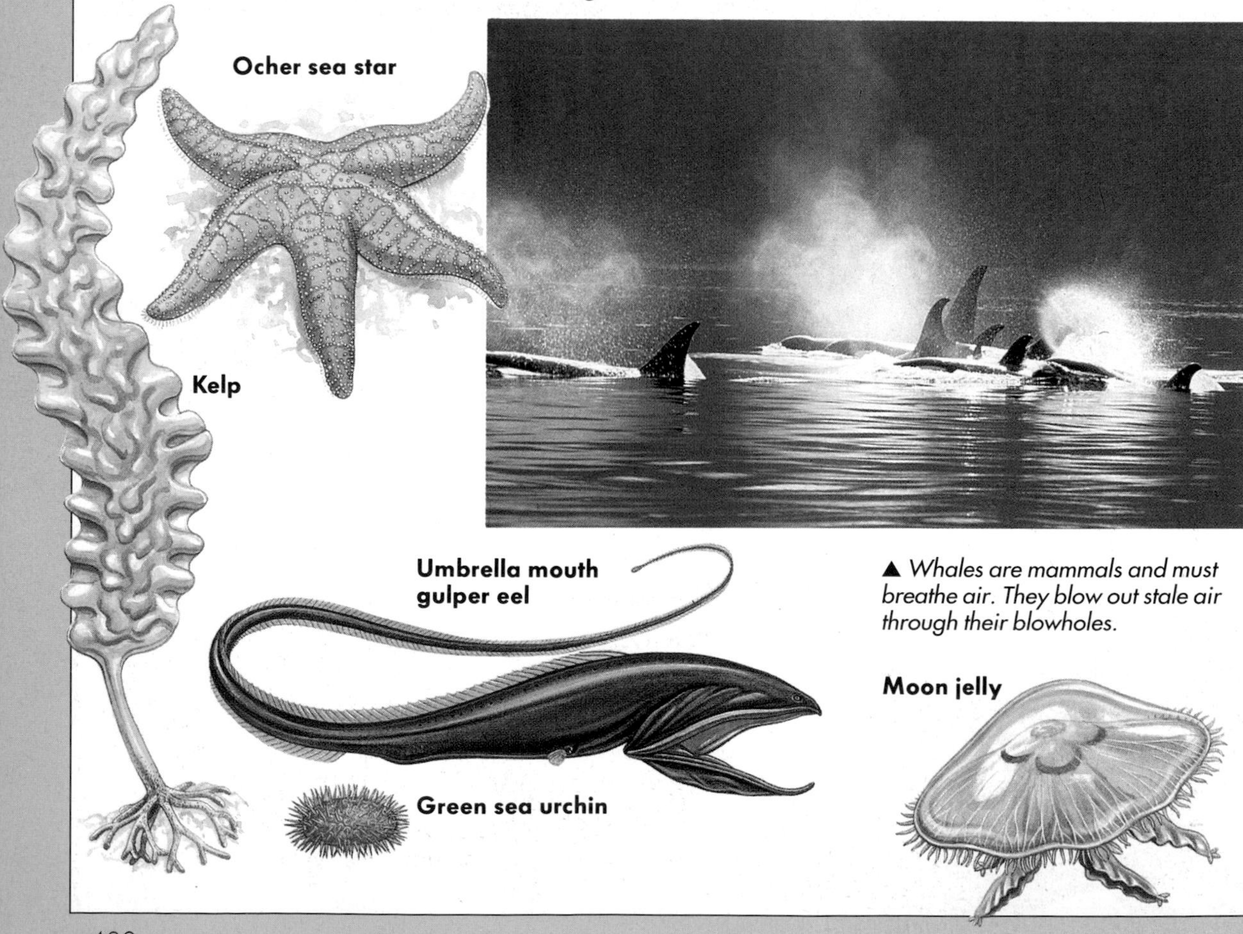


*▲ Whales are mammals and must breathe air. They blow out stale air through their blowholes.*

▲ *Tiny algae, such as these diatoms (highly magnified here), form the bottom of the food chain. Many fish use these as their only food source.*

▼ *Marine biologists carry out research into the way sea animals grow and develop. Here they are injecting a live lemon shark with a drug called* tetracycline.

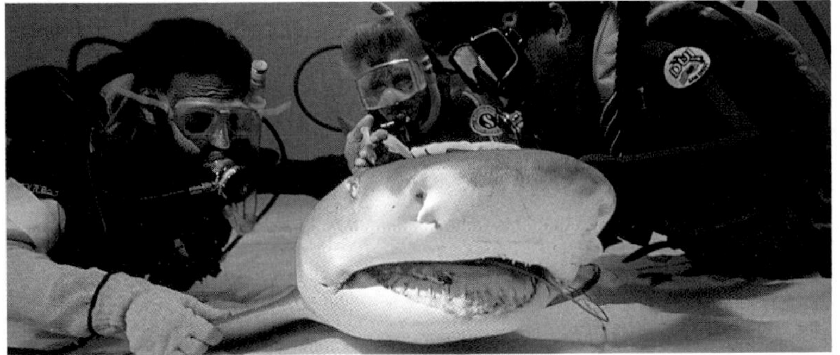

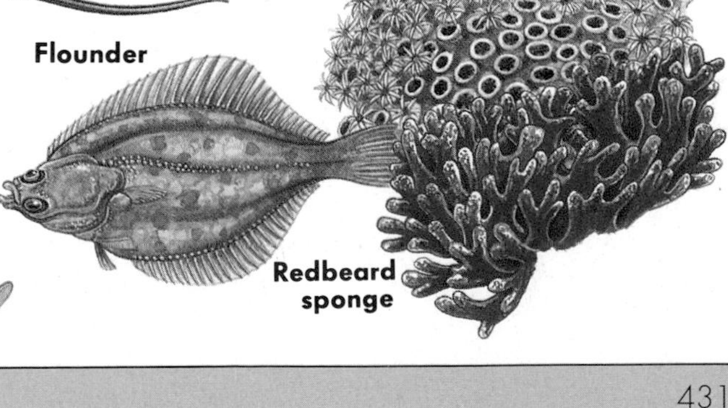

**Loggerhead turtle**

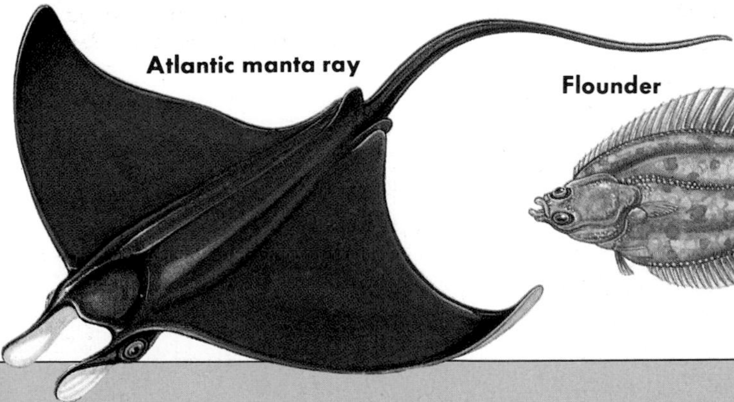

**Star coral**

**Atlantic manta ray**

**Flounder**

**Redbeard sponge**

▲ *Francis Marion's guerrilla-style attacks on British communication and supply ports helped to keep the pressure on the British in South Carolina.*

## MARION, Francis 

The cunning feats of Francis Marion (1732?–1795) during the American REVOLUTION caused the British to nickname him the Swamp Fox. Marion, a South Carolinian, was an officer in the colonial army. When the British forces defeated the American troops in South Carolina, Marion escaped into the backwoods with a small group of soldiers. They staged guerrilla raids against the British, attacking their camps and often rescuing American prisoners.

## MARQUETTE, Jacques 

Father Jacques Marquette (1637–1675) was a French missionary and explorer. Because he spoke a number of Indian languages, he was chosen to explore the MISSISSIPPI RIVER with Louis Jolliet. It was thought at that time that the river might flow into the Pacific Ocean. Marquette and Jolliet set off in canoes in 1673. Starting out in Lake Michigan, they went down the Mississippi as far as present-day Arkansas. They found that the river flowed south, not west, and did not flow into the Pacific Ocean. Jolliet's journal about the expedition was lost when a canoe overturned. But Marquette later wrote a book about their travels. Marquette and Jolliet were the first Europeans to explore the northern reaches of the Mississippi. Their discoveries added greatly to the geographical knowledge of the region.

◄ *Jacques Marquette encountered many Indian tribes as he traveled down the Mississippi. The peace pipe he holds aloft was a symbol of friendship.*

## MARSHALL, George C.

George Catlett Marshall (1880–1959) was a brilliant U.S. Army officer and statesman. He was born in Uniontown, Pennsylvania. After attending Virginia Military Institute he began a career in the U.S. Army. He served in the Philippines and in WORLD WAR I. Marshall became chief of staff of the Army in 1939 and helped formulate Allied military strategy during WORLD WAR II. After the war he became secretary of state under President Harry S. TRUMAN. He devised the European Recovery Plan, or Marshall Plan, to help European countries rebuild their war-torn economies. For this he was awarded the 1953 Nobel Peace Prize.

▲ *George Marshall was the first professional soldier to become secretary of state.*

## MARSHALL ISLANDS *See* Pacific Territories

## MARSHALL, John

John Marshall (1755–1835) was a Virginian who served as chief justice of the U.S. SUPREME COURT for 34 years (1801–1835). He established the right of the Court to interpret the U.S. CONSTITUTION and declare laws unconstitutional. Marshall believed in a strong central government, and he played a key role in persuading Virginia to ratify the Constitution in 1788. Some of his decisions gave Congress powers that were not spelled out in the Constitution. Others ruled that when federal and state laws conflicted, federal law should prevail. His contributions to constitutional law earned him the nickname the Great Chief Justice.

▼ *The Marx Brothers were Hollywood's favorite comedy team in the 1930s. Harpo (in the middle) never spoke in any of their movies.*

## MARX BROTHERS

The Marx Brothers were an American comedy team. The team was made up of Chico (1891–1961), Groucho (1890–1977), Harpo (1893–1964), and Zeppo (1901–1979). Before 1918 a fifth brother, Gummo (1894–1977), was also part of the team. They began as a VAUDEVILLE act in 1904. By the mid-1920s their plays were Broadway hits. In the late 1920s they began making films. Their best-known movies are *The Cocoanuts*, *Animal Crackers*, *Monkey Business*, *Duck Soup*, and *A Night at the Opera*. In the 1950s, Groucho was quizmaster of the television program "You Bet Your Life."

# MARYLAND

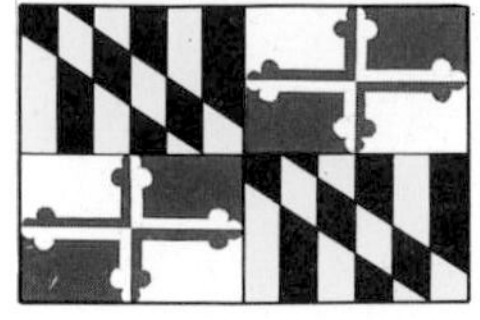

The mid-Atlantic state of Maryland is located on the eastern coast of the United States. CHESAPEAKE BAY divides the state into two parts, the Eastern Shore and the Western Shore. The Eastern Shore shares the long Delmarva Peninsula with Delaware and Virginia.

Most of Maryland's 4.2 million people live on the Western Shore, especially along the coastal strip. BALTIMORE, an important port and Maryland's largest city, is located here, as is ANNAPOLIS, the state capital. The U.S. Naval Academy is at Annapolis. A narrow strip of the Western Shore extends far to the west into the Appalachian Mountains. Coal mining is an important activity in this region.

Sir Cecil Calvert, 2nd Baron Baltimore, founded the colony of Maryland in 1632. He named the colony for Queen Henrietta Marie of England, and the city of Baltimore was later named for his family. Many Roman Catholics settled in Maryland because of its reputation for religious tolerance. Maryland did not see much fighting during the American Revolution. After the war it gave land to the government for the nation's new capital, the DISTRICT OF COLUMBIA. It was during the War of 1812 that Francis Scott KEY wrote "The Star-Spangled Banner" while he was being held prisoner on a British ship in Baltimore Harbor. Although Maryland was a slave state, it stayed in the Union during the Civil War. In the years that followed, it continued to expand its industries and to prosper.

Today, Maryland is an important agricultural and industrial state. It is a major producer of poultry and

**Places of Interest**

- Maryland's capital, Annapolis, is a fascinating seaport and home of the U.S. Naval Academy.
- Baltimore, the state's largest city, has many attractions clustered around its redeveloped Inner Harbor.
- Antietam National Battlefield, near Sharpsburg, was the scene of a fierce Civil War battle.

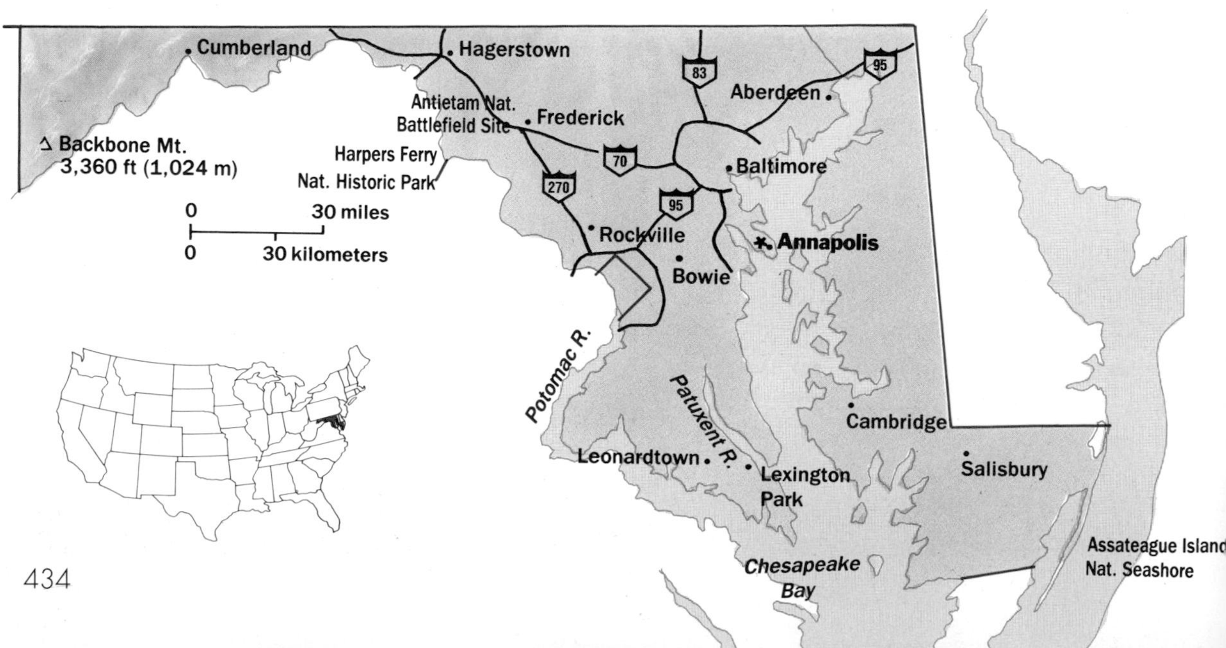

► *Baltimore is Maryland's largest city and its commercial center. In 1904 most of the downtown area was destroyed in the Great Baltimore Fire and had to be rebuilt.*

Maryland
**Capital:** Annapolis
**Area:** 12,407 sq mi (32,135 km$^2$). Rank: 42nd
**Population:** 4,781,468 (1990). Rank: 19th
**Statehood:** April 28, 1788
**Principal rivers:** Patapsco, Patuxent, Potomac, Susquehanna
**Highest point:** Backbone Mountain, 3,360 ft (1,024 m)
**Motto:** *Fatti Maschii, Parole Femine* (Manly Deeds, Womanly Words)
**Song:** "Maryland, My Maryland"

dairy products. Its major crops include corn, soybeans, and tobacco, which has been grown since Colonial times. Maryland crabs and oysters are prized as seafood. Maryland factories make food products, communications equipment, steel products, and other goods. The biggest employer, though, is the federal government. Many government workers in Washington, D.C., commute from their homes in Maryland.

▼ *The harbor of Annapolis provides a berth for many of the recreational boats cruising on Chesapeake Bay.*

# MASSACHUSETTS

The state of Massachusetts is located on the northeastern coast of the United States. It is the most populous of the New England states. More than 70 percent of the people live in the eastern part of the state, in the Greater BOSTON area. Boston is the capital and largest city. To the west, the Connecticut River flows north to south, creating rich farmland near the center of the state. And beyond the river, the beautiful Berkshire mountains rise along the western border with New York State.

Massachusetts has great historical importance. In 1620 the Pilgrims set up PLYMOUTH COLONY, the second permanent English settlement in the Americas. In the next century, the people of Massachusetts led the way in seeking American independence from Britain. The BOSTON MASSACRE and the BOSTON TEA PARTY took place here. So, too, did the battles of LEXINGTON AND CONCORD, where the opening shots of the American REVOLUTION were fired.

During the 1800s, the American Industrial Revolution began in Massachusetts. The first textile factory was in Waltham. Factories in the state soon produced textiles for the entire country. Today, Massachusetts is still a major industrial state. Its factories make computers and other high-tech products, as well as machinery, metal products, and books and other printed materials.

Massachusetts
**Capital:** Boston
**Area:** 10,555 sq mi (27,337 km$^2$). Rank: 44th
**Population:** 6,016,425 (1990). Rank: 13th
**Statehood:** February 6, 1788
**Principal rivers:** Charles, Connecticut, Merrimack
**Highest point:** Mt. Greylock, 3,491 ft (1,064 m)
**Motto:** *Ense petit placidam sub libertate quietam* (By the sword we seek peace, but peace only under liberty)
**Song:** "All Hail to Massachusetts"

► *An aerial view of the town of Provincetown on Cape Cod. The sandy beach in the foreground was where the Pilgrims first landed.*

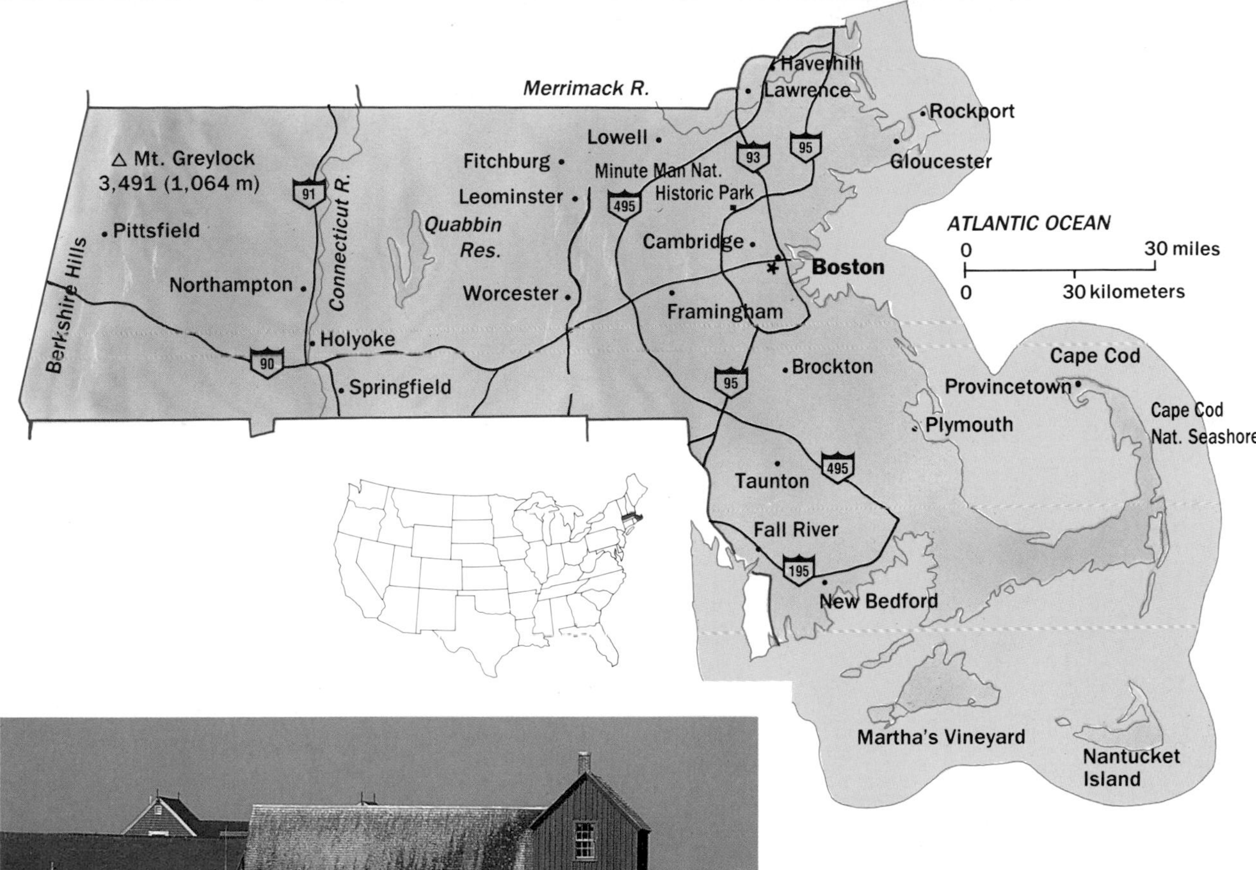


◀ *Rockport, located north of Boston, is a thriving fishing community. It also attracts many artists and tourists.*

Massachusetts' educational, cultural, and recreational facilities are known the world over. Harvard University, the first college in the American colonies, and Massachusetts Institute of Technology are among the nation's finest institutions of higher education. The Boston "Pops" Orchestra and the Boston Museum of Fine Arts draw many visitors to the state. So, too, do the many historic places, such as Paul REVERE's house, and the summer resorts along the Atlantic coast. The best known of these are the islands of Martha's Vineyard and Nantucket and the hook-shaped peninsula of CAPE COD which juts into the Atlantic Ocean.

**Places of Interest**

- The Freedom Trail, a walking tour of Revolutionary War sites, takes in many of Boston's attractions.
- Plimoth Plantation is a replica of the first Pilgrim settlement in Plymouth.
- The cobbled streets and old houses of Nantucket Island, south of Cape Cod, tell of its time as a whaling center.
- The Basketball Hall of Fame is located in Springfield, where the sport was invented.

## MASSASOIT

Massasoit (1580?–1661) was a chief of the Wampanoag Indians, a tribe that lived in what is now Massachusetts and Rhode Island. In 1621 he signed a treaty of peace and friendship with the Pilgrims of PLYMOUTH COLONY. Chief Massasoit helped the colonists learn how to survive in their new land. He is the chief who is supposed to have been at the first THANKSGIVING festival held by the Pilgrims in 1621.

Massasoit kept the peace for 40 years. But after his death, his son Metacomet, who was known as King Philip, attacked the colonists. A thousand colonists were killed during King Philip's War.

*▲ A statue of Massasoit stands in Plymouth, Massachusetts, where he helped the Pilgrims survive in the New World.*

*► Clouds shroud the top of the volcano Mauna Loa, which rises from a landscape made desolate by lava.*

## MAUNA LOA

The world's largest active VOLCANO, Mauna Loa is on the island of Hawaii, in Hawaii Volcanoes National Park. It is 13,677 feet (4,169 m) high. The dome is 75 miles (121 km) across at its widest point. The lava that has flowed out of it covers more than 2,000 square miles (5,120 km$^2$). In winter the volcano is often snowcapped. Since 1832 it has erupted on average every three and a half years. In 1855–1856 the eruption lasted a year and a half. Eruptions in 1926 and 1950 destroyed villages. The city of Hilo has been threatened by lava flows. In 1935, bombs were dropped by U.S. Army planes in the path of lava flowing toward the city.

**If measured from its base on the ocean floor, Mauna Loa would be taller than the tallest mountain on the surface of the earth. Mt. Everest in Asia rises 29,108 feet (8,872 m) above sea level. From its base to its peak Mauna Loa is about 30,000 feet (9,100 m).**

## MAYFLOWER *See* Plymouth Colony

## McCARTHY, Joseph

Joseph McCarthy (1908–1957) was a U.S. senator from Wisconsin. He first made headlines in 1950 by claiming that there were 205 Communists in the State Department. In those days many Americans thought that the government was not firm enough against Communist countries, and they were ready to believe that traitors were everywhere. McCarthy took advantage of these feelings. His investigating committee falsely accused hundreds of people—from top Army officers to college teachers—of disloyalty. Many careers were ruined. In 1954, the Senate stripped McCarthy of his power.

▲ *Joseph McCarthy's techniques gave the language a new word. "McCarthyism" has come to mean political accusations using sensational tactics and unsupported evidence.*

## McCORMICK, Cyrus

Cyrus Hall McCormick (1809–1884) invented the reaper. This grain-harvesting machine probably did more to improve agriculture than any other invention.

The son of a farmer, blacksmith, and inventor, McCormick spent much of his youth in his father's workshop. At the age of 22 he built his first reaper. But it had a number of defects. After 1837, McCormick set about improving his reaper. In 1841 he sold two reapers; three years later he sold 50; in 1847, after opening a factory in Chicago, he sold 800. After his death, his company merged with others to form the International Harvester Company.

**Cyrus McCormick's first horse-drawn mechanical reaper had one major fault—it was so noisy that slaves were needed to walk alongside to calm the frightened horses! An improved McCormick reaper became world famous. Emperor Napoleon III of France pinned the Legion of Honor to McCormick's chest. The French Academy of Sciences honored him as "having done more for the cause of agriculture than any other living man."**

◄ *The painter Andrew Wyeth captured the atmosphere of Cyrus McCormick's first demonstration of his reaping machine in 1831.*

# McKINLEY, William

William McKinley was the 25th president of the United States. During his term in office (1897–1901), the United States became a world power for the first time.

After serving in the Civil War, McKinley became a lawyer in his home state of Ohio. He served that state as a U.S. congressman and then as governor from 1892 to 1896. In 1896, McKinley ran for president. The main issue in the election was how to deal with the country's financial crisis. McKinley had the support of the businessmen, and he won the election after an exciting campaign. As president, his first action was to raise tariffs, or taxes, on foreign goods. He believed that this was necessary to protect American manufacturers.

▲ *The bombing of the battleship* Maine *triggered the Spanish-American War. The resulting American victory made McKinley very popular.*

Two years before McKinley's election, nearby Cuba had begun to revolt against the Spanish rulers of the island. After the U.S. battleship *Maine* was sunk in Havana Harbor in 1898, the United States went to war against Spain. The United States quickly won the war, known as the SPANISH-AMERICAN WAR. Cuba was given its independence. And the United States took control of the Spanish possessions of Puerto Rico, Guam, and the Philippines. Soon after, the United States also took over the Hawaiian islands. Suddenly the United States was a world power.

Some people said it was not right to take over these places. But McKinley had become very popular and he easily won the election in 1900. On September 6, 1901, at a reception held to honor him, a young man who hated all governments shot McKinley. He died eight days later.

William McKinley
**Born:** January 29, 1843, in Niles, Ohio
**Education:** Poland Seminary, Ohio
**Political party:** Republican
**Term of office:** 1897–1901
**Married:** 1871 to Ida Saxton
**Died:** September 14, 1901, in Buffalo, New York

## McLUHAN, Marshall

Marshall McLuhan (1911–1980) was a Canadian writer and educator. His special area of interest was modern communication. He believed that television, telephones, computers, and other communication *media* were changing the world and the way people think. He believed that the world was becoming a "global village," because communication was almost instantaneous. He also believed that the communication media themselves were even more important than the information they carried. He expressed this with the phrase "The medium is the message." McLuhan wrote several books, including *Understanding Media*.

▲ *Margaret Mead studied American Indians, as well as people of the Pacific Islands.*

## MEAD, Margaret

Margaret Mead (1901–1978) was a leading American anthropologist. (An anthropologist is a person who studies human beings and human cultures.) She spent some time living among the peoples of the Pacific islands, especially those in Samoa and New Guinea. Here she studied how the beliefs and customs of these societies affected the individuals, especially the children and young people. She described how people's behavior and even personalities varied according to the society they lived in. Mead's best-known books are *Coming of Age in Samoa* and *Growing Up in New Guinea*.

▼ *General George Meade commanded various military departments during his long career.*

## MEADE, George Gordon

General George Meade (1815–1872) was one of the leading Union commanders during the CIVIL WAR. His victory at the Battle of GETTYSBURG (1863) marked a turning point in the war.

Meade graduated from West Point in 1835 and became a military engineer. He served in the MEXICAN WAR (1846–1848). During the first year of the Civil War, Meade was engaged in building a fort near Washington, D.C. Beginning in 1862, he served with distinction in several important battles. His reputation as a stubborn fighter won him the command of the Army of the Potomac in 1863, just before the Battle of Gettysburg began. He kept this command until the end of the war, although from early 1864 onward he was subordinate to General Ulysses S. GRANT.

▲ *George Meany's attempts to rid the labor unions of corruption led to the expulsion of the powerful Teamsters Union from the AFL-CIO in 1957.*

## MEANY, George

George Meany (1894–1980) was one of the giants of the U.S. LABOR movement. In his early twenties, he was elected as a union official in New York. In 1934 he became president of the New York State Federation of Labor. The national labor movement split at this time. The two major organizations of unions were the American Federation of Labor (AFL) and the Congress of Industrial Organization (CIO). Meany rose through the ranks to become president of the AFL. His main aim as president was to reunite the AFL and the CIO. He achieved his goal in 1955. Today, some 13 million workers belong to the AFL-CIO.

## MEDICINE *See* Health

## MELVILLE, Herman

▼ *Herman Melville spent several years on whaling ships, where he heard tales of a great white whale. These stories led to his masterpiece* Moby Dick.

The novelist and poet Herman Melville (1819–1891) is best remembered for *Moby Dick*. Melville went to sea as a young man, and like many of his books, *Moby Dick* is about the sea. It is the story of a whaling voyage, but it also examines the nature of good and evil. Melville's early books were very popular. But his later, more difficult ones, including *Moby Dick*, were not. He became a customs inspector in New York and continued to write, but he found it difficult to support his family. He died in poverty. His last novel, *Billy Budd*, was not published until 1924, many years after his death. Melville is now considered one of America's greatest writers.

▲ *Memorial Day parades, such as this one in Churchtown, Pennsylvania, usually feature members of the armed forces.*

## MEMORIAL DAY 

Memorial Day is an American holiday in which the nation pays tribute to those who died in its wars. It was once called Decoration Day. Memorial Day was first observed after the Civil War. Today, the holiday honors those who have died in all of America's wars. It is a legal holiday in most states (schools, banks and most offices are closed) and takes place on the last Monday in May. Many towns and cities have parades. And many national cemeteries, where those who have served in the armed forces are buried, hold special ceremonies. On this day volunteers sell paper poppies and the money goes to help disabled veterans.

## MEMPHIS 

Memphis is the largest city in TENNESSEE, with a population of about 610,000 people. It is located in the southwestern corner of the state on the Mississippi River. Memphis is a major cotton and lumber port. Industrial and farm goods grown throughout much of the South pass through Memphis. Its huge stockyards make it the largest livestock center in the South. Its four bridges across the Mississippi link Tennessee with Arkansas. The famous Spanish explorer Hernando DE SOTO first saw the Mississippi from what is now Memphis. A Confederate stronghold during the Civil War, it was captured by Union forces in 1862.

▼ *Mud Island Park, a popular theme park, is connected to Memphis by a monorail.*

**The Amish farming communities of Pennsylvania and Ohio make up one of the strictest Mennonite groups. Old Order Amish are the most conservative. They dress in an old-fashioned plain style, and all men have beards. Old Order Amish ride in horse-drawn buggies instead of automobiles and ban electrical goods from their houses.**

## MENNONITES

Mennonites are members of a Protestant religious group that began in the early days of the Protestant Reformation, about 1530. They take their name from Menno Simons, one of their first leaders. Mennonites are peaceful and will not use weapons or swear oaths. They were persecuted for these beliefs. Many fled to America, the earliest settling in Pennsylvania in the 1600s. Forty percent of all Mennonites live in America. There are 9 main Mennonite churches with a combined membership of 364,739. The two largest, each with over 92,000 members, are the General Conference Mennonite Church and the Mennonite Church.

*► A group of Mennonites watch the parade of the Tulip Festival in Holland, Michigan.*

## MENOMINEES

The Menominee INDIANS are an Algonquian-speaking tribe from upper Michigan and Wisconsin. Long ago they were hunters, but wild rice was their staple food, and their name means "wild-rice people." During the War of 1812 the Menominees sided with the British, but they generally lived in peace with American settlers. In 1864 they were moved onto a reservation in Wisconsin. In 1961, however, the government wanted the Menominees to become integrated into society, so they took away their land's reservation status. This caused the Menominees great economic hardships. The government finally restored reservation status in 1974.

*▲ Menominee fisherman lured fish to the surface using blazing torches attached to their canoes. Then they would quickly spear them.*

## METHODISTS

The Methodists are one of the largest Protestant groups in America. There are eight Methodist churches with a total of about 12,650,000 members. The United Methodist Church is the largest group, with almost three quarters of the total. Methodists trace their roots to John Wesley, an 18th-century minister. His followers broke away from the more traditional Church of England. He stressed regular periods of Bible study and prayer. It was this serious method of study and sense of discipline that led to their being called "Methodists." Methodism grew quickly in the United States, largely because of the work of traveling preachers.

**John Wesley's Methodist movement began officially in England in 1738. But Wesley's inspiration came the year before during his brief role as chaplain to the colony of Georgia. There he met Christian missionaries who aimed to develop "spiritual holiness" with fewer ties to the Church of England.**

## MEXICAN HISTORY

Long before Christopher Columbus reached the New World in 1492, advanced American Indian cultures thrived in what is now Mexico. These included the Olmecs, Mayas, Toltecs, Zapotecs, and Aztecs. The Aztecs developed the most advanced civilization. They built large cities and were skilled at architecture and engineering. The Aztec Empire was at its peak in 1519, when the Spanish *conquistador* Hernán CORTÉS sailed from Cuba to Mexico with a force of 600 men. Cortés conquered the Aztecs in 1521 and established a Spanish colony called New Spain. It grew to include all of what is now Mexico and the American Southwest.

New Spain was governed for the benefit of Spain. Gold, silver, and crops were sent back to that country, but the Mexicans themselves, especially the Indians, were very poor. The Indians were treated as slaves. This situation lasted for 300 years. In 1821 the people of Mexico re-

**Mexicans celebrate September 16 as Independence Day. On that date in 1810, a priest, Miguel Hidalgo y Costilla, led the first Mexican uprising against the Spanish. He was excuted the following year, but Mexico gained its independence in 1821.**

◀ *The Temple of the Dwarf, at Uxmal on the Yucatán peninsula, was built by the Aztecs in the 1400s. The Aztec Empire covered most of Mexico at the time of the first Spanish* conquistadores *(conquerors) in 1519.*

▲ *This pottery figure is the work of the Olmec people.*

▼ *Toltec temples were guarded by stone statues of warriors.*

volted against Spanish rule, and their country became independent. But Mexico still faced many problems. American settlers in Texas revolted against Mexican rule in 1836 and declared their independence. Mexico lost even more land to the United States as a result of the MEXICAN WAR (1846–1848).

During this period, Mexico was ruled by dictators. In 1855, however, Benito Juárez overthrew the dictator Antonio López de Santa Anna. Civil war followed. In 1864, Emperor Napoleon III of France sent troops to Mexico and set up a short-lived monarchy. When it

### The Pre-Columbian Cultures of Mexico

The **Olmecs** established Mexico's first advanced civilization. They lived along the southern Gulf of Mexico coast and flourished between 800 B.C. and 400 B.C. They sculpted huge stone heads weighing many tons.

The **Zapotec** culture began to flourish around 100 B.C. They were farmers and developed a kind of hieroglyphic writing.

The **Mayan** culture was second only to that of the Aztecs. They lived in farming communities in southern Mexico. A peaceful people, they flourished between A.D. 250 and 950. They invented systems of writing and mathematics and developed a 365-day calendar.

The **Mixtecs** lived in southwestern Mexico, where their culture flourished between the 600s and 1300s. They had a system of hieroglyphic writing and made beautiful stone and metal carvings.

The **Toltecs** were a warrior people who flourished in central Mexico from the 900s to the 1100s. They worshiped the god Quetzalcoatl. The Toltecs dominated the Mayas but were in turn defeated by the Spanish.

The **Aztecs** of central Mexico created Mexico's most advanced Indian civilization. They were excellent artists and craftsmen and built stone buildings and temples. Their religion, based on human sacrifice, dominated their way of life. They were defeated by the Spanish, who built Mexico City on the site of the Aztec capital, Tenochtitlán.

collapsed in 1867, Juárez became president again. He built schools, encouraged the growth of industry, and tried in many ways to help the poor people of Mexico.

Porfirio Díaz was president of Mexico for most of the period from 1877 to 1911. Although he was a dictator, he did much to promote economic growth. But most of the people of Mexico continued to live in poverty. In 1910 a revolution broke out, led by Emiliano Zapata and Pancho Villa. Stability finally came to Mexico in 1917, when a new constitution was drafted. Among the many things guaranteed to the people were free education and workers' rights to form labor unions.

In 1929, what is now known as the Institutional Revolutionary Party was founded. Members of this party have ruled Mexico ever since. During the 1930s, the government distributed land to the peasants and greatly reduced the illiteracy rate. During and after World War II, the Mexican economy grew rapidly. This was helped along in the 1970s, when Mexico became a major exporter of oil. A strong middle class began to emerge at this time. But even today the peasants of Mexico remain poor. A hopeful sign for the future of Mexico is the growth of small industries, and the free-trade pact with the United States and Canada.

## MEXICAN WAR

The Mexican War (1846–1848) was fought between the United States and Mexico. It resulted from moves by the United States to expand its territory to include a vast region then belonging to Mexico, including California and New Mexico. Relations between the two countries had worsened because of the U.S. annexation of Texas in 1845. That same year, President James POLK attempted to buy California and New Mexico. This effort failed.

On April 25, 1846, American troops moved into a disputed area between Texas and Mexico. The Mexican army moved in also, and the United States declared war. In March 1847 an American force under General Winfield Scott landed at Veracruz, Mexico. Within a

**Highlights of Mexican History**

**1521** Hernán Cortés conquers the Aztec Empire and establishes the Spanish colony of New Spain.

**1821** Mexico declares its independence from Spain.

**1824** Mexico becomes a republic.

**1836** American settlers in Texas revolt and declare the independence of the Republic of Texas.

**1846–1848** The United States defeats Mexico in the Mexican War; Mexico loses its land north of the Rio Grande.

**1855** Benito Juárez becomes president and begins a reform movement.

**1864–1867** Maximilian, brother of Archduke Ferdinand of Austria, rules the short-lived Mexican Empire.

**1867** Benito Juárez becomes president again.

**1876–1911** Dictator Porfirio Díaz rules Mexico.

**1917** Mexico adopts a new constitution.

**1929** The Institutional Revolutionary Party is founded.

**1934** Land is distributed to poor farmers.

**1985** More than 7,000 people die in a Mexico City earthquake.

▼ *U.S. forces took Chapultepec, the last hills before Mexico City, on September 13, 1847. They had driven south from the United States, through territory that was claimed by both the United States and Mexico.*

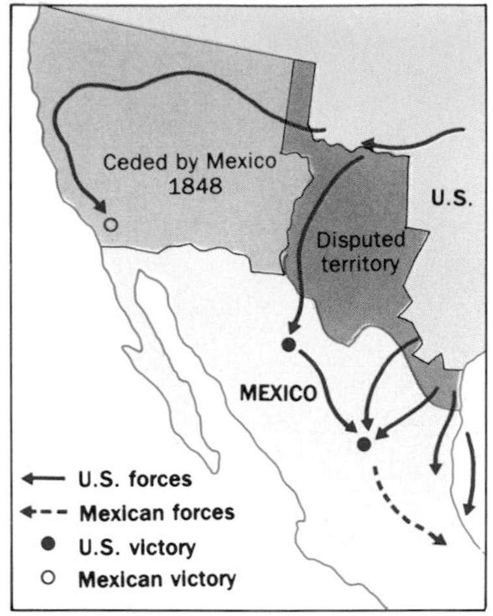


few weeks the capital, Mexico City, surrendered. The treaty of Guadalupe Hidalgo gave the United States all the territory now included in Utah, Nevada, and California, and parts of Arizona, New Mexico, Colorado, and Wyoming.

► *The Spanish influence remains in the architecture of Taxco, which is south of Mexico City.*

## MEXICO

Mexico is the southern neighbor of the United States. Its varied countryside contains tropical jungles, deserts, and the long Sierra Madre mountain ranges. Its population of 88 million is growing fast. Nearly 9 million Mexicans live in the capital, Mexico City. It has more people than any other city in the Western Hemisphere.

The official language of Mexico is Spanish. The country was Spain's first colony in the Americas. Spanish *conquistadores* (conquerors) arrived in Mexico in 1519. They fought and conquered the powerful Aztec Empire led by Emperor Montezuma. The colony of Mexico, called New Spain, was under Spanish rule until 1821, when it gained independence. In the 1840s, Mexico lost much of its land to the United States as a result of the MEXICAN WAR (1846–1848).

Mexico
**Capital:** Mexico City
**Official language:** Spanish
**Area:** 758,136 sq mi (1,963,564 km²)
**Population:** 92,400,000 (1992)
**Government:** Federal republic
**Highest point:** Orizaba, 18,701 ft (5,700 m)
**Principal rivers:** Balsas, Pánuco, Rio Grande, Santiago
**National Anthem:** *Mexicanos, al grito de guerra* (Mexicans to the Cry of War)

▲ *Mexico City is one of the world's largest and busiest cities. This photograph shows Avenida Lazaro Cardenas, with the Palace of Fine Arts in the foreground.*

Modern Mexico is a fascinating mixture of old and new. Peasants in remote areas still speak Nahuatl, the ancient Aztec language. At the same time, Mexico City faces the very modern problems of pollution and overcrowding. Mexico depends on its large oil reserves, farming, and tourism for its income.

**Mexico's population is growing rapidly. From about 15 million in 1910, the population grew to 34 million in 1960 and over 92 million in 1992. Mexico's population is expected to reach 109 million by the year 2000. Nearly half the people in Mexico are under 15 years of age.**

◀ *Corn is the staple crop of Mexican farms. These farmers in the Mesquital Valley are preparing cornstalks for cattle food.*

**A 1920s real estate boom in Miami crashed to a halt when a hurricane destroyed much of the city.**

## MIAMI

Miami is the second largest city in FLORIDA. With Miami Beach, it is one of the most popular tourist spots in the United States. Its warm climate and beautiful Atlantic coast beaches draw millions of visitors every year. Miami has a population of 358,000, and it continues to grow. Some of the new Miamians are northerners who have gone there to escape the cold. Hispanics, mainly Cubans, have also played a part in the rise of Miami. More than half of Miami's population is now Hispanic. There are Spanish TV stations, restaurants, and sports such as jai alai.

Miami was founded in 1870. It grew rapidly after 1895, when the first resorts were built.

▼ *Miami Beach is one of the country's most popular tourist resorts. Its hotels can provide rooms for more than 200,000 people.*

## MIAMIS

**The U.S. Army finally defeated the Miami Indians at the Battle of Fallen Timbers in 1794. The Miami defeat opened up much of the Ohio Valley to white settlers.**

The Miami INDIANS lived in what is now Ohio, Indiana, Illinois, and Wisconsin. Their name comes from the Chippewa word *omaumeg* (people who live on the peninsula). The Miamis spoke one of the Algonquian languages. In 1752 their chief Demoiselle was killed by Indians fighting for the French in the FRENCH AND INDIAN WAR. They fought against the British in the 1760s and against American settlers after the American Revolution. In the early 1790s, their chief Little Turtle organized a war. It took almost five years for the army to defeat them. During the War of 1812, the Miamis

◀ *The Miami Indians wore clothing made of hide and furs. To prepare the hide, it was cleaned, stretched, and rolled before being made into garments and moccasins.*

joined TECUMSEH and the Shawnees in support of the British. The Miamis were forced into the Indian Territory in the middle of the 19th century.

## MICHELSON, Albert

Albert Michelson (1852–1931) was a German-born American scientist. He lived in the United States from the age of two. He studied at the U.S. Naval Academy and in Germany.

In 1881, Michelson left the Navy and became a professor of physics at the University of Chicago. Most of his career was spent in developing instruments that would find exact measurements. He designed an instrument that could measure the speed of light with an accuracy that had never before been achieved. In 1907, Michelson was awarded the Nobel Prize for physics for his "optical precision instruments" and the investigations he carried out. He was the first American to win this prize.

**Albert Michelson's most famous invention was the *Michelson interferometer*, which he invented in 1881. With it he could measure light wavelengths to an accuracy of one millionth of an inch. He also used it to define the length of the standard meter to a previously impossible accuracy. In addition, Michelson invented the range finder and several other instruments for the U.S. Navy.**

## MICHENER, James

James Michener (1907–    ) is best known as the author of *Tales of the South Pacific*. This collection of stories, about American servicemen in the Solomon Islands during World War II, won him the Pulitzer Prize in 1948. And it inspired the Rodgers and Hammerstein musical *South Pacific*.

Michener was born in New York City and grew up in Pennsylvania. While in his teens he ran away from home. He later became an editor, and during World War II he was a naval historian in the Pacific.

Michener's novels, which include *Hawaii* and *Centennial*, are noted for their wealth of background detail about different regions and cultures.

▼ *James Michener has written detailed historical novels about Japan, Poland, and South Africa, as well as works on the United States and the Pacific islands.*

# MICHIGAN

Robin

Apple blossom White pine

The state of Michigan is in the eastern north-central part of the United States. It is made up of the Lower Peninsula and the Upper Peninsula, which are separated by Lake Michigan. The state also borders three other GREAT LAKES — Superior, Huron, and Erie.

Most of Michigan's 9.3 million people live in the Lower Peninsula. The state's major cities, DETROIT, Grand Rapids, Warren, Flint, and Lansing, are located in the southern part of the Lower Peninsula. This region is one of the United States' most important industrial areas. Detroit and the surrounding area is home to most

▲ *The Renaissance Center, a commercial and leisure development, has brightened the face of downtown Detroit.*

▼ *The Grand Traverse Peninsula, on the western edge of Michigan's Lower Peninsula, juts into Lake Michigan.*

Michigan
**Capital:** Lansing
**Area:** 96,810 sq mi (250,738 km$^2$). Rank: 11th
**Population:** 9,295,297 (1990). Rank: 8th
**Statehood:** January 26, 1837
**Principal rivers:** Detroit, Grand, Kalamazoo, St. Clair, St. Marys
**Highest point:** Mt. Curwood, 1,980 ft (604 m)
**Motto:** *Si quaeris peninsulam amoenam, circum spice* (If you seek a pleasant peninsula, look about you)
**Song:** "Michigan, My Michigan"

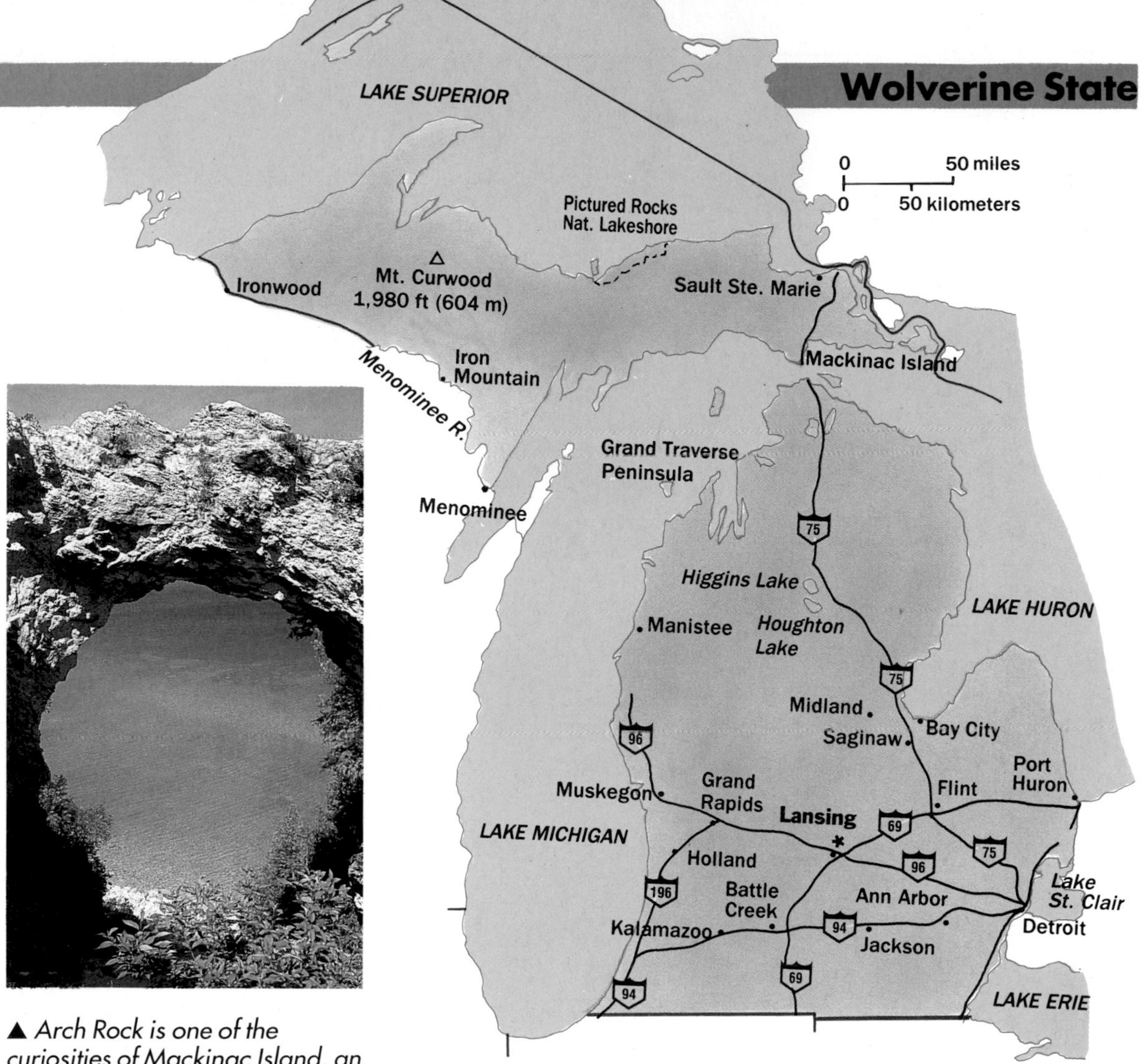


▲ *Arch Rock is one of the curiosities of Mackinac Island, an unspoiled attraction located between Lakes Michigan and Huron.*

U.S. automobile manufacturers. Factories here also produce motor vehicle parts, metal products, nonelectrical machinery, and food products. The northern part of the Lower Peninsula has fertile land. The farms here produce dairy products, corn, soybeans, wheat, and other crops. Cattle are also raised.

Michigan's Upper Peninsula is a beautiful land of lakes and pine forests. Sawmills and fishing provide some employment, but this is more an area for campers and vacationers. Long ago fur trappers caught so many wolverines here and in other parts of the state that Michigan's nickname is the Wolverine State.

The French were the first to settle Michigan. Father Jacques MARQUETTE founded Sault Ste. Marie, Michigan's first permanent settlement. And Antoine de la Mothe, Sieur de CADILLAC, founded what is now Detroit in 1701. Britain took over the territory in 1763. After the American Revolution, Michigan became a U.S. territory and then, in 1837, a state.

Places of Interest

- Detroit, Michigan's largest city, is the home of museums, four professional sports teams, and more than 200 parks.
- Pictured Rocks National Lakeshore, along Lake Superior, contains multicolored sandstone cliffs, beaches, and marshes.
- Mackinac Island, located between Michigan's Upper and Lower peninsulas, is a relaxing resort where automobiles are not allowed.
- Soo Canals, at Sault Ste. Marie, allow ships to pass between Lake Huron and Lake Superior.

## MICHIGAN, Lake *See Great Lakes*

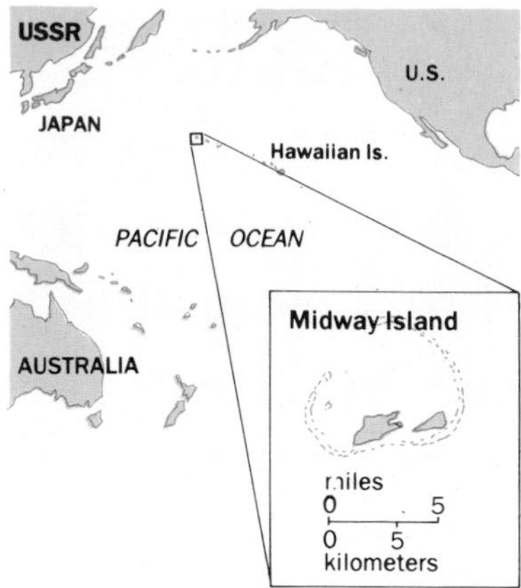


▲ *Midway Island is in the Pacific Ocean, 1,300 miles (2,090 km) northwest of Honolulu.*

► *The U.S.S.* Yorktown *was sunk by Japanese submarines during the Battle of Midway. By that time, however, the battle had swung in favor of the United States.*

## MIDWAY, Battle of

The Battle of Midway—on June 4–6, 1942—was one of the most important battles of World War II. It was the turning point of the war against the Japanese. The battle took place in the central Pacific, after carrier-based planes from the Japanese fleet had bombed the U.S.-controlled Midway Island. U.S. carrier-based planes sank four Japanese aircraft carriers and one heavy cruiser. The United States lost one carrier and one destroyer. But Midway Island was saved, and the Japanese advance in the Pacific was halted.

▼ *The Lake Shore Drive apartments in Chicago display Mies van der Rohe's clean and simple style of architecture.*

## MIES VAN DER ROHE, Ludwig

The architect Ludwig Mies van der Rohe (1886–1969) was born in Germany. From his father, a stonemason, he learned a great deal about craftsmanship and acquired a love of building materials. By the 1920s, Mies had become one of the most famous architects in Germany. He was one of the pioneers of modern architecture. This is the severely simple style of glass and steel buildings.

Mies was the head of the Bauhaus, a famous school of design, from 1930 to 1933. He left Nazi Germany in 1937 and settled in the United States. Here, he designed many important buildings. His work is known for its purity of line and lavish use of glass. Perhaps his most famous building is the Seagram Building in New York, on which he collaborated with Philip Johnson.

## MILLER, Arthur 

Arthur Miller (1915– ) is one of the foremost American playwrights. His plays often comment on social injustices. Because his father was financially ruined in the Depression, Miller had to work in a warehouse to put himself through the University of Michigan. His best-known play, *Death of a Salesman*, is a moving portrayal of a man having to face his own failure. It won a Pulitzer Prize. Miller's other plays include *The Crucible*, *A View from the Bridge*, and *After the Fall*. Miller's second wife was the actress Marilyn MONROE.

**Arthur Miller's marriage to the actress Marilyn Monroe provided some inspiration for his autobiographical play *After the Fall*.**

◀ *Arthur Miller's play* Death of a Salesman *was made into a powerful television drama starring Dustin Hoffman in the title role.*

## MILLER, Glenn 

Glenn Miller (1904–1944) was an American musical arranger, trombonist, and bandleader. After playing trombone in several well-known bands, Miller formed his first dance band in 1937, and a second a year later. By 1939 the Glenn Miller Orchestra was the most popular of all the big bands. During World War II, Miller was leader of the U.S. Army Air Force Band in Europe. In 1944, while flying from England to France, his plane disappeared. A movie about his life, *The Glenn Miller Story*, was released in 1953.

▼ *Glenn Miller's band was in constant demand for concerts and movies. Here they are seen on the set of the 1941 film* Sun Valley Serenade.

▲ *One of Robert Millikan's important discoveries was the measuring of the intensity of cosmic rays with balloons that carried special instruments.*

## MILLIKAN, Robert A.

Robert A. Millikan (1868–1953) was a very important American physicist and educator. He was born in Morrison, Illinois, and educated at Oberlin College and Columbia University. From 1896 until 1921 he taught physics at the University of Chicago. During this time he wrote some of the country's first textbooks on physics. He had a great ability to explain things clearly to students. In 1921 he took charge of the California Institute of Technology. There he measured the electrical charge of the electron and did research into cosmic rays. Millikan won the 1923 Nobel Prize for physics.

► *Milwaukee has become a major industrial center in the United States. Its modern buildings tower in the downtown area, which lies by the lakefront.*

## MILWAUKEE

Milwaukee is the largest city in WISCONSIN, with a population of more than 628,000. It is located in the southeast corner of the state, on Lake Michigan. Manufacturing and trade through the port provide most of the jobs in Milwaukee. Machinery, diesel engines, motorcycles, and outboard motors are important products. Milwaukee's most famous product is beer. Breweries have been a feature of Milwaukee since the first German settlers arrived in the mid-1800s. Milwaukee has had three Socialist mayors during this century.

**Milwaukee is one of the few major cities in the United States to have elected a Socialist mayor. Socialists held that post for a total of 38 years between 1910 and 1960. They pressed for labor reforms and more social benefits.**

## MINING INDUSTRY

Mining involves extracting useful minerals and other substances, such as fuels, from the earth. In the United States, about $170 billion worth of minerals and fuels are taken from the earth every year. The OIL INDUSTRY, which extracts crude oil and NATURAL GAS, and the coal mining industry account for about 86 percent of this total. Coal mining is one of the most important industries in the United States. The value of coal mined each year—about $22 billion—is about equal to the value of all industrial minerals and metals combined.

There are two major kinds of minerals, industrial minerals and metals. Industrial minerals include limestone, gravel, and sand, which are used to make cement. Other industrial minerals are phosphate rock, which is used in making fertilizer, and sulfur, which is used in many compounds. Among the valuable metals mined in the United States are copper, gold, iron ore, magnesium, silver, zinc, lead, and molybdenum.

**THE MOST IMPORTANT METALS MINED IN THE UNITED STATES (by value in $000s)**

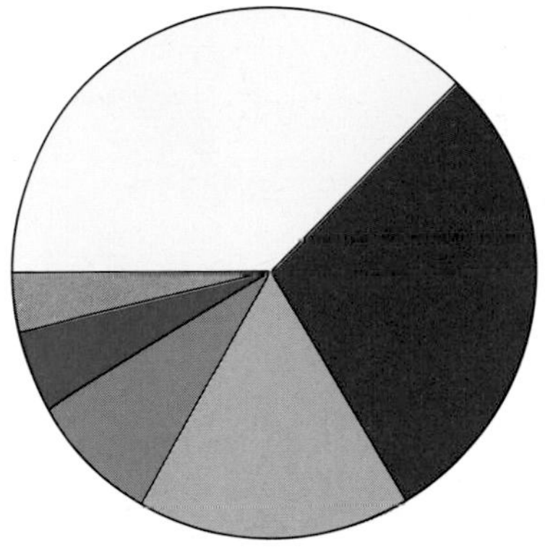

Zinc $847,000

Lead $481,000

Silver $336,000

**In one 1907 accident in West Virginia, 361 coal miners lost their lives. Disasters such as this tragedy led state and federal governmental bodies to impose strict safety regulations.**

◀ *An aerial view of a huge copper mine at Bingham Canyon, Utah. Copper ore may contain other minerals, such as nickel and gold. It then must be refined at mills and smelters.*

# MINNESOTA

Common loon

Pink and white lady's slipper

Norway pine

The state of Minnesota is located in the north-central part of the United States. It is noted for its great natural beauty. There are millions of acres of forests and thousands of lakes. Minnesota license plates have the inscription "10,000 Lakes," but there are probably more than 15,000.

The northeastern corner of Minnesota is on the edge of Lake Superior. Here, at the busy Great Lakes port of Duluth, timber and industrial goods are loaded aboard ships for transport along the St. Lawrence Seaway.

Minneapolis and St. Paul, which are known as the Twin Cities, are located in the southeastern part of the state. They straddle the Mississippi River, which has its source in Lake Itasca in northwestern Minnesota. Minneapolis is one of the most important manufacturing cities in the United States. Among the goods produced here are food products and electronic equipment. St. Paul is the state capital.

The prairies of southern Minnesota are dotted with farms. Corn, soybeans, sugar beets, and wheat and other grains are among the state's most important crops. Dairy products are also important, and Minnesota is sometimes known as the Bread and Butter State. Other Minnesota products include pulp for paper and iron

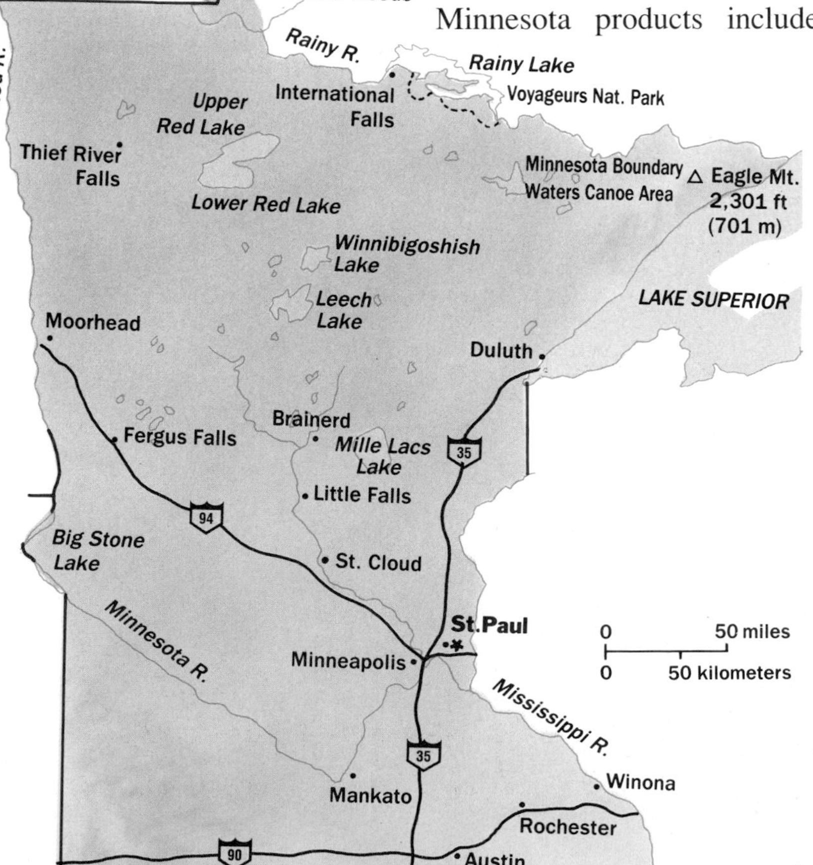


Minnesota

**Capital:** St. Paul
**Area:** 86,943 sq mi (225,182 km²). Rank: 12th
**Population:** 4,375,099 (1990). Rank: 20th
**Statehood:** May 11, 1858
**Principal rivers:** Minnesota, Mississippi, Rainy, Red River of the North
**Highest point:** Eagle Mountain, 2,301 ft (701 m)
**Motto:** *L'Etoile du Nord* (The Star of the North)
**Song:** "Hail! Minnesota"

ore. More than two thirds of the iron ore mined in the United States comes from Minnesota.

The part of Minnesota that is east of the Mississippi came under U.S. control in 1783. The land to the west came under U.S. control as a result of the LOUISIANA PURCHASE. Minnesota Territory was formed in 1849, and statehood was achieved in 1858. During the second half of the 1800s, many Scandinavian people from Norway, Sweden, Denmark, and Finland settled in Minnesota to work at mining and lumbering. In the 1900s, thousands of southern blacks moved there to work in the factories. Poles, Hispanics, Germans, Asians, and others who have immigrated to the state have added to Minnesota's ethnic mix.

► *The climate and soil of Minnesota were well suited to the Scandinavian farmers who settled there.*

**Places of Interest**

- Minnesota's capital, St. Paul, and its largest city, Minneapolis, are on opposite banks of the Mississippi River.
- Boundary Waters Canoe Area, north of Eagle Mountain, is reserved for canoeing.
- International Falls, on the Canadian border, frequently records the lowest temperatures in the United States.

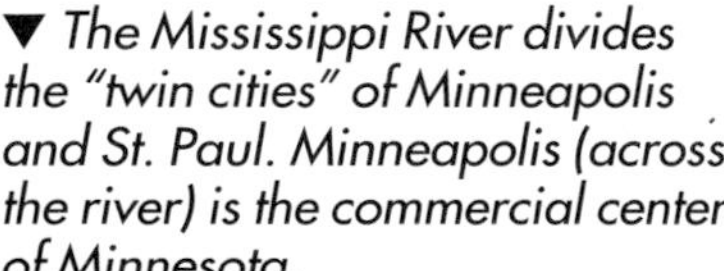

▼ *The Mississippi River divides the "twin cities" of Minneapolis and St. Paul. Minneapolis (across the river) is the commercial center of Minnesota.*

▼ *An ice sculpture presides over the St. Paul Winter Carnival, an annual event that is one of the state's major tourist attractions.*

▼ *Peter Minuit bought the island of Manhattan from the Canarsee Indians. They preferred the Dutch beads to gold or silver.*

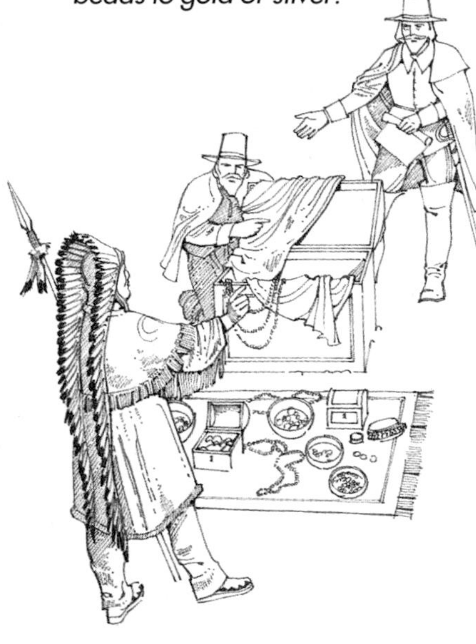

## MINUIT, Peter 

Peter Minuit (1580?–1638) was the Dutch colonial official who bought Manhattan Island from the Indians.

Minuit arrived in the colony of New Netherland in 1626. A few months later he was appointed its director general. Minuit then persuaded the local Indian chiefs to sell him Manhattan for an assortment of trinkets valued at about $24. Minuit built a fort on the southern tip of the island, establishing the settlement of New Amsterdam. After serving as its governor for four years, he was ordered back to Holland by the Dutch West India Company. In 1638, Minuit helped Swedish settlers to found a colony in what is now Delaware. That same year, he died in a hurricane during a voyage to the West Indies.

## MINUTEMEN 

The minutemen were colonial volunteers during the American REVOLUTION. They were said to be prepared to fight "at a minute's notice."

The first groups of minutemen were formed in Massachusetts. An act of the Provincial Congress that reorganized the Massachusetts militia stated that one-third of the regiments were to consist of minutemen. Some of these volunteers fought in the battles of LEXINGTON AND CONCORD in 1775. Other colonies also established companies of minutemen on the recommendation of the Continental Congress. When regular armies were formed, the minutemen were disbanded.

**The term "minutemen" was revived during World War I. It referred to volunteer speakers who addressed public gatherings to urge the purchase of the government's Liberty Bonds.**

► *During the American Revolution, colonists who had volunteered as minutemen dropped whatever they were doing to fight alongside the militia.*

*◀ Spanish Catholic missionaries were the first Europeans to settle California.*

**European missionaries were also important explorers in North America. Jacques Marquette, a Roman Catholic priest from France, traveled down much of the Mississippi River. A Spanish priest, Father Junípero Serra, founded the first white settlements in California.**

## MISSIONARIES

The earliest missionaries in North America were sent from Europe to convert the Indians to Christianity. Most of them were Roman Catholic priests from Spain and France. The Spanish were the first in the field. They established missions in Florida as early as the 1570s. Later more Spanish missions were established in the Southwest, including Franciscan outposts along the California coast between San Francisco and San Diego.

The French became active in the 1600s. They concentrated in the Great Lakes area and along the Mississippi River, where such missionaries as Jacques MARQUETTE were also pioneering explorers.

In the 1800s, American Protestant missionary groups sent men and women to bring the faith to Indians in the West and Polynesians in Hawaii. Today, American missionaries, both Protestant and Roman Catholic, are active in other countries.

*▼ Father Junípero Serra founded the mission of San Juan Capistrano, in San Juan Capistrano, California.*

**Missions to Visit**

- San Antonio de Valero is better known as the Alamo, the site of a famous battle in 1836. It is located in San Antonio, Texas.
- Santa Barbara is a beautiful Spanish mission in Santa Barbara, California
- San José was founded by the Franciscan missionaries in the early 1700s. It is now part of San Antonio Missions Historical Park, San Antonio, Texas.

# MISSISSIPPI

The Deep South state of Mississippi is located on the Gulf of Mexico. It has long, hot, humid summers, but the mild climate at other times of the year attracts many visitors to the beautiful beaches at Biloxi and other places along the Gulf coast.

The state is named for the Mississippi River, which forms the western border. The French were the first Europeans to establish a colony in Mississippi, in 1699. The area later came under English and then Spanish rule. It became a U.S. territory in 1789 and a state in 1817. Mississippi's economy was then based on cotton and the use of black slaves to work the cotton plantations. As the American CIVIL WAR approached in 1861, Mississippi became the second Southern state to secede from the Union. Jefferson DAVIS, a Mississippian, became president of the Confederate States of America. Many Civil War battles were fought in Mississippi, and the state suffered great hardships.

Mississippi remained a poor agricultural state after the war. And despite being freed, Mississippi blacks were still denied their basic rights. It wasn't until the CIVIL RIGHTS movement of the 1960s that blacks began to achieve equality with whites in education and other areas. Today, Black Americans make up about a third of Mississippi's population, a higher percentage than in any other state.

Mississippi
**Capital:** Jackson
**Area:** 48,434 sq mi (125,443 km²). Rank: 32nd
**Population:** 2,573,216 (1990). Rank: 31st
**Statehood:** December 10, 1817
**Principal rivers:** Big Black, Mississippi, Pearl, Yazoo
**Highest point:** Woodall Mountain, 806 ft (245 m)
**Motto:** *Virtute et Armis* (By Valor and Arms)
**Song:** "Go Mis-sis-sip-pi"

► *Stanton Hall, in Natchez, is a stately reminder of how plantation owners lived in Mississippi before the Civil War.*

**Places of Interest**

- The Old Capitol Building in Jackson houses the fascinating Mississippi State Historical Museum.
- Many visitors board the *Delta Queen*, an old-fashioned riverboat that stops at ports along the Mississippi River.
- Gracious mansions near Natchez are reminders of the life that plantation owners led before the Civil War.
- The Gulf port of Biloxi is famous for its seafood.

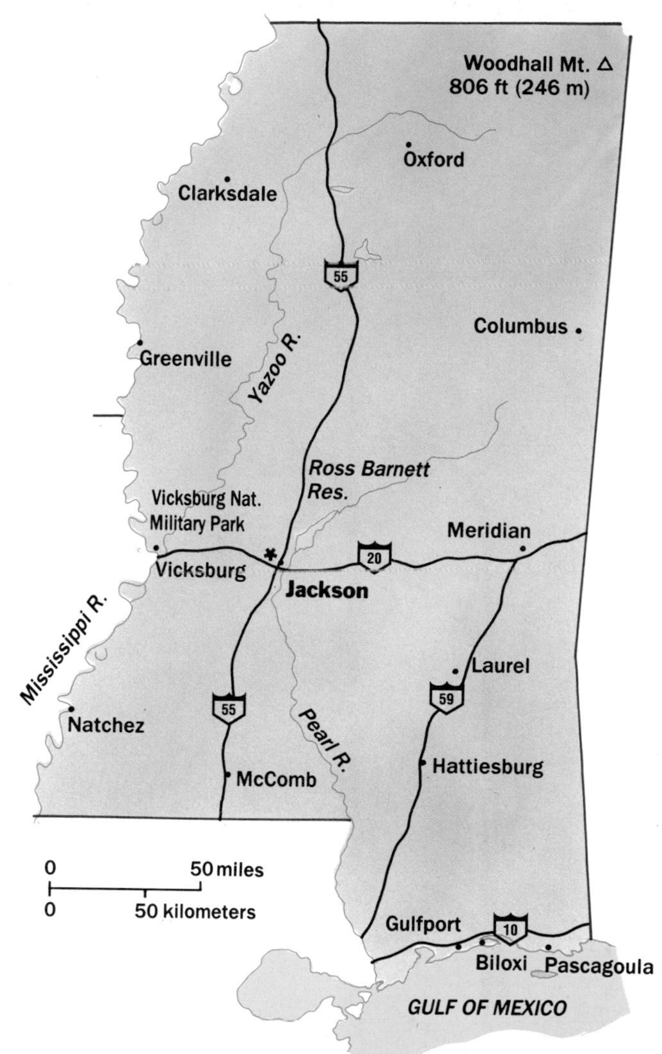

◀ *Peaceful moments can be spent fishing in Percy Quinn State Park.*

▼ *The military cemetery in Vicksburg is the final resting place for soldiers who died in one of the Civil War's bloodiest battles.*

Beginning in the 1930s, Mississippians worked hard to bring industry to their state. The discovery of oil at that time helped considerably. Petroleum refining is an important industry today. Textiles, transportation equipment, and electric and electronic goods are among the products produced in Mississippi factories. Jackson, the largest city and capital, is a center for the manufacture of furniture and chemical products. And cotton is still important, though many farms also grow rice, soybeans, and other crops. Fishing is also an important industry in Mississippi.

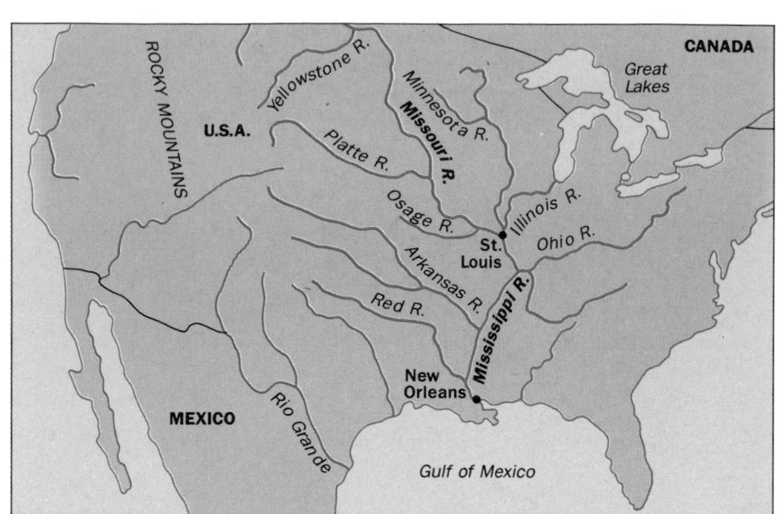


► *The Mississippi–Missouri river system and its major tributaries.*

**The Mississippi River is the longest river in the United States and has inspired poets, writers, and composers. Mark Twain used his own experiences to write *Life on the Mississippi.***

## MISSISSIPPI-MISSOURI RIVER SYSTEM 

The Mississippi-Missouri RIVER system is one of the longest waterways in the world. The Missouri, the second longest river in the United States, originates in the Rocky Mountains of southwestern Montana. The Mississippi, the country's longest river, originates in Lake Itasca in northwestern Minnesota. The Missouri, which flows in a generally southeastern direction, meets the Mississippi just north of St. Louis, Missouri. From here the Mississippi flows south to the Gulf of Mexico 100 miles (160 km) south of New Orleans, Louisiana. The course of the river is sometimes straight, sometimes meandering, and it forms many loops and bends. At its mouth, deposits of sediment have formed a delta, which extends farther into the Gulf of Mexico each year.

The Mississippi and Missouri rivers and their tributaries drain the heartland of the United States, from the Rockies in the west to the Appalachian Mountains in the east. Today there are 14 dams on the Missouri and another 60 on its tributaries. The Mississippi is dammed above St. Louis, and the Ohio, a major tributary, has many dams. Some provide water for irrigation and HYDROELECTRIC POWER. But most provide flood control. In 1993, however, the system of dams and levees failed, and the area suffered devastating floods.

Before the arrival of Europeans, many different Indian tribes lived along the two rivers. The Ojibways gave the Mississippi its name *Missi Sipi*, which means "Great River." The Missouri was named after the Missouri Indians. Settlers later nicknamed it the Big

Major Ports

Missouri River
Kansas City, Missouri
Omaha, Nebraska
Sioux City, Iowa

Mississippi River
Minneapolis–St. Paul, Minnesota
St. Louis, Missouri
Memphis, Tennessee
Baton Rouge, Louisiana
New Orleans, Louisiana

Major Tributaries of the Mississippi River
Minnesota River
Illinois River
Missouri River
Ohio River
Arkansas River
Red River

Muddy, because there is so much mud in the river.

The Spanish explorer Hernando DE SOTO was the first European to see the Mississippi. In 1541 he crossed the river near present-day Memphis, Tennessee. More than a century later, in 1673, the French explorers Jacques MARQUETTE and Louis Jolliet explored the upper reaches of the Mississippi as well as the mouth of the Missouri. The French explorer Robert Cavalier, Sieur de LA SALLE, traveled down the river in 1682. He went from Illinois to the Gulf of Mexico and claimed the entire area for France. The Frenchman Pierre Gaultier de Varennes, Sieur de La Verendrye, explored the upper Missouri in 1738.

▲ *The importance of the Mississippi-Missouri River System as a trade route was increased when steamboats were developed in the early 1800s.*

After the British defeated the French in the FRENCH AND INDIAN WAR (1763), the Mississippi formed the boundary between British lands to the east and Spanish lands to the west. The river formed the United States' western boundary after independence. With the LOUISIANA PURCHASE of 1803, the Mississippi and Missouri became American rivers. LEWIS AND CLARK explored both river basins during their historic expedition into the Louisiana Territory in 1804–1806. Soon the rivers became transportation routes for fur traders and for pioneer settlers heading west. Steamboats appeared on the rivers after about 1819, and the Mississippi and lower Missouri saw a boom in commerce.

Today, river transportation is not as important as it was in the past. However, more than 40 percent of all the freight shipped on the inland waterways of the United States is still shipped on the Mississippi and the lower Missouri.

▼ *Most freight on the Mississippi River is carried on large barges. Agricultural products, coal, and steel make up most of the cargo transported along the Mississippi.*

Missouri is an important farming and industrial state in the Midwest. Its history and economy have been shaped by the United States' two greatest rivers, the Mississippi and the Missouri. The Mississippi forms the state's eastern border. The Missouri forms its northwestern border. At Kansas City, Missouri's largest city, the Missouri River turns eastward and flows across the center of the state. It joins the Mississippi just north of ST. LOUIS. St. Louis, a busy river port, is known as the Gateway to the West.

The United States acquired Missouri from France in 1803 as part of the LOUISIANA PURCHASE. Soon, the invention of the steamboat and the use of these boats on the Mississippi and Missouri rivers made Missouri a center of commerce. In 1821, Missouri was admitted to the Union as a slave state under the terms of the Missouri Compromise. This compromise also brought Maine into the Union and thus kept the number of slave states and free states equal. Missouri remained loyal to the Union during the Civil War.

Today Missouri is a prosperous state with a diverse economy. Its factories make everything from aircraft, spacecraft, and cars to food and dairy products and beer. The McDonnell Douglas Aircraft Company is the state's largest employer. And Anheuser-Busch, the St. Louis–based maker of Budweiser and other beers, is the largest brewery in the world. Soybeans, corn, and other crops are grown on Missouri farms. Missouri leads all other states in lead production and is number two in zinc production. The scenic Ozark Mountains attract many vacationers.

Missouri
**Capital:** Jefferson City
**Area:** 69,709 sq mi (180,546 km²). Rank: 21st
**Population:** 5,117,073 (1990). Rank: 15th
**Statehood:** August 10, 1821
**Principal rivers:** Mississippi, Missouri, Osage
**Highest point:** Taum Sauk Mountain, 1,772 ft (540 m)
**Motto:** *Salus populi suprema lex esto* (The welfare of the people shall be the supreme law)
**Song:** "Missouri Waltz"

◀ *Dillard Mill is typical of Missouri's countryside, where traditional industries still employ a rural work force.*

▲ *The stainless steel Gateway Arch in St. Louis was built in 1965. Its height of 630 feet (192 m) makes it the tallest monument in the United States.*

▲ *Lake of the Ozarks is a popular recreational resort in the center of the state.*



**Places of Interest**

- The Gateway Arch is a monument to the pioneers who passed through St. Louis on their way west.
- Mark Twain Museum and Home, in Hannibal, is the childhood home of the famous writer.
- The Ozark Plateau in southern Missouri is an unspoiled region of caves, lakes, and forests.

▲ *At his court-martial, Billy Mitchell argued that his accusers displayed "criminal negligence" of U.S. defense interests because they did not appreciate air power.*

## MITCHELL, Billy

William "Billy" Mitchell (1879–1936) was a general in the U.S. Army. He was a combat pilot in WORLD WAR I and recognized the importance of air power. At that time pilots were under the control of the Army and the Navy. After the war, Mitchell fought to increase U.S. air power. He also wanted the air forces to be separate from the Army. His superiors did not agree with him, but Mitchell kept on fighting for this. Eventually the Army court-martialed him. Mitchell resigned from the Army. During World War II, the Army realized Mitchell had been right about the need to build a powerful U.S. air force, and he was posthumously awarded the Congressional Medal of Honor.

## MOCKINGBIRD

The mockingbird is found only in the Western Hemisphere. In the United States it lives mainly in the South. The North American species is the common, or northern, mockingbird. The bird has a loud, beautiful song. It imitates the songs of many other birds, which is the reason for its name. About 10.5 inches (27 cm) long, the mockingbird builds its nest in shrubs and low trees. It eats seeds, insects, and fruits.

▼ *The Mohawk Chief Joseph Brant was educated by the British, and he fought for them in the French and Indian War and the American Revolution.*

## MOHAWKS

The Mohawks are an IROQUOIS tribe who originally lived in eastern New York State and Ontario. They were one of the five tribes that formed the League of Five Nations (also called the Iroquois Confederacy). They fought over control of the fur trade with the MOHICANS. The two tribes made peace in 1664. The British sought their help in Queen Anne's War in the early 1700s. During the FRENCH AND INDIAN WAR, Mohawks under Chief Hendrick fought for the British against the French. In 1755 they won the battle of Lake George, but their chief was killed. In that battle, Mohawks fought against other members of the Iroquois Confederacy. During the American REVOLUTION, the Mohawks under Chief Joseph BRANT fought for the British. After the war, Brant and his fighters were given land in Canada. Many of their descendants live there today, as well as in Brooklyn, Buffalo, and Detroit.

## MOHICANS

The Mohican (or Mahican) Indians were a confederacy of Algonquian-speaking Indians. They originally lived between the upper Hudson River valley and Lake Champlain in New York State. In the 1600s, during the time of Dutch settlement, the Mohicans often fought with the Mohawks, their Iroquois neighbors, over the rights to hunt and sell fur in the area. This dispute was called the Beaver Wars. After being defeated in the early 1700s, most Mohicans migrated. Today a few hundred live in Wisconsin, where they call themselves Stockbridge Indians. The Mohicans have achieved a lasting fame in James Fenimore COOPER's *The Last of the Mohicans.*

▲ *The Mohicans prayed to Mother Earth to ensure success in cultivating crops and in hunting and battle.*

## MOJAVE DESERT

The Mojave, or Mohave, Desert is a dry region in southeastern California, covering about 25,000 square miles (65,000 km²). In the summer the temperature can reach 125°F (52°C). The Mojave receives less than 5 inches (13 cm) of rain a year. After the rains, many plants flower briefly. Otherwise, the principal plants are cacti, creosote bush, mesquite, and Joshua trees. Joshua Tree National Monument is located in the Mojave Desert. Irrigation makes it possible to grow alfalfa in parts of the desert, and cattle grazing is common in the northern part.

▼ *Boron and other minerals are mined in the Mojave Desert.*

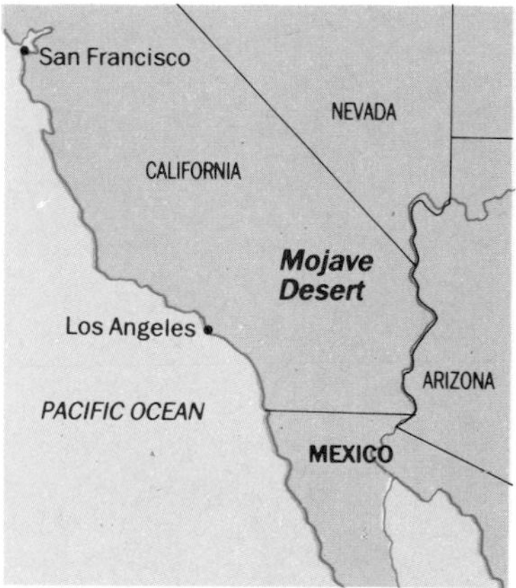


## MOLES AND SHREWS

Moles and shrews are small, burrowing animals that live underground. Almost blind, the mole has velvety fur and long claws. The common, or eastern, mole is found east of the Rockies. The star-nosed mole is found in the East. The smallest mole is the American shrew mole. Only 5 inches (13 cm) long, including the tail, it is found in the Northwest.

▼ *The short-tailed shrew poisons its prey with its saliva. Moles are common in eastern North America. The star-nosed mole (far left) has a ring of 22 tentacles on its nose. These help it search for food.*

**Short-tailed shrew**

**Star-nosed mole**

**Eastern mole**

**Masked shrew**

▼ *Some mollusks, such as the octopus, have no shell. Others, such as the abalone and snail, have a hard shell to protect their soft bodies.*

Like the mole, the shrew has a long, pointed snout. It looks somewhat like a mouse. A shrew can eat more than three times its weight each day. Many kinds of shrews give off an unpleasant odor when they are attacked. The masked shrew is found across northern North America. The northern water shrew is one of the largest shrews. The pygmy shrew is the smallest.

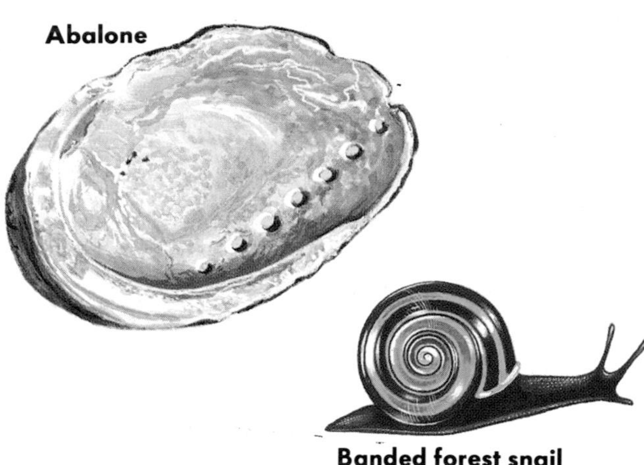


**Octopus**

## MOLLUSKS 

A mollusk is an animal with no backbone. Most mollusks have a hard shell to protect their soft bodies. One important class of mollusks includes limpets, snails, slugs, and whelks. Squid and octopus make up another important class.

The most commercially valuable mollusks are the bivalves—mollusks with two shells. They live in shallow salt water or fresh water. Bivalves include oysters, clams, mussels, and scallops. There are edible types of all these. The oyster industry is one of the most important U.S. fishing industries. The Virginia oyster is the most commercially important mollusk in the United States. Oysters are cultivated in oyster farms on the Pacific and Atlantic coasts and in the Gulf of Mexico. Soft shell clams and scallops are also cultivated. The dingy white shell is the most valuable Atlantic clam.

▼ *Wampum was made from shell beads that were woven together to make decorative belts or necklaces. Because coins were rare, wampum was used for money in Colonial times.*

## MONEY 

Before the American Revolution, colonists used English, French, Dutch, and Spanish coins to buy and sell goods. If these were not available they even used Indian beads, tobacco, and beaver skins. After independence, banks in different states issued money, but sometimes they would refuse money from another state. National banks were created and these came under control of the newly formed Federal Reserve System in 1913.

The Federal Reserve System acts as the central bank of the United States. It guarantees all U.S. paper money, called notes. Coins, produced at U.S. mints, are controlled by the U.S. Treasury Department. A special printing process is used to produce notes. Secret formulas are used for the paper and ink. About $20 billion of paper money is produced this way each year. Most of the money replaces old notes. A dollar bill has an average lifetime of 17 months.

▲ *The U.S. dollar as it appears today. George Washington appears on the front of the bill; the Great Seal appears on the back.*

## MONITOR AND MERRIMAC

The *Monitor* and *Merrimac* were two ironclad ships. The *Monitor*, a Union ship, and the *Merrimac*, a Confederate ship, fought the first battle between ironclad vessels on March 8, 1862. This CIVIL WAR battle took place at Hampton Roads, Virginia, at the mouth of the James River. The *Merrimac*—a U.S.-built ship that the Confederacy had taken and renamed the *Virginia*—was the larger of the two. But the *Monitor*, which was described as resembling "a cheesebox on a raft," was easier to maneuver. Neither ship was able to sink the other during the four-hour battle. But both sides found the results encouraging. The South believed that it now had a chance to break the Northern blockade of its ports—a belief that proved false.

**The *Monitor* sank off Cape Hatteras, North Carolina, in 1862. It was rediscovered by a team of archaeologists using special underwater equipment in 1973, but the ship was in too fragile a condition to be raised. Only its anchor was recovered.**

▼ *Following the battle between the* Monitor *and the* Merrimac, *the U.S. government ordered the building of more ironclad ships.*

# MONROE, James

**James Monroe**
**Born:** April 28, 1758, in Westmoreland County, Virginia
**Education:** College of William and Mary
**Political party:** Democratic-Republican
**Term of office:** 1817–1825
**Married:** 1786 to Elizabeth Kortright
**Died:** July 4, 1831, in New York City

James Monroe was the fifth president of the United States. Among his many accomplishments was the MONROE DOCTRINE, an important statement of U.S. foreign policy. It warned European countries not to try to set up new colonies in the Americas and not to interfere in the affairs of the countries in the Americas.

Monroe fought in the American REVOLUTION and later was a delegate from Virginia to the CONTINENTAL CONGRESS. As a U.S. senator in the early 1790s, he opposed the Federalists, who wanted a strong central government. Monroe later was a minister to France, Spain, and Great Britain and governor of Virginia. He also helped bring about the LOUISIANA PURCHASE in 1803 and was secretary of state and secretary of war under President James MADISON.

► *The Monroe Doctrine was the most important accomplishment of James Monroe's first term as president.*

Monroe was elected president in 1816. He served from 1817 until 1825, during a period of peace and prosperity known as the "era of good feeling." From the very beginning of his presidency there was a new feeling of national unity. In 1818, Missouri applied to join the Union as a slave state. This threatened to divide the nation, but in 1820 Congress passed the Missouri Compromise. Missouri was admitted as a slave state, and Maine as a free state. This compromise ended the nation's first crisis over the issue of slavery.

During Monroe's presidency, the United States and Britain agreed to reduce their armaments on the Great Lakes and later removed them altogether. The U.S.-Canadian border was established along the 49th parallel as far west as the Oregon Territory. In 1819, Florida was acquired from Spain. Monroe was re-elected in 1820.

▼ *Elizabeth Monroe became the first First Lady of the present White House in 1817. The British had burned the original White House during the War of 1812.*

◀ *Marilyn Monroe (with ukulele) displayed a talent for comedy in the movie* Some Like It Hot. *In earlier movies, she had played the role of "dumb blonde."*

## MONROE Marilyn

Marilyn Monroe (1926–1962), who was born in Los Angeles as Norma Jean Baker, was a famous movie actress. She studied with Lee Strasberg of the Actor's Studio in New York. Monroe had a gift for playing light comedy roles in films such as *Gentlemen Prefer Blondes* and *Some Like It Hot*. She also showed that she had fine dramatic talent in *Bus Stop* and in her last movie, *The Misfits*. She was married to the baseball star Joe DiMaggio and the playwright Arthur MILLER.

**Marilyn Monroe was working as a paint sprayer in a defense plant when she was discovered in 1944 by an army photographer. She became a photographer's model. In 1946, Monroe signed a contract with Fox Studios and went on to become one of the cinema's greatest stars.**

## MONROE DOCTRINE

The Monroe Doctrine of 1823 was a statement of foreign policy by President James MONROE. It was addressed to the European powers and declared that the American continents were "not to be considered as subjects for future colonization." It also stated that the United States would not intervene in European affairs and that European governments should not intervene in the affairs of the American nations. The doctrine was mainly a response to threats that France and Spain might attempt to retake the nations of Latin America, which had just won their independence, and that Russia might renew its claims along the Pacific coast.

Over the years the doctrine has been interpreted in various ways and, in expanded form, has even been used to justify U.S. intervention in Latin America.

**Some Landmarks of the Monroe Doctrine**

1824: U.S. announces its opposition to Russian expansion of North America.
1881: Monroe Doctrine extended to protect Hawaiian Kingdom.
1904: "Roosevelt Corollary" claims for United States a "policeman's" role in Central America.
1912: Doctrine extended to protect against non-European countries.
1928: U.S. drops Roosevelt Corollary; renews promises to protect Latin America.

# MONTANA

Ponderosa pine

Bitterroot

Western meadowlark

Montana, located in the northwestern United States, is the fourth largest state. But with a population of only 803,655, it has fewer people than many U.S. cities. Because Montana has wide open spaces and great natural beauty, one of its nicknames is Big Sky Country.

The name Montana comes from a Spanish word meaning "mountainous." The Rocky Mountains run through the western part of the state. The rest of the state is made up of the gently rolling northern Great Plains. The Missouri and the Yellowstone are Montana's two most important rivers.

Montana is an important grower of barley, wheat, and sugar beets. Cattle ranching is also important, as is mining. Another nickname, the Treasure State, reflects the fact that gold and silver were discovered there in the mid-1800s. Gold and silver are still mined, as is copper. The state is an important producer of lumber and wood products. It also has large reserves of oil and coal.

Tourism is important in Montana. Hunters, fishermen, and campers are among the vacationers who come to Montana. The southwest boundary of the state borders Yellowstone National Park. Glacier National Park, on Montana's border with Canada, has some of the country's most spectacular mountain scenery.

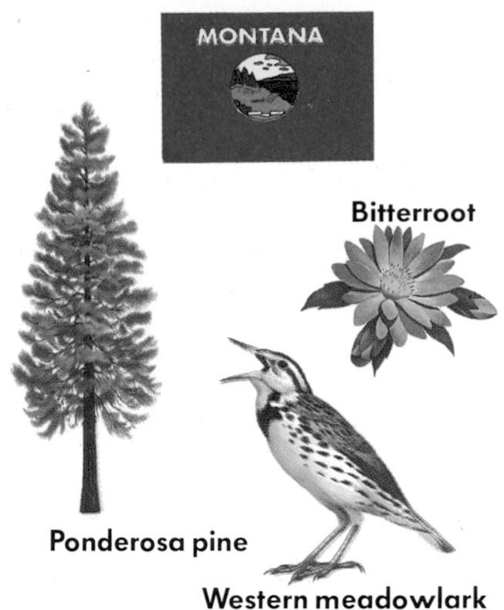

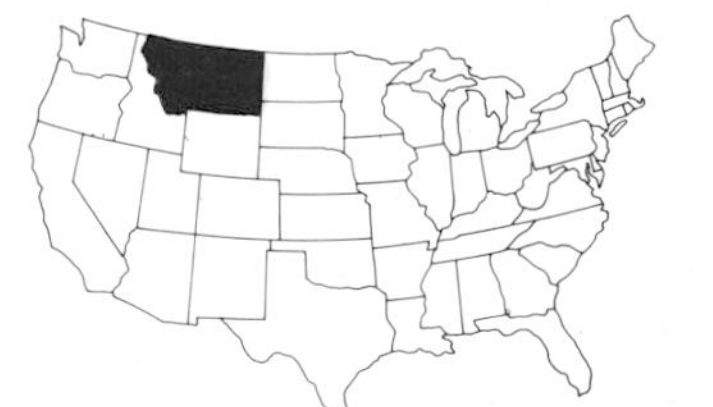

▼ *The scenery near Ronan, in western Montana, lives up to one of the state's nicknames, Big Sky Country.*

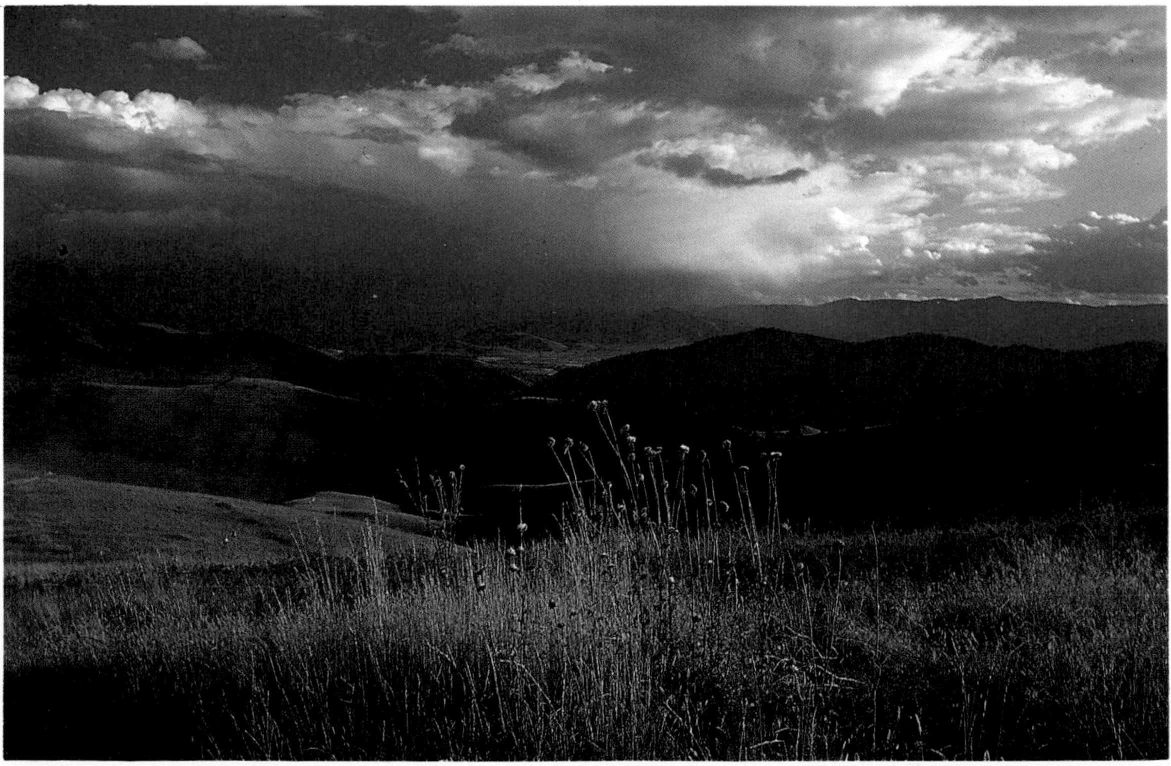

▲ *A quiet street scene in Livingston, in southern Montana. The state's open spaces are dotted with small cities and towns similar to Livingston.*

The United States obtained most of Montana in the LOUISIANA PURCHASE in 1803. Fur traders roamed the region and then were joined by gold miners in the mid-1800s. When they went on to Indian land, fighting broke out. The Battle of the Little Bighorn, or CUSTER's Last Stand, took place in Montana in 1876. More than 37,000 American Indians still live in Montana.

**Montana**
**Capital:** Helena
**Area:** 147,046 sq mi (380,850 km$^2$). Rank: 4th
**Population:** 799,065 (1990). Rank: 44th
**Statehood:** November 8, 1889
**Principal rivers:** Clark Fork, Kootenai, Missouri, Yellowstone
**Highest point:** Granite Peak, 12,799 ft (3,901 m)
**Motto:** *Oro y Plata* (Gold and Silver)
**Song:** "Montana"

**Places of Interest**

- Custer Battlefield National Monument, near Hardin, commemorates Custer's Last Stand.
- Glacier National Park, along Montana's border with Canada, has spectacular glaciers and mountain scenery.
- The Wild West gold mining town of Virginia City, near Dillon, has been restored to appear as it did in the 1800s.

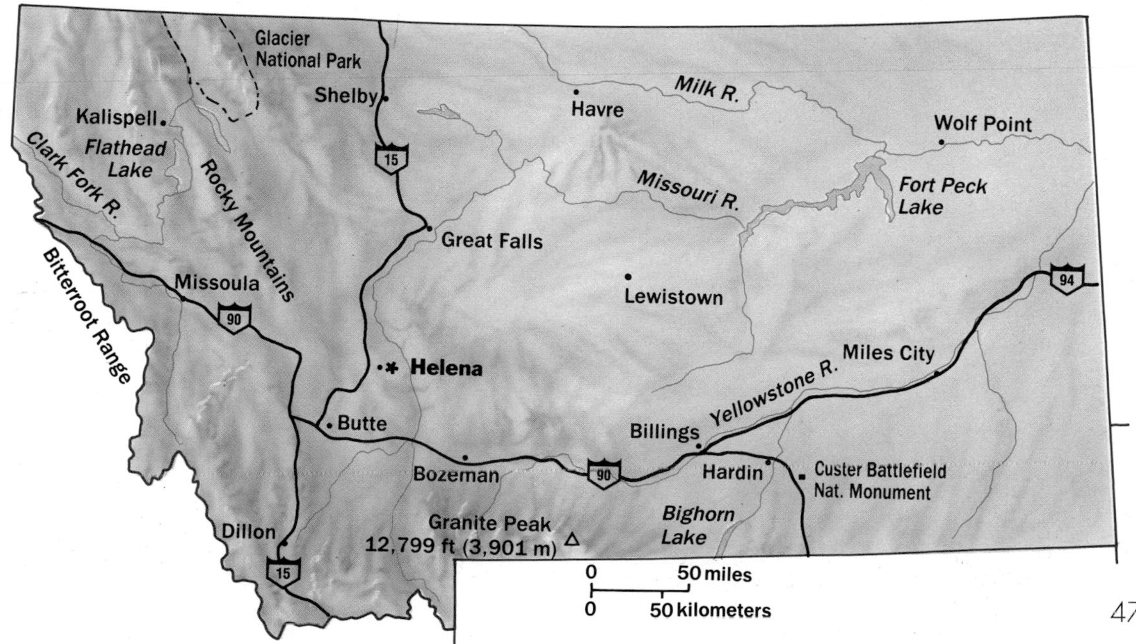

► *Parts of Montreal, such as Place Jacques Cartier, have sidewalk cafes and restaurants like those in France.*

**The Montreal International Airport (Mirabel), opened in 1975, covers 138 square miles (357 km$^2$). It is the largest airport in the world in total area.**

## MONTREAL

Montreal, with a population of just over 1 million, is the second largest city in Canada and the largest French-speaking city outside France itself. It was founded by the French in 1642. Montreal is situated on an island in the St. Lawrence River in the southern part of the province of QUEBEC. It is an important port and financial, industrial, and commercial center. French-speaking people make up the majority of the population, but there are sizable communities of English-speaking Canadians also. Parts of Montreal look and feel like any other busy North American city, but, with its restaurants and sidewalk cafes, it has a European atmosphere.

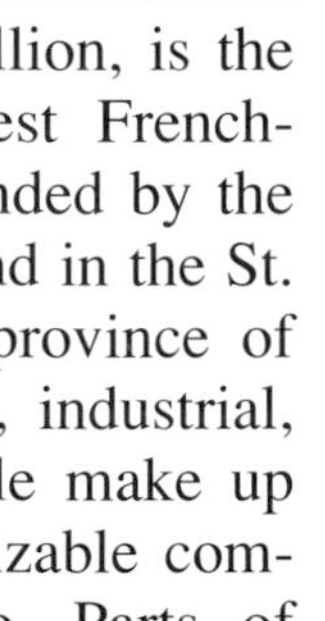

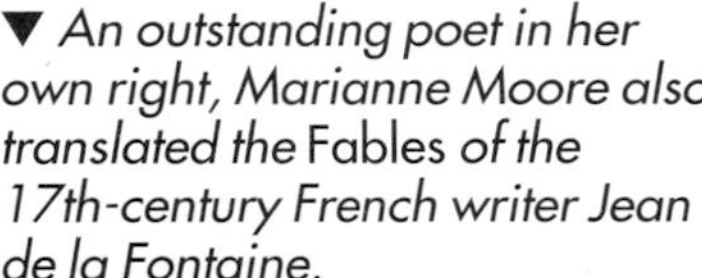

▼ *An outstanding poet in her own right, Marianne Moore also translated the* Fables *of the 17th-century French writer Jean de la Fontaine.*

## MOORE, Marianne

Marianne Moore (1887–1972) was one of the most important poets of the century. She was born in Kirkwood, Missouri, and graduated from Bryn Mawr College in Pennsylvania. After teaching at the Indian school in Carlisle, Pennsylvania, from 1911 to 1915, she moved to New York to write poetry. Her first volume, called *Poems*, was highly praised when it was published in 1921. By this time she was living in Brooklyn. She loved the Brooklyn Dodgers baseball team, and some of her poems conveyed the grace and strength of athletes. She also wrote poems about natural history subjects, such as birds and other wild animals. Her *Collected Poems* won her the Pulitzer Prize in 1952.

◀ *With its long legs, a moose can pick its way through woods in the winter or wade into swamps for food.*

## MOOSE

The moose is the largest member of the deer family. The biggest moose are found in Alaska. Most moose are 5 to 6.5 feet (1.5 to 2 m) tall at the shoulder and weigh up to 1,800 pounds (about 820 kg). Moose live in northern woodlands near water. In North America they are found mostly in Alaska, Canada, and the Rocky Mountain states. Nearly all the moose in the eastern United States were killed by hunters, but a few are found today in New England. Moose are now protected by law.

**The name "moose" is an American Indian word. In Europe, the moose is known by its old Germanic name, elk. To complicate things further, an elk (wapiti) in North America is an entirely different deer.**

## MORGAN, John Pierpont

John Pierpont Morgan (1837–1913) was a famous financier. Born in Hartford, Connecticut, he started out in business in his father's banking firm. In 1871 he helped found a firm that later became known as J. P. Morgan and Company. He then became involved in reorganizing railroads and other companies. He also formed large companies from a number of smaller ones. This is how he formed U.S. Steel in 1901. Morgan became very wealthy, and he gave a great deal of money to hospitals and schools. He also gave works of art to the Metropolitan Museum of Art in New York City.

▲ *J. P. Morgan saved the U.S. gold reserve during the Panic of 1907 by buying $65 million worth of gold himself.*

## MORMONS

Mormons are members of the Church of Jesus Christ of Latter-day Saints. Their beliefs are based on the Bible and the Book of Mormon. There are about 4 million

▲ *The Mormons faced natural hardships and hostility from other settlers on their way west. They finally settled in Utah, which was still part of Mexico.*

Mormons worldwide. Most live in the United States, especially the West.

The church was founded in New York State in 1830 by Joseph SMITH. Mormons believe that he was a modern prophet who received a series of revelations from God. During the 1830s the Mormons established communities in Kirtland, Ohio; Independence, Missouri; and Nauvoo, Illinois. In 1846, following anti-Mormon violence and Smith's murder, Brigham YOUNG led the Mormons to UTAH, where they settled. Salt Lake City, Utah, is the headquarters of the church today. The famous Mormon Tabernacle Choir is based there.

International Morse Code

| | | | |
|---|---|---|---|
| A | ·– | N | –· |
| B | –··· | O | ––– |
| C | –·–· | P | ·––· |
| D | –·· | Q | ––·– |
| E | · | R | ·–· |
| F | ··–· | S | ··· |
| G | ––· | T | – |
| H | ···· | U | ··– |
| I | ·· | V | ···– |
| J | ·––– | W | ·–– |
| K | –·– | X | –··– |
| L | ·–·· | Y | –·–– |
| M | –– | Z | ––·· |

## MORSE, Samuel F. B.

Samuel Finley Breese Morse (1791–1872) invented the first successful telegraph and the Morse code that is used to send telegrams. Morse was born in Charlestown,

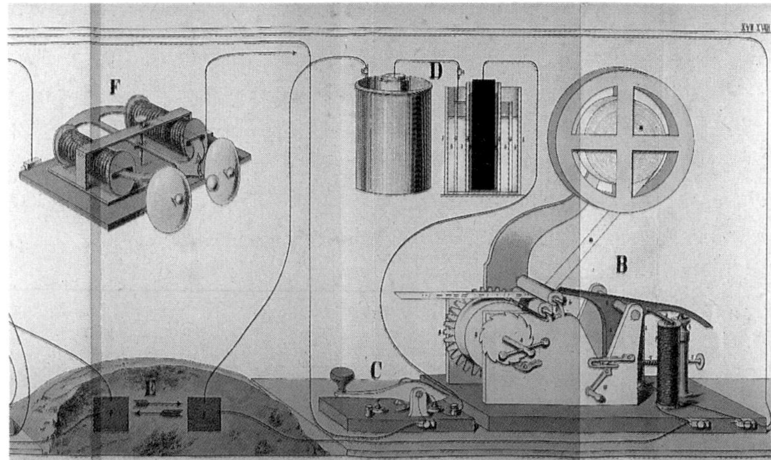


► *A telegraph receiver of the 1880s could transmit messages across the country and even to Europe. Messages could be received on tape (B), so that operators could leave the receiver.*

Massachusetts. He studied in England and went on to become a portrait painter.

In 1832, Morse became interested in the idea of using electricity for communications. His ideas led to the development of the first successful telegraph in the United States in 1843. In the following year he demonstrated the telegraph in the Capitol in Washington, D.C. Using the Morse code, which he had invented in 1840, he sent his famous message, "What hath God wrought?" It traveled over a telegraph line that had been built between Washington and Baltimore.

▲ *Samuel Morse's first telegraph message was "What hath God wrought?" It conveyed his sense of both awe and pride.*

## MOSES, Grandma

The painter Anna Mary Robertson ("Grandma") Moses (1860–1961) is the best known of all American folk artists. As a child, on a farm in New York State, she drew pictures and colored them with berry juice. Later she made pictures in embroidery. In her late seventies, unable to embroider because of her arthritis, she began to paint. Her brightly colored paintings show lively scenes of rural life and bear such titles as *Catching the Thanksgiving Turkey* and *Over the River to Grandma's House*.

In a little over 20 years, Grandma Moses painted more than 1,000 pictures.

**Grandma Moses did not have any art training and did not have her own one-artist show until 1940—when she was 80 years old.**

◀ *Grandma Moses' paintings were based on memories of her early life on a farm in New York State.*

# MOTION PICTURES

▲ *King Kong, made in 1933, updated the traditional story of Beauty and the Beast.*

Motion pictures, or movies, are one of the most popular forms of entertainment. People spend billions of dollars every year to watch them in movie theaters or at home with their VCRs.

Hollywood became the movie capital of the United States after the first film studio was established there in 1911. D. W. Griffith, the first great American film director, built his studio there. This pioneer of movie techniques produced such feature-length films as *The Birth of a Nation* and *Intolerance*. Cecil B. DeMille, Samuel Goldwyn, and other moviemakers produced many westerns, swashbuckling adventures, biblical spectacles, and comedies. *The Jazz Singer*, starring Al JOLSON, was the first major film to have sound. As sound techniques improved, movie studios began producing musicals, such as *The Gold Diggers of 1933*. Gangster movies were also very popular during the 1930s. The Civil War epic *Gone With the Wind* is considered the greatest movie of the 1930s. It is still popular today.

Movies reached the peak of their popularity during the 1930s and 1940s. But in the late 1940s, as a result of television, movie attendance began to decline. The movie studios responded by introducing the wide screen, lavish use of color, and stereophonic sound.

In recent years there have been great advances in film technology. The special effects in science fiction films and horror movies are bringing millions of people back to the movie theaters.

Among the most popular movies of recent times are *E.T.*, *Star Wars*, *Return of the Jedi*, *Batman*, *The Empire Strikes Back*, *Ghostbusters*, *Jaws*, and *Jurassic Park*.

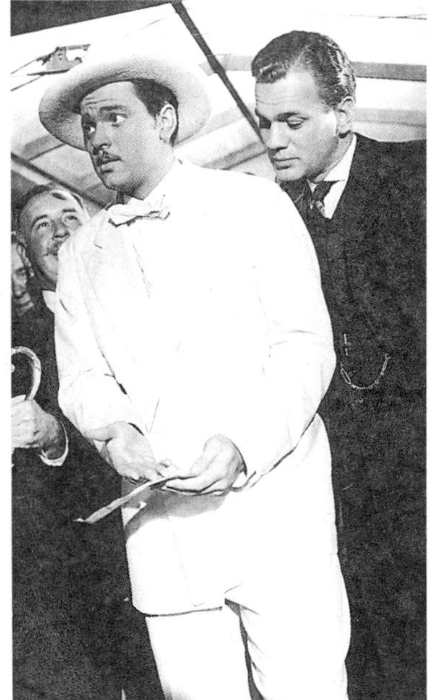

▲ *Orson Welles (left) directed and starred in Citizen Kane when he was only 25.*

► *Douglas Fairbanks, D. W. Griffith, Mary Pickford, and Charlie Chaplin set up the United Artists studio in 1919.*

◀ Gone With the Wind, *based on the Civil War, won four of the six major Oscars in 1939.*

▲ *Clint Eastwood played "the Man With No Name" in a series of westerns in the 1960s.*

**Who Does What in the World of Motion Pictures**

**Cinematographer:** the person in charge of the camera, sometimes called the director of photography.
**Designer:** the person who creates the clothing worn by actors and actresses, or the person who creates the scenery.
**Director:** the person who guides the actors and technicians, giving the motion picture its "feel."
**Extras:** actors who have nonspeaking roles, usually in battle or crowd scenes.
**Gaffer:** the chief electrician in charge of lighting.
**Grip:** the person in charge of equipment.
**Producer:** the person who looks after the business matters in paying for and making a motion picture.
**Scriptwriter:** someone who writes the screenplay (script) of a motion picture.

▼ *Harrison Ford starred in the action-packed* Indiana Jones and the Last Crusade *(1988).*

◀ *Dooley Wilson, Humphrey Bogart, and Ingrid Bergman in* Casablanca, *one of the world's most popular movies.*

► *Motorcycles in races such as the Daytona 500 can reach speeds of up to 170 miles per hour (310 km/hr).*

▼ *Motorcycles make ideal police vehicles because they are fast and can maneuver easily through traffic.*

## MOTORCYCLES

A motorcycle is a two-wheeled (or three-wheeled) vehicle that is powered by a gasoline engine. Motorcycles are used for recreation, transportation, work, and racing. People who use motorcycles for transportation do so because they are less expensive to buy and operate than automobiles. Even the largest motorcycle can travel up to 50 miles (80 km) on a gallon of gas.

Many people like the thrill of riding motorcycles, but they can be dangerous. Most states have strict laws regarding these vehicles. Riders are supposed to wear helmets and heavy clothing that will protect them in case of a spill.

## MOTT, Lucretia

Lucretia Mott (1793–1880) fought for an end to slavery and for women's rights during the 1800s. Born in Nantucket, Massachusetts, she grew up as a Quaker. Mott became an ABOLITIONIST and helped found the Anti-Slavery Convention of American Women in 1832. In 1840 she and other women were refused seats at an anti-slavery convention in England. Mott then devoted herself to the cause of women's rights, including the right of women to vote. In 1864 she helped found Swarthmore College in Pennsylvania.

**Lucretia Mott and Elizabeth Cady Stanton organized the first women's rights assembly in Seneca Falls, New York, in 1848. The 68 women and 32 men at the assembly listed 16 forms of discrimination against women. They demanded that women be given the right to vote and better opportunities for education and jobs.**

## MOUND BUILDERS

The Mound Builders were Indians who lived in central and eastern North America from about 1000 B.C. to A.D. 1500. Their villages were built around the Mississippi and Ohio rivers and their tributaries. These Indians built enormous mounds of earth. Some were used as places of burial. Others were the sites of large temples and places of worship and sacrifice. These mounds, or earthworks, were often in the shapes of circles, octagons, snakes, birds, and stars. One of the first of these Mound Builder groups is called the Adena culture, after the site in Adena, Ohio. Another important group was the Hopewell culture.

◀ *The Serpent Mound State Memorial in Ohio (left) preserves some of the Mound Builders' most elaborate work. Statues (above) recovered from such sites help experts discover the age and purpose of the mounds.*

## MOUNTAINS

The two major mountain ranges in the United States are the APPALACHIANS in the East and the ROCKIES in the West. The Appalachians stretch from Alabama to Maine and eastern Canada. The tallest peak is Mount Mitchell in North Carolina, which reaches 6,684 feet (2,037 m). The Rocky Mountains stretch from New Mexico northward into Canada. They are younger and higher than the Appalachians. Some have caps of snow and ice year-round. The highest is Mount Elbert in Colorado, which reaches 14,433 feet (4,399 m).

To the west of the Rockies are several mountain ranges, including the SIERRA NEVADA and the Cascades. The highest of the Sierra Nevada peaks is MOUNT WHITNEY in California, which reaches 14,494 feet

**The Rocky Mountains, the major mountain system of North America, are "young" mountains, having been pushed up in the late Cretaceous Period (65 to 100 million years ago). The Appalachians were formed about 250 million years ago.**

▲ *Most of North America's tallest mountains are in Alaska or western Canada. Mt. Mitchell, the tallest mountain east of the Mississippi, is only about a third as tall as Mt. McKinley.*

(4,418 m). The highest of the Cascades is Mount Rainier in Washington, at 14,410 feet (4,392 m).

Alaska has many high mountains in the Alaska Range. At 20,320 feet (6,194 m), MOUNT MCKINLEY is the highest mountain in North America. Hawaii's mountains rise from the ocean floor. MAUNA LOA (13,680 feet, or 4,169 m) is the world's largest active volcano.

## MOUNT McKINLEY

Mount McKinley is the highest mountain in North America. It is part of the Alaska Range and is located in south-central Alaska about midway between Anchorage and Fairbanks. The mountain has two peaks: South Peak (20,320 feet, or 6,194 m) and North Peak (19,470 feet, or 5,934 m). Mount McKinley was named for William MCKINLEY in 1896, the year before he became president of the United States. The mountain is the main attraction in Denali National Park. Denali, meaning "The Great One," or "The High One," is the Indian name for the mountain.

Highest U.S. Mountains (by region)

**Alaska**
Mt. McKinley
20,320 ft (6,194 m)
Mt. St. Elias
18,008 ft (5,489 m)
Mt. Foraker
17,400 ft (5,304 m)

**Rockies (lower 48 states)**
Mt. Whitney, California
14,494 ft (4,418 m)
Mt. Elbert, Colorado
14,433 ft (4,399 m)
Mt. Massive, Colorado
14,421 ft (4,396 m)

**Appalachians**
Mt. Mitchell, North Carolina
6,684 ft (2,037 m)
Clingmans Dome, Tenn.
6,643 ft (2,025 m)
Richland Balsam, North Carolina
6,410 ft (1,954 m)

## MOUNT RUSHMORE

Mount Rushmore National Memorial, in the Black Hills of SOUTH DAKOTA, is one of the most famous monuments in the United States. Carved into the granite of Mount Rushmore are the faces of four U.S. presidents, George Washington, Thomas Jefferson, Theodore Roosevelt, and Abraham Lincoln. The memorial was the creation of sculptor Gutzon Borglum. He, his son Lincoln, and others worked for 6½ years, using dynamite and drills, to create the faces. The monument was

◀ *The Mt. Rushmore busts are carved from the Black Hills of South Dakota. Mt. Rushmore National Monument is part of the National Park System.*

**Gutzon Borglum and others worked for 6½ years during a 12-year period to carve the four giant heads on Mt. Rushmore. The heads are about 60 feet (18 m) high — as high as a five-story building — and were carved with dynamite and pneumatic drills. Borglum died before the work was completed. His son Lincoln finished the memorial.**

completed in 1941. The memorial covers an area of almost 2 square miles (5 km$^2$). Each face is about 60 feet (18 m) high.

## MOUNT ST. HELENS

On the morning of May 19, 1980, Mount St. Helens volcano in WASHINGTON State erupted, killing about 60 people and causing billions of dollars in damage. The volcano, just 95 miles (152 km) south of SEATTLE in the Cascade Mountains, had been inactive since 1857. It had been emitting smoke and ash for weeks before the eruption, so most people living near it had been evacuated. But the eruption was more severe than predicted, and landslides and forest fires accounted for most of the deaths and property damage. A 60,000-foot (18,300-m) column of ash was sent into the sky. This ash settled over a huge area and even caused weather changes. The eruption reduced the height of the volcano by about 1,300 feet (400 m).

▼ *The shape of Mt. St. Helens (left) was completely changed when the volcanic explosion sent tons of ash and lava flying for miles. Afterward, only a crater (right) remained where the peak had been.*

**Mount Vernon, George Washington's family estate, was named for a British admiral, Edward Vernon, famed for his Caribbean exploits against the Spanish in 1740. Admiral Vernon was referred to by his men as "Old Grog" because he wore a grogram coat. (Grogram is a fabric of silk and wool.) His nickname "grog" was given to the rum-and-water mixture he issued to the sailors to control drunkenness.**

## MOUNT VERNON

Mount Vernon was the home of George WASHINGTON. It is in Fairfax County, Virginia, on the south bank of the Potomac River not far from Washington, D.C. The first president and his wife Martha are buried there.

After their deaths the house and estate gradually fell into decline. A group of people not only saved the property but restored it to its former state. Today the estate is maintained by the Mount Vernon Ladies' Association of the Union. It is a national shrine that is visited by more than a million tourists each year.

► *George Washington had lived 16 years as a gentleman farmer at Mount Vernon before getting the call to lead the new American army.*

▼ *The peak of Mt. Whitney towers above the timberline, the highest point where trees can survive on a mountain.*

## MOUNT WHITNEY

Mount Whitney is the highest mountain in the United States outside of Alaska. Located in central California, the 14,494-foot (4,418-m) peak is part of the SIERRA NEVADA range. Its granite walls rise sharply 10,000 feet (3,000 m) above the neighboring valley. The mountain, one of the toughest challenges for mountain climbers, was first climbed in 1873. Mount Whitney is named for the geologist Josiah Dwight Whitney, who worked for years in the Sierra Nevada and first measured the mountain's height in 1864.

## MOUSE

Mice are small RODENTS. House mice are the most familiar. They live near people and eat just about anything. White-footed, or deer, mice are found all over North America. American harvest mice live on the Pacific coast and in the Southeast, especially in grassy areas. They climb up plant stems to their nests. Harvest mice "harvest" seeds from plants.

Grasshopper mice are found in dry regions of the West. They live in the ground and eat grasshoppers and other insects. Pocket mice also live in dry regions. They have pouches on the outside of their cheeks. They use these "pockets" to carry seeds and other food for storage in their burrows.

▼ *Mice eat mainly seeds and nuts, but the common American house mouse will eat almost anything left behind by humans.*

## MUCKRAKERS

The muckrakers were writers who, in the early 1900s, drew attention to social problems and corruption in business and industry. They included novelists, historians, and journalists. Ida M. Tarbell, who exposed business corruption in her *History of the Standard Oil Company*, was a leader in the movement. Among other muckrakers were Lincoln Steffens, who attacked political corruption in *The Shame of the Cities*, and the novelist Upton SINCLAIR. Sinclair's novel *The Jungle* exposed appalling conditions in the meat-packing industry. It prompted the first U.S. pure-food laws.

**The term "muckraker" was coined by President Theodore Roosebelt, who said these writers were interested only in digging up dirt. But their work led to many social and political reforms, including government regulation of business and the direct election of U.S. Senators.**

## MURROW, Edward R.

Edward R. Murrow (1908–1965) was a radio and television broadcaster for CBS. His radio broadcasts from London to the United States during German bombing raids in World War II made him famous. After return-

▲ *Edward R. Murrow led a brave radio campaign against Senator Joseph McCarthy in 1954. Public opinion turned against the senator's bullying behavior.*

▼ *The National Air and Space Museum is one of the most popular attractions at the Smithsonian Institution in Washington, D.C.*

ing to the United States, he produced two popular television shows, *See It Now* and *Person to Person.* These relied on Murrow's news skills. From 1961 to 1963 he was director of the U.S. Information Agency.

## MUSEUMS

A museum is a permanent institution housing and displaying objects of artistic, scientific, or historical interest. The first in the American colonies was the collection of the Charleston (South Carolina) Library Society, founded in 1773. The 1846 act of Congress that created the SMITHSONIAN INSTITUTION founded what has become the largest museum complex in the world. Its units include the National Museum of Natural History and National Museum of Man, the National Museum of Technology, the National Gallery of Art, and the National Air and Space Museum, all in Washington, D.C. Other famous museums include New York City's American Museum of Natural History, Metropolitan Museum of Art, and Museum of Modern Art.

**Some of the United States' Varied Museums**

**The Art Institute of Chicago,** in Illinois, has paintings from all periods of European and American art.
**The Baseball Hall of Fame,** in Cooperstown, New York, honors the great players and teams of the national pastime.
**The Children's Museum,** in Boston, Massachusetts, is one of the country's oldest museums for young people.
**The J. Paul Getty Museum,** near Los Angeles, California, buys art treasures with money left by the famous billionaire.
**The Museum of Fine Arts,** in Boston, Massachusetts, has one of the best collections of Asian art in the world.
**The Museum of Science and Industry,** in Chicago, Illinois, has many exhibits that allow visitors to experiment.
**The Yale Gallery of Fine Arts,** in New Haven, Connecticut, was the first college art museum in the United States.

## MUSHROOMS

Mushrooms are a type of fungus. Many kinds are edible (can be eaten) but some are poisonous. Poisonous mushrooms are often called "toadstools." It is very difficult to tell edible mushrooms from poisonous ones, so only those bought at a store should be eaten.

The only mushroom that is widely grown for eating is the common, or field, mushroom. Edible wild mushrooms that are common in North America include the morel, chanterelle, inkcap, and oyster mushroom. The parasol mushroom is one of the largest edible mushrooms. Common in the East, it can be up to 16 inches (40 cm) tall.

The deadliest poisonous mushrooms are the amanitas. One amanita, the death cap, is the most poisonous mushroom known. The panther, another amanita, is the most common poisonous mushroom west of the Rockies. Like its relative, it can also cause death.

▲ *The poisonous death cap toadstool can be mistaken for an edible mushroom.*

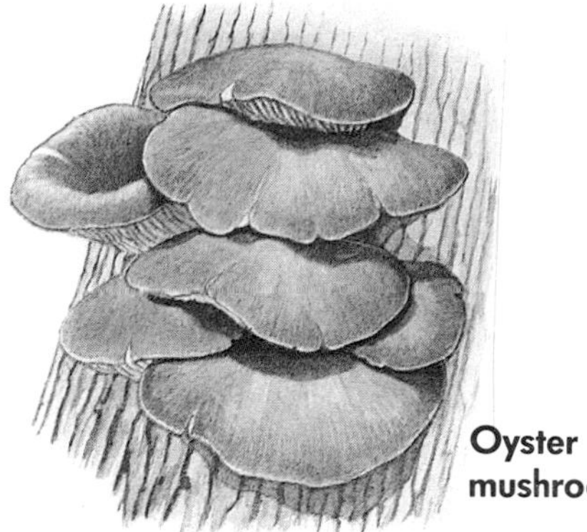


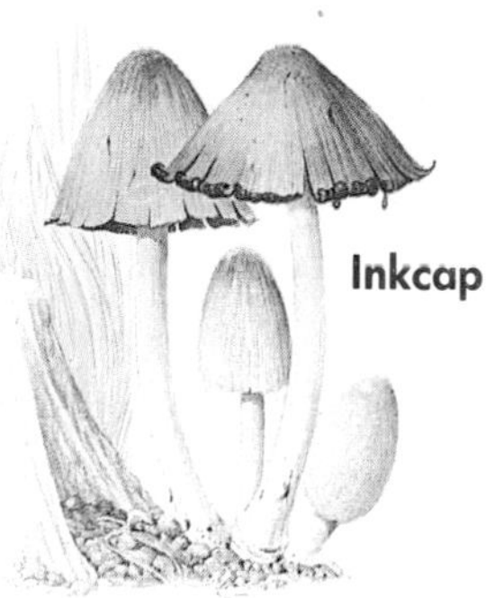


◀ *The oyster mushroom and the inkcap are just two of many edible North American mushrooms.*

## MUSIC

Both POPULAR MUSIC and classical music have a long history in America. Concerts of instrumental and vocal classical music were first performed in the American colonies in the 1730s. The first permanent symphony orchestra, the Philharmonic Society of New York, was formed in 1842. Now almost every major American city has a resident symphony orchestra. Some are among the best in the world. Many smaller cities also have symphony orchestras.

The first internationally recognized American composer was Louis Gottschalk (1829–1869). His work was

▼ *The violin is a good instrument for children because it is small and portable.*

**Some Common Musical Terms**

**Aria:** a song in an opera, usually sung by one person (solo) or two people (duet).
**Concerto:** a piece for one or more instruments and orchestra.
**Movement:** a section of a longer piece of music, such as a sonata or symphony.
**Overture:** the instrumental opening sequence of an opera or other vocal work.
**Sonata:** a work in several movements for piano, sometimes including other instruments.
**Symphony:** a work in several movements for the whole orchestra.

▲ *High school marching bands have been an American tradition for more than a century.*

influenced by black and Creole folk music. The music of later composers such as Charles Ives and Aaron COPLAND also has a "New World" flavor, including fragments of folk music, patriotic melodies, and hymn tunes. JAZZ clearly influenced the music of George GERSHWIN and Leonard BERNSTEIN. The work of other 20th-century American composers ranges from the rich melodies of Samuel Barber to the complex works of Elliott Carter and the innovations of John Cage.

Among other prominent native-born American musicians have been the conductors Eugene Ormandy, Sarah Caldwell, and James Levine; the pianists Van Cliburn and Andre Watts; the cellist Lynn Harrell; and the violinist Yehudi Menuhin.

► *Many musicians consider playing at New York City's Carnegie Hall to be the highlight of their career.*

▼ *Jessye Norman is one of America's leading opera stars. She was even chosen to sing the French national anthem at France's bicentennial celebration in 1989.*

Some 20th-Century American Composers

**Samuel Barber** (1910–1981) composed instrumental music as well as operas.

**Leonard Bernstein** (1918–1990) was a pianist, composer, and conductor who mastered many types of music.

**John Cage** (1912– ) is a controversial composer whose work changes with each performance.

**Aaron Copland** (1900–1990) composed all types of music, including several popular ballets.

**George Gershwin** (1898–1937) wrote popular songs as well as serious pieces using jazz as an influence.

**Charles Ives** (1874–1954) composed symphonies, chamber music, and choral music.

**Roger Sessions** (1896–1985) composed eight symphonies, a violin concerto, and other works. He also wrote several books on music.

◀ *The finale of* Jerome Robbins' Broadway, *which won most of the leading New York awards for best musical of 1989.*

Giants of the Musical Theater World (most famous works)

**Irving Berlin** (1888–1989), *Annie Get Your Gun*
**Leonard Bernstein** (1918–1990), *West Side Story*
**George Gershwin** (1898–1937), *Of Thee I Sing*
**Oscar Hammerstein II** (1895–1960), *Oklahoma!*
**Jerome Kern** (1895–1945), *Show Boat*
**Frank Loesser** (1910–1969), *Guys and Dolls*
**Cole Porter** (1893–1964), *Can Can*
**Richard Rodgers** (1902–1979), *The Sound of Music*
**Stephen Sondheim** (1930– ), *A Little Night Music*

## MUSICAL THEATER

There are many kinds of musical theater, including the opera. The kind that is most distinctively American is the musical comedy. This is a play in which the story is told through a combination of songs, dances, and spoken dialogue. The modern "musical" began to take shape in the early 1900s. Among those that have advanced the form are *Show Boat*, *Oklahoma!*, *West Side Story*, and *Pacific Overtures*. Composers of musicals have included Jerome KERN, Irving BERLIN, George GERSHWIN, Richard RODGERS, Cole PORTER, Leonard BERNSTEIN, and Stephen Sondheim. Among the notable choreographers have been Agnes de Mille, Jerome Robbins, Michael Kidd, and Bob Fosse. Performers have included Mary Martin, Ethel Merman, and Bernadette Peters.

## MUSKRAT

The muskrat, a type of RODENT, is found in most parts of North America. Muskrats live in burrows on the banks of streams, marshes, or shallow lakes, or in mounds of reed and grass in the water. They weigh about 4 pounds (1.8 kg) and are about 12 inches (30 cm) long, with a long, flat tail that they steer with when swimming. Their hind feet are partly webbed, to help them swim. Muskrats are named after the unpleasant musky smell they give off. Their fur is sold as "Hudson seal" and their meat as "marsh rabbit."

▼ *A muskrat's fur is covered with oily guard hairs, which keep it dry in winter.*

▲ *One myth of Pacific Coast Indians tells of how a young girl lived with an old man, who kept the moon hidden in a bag. When the girl grew up, a "trickster" raven turned himself into a man and married the girl. A son was born and the girl asked the old man to let her little boy play with the moon. As soon as the moon was released, the boy's father turned back into a raven and flew off with the moon.*

## MYTHS AND LEGENDS OF THE AMERICAN INDIANS

Myths and legends are a kind of FOLKLORE. They are stories that explain such things as how the world began—and how it might end. Myths originated long ago, before the time of history, and often tell about gods. Legends are often based on real events.

The American Indians have many wonderful myths and legends. Even today they use dances and ceremonies to tell how the world—and their tribe—began. According to one Navajo Indian myth, they live in the last of five worlds that had been created. Each of the first four worlds had had something wrong with it. In each of the five worlds, there is a First Woman, or the First People, much as Adam and Eve were the first people in the Western creation story.

Another myth about creation is told by the Pueblo Indians. The myth is about Awonawilona—the one who contains everything. He created light (the sun) and water (the sea). From the water he made land and sky, and everything else came from the land and sky.

Another theme in Indian myths is that of people who are really animals. Sometimes they have wives who are real people, but eventually the wives become snakes or other frightening creatures.

► *In a Blackfoot myth, thunder was a violent man who befriended the Blackfeet by offering them the first peace pipe. The same man could fire his bow and arrows to create lightning when he was angry.*

**A Shared Indian Myth about the Origin of Corn**

Soon after the first Indians were made, one man lived on his own, far away from any other Indians. He lived on roots, bark, and nuts because he had never seen fire. This life was tiresome, and the man became lonely. He grew tired of digging roots, lost his appetite, and lay dreaming in the sunshine. After several days he awoke to find a beautiful woman with long golden hair. At first he was frightened of the mysterious stranger. He called to her, but she stayed where she was. When the man went toward her she drew back. Then he sang to her of his loneliness and asked her never to leave him. She told the man that he would always have her with him as long as he did what she asked. The man agreed and followed the strange, beautiful woman.

She led him to a field of very dry grass and taught him to light the grass by rubbing two sticks together. Then she told him to take her by the hair and drag her over the burned ground. If he did this she would disappear, but a crop (corn) would grow up wherever he dragged her. It would remind him of her because he would see her hair coming out between its leaves. Its seeds would also feed him. He did what she told him and later found that she had kept her promise. To this day, whenever Indians see corn silk (hair), they know that she has not forgotten him. And they burn the corn in the fall so that she will return.

▲ *Plains Indians believe that fire was stolen from the gods by a "trickster" rabbit. The rabbit joined the gods in a dance around the sacred fire. The rabbit got closer and closer to the fire as it danced and then dipped its head into the flame. The top of the rabbit's head caught fire and the rabbit ran off to present the earth with the precious gift of fire.*

The Mandan Indians, farmers of the Great Plains, have a myth that tells how the founders of the human race were saved during a great flood. Relics of these founders are kept in a "medicine bundle," and a Sun Dance is performed around the bundle.

◀ *The Tlingit tribe of southern Alaska has a myth about the creation of many sea animals, such as seals and whales. Two giants had a daughter called Sedna. The little girl's appetite was enormous, and one night the giants woke to find Sedna about to eat them. The giants cut the girl into pieces and threw them from their canoe. Each piece turned into a sea animal as soon as it hit the water.*

## NADER, Ralph 

Ralph Nader (1934– ) is one of the foremost consumer champions in the United States. In 1965 he published *Unsafe At Any Speed.* This book led to the federal government's 1966 National Traffic and Motor Vehicle Safety Act, which gave Congress the power to enforce the car safety laws. Since then Nader has investigated the potential dangers of radiation from color TV, atomic energy, and X rays as well as health hazards in food and drugs.

## NATIONAL ANTHEM 

"The Star-Spangled Banner" was written in 1814. It became the official national anthem of the United States in 1931. The tune is English and dates from the late 1700s. By the time of American independence, there were already several versions of the tune with patriotic American words. The present version was written on the morning of September 14, 1814, during the War of 1812, by Francis Scott Key. He had been held on a British ship overnight while the British bombarded Fort McHenry in Baltimore, Maryland. His joy and relief to see the Stars and Stripes still flying the next morning led him to write the lyrics. By the mid-1800s it was the unofficial national anthem. A 1931 act of Congress made it official.

**"The Star-Spangled Banner" has four verses, but only one is usually sung at public events.**

► *"The Star-Spangled Banner" recalls Francis Scott Key's pride at seeing the U.S. flag still flying over Fort McHenry on the morning of September 14, 1814. The British Navy had been bombing the Baltimore fort all night.*

◄ *Reverend Martin Luther King, Jr., received the Spingarn Medal in 1957. The NAACP awards the medal annually for the highest achievement by a black American.*

**Membership of the NAACP is about 500,000, divided into some 1,800 chapters and 700 youth councils.**

## NATIONAL ASSOCIATION FOR THE ADVANCEMENT OF COLORED PEOPLE 

The National Association for the Advancement of Colored People (NAACP) is the largest CIVIL RIGHTS organization in the United States. It was founded in 1910, when W.E.B. DU BOIS's Niagara Movement merged with a group of concerned white people.

From its beginnings, the NAACP has been active in opposing segregation and securing constitutional rights for black people and other racial minorities. The 1954 Supreme Court ruling against segregation in public schools was the result of action by NAACP lawyers.

## NATIONAL GUARD 

The National Guard is a form of militia. There are two branches, the Army National Guard, with 444,000 members, and the Air National Guard, with 118,000 members. Members of the Guard drill regularly, usually one weekend a month. They are state military forces, but they are paid, equipped, and housed by the U.S. government. National Guard units are called to active duty only in times of emergency. Only the president or the state governors can call them to active duty. Guardsmen have been called to active duty to help control rioting and to patrol during and after natural disasters. In 1990, President George Bush called Guard units to active duty during the Persian Gulf crisis.

▼ *National Guard troops helped maintain order and clear Boston's roads after a blizzard in February 1978.*

# NATIONAL PARK SYSTEM

The United States has 50 national parks, covering some 47 million acres (19 million ha) of land. These areas are protected by law so that the beautiful or unusual scenery and the wildlife can be preserved. National parks generally allow some forms of recreation, such as camping, hiking, picnicking, or water sports. Private fishing is allowed, but commercial fishing, hunting, logging, mining, farming, and grazing are not.

Yellowstone National Park in Idaho, Montana, and Wyoming, established in 1872, was the world's first national park. It is famous for its hot springs and GEYSERS such as "Old Faithful." Wrangell–St. Elias in Alaska is the country's biggest national park. It has the largest collection of glaciers and peaks above 16,000 feet (4,900 m) in the United States. At the other extreme, Petrified Forest National Park in Arizona is an extremely hot, dry wilderness. The Painted Desert is located here. The world's tallest trees are preserved in California's Redwood, Sequoia, and Kings Canyon National Parks. Yosemite National Park, also in California, has spectacular mountain scenery with many waterfalls, including Yosemite Falls, the highest falls in the country. Oregon's Crater Lake National Park surrounds the nation's deepest lake. Carlsbad Caverns National Park in New Mexico is the largest area of caverns in the world.

Since the United States established Yellowstone National Park, more than 100 other countries have created their own national parks. Canada's national park system began in 1885, with the creation of Banff National Park in the province of Alberta. Today there are 32 Canadian national parks.

*▲ A volcanic eruption in 1912 reshaped the Valley of Ten Thousand Smokes in Katmai National Park, Alaska.*

*▼ Mammoth Springs is part of the oldest national park, Yellowstone. The park straddles three states — Idaho, Montana, and Wyoming.*

*► The sun sets over Manzanita Lake in California's Lassen Volcanic National Park.*

The National Park System of the United States is administered by the National Park Service, a division of the U.S. Department of the Interior. In addition to national parks, there are many other kinds of areas. These areas are shown in the table below.

Oldest Areas of the National Park System

| Type of Area | Name (State) | Year |
|---|---|---|
| International Historic Site | Saint Croix Island (Me.) | 1949 |
| National Battlefield | Stones River (Tenn.) | 1960 |
| National Battlefield Park | Kennesaw Mountain (Ga.) | 1935 |
| National Battlefield Site | Brices Cross Roads (Miss.) | 1929 |
| National Historical Park | Morristown (N.J.) | 1933 |
| National Historic Site | Salem Maritime (Mass.) | 1938 |
| National Lakeshore | Indiana Dunes (Ind.) | 1966 |
| | Pictured Rocks (Mich.) | 1966 |
| National Mall | National Mall (D.C.) | 1933 |
| National Memorial | Washington Monument (D.C.) | 1848 |
| National Military Park | Chickamauga (Ga.) and Chattanooga (Tenn.) | 1890 |
| National Monument | Custer Battlefield (Mont.) | 1879 |
| National Park | Yellowstone (Idaho/Mont./Wyo.) | 1872 |
| National Parkway | George Washington Memorial (Va./Md.) | 1930 |
| National Preserve | Denali (Alaska) | 1917 |
| National Recreation Area | Chickasaw (Okla.) | 1902 |
| National River | Ozark (Mo.) | 1964 |
| National Scenic River and Riverway | Saint Croix (Minn./Wisc.) | 1968 |
| National Scenic Trail | Appalachian (Me.–Ga.) | 1968 |
| National Seashore | Cape Hatteras (N.C.) | 1937 |
| Park | Rock Creek (D.C.) | 1890 |

▲ *The Washington Monument in Washington, D.C., was the first national memorial to be established.*

▲ *Traditional Appalachian buildings, such as this water mill, line the Blue Ridge Parkway in Virginia and North Carolina.*

◄ *The Chisos Mountains stand as a backdrop to blossoming prickly pear cactus at Big Bend National Park, Texas.*

**Natural gas is a popular heating source because it is less expensive to process than other fuels. Liquid and solid fuels need to be heated until they become gases before they can be burned. Natural gas has the advantage of being in that state already. Also, natural gas is often in a usable state when it is first extracted.**

## NATURAL GAS

Natural gas is a fuel consisting chiefly of methane. It is brought to the surface from wells, sometimes with crude oil, sometimes alone. The United States produces about a quarter of the world's natural gas. Two thirds of the U.S. total comes from Texas and Louisiana. Some of it is sold as bottled gas, but most is sent to consumers by pipeline. More than half of all U.S. homes are heated by gas, and a large number of homes use gas stoves for cooking. But two thirds of all U.S. natural gas goes to industrial customers. Some of this is used as fuel, but natural gas is also used in making chemical products such as plastics and drugs.

► *This pump in Oklahoma is equipped to reach pockets of natural gas 6 miles (10 km) under the Earth's surface.*

## NATURALIZATION

Naturalization is the process by which a person who is a citizen of one country becomes a citizen of another country. In the United States the first naturalization law was passed in 1790. It allowed only free white persons to become citizens. Blacks became eligible in 1870, American Indians in 1940, Chinese in 1940, and Indians and Filipinos in 1946. The Immigration and Nationality Act of 1952 ended all barriers to naturalization based on race. Naturalization laws are administered by the Immigration and Naturalization Service, a division of the U.S. Department of Justice.

From the Oath of Allegiance

I hereby declare, on oath, that I absolutely and entirely renounce and abjure all allegiance and fidelity to any foreign prince, potentate, state or sovereignty, to whom or which I have heretofore been a subject or citizen; that I will support and defend the Constitution and laws of the United States of America against all enemies, foreign or domestic; that I will bear true faith and allegiance to the same; that I will bear arms on behalf of the United States when required by law; . . . and that I take this obligation without any mental reservation or purpose of evasion; so help me God.

◀ *The last stage in naturalization is an oath of allegiance before a judge. Naturalized citizens must renounce their ties to other countries.*

**Naturalization in the United States confers all the rights of citizenship except the right to become president or vice president.**

To become a citizen of the United States, an alien must meet certain requirements. Applicants must be at least 18 years old and demonstrate a working knowledge of the English language. They must have lived legally in the United States for five years before applying (in most instances, husbands and wives of U.S. citizens must be residents for three years). They must have shown good moral character during this time. They must demonstrate a knowledge and understanding of U.S. history, government, and the Constitution. And, finally, they must swear an oath of allegiance to the United States and give up loyalties to other countries.

## NATURAL RESOURCES

Natural resources are those things available from nature that are useful to people. Land and water are natural resources, as are plants and animals. An area's or country's climate, including its sunshine, may also be considered a natural resource. Some natural resources, such as oil and coal, are used to power machinery and supply heat for homes and offices. Other resources, including timber, metal, and other minerals, are used to make various products.

Some countries, such as those in the arid regions of Africa, have very few natural resources. Others may have only one major natural resource—such as oil. This is the case with some small oil-producing countries in the Persian Gulf area. The United States, however, is a large country with a wealth of natural resources. It has

Leading States for Natural Resources

**Coal:** Wyoming, Kentucky, West Virginia, Pennsylvania
**Copper:** Arizona, New Mexico, Utah, Montana
**Gold:** Nevada, California, Utah, South Dakota
**Oil:** Alaska, Texas, California, Louisiana
**Silver:** Nevada, Idaho, Alaska, Montana
**Timber:** Oregon, Washington, California
**Water power:** Washington, Oregon

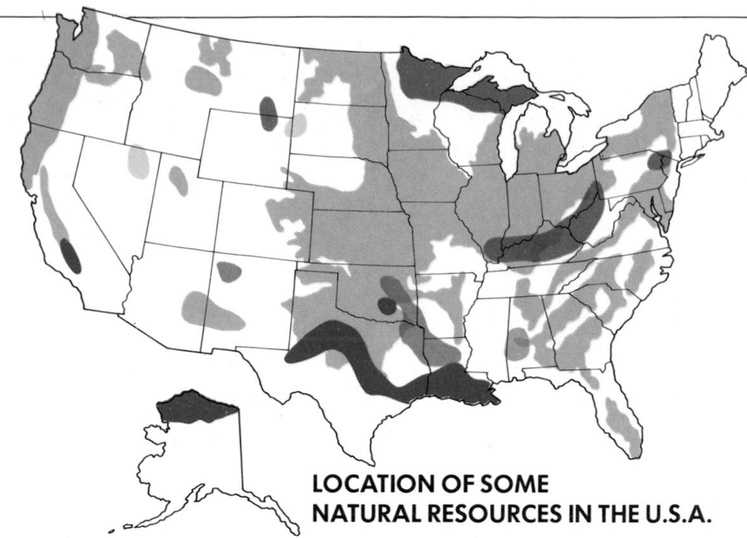


▲ *This map shows the distribution of natural resources in the United States. America's size provides it with a wider range of natural resources than most other countries.*

huge forests, vast areas of fertile farmland, and substantial deposits of oil, coal, and minerals. But the United States also uses very large quantities of natural resources—more than any other country in the world.

The overuse of natural resources is a major problem today. As the world population continues to increase, this problem will worsen. CONSERVATION of these resources is important. In the United States and elsewhere new trees are being planted. Aluminum cans and newspapers are being recycled. And scrap metal is being melted down to make new products. Only with everyone's help can natural resources be conserved.

## NAVAJOS

▼ *Traditional woven blankets provide Navajo Indians with a valuable source of income.*

The Navajos make up the largest American INDIAN tribe. There are more than 160,000 Navajos. About half of them live on the Navajo reservation, located primarily in Arizona but extending into New Mexico and Utah.

The Navajos originally lived in northwestern Canada. They migrated southward, settling in the southwestern part of what is now the United States about 500 years ago. In 1848, after the MEXICAN WAR, Navajo lands became part of the United States. In the early 1860s, Kit CARSON led a group of militiamen in forcing the Navajos to march 300 miles (480 km) to Fort Sumner in New Mexico. During this "Long Walk," 4,000 of the 12,000 Navajos died. In 1868 the Navajos were given their own reservation in Arizona. Since then, their numbers have increased dramatically. They work at mining, farming, and lumbering. But the Navajos are among the poorest of all the Native Americans.

# NAVY, United States

The mission of the U.S. Navy is to protect the nation's coastline and its merchant shipping, attack enemy naval forces and seaborne commerce, control vital sea lines of communication, land amphibious forces, and attack the interior of an enemy nation with aircraft and missiles.

In 1992 there were 572,000 naval personnel on active duty and 370 warships. These included 14 aircraft carriers and 96 nuclear attack submarines.

The Second (Atlantic) Fleet is based in Norfolk, Virginia, and the Third (eastern and central Pacific) Fleet in Pearl Harbor, Hawaii. The Sixth Fleet (Mediterranean) is based in Italy and the Seventh Fleet (western Pacific) in the Philippines. The Military Sealift Command provides transport for all the services. The Naval Academy, in Annapolis, Maryland, trains career officers, and the Naval War College, in Newport, Rhode Island, is for advanced study. The highest military commander is the chief of naval operations, and the highest civilian official is the secretary of the navy.

▲ *The American bald eagle perches on an anchor in the seal of the U.S. Navy.*

◀ *Naval uniforms have become simpler and more practical since the American Revolution. Female personnel, once unheard of, are now common in the Navy.*

The Continental Navy was founded on October 13, 1775, in the early months of the Revolutionary War. It fielded 27 armed vessels during the war. The Department of the Navy was established on April 30, 1798. Since 1947 it has been part of the Department of Defense. The United States MARINE CORPS is a separate service within the Department of the Navy.

▼ *The Navy's aircraft carriers are really mobile bases for air missions against a wide range of targets.*

# NEBRASKA

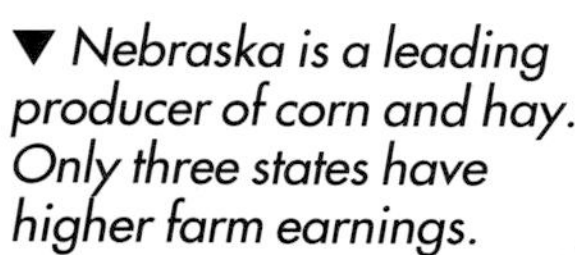

Located in the midsection of the United States, Nebraska is one of the most important farming states in the country. It ranks near the top in both the number of cattle and calves and the number of hogs raised. Nebraska is also among the leading states in growing corn and is called the Cornhusker State. Sorghum, winter wheat, and soybeans are other important crops grown on Nebraska farms.

Most of Nebraska is prairie land. However, near the western border with the mountain states of Colorado and Wyoming, the elevation reaches a mile high. The temperatures are extreme, and blizzards and windstorms often strike the state. Drought can also be a problem. Fortunately, farmers have two major rivers to tap for water. The Missouri River flows along the state's northern and eastern borders for about 450 miles (725 km). The Platte River runs east-west across the state.

**Nebraska**

**Capital:** Lincoln
**Area:** 77,358 sq mi (200,358 km$^2$). Rank: 16th
**Population:** 1,578,385 (1990). Rank: 36th
**Statehood:** March 1, 1867
**Principal rivers:** Missouri, Niobrara, Platte, Republican
**Highest point:** Johnson Township, 5,426 ft (1,654 m)
**Motto:** Equality Before the Law
**Song:** "Beautiful Nebraska"

**Places of Interest**

- Agate Fossil Beds National Monument, in northwest Nebraska, has a wide range of animal remains.
- Boys Town, the famous refuge for neglected children, is located near Omaha.
- Stuhr Museum of the Prairie Pioneer, near Grand Island, has a restored 19th-century railroad town with authentic buildings and furniture.

▼ *Nebraska is a leading producer of corn and hay. Only three states have higher farm earnings.*

Industry in Nebraska is usually related to farming. Omaha, the biggest city, is one of the country's leading meat-packing centers. Nebraskan factories also process grain into breakfast cereals. The industrial centers, like the best farmland, are in the eastern part of the state. Near Omaha is Offutt Air Force Base, the headquarters of the Strategic Air Command.

French and Spanish trappers and fur traders passed through Nebraska in the 1700s. The United States purchased it as part of the Louisiana Territory in 1803. The promise of cheap land under the Homestead Act of 1862 fostered settlement. Nebraska was admitted to the Union in 1867 as the 37th state.

▲ *The state capitol towers over the city of Lincoln. Nebraska is the only state with a single-house legislature. Every other state has two houses, like the U.S. Congress.*

◀ *Scottsbluff, a farming community on the North Platte River, was an important stop along the Oregon Trail in the 1800s.*

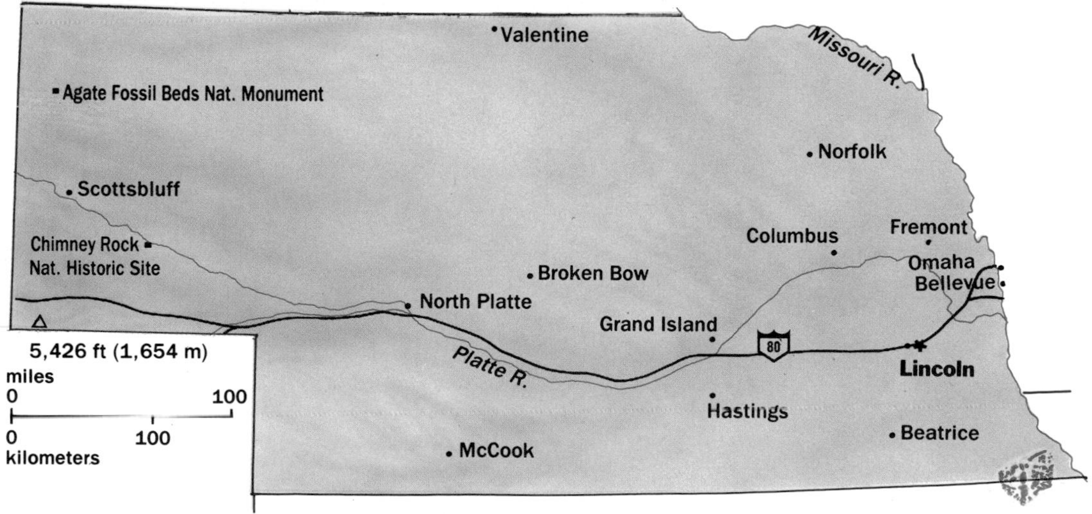

# NEVADA

Mountain bluebird

Sagebrush

Single-leaf piñon

Nevada, in the Southwest, is the driest state in the Union. Arid and mountainous, it cannot support many people. But its gold and silver once attracted prospectors hoping to strike it rich. Now tourists flock to hotel-casinos in Las Vegas and Reno for the same reason. The money they spend directly provides about one third of the jobs in the state.

Nevada receives an average of only 4 inches (10 cm) of rain and snow a year. So forbidding is the terrain that it was one of the last parts of the West to be explored. Eighty-six percent of its land is owned by the federal government. After World War II, the Atomic Energy Commission tested nuclear weapons there.

Important sources of income are the state's gold and silver mines. Nevada leads all states in the production of

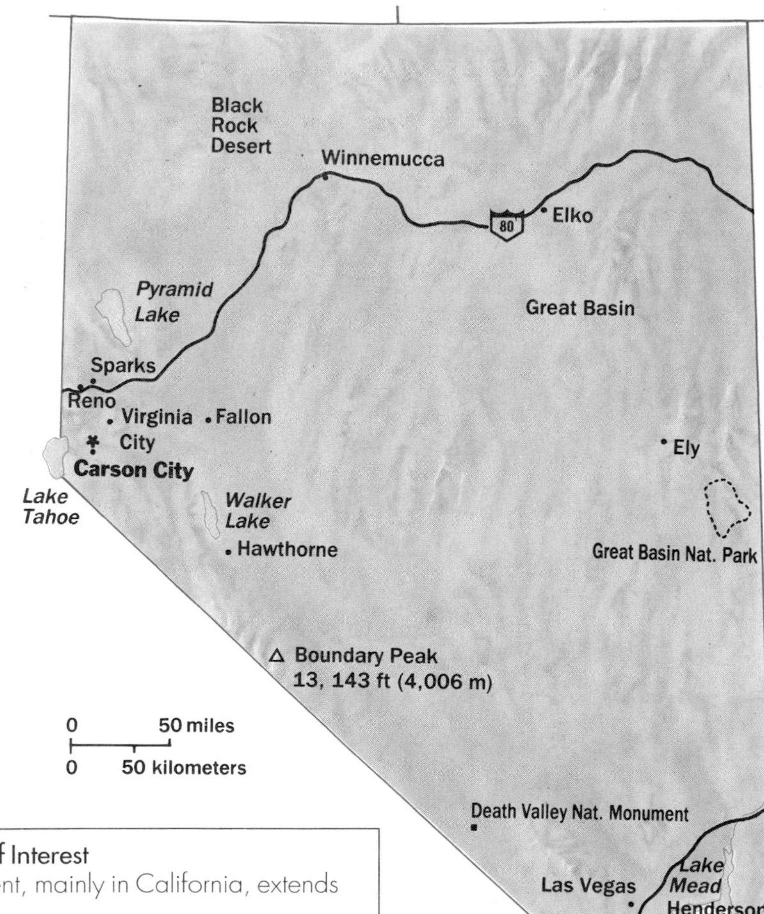


Nevada
**Capital:** Carson City
**Area:** 110,567 sq mi ($286,368 \text{ km}^2$). Rank: 7th
**Population:** 1,201,833 (1990). Rank: 39th
**Statehood:** October 31, 1864
**Principal rivers:** Columbia, Humboldt, Truckee
**Highest point:** Boundary Peak, 13,143 ft (4,006 m)
**Motto:** All for Our Country
**Song:** "Home Means Nevada"

Places of Interest

- Death Valley National Monument, mainly in California, extends into southwestern Nevada.
- Hoover Dam, near Las Vegas, is one of the world's largest hydroelectric dams.
- Lake Tahoe, on the border with California, is a four-season resort.
- Las Vegas, Nevada's largest city and gambling center, brings a neon rainbow of colors to the desert night sky.

these metals. The real wealth comes from tourism, however. The state's easy divorce laws started attracting visitors in the 1920s. Gambling was made legal in 1931. Then the building of Boulder (now Hoover) Dam on the Colorado River created Lake Mead and provided water and power for the growth of Las Vegas. This city became a major gambling and entertainment center after World War II. Lake Tahoe, on the California border, also attracts many visitors.

Mormons were the first whites to settle in Nevada, in the 1850s. In 1859 the discovery of the Comstock Lode, a huge deposit of gold and silver, brought thousands of fortune seekers. Nevada became a state in 1864. The population was only 110,000 in 1940, but it had grown to well over a million by 1990.

► *Casinos compete for business 24 hours a day in Las Vegas. Gambling is Nevada's largest source of income.*

▼ *Cathedral Gorge got its name from the natural clay towers that look like church spires.*

▼ *Virginia City is one of Nevada's most famous ghost towns. It was once a thriving gold-mining center.*

# NEW BRUNSWICK

Purple violet

New Brunswick is one of CANADA's four Atlantic provinces. It lies east of the state of Maine. The interior is chiefly a thick evergreen forest, with many lakes and rivers. The rocky and irregular coast borders two arms of the Atlantic Ocean, the Gulf of St. Lawrence and the Bay of Fundy. The Bay of Fundy has some of the highest tides in the world. The water level rises and falls as much as 60 feet (18 m) with each tide.

The main economic activities are lumbering and making paper and wood products. The largest city is Saint John, which lies at the mouth of the St. John River. It is an important seaport. Fredericton, the capital of the province, is also on the river, but upstream. To the east is Moncton, the second biggest city. The French explorer Samuel de Champlain mapped parts of New Brunswick's coast in the early 1600s. Later in that century and in the 1700s, many French settlers arrived. In 1763, after defeating the French in the French and Indian War, the British took over the area. Many people from New England then began to settle in New Brunswick. They were joined by about 12,000 Loyalists, who fled the United States after the American Revolution. New Brunswick was one of the four original provinces to join the Canadian confederation in 1867.

New Brunswick
**Capital:** Fredericton
**Area:** 28,355 sq mi ($73,440 \text{ km}^2$). Rank: 8th
**Population:** 723,900 (1991). Rank: 8th
**Entry into Confederation:** July 1, 1867 (one of the first four provinces)
**Highest point:** Mt. Carleton, 2,690 ft (820 m)

*▼ The Swallowtail lighthouse on Grand Manan Island protects shipping routes between New Brunswick, Nova Scotia, and Maine.*

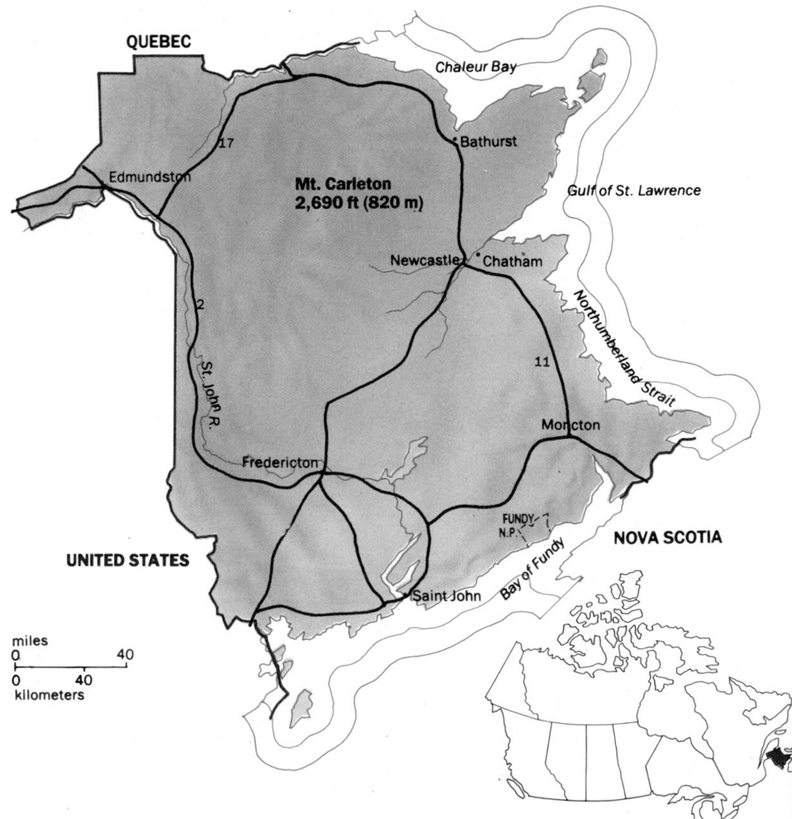

## NEW DEAL 

The New Deal was President Franklin D. ROOSEVELT's program to solve the economic problems caused by the Great DEPRESSION of the 1930s. The program had three main goals: to give *relief* to people suffering hardship; to help businesses *recover*; and to *reform*, or change, the practices of business, finance, industry, and agriculture, to prevent another depression.

Such new agencies as the Public Works Administration and the Works Progress Administration organized the building of bridges and other kinds of work to give jobs to unemployed people. Other agencies, such as the National Recovery Administration and the Agricultural Adjustment Administration, helped businesses and farmers to recover. Business reforms regulated banks and the stock market. The most important social reform was the introduction of social security, which provided unemployment insurance and old-age pensions. The New Deal was only a partial success. Military spending during World War II finally ended the Depression.

**Some New Deal Programs**

**CCC:** The Civilian Conservation Corps gave young people jobs on conservation projects.

**FCC:** The Federal Communications Commission was established to regulate radio, telegraph, and telephone systems.

**FDIC:** The Federal Deposit Insurance Corporation restored confidence in banks by insuring deposits.

**NRA:** The National Recovery Administration monitored working conditions and pricing policies in industry.

**REA:** The Rural Electrification Administration provided electricity for many farms.

**SEC:** The Securities and Exchange Commission was formed to regulate activity in stock markets.

◄ *The Works Progress Administration used civic projects such as road building to provide jobs under the New Deal.*

## NEW ENGLAND 

New England is a region in the northeastern corner of the United States. It is made up of six states: Maine, New Hampshire, Vermont, Massachusetts, Rhode Island, and Connecticut. Boston, the capital of Massachusetts, is the largest city. All of the states except Vermont border on the Atlantic Ocean.

▼ *New England was the center of the American Revolution.*

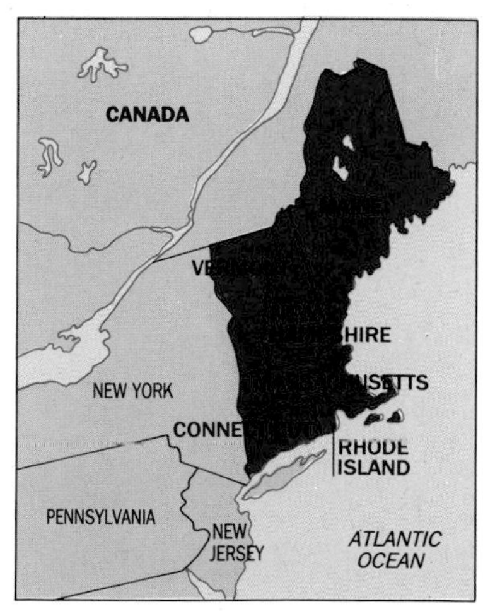

# NEWFOUNDLAND

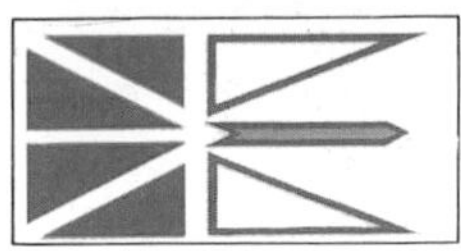

Pitcher plant

CANADA's Atlantic, or Maritime, province of Newfoundland is composed of the island of Newfoundland and the mainland region of Labrador. It is almost the same size as California, but it has only 3 percent of California's population and is the poorest province in Canada. All but 5 percent of the people live on the island of Newfoundland. St. John's, the capital, largest city, and chief seaport, is there.

The economy depends mainly on exploiting the island's natural resources—its forests and fishing grounds. Trees are cut down and converted to pulp, paper, and paper products. The fish are mostly canned or frozen. Labrador has two large mines that produce almost half of Canada's iron ore. Labrador also has the huge Churchill Falls complex for generating electricity.

The first white settlers in North America were Norse explorers who came to the island of Newfoundland about the year 1000. British and French fishermen arrived in the 1500s. Newfoundland was a British colony until 1949, when it voted to join Canada.

**Newfoundland**
**Capital:** St. John's
**Area:** 156,649 sq mi ($405,720 km^2$). Rank: 7th
**Population:** 568,474 (1991). Rank: 9th
**Entry into Confederation:** March 31, 1949 (10th province)
**Highest point:** Mt. Caubvick, 5,322 ft (1,622 m)

▲ *Historic homes built in the 1700s and 1800s run down to the waterfront of St. John's, Newfoundland's main port and capital.*

*◀ Jacques Cartier landed on the Gaspé Peninsula in 1534 and claimed the surrounding land in the name of France.*

## NEW FRANCE

New France was the name for France's North American colonies in the 1600s and 1700s. It was made up of three colonies—Canada, Acadia, and Louisiana. Canada and Acadia covered what is now Canada's eastern and Atlantic provinces. Louisiana made up a large part of the Mississippi River valley and extended south to the Gulf of Mexico.

Explorers, fishermen, and fur traders had claimed much of North America for the French in the 1500s. They entered North America through the Gulf of St. Lawrence, which Jacques CARTIER claimed for France in 1534. Samuel de CHAMPLAIN, an explorer, established the settlement of Quebec in 1608. Montreal was founded by Catholic missionaries 34 years later.

France's King Louis XIV made New France a French province in 1663. Louisiana became a colony in 1699, and the French built a string of forts along the Ohio River to link it with the other two colonies of New France. The British felt that New France blocked their chance to expand westward in North America. They also had had many disputes with the French about valuable fur-trading rights. After about 50 years of skirmishes, things came to a head with the FRENCH AND INDIAN WAR (1756–1763). British victory in that war ended France's colonial empire in North America.

Important Dates for New France

**1534:** Jacques Cartier claims St. Lawrence Valley for France.
**1604:** Acadia founded.
**1608:** Settlement established at Quebec.
**1642:** Ville-Marie (Montreal) founded.
**1663:** New France becomes a province of France.
**1682:** LaSalle claims Mississippi Valley for France, naming it Louisiana.
**1696:** Louisiana becomes a French colony.
**1713:** France loses Newfoundland and Nova Scotia to Britain.
**1762:** Louisiana is given to Spain.
**1763:** France loses Canada to Britain.

**During the 1600s and 1700s, the fur trade was the chief economic activity in New France. Furs were very valuable, largely because of the growing popularity of fur hats in Europe.**

# NEW HAMPSHIRE

New Hampshire is one of the six states of NEW ENGLAND in the northeastern corner of the United States. Its independent but democratic spirit is best expressed in town meetings, where everyone can vote on local issues. Every four years its early presidential primary elections attract candidates to the state.

From a narrow, 18-mile (29-km) Atlantic coastline, New Hampshire rises northward to the White Mountains. There are found the rock outcroppings that have given New Hampshire the nickname the Granite State. There also is Mount Washington, the highest peak (6,288 feet, or 1,917 m) in the Northeast. Mount Washington is one of the windiest places on earth. The Connecticut River forms most of the state's western border. More than 80 percent of New Hampshire is

◀ *Visitors find New Hampshire's covered bridges quaint, but they still perform their original duty—protecting travelers from harsh New England winters.*

▼ *Traditional New Hampshire buildings, such as the old village schoolhouse at Fitzwilliam, are built of wood. New Hampshire's other main building material, granite, is used for the curb in front.*

New Hampshire
**Capital:** Concord
**Area:** 9,351 sq mi (24,219 km²). Rank: 46th
**Population:** 1,109,252 (1990). Rank: 40th
**Statehood:** June 21, 1788
**Principal rivers:** Androscoggin, Connecticut, Merrimack
**Highest point:** Mt. Washington, 6,288 ft (1,917 m)
**Motto:** Live Free or Die
**Song:** "Old New Hampshire"

forested. The state is an all-year attraction for campers, skiers, fishermen, and hunters. The forests yield lumber, wood pulp, and paper products. The southern part of the state has most of the people and industry. The four biggest cities—Manchester, Nashua, Portsmouth, and Concord, the capital—are in southeastern New Hampshire. These cities once had many textile mills. Now they attract firms that produce high technology goods such as computer components and software. Many of these firms moved north from the Boston area because taxes are lower in New Hampshire.

English settlers first established themselves in New Hampshire in 1623. It was the first of the original 13 colonies to establish an independent government, six months before the Declaration of Independence.

▲ *Mt. Chocorua towers over New Hampshire's forested eastern border with Maine.*

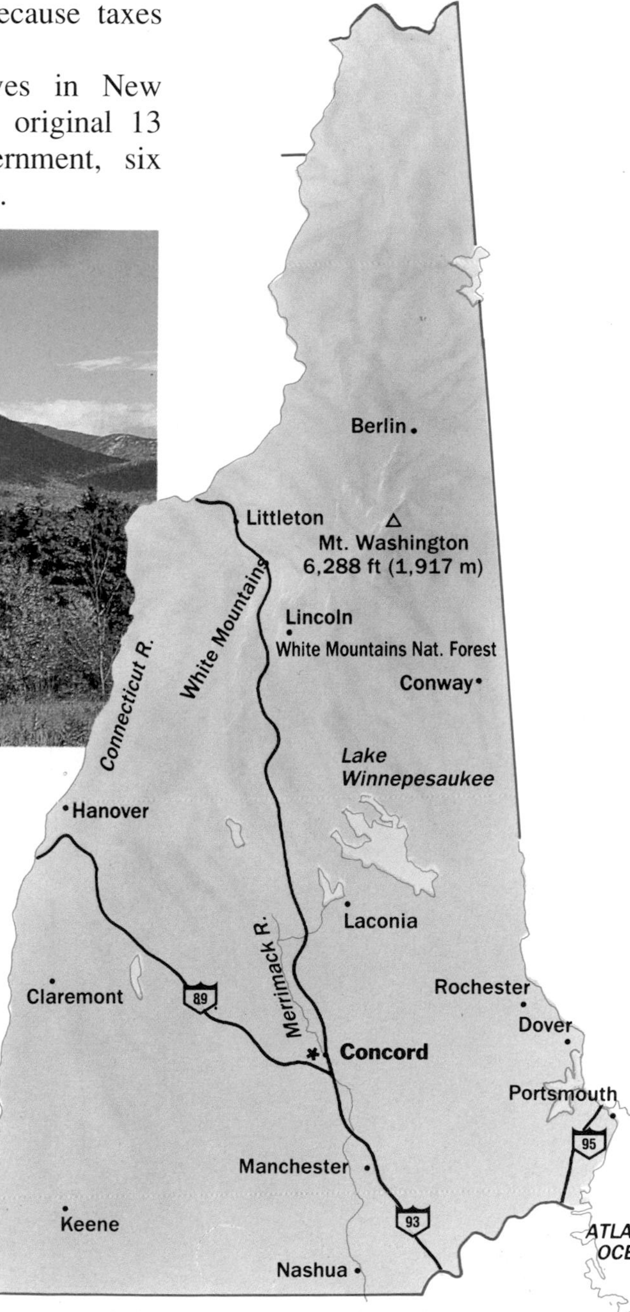


**Places of Interest**

- Dartmouth College Winter Carnival, held each February in Hanover, features ice sculptures and winter sports.
- You can climb, take a cog railway, or drive to the top of Mt. Washington, where the world's highest winds have been recorded.
- The Kancamagus Highway runs between Lincoln and Conway in the White Mountain National Forest.

## NEW JERSEY

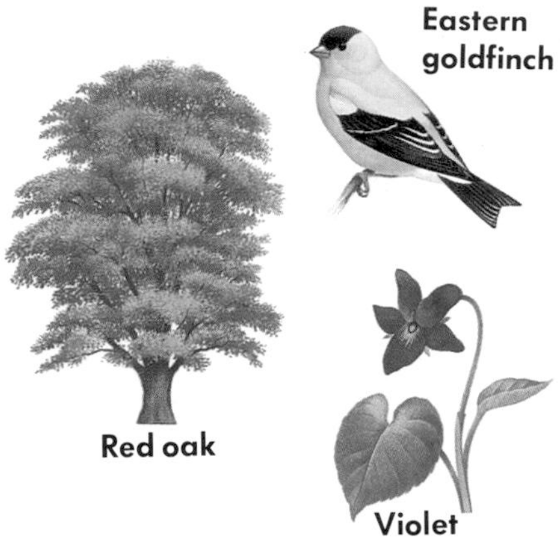

Eastern goldfinch

Red oak

Violet

New Jersey
**Capital:** Trenton
**Area:** 8,722 sq mi (22,590 km$^2$). Rank: 47th
**Population:** 7,730,188 (1990). Rank: 9th
**Statehood:** Dec. 18, 1787
**Principal rivers:** Delaware, Hudson
**Highest point:** High Point, 1,803 ft (550 m)
**Motto:** Liberty and Prosperity
**Song:** None

Places of Interest
- Atlantic City is a beach resort famous for its boardwalk, nightclubs, and gambling casinos.
- The Edison National Historic Site, in West Orange, preserves Thomas Edison's home and many of his models.
- Princeton University has an attractive campus in the town of Princeton, which is also home of Princeton Battlefield, scene of a decisive American victory in the Revolutionary War.

Benjamin Franklin called New Jersey "a rumkeg tapped at both ends" because it lies between Philadelphia on the west and New York City on the east. Some people see the state only while driving between these cities. The entire population is classified as living in metropolitan areas. Yet New Jersey has surprising variety.

The state is bounded on the west by the Delaware River and on the east by the Hudson River and Atlantic Ocean. Farms in central and southwestern New Jersey have given it the nickname the Garden State. The rich soil here is ideal for growing crops such as potatoes, peaches, and tomatoes. Along the Jersey shore are seaside resorts such as Atlantic City and Cape May. Atlantic City, long a convention center, has also become the site of gambling casinos. Also in southeastern New Jersey are the mysterious Pine Barrens. In central New Jersey is Princeton University, one of the nation's finest. The scenic Delaware Water Gap is in the northwest.

The northeast has the state's biggest city, Newark,

and most of its industry. New Jersey is a leader in producing pharmaceutical drugs, chemicals, and petroleum products. It was in this industrial part of New Jersey that Thomas Edison maintained his workshop. Newark and Elizabeth are major ports, and Newark is a center of the insurance industry.

The first Europeans in New Jersey were Dutch and Swedish settlers, but in 1664 the English took control. Five major Revolutionary War battles were fought in New Jersey. The state began to build many factories after the Civil War.

▲ *Atlantic City is famous for its long Boardwalk, which stretches 4½ miles (7.2 km) along the coast of the Atlantic Ocean.*



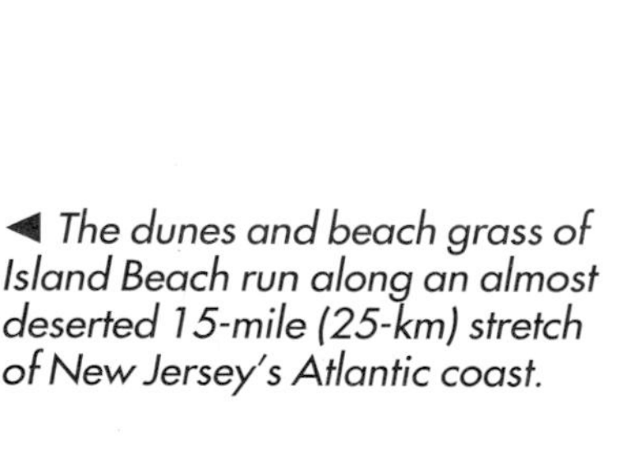

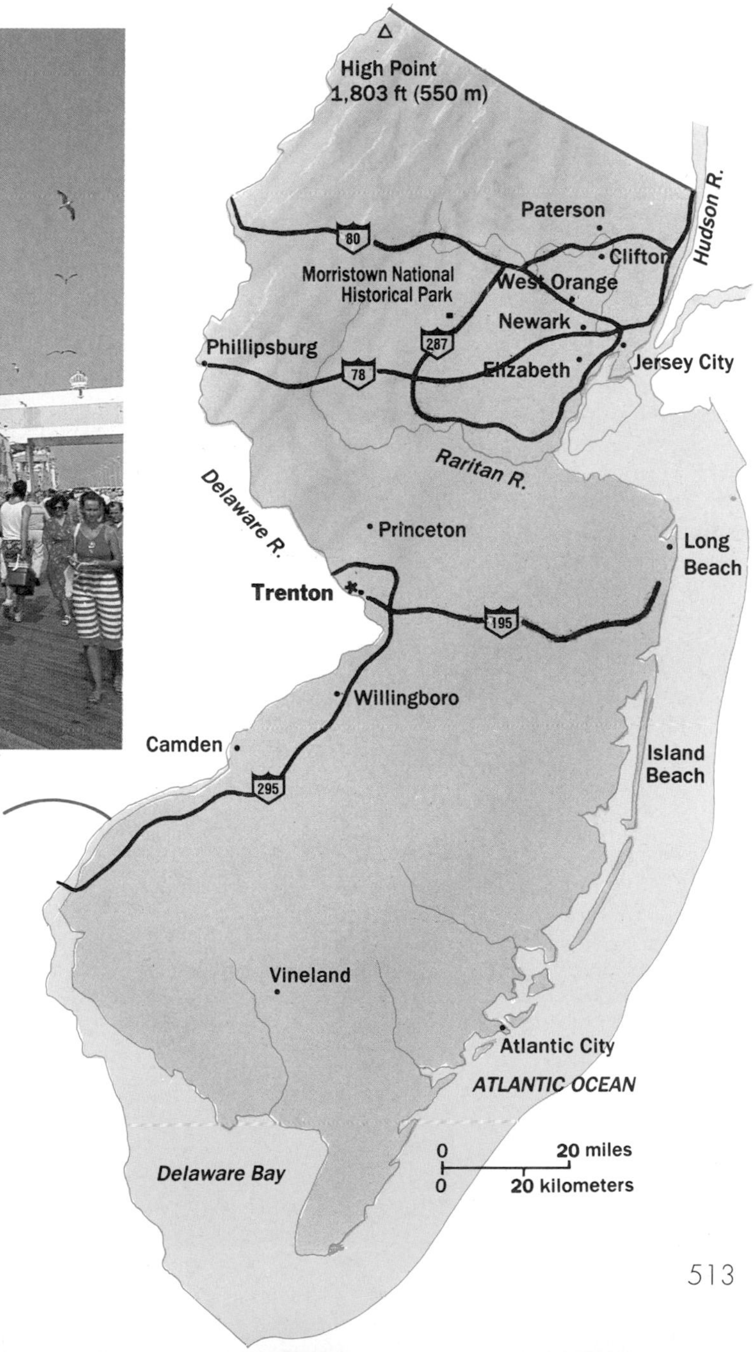

◀ *The dunes and beach grass of Island Beach run along an almost deserted 15-mile (25-km) stretch of New Jersey's Atlantic coast.*

# NEW MEXICO

New Mexico is a state in the Southwest. Its canyon walls, buttes, and mesas turn golden in the rays of the setting sun. Desert flowers bloom overnight after a sudden thunderstorm. The state's Indian pueblos (villages) and Hispanic heritage tell of a way of life distinct from "Anglo" culture. Truly New Mexico is, as its nickname proclaims, the Land of Enchantment.

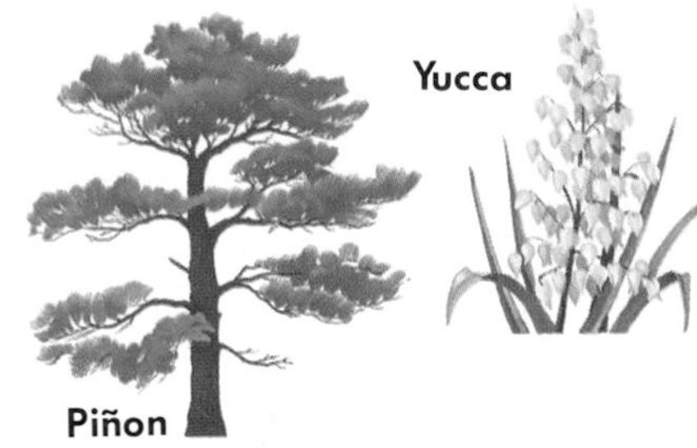


This lovely yet arid land is mostly mountainous, although the eastern third is a high plateau. The RIO GRANDE cuts through the center of the state, north to south. The main wealth is in minerals. New Mexico produces oil and natural gas. It is also a leader in the mining of potash, copper, silver, and uranium.

The metropolitan area that includes ALBUQUERQUE has about a third of the state's population and more

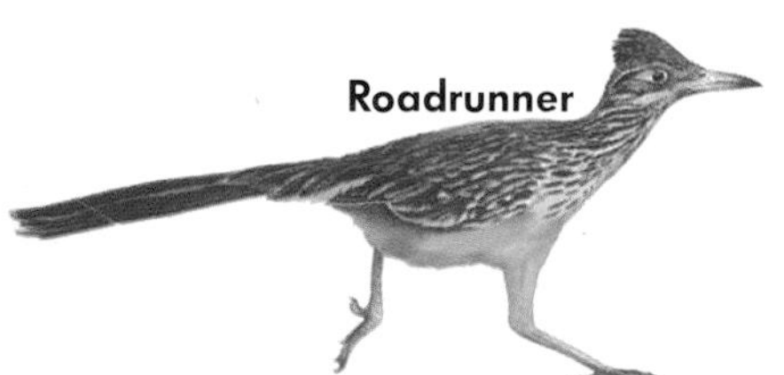

► *Mud-baked adobe pueblos, such as this one at Taos, can last for centuries in the dry New Mexican climate.*

▼ *The rock formations of El Morro National Monument are typical of the mesas (flat-top rocks) of New Mexico.*

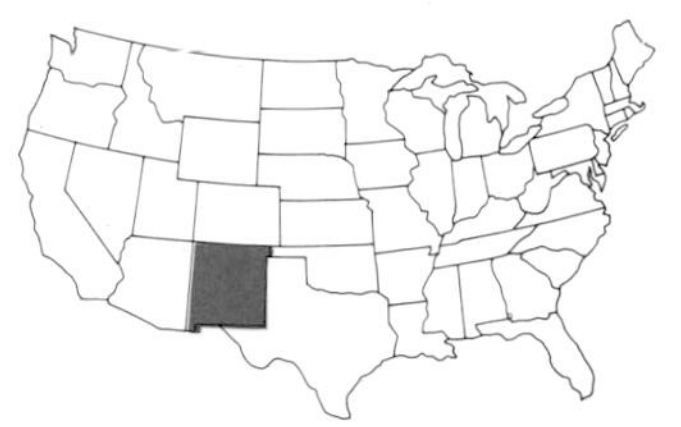

than half its manufacturing. SANTA FE, the charming state capital, was founded in 1609, 11 years before the Pilgrims landed at Plymouth Rock. It retains its colonial character, and its cultural life includes opera and theater. Taos has an artist's colony, set among the northernmost of the 18 Indian pueblos along the Rio Grande. Carlsbad Caverns, a huge underground labyrinth, is a national park. Another attraction is Los Alamos Scientific Laboratory, which developed the first atomic bomb. This device was successfully tested in the New Mexico desert in 1945.

Seeking gold and silver, the Spanish explorer Francisco CORONADO passed through New Mexico in 1540. Spanish colonization began in 1598. The area passed from Spain to Mexico in 1821 but was won by the United States during the MEXICAN WAR (1846–1848). It did not become a state until 1912.

► *The International Space Hall of Fame, in Alamogordo, honors pioneers in space travel.*

New Mexico
**Capital:** Santa Fe
**Area:** 121,598 sq mi (314,939 km$^2$). Rank: 5th
**Population:** 1,515,069 (1990). Rank: 37th
**Statehood:** January 6, 1912
**Principal rivers:** Gila, Pecos, Rio Grande
**Highest point:** Wheeler Peak, 13,161 ft (4,011 m)
**Motto:** *Crescit Eundo* (It Grows as it Goes)
**Song:** "O, Fair New Mexico"

Places of Interest

- Carlsbad Caverns National Park contains the world's largest caves.
- Bandelier National Monument, near Santa Fe, has Indian cliff dwellings built around A.D. 1000.
- Los Alamos Bradbury Science Hall and Museum displays the history of nuclear energy.
- Santa Fe was founded by the Spanish in 1609, 11 years before the Pilgrims landed in Massachusetts.

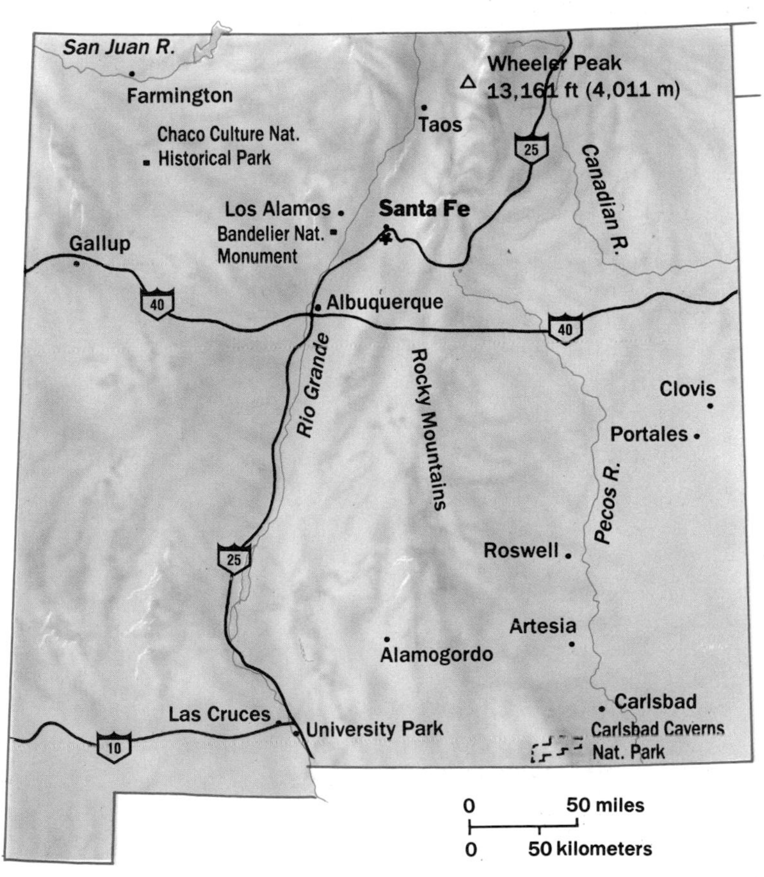

**About 20 languages were spoken in the colony of New Netherland. Many settlers were attracted to the Dutch colony, which was sponsored by a trading company.**

## NEW NETHERLAND

The colony of New Netherland was founded by the Dutch West India Company in 1624. It included parts of what are now the states of New York, New Jersey, Connecticut, and Delaware. In 1626 the Dutch bought Manhattan Island from the Indians and built New Amsterdam (now New York City) on its southern tip. The port of New Amsterdam prospered and attracted settlers from other countries. It was captured by the English in 1664 and renamed New York.

▲ *This building, with its balconies and iron grillwork, is typical of the architecture found in the French Quarter of New Orleans.*

## NEW ORLEANS

New Orleans is one of the liveliest cities in the United States. It is the largest city in LOUISIANA, with 496,938 people, and one of the country's busiest ports. It is located on the Mississippi River, about 110 miles (177 km) north of where it empties into the Gulf of Mexico.

Many different ethnic groups have contributed to the glamour of New Orleans. Two of them are the Creoles and the CAJUNS. The Creoles are descendants of the early French and Spanish settlers. The Cajuns are descendants of French-speaking people who were forced out of Canada by the British in the 1700s. The city's architectural style, its food, and many of its social customs come from these two groups. The blacks of New Orleans developed jazz there around the turn of the century.

New Orleans' greatest event is the Mardi Gras carnival. It attracts thousands of visitors who watch the costumed merrymakers dance and sing and parade through the streets. Tourism is an important part of the city's economy. The manufacture of petrochemicals is also a major activity.

## NEWSPAPERS

**The first regular American newspaper was the *Boston News-Letter*, published in 1704 by John Campbell. By 1770, the colonies had more than 30 newspapers.**

The United States has about 1,600 daily newspapers. Their total circulation is 62,700,000. In addition, there are 840 Sunday newspapers, with a total circulation of 61,500,000.

Only six newspapers are actually "national." Of these, by far the largest are the *Wall Street Journal* (circulation 1,931,000) and *USA Today* (1,677,000 on Monday–Thursday, 2,061,000 on Friday). Other nation-

◀ *Journalists and editors discuss the next edition of a newspaper during an editorial meeting.*

al newspapers are the *Christian Science Monitor, New York Times* (national edition), *Investor's Business Daily*, and *National* (a sports newspaper).

The remaining newspapers serve states, cities, or local regions. They report local news as well as state, national, and other world news. Nevertheless, some of these are also read in other parts of the country and also abroad. The best known of these papers are *The New York Times* (circulation 1,110,000), *Los Angeles Times* (1,177,000), *Chicago Tribune* (723,000), *Washington Post* (791,000), *San Francisco Chronicle* (553,000), and *Boston Globe* (504,000).

The Top 20 Daily Newspapers in the U.S. (by circulation)

1. *Wall Street Journal*
2. *USA Today*
3. *Los Angeles Times*
4. *New York Times*
5. *Washington Post*
6. *New York Daily News*
7. *Long Island Newsday*
8. *Chicago Tribune*
9. *Detroit Free Press*
10. *San Francisco Chronicle*
11. *Chicago Sun-Times*
12. *Boston Globe*
13. *Philadelphia Inquirer*
14. *Newark Star-Ledger*
15. *New York Post*
16. *Detroit News*
17. *Miami Herald*
18. *Cleveland Plain Dealer*
19. *Minneapolis Star-Tribune*
20. *Houston Chronicle*

◀ *A technician called a compositor arranges headlines, pictures, and text for the* Hartford Courant.

# NEW YORK

New York is located in the northeastern United States. It is second only to California in population. A leader in almost every field of human endeavor, New York is truly the Empire State.

New York's varied topography includes the ADIRONDACK MOUNTAINS, in the northeastern part of the state. Three lakes—Erie, Ontario, and Champlain—and two rivers—the St. Lawrence and Hudson—form part of its borders. Ships ply the St. Lawrence Seaway and the state's extensive canal system, linking New York to the Midwest and Canada. New York is an important fruit-growing and dairying state. Buffalo, Rochester, and Syracuse are important cities. The magnificent NIAGARA FALLS draws visitors, as do the Catskill Mountains, West Point, and the Thousand Islands. Populous LONG ISLAND has major industries, yet millions of people enjoy its sandy beaches.

NEW YORK CITY is the national center of banking, finance, trade, communications, arts, publishing, and fashion. It has one of the finest natural harbors in the world and remains an important port. Its music halls, museums, and theaters are world famous. New York

New York
**Capital:** Albany
**Area:** 54,475 sq mi ($141{,}089\ km^2$). Rank: 27th
**Population:** 17,990,455 (1990). Rank: 2nd
**Statehood:** July 26, 1788
**Principal rivers:** Hudson, Mohawk, Genesee
**Highest point:** Mt. Marcy, 5,344 ft (1,629 m)
**Motto:** *Excelsior* (Ever Upward)
**Song:** "I Love New York"

► *The Ausable River cascades through the Adirondack Mountains near Lake Placid in upstate New York.*

State's varied population includes more blacks, Puerto Ricans, and Roman Catholics than that of any other state. One third of all the nation's Jews live there.

The dutch colony of NEW NETHERLAND passed to the English in 1664 and was renamed New York. The Battle of Saratoga in 1777 is called the turning point of the Revolutionary War. Always a center of immigration, New York was the nation's most populous state by 1820, and it remained so until 1963.

Places of Interest

- Adirondack Park, covering 6 million acres (2.4 million ha) of mountains and forests, is the largest park in the country.
- Corning Glass Center, in Corning, displays the industry and history of glassmaking over 3,500 years.
- New York City, the nation's largest urban center, is a world leader in advertising, finance, theater, and many other areas.
- Niagara Falls, by the city of the same name, is one of the most famous and impressive waterfalls in the world.

▲ *Notre Dame church overlooks the quiet bandstand on the village green in the small town of Malone.*

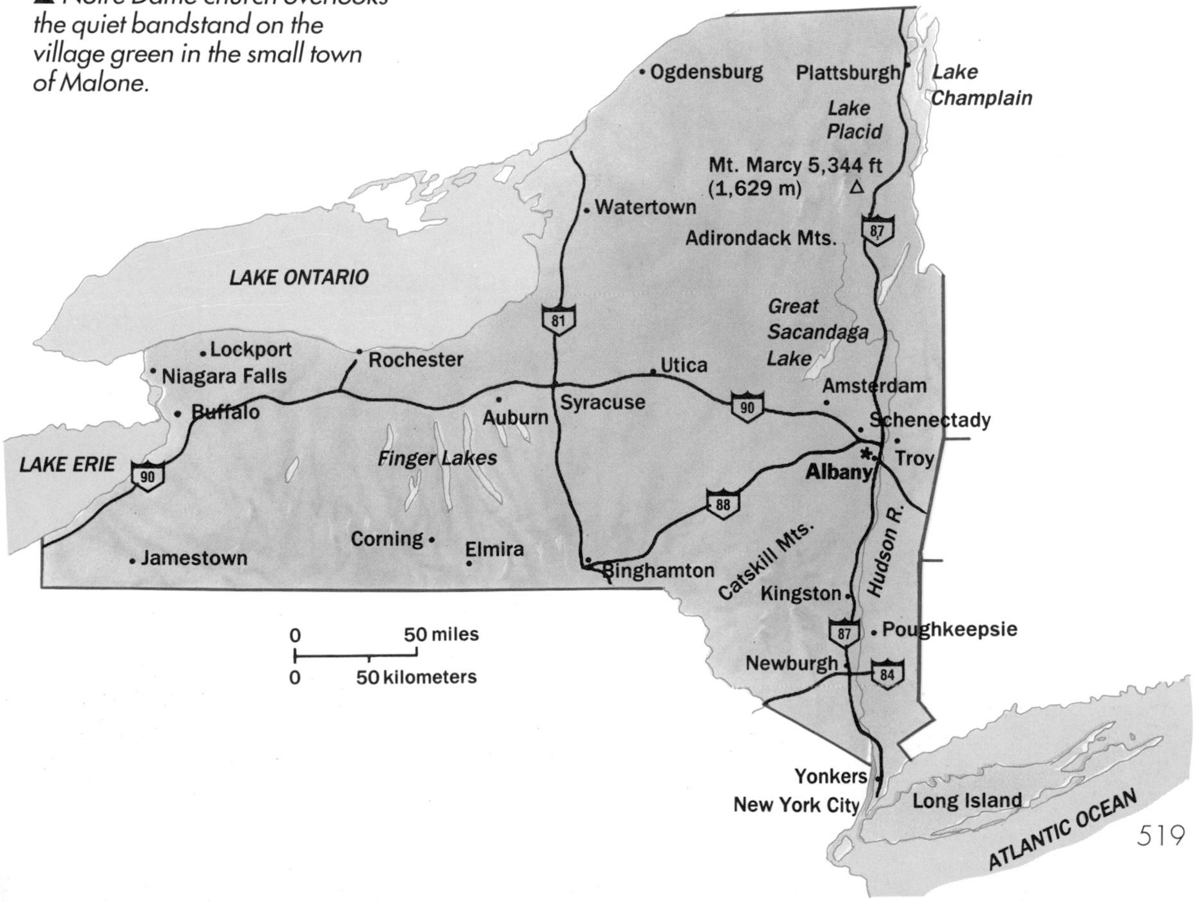

Ogdensburg
Plattsburgh
Lake Champlain
Lake Placid
Mt. Marcy 5,344 ft (1,629 m)
Watertown
Adirondack Mts.
87
LAKE ONTARIO
81
Great Sacandaga Lake
Lockport
Niagara Falls
Rochester
Utica
Amsterdam
Buffalo
Auburn
Syracuse
90
Schenectady
Troy
Albany
LAKE ERIE
90
Finger Lakes
88
Hudson R.
Catskill Mts.
Jamestown
Corning
Elmira
Binghamton
Kingston
0 50 miles
0 50 kilometers
87
Poughkeepsie
Newburgh
84
Yonkers
New York City
Long Island
ATLANTIC OCEAN

**One of the most famous ferry services in the world runs between Manhattan and Staten Island. Until 1972 the fare was kept at a nickel for the half-hour trip.**

## NEW YORK CITY

New York City is one of the world's greatest cities. With a population of 7,322,564, it is the largest city in the United States. It stands at the point where the Hudson and East rivers flow into the Atlantic Ocean. New York's importance as a port dates from the early 1600s when the Dutch bought Manhattan from the local Indians for $24. Manhattan is one of five boroughs that make up modern New York City. The other boroughs are Brooklyn, the Bronx, Queens, and Staten Island. Most New Yorkers live in these boroughs, but many work in Manhattan. In New York the streets seem to have a personality. Fifth Avenue represents wealth; Wall Street is the home of the stock market; Madison Avenue is the center of advertising; and Broadway is the nation's theater capital.

The Italian explorer Giovanni da VERRAZANO sailed into New York Bay in 1524. Henry HUDSON sailed up the Hudson River in 1609, and 15 years later the Dutch established the settlement of New Amsterdam on the southern tip of Manhattan. The British captured New Amsterdam in 1664 and renamed it New York. New York City became the first capital of the United States (1789–1790). During the late 1800s and early 1900s, millions of immigrants came to the United States. Many stayed in New York. Southern blacks and Puerto Ricans flocked to the city after World War II. Today, Asians, Latin Americans, Africans, and others are adding to the ethnic mix of the city.

## NEZ PERCÉ

The Nez Percé INDIANS lived along the Idaho-Washington-Oregon border. During the 1700s, they became fine breeders and trainers of horses. The Nez Percé had a peaceful relationship with white settlers until 1855, when they were forced to give up much of their land. They lost more land in 1863, after gold was discovered there. In 1877 the Nez Percé were ordered to move to a reservation. A war broke out, during which Chief JOSEPH tried to lead his people to Canada. In October 1877 he surrendered near the U.S.–Canadian border. Today about 2,000 Nez Percé live on or near a reservation in Idaho.

▲ *Peopes Tolict, a Nez Percé farmer, stands with his wife in front of their traditional tepee.*

## NIAGARA FALLS

The spectacular Niagara Falls is on the Niagara River, on the border between New York State and the Canadian province of Ontario. Halfway between Lake Erie and Lake Ontario, it is one of the most famous sights of North America. Millions of people visit it every year. Niagara Falls actually consists of two waterfalls, the American Falls—167 feet (51 m) high and 1,000 feet (305 m) across—in the United States and Horseshoe Falls in Canada. Below the falls is the Niagara Gorge. A 2.25-mile (3.6-km) stretch of this can be navigated by

▼ *The twin 110-story towers of the World Trade Center (left) tower over Manhattan's famous skyline.*

**The first European to sight Niagara Falls was a Roman Catholic priest, Father Louis Hennepin, in 1678. He wrote: "These waters foam and boil in a fearful manner. They thunder continually."**

boats. Here, the *Maid of the Mist* excursion boats take tourists along the base of the American Falls. Niagara Falls is one of North America's most important sources of hydroelectric power.

Niagara Falls was formed about 12,000 years ago, at the end of the last ice age. The water from the melting glaciers caused Lake Erie to overflow, creating the Niagara River, which flowed toward Lake Ontario. The falls formed where the river plunged over a cliff.

► *Loose boulders tumble off Niagara Falls because the churning waters eat into the base of the cliff.*

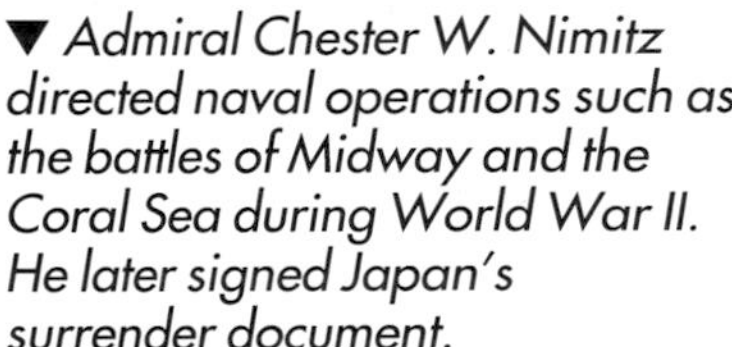

▼ *Admiral Chester W. Nimitz directed naval operations such as the battles of Midway and the Coral Sea during World War II. He later signed Japan's surrender document.*

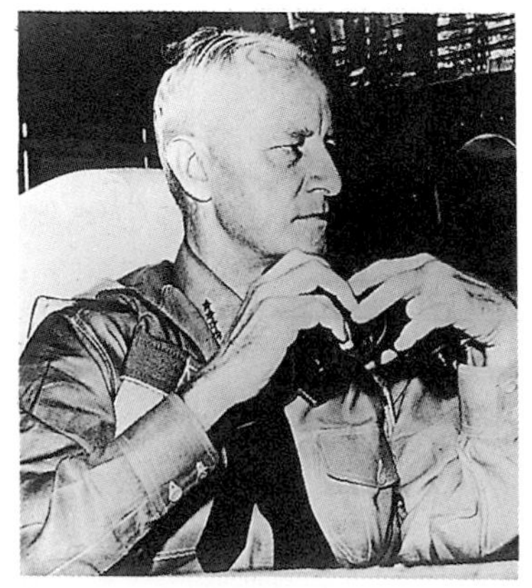

## NIMITZ, Chester W.

Admiral Chester W. Nimitz (1885–1966) planned and led the successful naval war against the Japanese in the Pacific during World War II. Born in Fredericksburg, Texas, Nimitz graduated from the U.S. Naval Academy in 1905. After the Japanese attack on PEARL HARBOR in December 1941, he was made commander of the U.S. Pacific Fleet. He directed American naval forces in many battles, including MIDWAY (1942), Leyte Gulf (1944), and IWO JIMA (1945). Nimitz signed the peace treaty for the United States when Japan surrendered in August 1945.

# NIXON, Richard M.

Richard Milhous Nixon was the 37th president of the United States. Nixon ended U.S. participation in the VIETNAM WAR and improved relations with the Soviet Union and China. He was the first president to resign from office.

After World War II service in the Navy, Nixon served in Congress from 1947 to 1952. There he won a reputation by pursuing charges of Communist subversion in government. He was elected vice president in 1952 and 1956 as running mate to Dwight D. EISENHOWER, the Republican candidate. In 1960, Nixon narrowly lost the presidential election to John F. KENNEDY. But, in another close race, against Democrat Hubert Humphrey, he was elected president in 1968.

**Richard Milhous Nixon**
**Born:** January 9, 1913, in Yorba Linda, California
**Education:** Whittier College
**Political party:** Republican
**Term of office:** 1969–1974
**Married:** 1940 to Thelma Catherine (Pat) Ryan

◀ *Richard Nixon was a guest of Chinese leader Mao Zedong in 1972, when he became the first U.S. president to visit China.*

Nixon ordered the heavy bombing of North Vietnam during the Vietnam War and extended the war to neighboring Cambodia while reducing the number of U.S. troops. A settlement reached in early 1973 resulted in the withdrawal of all American forces. His visit to China in 1972 began a process that later resulted in diplomatic ties with the Communist regime there. Also in 1972, he visited the Soviet Union and signed an agreement to limit nuclear weapons.

Nixon was re-elected by a landslide in 1972. In 1974, Congress began the process of removing him from office for his role in the Watergate scandal, which involved illegal campaign activities. He resigned and was succeeded by Gerald R. FORD.

▼ *An Air Force helicopter took President Nixon from the White House lawn on August 9, 1974. He was the first president to resign from office.*

**Sinclair Lewis**
**Nobel Prize for literature (1930)**

▲ *Sinclair Lewis was the first American to win the Nobel Prize for literature. William A. Fowler and Barbara McClintock joined American prizewinners in other fields.*

**William A. Fowler**
**Nobel Prize for physics (1983)**

**Barbara McClintock**
**Nobel Prize for physiology (1983)**

## NOBEL PRIZE

Nobel prizes have been awarded each year since 1901 in a number of fields. There have been many U.S. winners (there may be more than one in a single year): 35 for chemistry; 19 for economics (only given since 1969); 11 for literature, including Sinclair LEWIS, Eugene O'NEILL, William FAULKNER, Ernest HEMINGWAY, Isaac Bashevis SINGER, and Joseph Brodsky; 69 for physiology or medicine, including James WATSON in 1962 for his work with DNA; and 53 for physics. The special prize for contributions to world peace has been

Some U.S. Winners of Nobel Prizes

**Physics**

| | |
|---|---|
| 1988 | Leon M. Lederman, Melvin Schwarz, Jack Steinberger |
| 1989 | Norman F. Ramsay |
| 1990 | Jerome I. Friedman, Henry W. Kendall |
| 1993 | Joseph H. Taylor, Russell A. Hulse |

**Physiology or Medicine**

| | |
|---|---|
| 1985 | Michael S. Brown, Joseph L. Goldstein |
| 1986 | Stanley Cohen |
| 1988 | Gertrude B. Elion, George H. Hitchings |
| 1989 | J. Michael Bishop, Harold E. Varmus |
| 1990 | Joseph E. Murrary E. Donnal Thomas |
| 1992 | Edmond Fischer, Edwin Krebs |
| 1993 | Phillip Sharp |

**Chemistry**

| | |
|---|---|
| 1985 | Herbert A. Hauptman, Jerome Karle |
| 1986 | Dudley R. Herschbach, Yuan T. Lee |
| 1987 | Charles J. Pedersen, Donald J. Cram |
| 1989 | Sidney Altman, Thomas R. Cech |
| 1990 | Elias James Corey |
| 1992 | Rudolph Marcus |
| 1993 | Kary B. Mullis |

**Literature**

| | |
|---|---|
| 1930 | Sinclair Lewis |
| 1936 | Eugene O'Neill |
| 1938 | Pearl S. Buck |
| 1949 | William Faulkner |
| 1954 | Ernest Hemingway |
| 1962 | John Steinbeck |
| 1976 | Saul Bellow |
| 1978 | Isaac Bashevis Singer |
| 1980 | Czeslaw Milosz (Polish-U.S.) |
| 1993 | Toni Morrison |

**Peace**

| | |
|---|---|
| 1950 | Ralph J. Bunche |
| 1953 | George C. Marshall |
| 1962 | Linus Pauling |
| 1964 | Martin Luther King, Jr. |
| 1970 | Norman E. Borlaug |
| 1973 | Henry Kissinger |
| 1985 | International Physicians for the Prevention of Nuclear War |
| 1986 | Elie Wiesel |

**Economics**

| | |
|---|---|
| 1985 | Franco Modigliani (Italian-U.S.) |
| 1986 | James M. Buchanan |
| 1987 | Robert Solow |
| 1990 | Harry M. Markowitz, William F. Sharpe, Merton H. Miller |
| 1991 | Ronald H. Coase |
| 1992 | Gary Becker |
| 1993 | Robert W. Fogel, Douglass North |

awarded to 18 U.S. citizens. They include Presidents Theodore ROOSEVELT and Woodrow WILSON, Ralph BUNCHE, Rev. Dr. Martin Luther KING, Jr., Henry KISSINGER, and Elie WIESEL.

## NORTH AMERICA *See the special article on pages 526–527*

## NORTH ATLANTIC TREATY ORGANIZATION

The North Atlantic Treaty Organization (NATO) is a regional defense alliance of 16 member nations. These are Belgium, Canada, Denmark, France, Germany, Great Britain, Greece, Iceland, Italy, Luxembourg, the Netherlands, Norway, Portugal, Spain, Turkey, and the United States. Its governing body is the North Atlantic Council, with headquarters near Brussels, Belgium. There are three main military commands; the European command, Atlantic Ocean command, and the English Channel command. NATO was established in 1949 in response to fears that Soviet troops would overrun Western Europe.

**Elie Wiesel**
**Nobel Peace Prize (1986)**

▲ *Romanian-born Elie Wiesel contributed to world peace by teaching the public about the horrors of World War II.*

▼ *A U.S. naval landing craft takes part in a multinational NATO exercise on the Italian island of Sardinia.*

# NORTH AMERICA

North America includes Canada, the United States, Mexico, Central America, and the West Indian islands of the Caribbean Sea. It is the third largest continent in the world. Some geographers also include the island of Greenland, to the northeast of Canada, as part of North America.

The land and climate of North America vary greatly. In the far north, the land is permanently frozen and the temperatures are usually frigid. The climate is more temperate in southern Canada and in most of the United States. In southern Florida, the climate is subtropical, and farther south, in parts of Mexico and in Central America and the Caribbean, there are tropical rain forests. And deserts cover the southwestern United States and parts of Mexico.

Great mountain ranges extend along the western part of North America. These include the Rocky Mountains, the Sierra Nevada, and the Sierra Madre. The Appalachian Mountains are near the east coast. Between the Appalachians and the Rockies are the Central Plains and the Great Plains. North America has many large rivers. The largest, the Mississippi-Missouri, drains most of the center of the continent. The continent's plants and animals are as varied as the topography. (See the articles Plant Life and Animal Life.) Many areas have rich supplies of minerals.

People first entered North America at least 12,000 years ago. They came across a land bridge that connected Alaska and Siberia. The Eskimos (Inuits), Aleuts, and American Indians are descendants of the first Americans. European settlement began in the 1500s. Since then, millions of immigrants have come to North America from all over the world.

▲ *The Canadian city of Toronto, in the province of Ontario, is situated on the shores of Lake Ontario. The CN Tower dominates the skyline of the city.*

▼ *Water tumbles 2,425 ft (739 m) in three falls at Yosemite National Park in California.*

▼ *St. George's is the capital and largest city of Grenada, an island nation in the Caribbean Sea. Its economy is based mainly on tourism and agriculture. Grenada is a leading producer nutmeg and other spices.*

▲ *Denali National Park in Alaska is a rich wildlife area. The park contains Mt. McKinley, North America's highest peak.*

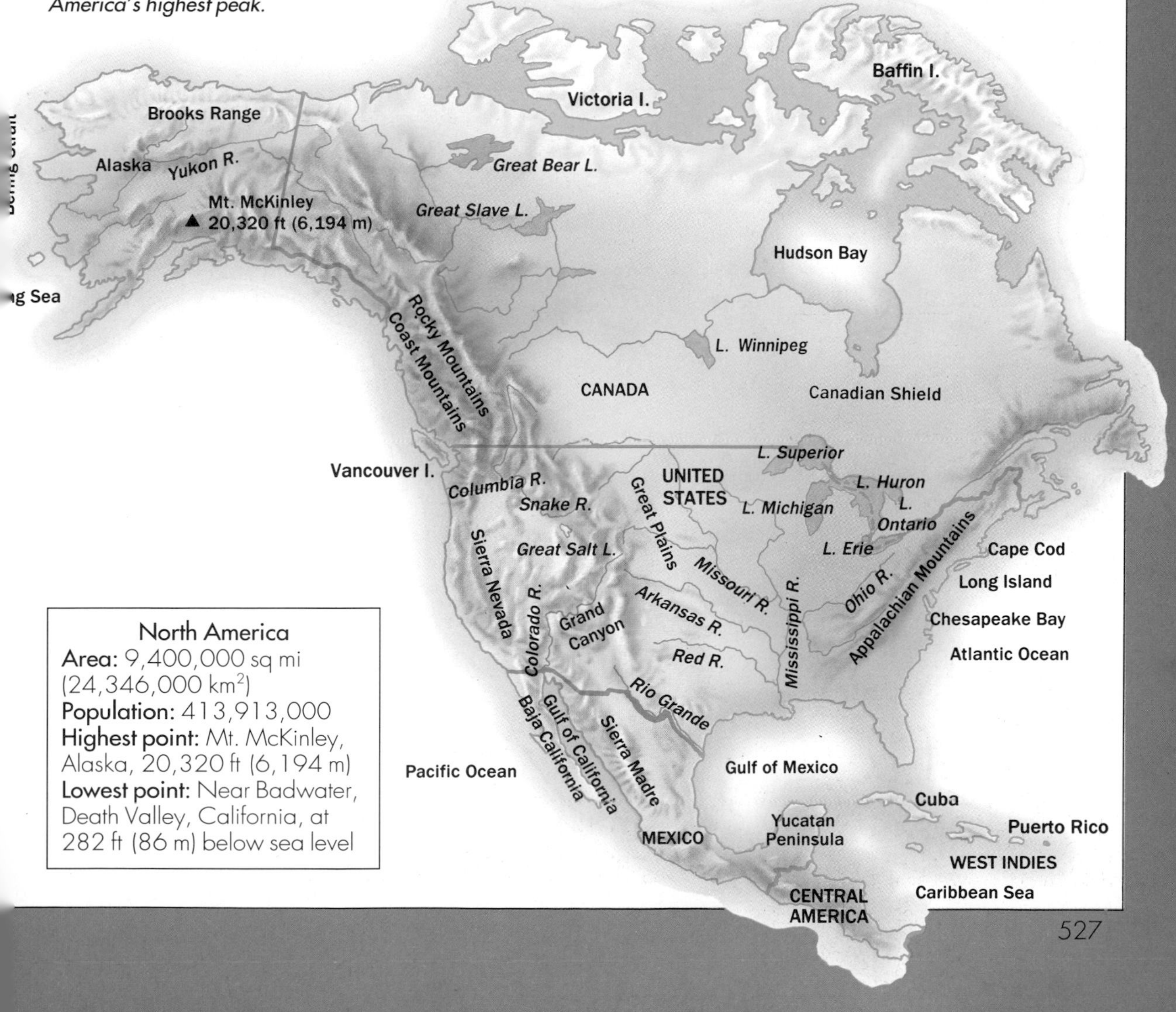

Baffin I.
Victoria I.
Brooks Range
Alaska
Yukon R.
Great Bear L.
Mt. McKinley
▲ 20,320 ft (6,194 m)
Great Slave L.
Hudson Bay
Rocky Mountains
Coast Mountains
L. Winnipeg
CANADA
Canadian Shield
L. Superior
Vancouver I.
Columbia R.
Snake R.
Great Plains
UNITED STATES
L. Michigan
L. Huron
L. Ontario
Sierra Nevada
Great Salt L.
L. Erie
Cape Cod
Missouri R.
Mississippi R.
Ohio R.
Appalachian Mountains
Long Island
Colorado R.
Grand Canyon
Arkansas R.
Chesapeake Bay
Red R.
Atlantic Ocean
Rio Grande
Baja California
Gulf of California
Sierra Madre
Pacific Ocean
Gulf of Mexico
Cuba
Puerto Rico
Yucatan Peninsula
MEXICO
WEST INDIES
CENTRAL AMERICA
Caribbean Sea

North America
**Area:** 9,400,000 sq mi ($24,346,000 km^2$)
**Population:** 413,913,000
**Highest point:** Mt. McKinley, Alaska, 20,320 ft (6,194 m)
**Lowest point:** Near Badwater, Death Valley, California, at 282 ft (86 m) below sea level

# NORTH CAROLINA

North Carolina is a state on the southeastern coast of the United States. It stretches from its Atlantic islands in the east to the Great Smoky Mountains in the west. North Carolina was the site of the LOST COLONY of the 1580s—the second English attempt at establishing a settlement in the New World.

The Outer Banks, narrow islands of shifting sandbars, lie off the coast of North Carolina. Hundreds of ships have foundered in these treacherous waters, especially off Cape Hatteras, the easternmost point of land. Also on the Outer Banks is Kitty Hawk, where the Wright brothers ushered in the age of powered flight. West of the islands is the coastal plain. Tobacco, North Carolina's most important crop, is grown here.

Farther west is the Piedmont, a rolling plateau that contains the state's chief population and industrial centers. Charlotte, the biggest city, is here. North Carolina leads all states in textiles and furniture output. High technology products are produced at Research Triangle Park, an area bounded by Durham, Raleigh (the state capital), and Chapel Hill. There scientists can draw on the expertise of the state's three major universities. The

North Carolina
**Capital:** Raleigh
**Area:** 48,843 sq mi (126,494 km²). Rank: 28th
**Population:** 6,657,630 (1990). Rank: 10th
**Statehood:** Nov. 21, 1789
**Principal rivers:** Neuse, Roanoke, Yadkin
**Highest point:** Mt. Mitchell, 6,684 ft (2,037 m)
**Motto:** *Esse Quam Videri* (To Be Rather Than to Seem)
**Song:** "The Old North State"

► *Bustling Charlotte, North Carolina's largest city, is one of the fastest-growing urban centers in the country.*

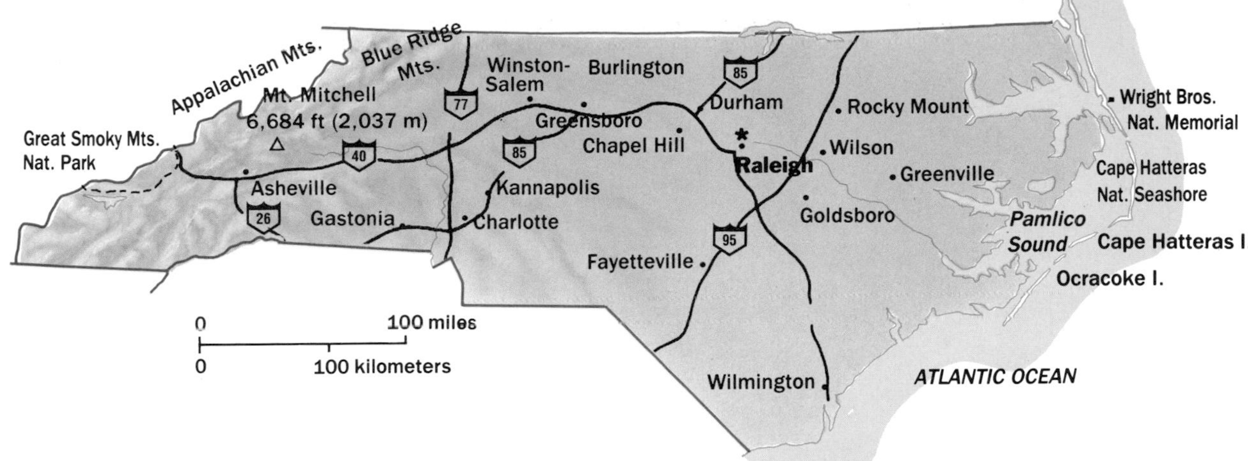


Piedmont also has most of the state's thriving poultry-raising industry. West of the Piedmont the land rises to the BLUE RIDGE MOUNTAINS. Farther west still, and higher, are the Great Smokies. This is the highest range east of the Mississippi and the site of a national park.

The permanent settlement of North Carolina did not begin until about 1650. It was the last state to join the Confederacy. However, it provided the South with more troops in the CIVIL WAR than any other state.

▼ *Sluggish bayous and mangrove swamps are common in the southeastern part of North Carolina.*

► *The restored Colonial village of Old Salem is a popular attraction at Winston-Salem, in western North Carolina.*

### Places of Interest

- Asheville was the hometown of writer Thomas Wolfe. Nearby is the Biltmore Estate, a mansion and grounds covering 12,000 acres (4,860 ha).
- The Blue Ridge Parkway, shared with Virginia, leads along the crest of the Appalachians to Great Smoky Mountains National Park.
- Ocracoke Island was once the hideout of the famous pirate Blackbeard. It is now part of the Cape Hatteras National Seashore.

# NORTH DAKOTA

Enormous farms on a treeless prairie, with no obstruction from horizon to horizon—that is what much of North Dakota looks like. It takes a special breed to thrive where temperatures can range from 120°F (50°C) to –60°F (–50°C) in a single year. Perhaps this is one reason why the state has only 641,000 people.

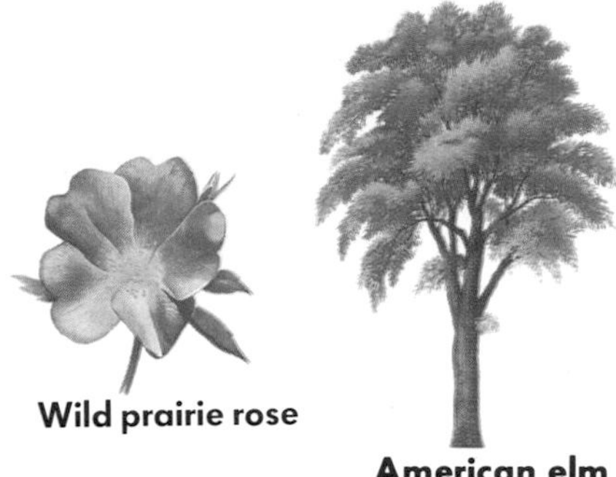

Wild prairie rose

American elm

North Dakota rises slowly from the prairie of the east to the high plateau of the west. The Red River of the north forms its eastern border. The Missouri River enters from the west and runs through the center of the state. Eastern North Dakota is good for farming, in spite of a short growing season and not much rain. The farms are huge, averaging more than 1,000 acres (405 ha). In some years, North Dakota leads all states in wheat production. Other important crops are barley, oats, and flaxseed. There is little manufacturing except for food products and farm machinery.

Western meadowlark

The western part of the state is too dry for farming, but beef cattle graze there on pastureland. The west also has oil fields and large deposits of lignite (soft coal). Power plants use some of this fuel to generate

North Dakota
**Capital:** Bismarck
**Area:** 70,704 sq mi (183,123 km²). Rank: 19th
**Population:** 638,800 (1990). Rank: 47th
**Statehood:** Nov. 2, 1889
**Principal rivers:** James, Missouri, Red
**Highest point:** White Butte, 3,506 ft (1,069 m)
**Motto:** Liberty and Union, Now and Forever, One and Inseparable
**Song:** "North Dakota Hymn"

► *The fertile Red River valley lies in the eastern part of North Dakota. The state is a leading producer of spring wheat.*

electricity for export. Also in the west is Theodore Roosevelt National Park. Here, in the so-called Badlands, are strange contours formed by the erosion of soft rock.

The fur trappers and traders who first arrived in the 1700s found mostly Sioux Indians. ("Dakota" was the word for an alliance of Sioux tribes.) White settlers arrived with the railroad in the 1870s, when Indian resistance was broken. In 1889 the territory was divided to create the states of North and South Dakota.

### Places of Interest

- The Badlands, in North Dakota's southwest, is a rugged area where wind and rain have carved the rock into unusual shapes.
- The International Peace Garden straddles the border with the Canadian province of Manitoba. It symbolizes the friendship between the two countries.
- Fort Abraham Lincoln State Park has preserved the fort that General George Armstrong Custer left on his way to the fateful Battle of Little Bighorn.

◄ *Agriculture is North Dakota's mainstay. Hogs are judged in an agricultural competition in Fargo.*

0 50 miles
0 50 kilometers
International Peace Garden
Williston
Minot
Rugby
Grand Forks
Sheyenne R.
Lake Sakakawea
Theodore Roosevelt Nat. Park
Missouri R.
Carrington
Mayville
Dickinson
Fort Abraham Lincoln State Park
Bismarck
94
Jamestown
Fargo
Red R.
29
Little Missouri R.
The Badlands
△ White Butte 3,506 ft (1,069 m)

## NORTHWEST ORDINANCE

The Northwest Ordinance, or Ordinance of 1787, created the Northwest Territory and set up procedures for sections of the territory to become states. The ordinance was passed by the Confederation Congress. Under its terms a territory with an adult male population of 5,000 could elect a legislature. When it had 60,000 people it could apply for admission to the Union as a state. Between 1803 and 1848, Ohio, Indiana, Illinois, Michigan, and Wisconsin became states.

The Northwest Ordinance marked the beginning of the westward expansion of the United States. It outlawed slavery in the Northwest Territory and guaranteed settlers such basic civil liberties as freedom of worship.

▼ *Many attempts were made to find the Northwest Passage, which people thought would provide an easy route to Asia. It was not until 1969 that a commercial ship, the* Manhattan, *sailed through the passage. By this time, the route was not considered useful for commercial purposes.*

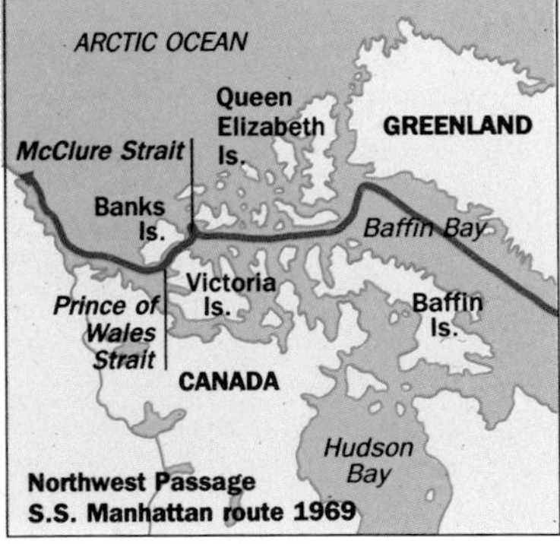


## NORTHWEST PASSAGE

The Northwest Passage is a water route between the Atlantic and Pacific oceans along the northern coast of North America. A short route from Europe to Asia was the goal of Henry HUDSON and other early explorers. In 1850, Sir Robert McClure sailed as far west as Banks Island in the Arctic Ocean. In 1906, Roald Amundsen completed the first crossing. In 1969 the icebreaker-tanker *Manhattan* traveled the passage. The route, however, is not useful for commerce.

▼ *The icebreaker-tanker* Manhattan.

# NORTHWEST TERRITORIES

CANADA's Northwest Territories covers more than one third of the country. It includes most of Canada's land north of latitude 60° north. The Northwest Territories has some of the world's harshest weather, with winter temperatures going as low as –63°F (–53°C). Most of the more than 1.3 million square miles (3.4 million km²) of land is north of the tree line. The soil there is locked in a frozen condition called permafrost.

More than 52,000 people live in the Northwest Territories. About half of them are Native Canadians—Inuits (Eskimos) and Indians. Many still follow the traditional way of life, which includes hunting and trapping for fur. Most white inhabitants live in the Mackenzie Valley. The Mackenzie, the longest river in Canada, flows out of Great Slave Lake in the southern part of the Northwest Territories and then flows northwestward to empty into the Arctic Ocean. Yellowknife, the capital of the Northwest Territories, is on the north shore of Great Slave Lake. It has a population of about 12,000.

Mining is the most important industry in the Northwest Territories. Lead, zinc, and gold are among the minerals taken from the earth.

Fur traders and prospectors were the first to visit this area. It was controlled by the Hudson's Bay Company from 1670 to 1870, then by the government of Canada.

Northwest Territories
**Capital:** Yellowknife
**Area:** 1,322,910 sq mi (3,426,320 km²)
**Population:** 57,649 (1991)
**Highest point:** Mt. Sir James MacBrien, 9,062 ft (2,762 m)

▼ *Many of the harbors along Baffin Bay lie north of the Arctic Circle and remain frozen throughout the year.*

# NOVA SCOTIA

▲ *Fishermen from Nova Scotian villages such as Peggy's Cove can spend weeks away from home in their search for cod and haddock.*

Nova Scotia is one of CANADA's four Atlantic provinces. It consists of Cape Breton Island and a mainland peninsula connected to the province of NEW BRUNSWICK. Halifax, its capital and chief city, is Canada's leading Atlantic port. About one third of Nova Scotia's nearly 900,000 people live in the Halifax metropolitan area. Fishing, forestry, and their products are important to the provincial economy. Aerospace industries have also been established in recent years. Cape Breton Island has coal mines and a steel mill.

The first white settlers in this region were French who came in the 1600s and called the region Acadie (Acadia). But the British expelled the French in 1755. Nova Scotia became part of Canada in 1867.

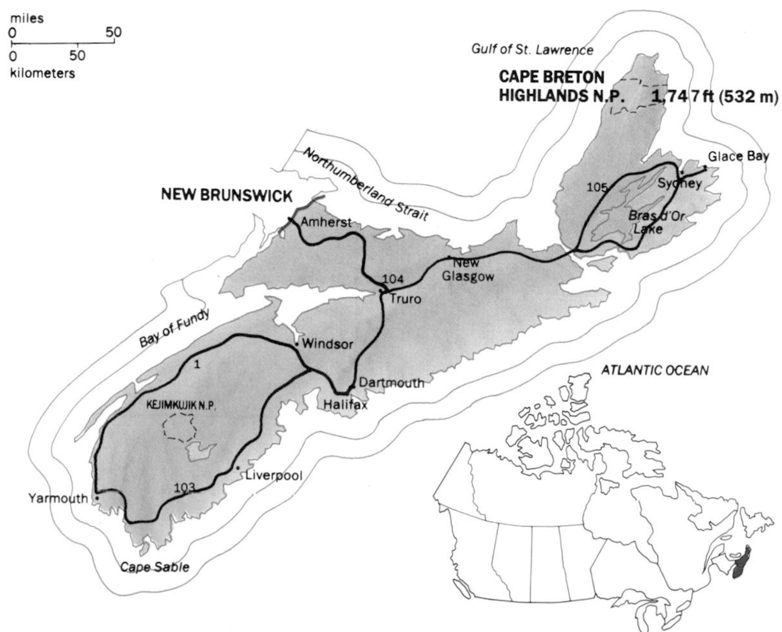


**Nova Scotia**
**Capital:** Halifax
**Area:** 21,423 sq mi ($55,490$ km$^2$). Rank: 9th
**Population:** 899,942 (1991)
**Entry into Confederation:** July 1, 1867 (one of the first four provinces)
**Highest point:** 1,747 ft (532 m), in Cape Breton Highlands National Park

## NUCLEAR POWER

The same enormous power released by atomic weapons is also used for peaceful purposes, especially to produce electricity. In most nuclear power plants, power comes from energy released by splitting the nucleus of an atom of uranium-235, which is a form of the mineral element uranium. The released energy heats water and produces steam. Steam drives the turbine generators that produce electricity. There are more than 100 such plants in the United States. They account for nearly one fifth of all electricity produced in the country.

The biggest advantage of nuclear power is that it produces electricity without burning oil or coal, fuels that are expensive and cause air pollution. However, splitting uranium-235 atoms releases radioactive materials—tiny particles that can damage living things. Power plants need to avoid accidents and radiation leaks that could cause harm. They also need to find a safe way to store the waste products of nuclear power, which remain radioactive. Nuclear waste is usually stored deep under the ground.

▲ *Engineers examine the dome-shaped main reactor building of the San Onofre Nuclear Power Plant in California.*

◄ *Researchers at the Oak Ridge National Laboratory in Tennessee conduct experiments to improve nuclear energy technology.*

States Producing Most Nuclear Power

1. Illinois
2. Pennsylvania
3. South Carolina
4. California
5. North Carolina
6. Georgia
7. Virginia
8. New Jersey
9. New York
10. Florida

## OAK

More than 50 kinds of oak trees are found in the United States. Oak trees vary dramatically in size and in the way they grow. Some oaks are very tall while others mature into small shrubs. The timber of the white oak, found as far west as Texas, is the most valuable. The bur oak, which grows in the central United States, is a popular shade tree.

The handsome red oak is an important timber tree. Common in the East, it is also planted as an ornamental. The black oak is found east of Texas, on slopes and ridges since it will not grow in shade. The California black oak grows in the West. The live oak is a handsome evergreen native to the Atlantic and Gulf coasts. Its timber is valuable, but it is also planted as an ornamental and for shade along avenues in the South.

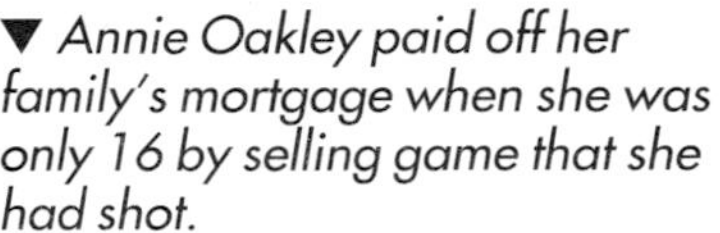

▶ *The leaves of different oak species can vary widely, but all oak acorns are partly covered by a scaly cap.*

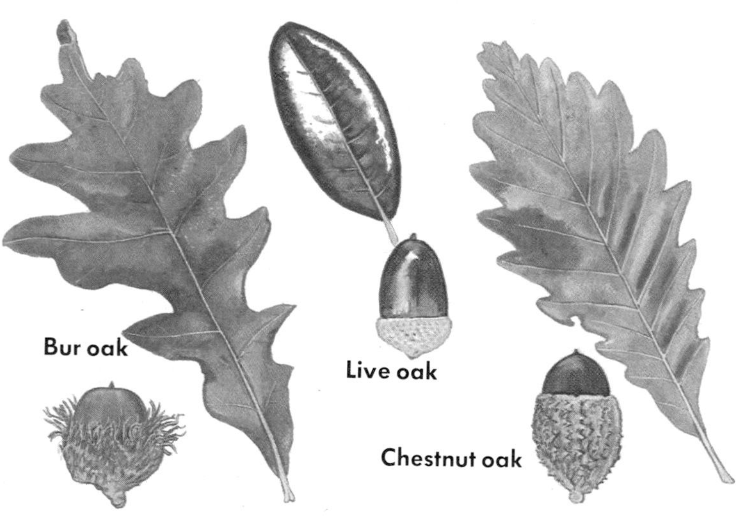



▼ *Annie Oakley paid off her family's mortgage when she was only 16 by selling game that she had shot.*

## OAKLEY, Annie

Annie Oakley (1860–1926) was an expert markswoman who became a star entertainer. As a young girl in Ohio she learned to shoot in order to help provide food after her father died. In 1879 she beat the well-known marksman Frank E. Butler in a shooting match in Cincinnati. They later married and toured a double act, joining Buffalo Bill's Wild West Show in 1885. Given top billing as the "Peerless Lady Wing-Shot," Annie amazed audiences by hitting the thin edge of a playing card at a distance of 30 paces. Her story served as the inspiration for the Irving Berlin musical *Annie Get Your Gun*.

▲ *The Very Large Array radio telescope contains 27 movable, steerable radio dishes spread over 13 miles (21 km) west of Socorro, New Mexico. Their combined images are ten times more detailed than any earth-based optical telescope.*

## OBSERVATORIES

Observatories are places where astronomers study the stars and galaxies that make up the universe. Optical observatories house telescopes that magnify the images seen by the naked eye. They are located on top of mountains, where conditions are best for viewing. The largest of these instruments, a 393.7-inch (1,000-cm) reflecting telescope, is being built atop Mauna Kea, Hawaii's highest volcano. More recent are observatories that house radio telescopes. These dish-shaped antennas pick up radio waves that come from distant stars and galaxies. The largest dish-type radio telescope is near Arecibo, Puerto Rico. The most powerful radio telescope is west of Socorro. New Mexico. Space observatories carry telescopes in earth-orbiting satellites to avoid interference from the earth's atmosphere. The 94.5-inch (240-cm) Hubble Space Telescope was launched in 1990.

## OCEANOGRAPHY

Oceanography is the study of the world's oceans. This includes the water itself; waves, currents, and tides; the plants and animals found in the oceans; and the ocean floor. Research tools include diving vessels, surface ships, floating devices like bouys, and airborne craft such as balloons and earth satellites.

Oceanographers are trained in such disciplines as biology, geology, and meteorology. The National Oceanic and Atmospheric Administration explores, maps, and charts the ocean and its resources. The United States is taking part in the World Ocean Circu-

▼ *Oceanographers can use their findings to plot undersea mineral deposits. These California scientists are mapping manganese nodules.*

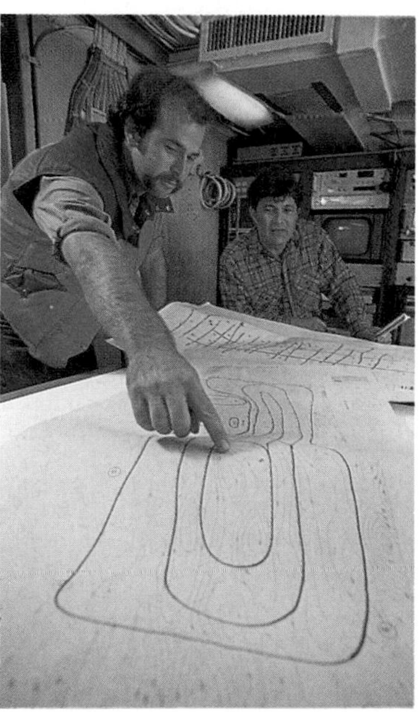

▲ *Sensitive equipment such as this current flow meter can chart the movement of the ocean's waters.*

lation Experiment, which began in 1990. This cooperative research effort will involve 44 countries.

## OCELOT

Ocelots are wild CATS. They are native to North and South America, but in the United States, they are confined to forest areas of Arizona, New Mexico, and Texas. Ocelots grow to be 4 feet (120 cm) long, including a 15-inch (38-cm) tail. The color of ocelots' fur ranges from reddish to almost cream. All ocelots are covered with spots. The combination of fur color and spots helps ocelots blend into their surroundings as they hunt mice, rabbits, lizards, and even small deer. Laws in the United States protect ocelots from hunters.

► *The ocelot's light and dark coloring lets it blend in perfectly with its surroundings.*

▼ *Adolph Ochs believed that a newspaper's main responsibility was to its readers, rather than to political parties or business interests.*

## OCHS, Adolph

Adolph Ochs (1858–1935) was a successful newspaper publisher. He was born in Cincinnati, Ohio, and grew up in Tennessee. When he was 14 he became an office boy for the *Knoxville Chronicle*. Ochs quickly learned the skills of journalism and finance, and when he was only 20 he bought controlling interest in the *Chattanooga Times*. He built it into a leading southern newspaper. Ochs then moved to New York, where in 1896 he bought control of *The New York Times*. He gave it a motto—"All the News That's Fit to Print"—and built it into one of the world's greatest newspapers.

## O'CONNOR, Flannery

Flannery O'Connor (1925–1964) was a novelist and short-story writer. She was born Mary Flannery O'Connor to a devoutly Catholic family in Savannah, Georgia. Religion and the South's unique qualities were important themes in all her writing.

Forced by ill health to observe society from a distance, O'Connor sympathized with others who felt themselves to be different. Her two novels, *Wise Blood* and *The Violent Bear It Away*, deal with people who are mentally or physically crippled. A collection of her short stories was published seven years after her death. *Flannery O'Connor: The Complete Stories* won the 1972 National Book Award for fiction.

*▼ Sandra Day O'Connor won a unanimous vote of confirmation in the U.S. Senate in September 1981. The Arizona judge then took her place as the first female member of the U.S. Supreme Court.*

## O'CONNOR, Sandra Day 

Sandra Day O'Connor (1930– ) was the first woman to be appointed a justice of the Supreme Court of the United States. Born in El Paso, Texas, O'Connor graduated from Stanford University Law School. After working as a lawyer for the U.S. Army in Germany, she set up a law practice in Phoenix, Arizona. From 1965 to 1974, O'Connor served as assistant attorney general of Arizona and as a state senator. She was elected judge of the superior court in Phoenix in 1974, and in 1979 she became a judge of the Arizona Court of Appeals. President Ronald Reagan nominated her as a Supreme Court justice in 1981.

## OGLETHORPE, James Edward 

James Oglethorpe (1696–1785) was the founder and first governor of the colony of Georgia. Born in London, England, he was elected to Parliament in 1722. He became a leader in the movement for prison reform. Oglethorpe was especially concerned about people who had been sent to prison for debt. In 1732 he obtained a charter for a colony where such people could start a new life. The following year, more than 100 settlers arrived in Georgia. Oglethorpe founded the town of Savannah and was the governor of the colony for the next ten years. During his rule, Georgia was a buffer between Spanish Florida and the British colonies to the north. In 1743, Oglethorpe returned to England.

*▼ James Oglethorpe originally saw his colony of Georgia as a refuge where European debtors could start a new life.*

## OHIO

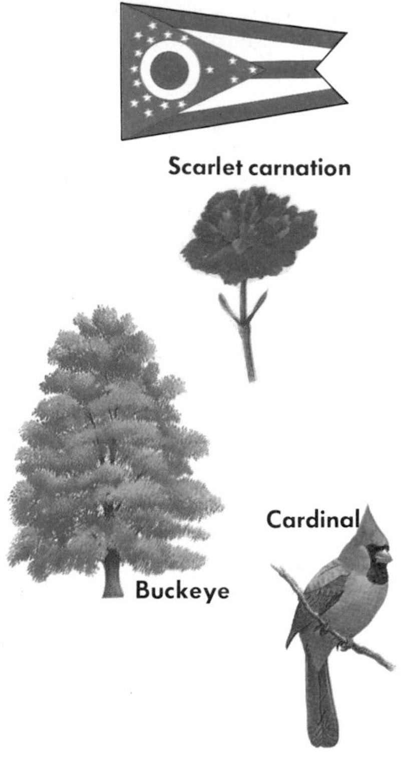


Ohio is one of the leading industrial states. Steel, automobiles and aircraft, tires and other rubber products, petroleum products, plastics and chemicals, and office equipment are made there. Some of the factories producing these goods closed in the 1970s and 1980s. Now Ohio is looking for service and high technology industries to fuel its economy.

Lake Erie forms Ohio's northern border, and the Ohio River forms its southern boundary. Ships and barges carry bulk cargo such as coal and iron ore to and from Ohio ports. The Ohio River flows into the Mississippi, and Lake Erie connects to the Atlantic Ocean by means of the St. Lawrence Seaway. These waterways, and the canals connecting them, helped Ohio to develop. Agriculture is also important, and coal is mined in mainly rural southeastern Ohio.

Ohio's largest cities are CLEVELAND, Cincinnati, and COLUMBUS. The first two cities were among Ohio's oldest settlements and are noted for cultural attractions such as their art museums and symphony orchestras. Columbus has Ohio State University, the state's biggest. Other important cities in Ohio include Toledo, Akron, and Dayton.

Marietta, the first permanent settlement in Ohio, was founded in 1788. New Englanders mainly settled northern Ohio, and people from Virginia and Kentucky settled the south. The population grew rapidly and Ohio became the 17th state in 1803. Seven United States presidents—all Republicans—were born in Ohio.

### Places of Interest

- Mound City Group National Monument, in Chillicothe, preserves the mysterious burial mounds built by some of Ohio's earliest Indian inhabitants.
- The Neil Armstrong Air and Space Museum, in Wapakoneta, honors one of Ohio's most famous natives with displays on aircraft and space travel.
- The Pro Football Hall of Fame is located in Canton.
- The Toledo Museum of Art has one of the Midwest's finest collections of fine arts.

► *Beaver Pond is a tranquil wildlife habitat near the industrial city of Akron in northeast Ohio.*

◀ *Farm stands line the roads of rural Ohio, especially in the autumn.*

Ohio
**Capital:** Columbus
**Area:** 44,828 sq mi (116,103 km$^2$). Rank: 34th
**Population:** 10,847,115 (1990). Rank: 7th
**Statehood:** March 1, 1803
**Principal rivers:** Ohio, Cuyahoga, Miami, Sandusky
**Highest point:** Campbell Hill, 1,550 ft (472 m)
**Motto:** With God, All Things Are Possible.
**Song:** "Beautiful Ohio"

▲ *A blast furnace at Republic Steel in Cleveland burns coke from eastern Ohio to melt iron ore.*

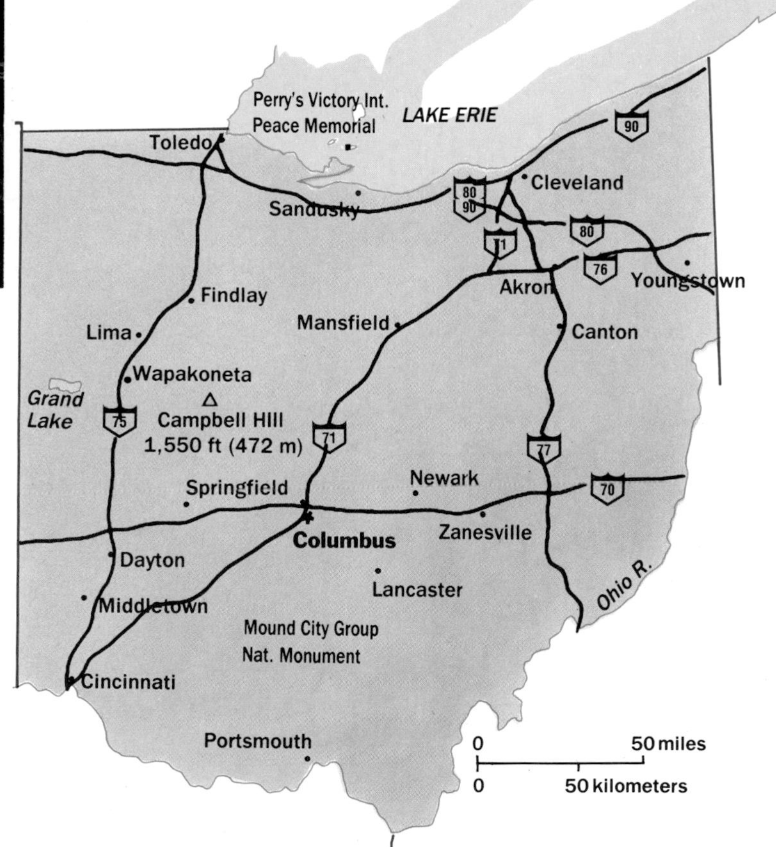

*► Oil refineries, such as this plant in El Segundo, California, turn crude oil into valuable commercial products.*

| Leading Oil-Producing States (million barrels/year) |
|---|
| 1. Texas (674) |
| 2. Alaska (658) |
| 3. California (322) |
| 4. Louisiana (148) |
| 5. Oklahoma (117) |
| 6. Wyoming (103) |
| 7. New Mexico (66) |
| 8. Kansas (59) |
| 9. North Dakota (39) |
| 10. Colorado (31) |

## OIL INDUSTRY

The oil, or petroleum, industry is one of the largest industries in the United States, employing more than 1.5 million people. Once petroleum is extracted, it is refined into a variety of products. The 205 U.S. oil refineries produced almost half of all the world's gasoline in 1990. Other petroleum products include fuel oil and kerosene. Petroleum is a raw material used in the manufacture of numerous products, including plastics, medicines, fertilizers, foods, and building materials.

The oil industry began with the drilling of an oil well in Titusville, Pennsylvania, in 1859. Soon wells were being drilled in Kentucky, Ohio, Illinois, Indiana, Texas, California, Oklahoma, and Louisiana. A major oil field was discovered along the Arctic coast of Alaska in 1968. The major petroleum refining companies in the United States are Exxon, Mobil, Texaco, and Chevron.

*▼ Two workers keep a steady hand on the drilling platform of an oil rig in the Gulf of Mexico.*

## OJIBWA *See* Chippewas

## O'KEEFFE, Georgia

Georgia O'Keeffe (1887–1986) was a painter who found inspiration in the natural world of the American Southwest. She was born in Sun Prairie, Wisconsin, and studied art in Chicago and New York City. In 1912 a teaching job took her to Amarillo, Texas. The desert landscape became the subject of most of her paintings. In 1918 she devoted herself full-time to painting. Desert flowers, animal bones, and burned hillsides began to figure in most of her work. In 1924 she married the New York photographer and art dealer Alfred STIEGLITZ. He introduced O'Keeffe's works to the art world, which immediately saw their value. In 1949, Georgia O'Keeffe settled in Taos, New Mexico, in the countryside she loved to paint. O'Keeffe continued with her large, boldly colored paintings well into her old age.

**In her later years, Georgia O'Keeffe began painting a series of works based on the sky and clouds as seen from an airplane. Her *Sky About Clouds IV* is an immense painting— 24 feet (7.3 m) wide.**

◀ *Georgia O'Keeffe's* The Red Poppy *shows how her devotion to nature and color can produce an almost abstract design.*

## OKEFENOKEE SWAMP

Okefenokee is a huge SWAMP in southeastern Georgia and northeastern Florida. It has an area of more than 600 square miles (1,550 km$^2$). Much of it is protected as a wildlife refuge and tropical wilderness. It is home to a wide variety of animals, including at least 200 species of birds, 50 species of fish, ALLIGATORS, OTTERS, OPOSSUMS, RACOONS, BEARS, and DEER. The swamp consists of wet grasslands, lakes and winding channels of water, and small islands that seem to float in the marsh. Bald cypress, pine, magnolia, and red bay trees grow in the swamp, as do many exotic flowers, including rare orchids. The swamp drains into the Suwannee and St. Marys rivers, which flow into the Atlantic Ocean.

▼ *Much of the Okefenokee Swamp is a national wildlife refuge, where rare plants, alligators, birds, and deer are protected.*

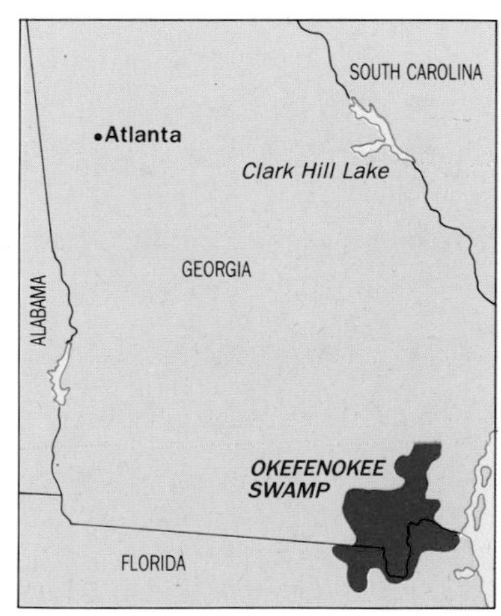

# OKLAHOMA

Scissor-tailed flycatcher

Oklahoma is a Choctaw Indian word meaning "red people," and at one time it was meant to be occupied only by Indians. That all changed on April 22, 1889, when homesteaders were allowed to cross the border and stake land claims. By nightfall, 20,000 had done so. But some jumped the gun and were named "Sooners." Now Oklahoma is called the Sooner State.

Oklahoma is generally shaped like a rectangle, except for a long panhandle on the western end. Most of it is gently rolling prairie. The Red River forms most of the southern border. The Arkansas River and its tributaries, including the Cimarron and Canadian rivers, run through the state.

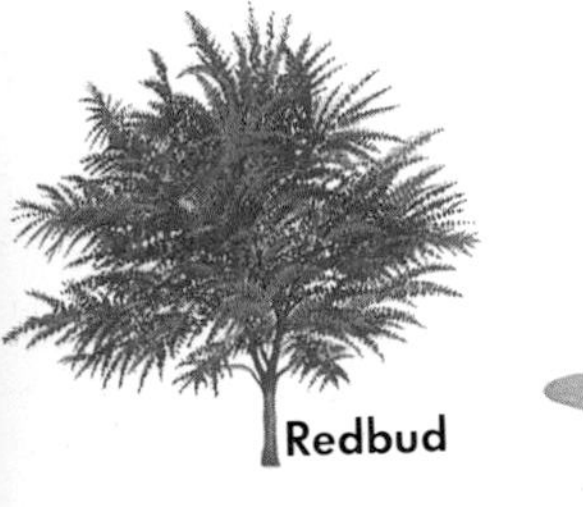

Redbud

Mistletoe

Wheat growing and cattle raising are important sources of income. Even more valuable are the state's

► *Oklahoma City is the largest city in the state and one of the chief oil-producing centers in the country.*

▼ *Successful irrigation techniques have helped Oklahoma farmers to diversify. Here a peanut farm extends to the horizon.*

plentiful oil and natural gas wells. Manufacturing includes food processing, oil refining, and the making of nonelectrical machinery. More than half the people live in the Tulsa or OKLAHOMA CITY urban areas.

In 1830 five Indian tribes of the southeastern United States were forced to leave their homes. These five peoples—the Cherokees, Chickasaws, Choctaws, Creeks, and Seminoles—were sent to what was called Indian Territory. They were told the land was theirs "as long as the grass grows and the waters run." But the central and western parts were thinly populated and sought after by whites. They were bought by the federal government for settlement. Oklahoma became a state in 1907. It has more Indians than any other state except California—about 5 percent of the population.

▲ *The City of Faith Clinic Tower rises 60 stories above Tulsa. It forms part of one of the country's most modern medical centers.*

Oklahoma

**Capital:** Oklahoma City
**Area:** 69,903 sq mi (181,049 km$^2$). Rank: 20th
**Population:** 3,145,585 (1990). Rank: 28th
**Statehood:** November 16, 1907
**Principal rivers:** Arkansas, Canadian, Red
**Highest point:** Black Mesa, 4,973 ft (1,516 m)
**Motto:** *Labor Omnia Vincit* (Work Conquers All Things)
**Song:** "Oklahoma!"

Places of Interest

- American history comes alive at the American Indian Hall of Fame, in Anadarko, and the National Cowboy Hall of Fame, in Oklahoma City.
- The Chickasaw National Recreation Area, in southern Oklahoma, features cascading streams and mineral springs.
- Sequoyah State Park is a popular vacation area in the Ozark region in the northeast. It was once a hideout for bandits.

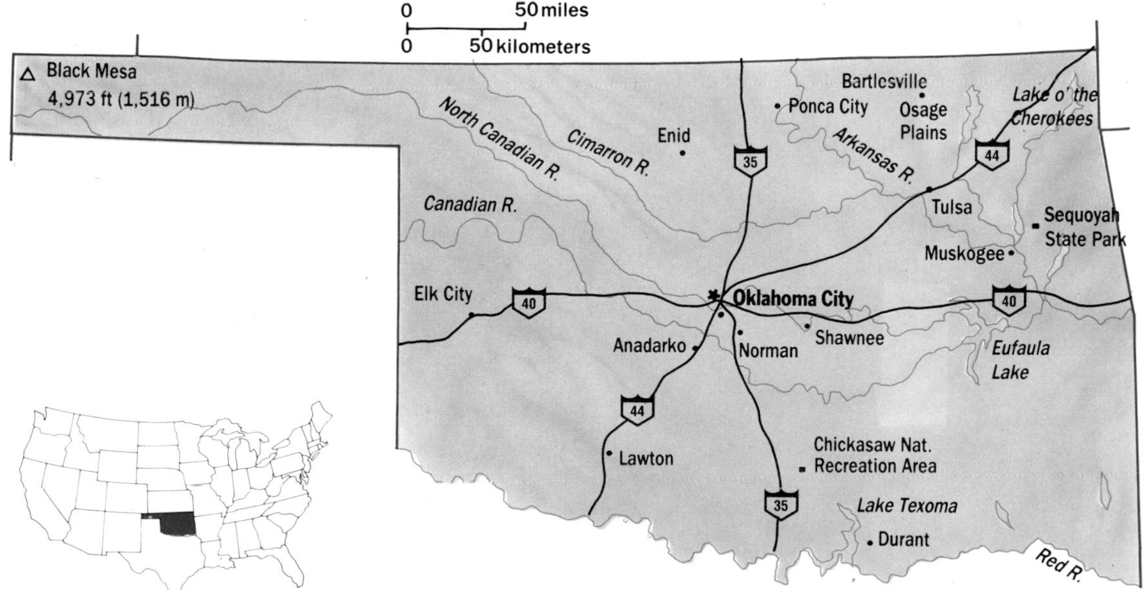

▲ *The City Place and Globe Life buildings tower over Oklahoma City's commercial district. The city's role as state capital also provides employment.*

## OKLAHOMA CITY

Oklahoma City is the capital of OKLAHOMA and its largest city. It has a population of 444,719. The city was founded in 1889, and it became the capital in 1910, soon after the local oil industry was established.

Oil production is Oklahoma City's main industry. But its factories also produce steel, electronic equipment, and computers. Tinker Air Force Base, located nearby, is the city's largest employer. Oklahoma City's location near the center of the state has made it an important transportation and distribution center for the state's agricultural products.

## OLYMPIC GAMES

The United States has competed in the Summer Olympic Games since they were started in 1896. These games have been held in the United States three times, in St. Louis (1904) and in Los Angeles (1932 and 1984). The Winter Olympics, which originated in 1924, have also been held in the United States three times, in Lake Placid, New York (1932 and 1980), and in Squaw Valley, California (1960). United States Olympic teams have excelled at such events as boxing, track sprints, and basketball. At the 1992 Summer Olympic Games, held in Spain, American athletes won 108 medals, compared with 12 for members of the Unified Team, which was made up of athletes from the former Soviet Union.

▼ *Eugene O'Neill's plays dealt with American themes but had universal appeal. He won the Nobel Prize for literature in 1936.*

## O'NEILL, Eugene

Eugene O'Neill (1888–1953) was one of America's greatest playwrights. He wrote 45 plays, won the Pulitzer Prize four times, and was the first American playwright to win the Nobel Prize for literature (1936).

O'Neill was born in New York City. His parents were actors who traveled all the time, and O'Neill had a very unhappy childhood. This unhappiness was reflected in most of his plays. Many of them deal with people who are constantly searching for meaning in life. O'Neill's four Pulitzer Prize–winning plays are *Beyond the Horizon*, *Anna Christie*, *Strange Interlude*, and *Long Day's Journey into Night*. Other memorable plays are *Desire Under the Elms*, *Mourning Becomes Electra*, and *The Iceman Cometh*.

# ONTARIO

▲ *St. Brendan's Catholic Church, in Rockport, stands on the Rocky Canadian Shield, which extends through Ontario.*

Ontario is the heart of CANADA and its economic powerhouse. Second in size only to Quebec, the province borders four of the five Great Lakes. It has more than 9 million people, or more than one third of Canada's population. Family income is the highest, and unemployment the lowest, in Canada. Ontario also leads the nation in almost every major kind of manufacturing. Especially important is the assembly of motor vehicles. About 90 percent are exported, almost all to the United States. Ontario leads all other provinces in agriculture and metals mining. Forestry in the northwestern area of the province is important, too.

OTTAWA, the national capital, is on the border with Quebec. Most of the other big cities are situated on Lake Ontario. With about 3.5 million people, the TORONTO metropolitan area is the largest in Canada. Toronto is the center of publishing and communications in English-speaking Canada. Bay Street in Toronto is the financial and banking capital of Canada.

The French were the first to explore Ontario, in the early 1600s. The British won it in 1763. Ontario became part of the Canadian confederation in 1867.

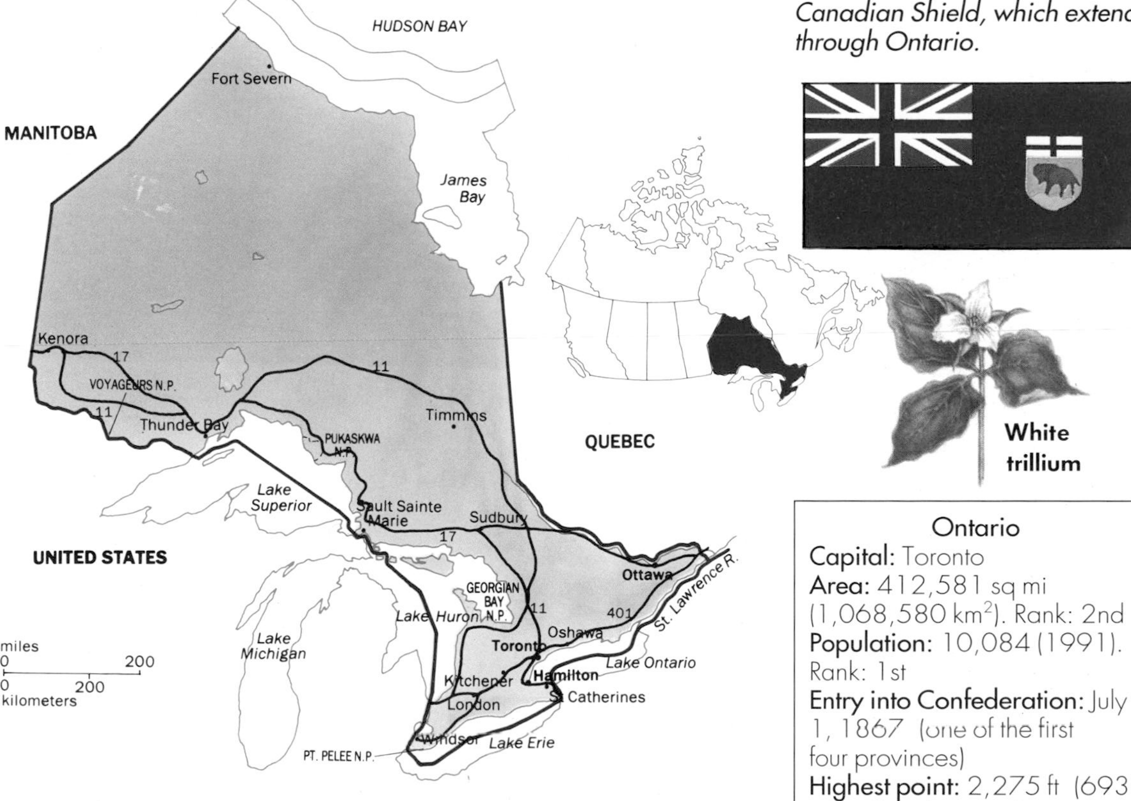


**White trillium**

**Ontario**
**Capital:** Toronto
**Area:** 412,581 sq mi (1,068,580 km²). Rank: 2nd
**Population:** 10,084 (1991). Rank: 1st
**Entry into Confederation:** July 1, 1867 (one of the first four provinces)
**Highest point:** 2,275 ft (693 m), in Timiskaming District

Some U.S. Opera Singers

Licia Albanese (1913– ): soprano.
Marian Anderson (1902–1993): contralto.
Marilyn Horne (1934– ): mezzo-soprano.
Robert Merrill (1919– ): baritone.
Roberta Peters (1930– ): coloratura soprano.
Leontyne Price (1927– ): soprano.
Beverley Sills (1929– ): soprano.
Helen Traubel (1899–1972): soprano.
Richard Tucker (1914–1975): tenor.

## ONTARIO, Lake *See* Great Lakes

## OPERA

An opera is a form of musical theater in which all or most of the dialogue is sung rather than spoken. New York City's Metropolitan Opera is the leading opera company in the United States. Other cities, including Chicago, San Francisco, and Houston, have their own companies. Notable operas by American composers include Deems Taylor's *Peter Ibbetson*, Virgil Thomson's *Four Saints in Three Acts*, George Gershwin's *Porgy and Bess*, Gian Carlo Menotti's *Amahl and the Night Visitors*, and Philip Glass's *Akhnaten*.

► *Pearl Bailey and Sidney Poitier led an all-star cast in the movie version of* Porgy and Bess. *The opera was written by George Gershwin.*

## OPINION POLL

Opinion polls are used to find out what people think about different subjects. They are also called public opinion polls. Such polls are often used to see which candidate voters will choose in an election. They are also used in marketing, to find out if people like or would buy a certain product. In a poll, a group of carefully chosen people are asked questions. Poll takers pick these people so that they reflect society as a whole. Questions are also carefully chosen. There are many companies that specialize in polling. The oldest and best-known polls are those developed by George GALLUP and Elmo Roper.

**One of the most famous opinion poll upsets occurred in 1948 when the polls predicted that Thomas Dewey would easily defeat President Harry Truman. Truman won the election with some ease. The pollsters learned from this embarrassment, and polls are now much more reliable.**

◀ *Opossums can use their long tails to hang from trees. They are nocturnal (nighttime) hunters and will eat almost anything.*

**When an opossum is in danger, it pretends to be dead, so that its enemy (which prefers live prey) will leave it alone. This is where the expression "playing 'possum" comes from.**

## OPOSSUM 

The common opossum is a marsupial, an animal, like the kangaroo, that carries its young in a pouch on its abdomen. It is the only marsupial in North America. It is most common in the central and eastern parts of the United States.

The opossum has more teeth—50—than any other North American mammal. It often kills chickens and other poultry, so it is hunted by farmers. It is also hunted for its fur and meat. Coyotes, bobcats, hawks, and owls prey on opossums.

## OPPENHEIMER, J. Robert 

J. Robert Oppenheimer (1904–1967) was known as the "father of the atomic bomb." From 1942 to 1945 he was director of the Los Alamos Laboratory in New Mexico, where the first atomic bomb was made. In 1946 he was named chairman of the general advisory committee of the U.S. Atomic Energy Commission (AEC). And a year later he became head of the Institute for Advanced Studies in Princeton, New Jersey.

Oppenheimer spoke out about the dangers of atomic weapons. In 1953, during a time when many people were accused of disloyalty, he was judged a security risk. He was no longer allowed to take part in government research. Many scientists protested the government's action. In 1963 the AEC awarded Oppenheimer its highest award, the Fermi Award.

▼ *J. Robert Oppenheimer helped write the first U.S. proposal for international control of nuclear energy.*

# OREGON

The Pacific Northwest state of Oregon is a land of striking scenery and vast forests. The rocky Pacific coast, with its pounding surf and mysterious mists, is a popular attraction for visitors. The Cascade Mountain range includes majestic Mount Hood, a dormant volcano, and Crater Lake, which rests in the cone of a collapsed volcano. Oregon is also known for its vast forests. The state contains more standing commercial timber than any other and is the leading state in timber production.

Water bounds much of the state. The Pacific Ocean is on the west. The COLUMBIA RIVER forms most of the northern border, and the Snake River part of the eastern boundary. The Coast and Cascade mountains run parallel to the coast. Most of the state's extensive forests are found on their slopes. These are almost entirely evergreens, including large tracts of Douglas fir. The climate is mild and moist. But two thirds of the state lies east of the Cascades. This part is dry, and the climate is more extreme. Wheat is grown and cattle raised there.

Three of every four Oregonians live in the Willamette Valley, which includes PORTLAND (the biggest city), Salem (the capital), and Eugene. Most of the state's industry is there. Lumber, wood, and paper products are the chief industry. Food processing is also important, and there are a growing number of computer and electronics firms.

The explorers LEWIS AND CLARK reached the

**Places of Interest**

- Crater Lake, centerpiece of a national park, is the deepest lake in the Unites States.
- Fort Clatsop National Memorial, near Astoria, was the winter camp of the Lewis and Clark Expedition when it reached the Pacific Ocean.
- John Day Fossil Beds National Monument, in northern Oregon, has an astonishing variety of animal and plant fossils, as well as ancient Indian pictures.
- Oregon Dunes is a 50-mile (80-km) stretch of empty beaches and towering sand mounds.

► *Lumbering is an important industry in Oregon. Redwood grown in the state is valuable in construction.*

◀ *Water cascades over the moss-covered rocks of Proxy Falls in western Oregon.*

**Oregon**
**Capital:** Salem
**Area:** 98,386 sq mi (254,819 km$^2$). Rank: 9th
**Population:** 2,842,321 (1990). Rank: 29th
**Statehood:** Feb. 14, 1859
**Principal rivers:** Columbia, Deschutes, Willamette
**Highest point:** Mt. Hood, 11,235 ft (3,424 m)
**Motto:** The Union
**Song:** "Oregon, My Oregon"

mouth of the Columbia River in 1805. The OREGON TRAIL brought many white settlers in the 1840s. Oregon became a territory in 1849 and a state in 1859.

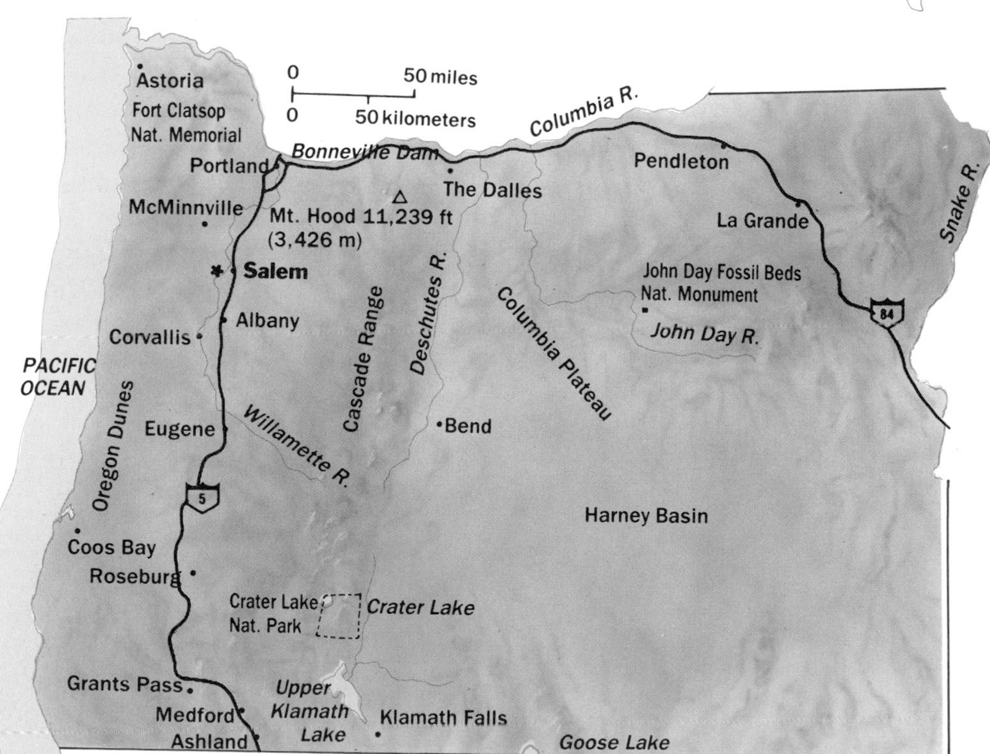

*► The Rockies (right) were the biggest obstacle for the pioneers along the Oregon Trail. Some of the guides were the former trappers who had first mapped the region. The Lewis and Clark Expedition covered much of the region west of what became Fort Bridger.*

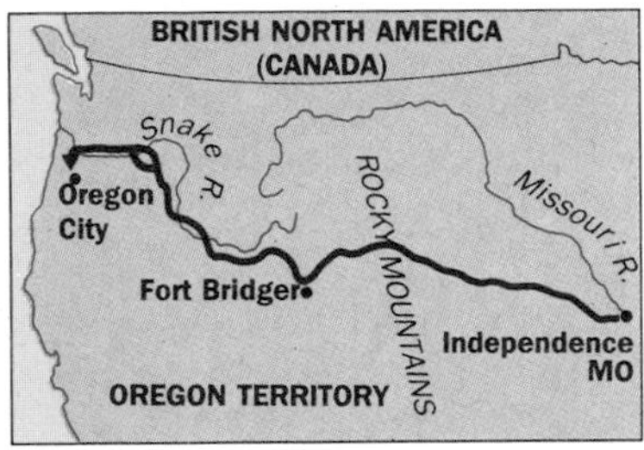

## OREGON TRAIL 

The Oregon Trail was an important route for settlers making their way west during the 1840s. It was 2,000 miles (3,200 km) long and stretched from Independence, Missouri, across the Great Plains and Rocky Mountains to the Oregon country.

Trappers and traders established part of the Oregon Trail in the early 1800s. They were followed by missionaries, and it soon became known that Oregon's Willamette Valley had an abundance of fertile land. In 1843 some 1,000 pioneers began a six-month journey in covered wagons. In the years that followed, thousands more braved Indian attacks, floods, storms, and hunger to reach the west. By 1846 there were so many Americans in the Oregon country that the British gave up all claims to the land south of the present border between Washington State and Canada. The Oregon Territory was established two years later.

## ORGANIZATION OF AMERICAN STATES 

The Organization of American States (OAS) is an organization of 35 Western Hemisphere countries. Its major goals are to promote peace and cooperation among its members. OAS members also have a mutual defense treaty. The OAS, which grew out of the Pan-American Union, was set up in 1948. Its headquarters are in Washington, D.C. A meeting of the organization's General Assembly is held once a year.

**Organization of American States (member countries)**

| | |
|---|---|
| Antigua and Barbuda | Haiti |
| Argentina | Honduras |
| Bahamas | Jamaica |
| Barbados | Mexico |
| Belize | Nicaragua |
| Bolivia | Panama |
| Brazil | Paraguay |
| Canada | Peru |
| Chile | St. Kitts and Nevis |
| Colombia | St. Lucia |
| Costa Rica | St. Vincent and the Grenadines |
| Cuba | Suriname |
| Dominica | Trinidad and Tobago |
| Dominican Republic | United States |
| Ecuador | Uruguay |
| El Salvador | Venezuela |
| Grenada | |
| Guatemala | |
| Guyana | |

Much of the organization's work concerns economic development and cooperation. In 1965, however, the OAS authorized the United States to send troops to the Dominican Republic to restore order after a revolt. In 1962, Cuba was accused of inciting revolts in other OAS countries and was banned from active membership, but it still remains in the OAS.

## ORIOLE

American orioles are perching birds that are related to blackbirds, bobolinks, and meadowlarks. The best known is the Baltimore oriole, which breeds east of the Rocky Mountains. A very similar bird found in the West is Bullock's oriole. Another, the orchard oriole, lives in the East, farther south than the Baltimore oriole. Orioles live in woodlands. During the nesting season the male's loud, flutelike song can be heard. Orioles build deep, hanging nests in the forked branches of trees.

▲ *Bird-watchers find it easy to identify orioles because of their bright orange and black plumage and their distinctive call in mating season.*

## OSCEOLA

Osceola (1804?–1838) was a SEMINOLE warrior. The United States government told the Seminoles to give up their lands in Florida and move to Indian Territory (present-day Oklahoma) by 1835. Osceola refused. He began a rebellion that went on for seven years and became known as the Second Seminole War. The Seminoles fought from their hideouts in the Everglades, and the U.S. Army was unable to defeat them. General T. S. Jesup finally tricked Osceola—he invited him to a peace conference in 1837 and then took him prisoner. Osceola died in prison a year later.

▲ *The eight-year war waged by Osceola cost the lives of 1,500 U.S. soldiers before the Seminoles were forced to the Oklahoma Territory.*

## OTTAWA

Ottawa is the capital of CANADA. It is located on the Ottawa River in southeastern ONTARIO. The Quebec city of Hull is just across the river. Ottawa was chosen as the capital of the Province of Canada in 1857 and became the capital of the independent Dominion of Canada in 1867. It was seen as a compromise between the larger cities of Toronto and Montreal.

Like Washington, D.C., Ottawa relies on the federal government for most of its jobs. About 100,000 people, or about one third of the city's population, are em-

► *A popular skating track in Ottawa leads right by the Canadian Houses of Parliament (left).*

**Ottawa grew around the construction site of the Rideau Canal, which links the Ottawa River and Lake Ontario. Originally called Bytown, the city's name was changed to Ottawa, taken from the Algonquin word that means "to trade."**

ployed by the Canadian government. Being a center of government helps tourism too. Each year, thousands come to see the Canadian Parliament buildings. The National Arts Centre, the National Gallery, the National Library, and the Royal Canadian Mint are also located in Ottawa.

## OTTER

The otter is a type of WEASEL. It spends much of its life in the water and is a very good swimmer. It has webbed feet, and it uses its paws to handle things, such as shellfish. Intelligent and friendly, otters are much more playful than other wild animals. They communicate with each other using a variety of sounds. The North American, or river, otter digs its burrow in banks of lakes and large rivers. The entrance is underwater.

The sea otter lives near kelp beds on the Pacific Ocean. It was nearly extinct because it was hunted for its fur. Now it is protected by law, and the numbers are slowly increasing.

**Otters can swim underwater for a quarter of a mile (400 m) without coming up for air. The sea otter floats on its back, sometimes carrying a stone on its chest, against which it smashes clams and other mollusks. It also carries its young in this way.**

► *Otters thrive in the countless waterways of North America. In other parts of the world, such as Europe, they are nearly an endangered species.*

## OWENS, Jesse

Jesse Owens (1913–1980) was a great athlete. He was born in Oakville, Alabama, and was raised in Cleveland. In college he broke three world records and tied a fourth in track-and-field events. Owens is best remembered for his superior performance at the Olympic Games held in Berlin, Germany, in 1936. He won gold medals in the 100- and 200-meter dashes and the long jump and was on the team that won the 400-meter relay. He devoted much of the rest of his life to working for athletics and against racism.

▲ *Jesse Owens's four gold medals at the 1936 Berlin Olympics were a source of pride for Americans, particularly black Americans.*

**Snowy owl**

**Great horned owl**

◀ *Owls have coloring to adapt to many habitats. But all species share excellent eyesight and nocturnal (nighttime) hunting habits.*

## OWL

The owl is a BIRD OF PREY with a powerful beak and sharp claws. It eats rodents and other small mammals, snakes, and insects. Owls, which hunt at night, have broad heads and large eyes that make them look intelligent. This gave rise to the saying "as wise as an owl."

A number of species of owls live in North America. The largest is the barred owl, which lives in wooded areas in eastern North America. It can grow up to 30 inches (76 cm). The smallest, the elf owl, is only about 5 inches (12 cm). It lives in the deserts of the Southwest, where it builds nests in holes in cactuses. Other North American owls include the burrowing owl, barn owl, screech owl, hawk owl, short-eared owl, and snowy owl of the Arctic.

**Barn owl**

## PACIFIC TERRITORIES OF THE UNITED STATES

The United States governs a number of islands in the Pacific Ocean (in addition to the islands that form the state of Hawaii). The largest of these is Guam, which has commonwealth status and elects its own governor and legislature. American Samoa also elects its own governor and legislature. In World War II the United States won four island groups from Japan and took control of them as a trust territory of the United Nations. The Northern Mariana Islands became a commonwealth in 1986. The Marshall Islands and the Federated States of Micronesia have signed compacts of free association with the United States. They are completely self-governing except that Washington remains responsible for their defense in emergency situations. The Republic of Palau has signed but not ratified this compact.

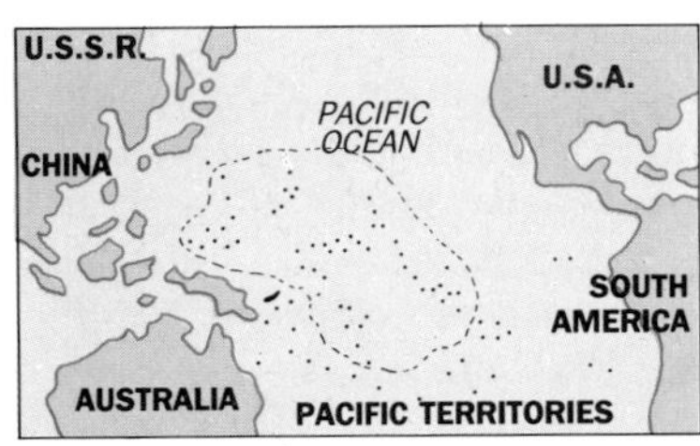


▲ *The U.S. Pacific Territories are located in a large area that is sometimes described as "Micronesia" (tiny islands). The territory's overall area covers 3 million sq miles (7.7 million km²) of the Pacific Ocean. But the land area of all the islands is only 716 sq miles (1,833 km²), less than half the size of Rhode Island.*

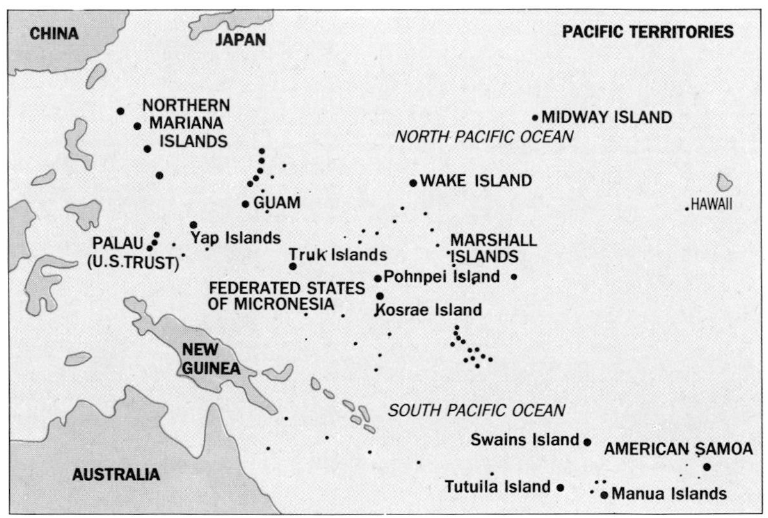


## PACK RAT

The pack rat is a wild RODENT sometimes called the wood, bush, or trade rat. It is similar to the house rat but has larger eyes and longer, softer fur. Its length is 6 to 9 inches (15 to 23 cm), not counting the tail, which is nearly as long. The pack rat can be found from Canada to Nicaragua. Some rats live in the mountains and others on the deserts. It feeds on plant material, usually at night. It gets its name from its habit of collecting shiny objects for its den, such as coins and pebbles.

## PAINE, Thomas 

Thomas Paine (1737–1809) was a political writer and a crusader for democratic rights during the late 1700s.

Born in England, Paine moved to the American colonies in 1774 with the help of Benjamin FRANKLIN. In January 1776 he published a pamphlet called *Common Sense*. It called for American independence from Britain and influenced the men who soon wrote the DECLARATION OF INDEPENDENCE. Paine later wrote a series of pamphlets called *The American Crisis*. These helped boost the morale of the colonial troops.

Paine returned to England in 1787, where he wrote *The Rights of Man*. This book, which supported the French Revolution (1789) and the republican form of government, angered the British government. Paine fled to France, but radical French revolutionaries put him in jail. While there he began to write *The Age of Reason*, which rejected established religion. Paine returned to the United States in 1802.

▲ *At the end of the Revolutionary War in 1783, Thomas Paine wrote that "the times that tried men's souls are over."*

## PAINTED DESERT 

The Painted Desert is an area of beautifully colored rocks in the plateau region of north-central ARIZONA. It is a wasteland of mesas, buttes, rock pinnacles, and valleys. But thousands of visitors are drawn to the area, where the pastel colors of the rocks range from red and chocolate to yellow and green.

▼ *The Painted Desert extends for 150 miles (240 km) along Arizona's high plateau. Brightly colored cliff faces give the desert its name.*

▲ *Charles Gilbert Stuart's unfinished portrait of George Washington was painted in 1796. It is considered the most famous portrait in the United States.*

► Yellow Islands *by Jackson Pollock is an example of abstract expressionism. The artist expresses his feelings by abandoning attempts to depict things realistically.*

▼ *Grant Wood's* American Gothic, *painted in 1930, captures the atmosphere of the Midwest at that time.*

## PAINTING

American painting has a history of almost three hundred years. The most popular kind of painting during and following the Colonial period was the portrait. As the country expanded westward in the 1800s, many painters turned their attention to magnificent landscapes and life along the frontier. Toward 1900 prominent American artists drew on European influences to produce realistic paintings. Since the 1930s, however, painters have turned to abstract art.

This encyclopedia contains biographies of many important American painters. Some of them are listed below. You may look up others in the Index.

Some Important Painters of the United States

*Thomas Hart Benton
Albert Bierstadt
George Caleb Bingham
*Mary Cassatt
George Catlin
*John Singleton Copley
Willem de Kooning
Thomas Eakins
*Winslow Homer
*Edward Hopper
*Jasper Johns
*Rockwell Kent
Roy Lichtenstein
*Grandma Moses
*Georgia O'Keeffe
Jackson Pollock
Frederic Remington
*Norman Rockwell
*Mark Rothko
*Albert Pinkham Ryder
*John Singer Sargent
Frank Stella
John Trumbull
*Andy Warhol
Benjamin West
James A. M. Whistler
Grant Wood
Andrew Wyeth

*See individual entries

◀ *The Paiutes are skilled gatherers of wild fruits and berries. In this photograph, taken early in the 20th-century, Jigger Bob, a 103 year-old Paiute, helps his wife and son to prepare wild cherries.*

## PAIUTES

The Paiute INDIANS lived in the Great Basin—that area between the Sierra Nevada in the west and the Rocky Mountains in the east. There were two groups of Paiutes, the Southern Paiutes and the Northern Paiutes. The lands of the Southern Paiutes were arid. They lived by gathering seeds, berries, and fruits and by hunting small animals. The lands of the Northern Paiutes were more fruitful. In addition to gathering food and hunting, they also fished. Beginning in the mid-1800s, the Northern Paiutes resisted the white settlers who came to their land. They and the Southern Paiutes were forced onto a number of small reservations in the 1860s and 1870s. Today there are about 5,000 Paiutes.

**A Paiute chief called Wovoka had a vision in 1890. It told him to perform a ceremony called the Ghost Dance in order to rid his lands of white people and to fill the plains with buffalo once more. The Ghost Dance movement spread to many other tribes but died out later in 1890 when 200 Indians were wiped out at the Battle of Wounded Knee.**

## PANAMA CANAL

The Panama Canal links the Atlantic and Pacific oceans. It crosses Central America at its narrowest point, the Isthmus of Panama. Many people in the 1800s had called for a canal so that ships traveling between San Francisco and New York would no longer have to go around the tip of South America. The canal, which opened in 1914, cut about 8,000 miles (13,000 km) from this voyage. The United States built the canal under an agreement with Panama, which had just gained its independence from Colombia. This same agreement, signed in 1903, gave the United States the right to operate the canal and a Canal Zone around it. In 1977, President Jimmy Carter signed a new treaty with Panama. This promised to pass control of the canal to Panama on December 31, 1999.

▼ *The Panama Canal was built across the Isthmus of Panama, one of the narrowest points between North and South America. Engineers reduced the need for digging by running the canal through Lake Gatun.*

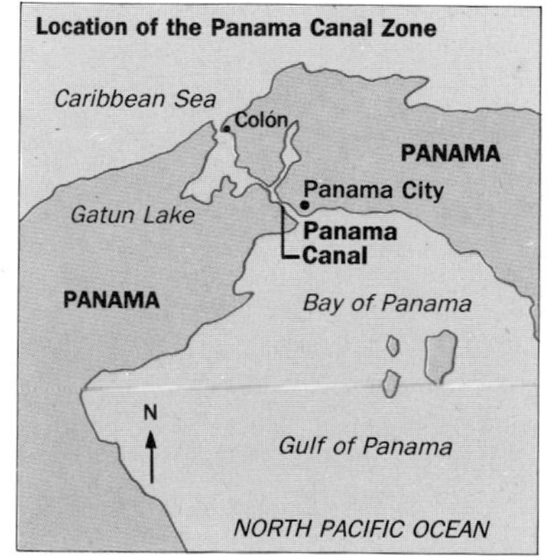

▶ *Dorothy Parker was a noted poet and short-story writer. But many people remember her for her sparkling wit, which typified the lively spirit of the 1920s.*

**Dorothy Parker had problems falling asleep but refused some advice that friends gave her. "I really can't be expected to drop everything and start counting sheep at my age. I hate sheep."**

## PARKER, Dorothy

Dorothy Parker (1893–1967) was a literary critic, poet, and short-story writer. Born in West End, New Jersey, she became drama critic for *Vanity Fair* and a book reviewer for the *New Yorker*. Parker was also a member of the Algonquin Round Table. This group of literary and theatrical people met for lunch and witty conversation at New York City's Algonquin Hotel. Parker's short stories appear in *Here Lies* and other collections. Among her volumes of poetry is *Enough Rope*. This book contained one of her wittiest bits of verse: "Men seldom make passes/At girls who wear glasses."

## PARKMAN, Francis

Francis Parkman (1823–1893) was a major American historian. His first book, *The Oregon Trail*, was based on his own travels, during which he lived with the Sioux Indians. Despite poor health and weak eyesight, Parkman wrote a multivolume history called *France and England in North America*. This series described the English–French struggle for control of the continent, as well as the role played by American Indians in this struggle. Parkman used original documentation in writing these books.

▼ *A passport is an important proof of U.S. citizenship. People should always report a lost or stolen passport.*

## PASSPORT

A passport is an official government document. It identifies the holder as a citizen of a particular country and allows him or her to travel from one country to another. In the United States, passports are issued by the Passport Services, Bureau of Consular Affairs, U.S. Department of State. It is not necessary to have a passport to visit some countries, such as Canada and Mexico. Other countries may require a *visa*. This is a document or stamp placed in the passport stating that the passport holder's entry has been approved.

## PATENTS AND COPYRIGHTS

Governments issue patents to protect the legal and financial rights of inventors. Copyrights protect the rights of creators of literary, musical, and artistic works.

An inventor must apply to the Patent and Trademark Office of the U.S. Department of Commerce. Patents are granted to the first person who actually created the invention. Patents give inventors exclusive rights for 17 years. Only an Act of Congress can renew a patent beyond 17 years.

Authors have copyright for the whole of their lifetime. This is extended for another 50 years after their death. This allows heirs to benefit from payments for the work. For works created before 1978, the copyright

| Patents Issued (1982–1990) | |
|---|---|
| 1982 | 63,300 |
| 1983 | 62,000 |
| 1984 | 72,700 |
| 1985 | 77,200 |
| 1986 | 76,900 |
| 1987 | 89,400 |
| 1988 | 84,300 |
| 1989 | 102,500 |
| 1990 | 99,100 |

Top Copyrights
1. Musical works
2. Computer software
3. Works of visual art
4. Renewals

**The first U.S. patent was issued in 1790 to Samuel Hopkins of Vermont for making "pot ash and pearl ash by a new apparatus and process." Since then more than 4 million patents have been issued— about 70,000 a year. Thomas Edison obtained more than 1,000 patents.**

◄ *Elisha Otis built the first elevator with protective safety devices. He demonstrated his invention at a fair in New York City in 1854.*

is 28 years and can now be renewed for another 47 years. Copyrights are registered by the Copyright Office of the LIBRARY OF CONGRESS.

**In the 1930s, Alice Paul worked with several international women's organizations. In 1938 she founded the World Women's Party.**

## PAUL, Alice

Alice Paul (1885–1977) was a leader of the American WOMEN'S RIGHTS movement. Born in Moorestown, New Jersey, she lived in England from 1907 to 1910. While there she became involved in the British suffragette movement. Upon returning to the United States, Paul organized marches and protest meetings, demanding that women be allowed to vote. She founded and was chairperson of the National Woman's Party. After the passage, in 1920, of the Nineteenth Amendment, which gave women the right to vote, Paul continued working for another amendment to give women equal rights in other areas. She submitted the first version of this amendment to Congress in 1923 and continued working for women's rights into the 1960s.

## PAULING, Linus

The chemist Linus Pauling (1901– ) was the second person (after Marie Curie) to win two Nobel Prizes. He won the 1954 Nobel Prize for chemistry for his work on the structure of molecules, the basic units of chemical compounds, and the forces that bind them together. He also won the 1962 Nobel Peace Prize for campaigning against the testing of atomic weapons. Pauling advocates the use of high doses of vitamin C to combat the common cold. Many consider this treatment to be controversial. Born in Portland, Oregon, Pauling taught at the California Institute of Technology.

*▼ Religion was very important to the Pawnees. One annual ceremony involved sacrificing a young woman. She was meant as a gift and to carry messages to the gods. According to legend, this ritual stopped when Petalshara, a Pawnee, rescued a Comanche girl who was meant to be sacrificed and took her back to her own tribe. When he returned, unharmed, he proved to the Pawnee tribe that human sacrifice was not necessary.*

## PAWNEES

The Pawnees once lived along the Platte River in Nebraska. They were farmers, growing crops of maize (corn) and beans, but twice a year they hunted buffalo on the plains. In 1857 the Pawnees moved onto a reservation in Nebraska. But they soon faced pressure from white settlers and attacks by hostile Indian tribes. They were moved to Indian Territory (Oklahoma) in 1875. Today there are about 2,000 Pawnees. Many live in and around Pawnee, Oklahoma.

## PEACE CORPS

The Peace Corps is an independent agency of the United States government. Its most important goal is to help developing countries train people in such areas as agriculture, health, education, natural-resource conservation, and the development of small businesses. By doing this, the Peace Corps helps promote world peace and friendship and increases understanding between the United States and the host countries. John F. Kennedy promised to develop a Peace Corps when he ran for president. Its establishment, in March 1961, was one of his first acts as president. Today there are more than 7,000 Peace Corps volunteers in 94 countries in Latin America, Africa, Asia, the Pacific, and parts of Eastern Europe. Before being sent overseas, volunteers are trained for 9 to 14 weeks.

▲ *A U.S. Peace Corps volunteer helps install an irrigation system in Senegal. During his two years of service he will pass on his knowledge so local people can take over from him.*

## PEANUT

The peanut is not a nut but a type of pea. It is an important crop, and the United States is one of the world's leading producers. Peanuts grow only in warmer regions. Georgia is the largest peanut-growing state. Alabama, North Carolina, Texas, and Virginia are also important producers. About half of the U.S. harvest is used to make peanut butter. About a quarter is sold as roasted nuts. Only a small proportion is crushed for oil, although this is the main use for peanuts outside the United States. Peanuts are also used as livestock feed. George Washington CARVER discovered many uses for the peanut.

▼ *Peanuts have many uses. They can be cooked to prepare foods such as peanut brittle and peanut butter. Processing (breaking up) peanuts releases oil that can be used for shampoo and even paint.*

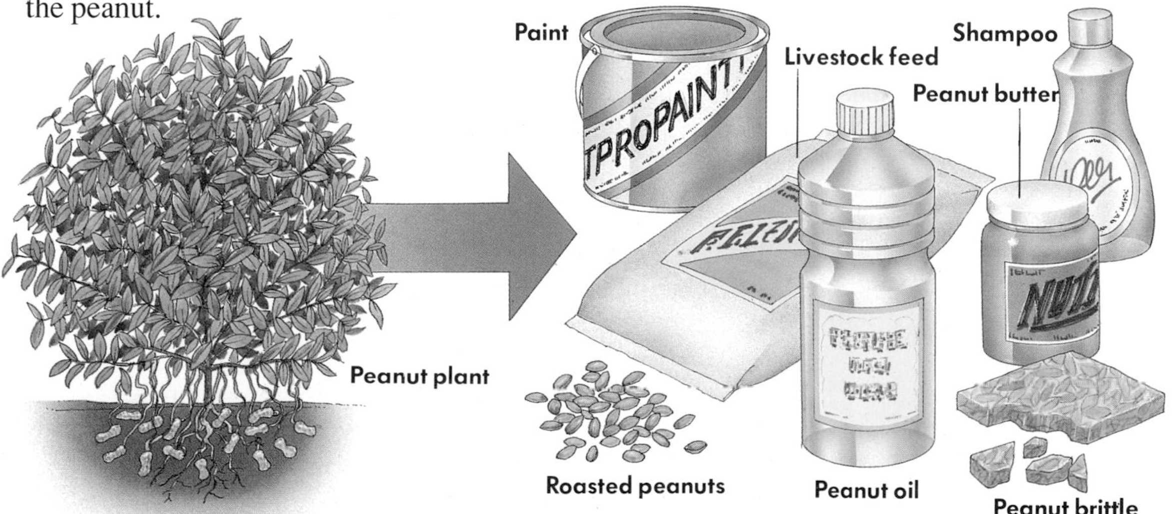

► *Eight battleships were destroyed when Japanese airplanes bombed the U.S. naval base at Pearl Harbor on December 7, 1941. Some 2,400 U.S. sailors and soldiers died in the attack.*

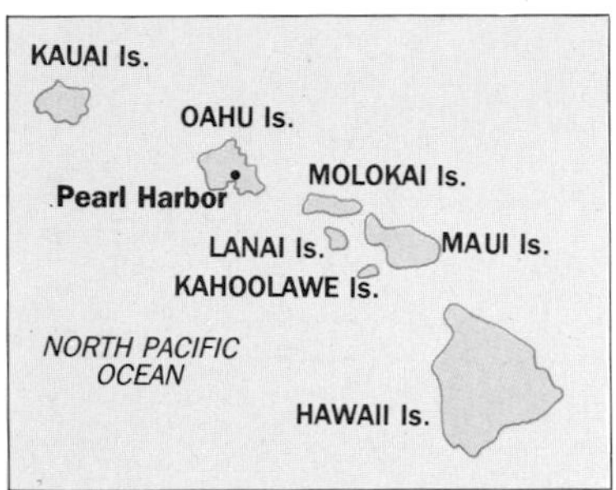

## PEARL HARBOR

Pearl Harbor, located on the island of Oahu, Hawaii, has been the home base of the United States Pacific Fleet since 1940. In the early morning hours of December 7, 1941, Japanese carrier-based airplanes attacked Pearl Harbor. More than 2,400 American soldiers and sailors were killed, and 18 major ships were destroyed or seriously damaged. The Japanese lost fewer than 100 men. On the following day, after President Franklin D. ROOSEVELT called December 7 "a date which will live in infamy," the Congress declared war on Japan, and the United States entered WORLD WAR II. "Remember Pearl Harbor!" was the United States' rallying cry until the defeat of Japan in 1945.

▼ *Robert E. Peary set off for the North Pole in 1909 from Ellesmere Island in northern Canada. He and his team built an igloo when they reached the North Pole on April 6, 1909.*

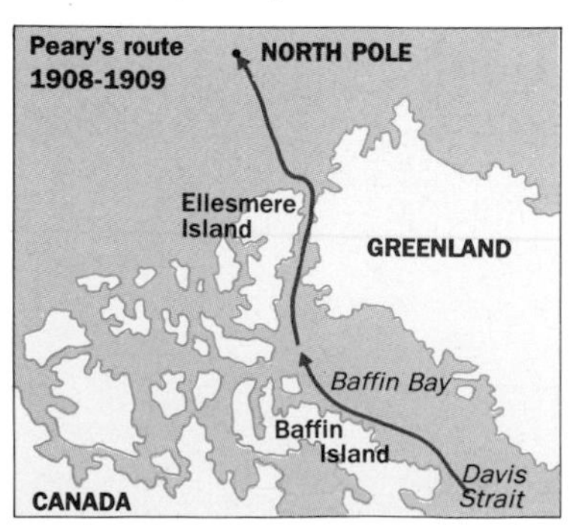


## PEARY, Robert E.

Admiral Robert Peary (1856–1920) led the first expedition to reach the North Pole. During the late 1880s and early 1890s, he made five trips to Greenland. On one expedition, he traveled by sledge over 1,300 miles (2,100 km) of ice and snow and proved that Greenland was an island. He then made several attempts to reach the Pole, finally succeeding in 1909 along with his black companion Matthew Henson and four Eskimos. Peary wrote several books about his expeditions, including *The North Pole* and *Secrets of Polar Travel.*

## PECOS BILL

Pecos Bill is a legendary cowboy hero. He was created by the writer Edward O'Reilly in 1923. The character soon became a hero of American FOLKLORE. It was said that Pecos Bill was born in Texas in the 1830s and was reared by coyotes along the Pecos River. According to legend, he invented all the cowboys' techniques, including roping and branding. Among the tall tales told about him is how he once rode a tornado from Oklahoma to California, where he crash-landed, creating Death Valley. The heavy rain that washed away the tornado was said to have formed the Grand Canyon.

▲ *The legendary western character Pecos Bill could ride a tornado as he would ride a bucking bronco. According to the story, Death Valley was formed from the hole where he crashed.*

## PELICAN

A WATER BIRD, the pelican is one of the largest birds with webbed feet. It nests in large colonies on rivers, lakes, and coasts. The American white pelican is common in western North America, nesting on islands in lakes from Canada south to Texas. It spends the winter on the California coast, on the Gulf coast, in the South, or in the Caribbean. The brown pelican is found in coastal regions of the Southeast and California, particularly in reserves such as Pelican Island in Florida.

## PENN, William

William Penn (1644–1718) was the founder of the colony of PENNSYLVANIA. Throughout his life, he was a supporter of civil and religious rights.

Penn was born in London, England. His father was a vice admiral of the English fleet and a member of the ruling classes. Penn, however, joined the Quakers (see FRIENDS, SOCIETY OF) while in his early twenties. In England, at that time, Quakers were persecuted, and Penn spent some time in prison.

In 1681, to pay off a debt to Penn's father, King Charles II gave Penn a charter for a colony in the Americas. It was named Pennsylvania after Penn's father. Penn took Quakers and other settlers there in 1682 and built a prosperous colony. There was religious freedom in the colony, and the people set up a representative assembly. Penn established friendly relations with the Indians in the area. He lived in Pennsylvania from 1682 to 1684 and 1699 to 1701.

▼ *William Penn was granted the land that became Pennsylvania because British King Charles II owed Penn's father money. The king was relieved when Penn took other Quakers with him to America.*

# PENNSYLVANIA

Mountain laurel

Ruffed grouse

Hemlock

Pennsylvania is a state in the northeastern United States. It borders Lake Erie and is an important industrial, agricultural, and mining state. It is also a historic one. Pennsylvania was one of the original 13 colonies and the second state to join the Union. Because of its central location in the new American nation—six states were to the north and six to the south—Pennsylvania was nicknamed the Keystone State.

The Appalachian Highlands cover most of Pennsylvania, but there are many areas of plains and valleys with farms. Corn, oats, soybeans, and mushrooms are important agricultural products. Among the state's manufactured goods are petroleum products, drugs, motor vehicles, and electronic goods. But the state is best known for its steel. Pittsburgh, in the western part of the state, is the leading steel city in the United States. Pennsylvania's mineral products include portland cement, stone, pig iron, and lime. Philadelphia, the largest city, is a major port on the Delaware River.

The colony of Pennsylvania was founded in 1682 by William Penn as a haven for Quakers. For this reason, Pennsylvania is sometimes called the Quaker State. The Continental Congress met in Philadelphia and directed the American Revolution from there. The Battle of Gettysburg and other battles were fought in Pennsylvania during the Civil War. It was also at Gettysburg that President Abraham Lincoln gave his famous Gettysburg Address.

Pennsylvania
**Capital:** Harrisburg
**Area:** 46,058 sq mi ($119,291\ km^2$). Rank: 33rd
**Population:** 11,881,643 (1990). **Rank:** 5th
**Statehood:** Dec. 12, 1787
**Principal rivers:** Allegheny, Susquehanna, Delaware, Ohio
**Highest point:** Mt. Davis, 3,213 ft (979 m)
**Motto:** Virtue, Liberty, and Independence
**Song:** None

► *An Amish buggy travels along a road near Lancaster, in the heart of Pennsylvania Dutch country. The Amish believe that it is wrong to use many modern inventions.*

▲ *Cable cars in Pittsburgh take passengers up and down the steep hills by the riverbank.*

### Places of Interest

- Gettysburg National Military Park was the scene of the famous Battle of Gettysburg during the Civil War and the place where Abraham Lincoln delivered his Gettysburg Address.
- Philadelphia, originally the country's capital, is full of interesting sites. The Declaration of Independence and the Constitution were both adopted in the historic Independence Hall.
- The Appalachian Mountains run through the state and provide sites for many activities, including camping, fishing, and skiing.

▲ *Freshly harvested pumpkins are prepared for shipment. Pennsylvania is one of the leading farming states east of the Mississippi River.*

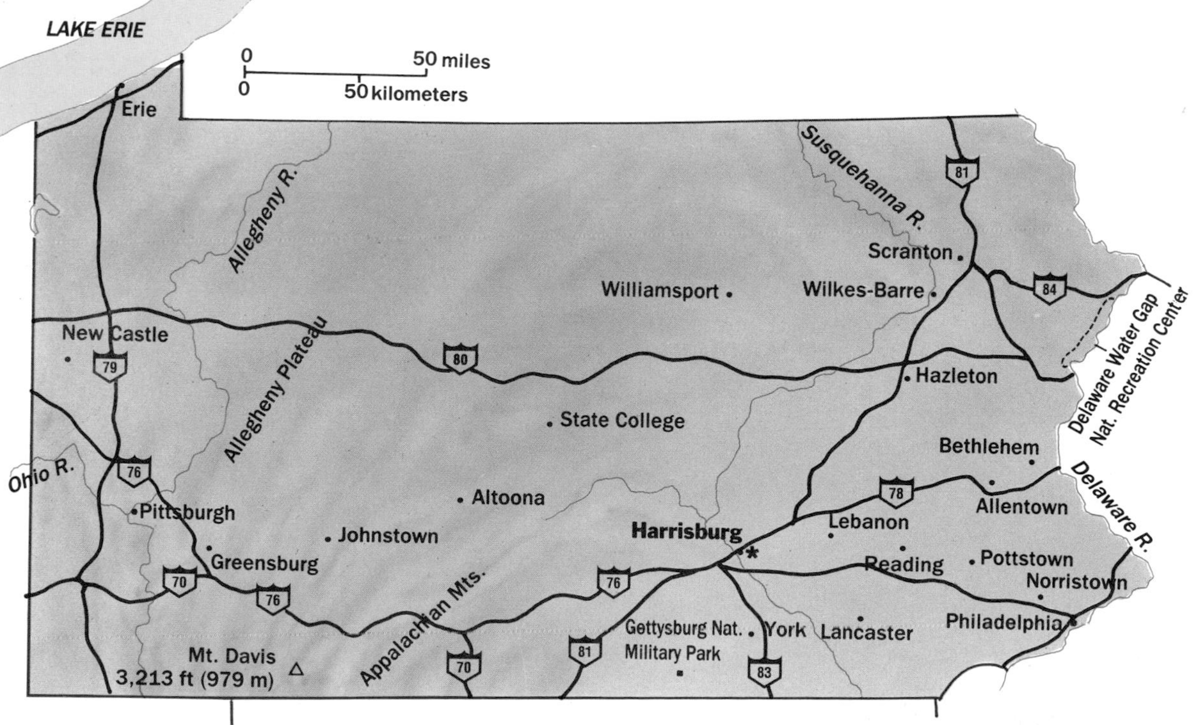

▲ *During the Battle of Lake Erie, in the War of 1812, Oliver Perry's ship, the* Lawrence, *was severely damaged. Perry rowed to another ship in his fleet, the* Niagara. *Under Perry's command the* Niagara *quickly defeated the British ships.*

▼ *General John Pershing was known as "Black Jack" because he led black troops during the Mexican campaign of 1916.*

## PERRY, Matthew C. and Oliver H.

Matthew C. and Oliver Hazard Perry, brothers, were famous American naval officers. Oliver (1785–1819), the eldest, fought in the WAR OF 1812. He commanded a naval force on Lake Erie, where his fleet defeated the British. Perry sent a famous message to his commander, announcing, "We have met the enemy and they are ours." Matthew Perry (1794–1858) is known as the man who opened Japan to the rest of the world. In 1853 he sailed a fleet of American ships into Tokyo Bay. In the following year he signed a treaty with Japan that gave the United States trading rights with that country.

## PERSHING, John J.

John Joseph "Black Jack" Pershing (1860–1948) was the commander of the American Expeditionary Forces (AEF) in WORLD WAR I. Pershing was born in Laclede, Missouri. He graduated from West Point in 1886 and became a cavalry officer. His first battle experience was against the Apache Indians. He later fought in the Spanish-American War (1898) and in the Philippines. In 1916, Pershing led U.S. troops against the Mexican revolutionary leader Pancho Villa, who had raided some American towns. In 1917, Pershing was named commander of the AEF. His 2 million troops played an important part in defeating Germany in World War I. After the war he was promoted to the newly created rank of general of the armies.

## PERSIAN GULF WAR 

The 1991 Persian Gulf War pitted Iraq against a U.S.-led coalition. These allied forces were commanded by U.S. General H. Norman SCHWARZKOPF. The war forced Iraq to withdraw from Kuwait, which it had invaded and occupied on August 2, 1990. Allied air attacks on Iraqi targets began on January 16, 1991. The ground war started on February 23. Iraq was defeated in four days. Sophisticated electronic weapons systems played a major role in the war. The allied military death toll was less than 200. Iraq lost 25,000 to 50,000 troops.

**The Persian Gulf War started one day after the deadline President George Bush set for an Iraqi withdrawal from Kuwait. President Bush called the January 15 deadline "a line drawn in the sand." Iraq stepped across that line—and brought on the fighting—by continuing to occupy Kuwait.**

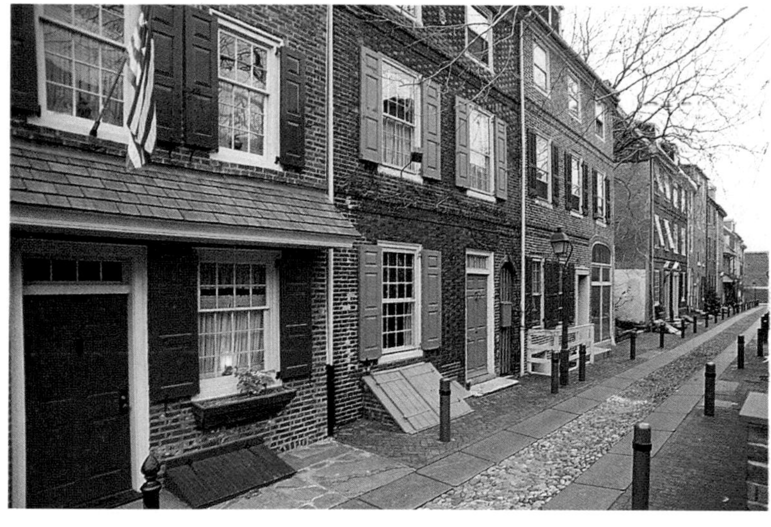

◀ *Elfreth's Alley in Philadelphia. Many streets in the city's older districts look unchanged from the 1790s, when Philadelphia was the nation's capital.*

## PHILADELPHIA 

With a population of almost 1.6 million, Philadelphia is the largest city in PENNSYLVANIA and the fifth largest city in the United States. It is known as the birthplace of the nation. The DECLARATION OF INDEPENDENCE was signed there. The U.S. CONSTITUTION was drafted there. And the LIBERTY BELL, symbol of American independence, is in Liberty Bell Pavilion in Independence National Historical Park.

Philadelphia was founded by William PENN in 1682. It was the capital of the United States from 1790 to 1800. Today, as in Colonial times, it is an important port on the Delaware River, in southeastern Pennsylvania. It is also an important commercial, banking, and educational center. Textiles, chemicals, and petroleum products are among the city's manufactures.

**Philadelphia's population of almost 1.6 million makes it the fifth largest city in the United States. But, like other major East Coast cities, it is not growing as fast as those in the Sun Belt. Philadelphia was ranked third in 1950: since then it has been overtaken by Los Angeles and Houston.**

*▼ The architecture of St. Mary's Basilica in Phoenix shows the Spanish influence on the American Southwest.*

## PHOENIX

Phoenix is the capital of ARIZONA and its largest city. It has a population of 983,000. The city is located on the Salt River, in the south-central part of the state.

Gold prospectors who arrived in 1867 were the first white settlers. The city experienced a boom after World War II, when air-conditioning made life easier in the hot climate. Today, Phoenix's clean, dry air and sunny days attract many new settlers. The city is an important center for the manufacture of aerospace and electronic equipment.

## PHOTOGRAPHY

Photography is the art of taking pictures with cameras. These pictures, called photographs, have many uses. One of their most important uses is to communicate information. Photographs used in books, magazines, and newspapers, as well as in advertisements, are among this type. Many photographs are considered works of art, just like paintings.

Photography developed primarily in France and England during the early 1800s. But it was the American inventor George EASTMAN who made picture taking simple enough for amateurs. In 1888 he invented the Kodak box camera, the first camera to use rolls of film. Before that, pictures were taken using glass plates.

**Important American Photographers**

Berenice Abbott
*Ansel Adams
Diane Arbus
Richard Avedon
*Margaret Bourke-White
*Mathew Brady
Harry Callahan
Robert Capa
Walker Evans
Robert Frank
Lee Friedlander
Ernst Haas
William Jackson
Dorothea Lange
Irving Penn
Eliot Porter
Jacob A. Riis
W. Eugene Smith
*Edward Steichen
*Alfred Stieglitz
Jerry Velsmann
Edward Weston
Minor White
Garry Winogrand

*See individual entries

*► Dorothea Lange's photographs documented some of the hardest times in the Depression.*

American photographers were active during the mid-1800s. William Henry Jackson photographed the American West. Mathew BRADY became famous for his Civil War photographs. One of the most famous war photographers of this century was Robert Capa, who photographed some of the battles of World War II. Some photographers have used the camera to point out social problems. Dorothea Lange's pictures of migrant workers during the Great Depression are among the outstanding examples of this.

Alfred STIEGLITZ, Edward STEICHEN, and Ansel ADAMS are among the many photographers who have explored the artistic possibilities of the camera.

*▲ Young photographers discover that using a camera can be exciting and fun. Many schools have camera clubs where students can learn new techniques and even develop their own pictures.*

*◀ This Walker Evans photograph captured the spirit of a southern dry goods store in the 1930s.*

## PICKFORD, Mary

Mary Pickford (1893–1979) was a silent movie star. She was born in Canada but spent most of her life in Hollywood. Pickford was widely liked and became known as "America's Sweetheart." She was in 194 motion pictures from 1909 until her retirement in 1933. In 1929 she won the ACADEMY AWARD for best actress for her role in *Coquette*. Her other popular films included *Rebecca of Sunnybrook Farm*, *Pollyana*, *Little Lord Fauntleroy*, and *Little Annie Rooney*. She was one of the founding members of the United Artists movie studio. Mary Pickford married Douglas FAIRBANKS, Sr., in 1920.

*▼ Mary Pickford kept her popular screen image as an innocent beauty. In real life she was an able businesswoman and helped found United Artists, a major movie studio.*

# PIERCE, Franklin

Franklin Pierce was the 14th president of the United States. He served from 1853 to 1857, a period of worsening relations between the North and South over the issue of slavery.

Pierce, a Democrat and a lawyer, served in the New Hampshire legislature from 1829 to 1833 and in the U.S. House of Representatives and Senate from 1833 to 1842. In 1852 the Democrats chose Pierce as a compromise candidate for the presidential nomination. He was a Northerner, but Southerners also trusted him because he had supported the Compromise of 1850, including the Fugitive Slave Law. In the election, Pierce defeated his Whig opponent Winfield Scott.

As president, Pierce supported the Kansas-Nebraska Act (1854). It created two new territories—Kansas and Nebraska—and allowed settlers to choose whether or not they wanted slavery in the territory. Soon, pro- and anti-slavery groups in Kansas were fighting bitter battles, and the United States moved closer to civil war.

▲ *The Kansas-Nebraska Act caused heated discussions and violence among the people of those states.*

Pierce followed an aggressive foreign policy. He called for the annexation of Hawaii and the takeover of Cuba. His major accomplishment was the GADSDEN PURCHASE (1853). The United States acquired a strip of land from Mexico that forms the southern parts of Arizona and New Mexico. In 1854 the United States and Japan signed a treaty opening Japanese ports to American trade.

Pierce's handling of the slavery issue made him very unpopular. He was not chosen as the Democratic candidate in the 1856 presidential election.

Franklin Pierce
**Born:** November 23, 1804, in Hillsboro, New Hampshire
**Education:** Bowdoin College
**Political party:** Democratic
**Term of office:** 1853–1857
**Married:** 1834 to Jane Appleton
**Died:** October 8, 1869, in Concord, New Hampshire

## PIGEON

Of the 300 species of wild pigeons in the world, 11 are found in the United States and 3 in Canada. Smaller pigeons are known as doves. One of the smallest is the American ground dove, which is about 6 inches (15 cm) long. The largest wild pigeon in the United States is the band-tailed pigeon, a favorite game bird in the West. The most common is the mourning dove; its name refers to the male's mournful, cooing love song.

A number of breeds of domestic pigeons are bred as a hobby or business. The most popular breed for meat is the white king pigeon. Homing pigeons are bred for racing and carrying messages. Carrier pigeons also carry messages. Fancy breeds raised for shows include the pouter pigeon. The street pigeons found in cities are descended from domestic breeds.

▲ *The feathers of most pigeons are dull black, blue, brown, or gray. Pigeons are strong fliers and are sometimes used to carry messages to faraway places.*

## PIGS AND HOGS

In the United States pigs weighing more than 120 pounds (50 kg) are called hogs. The United States is one of the top three pig- and hog-raising countries. Iowa is the leading pig- and hog-raising state. Because corn is their main food, more than two thirds of pigs and hogs produced in the United States are raised in the Corn Belt states of the Midwest. About 20 breeds of pigs are raised, most of which were developed in the United States.

The only wild pig or hog found on the continent is the razorback hog, from the swamps of the South.

▼ *Some breeds of pigs are well suited to the American climate and eating habits. There are more than 53 million pigs on U.S. farms.*

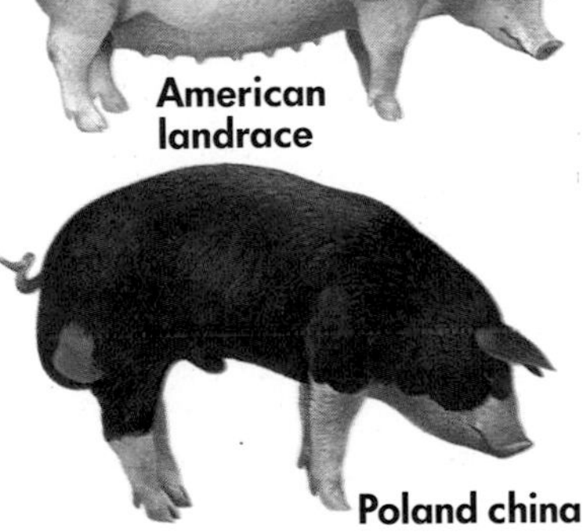

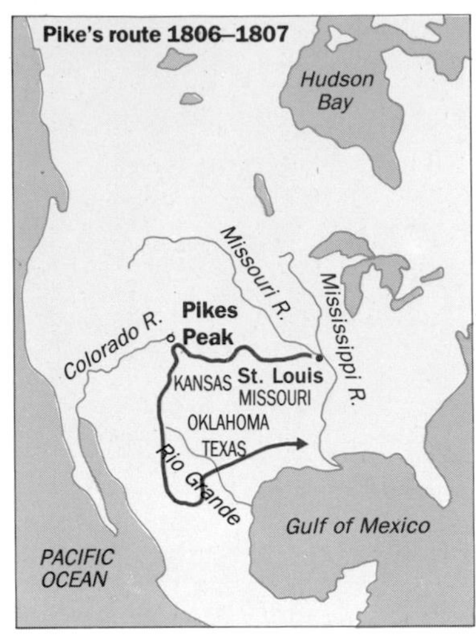


▲ *Zebulon Pike's explorations helped to open up the Southwest.*

## PIKE, Zebulon 

Zebulon Pike (1779–1813) was a U.S. Army officer and an explorer who discovered Pikes Peak in Colorado's Rocky Mountains. In 1805, Pike traveled from St. Louis, Missouri, to Minnesota, searching unsuccessfully for the source of the Mississippi River. In the following year he was sent to explore the Southwest. It was during this trip that he discovered Pikes Peak, which he tried but failed to climb. He then continued his journey into New Mexico. Pike's report helped to encourage Americans to move into the Southwest. Pike was killed during the War of 1812.

## PILGRIMS *See* Plymouth Colony; Puritans

## PINE 

About a third of the world's 100 species of pine trees grow in the United States. They are most common in the mountains of the West and the Southeast. The largest is the sugar pine, from the Sierra Nevada; it also has the largest cones. Some BRISTLECONE PINES are thousands of years old. Pine is the most important source of lumber in the world. In addition, it is a major source of pulp for paper. The eastern white pine was the tree that originally started the U.S. lumber industry. The ponderosa pine, from the West, and the loblolly pine, from the South, are particularly important today.

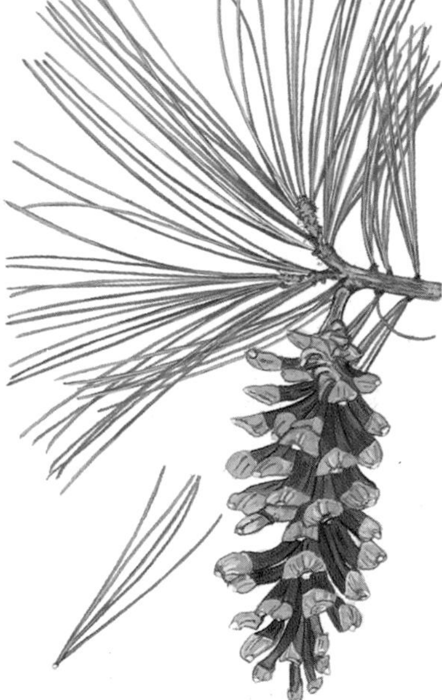

▲ *A white pine is easy to identify. Its needles are clustered in groups of five, matching the number of letters in the word* white.

► *This Californian pine forest has been cleared after a storm. Some types of pine trees have shallow roots and are easily overturned by strong winds.*

## PIONEERS

Pioneers are people who are the first to settle in a particular territory. In United States history, the word *pioneer* is especially used to describe those people who were part of the WESTWARD MOVEMENT. During this movement, which began in the mid-1700s and ended more than a century later, people from the East moved west to settle the rest of the continent.

Even as American colonists were fighting the British at the battles of LEXINGTON AND CONCORD, Daniel BOONE was blazing a trail across the Appalachian Mountains. Soon, pioneers were crossing the mountains to settle in Kentucky, Tennessee, and the Ohio Valley. The second great wave of pioneers began to make their way west after the War of 1812. By the 1840s, using the OREGON TRAIL and other trails, they were crossing the

Great Plains in record numbers. The destination for many of them was the west coast—California and Oregon. This dangerous journey of 2,000 miles (3,200 km) often took six months. These pioneers, many of them in wagon trains, faced Indian attacks, diseases, and other hardships. But the lure of fertile farmland and a new life drew them to the West.

Newcomers at a frontier settlement often lived in the stockade—a wooden fort—until they could build their own log cabins and clear the land to make farms.

The era of the pioneers ended around 1890, when Oklahoma was opened to homesteaders.

▲ *Decorative Dutch ceramic tiles depicted the Pilgrims' voyage of 1620. Many of the Pilgrims had first moved to Holland to escape religious conflict in England.*

◀ *Pilgrims believed in the importance of Bible studies. Families devoted much of their time to Scripture study and prayers.*

▼ *Clearing a plot of land out of woods was the first job of the earliest pioneers. The timber could then be used to build log cabins.*

► *Pirates would take their stolen cargoes to hideouts along the southeast coast of America. Even today people search for buried pirate treasure on the islands off the coast of South Carolina and Georgia.*

**Pittsburgh has over 720 bridges—more than any other U.S. city. Radio station KDKA of Pittsburgh began broadcasting in 1920, the first regular commercial radio station in the United States.**

## PIRATES AND BUCCANEERS 

During the period of colonization in the New World, many pirates, or buccaneers, preyed on ships and settlements in the Americas. The most famous of them was the British buccaneer Henry Morgan (1635–1688), who led raids on town in the West Indies and South and Central America. Another British pirate was Edward Teach (?–1718), known as Blackbeard, who attacked towns along the coast of Virginia and the Carolinas.

In the late 1700s, American merchant ships in the Mediterranean were sometimes captured by the Barbary pirates of Tripoli and other North African states. Between 1801 and 1805 the United States and Tripoli fought a naval war over the issue. The most famous American pirate was Jean Laffite (1780?–1825?). During the War of 1812, he and his band of pirates and smugglers helped Andrew JACKSON defeat the British at the Battle of New Orleans.

## PITTSBURGH 

With a population of 369,879, Pittsburgh is the second largest city in Pennsylvania. It is located in the western part of the state, where the Monongahela and Allegheny rivers join to form the Ohio River.

Pittsburgh is an important industrial and transportation center and the steel capital of the United States since the late 1800s. Pittsburgh factories also produce glassware, machinery, oil products, and chemicals.

▼ *A modern greenhouse flanks the base of One PPG Place, which rises 635 feet (193 m) above Pittsburgh's commercial district.*

## PLAINS INDIANS

The Plains INDIANS lived on the grasslands of North America for thousands of years. This vast area stretched from the Mississippi River in the east to the Rocky Mountains in the west and from Canada in the north to Texas in the south.

Until the 1600s, many Plains tribes were farmers. They grew maize (corn), beans, and other foods, but they also hunted buffalo on foot, using bows and arrows. Beginning in the 1600s, the Indian way of life on the plains was changed when the Spanish introduced the horse. With horses, the Indians could follow the buffalo with ease. The buffalo provided the Indians with meat. Tools and weapons were made from the animals' bones. And tepees and clothing were made from their skins.

As the use of horses became more widespread, many nomadic hunting tribes, such as the APACHES, CHEYENNES, COMANCHES, and SIOUX, entered the plains to hunt buffalo. They fought each other and the tribes that had farmed on the plains. And, beginning in the 1840s, they fought American settlers who were heading west across the Indian hunting grounds.

In the late 1800s, American hunters killed millions of buffalo. The Indians, without their main source of food, suffered greatly. Fierce battles with American soldiers resulted in the deaths of thousands of Plains Indians. Their last battle was the Battle of Wounded Knee in South Dakota in 1890. U.S. soldiers slaughtered 200 Sioux. Soon, the Indians were moved onto reservations. The way of life of the Plains Indians was over.

◀ *Plains Indian hunters often wore coyote skins in order to sneak up to a herd of buffalo without startling them.* Sioux Hunting the Buffalo, *by George Catlin, captures the tension of the hunt.*

**Tribes of the Great Plains**

Arapaho
Assiniboin
Atakapa
Blackfoot
Caddo
Cheyenne
Comanche
Crow
Gros Ventre
Iowa
Kiowa
Mandan
Osage
Pawnee
Ponca
Quapaw
Sioux
Wichita

**Many Plains Indians tribes had had 250 years of contact with the Spanish by the time the first Americans entered their territory. The Indians' fighting tactics and good horsemanship helped them secure some notable victories against the U.S. Army.**

# PLANT LIFE

▲ *Grasslands like these in Missouri once covered the land that became the rich farming regions of the Midwest.*

▼ *Bear grass thrives on the upper slopes of Glacier National Park in Montana. Few other plants can survive the harsh climate and short growing season.*

There are about 400,000 kinds of plants in the world. Many thousands of these are native to North America.

Forests cover about 728 million acres (295 million ha) of land in the United States. In the East, forests contain both hardwood and softwood trees, including PINE, OAK, birch, beech, walnut, hickory, and MAPLE. Oak, maple, hickory, walnut, and ash trees grow in some parts of the central United States. Grassland once covered much of the central United States—the PRAIRIES and the GREAT PLAINS. Now much of this land is used for farming and for grazing cattle.

Along the Gulf coast, pine, hickory, pecan, gum, sycamore, and birch trees are common. Southern Florida, especially, has tropical trees such as the palm. Giant redwoods and SEQUOIAS and Douglas firs grow along the Pacific coast. CACTUSES, yucca, and Joshua trees survive in the dry areas of the Southwest.

WILDFLOWERS grow in almost all areas. The lady's slipper and the JACK-IN-THE-PULPIT are common woodland flowers. Daisies, pink roses, black-eyed Susans, and Queen Anne's lace are found in meadows. And flowers of the prairies include poppies, sunflowers, and verbena. Phlox and harebells grow high up in the mountains, and the deserts are home to desert marigolds, desert lilies, Arizona poppies, and the flowers of various cactuses. Among the water plants in the United States are water lilies, marsh marigolds, and cattails. And in the far north, poppies and other hardy flowers appear during the brief spring.

▲ *Cactuses cover desert areas in the Southwest. Some cactuses produce strikingly beautiful flowers.*

**Natural Plant Life of U.S. Regions**

**East:** Mainly deciduous forest; pine forests in Southeast; tropical swamps in Florida.
**Midwest:** Grasslands in the Corn Belt and Plains states; coniferous forests in north.
**Southwest:** Desert plants such as cactuses and deep-rooted shrubs.
**Rockies:** Mixture of all types, depending on elevation.
**West Coast:** Ranges from evergreen forests in north to subtropical plants in south.
**Hawaii:** Rain forests, coconut palm groves.
**Alaska:** Tundra in north; evergreen forests in south.

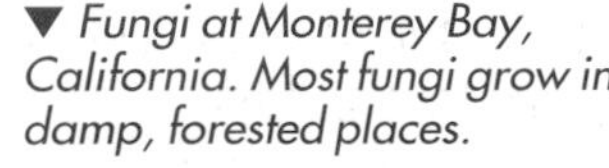

▼ *Fungi at Monterey Bay, California. Most fungi grow in damp, forested places.*

▼ *Water lilies grow from the mud bottom of shallow water. They grow in both temperate and hot climates.*

▲ *Plimoth Plantation in Massachusetts is a reconstruction of the first Pilgrim settlement. The* Mayflower II, *a replica of the original* Mayflower, *is moored in the background.*

## PLYMOUTH COLONY 

Plymouth Colony was the second permanent English colony in America. It was founded in 1620 by PURITANS who sailed from England aboard the *Mayflower*. They landed at the site of the famous Plymouth rock in Massachusetts. These Puritans—who called themselves Pilgrims—were seeking religious freedom. The first year in America was a difficult one for the Pilgrims. But things improved when MASSASOIT, chief of the local Wampanoag Indians, befriended them. In 1621 the Pilgrims and Indians celebrated the first American THANKSGIVING together. William Bradford was governor of the colony between 1621 and 1656. In the 1670s, however, Massasoit's son began what is known as King Philip's War. More than a thousand New England colonists were killed. In 1692, Plymouth Colony became part of the Massachusetts Bay Colony.

## POCAHONTAS 

Pocahontas (1595?–1617) was the daughter of the Indian chief POWHATAN. According to John Smith, one of the founders of the JAMESTOWN Settlement in Virginia, Pocahontas saved his life. Powhatan was about to kill him. In 1613, Pocahontas was taken captive by the Jamestown colonists. During her captivity she became a Christian and took the name Rebecca. The following year she married James Rolfe, a tobacco planter. This began a period of peace between the Indians and colonists. Pocahontas traveled to England with her husband in 1616. She became ill and died there the following year.

▼ *Published editions of Edgar Allan Poe's works often contained vivid illustrations. This woodcut appeared in a version of* The Raven.

## POE, Edgar Allan 

The poet and story writer Edgar Allan Poe (1809–1849) is best known for his tales of mystery and horror.

Born in Boston, Poe was educated in England and Virginia. He worked as an editor and writer on several literary magazines. It was in one of these that his story "The Fall of the House of Usher" first appeared in 1839. His detective story "The Murders in the Rue Morgue" was first published in another. Among Poe's best horror stories are "The Tell-Tale Heart" and "The Pit and the Pendulum." One of his best poems is "The Raven."

## POETRY

Much of American poetry has changed with the course of American history. During the Colonial period, those seeking religious freedom in the New World wrote about religious subjects. Patriotic poems, such as Joel Barlow's *The Vision of Columbus*, were popular during and after the Revolutionary War period. And poems about nature by William Cullen BRYANT and other poets were popular during the first half of the 1800s.

American themes were the subjects of poems written as the nation expanded westward during the middle to late 1800s and civil war erupted. Among them were Henry Wadsworth LONGFELLOW's *Song of Hiawatha* and John Greenleaf WHITTIER's anti-slavery collection of poems, *Voices of Freedom*. Ralph Waldo EMERSON and Walt WHITMAN were others whose poetry was about America and Americans. Whitman's collection of poems, *Leaves of Grass*, is considered one of the world's most important literary works.

The 1900s brought new subjects to American poetry. Some poets began writing about things European, and black Americans such as Countee CULLEN and Langston HUGHES created poetry about the black experience in America. More recently, some American poets, such as Robert LOWELL and Sylvia Plath, have tended to write poems about personal experiences.

Some Important American Poets

Conrad Aiken
W. H. Auden
*Steven Vincent Benét
John Berryman
*Gwendolyn Brooks
William Cullen Bryant
Countee Cullen
E. E. Cummings
*Emily Dickinson
*Ralph Waldo Emerson
*Robert Frost
*Frances Harper
*Oliver Wendell Holmes
*Langston Hughes
Vachel Lindsay
*Henry Wadsworth Longfellow
Amy Lowell
*James Russell Lowell
Robert Lowell
Archibald MacLeish
Edna St. Vincent Millay
*Marianne Moore
Ogden Nash
*Dorothy Parker
Sylvia Plath
*Edgar Allan Poe
*Ezra Pound
John Crowe Ransom
Adrienne Rich
James Whitcomb Riley
*Edwin A. Robinson
Theodore Roethke
*Carl Sandburg
*Wallace Stevens
John Updike
Robert Penn Warren
*Walt Whitman
*John Greenleaf Whittier
Richard Wilbur
William Carlos Williams

*See individual entries

▼ *Three great American poets of the 20th century. Carl Sandburg won the 1951 Pulitzer Prize for poetry; Sylvia Plath and Ezra Pound produced personal visions that touched readers around the world.*

**Carl Sandburg**

**Sylvia Plath**

**Ezra Pound**

| Some Poisonous Plants |
|---|
| Holly berry |
| Jimsonweed |
| Poison hemlock |
| Poison ivy |
| Poison oak |
| Poison sumac |
| Spider lily |
| Star-of-Bethlehem |
| Tiger lily |
| **Some Venomous Animals** |
| Black widow spider |
| Copperhead snake |
| Portuguese man-of-war |
| Rattlesnake |
| Scorpionfish |
| Tick |
| Water moccasin snake |

## POISONOUS PLANTS AND ANIMALS 

About 700 kinds of plants found in North America are poisonous. Some are deadly. Others just cause illness. Some are poisonous when eaten. Among the poisonous North American plants are aconite, belladonna (deadly nightshade), water hemlock, LOCOWEED, and poisonous MUSHROOMS. Even some garden plants are poisonous. Some of these are daphne, foxglove, mountain laurel, larkspur, hydrangea, lily of the valley, wisteria, and rhododendron. Some plants, such as poison ivy, poison oak, poison sumac, and poinsettias, are poisonous when they are touched.

North American animals that have poisonous bites or stings include BEES, wasps, and hornets; some scorpions; the brown recluse spider and black widow spider; certain ANTS; the Gila monster; copperheads, RATTLESNAKES, and water moccasins; and the short-tailed shrew.

► *Some poisonous plants and animals, such as the foxglove and the copperhead snake, can cause death. A poison ivy rash or a tarantula bite is painful but not fatal.*

## POITIER, Sidney 

Sidney Poitier (1927– ) is an important movie actor. Born in Miami, Florida, and raised in the Bahamas, he moved to New York in the 1940s and studied acting. His fine talent on the stage soon brought him to Hollywood. Many of his films center around the problems of being black in the United States. In *Guess Who's Coming to Dinner* his character meets the parents of the white woman to whom he is engaged. In the film *In the Heat of the Night* he plays a northern policeman in a bigoted southern town during a murder investigation.

▼ *In the movie* In the Heat of the Night, *Sidney Poitier played a policeman who had to work with a white racist colleague.*

## POLAR REGIONS 

The polar regions are the regions around the North Pole and South Pole. They are the two coldest areas in the world.

The north polar region consists of the land and water within the Arctic Circle. In North America, it includes the northern parts of Alaska and Canada's Yukon Territory and Northwest Territories. Few people other than Inuits (Eskimos) and miners live in these lands. But the north polar region is rich in minerals. And most of Alaska's oil is from its Arctic coastline.

The south polar region consists of the area south of the Antarctic Circle. Most of this area is taken up by the frozen continent of Antarctica. The United States, as well as other countries, has year-round scientific stations there. In 1959 the United States and other countries signed the Antarctic Treaty. They promised that "Antarctica shall be used for peaceful purposes only."

▲ *The polar ice cap, made up of frozen water of the Arctic Ocean, covers the North Pole. The South Pole is covered by Antarctica, one of the seven continents.*

◀ *U.S. polar research stations, such as the Amundsen-Scott Station in Antarctica, measure wind speeds, temperature, and snowfall. They contribute valuable information about the earth's climate and atmosphere.*

## POLICE 

The job of the police is to maintain public order. Police, or law enforcement, officers prevent crimes, protect people and their property, and enforce laws. There are more than 15,000 law enforcement agencies and about 780,000 law enforcement officers in the United States.

The FEDERAL BUREAU OF IVESTIGATION (FBI) is the best known federal law enforcement agency. There are more than 74,000 state police officers. They patrol state highways. The 683,000 local police officers work for counties, cities, and other municipalities.

▼ *A policewoman patrols 42nd Street, one of the busiest areas of New York City.*

Some Third Parties in United States History

**Prohibition Party** (founded 1869) fought to outlaw the use of alcoholic drinks.
**Greenback Party** (1876) called for the increased circulation of paper money to help the nation prosper.
**Populist Party** (1891) worked to help farmers.
**Socialist Party** (1901) wanted greater public control of the nation's means of production.
**Progressive Party** (1912), also known as the Bull Moose Party, was an offshoot of the Republican Party and called for social and economic reform. Theodore Roosevelt was its unsuccessful presidential candidate.
**Communist Party** (1919) supported the cause of communism.
**Dixiecrat Party** (1948), or the States' Rights Democratic Party, broke away from the Democratic Party because of its pro–civil rights platform.

# POLITICAL PARTIES

A political party is an organized group of individuals whose goal is to obtain political power. In some countries, especially dictatorships, there is only one party. In other countries there may be many different political parties. This multiparty system is common in many countries of Western Europe, Asia, and Latin America.

The United States has a two-party system. There are two major political parties, the DEMOCRATIC PARTY and the REPUBLICAN PARTY. These parties compete in national, state, and local elections. Every four years they hold national conventions to choose their presidential and vice presidential candidates.

The FEDERALIST Party was the first U.S. political party. Federalists wanted a strong central government. This party began to form in 1787, even before George Washington became the country's first president. The Federalists were opposed by the Democratic-Republicans, who wanted a weak central government. In the 1820s, the Democratic-Republicans, led by Andrew JACKSON, changed the name of their party to the Democratic Party. The Republican Party was formed in 1854 as an anti-slavery party.

Throughout its history, the United States has had many "third parties." But none of these has ever been strong enough to win a presidential election.

The two major political parties in Canada are the Progressive Conservative Party and the Liberal Party.

► *Bill Clinton and Al Gore were nominated as candidates for president and vice president at the 1992 Democratic National Convention in New York City. Each party has a convention to choose candidates and to approve ideas for the campaigns.*

# POLK, James K.

James Knox Polk was the 11th president of the United States. During Polk's presidency, California and much of the Southwest became part of the United States.

Polk, a lawyer, was elected to the U.S. House of Representatives from Tennessee in 1835. He served there until 1839, when he was elected governor of the state. In 1844, Polk won the Democratic presidential nomination and went on to defeat Henry CLAY in the presidential election.

Polk was one of the strongest presidents of the 19th century. He believed in MANIFEST DESTINY—the right of the United States to expand westward across the continent. He demanded—and got—the annexation of Texas. He also urged Congress to declare war on Mexico. As a result of the MEXICAN WAR (1846–1848), the United States acquired what are now California, Nevada, Utah, and parts of Arizona, New Mexico, Colorado, and Wyoming. Polk also settled a controversy with Britain over the Oregon Territory. The two countries agreed to set the northern boundary of Oregon at the 49th parallel.

▲ *Under President Polk, the United States defeated Mexico in a war over territory.*

Polk was very skillful at influencing Congress, and he was able to achieve two other important goals. He reduced the tariff—tax on goods brought into the country. And he re-established an independent treasury.

Polk was the first president not to seek re-election. His four years in office had exhausted him, and he died three months after leaving office.

James Knox Polk
**Born:** November 2, 1795, near Pineville, North Carolina
**Education:** University of North Carolina
**Political party:** Democratic
**Term of office:** 1845–1849
**Married:** 1824 to Sarah Childress
**Died:** June 15, 1849, in Nashville, Tennessee

**Pollutants may be carried by the wind from one country to another, sometimes over a distance of thousands of miles. Lakes in eastern Canada have been poisoned by acid rain that originated in the United States.**

## POLLUTION

Pollution is the discharge of harmful materials into the environment. There are three main kinds of pollution—air, soil, and water. Air pollution is caused by the discharge of certain gases into the air. The burning of coal to run factories and produce electricity and the burning of gasoline to power cars and trucks causes air pollution. Besides harming health, air pollution causes acid rain in which rain and snow carry toxic chemicals. Pollution from one country can travel hundreds of miles to create acid rain in a neighboring country.

Soil and water pollution are caused mostly by manufacturing plants and farming. Harmful chemicals and fertilizers get into the ground, as well as rivers, lakes, and the ocean. This contaminates drinking water and kills birds and other animals. Fish become contaminated, and this can be harmful to the people who eat them. Waste is another major pollution problem.

The Environmental Protection Agency, a governmental agency, leads the fight to control pollution.

► *Chemical factories line the waterfront at Tacoma, Washington. Air and water pollution are still hazards, despite federal, state, and local laws to protect the environment.*

▼ *Ponce de León failed to discover a fountain of youth, but his exploration led to Spanish settlement of Florida.*

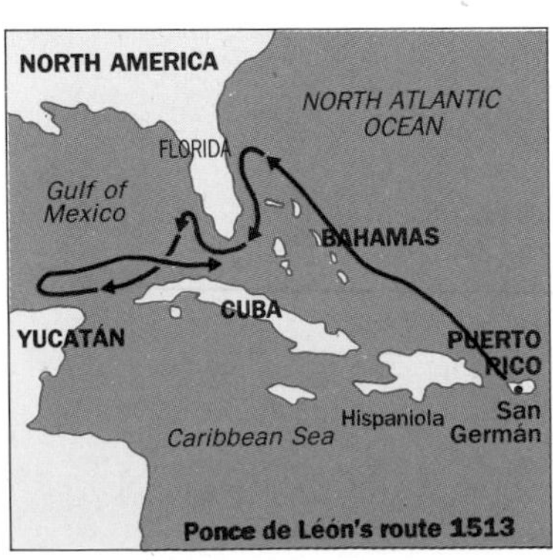


## PONCE DE LEÓN, Juan

Juan Ponce de León (1460–1521) was the Spanish explorer who discovered Florida. He sailed with Christopher Columbus on his second voyage to the Americas in 1493. After defeating the Indians on the island of Hispaniola, he was made its governor. He soon began to seek the legendary "Fountain of Youth." This led him to the land he called Florida ("full of flowers"). In 1513 he became the first European to set foot there.

## PONTIAC 

Pontiac (1720?–1769) was an Ottawa Indian chief. During the FRENCH AND INDIAN WAR he fought alongside the French against the British. After France's defeat in 1763, the British began settling on Indian land. An angry Pontiac led the Ottawas and other Algonquian tribes in what is known as Pontiac's Rebellion, or Conspiracy. They attacked and captured nine British forts in the Great Lakes region. Only Detroit and Fort Pitt in Pennsylvania held out. The Indians were finally defeated in 1765. Pontiac then helped the British defeat bands of Indians who had not given up. This caused great hostility, and a Peoria Indian assassinated Pontiac.

▲ *In 1763, Pontiac picked up the war hatchet to begin the Ottawa Indian struggle to drive out the British. He told an Indian gathering: "We must exterminate from our land the nation whose only object is our death."*

## PONY EXPRESS 

The pony express was a system of delivering mail by horseback. It operated between St. Joseph, Missouri, and Sacramento, California, from April 1860 to October 1861. It used relays of riders—about 80 in all—and 400 horses, which were kept in readiness at the 157 stations along the 2,000-mile (3,200-km) route. When a rider reached a station he dismounted, changed to a fresh horse, and continued on his way.

The opening of the transcontinental telegraph service in October 1861 made the pony express unnecessary, and it closed down.

▼ *Teams of pony express riders could carry mail from St. Joseph, Missouri, to Sacramento, California, in ten days. That was less than half the time mail took by stagecoach.*

► *Diana Ross has remained popular during the many changes in the world of popular music.*

▼ *Stephen Foster wrote some of America's best-loved songs. Tunes such as "Oh! Susanna!" have become part of American culture.*

▼ *Nat King Cole was a respected jazz pianist who became even more famous as a singer. In the 1950s he became the first black person to host his own television program.*

## POPULAR MUSIC

Many kinds of music are considered popular music. ROCK MUSIC, JAZZ, and music for musical comedies are forms of popular music. Popular music is distinct from classical, or serious, music, such as music for symphony orchestras, operas, and ballet.

Popular music in the United States is as old as the country itself. "Yankee Doodle," for example, dates from the time of the American Revolution. During the Civil War, Julia Ward HOWE's "Battle Hymn of the Republic" was the most popular song in the North. "Dixie" was the favorite tune in the South. Love was—and is—another major theme of popular songs. "Let Me Call You Sweetheart" was but one example from the early 1900s. New types of popular music began around this time, such as the blues. W. C. HANDY's "St. Louis Blues" is still popular. The blues were important in the development of jazz.

Popular music reached new heights of popularity in the 1920s and 1930s. This was brought about by radio, motion pictures, and sound recordings. Al JOLSON, Kate Smith, Bing Crosby, and other singers became celebrities. After World War II, Frank SINATRA, Nat King Cole, Dinah Shore, and Peggy Lee were among those who sang to America.

The world of popular music changed dramatically in the 1950s. Rock and roll was born. Elvis Presley and the Beatles from England sang a form of popular music that appealed especially to young people. Rock is still the dominant form of popular music.

## PORCUPINE

The porcupine is a RODENT. The North American porcupine can weigh as much as 40 pounds (18 kg). Porcupines live in burrows or hollow trees in wooded areas. They travel about at night, searching for plants to eat. During the winter especially, porcupines will peel the bark off trees to eat the tender tissue underneath. Porcupines are covered with long, sharp quills. These serve as protection.

▲ *A porcupine's quills are its best defense. They fan out when the porcupine is threatened. Some porcupines have as many as 30,000 quills.*

## PORTER, Cole

Cole Porter (1892–1964) was one of the most gifted songwriters of the 20th century. He wrote not only the music of his songs but also the lyrics, which are witty and sophisticated. Among his best-known songs are "I Love Paris," "Night and Day," "Begin the Beguine," and "Anything Goes."

Porter was born into a wealthy family and began studying music as a child. At the age of ten he composed an operetta. His first Broadway hit show, *Fifty Million Frenchmen*, was followed by many other successes, including *Kiss Me Kate*, based on Shakespeare's *The Taming of the Shrew*. He also wrote songs for films.

▲ *Cole Porter wrote some of the wittiest songs of the 1930s and 1940s. Many of his songs were for musical comedies.*

## PORTLAND

Portland is the largest city in OREGON. Located on the Williamette River near where it meets the Columbia River, Portland is the most important port in the Northwest. About 110 miles (177 km) from the Pacific Ocean, its docks can handle oceangoing ships. Portland's factories produce wood products, processed

◀ *Portland is a busy American city and an important port. Portland also has 148 parks, including Forest Park, which covers 6,000 acres (2,400 ha).*

foods, and metal products, among other goods.

Portland was founded in 1845 and named for Portland, Maine. It grew rapidly during World War II, when shipbuilding yards were built there. Today the city has a population of about 437,000, and its mild climate continues to draw many settlers.

Busiest Ports and Harbors in the United States (by tons of cargo)

1. South Louisiana
2. Houston, Texas
3. New York, New York
4. Valdez Harbor, Alaska
5. Baton Rouge, Louisiana
6. New Orleans, Louisiana
7. Corpus Christi, Texas
8. Port of Plaguemine, Louisiana
9. Norfolk Harbor, Virginia
10. Long Beach, California

## PORTS AND HARBORS

The first American cities in Colonial times were ports built around natural harbors. Boston, New York, and Charleston, South Carolina, all have deep natural harbors. Philadelphia, a river port on the Delaware River, is linked to the Atlantic Ocean by way of Delaware Bay. Over the past 200 years the importance of these eastern ports has declined, except for New York. As the U.S. population has shifted westward and southward, ports in the South, Midwest, and West have become busier. Freshwater ports along the Great Lakes—Buffalo, Chicago, and Detroit—were some of the first to rival the old Atlantic ports. Busy Gulf of Mexico ports include Galveston, Texas; New Orleans, Louisiana; Mobile, Alabama; and Tampa, Florida.

Each year more than $250 billion worth of goods arrive at U.S. ports. About $103 billion worth are

▼ *The port of Houston is the processing and transport center of the important Texas oil industry. It is the third busiest U.S. port, handling more than 112 million tons of cargo each year.*

shipped as exports. Experts predict that in the next century Asian and Pacific nations will become more important trading partners than European nations. This should signal even more growth in West Coast ports such as Los Angeles and Long Beach, California; Portland, Oregon; Seattle, Washington; and Anchorage, Alaska.

**A New England postal clerk in the early 1800s once had to forward a letter with the address:**
**HILL**
**JOHN**
**MASS**
**It took him only a few moments to realize that the letter should go to John Underhill, Andover, Massachusetts.**

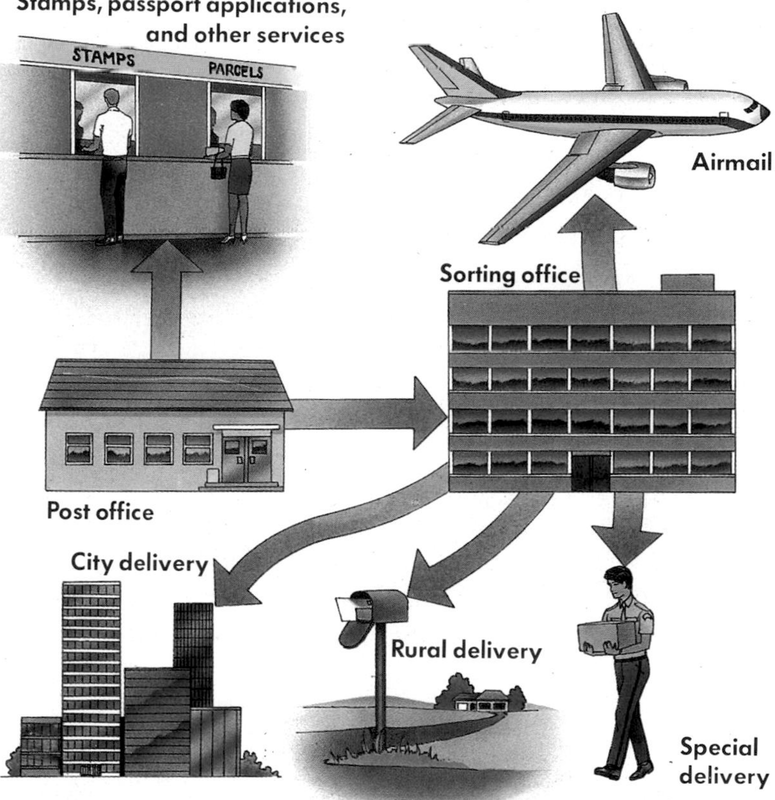


*◄ The U.S. Postal Service handles about 166 billion pieces of mail each year.*

## POSTAL SERVICE 

The U.S. Postal Service is an agency of the United States government. It operates the largest postal system in the world. It has almost 800,000 employees working in more than 30,000 post offices.

The Continental Congress created the first U.S. postal service in 1775. Benjamin Franklin was the first postmaster general. In 1789, Congress gave the federal government complete control of the postal system. U.S. postal stamps were first issued in 1847. In 1860 the PONY EXPRESS began carrying mail from Missouri to California. It ended the following year, however, when a coast-to-coast telegraph system was established. Soon trains began carrying the mail, and in this century airplanes have taken on much of the work.

Notable Dates in U.S. Postal Service History

1639 First official postal system established in Boston.
1775 Benjamin Franklin becomes the first postmaster general.
1789 Congress creates the U.S. Post Office Department.
1847 First postage stamps issued.
1860–61 The pony express service operates between Missouri and California. It became a popular way of mail transport.
1918 The first regular airmail route is established between Washington, D.C., and New York City.
1939 First transatlantic airmail flight.
1943 Major cities divided into numbered postal zones.
1963 ZIP (Zoning Improvement) codes introduced.
1971 The U.S. Postal Service replaces the U.S. Post Office Department.

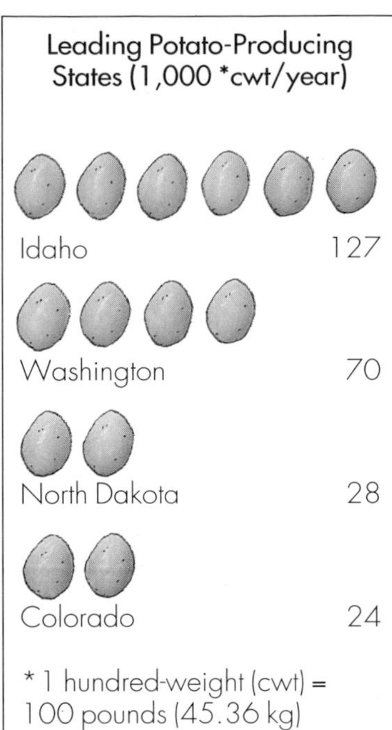


## POTATO

The potato is one of the world's main food crops, and the United States is one of the leading producers. Idaho is the principal potato-growing state, followed by Washington, Maine, Oregon, North Dakota, California, Wisconsin, and Colorado. The most popular varieties are the Russet Burbank, Norchip, Kennebec, and Katahdin. These account for more than two thirds of all the potatoes grown in the United States. Most are processed into french fries and potato chips.

Spanish explorers discovered the potato in Peru in the 1500s. It was an important part of the diet of the Incas. The Spanish took the potato to Europe. Immigration later brought it to the English colonies in North America, where it was first grown in the early 1700s.

## POUND, Ezra

Ezra Pound (1885–1972) was one of the most important and controversial figures in modern literature. Born in Hailey, Ohio, he moved to Europe when he was in his early twenties. He edited poetry magazines and helped many younger writers, including Frost and Ernest Hemingway. His own poetry included *Cantos*, an epic poem that traced the growth of civilization.

Pound was disillusioned with the American way of life. During World War II he made pro-Fascist radio broadcasts from Italy. He was captured by American troops after the war and sent to the United States. He was tried for treason but judged to be insane and sent to an asylum. He was released after 12 years and then returned to Italy.

*▼ Adam Clayton Powell retained the loyalty of his constituents in Harlem though he was not always popular among fellow congressmen.*

## POWELL, Adam Clayton, Jr.

Adam Clayton Powell, Jr. (1908–1972), was a congressman from Harlem in New York City. He was born in New Haven, Connecticut. In 1936, Powell became pastor of the Abyssinian Baptist Church in New York. He began to speak out against racism, and this led to his going into politics. In 1944, he entered the House of Representatives. Powell was always popular with the voters, but in the late 1960s, congressmen accused him of dishonesty and betraying public trust. He left politics in 1970.

## POWELL, Colin L.

Colin L. Powell (1937– ) was the first black and the youngest U.S. Army officer to become chairman of the Joint Chiefs of Staff, the group that oversees all U.S. military matters. Born in New York City, Powell entered the Army in 1958. He was wounded in combat during the Vietnam War and later held increasingly important commands. He also served as President Ronald Reagan's national security adviser. Powell was promoted to the rank of four-star general in January 1989 and became the head of the Joint Chiefs in August of that year. He retired from the military in 1993.

▲ *General Colin L. Powell became chairman of the Joint Chiefs of Staff in 1989. Only the president, as commander in chief, was his military superior.*

## POWHATAN

Powhatan (?–1618) was the name that English settlers at Jamestown, Virginia, gave to the Indian chief Wahunsonaock. He was the head of a group of tribes called the Powhatan Confederacy. His daughter, POCAHONTAS, married the English colonist John Rolfe. Powhatan and the English colonists lived together in peace. But four years after his death a war broke out.

## PRAIRIE

A prairie is an area of flat or rolling grassland. The world's largest prairie is in central North America. At one time the prairie was covered with wild grasses, but

▼ *Contour farming, seen here in Nebraska, means planting crops in varying levels along the rolling prairies.*

most of it has now been turned into farmland or grazing land. Hot summers, cold winters, moderate rainfall, and rich soil characterize the prairie.

In the eastern part of the North American prairie, which receives the most rainfall, tall grasses grow naturally, and corn is the principal crop. West of this are the GREAT PLAINS, a dry area of short bunchgrass, mostly used for grazing. Between the two regions is the mixed-grass prairie, where wheat is the main crop.

**Prairie dogs were once very common, but ranchers regard them as pests and have poisoned large numbers of them. This has reduced not only the number of prairie dogs but also the animals who prey on them (such as the black-footed ferret, which is now threatened with extinction, and the burrowing owl).**

## PRAIRIE DOG

The prairie dog is a type of GROUND SQUIRREL. It lives in burrows in the ground, in large groups known as colonies or "towns." Gentle and sociable, prairie dogs groom one another and appear to kiss. If an enemy such as a COYOTE or RATTLESNAKE approaches, the prairie dogs will warn the others in the colony with their loud, sharp, barking call.

The animals are up to about 17 inches (43 cm) long, including the tail, and weigh about 1 to 2 pounds (0.5 to 1.0 kg). There are two main types. The black-tailed prairie dog is found in the GREAT PLAINS. The white-tailed prairie dog lives at higher elevations, from southern Montana to northern Arizona and New Mexico.

▼ *The holes leading to the burrows of black-tailed prairie dogs are surrounded by mounds of earth to prevent the burrows from flooding. The prairie dogs maintain the mounds very carefully.*

▲ *Remains of many prehistoric mammals were found in Los Angeles's famous La Brea tar pits. The animals — including the saber-toothed tiger, ground sloth, mastodon, and mammoth — had been trapped in the tar as they attempted to drink the rainwater underneath.*

## PREHISTORIC ANIMALS

Prehistoric animals are those that lived more than 5,000 years ago. Many animal fossils (preserved remains) have been found in North America, particularly in Texas, New Mexico, Kansas, Utah, Arizona, Wyoming, and Colorado. Some are hundreds of millions of years old.

Many prehistoric animals were similar to today's animals; others were very different. The first animals with backbones to live on land were AMPHIBIANS. REPTILES evolved from them, with DINOSAURS dominating the world for 140 million years. The first INSECTS and BIRDS appeared at about the same time.

When the dinosaurs disappeared, mammals began to rule the earth. The first HORSE, Hyracotherium, and, later, the ancestors of the camel, lived in North America. Still later, Brontotheres, which looked rather like rhinoceroses, ranged across the continent. After that, saber-toothed tigers and bear-dogs appeared. Ancestors of the PRONGHORN and then ancestors of PIGS, SHEEP, and cattle grazed in the grasslands. Mastodons and mammoths (early elephants) were relatively recent—they died out "only" about 10,000 years ago.

**Scientists still cannot agree on the reason the most famous prehistoric animals, the dinosaurs, died out. Some say that a huge meteor crashed into the earth, throwing up dust that choked the dinosaurs. Others say they died out more slowly, as a result of gradual climate change.**

## PRESBYTERIANS

Presbyterians follow a form of PROTESTANTISM. Their religious practices had their beginnings in the teaching of John Calvin. He was a religious reformer during the Protestant Reformation of the 1500s. Presbyterians

**The Presbyterian Church (U.S.A.) has about 3.8 million members and almost 12,000 congregations. The congregations are organized into larger groups called presbyteries, and the presbyteries into still larger units called synods.**

**Many people consider the president of the United States to be the most powerful elected leader in the world. As chief executive, the president is responsible for enforcing federal laws, developing national policies, preparing the budget, and appointing federal officials. As chief of state, he attends many ceremonial occasions. As commander in chief of the armed forces, he is responsible for the country's defense. He is also in charge of foreign policy.**

practice a simple form of worship. They consider the Bible to be the final authority in matters of religion. Their services are conducted by elders, or presbyters. In non-English-speaking countries, Presbyterian churches are known as Reformed churches. The largest Presbyterian group in the United States is the Presbyterian Church (U.S.A.), with 3.8 million members.

## PRESIDENT OF THE UNITED STATES

According to Article II of the CONSTITUTION of the United States, "The executive power shall be vested in a president of the United States of America." In the 200 years since the founding of the nation, there have been 40 presidents.

The president must be a natural-born citizen of the United States, at least 35 years old, and a resident of the United States for at least 14 years. Presidents are elected for a four-year term. Franklin D. ROOSEVELT, who was elected four times, was the longest-serving president (1933–1945). The Twenty-second Amendment to the Constitution (1951) provided that no one could be elected to the office more than twice.

The president is the head of state, the chief executive officer of the government, and the commander in chief of the armed forces. In carrying out his duties, he is advised by his CABINET. If the president dies in office, the vice president becomes president.

▼ *The Seal of the President of the United States is a symbol of the nation's highest office.*

► *The president's daily duties are carried out in the Oval Office of the White House. Special advisers go there to keep the president informed about national and international events.*

## Presidents and Vice Presidents of the United States

| President | Party | Served | Vice President |
|---|---|---|---|
| George Washington (1732–1799) | None | 1789–1797 | John Adams |
| John Adams (1735–1826) | Federalist | 1797–1801 | Thomas Jefferson |
| Thomas Jefferson (1743–1826) | Democratic-Republican | 1801–1809 | Aaron Burr<br>George Clinton |
| James Madison (1751–1836) | Democratic-Republican | 1809–1817 | George Clinton<br>Elbridge Gerry |
| James Monroe (1758–1831) | Democratic-Republican | 1817–1825 | Daniel Tompkins |
| John Quincy Adams (1767–1848) | Democratic Republican | 1825–1829 | John Calhoun |
| Andrew Jackson (1767–1845) | Democratic | 1829–1837 | John Calhoun<br>Martin Van Buren |
| Martin Van Buren (1782–1862) | Democratic | 1837–1841 | Richard Johnson |
| William H. Harrison (1773–1841) | Whig | 1841 | John Tyler |
| John Tyler (1790–1862) | Whig | 1841–1845 | |
| James K. Polk (1795–1849) | Democratic | 1845–1849 | George Dallas |
| Zachary Taylor (1784–1850) | Whig | 1849–1850 | Millard Fillmore |
| Millard Fillmore (1800–1874) | Whig | 1850–1853 | |
| Franklin Pierce (1804–1869) | Democratic | 1853–1857 | William King |
| James Buchanan (1791–1868) | Democratic | 1857–1861 | John Breckinridge |
| Abraham Lincoln (1809–1865) | Republican | 1861–1865 | Hannibal Hamlin<br>Andrew Johnson |
| Andrew Johnson (1808–1875) | Natl. Union | 1865–1869 | |
| Ulysses S. Grant (1822–1885) | Republican | 1869–1877 | Schuyler Colfax<br>Henry Wilson |
| Rutherford Hayes (1822–1893) | Republican | 1877–1881 | William Wheeler |
| James Garfield (1831–1881) | Republican | 1881 | Chester Arthur |
| Chester Arthur (1829–1886) | Republican | 1881–1885 | |
| Grover Cleveland (1837–1908) | Democratic | 1885–1889 | Thomas Hendricks |
| Benjamin Harrison (1833–1901) | Republican | 1889–1893 | Levi Morton |
| Grover Cleveland (1837–1908) | Democratic | 1893–1897 | Adlai Stevenson |
| William McKinley (1843–1901) | Republican | 1897–1901 | Garret Hobart<br>Theodore Roosevelt |
| Theodore Roosevelt (1858–1919) | Republican | 1901–1909 | Charles Fairbanks |
| William Taft (1857–1930) | Republican | 1909–1913 | James Sherman |
| Woodrow Wilson (1856–1924) | Democratic | 1913–1921 | Thomas Marshall |
| Warren Harding (1865–1923) | Republican | 1921–1923 | Calvin Coolidge |
| Calvin Coolidge (1872–1933) | Republican | 1923–1929 | Charles Dawes |
| Herbert Hoover (1874–1964) | Republican | 1929–1933 | Charles Curtis |
| Franklin D. Roosevelt (1882–1945) | Democratic | 1933–1945 | John Garner<br>Henry Wallace<br>Harry Truman |
| Harry Truman (1884–1972) | Democratic | 1945–1953 | Alben Barkley |
| Dwight Eisenhower (1890–1969) | Republican | 1953–1961 | Richard Nixon |
| John Kennedy (1917–1963) | Democratic | 1961–1963 | Lyndon Johnson |
| Lyndon Johnson (1908–1973) | Democratic | 1963–1969 | Hubert Humphrey |
| Richard Nixon (1913– ) | Republican | 1969–1974 | Spiro Agnew<br>Gerald Ford |
| Gerald Ford (1913– ) | Republican | 1974–1977 | Nelson Rockefeller |
| Jimmy Carter (1924– ) | Democratic | 1977–1981 | Walter Mondale |
| Ronald Reagan (1911– ) | Republican | 1981–1989 | George Bush |
| George Bush (1924– ) | Republican | 1989–1993 | Dan Quayle |
| Bill Clinton (1946- ) | Democratic | 1993– | Albert Gore |

▲ *Lester B. Pearson, Canadian prime minister from 1963 to 1968, received the 1957 Nobel Peace Prize.*

## PRIME MINISTER OF CANADA

The prime minister of Canada is the head of the Canadian GOVERNMENT, but the British monarch is the Canadian head of state. This system differs from that of the United States, where the president is the head of government and state. Canada has a parliamentary system of government. Every political party has a leader to represent it in the House of Commons, the lower house of the Canadian Parliament. If a party has a majority of seats in this house, its leader automatically becomes prime minister. Most Canadian prime ministers have come from either the Liberal Party or Progressive Conservative Party. The first prime minister was Sir John A. MACDONALD, one of the founders of independent Canada. The prime minister lives in an official residence in the Canadian capital of OTTAWA.

Prime Ministers of Canada

| Name | Served | Political Party |
|---|---|---|
| Sir John A. Macdonald | 1867–1873 | Conservative |
| Alexander Mackenzie | 1873–1878 | Liberal |
| Sir John A. Macdonald | 1878–1891 | Conservative |
| Sir John Abbott | 1891–1892 | Conservative |
| Sir John Thompson | 1892–1894 | Conservative |
| Sir Mackenzie Bowell | 1894–1896 | Conservative |
| Sir Charles Tupper | 1896 | Conservative |
| Sir Wilfred Laurier | 1896–1911 | Liberal |
| Sir Robert Borden | 1911–1917 | Conservative |
| Sir Robert Borden | 1917–1920 | Unionist |
| Arthur Meighen | 1920–1921 | Unionist |
| W. L. Mackenzie King | 1921–1926 | Liberal |
| Arthur Meighen | 1926 | Conservative |
| W. L. Mackenzie King | 1926–1930 | Liberal |
| Richard Bennett | 1930–1935 | Conservative |
| W. L. Mackenzie King | 1935–1948 | Liberal |
| Louis St. Laurent | 1948–1957 | Liberal |
| John Diefenbaker | 1957–1963 | Progressive Conservative |
| Lester B. Pearson | 1963–1968 | Liberal |
| Pierre E. Trudeau | 1968–1979 | Liberal |
| Charles Joseph Clark | 1979–1980 | Progressive Conservative |
| Pierre E. Trudeau | 1980–1984 | Liberal |
| John Turner | 1984 | Liberal |
| Brian Mulroney | 1984–1993 | Progressive Conservative |
| Kim Campbell | 1993 | Progressive Conservative |
| Jean Chrétien | 1993– | Liberal |

▼ *Quebecois Jean Chrétien, of the Liberal party, was elected as Canada's prime minister in 1993.*

# PRINCE EDWARD ISLAND

▲ *Prince Edward Island's population lives mainly on farms. Potatoes are the province's most important crop.*

Prince Edward Island is the smallest Canadian province. It is one of Canada's four Atlantic provinces and the only province that is an island. It was discovered in 1534 by the French explorer Jacques CARTIER and claimed for France in 1603 by Samuel de CHAMPLAIN. In 1763, following the French and Indian War, it became British along with most of present-day Canada. For six years it was part of neighboring Nova Scotia, but in 1769 it became the Colony of St. John's Island. Its name was changed to Prince Edward Island in 1799.

Prince Edward Island, or "P.E.I." as it is known locally, lies in the Gulf of St. Lawrence. Farming and fishing are the principal industries. Warm currents keep the climate relatively mild. The waters around Prince Edward Island are said to be warmer than any on the east coast of North America north of Virginia. Uncrowded, sandy beaches and the promise of excellent seafood (particularly lobster) attract thousands of tourists each year.

**Lady's slipper**

| Prince Edward Island |
|---|
| **Capital:** Charlottetown |
| **Area:** 2,185 sq mi (5,660 km$^2$). Rank: 10th |
| **Population:** 129,765 (1991). Rank: 10th |
| **Entry into Confederation:** July 1, 1873 (7th province) |
| **Highest point:** Queens County, 465 ft (125 m) |

*► Revenue agents display cases of liquor recovered after a raid on a speakeasy (secret barroom) in Washington, D.C., during Prohibition.*

**Prohibition was sometimes called the Noble Experiment by its supporters. It began in 1919, shortly after World War I had ended. The end of the war had caused many people to look for dramatic measures to improve life and guarantee peace. The experiment of banning alcohol was one such action.**

## PROHIBITION

Prohibition is the legal forbidding of the manufacture, sale, and transportation of alcoholic beverages. In the late 1800s and early 1900s, the Women's Christian Temperance Union (WCTU) and other groups fought for prohibition. They argued that alcohol is a dangerous drug that destroys family life and leads to crime.

Their efforts led to the Eighteenth Amendment to the U.S. Constitution, which went into effect in 1920. It banned the manufacture, sale, and transportation of alcoholic beverages in the United States. The Volstead Act of 1920 provided for the enforcement of prohibition. But enforcement was difficult. Gangsters set up illegal saloons called speakeasies, where they sold bootleg, or illegal, liquor. Gang warfare also became commonplace. When it was realized that the enforcement of prohibition would not work, the Twenty-first Amendment was passed. The Eighteenth Amendment was repealed, and prohibition ended.

## PRONGHORN

The pronghorn is one of North America's fastest mammals. It is often called the American antelope, but it is not a true antelope. It is a unique animal with no close relatives. Both the male and female have unusual horns with two prongs. Bands of pronghorns live in open grassland, gathering into larger herds in the winter. At one time they were found all over the central and western United States, but they were hunted so much that their numbers dwindled. The pronghorn is now protected by law.

*▼ The pronghorn is about 3 feet (90 cm) tall at the shoulder. It can run at 44 miles per hour (70 km/hr), so that it usually escapes from wolves and coyotes.*

## PROTESTANTISM

Protestantism is a form of CHRISTIANITY. Protestants generally trace their origins back to the Reformation, the religious reform movement that began in the Roman Catholic Church in Europe in the early 1500s. Many of the early Protestants came to the New World seeking the freedom to worship in their own way. Some churches, such as the Church of Jesus Christ of Latter-day Saints (Mormons), began in the United States itself. There are about 87 million Protestants in the United States. The Baptists are the largest group, with about 31 million members. Other groups include the Methodist (about 12.5 million), Lutheran (8.3 million), Pentecostal (3.3 million), and Presbyterian (4.2 million). The Episcopal Church (2.5 million) is part of the large worldwide Anglican Communion.

**Leading Protestant Churches in the United States (millions of members)**

1. Southern Baptist Convention (15.04)
2. United Methodist Church (8.90)
3. National Baptist Convention, U.S.A (7.80)
4. Evangelical Lutheran Church in America (5.24)
5. Church of Jesus Christ of Latter–day Saints (4.46)
6. Presbyterian Church (U.S.A.) (3.79
7. National Baptist Convention of America (2.67)
8. Lutheran Church – Missouri Synod (2.60)
9. Episcopal Church in the U.S.A. (2.45)
10. African Methodist Episcopal Church (2.21)

◀ *The Congregational Church in South Newfane, Vermont, is typical of many Protestant churches in New England. Its simple design reflects the plain faith of the worshipers.*

## PUBLIC HEALTH

Public health is the organized community effort to protect the health of the members of the community. The provision of clean water, nutritional food, and

**Many voluntary organizations are active in the public health field. These include the Red Cross, American Cancer Society, and American Heart Association.**

proper sanitation is an important aspect of public health. Public health services also formulate laws regarding health. They set up programs to prevent or control diseases. These services also provide health care for the needy.

In the United States, there are local, state, and national public health services. State and local governments are the main public health providers. The United States government is involved primarily through the U.S. Public Health Service, a division of the Department of Health and Human Services. The most important international group is the World Health Organization (WHO), an agency of the United Nations.

► *Young people join in a parade in Willcox, Arizona to promote D.A.R.E., an anti-drug project.*

## PUBLIC UTILITIES 

A public utility is an industry that supplies certain essential services to the public. Such services include electricity, natural gas, water, garbage disposal, telephone and telegraph communication, and public transportation.

In most countries public utilities are owned by the government. In the United States they are regulated by the government rather than owned. One notable exception in the United States is the Tennessee Valley Authority (TVA), a hydroelectric system that is a government-owned corporation. And cities in the United States usually own and operate public transportation systems and water and sewer services.

Top Public Utilities on the New York Stock Exchange

American Electric Power
Centerior Energy
Columbia Gas System
Commonwealth Edison
Consolidated Edison
Consolidated Natural Gas
Detroit Edison
Houston Industries
Niagara Mohawk Power
Pacific Gas & Electric
Panhandle Eastern
Peoples Energy
Philadelphia Electric
Public Service Enterprises
SCE

◀ *Pueblo Indian women make and sell pottery at a backstreet stall. Pueblo pottery designs are more than 1,000 years old.*

## PUEBLOS

The Pueblo INDIANS have lived in the Southwest for many centuries. Their homes are called *pueblos*, which means "town" in Spanish. Many of these homes look like multi-storied apartment buildings. Long ago the ancestors of the Pueblo Indians built their homes into cliffs, and they were known as CLIFF DWELLERS.

There are a number of groups of Pueblo Indians in Arizona and New Mexico, including the HOPI, Zuni, Tewa, Tiwa, Towa, and Keresan. Spanish explorers discovered them in the 1500s. They used them as forced labor and tried to destroy their ancient religion. This led to a number of revolts in the late 1500s and again in the late 1600s. The Pueblos also revolted against American rule in the late 1840s. There are more than 48,000 Pueblos today. They are known for their beautiful pottery, woven baskets, and silverwork.

**The Spanish conquistador Francisco de Coronado was the first European to come across the Pueblo culture. During a mission in 1542 he sent a scout ahead to examine the Pueblo town of Acoma. The scout described the cliff-top settlement as "a great city in the sky...the strongest position ever seen in the world."**

## PUERTO RICO

Puerto Rico is a self-governing part of the United States. It is a beautiful island in the Caribbean Sea, and tourism is important to its economy. Each year, about 1.5 million visitors enjoy its sandy beaches and pleasant climate. Agriculture is also important; sugarcane, coffee, and bananas are among the major crops. Puerto Rican factories turn out many products, including

▼ *San Juan is the capital of Puerto Rico and its largest city. The city combines modern and historical architecture in a beautiful setting.*

▲ *Casimir Pulaski's cavalry leadership helped secure many American successes during the Revolutionary War.*

pharmaceuticals, chemicals, petroleum products, machinery, clothing, and textiles.

Christopher COLUMBUS discovered Puerto Rico in 1493. The first Spanish settlement was built there in 1508. It remained a Spanish colony until 1898, when the United States took control following the SPANISH-AMERICAN WAR. The island became a commonwealth in 1952. Today there are 3.7 million Puerto Ricans on the island. About half of them live in and around San Juan, the capital. Another 2 million Puerto Ricans live on the U.S. mainland. The Puerto Rican people continue to debate the status of their homeland. Many want Puerto Rico to remain a commonwealth associated with the United States. Others want it to become the 51st state. And still others want it to become independent.

## PULASKI, Casimir

Casimir Pulaski (1747–1779) was a Polish patriot and soldier who helped the American colonists win their independence from Britain. Forced to leave Poland because of his part in armed rebellions against its Russian conquerors, Pulaski went to the colonies in 1777 and joined the Continental Army. In 1778 he formed Pulaski's Legion, a corps of cavalrymen and infantrymen. In May 1779, Pulaski's Legion prevented the British from capturing Charleston, South Carolina. Pulaski was fatally wounded during the siege of Savannah soon afterward.

## PULITZER PRIZES

▼ *Money that Joseph Pulitzer left to Columbia University in 1911 became the basis for the Pulitzer Prizes. Each year the university presents Pulitzer Prizes for 21 categories of journalism, writing, and music.*

The Pulitzer Prizes are awarded each year for outstanding achievements in American journalism, literature, and music. The prizes were established in 1917, with funds left by the late newspaper editor Joseph Pulitzer (1847–1911). Pulitzer also left funds to establish a school of journalism at Columbia University.

The trustees of Columbia University make the awards. There are 14 prizes in journalism. They include prizes for local, national, and international reporting and editorial writing. Awards are also made for political cartoons and news photography. The literature awards are for fiction, drama, history, biography or autobiography, poetry, and general nonfiction. The music award, for composition, has been awarded since 1943.

## PURITANS 

The Puritans were originally members of the Church of England. But they believed in simple ways of worshiping and in a simple church organization. They did not like some of the church's elaborate ceremonies, music, or even the dress of the church officials. They wanted to purify the church of these things. Some Puritans—called Separatists—even left the church. One group of Separatists, known as the Pilgrims, founded PLYMOUTH COLONY in 1620.

Thousands of Puritans followed the Pilgrims to the New World. In 1630 they founded Massachusetts Bay Colony. As other colonies were founded, the Puritans came to dominate the political and cultural life in New England. At that time, church and state were not separate, as they are today. The Puritans allowed only church members to vote in the affairs of the Massachusetts Bay Colony. The Puritan administration abolished many traditional English holidays, such as May Day and St. Valentine's Day. They considered such holidays frivolous and not in keeping with the simple Puritan faith. Roger WILLIAMS, the founder of Rhode Island, was a Puritan. But he was forced out of Massachusetts because he attacked the Puritan leaders for not practicing religious toleration.

Puritanism was an important force in New England even into the 1800s.

**The first Puritan settlers knew nothing about how to live in the wilderness that was America. They spent their first winter in sailcloth tents. Nearly a quarter of them died from hunger, exposure, and disease before a ship from England brought fresh supplies.**

▼ *Puritans faced many difficulties in their new country. Establishing settlements meant that land had to be cleared for building—even in the harsh New England winter.*

## QUAIL

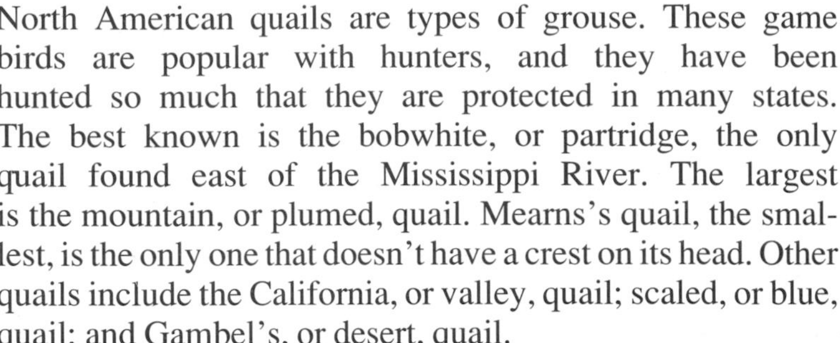

North American quails are types of grouse. These game birds are popular with hunters, and they have been hunted so much that they are protected in many states. The best known is the bobwhite, or partridge, the only quail found east of the Mississippi River. The largest is the mountain, or plumed, quail. Mearns's quail, the smallest, is the only one that doesn't have a crest on its head. Other quails include the California, or valley, quail; scaled, or blue, quail; and Gambel's, or desert, quail.

► *Quails are easy to identify because of their plume, neck, and small beak. They are a popular game bird, especially in the South.*

## QUAKERS *See* Friends, Society of

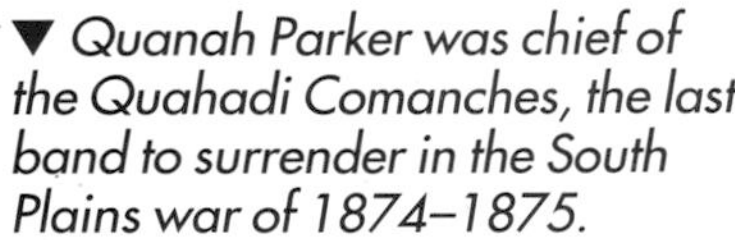

▼ *Quanah Parker was chief of the Quahadi Comanches, the last band to surrender in the South Plains war of 1874–1875.*

## QUANAH PARKER

Quanah Parker (1845?–1911) was a COMANCHE Indian chief. His mother, Cynthia, was a white woman who had been captured by the Comanches as a child. She later married Nokoni, a Comanche chief. When Nokoni died, Quanah became chief. In the 1870s, white settlers continued to invade Indian lands, slaughtering the buffalo. In 1874, Quanah led a band of Comanches, Cheyennes, and Kiowas against the Adobe Walls fort in Texas. Quanah surrendered in 1875. He became an able businessman and encouraged his people to go to school.

# QUEBEC

Quebec is the largest province in Canada. It stretches from the St. Lawrence River in the south to Hudson Strait in the north. Much of northern Quebec is a forested wilderness. Most people live in the south, in such cities as MONTREAL and QUEBEC CITY, the capital. Quebec has more people than any other province except neighboring Ontario. The province is the center of French culture in Canada.

Jacques CARTIER claimed the Quebec region for France in 1534. Quebec City was founded in 1608 by Samuel de CHAMPLAIN. This was the start of the colony of NEW FRANCE. In 1763, however, after France was defeated by Britain in the FRENCH AND INDIAN WAR, it was forced to give up its North American colonies. Quebec joined the Canadian confederation in 1867. During the 1900s, some French Canadians have sought to separate their province from the rest of Canada. But in 1980 the people of Quebec voted against a plan to make their province politically independent.

Quebec's factories make automobiles, aircraft, machinery, chemical and petroleum products, food products, and many other kinds of goods. Its vast northern region is a treasure trove of minerals. Tourism and lumbering are other important industries.

▲ The church of St. Saveur nestles in the wooded foothills of the Laurentides of Quebec. Most French-speaking Quebecers belong to the Roman Catholic Church.

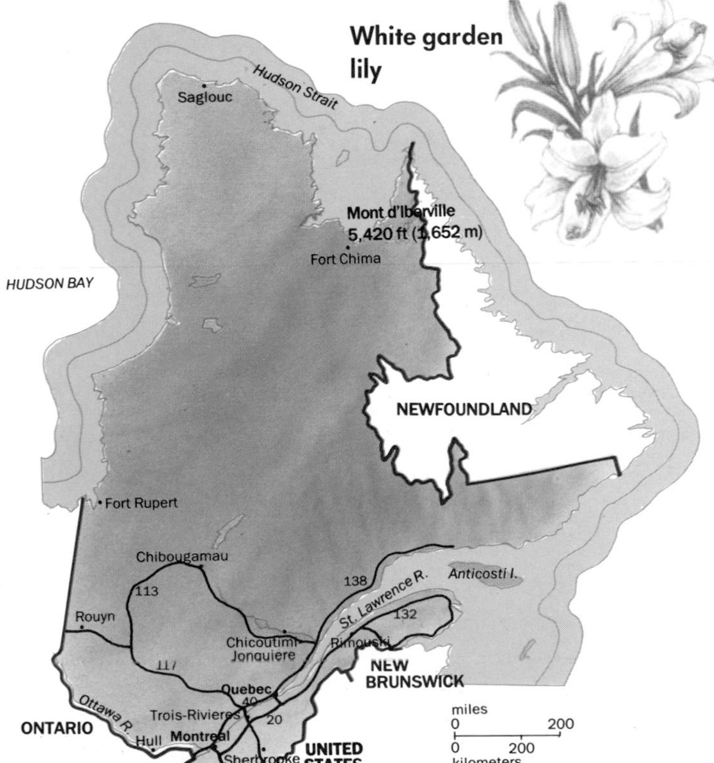

**Quebec**
**Capital:** Quebec City
**Area:** 594,860 sq mi (1,540,680 km²). Rank: 1st
**Population:** 6,895,963 (1991). Rank: 2nd
**Entry into Confederation:** July 1, 1867 (one of the first four provinces)
**Highest point:** Mont d'Iberville, 5,420 ft (1,652 m)

**At the time of the Battle of Quebec, about 2 million British colonists were living along Canada's eastern seaboard. About 60,000 French people lived in North America, mostly in Canada.**

## QUEBEC, Battle of

The Battle of Quebec was the most important battle of the FRENCH AND INDIAN WAR. The decisive British victory over French troops forced France to give up its American colonies.

QUEBEC CITY is located high above the St. Lawrence River. This position makes it difficult to attack. But on the night of September 12–13, 1759, the British general James WOLFE secretly landed 4,000 troops just west of the city on the Plains of Abraham. The French commander, the Marquis de Montcalm, did not expect an attack here, and the British won a decisive victory. Both Wolfe and Montcalm were killed in the battle.

► *This British print, based on eyewitness accounts, depicts the Battle of Quebec in 1759.*

## QUEBEC ACT

The Quebec Act was passed by the British Parliament in 1774. It guaranteed the use of the French language in QUEBEC and recognized the Roman Catholic religion there. It also enlarged Quebec to include much of what is now the midwestern United States. The British passed this act in the hope that the French Canadians would help them or remain neutral if the 13 American colonies revolted.

In 1774 the British also passed what are known as the Intolerable Acts. These closed the port of Boston and forced the colonists to house and feed British soldiers. The colonists believed that the Quebec Act was just one more Intolerable Act. These acts helped unite the American colonies in their desire to end British rule.

**In April 1775, shortly after the passing of the Quebec Act, the Americans invaded Quebec but were turned back. Nearly all French Canadians remained neutral during the invasion. They considered it a quarrel between the British colonies and the British.**

◀ *The Chateau Frontenac (background), a hotel built in the 1800s in the French style, stands on the highest point of Quebec City.*

**Quebec City was the scene of two important meetings between President Franklin D. Roosevelt and the British prime minister, Winston Churchill, during World War II. The first meeting, in 1943, discussed plans for the European offensive later known as D Day. The second, in 1944, planned war efforts in the Pacific Ocean.**

## QUEBEC CITY

Quebec City is the capital of the Canadian province of QUEBEC. It is located in the southern part of the province, on the northern bank of the St. Lawrence River. The city is the center of French Canada, and 96 percent of the people speak French.

Quebec City has two distinct areas, Upper Town and Lower Town. Upper Town is located on top of a cliff overlooking the St. Lawrence. Its business and residential areas are surrounded by stone walls that were built in the 1600s. This area has an Old World flavor. The Lower Town stretches along the river. This section is the city's business and industrial center.

Samuel de CHAMPLAIN founded Quebec City in 1608 as a fort and trading post. It is the oldest city in Canada. It became the capital of NEW FRANCE in 1663. The British captured the city in 1759 during the FRENCH AND INDIAN WAR. Today it is an important industrial center and one of Canada's most important ports.

▼ *A view of Quebec City's harbor. The city's location on the St. Lawrence River makes it an important port.*

▼ *Rabbits and their larger relatives, hares, use their coloring to blend into surroundings and escape from enemies.*

## RABBITS AND HARES 

The wild rabbits found in North America are cottontails, or New World rabbits. They have fluffy tails that are white or light-colored on the underside. Cottontails usually live on open land. The eastern, or Florida, cottontail is the most common. It is found east of the Rocky Mountains, as well as in southeastern Canada and eastern Mexico. There are also desert, mountain, and New England cottontails.

The JACKRABBIT (which is a hare, not a rabbit) and the snowshoe hare are both North American hares.

▲ *A raccoon's black "mask" and striped tail make it easy to identify in daylight. But raccoons are nocturnal and scavenge mainly at night.*

**The American Indians hunted raccoons before the white people came. After the arrival of the settlers, they exchanged raccoon skins for guns and other items. The settlers also used raccoon furs as money before a currency was established.**

## RACCOON 

A relative of the panda, the raccoon is up to 3 feet (90 cm) long, including the tail. The species known as the northern raccoon is found almost all over the United States and in parts of Canada and Central America.

The raccoon prefers to make its home in woods near water. A good climber, it usually sleeps in a den in a hollow tree or log. In areas with no trees, it may make its nest in tall grass or in an abandoned building. The raccoon sleeps by day and comes out at night to hunt for food. It eats crabs, crayfish, small animals, and fruit. The raccoon is widely hunted for its fur and meat.

## RACHMANINOFF, Sergey 

Sergey Rachmaninoff (1873–1943) was a Russian-born composer, pianist, and conductor. He wrote some of the most richly melodic music of the 20th century. In the year of his graduation from the Moscow Conservatory (1892) he produced one of his most popular compositions, the Prelude in C-Sharp Minor. His lushly romantic Second Piano Concerto was first performed in 1901.

Rachmaninoff settled in the United States in 1917. There, he had an active career as a concert pianist, while continuing to compose. The *Rhapsody on a Theme of Paganini* is a famous piece from this period.

## RACIAL DISCRIMINATION *See* Civil Rights

## RADIO BROADCASTING

There are more than 9,000 radio stations in the United States. About 90 percent of them are commercial stations that broadcast music. These stations arc regulated by the Federal Communications Commission. It assigns radio frequencies and approves the stations' call letters. The call letters of stations east of the Mississippi River begin with the letter W, as in WCBS. Those west of the Mississippi begin with the letter K.

Before television started in the early 1950s, the radio was the chief source of entertainment and news for most people. Regular radio broadcasting started about 1920. The period from 1920 until the 1940s was known as the Golden Age of Radio. People would sit for hours listening to such programs as "Gangbusters," "The Lone Ranger" and "Superman."

**The power of radio at its peak became known on the night of October 30, 1938. The actor Orson Welles, then only 23 years old, broadcast a reading of the novel *War of the Worlds*, by H. G. Wells. Millions of people were swept into panic and confusion by the tale of Martians landing in New Jersey. Many Americans believed it was a real news broadcast. They never heard Welles admit that it was a Halloween spoof.**

◄ *A disc jockey and a radio advertiser check a day's playlist. The playlist shows the music and advertising schedule.*

► *Railroad posters of the 1800s confidently predicted that trains would link some of the continents.*

**Important Dates in U.S. Railroad History**

**1831** The United States' first regular steam-powered railroad begins operating in South Carolina.
**1859** George Pullman builds the first sleeping car.
**1869** The Union Pacific and Central Pacific railroads complete the world's first transcontinental railroad line.
**1887** The Interstate Commerce Commission is formed to regulate railroad rates.
**1970** Amtrak is created to operate intercity passenger trains in the United States.

## RAILROADS

The railroad is an important means of transportation. In the United States, railroads carry about 4 million passengers and 1.4 billion tons of freight each year.

At first, railroad cars were pulled along tracks by horses. Steam-powered LOCOMOTIVES were first used in England in 1825. The first American steam-powered railroad was built in South Carolina in 1831. By 1860 there were 30,000 miles (48,000 km) of track in the United States, and the United States and Canada were rushing to complete transcontinental railroad lines. The Union Pacific Railroad built its track west from Omaha, Nebraska. The Central Pacific Railroad built east from

**The completion of the transcontinental railroad line in 1869 led to a rise in daring, violent train robberies in the West. Gangs led by hardened criminals such as Jesse James and Sam Bass attacked trains carrying mail, gold, and bank deposits. In one train robbery in 1899, Butch Cassidy and his "Wild Bunch" made off with $60,000 in cash.**

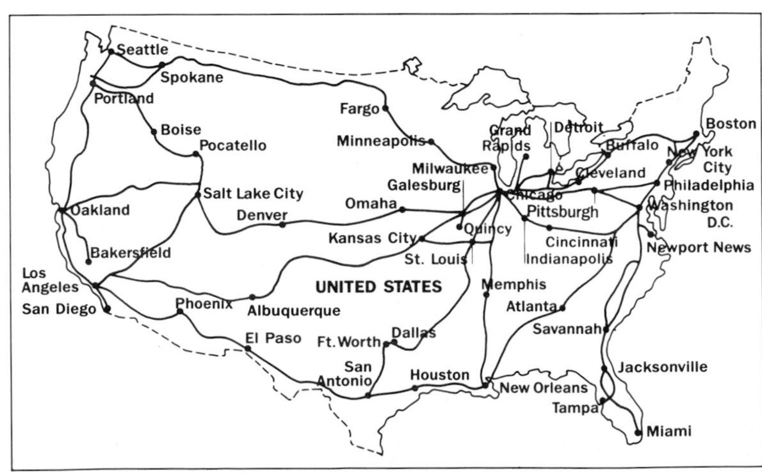


► *Train lines connect cities all across the United States. Train travel from the Atlantic Ocean to the Pacific has been possible since 1869.*

◀ *A Southern locomotive flies the Confederate flag during the Civil War. Railroads played an important role in the war. The South's railroad network could not compete with the North's.*

Sacramento, California. The two lines met in Promontory, Utah, in 1869. Sixteen years later the Canadian Pacific Railroad completed a line from Montreal, Quebec, to Vancouver, British Columbia. These rail lines opened the way for settlement of the American and Canadian west.

By 1916, United States railroads had 254,000 miles (406,000 km) of lines. But soon, automobiles, trucks, and airplanes began to compete with railroads for passenger and freight traffic. Railroads went into a decline. In 1970 the U.S. government was forced to take over the operation of most intercity railroads. It established the National Railroad Passenger Corporation (Amtrak) to operate the lines. Today, railroads carry almost as much freight as airlines, trucks, and barges combined. See also SUBWAYS.

▲ *A freight train carries cargo through the wilderness of the United States.*

◀ *Trains carry passengers through the snowy Colorado landscape.*

▲ *Sir Walter Raleigh's American explorations brought him great fame at home in England. He was one of the first people to suggest an English empire in America.*

## RALEIGH, Sir Walter

Sir Walter Raleigh (1554?–1618) was an English writer, soldier, and explorer. He was among the first to try to establish an English colony in America.

Raleigh was a favorite of Queen Elizabeth I, and she made him a knight. In 1585, Raleigh sent a group of settlers to what is now North Carolina. They found life there too difficult and returned to England the following year. A second group of colonists, sent by Raleigh in 1588, disappeared, and their colony has become known as the LOST COLONY.

Raleigh fought bravely during England's wars with Spain in the late 1500s. When Queen Elizabeth died in 1603, James I, an enemy of Raleigh's, became king. He accused Raleigh of treason and kept him a prisoner in the Tower of London for 12 years. Raleigh was freed to search for gold in South America, but in 1618 James had him executed.

► *Many modern ranchers still use the traditional cowboy skills of roping cattle with a lasso during a roundup.*

**American ranch life has always centered around the cowboy, the hero of many movies, books, and songs. He first appeared in Texas around 1836, and soon ranches spread to almost every part of the West. Cowboys' lives centered on the cattle drive every spring and autumn when great herds were driven over vast areas to the nearest railroad terminal. During these drives the men were often on horseback for 15 hours a day.**

## RANCHING

Ranching is the raising of cattle or other animals, such as sheep, on ranches, or large farms. In the United States there are about 95 million head of cattle. Most ranches are in the West and Southwest.

The first ranches were established in the mid-1800s. Cattle ranchers allowed their herds to graze on the wide-open ranges of the West. COWBOYS looked after the herds of cattle, protecting them from rustlers. They also drove the herds to railheads in Kansas and Nebraska. Here they were loaded aboard the trains for shipment to markets in the East.

Today ranches are much smaller than they were during the heyday of cattle ranching in the years after the Civil War. Jeeps and helicopters have largely replaced the legendary cowboys on horseback.

## RANDOLPH, A. Philip

A. Philip Randolph (1889–1979) was an American labor leader. He played a major part in bringing black workers into the labor movement. Randolph first became interested in this cause while working his way through college in New York City. His efforts to organize black workers finally began to succeed in 1925, when he founded the Brotherhood of Sleeping Car Porters. At the beginning of World War II he prevailed on President Franklin D. Roosevelt to end discrimination against blacks in government jobs and in defense industries. Randolph also took an active part in the CIVIL RIGHTS movement of the 1960s.

▲ *In the 1920s, A. Philip Randolph organized the first labor union representing black employees. He was still active in the civil rights movement of the 1960s.*

## RANKIN, Jeanette

Jeanette Rankin (1880–1973) was the first woman elected to the U.S. Congress. She was born in Montana and graduated from the University of Montana in 1902. She soon became a fighter for women's SUFFRAGE, the right of women to vote. In 1916, Rankin, a Republican, was elected to the U.S. House of Representatives from Montana. She served one term, during which she opposed U.S. entry into World War I. From 1918 to 1940, Rankin was a social worker. She became a Montana congresswoman again in 1941, serving until 1943. She cast the only congressional vote against U.S. entry into World War II.

## RAT

A rat is a RODENT (gnawing mammal). There are more than 100 types of rats in the world. The only two that live near people are the black rat and the brown, or Norway, rat. The brown rat is found all over the United States. It is larger—up to 10 inches (25 cm) long—and fiercer than the black rat and is a good swimmer. The white rat is a domesticated variety of brown rat. In the United States the black rat is found near ports. It is up to 8 inches (20 cm) long.

▼ *The Norway rat, sometimes called the house rat, is found around the world.*

Rats live in large groups, making nests in or near buildings. They feed mostly at night and will eat practically any plant or animal. Rats can produce up to seven litters a year, each containing 6 to 22 young. They cause great damage, by destroying poultry, lambs, crops, and stored grain and by passing on many diseases.

▶ *The rattling of a rattlesnake's tail is a warning to stay away. Most rattlesnake bites are not fatal (deadly), but they are always painful.*

**The Mojave rattlesnake is one of the deadliest snakes in North America. Its bite can paralyze a person's limbs or even cause death, unless the victim is treated quickly with antivenin, a drug made from the snake's poisonous venom.**

## RATTLESNAKE

The rattlesnake is a poisonous SNAKE with a rattle on its tail. Often it gives a warning before it strikes, by lifting its tail and shaking the rattle, but some of the larger ones do not always rattle before biting.

Rattlesnakes are found from Canada to South America, generally in dry regions. The greatest number live in the southwestern United States and Mexico. The largest and most dangerous of the U.S. rattlesnakes are the diamondbacks. The eastern diamondback is up to 8 feet (2.5 m) long. The sidewinder is one of the smallest. About 18 inches (45 cm) long, it gets its name from the S-shaped curve it makes when moving across the desert.

▼ *Sam Rayburn had three terms as Speaker of the House of Representatives between 1940 and 1961. He held the position for 17 years, longer than anyone else in history.*

## RAYBURN, Sam

Sam Rayburn (1882–1961) was a member of the U.S. House of Representatives for almost 49 years. He was born in Roane County, Tennessee, but spent almost his whole life in Texas. Rayburn studied law at the University of Texas and was a lawyer for a short time. But he quickly became interested in politics, and in 1912 he was elected to the U.S. House of Representatives. He was re-elected 24 times. Rayburn held the powerful position of Speaker of the House for 17 years.

## REAGAN, Ronald W.

Ronald Wilson Reagan was the 40th president of the United States. He served two terms, from 1981 to 1989, and was one of the most popular presidents in U.S. history.

Starting his career as a sports announcer, Reagan turned to acting in 1937. He appeared in more than 50 films. Originally a liberal, Reagan joined the Republican Party in 1962. Five years later he won the governorship of California. He served for eight years. In 1980 the Republican Party chose him as its presidential candidate. Reagan easily defeated Democrat Jimmy CARTER. Two months after his inauguration, Reagan was injured in an assassination attempt.

As president, Reagan reduced government spending on domestic programs, but he increased defense spending. And he maintained a strongly anti-Soviet and anti-Communist stand. He ordered U.S. troops to invade the Caribbean nation of Grenada in 1983 to oust a pro-Communist government. He supported guerrilla forces that opposed the Communist government in Nicaragua. He supplied weapons to rebel forces in Afghanistan that were fighting against the Soviet-backed government. And in 1986 he ordered U.S. planes to bomb Libya because that North African country supported terrorism. In 1987, however, Reagan and Soviet leader Mikhail Gorbachev signed a treaty eliminating short- and medium-range missiles from Europe.

◄ *Reagan is seen here accompanied by his vice president, George Bush, and Soviet leader Mikhail Gorbachev. Reagan's meetings with Gorbachev eased tensions between the United States and the USSR. In 1987 the two leaders signed a treaty that led to the reduction of nuclear arms.*

In domestic affairs, Reagan's presidency was marked by increasing budget deficits and trade deficits. But the U.S. economy was strong during his eight years in office.

**Ronald Reagan**
**Born:** February 6, 1911, in Tampico, Illinois
**Education:** Eureka College
**Political party:** Republican
**Term of office:** 1981–1989
**Married:** 1940 to Jane Wyman (divorced 1948); 1952 to Nancy Davis

▲ *The Reconstruction period after the Civil War gave many former slaves their first taste of education. This illustration from the period shows how young and old attended the same classes.*

## RECONSTRUCTION

Reconstruction was the process of bringing the former CONFEDERATE STATES back into the Union after the CIVIL WAR. The Reconstruction period lasted from 1865 to 1877. President Andrew JOHNSON wanted to follow President Abraham LINCOLN's policy of dealing leniently with the South. He was opposed by Radical Republicans in Congress. They wanted the South dealt with harshly.

Three amendments to the U.S. Constitution were ratified during Reconstruction. The Thirteenth Amendment abolished slavery. The Fourteenth Amendment gave citizenship to former black slaves. And the Fifteenth Amendment gave blacks the right to vote. But the southern states did not want to give blacks equality. They passed the Black Codes to keep blacks "in their place." As a result, Congress passed the Reconstruction Acts of 1867. Federal troops were sent to the South, and new state governments were set up. They were run mainly by northerners (carpetbaggers), their southern collaborators (scalawags), and blacks. Some blacks also represented southern states in Congress.

By 1870, the southern states were re-admitted to the Union. But the KU KLUX KLAN terrorized and killed

**The Reconstruction Years**

**1865** War Department sets up Freedmen's Bureau to help freed slaves. Congress forms Committee on Reconstruction. Thirteenth Amendment bans slavery.

**1866** Blacks granted citizenship. Ku Klux Klan spreads through the South; race riots in southern cities.

**1867** Congress divides South into five regions and appoints military governors. "Carpetbaggers" arrive from the North.

**1868** 4th Reconstruction Act strengthens blacks' rights.

**1877** Federal troops withdrawn from South.

many blacks. After federal troops were withdrawn in 1877, southern whites regained control of their state governments. They established a system of segregation (racial separation) that lasted for almost a century.

## RED CROSS

The American Red Cross is a voluntary relief organization. It is best known for providing help in times of disasters and emergencies. The Red Cross has a large blood donor program. It provides assistance for members of the armed forces and their families. And it gives courses in first aid, home nursing, water skills, parenting and child care, and home hygiene.

The American Red Cross is one of 126 national organizations that make up the international Red Cross, which was founded in 1863. The American Red Cross was founded in 1881 by Clara BARTON.

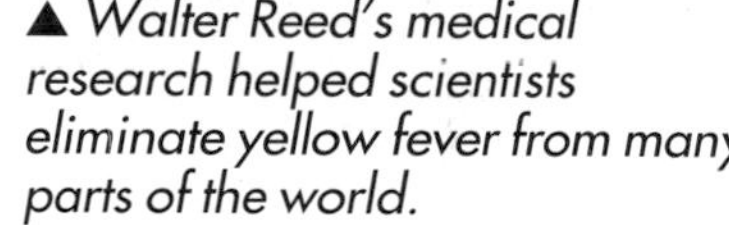

▲ *Walter Reed's medical research helped scientists eliminate yellow fever from many parts of the world.*

## REED, Walter

The work of Dr. Walter Reed (1851–1902) led to the control of yellow fever, a deadly disease.

Born in Virginia, Reed studied medicine at the University of Virginia and at Bellevue Hospital Medical College in New York City. He joined the U.S. Army as a surgeon in 1875. In 1900, Reed was sent to Cuba to deal with an outbreak of yellow fever among American soldiers stationed in that country since the Spanish-American War. He determined that the disease was carried and spread by a certain mosquito. With that knowledge, soldiers were sent to kill the mosquitoes and destroy their breeding grounds. The disease was brought under control. The Walter Reed Army Medical Center near Washington, D.C., is named for him.

## RELIGIONS

Almost 63 percent of people in the United States, about 156 million, are members of a religious group. A large majority, some 96 percent (150 million people) belong to Christian churches. The largest group of non-Christians are Jews, with almost 4 percent of all religious worshipers (just under 6 million). Some 2.6 million people, or 1.7 percent, are Muslims. Finally there is a tiny number of Buddhists and other non-Christians.

▼ *Roman Catholics form the largest single religious group in the United States, but the combined Protestant total is larger. Four out of every ten Americans attend religious services at least once a week.*

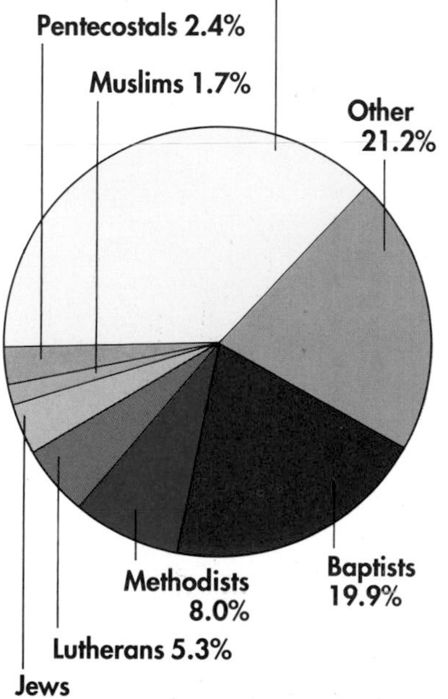

► *The crocodile uses its powerful tail to swim and is recognizable by its long, pointed snout.*

▼ *Reptiles are cold-blooded and spend hours absorbing warmth from the sun. Special coloring and other devices, such as the turtle's shell, protect them from enemies.*

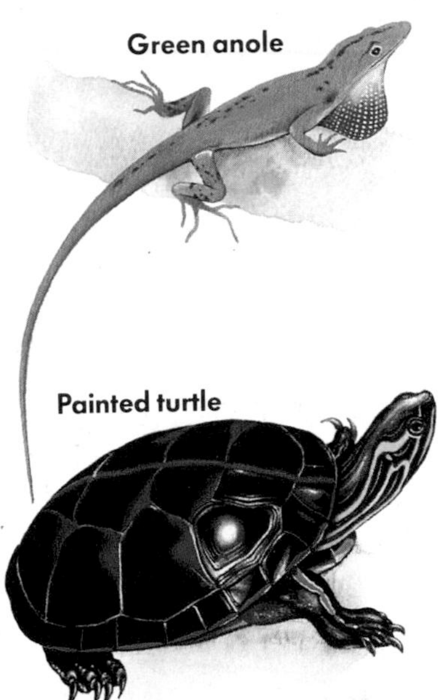

## REPTILES

Reptiles are vertebrates—animals with backbones. They have dry, scaly skin and breathe air through their lungs. Reptiles found in the United States include LIZARDS, SNAKES, TURTLES, ALLIGATORS, and crocodiles. A reptile is cold-blooded—its body temperature changes with the temperature of its surroundings. For that reason there are more reptiles in the warmer parts of the United States, in particular the Southeast and the Southwest.

Most reptiles are harmless. Only a few are poisonous. The Gila monster is the only poisonous U.S. lizard. Poisonous snakes include the RATTLESNAKE, copperhead, and water moccasin. The alligator snapping turtle, one of the largest freshwater turtles, is not poisonous, but its massive, sharp jaws can wound a person. The largest U.S. reptile is the American crocodile, found on the coast of Florida. It is now an endangered species because, like many other reptiles, the crocodile was hunted for its skin.

## REPUBLICAN PARTY

The Republican Party is one of two major POLITICAL PARTIES in the United States. Its symbol is the elephant. The nickname of the Republican Party is the G.O.P., or Grand Old Party.

The Republican Party was formed in 1854 as an antislavery party, but it soon broadened its appeal. The founders called themselves Republicicans because they favored national interests over states' rights. From their first victory in 1860, when Abraham LINCOLN won the presidency, the Republicans were in power for 56 of the next 72 years. In 1912 former president Theodore Roosevelt temporarily split the party when he formed the Progressive Party. The Democratic Party won that election.

The Party was described as the "party of prosperity" during the 1920s. But as a result of the economic Depression that followed, the Republicans lost the 1932 election to the Democrats. They did not regain control until 1952, when General Dwight Eisenhower won the presidential election. The Republicans were in power for 28 of the next 40 years.

**The Republican Party was founded in 1854 by anti-slavery forces and Free Soil forces (a group founded in New York). In the congressional elections of that year, 44 Republicans were elected to the House of Representatives. They won control of the House in 1858. The Republicans ran their first presidential candidate, John C. Frémont, in 1856. He was defeated by James Buchanan.**

## REUTHER, Walter

Walter Reuther (1907–1970) was an important U.S. labor leader. Born in Wheeling, West Virginia, he organized a workers' protest when he was still a teenager. In 1935 he became president of a local chapter of the newly formed United Automobile Workers (UAW) union. He became UAW president in 1946, serving until his death in 1970. Reuther was also president of the Congress of Industrial Organizations (CIO) from 1952 to 1955, and a leader of the AFL-CIO from 1955 to 1968. During his career, Reuther fought for higher wages and better working conditions for workers. He also fought against union corruption.

## REVERE, Paul

Paul Revere (1735–1818) was a patriot and hero of the American Revolution. He is most famous for his ride on horseback on April 18, 1775, to warn the minutemen of Lexington and Concord, Massachusetts, that the British were coming. Henry Wadsworth Longfellow wrote a poem about this feat, called "Paul Revere's Ride."

Revere was born in Boston. Like his father, he was a silversmith. His copperplate engraving of the Boston Massacre helped to stir up patriotic anger against the British. Revere took part in the Boston Tea Party and was a leader of the Sons of Liberty. During the war, he served as a lieutenant colonel.

Revere prospered after the war. He set up a mill for the manufacture of sheet copper, some of which was used on the hull of the U.S.S. Constitution. He also continued to design silver.

*▼ Paul Revere knew that his mission was urgent. The British would have captured the patriots' weapons unless he could warn the minutemen.*

# REVOLUTION, AMERICAN

The American Revolution, or Revolutionary War (1775–1783), was fought between Great Britain and its 13 American colonies. The American victory resulted in the independence of the United States of America.

The causes of the American Revolution were both political and economic. For the most part the American colonies were self-governing. But after the British defeated the French in the French and Indian War (1754–1763), the British did many things to assert their control. They decided to station large numbers of troops in the colonies—and to make the colonists pay for this. They also tried to prevent the colonists from settling on land west of the Appalachian Mountains. They told the colonists they could trade only with the British. And they passed such acts as the STAMP ACT. It seemed to the Americans that the British were trying to govern the colonies for the benefit of Britain—not the colonies.

American anger deepened when a number of them were killed by British troops in the BOSTON MASSACRE in 1770. When the British placed a tax on tea, the colonists responded with the BOSTON TEA PARTY, in which British tea was destroyed. To punish the Americans, the British passed what the colonies called the "Intolerable Acts" in 1774. One of these acts closed the port of Boston.

▲ *The Americans defeated British General John Burgoyne near Saratoga, New York, on October 17, 1777. Burgoyne and his 6,000 Redcoats had been trying to cut off New England from the other colonies. The victory convinced France to support the American cause.*

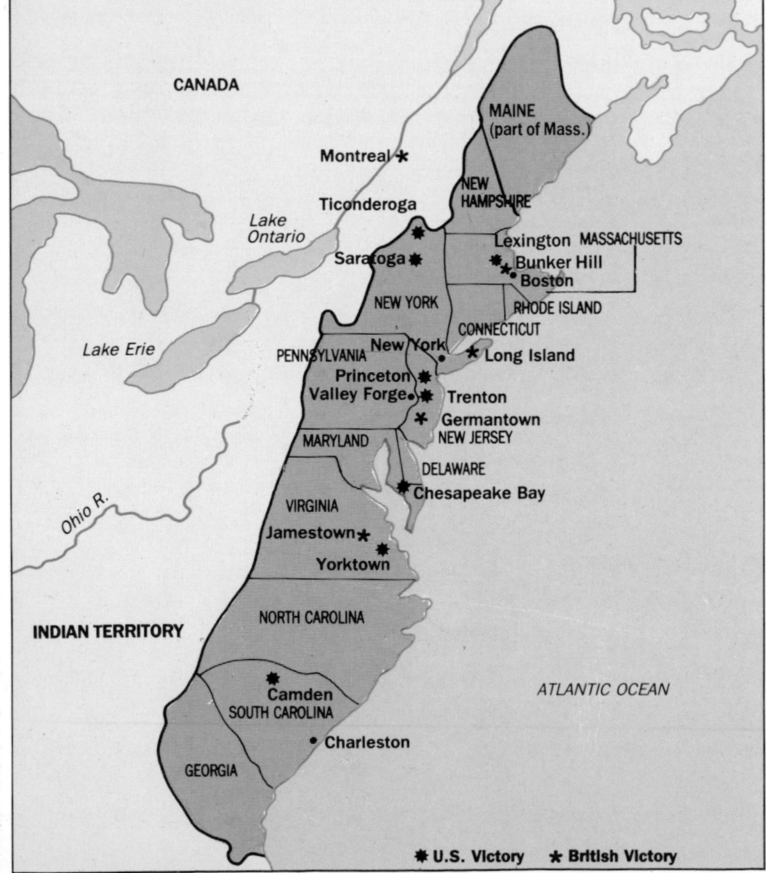


**George Washington was an excellent choice for commander of the Continental Army. Until his appointment, most of the fighting had been confined to the state of Massachusetts. With General Washington, a Virginian, in overall command, the Americans could prove that the Revolution had united both northern and southern colonies in their dispute with the British.**

◀ *American troops held off a British attack at the Battle of Guildford Courthouse, North Carolina, on March 15, 1781. British troops were forced from the state after the battle.*

The colonists now convened the First CONTINENTAL CONGRESS. They denounced the British laws and said they would not trade with Britain. Most colonists wanted fairness, but not independence. Nevertheless, colonial militias were formed. When the British sent troops to destroy the militias' arms at Concord, Massachusetts, the Americans fought back. The battles of LEXINGTON AND CONCORD marked the beginning of the American Revolution.

In July 1775, the Second Continental Congress named George WASHINGTON commander of the Continental Army. A year later, on July 4, 1776, the DECLARATION OF INDEPENDENCE was adopted.

Many battles were fought, with neither side gaining a definite advantage. The turning point came in 1778, when France signed an alliance with the United States and sent troops and ships to help. The British commander, Lord Charles Cornwallis, was forced to surrender to American forces at Yorktown, Virginia, on October 19, 1781. There was little fighting after this, and on September 3, 1793, under the terms of the Treaty of Paris, Britain recognized the independence of the United States of America.

### Major Battles of the American Revolution

**1775** The American Revolution starts with the battles of Lexington and Concord (April 19). The British win the Battle of Bunker Hill (June 17).

**1776** The colonists are forced to retreat from Long Island (August 27). The patriots win a major victory at Trenton, New Jersey (December 26).

**1777** The British suffer heavy losses near Bennington, Vermont (August 16). The British win the Battle of Brandywine and occupy nearby Philadelphia (September 11). The British win the Battle of Germantown, Pennsylvania (October 4).

**1779** Victory at Vincennes enables the Americans to gain control of most of the Northwest Territory (February 25).

**1780** The British capture Charleston, South Carolina (May 12).

**1781** The British suffer a major defeat at Cowpens, South Carolina (January 17). The British surrender at Yorktown, Virginia, virtually ending the American Revolution (October 19).

◀ *The Battle of Bunker Hill in Charlestown, Massachusetts, was fought on June 17, 1775. The British attacked from nearby Boston. They were victorious but suffered 1,000 dead and wounded.*

# RHODE ISLAND

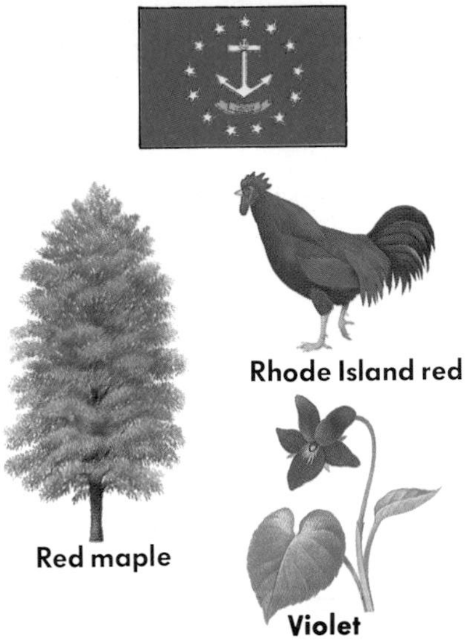


Places of Interest

- Newport is a leading resort center. It offers swimming, boating, and fishing. Also in Newport is the beautiful Cliff Walk, a 3-mile (5-km) path that passes by the seaside mansions and along the coast of the Atlantic Ocean.
- Block Island, 10 miles (16 km) off the mainland, is a famous resort area.
- Slater Mill, in Pawtucket, was one of the first textile mills in North America. The mill is now a museum.

Rhode Island is one of the six NEW ENGLAND states. It borders Connecticut on the west, Massachusetts on the north and east, and the Atlantic Ocean on the south. Its nickname is the Ocean State. Rhode Island is the smallest state. And its population density is second highest in the nation. Providence, with a population of 160,000, is the largest city and capital. It is located in the eastern part of the state, at the head of Narragansett Bay.

Rhode Island was founded in 1636 by Roger WILLIAMS. He had been expelled from the colony of Massachusetts for promoting religious and political freedom. In May 1776, Rhode Island became the first colony to formally declare its independence from England. But it was the last of the 13 original colonies to join the Union.

The new state of Rhode Island developed the textile industry that had begun during Colonial times. With the large markets of New York City and Boston nearby, the factory towns of Pawtucket, Woonsocket, Cranston, and Warwick prospered. The manufacture of textiles is still important to Rhode Island. The state's other products include jewelry, silverware, machinery, metal goods, and rubber products.

Tourism is also important to Rhode Island. The islands in Narragansett Bay, and the area around the bay, are known for their beautiful beaches. The city of Newport, with its magnificent seaside mansions, attracts many visitors. There are more than 300 colonial buildings in the city. One of them, Touro Synagogue, is the oldest synagogue in the United States.

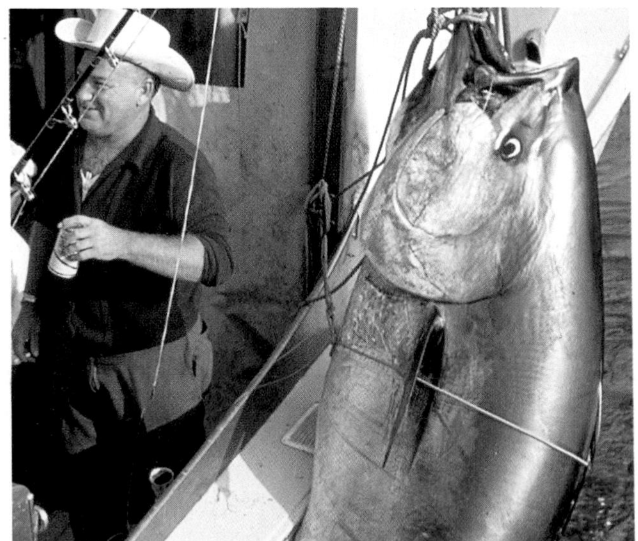

◀ *Sport fishing is popular in the Ocean State. The waters off Rhode Island provide large fish such as tuna (left), as well as smaller fish such as mackerel, bluefish, and bass.*

▲ *America's richest families built summer homes along the coast in Newport, Rhode Island, at the turn of the century. These houses are called "cottages" but are really huge mansions.*

Woonsocket
295
Pawtucket
**Providence**
Jerimoth Hill
812 ft (247 m)
*Scituate Res.*
Cranston
*Flat River Res.*
Warwick
95
*Narragansett Bay*
*Rhode Island*
*Rhode Island Sound*
Middletown
Newport

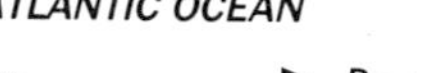


*ATLANTIC OCEAN*

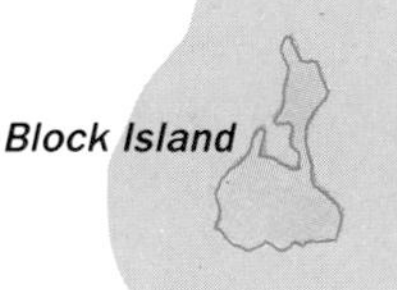


**Rhode Island**
**Capital:** Providence
**Area:** 1,545 sq mi (4,002 km$^2$). Rank: 50th
**Population:** 1,003,464 (1990). Rank: 43rd
**Statehood:** May 29, 1790
**Principal rivers:** Blackstone, Providence
**Highest point:** Jerimoth Hill, 812 ft (247 m)
**Motto:** Hope
**Song:** "Rhode Island"

► *Beechwood Cottage, built by the Astor family, is a Newport attraction. Like most Newport cottages it is built in the European style.*

▲ *Eddie Rickenbacker was the leading American combat pilot in World War I. He shot down 22 enemy airplanes and 4 observation balloons.*

## RICKENBACKER, Eddie

Edward ("Eddie") Rickenbacker (1890–1978) was a World War I fighter pilot and later an airline executive. He was born in Columbus, Ohio. His first interest was in automobiles and car racing. He joined the U.S. Army during World War I and became the country's leading ace pilot, shooting down 22 enemy planes. After leaving the Army, he went back to working with racing cars—he owned the famous Indianapolis Speedway. From 1938 to 1963 he was president and then chairman of the board of Eastern Airlines. During World War II, Rickenbacker was an adviser to the government.

## RIDE, Sally

Sally Ride (1951– ) was the first American woman to travel in space. Born in Los Angeles, she received a Ph.D. in physics from Stanford University in 1977 and soon became an astronaut. In 1983 she rocketed into space aboard the space shuttle *Challenger*. A year later she made another flight on the shuttle. In both flights important experiments were carried out by the crew. In 1987, Ride left the space program to accept a position with Stanford.

▼ *Louis Riel's two uprisings led to his execution for treason in 1884. Many Canadians now view him as a hero who fought for the rights of native-born Canadians.*

## RIEL, Louis

Louis Riel (1844–1885) led two rebellions against the Canadian government. Born in St. Boniface, Manitoba, he was a méti, a person of mixed white and Indian ancestry. He and his followers fought to prevent their land from being taken over by new settlers. In 1869 he led the First Riel Rebellion, also known as the Red River Rebellion. Canadian soldiers forced Riel to flee. In 1885 the métis turned to Riel for help again, after they had moved to what is now Saskatchewan. Once again Canadian soldiers defeated Riel. He was captured and hanged.

## RIO GRANDE

The Rio Grande is the fifth longest RIVER in North America. It flows for 1,760 miles (2,832 km), forming the entire boundary between Texas and Mexico. The river begins on the CONTINENTAL DIVIDE in the

ROCKY MOUNTAINS of Colorado. It flows through the spectacular Rio Grande Gorge, then through New Mexico and along the Texas border to the GULF OF MEXICO. One of the wildest areas of the United States is found along the Big Bend of the river in Big Bend National Park.

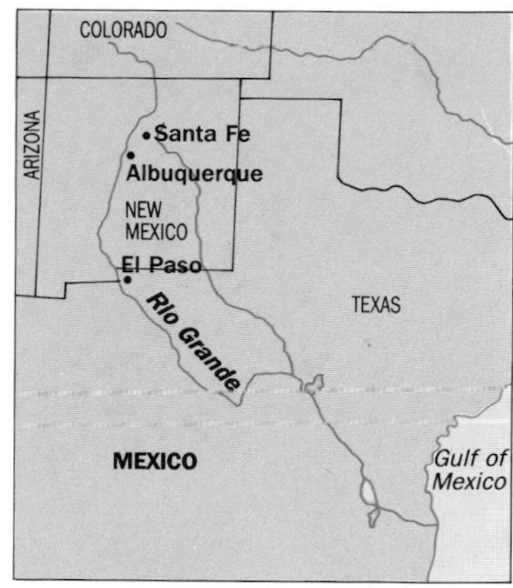


▲ *The Rio Grande forms the boundary between Texas and Mexico.*

◀ *The Rio Grande is one of the longest rivers in North America, but it is too shallow to navigate. It has cut deep canyons into the surrounding cliffs over hundreds of thousands of years.*

## RIVERS

From Colonial times until the present, rivers in the United States have served as avenues of transportation. Rivers also provide water for farmland, for industry, and for drinking. Waterfalls and dams along rivers provide the power for hydroelectricity.

The longest river system in the United States is the MISSISSIPPI-MISSOURI RIVER SYSTEM. It drains the vast interior of the country and empties into the GULF OF MEXICO. Another major river, the RIO GRANDE, also flows into the Gulf of Mexico. The rivers of the West, such as the COLORADO RIVER and COLUMBIA RIVER, flow into the Pacific Ocean or one of its arms. In the East, such rivers as the HUDSON RIVER and the Potomac River empty into the Atlantic Ocean. One of the most important rivers in the East is the St. Lawrence. The river makes up part of the ST. LAWRENCE SEAWAY, which connects the GREAT LAKES with the Atlantic Ocean.

**Longest U.S. Rivers (miles/km)**

1. Mississippi (2,340/3,766)
2. Missouri (2,315/3,725)
3. Rio Grande (1,760/2,832)
4. Arkansas (1,459/2,348)
5. Colorado (1,450/2,333)
6. Ohio (1,310/2,108)
7. Red (1,290/2,076)
8. Columbia (1,243/2,000)
9. Snake (1,038/1,670)
10. Pecos (926/1,490)

**The first automobile trip across the United States took more than two months in 1903. Nowadays, using interstate highways, the same 2,934-mile (4,722-km) ride from San Francisco to New York City would take less than a week.**

## ROADS AND HIGHWAYS

There are almost 3.9 million miles (6.3 million km) of roads and highways in the United States. Most of these roads are under state or local control. The federal government pays some or all of the funds for those highways called Federally Aided Highways. Among them are interstate highways. There are 44,000 miles (71,000 km) of interstate highways in the United States. About 90 percent of all U.S. roads are surfaced. Texas has more roads (286,000 miles, or 460,000 km) than any other state in the nation. Hawaii, with 4,100 miles (6,600 km), has the least.

► *A freeway junction at San Jose, California, appears as a geometric design when seen from the air.*

## ROBESON, Paul

Paul Robeson (1898–1976) was a singer, actor, and civil rights advocate. Born in Princeton, New Jersey, he graduated from Rutgers University. He also earned a law degree from Columbia University but soon turned to acting. Robeson became famous for his performance in the title role of Eugene O'Neill's play *The Emperor Jones*. His beautiful bass-baritone voice created a memorable interpretation of the song "Ol' Man River" in Jerome Kern's *Showboat*. He also appeared on radio and made records and movies.

After World War II, Robeson fought for civil rights for blacks. But his friendship with the Soviet Union resulted in a campaign against him. For many years he lived and worked in Europe.

▼ *Paul Robeson played the title role in the 1943 production of* Othello*, which ran for a record 196 performances. His acting in this play earned him several awards.*

◄ *The robin is one of North America's hardiest birds. Crocus blossoms of early spring welcome this robin after a winter searching for food.*

**The first English settlers in Colonial America gave the robin its name. Seeing a local bird with red markings on its chest, they were reminded of the English robin, or robin redbreast. However, the two birds are unrelated; the English robin is only about half the size of the American robin.**

## ROBIN

One of the best-known North American birds, the American robin is a type of thrush. It is about 10 inches (25 cm) long and has a beautiful song. The male has a rust-colored breast; the female's coloring is less bright. It breeds all over North America. Robins from northern regions usually fly south in winter. The robin builds its nest in a tree or sometimes a barn or other building. A pair will rear two or even three broods in the spring and summer. The robin eats berries, insects, and worms.

## ROBINSON, Edwin Arlington

Edwin Arlington Robinson (1869–1935) was an important poet of the early 20th century. He won three Pulitzer Prizes. Many of his early works were about unhappy people, such as "Luke Havergal," "Richard Cory," and "Miniver Cheevy." In 1921 his *Collected Poems* won the first Pulitzer Prize for poetry. Among his works from these later years are several long narrative poems based on the King Arthur legends: *Merlin*, *Lancelot*, and *Tristram*.

▼ *Edwin Arlington Robinson's first volumes of poetry contain character sketches of townspeople from an imaginary place called Tilbury Town. The community is based on the town of Gardiner, Maine, where Robinson had lived as a child.*

## ROBINSON, Jackie

Jack Roosevelt (Jackie) Robinson (1919–1972) was the first black to play baseball in the major leagues. Born in Cairo, Georgia, he attended the University of California. There he starred in baseball, football, basketball, and track. After college, Robinson played in baseball's minor leagues. In 1947, Robinson joined the Brooklyn

▲ *The father-and-son team of John D. Rockefeller, Sr. and Jr., represented a large proportion of America's wealth.*

Dodgers as a second baseman and was named the National League's rookie of the year. During his ten years with the Dodgers, they won six pennants and one World Series. He was elected to the National Baseball Hall of Fame in 1962.

## ROCKEFELLER FAMILY

The Rockefeller family is noted for its activities in business, politics, and philanthropy. John D. Rockefeller, Sr. (1839–1937), founded the Standard Oil Company in 1870. By 1882 his company controlled most of the oil business in the United States, and he became a multimillionaire. He and his descendants contributed much of their fortune to good causes. For example, a gift from John D. Rockefeller, Sr., made possible the founding of the University of Chicago. His son, John D. Rockefeller, Jr. (1874–1960), funded the restoration of Colonial Williamsburg, Virginia.

John D. Rockefeller, Jr., had five sons. John D. Rockefeller III (1906–1978) helped create Lincoln Center in New York City. Nelson Rockefeller (1908–1979) was a governor of New York and vice

**John D. Rockefeller, Sr., was the son of a peddler. At the age of 16 he started work in a small produce firm. He entered the oil business at 23 and became the world's richest man before he was 40. He gave away $550 million during his lifetime.**

► *Rockefeller Center, in New York City, comes ablaze each year with its Christmas decorations.*

president under Gerald Ford. Lawrence Rockefeller (1910– ) is an active conservationist. Winthrop Rockefeller (1912–1973) was a governor of Arkansas. David Rockefeller (1915– ) was the head of Chase Manhattan Bank. Among the other noted Rockefellers is John D. Rockefeller IV (1937– ), who has served as West Virginia governor and U.S. senator.

## ROCKETS AND MISSILES 

A rocket is a kind of engine. Rockets burn fuel that turns into hot gases. As the gases expand, they shoot out of the open end of the rocket, and the rocket is pushed forward. Rockets are used to launch artificial satellites, manned spacecraft, space probes, and military missiles.

The Chinese invented rockets in the 1200s. During World War II, the Germans built rockets to bombard London. After the war, the German rocket scientist Wernher VON BRAUN led a team that helped the United States to build the first Saturn rocket. A Saturn V rocket was used to send the first man to the moon. The space shuttle uses rockets to achieve space orbit.

Rockets are used to launch military missiles. Some missiles can travel up to 5,000 miles (8,000 km).

▲ *A U.S. Navy Harpoon missile is launched from the U.S.S.* New Jersey. *Missile boats can carry up to eight guided missiles that can be fired accurately at distant targets.*

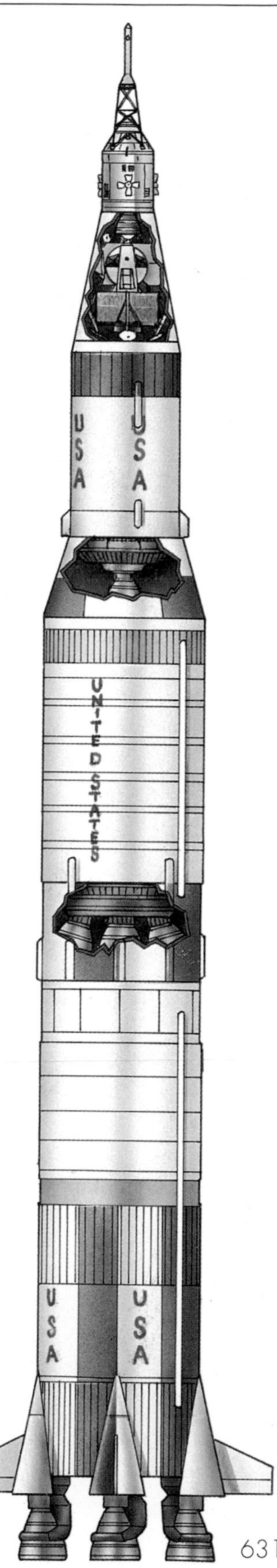


► *More than nine tenths of a rocket is discarded after it projects its capsule into orbit. Huge amounts of thrust are needed to achieve the speed necessary to gain earth orbit.*

► *Chuck Berry became one of the first rock music stars. His energetic singing and guitar playing has influenced many other performers.*

▼ *Elvis Presley rose from his poor Mississippi childhood to become the world's best-known singer.*

▼ *Madonna has entered the 1990s as one of the rock world's most popular performers. Her records and movie appearances have made her a star around the world.*

## ROCK MUSIC

Rock music is the most popular type of music in the United States and in many other countries. The term "rock" is short for "rock and roll." The music's fast, strong beat has a strong appeal for young people.

Rock and roll developed in the mid-1950s. It was a mixture of black rhythm and blues music and country and western music. The first rock stars, such as Little Richard and Chuck Berry, had already been playing their music in black nightclubs. They were joined by white singers such as Bill Haley, Elvis Presley, and Buddy Holly in the late 1950s. The Beatles, an English group, widened the appeal of rock when they first visited the United States in 1964.

During the 1960s, rock music was the music of protest. It was taken up by people in the civil rights movement and by anti–Vietnam War protesters. Its popularity was evident when 500,000 people attended a three-day rock festival at Woodstock, New York, in 1969.

In recent years, rock has gone through many changes. It no longer has one sound. Folk rock, country rock, soul rock, punk rock, and other forms attract different audiences. And rock stars, such as Michael Jackson, Madonna, Bon Jovi, Prince, and New Kids on the Block, continue to sell millions of records.

## ROCKNE, Knute

Knute Rockne (1888–1931) was one of the greatest college football coaches in the United States. Born in Norway, he came to the United States with his parents when he was five years old. He studied chemistry at the University of Notre Dame and played on the school's football team. In 1918, Rockne became the coach of the Notre Dame football team. Between then and 1931 his team won 105 games, lost 12, and tied 5. The team went five seasons without a single defeat. Rockne's *Autobiography* was published in 1931, soon after he died in a plane crash.

▲ *Knute Rockne's football teams at Notre Dame University built their fearsome reputations on tough practice and loyalty. Rockne introduced many modern coaching techniques to the sport.*

## ROCKWELL, Norman

Norman Rockwell (1894–1978) was a famous illustrator. He is best known for the covers he painted for the *Saturday Evening Post.* Over a period of half a century he produced 317 *Post* covers, depicting scenes of small town and family life with sympathetic humor and a wealth of realistic detail. Rockwell's first illustrations were done for children's magazines such as *Boy's Life* and *St. Nicholas.*

During World War II, Rockwell's paintings representing the Four Freedoms (freedom of speech and religion and freedom from want and fear) were reproduced and distributed throughout the United States.

▼ *Norman Rockwell's* The County Agricultural Agent *shows the artist's ability to capture everyday life in a realistic and understanding way.*

# ROCKY MOUNTAINS

The Rocky Mountains form the largest mountain system in North America. They stretch for 3,000 miles (4,800 km), from New Mexico in the south to Alaska in the north. There are five major sections of the Rockies. The Southern, Central, and Northern Rockies are in the United States. The Canadian Rockies are in Canada. The Brooks Range is in Alaska. The crest of the Rockies forms the CONTINENTAL DIVIDE.

There are more than 50 Rocky Mountain peaks that are more than 14,000 feet (4,300 m) above sea level. The highest, Mount Elbert (14,431 feet, or 4,399 m), is in Colorado. Many rivers rise in the Rockies, including the COLORADO, COLUMBIA, Missouri, and RIO GRANDE.

During the early 1800s, the LEWIS AND CLARK expedition and Zebulon PIKE and other explorers crossed the Rockies. But the mountains were a barrier to American westward expansion. Among the first people to live there were fur traders. In the mid-1800s, prospectors flocked to the Rockies to search for gold.

Today gold, silver, lead, coal, copper, and other minerals are mined in the Rockies. Lumbering is another important industry, as is tourism. Each year, hundreds of thousands of people visit the Rockies to fish, hunt, hike, and ski and to explore the beauty of the many national parks in the mountains. United States parks include YELLOWSTONE, Mesa Verde, GRAND CANYON, Grand Teton, Rocky Mountain, and Bryce Canyon. Canada's Rocky Mountain national parks include Banff, Jasper, and Kootenay.

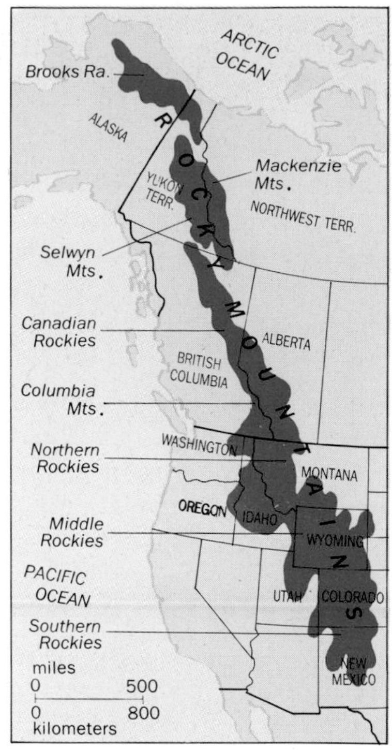


▲ *The Rocky Mountains are made up of several ranges, from the Southern Rockies to the Brooks Range, which extends north of the Arctic Circle.*

◀ *Ear Mountain is typical of the Rocky Mountains of Montana. The terrain is well above the tree line, and only hardy grasses grow by the cold lakes.*

**The Rocky Mountains were the most daunting obstacle facing the pioneers on their way west. Settlements had been established in the Great Plains as early as 1810, but it took more than 50 years for the Oregon Trail to open a route through the Rocky Mountains.**

▼ *The Teton Range in Wyoming is one of the most spectacular sections of the Rockies. Grand Teton National Park features dramatic mountain scenery and giant glaciers.*

▲ *Rodents use their long front teeth to gnaw through nuts and wood for food and shelter.*

## RODENTS

Rodents are mammals that have front teeth that are ideal for gnawing. There are more rodents than any other kind of mammal in the world. In North America, rodents include the BEAVER, CHIPMUNK, gerbil, GOPHER, GROUNDHOG, GROUND SQUIRREL, guinea pig, hamster, MOUSE, MUSKRAT, PACK RAT, PORCUPINE, PRAIRIE DOG, RAT, and SQUIRREL.

Many rodents, such as the gopher, groundhog, and prairie dog, live in burrows in the ground. A few, such as the beaver and muskrat, live in fresh water.

## RODEO

A rodeo is a form of entertainment and a sporting event for cowboys and cowgirls, who demonstrate their riding and roping skills. There are five main events in rodeos: bareback bronc riding, saddle bronc riding, bull riding, calf roping, and steer wrestling, or bulldogging. Another event, a horse race known as barrel racing, is primarily for cowgirls. In all-girl rodeos, however, the cowgirls compete in bareback bronc riding, bull riding, calf roping, and other events.

A major U.S. rodeo is the National Finals Rodeo in Oklahoma City, Oklahoma. The Stampede in Calgary, Alberta, is Canada's most important rodeo.

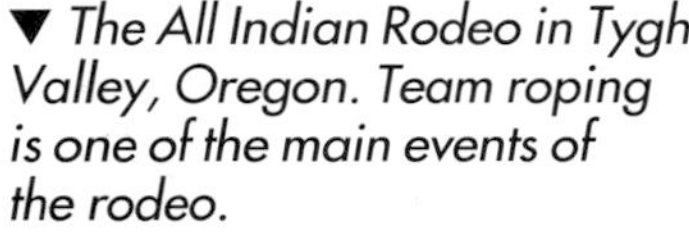

▼ *The All Indian Rodeo in Tygh Valley, Oregon. Team roping is one of the main events of the rodeo.*

◀ *Richard Rodgers wrote the music for* The Sound of Music, *one of the most popular movies ever made.*

## RODGERS, Richard 

Richard Rodgers (1902–1979) composed the music for many Broadway hit shows. His first collaborator was Lorenz Hart. Hart wrote the words and Rodgers the music for such shows as *On Yours Toes* and *Pal Joey*.

After Hart's death in 1943, Rodgers worked with Oscar Hammerstein II. Among their many hits were *Oklahoma!* and *South Pacific*, both of which won Pulitzer Prizes, *The King and I*, and *The Sound of Music*. Rodgers's most memorable songs include "My Funny Valentine" (with Hart) and "Some Enchanted Evening" (with Hammerstein).

**Richard Rodgers won many awards for his work. He received the Pulitzer Prize in drama for *South Pacific* and a special Pulitzer citation for *Oklahoma!***

## ROGERS, Will 

Will Rogers (1879–1935) was a famous humorist, actor, and entertainer of the early 1900s. His stage act consisted of cowboy rope tricks, which he had learned while working on his father's ranch in Oklahoma, accompanied by a humorous commentary on current events. Beginning in 1922 he also wrote a weekly column for *The New York Times*, which was syndicated in 350 newspapers. He acted in many movies, including *A Connecticut Yankee*. In 1926, President Calvin Coolidge sent Rogers on a tour of Europe as an "ambassador of good will." He died in a plane crash in Alaska.

▼ *Will Rogers summed up his view of life with the phrase "I've never met a man I didn't like."*

## ROLLER SKATING 

Roller skating is both a sport and a form of recreation. Skaters use special shoes that have wheels attached. Each skate has two pairs of wheels, one in front and one

▲ *Roller skaters participate in speed skating at the Pan Am Games, held every four years.*

in back. In the past the wheels were made of wood or metal. Today most wheels are hard plastic. In recent years, a new kind of roller skating—roller-blading—has become very popular. Roller-blades have three, four, or five wheels lined up one behind the other.

In the sport of roller skating, skaters compete in speed races, figure skating, roller dancing, and roller hockey. In the United States the sport is regulated by the U.S. Amateur Confederation of Roller Skating.

The first roller skate was invented in Europe in the 1700s. James Plimpton, an American, invented the "rocking skate" in 1863, which enabled people to skate on a curve, instead of just in a straight line.

## ROMAN CATHOLIC CHURCH

The Roman Catholic Church is the largest religious body and Christian denomination in the United States. It has about 59 million members, or 23 percent of the population of the United States. New York, California, Illinois, and Texas are the states with the most Catholics. The Catholic Church has the nation's largest private school system, educating more than 3 million students. It also operates a large number of charitable institutions, including more than 600 hospitals. The head of the church is the pope, who is the bishop of Rome. The basic administrative unit is the diocese, headed by a bishop.

U.S. Cities with Roman Catholic Cardinals

- Boston
- Chicago
- Detroit
- New York
- Philadelphia
- Saint Louis
- San Juan (Puerto Rico)
- Washington, D.C.

## ROOSEVELT, Eleanor

Eleanor Roosevelt (1884–1962) was a distinguished U.S. public figure who worked tirelessly for social justice. While her husband, Franklin D. ROOSEVELT, was president, she worked closely with him. The most active first lady in American history, she traveled a great deal and was involved in child welfare, slum clearance, and minority rights. After her husband's death, she became a U.S. delegate to the UNITED NATIONS. She was chairman of the UN Commission on Human Rights and helped prepare the Universal Declaration of Human Rights. She also wrote a daily column for many newspapers, entitled "My Day."

Eleanor Roosevelt was born in New York City. She was the niece of President Theodore ROOSEVELT and a distant cousin of her husband, Franklin.

▼ *Eleanor Roosevelt was a special representative to the United Nations.*

## ROOSEVELT, Franklin D.

Franklin Delano Roosevelt was the 32nd president of the United States. He steered the United States out of the deepest DEPRESSION and costliest war in its history. He was the only president to serve more than two terms. Under his leadership, the federal government assumed a much larger role in the country's economic life. His opposition to the Axis powers helped forge the alliance that won WORLD WAR II.

A Democrat, Roosevelt became president in 1933, when the Depression was at its worst. He immediately began his NEW DEAL program. In the first 100 days of his administration, Congress overhauled the banking system and established a program to aid farmers. It also provided money for roads, dams, and other public projects. The "second New Deal" of 1935 established a work-relief program, Social Security, and unemployment insurance. Roosevelt's GOOD NEIGHBOR POLICY improved relations with Latin America. In 1936, Roosevelt was re-elected by a landslide. Four years later, he was the first president to be elected to a third term in office.

◀ *In February 1945, with victory in sight, Franklin Roosevelt met fellow World War II leaders: Britain's Winston Churchill (left) and Joseph Stalin of the Soviet Union. The conference, held at the Soviet city of Yalta, helped shape events after the war.*

The Depression did not truly end until World War II began in 1939. At first the United States tried to remain neutral. Roosevelt helped the British through LEND-LEASE and other aid. After the Japanese attack on PEARL HARBOR on December 7, 1941, the United States entered World War II. Roosevelt and the British and Soviet leaders, Winston Churchill and Joseph Stalin, led the Allies. Roosevelt was elected to a fourth term in 1944 but died before the war ended in 1945.

**Franklin Roosevelt**
**Born:** January 30, 1882, in Hyde Park New York
**Education:** Harvard and Columbia universities
**Political party:** Democratic
**Term of office:** 1933–1945
**Married:** 1905 to Eleanor Roosevelt
**Died:** April 12, 1945, in Warm Springs, Georgia

# ROOSEVELT, Theodore

Theodore Roosevelt, the 26th president of the United States, was the youngest president ever and a man of action. He believed in strong leadership and reform at home and in an assertive foreign policy.

A Republican, Roosevelt was vice president when President William McKINLEY was shot and killed. He was only 42 when he succeeded McKinley. With characteristic energy, Roosevelt promised what he called a "square deal" for the public. This involved reforms such as tightening federal regulation of railroads. He also challenged big business combines, called trusts. He also preserved vast areas of forests and mineral lands for public use by forbidding their sale to private owners. At the next election he won a full term in office.

► *Theodore Roosevelt inspected the digging of the Panama Canal in 1906.*

| Theodore Roosevelt |
| --- |
| **Born:** October 27, 1858, in New York City |
| **Education:** Harvard |
| **Political party:** Republican |
| **Term of office:** 1901–1909 |
| **Married:** 1880 to Alice Hathaway; 1886 to Edith Carow |
| **Died:** January 6, 1919, in Oyster Bay, New York |

Roosevelt said he believed in "speaking softly and carrying a big stick." This was especially true in foreign affairs. He increased the size of the Navy and announced that the United States would intervene in Latin America if necessary. This became known as the "Roosevelt Corollary" to the MONROE DOCTRINE. Roosevelt began the construction of the PANAMA CANAL. He also mediated a settlement of the Russo-Japanese War. He won the Nobel Peace Prize for this.

Roosevelt left office in 1909 but soon quarreled with his handpicked successor, William Howard TAFT. He helped establish the Progressive Party and ran for the presidency as its candidate in 1912. Although Roosevelt outpolled Taft, he lost the election to the Democratic candidate, Woodrow WILSON.

▼ *This 1902 cartoon shows how Roosevelt refused to shoot a bear cub on a hunting trip. The incident was the origin of the term "teddy bear."*

## ROOT, Elihu

The statesman Elihu Root (1845–1937) served as secretary of war under William McKinley (1899–1904) and secretary of state under Theodore Roosevelt (1905–1919). As secretary of war, he achieved a number of reforms in the Army and created the Army War College (1901). As secretary of state and, later, as a Republican senator from New York (1909–1915), Root worked for peace. He established treaties with many European nations providing for arbitration in case of disputes. And he worked to establish good relations with Japan. In the Root-Takahira Agreement (1908), the two countries agreed not to take over territories in the Pacific. Root was also a strong supporter of the League of Nations and of U.S. membership in the Permanent Court of International Justice (World Court). For his achievements on behalf of world peace, Root was awarded the Nobel Peace Prize in 1912.

**Elihu Root first gained national prominence as a lawyer. He earned huge fees by successfully representing large companies. But these triumphs hurt his political career. Root lost any chance of winning the Republican Party's nomination for president because his business links were too close.**

## ROSS, Betsy

According to legend, Betsy Ross (1752–1836) made the first official American flag. Born in Philadelphia, she became a skilled seamstress and made a number of colonial flags. Her story of the first Stars and Stripes was written down by her grandson William J. Canby in 1870. It tells of how she was visited in June 1776 by some Revolutionary War leaders, including General George Washington, who brought a rough design of the flag for her to copy. Her own contribution to the design was to suggest stars with five points instead of six.

**The Arch Street shop in Philadelphia, where Betsy Ross carried on her late husband's upholstery business, still stands. Thousands of people visit it each year. Betsy was married three times and had seven children—all daughters.**

▼ *The legend of Betsy Ross is popular, but historians have been unable to prove that she was ever asked to sew a flag.*

▲ *Mark Rothko's* Blue, Orange, Red, *painted in 1960, uses uneven shapes of color to convey a sense of calm.*

## ROTHKO, MARK 

Mark Rothko (1903–1970) was a leading member of the abstract expressionist school of painters. Born in Russia, Rothko moved to the United States with his family at the age of 10. He took up painting, with only a little formal training, in the 1920s. His early paintings were done in a realistic style. They include a series called "Subway," which depicts the loneliness of city life. Later, Rothko developed his own form of abstract expressionism, known as color field painting. These paintings consist of large rectangles of vibrant color that interact in subtle yet powerful ways.

## ROUGH RIDERS 

The Rough Riders was the popular name of the First United Volunteer Cavalry. Its members, around 1,000, had been chosen for their riding and shooting skills. They were first commanded by Colonel Leonard Wood. But it was under the command of Colonel Theodore Roosevelt that they achieved their fame. In 1898, during the SPANISH-AMERICAN WAR, Roosevelt led his men on a charge in the battle of San Juan Hill in Cuba. There were many losses, but the American forces won the day, even though they were on foot—their horses had been left behind in Florida.

▼ *Theodore Roosevelt and his Rough Riders posed for photographers on San Juan Hill, Cuba, in 1898.*

## ROYAL CANADIAN MOUNTED POLICE 

The Royal Canadian Mounted Police (RCMP) is the federal police force of Canada. Set up in 1873, it was first called the North-West Mounted Police (NWMP). Its duties were mainly to keep the peace in Canada's western plains, an area then known as the Northwest Territories. Traders there had caused tension between Indians and white settlers. Later the NWMP helped to police the Klondike during the gold rush. In 1885 it helped end a rebellion led by Louis RIEL in Saskatchewan. Gradually it began to operate in more areas of Canada. In 1920, it was joined with the Dominion Police and became the national police force known as the Royal Canadian Mounted Police. Members of the RCMP are known as "Mounties" because they used to travel on horseback. Today the more than 20,000 Mounties are more likely to use cars or snowmobiles. The RCMP was involved in Canadian security (like the FBI in the United States) until 1981.

◀ *Members of the Royal Canadian Mounted Police, in full dress uniform, perform a musical ride at Thunder Bay, Ontario.*

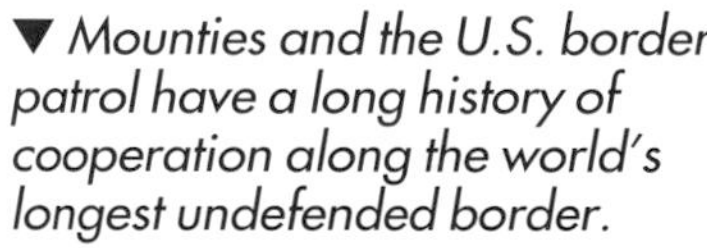

▼ *Mounties and the U.S. border patrol have a long history of cooperation along the world's longest undefended border.*

## RUNYON, Damon 

The journalist and short-story writer Damon Runyon (1881–1946) is known for his stories of life in New York City's underworld. In such collections as *Guys and Dolls* and *Blue Plate Special*, Runyon relates the adventures and misadventures of assorted gamblers, gangsters, and

► *Damon Runyon's* Guys and Dolls *has been made into a Broadway musical.*

other Broadway characters, including Harry the Horse and Nathan Detroit. The stories are written in the present tense and are full of Broadway slang.

Born in Manhattan, Kansas, Runyon began his career as a newspaper writer.

▼ *Babe Ruth powered his way to 12 Major League home run titles —more than any other player in baseball history.*

## RUTH, Babe

George Herman "Babe" Ruth (1895–1948) was one of baseball's best-loved stars. He began his professional career as a pitcher, but his power hitting got him a place playing first-base when he was not pitching. In 1920 he was sold to the New York Yankees. He played right field for them. In 1927 he hit 60 home runs. During his career he hit a total of 714 home runs, a record that stood until 1974, when Hank Aaron broke it. During Ruth's years with the Yankees, the team won seven American League pennants and four World Series. Ruth was elected to the Baseball Hall of Fame in 1936, the year after his retirement.

▼ Roadside Meeting *by Albert Pinkham Ryder gives a sense of mystery to an ordinary event.*

## RYDER, Albert Pinkham

Albert Pinkham Ryder (1847–1917) was one of the most imaginative of artists in the United States. He was born in the busy port of New Bedford, Massachusetts, and retained a love of the sea throughout his life. Ryder taught himself to paint. He spent most of his life in New York City, although he avoided contact with other artists living there. Ryder relied on his imagination to inspire a sense of mystery in his paintings.

## SACAGAWEA

The Shoshoni Indian woman Sacagawea (1787?–1812?) was an important member of the LEWIS AND CLARK EXPEDITION (1804–1806). As a young girl, Sacagawea, whose name means "Bird Woman," was captured and sold to a fur trader, Toussaint Charbonneau. When Lewis and Clark hired Charbonneau as an interpreter, his wife Sacagawea joined the party as its guide. Carrying her baby son on her back, she traveled from North Dakota to the Pacific Northwest. Her presence eased the party's passage through Indian territory.

◀ *When she was a young girl, Sacagawea was captured by Hidatsa Indians and sold to a French Canadian fur trader. She later proved invaluable as a guide on the Lewis and Clark Expedition.*

## ST. AUGUSTINE 

St. Augustine in FLORIDA is the oldest city in the United States. It was founded by the Spanish in 1565. It is located in northeastern Florida on a peninsula jutting into the Atlantic Ocean about 40 miles (65 km) south of Jacksonville. Its harbor is now home to a fleet of fishing boats. The main catch is shrimp. St. Augustine also has an important aeronautics industry as well as a number of companies that process food grown locally. Tourism is another source of income. St. Augustine's mild climate and historical attractions make it a popular vacation spot.

▼ *St. Augustine's famous Lightner Museum is built in a Spanish style that recalls the city's colonial past.*

**Augustus Saint-Gaudens's reputation was based on his large sculptured monuments of great Americans such as Abraham Lincoln and Admiral David Farragut. His career began, though, with six years of cameo work, making intricate engravings on small gems.**

## SAINT-GAUDENS, Augustus

Most people consider Augustus Saint-Gaudens (1848–1907) to have been the finest American sculptor of the 19th century. Born in Ireland, to a French father and and Irish mother, Saint-Gaudens was taken to the United States as a child.

He worked as a cameo cutter and later studied art in Paris and Rome. After settling in New York City in 1875 Saint-Gaudens produced many fine sculptures including the statues of Abraham Lincoln in Lincoln Park, Chicago, and General William Tecumseh Sherman in Central Park, New York City.

► *A detail of Augustus Saint-Gaudens's Shaw Memorial brings to life the famous Civil War story of the courageous black regiment from Massachusetts.*

## ST. LAWRENCE SEAWAY

The St. Lawrence Seaway is an international waterway that connects the GREAT LAKES with the Atlantic Ocean. The seaway forms part of the U.S.-Canadian border. The total length of the St. Lawrence Seaway–Great Lakes system is 2,340 miles (3,765 km). The completion of the seaway in 1959 enabled the United States and Canada to ship goods from the interior of North America to Europe. Most of the cargo consists of raw materials, such as iron ore, grain, and coal, and manufactured goods, such as steel and motor vehicles.

▼ *The St. Lawrence Seaway's three canals and seven locks provide a shipping route from Montreal to Lake Ontario.*

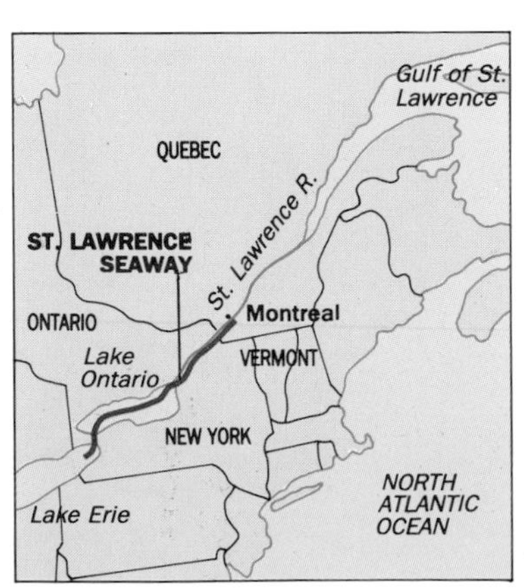

## ST. LOUIS

With a population of 396,685, St. Louis is the second largest city in MISSOURI. Only Kansas City is larger. St. Louis is also the most important inland port along the Mississippi River. It is located 10 miles (16 km) south of where the Missouri River meets the Mississippi on Missouri's eastern border. Mainly an industrial city, it is a leading producer of automobiles and beer. The 630-foot (192-m) Gateway Arch, standing along the river, honors the city's role as "Gateway to the West." Thousands of pioneers, and one of the first transcontinental railroads, set off from St. Louis.

▲ *St. Louis's historic Old Courthouse is flanked by modern fountains and the famous Gateway Arch.*

## SALEM WITCHCRAFT TRIALS

The Salem witchcraft trials took placc in the Puritan town of Salem, Massachusetts, in 1692, a time when many people believed in witches. The trials began when several young girls claimed that they had been bewitched by a West Indian slave, Tituba, and two other Salem women. A special court was set up by the colony's governor, Sir William Phips, to hear the evidence. A wave of fear and hysteria swept through Salem and other Massachusetts towns. Belief that the devil was trying to destroy their devoutly Christian community caused people to panic; they denounced their neighbors on the slightest trace of unconventional behavior. In all, 19 people were hanged for witchcraft, and one man was pressed to death. When some church officials criticized the trials, they were stopped, and in May 1693 the remaining prisoners were released.

▼ *Most of the evidence of the Salem witchcraft trials was based on rumors and gossip.*

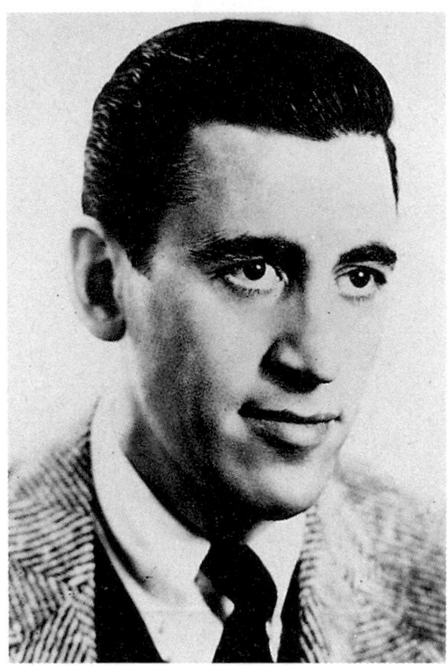

▲ J. D. Salinger was able to give a sense of what young people really felt in the years after World War II.

## SALINGER, J. D.

Jerome David Salinger (1919– ) is an American novelist and short-story writer. Many of his stories are concerned with troubled young people. His best-known work is *The Catcher in the Rye*, with its sensitive young hero, Holden Caulfield.

Many of Salinger's stories appeared first in *The New Yorker* magazine. One of them, "A Perfect Day For Bananafish," introduces Seymour Glass, whose family figures in some of Salinger's later novels.

## SALK, Jonas

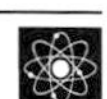

Jonas Salk (1914– ) developed a vaccine that prevents poliomyelitis, a terrible crippling disease. Born in New York City, Salk graduated from the New York University School of Medicine. He then worked in research at the University of Pittsburgh. Salk was interested in diseases caused by viruses. By the early 1950s he spent all his energy seeking to destroy the polio virus. In 1954, Salk's polio vaccine was tested on almost 2 million children. It proved effective. In 1963 he became director of the Salk Institute for Biological Studies at La Jolla, California.

## SALT LAKE CITY

Salt Lake City is the capital of UTAH and its largest city. It has a population of 159,936. The city is nestled in the foothills of the lofty Wasatch Range of the Rockies.

▼ The Mormon Temple, in Temple Square, is at the heart of Salt Lake City.

Salt Lake City was founded in 1847 by Brigham YOUNG, one of the greatest leaders of the Church of Jesus Christ of Latter-day Saints (MORMONS). The Mormon influence is still felt. More than half the city's population belongs to the religion, and many of its most important buildings are owned by the church. The Mormon Tabernacle is the home of one of the world's most famous choirs. Salt Lake City is an industrial center thanks to the mineral resources found nearby. The chemical industry mines and processes copper, magnesium, and chloride. Electrical and metal manufacturing also provides jobs, and the ski slopes a few miles away make the area a popular winter resort.

▲ *Salvation Army musicians and volunteers provide comfort and inspiration for the inner-city poor.*

## SALVATION ARMY 

The Salvation Army is a religious and charitable organization. It was founded in England in 1865 by the Methodist minister William Booth. Its international headquarters are in London. The Salvation Army has over 430,000 members in the United States. Its U.S. headquarters are in Verona, New Jersey. It is a church set up along military lines. Each center is a small unit run by a "commander." Individual members are "soldiers." The Salvation Army does much charitable work. It operates hostels, day-care centers, and clubs for senior citizens. It also provides meals for the poor and needy and offers family counseling and helps alcoholics and drug abusers.

## SAMOA, American *See* Pacific Territories

## SAN ANDREAS FAULT 

The San Andreas Fault stretches north to south about 750 miles (1,200 km) in the state of California. The places along this fault line are more likely to experience EARTHQUAKES than any others in North America. Faults lie on the boundary between large sections of the earth's crust known as plates. The San Andreas Fault is located where the Pacific Plate is slowly sliding against the North American Plate. The strains on rocks caused by this sliding motion produce earthquakes. In 1906 an earthquake destroyed much of San Francisco. Another major earthquake took place in 1989.

▼ *The San Andreas Fault runs parallel to California's Pacific coast and crosses San Francisco, the site of several major earthquakes.*

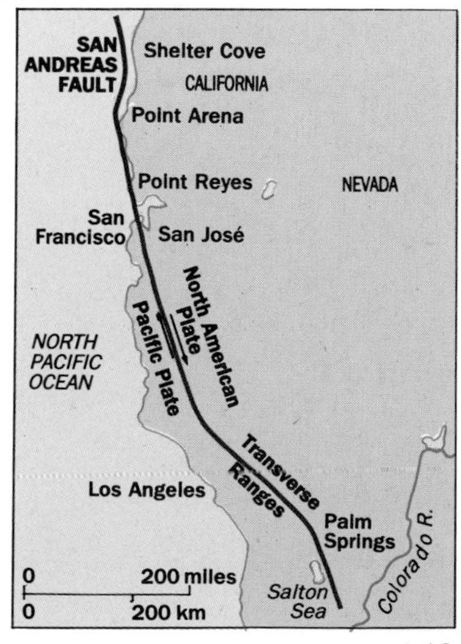

▲ *The Lone Star flag of Texas flies over the historic Alamo, where 187 Texans died defending San Antonio from the Mexicans in 1876.*

## SAN ANTONIO

San Antonio is the third largest city in TEXAS. It has a population of 935,933. The city is located along a bend of the San Antonio River in south-central Texas. San Antonio, founded by the Spanish in 1718, is the site of the Alamo, a Spanish mission. When Texas was fighting for its independence from Mexico in 1836, the Texan defenders of the Alamo fought bravely to the death. The cry of "Remember the Alamo" still inspires Texans with strong feeling. Modern San Antonio still has close links with the military. Fort Sam Houston, headquarters of the U.S. Fifth Army, and four Air Force bases provide about 80,000 jobs in and around San Antonio. Electronic equipment, aircraft parts, chemicals, and clothing are produced in San Antonio factories.

## SANDBURG, Carl

Carl Sandburg (1878–1967) was one of the most important American poets and historians. In his writing he expressed a deep love of the United States, its landscape, its folklore, and its people.

Born in Illinois, Sandburg settled in Chicago in 1913. There, he worked on a newspaper and began to publish poems. *Chicago Poems* included his most famous poem, "Chicago," which celebrates in free verse the vitality and industry of that city.

Among Sandburg's many other works are *Abraham Lincoln: The Prairie Years* and *Abraham Lincoln: The War Years*, which won a Pulitzer Prize. He also wrote stories for children.

▼ *Spanish colonial architecture forms a backdrop to the palms and lily pond of Balboa Park in San Diego.*

## SAN DIEGO

With a population of 1,110,549, San Diego is the second largest city in CALIFORNIA. It is just 12 miles (20 km) from the Mexican border. San Diego has one of the best deep-water harbors in the world. It is home to many U.S. Navy vessels and a huge fishing fleet. San Diego's factories produce high-tech electronics and computer goods, aircraft and aerospace equipment. The Spanish founded San Diego in 1769. American forces captured the city in 1846, during the Mexican War. Today the city is popular with tourists. The San Diego Zoo attracts more than 3 million visitors each year.

◀ *San Francisco's bustling Chinatown is the most important Chinese community in North America.*

**One of the most famous quotes about San Francisco came from the poet Rudyard Kipling. He said, "San Francisco has only one drawback — 'tis hard to leave."**

## SAN FRANCISCO

San Francisco, CALIFORNIA, is a beautiful port city with a population of 723,959. It occupies the tip of a peninsula that separates San Francisco Bay from the Pacific Ocean. The channel into the bay is known as the Golden Gate. Hills, cable cars, and attractive wooden houses give San Francisco a unique charm. Its Chinatown is one of the largest outside Asia. The city is a center for banking, finance, and international trade.

The Spanish were the first to settle in San Francisco, building a fort and a Catholic mission in 1776. In 1848, the United States won California in the MEXICAN WAR. Gold was discovered the same year, and San Francisco became a major supply point and port for the prospectors. Because the SAN ANDREAS FAULT runs near San Francisco, the city is subject to earthquakes. The 1906 earthquake and fire destroyed much of the city. A 1989 earthquake also caused damage.

## SAN JOSE

The fast-growing industrial city of San Jose, CALIFORNIA, is located in the fertile Santa Clara Valley, about 50 miles (80 km) south of San Francisco. It has a population of 782,248. San Jose is the southern end of the famous "Silicon Valley," a collection of high-tech industries. San Jose produces computers, space and electronic equipment, plastics, food products, and wine. San Jose was founded in 1777 and was the state's first capital (1849–1851).

▼ *San Jose was first named Pueblo de San Jose de Guadalupe, but the name was later shortened.*

## SANITATION 

Sanitation protects public health by preventing disease. Garbage and other solid refuse are burned or dumped. A landfill, in which the waste is covered with earth, is more sanitary than an open dump. Sewage disposal employs water to carry away domestic or industrial waste. Flush toilets, for example, carry human waste either to private underground septic tanks or to sewer mains that connect to treatment plants. Government agencies check to make sure that foods sold to the public meet sanitary standards. Drinking water is treated to make sure harmful germs are eliminated.

▲ *New York City's sanitation department disposes of millions of tons of waste each year in landfills such as this one in the borough of Queens.*

## SANTA FE TRAIL 

The Santa Fe Trail was the main overland route to the Southwest before the coming of the Atchinson, Topeka, and Santa Fe Railroad in 1880. First traced by explorer and trader William Becknell in 1820–1821, the trail ran from Independence, Missouri, to Santa Fe, New Mexico. At Cimarron, Kansas, the trail divided into three routes. The shortest, called the Cimarron Cutoff, was the most often used, even though Indian attacks made it the most dangerous.

It took a wagon train between 40 and 60 days to cover the distance of about 780 miles (1,260 km). Traders took manufactured goods to Santa Fe (under Mexican rule until 1848) and returned with gold, silver, and furs. After the United States acquired New Mexico, travel on the trail increased; by the late 1860s, about 5,000 wagons a year were using it.

▼ Mrs. Knowles and Her Children *is an example of John Singer Sargent's many portraits of wealthy families.*

## SARGENT, John Singer 

The painter John Singer Sargent (1856–1925) won fame for his portraits of elegant ladies and gentlemen. Although an American, Sargent was born in Florence, Italy, and spent most of his life in Europe. He studied art in Paris. There, in 1884, his *Portrait of Madame X* in a low-cut black dress caused a scandal. Moving to London, Sargent soon became the most fashionable portrait painter of his day. Later he turned to painting landscapes. Between 1890 and 1910 he worked on a series of murals for the Boston Public Library, depicting the history of Judaism and Christianity.

# SASKATCHEWAN

The prairie province of Saskatchewan is often called Canada's Breadbasket because it produces 60 percent of the country's wheat. Saskatchewan is situated north of the U.S. states of North Dakota and Montana, west of Manitoba, and east of Alberta. It has a population of more than 1,000,000.

Among the wheat fields of the southern half of the province are found oil fields that account for more than 10 percent of Canada's petroleum production. Here, too, are potash mines that provide a quarter of the world's demand for this natural fertilizer. All of the province's cities are in the south, including Regina (the capital) and Saskatoon. The province's manufacturing industries are centered in the south, too. They include petroleum refining, metal fabricating, and food processing. Northern Saskatchewan is a rocky land of forests, lakes, and rivers. Rich ore deposits here make Saskatchewan the world's leading exporter of uranium.

Chipewyan, Assiniboin, and Cree Indians lived in the area before the arrival of Europeans. The first Europeans were fur traders. Many worked for the Hudson's Bay Company, which had title to the land. Canada bought the area from the company in 1870. Settlement began with the arrival of the railroad in 1883. In 1885 the Métis, led by Louis RIEL, rebelled against the Canadian government. These people, of mixed Indian and French ancestry, feared that the settlers would kill all the bison. Saskatchewan became a province in 1905.

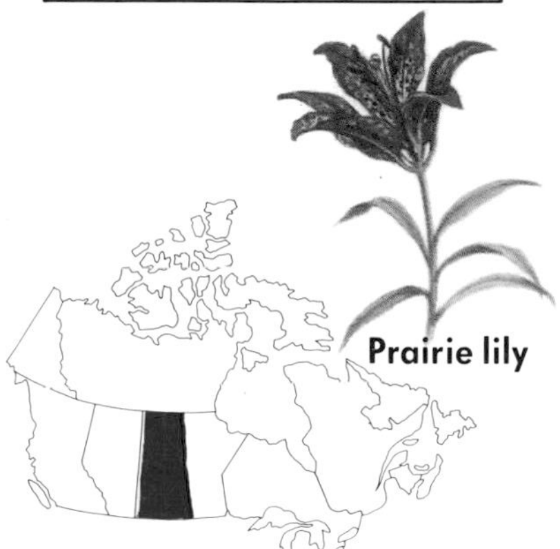

▲ *Grain elevators at Estlin store some of Saskatchewan's rich wheat harvest.*

Saskatchewan
**Capital:** Regina
**Area:** 220,348 sq mi (570,657 km²). Rank: 5th
**Population:** 988,928 (1991). Rank: 6th
**Entry into Confederation:** September 1, 1905, with Alberta as 8th and 9th provinces
**Highest point:** Cypress Hills, 4,567 ft (1,382 m)

► *Environmental Satellite 4076 gathers data and supplies pictures of the earth's continents.*

**U.S. Satellite Landmarks**

**1958** Explorer I discovers Van Allen Belts (bands of magnetic radiation).
**1959** Vanguard II sends first weather information from space.
**1962** Telstar I relays television pictures between the United States and Europe.
**1967** Intelsat IIB becomes first satellite to achieve a stationary orbit. (Its orbital speed matches that of the rotating earth, so it stays over one place.)
**1968** OAO-II is first orbiting solar observatory.
**1978** GOES-3 provides day and night weather pictures for more accurate forecasting and records.
**1990** The Hubble Space Telescope begins taking pictures of the universe.

## SATELLITES, Artificial

A satellite is an object that revolves around another. The moon is a natural satellite of the earth. Artificial satellites are man-made objects rapidly orbiting the earth. A satellite remains in orbit because the earth's gravity causes it to follow a curved path instead of flying off into space. If it traveled slowly, gravity would curve its path enough to bring it back to earth.

The first artificial satellite, the original Sputnik, was put into orbit by the Soviet Union in 1957. The United States launched its first one in 1958. Hundreds of satellites have been put into orbit since then. Communications satellites relay telephone calls and television images. Weather satellites gather data on the earth's atmosphere. Navigation satellites send signals to help aircraft and ships determine their positions. "Spy satellites" check the military potential of other countries.

## SCHLESINGER, Arthur, Sr. and Jr.

Arthur Schlesinger, Sr. (1888–1965), was a historian with a special interest in American social and urban history. In 1924 he became professor of history at Harvard University. Among his many books are *The Rise of the City 1878–1898*.

Like his father, Arthur Schlesinger, Jr. (1917– ), also taught history at Harvard. He left Harvard in 1961 to become a special assistant to President John F. Kennedy. After Kennedy's assassination, Schlesinger wrote an account of his presidency, *A Thousand Days*, which won a Pulitzer Prize and a National Book Award.

**Arthur M. Schlesinger, Sr., believed that the study of history should be impartial, or free from personal opinions.**

## SCHOOLS 

Enrollment in school is generally required by law in the United States for persons between the ages of 7 and 16. While the states are responsible for public schools, the schools are usually run by local school districts. These bodies levy taxes to pay for education. School construction is often financed by bond issues. Public education below the college level is free, but private schools charge tuition fees. There are almost 85,000 public schools and more than 26,000 private schools in the United States. Total enrollment, from kindergarten through graduate school at universities, is almost 60 million. In 1940, only one of four adults 25 years of age and older had graduated from high school, but by 1987 three out of four had done so.

**States with Fewest Public School Pupils per Teacher**

Vermont (13.2)
Connecticut (13.6)
New Jersey (13.6)
Maine (13.9)
Wyoming (14.5)
Rhode Island (14.6)
Nebraska (14.6)
New York (14.7)
Kansas (15.0)
West Virginia (15.0)

**Highest Rates of High School Graduates**

Vermont (91.6%)
Minnesota (89.7%)
North Dakota (88.1%)
Iowa (87.5%)
Hawaii (86.8%)
South Dakota (85.7%)
Nebraska (85.5%)
Wisconsin (84.2%)
Montana (83.3%)
Utah (83.1%)

◄ *Schools still rely on dedicated teachers to train children to succeed in the changing modern world.*

## SCHWARZKOPF, H. Norman 

H. Norman Schwarzkopf (1934– ), a four-star U.S. Army general, became a national hero as field commander of the U.S.-led multinational coalition that ousted Iraq from Kuwait in the 1991 PERSIAN GULF WAR. The son of a general, he graduated from the U.S. Military Academy in 1956. He rose through army ranks to became deputy chief of staff for operations and plans in 1987. Schwarzkopf served two tours of duty in Vietnam. He was deputy commander of the U.S. invasion of Grenada in 1983. Schwarzkopf retired from the military in 1993.

▲ *General Norman Schwarzkopf answered reporters' questions at regular press conferences during the Persian Gulf War.*

# SCIENCE

There are many branches of science. These include astronomy, biology, botany, chemistry, geology, mathematics, medicine, physics, and zoology. American scientists have distinguished themselves in all of these fields. Some of these scientists, and their work, are shown on these pages. The biographies of many others appear throughout this encyclopedia. You may want to look them up in the Index.

▲ *German-born physicist Albert Einstein showed new ways of understanding space and time with his theory of relativity.*

▲ *George Washington Carver's experiments with peanuts and other crops helped develop more than 300 products for scientific purposes and everyday use.*

▼ *American scientists and electronics firms have used tiny integrated circuits to reduce the size – and cost – of computers and other equipment.*

▼ *Percy Julian's chemical research led to medical breakthroughs and saved thousands of lives during World War II.*

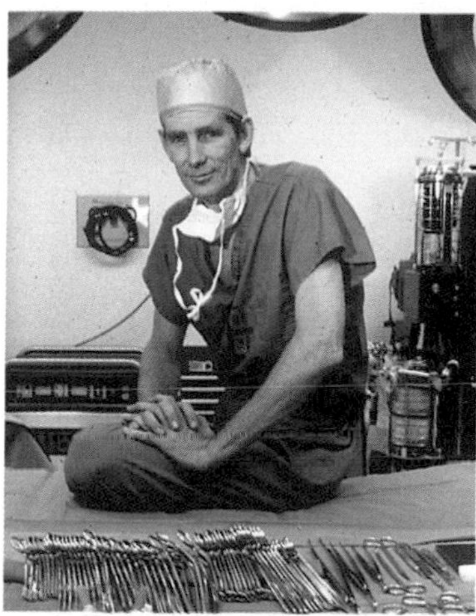

◀ *Dr. William C. DeVries transplanted the world's first artifical heart in Salt Lake City, Utah, in 1982.*

▼ *Rosalyn Yalow received the Nobel Prize for Medicine after her breakthroughs using radioactive substances to test body fluids.*

▼ *Dr. Paul Chu of the University of Houston displays his experimental superconductor, which could reduce the world's future energy needs by nearly one half.*

▲ *NASA biologists developed many features of the Biosphere experiment. Seven scientists will live and work for two years in an enclosed space station in the Arizona desert.*

**Some of America's first science fiction authors began by writing short stories in magazines during the 1930s. Hugo Gernsback, founder of *Amazing Stories* magazine in 1926, was the first person to popularize the term "science fiction." John W. Campbell, Jr., attracted many authors to his *Astounding Science Fiction* magazine in the 1930s. Among his writers were Poul Anderson, Isaac Asimov, L. Sprague de Camp, and Robert A. Heinlein.**

## SCIENCE FICTION

Science fiction is a form of literature that combines science and fantasy. Most science fiction stories take place in the future. In the late 1800s, for example, Jules Verne wrote about trips to the moon, spaceships, and powered submarines—long before these were realities. Verne is considered the "father of science fiction." Another great early science fiction writer was H. G. Wells. In the 1890s he wrote about traveling to the future in *The Time Machine* and about a Martian invasion of earth in *The War of the Worlds.*

Among the leading modern science fiction writers are Isaac Asimov, Ray Bradbury, Arthur Clarke, and Robert Heinlein. Clarke's *2001, A Space Odyssey* and Bradbury's *Star Trek* were made into motion pictures. The three *Star Wars* films have brought many new fans to science fiction.

## SCOUTS

Scouting is a worldwide group of organizations for young people. Its goal is to help boys and girls develop character, citizenship, and physical and mental fitness. The two main scouting groups are the Boy Scouts and Girl Scouts. The Boy Scouts was founded in England by Sir Robert Baden-Powell in 1908. The Boy Scouts of America was started two years later by William Boyce. Its headquarters are in Irving, Texas. Today it has almost 5 million members. The Girl Scouts of America was founded in 1912 by Juliette Low. Its headquarters are in New York City. It has almost 3 million members.

▲ *Scouts from West Redding, Connecticut, stand at attention to make the Girl Scout pledge.*

► *A Cub Scout honor guard holds flags identifying its troop at a parade in New York State.*

## SCULPTURE

The earliest examples of American sculpture include Indian totem poles and tombstones and woodcarvings by the colonists. Around 1800, American artists trained in Italy began making marble statues of public figures in the formal neoclassical style inspired by ancient Greece and Rome. Later in the century sculptors like Augustus SAINT-GAUDENS and Daniel Chester French produced more expressive works. In the 20th century, many sculptors have become interested in creating abstract sculpture. Works are likely to be made of welded metal rather than stone or bronze.

Noted American Sculptors

**Aleksandr Archipenko** (1887–1964): Abstract sculpture
**Gutzon Borglum** (1871–1941): Monuments; Mt. Rushmore
**Alexander Calder** (1898–1976): Mobiles
**Joseph Cornell** (1903–1972): Three-dimensional collages
**Gaston Lachaise** (1887–1935): Large female nudes
**Jacques Lipchitz** (1891–1973): Cubist sculpture; religious themes
**Louise Nevelson** (1900– ): Assemblages
**Isamu Noguchi** (1904– ): Abstract sculptures
**Claes Oldenburg** (1929– ): Pop art sculptures
**Frederic Remington** (1861–1909): Western subjects
**David Smith** (1906–1965): Welded metal objects

▲ *Claes Oldenburg's* Trowel *is part of his series of giant statues of everyday objects.*

▲ *Christo's* Surrounded Islands *shows how he turns places into sculpture by using acres of colorful material.*

► *Frederic Remington's sculpture, such as* The Bronco Buster, *captured the exciting feeling of the Wild West.*

▲ *The California sea lion, a native of the Pacific coast, can grow up to 10 feet (3 m) long.*

## SEALS AND SEA LIONS

Seals and sea lions are mammals that live most of their lives in the sea. They are closely related to the WALRUS. All of these animals are called *pinnipeds*, or fin-footed mammals. Their front and hind limbs are flippers, or fins, that enable them to swim speedily through the water. Because so many have been killed for their fur, meat, and hides, they are now protected in the United States and other countries.

There are many different kinds of seals in the waters around North America. The smallest, the ringed seal, lives in Alaskan waters. The largest, the elephant seal, lives along the west coast of North America. This giant animal can weigh as much as 3.5 tons.

Sea lions differ from true seals in that they have external ears. The California sea lion and Stellar's sea lion live off the west coast of North America. The Alaskan, or northern, fur seal and the Guadalupe fur seal are in the same family as sea lions; they too have external ears.

## SEATTLE

The important port and manufacturing city of Seattle is the largest city in WASHINGTON State. It has a population of 516,259. Seattle is located on the shores of Puget Sound, about 125 miles (200 km) east of the Pacific Ocean. It is a hilly city and is sandwiched between the Olympic Mountains to the west and the Cascade Range to the east. Seattle's port handles most of Alaska's trade to and from the lower 48 states. Aircraft manufacturing is Seattle's most important industry. Boeing, one of the world's largest aircraft producers, has its headquarters in the city. Seattle processes much of the timber from the Pacific Northwest.

▼ *A view of the Lake Union harbor in Seattle. Mount Rainier lies in distance.*

## SECRET SERVICE

The Secret Service is a branch of the U.S. Department of the Treasury. It was founded in 1865 to combat counterfeiting, and the Secret Service still provides this service. More people associate it with its role as guardian of the president's safety. Secret Service agents guard the president and vice president and their families, as well as other prominent Americans or visiting foreign officials.

## SEMINOLES

The Seminole INDIANS were originally CREEK Indians. When white settlers moved onto their lands in Georgia in the 1700s, they fled to Florida. Here they intermarried with other Indians and escaped black slaves. When American settlers moved onto their lands again, the Seminoles fought back. In 1817–1818, Andrew JACKSON led American troops against them in the First Seminole War. In the Second Seminole War (1835–1842), the Indians were led by the great chief OSCEOLA. He was defeated, however, and most Seminoles were forced to move to Indian Territory (Oklahoma). About 4,000 live in Oklahoma today. Another 1,500 live near Lake Okeechobee in Florida's Everglades.

▲ *A Seminole woman does the family wash. Each year of her life she will add another bead necklace.*

## SENATE

In the United States and some other countries, one of the two houses of a legislative body is called the Senate. It is often called the upper house because it has fewer members, serving for longer terms, than the other house. The U.S. Senate, one of the two houses of CONGRESS, has 100 members, two from each state. They serve six-year terms. The Senate must approve certain appointments by the president, such as Cabinet members and federal judges. The Senate must also approve treaties by a two-thirds vote for them to become law. It also tries IMPEACHMENT cases, which require a two-thirds vote for conviction.

▼ *A grown man is dwarfed by these sequoia tree trunks in Redwood, California.*

## SEQUOIAS

The evergreen trees known as sequoias are some of the oldest and largest of living things. They are named for the Cherokee Indian SEQUOYA. There are two kinds. Redwoods, or coast redwoods, grow along the Pacific coast from southern Oregon to central California. They are the tallest trees in the world. Many are over 300 feet (90 m) high. Giant sequoias—also known as big trees or Sierra redwoods—grow on the western slopes of California's Sierra Nevada mountain range. Though not as tall as redwoods, they are the largest of all trees in volume. Redwoods are important to the lumber industry, but giant sequoias are too big to log and the wood is too brittle. The larger sequoias are protected law.

▲ *Sequoya found the time to devise the Cherokee written alphabet after he was crippled in a hunting accident.*

## SEQUOYA

Sequoya (1770–1843) was a CHEROKEE Indian scholar from Tennessee. He knew a great deal about the history and customs of his tribe. To keep a lasting record, Sequoya invented a system of writing for the Cherokee language. This system was made up of 86 characters. These characters were adapted from the English, Hebrew, and Greek alphabets. Soon, thousands of Cherokees learned to read and write, using their own language. Sequoya's system of writing was used for a tribal newspaper, the *Cherokee Phoenix*, first published in 1818. Sequoya himself became a spokesperson for Indian rights. The SEQUOIA tree is named for him.

## SERVICE INDUSTRIES

In the broadest definition, service industries are all income-earning activities that provide services rather than products. Doctors, lawyers, teachers, bankers, and airline pilots are service workers. By this measure, the U.S. labor force has about 40 million service workers. However, the federal government sometimes uses a narrower definition. In calculating the gross national product, government is listed separately, as are other service-related segments of the economy, such as utilities, transportation, communications, trade, and finance, insurance, and real estate. Even by this definition, the service sector is large and growing rapidly.

Health services, the biggest service industry, includes hospitals and nursing homes. Business services includes employment and advertising agencies and companies providing data processing and computer software. Other service industries include legal and accounting firms, hotels, caterers, garages, laundries, and beauty and barber shops. Economists say the increase in the service sector reflects the nation's growing prosperity.

**In 1960, U.S. service industries earned just under $47 billion, or about one tenth of overall industrial earnings. Since then their share of the total has increased dramatically. In 1975 they earned $182 billion, or about one sixth of the industrial total. In 1991 the service industry total of $1,002 billion was more than a fifth of overall industrial earnings.**

## SHEEP

Sheep are raised all over the world for their meat and wool. There are almost 11 million sheep in the United States. Sheep are usually kept in large herds on open rangeland in the West. There may be as many as a thousand sheep in a herd. Among the breeds raised for wool in the United States are the Merino, Cheviot, Cor-

States with Most Sheep

1. Texas (1.8 million)
2. California (955,000)
3. Wyoming (837,000)
4. Colorado (825,000)
5. Utah (600,000)
6. South Dakota (590,000)
7. New Mexico (578,000)
8. Montana (568,000)
9. Oregon (475,000)

◀ *During sheepshearing, seen here on an Oklahoma ranch, the winter wool is clipped from sheep as the weather gets warmer.*

**The American taste for mutton (the meat from adult sheep) has declined over the past 50 years. In 1940 the nation consumed 873 million pounds; the 1989 figure was only 406 million pounds.**

riedale, Columbia, Panama, Leicester, Cotswold, and Lincoln. Wild sheep, known as BIGHORN, are found in the mountains of western North America.

## SHEPARD, Alan B., Jr.

Alan Shepard (1923– ) was the first U.S. astronaut to be launched into space. Born in East Derry, New Hampshire, Shepard graduated from the U.S. Naval Academy in 1944. He became a Navy test pilot and in 1959 joined the astronaut program. On May 5, 1961, aboard the *Freedom 7* space capsule, he made his historic 15-minute suborbital flight. The flight reached an altitude of 115 miles (185 km) before splashing down in the Atlantic Ocean. In 1971, Shepard became the fifth astronaut to walk on the moon. He retired in 1974.

## SHERIDAN, Philip Henry

Philip Sheridan (1831–1888) was a brilliant Union cavalry officer in the CIVIL WAR. A graduate of West Point, Sheridan came to the attention of General Ulysses S. GRANT after his successful assault on Missionary Ridge during the Battle of Chattanooga, Tennessee, in 1863. Sheridan was then given command of the cavalry of the Army of the Potomac. In 1864, as commander of the Army of the Shenandoah, in Virginia, he defeated Confederate troops in three major battles. During the Union's final offensive in April 1865, he blocked the Confederate retreat, forcing General Robert E. LEE to surrender.

▼ *Alan Shepard trained for America's first astronaut launch at the Manned Spacecraft Center in Houston, Texas.*

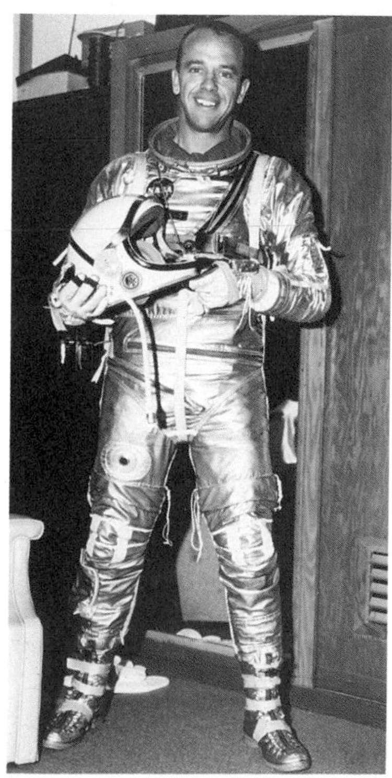

▼ General William Tecumseh Sherman led a fierce march through Georgia during the Civil War, but he opposed harsh measures against the South after the war.

## SHERMAN ANTITRUST ACT

The Sherman Antitrust Act (1890) was the first federal law making it illegal to restrain trade by limiting the availability of a product and thereby fixing prices. The intention was to regulate certain business combines—called trusts—such as John D. Rockefeller's Standard Oil Company, which controlled almost all oil refining and marketing. The U.S. Supreme Court ruled in 1911 that the Standard Oil Company of New Jersey must be broken into 38 separate parts. The law was applied to labor unions as well as businesses. In 1914 it was supplemented and strengthened by the Clayton Act.

## SHERMAN, William Tecumseh

William Tecumseh Sherman (1820–1891) was one of the leading generals of the CIVIL WAR. A graduate of West Point, Sherman became a colonel in the Union Army at the start of the war. He was promoted to major general in 1862, and in the following year he played important parts in the capture of Vicksburg, Mississippi, and the Battle of Chattanooga, Tennessee.

In the fall of 1864, Sherman captured Atlanta, Georgia, and burned it to the ground. He then began his "March to the Sea." In this month-long campaign (November–December), Sherman led a force of 60,000 men from Atlanta to the port of Savannah. They destroyed railroads, houses, factories, and everything else that might have been useful to the Confederate Army.

After the war, in 1869, President Ulysses S. Grant, who had been Sherman's commander in the Civil War, appointed Sherman commanding general of the Army. He held that post until 1883.

▼ An oceangoing tanker uses the St. Lawrence Seaway to connect the Great Lake ports with the Atlantic Ocean.

## SHIPS AND SHIPPING

The American shipping industry dates from Colonial times. Shipbuilding was a major industry, especially in New England, and American sailing ships plied the Atlantic Ocean. By 1850, fast American clipper ships were sailing the Pacific as well, and New England whaling vessels roamed the seven seas. Regular steamship service in vessels made of iron began about 1870. While passenger-carrying liners have given way to air traffic, cargo ships have become larger. Goods are

often sealed in containers loaded directly from trains or trucks. Enormous tankers carry petroleum and other liquid cargoes. More than 2 billion tons of goods leave or enter U.S. ports each year. There are 635 U.S. registered merchant vessels of 1,000 tons or more.

▲ *Machines, such as this crane at the Tacoma, Washington, container post, now unload cargo ships. Dockworkers called longshoremen or stevedores did the work by hand up until 20 years ago.*

## SHOCKLEY, William B.

William Bradford Shockley (1910–1989) was a scientist who helped invent the transistor in 1948. The transistor is the common name for a group of electronic devices that have allowed radios, television sets, computers, and other electronic instruments to take up much less space than they did before. Shockley and two other Bell Telephone Laboratory scientists shared the 1956 Nobel Prize for physics for their work on transistors. Shockley started a controversy in the 1970s when he said that black people were not, on average, as intelligent as whites because of differences in their genetic makeup.

## SHOSHONIS

The Shoshoni, or Shoshone, INDIANS lived in the semi-desert areas of the western United States. They were a nomadic people who traveled from place to place in search of food. SACAGAWEA, who acted as a guide for

**Among the most famous Shoshoni Indians was Sacagawea (Bird Woman), who was the interpreter for the Lewis and Clark Expedition to the Pacific Ocean in 1804 and 1805. She has been honored by having a mountain peak, a mountain pass, and a river named for her.**

▲ *Fannie Tayonix, a young Shoshoni girl with a traditional bead necklace, posed with freshly picked sunflowers at the beginning of the 20th century.*

the LEWIS AND CLARK EXPEDITION of 1804–1806, was a Shoshoni Indian.

The Shoshonis, like other Indians, fought to keep white settlers out of their lands in the 1800s. But eventually they were forced to live on reservations. Today there are about 8,000 Shoshonis on reservations in Wyoming, Idaho, Nevada, and Utah.

## SHULTZ, George

George Pratt Shultz (1920– ), a public servant and economist, was secretary of state under President Ronald Reagan. Born in New York City, Shultz was a professor and dean of the Graduate School of Business at the University of Chicago before entering public service. Under President Richard Nixon, Shultz served as secretary of labor, director of the Office of Management and Budget, and secretary of the treasury. He was president of the Bechtel Group, an engineering firm, from 1975 to 1982, when Reagan chose him to be secretary of state. He served in this position until 1989.

## SIERRA NEVADA

**The Sierra Nevada range stops the moist Pacific Ocean air from reaching the semi-desert regions of Nevada and Utah. As the air moves east from the sea, it provides rain for California's fertile Central Valley. This rain turns to snow when it reaches the barrier of the Sierra Nevadas.**

The Sierra Nevada is a North American MOUNTAIN range. It runs for about 400 miles (640 km) through eastern California, from the Cascade Range in the north to the MOJAVE DESERT in the south. MOUNT WHITNEY, in the Sierras, is the highest peak in the United States outside of Alaska. To the east of the Sierras is the GREAT BASIN. The large streams of the

► *The snowcapped Sierra Nevada rises up behind the tuga (limestone) towers of California's Moro Lake.*

more gentle western slopes drain into the fertile farming country of the Central Valley of California. SEQUOIA trees grow on these western slopes of the Sierra Nevada. Sequoia, Kings Canyon, and Yosemite national parks are in the Sierras.

◀ *Igor Sikorsky enjoyed hands-on testing of his own designs, such as this early helicopter in the 1930s.*

**In 1913, Igor Sikorsky built and piloted the world's first four-engine airplane, called *Le Grand*. It had a completely enclosed cabin for the pilots and passengers, something not adopted elsewhere until the mid-1920s.**

## SIKORSKY, Igor 

Igor Ivanovich Sikorsky (1889–1972) was one of the world's most inventive aircraft designers. Born in Russia, he built four-engine bombers for the Russian military during World War I. He left his homeland during the Russian Revolution and settled in the United States in 1919. Beginning in 1923 he set up companies that built passenger planes and flying boats. In 1939, Sikorsky developed the first single-rotor helicopter. Sikorsky helicopters soon became known for their good design and reliability.

## SINATRA, Frank 

Francis Albert "Frank" Sinatra (1915– ) is one of the most popular American entertainers. Born in Hoboken, New Jersey, he began singing in 1939 with Harry James's band. After singing with the Tommy Dorsey band from 1940 to 1942, he began a highly successful career as a solo singer. Sinatra also made many motion pictures, including *From Here to Eternity*, for which he won the 1953 Academy Award for best supporting actor. His other films include *Guys and Dolls*, *High Society*, and *The Manchurian Candidate*. Sinatra continues to record and to appear in concerts.

▼ *This 1958 album cover photograph captured the jaunty, well-dressed image of Frank Sinatra.*

## SINCLAIR, Upton

The novelist and journalist Upton Sinclair (1878–1968) wrote some 80 books. His specialty was the documentary novel, in which the story is combined with journalistic reporting on some topical issue. Sinclair's most successful novel, *The Jungle*, was about the terrible conditions in Chicago's stockyards. It aroused concern about the quality of processed meat and contributed to the passage of the Pure Food and Drug Act (1906). Sinclair's novel *Dragon's Teeth* won the 1943 Pulitzer Prize for fiction.

## SINGER, Isaac Bashevis

**Isaac Singer's writing is most widely known in English. He always wrote in Yiddish and then carefully oversaw the English translation.**

The Polish-born writer Isaac Bashevis Singer (1904–1991) was the author of many novels and short stories about Jewish life. He lived in the United States from 1935. Singer's novels include *The Magician of Lublin* and *Enemies, a Love Story*. Among the collections of his stories are *Gimpel the Fool* and *The Seance*. Singer also wrote stories for children, including *Zlateh the Goat*. He won the 1978 Nobel Prize for literature.

## SIOUX

The Sioux are a Great Plains tribe. They are divided into three main groups, the Lakota (or Teton), Dakota, and Nakota. The Sioux lived mainly in what are now

**Crazy Horse, a Sioux chief, used his tribe's skilled horsemanship to develop a fighting strategy against the U.S. Army. He knew that Sioux horsemen would be wiped out if they faced the army head-on. So he sent his men riding back and forth to find the army's weakest point. The plan was used at Custer's Last Stand in 1876.**

► *Frederic Remington's sketch* Going to the Dance *portrayed a Sioux community on the way to a tribal ceremony.*

the states of Minnesota, South Dakota, and Nebraska. The Sioux sided with the British during the American Revolution and the War of 1812. And they fought American settlers who tried to take their lands during the 1860s and 1870s. Among their greatest chiefs were CRAZY HORSE, Red Cloud, and SITTING BULL. The Sioux, along with the Cheyenne, killed George CUSTER and his troops at the Battle of the Little Bighorn in 1876. The Sioux were finally defeated in 1890 at Wounded Knee in South Dakota. Soldiers massacred about 200 men, women, and children. Today about 50,000 Sioux live on and near reservations in Minnesota, North and South Dakota, Nebraska, and Montana, as well as in Manitoba and Saskatchewan, Canada.

▲ *Young skateboarders take on the track at Monster Bowl State Park, in Seaside Heights, New Jersey.*

## SKATEBOARDING

The sport of skateboarding developed in California in the late 1950s. It combined two sports that were very popular at the time, surfing and roller skating. The first skateboards were made of wood and had metal wheels. The method of making skateboards has changed with the sport itself. Modern boards are made of hard plastic or fiberglass. Urethane plastic wheels make the boards safer and easier to steer. Skateboarding can be dangerous if done without supervision or protective pads. Many cities and towns have special skateboard parks where skateboarders are not a danger to themselves or others.

## SKIING *See* Winter Sports

## SKUNK

The skunk is a small mammal related to the WEASEL. It is known for the foul-smelling liquid it sprays when in danger. Skunks live only in the Western Hemisphere. They live mostly in burrows, coming out at night to hunt for small animals and other food. All skunks are black and white. Most have stripes, but some are spotted. The striped skunk, the most common, is found all over North America. The hooded and hog-nosed skunks are found mostly in the Southwest. The spotted skunk, the only skunk that can climb, often lives in hollow trees in the South and West.

▼ *A skunk can often scare off an intruder merely by raising its tail to threaten spraying.*

▲ *Chicago's Sears Tower, standing 1,454 feet (443 m) high, is the world's tallest skyscraper. Chicago is the birthplace of the skyscraper.*

## SKYSCRAPERS

Skyscrapers are tall buildings. Most contain offices for businesses, but some also have apartments for people to live in. Skyscrapers were not possible until the late 1800s, when Elisha OTIS developed the elevator and builders began to use steel girders.

Chicago was the first city to have skyscrapers. In the late 1800s, a building above six stories was considered a skyscraper. The first skyscraper to use steel girders was the ten-story Home Insurance Building, built in Chicago in 1884. Today the tallest building in the world, the Sears Tower, is also in Chicago. It is 110 stories and rises 1,454 feet (443 m). Among the many notable skyscrapers in New York City are the 110-story World Trade Center (1,350 feet, or 411 m) and the 102-story Empire State Building (1,250 feet, or 381 m).

## SLAVERY

The first African slaves arrived in Virginia in 1619. By 1700 slavery was firmly established in the colonies, especially on the large plantations of the South. Most slaves who were not field hands worked as domestic servants. A few were taught crafts, such as carpentry. They had few, if any, legal rights. They could be sold at auction, and families were often broken up.

In 1808, the United States banned the importing of slaves. By then, many Northern states had outlawed slavery. But slaves were still held in the South. In 1860,

Some Dates in the History of American Slavery

**1619** First black laborers arrive in Virginia.
**1650** Slavery legalized.
**1712** Slaves revolt in New York City.
**1774** Rhode Island abolishes slavery.
**1783** Massachusetts abolishes slavery.
**1808** U.S. bans slave importing.
**1820** Missouri Compromise limits spread of slave states.
**1850** Fugitive Slave Bill passed; Underground Railroad helps slaves escape.
**1863** Emancipation Proclamation frees slaves in the South.
**1865** Thirteenth Amendment outlaws slavery.

► *Families were often split up and their members sold separately at slave auctions in the South.*

just before the CIVIL WAR, there were nearly 4 million slaves. Slavery was the main issue of the Civil War. Abraham Lincoln's EMANCIPATION PROCLAMATION, issued during the war, freed slaves in the South. Slavery was abolished throughout the nation by the Thirteenth Amendment to the Constitution (1865).

## SMITH, John *See* Pocahontas

## SMITH, Joseph

Joseph Smith (1805–1844) was a prophet and founder of the Church of Jesus Christ of Latter-day Saints. Members of the church are called MORMONS. At the age of 14, Smith had a vision that he claimed led him to some inscribed golden plates. Translated by Smith as *The Book of Mormon*, these texts were to form the basis (along with the Bible) of the Mormon faith.

Smith established his church in Fayette, New York, in 1830. However, he and his followers had to move twice because of their neighbors' hostility. They finally settled in Commerce, Illinois, which Smith renamed Nauvoo. For a while they prospered, but the church split into two opposing camps. In the resulting violence, Smith and his brother were murdered. Brigham YOUNG became leader and led the Mormons to Utah.

▼ *Joseph Smith's memory and guidelines kept the Mormon faith alive after his assassination in 1844.*

## SMITHSONIAN INSTITUTION

The Smithsonian Institution is a nonprofit cultural and scientific institution. Based in Washington, D.C., it is sponsored by the United States government. It was established by an act of Congress in 1846 after a British scientist, James Smithson, left funds for it in his will. The Smithsonian is run by a board that includes the chief justice of the United States, the vice president, three senators, and three representatives.

The Smithsonian conducts scientific research and publishes scientific information. It also maintains numerous art collections and preserves and displays items relating to science, natural history, aeronautics, and space technology. Among the hundreds of thousands of items in its various centers are Charles Lindberg's plane the *Spirit of St. Louis*, Samuel Morse's telegraph, and a lunar module.

▼ *The Smithsonian Institution preserves America's past with exhibits such as this working replica of a 19th-century post office.*

▲ *The cottonmouth snake, or water moccasin, is a venomous snake living in southern wetlands. Its bite is painful and sometimes fatal.*

## SNAKES 

Snakes, like turtles, lizards, and crocodiles and alligators, are REPTILES. They are found in most areas of North America. Most snakes are harmless, but some kinds are poisonous. Among the harmless snakes in North America are garter snakes and rat snakes. Rat snakes hunt rats and mice. The blind snake is another harmless snake. Most snakes live in trees, in the water, and on the ground.

Four kinds of poisonous snakes live in North America. The coral snake lives in the southern part of the United States. Copperheads and cottonmouths live in the Southeast. Cottonmouths are also known as water moccasins. The RATTLESNAKE is the most widespread poisonous snake in North America.

## SOAP BOX DERBY 

A soap box derby is a race for handmade cars with no engines. Youngsters from 9 to 16 years of age can compete as long as they have built the car themselves, or with the help of a family member. The first cars used wooden soap boxes as seats. This gave the sport its name. The national championships, known as the All-American Soap Box Derby, are held in Akron, Ohio, each August. All racers can enter the Kit Car Division. The Master's Division, with faster and sleeker cars, is for those between the ages of 11 and 16.

▼ *The overall length and width of a soccer field can vary, but measurements within the field must be the same.*



## SOCCER 

The team sport of soccer is the world's most popular sport. The basic rules are very simple: two teams of 11 players each try to score goals by getting the soccer ball into the other team's net. The goalkeeper, or goalie, is the only player who can touch the ball with his or her arms or hands. Most goals and passes are kicked or "headed" past the opposing players. Until recently, soccer was not very popular in the United States. Several attempts to establish a professional league failed. The sport has grown, however, because of the many school-age players. Soccer's biggest event is the World Cup, held every four years. National teams from all over the world compete for the championship. The United States will host the 1994 World Cup.

## SOCIAL WELFARE 

Social welfare is a term for financial or other assistance to individuals. Social Security provides monthly cash benefits and health insurance (Medicare) for retired and disabled workers and their eligible survivors. Other work-related programs include unemployment insurance and workers' compensation. A Social Security-related federal program provides income for the needy aged, blind, and disabled. Others include food stamps for people with low income and special aid to veterans. Medicaid and Aid to Families with Dependent Children are programs for the poor.

▲ *A good softball batter needs keen eyesight, good timing, and powerful arms.*

## SOFTBALL 

Softball is one of the most popular team sports in the United States. The rules of softball are like those of BASEBALL, except the field is smaller, pitching is underhand, and an extra fielder can be allowed. Also, a softball is larger than a baseball. There are two types of softball, slow-pitch and fast-pitch. Most people play slow-pitch. Championships are organized by the American Softball Association. International competition is supervised by the International Softball Federation.

**People usually think of softball as a friendly, slower version of baseball. But in fast-pitch softball competitions, batters have to keep their eye on a ball traveling 90 miles per hour (150 km/hr) toward home plate.**

## SONS OF LIBERTY 

The Sons of Liberty were groups of colonial American patriots in the period before the American Revolution. They were first formed after the passage of the hated STAMP ACT in 1765. They circulated petitions, arranged public meetings, and sometimes stirred up riots and attacks on British officials. They later demanded American independence.

## SOUSA, John Philip 

The composer and bandleader John Philip Sousa (1854–1932) was known as the March King. He wrote about 140 military marches, including such classics as "The Washington Post March" and "The Stars and Stripes Forever." Sousa joined the U.S. Marine Band in 1868 and became its conductor in 1880. In 1892 he formed his own band, which played symphonic music as well as the famous Sousa marches.

**John Philip Sousa's rousing marches echoed the optimistic mood of the country in the 1890s. Sousa believed that "a march should make a man with a wooden leg want to step out."**

# SOUTH CAROLINA

South Carolina was one of the original 13 states and was also the first southern state to secede from the Union just before the CIVIL WAR. The war ended a gracious way of life for those who profited from the cotton, rice, and indigo plantations tended by slave labor. Traces of the Old South survive in the historic district and lush gardens of Charleston and in the state's American Revolution and Civil War battlefields. The Atlantic resorts of Myrtle Beach and Hilton Head Island also attract many visitors.

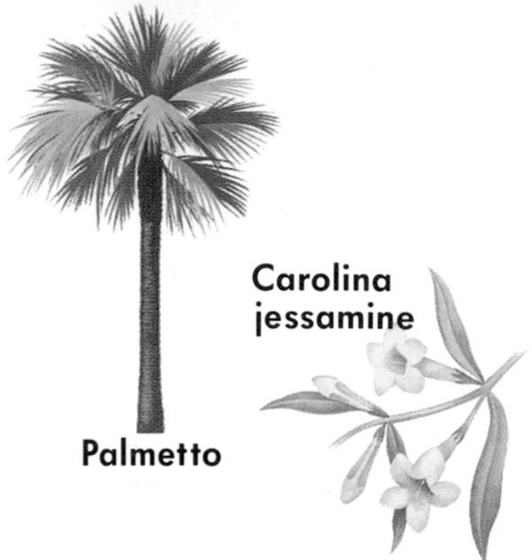


Charleston is a busy port and the biggest city in the eastern lowland area. This region has most of the state's productive farms. The chief crops are tobacco and soybeans. Farther west is the Piedmont, a gently rolling plateau. This is the state's manufacturing center. Textiles are South Carolina's most important product. Other important industrial goods are chemicals, machinery, paper products, food products, clothing, and electrical and electronic equipment. The BLUE RIDGE MOUNTAINS, in the western corner of the state, have a cool summer climate and are popular with vacationers.

Charleston was the first permanent settlement in what is now South Carolina. It was founded in 1670 and was moved to its present site in 1680. The many battles fought here during the American Revolution included King's Mountain and Cowpens in 1780–1781. The Civil War began in 1861 when South Carolina forces opened fire on Fort Sumter, in Charleston Harbor. Four years later, with the war drawing to a close, the Union Army occupied the state, causing great destruction.

South Carolina
**Capital:** Columbia
**Area:** 32,007 sq mi (82,898 km²). Rank: 40th
**Population:** 3,486,703 (1990). Rank: 25th
**Statehood:** May 23, 1788
**Principal rivers:** Santee, Edisto, Savannah
**Highest point:** Sassafras Mountain, 3,560 ft (1,085 m)
**Motto:** *Dum Spiro Spero* (While I Breathe, I Hope)
**Song:** "Carolina"

► *Many of the old houses in the restored Charleston Harbor area were built in the 1700s for sea captains and merchants.*

▲ *A mountain lake in northwest South Carolina reflects Table Rock, part of the Blue Ridge chain of the Appalachians.*

Places of Interest

- Char!eston Museum, established in 1773, is the oldest museum in the United States.
- For Sumter, in Charleston Harbor, is the place where the Civil War began in 1861.
- The beautiful seaside resort of Myrtle Beach offers a variety of outdoor activities.
- Middleton Place Gardens, begun in 1741, are the oldest landscaped gardens in the United States.

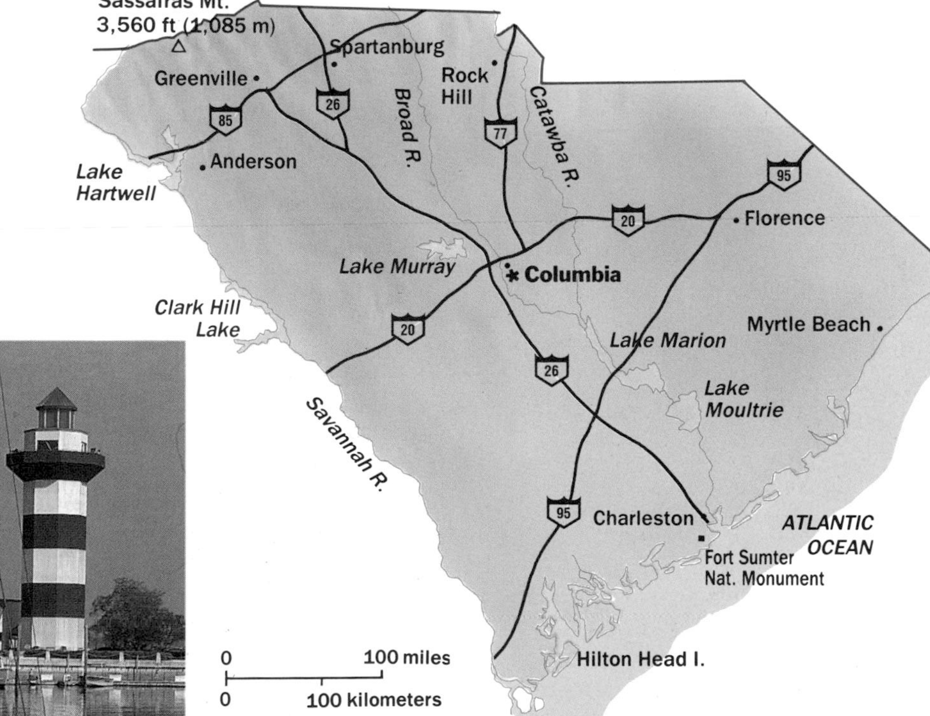


▼ *Hilton Head Island is one of the most popular luxury resorts on the U.S. east coast.*

# SOUTH DAKOTA

South Dakota is one of the states where the fertile Midwest prairie meets the higher Great Plains to the west. Lying roughly between the two is the mighty Missouri River, which flows southward through the center of the state. South Dakota's highest region is the Black Hills of the southwest. These hills are granite peaks that rise 4,000 feet (1,200 m) above the surrounding plains. Neighboring the Black Hills is the spectacular BADLANDS, a region of jagged cliffs and ravines.

There is a feeling of open space throughout this sparsely populated state. East of the Missouri, farmers grow corn, wheat, soybeans, and alfalfa. But the advantages of the rich soil are often offset by drought, blizzards, and frosts. Livestock raising, particularly of beef cattle, is more important in western South Dakota. Industry is mostly confined to producing meat products. Near Lead, in the Black Hills, is the Homestake Mine, one of the most productive gold mines in North America. The Black Hills and Badlands are popular for camping. The heads of presidents Washington, Lincoln, Jefferson, and Theodore Roosevelt are carved from a side of MOUNT RUSHMORE in the Black Hills.

French fur traders were the first whites to visit this region. "Dakota" was what the Sioux Indians called themselves and their allies. The United States gained the area from France as part of the LOUISIANA PURCHASE of 1803, but there were few settlers until gold was discovered in the Black Hills in 1874. South Dakota became a state in 1889.

South Dakota
**Capital:** Pierre
**Area:** 77,121 sq mi ($199,745 km^2$). Rank: 17th
**Population:** 696,004 (1990). Rank: 45th
**Statehood:** November 2, 1889
**Principal rivers:** Cheyenne, White, Missouri
**Highest point:** Harney Peak, 7,242 ft (2,207 m)
**Motto:** Under God the People Rule
**Song:** "Hail, South Dakota"

► *The tracks of contour farming weave around trees in South Dakota's fertile prairie land.*

► *Visitors to Hot Springs, South Dakota, can see mammoth bones that have been preserved for 10,000 years.*

Places of Interest

- Badlands National Park provides breathtaking beauty for its many visitors.
- The Black Hills, where the famous Passion Play is performed every year
- Custer State Park, where bison still roam.
- Mt. Rushmore National Memorial, near Rapid City, a spectacular tribute to presidents Washington, Jefferson, Theodore Roosevelt, and Lincoln.

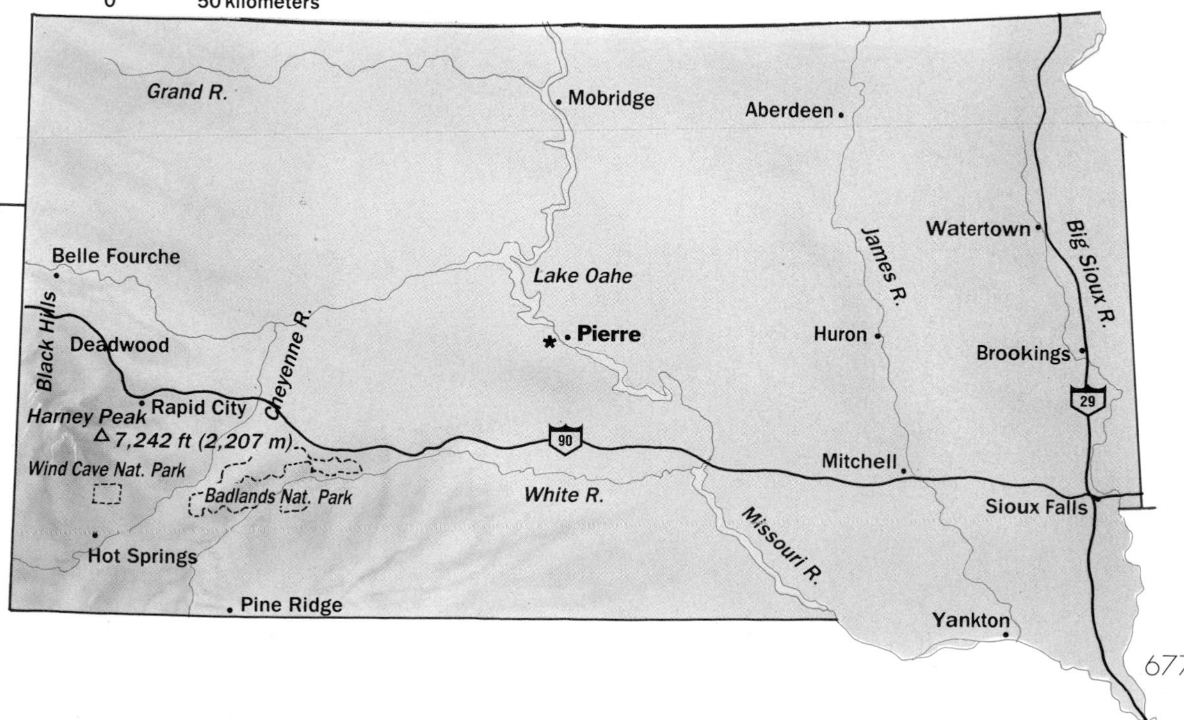

# SPACE PROGRAM

The conquest of space has been one of humankind's greatest accomplishments in this century. It began when the Soviet Union sent the first Sputnik into orbit around the earth in 1957. In 1959 a Soviet space probe hit the moon. Since then a variety of unmanned vehicles have landed on the moon and planets or have orbited these bodies as well as the earth and sun. Manned space travel began when the Soviet Union sent a cosmonaut — the Russian term for astronaut — into earth orbit in 1961. The United States followed in 1962. The U.S. goal of putting a man on the moon before the end of the 1960s was achieved on July 20, 1969, when two of the three crew members of *Apollo II* touched down. The third remained in orbit around the moon.

In the 1970s the Soviet Salyut and U.S. Skylab space stations orbited the earth for long periods. They served as bases for vehicles and their crews, who conducted a variety of experiments. In 1981 the United States successfully tested the first re-usable space vehicle. These maneuverable manned space shuttles conduct experiments in earth orbit and then return intact.

In 1990, U.S. President George Bush promised to land an astronaut on Mars before 2019, the 50th anniversary of the first manned lunar landing. The National Aeronautics and Space Administration (NASA), a civilian agency, accounted for most launches in the early years of the U.S. space program. In recent years however, the military has received a greater percentage of the space budget than NASA.

**Milestones in the U.S. Space Program**

**1958** First U.S. satellite (Explorer I) is launched.
**1961** Alan B. Shepard, Jr., is first American in space.
**1962** John H. Glenn becomes first American to orbit the earth. President John F. Kennedy promises to land an American on the moon by 1970.
**1969** Neil A. Armstrong and Edwin E. Aldrin, Jr., become first to land on the moon.
**1975** Apollo 18 links with Soyuz 19 in a joint U.S.-Soviet mission.
**1983** On separate space shuttle missions, Sally K. Ride and Guion Bluford become first American woman and first black person in space.
**1990** The Hubble Space Telescope is put in orbit.

◀ *In 1965, Edward H. White II became the first American to walk in space.*

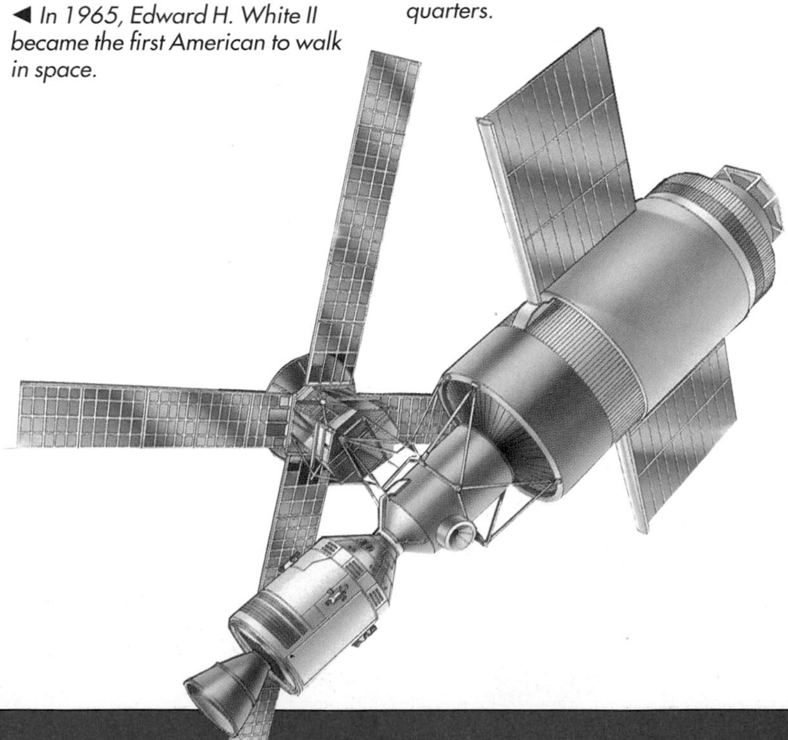

▼ *The Skylab space station contained experiments, work stations, food stores, and living quarters.*

▲ *Mae Jemison, now a fully trained astronaut, sits in an ejection seat during her year-long training course at Vance Air Force Base.*

**The moon landing in 1969 fulfilled the promise made by President John F. Kennedy in 1961. He called for a manned moon landing "before the decade is out."**

### Types of U.S. Piloted Spacecraft

**Mercury:** The first American spaceflights carried only one astronaut. Successes included the first American in space (1961), to orbit the earth (1962), and to spend more than 24 hours in space.

**Gemini:** These two-man orbital flights were much longer than Mercury missions (up to two weeks). Gemini missions pioneered the space walk (outside the capsule) and developed new methods of navigation.

**Apollo:** The three-man Apollo missions put the first astronauts on the moon (1969). The six Apollo moon landings conducted scientific research, took a vehicle to the moon, and brought back 850 pounds (386 kg) of lunar rocks.

**Skylab:** This space station orbited the earth between 1973 and 1979. The three-man crews conducted scientific research, particularly on the prolonged effects of weightlessness. In other experiments, Skylab astronauts grew metal crystals on board and improved satellite techniques for observing the earth. The third and longest mission spent 84 days in orbit.

**Space Shuttle:** These re-usable spacecraft can orbit the earth then land on a runway like an airplane. Space shuttle missions have up to eight crew members. Achievements include the first American woman in space, the first black person in space, repairs or orbiting satellites, and the launch of the Hubble Space Telescope (1990). Scientific, industrial, and military missions have been carried out by space shuttle crews.

▼ *Space shuttles carry satellites and laboratories.*

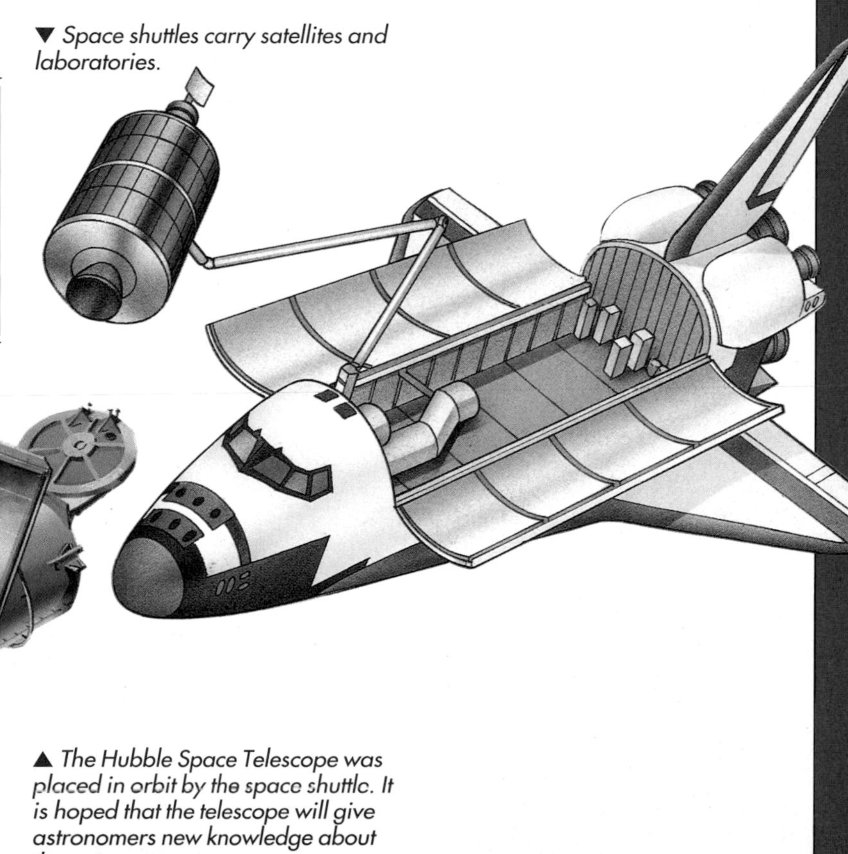

▲ *The Hubble Space Telescope was placed in orbit by the space shuttle. It is hoped that the telescope will give astronomers new knowledge about the universe.*

▲ *During the Spanish-American War, Lieutenant Colonel Theodore Roosevelt led his Rough Riders to victory at San Juan Hill in Cuba in 1898.*

## SPANISH-AMERICAN WAR 

The Spanish-American War was fought between the United States and Spain in 1898. There were a number of causes of the war. The people of Cuba, a Caribbean island about 100 miles (160 km) from Florida, were fighting for their independence from Spain. Many Americans supported their cause. Also, some newspapers in the United States—the "yellow press"—whipped up anti-Spanish feelings. Those feelings increased after the U.S. battleship *Maine* was sunk in the harbor of Havana, Cuba, on February 15, 1898. The yellow press blamed the Spanish, but that charge has never been proved.

The United States demanded that Spain get out of Cuba on April 19, and in the next week Congress declared war. The war was short. On May 1, Admiral George DEWEY destroyed a Spanish fleet in Manila Harbor in the Philippines, a Spanish colony in the Pacific Ocean. On July 3 another Spanish fleet was destroyed in the harbor of Santiago, Cuba. Meanwhile, U.S. troops had landed in Cuba at the end of June. Led by Theodore Roosevelt's ROUGH RIDERS, they forced the Spanish to surrender on July 17. An armistice was declared on August 12.

The Treaty of Paris, signed on December 10, ended the war. Cuba won its independence, but the U.S. military controlled the island until 1902. The United States took over the Philippines, PUERTO RICO, and the Pacific island of GUAM and became as a result a world power.

**President William McKinley reacted cautiously after the *Maine* blew up in Cuba in 1898. Many Americans criticized the president's efforts to avoid war. Theodore Roosevelt, who was Assistant Secretary of the Navy at the time, said privately that the president was weak and had "no more backbone than a chocolate eclair."**

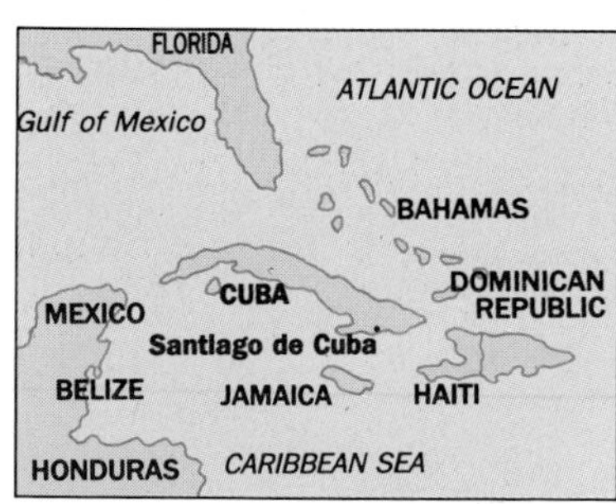


▲ *The U.S. victory in the Spanish-American War ended Spanish control of Cuba.*

## SPERRY, Elmer

Elmer Ambrose Sperry (1860–1930) was an inventor who changed the world of ship navigation. He used the spinning power of a gyroscope to build an accurate compass for ships. The gyrocompass, as it was called, did not rely on the magnetic north pole to give its reading, so the steel in the ship's hull would not affect it. This invention led to automatic pilot devices for ships and accurate aiming mechanisms for torpedoes. Sperry set up the Sperry Gyroscope Company in 1910; it was the forerunner of today's Sperry Rand Corporation.

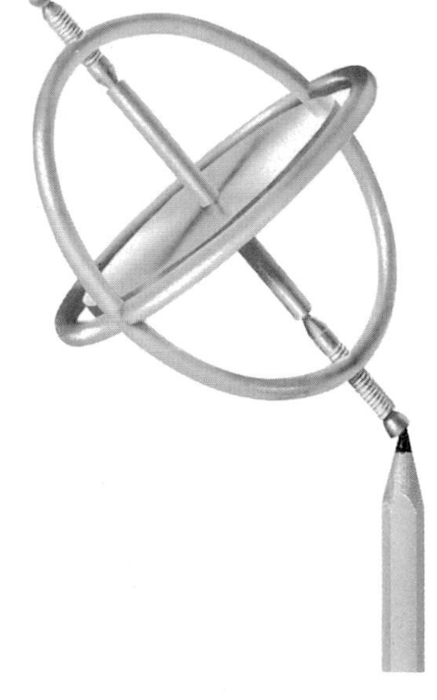

▲ *Gyroscopes are kept stable by their spinning. They seem to defy gravity by staying "locked" onto a pencil point.*

## SPIDERS

Spiders are very small animals that look like insects. They are related to scorpions, daddy longlegs, ticks, and mites. Spiders spin silk threads, often in the form of webs. Many spiders use these webs to catch insects. Most spiders have poison glands, but only a few North American spiders are poisonous to humans. These include the black widow and the brown recluse spider. The largest spiders are the tarantulas. North American tarantulas, which are up to 3 inches (7.5 cm) long, are common in the Southwest. Among the smallest is the dwarf spider, which is less than $\frac{1}{20}$ inch (1.3 mm) long.

▼ *Unlike insects, which have six legs, spiders and scorpions have eight legs. Some, such as the Arizona scorpion and the black widow spider, are venomous.*

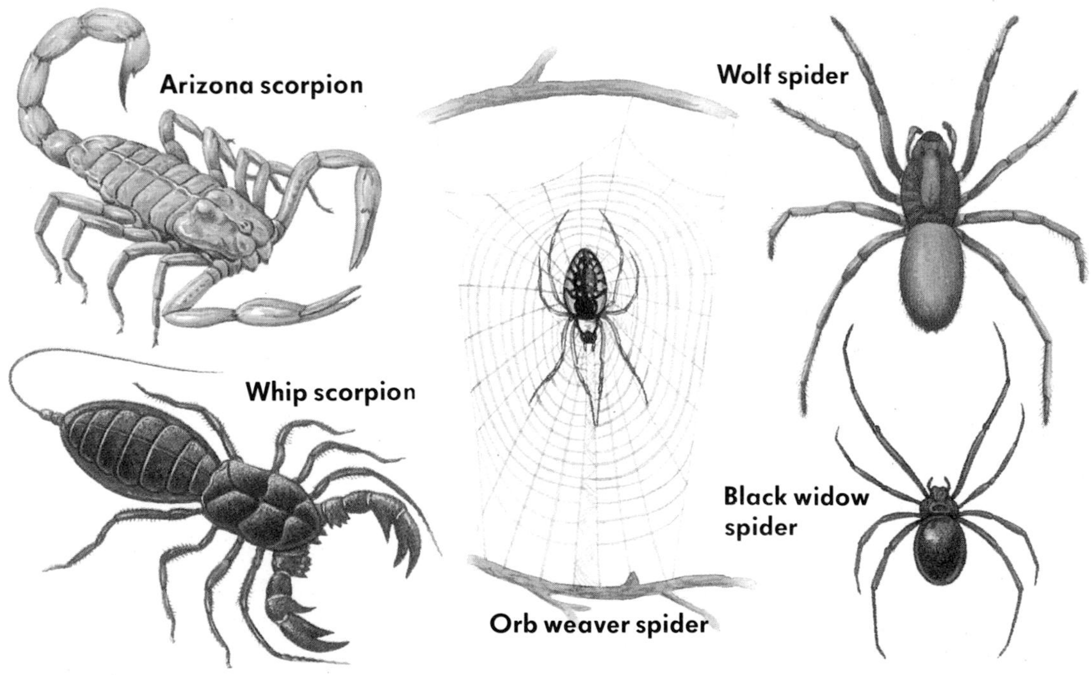

| Year | Name and Area of Achievement |
| --- | --- |
| 1993 | Dorothy Height (civil rights) |
| 1992 | Barbara Jordan (law; politics; government) |
| 1991 | Gen. Colin L. Powell (military) |
| 1990 | L. Douglas Wilder (government) |
| 1989 | Jesse Jackson (government) |
| 1988 | Frederick Patterson (education) |
| 1987 | Percy E. Sutton (law; politics; business) |
| 1986 | Benjamin L. Hooks (civil rights) |
| 1985 | Bill Cosby (entertainment; education) |

Some Recent Winners of the Spingarn Medal

## SPINGARN, Joel Elias 

Joel Elias Spingarn (1875–1939) was an educator and social reformer. Born in New York City, he became a professor of literature at Columbia University. Spingarn wrote several important works on the history of literary criticism. Early in his life he became interested in the contribution of blacks to American culture. He was active in the NATIONAL ASSOCIATION FOR THE ADVANCEMENT OF COLORED PEOPLE, serving as its president from 1930 to 1939. In 1914, Spingarn created an annual award to acknowledge outstanding black Americans. Langston HUGHES, Ralph BUNCHE, Martin Luther KING, Jr., Leontyne Price, and Bill Cosby are among its winners.

## SPOCK, Benjamin 

Dr. Benjamin Spock (1903– ) is a world-known pediatrician (children's doctor) and author. Born in New Haven, Connecticut, he received a medical degree from Columbia University. His books, including the best-selling *Common Sense Book of Baby and Child Care*, have given practical advice to parents since 1946. Several of his later books dealt with specific areas, such as the problems of coping with the special needs of a disabled child. Spock was a man who took strong stands. He became involved with the movement against the Vietnam War during the 1960s.

▼ *The New York Marathon, like many other sporting events, has a special wheelchair competition for disabled racers.*

## SPORTS 

Sports are activities, usually undertaken for pleasure, that generally involve some sort of physical exercise. The most popular spectator sports in the United States are the team games of BASEBALL, FOOTBALL, and BASKETBALL. But such games are not necessarily good participant sports because they are not for all ages, are difficult to organize, and often require special equipment. The top three participant sports for adult Americans are SWIMMING, bicycling, and BOWLING. The top three for young Americans are swimming, bicycling, and basketball. Other popular participant sports include running, TENNIS, GOLF, hunting, and fishing. Doctors welcome the popularity of participant sports because they contribute to physical fitness.

| Popular Spectator Sports | Some Participant Sports |
|---|---|
| *Automobile racing | Archery |
| *Baseball | Badminton |
| *Basketball | *Bowling |
| *Bowling | Croquet |
| *Boxing | Darts |
| *Field hockey | Fencing |
| *Golf | *Gymnastics |
| *Horse racing | Hiking |
| Jai alai | Horseshoe throwing |
| *Lacrosse | Martial arts |
| *Rodeo | Mountain climbing |
| Roller derby | Racquetball |
| *Soccer | *Roller skating |
| *Softball | Shuffleboard |
| *Tennis | Squash |
| *Track and field | *Swimming |
| *Volleyball | *Tennis |
| Water polo | Weight lifting |

* See individual entries

**The most popular sports in the United States until the 1880s were frontier pursuits—rifle shooting, rowing, and walking. More than 100,000 people attended a rifle-shooting contest on Long Island, New York, in 1873.**

## SQUARE DANCING

The square dance is an American folk dance, performed to music by four couples arranged in a square. In a singing patter, a caller announces the figures, or movements, to be performed, improvising the sequence at will. Square dancing developed during the early 1800s. It was derived from English country dancing and from two French dances, the cotillion and the quadrille. Music for square dancing is usually provided by fiddles, banjos, guitars, or accordions.

*▼ A happy group square dances into the night at the Big 4 Ranch at Carbondale, Colorado.*

## SQUIRRELS

Squirrels are RODENTS with long, furry tails. There are two kinds, GROUND SQUIRRELS and tree squirrels. Chipmunks, PRAIRIE DOGS, and woodchucks are ground sqirrels. North America has three types of tree squirrels—gray squirrels, red squirrels, and flying squirrels. The largest gray squirrel is the fox squirrel. The two other North American species are the eastern gray squirrel and the western gray squirrel.

Red squirrels are smaller, more active, and noisier than gray squirrels. They live in evergreen forests, where they collect pine cones. The two species are the Douglas squirrel and the common red squirrel.

Flying squirrels, found all over the continent, are the smallest tree squirrels, they have furry flaps of skin

*▼ A squirrel seems poised for a quick escape even when it has stopped to eat some nuts or grain.*

stretching from their front legs to their back legs that enable them to glide from tree to tree.

▲ *The flying squirrel gets its name from the way it spreads two wide folds of skin to make long, gliding leaps.*

## STAMP ACT

The Stamp Act was passed by the British Parliament in 1765. It placed a tax on documents, licenses, newspapers, almanacs, playing cards, and dice in the American colonies. The purpose of the Stamp Act was to raise money to pay for the stationing of British troops in the colonies. It was a heavy tax, which had to be paid in British currency, and the colonists, who were not represented in Parliament, resented this "taxation without representation." Many people simply refused to buy the stamps; in some places there were riots. Although the act was repealed the following year, it had already stimulated a spirit of independence in the colonies that was to become ever stronger.

**Today people would not think twice about paying a stamp tax on items included in the Stamp Act. Liquor, playing cards, and cigarettes all have revenue (tax) stamps. The difference, though, is that Americans now have a say in how the money raised is spent—colonists were denied that right.**

## STAMPS AND STAMP COLLECTING

Stamps are adhesive labels that must be put on letters, packages, and other items sent through the mail. The world's first postage stamp was issued in England in 1840. Seven years later the United States government issued 5-cent stamps with a picture of Benjamin Franklin, the country's first postmaster general, and 10-cent stamps with a picture of George Washington.

The United States POSTAL SERVICE sells more than $7 billion worth of stamps each year. Some of these have become very valuable. An airmail stamp issued in 1918, for example, is worth perhaps $200,000, because the airplane on the stamp was printed upside down. People who collect stamps like this, and other stamps, are called philatelists. Stamp collecting is a popular and enjoyable hobby. Some people collect stamps from one

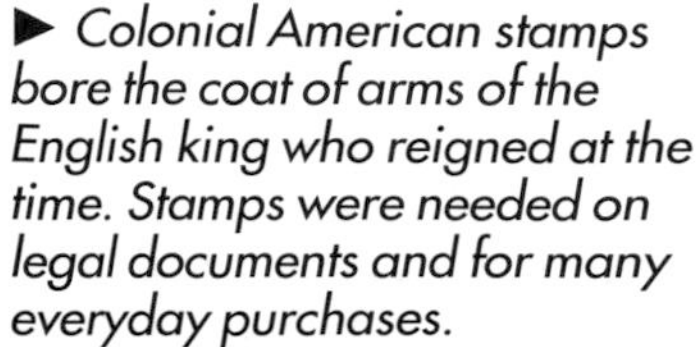

► *Colonial American stamps bore the coat of arms of the English king who reigned at the time. Stamps were needed on legal documents and for many everyday purchases.*

◀ *U.S. postage stamps come in many denominations and honor famous people and events, charitable causes, and great works of art.*

country or from groups of countries. Others enjoy topical collecting—collecting stamps about one topic, or subject, such as animals, flags, sports, or maps.

**Some of the rarest—and most expensive—stamps are those on which mistakes appear. U.S. stamp collectors are always looking for the 15 cent, 24 cent, and 30 cent, stamps from 1869; the center picture was inverted (printed upside down) on some of these.**

## STANLEY, Sir Henry Morton

Sir Henry Morton Stanley (1841–1904), a journalist and explorer, was a colorful figure in American history. He was born in Wales and led the life of an adventurer. He sailed to New Orleans as a ship's cabin boy when he was 17. During the Civil War he managed to serve in both the Union and Confederate armies. His taste for excitement led him to become a newspaper reporter. In 1869 the *New York Herald* sent him to Africa to find David Livingstone, a British explorer who had been missing for several years. After a long and difficult expedition, Stanley found Livingstone in 1871 near Lake Victoria. His words on meeting him became famous: "Doctor Livingstone, I presume?" Stanley later made three other expeditions to Africa.

▲ *Henry Morton Stanley spent months searching the African jungle before he could make his famous introduction, "Dr. Livingstone, I presume."*

## STANTON, Elizabeth Cady

Elizabeth Cady Stanton (1815–1902) was a leader in the WOMEN'S RIGHTS movement. In 1848 she joined with Lucretia MOTT in organizing the first women's rights convention in the United States, which took place in Seneca Falls, New York. Working with Susan B. ANTHONY, she continued the fight for women's suffrage (the right to vote) and other rights for the rest of

**Elizabeth Cady Stanton and her partner, Susan B. Anthony, were an ideal team to lead the U.S. women's movement. Stanton did most of the writing, in publications such as the newspaper *The Revolution*, while Anthony handled the business affairs.**

her life. She and Anthony edited a newspaper, *The Revolution*, and from 1869 to 1890, Stanton was president of the National Woman Suffrage Association.

## STAR-SPANGLED BANNER *See* National Anthem

## STATE DEPARTMENT *See* Government, U.S.

## STATE GOVERNMENT

The governments of the 50 U.S. states are similar to that of the federal government. In all of them, there is a separation of the executive, legislative, and judicial powers. The U.S. Constitution forbids the states certain activities, such as coining money or engaging in war. But the Tenth Amendment reserves "to the States respectively, or to the people" all powers not delegated to the federal government by the Constitution. Many of those powers, such as maintaining law and order and running public school systems, are in turn partly delegated to local governments. The federal government now shares with the states responsibility in such areas as public health and welfare and the regulation of business and labor.

## STATUE OF LIBERTY

The Statue of Liberty is a symbol of American liberty and freedom. Its real name is Liberty Enlightening the World. The statue stands on Liberty Island (formerly Bedloe's Island) in Upper New York Bay. The statue, which was unveiled in 1886, was given to the United States by the people of France. The enormous copper figure was designed and created by the French sculptor Frederic Auguste Bartholdi. In the years after 1886, millions of immigrants came to the United States. Most came by ship to the immigration center on Ellis Island, a short distance from the statue. The first thing they saw was Lady Liberty, with her hand and torch raised high in welcome. The statue, which is 151 feet (46 m ) high, is part of the Statue of Liberty–Ellis Island National Monument. In 1986, for its 100th birthday, it was restored and given a new torch.

▼ *A strong steel skeleton, containing an elevator, stairs, and ventilation shafts, supports the Statue of Liberty.*

## STEICHEN, Edward

Edward Steichen (1879–1973) was one of the greatest American photographers. He and Alfred STIEGLITZ helped to establish photography as an art form. Steichen, who was born in Luxembourg, trained as a painter. During the 1920s and 1930s he worked as a fashion photographer. He also took many outstanding photographs of celebrities, such as Greta Garbo and Charlie Chaplin. Between 1947 and 1962, Steichen was director of the photography department of the Museum of Modern Art, in New York City. There, he organized the famous exhibition "The Family of Man," which consisted of photographs on the theme of the brotherhood of mankind.

▲ *Edward Steichen (right) is shown here with his poet friend Carl Sandburg. Steichen and Sandburg were both 81 when this photograph was taken.*

## STEIN, Gertrude

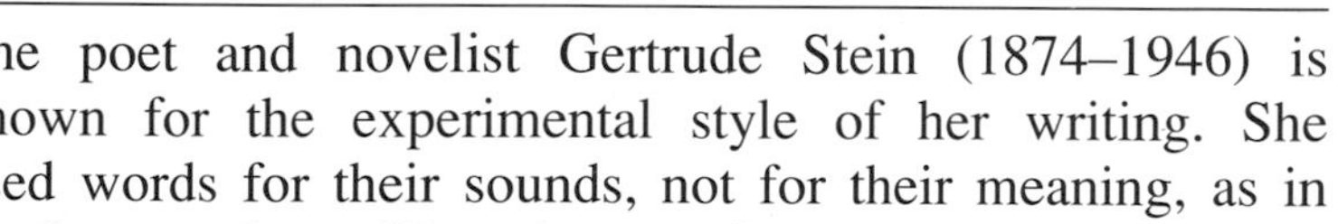

The poet and novelist Gertrude Stein (1874–1946) is known for the experimental style of her writing. She used words for their sounds, not for their meaning, as in her famous phrase "Rose is a rose is a rose is a rose."

Stein was born in Allegheny, Pennsylvania. She moved to Paris in 1903. Stein helped many artists and writers, including Pablo Picasso and Ernest Hemingway. In 1909 she published her first book, *Three Lives*, sympathetic stories of three working-class women. Her famous autobiography was titled *The Autobiography of Alice B. Toklas*. Toklas was her lifelong companion.

## STEINBECK, John

The novels of John Steinbeck (1902–1968) are noted especially for their sympathetic portrayal of poor people. In his finest book, *The Grapes of Wrath* (1939, winner of the Pulitzer Prize), Steinbeck tells the story of an Oklahoma family, the Joads, and their struggle against economic disaster and a hostile society.

Many of Steinbeck's books, including *Of Mice and Men* and *East of Eden*, are set in his native California. *Travels with Charley* was an account of a trip across the United States with his pet poodle. John Steinbeck was awarded the 1962 Nobel Prize for literature.

▼ *John Steinbeck, seen here judging a whaleboat race in his later years, experienced many of the difficulties that became the subject of his writing.*

**STEEL** *See* Iron and Steel Industry

▲ *Baron von Steuben's experience as Prussian military commander helped George Washington plan his strategy against the British.*

## STEUBEN, Baron von

The German officer Friedrich Wilhelm von Steuben (1730–1794) helped the American colonists to win independence by molding their army into an effective fighting force. Steuben was born into an elite Prussian family and while in his teens entered the Prussian Army. In 1777, on the recommendation of Benjamin Franklin, von Steuben went to America and was appointed by Congress to train the Colonial troops. At Valley Forge he formed a drill company that served as a model for other companies.

## STEVENS, Wallace

Wallace Stevens (1879–1955) is one of the most important American poets of the 20th century. Many of his poems are concerned with the relationship between reality and the imagination.

Steven's first book of poems, *Harmonium*, sold fewer than 100 copies, but it was later re-issued, and many of its poems are now considered among his finest. These include "Sea Surface Full of Clouds." His *Collected Poems* won the 1955 Pulitzer Prize for poetry.

▼ *James Stewart has built a reputation for honesty and dependability in a film career lasting more than 50 years.*

## STEVENSON, Adlai E.

Adlai Stevenson (1900–1965) was a U.S. diplomat and political leader. Born in Los Angeles, he obtained a law degree in 1926. Stevenson held a number of government posts during the 1930s and 1940s. In 1948 he was elected governor of Illinois, serving until 1953. In 1952 and 1956, Stevenson, a gifted and witty speaker, was the Democratic candidate for president. In both elections he lost to the Republican candidate, Dwight D. EISENHOWER. He later served as U.S. ambassador to the United Nations (1961–1965). Stevenson's grandfather, the first Adlai E. Stevenson, was vice president under Grover Cleveland. His son, Adlai E. Stevenson III, was a U.S. senator from Illinois.

## STEWART, James

James Stewart (1908– ) is a famous film actor. In 1939 he won the New York Film Critics' Award for best actor in *Mr. Smith Goes to Washington*. The next year he won the Academy Award for best actor in *The Philadelphia Story*. Stewart starred in four thrillers directed by Alfred HITCHCOCK—*Rope, Rear Window, The Man Who Knew Too Much,* and *Vertigo*—and in Otto Preminger's *Anatomy of a Murder*. His later films were mainly westerns.

**The great movie director Alfred Hitchcock enjoyed casting James Stewart in his famous thrillers. Stewart's decency and innocence always attracted the audience's sympathy as he faced mysterious villains and complicated plots.**

## STIEGLITZ, Alfred 

The photographer Alfred Stieglitz (1864–1946) played a major part in winning public acceptance of photography as an art. He also introduced modern art in the United States. In 1902, he helped found the Photo-Secession Group of photographers, dedicated to raising standards in this medium. His own work was technically far ahead of its time. Around the turn of the century, he was producing photographs in rain and snow and at night. Some of his finest photographs were a series of portraits of his wife, the painter Georgia O'KEEFFE.

◀ Steerage, *a 1911 photograph by Alfred Stieglitz, captures the crowded conditions poor immigrants faced on their ocean voyage to the United States.*

**Alfred Stieglitz believed in "straight" photography, relying on camera technique and good observation rather than artificial lighting. Stieglitz's studies of light and dark led to the first successful photographs of snow.**

| Shares Traded on the New York Stock Exchange (billions) | |
|---|---|
| 1982 | 16.5 |
| 1983 | 21.6 |
| 1984 | 23.1 |
| 1985 | 27.5 |
| 1986 | 35.7 |
| 1987 | 47.8 |
| 1988 | 40.4 |
| 1989 | 41.7 |
| 1990 | 39.7 |
| 1991 | 45.4 |
| 1992 | 51.4 |

## STOCK MARKETS

To raise money, business companies sell stocks. These are certificates representing shares of ownership in a company. These stock shares entitle the owner to a share in the company's profits, in the form of dividends. Stocks are bought and sold at licensed stock exchanges, or stock markets. The market value of all stocks sold on U.S. exchanges in 1990 was nearly $1.8 trillion. Of this total, the New York Stock Exchange accounted for 80 percent. Other important stock exchanges are the American (New York), Midwest (Chicago), Pacific (San Francisco and Los Angeles), Philadelphia, and Boston.

**The first New York stock market was an informal group of 24 traders in the years just after U.S. independence. They conducted business under a buttonwood tree near the present site of Wall Street in New York City.**

## STONE MOUNTAIN

Stone Mountain is the largest stone mountain in the United States. Colossal sculptures of the Confederate heroes Jefferson DAVIS, Robert E. LEE, and Stonewall JACKSON are carved in the stone on the mountain's northern face. Gutzon Borglum, the sculptor of MOUNT RUSHMORE, began the project in 1917. It was completed in 1968 by Walter Kirtland Hancock. The mountain, near Atlanta, Georgia, is part of a state park.

## STOWE, Harriet Beecher

Harriet Beecher Stowe (1811–1896) is best known as the author of the anti-slavery novel *Uncle Tom's Cabin.* The book aroused great public anger against slavery and strengthened the cause of ABOLITIONISTS. Stowe came from an intellectual family. Her father, Lyman Beecher, and brother Henry Ward Beecher both were well-known clergymen. When President Abraham Lincoln met Harriet Beecher Stowe during the Civil War, he said to her, "So you're the little lady who wrote the book that caused this great war."

▼ Uncle Tom's Cabin, *by Harriet Beecher Stowe, sold more than 2 million copies in the years before the Civil War.*

## STRAVINSKY, Igor

Igor Stravinsky (1882–1971) was one of the greatest composers of the 20th century. Born near St. Petersburg (now Leningrad), Russia, into a musical family, Stravinsky studied composition under Rimsky-Korsakov. In the first phases of his long career he wrote several ballets for the Paris-based Ballets Russes, including *The Firebird*, *Petrushka*, and *The Rite of Spring*. All of these have a colorful, strongly Russian character.

After the Russian Revolution, Stravinsky moved to France, where he wrote in a style known as "neoclassical," because of its resemblance to 18th-century music. In 1939 he settled in the United States. Among his outstanding works of this period are the opera *The Rake's Progress* and a mass, the *Requiem Canticles*.

▲ *Igor Stravinsky's modern music drew fierce criticism in his native Russia, so he settled in the United States and became a U.S. citizen.*

## STUART, J.E.B.

"Jeb" (James Ewell Brown) Stuart (1833–1864) was a Confederate cavalry officer during the CIVIL WAR.

Born in Virginia, Stuart graduated from West Point in 1854. After fighting with bravery at the First Battle of Bull Run (1961), he was made a brigadier general and given command of the cavalry of the Army of Northern Virginia. In several campaigns Stuart provided General Robert E. Lee with intelligence that helped to secure a Southern victory; Lee called him the "eyes of the army." But at Gettysburg, Stuart went off on a raid and thus failed to provide vital information—one cause of the Confederate defeat. The next year, during fighting in Virginia, he was fatally wounded.

▼ *Peter Stuyvesant, who had earlier lost a leg in the service of the Dutch West India Company, was forced to surrender the Dutch colony of New Amsterdam to the British.*

## STUYVESANT, Peter

Peter Stuyvesant (1610–1672) was governor of the Dutch colony of New Netherland from 1646 to 1664. He was a harsh ruler and opposed political and religious freedom. In 1655 he increased the size of New Netherland by taking over the colony of New Sweden, which included parts of what are now New Jersey, Pennsylvania, and Delaware. In 1664, Stuyvesant was forced to surrender New Netherland to the British, who renamed it New York. Stuyvesant spent the rest of his life on his farm, the Bouwery, in the southern part of Manhattan.

## SUBMARINES

A submarine is a ship that can travel underwater. Submarines can be used for military or scientific purposes. The first American submarine was built by David Bushnell during the American Revolution. It held one man, who used hand and foot cranks to move the craft. Robert FULTON also built a submarine with hand

▲ *The nuclear submarine U.S.S. Snook takes on supplies at Point Loma Naval Reservation in San Diego, California.*

cranks in 1801. And during the Civil War, a Confederate submarine, *The Turtle*, sank a Federal ship, but it also sank. The first practical submarine was built for the U.S. Navy in 1900 by John Holland. His submarine, the *Holland*, was powered by gas and electricity. Submarines were used in both World War I and World War II.

The first nuclear-powered submarine, the USS *Nautilus*, was launched in 1954. Today, most military submarines are nuclear-powered. Attack submarines hunt out enemy submarines. Ballistic-missile submarines can launch nuclear missiles at an enemy. Many small submarines are used to gather scientific information and samples from the ocean floor.

## SUBWAYS

Subways are underground railroads built in busy cities to help the flow of traffic. The first subway was built in London, England, in 1863. Boston was the first city in North America to build a subway. The first line opened

▶ *New York City subway riders travel through Manhattan. There would be "standing room only" on this train during the morning or evening rush hours.*

in 1897. New York City followed in 1904. The New York subway system is one of the world's largest. Subway lines connect Manhattan with Long Island and the New Jersey mainland. Other U.S. cities with subways are Chicago, San Francisco, Baltimore, Atlanta, and Washington, D.C. Montreal, Canada, and Mexico City also have subway systems.

**A woman suffrage amendment was first put before Congress in 1878. Congress threw it out, but it was reintroduced in every session of Congress for the next 40 years. In 1918 the House of Representatives approved an amendment, but it was defeated in the Senate. In 1919 the Senate finally passed the suffrage amendment, and in 1920 it was ratified as the Nineteenth Amendment. Women could at last vote.**

## SUFFRAGE

Suffrage is the right to vote. In general, only white male Protestants who owned a certain amount of property or paid a certain amount of taxes could vote in Colonial times. After independence, each state determined who could vote. Federal action began with the Fifteenth Amendment to the U.S. Constitution (1865), which tried to extend suffrage to black males. The Nineteenth Amendment (1920) extended it to women. The Twenty-fourth Amendment (1964) forbade denying suffrage for failure to pay a tax, and the Twenty-sixth Amendment (1971) lowered the minimum age to 18.

## SUGAR

Sugar is a food that provides a quick source of energy. Most sugar comes from sugarcane and sugar beets. Maple syrup, honey, milk, grapes, and corn are other sources of sugar. Sugar beets grow in temperate (mild) or cold climates. The United States is one of the leading producers of sugar beets. Sugarcane is grown in the tropical and subtropical areas of the United States.

**Leading Sugar-Producing States (by tons)**

Florida (1.2 million)

Hawaii (1 million)

Louisiana (600,000)

Minnesota (590,000)

California (500,000)

## SULLIVAN, Louis Henry

Louis Sullivan (1856–1924) is sometimes considered to be the father of modern ARCHITECTURE in the United States. He believed that a building's design should express the architect's view of nature and civilization. His own designs combined simple forms with rich decoration. His most successful period was when he was in partnership in Chicago with Dankmar Adler, from 1879 to 1895. The ten-story Wainwright Building, in St. Louis, Missouri, was Sullivan's most important design. The 16-story Guaranty (now Prudential) Building in Buffalo, New York, is another of his greatest works.

**Louis Sullivan was the first American architect to design buildings from the inside out. Other architects were busy copying traditional European styles, but Sullivan concentrated on a building's metal frame. He then designed according to the principle "Form follows function," meaning that the look of a building should reflect its purpose.**

◀ *Chicago's Auditorium, seen here in the 1890s, was one of architect Louis Sullivan's largest and most famous buildings.*

▲ *Expert surfers can reach speeds of 55 miles per hour (34 km/hr).*

## **SUPERIOR, Lake** *See* Great Lakes

## SUPREME COURT

The Supreme Court is the highest court in the United States. It is composed of a chief justice and eight associate justices, and it sits in Washington, D.C. The members are nominated by the president but must be approved by the Senate. They serve for life and can only be removed by IMPEACHMENT and conviction. The main function of the Supreme Court is to hear appeals from the decisions of lower federal courts and the highest state courts. It is often asked to rule whether a law or executive directive is in conflict with the U.S. Constitution. When the court so rules, the offending law or executive action cannot be enforced.

## SURFING

Surfing is a popular WATER SPORT. Most surfing is done with surfboards, but body surfing (using no board) is also a popular sport. Surfers paddle out into the ocean and then "ride" the front of a wave as it rushes to shore. Surfing began in Hawaii centuries before any white explorers arrived there. The Pacific state now has a rival in California as the center of the sport. The International Surfing Committee organizes championships each year.

▼ *Foul-smelling skunk cabbage, seen here in Clackamas County, Oregon, grows in swamps across the United States.*

## SWAMPS

Swamps are wetlands—areas of land that are covered with water for long periods of time. Marshes are another kind of wetland. They contain mainly grasses. Swamps, however, contain trees and tall shrubs. The EVERGLADES, in Florida, and the OKEFENOKEE Swamp, in Georgia and Florida, are mixtures of swamp and marshland.

Many kinds of plants and animals are found in swamps. The red maple is a common swamp tree in the northern United States, while the bald cypress grows in southern swamps. Other kinds of plant life include algae, moss, and wildflowers. Many species of amphibians, reptiles, birds, and fish make their homes in swamps, as do raccoons, beavers, and other mammals.

## SWEET POTATO

The sweet potato is a VEGETABLE. A type of morning glory, it is not related to either the potato or the yam. The sweet potato vine grows along the ground. The part that is eaten is the fleshy root, which is rich in vitamins A and C.

Sweet potatoes need at least four months of warm weather. In the United States, the sweet potato is grown mainly in the southern states. North Carolina, Louisiana, Texas, Virginia, and California are the leading producers. The main varieties are Yellow Jersey, Triumph, Porto Rico, and Centennial.

▲ *The edible part of a sweet potato plant is the fleshy root.*

## SWIMMING

Swimming is one of the most popular sports and recreational activities in the United States. Most cities and towns have municipal pools and organized programs for swimming instruction and water safety. The American Red Cross has a program that helps young people develop as swimmers and qualify as lifeguards. Swimming competitions are popular throughout the country. The best swimmers are chosen to represent the United States at the Summer Olympic Games. American swimmers such as Don Schollander, Mark Spitz, Matt Biondi, and Janet Evans have won many Olympic events. American men won four gold medals at the 1988 Olympics, and American women won three.

Some World Records Held by U.S. Swimmers

Men
**100-m freestyle:** Matt Biondi (0:48.42)
**200-m breaststroke:** Mike Barrowman (2:10.16)
**100-m butterfly:** Pablo Morales (0:52.84)
**200-m butterfly:** Melvin Stewart (1:55.69)
**100-m backstroke:** Jeff Rouse (0:53.86)

Women
**100-m butterfly:** Mary T. Meagher (0:57.93)
**200-m butterfly:** Mary T. Meagher (2:05.96)
**200-m breastroke:** Anita Nall (2:25.92)
**400-m freestyle:** Janet Evans (4:03.85)
**800-m freestyle:** Janet Evans (4:03:85)
**1,500-m freestyle:** Janet Evans (15:52.10)

◀ *Competitive swimmers race in lanes marked by floats. They wear bathing caps for speed and goggles to see underwater.*

## TABLE TENNIS

Table tennis is an indoor sport played by two people (singles) or by four (doubles). Players use small wooden paddles to hit a light ball back and forth across a net that divides the table. A player scores a point when his or her opponent fails to hit the ball back across the table. One player serves for five points, the other player for five points, and so on. The first player to reach 21 points, with a two-point lead, wins. National championships are organized by the United States Table Tennis Association. The International Table Tennis Federation supervises international tournaments.

## TAFT, Robert A.

Robert Alphonso Taft (1889–1953) was a U.S. political leader and a spokesman for many conservatives. Taft was the son of President William Howard TAFT. He attended Yale University and Harvard Law School before starting a law practice in Cincinnati, Ohio, in 1916. Taft was elected to the House of Representatives as a Republican in 1921 and served until 1926. He then returned to law and politics in his home state. In 1938, Taft was elected U.S. senator and was re-elected twice. In 1947 he co-sponsored the Taft-Hartley Act, which reduced the power of LABOR UNIONS. Taft tried and failed three times to gain the Republican nomination for president—in 1940, 1948, and 1952.

**Robert A. Taft argued against U.S. involvement in foreign wars until the United States entered World War II. This "isolationism" hurt Taft politically in 1948 and 1952. The Republican Party chose Thomas Dewey and Dwight Eisenhower, both convinced "internationalists," as presidential candidates instead of Taft.**

► *Busy Senator Robert A. Taft always had his local Ohio newspapers sent to his Washington, D.C., offices.*

## TAFT, William H.

William Howard Taft was the 27th president of the United States. He really wanted to be appointed to the Supreme Court rather than run for president. But, with the backing of President Theodore ROOSEVELT, he was easily elected in 1908 as the Republican candidate. Four years later, Roosevelt wanted his job back, but Taft refused to make way. Both lost the election to the Democratic Party candidate, Woodrow WILSON.

Taft was not a forceful president. He was unable to heal the breach between conservative Republicans and Roosevelt's progressive wing. In 1909, Congress passed a bill that did not reduce the overall level of tariffs (taxes on imported goods). The progressives were angered when Taft signed the bill into law, even though he claimed to favor lower tariffs. They were also upset when he fired Gifford Pinchot, the conservation-minded chief of the U.S. Forest Service and a friend of Theodore Roosevelt's.

▲ *The famous flowering cherry trees of Washington, D.C., were a gift from Japan to President Taft and the American people.*

In some respects, Taft followed Roosevelt's policies. His administration prosecuted business trusts (monopolies). John D. Rockefeller's Standard Oil Company of New Jersey was broken up while Taft was president. Telephone, telegraph, cable, and wireless companies were placed under federal regulation. Taft also took the first steps toward an annual federal budget. Eight years after leaving office, Taft was appointed chief justice of the United States the position he had always wanted. Under his leadership the Supreme Court favored business and was hostile to unions. Taft retired from the Supreme Court in February 1930.

William H. Taft
**Born:** September 15, 1857, in Cincinnati, Ohio
**Education:** Yale College
**Political party:** Republican
**Term of office:** 1909–1913
**Married:** 1886 to Helen Herron
**Died:** March 8, 1930, in Washington, D.C.

▲ *This 1859 engraving shows the wild celebration and excitement that would sweep through Tammany Hall on election night.*

## TAMMANY HALL

Tammany Hall was the name given to the Democratic Party leadership that usually controlled New York City's government between 1854 and 1933. The Tammany Society originally was national in scope and opposed the Federalist Party in the early days of the republic. It soon became confined to New York, where its leaders included Aaron Burr and Martin Van Buren. Under William Marcy ("Boss") Tweed, Tammany became a byword for political corruption. Shortly after 1961, Manhattan's Democrats dropped the name.

## TAXES

In the United States, taxes are imposed by the local, state, and federal governments and are used to pay for most services. The major forms of taxation are taxes on income, sales, and property. The income tax is most commonly imposed by the federal and state governments, the sales tax by the states, and the property tax by local governments. In 1990 the federal, state, and local governments took in a total of $1,134 billion in taxes, or $4,559 per person. Of this amount, income taxes accounted for 61 percent, sales taxes 20 percent, and property taxes 14 percent. The federal government took in 56 percent, the states 26 percent, and the localities 18 percent. Taxes have never been popular. The major cause of the American Revolution was taxation imposed on the colonies by Great Britain in the 1700s.

▼ *The federal government uses taxes (left) to raise most of the money it needs to spend on its various projects (right).*

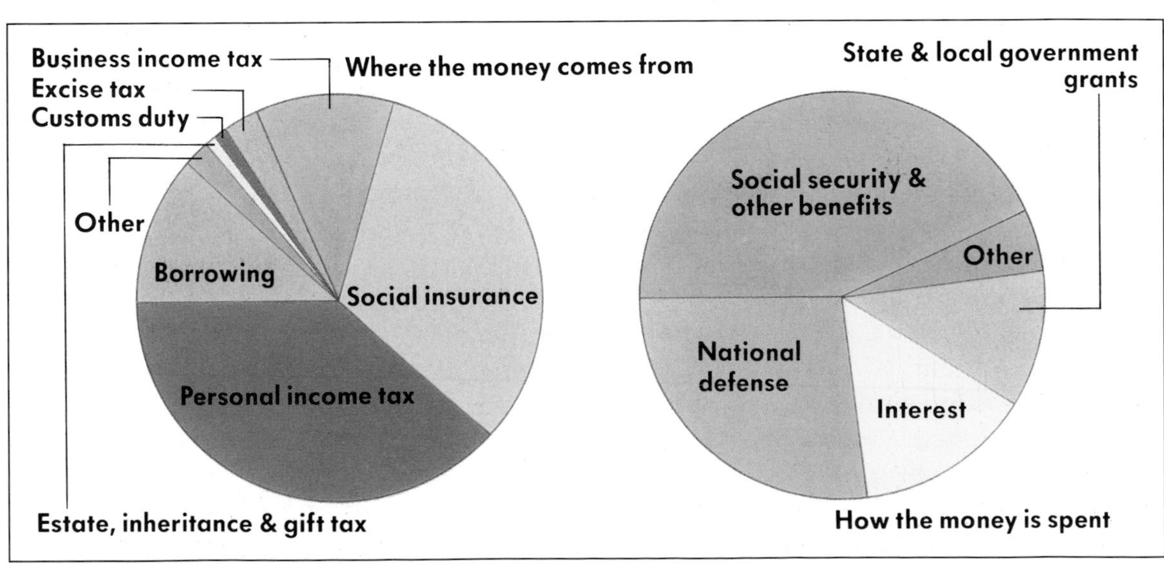

## TAYLOR, Zachary

Zachary Taylor was the 12th president of the United States. He was elected president in 1848 because he was a military hero, but he died just 16 months after taking office.

Born in Virginia, Taylor joined the army in 1808 and served for 40 years. He fought in the WAR OF 1812 and in the INDIAN WARS and was promoted to brigadier general after defeating the SEMINOLE INDIANS in southern Florida. In the MEXICAN WAR, Taylor led his troops to several notable victories. His defeat of the much larger Mexican forces at Buena Vista made him a national hero. He was popular with his men, and his nickname was Old Rough and Ready.

Although Taylor had never joined a political party—or even voted—the Whigs made him their presidential candidate in 1848. The Democratic Party was split, and Taylor won the election.

▲ *The California Gold Rush of 1849 was a major event during Zachary Taylor's term of office. Thousands of prospectors struggled across the country to seek their fortune.*

The main problem Taylor faced as president was the slavery issue. California and New Mexico had been acquired when the United States won the Mexican War. Taylor said the people there, rather than Congress, should decide whether or not to allow slavery. California then adopted a constitution prohibiting slavery. When Taylor asked Congress to admit California as a state, the South was angered because its admission would put the slave states in the minority. The South was especially angry because Taylor was a Southerner. Before the issue was decided by what became known as the Compromise of 1850, Taylor suddenly died.

**Zachary Taylor**
**Born:** November 24, 1784, near Barboursville, Virgina
**Education:** Little formal education
**Political party:** Whig
**Term of office:** 1849–1850
**Married:** 1810 to Margaret Smith
**Died:** July 9, 1850, in Washington, D.C.

▲ *During the War of 1812, British troops fought with Tecumseh's Indian alliance against the U.S. Army.*

## TECUMSEH

Tecumseh (1768–1813) was a great chief of the Shawnee Indians. He tried to unite the Indian tribes of the Ohio River valley in the fight against white settlers. In 1811, however, Tecumseh's brother, the Shawnee prophet, was defeated in the Battle of Tippecanoe in Indiana Territory. This ended Indian resistance. During the War of 1812, Tecumseh and his warriors fought alongside the British against American forces. He was killed during the Battle of the Thames, in Ontario, Canada, in 1813.

## TELEGRAPH

The telegraph was the first device to use electricity to send messages. It was invented in 1837 by Samuel F. B. MORSE in the United States and Sir Charles Wheatstone and Sir William F. Cooke in Great Britain. The wires strung by the Western Union Telegraph Company in the 1850s were vital in the westward expansion of the United States. Communication with Europe was enhanced when the first cable across the Atlantic Ocean became permanently operational in 1866. Later services by telegraph companies have included teletype, telex, electronic mail, facsimile reproduction, and microwave transmissions.

**Important Dates in the History of the Telegraph**

**1837** Samuel F. B. Morse demonstrates his telegraph system.
**1843** Congress pays Morse $30,000 to link Washington, D.C., with Baltimore.
**1844** Telegraph news of the presidential nomination reaches Washington 90 minutes before the same news by train.
**1850s** The Western Union Company builds telegraph lines along new train routes.
**1861** Transcontinental link achieved by Western Union.
**1866** Transatlantic cable laid on the floor of the Atlantic Ocean.
**1874** Thomas A. Edison develops a system to send four messages at once.

► *An 1868 woodcut shows that congressional reporters had already come to rely on the telegraph to file their stories.*

## TELEPHONE

A telephone is an instrument that transmits and receives sound through electricity and magnetism. Sounds entering a telephone are converted into electrical impulses that travel along wires. The impulses are reconverted into sounds at the other telephone. Some telephones, such as the cellular (mobile) phones used in automobiles and ships, are cordless. They use radio waves and magnetism to transmit sound. The telephone was invented by Alexander Graham BELL in Boston in 1876. About 95 percent of all households in the United States have telephones. On an average business day Americans talk on the phone for 9.5 billion minutes.

▲ *Modern telephone equipment undergoes many engineering tests before it can be sold.*

◀ *By 1908 even small towns such as Hamburg, New York, had their own telephone exchanges.*

## TELESCOPE *See* Observatories

## TELEVISION

Television has become the most popular form of communication and entertainment in the United States. About 98 percent of all households have at least one television set, and the average household has two sets. Almost half of all households subscribe to cable systems, in addition to receiving over-the-air telecasting. There are almost 1,500 television stations in the United States. Some are educational stations belonging to the nonprofit Public Broadcasting Service (PBS). Most are commercial businesses relying on advertising to make a profit. The vast majority of these receive most of their programming from the "Big Three" networks—NBC, CBS, and ABC. A significant number,

▼ *More than 600 million television viewers around the world watched the first moon landing on July 20, 1969.*

► *Hollywood star Danny DeVito joins Big Bird, Ernie, and the rest of the* Sesame Street *regulars.*

Some Dates in U.S. Television History

**1929** Vladimir Zworykin demonstrates a workable television system.
**1939** First commercial broadcast (NBC).
**1951** First coast-to-coast broadcast.
**1953** Color television introduced.
**1960** First televised presidential debates (Kennedy vs. Nixon).
**1969** The world watches the first moon landing.
**1979** Congress allows television broadcasts of its sessions.

however, are independent stations. And many smaller networks now reach people across the United States on cable systems.

Vladimir ZWORYKIN is credited with demonstrating the first practical television set in 1929. In the years from 1945 to 1960, the number of television sets in the United States rose from 10,000 to 60 million.

Television is not only an entertainment medium. Televison cameras aboard spacecraft transmit information about the earth, moon, and planets. Closed circuit television is used in business meetings and in operating rooms in hospitals.

▼ *Tom Brokaw is the main presenter, or anchorman, of the NBC Nightly News.*

Television in the United States – Some Facts

- 98 percent of all households have at least one television set.
- Two thirds of American households have two or more television sets.
- Only 2 percent of households have only black-and-white television sets.
- More than 80 million Americans watch some major television programs such as the Superbowl.
- More than 60 percent of all households receive cable television channels.
- The largest ever television audience – 1.5 billion people worldwide – watched the "Live Aid" concert in 1985.
- Roughly 60 percent of all households have videocassette recorders (VCRs).
- There are more than 1,000 commercial television stations in the United States.
- American children watch an average of 30 hours of television each week.

## TELLER, Edward

Edward Teller (1908– ) is an important American physicist. He is best known for his work on nuclear fusion, and he is sometimes called the "father of the hydrogen bomb." Teller was born in Hungary and moved to the United States in the 1930s. During World War II he helped develop the atomic bomb. After the war, he began working on nuclear fusion and was responsible for the development of the hydrogen bomb in 1952. Teller taught at many American universities, including the University of California. In 1962 he received the Atomic Energy Commission's Fermi Award.

▲ *Much of Edward Teller's later work was concerned with the theory of nuclear fission and its application to peaceful uses.*

## TEMPLE, Shirley

Shirley Temple (1928– ) was the most famous child star in the history of motion pictures. Born in Santa Monica, California, she made her first movie when she was only three. Six years later, she became a star in *Stand Up and Cheer*. Shirley Temple appeared in about two dozen movies including *Heidi, Rebecca of Sunnybrook Farm*, and *The Little Princess*. Many were musicals in which she sang and danced. She retired in 1949. During the 1960s and 1970s, as Shirley Temple Black, she became a diplomat. She served as a U.S. delegate to the United Nations, U.S. ambassador to Ghana, and U.S. chief of protocol.

◀ *Shirley Temple's innocent appeal won her many movie parts. She also appeared in advertisements, such as this one for Sunfreze ice cream.*

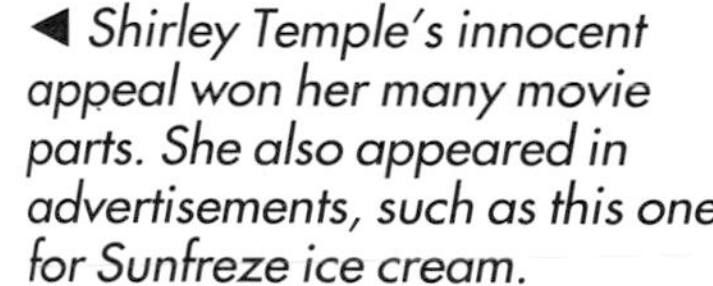

**Shirley Temple received an Academy Award in 1934, when she was only six years old. The award honored her because "she brought more happiness to millions of children and millions of grownups than any other child in the history of the world."**

In many ways the state of Tennessee is the crossroads of the South. It lies near the center of the Old Confederacy and is bordered by eight states. It was a battleground between the North and South in the CIVIL WAR. And Tennessee is both the birthplace of the blues and the capital of country and western music.

Tennessee stretches westward from the Blue Ridge Range of the Appalachian Mountains to the Mississippi River. The development of eastern Tennessee has been shaped by its coal mines and by the Tennessee Valley Authority. This federal project tamed the Tennessee River and provides plentiful power for industry. Here, too, is Oak Ridge, a federal laboratory that produced enriched uranium for the first atomic weapons. It remains an important center for nuclear research.

Nashville, the state capital, is in central Tennessee. It is the home of the Country Music Hall of Fame and Museum and of the famed Grand Ole Opry concert hall—now located in "Opryland, U.S.A.," an amusement park. Near Nashville are two large motor vehicle plants

**Tennessee**
**Capital:** Nashville
**Area:** 42,146 sq mi (109,158 km$^2$). Rank: 36th
**Population:** 4,877,185 (1990). Rank: 17th
**Statehood:** June 1, 1796
**Principal rivers:** Tennessee, Mississippi
**Highest point:** Clingmans Dome, 6,643 ft (2,025 m)
**Motto:** Agriculture and Commerce
**Song:** "The Tennessee Waltz"

▲ *American lotus blossoms cover the water at Reelfoot Lake State Park.*

◄ The Memphis Queen, *an old-style Mississippi riverboat, serves the modern riverfront district in Memphis.*

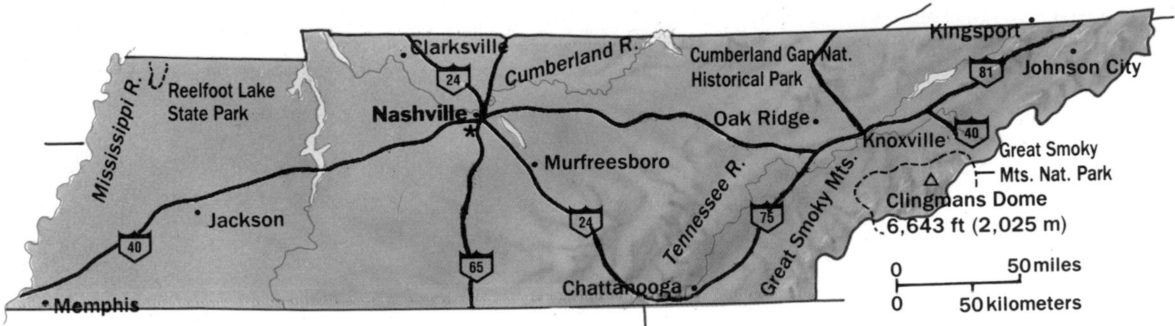


built in recent years. Farms in this region produce tobacco, cattle, and the Tennessee walking horse.

The rich bottom land of western Tennessee, adjoining the Mississippi, yields soybeans and cotton. MEMPHIS, a major port, lies along the river. Tourists come to see Beale Street, the home of the blues and of blues composer W. C. HANDY. They also visit Graceland, Elvis PRESLEY's mansion.

The first permanent settlement by Europeans began in the 1760s, and Tennessee became a state in 1796.

Places of Interest

- The Grand Ole Opry House, near Nashville, is widely considered the home of country music.
- The Cumberland Gap National Historical Park is the place where Kentucky, Virginia, and Tennessee meet.
- The home of President Andrew Jackson, The Hermitage, is located near Nashville.
- Graceland, the former home of Elvis Presley, is a vast estate in Memphis.

▼ *Clouds sweep over the crest of the Great Smokies at the Cumberland Gap National Historical Park.*

▲ *Helen Wills Moody dominated women's tennis tournaments in the 1920s and early 1930s.*

▼ *Bill Tilden won seven U.S. Open singles titles in the 1920s.*

## TENNIS

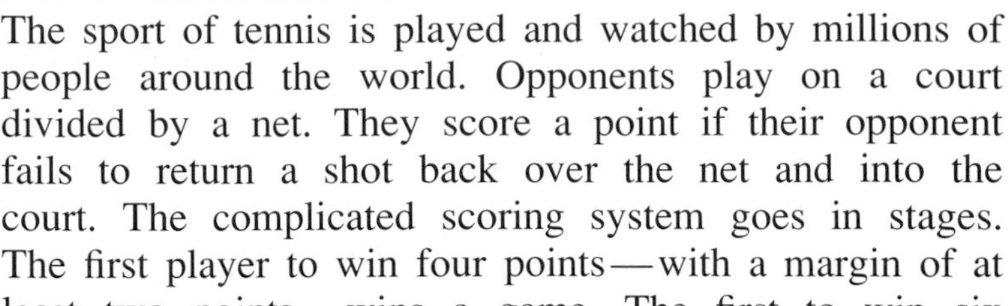

The sport of tennis is played and watched by millions of people around the world. Opponents play on a court divided by a net. They score a point if their opponent fails to return a shot back over the net and into the court. The complicated scoring system goes in stages. The first player to win four points—with a margin of at least two points—wins a game. The first to win six games—again with a margin of at least two—wins a set. Matches are the best of three or five sets.

The United States Tennis Association organizes the sport nationally. Many professional tournaments are managed by the International Tennis Federation and the Association of Tennis Professionals. American players play in these tournaments and sometimes represent their country in the Davis Cup team competition.

U.S. Open Champions

| Men's Singles | | Women's Singles |
|---|---|---|
| Year | Name | Name |
| 1993 | Pete Sampras | Steffi Graf |
| 1992 | Stefan Edberg | Monica Seles |
| 1991 | Stefan Edberg | Monica Seles |
| 1990 | Pete Sampras | Gabriela Sabatini |
| 1989 | Boris Becker | Steffi Graf |
| 1988 | Mats Wilander | Steffi Graf |
| 1987 | Ivan Lendl | Martina Navratilova |
| 1986 | Ivan Lendl | Martina Navratilova |
| 1985 | Ivan Lendl | Hana Mandlikova |
| 1984 | John McEnroe | Martina Navratilova |
| 1983 | Jimmy Connors | Martina Navratilova |

► *Martina Navratilova's dedication and athletic style made her almost unbeatable in the 1980s.*

## TERRORISM

Terrorism is the use of violence to gain some goal. Today acts of terrorism happen all over the world. Terrorist groups hijack airplanes, assassinate people, kidnap hostages, and plant bombs. In 1979, dozens of Americans were taken hostage at the U.S. Embassy in Iran. In 1988, a Pan-American flight with 259 people aboard was blown up. In 1993, terrorists set off a bomb in one of the twin towers of the World Trade Center in New York City. Most countries try not to deal with those who commit acts of terrorism. They feel that if they give in to terrorist demands, it will only encourage other terrorists to commit violence.

The Most Common Forms of International Terrorism

1. Bombing
2. Arson
3. Armed attack
4. Kidnapping
5. Assault
6. Sabotage
7. Extortion
8. Non-air hijacking
9. Skyjacking
10. Theft

◀ *Modern equipment, such as this X-ray screen at Honolulu Airport, guards against terrorist weapons being smuggled onto aircraft.*

**Terrorists get their name because they rely on surprise to create fear. They attack people who cannot fight back. In 1983, terrorists bombed the headquarters of an international peacekeeping force in Lebanon. Nearly 200 American and French soldiers were killed; many had been asleep in their barracks.**

## TESLA, Nikola

Nikola Tesla (1856–1943) was a famous physicist, electrical engineer, and inventor. He was born in Smiljan in what is now Yugoslavia and moved to the United States in 1884. He had already invented an electric motor that produced alternating current. By 1888 he had patented the invention and sold his idea to George WESTINGHOUSE, who used it profitably in his own company. In 1900, Tesla set up his own laboratory, where he worked as an inventor and researcher for the rest of his life. He specialized in high-voltage and high-frequency inventions to be used in industry, communications, and lighting.

**Nikola Tesla improved on a design by Thomas Edison to invent a machine to produce hydroelectric power from flowing water. The water power of Niagara Falls was harnessed under Tesla's system in 1895.**

Texas is the second largest state in the United States. Only Alaska is larger.

In 1901, the eruption of a huge gusher uncovered one of the most productive oil fields in the world. Today Texas leads all other states in the production of its most important natural resources—petroleum and natural gas. Texas also leads all states in livestock and cotton.

The HOUSTON metropolitan area is the nation's leader in the manufacture of petrochemicals and oil field equipment. It also has the largest U.S. steelworks. The port of Houston is one of the country's busiest. DALLAS is the banking center of the Southwest and has more than 200 insurance companies. The Dallas–Fort Worth area is a center for manufacturing, aerospace and electronics equipment.

Each area of the state has its special attractions. In SAN ANTONIO, a center of the state's large Hispanic population, is the Alamo. Houston has the Johnson Space Center, "mission control" for U.S. manned space flights. A favorite with fishermen, sailors, and sun worshipers is Padre Island, a 117-mile-long (189-km) Gulf coast sandbar. Western Texas has the Big Bend and Guadalupe Mountains national parks.

Six flags have flown over Texas since Spanish explorers arrived in 1519. These were the flags of Spain, France, Mexico, the Republic of Texas, the United States, and the Confederacy. American colonists won independence from Mexico in 1836 and created a republic before joining the United States in 1845.

▲ *Palm trees line the downtown streets of Galveston, a busy port on the Gulf of Mexico.*

► *Farm hands load some of the winter cabbage crop at McAllen in southern Texas.*

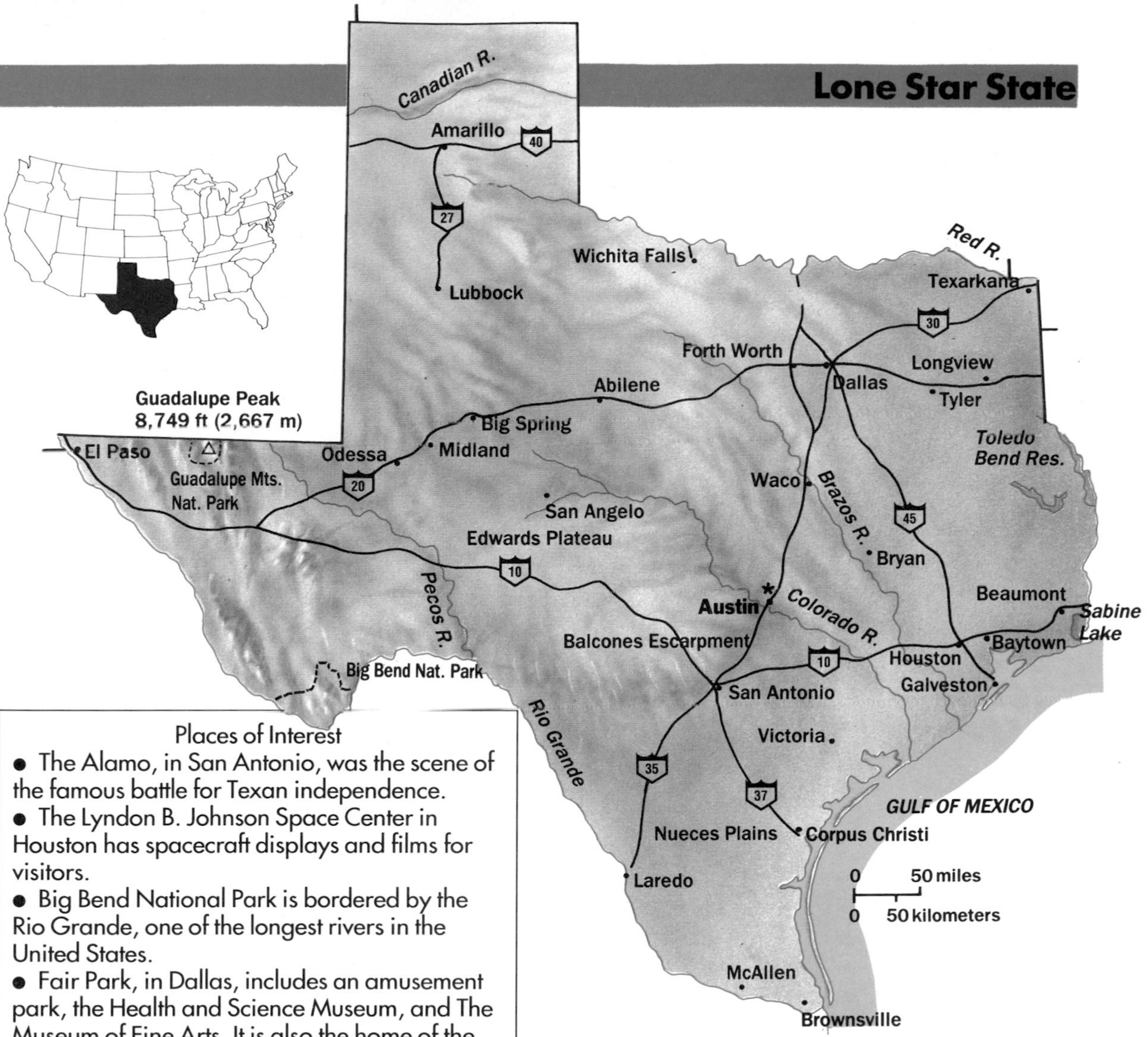

Canadian R.
Amarillo
40
27
Lubbock
Wichita Falls
Red R.
Texarkana
30
Forth Worth
Longview
Dallas
Tyler
Abilene
Guadalupe Peak
8,749 ft (2,667 m)
Big Spring
Toledo Bend Res.
El Paso
Odessa
Midland
Guadalupe Mts. Nat. Park
20
Waco
Brazos R.
San Angelo
Edwards Plateau
45
Bryan
10
Pecos R.
Austin
Colorado R.
Beaumont
Sabine Lake
Balcones Escarpment
Baytown
Houston
10
Big Bend Nat. Park
Galveston
San Antonio
Rio Grande
Victoria
35
37
GULF OF MEXICO
Nueces Plains
Corpus Christi
Laredo
0 50 miles
0 50 kilometers
McAllen
Brownsville

Places of Interest

- The Alamo, in San Antonio, was the scene of the famous battle for Texan independence.
- The Lyndon B. Johnson Space Center in Houston has spacecraft displays and films for visitors.
- Big Bend National Park is bordered by the Rio Grande, one of the longest rivers in the United States.
- Fair Park, in Dallas, includes an amusement park, the Health and Science Museum, and The Museum of Fine Arts. It is also the home of the State Fair of Texas.

◀ *The rocky peaks of the Chisos Mountains tower over Big Bend National Park, located along the Rio Grande.*

Texas

**Capital:** Austin
**Area:** 268,601 sq mi (695,676 km$^2$). Rank: 2nd
**Population:** 16,986,510 (1990). Rank: 3rd
**Statehood:** December 29, 1845
**Principal rivers:** Rio Grande, Red, Brazos
**Highest point:** Guadalupe Peak, 8,751 ft (2,667 m)
**Motto:** Friendship
**Song:** "Texas, Our Texas"

▲ *Wampanoag Indians joined the Pilgrims for the first Thanksgiving. Without Indian advice on farming and fishing, the Plymouth settlement would not have survived.*

**The first Thanksgiving in New England was celebrated in 1621. It lasted three days and the food was eaten outdoors. The hunters had shot geese, turkeys, and ducks. The menu also included eel, clams, leeks, plums, and corn bread. Some Indians attended the feast, bringing deer meat to add to the celebration.**

## THANKSGIVING DAY

Thanksgiving Day is a national HOLIDAY in the United States and Canada. Families get together for a large dinner to give thanks for the blessings of the past year. It began as a harvest festival, like those celebrated around the world. The first Thanksgiving was in 1621, when the Pilgrims in PLYMOUTH COLONY gave thanks to God for their first corn harvest. After 1630 the custom slowly spread throughout New England and eventually around the rest of North America. In 1863, President Abraham Lincoln proclaimed Thanksgiving a national holiday. It was held on the last Thursday of November in the United States. In 1941 it was officially changed to the fourth Thursday in November. In Canada it is held on the second Monday in October. For the first Thanksgiving the Indians brought wild turkeys, and turkey is still traditionally served today.

## THEATER

Theater has been a popular form of entertainment in North America since the mid-1700s. During much of the 19th century, every major city had its resident company. Traveling companies reached small communities as well. Most of the productions were crude melodramas, minstrel shows, or burlesque (musical parodies). Some were imports with English casts. However, there were also outstanding American actors such as Edwin Booth, Charlotte Cushman, and Edwin Forrest.

Musical comedies first appeared in the early 1900s. For serious drama, the American theater still relied on European playwrights, such as Henrik Ibsen and George Bernard Shaw. The period since the 1920s, however, has produced major American dramatists, especially Eugene O'NEILL, Tennessee WILLIAMS, and Arthur MILLER.

The center of the American theater is BROADWAY in New York City, where big, expensive productions are mounted. Some of the most interesting productions originate "off-Broadway" or "off-off Broadway"—smaller theaters elsewhere in Manhattan. In addition, more than 50 major institutions and countless smaller companies bring live theater to audiences outside New York. Almost every large city has a resident company. Summer and community theater, and college and university productions, are held not only in playhouses but also in barns, tents, and the open air.

**Longest-Running Plays on Broadway**

| Play | Performances |
|---|---|
| Chorus Line | 6,137 |
| Oh, Calcutta (revival) | 5,959 |
| *Cats | 4,485 |
| 42nd Street | 3,486 |
| Grease | 3,388 |
| Fiddler on the Roof | 3,242 |
| Life with Father | 3,224 |
| Tobacco Road | 3,182 |
| Hello Dolly | 2,844 |
| My Fair Lady | 2,717 |
| Annie | 2,377 |
| Man of La Mancha | 2,328 |
| Abie's Irish Rose | 2,327 |
| Oklahoma! | 2,212 |
| *Les Miserables | 2,572 |

*still running May 1994

## THIRTEEN COLONIES 

The Thirteen Colonies were the British colonies in North America that declared their independence in 1776 and became, after the American REVOLUTION, the original thirteen states of the Union. They were Connecticut, Delaware, Georgia, Maryland, Massachusetts, New Hampshire, New Jersey, New York, North Carolina, Pennsylvania, Rhode Island, South Carolina, and Virginia.

The colonies were founded in various ways. Some, such as Virginia (the oldest, founded in 1607) and the Massachusetts Bay Colony, were founded and financed by groups of investors.

In time, these were taken over by the British Crown, becoming royal colonies. Others, such as Maryland and Pennsylvania, were proprietary colonies, established by a single individual who had been granted the land by the king. Still others, such as Rhode Island and Connecticut, were founded by colonists who moved away from established colonies.

Some of the colonies had been founded for the purpose of providing religious freedom—for Puritans (Massachusetts), for Catholics (Maryland), and for Quakers (Pennsylvania). Others, such as Virginia and New York (originally New Netherland), were settled by people seeking greater prosperity.

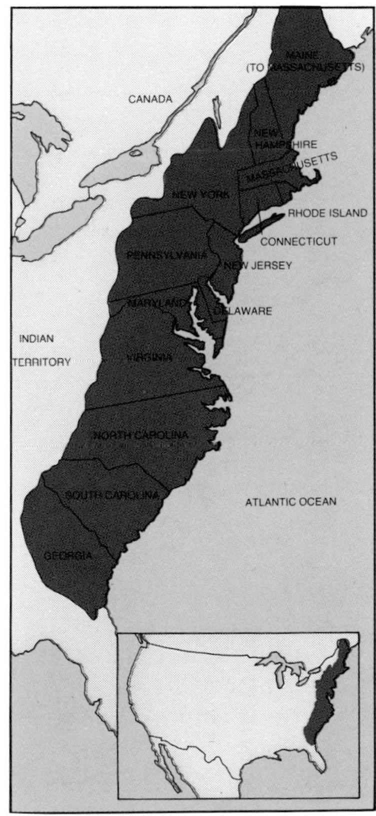


▲ *The Thirteen Colonies stretched 1,300 miles (2,100 km) down the Atlantic coast and westward as far as the Appalachians.*

On the eve of the Revolution the population of the Thirteen Colonies was 2.5 million. The largest city was Philadelphia, with a population of nearly 54,000.

## THOREAU, Henry David

▲ *Henry David Thoreau's masterpiece,* Walden, *continues to inspire readers to value nature and individuality.*

Henry David Thoreau (1817–1862) was an important thinker and author of the 1800s. His writings have had a great influence on American thought.

Thoreau was born in Concord, Massachusetts, where he remained for most of his life. There he became friendly with the writer Ralph Waldo EMERSON. Emerson gave Thoreau some land near Concord. For two years (1845–1847), he lived alone there, in a cabin on Walden Pond. Thoreau kept a journal, which provided material for his best-known book, *Walden; or, Life in the Woods*. It told about his belief in the importance of an individual's conscience and in living a simple life close to nature.

Thoreau also had strong political convictions. He opposed the Mexican War, and refused to pay the poll tax as a protest against slavery, which was an issue in the War. He spent a night in jail as a result. He explained his views in an essay entitled "Civil Disobedience." Thoreau was an ABOLITIONIST. In the years before the Civil War, he helped slaves make their way to freedom by way of the UNDERGROUND RAILROAD.

## THURBER, James

**James Thurber continued writing until his death, but his work with cartoons ended as his eyesight failed. He was blind for the last ten years of his life.**

James Thurber (1894–1961) was one of America's greatest humorists. He wrote short stories and essays, many of them illustrated with his own comical drawings. Thurber was born in Columbus, Ohio. In 1927, after moving to New York City, he began writing for the *New Yorker* magazine. He often illustrated his own stories with simple line drawings that achieved wonderfully comical effects in a few strokes.

Some of the characters in Thurber's books, such as in *My Life and Times*, are based on Thurber's own family. His most famous character, though, is the fictional Walter Mitty, who appeared in the story "The Secret Life of Walter Mitty." This character escapes into various fantasy worlds in which he is always the hero—until his wife wakes him up to do some household chores. Thurber also wrote a children's story, *The 13 Clocks*.

## TOBACCO

The United States is the second most important tobacco-producing country, after China. North Carolina is the principal tobacco-growing state. Other states include Kentucky, South Carolina, Virginia, Tennessee, and Georgia. The leaves of the tobacco plant are first *cured* (dried) and then used mainly in cigarettes. Tobacco is also used in cigars, pipe tobacco, chewing tobacco, and snuff.

American Indians smoked tobacco as a sacred herb long before the arrival of European settlers. In the early 1600s the colonists of Virginia and Maryland began growing tobacco to sell. It was North America's first commercial crop. After the American Revolution, other states also began producing it, mainly to sell to England.

▲ *Clusters of star-shaped blossoms identify a tobacco plant. Its matured leaves are cured (dried) for use in cigarettes, cigars, and pipe tobacco.*

◀ *A tornado descends on Mitchell, Nebraska. "Twisters" have wind speeds of up to 300 miles per hour (500 km/hr).*

## TORNADO

A tornado is the most violent windstorm on earth. Tornadoes are much stronger and more frequent in the United States than elsewhere in the world. About 700 to 800 are reported every year in the country. They rarely occur west of the Rockies. They strike most often in the tornado belt of the Great Plains and the Southeast, particularly western Texas, Oklahoma, Arkansas, Missouri, and Kansas. Tornadoes develop from severe thunderstorms, usually in the spring (especially May) during the late afternoon. The winds are so fierce that they can lift railroad cars into the air and cause small buildings to explode. Tornadoes often arrive with almost no warning. The National Weather Service issues tornado warnings when possible.

**The National Weather Service advises people to open doors and windows in their houses before taking shelter from an approaching tornado. This is because tornadoes have low air pressure and a house with normal air pressure (locked in behind closed doors and windows) can sometimes explode.**

*▼ Toronto's CN Tower, at 1,821 ft (555 m), is the world's tallest self-supporting structure.*

## TORONTO 

Toronto is the capital of the Canadian province of Ontario. With a population of over 700,000, it is the second largest city in Canada, after Montreal. Toronto is an important financial, manufacturing, and cultural center. Most of Canada's major newspapers, publishing houses, banks, insurance companies, and leading manufacturing companies are located in the city. It owes its importance to its location on the shore of Lake Ontario. The city's most important products are textiles, fabricated metals, machinery, chemicals, transportation equipment, and processed foods. Toronto's Lester B. Pearson Airport is the busiest in Canada. The CN Tower in the heart of Toronto is the highest (1,815 feet, or 553 m) freestanding structure in the world.

Toronto began as a French and Iroquois fur trading post in the early 1700s. It became York, and then Toronto, after the British gained control of Canada. It became the capital of the colony of Upper Canada, which became the province of Ontario after the Canadian Confederation was established in 1867.

## TRACK AND FIELD 

**International track events are nearly all measured over metric distances — 100 meters, 400 meters, and so forth. The only exception is the mile, considered the ultimate distance by many track observers.**

Track and field consists of athletic events that involve running, jumping, and throwing. Track, or running,

*► U.S. hurdler Edwin Moses dominated the 400-m hurdles from 1976 to 1988, setting the world record and winning two gold and one silver Olympic medals.*

events are foot races along an oval track that is usually 400 meters (440 yards) long. The shortest, called sprints, are run at top speed for less than one lap of the track. Longer events, up to 30,000 meters (18.6 miles), call for strategy and stamina. Field events are usually held inside the track area. They involve throwing and jumping. The pole vault, the long jump, the high jump, the shot put, the discus throw, and the javelin throw are field events. The longest-standing track-and-field world record—8.9 meters (more than 29 feet) for the long jump—was set by American Bob Beamon at the 1968 Olympics. The International Amateur Athletic Federation governs track and field and monitors world records.

## TRADE

Trade is the exchange—or buying and selling—of goods and services. There are two kinds of trade, domestic and foreign. Domestic trade takes place within a country. Foreign trade takes place between countries.

Domestic trade within the United States totals about $3.5 trillion each year. Retail sales, in such places as supermarkets and department stores, account for more than half of the trade. Wholesale trade accounts for just under one half.

In 1991, the United States' foreign trade amounted to $908.8 billion. It sold $421.7 billion worth of goods to other countries, and it bought $487.1 billion worth. American exports include agricultural goods, such as corn, wheat, and soybeans, and manufactured goods, such as computers, airplanes, and machinery. United States imports include petroleum, clothing, automobiles, and such items as television sets and videocassette recorders.

The difference between what a country exports and what it imports is called the trade balance. The United States has long had a trade deficit. This means that it buys more from other countries than it sells.

## TREES

More than 1,000 kinds of trees grow in the United States. One of the greatest forest belts in the world once covered much of the eastern United States. Many of the trees have been cut down, but more than 200 kinds of broadleaf trees and about 30 kinds of needleleaf trees

▼ *Jackie Joyner-Kersee of the United States won the women's long jump at the 1988 Olympics in Seoul, South Korea.*

U.S. Trading Partners
($ billion: 1991)

Exporters to U.S.
1. Japan (91.5)
2. Canada (91.1)
3. Germany (26.1)
4. Taiwan (23.0)
5. China (19.0)
6. South Korea (17.0)
7. Italy (11.8)

Importers of U.S. Goods
1. Canada (85.1)
2. Japan (48.1)
3. Germany (21.3)
4. South Korea (15.6)
5. Taiwan (13.2)
6. Singapore (8.8)
7. Italy (8.6)
8. Hong Kong (8.1)

► *Evergreens get their name because they keep their green needles, even in winter.*

are still found there. Tropical trees such as the PALM, mahogany, cypress, and mangrove grow near the Gulf of Mexico. Needle-leaf forests with some broadleaf trees run through the western mountains. The forests of the West Coast are one of North America's last major sources of lumber (see LUMBER INDUSTRY.)

Familiar broadleaf trees of the United States include the ash, beech, elm, holly, MAPLE, OAK, walnut, and willow. Familiar U.S. needle-leaf trees include the cedar, fir, hemlock, juniper, PINE, redwood, and spruce. The world's largest tree, the SEQUOIA, and the world's oldest tree, the BRISTLECONE PINE, are found in the United States.

Valuable products from trees include lumber and wood pulp and many kinds of FRUITS and nuts.

Common Trees in North American Forest Regions

**Northern:** spruces, firs, eastern white pine, oaks, sugar maple, American beech, American elm
**Southeastern:** pines, magnolias, tupelos, cedar elm, pecan, hickories, oaks
**Central:** black walnut, American sycamore, yellow poplar, oaks, maples, ashes
**Rockies:** pines (Ponderosa, limber, pinyon), spruces, firs, western larch, quaking aspen, junipers
**Subtropical:** mahogany, mangroves, sapodilla, palms
**Pacific Coast:** firs, hemlocks, cedars, pines, western larch, Redwood, giant sequoia, quaking aspen, oaks, bigleaf maple, Oregon ash

▼ *Some common North American trees.*

▲ *Eighteen-wheelers carry refrigerated meat, fish, and dairy products to major U.S. cities nearly every day.*

## TRUCKS

Trucks are an important way of transporting goods. Each year more than $113 billion is spent in the United States on sending cargo by truck. There are many kinds of trucks. Each has a different purpose. A dump truck, for example, has a cargo hold that tilts back to allow sand or gravel to flow out easily. Industry is the largest user of trucks in the United States. Farms also use trucks for transportation and other agricultural uses. The government uses trucks, such as the 750,000 trucks used by the Postal Service. About 45 million trucks are registered in the United States.

## TRUDEAU, Pierre Elliott

Pierre Trudeau (1919– ) was prime minister of Canada from 1968 to 1979 and from 1980 to 1984. His colorful personality and progressive ideas made him a popular prime minister. A Liberal, Trudeau worked hard to preserve national unity. He resisted demands for Quebec, the French-speaking province, to become separate from Canada. A French Canadian himself, Trudeau took a firm stand against separatist terrorists. Other problems he had to deal with were rising prices and unemployment. Trudeau's greatest achievement was reforming the Canadian constitution and obtaining formal independence from the British Parliament.

▼ *Prime Minister Pierre Trudeau's ease with Canada's English and French traditions earned him a national following.*

# TRUMAN, Harry S.

Harry S. Truman
**Born:** May 8, 1884, in Lamar, Missouri
**Education:** High school; law studies in Kansas City
**Political party:** Democratic
**Term of office:** 1945–1953
**Married:** 1919 to Elizabeth Wallace
**Died:** December 26, 1972, in Kansas City, Missouri

Harry S. Truman was the 33rd president of the United States. He served from 1945 to 1953. During this period, WORLD WAR II ended and the KOREAN WAR began. And a long struggle between the United States and the Soviet Union, called the COLD WAR, also began.

Truman, a Democrat, was vice president when President Franklin D. ROOSEVELT died in office. His first major decision as president was to authorize dropping the new atomic bomb on Japan, an action that quickly ended World War II. By 1947, Truman was determined to halt Soviet expansion. The Truman Doctrine promised U.S. aid to any country resisting communism. The Marshall Plan provided U.S. aid to help Europe recover from the war.

Truman won the 1948 election even though most experts said he would lose. He then proposed a "Fair Deal" program of liberal reforms, many of which were blocked by Congress. Truman also ended segregation (the separation of the races) in the armed forces.

► *President Harry S. Truman joined wartime allies Winston Churchill of Great Britain and Joseph Stalin of the Soviet Union at the Potsdam Conference in 1945.*

▼ *Harry S. Truman enjoyed surprising the newspaper polls when he defeated Thomas E. Dewey in the 1948 presidential election.*

In April 1949, the United States and 11 other countries established the NORTH ATLANTIC TREATY ORGANIZATION (NATO), a military alliance. This alliance committed the United States to fight in Europe should the need arise.

In 1950, Truman sent U.S. troops to stop the invasion of South Korea by Communist North Korea. He fired the commander in Korea, General Douglas MACARTHUR, for ignoring orders. Truman did not run for re-election in 1952.

## TRUTH, Sojourner

Sojourner Truth (1797?–1883) was an American preacher and crusader for human rights. She was born a slave in New York State but was freed in 1827. She then became involved with an evangelical movement. In 1843 she began preaching in the streets and at revival meetings. Truth also worked for the ABOLITIONIST movement and the WOMEN'S RIGHTS movement. During the CIVIL WAR she collected supplies for black Union Army regiments and worked for the National Freedmen's Relief Association as a counselor. After the war she continued to help freed slaves.

## TUBMAN, Harriet

Born into slavery, Harriet Tubman (1820?–1913) became known as the "Moses of her people." In 1849, she escaped from a Maryland plantation and headed north along the UNDERGROUND RAILROAD. Over the next ten years she helped more than 300 other slaves to escape, including her parents. Tubman made 19 rescue trips in all. During the CIVIL WAR she was a spy for the Union forces in South Carolina. After the war she settled in Auburn, New York, where she founded the Harriet Tubman Home for Aged Negroes.

Sojourner Truth

Harriet Tubman

▲ *Abolitionists Sojourner Truth and Harriet Tubman.*

## TULSA

Tulsa is the second largest city in Oklahoma, after Oklahoma City, with a population of 367,302. It is located in the northeastern part of the state, on the Arkansas River. Tulsa was first settled in 1836, by the Creek Indians. Many white settlers moved to the area after the railroad arrived in 1882. Tulsa then became a center for the shipment of cattle. After oil was discovered in 1901, the city became a center of the petroleum industry. Today, Tulsa's factories make machinery, aerospace equipment, and fabricated metals, but oil is still the major industry.

▼ *Boston Avenue Methodist Church in Tulsa was designed by Bruce Goff, a student of Frank Lloyd Wright.*

## TUNNELS

Tunnels are underground or underwater passages. They are used for the transportation of people and goods. Railroads, subways, and motor vehicles travel through

► *Second Street Tunnel in Los Angeles, California, was built to help the city cope with more than 5 million automobiles.*

Longest Underwater Tunnels in the United States

1. **Bart Trans-Bay Tubes**, San Francisco, California
Length: 3.6 miles (5.8 km)
2. **Brooklyn-Battery Tunnel**, New York, New York
Length: 9,117 ft (2,779 m)
3. **Holland Tunnel,** New York, New York
Length: 8,557 ft (2,608 m)
4. **Lincoln Tunnel**, New York, New York
Length: 8,216 ft (2,504 m)
5. **Thimble Shoals Channel**, Newport News, Virginia
Length: 8,187 ft (2,495 m)

hundreds of tunnels in the United States. The 7.8-mile (12.6-km) Cascade Tunnel in Washington is the longest railway tunnel in the United States. In New York City, three tunnels for motor vehicles—the Lincoln, Holland, and Brooklyn-Battery tunnels—connect Manhattan with surrounding areas.

Tunnels are also used to transport water and sewage. A water tunnel that runs for 105 miles (169 km) from the Catskill Mountains in New York State to the northern edge of New York City is the longest tunnel of any kind in the world.

## TURKEY

The turkey is a game bird traditionally served for THANKSGIVING and Christmas dinners. The wild turkey is native to North America. It lives in woodlands in parts of the central, southern, and eastern United States. Domestic turkeys are bred in many states, particularly North Carolina, Minnesota, and California.

▼ *Benjamin Franklin proposed the turkey as the national bird. In a congressional vote the turkey was just beaten by the bald eagle.*

## TURNER, Nat

The black slave Nat Turner (1800–1831) led the most serious revolt in the history of American SLAVERY. As a youth in Virginia, Turner acquired a strong, mystical religious faith. He began to see himself as the savior of his people. On the night of August 21, 1831, Turner and seven other slaves murdered his master, Joseph Travis, and Travis's family. They then set off for the county seat, called Jerusalem, where they intended to capture the armory. Over the next two days, Turner and his followers, who eventually numbered 75, killed another 57 whites. The state militia and armed white civilians quickly crushed the uprising, killing many slaves, including innocent ones. Turner was tried and hanged.

▲ *Nat Turner and his fellow slaves had to use small knives and farm tools as weapons in their revolt.*

## TURTLES

Turtles are REPTILES with shells. The largest are the sea turtles, which live in the sea but lay their eggs on beaches. Some weigh as much as 1,500 pounds (680 kg). Most species of sea turtles are now endangered. Snapping turtles and many other North American turtles live in fresh water. These include the box turtle, another endangered species, terrapins, and the diamondback.

Tortoises are slow-moving turtles that live entirely on land. In the United States they live in the Southeast and in Texas and other parts of the Southwest.

◀ *A snapping turtle can bite off a person's fingers with its powerful jaws.*

## TWAIN, Mark

Mark Twain (1835–1910) is generally considered the greatest American humorist. His real name was Samuel Langhorne Clemens. Clemens's boyhood, spent in Hannibal, Missouri, on the Mississippi River, inspired two of his best-loved books, *Tom Sawyer* and *Huckleberry Finn.* As a young man, he worked on the Mississippi as a steamboat pilot. From this experience he got his pen name ("mark twain" is a riverman's term for "two fathoms" deep) and the material for his book *Life on the Mississippi.*

Twain's first published writings were stories and articles for newspapers. A series of humorous accounts of a visit to Europe and Palestine, published in one volume as *The Innocents Abroad,* made him famous.

Twain enjoyed great success not only as a writer but also as a lecturer, both in the United States and abroad.

▼ *Mark Twain posed in his Hartford, Connecticut, living room for this 1905 photograph. He died five years later.*

# TYLER, John

John Tyler was the tenth president of the United States. He was the first vice president to succeed to the presidency after the death of a president.

Like his father before him, Tyler was governor of Virginia. He served from 1825 to 1826. From 1827 to 1836 he was a U.S. senator from Virginia. Originally a Democrat, Tyler became allied with the Whig Party in the late 1830s. In 1840 the party chose him as a compromise vice presidential candidate to run with presidential candidate William Henry HARRISON. The Whigs won the election easily. But Harrison died after only one month in office, and Tyler became president.

In office, Tyler brought an end to the Second Seminole War in 1842. He also improved relations with Great Britain. The Webster-Ashburton Treaty of 1842 settled a long-standing border dispute between Maine and Canada, which was then under British control.

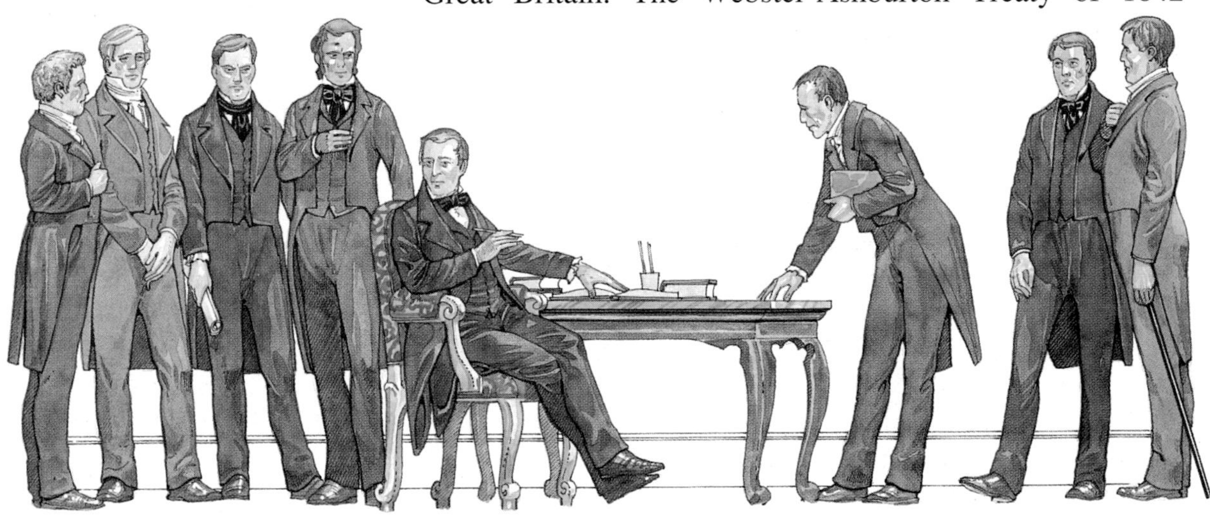

▲ *President John Tyler signed the resolution annexing Texas on March 1, 1845. Texas became a state ten months later.*

At home, however, the Whigs soon found that Tyler was not one of them. They thought Tyler supported the creation of a new national bank. But when Congress passed new bank bills, Tyler vetoed them. He felt the bank should not be able to open a branch in each state without the state's consent. After Tyler's second veto, his entire Cabinet resigned, except for Secretary of State Daniel WEBSTER.

A man without a party, Tyler wanted to run for a full term as president, but he lacked support. His greatest achievement came three days before he left office. On March 1, 1845, he signed into law a joint resolution of Congress providing for the annexation of Texas, a measure he had long supported.

John Tyler
**Born:** March 29, 1790, in Charles City County, Virginia
**Education:** William and Mary College
**Political party:** Whig
**Term of office:** 1841–1845
**Married:** 1813 to Letitia Christian; 1844 to Julia Gardner
**Died:** January 18, 1862, near Charles City, Virginia

## UNCLE SAM

Uncle Sam is a figure that serves as a symbol of the United States. He often appears in cartoons and is shown as a long-legged gentleman with white hair and whiskers, wearing a top hat decorated with stars and stripes, a tailcoat decorated with stars, a vest, and striped trousers. The name Uncle Sam is believed to have originated with a New York State businessman named Sam Wilson, who supplied beef to the U.S. Army during the War of 1812. The barrels were stamped "U.S." to show that they were government property. Because Wilson was familiarly called "Uncle Sam," his identity and that of the nation became linked.

## UNDERGROUND RAILROAD

The Underground Railroad was a system for helping slaves escape to freedom in the years before the Civil War. It operated in the northern states and extended to Canada. In Canada, escaped slaves were beyond the reach of the fugitive slave laws, which gave slaveowners the right to recapture their slaves in free states.

It was not a real railroad, but the people who worked for it (who included both blacks and whites) used railroad terms to describe the system. For example, the people who accompanied the slaves were called "conductors." The term "underground" referred to the secrecy of the operation. As many as 100,000 slaves may have been helped to freedom by the Railroad.

**All kinds of tricks were used to help fugitive slaves along the Underground Railroad. One slave from Virginia had a friend seal him into a box and ship him to an anti-slavery group in Philadelphia.**

▼ *Slave families considered themselves lucky to have a roof over their heads when they paused on their journey north along the Underground Railroad.*

**A very large number of United Empire Loyalists were not even of English origin. Thousands of Scots, Dutch, Germans, and French Huguenots remained loyal to Great Britain and moved to Canada. So, too, did large numbers of blacks and Indians. The Mohawk chief Joseph Brant led his people and other members of the Iroquois League to a reservation in Upper Canada.**

## UNITED EMPIRE LOYALISTS

During and after the American REVOLUTION, about 500,000 colonists remained loyal to Great Britain. Known as Loyalists, they were frequently abused by those colonists who fought for independence. Some were beaten, others were jailed, and many had their property taken away. After the war, about 100,000 Loyalists left the United States. Of these, about 40,000 moved to Canada, where they were offered free land. These people were known as United Empire Loyalists. Most of them settled in Nova Scotia and Quebec. Others helped establish the colonies of New Brunswick and Upper Canada (Ontario).

► *Each of the 159 member states of the United Nations has one vote in the UN General Assembly in New York City.*

## UNITED NATIONS

The United Nations (UN) is an international organization. Its goals are to promote world peace and to help solve economic, social, cultural, and humanitarian problems. The UN was set up in 1945 by the countries that fought against Germany, Italy, and Japan in WORLD WAR II. It replaced the LEAGUE OF NATIONS. Today, 184 nations—most of the countries in the world—are members of the UN. The UN headquarters is in New York City.

▼ *The United Nations insignia depicts the world protected by the laurel leaves of peace.*

All member states are represented in the General Assembly. Important issues are discussed in the General Assembly, which can then recommend courses of action. The UN Security Council is responsible for maintaining world peace. There are 15 members of the Security Council. Ten are elected by the General Assembly. The other five—the United States, the USSR, France, Great Britain, and China—are permanent members. The other major organs of the UN are the Secretariat (headed by the secretary general), the Economic and Social Council, the International Court of Justice, and the Trusteeship Council.

Many specialized agencies are connected with the UN. These include the World Bank; United Nations Educational, Scientific and Cultural Organization (UNESCO); World Health Organization (WHO); and UN Children's Fund (UNICEF).

## UNITED STATES OF AMERICA

The United States of America is the fourth largest country in the world in both population and area. It consists of 50 states and the DISTRICT OF COLUMBIA. Forty-eight of the states are in the center of NORTH AMERICA. The state of ALASKA is in the northwest corner of North America. HAWAII is an island state in the Pacific Ocean. (See individual entries on states.) The United States also has a number of PACIFIC TERRITORIES, and possessions in the Caribbean Sea. (See PUERTO RICO and the VIRGIN ISLANDS.)

The United States is bounded by CANADA on the north, the Atlantic Ocean on the east, and the Pacific Ocean on the west. MEXICO and the Gulf of Mexico lie to the south. Its topography ranges from icy glaciers and lofty MOUNTAINS to DESERTS, SWAMPS, and vast plains. Running north to south through the heart of the nation is the mighty MISSISSIPPI-MISSOURI RIVER SYSTEM. The GREAT LAKES, the largest body of fresh water in the world, straddle part of the border between the United States and Canada. (See GEOGRAPHY for map and further information.)

The land that is now the United States was first settled thousands of years ago by the ancestors of the American INDIANS. European settlement began after Christopher COLUMBUS made his first voyage to the New World in 1492. The British, French, Spanish, and other Europeans all fought for control of the land. The British succeeded, but their American colonies revolted and declared their independence as the United States of America on July 4, 1776. In the more than 200 years since, the United States has become the most powerful country in the world—and one of the wealthiest.

**United States**
**Capital:** Washington, D.C.
**Area:** 3,787,425 sq mi (9,809,431 km²)
**Population:** 248,709,873 (1990)
**Highest point:** Mt. McKinley, Alaska, 20,320 ft (6,194 m)
**Lowest point:** Death Valley, California, 282 ft (86 m) below sea level
**Major rivers:** Missouri, Mississippi, Arkansas, Colorado, Ohio, Red, Rio Grande, Snake
**Motto:** In God We Trust
**National anthem:** "The Star-Spangled Banner"
**National symbol:** Bald eagle

▲ *People of many different cultural backgrounds make up the population of the United States.*

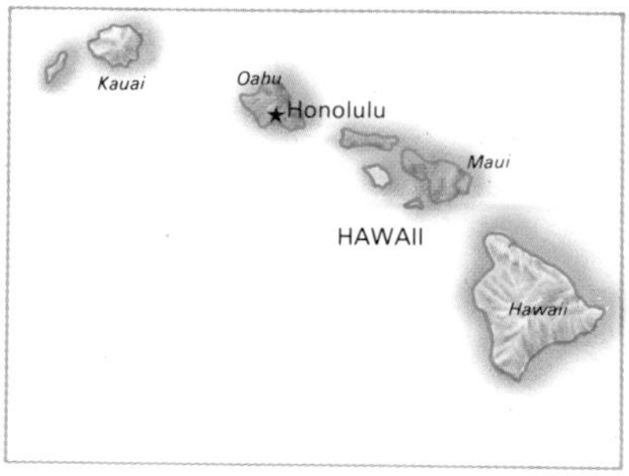

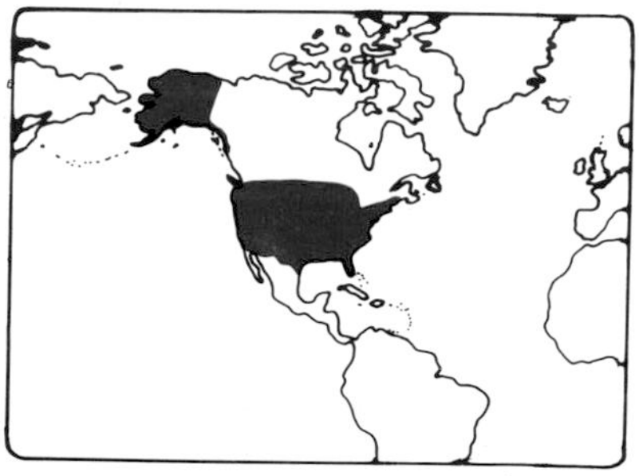

◀ *A view of Baltimore Harbor, Maryland, as it is today. During the War of 1812, an attack was made on Fort McHenry, which then overlooked the harbor. The sight of this bombardment inspired Francis Scott Key to write "The Star-Spangled Banner."*

▼ *The winters in Alaska are very long, but spectacular sights can be viewed by visitors to this northern state.*

You will find information about the United States throughout this encyclopedia. See the articles on individual states and territories; AMERICAN HISTORY; CLIMATE; ETHNIC GROUPS; GOVERNMENT OF THE UNITED STATES; LAWS AND LEGAL SYSTEM; ART, MUSIC, and LITERATURE; and PLANT and ANIMAL LIFE. Consult the Index for articles on the branches of government and the military, cities, presidents and other famous Americans, important events in history, individual ethnic groups, industries, and major geographical features.

# UTAH

Utah
**Capital:** Salt Lake City
**Area:** 84,904 sq mi (219,902 km$^2$). Rank: 13th
**Population:** 1,722,850 (1990). Rank 35th
**Statehood:** January 4, 1896
**Principal rivers:** Colorado, Green
**Highest point:** Kings Peak, 13,528 ft (4,123 m)
**Motto:** Industry
**Song:** "Utah, We Love Thee"

The story of Utah is largely that of the Church of Jesus Christ of Latter-day Saints, or MORMONS. In order to practice their religion in peace, the Mormons came by wagon train from the East. In 1847 they arrived at what is now SALT LAKE CITY. Even now, Mormons make up two thirds of the state's population.

Most of Utah is either mountainous or semidesert. The arid Great Basin, which includes Great Salt Lake, occupies the western third. The rest of the state consists of Rocky Mountain ranges in the north and the Colorado Plateau in the south. Mineral production is important to the economy and includes oil, natural gas, coal, copper, iron ore, gold, and silver. The chief manufacturing activities are steel making, copper smelting, and oil refining. Utah's farmers and ranchers raise cattle and sheep and market dairy products.

Salt Lake City is a gateway to some of the country's best skiing. Here also are the Mormons' six-spired Temple and Mormon Tabernacle, with its famous choir. Five national parks offer a spectacular view of mountains, canyons, and desert.

Mountain men and fur trappers were the first whites to visit the area, which is named for the UTE Indians. In 1848, a year after the Mormons arrived, Utah became part of the United States as a result of the MEXICAN WAR. Utah Territory was created in 1850, with Brigham YOUNG, the Mormon leader, as governor. In 1890 the church renounced the Mormon practice of polygamy (multiple marriage). This opened the way for Utah to become a state in 1896.

► *Newspaper Rock Historical Monument contains ancient Indian pictographs.*

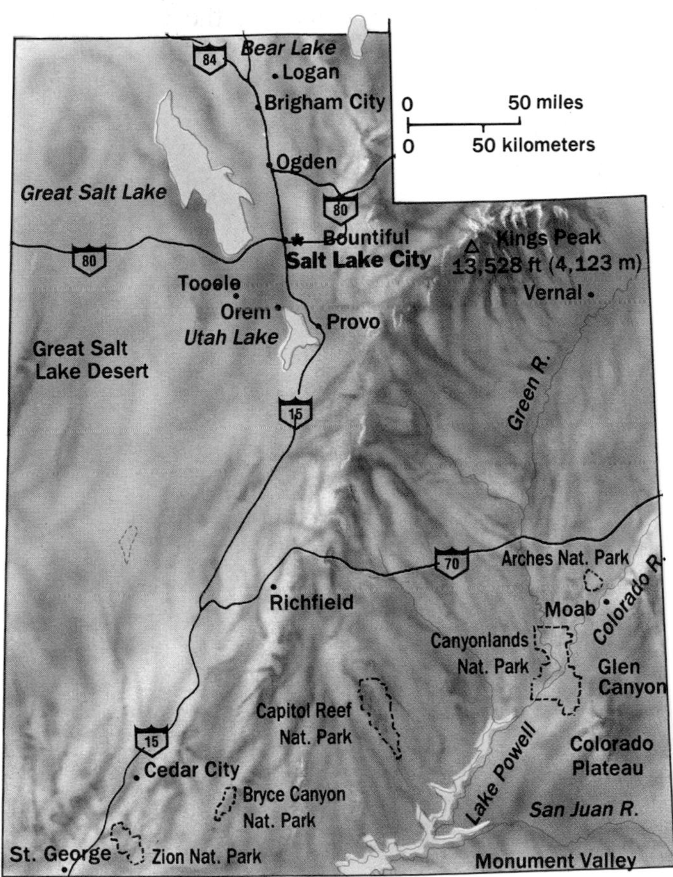

*▲ The Mormon Temple, an impressive architectural feat that took 40 years to complete, stands in Temple Square, Salt Lake City.*

*▼ The snowcapped Rocky Mountains that run through Utah attract millions of skiing enthusiasts and tourists every year.*

**Places of Interest**

- Bryce Canyon National Park, in the southern part of the state, is one of the most spectacular canyons in the United States.
- Monument Valley, in the southeast, has red sandstone formations that rise up to 1,000 feet (300 m).
- The Mormon Tabernacle, Salt Lake City, is the home of the famous Mormon Tabernacle Choir.
- Great Salt Lake, is the largest natural lake west of the Mississippi, and it is saltier than any ocean.

**The best-known Ute chief was Ouray. He became a great diplomat, speaking English, Spanish, and several Indian languages. Ouray settled disputes between the Utes and the white settlers, and also between the Utes and the government.**

## UTES

The Utes are an important North American INDIAN tribe that originally occupied land by the Rocky Mountains in what is now Colorado. They were often at war with their southern neighbors, the APACHES and NAVAJOS. Sometimes they even joined Spanish and, later, American soldiers in battles against their traditional enemies. The Utes lost most of their best lands when precious minerals were discovered in Colorado during the 1860s. A treaty with the United States in 1863 reduced the Ute territory. In 1881 the Utes were moved from Colorado to reservations in Utah. Today there are almost 10,000 Utes, living mainly on reservations in Utah and Colorado.

► *This photograph, taken at the beginning of the 20th century, shows a Ute baby wrapped in a traditional backpack.*

**The Uto-Aztecan language group has given a number of words to English. The state names Utah and Arizona both come from that source. Nahuatl, the language of the Aztecs, has given us the words *chocolate, avocado, tomato, chile,* and *coyote.***

## UTO-AZTECAN LANGUAGES

The term Uto-Aztecan describes a family of languages used by INDIANS living west of the Rocky Mountains. Languages within this group share certain sounds, words, or elements of grammar in the same way that English has some links with Spanish, German, and other European languages. The Uto-Aztecan language group takes its name from the tribes at the extremes of its territory—the UTES in the north and the Aztecs of MEXICO in the south. Other tribal languages within the family include HOPI, COMANCHE, and SHOSHONI.

## VALENTINO, Rudolph

Rudolph Valentino (1895–1926) was a motion-picture actor of the 1920s. He was adored by countless women for his image as the great romantic lover and was the idol of the silent screen. Born in Italy, Valentino came to the United States in 1913. He began his film career as a dancer in 1918. In 1921 he shot to fame with *The Four Horsemen of the Apocalypse*. He appeared in 15 more films, including *The Sheik*, *Blood and Sand*, *The Eagle*, and *The Son of the Sheik*. When Valentino died at the age of only 31, women all over the world grieved.

## VALLEY FORGE

Valley Forge is the place where General George WASHINGTON and the Continental Army set up camp from December 1777 to June 1778. It is located in Pennsylvania, about 22 miles (35 km) northwest of Philadelphia. The winter of 1777–1778 was an unusually cold one, and the army was desperately short of food and supplies. Of the 11,000 troops stationed at Valley Forge, 4,000 had no blankets. A similar number had no shoes. About 2,500 died of disease. Moreover, the war had been going badly for the Americans; and Philadelphia itself was occupied by the British. Despite the hardships, however, morale remained relatively high, thanks mainly to the inspiring leadership of Washington. During that winter the troops were also reorganized and trained by Baron von STEUBEN and were better prepared to resume fighting in the spring. Today Valley Forge is a national historical park.

▼ *George Washington decided to remain all winter with his soldiers at Valley Forge. Their fighting spirit would have been damaged if he had taken more comfortable living quarters.*

## VAN ALLEN, James

James Van Allen (1914– ) is a physicist who made an important contribution to the field of astronomy. Born in Mount Pleasant, Iowa, Van Allen became head of the Department of Physics and Astronomy at the University of Iowa in 1951. In 1958, using data gathered by the Explorer I satellite, Van Allen discovered a double layer of electrically charged particles surrounding the Earth. These layers of particles are known as the Van Allen Belts. Scientists are still studying these belts, which cause auroras (bands of light in the sky) and affect radio waves and electrical power.

# VAN BUREN, Martin

Martin Van Buren was the eighth president of the United States. He served from 1837 to 1841, a time when the United States was suffering a great economic depression.

Van Buren, a New York lawyer, was elected to the U.S. Senate in 1821. He helped organize the Democratic Party and also played an important role in getting Andrew JACKSON elected president in 1828. Van Buren became Jackson's secretary of state and his closest friend and adviser. In 1832 he was elected Jackson's vice president. Jackson soon chose Van Buren as his successor. In 1836, Van Buren won the Democratic presidential nomination and the presidential election.

By the time Van Buren took office, the Panic of 1837 had broken out. Every bank in the country was forced to close. Thousands of people were put out of work, and they hoped that the government would help. But Van Buren believed that the government should not interfere in the economy. He believed that private business could best end the depression. Van Buren did, however, get Congress to pass the Independent Treasury Act of 1840. This act separated the U.S. Treasury from the banks in the country.

▲ *Soup kitchens were the only source of food for many people who lost their savings in the Panic of 1837. This financial collapse occurred in the first year of Martin Van Buren's presidency.*

The depression spoiled Van Buren's reputation as a friend of labor and the working person. In addition, he was distrusted by Southern Democrats. They suspected, correctly, that he did not want slavery extended to the western territories. Van Buren lost the 1840 election to William Henry HARRISON, the Whig candidate. He ran again unsuccessfully in 1848 as the candidate of the anti-slavery Free Soil Party.

Martin Van Buren
**Born:** December 5, 1782, in Kinderhook, New York
**Education:** Law studies in New York City
**Political party:** Democratic
**Term of office:** 1837–1841
**Married:** 1807 to Hannah Hoes
**Died:** July 24, 1862, in Kinderhook, New York

## VANCOUVER

Vancouver is CANADA's busiest port and the largest city in the province of BRITISH COLUMBIA. It is known as "Canada's Gateway to the Pacific." It handles most of the country's trade with Asia and the U.S. West Coast. Vancouver's large natural harbor is protected by mountains, so it never freezes. The same mountains, as well as Vancouver Island across the Strait of St. George, are major tourist attractions. Vancouver, with a population of over 470,000, is Canada's eighth largest city. It began as a lumber camp in 1865. Today shipping is the city's most important industry. Other industries include food processing, petroleum refining, and the production of lumber and paper products.

▲ *A steam clock tells the time in Gastown, one of Vancouver's attractive pedestrian districts.*

## VANDERBILT FAMILY

The Vanderbilts are one of the most important families in the history of American business and finance. Cornelius Vanderbilt (1794–1877), who was known as "Commodore," developed a fleet of ships. When this business became successful, he sold it and bought into railways in the 1860s. Eventually he became one of the richest men in the country and controlled some of the largest railways in the East, Midwest, and Canada, including the New York Central Railroad. His son, William Henry (1821–1885), took control of the family business on his father's death. William's son, Cornelius II (1843–1899), followed into the business, running part of it under his father. By 1883, Cornelius controlled three of the nation's major railways.

## VEGETABLES

The United States is the third most important vegetable-growing country in the world. Because of the country's wide variety of climates, many different vegetables can be grown. Cool-season vegetables, such as broccoli, carrots, cauliflower, celery, lettuce, peas, and POTATOES, are grown in the northern states. Warm-season vegetables, such as cucumbers, peppers, squash, and SWEET POTATOES, are grown in the southern states. California is the leading vegetable-growing state. Other important vegetable-producing states are Illinois, Iowa, Minnesota, Missouri, Indiana, and Idaho.

▼ *Different parts of different vegetables are used for food.*

**Cauliflower (flower clusters)**

**Onion (bulb)**

**Tomato (fruit)**

**Cabbage (leaves)**

**Carrot (root)**

**Corn (seeds)**

**Potato (tuber)**

Red clover

Sugar maple

Hermit thrush

Named for the Green Mountains that run lengthwise through the state, Vermont offers great scenic beauty. It fills with summer campers, winter skiers, and "leafers" who drive through in fall to watch the wooded slopes burst into red and gold. Roadside stores and stands sell antiques, quilts, cheeses, apples, and maple syrup. On a given weekend the tourists may outnumber the natives. But Vermont retains its Yankee virtues of thrift and self-reliance.

Vermont is the most rural state. Close to two thirds of its population lives in the country. Yet only a few thousand farms remain. Most of them border Lake Champlain in the northwest or lie along the Connecticut River, which forms the state's eastern boundary. Milk from dairy cows is the chief farm product. Burlington, on Lake Champlain, is the biggest city and center of industry. Computer components and machine tools are the chief manufactured goods. Forest products, especially paper, are another important source of income for the state.

In 1609 the French explorer Samuel de CHAMPLAIN discovered the lake that bears his name. The French later built a fort by the lake, but they lost the area to the British in the French and Indian War. Soon after, Ethan Allen's Green Mountain Boys ousted the British in the American REVOLUTION in a series of daring battles. Vermont became an independent republic in 1777. It adopted a constitution that abolished slavery and gave the vote to all men. In 1791 it became the first state after the original 13 to join the Union.

Vermont
**Capital:** Montpelier
**Area:** 9,615 sq mi (24,903 km$^2$). Rank: 45th
**Population:** 562,758 (1990). Rank 48th
**Statehood:** March 4, 1791
**Principal rivers:** Connecticut, West, Otter
**Highest point:** Mt. Mansfield, 4,393 ft (1,339 m)
**Motto:** Freedom and Unity
**Song:** "Hail, Vermont"

► *Forests cover much of Vermont and provide for its thriving lumber industry.*

▼ *The lonely steeple of a wooden church rises above the trees in East Orange, Vermont.*

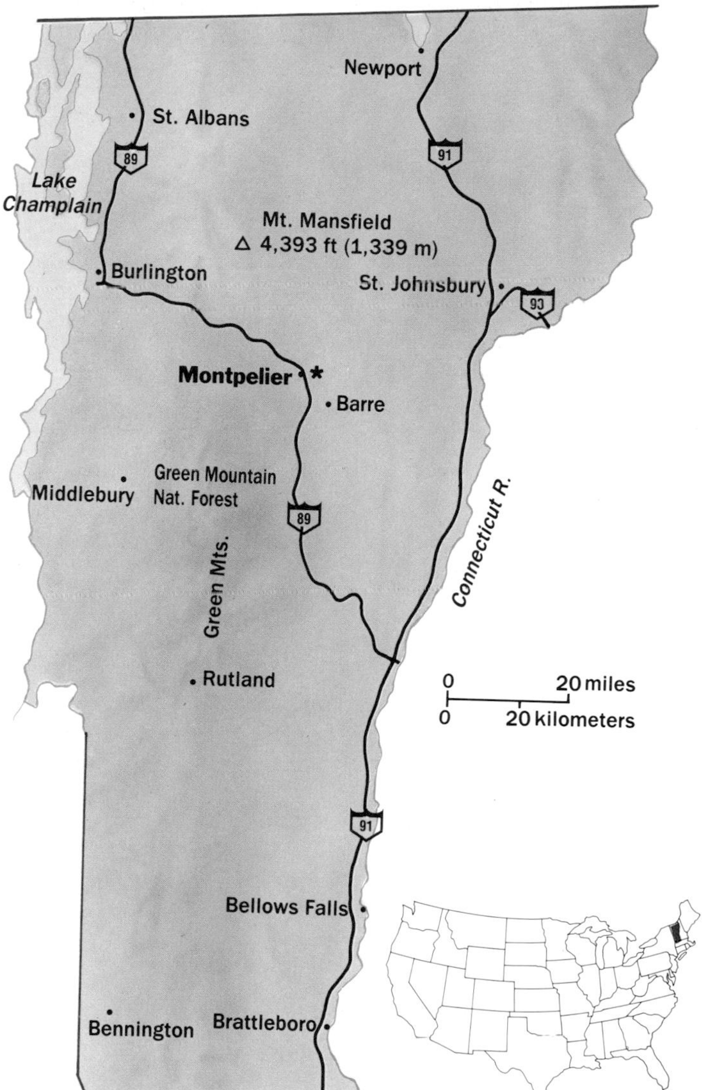


Places of Interest

- The Green Mountains, which run through the center of Vermont, offer visitors a range of activities, from hiking and camping in the summer to skiing in the winter.
- Visitors to St. Albans Maple Festival can watch syrup being made from maple sap.
- Shelborne Museum, in Shelborne, is a reconstructed early American village. It houses many items from Colonial times.

► *Skiers take on the tree-lined slopes of Jay Peak, one of the 56 ski areas in Vermont.*

**Giovanni da Verrazano had been hired to find a trading route to the Orient for French silk traders. The French considered his detailed explorations of Chesapeake Bay, New York Harbor, and the Hudson River failures because none of these led to the Far East.**

## VERRAZANO, Giovanni da

The explorer Giovanni da Verrazano (1485–1528) made at least two voyages to the New World. He explored the Atlantic coast of North America between North Carolina and Maine. Verrazano was born in Italy, but as an adult he joined the French Navy. In 1524, King Francis I of France sent him to find a short route to China. Verrazano sailed west, reaching the coast of North Carolina, and then north, exploring New York and Narragansett bays. He found that neither of these offered a passage to Asia. On his last voyage, in 1528, Verrazano was killed by Indians, possibly in Brazil.

▼ *Amerigo Vespucci's exploration of the American coastline convinced him that it was a New World.*

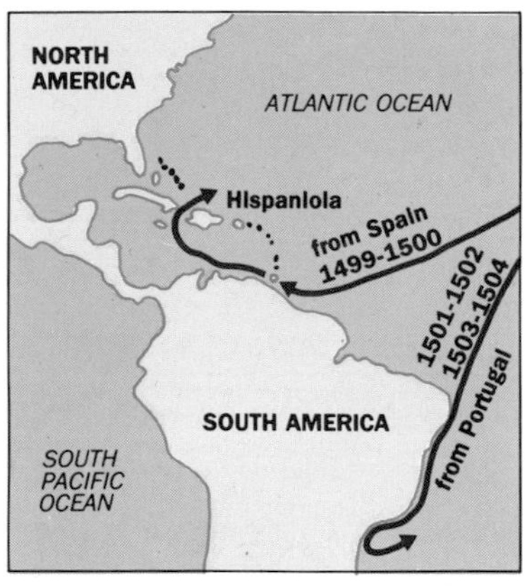


## VESPUCCI, Amerigo

The Italian navigator and explorer Amerigo Vespucci (1454–1512) was the man after whom AMERICA was named. Vespucci made at least two and possibly four voyages to the New World, serving as navigator. On a voyage made in 1499–1500 he traveled along the coast of Venezuela and northern Brazil. On his second voyage (1501–1502), which ventured farther south, he became convinced that this land was not part of Asia, as had been thought, but a new continent. In 1507 a German mapmaker named Martin Waldseemuller wrote about Vespucci's voyages and made a map of the area that Vespucci had explored. He used the name America for that area.

▼ *An honor guard carries state and national flags in a Veterans Day parade in Nashville, Tennessee.*

## VETERANS DAY

Veterans Day is a national holiday in the United States. Held on November 11, it honors those who served in the U.S. armed services during war (known as veterans). Parades are held, and the graves of those who died in the armed services are decorated with flowers. The occasion was originally called Armistice Day, in memory of the armistice that ended World War I on November 11, 1918. It became a national holiday in 1939. In 1954, after the Korean War, the name was changed to Veterans Day, to honor U.S. veterans of all wars.

## VICE PRESIDENT *See* President of the United States

## VIETNAM WAR

The Southeast Asian country of Vietnam was part of a colony known as French Indochina from the 1860s until World War II, when the Japanese took control. After the war, France took control again, but the Vietnamese people began to fight for their independence. The French were defeated and forced to pull out in 1954. They left the country divided. North Vietnam was a Communist country supported by China and the Soviet Union. South Vietnam looked to the West for support.

Beginning in 1957, North Vietnam gave aid to South Vietnamese Communists called the Viet Cong. They tried to overthrow the South Vietnamese government. The United States, which wanted to stop Communist aggression began to aid South Vietnam. Troops were sent beginning in 1965. By 1969, at the end of Lyndon JOHNSON's term as president, there were 540,000 U.S. troops in Vietnam. After Richard NIXON became president in 1969, he began to withdraw U.S. troops. In 1973 a cease-fire was signed, and U.S. troops were withdrawn. But in 1975 the Communists mounted a strong offensive, and South Vietnam was forced to surrender on April 30, 1975. The neighboring countries of Laos and Cambodia also fell to the Communists. Vietnam was reunited under Communist rule in 1976. Pro- and anti-war sentiments in the United States caused a great deal of conflict in the nation.

▲ *Civilians fled with all the possessions they could carry as North Vietnamese forces closed in on Saigon in 1975.*

◀ *The Vietnam War Memorial, in Washington, D.C., is inscribed with the names of the more than 57,000 Americans who died or remain missing in Vietnam.*

**Important Events of the Vietnam War**

**1957** Viet Cong begin to rebel against the South Vietnamese government (under President Diem).

**1963** Diem government is overthrown by South Vietnamese rebels; Diem is killed.

**1965** President Lyndon Johnson sends U.S. Marines to South Vietnam.

**1969** President Richard Nixon announces the beginning of the withdrawal of U.S. troops from Vietnam.

**1973** The United States, North and South Vietnam, and the Viet Cong sign a cease-fire agreement.
The last U.S. ground troops leave Vietnam.

**1975** South Vietnam surrenders.

## VIKINGS *See* Ericsson, Leif

# VIRGINIA

**Flowering dogwood**

Virginia
**Capital:** Richmond
**Area:** 42,769 sq mi (110,771 km²). Rank: 35th
**Population:** 6,187,358 (1990). Rank: 12th
**Statehood:** June 25, 1788
**Principal rivers:** James, Rappahannock, Potamac, Shenandoah
**Highest point:** Mt. Rogers, 5,729 ft (1,746 m)
**Motto:** *Sic Semper Tyrannis* (Thus Always to Tyrants)
**Song:** "Carry Me Back to Old Virginia"

Virginia is steeped in history. Called the Old Dominion, it was the first colony in English North America. Its capital, Richmond, was the capital of the CONFEDERATE STATES OF AMERICA in the CIVIL WAR. Virginia has given the nation eight presidents, including George WASHINGTON and Thomas JEFFERSON.

Tobacco, peanuts, corn, and sweet potatoes are some of the crops grown in the state. Virginia farms are also noted for poultry and hams. Richmond has diversified manufacturing. The Port of Hampton Roads handles much of the region's shipping. Norfolk is headquarters for the U.S. Navy's Atlantic Fleet, and Newport News produces naval warships. Coal is mined in the state's Appalachian region, and the state's forests yield lumber for paper and furniture. But Virginia's growth industry is the federal government. The state has the Pentagon and numerous military bases. And many Virginians commute to federal offices in Washington.

JAMESTOWN, England's first permanent settlement in North America, was founded in 1607. Virginia was the most populous of the original 13 colonies. The British surrender at Yorktown, Virginia, in 1781 virtually

► *The Governor's Mansion in Colonial Williamsburg is a well-preserved example of 17th-century architecture.*

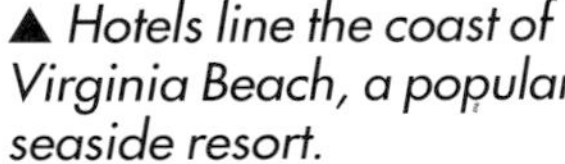

▲ *Hotels line the coast of Virginia Beach, a popular seaside resort.*

► *South River Falls in Virginia's picturesque Shenandoah National Park.*

ended the American REVOLUTION. The state was the principal battlefield of the Civil War, a struggle that left it devastated.

Virginia abounds with historical attractions, including its many battle sites, the Colonial Williamsburg restoration, Washington's home at MOUNT VERNON, Jefferson's home at Monticello, and Arlington National Cemetery. Also popular are its beaches, Shenandoah National Park, and two scenic roads—the Blue Ridge Parkway and Skyline Drive—that run along the crest of the APPALACHIAN MOUNTAINS.

**Places of Interest**

- James Fort, in Jamestown Festival Park, is the reconstruction of the first English settlement of 1607.
- Mount Vernon, near Alexandria, was the home of George Washington.
- Monticello, where Thomas Jefferson lived, is near Charlottesville.
- Williamsburg, one of the oldest settlements in the country, has been restored to look as it did in the 1700s.

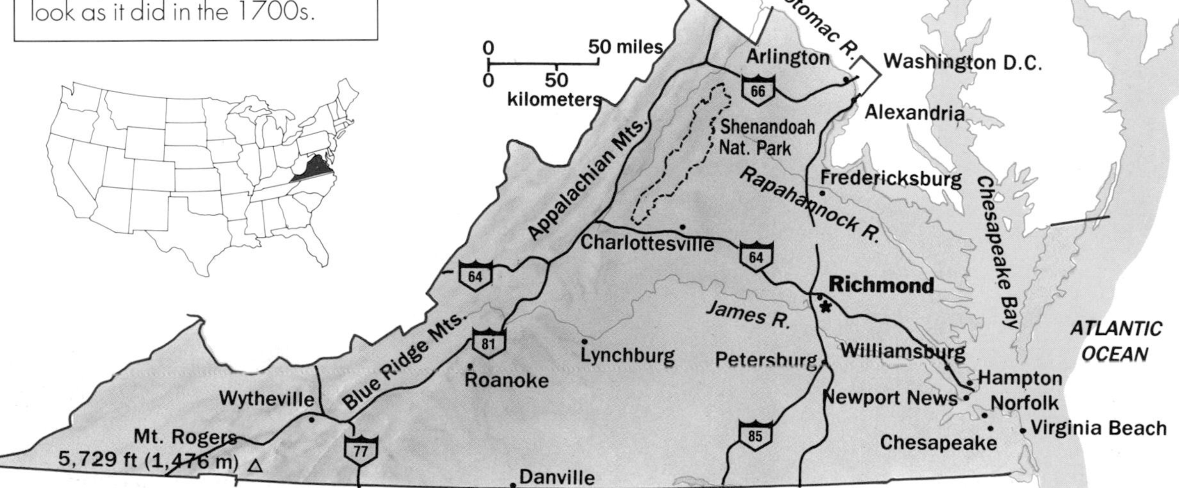

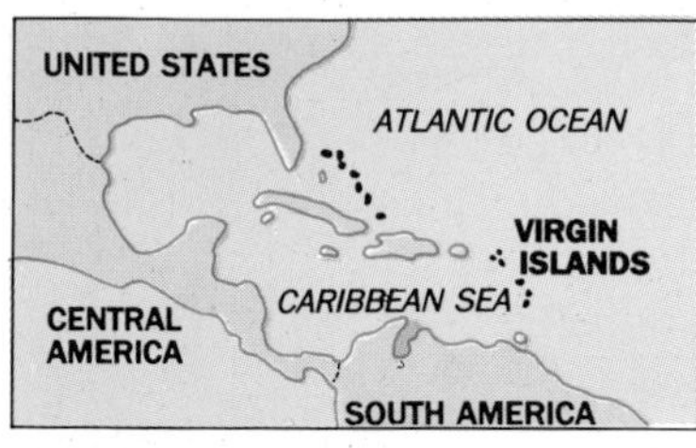


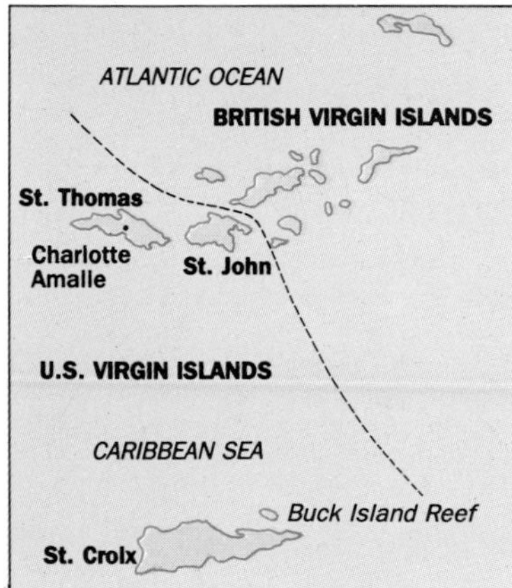


▲ *Most U.S. Virgin Islanders live on St. Thomas, St. John, or St. Croix. The British Virgin Islands, to the north and east, have a much smaller population.*

## VIRGIN ISLANDS

The Virgin Islands are a group of islands in the CARIBBEAN SEA east of PUERTO RICO. They comprise the Virgin Islands of the United States and the British Virgin Islands. The U.S. group was purchased from Denmark in 1917. The largest of this group's many islands are St. Thomas, St. John, and St. Croix. The capital, Charlotte Amalie, is a seaport on St. Thomas. Tourism is the major industry of the Virgin Islands. Each year they receive more than a million visitors, about ten times their population.

## VOLCANO

A volcano is a mountain where hot, melted rock has erupted, or burst through an opening in the earth's surface. Extinct volcanoes (those that have not erupted since the beginning of recorded history) are found in many regions of the United States.

The world's largest volcano, MAUNA LOA, is in Hawaii. Hawaii and Alaska each have several active volcanoes. The only other U.S. volcanoes that are not extinct are in the Cascade Range of Washington, Oregon, and northern California. This chain of volcanoes is part of the "Ring of Fire"—the volcano-and-earthquake belt that runs around the rim of the Pacific Ocean.

MOUNT ST. HELENS, in Washington, had been dormant, or "sleeping," for 123 years when it erupted in 1980. Other dormant volcanoes include California's Lassen Peak and Washington's Mount Baker.

Volcanoes in the United States

**Mauna Loa**, Hawaii, 13,680 ft (4,170 m)
**Redoubt**, Alaska, 10,197 ft (3,108 m)
**Iliamna**, Alaska, 10,016 ft (3,053 m)
**Shishaldin**, Aleutian Islands, Alaska, 9,387 ft (2,861 m)
**Mt. St. Helens**, Washington, 8,300 ft (2,530 m)
**Kilauea**, Hawaii, 4,077 ft (1,243 m)

► *Kilauea is an active volcano on the island of Hawaii. It last erupted in 1990 after several dormant years.*

## VOLLEYBALL 

Volleyball is a popular team sport played indoors or out, often on beaches. The object is to hit a ball over a net so that the opposing team cannot return it. Players can hit the ball with their fists or palms. There are six players on a team. One side serves to start play. If it wins a point, then the point is scored. If the receiving side wins the point, it is not scored, but it gets the serve and the chance to score. Games are played until one side gets 15 points and wins by two.

Volleyball was invented by William G. Morgan, a gym teacher in Holyoke, Massachusetts, in 1895. The International Volleyball Federation organizes tournaments. Volleyball has been an Olympic sport since 1964.

▲ *The U.S. men's volleyball team defeated the Soviet Union to win the gold medal at the 1988 Seoul Olympic Games.*

## VON BRAUN, Wernher 

Wernher Von Braun (1912–1977) was a rocket engineer. He led the teams of engineers who built the rockets that put U.S. astronauts on the moon. Von Braun was born in a part of Germany that is now in Poland. During World War II he helped the Germans develop rockets. At the end of the war he surrendered to the Americans and was sent to the United States in 1945. Von Braun and other German scientists helped the United States develop rocket power. In 1950 his team, based in Huntsville, Alabama, helped build the first U.S. guided missile. In the late 1950s and throughout the 1960s he supervised the building of the Jupiter and Saturn rockets. The Jupiter rocket put the first U.S. satellite into orbit. The Saturn put the first astronauts on the moon.

## VULTURE 

The vulture is a bird of prey that lives on carrion (dead animals). Three species are found in North America. The California CONDOR is the largest; it is in danger of becoming extinct. The smallest is the black vulture, or black buzzard. The turkey vulture, or buzzard, is one of the most common North American birds of prey. Vultures roost and nest on cliffs and in tall trees. They can often be seen at the roadside or circling overhead. Vultures are found in rocky regions, deserts, fields, and even cities.

▼ *The turkey vulture is one of the most common North American vultures. They usually scavenge for dead animals but sometimes swoop down and catch live prey.*

## WALL STREET

Wall Street is the financial capital of the United States. It is a short street in the southern end of Manhattan in NEW YORK CITY. Many investment companies are based on Wall Street in order to compete in the STOCK MARKET. Stocks are traded on the New York Stock Exchange and the American Stock Exchange, which are located in the Wall Street district. Banks, insurance companies, and other financial firms are also located along Wall Street. The term "Wall Street" is also used to describe the world of finance in general.

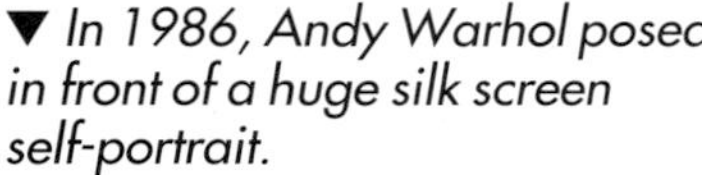

► *The walrus is distinctive because of its large, white tusks. It is the only seal to have this characteristic.*

▼ *In 1986, Andy Warhol posed in front of a huge silk screen self-portrait.*

## WALRUS

The walrus is a large sea mammal. It is related to the SEAL. It lives on beaches and ice floes in the Arctic. A good swimmer, it spends much of its life in the sea, looking for clams and other food. The male is up to 13 feet (3.7 m) long and weighs up to 3,500 pounds (1,600 kg). Walruses usually live in large herds. They are hunted by the ESKIMOS (Inuits) and by commercial hunters for their long ivory tusks; their blubber (body fat), which can be turned into oil; and their hides.

## WARHOL, Andy

The artist Andy Warhol (1930–1987) was one of the leading figures of the Pop Art movement. In the early 1960s, he began to produce large paintings showing such comic strip characters as Popeye. He later produced silk screen paintings of such objects as Campbell Soup cans and dollar bills, as well as colored portraits of movie stars and popular singers. He also made a number of experimental films.

## WAR OF 1812

The War of 1812 (1812–1815) was fought between the United States and Great Britain. Before it broke out, the British Navy seized a number of American ships and forced the sailors into British naval service. American anger was increased by evidence that the British were supplying arms to Indians to prevent American expansion into the Northwest. The United States declared war on June 18, 1812.

American attempts to invade Canada in the first year of the war were a failure; but the small American Navy scored several victories. On September 10, 1813, Commander Oliver PERRY's fleet defeated a British fleet on Lake Erie, thus securing control of the Great Lakes. However, the British Navy launched a series of raids on American coastal cities.

In August, 1814 the British captured Washington, D.C. and burned most of the government buildings including the Capitol and the White House. But the British navy and armed forces were then driven back at Baltimore, an encounter that was to inspire Francis Scott Key to write the words to "The Star Spangled Banner."

By the end of 1814, Britain was ready to make peace. The two sides signed the Treaty of Ghent (Belgium) on December 24, 1814. News of the peace treaty arrived too late, however, to prevent the Battle of New Orleans (January 8, 1815), in which a British invasion force was overwhelmingly defeated by General Andrew JACKSON.

**The states of New England opposed the idea of fighting Great Britain in the War of 1812. Those states feared that a war would disrupt sea trade and would destroy their livelihood. Some New England states held back money and soldiers during the war.**

Important Events of the War of 1812

June 18, 1812: The United States declares war on Great Britain.

October 13, 1812: The Battle of Queenston Heights is won by British forces.

September 10, 1813: American forces win the Battle of Lake Erie.

August 24, 1814: British forces invade Washington, D.C., and burn the Capitol and the White House.

September 11, 1814: American forces win the Battle of Lake Champlain.

December 24, 1814: Peace treaty signed in Ghent, Belgium.

January 8, 1815: American forces win the Battle of New Orleans, before news of peace reaches the United States.

◄ *English forces suffered a severe defeat from the American forces under General Andrew Jackson in New Orleans in 1815.*

# WASHINGTON

The scenic state of Washington is located on the Pacific coast. It is a land of majestic forests and mountains on the rim of the Pacific Ocean.

Most of Washington's people live along the shores of Puget Sound, an inlet of the Pacific flanked by the Coast and Cascade mountain ranges. Among the volcanic Cascades are scenic Mount Rainier and MOUNT ST. HELENS, which erupted violently in 1980. East of the Cascades is the flat, dry Columbia Plateau. The mighty COLUMBIA RIVER, joined by the Snake, cuts through eastern Washington and forms the border with Oregon as it bends westward.

Western Washington's mild, damp climate is ideal for growing fruit, nuts, and berries. Washington is the leading apple-growing state. The thick forests of Douglas fir, cedar, and spruce that cover the mountains make the state second only to Oregon in lumbering. Eastern Washington has cattle ranches and irrigated wheat lands. The ten major dams on the Columbia and Snake include Grand Coulee, one of the largest in the world. SEATTLE is Washington's largest city. Its metropolitan area has five Boeing plants turning out aircraft and aerospace equipment. Another important industry is aluminum refining.

Washington's population growth did not begin until the Pacific Northwest border with Canada was agreed on in 1846. Seattle grew rapidly in the 1890s as the jumping-off point to the Alaskan oil fields.

Washington
**Capital:** Olympia
**Area:** 71,303 sq mi (184,674 km$^2$). Rank: 18th
**Population:** 4,866,692 (1990). Rank: 18th
**Statehood:** Nov. 11, 1889
**Principal rivers:** Columbia, Snake, Spokane
**Highest point:** Mt. Rainier, 14,410 ft (4,392 m)
**Motto:** *Alki* (By and By)
**Song:** "Washington, My Home"

► *The 607-ft (185-m) Space Needle is the most famous feature of Seattle's skyline. It was built for the world's fair held in 1962.*

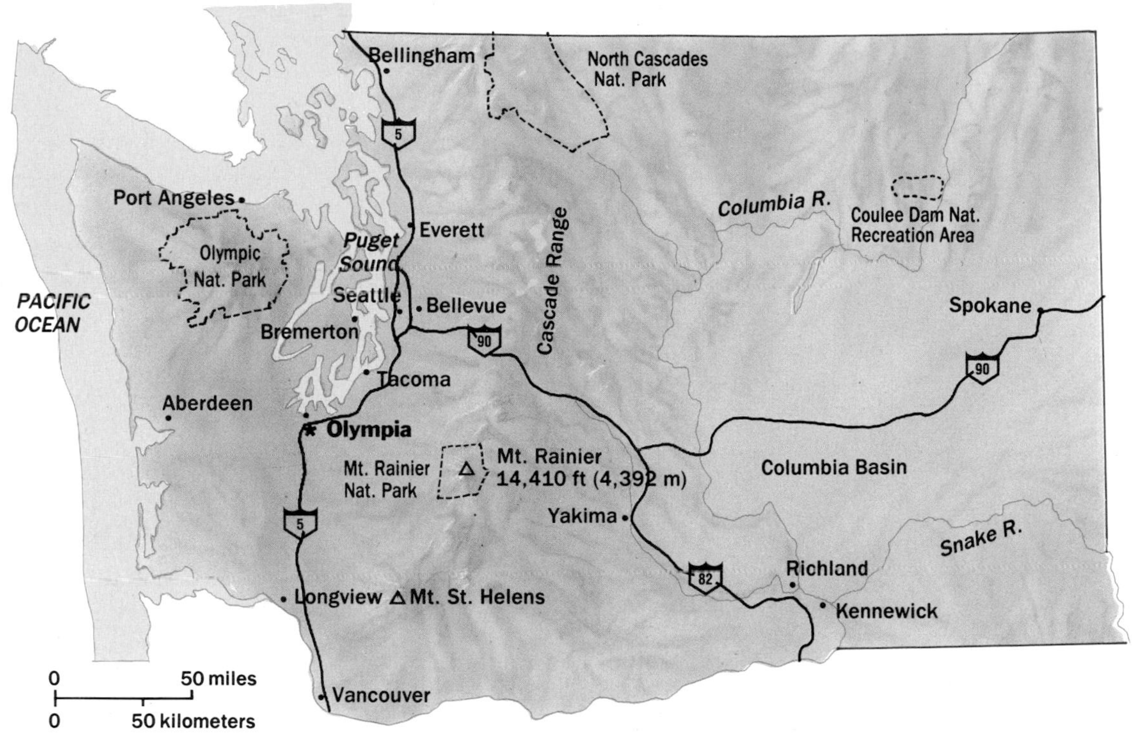


Places of Interest

- Grand Coulee Dam, west of Spokane, is the largest concrete dam in the United States.
- Mt. Rainier, southeast of Seattle, is one of the highest mountains in the United States.
- Seattle is the largest city in Washington. The Pacific Science Center is found there, and the Seafair, held every summer, is one of the highlights of the year.
- Mt. St. Helens National Volcanic Monument, is the site of the volcanic eruption of 1980.

► *The burned and broken remains of Douglas firs are "exhibits" at the Mt. St. Helens Volcanic Monument. Mt. St. Helens erupted in 1980, killing 60 people.*

▲ *Booker T. Washington influenced two U.S. presidents and other national figures, but he clashed with black leaders who demanded rapid improvements in civil rights.*

## WASHINGTON, Booker T.

Booker T. Washington (1856–1915) was a black American educator. After he and his family had been freed from slavery at the end of the Civil War, they moved from Virginia to West Virginia. Washington studied and became a teacher at a school that taught industrial trades to black students. As a result of his experience, Washington became convinced that gaining practical and industrial skills was the best way for the black population to gain financial security—and a political voice. In 1881 he helped found and became the first principal of Tuskegee Institute. He wrote about his beliefs in *Up From Slavery*, published in 1901. Washington was active as a spokesman for black rights.

► *The Lincoln Memorial is mirrored in the waters of the Reflecting Pool, one of the many landmarks of Washington, D.C.*

## WASHINGTON, D.C.

The city of Washington is the capital of the United States. It takes up all of the DISTRICT OF COLUMBIA. It is named for President George WASHINGTON, who chose the site—between Maryland and Virginia—in 1791. The French engineer Pierre Charles L'Enfant planned and built much of the city.

Washington is the headquarters of the federal government. About 375,000 federal employees work there. The city's population is 609,900.

Many tourists visit government and other buildings and sites in Washington. Among the most popular are the WHITE HOUSE, CAPITOL, LIBRARY OF CONGRESS, SMITHSONIAN INSTITUTION, National Gallery of Art, Kennedy Center for the Performing Arts, Lincoln Memorial, and Vietnam Memorial.

**When the city of Washington was established in 1791, the site was a swamp in a bowl formed by hills to the north and south. For the first hundred years Washington grew very slowly because the hot, humid summers and the nearby swamps brought various diseases. It was not until the 1870s that the city's streets were paved and sewer pipes were laid.**

# WASHINGTON, George

George Washington was the first president of the United States. Called the "father of his country," he was already a national hero when he was elected. As commander in chief of the Continental Army, he had led the United States to victory over Great Britain in the American REVOLUTION. After the war Washington presided over the convention that wrote the U.S. CONSTITUTION.

Washington was elected president in 1789 and was re-elected in 1792. Both times he received every vote cast by the electors. He united the country as no other could have done.

Washington did not want political parties to develop, yet two rival parties soon appeared. Washington preferred not to take sides, but he believed in strong central government and so decided several issues in favor of the FEDERALISTS.

Soon after Washington took office, the BILL OF RIGHTS was adopted. Washington sent troops to crush an armed rebellion by backwoods farmers who objected to paying a tax on whiskey. Treaties were signed with Britain, Spain, and Indians on the western frontier. Five new states joined the Union. The United States avoided involvement in a war between France and nations opposed to the French Revolution, including Britain. Washington set a precedent that lasted almost 150 years by refusing to run for a third term. After his death the new capital being built near his Virginia home was named Washington in his honor.

George Washington
**Born:** February 22, 1732, in Westmoreland County, Virginia
**Education:** Little formal schooling
**Political party:** None
**Term of office:** 1789–1797
**Married:** 1759 to Martha Custis
**Died:** December 14, 1799, at Mount Vernon

▼ *The German-born artist Emanuel Leutze commemorated a turning point in the American Revolution with his famous* Washington Crossing the Delaware, *painted in 1850.*

▶ *Water birds vary enormously in size and shape. But most have webbed feet and feathers that let water "roll off."*

| Some Famous Waterfalls in the United States | |
|---|---|
| Name | Height |
| Ribbon, California | 1,612 ft (491 m) |
| Multnomah, Oregon | 620 ft (189 m) |
| Alaka, Hawaii | 442 ft (135 m) |
| Sluiskin, Washington | 300 ft (91 m) |
| Shoshone, Idaho | 212 ft (65 m) |
| Niagara, New York | 182 ft (55 m) |

## WATER BIRDS

Water birds live by lakes, rivers, ponds, marshes, or the sea. They include DUCKS AND GEESE. Many seabirds—including guillemots, puffins, petrels, and GULLS AND TERNS—are found on both the Atlantic and Pacific coasts of North America. The brown PELICAN is also found along the Gulf of Mexico coast. Some species, such as certain HERONS, live all over the continent. The swamps of the southeastern states are home to a number of unique water birds, including the wood stork, the only North American stork.

## WATERFALLS

A waterfall is the sudden descent of a stream of water from a higher to a lower level. The highest waterfalls usually have a relatively small volume of water. These are called cascades. California's Silver Strand and Ribbon falls are cascades. By contrast, more water passes over the famous NIAGARA FALLS than any other in North America, yet Niagara Falls is quite low. Waterfalls with a large volume of water are called cataracts.

Most of North America's major waterfalls are in mountainous regions where there once were glaciers. These include the SIERRA NEVADA and ROCKY MOUNTAINS regions. There are many waterfalls around Yosemite Valley. These include the Bridalveil, Vernal, Nevada, and Illilouette falls. Wyoming's Rockies contain the spectacular Yellowstone Falls.

▼ *Bridalveil Falls is one of many waterfalls that lie along the Colorado River.*

## WATER SPORTS 

Water sports include boating, SWIMMING, diving, rafting, rowing, FISHING, skin diving, surfing, water polo, and waterskiing. Some, like swimming, require little or no equipment. Others, like yacht racing, are very expensive. Swimming, diving, rowing, canoeing, sailing, and water polo are Olympic sports. The AMERICA'S CUP race, held every four years, is an international sailboat racing competition among yachts of the 12-meter (39.4-ft) class. New water sports are constantly being developed. Windsurfing and parasailing were unheard of only 25 years ago. Even surfing was hardly known outside Hawaii and California until about 1960.

▲ *Windsurfing, also called sailboarding, has become one of America's most popular water sports in the 20 years since its invention.*

◀ *California aqueducts pass through hundreds of miles of desert to supply Los Angeles with its water.*

## WATER SUPPLY 

The United States has an excellent system of water supply. Most cities are located near a body of fresh water, such as a lake or river. Larger cities build reservoirs to hold water during times when their normal supplies start to run dry. Smaller communities often get their water from underground wells. Slightly more than half of U.S. water consumption is by industry. Irrigation for farmland accounts for about 40 percent of the total. Some of the rest goes for SEWAGE DISPOSAL. Households use water for drinking, showering and bathing,

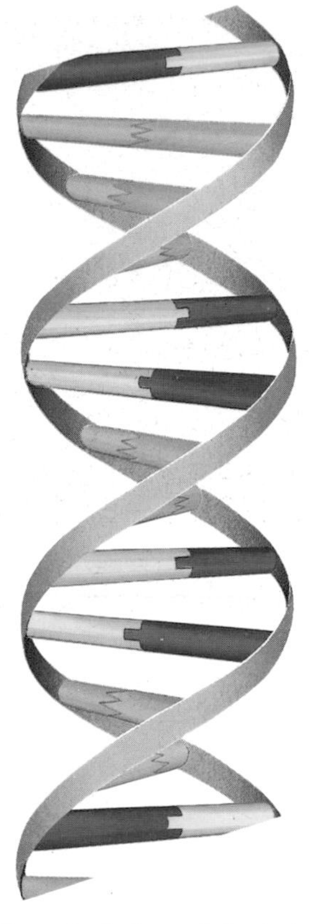

▲ *The spiral-shaped depiction of the DNA molecule is known to biologists as the Watson-Crick model.*

▼ *Anthony Wayne's victory at Stony Point, New York, in 1779 secured American control of a valuable fort along the Hudson River.*

flushing toilets, and cleaning clothes and dishes. People now realize that water pollution is a problem because the supply of fresh water is limited.

## WATSON, James Dewey

James Dewey Watson (1928– ) made one of the most important discoveries in the history of biology. Scientists knew that deoxyribonucleic acid (DNA) was the substance that determines the traits living organisms pass on to their offspring. In 1953, Watson and English biologist Francis Crick found that the DNA molecule is composed of two long strands in the form of a double helix. The structure resembles that of a long, spiral ladder. This discovery is fundamental to contemporary understanding of genetics. Watson shared the 1962 Nobel Prize for physiology or medicine with Crick and another English biologist, Maurice Wilkins.

## WAYNE, Anthony

Anthony Wayne (1745–1796) was a famous general in the American REVOLUTION. A Pennsylvania landowner, Wayne was commissioned a colonel at the start of the war and was later promoted to brigadier general. He played an important part in several battles. In July 1779 he led a brilliant surprise attack on the British fort at Stony Point, New York. This victory greatly helped to boost American morale. Wayne also participated in the Battle of Yorktown. After the war, Wayne led an expedition against the Indians in the Old Northwest. His defeat of

the Indians resulted in the Treaty of Greenville (1795), which opened more western lands to white settlement. Wayne was known as Mad Anthony by his troops because of his rashness.

## WAYNE, John

John Wayne (1907–1979) was an American film actor who was famous for his roles as the strong, silent type, particularly in westerns. Wayne began his film career in 1928 and had his first leading role in *The Big Trail* in 1930. In 1939, *Stagecoach* made him a star. Wayne made more than 250 motion pictures. Some of his best performances were in *Red River*, *The Quiet Man*, *Rio Bravo*, and *The Man Who Shot Liberty Valance*. In 1969, Wayne won an Academy Award for his performance as an aging marshal in *True Grit*.

▲ *John Wayne starred in the popular western* Red River, *made in 1948.*

## WEASELS

The weasel family consists of many fur-bearing animals. North American weasels include the least weasel, short-tailed weasel, or stoat, and the long-tailed weasel. The fur of weasels living in cold climates changes to white in winter. When this happens, the animals are known as ermine. Ermine fur is very valuable.

The North American mink and the American marten, or sable, are two other weasels whose fur is highly prized. The fisher has been trapped for its fur to the point of extinction. Another weasel, the black-footed ferret, is also on the verge of extinction.

Other North American animals in the weasel family are the BADGER, OTTER, SKUNK, and wolverine.

## WEATHER FORECASTING

Accurate predictions of the weather are important for pilots, sailors, and farmers, as well as for people planning their weekends. Weather forecasting is part of meteorology, the study of the earth's atmosphere. A federal agency, the National Weather Service, gathers information from ground stations, earth satellites, airplanes, ships, buoys, and balloons. The data gathered include wind direction and speed, temperature, precipitation, and air pressure. Computers process and analyze this information, and detailed weather maps are created.

▼ *A meteorologist studies a computer display of a weather satellite image at the U.S. National Weather and Hurricane Service.*

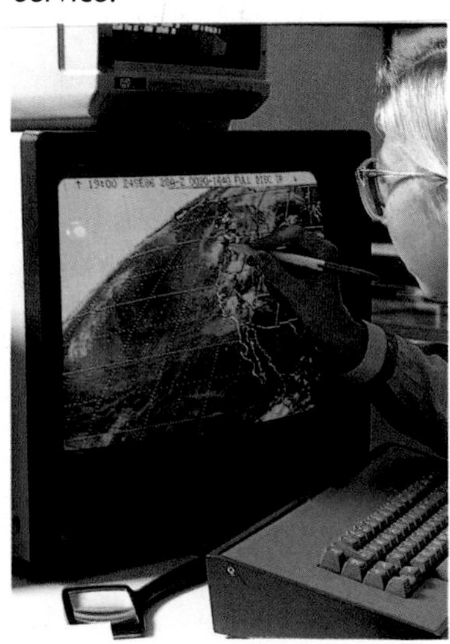

▲ *Daniel Webster was an important member of the Whig Party, and his career in government was a long and impressive one. His dream of the presidency, however, was never realized.*

Simpler versions of these maps appear in newspapers and on television.

The National Weather Service updates its short-term forecasts (18 to 36 hours ahead) about three times daily. Longer-term forecasts contain fewer details and are updated less often. Since weather patterns cross national boundaries, international cooperation is important in predicting the weather. The World Meteorological Organization, a United Nations agency, gathers information from 140 countries.

## WEBSTER, Daniel

Daniel Webster (1782–1852) is considered one of the greatest orators in U.S. history. He was an important figure in American politics for four decades—from 1812 until the end of his life.

Webster studied law at Dartmouth College, where he first began to acquire a reputation as a public speaker. He later became a highly successful lawyer. Beginning in 1812, Webster was twice elected to the House of Representatives and twice to the Senate. He also served as secretary of state under presidents William Henry HARRISON, John TYLER, and Millard FILLMORE. In 1842 he negotiated the Webster-Ashburton Treaty with Britain, which fixed the northern boundary of Maine.

Webster strongly supported the American Union and the supremecy of the federal government over states' rights. In a debate in 1830, he uttered his most famous phrase, "Liberty, *and* Union, now and forever, one and inseparable!"

▼ *In 1803, Noah Webster set aside successful work in law, teaching, and politics to devote the rest of his life to compiling dictionaries.*

## WEBSTER, Noah

Noah Webster (1758–1843) compiled the first American dictionary. Published in 1828, the 70,000-entry *American Dictionary of the English Language* has been revised several times since then. In this book, and in his *American Spelling Book*, which sold millions of copies, Webster standardized and simplified American spelling. He eliminated many silent letters and difficult spellings that remain in British English.

Webster was a graduate of Yale University. He taught school, practiced law, founded two newspapers, and was active in local politics. He was also one of the founders of Amherst College.

## WEIGHTS AND MEASURES

An accurate and accepted system of weights and measures is the best method for determining the size of things. Nearly everything we buy is measured in some way. It is therefore important that buyers, sellers, and producers of goods agree on a system.

The system used in the United States is called the English system of measurements. It is confusing for some people, because the units are divided differently. For example, there are 12 inches in a foot, but 16 ounces in a pound. Most other countries use the metric system, in which everything can be divided by 10, 100, or 1,000. There are 1,000 millimeters in a meter (a unit of length) and 1,000 milliliters in a liter (volume). In 1975 the U.S. Congress passed the Metric Conversion Act. It called for a voluntary changeover from English measurements to metric. So far there has been little response from industry.

Metric Conversion Table

| Unit | Multiply by | Metric |
|---|---|---|
| inches | 25.4 | millimeters |
| feet | 30.5 | centimeters |
| yards | 0.914 | meters |
| miles | 1.61 | kilometers |
| square miles | 2.59 | square kilometers |
| acres | 0.405 | hectares |

## WELLES, Orson

Orson Welles (1915–1985) was one of the most important figures in the history of motion pictures. Born in Kenosha, Wisconsin, Welles was a director in the early days of radio drama. His production of *War of the Worlds* in 1938 was so realistic that thousands of listeners believed the Martians had landed in New Jersey. His first film, *Citizen Kane*, in which he also starred, is a classic and has had influence worldwide. Welles acted and directed all his life.

▲ *Orson Welles co-wrote, directed, and stared in* Citizen Kane. *It was made in 1940, when Welles was only 25 years old.*

## WESTINGHOUSE, George

George Westinghouse (1846–1914) was an American inventor and businessman. He patented about 400 inventions, including the air brake for railroad trains. Born in Central Bridge, New York, Westinghouse began his career when he was only a teenager. He devoted much of his creative energy to trains. By the time he was 20, he had invented two major pieces of railway equipment. In 1869, he patented his famous air brake—an important safety device. Westinghouse set up a company to manufacture the air brake. Of the dozens of companies he headed, the Westinghouse Electric Company (founded 1884) is the best known.

# WEST VIRGINIA

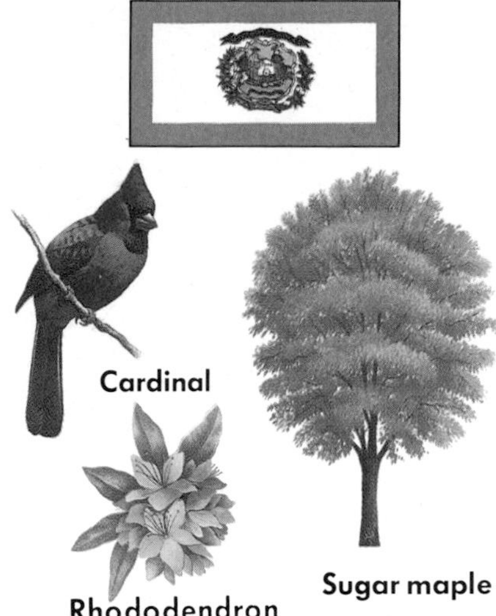


West Virgina
**Capital:** Charleston
**Area:** 24,231 sq mi (62,759 km$^2$). Rank: 41st
**Population:** 1,793,477 (1990). Rank: 41st
**Statehood:** June 20, 1863
**Principal rivers:** Ohio, Guyandotte, Greenbrier
**Highest point:** Spruce Knob, 4,863 ft (1,482 m)
**Motto:** *Montani Semper Liberi* (Mountaineers Are Always Free)
**Song:** "The West Virginia Hills"

Places of Interest

- Harpers Ferry National Historical Park lies southeast of Martinsburg on the border between West Virginia and Maryland. Harpers Ferry is famous in Civil War history.
- The town of Cass, which lies in the scenic Appalachian Mountain country, has a steam-powered train that takes visitors through the area on a former logging railroad.

West Virginia is called the Mountain State because it has the highest average elevation east of the Mississippi River. The slopes of its heavily wooded Appalachian Range, divided by deep valleys and gorges, offer great natural beauty. But its isolation from major economic markets has created many economic problems for the people of West Virginia. Two thirds of the population live in rural areas, often without access to good roads.

Coal mining is the state's most important industry. West Virginia ranks among the top two or three states in coal production. Most of the biggest mines are in the southwestern part of the state. The industry has experienced many bitter strikes. Violence between miners and company guards took many lives.

With little level, fertile soil, West Virginia has fewer than 20,000 farms. The chief sources of farm income are livestock and livestock products. Industry is mostly concentrated around Charleston or near the Ohio and Pennsylvania borders. The main products are chemicals, steel, and glass products. Another source of income is tourism. Mineral springs such as White Sulphur Springs and Webster Springs have been attracting visitors for more than 150 years.

West Virginia was originally part of Virginia. When Virginia seceded from the Union in 1861, to join the Confederacy, the western counties voted to remain in the United States. West Virginia was granted statehood in 1863. Since 1950, many West Virginians have migrated to other parts of the United States.

► *The Blue Ridge Range of the Appalachians helps give West Virginia its nickname, the Mountain State.*

▲ *West Virginia ranks third in U.S. coal production. This mine in Prenter is one of several found all over the state.*

▲ *The Ohio River forms West Virginia's western border and provides an important trade route for the state's commerce.*

Wheeling
Ohio R.
Morgantown
Fairmont
Potomac R.
Martinsburg
Parkersburg
Clarksburg
79
Spruce Knob
4,861 ft (1,482 m)
77
0 30 miles
0 30 kilometers
64
Huntingdon
Charleston
Appalachian Mountains
64
77
64
Beckley
77
Bluefield

# WESTWARD MOVEMENT

In Colonial times, most Americans lived along the Atlantic coast. By the late 1800s, however, the entire area of the United States, from the Atlantic Ocean to the Pacific, was settled. This came about as a result of the westward movement of pioneering settlers across the continent.

People were making their way west even before the United States gained its independence. Their first great obstacle was the Appalachian Mountains. In 1775, however, Daniel BOONE blazed the WILDERNESS ROAD through the mountains. Soon, thousands of settlers used this trail and others to make their way to Kentucky and beyond.

On the western side of the Appalachians, the pioneers came into conflict with the Indians, who fought to protect their lands. But the settlers, aided by the Army, kept pushing the Indians farther and farther west—and later onto reservations. By 1840 millions of people had moved into the area between the Appalachians and the Mississippi River. Some had even ventured west of the Mississippi.

The next great wave took place between 1840 and 1860. These pioneers crossed the Great Plains in wagon trains. They braved Indian attacks and other dangers to reach the fertile farmland of the Far West. The California GOLD RUSH of 1848 brought miners to the West. The MORMONS, seeking a place to practice their religion in peace, settled in Utah.

The last part of the United States to be settled was the Great Plains. Many called this arid area the Great American Desert. But after the HOMESTEAD ACT of 1862, farmers flocked to the region. The completion of the country's first transcontinental railroad in 1869 spurred more migration. By 1890, the great westward movement was at an end.

**Many early settlers were ill-suited for the fearful adventure ahead. They knew little or nothing about the wilderness, the Indians, or the animals they would encounter. Few had ever seen a firearm.**

▼ *The different colors on the map below show how the United States expanded westward.*

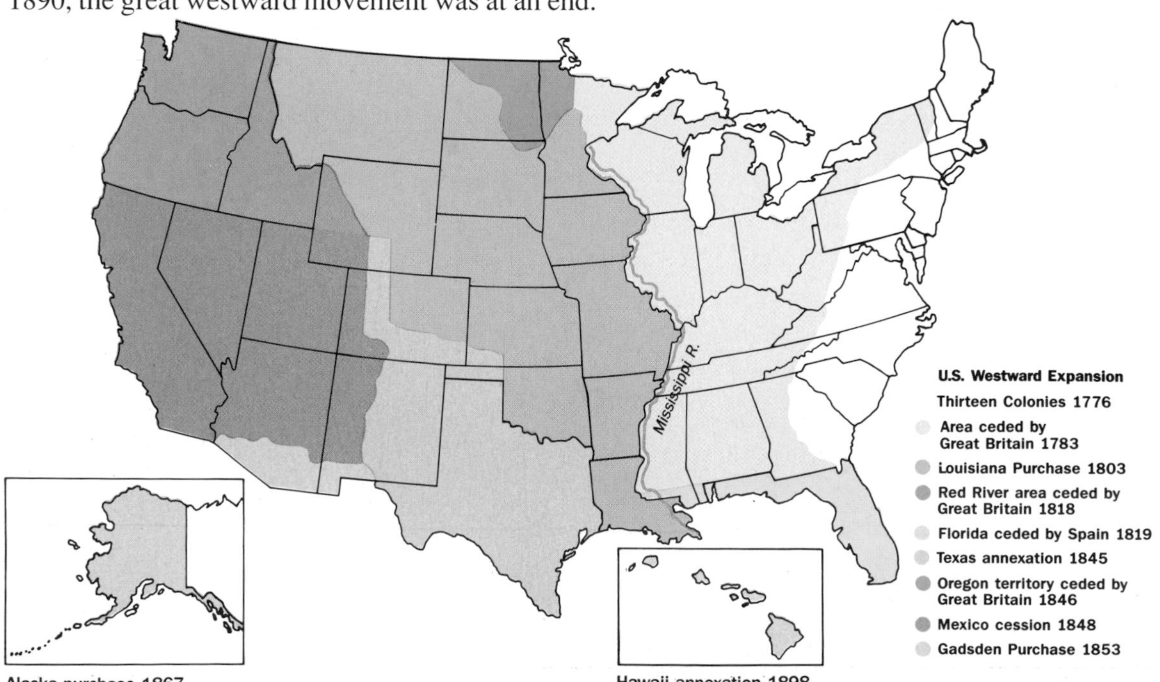

▲ *The title of Emanuel Leutze's mural,* Westward the Course of Empire Takes Its Way, *reflected the nation's pride in its pioneer tradition. The mural is in the U.S. Capitol.*

**The Wilderness Road, pioneered by Daniel Boone in 1775, was a rocky trail menaced by unfriendly Indians. But by 1800 about 200,000 settlers had traveled west along it.**

▼ *The first railroad routes to the West Coast followed pioneer trails blazed during the westward movement. Some of these trails, such as the Oregon Trail, went straight through the Rocky Mountains and proved too steep for trains.*

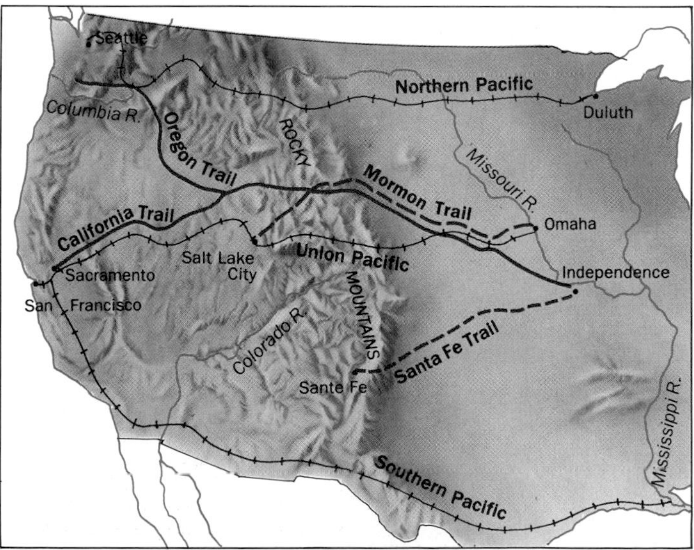


### Westward Movement

**1607:** Jamestown established as the first permanent English settlement.
**1763:** British victory at the end of the French and Indian War gains French territory; Proclamation of 1763 forbids settlement west of the Appalachians by colonists.
**1775:** Daniel Boone opens the Wilderness Road.
**1783:** The United States receives British lands extending west to the Mississippi, north to Canada, and south to Florida following the Revolutionary War.
**1785:** Ordinance of 1785 provides a system of government buying and selling of land.
**1787:** The Northwest Ordinance provides a government for the Northwest Territory.
**1803:** The Louisiana Purchase extends the U.S. border to the Rocky Mountains.
**1845:** The United States annexes Texas.
**1846:** Southern part of Oregon region ceded to the United States by Great Britain.
**1848:** The United States acquires California and the Southwest as a result of the Mexican War; the Gold Rush leads prospectors to California.
**1862:** Homestead Act provides free land to settlers in the West.
**1869:** First transcontinental railway is completed.
**1890:** Bureau of the Census declares that the frontier as a line of settlement on the Census map no longer exists.

► *A gray whale surfaces for air off the Californian coast. Gray whales grow up to 50 feet (15 m) long and feed on small animals that live on the ocean floor.*

**A New England whaling industry flourished in the 1700s and early 1800s. Oil from sperm whales was used for lamps; each whale provided about 2,500 gallons of oil.**

## WHALES

Many kinds of whales are found in the waters off North America. These include the right, gray, humpback, and pilot whales. The bowhead, or Greenland, whale lives in the Arctic Ocean. The largest is the blue whale, which is now rare. Up to 100 feet (30 m) long, it is the largest animal that has ever lived—longer than even the largest dinosaur. Dolphins and porpoises, which are types of whales, also live in North American waters.

Whales have long been hunted by people. They have been hunted so much in the 1900s that many species are endangered. In 1946 the principal whaling countries set up the International Whaling Commission (IWC). It banned the killing of endangered species and limited the numbers of other whales that might be killed. Commercial whaling was banned by the IWC from 1986 to allow the number of whales to increase.

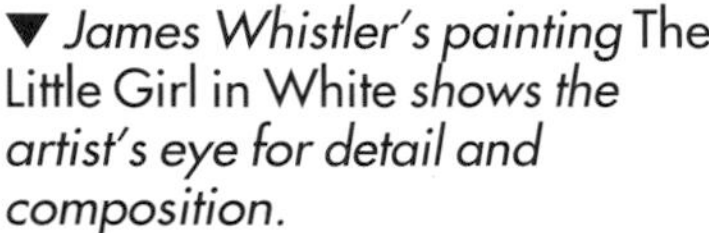

▼ *James Whistler's painting* The Little Girl in White *shows the artist's eye for detail and composition.*

## WHISTLER, James A. McNeil

James Abbott McNeil Whistler (1834–1903) was a famous American painter. Born in Massachusetts, he spent much of his life in London, England. Whistler was noted especially for his portraits. The best known of these is the seated profile portrait of his mother. It is commonly known as "Whistler's Mother." Later in life he produced many fine etchings and lithographs, including a remarkable series of Venetian scenes.

## WHITE, E. B.

Elwyn Brooks White (1899–1985) was a noted author. He wrote three classic books for children, *Stuart Little*, *Charlotte's Web*, and *The Trumpet of the Swan*.

After graduating from Cornell University, White became a journalist. In 1927 he joined the staff of *The New Yorker* magazine. He had a great influence on the magazine's style and content. Among his books or essays are *The Second Tree from the Corner* and *Points of My Compass*. White also produced a revised edition of William Strunk's guide to writing, *The Elements of Style*.

**As editor of *The Elements of Style*, E. B. White stressed the importance of clear and concise writing. He used this skill for children's books, such as *Charlotte's Web*, as well as in his sophisticated articles for *The New Yorker* magazine.**

## WHITE HOUSE

The White House has been the official home of the president of the United States since 1800. Most of the original building was destroyed by the British during the War of 1812. It was then rebuilt and enlarged several times. The White House contains the president's office as well as his living quarters. The famous Oval Office is in the west wing, as are the offices of the president's staff. Military advisers are in offices in the east wing. Many of the rooms are open to the public—the State Dining Room, the Red Room, and the Blue Room (the reception room for presidential guests).

**During Theodore Roosevelt's term of office, the White House was restored and enlarged. The East Room, which had been used for only the most formal occasions, was temporarily used by Roosevelt's children for roller-skating contests!**

▼ *The south portico (porch) of the White House is elegantly curved with tall columns.*

▲ *Walt Whitman had a great love for his country. He once wrote that "the United States are essentially the greatest poem."*

## WHITMAN, Walt 

Walt Whitman (1819–1892) was the greatest American poet of the 19th century. He is best known for his *Leaves of Grass*, a collection of poems that he revised and added to over nearly 40 years.

Born on Long Island, New York, Whitman learned the printing trade and then worked as a teacher and a journalist.

The first edition of *Leaves of Grass* was published in 1855. Its longest poem, "Song of Myself," contains the major themes of Whitman's poetry: a celebration of himself and of life, freedom, and equality of all people and the cyclical rebirth of nature. Like all of Whitman's poetry, it is written in free verse.

During the CIVIL WAR , Whitman served as a volunteer nurse in a Washington hospital. His grief at the death of President Abraham LINCOLN was expressed in two of his finest poems, "When Lilacs Last in the Dooryard Bloom'd" and "O Captain! My Captain!"

▲ *Eli Whitney's cotton gin could clean as much cotton in a day as 50 people could by hand.*

## WHITNEY, Eli 

Eli Whitney (1765–1825) was the inventor of the cotton gin. Born in Westborough, Massachusetts, he graduated from Yale College in 1792. Whitney then went to Georgia, where he saw the difficulties of harvesting cotton. He designed and built the cotton gin, a machine that quickly removed the seeds from cotton. His invention enabled farmers to grow cotton in much larger quantities. Whitney patented the cotton gin in 1794.

## WHITTIER, John Greenleaf 

John Greenleaf Whittier (1807–1892) was both a poet and a noted ABOLITIONIST writer. He was born into a Quaker family, on a Massachusetts farm. Later in life he would portray rural life in his poems, including his best known, "Snow-Bound." As a young man, however, he wrote mainly prose. His first book, *Legends of New England in Prose and Verse*, was published in 1831.

Whittier believed strongly in the abolition of slavery. He wrote essays, articles, and poems on the subject. From the 1840s onward, Whittier's poetry became very popular. Other successes, in addition to "Snow-Bound," were "Maud Muller" and "The Barefoot Boy."

## WIESEL, Elie 

Elie Wiesel (1928– ) is a well-known author and educator. He was born in Romania, and his parents died in Nazi concentration camps during WORLD WAR II. After the war, Wiesel lived and studied in France. In 1976, he settled in the United States and became a citizen. Wiesel has written several books about the Nazi camps and their survivors, including his own story, *Night*. His lifework is to let people know what happened under the Nazis. He speaks out on behalf of all who suffer from hatred and racism. In 1986, Elie Wiesel was awarded the Nobel Peace Prize.

## WILDER, Thornton 

Thornton Niven Wilder (1897–1975) was an award-winning playwright and novelist. He was born in Madison, Wisconsin, and even as a child he knew he wanted to write plays.

He began writing for the stage in 1915, but his first real success came from his novel *The Bridge of San Luis Rey*. The novel won him the first of three PULITZER PRIZES. The other two were for his plays *Our Town* and *The Skin of Our Teeth*. Wilder's writing captured the feel of American life and speech at a time when the country was outgrowing its small-town origins and becoming a world power.

▲ *Thornton Wilder's plays could poke fun at people's failings while still retaining a sympathetic tone.*

## WILDERNESS ROAD 

The Wilderness Road was an important pioneer route through the Appalachian Mountains. Its opening was one of the first important chapters of the WESTWARD MOVEMENT. The Wilderness Road was a 300-mile (500-km) route from eastern Virginia through the Cumberland Gap to Kentucky. It ended at the Ohio River. The route was first explored by Daniel BOONE in 1769. In 1775, Boone and 30 other pioneers cut down trees and rolled away boulders to mark it as a trail. By 1790, more than 100,000 pioneers had traveled along the Wilderness Road to settle Kentucky and eastern Tennessee. These settlers had to make their way on foot because the Wilderness Road was not widened for wagons until 1795. Even then, pioneers risked attacks from hostile Indians.

▼ *Pioneers traveling along the Wilderness Road had to be well armed to protect themselves from hostile Indians.*

## WILDFLOWERS 

▼ *Wildflowers demonstrate the richness of American plant life. Some species, such as the lady's slipper, are protected, which means that they cannot be picked.*

Wildflowers are flowering plants that have not been deliberately planted. There are about 10,000 species, or types, of wildflowers in North America. Each grows in the habitat, or natural home, that suits it best.

Wildflowers thrive in the mild climate of the southern California chaparral and also in the grasslands of central California and eastern Washington and Oregon.

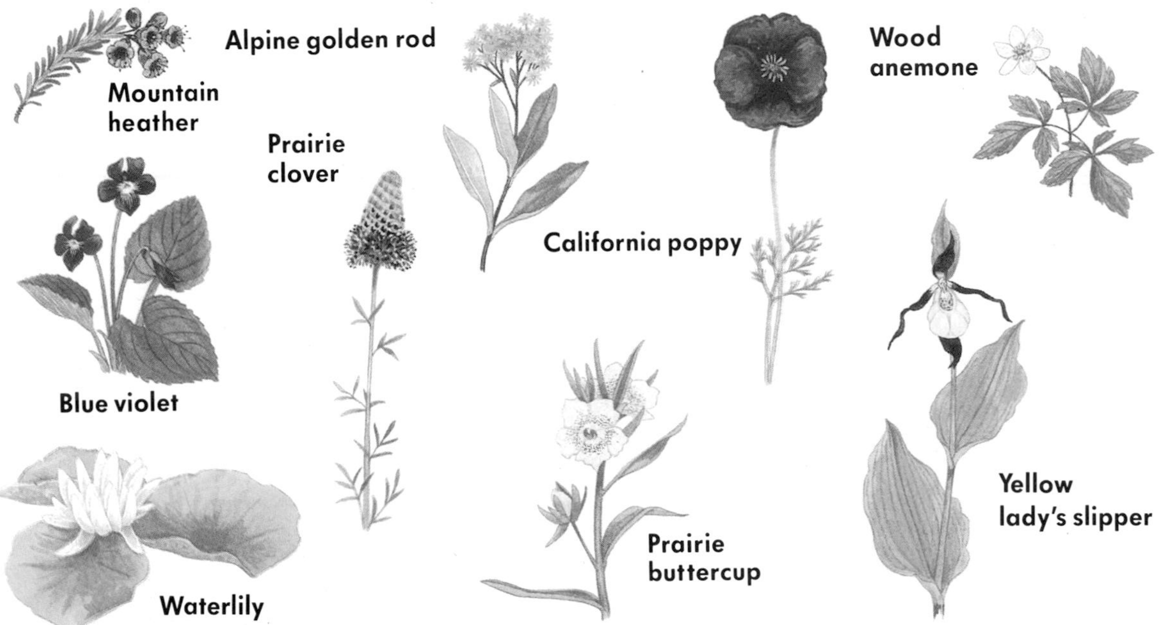


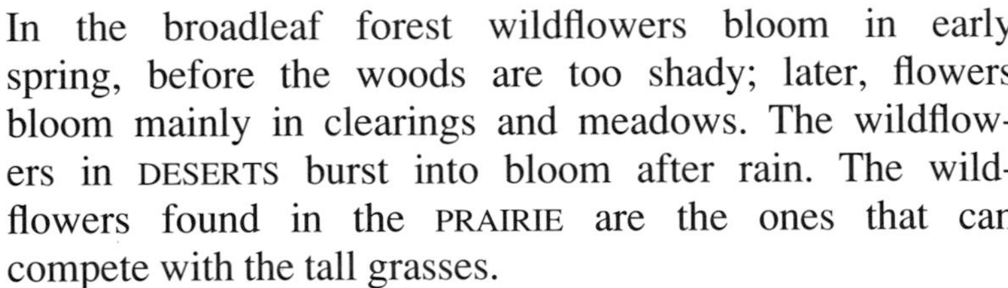

In the broadleaf forest wildflowers bloom in early spring, before the woods are too shady; later, flowers bloom mainly in clearings and meadows. The wildflowers in DESERTS burst into bloom after rain. The wildflowers found in the PRAIRIE are the ones that can compete with the tall grasses.

▼ *Roy Wilkins's lifetime efforts to promote racial equality earned him the nickname Mr. Civil Rights.*

## WILKINS, Roy 

The black CIVIL RIGHTS leader Roy Wilkins (1901–1981) was executive director of the NATIONAL ASSOCIATION FOR THE ADVANCEMENT OF COLORED PEOPLE (NAACP) from 1955 to 1977.

Wilkins was born in St. Louis, Missouri, and graduated from the University of Minnesota. He first worked in journalism, as managing editor of a black newspaper, the *Kansas City Call*. After joining the NAACP in 1931, he directed its nationwide anti-discrimination program.

During the 1960s he kept the organization focused on achieving black rights through legal means. Wilkins was awarded the U.S. Medal of Freedom in 1968.

## WILLIAMS, Roger 

Roger Williams (1603?–1683) was the founder of the colony of Rhode Island. He was born in England and educated at Cambridge University. Although ordained in the Church of England, he became a Puritan and settled in the Massachusetts Bay Colony in 1630. There, he came into conflict with the colony's strict government, and in 1636 he was banished. He settled on some land purchased from the Narragansett Indians, with whom he established friendly relations (even learning their language), and founded the town of Providence. Other refugees from Massachusetts settled in this area, eventually forming the colony of Rhode Island, with Williams as its leader. Williams's policy of religious tolerance made Rhode Island a haven for many people.

**The colony that Roger Williams set up in Providence, Rhode Island, was the first true democracy in America. Religious liberty was guaranteed for all, and the Indians were treated fairly.**

## WILLIAMS, Tennessee 

Tennessee (born Thomas Lanier) Williams (1911–1983) was an important American playwright. He was born in Mississippi and most of his plays are set in his native South. Williams began writing plays while at college in Missouri and Iowa. His first major success, *The Glass Menagerie* is about a shy, crippled girl and her mother's unrealistic ambitions for her. In later plays, such as *A Streetcar Named Desire*, *Cat on a Hot Tin Roof* (both PULITZER PRIZE winners), and *The Night of the Iguana*, Williams dealt frankly but sympathetically with people's frustrations and their violent natures.

▼ *Tennessee Williams, seen here on the S.S.* Liberty *on his way to London, had his plays performed around the world.*

## WILSON, Edmund 

Edmund Wilson (1895–1972) was an important 20th-century writer and literary critic.

Wilson, who was born in Red Bank, New Jersey, wrote about many subjects, including literature, history, politics, and religion. Many of his writings appeared in *The New Yorker* magazine. He was a brilliant man who learned Russian and Hebrew for his research. His better known works include *Axel's Castle*, *Scrolls from the Dead Sea*, and *To the Finland Station.*

# WILSON, (Thomas) Woodrow

Woodrow Wilson was the 28th president of the United States. He was a man of high ideals. He worked toward the creation of a world that was at peace. As president, he led the United States to victory in WORLD WAR I. But Congress rejected the peace he negotiated as well as U.S. membership in the LEAGUE OF NATIONS.

Wilson had been a professor, university president, and governor of New Jersey before he was elected president in 1912. A Democrat, he won without polling a majority of popular votes because the Republicans were split. Once in office, he announced a program of liberal reforms. A new central banking system was established, and the tariff was lowered. The Clayton Anti-Trust Act and New Federal Trade Commission attempted to curb unfair practices by big business.

▲ *President Woodrow Wilson introduced his Fourteen Points as a way of ending World War I honorably and of setting up the League of Nations.*

Wilson believed the United States should support democracy abroad. He opposed the Mexican dictator Victoriano Huerta and narrowly avoided war. He tried to keep the country neutral in World War I and was re-elected on the slogan "He kept us out of war." Soon after, Germany resumed sinking American ships carrying supplies to Britain and France. At Wilson's request, Congress declared war. His FOURTEEN POINTS advanced the principle of the self-determination of nations and were intended as the basis for a peace settlement. But the Republican-dominated Congress rejected the Treaty of Versailles, which involved American participation in the League of Nations. In late 1919, Wilson suffered a stroke. He was an invalid for the rest of his presidential term.

Woodrow Wilson
**Born:** December 29, 1856, in Staunton, Virginia
**Education:** Princeton University
**Political party:** Democratic
**Term of office:** 1913–1921
**Married:** 1885 to Ellen Axson
**Died:** February 3, 1924, in Washington, D.C.

## WINNIPEG

Winnipeg is the capital of MANITOBA, Canada's eastern most Prairie Province. With a population of over 600,000 it is the fourth largest city in Canada. Winnipeg's location in the heart of the Canadian prairie makes it the country's main market for grain. This same central location, midway between the Atlantic and Pacific oceans, accounts for its nickname, the Gateway to the West. The city's chief products are food products, furniture, clothing, buses, farm tools, and aircraft equipment.

Winnipeg was established in 1738 as Fort Rouge and became the provincial capital in 1870. Its growth began in 1885, when the Canadian Pacific Railroad arrived.

▲ *Old and modern business buildings form the heart of Winnipeg's downtown "exchange district."*

## WINTER SPORTS

The popular winter sports of SKATING, SKIING, and ICE HOCKEY were once confined to the northern United States. Now, with the development of skating rinks and dry ski slopes, people from most parts of the country can take part. Most of these sports are recreational; people participate mainly for enjoyment or amateur prizes. However, ice hockey's professional league offers top salaries to some of its best players, such as Wayne Gretzky. The Winter Olympics, held every four years, are the ultimate test for winter sportsmen and women.

▼ *The exhilarating sport of downhill (or Alpine) skiing requires good balance and physical fitness.*

## WINTHROP, John

John Winthrop (1588–1649) was a leader of the Massachusetts Bay Colony. He served as its governor for 12 years between 1629 and 1648.

Winthrop was born into a wealthy English family. He studied law at Cambridge University and in 1627 obtained a position in the government. A devout Puritan, Winthrop lost this position in 1629 because of King Charles I's anti-Puritan policy. He then joined the Massachusetts Bay Company and sailed with his family to America.

As the Puritan colony's first governor, Winthrop played a major role in organizing it, establishing towns along strict religious lines. Although some colonists opposed Winthrop's authoritarian rule, the majority respected him. At their annual elections, the voters reelected him 11 times.

# WISCONSIN

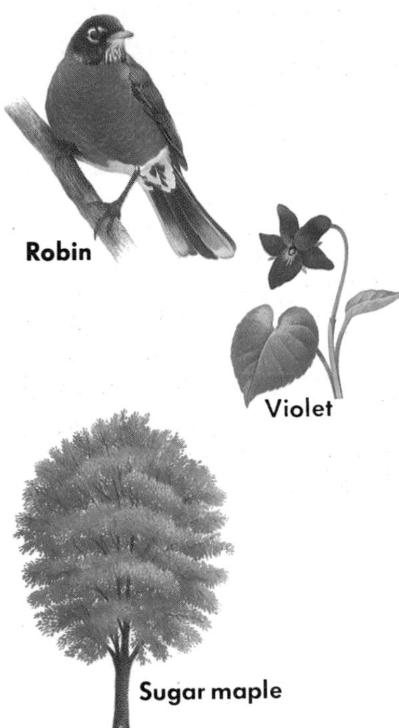


The midwestern state of Wisconsin is one of the country's leading producers of dairy goods. Wisconsin raises more dairy cows than any other state, and one of its nicknames is America's Dairyland. Wisconsin leads the nation in milk, butter, and cheese production. The chief farm crop is corn.

Processing of dairy goods is just one part of Wisconsin's healthy manufacturing sector. The processing of vegetables and fruit canning are also important. Factories produce electrical goods, paper products, machinery, household goods such as kitchen equipment, and motor vehicles. The state's rich forests provide the raw materials for a thriving paper-making industry. The state's largest city, Milwaukee, is one of the world's most important beer producers.

Wisconsin borders Lake Michigan and Lake Superior. The Lake Michigan ports of Green Bay, Milwaukee, Kenosha, and Racine ship agricultural and manufactured goods to the East by way of the ST. LAWRENCE SEAWAY or by truck and rail. The Mississippi River forms much of the state's western border with Iowa. Wisconsin's Northern Highland region, near Lake Superior, attracts many tourists to its wooded hills and thousands of lakes.

French explorers, fur traders, and missionaries were the first to visit Wisconsin, in the 1600s. It passed to the British in 1763 and to the United States in 1783. Settlers from the East and immigrants from Europe arrived between 1830 and 1850.

**Places of Interest**

- Visitors to the Milwaukee Public Museum can view some of the best natural-history exhibits in the United States.
- The Wisconsin River winds through the Wisconsin Dells, one of the most beautiful areas in the state.
- The Circus World Museum, in Baraboo, north of Madison, houses displays of equipment used by U.S. circuses. Visitors can see circus acts there every day during the summer.

► *Racine, Wisconsin's fourth largest city, has an attractive shoreline along Lake Michigan.*

◀ *The Dairy Shrine, located in Fort Atkinson, houses an impressive collection of Indian arrowheads.*

**Wisconsin**
**Capital:** Madison
**Area:** 65,503 sq mi (169,653 km²). Rank: 23rd
**Population:** 4,891,769 (1990). Rank: 16th
**Statehood:** May 29, 1848
**Principal rivers:** Wisconsin, Mississippi, Chippewa
**Highest point:** Timms Hill, 1,952 ft (595 m)
**Motto:** Forward
**Song:** "On, Wisconsin!"

▲ *Milwaukee is the largest city in Wisconsin and a major port on Lake Michigan.*

▲ *The wolf's skill as a hunter derives from its acute sense of smell, sight, and hearing.*

## WOLF

The wolf is the largest member of the DOG family. The wolf found in the United States is the timber wolf, a type of gray wolf. It was once found all over North America, but its numbers have been greatly reduced by hunting. Today it is an endangered species (in danger of dying out completely) except in Alaska and Minnesota.

The red wolf once lived all over the South. Today it is found only on the Texas-Louisiana border. Like the timber wolf, it is an endangered species.

## WOLFE, Thomas

Thomas Wolfe (1900–1938) was a major 20th-century writer. He is best known for his novel *Look Homeward, Angel.* Like most of his work, it is strongly autobiographical. It tells the story of a boy growing up in the town of Altamont, North Carolina (based on his native Asheville). Time and memory are favorite themes in Wolfe's writing. On his early death, Wolfe left a huge pile of manuscripts. From this his editor, Edward Aswell, drew several works, including the novels *The Web and the Rock* and *You Can't Go Home Again.*

## WOMEN'S RIGHTS

Women's struggle for social, political, and educational equality with men in the United States began in the 1800s. A women's rights convention in 1848 was organized by Lucretia MOTT and Elizabeth Cady STANTON. They demanded the right to vote (SUFFRAGE) and equal economic opportunity. Women finally received the right to vote in 1920, when the Nineteenth Amendment to the U.S. Constitution was passed.

The women's rights movement took on new life in the 1960s. In 1964, job discrimination on the basis of sex was forbidden by federal law. The National Organization for Women, founded by Betty Friedan in 1966, called for an end to all discrimination against women. Feminists fought for the passage of the Equal Rights Amendment. They failed in this effort. But women have made advances, nevertheless. In the 1830s, for example, women had limited access to college. Today, they make up more than 50 percent of the student body. Still, much remains to be done in other areas.

**In 1972 Congress passed the Equal Rights Amendment (ERA) to the Constitution, but it had to be approved by three fourths of the individual state legislatures. The bill narrowly missed this target in 1982. Supporters of women's rights still view this as a setback rather than a defeat.**

## WORLD WAR I

World War I began in 1914 as a conflict between the Entente Powers, or Allies (chiefly Britain, France, and Russia), and the Central Powers (chiefly Germany, Austria-Hungary, and Turkey). Most Americans wanted to stay neutral. However, Britain and France ordered large amounts of American goods for the war effort. Germany could not obtain those goods because of the British sea blockade. To keep them from reaching Britain and France, it ordered its submarines (U-boats) to sink merchant ships on sight. Because of these assaults, the United States went to war on April 6, 1917.

The U.S. Navy helped the British to reduce the German U-boat menace. The American Expeditionary Force (AEF), led by General John PERSHING, was sent to France beginning in 1917. An armistice on November 11, 1918, ended the war. U.S. battle casualties included about 53,000 men killed.

▲ *This World War I recruiting poster was painted by John Thomason, Jr., who was a U.S. marine.*

◀ *The American Expeditionary Force in France numbered more than 1 million men. Among the battles they fought were Chateau-Thierry, Belleau Wood, St. Mihiel, and the Argonne Forest.*

**Important Events of World War I**

**1914:** Assassination of Austrian Archduke Franz Ferdinand triggers war between the Allies (France, Great Britain, and Russia) and the Central Powers (Germany and Austria-Hungary); German advance stalls just east of Paris; Turkey joins the Central Powers.

**1915:** 128 U.S. passengers die when Germans sink the British ship *Lusitania*; poison gas used in battle for the first time; Italy declares war on Austria-Hungary.

**1916:** United States aids Allies with trade and loans; millions of soldiers die in trench warfare.

**1917:** United States declares war on Germany (April 6); first U.S. troops arrive in Europe (October).

**1918:** More than a million U.S. troops in Europe; Russia leaves the war (March); final Allied attack forces German and Austrian surrender (November 11).

**U.S. infantrymen in World War I were given the unusual nickname "doughboys." Some historians say that the round brass buttons on infantry uniforms reminded the men of balls of dough. Others suggest that the name came from the dough-like clay that infantrymen used to clean their white belts.**

▲ *Jubilant French children and adults greeted U.S. soldiers when the Germans were driven from Paris in 1944.*

## WORLD WAR II

World War II began on September 1, 1939, when Britain and France declared war on Germany after it invaded Poland. By mid-1941 the war was truly worldwide. Japan and Italy had joined Germany to form the Axis Powers. The Soviet Union and other nations had joined the Allies because of Axis aggression. Following the Japanese attack on PEARL HARBOR, Hawaii, on December 7, 1941, the United States declared war on Japan. The other Axis powers then declared war on the United States.

The Allied war effort concentrated on defeating Germany first. By early 1943 the U.S. and British navies had reduced the German submarine threat to North Atlantic shipping. In the meantime, U.S. forces landed in North Africa, where they defeated Axis troops in May 1943. The invasion of Italy followed. On June 6, 1944—D DAY—Allied forces crossed the English Channel and landed in western France. Meanwhile, Soviet troops were advancing on Germany from the east. The Germans surrendered on May 7, 1945.

The war against Japan was led by the United States. The U.S. victory in the naval Battle of MIDWAY, June 3–6, 1942, made it possible to begin retaking islands in the Pacific Ocean. Atom bombs dropped on Hiroshima and Nagasaki forced Japan to surrender on August 14, 1945. On September 2, 1945, aboard the U.S. battleship *Missouri*, the surrendered was signed, and the war ended.

**Many American "isolationists" opposed U.S. entry into World War II, which they considered a "foreign war." It took the Japanese attack on Pearl Harbor for President Franklin D. Roosevelt to convince all of the country that the war was a battle to preserve freedom.**

Important Events of World War II

1939: Germany invades Poland; Great Britain and France declare war on Germany.

1940: Germany defeats Denmark, Norway, Belgium, the Netherlands, Luxembourg, and France; the Battle of Britain limits German air power; Italy joins the war on Germany's side.

1941: Germany invades Russia (June 22); Japanese attack Pearl Harbor in Hawaii (December 7); the United States enters World War II.

1942: U.S. naval victory at Midway turns back Japanese advance; Germans reach outskirts of Leningrad and Moscow.

1943: Soviet troops begin to push Germans back; U.S. marines defeat Japanese at Guadalcanal; Allies invade Italy.

1944: Allies attack occupied France on D Day (June 6); massive U.S. Air Force bombing raids on Japan.

1945: Allied troops invade the Japanese-held Philippines; Allied troops fight in Germany (spring); Germany surrenders (May 7); 2 atomic bombs dropped on Japan; Japan surrenders (August 14).

**The mass-production techniques pioneered by Henry Ford helped the United States build its naval fleet and air force. One factory in Willow Run, Michigan, turned out 8,760 airplanes a year or one an hour, 24 hours a day.**

## WRESTLING

Wrestling is a sport in which one opponent tries to pin the other opponent's shoulders to the floor. There are two main kinds of wrestling. In freestyle wrestling, the wrestlers can use their legs to force their opponents to the floor. This type of wrestling is popular in the United States. In Greco-Roman wrestling, the legs cannot be used. Both types of wrestling are featured in the Olympic Games.

▲ *An amateur wrestler (in red) uses his head to avoid being pinned by his opponent. Defensive tactics are important in wrestling.*

## WRIGHT, Frank Lloyd

Frank Lloyd Wright (1867–1957) is considered the greatest of all American architects. He designed many office buildings in Chicago. Later, he developed the "prairie house," a style of house especially suited to the Midwest. It was low and spreading. Wright's best-loved building is probably Falling Water. This concrete house, built on a wooded site near Bear Run, Pennsylvania, seems to hover over the waterfall that inspired its name. Wright also designed the Guggenheim Museum in New York City.

**Frank Lloyd Wright had a wonderful sense of humor. He once said that "the physician can bury his mistakes but the architect can only advise his clients to plant vines."**

## WRIGHT BROTHERS

The Wright brothers, Wilbur (1867–1912) and Orville (1871–1948), invented the first successful airplane. On December 17, 1903, at Kitty Hawk, North Carolina, they flew their aircraft four times. The flights ranged from 120 to 852 feet (36 to 260 m) and lasted no longer than a minute. People began to take air flight seriously in 1908 when Orville flew a one-hour flight. They set up companies to manufacture airplanes in the United States and Europe. Today, the original plane is in the National Air and Space Museum in Washington, D.C.

► *Only five people witnessed the world's first powered airplane flights, on December 17, 1903. Orville Wright piloted the first, and shortest, flight. His brother Wilbur made the longest flight, of just under a minute, later that day. It took nearly five years for the public to recognize their accomplishment.*

# WYOMING

Wyoming
**Capital:** Cheyenne
**Area:** 97,818 sq mi (253,349 km$^2$). Rank: 10th
**Population:** 453,588 (1990). Rank: 50th
**Statehood:** July 10, 1890
**Principal rivers:** Bighorn, Green, North Platte
**Highest point:** Gannett Peak, 13,804 ft (4,207 m)
**Motto:** Equal Rights
**Song:** "Wyoming"

Wyoming is a land of wide open spaces. It is the ninth largest state but is the one with the fewest people. Nearly half the land is owned by the federal government. These holdings include Yellowstone, the oldest and largest of the national parks.

Next to Colorado, Wyoming is the highest state. It has an average elevation of 6,700 feet (2,040 m). The eastern third is part of the GREAT PLAINS, but even here the lowest point is 3,100 feet (945 m). The rest of the state consists of ROCKY MOUNTAIN ranges, divided by the Wyoming Basin. Cattle and sheep, which outnumber people five to one, graze on about half of Wyoming's land. The state's minerals, however, are its chief source of income. Wyoming is among the nation's leading states in the production of coal, oil, natural gas, and uranium. Six of the nation's seven biggest coal mines are there. Industries convert these raw materials into petroleum products, chemicals, and fertilizer.

The harsh, arid climate, with its extremes of heat and cold, has always made Wyoming hard for settlers. Pioneers passed through on their way to California and Oregon, but few chose to stay. In 1867, however, the

*► Devils Tower, in northeastern Wyoming, became the country's first national monument in 1906. It is a sheer tower of volcanic rock, rising 865 feet (264 m) from its base.*

*▼ An archway made of elk antlers marks the center of Jackson Hole, a popular skiing and fishing center in Wyoming.*

◀ *Wyoming is one of the leading producers of oil in the United States.*

Union Pacific Railroad crossed Wyoming, and towns grew up overnight by the tracks. In 1869 the women of Wyoming became the only ones in the nation with the right to vote. This left an impression, and when Wyoming won statehood in 1890, it was called the Equality State. Nellie Tayloe Ross became governor in 1925—the first woman governor of a state.

**Places of Interest**

- Fort Laramie National Historic Site is a restored fort by the North Platte River. A former fur-trading center, the fort helped to protect pioneers along the Oregon Trail.
- Devils Tower, a volcanic tower northeast of Gillette, was established as the first national monument in the United States in 1906.
- Yellowstone National Park is the world's oldest national park. The spectacular gesyer Old Faithful is a popular attraction.

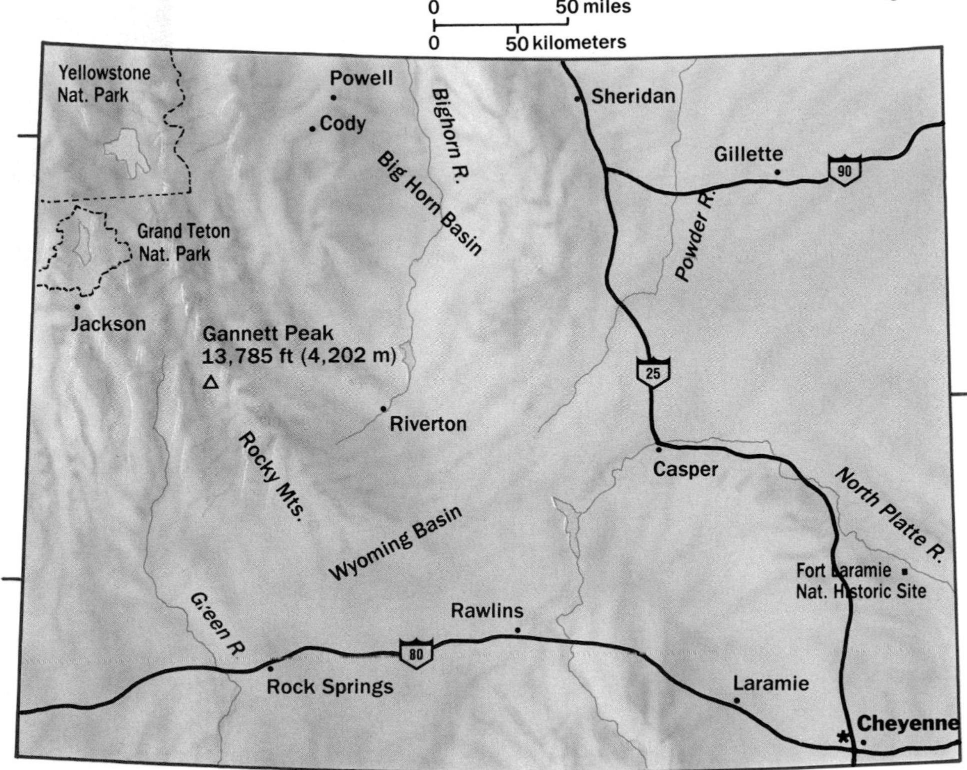

## YOUNG, Andrew 

Andrew Jackson Young, Jr. (1932– ), is an outspoken civil rights leader and a politician. Born in New Orleans, he became a minister in the United Church of Christ. He worked with Martin Luther King, Jr., in the civil rights movement, becoming executive director of the Southern Christian Leadership Conference in 1964. Young was elected to the U.S. House of Representatives from Georgia in 1972 and re-elected in 1974 and 1976. From 1977 to 1979 he was the U.S. ambassador to the United Nations, the first black to hold that position. From 1981 to 1989 he was mayor of Atlanta, Georgia.

## YOUNG, Brigham 

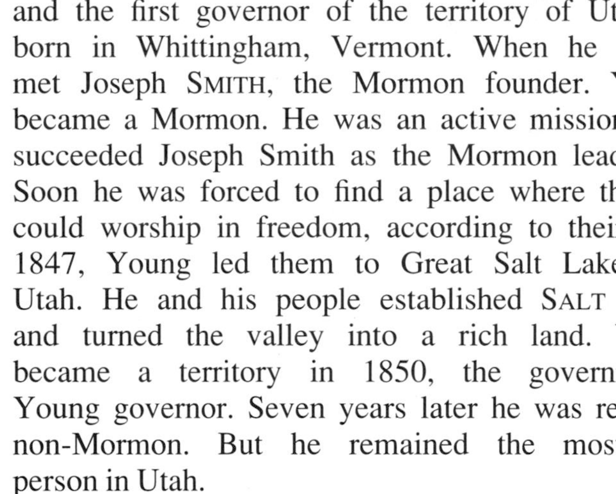

Brigham Young (1801–1877) was a Mormon leader and the first governor of the territory of Utah. He was born in Whittingham, Vermont. When he was 28, he met Joseph Smith, the Mormon founder. Young soon became a Mormon. He was an active missionary. Young succeeded Joseph Smith as the Mormon leader in 1844. Soon he was forced to find a place where the Mormons could worship in freedom, according to their beliefs. In 1847, Young led them to Great Salt Lake Valley in Utah. He and his people established Salt Lake City and turned the valley into a rich land. When Utah became a territory in 1850, the government made Young governor. Seven years later he was replaced by a non-Mormon. But he remained the most important person in Utah.

▲ *Six days after arriving in Utah, Brigham Young issued decrees that the land would be neither bought nor sold. Instead it was assigned to Mormon settlers according to their skills. Young's plan turned the desert into some of the most fertile land in the western United States.*

## YOUNG, Whitney M., Jr. 

Whitney Moore Young, Jr. (1921–1971), was an educator, a social worker, and a civil rights leader who urged blacks and whites to cooperate. Born in Lincoln Ridge, Kentucky, Young spent his life improving the lives of young blacks. He saw education as the key to getting jobs and building careers. He felt the problem started when people were very young. So he became active in the Head Start program, which gave special attention to pre-school children. From 1961 to 1971, Young was the director of the National Urban League. This organization worked to improve employment opportunities for blacks.

## YOUTH ORGANIZATIONS 

Organizations for young people provide a chance to make new friends, learn crafts, and become aware of civic responsibilities. They help members build character and mature. Among the leading youth organizations are the Boy SCOUTS and Girl Scouts. They provide young people with a wide range of activities, as does BOYS' Clubs of America. Other organizations have more specific aims. The 4-H CLUBS, for example, use farming and agricultural experiences to build self-reliance and good citizenship in their members.

**U.S. Youth Organizations and Membership**

Boys' Clubs of America 1.2 million
Boy Scouts of America, 3.8 million
Camp Fire Boys & Girls, 600,000
4-H Clubs, 5.8 million
Girls' Clubs of America, 250,000
Girl Scouts of the U.S.A., 3.2 million

▲ *The 450-mile (725-km) Dempster Highway winds through spectacular scenery to join the Yukon with Inuik in the Northwest Territories.*

## YUKON TERRITORY 

The Yukon Territory is in the northwestern corner of CANADA. It is an area of beautiful scenery and very harsh climate. During the winter, temperatures in the Yukon can go as low as –87°F (–63°C).

Mining is the Yukon's most important industry. Lead, zinc, gold, silver, and copper are the most important mineral ores. The discovery of gold in the Klondike region in 1896 brought thousands of prospectors to the Yukon. Preserved towns from this gold rush era are now tourist attractions.

Mountains cover most of the Yukon. Mount Logan (19,524 feet, or 5,951 m) is the highest peak in Canada. It is in the southwestern corner of the territory. The capital of the territory, Whitehorse, is also in the southwest. More than 60 percent of the Yukon's 25,000 people live in and around Whitehorse.

**Yukon Territory**
**Capital:** Whitehorse
**Area:** 1,271,442 sq mi (3,292,780 km²)
**Population:** 27,797 (1991)
**Highest point:** Mt. Logan, 19,524 ft (5,951 m)

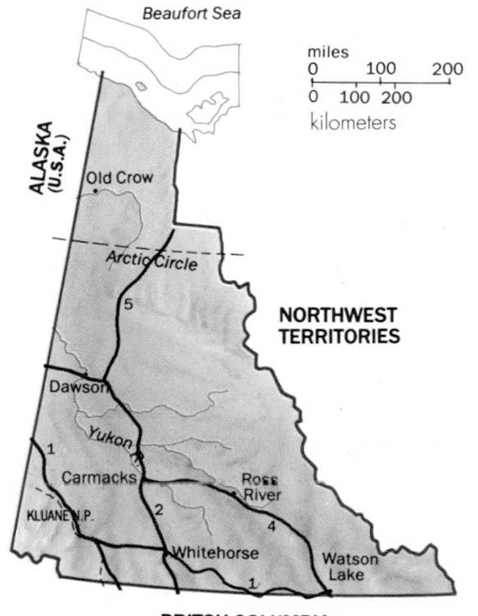

| Leading U.S. Zoos (by attendance) |
|---|
| Lincoln Park, Chicago |
| San Diego |
| National, Washington, D.C. |
| St. Louis |
| Bronx, New York City |
| Houston |
| Los Angeles |
| Cincinnati |
| Milwaukee |

▼ *The Weeki Watchee Springs Zoo in Florida is a small theme park where young people can approach and touch animals as well as observe them in a beautifully preserved setting.*

## ZENGER, John Peter 

John Peter Zenger (1697–1745) was an American journalist who fought for freedom of the press. Born in Germany, he moved to New York, where he published the New York *Weekly Journal.* After attacking the British governor in some articles, Zenger was thrown in jail for almost a year. His lawyer Andrew Hamilton argued that Zenger's articles were based on the truth and that he had committed no crime. Zenger was acquitted. His case helped establish the principle of freedom of the press in America.

## ZIEGFIELD, Florenz 

Florenz Ziegfield (1869–1932) was a theatrical producer. Born in Chicago, he started to produce a yearly show called the *Ziegfield Follies* in 1907. The show featured talented singers and dancers as well as beautiful chorus girls. Ziegfield girls often went on to become famous actresses. The last *Follies* was in 1931. Ziegfield also produced *Show Boat* and other musicals.

## ZOO 

A zoo is a place where wild and tamed animals are kept. The word *zoo* is short for "zoological garden." In many zoos, animals live in park areas that look like the animals' wild habitat. Here, people can enjoy watching the animals, and scientists can study them. An important function of zoos is to help keep endangered species of animals from dying out. The Central Park Zoo in New York City, which opened in 1864, was the first zoo in the United States. The National Zoological Park in Washington, D.C., was established in 1889.

## ZWORYKIN, Vladimir 

Vladimir Zworykin (1889–1982) was a physicist and electronics engineer. He is known as the father of television. Born in Russia, Zworykin moved to the United States in 1919. He worked for the Westinghouse Electric Company, where he developed the iconoscope. This special tube turns light rays into radio waves that can be transmitted for television images. Zworykin later helped develop the electron microscope.

# INDEX

The information in this encyclopedia concentrates on the United States, but you can also find information on Canada, Mexico, and the Caribbean. No encyclopedia can have entries on every subject, however, so there is a vast amount of infor mation that can only be found by looking in the Index. There is no entry for Astronomy, for example, but if you look in the Index you will be directed to entries for Edwin **Hubble**, **Observatories**, and other helpful articles.

Page numbers in **boldface type** (heavy and dark) indicate where the main reference to the subject can be found. Page numbers in *italic type* (slanting) refer to pages on which illustrations will be found.

Take the entry on Charles Lindbergh, for example:

**Lindbergh, Charles** 52, 104, *104*, **404**, *404*, 671

The main entry on the flight pioneer is on page 404, and a picture will also be found on this page. On page 104, under the entry on Richard **Byrd**, there is another picture of Charles Lindbergh--shaking the hand of the famous Arctic explorer. On pages 52, 104, and 671, listed in medium type, you can find information on Lindbergh in the main or boxed text of the entries on **Byrd**, **Aviation**, and the **Smithsonian Institution**. After the main index you will find a **Subject Index**. In this, all the entries in the encyclopedia are divided up by subject. The entries are alphabetical within each subject. Refer to the main index for page references.

## Aa

# Dd

# Gg



# Hh

# Ii



# Jj



# Kk

# Nn



# Oo

# Pp

# Qq



# Rr



# Ss

# Tt

# Uu



# Vv



# Ww

# Yy



# Zz

# Subject Index

## Animals, Plants, and Food



## Countries and Places



## Geography



## Government and Law



## History

French and Indian War
Fur Trade
Gadsden Purchase
Gallatin, Albert
Garrison, William Lloyd
Geronimo
Gettysburg Address
Gettysburg, Battle of
Gold Rush
Hale, Nathan
Hamilton, Alexander
Hancock, John
Henry, Patrick
Hessians
Hiawatha
Hickock, James 'Wild Bill'
Houston, Samuel
Howe, Julia Ward
Hudson, Henry
Hudson's Bay Company
Independence Day
Independence Hall
Indian Wars
Industrial Revolution
Iwo Jima, Battle of
Jackson, Thomas Jonathan 'Stonewall'
James, Jesse
Jamestown Settlement
Jolliet, Louis
Jones, John Paul
Joseph, Chief
Kamehameha I
Korean War
Kosciuszko, Tadeusz
Lafayette, Marquis de
La Salle, Robert Cavelier, Sieur de
Lee, Robert E.
Lewis and Clark Expedition
Lexington and Concord, Battles of
Liberty Bell
Liliuokalani, Lydia
Longstreet, James
Lost Colony
MacArthur, Douglas
Mackenzie, Sir Alexander
Manifest Destiny
Marion, Francis
Marquette, Jacques
Marshall, George C.
Massasoit
Meade, George Gordon
Mexican History
Mexican War
Midway, Battle of
Minuit, Peter
Minutemen
Mitchell, Billy
Monitor and Merrimace
New France
New Netherland
Oakley, Annie
Oglethorpe, James Edward
Paine, Thomas
Parkman, Francis
Pearl Harbor
Peary, Robert E.
Penn, William
Perry, Matthew C. and Oliver H.
Pershing, John J.
Persian Gulf War
Pike, Zebulon
Pioneers
Pirates and Buccaneers
Plymouth Colony
Pocahontas
Ponce de Leon, Juan
Pontiac
Pony Express
Powhatan
Prohibition
Pulaski, Casimir
Puritans
Quanah Parker
Quebec, Battle of
Quebec Act
Raleigh, Sir Walter
Reconstruction
Revere, Paul
Revolution, American
Rickenbacker, Eddie
Riel, Louis
Ross, Betsy
Rough Riders
Sacagawea
Salem Witchcraft Trials
Sante Fe Trail
Sequoyah
Sheridan, Philip Henry
Sherman Antitrust Act
Sherman, William Tecumseh
Slavery
Sons of Liberty
Spanish-American War
Stamp Act
Stanley, Sir Henry Morton
Steuben, Baron von
Stuyvesant, Peter
Tecumseh
Thirteen Colonies
Truth, Sojourner
Tubman, Harriet
Turner, Nat
Underground Railroad
United Empire Loyalists
Valley Forge
Verrazano, Giovanni da
Vespucci, Amerigo
Vietnam War
War of 1812
Wayne, Anthony
Webster, Daniel
Webster, Noah
Westward Movement
Wilderness Road
Williams, Roger
Winthrop, John
World War I
World War II
Zenger, John Peter

## Industry and Technology

Aerospace industry
Advertising
Agriculture
Air transportation
Automobile industry
Aviation
Banks and banking
Boeing, William E.
Bridges
Cable car
Canals
Carnegie, Andrew
Chevrolet, Louis
Cochran, Jacqueline
Communications industry
Computer industry
Construction industry
Corporation
Curtiss, Glenn Hammond
Dairy industry
Dams
Debs, Eugene V.
Douglas, Donald W.
Du Pont, Éleuthère
Duryea, Charles E. and J.F.
Earhart, Amelia
Erie Canal
Eastman, George
Electric power
Field, Marshall
Firestone, Harvey
Fishing industry
Food industry
Ford, Henry
Forests and forestry industry
Getty, J. Paul
Goethals
Goodyear, Charles
Gould, Jay
Guns
Hearst, William Randolph
Helicopter
Hilton, Conrad
Howe, Elias
Hydroelectric power
Insurance industry
Iron and steel industry
Lighthouses
Lindbergh, Charles
Locomotive
Lumber industry
Manufacturing
Mining industry
McCormick, Cyrus
Morgan, John Pierpont
Motorcycles
Natural gas
Natural resources
Oil industry
Panama Canal
Ports and harbors
Railroads
Ranching
Reuther, Walter
Roads and highways
Rockefeller family
Service industries
Ships and shipping
Sikorsky, Igor
Skyscrapers
Stock markets
Submarine
Subways
Telegraph
Telephone
Tesla, Nikola
Trade
Trucks
Tunnels
Vanderbilt family
Von Braun, Wernher
Wall Street
Water supply
Weights and measures
Whitney, Eli
Wright brothers

## Literature and the Arts

Academy awards
Adams, Ansel
Ailey, Alvin
Alcott, Louisa May
Alger, Horatio
Anderson, Marian
Architecture
Armstrong, Louis
Art
Asimov, Isaac
Astaire, Fred
Audubon, John James
Balanchine, George
Baldwin, James
Ballet
Barnum and Bailey
Barrymore Family
Basie, Count
Baum, L. Frank
Bellow, Saul
Benét, Stephen Vincent
Bennett, James Gordon
Benton, Thomas Hart
Berlin, Irving
Bernstein, Leonard
Bogart, Humphrey
Booth, Edwin
Bourke-White, Margaret
Brady, Mathew
Brando, Marlon
Brooks, Gwendolyn
Buck, Pearl S.
Burroughs, Edgar Rice
Cage, John
Cagney, James
Calder, Alexander
Cassatt, Mary
Cather, Willa Sibert
Chandler, Raymond
Chaplin, Charlie
Circus
Cody, William F.
Cohan, George M.
Comics
Cooper, James Fenimore
Copeland, Aaron
Copley, John Singleton
Country music
Crane, Stephen
Crosby, Bing
Currier and Ives
Dance
Davis, Bette
Dickinson, Emily
Disney, Walt
Dreiser, Theodore
Duchamp, Marcel
Duncan, Isadora
Eliot, T.S.
Ellington, Duke
Emerson, Ralph Waldo
Fairbanks, Douglas
Fashion
Faulkner, William
Ferber, Edna
Fields, W.C.
Fitzgerald, F. Scott
Folk art, American
Folklore, American
Folk music
Fonda, Henry
Foster, Stephen
Frost, Robert
Furniture
Gable, Clark
Garland, Judy
Gershwin, George and Ira
Goodman, Benny
Graham, Martha
Greeley, Horace
Hammerstein, Oscar II
Handy, William Christopher
Harper, Frances
Harris, Joel Chandler
Hawthorne, Nathaniel
Hemingway, Ernest
Henry, O.
Hepburn, Katharine
Holiday, Billie
Hollywood
Holmes, Oliver Wendell
Homer, Winslow
Hopper, Edward
Houdini, Harry
Hughes, (James) Langston
Jackson, Mahalia
James, Henry
Jazz
Johns, Jasper
Jolson, Al
Joplin, Scott
Journalism
Kahn, Louis
Keaton, Buster
Kelly, Gene
Kelly, Grace
Kent, Rockwell
Kenton, Stan
Kern, Jerome
Kerouac, Jack
Lardner, Ring
Laurel and Hardy
Lewis, Sinclair
Literature
Lloyd, Harold
London, Jack
Longfellow, Henry Wadsworth
Lowell, James Russell
Magazines
Marx brothers
Melville, Herman
Michener, James
Mies van de Rohe, Ludwig
Miller, Arthur
Miller, Glenn
Monroe, Marilyn
Moore, Marianne
Moses, Grandma
Motion pictures
Muckrakers
Murrow, Edward R.
Museums
Music
Musical theater
Newspapers
Ochs, Adolph
O'Connor, Flannery
O'Keeffe, Georgia
O'Neill, Eugene
Opera
Painting
Parker, Dorothy
Photography
Pickford, Mary
Poe, Edgar Allan
Poetry
Poitier, Sydney
Popular music
Porter, Cole
Pound, Ezra
Pulitzer prize
Rachmaninoff, Sergey
Radio broadcasting
Robeson, Paul
Robinson, Edward Arlington
Robinson, Jackie
Rock music
Rockwell, Norman
Rodgers, Richard
Rogers, Will
Rothko, Mark
Runyon, Damon
Ryder, Albert Pinkham
Saint-Gaudens, Augustus
Salinger, J.D.
Sandburg, Carl
Sargent, John Singer
Science fiction
Sculpture
Sinatra, Frank
Sinclair, Upton
Singer, Isaac Bashevis
Sousa, John Philip
Steichen, Edward
Stein, Gertrude
Steinbeck, John
Stevens, Wallace
Stewart, James
Stieglitz, Alfred
Stowe, Harriet Beecher
Stravinsky, Igor
Stuart, J.E.B.
Sullivan, Louis Henry
Television
Temple, Shirley
Theater
Thoreau, Henry David
Thurber, James
Twain, Mark
Valentino, Rudolph
Warhol, Andy
Wayne, John
Welles, Orson
Whistler, James A. McNeil
White, E.B.
Whitman, Walt
Whittier, John Greenleaf
Wilder, Thornton
Williams, Tennessee
Wilson, Edmund
Wolfe, Thomas
Wright, Frank Lloyd
Ziegfeld, Florenz

## People and Culture

Abernathy, Ralph
Abolitionists
Addams, Jane
Aleuts
Algonquins
American Legion
Apaches
Appleseed, Johnny
Arapahos
Arbor Day
Barton, Clara
Bethune, Mary McCleod

Black Americans
Blackfoot
Blackwell, Elizabeth
Caddos
Cajuns
Carmichael, Stokely
Census
Cherokees
Cheyennes
Chinooks
Chippewas
Choctaws
Citizenship
Civil rights
Cliff dwellers
Colleges and universities
Comanches
Community colleges
Conservation
Consumer protection
Cowboy
Crees
Creeks
Crime
Crows
Darrow, Clarence
Decorations and medals
Dewey, John
Drug abuse
Du Bois, W.E.B.
Education
Environmental protection
Eskimo
Ethnic groups
Flanagan, Edward J.
Galbraith, John Kenneth
Gallup, George
Garvey, Marcus
Gompers, Samuel
Hall of Fame
Halloween
Health
Hispanic-Americans
Hopis
Housing
Hurons
Indians, American
Iroquois League
Juvenile delinquency
Keller, Helen
King, Martin Luther, Jr.
Kiowas
Ku Klux Klan
Labor Unions
Language
Lewis, John L.
Libraries
Malcolm X
Mandans
Mann, Horace
McLuhan, Marshall
Mead, Margaret
Meany, George
Memorial Day
Mennonites
Menominees
Miamis
Missionaries
Mohawks
Mohicans
Mott, Lucretia
Mound builders
Nader, Ralph
National anthem
National Association for the Advancement of Colored People
Naturalization
Navajos
Nez Percé
Nobel Prize
Opinion Poll
Osceola
Paiutes
Passport
Paul, Alice
Pawnees
Plains Indians
Pollution
Public health
Public utilities
Pueblos
Randolph, A. Philip
Red Cross
Roosevelt, Eleanor
Salvation Army
Sanitation
Schlesinger, Arthur Sr. and Jr.
Schools
Scouts
Seminoles
Shoshonis
Sioux
Smithsonian Institution
Social welfare
Spingarn, Joel Elias
Stanton, Elizabeth Cady
Suffrage
Terrorism
Thanksgiving Day
Uncle Sam
United Nations
Utes
Uto-Aztecan languages
Veterans Day
Washington, Booker T.
Wiesel, Elie
Wilkins, Roy
Women's rights
Young, Andrew
Young, Whitney M., Jr.
Youth organizations

## Religion, Philosophy, and Myth

Baptists
Bunyan, Paul
Christianity
Christian Science
Eddy, Mary Baker
Episcopalians
Friends, Society of
Graham, Billy
James, William
Jews and Judaism
Lutherans
Methodists
Mormons
Myths and Legends of the American Indians
Pecos Bill
Presbyterians
Protestantism
Religions
Roman Catholic Church
Smith, Joseph
Young, Brigham

## Science and Space

Agassiz, Louis
Aldrin, Edwin Jr.
Alvarez, Louis
Armstrong, Neil
Baekeland, Leo
Banneker, Benjamin
Banting, Sir Frederick
Bardeen, John
Bell, Alexander Graham
Bowditch, Nathaniel
Brattain, Walter
Burbank, Luther
Cape Canaveral
Carver, George Washington
Collins, Michael
De Forest, Lee
Eckert, John P., Jr.
Edison, Thomas Alva
Einstein, Albert
Fermi, Enrico
Fuller, Buckminster
Fulton, Robert
Glenn, John H.
Goddard, Robert H.
Hubble, Edwin
Inventions
Jansky, Karl
Land, Edwin Herbert
Langley, Samuel Pierpont
Langmuir, Irving
Lawrence, Ernest O.
Maiman, Theodore
Michelson, Albert
Millikan, Robert A.
Morse, Samuel F.B.
Nuclear power
Observatories
Oceanography
Oppenheimer, J. Robert
Pauling, Linus
Reed, Walter
Ride, Sally
Rockets and missiles
Salk, Jonas
Satellite, artificial
Science
Shepard, Alan B., Jr.
Shockley, William B.
Space program
Sperry, Elmer
Spock, Benjamin
Teller, Edward
Van Allen, James
Watson, James Dewey
Weather forecasting
Westinghouse, George
Zworykin, Vladimir

## Sports and Pastimes

Ali, Muhammed
America's Cup
Automobile racing
Baseball
Basketball
Bowling
Boxing
Dempsey, Jack
Field hockey
Football
4-H Clubs
Golf
Gymnastics
Holidays
Horse racing
Hotels and motels
Ice hockey
Ice skating
Jones, Bobby
Kentucky Derby
Lacrosse
Little League
Louis, Joe
Olympic Games
Owens, Jesse
Rockne, Knute
Rodeo
Roller skating
Ruth, Babe
Skateboarding
Soap box derby
Soccer
Softball
Sports
Square dancing
Stamps and stamp collecting
Surfing
Swimming
Table tennis
Tennis
Track and field
Volleyball
Water sports
Winter sports
Wrestling

## States and Cities

Alabama
Alaska
Albuquerque
Annapolis
Arizona
Arkansas
Atlanta
Austin
Baltimore
Boston
Broadway
California
Chicago
Cities
Cleveland
Colorado
Columbus
Connecticut
Dallas
Delaware
Denver
Detroit
District of Columbia
El Paso
Florida
Fort Worth
Georgia
Guam
Hawaii
Houston
Idaho
Illinois
Indiana
Indianapolis
Iowa
Jacksonville
Kansas
Kansas City, Missouri
Kentucky
Long Beach
Long Island
Los Angeles
Louisiana
Maine
Maryland
Massachusetts
Memphis
Miami
Michigan
Milwaukee
Minnesota
Mississippi
Missouri
Montana
Mount Rushmore
Mount Vernon
Nebraska
Nevada
New England
New Hampshire
New Jersey
New Mexico
New Orleans
New York
New York City
North Carolina
North Dakota
Ohio
Oklahoma
Oklahoma City
Oregon
Pacific Territories of the United States
Pennsylvania
Philadelphia
Phoenix
Pittsburgh
Portland
Rhode Island
St. Augustine
St. Louis
Salt Lake City
San Antonio
San Diego
San Francisco
San Jose
Seattle
South Carolina
South Dakota
Statue of Liberty
Stone Mountain
Tennessee
Texas
Tulsa
United States of America
Utah
Vermont
Virginia
Virgin Islands
Washington
Washington, D.C.
West Virginia
Wisconsin
Wyoming

# Acknowledgments

The publishers would like to thank the following for supplying photographs for this book:

Page 2 Rex Features; 3 Hulton (top), Popperfoto (bottom); 4 Maryland Historic Society; 6 P. Newark Pictures; 7 P. Newark Pictures (bottom); 8 Lockheed (bottom); 9 Boeing (top), A. Ronan Pictures (bottom); 12 American Dance Theatre; 14 TWA; 15 TWA; 17 Spectrum (top); 21 NASA (bottom); 22 P. Newark Pictures; 23 Allsport; 25 Bridgeman Art Library; 26 Canadian High Commission (top), Mary Evans Pictures (left), P. Newark Pictures (bottom); 27 P. Newark Pictures (top), Illustrated London News (middle top), Camera Press (middle bottom), The White House (bottom); 28 Allsport; 29 Bruce Coleman (top), Hulton (bottom); 31 U.S. Naval Academy; 32 Bettmann; 34 University of Oklahoma Library (top); 36 and 37 The Architectural Association; 42 NASA; 44 Bridgeman Art Library (middle), Bath Museum (right), P. Newark Pictures (bottom); 45 Art Resource (top left and middle), Bridgeman Art Library (top and bottom left); 47 National Film Archive; 48 Hulton (top); 49 P. Newark Pictures; 50 Ford Motors (bottom); 51 Ford Motors (top), Michael Brown (bottom); 52 P. Newark Pictures (bottom); 54 Martha Swope; 55 Hulton (top), Martha Swope (bottom); 56 Robert Harding; 59 P. Neward Pictures (top), Allsport (bottom); 65 Bruce Coleman; 67 Hulton; 68 Camera Press (top), P. Newark Pictures (bottom); 69 © Thomas Hart Benton/DACS, London/VAGA, New York 1992; 70 Bettmann (top), Hulton (bottom); 72 Bruce Coleman; 75 Bruce Coleman; 77 P. Newark Pictures (top), Popperfoto (left), Virago (right); 78 Mansell Collection; 80 Ronald Grant Archive; 81 Bettmann; 82 P. Newark Pictures (top); 85 Bourke-White Collection; 86 P. Newark Pictures; 87 Allsport; 88 National Film Archive; 90 Bruce Coleman (left); 91 Valan; 93 Bettmann; 96 Bettmann; 100 National Film Archive; 101 The White House; 103 Bruce Coleman; 104 Bettmann; 105 Rex Features; 109 Ronald Grant Archive (top), Louisiana Office of Tourism (bottom); 110 Bettmann (top); 116 P. Newark Pictures (top), Bridgeman Art Library (bottom); 122 Poperfoto (bottom); 123 Bettmann (top), Gamma-Liaison (middle); 124 Jimmy Carter Library; 125 Bettmann (top), Wichita Art Museum, Roland P. Murdock Collection (bottom); 128 Bridgeman Art Library; 129 National Film Archive (top), P. Newark Pictures (bottom); 130 P. Newark Pictures; 131 Bruce Coleman (top); 132 P. Newark Pictures; 134 P. Newark Pictures; 136 P. Newark Picutres (top); 137 Bridgeman Art Library (top); 139 Gamman Liaison; 140 P. Newark Pictures; 141 P. Newark Pictures (top and right), Hulton (left); 142 NHPA/S.Kraseman; 144 Bettmann; 146 Frank Spooner Pictures (left), Rex Features (bottom); 147 Bettmann; 148 P. Newark Pictures; 149 The White House (bottom); 151 Tulane University (top, NASA (bottom); 154 P. Newark Pictures (left); 155 Hulton (bottom); 156 P. Newark Pictures;157 Peanuts, Charles Schultz (top), NASA (bottom); 161 P. Newark Pictures; 165 John Blake (bottom); 168 David McGill (top); 170 Library of Congress; 172 Mary Evans Pictures (top), Bettmann (middle); 175 P. Newark Pictures (bottom); 176 Rex Features (middle); 179 P. Newark Pictures; 181 P. Newark Pictures (top), Ronald Grant Archive (bottom); 182 Bruce Coleman; 183 P. Newark Pictures; 184 P. Newark Pictures; 187 The Dance Library/D. Williams (left), Ronald Grant Archive (right); 188 National Film Archive (top), P. Newark Pictures (bottom); 189 Popperfoto (right), Bruce Coleman (left); 190 Bettmann (left), P. Newark Pictures (right); 193 Dept. of Defense; 196 Bettmann (top); 197 Bettmann; 201 Bettmann; 202 Dinosaur National Museum, Utah; 203 P. Newark Pictures (top left), Ronald Grant Archive (right and bottom); 208 David Simson (middle), Bettmann (bottom); 209 Philadelphia Museum of Art: Louise and Walter Arensberg Collection © ADAGP, Paris and DACS, London 1992; 210 Hulton; 211 Bettmann; 212 Bettmann; 214 Kodak Library; 215 Associated Press; 216 Bettmann; 217 Valan (right), P. Newark Pictures (left); 219 Bettmann (bottom); 220 Dwight D. Eisenhower Library; 222 Bettmann (bottom); 223 P. Newark Pictures (bottom); 224 NHPA/S. Krasemann (right); 225 Exxon Co. USA; 227 Valan (right); 230 British Library; 232 Bettmann; 233 Donna Karan; 234 P. Newark Pictures (bottom); 235 Bettmann (top) FBI (bottom); 236 Ronald Grant Archive; 238 Ronald Grant Archive; 241 Firestone; 242 Valan; 243 Bettmann (bottom); 252 Rex Features; 253 Ronald Grant Archive; 254 P. Newark Pictures; 255 Allsport; 256 Gerald Ford Library; 262 P. Newark Pictures; 269 Johnson Wax; 270 National Film Archive; 271 Bettmann; 272 Ronald Grant Archive; 272 NASA; 278 Bettmann (top, Ronald Grant Archive (bottom); 282 NASA; 282 Bettmann; 283 The White House; 290 Camera Press (top), Bettmann (bottom); 292 Bettmann; 293 Valan; 299 Supersport; 301 Bettmann; 302 Valan (top), Bettmann (bottom), 303 Bettmann (top), P. Newark Pictures (bottom); 304 Bettmann; 306 Bettmann; 307 Bettmann (top), P. Newark Pictures (bottom); 313 P. Newark Pictures (top); 314 Hulton; Frontispiece Werner Forman Archive; 317 P. Newark Pictures; 318 Valan; 319 Unicorn Stock Photos; 322 The Butler Institute of American Art; 324 FBI; 325 The Butler Institute of American Art (top); 327 P. Newark Pictures (bottom); 331 Bettmann; 332 Canadian High Commission (top), N.O.A.A. (bottom); 333 Trip/Eye Ubiquitous; 335 Michael Dent (top), Allsport (bottom); 340 Bettmann; 342 Picturepoint; 347 Hutchinson Library; 348 Derek Widdicombe; 349 Bettmann; 351 Bruce Coleman; 358 Valan; 360 Camera Press; 361 Valan (top), Bettmann (bottom); 363 Bettmann; 364 Hulton (top left), P. Newark Pictures (top right), Bettmann (middle), Redferns (bottom); 365 P. Newark Pictures (top left), Bettmann (top right), David Simson (bottom); 366 P. Newark Pictures © Jasper Johns/DACS, London/VAGA, New York 1992; 372 P. Newark Pictures; 373 The Salk Institute; 376 Ronald Grant; 378 Ronald Grant Archive (right), Popperfoto (left); 379 Popperfoto (top and middle), Bettmann (bottom); 380 John F. Kennedy Library (right), Popperfoto (left); 381 Bridgeman Art Library (left), Popperfoto (right); 383 Valan (right); 384 Hulton; 385 Popperfoto; 386 National Archives; 387 Hulton; 388 Hulton; 389 Gamma-Liaison (top), Popperfoto (bottom); 391 P. Newark Pictures (top); 392 Bettmann; 393 The Nobel Foundation; 395 National Film Archive; 403 Bettmann; 404 Bettmann; 405 Bettmann (top and bottom left), P. Newark Pictures (top right), Mary Evans Pictures (middle and bottom right); 407 National Film Archives; 409 Bettmann; 410 Mary Evans Pictures (bottom); 411 Valan (left), P. Newark Pictures (right); 418 Robert Hunt Library; 419 P. Newark Pictures (left), Bettmann (right); 420 Bettmann (right), Mary Evans Pictures (left); 422 Spectrum; 423 Robert Harding (bottom); 424 Popperfoto (top), P. Newark Pictures (bottom); 425 Michael Dent; 428 Valan; 431 Science Photo Library (top), Planet Earth (bottom); 433 Bettmann (top), National Film Archives (bottom); 435 Robert Harding (top); 437 Valan; 438 Bettmann (left), Bruce Coleman (left); 439 Bettmann (top), P. Newark Pictures (bottom); 441 P. Newark Pictures; 446 Werner Forman Archive; 449 South American Pictures; 451 Hulton; 454 P. Newark Pictures (top), Architectural Association (bottom); 455 CBS (left), Bettmann (right); 456 Bettmann (top); 461 P. Newark Pictures (top), Unicorn Stock Photos (bottom); 465 P. Newark Pictures (top), Unicorn Stock Photos (bottom); 468 Bettmann (top), Canadian High Commission (bottom); 469 Art Resource; 472 Bettmann; 473 Ronald Grant Archive; 474 Valan; 476 Valan (top), Camera Press (bottom); 478 Mary Evans Pictures; 479 Camera Press; 480 Ronald Grant Archive (top and bottom), Hulton (middle); 481 Ronald Grant Archive (top left), P. Newark Pictures (top right), Hulton (bottom left), Lucas Film (bottom right); 483 Museum of the American Indian; 488 Bettmann (top), Paul Bahn (bottom); 489 Gamma-Liaison; 490 Rex Features (bottom); 491 Martha Swope; 494 P. Newark Pictures; 495 NAACP Public Relations (top); Gamma-Liaison (bottom); 496 Frances Valdes (bottom left); 499 Department of Justice; 506 Valan; 507 Bettmann; 508 Valan; 509 P. Newark Pictures; 510 Vlan (bottom); 513 Unicorn Stock Photos; 515 Valan; 516 Valan; 517 Hartford Courant; 518 and 519 Valan; 521 Idaho State Historical Society (top); 522 Valan (left), Popperfoto (right); 523 Nixon Presidential Library; 525 Gamma-Liaison; 526 Unicorn Stock Photos (top and bottom left); 531 Fargo Chamber of Commerce; 532 Shell; 536 Bettmann; 537 Science Photo Library (top); 538 New York Times (bottom); 539 Camera Press; 543 Art Resource; 544 J. Allan Cash (bottom); 546 Gamma-Liaison; 547 Valan; 548 Ronald Grant Archive; 549 NHPA/J.Shaw (top), Bettmann (bottom); 554 Valan; 555 Bettmann; 558 P. Newark Pictures (top), Bridgeman Art Library (middle), The Art Institute of Chicago (bottom) © Grant Wood/DACS, London/VAGA, New York 1992; 559 Popperfoto; 560 Bettmann; 563 Gamma-Liaison; 564 and 565 P. Newark Pictures; 567 Valan; 568 Bettmann; 570 Bettmann (bottom); 571 Unicorn Stock Photos (top), Library of Congress Collection (middle), Bettmann (bottom); 575 P. Newark Pictures; 577 Mary Evans Pictures; 579 Bruce Coleman (bottom right); 580 Bettmann (bottom); 582 Ronald Grant Archive; 583 Derek Widdicombe/M. Thomas (left), Valan (right); 584 Frank Spooner Pictures; 587 P. Newark Pictures; 588 Redferns (top), Bettmann (middle), Ronald Grant (bottom); 589 Frank Lane Pictures (top), Bettmann (middle); 592 Bettmann; 593 U.S. Army (top); 595 Paul Bahn; 596 The White House; 598 Frank Spooner Pictures; 600 Bettmann; 601 John Blake; 602 Frances Valdes; 603 Popperfoto (top), Valan (bottom); 607 Valan; 608 P. Newark Pictures; 609 Valan (bottom); 612 Library of Congress; 614 P. Newark Pictures (top); 616 Bettmann; 617 The White House; 618 and 619 Bettmann; 620 Spectrum; 622 and 623 P. Newark Pictures; 624 Rhode Island Tourist Board; 625 Valan; 626 U.S. Airforce (top), P. Newark Pictures (bottom); 629 Bettmann (bottom); 630 Bettmann (top); 632 Redferns (top), Rex Features (middle and bottom); 633 Bridgeman Art Library; 635 Valan; 636 Bruce Coleman; 637 Ronald Grant Archive (top), Bettmann (bottom); 638 Allsport (top), Bettmann (bottom); 639 Imperial War Museum; 640 P. Newark Pictures; 642 Art Resource (top), Bettmann (bottom); 643 Valan; 644 Martha Swope (top), Bettmann (middle), The Butler Institute of American Art (bottom); 645 Valan; 646 Art Resource; 648 Penguin Books (top); 650 J. Edmanson (bottom); 651 J. Edmanson (top); 652 The Butler Institute of American Art (bottom); 653 Valan; 655 Rex Features (bottom); 656 Bettmann (top and middle); 657 Bettmann (top, middle and bottom left), Science Photo Library (bottom right); 659 Art Resource (top), Wolfgang Volz/Christo 1983 (middle), P. Newark Pictures (bottom); 660 Valan (top); 661 Bettmann (top); 663 Nasa (bottom); 664 Valan (bottom); 666 Idaho State Historical Society (top); 667 Popperfoto (top), P. Newark Pictures (bottom); 668 Mary Evans Pictures; 670 Paul Bahn (top), P. Newark Pictures (bottom); 671 Smithsonian Institue; 672 Valan; 675 South Carolina Dept. of Commerce (bottom); 677 Paul Bahn; 678 P. Newark Pictures; 679 NASA; 682 Michael Dent; 687 Popperfoto; 688 Popperfoto; 689 Metropolitan Museum of Art; 690 Bettmann; 693 P. Newark Pictures; 694 Joseph Bailey (bottom); 696 Bettmann; 698 P. Newark Pictures; 700 Bettmann; 701 Bettmann (middle), NASA (bottom); 702 Children's Television Workshop (top), The National Broadcasting Company, Inc. (bottom); 703 Bettmann; 704 Valan (middle); 706 Hulton (top and middle), Allsport (bottom); 708 Valan; 714 Allsport (bottom); 715 Allsport; 716 Valan; 718 Harry S. Truman Library (right), P. Newark Pictures (left); 721 Bettmann; 724 UN Photos; 728 Paul Bahn; 729 Salt Lake Valley Convention & Visitors Bureau; 730 Utah State Historical Society; 733 Paul Bahn; 734 Vermont Tourist Office; 735 Valan; 737 Popperfoto (top); 739 Valan (top right); 741 Allsport; 742 Popperfoto; 743 Mansell Collection; 745 Valan; 746 J. Edmanson; 747 P. Newark Pictures; 749 Judyth Platt (left); 751 Ronald Grant Archive (top), Science Photo Library (bottom); 752 Bettmann; 753 Ronald Grant Archive; 755 West Virginia Governor's Office (top left); 757 P. Newark Pictures; 758 Nature Photographers (top), Tate Gallery, London (bottom); 761 Bettmann; 763 Bettmann; 765 Valan (top); 768 NHPA/S. Kraseman; 769 P. Newark Pictures (top); 770 Imperial War Museum; 772 Paul Bahn (left); 776 David Phillips.

All other photographs by ZEFA